Sherman's
Civil War

CIVIL WAR

AMERICA

Gary W. Gallagher,

editor

Sherman's

SELECTED CORRESPONDENCE OF

Civil War

William T. Sherman, 1860–1865

EDITED BY BROOKS D. SIMPSON

AND JEAN V. BERLIN

The University of North Carolina Press   Chapel Hill & London

© 1999
The University of North Carolina Press

Book Club Edition

Manufactured in the
United States of America
The paper in this book meets the guide-
lines for permanence and durability of the
Committee on Production Guidelines for
Book Longevity of the Council on Library
Resources.
Library of Congress
Cataloging-in-Publication Data
Sherman, William T. (William Tecumseh),
1820–1891.
Sherman's Civil War : selected correspondence
of William T. Sherman, 1860–1865 / edited by
Brooks D. Simpson and Jean V. Berlin.
    p. cm. — (Civil War America)
Includes bibliographical references and index.
ISBN 0-8078-2440-2 (alk. paper)
1. Sherman, William T. (William Tecumseh),
1820–1891—Correspondence.   2. Generals—
United States—Correspondence.   3. United
States. Army—Biography.   4. United States—
History—Civil War, 1861–1865—Personal
narratives.   5. United States—History—Civil
War, 1861–1865—Campaigns.   I. Simpson,
Brooks D.   II. Berlin, Jean V. (Jean Vance),
1962–   .   III. Title.   IV. Series.
E467.1.S55A4   1999
973.7'092—dc21   98-5621
[B]   CIP

03   02   01   00   99   5   4   3   2   1

For Rebecca and Emily

Contents

Introduction, *xi*

Acknowledgments, *xv*

Editorial Method, *xvii*

Symbols and Abbreviations, *xix*

1　November 3, 1860–February 25, 1861, *1*

2　March 9, 1861–July 14, 1861, *59*

3　July 15, 1861–December 12, 1861, *112*

4　December 18, 1861–May 26, 1862, *166*

5　May 31, 1862–August 25, 1862, *229*

6　August 26, 1862–January 25, 1863, *289*

7　January 25, 1863–March 16, 1863, *370*

8　April 3, 1863–July 4, 1863, *435*

9　July 5, 1863–December 30, 1863, *498*

10　January 6, 1864–May 4, 1864, *581*

11　May 20, 1864–September 4, 1864, *635*

12　September 7, 1864–November 12, 1864, *702*

13　December 13, 1864–February 24, 1865, *759*

14　March 12, 1865–April 9, 1865, *821*

15　April 12, 1865–May 30, 1865, *856*

Chronological List of Letters, *911*

List of Letters by Recipient, *925*

Index, *933*

Maps and Illustrations

MAPS

Washington, D.C., and Northeastern Virginia, *102*

Central Kentucky, *139*

Western Tennessee, *232*

Mississippi, Louisiana, and Arkansas, *374*

Chattanooga to Atlanta, *637*

Savannah to Durham Station, *812*

ILLUSTRATIONS *Following page 424*

William Tecumseh Sherman and Thomas Ewing Sherman

Ellen Ewing Sherman and Thomas Ewing Sherman

William Tecumseh Sherman Jr., "Willy"

Thomas Ewing Sr.

The four Sherman girls: Lizzie, Rachel, Elly, and Minnie

John Sherman

The four Ewing brothers: Hugh, Philemon, Thomas, and Charles

James B. McPherson

Ulysses S. Grant

Henry W. Halleck

William T. Sherman, commanding the Military Division of the Mississippi,
and his generals

Major General William T. Sherman at Atlanta

Introduction

In October 1864, William T. Sherman reflected on the flood of correspondence that had descended upon him in the aftermath of his capture of Atlanta, Georgia, the previous month. He admitted to his wife that at times he wrote "imprudent letters" (one might add that some were also impudent). "It seems that my letters now even are sought after like hot cakes"; he hoped that "none will be published as sample of literary composition." In words heartily endorsed by this editorial team, he added: "You can read my letters & guess at the meaning, but judging from my Copy clerks, some readers would make an awful jumble of my letters, written usually in the small hours of the night, by a single candle on a box."[1]

The letters Sherman left behind have proven a treasure trove for biographers, scholars, and students of the Civil War. Not all of what he said can be taken at face value, for usually Sherman's bark was worse than his bite. Often the general wielded his pen rather than his sword in an effort to blow off steam or to outline vivid images he never intended to make real. At the same time, however, the emotion revealed in such correspondence tells much about the general's personality and psyche, his joys and sorrows, and the intensity with which he felt anger, disappointment, shame, vindication, and triumph. Say what one might about the man and the general, it remains that he was never boring, least so in his letters.

Sherman's Civil War: Selected Correspondence of William T. Sherman, 1860–1865 is a selected edition of the personal and official correspondence of one of the major figures of the Civil War era. This volume is intended to serve a wide audience: biographers and other students of Sherman's career, readers interested in the Civil War, military historians, and political historians. The greatest strength of *Sherman's Civil War* lies in the letters themselves: lively, frank, opinionated, discerning, and occasionally extremely wrongheaded, they mirror the colorful personality and multifaceted mentality of the man who wrote them. It is close to being a "life through letters," enabling readers to see the Civil War through Sherman's eyes. They touch on such diverse issues as Northern politics, the pressure of popular expectations on military operations, the role and responsibilities of the press, the nature and intensity of Confederate resistance, justifications for the treatment of civilians in occupied areas, women's participation in the conflict, slavery, emancipation, the

---

1. WTS to EES, October 21, 1864.

enlistment of blacks in the Union army, and the problems of peacemaking and reconstruction, all important to a broader understanding of the American Civil War. And Sherman had more than enough to say about such prominent individuals as Ulysses S. Grant, Abraham Lincoln, and George McClellan, as well as a host of lesser figures.

The necessity for a new, more complete, and more extensive edition of Sherman's correspondence has been clear for some time. While historians and others have relied on Walter L. Fleming, ed., *General Sherman as College President* (1912), Rachel Sherman Thorndike, ed., *The Sherman Letters: Correspondence between General and Senator Sherman from 1837 to 1891* (1894), and Mark A. DeWolfe Howe, ed., *Home Letters of General Sherman* (1909), a comparison of their texts with the originals reveals significant discrepancies and excisions in the published versions (as well as variations between the various editions). The editors excised or altered some of Sherman's more colorful or pointed expressions of opinion, omitted descriptions of military operations, and silently corrected the general's grammar, as well as standardizing his spelling, capitalization, and punctuation. The result is a rather sanitized and somewhat misleading version of Sherman's views and statements as embodied in these letters. Scholars have noted the inaccuracies and warned against too great a reliance on the printed versions.[2]

In addition, the vast majority of the correspondence reprinted, especially in the last two editions mentioned above, was between Sherman and his wife, Ellen Ewing Sherman, and his brother, Republican politician John Sherman. A large number of Sherman letters both to these individuals and to others remained unpublished or unavailable to the general reader. Among these letters is Sherman's correspondence with Ulysses S. Grant (best available through a careful perusal of the annotation to Grant's letters in John Y. Simon, ed., *The Papers of Ulysses S. Grant* [22 vols. to date, 1967–   ]) and with other generals, politicians, associates, friends, and citizens. Two major collections of Sherman material, at the Library of Congress and the University of Notre Dame, are available on microfilm, but Sherman material in other collections at the Library of Congress, the National Archives, the Huntington Library, the Ohio Historical Society, and other repositories, including private owners, remains solely in manuscript form.

Since the focus of this volume is Sherman, only letters *from* Sherman were considered for publication in full. To merit serious consideration for inclusion, a letter had to contain material that would help readers understand

2. John F. Marszalek, *Sherman's Other War: The General and the Civil War Press* (Memphis, 1981), 217, and George C. Rable, "William T. Sherman and the Conservative Critique of Radical Reconstruction," *Ohio History* 93 (Autumn 1984): 148 n.3.

Sherman and his war. Letters that revealed Sherman the husband, the father, the general, or his opinions about politics, military operations, opposing generals, the South, slavery and emancipation, his fellow officers, or other aspects of warfare are included. Complete and accurate versions of virtually all the letters in Fleming, Thorndike, and DeHowe are included, along with other correspondence to John Sherman and Ellen Ewing Sherman not published in previous collections and letters to other family members. Some correspondence that brought to light aspects of military and political affairs is also included. Routine correspondence, requisitions, reports, and orders, usually to be found in the *Official Records*, were excluded, although information from them was used in annotation. Aware that a virtually complete collection of the correspondence between Sherman and Grant is available in some form in *The Papers of Ulysses S. Grant*, the editors decided to include those letters which best shed light on the themes featured in this volume.

A good number of these letters have never been published before; others in their entirety are inaccessible to all but the most dedicated researcher. Many may disagree with the inclusion or exclusion of a particular document, but the constraints of a one-volume selected edition designed for both a general and a scholarly audience dictated many choices. Any serious scholar of Sherman and his time will inevitably consult the *Official Records* and various manuscript collections.

Sherman's Civil War opens in November 1860 with his ruminations on the coming election. Sherman was the superintendent of the Louisiana State Seminary and Military Academy in Alexandria, Louisiana, the most satisfying job he had held in some time. Ironically, Sherman had always found the South a congenial place to live. The volume ends on May 30, 1865, the date of Sherman's Special Field Order No. 76, a farewell to his army. This was the end, in Sherman's eyes, of his Civil War service.

Acknowledgments

First on our list of thank yous is Richard N. Sheldon of the National Historic Publications and Records Commission. It was under his watchful eye that each of us got our introduction to documentary editing, one as an assistant editor at The Papers of Andrew Johnson, the other as a NHPRC Fellow at The Papers of William Thornton. Dick united this editorial team at Camp Edit in Madison, Wisconsin, in June 1986, although even he probably could not have predicted the consequences of his actions. Other friendships formed or reinforced there have helped to sustain us in our endeavors, and so we thank John Muldowny, Virginia Laas, and Betsy Hughes.

Three people deserve especial thanks for inspiring us to persist in our work: John Y. Simon, Mary Guinta, and Charles "Monty" Harris. After talking with them about this project we emerged determined to overcome any obstacle we encountered as we worked on this volume, for we knew how they would feel when they saw the finished product.

Other people affiliated with documentary editing assisted us by locating documents, responding to questions, and welcoming us on visits to the National Archives. Timothy Connelly and Donald Singer were especially helpful. So was Sara D. Jackson, who once cheered us on by declaring, "Let Sherman march!" We miss you, Sara.

Archivists and librarians offered us assistance, answered our queries, and forwarded documents and illustrations. Our thanks go to Gary J. Arnold, Ohio Historical Society; Daniel H. Woodward, Huntington Library; Charles Lamb and Peter J. Lysy, University of Notre Dame; Richard J. Sommers, U.S. Army Military History Institute; Susan M. Swasta and Robert S. Cox, William L. Clements Library, University of Michigan; Roger D. Bridges, Rutherford B. Hayes Presidential Center; Patricia J. Cable and Marion O. Smith, Andrew Johnson Papers; R. Douglas Parsons, Rosenbach Museum and Library; Leslie A. Morris and Emily C. Walhout, Houghton Library, Harvard University; Jean F. Preston, Firestone Library, Princeton University; Mary Ellen Sinko, *Forbes* magazine; Sandra M. Trenholm, Gilder-Lehrman Institute; Alexandra S. Gressit, Indiana Historical Society; Thomas Knoles, American Antiquarian Society; Phyllis Kuhn, Fairfield Heritage Association; and Jonathan P. Cox, Historical Society of Pennsylvania. We would also like to extend our thanks to the following individuals who made copies of letters in their possession available to us: C. Parke Day of Atlanta, Georgia; Joseph H. Ewing of Wheaton, Maryland; and Walter Lord of New York City.

Several institutions provided funds for travel, the acquisition of microfilm and other material, and other purposes. Wofford College supported the project between 1987 and 1990, allowing us to set up an office in the college library: we thank Dan Maultsby and Oakley Colburn for their interest and assistance. Since 1990 Arizona State University has supplied support through the Faculty Grant-in-Aid Program, the College of Liberal Arts and Sciences MiniGrant Program, and several other awards.

Members of the Sherman family graciously gave us permission to reprint the general's letters. Thanks to Rachel Achenbach, Frederic S. Cauldwell, William T. Hamlen, Elizabeth C. Klein, Erik A. Ruud, Karen E. Ruud, Paul Ruud, Peter J. Ruud, John Sherman Jr., Alexander M. Thackera, James J. Thackera, and Thomas E. Thackera.

Lew Bateman has been patient with us as we missed deadlines and found ourselves overwhelmed by other responsibilities, personal as well as professional. From the beginning he was confident that one day this volume would appear; his encouragement and good humor were (and are) much appreciated. Gary W. Gallagher and John F. Marszalek have long taken an interest in our work, and their reviews of the manuscript have done much to improve it. Ron Maner and Trudie Calvert did a fine and thorough job of preparing the manuscript for publication.

Chet and Anne Berlin took their daughter to Gettysburg before she knew she was interested in the Civil War. Auntie (Elizabeth Devenay Johnston) shared tales of her grandfather Charles McCann, who was present at John Brown's execution and served with the Army of Northern Virginia, surrendering at Appomattox. Uncle (William Kemp Johnston) saved the old family letters of Private Frederick Whitehead, Tenth Iowa, Army of the Tennessee—Sherman's own army. Both contributed to their grandniece's love of history. Little did John and Adelaide Simpson know when they gave their son a Sherman autograph some thirty years ago that they were simply acquiring the first of many documents for the project.

Over the last eleven years the coeditors have worked together on several projects. The most rewarding ones have been (and continue to be) Rebecca and Emily. This is for them.

Editorial Method

Anyone who has worked with Sherman's writings in manuscript is well aware of the challenges they present. Sherman's handwriting is notoriously difficult to decipher, and when he was angry or depressed it became worse. His punctuation is sometimes nonexistent, and he frequently used capitalization for emphasis. His spelling, however, was generally consistent, with a few notable and nearly invariable errors, such as "Mississipi" for "Mississippi." In transcribing the letters we placed an emphasis on producing both an accurate and a clean text, as anyone particularly interested in the intricacies and peculiarities of Sherman's orthography would want to use the originals. Following is a list of the rules used in producing our transcriptions.

Headings and closings on letters have been placed uniformly, with all addresses at the left margin and all locations and dates right of center. Canceled text and insertions have not been reproduced; Sherman changed his letters only to correct misspellings and place or name errors or to make minor changes in style. Paragraphs have been indented even though Sherman did not always indent them; he would occasionally end one sentence halfway along a line and then begin a new paragraph flush against the left margin.

Sherman's punctuation has been retained. In those clear cases when a large space between two independent clauses indicates two sentences, a period in brackets has been inserted. When commas are needed for the sake of clarification, they are added in brackets. When both a period and a dash follow the end of a sentence, the period has been kept and the dash dropped. When both a comma and a dash follow the end of a phrase, the comma has been kept and the dash dropped. Commas have been inserted in numbers of five figures or more (i.e., 50,000 for 50000) for the sake of clarity; in those cases where Sherman used a period to mark a number, it has been retained (for example, 50.000). Those words Sherman underlines are italicized in the printed text.

Sherman's spelling and capitalization have been retained with a few exceptions. All proper names of individuals have been standardized, as Sherman's inconsistent or incorrect spelling of these names could lead to confusion. Both "north" and "south" have been consistently capitalized when he referred to them as geographic and political regions; he did so himself most of the time. Certain consistent misspellings in letterbook copies—"poeple," for instance, or "then" for "than"—have been silently corrected.

In the case of abbreviations, periods have been added for the sake of clarity. When Sherman himself indicated the use of a contraction with an apostrophe (as in the case of Gen'l), no period has been added. Superscripts following numbers and used in titles (i.e., "Gen¹." or "3ʳᵈ") have been brought down to the line. ( ) denotes illegible or damaged areas in a manuscript; when the text for that area is extant elsewhere, it is inserted in the angle brackets and that source cited in the document's source line. { } indicates conjectured readings. [ ] have been used to mark material added to make sense of the narrative— inserted periods and commas, added letters, and so on.

When we have reproduced printed sources, we decided not to intervene with the text, except in rendering headings and closings according to the rules outlined above. In reprinting these texts, we wish to caution readers that sometimes they differ—occasionally a great deal—from the original text (and thus, where possible, we have printed the original text). Source notes indicate the location of printed versions of letters in the *Official Records*.

Annotation has been kept to a minimum; Sherman's letters illuminate each other and need few or no notes. We have forgone the practice favored by other documentary editions of providing capsule biographies of important military and civilian leaders and instead direct interested readers to consult the usual reference resources, which are designed for that purpose. Introductory essays at the beginning of each chapter provide the necessary context for the following documents. Sources for biographical information in footnotes, culled from diverse and sometimes obscure sources, have not been cited. When possible and desirable, the correspondence that preceded or followed a letter has been summarized and quoted. In many cases, Sherman's style of letter writing leaves no doubt as to the nature of the communication to which he is responding.

Symbols and Abbreviations

DESCRIPTIVE SYMBOLS FOR MANUSCRIPTS

AD   Autograph Document
ADS   Autograph Document Signed
ADf   Autograph Draft
ADfS   Autograph Draft Signed
AL   Autograph Letter
ALS   Autograph Letter Signed
D   Document
DS   Document Signed
Df   Draft
DfS   Draft Signed
Lbk   Letterbook
LbkS   Letterbook Signed
L   Letter
LS   Letter Signed

ABBREVIATIONS

Manuscript Repositories
CSmH   Henry E. Huntington Library, San Marino, Calif.
DLC   Library of Congress, Washington, D.C.
DNA   National Archives, Washington, D.C.
InHi   Indiana Historical Society, Indianapolis, Ind.
InNd   University of Notre Dame, Notre Dame, Ind.
MH   Houghton Library, Harvard University, Cambridge, Mass.
MHi   Massachusetts Historical Society, Boston, Mass.
MiU-C   William L. Clements Library, University of Michigan,
            Ann Arbor, Mich.
NjP   Princeton University, Princeton, N.J.
NHi   New-York Historical Society, New York, N.Y.
OFH   Rutherford B. Hayes Library, Fremont, Ohio
OHi   Ohio Historical Society, Columbus, Ohio
PCarlA U.S. Army Military History Institute, Carlisle Barracks, Pa.
PHi   Historical Society of Pennsylvania, Philadelphia, Pa.
PPRF   Rosenbach Foundation, Philadelphia, Pa.

Manuscript Collections

DLC:

  WTS   William T. Sherman Papers, Library of Congress, Washington, D.C.

SFP   Sherman Family Papers, University of Notre Dame,
            Notre Dame, Ind.

Published Works

CWAL   Roy P. Basler, Marion Dolores Pratt, and Lloyd A. Dunlap, eds.,
              The Collected Works of Abraham Lincoln (New Brunswick, 1953–55).

HL   M. A. DeWolfe Howe, ed., *Home Letters of General Sherman*
              (New York, 1909).

OR   *The War of the Rebellion: A Compilation of the Official Records of the
              Union and Confederate Armies* (Washington, D.C., 1880–91).

PM   William T. Sherman, *Personal Memoirs of Gen. W. T. Sherman*,
              4th ed., 2 vols. (New York, 1891).

PUSG   John Y. Simon, ed., *The Papers of Ulysses S. Grant*
              (Carbondale and Edwardsville, 1967–).

Personal Names

EES   Ellen Ewing Sherman
HWH   Henry Wager Halleck
JS   John Sherman
TESr   Thomas Ewing Sr.
USG   Ulysses S. Grant
WTS   William T. Sherman

Sherman's Civil War

CHAPTER 1

November 3, 1860–February 25, 1861

F or William T. Sherman, the breakup of the United States in the secession crisis of 1860–61 could not have come at a worse time. After years of struggling in various civilian pursuits following his resignation from the United States Army in 1853, he had finally found success as the superintendent of the Louisiana State Seminary and Military Academy in Alexandria. Since his arrival in Louisiana in the fall of 1859, he had done much to put the military academy on a sound footing, supervising construction, purchasing books, and overseeing the education and training of a growing student body. Not even the promise of a position as a banker in faraway London, tempting as it was, could pull him away from his new post; rather, he had been looking forward to the day when he could bring the rest of his family to Alexandria. He had spent far too much time away from his wife, Ellen, and his children, who had been residing in Lancaster, Ohio, with Ellen's father (and Sherman's foster father), Thomas Ewing Sr. Now, however, all was jeopardized by national events. "It does seem that the whole world conspires against us," Sherman sadly remarked.[1]

It had not always been this way. Born February 8, 1820, in Lancaster, the sixth child of Charles and Mary Sherman, Tecumseh Sherman was nine years old when his father died. Thomas Ewing, a prominent lawyer and politician who lived up the street from the Shermans, took in the boy; unhappy with the youth's name—it seemed somehow unfitting to be named after an Indian warrior—the Ewings made sure that he was baptized "William." Two years later, Ewing won election to the United States Senate; the clout that came with this position proved helpful in securing an appointment at the United States Military Academy at West Point for the boy known to his friends as Cump. Sherman entered the academy in 1836; upon his graduation in 1840, he ranked sixth in his class and would have ranked even higher but for his indifference to the demerit system. He accepted a commission as a second lieutenant of artillery and over the next six years saw service in Florida during the Second Seminole War followed by tours of duty in Alabama and South Carolina. Transferred to California at the beginning of the Mexican-American War, Sherman failed to see action in the conflict but gained a small slice of immortality as the officer who confirmed the discovery of gold in 1848. On May 1,

1850, he married Ellen Ewing, Thomas Ewing's daughter, in a Washington ceremony attended by many of the nation's most prominent political leaders, who no doubt welcomed the respite from the ongoing debate over sectional issues that culminated in a grand compromise agreement later that year.[2]

The next decade proved a trying one. Ellen did not care for army life and soon decided to return to Lancaster, taking the couple's daughter, Maria (affectionately known as Minnie), with her; soon they were joined by a second girl, Mary Elizabeth (called Lizzie). Sherman cared little for the arrangement, but it soon became evident that he would have to choose between his career and his family and in 1853 he resigned his commission. His first step as a civilian took him back to California, where he engaged in banking. Determined to make it on his own, he resisted his father-in-law's efforts to bring him—or, more accurately, Ellen—back to Ohio; he also welcomed the arrival of his first son, William, in 1854. Financial chaos, the appearance of vigilante violence, and Ellen's desire to return to Lancaster, however, led him to welcome the opportunity to relocate to New York in 1857, only to find himself the victim of the financial panic that spread over the land that fall. Crestfallen, he accepted his father-in-law's offer to manage a coal and saltworks, then took a turn as a lawyer in Kansas while trying to find other ways to make money, secure his independence, and reunite his family (now grown to four children with another boy, Thomas) under his own roof. "I am doomed to be a vagabond," he remarked. "I look upon myself as a dead cock in the pit, not worthy of further notice."[3] It was at this point that the offer of the superintendency promised a solution to his problems.

It was not as if Sherman was unaware of the storm clouds of secession. He had sat in the galleries as Congress debated the terms of the Compromise of 1850 and at one point secured admission to the floor to hear Daniel Webster's farewell address to the Senate. While in California, he had provided pointed commentary on events in Kansas, where proslavery and antislavery forces clashed. That his brother John was making a mark as a member of the new Republican party as a congressman only added to his interest. Cump shared none of his brother's antipathy toward slavery; he despised secessionist fire-eaters and abolitionists alike, even though Ellen's brother Thomas Ewing Jr. practiced antislavery politics. No sooner had he arrived in Louisiana than he found himself an object of suspicious curiosity, for John Sherman had just endorsed Hinton Rowan Helper's tract against slavery, *The Impending Crisis of the South*. Southern congressmen seized on this gaffe to deny Sherman the speakership of the House of Representatives. Cump stuck by his brother but only after reassuring anyone who would listen that John had never read the book.

Sherman had no problem with slavery. "I would not if I could abolish or modify slavery," he told Tom Ewing Jr. "I don't know that I would materially change the actual relation of master and slave. Negroes in the great numbers that exist here must of necessity be slaves"—a remark remarkable for its ignorance of the free black population in New Orleans. Blacks, he argued, would not work except under coercion; they could never claim equality with whites. "All the congresses on earth can't make the negro anything else than he is," he declared. "He must be subject to the white man, or he must amalgamate or be destroyed." He suggested that slave owners might enhance the acceptability of the peculiar institution by adopting reforms to preserve slave families and promote the education of slaves. He even contemplated the purchase of a few slaves as servants for his new home.[4]

But for secession Sherman harbored only hostility. He assailed those Southern politicians who constantly raised the threat of disunion, claiming that they had exaggerated the extent of support for secession in the North. He pledged to resign his post and leave Louisiana should that state leave the Union. In the presidential contest of 1860 he expressed his preference for the candidacy of the Constitutional Unionist John Bell, although in the end he did not vote.

The triumph of Republican nominee Abraham Lincoln, Sherman observed, made secession inevitable, for many Southern whites believed that the new president espoused abolitionist principles. The prospect of disunion, war, and chaos depressed him. Despite the "General Anarchy" that would ensue, a "mad foolish crowd" was determined to destroy the nation. Although Sherman was determined to leave the state should Louisiana secede, he did not know what the future held for him. "I see every chance of long, confused and disorganized Civil war, and I feel no desire to take a hand therein," he remarked. Indeed, he was not sure whether it would be wise to resist secession: only if the states bordering the Mississippi River joined the disunion movement was there a sufficient reason for a war.[5]

Passion and ignorance ruled the day. To one of his instructors at the academy, David F. Boyd, Sherman railed against the insanity of secession. "You, you the people of the South, believe there can be such a thing as peaceable secession. You don't know what you are doing. . . . The country will be drenched in blood. . . . Oh, it is all folly, a crime against civilization." War would be costly, especially to the South. "The North can make a steam-engine, locomotive or railway car; hardly a yard of cloth or shoes can you make. You are rushing into war with one of the most powerful, ingeniously mechanical and determined people on earth—right at your doors. You are bound to fail. Only in your spirit and determination are you prepared for war. In all else you are totally unprepared, with a bad cause to start with. . . . If your people would but stop and think, they must see that in the end you will surely fail."[6]

But the time for sober reflection had passed. "When People believe a delusion they believe it harder than a real fact," Sherman told Minnie. "Men have ceased to reason, and war seems to be courted by those who understand not its costs, and demoralizing results," he observed as Louisiana prepared to secede. "Civilians are far more willing to start a war than Military men and so it appears now." Yet it was also obvious to him that if the politicians had helped bring on the crisis, they would not be able to manage it. "My notion is that this war will ruin all Politicians & that military Leaders will direct the events," he predicted. With that in mind, he left Louisiana on February 24. When next he returned, he would be wearing the uniform of a major general in the United States Army.[7]

1. WTS to EES, December 23, 1860.

2. The best full biographies of Sherman are John F. Marszalek, *Sherman: A Soldier's Passion for Order* (New York, 1993), and Lloyd Lewis, *Sherman: Fighting Prophet* (1932; reprint, Lincoln, Neb., 1993). Michael Fellman's *Citizen Sherman* (New York, 1995) provides an incisive and provocative analysis of Sherman's personality, mentality, and character.

3. Marszalek, *Sherman*, 119.

4. Lewis, *Sherman*, 119, 120, 129.

5. WTS to EES, November 3, 23, 1860, January 8, 1861; WTS to JS, December 9, 1860.

6. Lewis, *Sherman*, 138.

7. WTS to Minnie Sherman, December 15, 1860; WTS to George M. Graham, January 16, 1861; WTS to JS, January 18, 1861.

TO ELLEN EWING SHERMAN

Louisiana State Seminary of Learning
and Military Academy.
Alexandria, Novr. 3, 1860

Dearest Ellen,

This is Saturday evening, and I am seated at the office table where the Academic Board has been all week examining Cadets[.] We have admitted in all some eighty and rejected about a dozen, for want of the elementary knowledge required for admission.[1] Tonight Saturday we close the business and on Monday Recitations begin. Still Many more will straggle in, and I expect we will settle down to about a hundred and twenty, less than we had reason to expect, but quite enough for comfort.

Joe[2] got here on Monday last and is here, helping receive, unpack and distribute stores, and he helps blow the calls—a Bugler I picked up in New Orleans, a kind of circus man. I hardly know what to do with Joe and he will be on my hands till something turns up. I had him make a list of the contents of some boxes, but his spelling is so bad that I cannot get him to help me in writing—I will take two of the Cadets for that purpose but what with treasurers accounts and the voluminous Correspondence I fear I will not be able to take reasonable exercise.

Poor Clay has fallen away much and I have him fed on oats at about a dollar a bushel, & hay $60 a ton but he dont appear to appreciate it—I have not had a chance to ride him this week, but made Joe take him to exercise this afternoon. Tomorrow Sunday also I must write all the day and Same next week, but then I hope to take some relief. Our House has now the 2nd coat of plaster all save the lower hall and as the scaffolding is removed it looks very well. The house will be good in every respect, and I hope to drive the Plasterer away in ten days—the Carpenter can finish up in ten more days and the painting ought not to take more than a month, so that by Christmas it will be done. A fence has to be built—I intend if affairs move along slowly—to furnish it in part, and occupy it by January—At present we have our old mess which smacks of the same old pork Grease—The Country is very poor and nothing can be bought here but stewed beef & pork—vegetables are out of the question save Potatoes at about $5 the barrel. Professors Vallas[3] & St. Ange[4] still are ugly, but I dont expect much trouble—only as the Board have divided my authority I will take less interest in details. People here now talk as though Disunion was a fixed thing—men of property say that as this constant feeling of danger of abolitionism exists they would rather try a Southern Confederacy—Louisiana would not secede but should South Carolina secede, I fear other Southern states will follow, and soon General Anarchy will prevail—I say but little, try & mind my own business, and await the issue of Events.

Sunday—here I was interrupted and occupied till bedtime and postponed balance to this Sunday—The day is beautiful—I have taken a long stroll embracing the new Houses which more & more please me on each visit—I think them admirably planned, and adapted to the circumstances & climate. Joe has gone to church and so have the Professors and many of the Cadets. Bye the way—Dr. Clark[5] our Surgeon a young gentleman (engaged to Miss Boyce[6] en confidence) has asked me to convey to you the assurances of his distinguished respect & consideration, and his wish that you Shd. hurry down—he says on his way south he fell in with Wash Young,[7] and by a mere accident they found we were mutual acquaintances—Wash of course spoke well of me, but of you he deal in panegyric especially on the Subject of Eucre,[8] and Dr. Clark says of all things Eucre is his delight—he is very young say 23—a real London Cockney in dress and manner, but withal a well bred Gentleman a la Paris. We dont play cards in the College Building, so you may count on as much Eucre as you please of evenings. I think our house will be ready Christmas but with the Exception of general preparation, I ask nothing till November is passed. I think Joe is disposed to be well pleased, and every body here likes his appearance. He thinks his sister would be benefitted by this climate. I feel very well indeed—and am free of cold or asthma—I notice with much pleasure what you say of the children. Affectionately,

W. T. Sherman

ALS, InND: Sherman Family Papers.

1. This was the beginning of the second year of the academy's operations.

2. Joe Miller had come to Alexandria from Lancaster, Ohio, as WTS's servant.

3. Anthony Vallas, a Hungarian who had fled his country during the revolution of 1848, was professor of mathematics and philosophy at the academy.

4. E. Berte St. Ange, a former marine in the French navy, was professor of French and modern languages.

5. Powhatan Clark was assistant professor of chemistry.

6. Louise Boyce was the daughter of Henry Boyce, an old friend of Sherman's who had been made the United States district judge for western Louisiana in 1850.

7. Possibly George Washington Young, Maryland's largest slaveholder and Hugh Boyle Ewing's father-in-law.

8. A card game.

TO ELLEN EWING SHERMAN

Louisiana State Seminary of Learning and Military Academy.
Alexandria, Novr. 10, 1860

Dearest Ellen,

We have had a week of cold stormy rains, but it has cleared off and today is bright and warm. I am going into town today and will leave this at the Post office—The Election came off on Tuesday and resulted in Alexandria for a majority for Breckinridge[1]—next Bell[2]—next Douglas[3]—Of course there were no votes for Lincoln[.][4] Indeed he has no ticket in this State—I received a note from a friend advising me to vote[5]—I thought the matter over, and concluded I would not vote—Technically I was entitled to a vote, as I entered Louisiana just a year ago, but I thought I ought not to vote in this election, and did not— I would have preferred Bell, but I think he has no chance, and I do not wish to be subject to any political conditions[.] If I am to hold my place by a political Tenure I prefer again to turn vagabond—I would not be surprised to learn that my not voting was construed into a friendly regard for Lincoln, and that it might result in my being declared a public Enemy. I Shall however rest under a belief that now as the Election is over, all this hard feeling will subside and peace once more settle on the Country. We have no Returns as yet— Maybe the mail tonight will bring some returns from New York, Pennsylvania & Ohio, those large states that determine this Election, but I do not count on any clear Knowledge till next Monday.

We began our Recitations last Monday and things have settled down into order & system. Joe is with me, and occasionally blows a call, but generally is employed as about my office—his expenses are at my cost, and I hardly know how to place him.

The plastering of the houses was much delayed by the stormy weather, but hope this will be done in ten days. As many more will enable the Carpenters to finish the Interior, and the painter will occupy as much more—allowing for delays and usual interruptions I think the House will be ready before Christmas—Before December 1, I will tell you exactly what is best to be done—I hate to have you come as it were on a mere visit but I dont know but that is the wisest course—we have been too much separated already and its Effect has not been good, but that is past and cannot be helped.

No matter which way we turn there arises difficulties which seem insurmountable—In case Lincoln is elected, they Say S. Carolina will secede and that the Southern States will not see her forced back—Secession must result in Civil War, anarchy and ruin to our present form of Government—but if it is attempted it would be unwise for us to be here: But I still hope for quiet.

All the cadets are now quartered, clothed and at their lessons. I can now give more of my time to our private interests—I enclose a slip from a tax receipt which gives a description of that 40 acre piece in Illinois. I know the Deed is recorded, and I feel certain I sent it to St. Louis to either Obear or Sherman, for you remember they once effected a sale, and you would not execute the Deed. I have looked everywhere for the Deed, and though I find a sketch, and other description of it, I know I had the Deed at Leavenworth. Let Phil[6] prepare for you such a deed as will ensure the property to you, and either send it to me for execution or bring it as you may think best.

Give my love to all the Children I am quite well. affectionately yrs.

W. T. Sherman

ALS, InND: Sherman Family Papers.

1. John C. Breckinridge (1821–75) of Kentucky, vice president of the United States (1857–61), ran for president on the Southern Democratic ticket.

2. John Bell (1797–1869) of Tennessee ran as a Constitutional Unionist.

3. U.S. senator Stephen A. Douglas (1813–61) of Illinois was the Northern Democratic candidate.

4. Republican candidate Abraham Lincoln (1809–65) won the presidential election of 1860 without carrying a single slave state.

5. George Mason Graham wrote to Sherman on November 5 to urge him to vote, saying that others would think he supported Lincoln if he did not cast a vote for someone else. SFP.

6. Philemon Beecher Ewing (1820–96) was Ellen Sherman's brother and a lawyer in Lancaster, Ohio.

Louisiana State Seminary of Learning
and Military Academy.
Alexandria, Novr. 23, 1860

My Dearest Ellen,

We are having a cold raw day, and I avail myself of it to do a good deal of indoor work. I was out for some hours directing the making of the fence around our new house, but the work within perused very slowly indeed—Our House is all plastered, and the Carpenters are putting in the doors, windows and casings. Also the Painter is tinkering around, but at present rate, the building will not be ready before Christmas. I now have all arrangements made for your coming down about that time, but prudence dictates some caution, as political events do seem portentous. I have a letter from the Cashier that he sent you the First of exchange, the second I now enclose to you for $290. But by the very mail which brought it came the rumor that the Banks were refusing exchange on the North, which cannot be true. Also that Goods were being destroyed on the Levee in New Orleans and that the Custom House was closed. I also notice that many Gentlemen, who were heretofore moderate in their opinions now begin to fall into the popular current and go with the mad foolish crowd that Seems bent on a dissolution of this Confederacy—The extremists in this Quarter took the first news of the election of Lincoln so coolly, that I took it for granted all would quietly await the issue— but I have no doubt that Politicians have so embittered the feelings of the People, that they think the Republican party is bent on abolitionism and they cease to reason or think of consequences. We are so retired up here, so much out of the way of news, that we hear nothing but stale exaggerations, but I feel that a change is threatened, and I will wait patiently for a while. My opinions are not changed. If the South is bent on dissolution of course I will not ally our fate with theirs, because by dissolution they do not escape the very danger at which they grow so frantically mad. Slavery is in their midst and must continue but the interest of slavery is much weaker in Missouri, Kentucky, Virginia & Maryland than down here. Should the Ohio River become a Boundary between the two new Combinations, then will begin a new change. The extreme South will look on Kentucky & Tennessee as the North, and in a very few years the Same confusion & disorder will arise, and a new dissolution, till each state, and may be each county will claim separate Independence. If South Carolina precipitate this Revolution, it will be because she thinks by delay Lincoln's friends will kind of reconcile the middle wavering states, whereas now they may raise the cry of abolition and unite all the slave states. I had no idea that this would actually begin so soon, but the news from that

Quarter does look as though she certainly would secede, and that Alabama, Georgia, Florida & Texas would follow suit—all these might go, and Still leave a strong rich Confederated Government—but then comes Mississipi and Louisiana. As these rest on the Mississipi and control its mouth, I know that the other States north will not submit to any molestation of the navigation by foreign states—If these two States go and Arkansas follows suit, then there must be war—fighting, and that will continue till one or the other party is subdued. If Louisiana call a convention I will not move, but if that convention resolves to secede on a contingency that I can foresee, then I must of course quit. It is not to be expected that the State would consent to trust me with arms & command if I did not go with them full lengths—I dont believe Louisiana would of herself do anything—but if S. Carolina, Georgia, Alabama, Mississipi & Texas resolve no longer to wait, then Louisiana will do likewise. Then of course you will be safe where you are. As to myself I might have to go to California, or some foreign Country, where I could earn the means of living for you & myself. I see no chance in Ohio for me. A man is never a prophet in his own land and it does seem that nature for some wise purposes, may be to Settle wild lands does ordain that men shall migrate, clear out from the place of their birth.

I did not intend to write so much but the day is gloomy, and the last news from New Orleans, decidedly so, if true—Among ourselves it is Known that I am opposed to disunion in any manner or form—Prof. Smith[1] d[itt]o, unless Lincoln should actually encourage abolitionism after installed in office—Mr. Boyd[2] thinks the denial to the Southern People of access to new Territories is an insult to which they cannot submit with honor, and Should not let the consequences be what they may[.] Dr. Clark is simply willing to follow the fortunes of the South, be they what they may. Vallas & St. Ange, Foreigners dont care—but will follow their immediate self interests.

Thus we stand, about a fair sample of a mixed crowd—but tis now said all over the South this issue is made, and better secession now, when they can, then wait till it is too late. This is a most unfortunate condition of things for us, and I hardly know how to act with decency and firmness, and like most undecided men, will wait awhile to See what others do. If feeling in S.C. continues, they must do something, else they will be the laughing stock of the world—and that is what they dread, for of all the States they can least afford to secede, as comparatively she is a weak & poor state. This on the contrary is destined to be a Rich & powerful one. Love to all,

W. T. Sherman

ALS, InND: Sherman Family Papers.
1. Francis W. Smith, a graduate of the Virginia Military Institute and the University of

Virginia, was professor of chemistry at the academy; he would serve in the Confederate army and was killed in April 1865 during Lee's final retreat from Richmond.

2. Professor David F. Boyd taught French and other modern languages.

TO ELLEN EWING SHERMAN

> Louisiana State Seminary of Learning
> and Military Academy.
> Alexandria, Novr. 26, 1860

Dearest Ellen,

I commenced writing a letter last night to Minnie, but a friend sent us out a newspaper of New Orleans Nov. 22, which had come up from New Orleans in a Boat. For some reason the papers come to us very irregularly. The stage whenever it has passengers leaves behind the Paper mail, and only brings the Bags when there are few or no passengers. Well of late though letters come about as usual our papers come along very straggling—well this newspaper so received brings inteligence how true I know not of a panic in New York— Baltimore Virginia and every where.¹ Of Course panics are the necessary consequence of the Mammoth Credit System, the habit of borrowing which pervades our Country, and though panics transfer losses to the wrong shoulders still they do good.

But along with this comes the Cause, the assertion that South Carolina will secede *certain*, Georgia do. and Alabama. Mississipi will of course and with her Arkansas & Texas. This will leave Louisiana no choice. If these premises be true, then indeed is there abundant cause for panic, disorder, confusion Ruin & Civil War. I am determined not to believe it, till to withold belief would be stupidity—This paper also announces that Governor Moore² has called the Legislature together for Decr. 10, and specially to consider the crisis of the Country, and to Call a Convention.

You know that the Theory of our Government is, as construed by southern Politicians that a state, one or more may withdraw from the Union, without molestation, and unless excitement abates Louisiana will follow the lead of her neighbors—You will hear by Telegraph the action of the Conventions of South Carolina & Alabama—Should they assert their right to Secede, and initiate measures to that end, then you may infer that I will countermand my heretofore preparations for a move—Then it would be unsafe even for you to come south. For myself I will not go with the South in a Disunion movement, and as my position at the head of a State Military College would necessarily infer fidelity and allegiance to the State as against the United States, my duty will be on the first positive act of Disunion to give notice of my purpose.

December 10 the Legislature meets[.] It is hardly possible a Convention will be called before January, and until the Convention acts, the State is not committed. Still I think the tone of feeling in the Legislature will give me a Clue to the future.

I confess I feel uneasy from these events, and more so from the fact that the inteligence comes so piecemeal and unsatisfactory. Yrs. affectionately,

W. T. Sherman

ALS, InND: Sherman Family Papers.
1. There had been a financial panic in New York City on November 12 causing heavy selling on the New York Stock Exchange with a steep decline in prices.
2. Thomas O. Moore (1803–76) had been elected governor of Louisiana earlier that year.

TO ELLEN EWING SHERMAN

Louisiana State Seminary of Learning
and Military Academy.
Alexandria, Novr. 29, 1860

Dearest Ellen,

This is a Holiday—Thanksgiving & prayer, but holidays & Sundays are my worst days as then the Cadets are idle and mischievous.

Governor Moore has issued his proclamation calling the Legislature together for Decr. 10, and the Proclamation is couched in ugly language, different from his usual more conservative tone. It is manifest to me now that the Leading Politicians of the State have conferred together and have agreed to go out of the Union, or at all events to favor the new Doctrine of Secession—The Legislature will determine the call of a convention, and the convention will divide very much according to the other events that may occur in the meantime—This imposes on us a change of purpose and it will not do for you or any one to come south unless this state of feeling changes—I know the Governor and believe him an Excellent thermometer of the political Atmosphere of Louisiana—I hear that business is dead in New Orleans, all of which is an evidence that the abolitionists have succeeded in bringing on that "Irresistible Conflict."

I am sick of this everlasting subject[.] The truth has nothing to do with this world—Here they know that all you in Ohio have to do is to steal niggers and in Ohio though the people are quiescent yet they believe that the South are determined to enlarge the area of niggers—Like Burton in Toodles I say Damn the Niggers—I wish they were anywhere or be kept at their work.

I observe more signs of a loosened discipline here—Boys are careless and last night because the Supper did not please them, they smashed the crockery & made a riot generally—Pistols were fired which scared Joe very much—his education has been neglected, but I think he will get used to it—We have dismissed five Cadets and others must share their fate—I fear the Institution is in danger from causes which arose after I left last summer.[1] The alterations made after I left were wrong in principle causing Genl. Graham[2] to resign, and since then he will take no interest in our affairs. Govr. Moore is intent on Politics, same of Dr. Smith[3]—so we are left to the chances of the caprices of a panel of wild Boys. Still this is a small matter susceptable of remedy, but the Secession movement underlays the very safety of everything.

I have just received your letter about the vulgarities practiced at the Common schools.[4] I regret the imperfections of these Schools, but the Question is—have you any better—Education is in part compulsory, and can only be imparted early—If the boys in Lancaster are not worse than other boys, what you say wont happen long, for some boy will take the matter up and thrash the offenders. As to the morals & religion of boys, you must guard that at home—same of Girls—I wish we had a choice, but I see none—If we ultimately settle here, we will have no schools at all, and the boys here are a hundred times worse than in Lancaster.

Every servant Girl you get will be carried off by siege in three months, and even Children are liable to be corrupted. I was in hopes, in Lancaster boys had not reached that progress in Civilization & Christianity but it seems they Keep up with the Times. I can only say that I know our Children will soon have to shift for themselves—it is in the order of nature—with some education they Stand a better chance, than without. If to avoid contact with immoral & vulgar boys you deprive them of the opportunity to read. . . .

AL (incomplete), InND: Sherman Family Papers.

1. Vallas and St. Ange had been successful in changing the academy's curriculum to a more liberal arts–oriented program than the traditional military one with the backing of parents who thought Sherman was too strict with cadets.

2. George M. Graham, half-brother of Richard B. Mason, Sherman's army commander and friend in California, had been on the original Board of Supervisors for the academy. A supporter of both Sherman and a military curriculum, he had resigned in the wake of the recent changes at the institution.

3. Dr. S. A. Smith (died ca. 1874), a member of the state senate, had replaced Graham on the Board of Supervisors; he would become a surgeon in the Confederate army and medical director of the Trans-Mississippi Department by the end of the war.

4. EES to WTS, November 21, 1860, SFP. The boy who sat next to Sherman's daughter Minnie at the school in Lancaster had been making "the *most indecent exposure of his person*" to her. Also, boys were urinating on girls through a hole in the fence as they went to their bathrooms, and a teacher of the older girls made passes at his students and had allegedly impregnated one. Ellen wanted Sherman's opinion as to whether she should withdraw their children and teach them at home, since he had wanted them to attend the public school; implied was the argument that such behavior would not be tolerated at a Catholic school.

TO THOMAS EWING SR.[1]

Louisiana State Seminary of Learning
and Military Academy
Alexandria, Decr. 1, 1860

Hon. Thos. Ewing

Dear Sir

Since I last wrote you I have observed a marked change in public opinion here—I was in town all day yesterday, with a Dr. Smith, Senator in the State Legislature, who is the Vice President of our Board of Supervisors and who is just from New Orleans—He is originally from Kentucky, but was an active supporter of Breckinridge in this state. He tells me he was surprised at the tone of feeling in New Orleans, which he described, and which I find corroborated by the Editorials of all the leading City papers. All go to the effect that secession is a sure thing, the only questions being the times when and how. Immediate Secession, unqualified and unconditional is the prevailing sentiment, the Bell party going even further than the Breckinridge adherents. Dr. Smith will attend the Session of the Legislature next week, the 10th inst, and says the calling of a convention will be the first and inevitable step—this will be he says unanimous—next the arming of the state, and putting herself in an attitude of defense—to this he says there will be no opposition. The convention will meet in January and the Questions submitted to them will be immediate Secession, or a General convention of all southern states, Louisiana to instruct her Delegates, to demand that the Northern States shall repeal the Laws adverse to slavery, and give pledges of future good behavior—Dr. S. thinks it will be all the Conservative men of this state will attempt, to carry this latter alternative against the adherents of the immediate secession: but I told him that for the South to demand of the North such conditions would be idle. The machinery of a Democratic Government is too slow, to bring about such pledges under a pressure when public feeling cannot be moulded by men—It occurs to me that Texas might withdraw from the Confederation, resuming her status as before the Treaty[2]—It might be that S. Carolina, Georgia Alabama and Florida might also fall out, & arrange by Treaty for the break of our Commercial Sea bond, but the moment Mississipi Arkansas, & Louisiana declare an independence, sovereign & complete, with a right to control, interrupt or tax the Commerce of the Mississipi, justly and fairly a storm would arise in those states bordering on the Territories, that would be fearful as compared with anything heretofore known on this Continent. They argue, however as their policy will be free trade, no possible interruption can occur to the usual navigation: but however they may start, some tax and obstruction will result, and then of course retaliation & war.

Now for myself I have told the Governor & all in Authority that as long as Louisiana is a part of the United States I will serve here in my present sphere, and moreover in case of domestic insurrection or molestation from without, I will head the Cadets under my Command, but that I will do no act inconsistent with my allegiance to the General Government: that as long as the form of Govt. indicated by the Constitution of the U.S. is in existence, that I will stand by it—As I have no other means of existence now save this, I will stay here till the Convention meets and does some act of Treason. Then I shall quit—but when to go is a question I cannot solve, and must trust to the confusion that must result from the dissolution of this Govt. I must therefore change my whole plan, and leave Ellen where she is, till this storm either subsides, or passes away, or until I can do something else: If I leave here suddenly & unexpectedly, I will fetch up at St. Louis—Clay has been very sick, is so still, but I begin to have hopes. Give Ellen the benefit of your advice as to probabilities &c—I am in good health but must have continuous and active employment. as ever with respect,

W. T. Sherman

ALS, DLC: Thomas Ewing and Family Papers.

1. Thomas Ewing Sr. (1789–1871), Ellen's father and Sherman's foster father, was a former United States senator and cabinet member in several administrations who still practiced law before the Supreme Court.

2. WTS is thinking of the annexation treaty entered into between Texas and the United States, designed to bring Texas into the Union. Although President Tyler signed it in 1844, the Senate turned it down. Its terms, however, formed the basis for the annexation resolution granting Texas statehood, which was passed by Congress in March 1845 and implemented the following December.

TO JOHN SHERMAN[1]

Louisiana State Seminary of Learning
and Military Academy.
Alexandria, Decr. 1, 1860.

Dear Brother,

When I last wrote you I had observed what I thought a general quiet, and determination to submit as heretofore to the General Election of Lincoln,[2] and as the House which has been under construction for me was drawing to a completion I gave Ellen notice to hold herself ready to start about the 15 instant with all the family, so as to get out of Ohio before the close of the River, and to take advantage of the present condition of Red River. But the whole case has changed. The quiet which I thought the usual acquiescence of the People was merely the prelude to the storm of opinion that now seems irresistable—Politicians have by hearing the prejudices of the people, and moving with the current have succeeded in destroying the Government—It cannot be stopped now I fear—I was in Alexandria all day yesterday, and had a full and unreserved conversation with Dr. S. A. Smith, State Senator, who is a man of education, property, influence and qualified to Judge—He was during the canvas a Breckinridge man, but though a Southern in opinion is really opposed to a dissolution of our Government. He has returned from New Orleans where he says he was amazed to See evidences of Public sentiment which could not be mistaken—The Legislature meets Dec. 10—at Baton Rouge—the calling a Convention forthwith is to be unanimous—the Bill for arming the State ditto—The Convention will meet in January, and only two questions will be agitated—Immediate dissolution, a declaration of State Independence, a General Convention of Southern States with instructions to demand of the Northern States to repeal all laws hostile to Slavery, and pledges of future good behavior.

Of course this latter demand cannot from the nature of an anarchical Democratic Government ever be entertained & therefore if these things be so, and all the Public prints of New Orleans confirm these views of Dr. Smith, Uncle Sam is already a Sick old man—whether the South or North be benefitted is a question that no man can solve—If Texas would draw off, no great harm would follow—Even if S. Carolina, Georgia, Alabama & Florida would cut away, it might be the rest could get along, but I think the secession of Mississipi, Louisiana and Arkansas will bring war—for though they now say that Free trade is their Policy yet it wont be long before steamboats will be taxed and molested all the way down. Therefore when the Convention meets in January, as they will assuredly do, and resolve to secede, or to elect members to a General Convention with instructions inconsistent with the nature of things I must quit this place for it is neither right for me to Stay nor would the Governor be justified in placing me in this position of Trust for the moment Louisiana assumes a position of hostility then this becomes an arsenal & fort. I wont move however until the last moment for I am at a loss what else to do. I will watch the proceedings of Congress with deep interest, and catch at the first chance of reconciliation—Let me hear the moment you think dissolution is inevitable. What Mississipi and Georgia do, this State will do likewise. Affectionately,

W. T. S.

ALS, DLC: William T. Sherman.

1. John Sherman (1823–1900), WTS's brother and closest sibling, was a Republican congressman from Ohio at this time.

2. On October 23, WTS had written JS, "If Lincoln be elected, I dont apprehend resistance, and if he be as Mr. Ewing say a reasonable moderate man things may move on, & the South become gradually reconciled." Still, Ewing's and JS's identification with Lincoln

would make WTS more "'Suspect'" in Louisiana. WTS would leave the state if he could, but in the absence of other opportunities he planned to stay, keeping a low profile and concentrating on his work. DLC: WTS.

TO JOHN SHERMAN

Louisiana State Seminary of Learning
and Military Academy.
Alexandria, Dec. 9, 1860

Dear Brother,

I am in receipt of yours from Mansfield.[1] I have also just seen an extract of the Presidents message—mails are very irregular and we have a foretaste of that confusion that will follow the disruption of our Government. Our whole Government is based on the idea that the People are always good & virtuous. Consequently it has always been the case that prejudice and popular caprices could overrule and override the Law. In the North you cannot enforce the fugitive slave law—in the South you cannot punish a man or set of men who hang another on a naked suspicion of being unsound on the Slavery question, or on a Filibustering scheme—These are mere illustrations of the same fact that you cannot enforce the Laws when in the locality there is a prejudice. I have an idea that all attempts at Reconciliation will fail—that S. Carolina will secede, and that other States will follow and that a change of violence is to begin not affecting the Slavery alone, but all other interests, property, representations &c.

I think it would be folly to liberate or materially modify the condition of the Slaves. Their labor & its fruits are necessary to the civilized world, and American slavery is the most modified form of compulsory labor. Any tampering with it is unkind to the negros, and causes the very natural outburst of passion of the whites—But if States secede on this pretext, it will be of course only the beginning of the end. Slavery is common to all Southern States—Let secession once take place on that point, and let these States attempt to combine they will discover that there are other interests not so easily reconciled—and then their troubles will begin[.] For this reason I will not stay South if Louisiana secedes from the Union—as long as she is in the Union I will presume she will remain, but the moment she cuts loose even by a Declaration, I must settle up my affairs here and start again, the fourth time in the last four years. Each time from Calamity—California, New York, Leavenworth & now Louisiana but the recent Financial affairs make me more & more content that I am unconnected with Banking & Credit, the most disastrous of all vocations. If Louisiana Secede I will quietly settle up here, and proceed by steamboat to St. Louis. The Legislature is now in session—The Convention will be called in January, and if some great Change do not occur in the meantime, or unless I am wrongly informed this State will follow S. Carolina, Georgia, Alabama & Mississipi. This will disorganize the whole army, and resignations without number will occur: if a chance offer got me a place in the Inspector Genl. Dept. or in the Adjut. Generals Department—If these States slide off, better let them go—reorganize the East Middle & West, but not west of the Rocky Mountains in a Compact strong Republic. Let California Oregon (damaged) & New Mexico slide into their original obscurity—if S. Carolina alone secede we might depend on her feeling the absurdity of her position and coming back humbled & subdued—but if all the Southern States Secede, twould be folly to coerce. The only feasible plan would be to make a compact confederacy of states, that have common binding self interests to hold them together. I will not send for Ellen as long as this condition of things lasts, and I would not stay here long if I had employment elsewhere that would maintain my family. Colonel Jo. Taylor,[2] Brother of Zachary, was very friendly to me in Washington. He married Judge McLean's[3] daughter I think—but he may go with the South in this question, as I hear his nephew, the Generals son[4] who owns a plantation in this State is firm for secession. Many of my personal friends here say that this Slavery Question *must* be settled *now*, and they demand certain promises from the northern Legislatures that I do not believe can be obtained by coaxing or force, & therefore that Such conditions cannot be had, they think they ought to combine for common safety. Maj. Townsend,[5] Buell,[6] and Shiras[7] are all friendly and would give you notice of any opening, but if we are on the eve of Revolution—the past will all be buried, and new men & new leaders will arise, to be swept away by succeeding tides. I (damaged) wish I were where I could watch events, but I cannot offer to give up present means of livelihood—Yrs.

W. T. Sherman

ALS, DLC: William T. Sherman.

1. On November 26, JS wrote discussing the election results, which he had predicted, and secession, declaring that the South should submit to electoral will. He also offered to do what he could with the new secretary of war to get WTS back into the regular army. DLC: WTS.

2. Lieutenant Colonel Joseph P. Taylor (1796–1864), brother of the late president, stayed with the Union. He had been serving in the U.S. Army since 1841 as assistant commissary general and became commissary general in 1861 and brigadier general in 1863.

3. John McLean (1785–1861) of Ohio had served in Congress, on the Ohio State Supreme Court, and as postmaster general before President Andrew Jackson appointed him to the Supreme Court in 1830.

4. Richard Taylor (1826–79) would vote for secession at the Louisiana Convention the next month; he then joined the Confederate army and reached the rank of lieutenant general in May 1864. Both he and his uncle had welcomed WTS to Louisiana.

5. Edward D. Townsend (1817–93) of the Adjutant General's Office, who would become General Winfield Scott's chief of staff in March 1861.

6. Don Carlos Buell (1818–98) was also in the Adjutant General's Office at this time.

7. Alexander E. Shiras (1812–75), a former instructor at West Point, was in the Commissary General's Office. He served there through the war and was also on the United States Sanitary Commission.

TO MARIA BOYLE EWING SHERMAN[1]

> Louisiana State Seminary of Learning
> and Military Academy.
> Alexandria, Dec. 15, 1860

Dearest Minnie

I have been intending to write you a good long letter and now I wish I could send you all something for Christmas—but I all along thought Mama, and you and Lizzy, Willy Tom & all[2] would be here in our New House, by New Years day. The House is all done, only some little painting to be done. The stable is finished but Poor Clay has been very sick. He is very poor. Sometimes I think he looks better & then again worse—All animals coming from the North to the South have to undergo a change. I thought that was what ailed Clay, but I know now he has distemper, and may be {Glanders}. At all Events I am afraid Clay will never live in the new stable which I built for him. He is still in the Old Stable belonging to the Seminary, whereas the new one is near the New House about four hundred yards distant. I have just had finished a plain board fence around the New House, 200 feet front by 330 deep. In the middle of which stands the House. In the front yard are growing some small oak trees to give shade in the hot summer days. Now however it is raw and cold, the leaves are off, and it looks like winter though thus far we have had no snow. Maybe we will have snow at Christmas. In the back yard I have prepared for a Small Garden, but the soil is poor and will not produce much except early peas, lettuce, turnips and sweet potatos. The House itself looks beautiful, two Front porches, and one back—All the windows open down to the floor like doors, so that you can walk out on the Porch, Either up stairs or down stairs. I Know you would all like the House so much—but my Dear little Minnie, Man proposes and God disposes—What I have been planning so long and patiently, and thought we were all on the point of realizing, the dream and hope of my life, that we could all be together once more, in a home of our own, with peace, and quiet & plenty around us, all I fear is about to vanish and again I fear I must be a wanderer leaving you all to grow up at Lancaster without your papa. Men are blind & crazy, they think all the people of Ohio are trying to steal their slaves & incite them to rise up and kill their masters. I know this is a delusion—but when People believe a delusion they believe it harder than a real fact, and these People in the South are going for this delusion, to break up the Government under which we live. You Cannot understand this but Mama will explain it to you—Our Governor here has gone so far now that he cannot change—and in a month maybe you will be living under one Government, and I another—This cannot last long, and as I know it is best for you all to stay in Lancaster, I will not bring you down here at all, unless some very great change takes place. If this were only a plain college I could stay with propriety, but it is an arsenal with guns and powder, and balls—and were I to Stay here I might have to fight for Louisiana & against Ohio. That would hardly do—You would not like that I know—and yet I have been asked to do it. But I hope still this will yet pass away, and that our House and garden will yet see us all united here in Louisiana.

Mama tells me you have sore throat but I hope it will be well long before this gets to Lancaster, and that you will have nice times at Christmas. Tell Lizzie & Willy and Tommy that Mama tells me all about them in her letters. Your loving Papa—

W. T. Sherman

ALS, OHi: William T. Sherman Papers.
1. Maria Boyle Ewing Sherman (1851–1913) was WTS's eldest child.
2. Mary Elizabeth Sherman (1852–1925), William Tecumseh Sherman Jr. (1854–63), Thomas Ewing Sherman (1859–1915), and Eleanor Mary Sherman (1859–1915), Sherman's other children at this time.

TO HUGH B. EWING[1]

Louisiana State Seminary of Learning
and Military Academy.
Alexandria, Dec. 18 1860

Dear Hugh

I have received your letter which is in my office not sixty steps off, but I am too old Fogyish to pass along the Gallery in view of a sentinel in my gown and Slippers & therefore answer it without a second Reading.

Your fathers guarantee is better than that 2nd mortgage, and therefore merits no objection from me. But the money is Ellen's; and I know she cannot afford to risk anything and therefore I must say that for her sake I prefer that note should not pass into third hands *now*.

This state, & Mississipi and Arkansas will secede from the Union in all January. St. Louis will feel the blow as much as any City in our country. The makers of that note Hanencamp & Hines, may prefer to let the note go by default & with it the property—Now Ellen holds two other notes, and if this note of the series falls into third hands, they may obtain all the security, viz. the 7 Morgan Street lots—You cannot imagine such a catastrophe—I can—and I say it is not only possible but probable.

It seems to me either we are all dreaming, the people are dreaming, the Legislature is mad or Louisiana will declare herself independent within 40 days. The convention meets Jan. 23. & those who were in the Legislature last week were almost unanimous for secession.[2] They appropriated unanimously half a million for arms, and this is one of the arsenals, and if I Stay here after she declares herself independent & hostile, then I am in the nature of a Traitor to Uncle Sam. Poverty may drive a man to any extreme, but I hope I may feel able to escape that fate. I shall hold on to the last minute solely for the pay. You & Your father also take to borrowing so easily, that I fear you will be illy prepared for the crash that must follow the general chaos. I did have hope till I noticed that Buchanan failed to reinforce Anderson.[3] Had he sent thither a large force, instead of being a threat, it would have made Southern states respect a Government, which they now regard as too pusillanimous to be worth saving. To abandon Robt. Anderson at Fort Moultrie is fatal, and no doubt Genl. Cass so regarded it.[4] It has the same effect as Johnsons abandoning the Jail in San Francisco.[5] I feel deeply the absolute importance of protecting Ellens means as far as possible, for I know not where I will turn up again, or how long it may be before I can again provide the means she must have for the support of herself & children. If you must use that note, why so be it—if you can possibly hold on to maturity, only some weeks now, do so for mercy's sake, lest it should not be paid. If not paid it could be a *first* lien, and I see no chance of saving the balance. In case of a general break up, the makers of that note however solvent will ask themselves—is the Property worth what remains due—some $6000? and their conclusion may be, it is not—I Know you regard me as an alarmist but I think I have reason.

I thought I had saved something here, as I failed to ask for a $500 due me as "Supt. in charge" of this arsenal, till I wanted it for my new House—when I did ask for it at Baton Rouge I discovered that though the Salary was created by law, the money was not specifically appropriated, and therefore I cannot draw it until the close of the next Legislature which will not be till next spring, when the State will have drained her Treasury for defences & arms, and therefore I regard it as a very bad egg.

Clay is fast sinking of a distemper—I will try the desperate remedy of tracheaotomy tomorrow, but there is not one chance in ten of recovery now. I have done all in my power to save him. Money matters are very bad here and every where. The universal system of credit is as fatal as the anarchical form of all our Governments. They will require a terrible remedy—Congratulate yourself that at least you & yours are in a snug retired Corner, where personal danger cannot come—Love to Henrietta[6] Yrs. affectionately

W. T. Sherman

ALS, OHi: William T. Sherman Papers.

1. Hugh Boyle Ewing (1826–1905), Ellen's brother, was a lawyer.

2. On December 10, 1860, the Louisiana state legislature had called for a secession convention to begin meeting on January 23, 1861.

3. Major Robert Anderson (1805–71) had been asking for reinforcements to Fort Moultrie and garrisons for Fort Sumter since he assumed command there in November. After a December 10 meeting with President James Buchanan, the South Carolina congressional delegation was reporting that the Federal government would not act on Anderson's requests.

4. Secretary of State Lewis Cass had resigned from James Buchanan's cabinet on December 12, 1860, in protest of the president's refusal to reinforce Anderson.

5. In May 1856, California governor J. Neely Johnson proved unable to prevent the San Francisco Vigilance Committee from taking justice into its own hands when its members broke into the city jail, seized James Casey, a newspaper editor who had killed a rival editor who had revealed Casey's criminal record, and lynched him. At the time Sherman headed the city's militia.

6. Henrietta Young Ewing had married Hugh in 1858.

TO ELLEN EWING SHERMAN

> Louisiana State Seminary of Learning
> and Military Academy.
> Alexandria, Dec. 18, 1860

Dearest Ellen,

I have just finished a letter to Boyle,[1] in answer to one from him asking my consent to use that note you gave him of Hanenkamp & Hines due next February, and to substitute your fathers guarantee in lieu of the mortgage in St. Louis. I write him that if possible that note Should not be parted with now—for this reason—You have two others—If Disunion takes place, Hanenkamp & Hines will not pay that note, but will let the property slide—Then you would have to pay the note to save the other two, and that you cannot do, and all would be lost before times mend—Still you sold the note, & Hugh can dispose of it, and if he insists on it, please ask him & your father to make a new transaction, surrender the two notes you hold of Hughs—take a new one from him endorsed by your father, and ask Phil to have it secured like the loan to your father last summer by the mortgage on the Farm. I understand from Hughs letter that your father wants the money—This whole system of borrowing is about to explode with the same fatal effects as in San Francisco, & Hughs speculations in Cincinati & Leavenworth will vanish like a dream. I will probably lose the $500 per annum as Supdt. of the Arsenal here, as the Legislature must appropriate & cannot do so till in the spring, before which I fear I will be driven from here. I cannot remain here much beyond January 23, the time set for the state convention to dissolve the connection of this state with the U.S. The Legislature only sat three days & passed unanimously the Bills for arming the State & calling a convention. That Convention has only to decree what has already been resolved on and proclaimed by the Governor, that Louisiana cannot remain under a Black Republican President. The opinion is universal that Disunion is resolved on, and the only open questions are what states will compose the Southern Confederacy. I regard the failure of Buchanan to strengthen Maj. Anderson at F. Moultrie as absolutely fatal, as the evidence of contemptible pusillanimity of our Genl. Govt., almost convincing me that the Government is not worth saving. No wonder Genl. Cass forthwith resigned. The Banks in New Orleans continue good, and I will endeavor to Send you a months pay at the close of this month, but for mercy's sake be close & mean, for I cannot say how soon all my supplies will come to a conclusion. I have not a list of your notes, & Know not whether you have any soon to mature, but I hope we may avoid the necessity of using any of them—I almost feel forced to stay here for the sake of the pay, though it would be awful to feel that I am a party to what I deem Treason to Uncle Sam. Clay is a heavy source of expense to me, but poor fellow—he will soon be food for the crows.

A Boy came to my office today, saying his name is John Keating from Lancaster.[2] He says he left after the Election, and has been a waiter on a Steamboat which is laid up—that he once worked for you—Joe knows him. He is an estray,[3] and I will get the steward to employ him as a waiter in the Mess Hall.

Did I not mention the receipt of the apple butter?[4] It came promptly & the expense was only about $4—I gave one to Governor Moore, one to General Graham, and one to Capt. Jarreau,[5] in whose family I board—and where we have it daily on the table—The two barrels of preserves are yet unopened—and I will leave them so till Events show some certain conclusions, when I will either use them or sell them. If I could hear of any thing in St. Louis or Ohio I could do, for a bare maintenance—I would forthwith quit here—but to depart without any chance would be wrong, but to stay after Louisiana secedes would cut me off forever from the Northern states—It would be unsafe here for a family, though insurrection on the part of the negros is not apprehended— Indeed Dissolution is regarded as the cure for any such danger—I am very well[.] Love to all, Yrs. ever

W. T. Sherman

ALS, InND: Sherman Family Papers.

1. WTS to Hugh Boyle Ewing, December 18, 1860, above.

2. EES replied to WTS on December 31 that "*as a particular favor* . . . you will not expend one *five cent* piece on him but *let him rather go to the poor house* or *beg or steal of other people.*" He had not worked for her, although she had fed and clothed him for several months before concluding he was "a brainless thankless vagabond." SFP.

3. An archaic form of the word "stray."

4. EES to WTS, November 24, 1860, expressed concern that he had not received a shipment of apple butter she had sent him. SFP.

5. Jarreau was the steward of the academy.

TO JOHN SHERMAN

Louisiana State Seminary of Learning
and Military Academy.
Alexandria, Dec. 18, 1860

Dear Brother,

Events here seem hastening to a conclusion. Doubtless you know more of the Events in Louisiana than I do, as I am in an out of the way place. But the Special Session of the Legislature was so unanimous in Arming the State and calling a convention, that little doubt remains that Louisiana will on the 23 of January follow other seceding states. Govr. Moore takes the plain stand that the State must not submit to a Black Republic President. Men here have ceased to reason—They seem to concede that Slavery is unsafe in a Confederacy with Northern States, and that now is the time—No use of longer delay—all concession, all attempts to reconstruct seem at an end. I regard Buchanans refusal to reinforce Maj. Anderson—my old Captain—at my old Fort Moultrie as a pusillanimous act—He should have been promptly reinforced—3000 men in Forts Moultrie, Sumpter & Johnson, with one or two steam Frigates would be beyond the danger of attack from South Carolina—and as to exasperating the People, it would have caused less fatal effects than the pusillanimous abandonment of a brave officer & his Command—Fort Moultrie is weak—Sumpter in mid-channel is strong—very much so, and with the command of the water no force would attack it—Uncle Sam certainly has a right to defend her own property, and her title may not be questioned. Buchanan ought to have taken this stand, and it would afford the very time all are struggling for, for the cool thoughts and determination of the property holders who will have to bear the brunt of these war expenses.

This is not only a college, but a military college—Moreover it was created by Law an arsenal—I obtained in Washington last summer about 160 arms which with other arms & ammunition are stored here—as long as Louisiana is in the Union I will be bound in honor to Serve her—but when she quits the Union I must either quit this Post, for it is a military post, or be hostile to the United States. Though necessity presses me almost to extremity, still I cannot bear the idea of being opposed to Uncle Sam, and I have openly on all proper occasions so expressed myself. As $500,000 have been appropriated for the purchase of arms for the State, and as some of them will be deposited here my fidelity to the

State should be assured; and I have no doubt the Governor will feel bound as he should, to demand of me my Sentiments. These I shall not withhold—The right of secession is absurd, but the right of revolution always exists, but in my judgment there is not a shadow of justification for Rebellion. The Fugitive Slave law ought to be enforced honestly & faithfully—but I fear the South is now so far gone, that even this would be scorned as insufficient—I know not, but that if all the Southern States insist the old Confederation must go—and new combinations made—There are other elements of weakness that will now thrust themselves forward—This universal system of Credit & worthless Bank paper—This reckless taxation of Real property, by non property owners—this right of mob law, for any state, county, town, or village to do as they d——n please, hang, steal & rob, and call it the Peoples Law. Sewards Higher Law—Southern mob law, and California Vigilance Committees are all now the common Law of the United States taking precedence of the Enactments of Legislatures, or Judgments of courts—The United States was the only semblance of a Govt. in America, and that seems melting away like a Snow Ball in the sun—I feel needy—my family requires money, & that a good deal, as much as I can possibly earn; but I fear I must cast loose again with nothing, as I look on secession here as a mere question of Time. If possible get me something to do in Ohio or St. Louis even for a time to let me learn new habits, I observe with great pleasure that you keep business going—the machine moving on That is the only hope—Discussion is useless—

S.

ALS, DLC: William T. Sherman.

TO ELLEN EWING SHERMAN

Louisiana State Seminary of Learning
and Military Academy.
Alexandria, Dec. 23, 1860

Dearest Ellen,

I have received yours of the 13th[1]—They say the Post office Clerks in New Orleans get no pay and consequently work or not as they please, and that this accounts for the irregularity of the mails so you must not be *concerned* if mine do not come regularly—You seem to be afraid that some damage may occur to Minnie's picture and your Books. I'll watch out for them. There certainly are symptoms of a general breaking up or dissolution of all Government, everywhere. The People of the Parish on the other side of Red River have constituted themselves into a kind of vigilance committee with powers to execute their own sentence on Suspected parties. These are the best Gentlemen of the country, and though I never can approve of organizations that may as easily be adopted by the evil disposed as the well disposed, yet they show the tendency towards a general anarchy here as well as all over the United States[.] I take it for granted South Carolina has "seceded" and that other Southern States will follow, and that Louisiana will be precipitated along—Her convention will meet Jan. 23, and I will await partially her action. If she secede and assumes a hostile attitude towards the other states I will resign here, but then the trouble begins. Your necessities are great and you need a deal of money, and where it is to come from I know not. This state will owe me $500 and I must wait till the Legislature can appropriate it, which may further delay me till March—but if I could hear of anything to do in St. Louis or Ohio I would leave that in the hands of some friend for me. Why did not Hugh go down Hocking? What is he doing? Is he living on borrowed money? How can he go on without occupation? It is easy enough to talk about packing up & marching—I can do that quick enough, but who is to pay the Bills? If a general break up occur all over the Country confusion must reign, and what new combinations will be formed will depend on circumstances that no one can foresee, and it will be a thankless task to Serve during civil wars—When the time for reconstruction comes, then a person may enter safely the game of war. You say you have rented Mrs. White's House—I fear this will be a new outlay in the way of furniture but still I dont object to anything in reason that will increase your personal Comfort—only be prepared for the hardest kind of times. If Hugh does not intend to go down Hocking, and if nothing better offers I would go down there, leaving you in Lancaster, or if the worst comes to the worst I will rent your fathers farm and pitch in for bread & butter. We have been too much separated, and I feel deeply at times the absence of you all, and had looked forward to our all being together anywhere that this new disappointment breaks me down. It does seem that the whole world conspires against us. Was it not for my wish to secure the $500 due me by the state I would prepare to quit here as soon as the convention declares the secession of the State, but I cant afford to lose that money—we will need every cent of it. Joe got a letter from his sister[2] today and tells me she wants to come down— Dont advise one way or the other—even if I leave I can secure Joe employment here and he would never be molested—Indeed I do not apprehend any difficulty up here in this out of the way place—but on the Mississipi Collisions are sure to follow secession. Though the policy of free Trade is announced, and will most likely be attempted it cannot last long, and the states lying on the upper Rivers will never consent to the mouth being in possession of an hostile state. I was glad to hear of Minnies recovery, and that Lizzie thrives so well this winter. Willy & Tom will make a strong pair of colts. I hope they will all have a nice Christmas—Mine will be dull enough—I have an invitation to Dr. Luck-itts,[3] but cannot go—Smith & Dr. Clark have gone up to Judge Boyces to see Miss Louise who has got back home. Clay is about the Same[.] He hold out wondrously, and I hope yet he may recover. My love to all yrs. affectionately

W. T. Sherman

ALS, InND: Sherman Family Papers.

1. EES to WTS, December 13, 1860, expressed her concern for both his personal safety and their property in Louisiana. SFP.

2. Gertrude was a servant in EES's household.

3. Dr. L. Luckitt to WTS, December 20, 1860, DLC: WTS.

TO GEORGE MASON GRAHAM

Seminary, Christmas, 1860.

Dear General,

Your Kind note of the 23rd instant reached me yesterday, after I had sent for the mail. Else I should have sent for the cartridges on yesterday. As it is I will send for them on Thursday. They are a most appropriate present and I hope they may all be used for holiday salutes or mere practice. As you request I will not put them on my returns, else they would have certainly gone on the books.

Where did you get Cartridges? I could procure none in Washington or in New Orleans, and when the Parish Jury appropriated $250 for ammunition to be stored here, I invested the money in 20 kegs of powder, lead and 15,000 percussion caps, and now wait for the return of the Rapidas for balls and buckshot, intending if necessity should arise to use our powder flasks and pouches till we have leisure for making cartridges. The mere fact of our having here these arms and munitions will be a great moral fact. Still should unfortunately an occasion arise I could leave a strong guard here and with a part of the Cadets could move promptly to any point.

I have to Gov. Moore, Dr. Smith and to the Magistrate of this Precinct defined my position—As long as Louisiana is *in* the Union, and I occupy this post, I will serve her faithfully against internal or external enemies. But if Louisiana secede from the Genl. Government *that* instant I stop—I will do no act, breathe no word, think no thought hostile to the Government of the United States. Weak as it is, it is the only semblance of strength and justice on this continent, as compared with which the State Governments are weak and trifling. If Louisiana join in this unhallowed movement to dismember our old Government, how long will it be till her parishes and people insult and deride her? You now profess to have a state government and yet your people, your neighbors, good, intelligent, and well-meaning men have already ignored the laws and courts, and given to an unknown, irresponsible body of citizens the right to try, convict, and execute suspected persons. If gentlemen on Rapides Bayou have this absolute right and power to try and hang a Stranger, what security have you or any stranger to go into those pine woods where it may become a popular crime to own a good horse and wear broadcloth.

My dear General, we are in the midst of sad times—It is not slavery—It is a tendency to anarchy everywhere—I have seen it all over America, and our only hope is in Uncle Sam. Weak as that Government is, it is the only approach to one—I do take the Intelligencer[1] and read it carefully—I have read all the items you call my attention to and have offered them to Cadets but they seem to prefer the Delta. I do think Buchanan made a fatal mistake. He should have reenforced Anderson, "My old Captain, at my old post Fort Moultrie" and with steam frigates, made Fort Sumpter impregnable: This instead of exciting the Carolinians would have *forced* them to pause in their mad career. Fort Sumpter with 3000 men and the command of the seas would have enabled the Government to execute the Revenue Laws, and to have held S. Carolina in check till Reason could resume its sway—whereas now I fear they have a contempt for Uncle Same, and will sacrifice Anderson. Let them hurt a hair of his head in the execution of his duty, and I say Charleston must be blotted from existence. 'Twill arouse a storm to which the slavery question will be as nothing, else I mistake the character of our people. Of course I have counter-manded my orders for Mrs. Sherman to come South, and I feel that my stay here is drawing to a close. Still I will not act, till I conceive I must and should, and will do all that a man ought, to allow time for a successor.

Smith and Dr. Clark are up at Judge Boyce's—St. Ange lives in Alexandria—Boyd and I are alone. I had provided for a Christmas dinner to the Cadets, Still your present to them is most acceptable, and what was provided by Jarreau can be distributed along. A Happy Christmas to your family circle.

W. T. Sherman

Copy, InND: Sherman Family Papers; docketed "A true copy. D. F. Boyd."
1. The *National Intelligencer* of Washington, D.C.

TO JOHN SHERMAN

Seminary, Louisiana
Dec. 29, 1860

Dear Brother,

I have received your letter[1] and admit the seeming impropriety of a longer stay here, if I could afford it. But, Ellens expenses are heavy and the demands of women & children cannot be satisfied with any thing but money, so patriotism aside I cannot afford to give up the means of livelihood I now have, until others are at my disposal.

If Buchanan had made Fort Sumpter impregnable with an adequate force backed by a couple first class Steam Frigates—he would have checkmated this movement, and allowed time for adjusting the differences. But S. Carolina is out and I do fear that Louisiana will also go. I see you also think so—but the question occurs to me can Hostile relations spring up between Ohio & Louisiana at once? I think not but that ultimately they will, there is no room for doubt. Now it so happens that the State owes me $500, which cannot be paid by the Treasurer till the legislature meets and appropriates, and that cannot be till after the Convention meets, acts and adjourns, and it is doubtful if they would appropriate should it be known that I had pronounced against them. I will not therefore throw up this place till the last moment. If the State secedes, they will demand of all, to swear a new allegiance and of course I will swear no allegiance to Louisiana so long as the United States retains the form of a Government—nor if the result be as some suppose a general break up—each state sovereign & independent like Mexico, then of course I should not bring my family south.

If however at any time you see a good chance for me in the new army that must be reconstructed, use my name, give me notice and I will act as promptly as any body, only, now I cannot be thrown out of employment even for a month. I only receive $500 per annum from the State and $4000 from this Institution which is a Body Corporate, so that I owe no allegiance to the State, Have never voted here, or done any act to compromise me. I continue on the most friendly relations with the Board of Supervisors who appreciate fully the delicacy of my position and will I think allow me to choose my own Course.

People all over the Country have ceased to reason, and all attempts to allay excitement by Legislation appear useless—I think you are acting exactly right—Keep the General Government moving and well Supplied, that it may act energetically at the right time. By these concessions the State Governments are emboldened—To coerce the People of a State is fruitless—but to hold the public property by force, and to execute all laws by force when resisted is necessary, and will command the respect even of the rebellious.

A Rumor says that Major Anderson my old Captain, (brother of Charles Anderson now of Texas formerly of Dayton & Cincinati—Larz, William & John all of Ohio) has spiked the Guns of Fort Moultrie, destroyed it and taken refuge in Sumpter. This is right—Sumpter is in mid channel, approachable only in boats, whereas Moultrie is old, weak and easily approached under cover—if Maj. Anderson can hold out, till relieved, and supported by Steam

Frigates, S. Carolina will find herself unable to control her commerce and will feel for the first time in her existence that she cant do as she pleases.

I would like much to be in Ohio now, but I cannot afford it, and therefore must stay here some time yet—

Dont fail to let me know anything important—a telegraph despatch addressed to me at Alexandria, could be mailed at New Orleans and reach me in three days from Washington.

My love to Cecilia[2] if with you and believe me yr. affectionate Brother

W. T. Sherman

ALS, DLC: William T. Sherman.

1. On December 15, JS had written to his brother to urge him to leave Louisiana for the sake of both his honor and his personal safety. War was inevitable and the North could not allow the South to take control of the Mississippi. DLC: WTS. Relevant passages also reprinted in Rachel Sherman Thorndike, ed., *The Sherman Letters: Correspondence between General Sherman and Senator Sherman from 1837 to 1891* (1894; reprint, New York, 1969), 90–91.

2. Margaret Cecilia Stewart Sherman (d. 1900) was JS's wife.

TO GEORGE MASON GRAHAM

La. State Seminary of Learning
And Military Academy.
Alexandria Jan. 5, 1861.

Genl. G. M. Graham,
Sir,

I have not acknowledged the receipt of the four Kegs of cartridges—They are old, unserviceable, and much decayed—The powder is all caked and even the balls are partially damaged by the corrosion of the nitre. Still these balls can be used for our practice in the spring, provided the Parish Jury, will assent to the use of some of the powder which I have on hand purchased with their money.

I have made my Annual Report accompanied by statements of finance, property &c. &c. all of which I know will interest you much. I went to Alexandria on Thursday to deliver them to Dr. Smith but he had gone up to Mr. McMitts and I left them with Mr. Manning. If you go to Alexandria and have leisure I would be pleased to hear you have given them a careful perusal. My report may seem to you rather short—I did feel much tempted to avail myself of that opportunity to point out the inconsistent parts of our Regulations and also to demonstrate that we have undertaken a course of study so voluminous, as to result in superficial education; but our country is so agitated by political questions calculated to break down all governments, that those things might seem out of place. My duty here is plain, simple, but not so easy as one would suppose. I think by keeping our studies and duties progressing without pause or interruption that I will do my share to sustain the principle of Government that is fast giving away all over the land, the only principle that can save us from a general anarchy. My only hope for the salvation of the Constitution of the country is in the army. The law is or should be our King, we should obey it, not because it meets our approval, but because it is the law, and because obedience in some shape is necessary to every system of civilized government. For years this tendency to anarchy has gone on till now every State, and county, and town through the instrumentality of Juries, either Regular or Lynch make and enforce the local prejudices as the Law of the Land.

This is the real trouble, it is not slavery, it is the Democratic spirit which substitutes mere popular opinions for law. But I know you have bores enough to trouble you, and I won't add my Share: but you will do justice to the difficulties that envelope me in my private relations. With great respect, Your friend

W. T. Sherman

(I had my only horse shot today by reason of Distemper)

Copy, InND: Sherman Family Papers; docketed "A true Copy D. F. Boyd."

TO ELLEN EWING SHERMAN

Louisiana State Seminary of Learning
and Military Academy.
Alexandria, Jan. 5, 1861

Dearest Ellen,

I have finished my Report, and placed all the papers in the hands of Dr. Smith Vice President. I walked into town the day before yesterday—poor Clay being dead & buried. Dr. Smith was away, and I only remained a few hours. Alexandria at best is not a cheerful town, but now decidedly the reverse— everybody naturally feels the danger which envelops us all in our common cause. I have had nothing said to me at all, and I discuss the questions of the day freely with my equals, and try & keep my peace with loungers about the street corners & ferry boat landing. I always say what is my real belief, that though the Slavery question seems to be the question, that soon it will sink into insignificance. Our country has become so democratic, that the mere popular opinion of any town or village rises above the Law—men have ceased to look to Constitutions and Law Books for their guides, but have studied popular opinion in Bar Rooms and village newspapers and that was & is law— The old Women & Grannies of New England, reasoning from abstract principles, must defy the Constitution of the Country, the people of the South not relying on the Federal Govt. must allow their people to form filibustering expeditions against the Solemn treaties of the Land—and every where from California to Maine any man could do murder, Robbery or arson if the People's prejudices lay in that direction—and now things are at such a pass that no one section believe the other, and we are beginning to fight—The right of secession is but the beginning of the end—it is utterly wrong, and the President ought never for one moment to have permitted the South Carolinians to believe he would not enforce the Revenue Laws, and hold the public Property in Charleston Harbor—Had he promptly reinforced Maj. Anderson, the Charlestonians would have been a little more circumspect: My only hope is that Maj. Anderson may hold out—that reinforcements may reach him, and that the People may feel that they Cant always do as they please. Or in other words, that they aint so free and independent as they think—In this view I am alone here—but I do so think and will say it.

As to our own situation it is too bad to think of. I have got pretty near to the end of my rope—I have neither health, strength or purpose to start out life anew—Nor can you afford it—when you know that any day might throw me out of employment, and when necessity may force me to go abroad to Seek a mere maintenance you engage a new house, and begin steps that will result in spending a few more hundred dollars. I wont find fault because I admit that your reasons are good: but it would have been more prudent to wait a while— we are bound for the Martin House till September. If still this Civil broil should pass on, I shall require you all to come down, regardless of consequences—for here I must stay summer & winter, or else give it up—and here I may maintain you in comparative comfort, whereas in Ohio it is out of the question. I have never seen the faintest hope of doing so there—St. Louis will be paralized with Civil War, and California will be a foreign country. My only hope is that bad as things now look, there may occur some escape—or if dissolution is inevitable that Ohio & Louisiana may belong to the same Confederacy. I am so far out of the current here that I can only judge by newspapers and they all indicate a bias—The Louisiana Convention will surely secede, but then the reconstruction—at all events I cannot do anything till that is over—if they turn me out I must stay & get my dues: and I will send you every cent I can—The House is now done, and the Carpenters leave it today for good—People begin to wonder why you dont come down, and the fact is operating to my prejudice, but at this time it would be imprudent to do so— maybe a change may yet occur. Yrs. affectionately

W. T. S.

ALS, InND: Sherman Family Papers.

TO THOMAS EWING SR.

Louisiana State Seminary of Learning
and Military Academy
Alexandria, Jan 8, 1861

Hon. Thomas Ewing
Dear Sir.

Yours of Dec. 4 did not reach me till the 5th instant, a full month by the way. It was postmarked "Henderson Ky., Missent."

My position is complicated, and it is proper you should understand it. The Election for Members of the Convention took place yesterday, and the Convention itself will meet Jan 23. There is not the Shadow of a doubt that Louisiana will secede. All people now say that the Question is beyond mending. Of course I regard this as all madness, all folly. It however has clearly illustrated the weakness of our Government and bodes some change—and that change must be violent. From the best information that reaches me it also seems probable that even the middle states of Tennessee, Kentucky, Virginia & Maryland will fall off. Even if they do not join the Southern Confederacy, will at least quit the Union, and then the new Combinations—all this is in the future, and I doubt if any living man foresees the End. I am now satisfied that Slavery is not the Cause but the pretext, and that when these important defections take place, what will be the new Combinations? I owe no allegiance to Louisiana. I am working like any laboring man for my hire. I need that hire to maintain my family. If they were in personal danger it would be my duty to be near them, but they are in no danger. If I am, I am paid for it, and there is no personal danger that I would weigh in the Scale with the mortification of hanging about loose and unemployed. I never saw the Shadow of a chance of employment in Ohio. I would then be out of place & necessity would force me away, and where could I go, unless to some state, may be as foreign as this. Therefore so long as I can remain here with honor, it does seem Suicidal to quit—I know I stand well with the best men here—they respect me none the less for being attached to the Union, and I have never concealed my opinion that the Union should be maintained by force if necessary, & possible. Gov. Moore has heard me say this. Gen. Graham is familiar with my opinions. So is Col. Bragg[1] and Dr. Smith the President of the Board. I have told them all, and yet they want me to remain. I will engage in no act hostile to the U.S. unless being here is an act of hostility and I think my necessities justify my hesitation. After Disunion it may be this Discretion will not be left me. Another hold is that the Legislature failed to appropriate for my salary in charge of the arsenal—$500 will be due me in March—The Legislature meets the 3rd Monday in January, and will appropriate and I cannot afford to lose this sum.

Dr. Smith is a member of the Legislature[.] I have been in town today and he tells me he is unwilling I should leave, he is unwilling any of the Professors here should be Superintendent, and he knows no one in the State to succeed me.

I cannot afford to leave here unless I Know I can do something right away— although I feel more a stranger in Ohio, than in any other part of the United States, Still if I could find employment I would come—but I repeat I know nothing there to do.

John Sherman also writes for me to come away, and that quick—I write him as I do you, that I cannot afford to leave my pay, but that if he can procure for me decent employment I will act with all promptitude.

As I intimate even this choice may not be left me long, but I hope I can hold to my present post for a couple months longer. From present appearances— Washington will be a scene of strife and contention in February, if Maryland and Virginia espouse the cause of the South. I will gladly be advised by you[.] affectionately yours,

W. T. Sherman

ALS, DLC: Thomas Ewing and Family Papers.

1. Braxton Bragg (1817–76) was running his Louisiana plantation, helping to set up the academy, and holding the position of colonel in the state militia at this time.

TO ELLEN EWING SHERMAN

Louisiana State Seminary of Learning
and Military Academy.
Alexandria, January 8, 1861

Dearest Ellen,

Things are moving along with the rapidity of Revolutions—The papers announce that the People of Alabama have seized the arsenals at Mobile Point Fort Morgan, and above Mobile. I think similar steps will soon follow at the Forts at the mouth of the Mississipi, and Lake Ponchartrain. I have been in town today and had a long talk with Dr. Smith who goes next week to Baton Rouge to attend the meeting of the Legislature & Convention. He knows well my opinions—I have not concealed them, that I cannot do any act hostile to the United States. He know that I hold on simply for pay. This may be an unworthy motive. We need money, and money we must have, and where else to procure it I know not—I cannot unless compelled come to Lancaster to hang about loose and unemployed. It would be neither a satisfaction to you or to me. I got a letter from your father, written at Lancaster Dec. 4 which was a month on its way, in which he advises me to come away, and intimates that I can get employment in Ohio, I think he is mistaken—I tried at New York and Cincinati, but you know that it is hard for anybody to get employment who has no particular profession, and in Ohio I am really more of a stranger than in any other part of the U. States. I would have to start forth again on some wild goose chase resulting in disappointment.

Again by a Revolution of the Board our salaries are not paid but Quarterly, so I cannot draw any money for three months. Nor can I expect the Legislature which meets the 3rd Monday in January to appropriate the $500. due me, till some time in March—I cannot abandon these Claims.

The Board is unwilling to entrust the management here to any one of the other Professors. It takes me all I can do to suppress disorder and irregularity—I had a cadet threaten me yesterday with a loaded pistol, because I detected a Whisky Jug in his Room, & threatened him with dismissal. He did not await trial but went off. Although a large majority of the Cadets are good boys, still we have some hard cases.

From what I see in the New Orleans papers, Anderson is still in possession of Fort Sumpter, and the Genl. Government has failed to reinforce him and will wait till he is attacked—This disgusts me, and I would not serve such a pusillanimous government. It merits dissolution. This fact will increase the chances of an attempt to prevent Lincolns installation into office, and then we shall see whether the wide awakes will fight as well as carry cheap lamps of a night Zig Zagging down the streets.

I see every chance of long, confused and disorganizing Civil war, and I feel no desire to take a hand therein. When the time comes for reorganization, then will be the time—I feel anxious for your comfort and safety, but these cannot be threatened. I hope your investments are safe, and I will feel much relieved to hear Hugh did not part with that note, but holds it for application to his mortgage debt in St. Louis—If he parts with it I shall feel very uneasy about it till I know it is paid Feb. 23. next. In Missouri there must be a struggle, and St. Louis must feel it intensely, and the date when that note falls due will be about the Crisis. I still hope for some favorable change, & that I may still be able to Send for you all—write me more frequently for the mails are very irregular and will become more so when Mississipi & Louisiana secede. They now hardly think of the confusion these must cause.

Give my love to all. I think of you & the children far more than you will ever give me credit for. Yrs. truly

W. T. Sherman

ALS, InND: Sherman Family Papers.

TO HUGH B. EWING

Seminary January 12, 61

Dear Hugh,

Yours of January 2, is received, and I cannot withhold the expression of my regret that that note has been parted with, but as it went for your father I can not complain. The reasons for guarding Ellen's resources are so cogent that I feel bound to guard their safety by every caution. Should the note go to protest, I will have no possible means of taking it up, or to protect the property from the consequences.

Notwithstanding your opinion Louisiana will secede. The Election for Delegates has resulted in the Success of the Candidates pledged to immediate Secession. I have reason to believe ere this that the New Orleans volunteers are in possession of Forts Jackson & St. Philip at or near the mouth of the Mississipi, and Forts Pike and Wood at the Outlets of Lakes Borgne and Ponchartrain.[1] There are no troops there. One company Haskins[2] is at the arsenal at Baton Rouge, but it is a mess open Barracks, indefensible against large odds, and the arms & munitions of war there will be taken soon after the Secession which will occur towards the close of this month—the appropriation of ½ million by the Legislature was made out of money on hand in the Treasury. The State needs no loan. The annual yield of ½ million bales of cotton, with sugar & other productions give Louisiana an income of about 60 millions of Dollars. A tax of 5 per cent on which gives her three millions, which being paid by large planters is easily & cheaply collected. Strange to say cotton is high and meets prompt sale, and the Large Planters are favorable to Secession, because they believe that the North proposes to gradually undermine their Slavery property, which is their active capital. Seward being named as Secretary of State,[3] confirms them in their hitherto naked assertion that the Republican party is identical with the abolition party. I think myself such men as Seward & Chase[4] ought not to be in the Cabinet. Of course the dilly dallying policy of Buchanan has helped to bring the General Government into Contempt which may prove fatal, and positive men should now be called to rule, but Seward & Chase are too offensive to the Middle States on which now so much depends—The Cotton States are gone.

Our news from New Orleans are to the 10th—Anderson still held Fort Sumpter, but the *Star of the West* had been fired at with ten Shots which compelled her to retire.[5] There are two channels into Charleston Bay, one along the southern {line} near Morriss Island—and one near Sullivans Island—a vessel entering must receive the fire of one or the other Batteries. I know not what calibre of Guns they have, but I wonder that Genl. Scott[6] should have sent reinforcements and provisions in a frail ship like the *Star of the West*—

half a dozen strong frigates, half of them Steam should have gone. A Repulse you know gives great cause at rejoicing. It is strange to hear and see people charmed at an insult to Uncle Sam, but I am compelled to swallow the bitter pill. It is easy enough to say come away, but I must bear insult and everything to earn money. The wants & necessities of my family are such that Patriotism must be a secondary matter. I am compelled to stay here till I am turned off, and that will be next month I expect. I know that you & your father have your hands full to take care of yourselves and I cannot lean on you. As to hanging about Lancaster unemployed, like many others would be intollerable—so that when I leave here I will have to seek some more obscure place to hide myself. If we could get employment at the salt wells, without being mere superfluous mouths to feed, it might do for want of a better place, but I do confess I hate to raise my Children down there. The fate of the {Dunnans,} rises up as a warning.

Clay is dead—he became so bad I had him shot—he communicated his disease to the Seminary mule which died also—and now the mare of Dr. Clark is following the Same down hill road. It was glanders, though for a long time I thought it Distemper.

Whenever any thing turns up I will act with promptness enough—but I cannot like Mr. Micawber wait for their turning up[7]—They must turn up first.

I am always affectionately your Brother
W. T. Sherman

Russell is in a bad Box, aint he?

ALS, OHi: William T. Sherman Papers.

1. Governor Moore had ordered these actions on the strength of advice from U.S. senators Judah P. Benjamin and John Slidell. On January 10, state troops had captured the U.S. arsenal at Baton Rouge and Forts Jackson and St. Philip; Fort Pike would be taken on January 14.

2. Joseph A. Haskin (1817–74), a Mexican War veteran who had lost his arm in service, would spend most of the war working on Washington's defenses.

3. William H. Seward (1801–72), a former governor of New York, had been a U.S. senator until joining Lincoln's cabinet as secretary of state in March 1861.

4. Salmon P. Chase (1808–73) of Ohio had been in the United States Senate until he became secretary of the treasury in March 1861.

5. This happened on January 9, when the ship approached Charleston Harbor with supplies and reinforcements for Anderson. The *Star* left before sustaining damage.

6. Winfield Scott (1786–1866) had been general in chief of the U.S. Army since 1841.

7. This remark from the character Wilkins Micawber of Charles Dickens's novel *David Copperfield* was often used in the 1860s.

TO GEORGE MASON GRAHAM

Louisiana State Seminary of Learning
And Military Academy,
Alexandria Jan. 16, 1861

Dear General,

It was my purpose to wait patiently for the development of events, but my mind was firmly resolved to do no act hostile to the United States.[1] I had given full notice of such resolution to Dr. Smith and Governor Moore.

The seizure of the Forts and worse than all the capture of the company of U.S. soldiers at Baton Rouge where they were stationed by invitation of the State authorities for the protection of the arms and munitions of war placed there for the safety of the State, and regarded by me as acts of war and a breach of common decency. I forthwith repaired to Alexandria, and notified Dr. Smith of my opinion and that my longer stay here was wrong. He thinks Governor Moore had reasons for his conduct not known to the public, and as he is on the point of going to Baton Rouge he asked me to forbear till he could consult and see what is to be done. He says that he has consulted with many and that all understand my opinions, that as I am entrusted with the moneys and management of the institution he cannot arrange for my relief till time is given to provide a successor. He is unwilling that Vallas should succeed to my powers as Superintendent—or that any one else to the care of the moneys. But he pledged me his word that I should in no wise be compromised in any act of hostility to the General Government. If I had in view any occupation by which I could maintain my family I would not stay, but as I have no such employment in view and as I cannot receive the compensation fixed by law for me as Superintendent of the Central Arsenal, and as I have laid by little or nothing I have consented to await awhile, to allow the Legislature to appropriate the $500 due for last year and for a little salary to accumulate, to give me the means of returning to Ohio, and cast around for some means of support. These are my reasons. They may be improper and unsuited to the occasion, but such they are. But I do think that the haste with which this resolution is pushed must produce sad and bitter fruits. I feel no wish to take part in the civil strife that seems inevitable. I would prefer to hide myself, but necessity may force me to another course. Here in Louisiana you must sustain a large army, and its commander will soon dispose of your Governor and Legislature and will keep them to the simple task of providing "ways and means." Then Gov. Moore will it may be see that it is not so simple a game to play. Our Friend Bragg seems to be about, and most likely he will soon be your King. You could not have a better. However secession may be regarded as to South Carolina, it becomes a far more serious matter, when we know that some of the most populous states are on the tributaries of the Mississippi whose mouth is now held by a foreign and hostile State. This of itself will turn their commerce by Lakes and rail-roads eastward, and moreover a new feeling of interest will arise in New York and Baltimore to embarrass the exports from New Orleans. The facility of closing the Mississippi by a single frigate or by the possession of Key West or the Tortugas will and must paralyze the trade of New Orleans.

It may be that Louisiana's honor compelled her to this course, but I see it not, and must think it is the rash result of excited men.

Men have ceased to reason, and war seems to be courted by those who understand not its cost, and demoralizing results. Civilians are far more willing to start a war than Military men and so it appears now. With great respect.

W. T. Sherman

Copy, InND: Sherman Family Papers; docketed "A true copy. D. F. Boyd."

1. On January 4, Graham had written to WTS to bemoan the South's precipitous rush to secession and to express his belief that the course of action WTS had chosen was the right one. SFP.

TO ELLEN EWING SHERMAN

Louisiana State Seminary of Learning
and Military Academy.
Alexandria, Dec. 16, 1860 [Jan. 16, 1861][1]

Dearest Ellen,

The Telegraph has announced to you ere this that Governor Moore hurried on by the wild enthusiasm which now pervades the Southern mind, has caused the Forts at the mouth of the Mississipi to be occupied by volunteers from New Orleans. Also those at the outlets of Lakes Ponchartrain & Borgne, and moreover that he has caused a large force to Surround the Barracks at Baton Rouge, and the Garrison to Surrender[.] Maj. Haskin will be much blamed but he is a plain brave man, lost an arm in Mexico, but he had only a single company, in an open barracks, and was stationed there as among friends to protect the arsenal not against the People, but against the negros— All these are acts of hostility and war. The News will cause intense feeling in the North & West. They were entirely too precipitate, and Govr. Moore is even censured here. Still the fact is manifest that the People of the South are in open Rebellion against the Government of the United States.

I went to Alexandria in a hard rain yesterday, and Saw Dr. Smith, Mr. Elgee[,] Wise and others, members of the Convention and Legislature and spoke my mind fully & clearly, that these were acts of unjustifiable war, and that I could no longer remain Silent. I asked to be relieved—But there is no one here to take my place—All are unwilling that Vallas, a hypocritical foreigner who would serve the Devil for his pay, should succeed me. Nor will Dr. Smith consent to entrust the monies of the Institution to any other of the Professors. They all go to Baton Rouge this week and pledged their words, that my position should be respected, and that in no event should I be compromised.

If I knew of any occupation awaiting me I should get away any how, but as I know of nothing I have done all I can. I have written to John Sherman to the Same Effect—Still so weak and vacillating has our Government been, that I would hardly be willing to accept a Commission under it. Any Government that has treated Anderson as ours has, cannot expect much Zeal of the part of its officers—I am clear now that the old U.S. is gone—that new combinations must be made—or a new Government organized with stronger executive powers, and an Army adequate to the compulsory enforcement of Laws in all parts of the country.

Every day the breach of feeling is widening—I met Miss Louise Boyce & her sister Mrs. Ketchum in town, and they were for "Secession"—the cruel fanatic North, came from their lips as easily, as though they had not just come from Ohio. And so it is everywhere, the people born & reared at the North are more enthusiastic in this Revolution than those native to the Soil.

If you want me to come away, you must move to get me something to do—I Know it is ridiculous for me to ask this of you, but on the other hand I would not stay in Ohio ten days without Employment—I wrote you last that you might visit Louisiana this winter with Lizzie & Willy—but these events are hurrying along too fast to make arrangements ahead—Still I doubt not I shall be here, into February and maybe March—Though when Govr. Moore receives my message he may think it wise to get me away—Smith on the contrary wants to prove to me that here in Louisiana we shall have more peace and prosperity than in Ohio—Turner[2] has written me that he should take his family to Europe for safety, and return to fight in the Sacred Cause of his Country South, against the invasion of the Fanatic North—So you see what force Religion & Charity has upon the minds of mankind. I know millions are sincere in the belief that the People of the north have done a barbarous deed in voting for Lincoln.

General Graham lays low & says nothing in these times, but I know he is much distressed at the hasty manner in which things are pushed[.] Yrs. truly,
W. T. Sherman

ALS, InND: Sherman Family Papers.

1. The events described in this letter took place in early January 1861. EES to WTS, January 29, 1861, answers Sherman's comments on Turner from this letter, further supporting the notion that the letter's true date should be January 16, 1861.

2. Henry S. Turner (1811–81), an old army associate and a founding partner in the California bank where Sherman had worked, now lived in St. Louis.

TO JOHN SHERMAN

Seminary, January 16, 1861

My Dear Brother,

I am so much in the woods here that I cant Keep up with the times at all. Indeed you in Washington hear from New orleans two or three days sooner than I do. I was taken back by the news that Governor Moore had ordered the forcible seizure of the Forts Jackson & St. Philip at or near the mouth of the Mississipi, also of Forts Pike and Wood at the outlets of lakes Borgne & Ponchartrain. All these are small forts, and have rarely been occupied by troops—They are designed to cut off approach by sea to New Orleans, and were taken doubtless to prevent their being occupied by order of General Scott. But the taking the arsenal at Baton Rouge is a different matter—It is merely an assemblage of store houses, barracks and dwelling houses designed for the healthy residence of a Garrison to be thrown into one or other of the Forts in case of war—The arsenal is one of minor importance, yet the Stores were kept there for the moral effect and the Garrison was there at the instance of the people of Louisiana. To surround with the military away, to demand surrender, and enforce the departure of the Garrison was an act of war. It amounted to a Declaration of War and defiance, and was done by Govr. Moore without the authority of the Legislature or Convention. Still there is little doubt but that each of these bodies to assemble next week will ratify & approve these violent acts, and it is idle to discuss the subject now. The People are mad on this question. I had previously notified all that in the event of secession I should quit. As soon as a knowledge of these acts reached me I went to the Vice President Dr. Smith in Alexandria and told him that I regarded Louisiana as at war against the Federal Govt. and that I must go. He begged me to wait till some one could be found to replace me. The supervisors feel the importance of system & discipline & seem to think that my departure will endanger the success of this last effort to build up an Educational Establishment in Louisiana—Dr. Smith is a member of the State Senate, goes down this week to Baton Rouge, and pledged me that in no event should I be asked to compromise my national character—He promised in the event of secession which is almost certain, to see about a successor—and asks me as a personal favor to wait; I can so ill afford to lose my wages, and hate to hang about Lancaster unemployed, that I yield more than I should, but you may assert that in no event will I forego my allegiance to the U.S. as long as a single state is true to the Old Constitution, and if an opportunity of employment offers I will not be influenced by the wishes of third parties or the interest of this Institution. I delay also to secure if possible the $500 due me under existing laws, but which by an oversight was not included in the old appropriation Bill.

I would not in civil war, engage in petty warfare, and would not reenter the army except with a high commission. In such times I would prefer civil appointment—such as an asst. Treasurer at St. Louis, or other City, as a Rail Road agency of some kind. If I leave here I cannot come down to just principles for however willing Ellen may be in theory, yet in practice she must have an array of servants and other comforts that money alone can give. If I leave here I fear I may be forced by necessity to go down Hocking, or get on a Farm, and it requires more strength than I possess. When I was an army officer at St. Louis I prospered well, but that Bank adventure cleaned me out entirely, and though Mr. Lucas[1] offered to help me to a business I did not want to put myself under obligations to him, for reasons which were good, but if I could once more get a foothold then I think I could again build myself up—I have made myself a good berth here, and all are anxious for me to remain, but I know the manifest impropriety of my staying after Louisiana secedes. But as I wrote before necessity compels me to act with caution, though I have taken good care that my opinions should be known to all in authority. If you know the new Secretary of the Treasury, and could get for me the offer of the St. Louis Treasury, I could get the Bonds, and in the Four years I could reestablish myself there in safety. Otherwise I fear I am doomed to the salt wells. Missouri will be a scene of strife, but I suppose its alternate fate is certain. Yrs.

W. T. Sherman

I think Senator Baker[2] is a good friend of mine.

ALS, DLC: William T. Sherman.

1. James H. Lucas (ca. 1805–73) was one of the founding partners of Lucas, Turner, & Co., WTS's bank in California, and lived in St. Louis.

2. Edward D. Baker (1811–61) was a U.S. senator from Oregon, a lawyer from San Francisco, and a friend of Lincoln's. He accepted a commission as a colonel in the Seventy-first Pennsylvania and was killed at Ball's Bluff in October.

TO THOMAS O. MOORE

Louisiana St. Seminary of Learning
& Mil. Academy,
Jany. 18, 1861

Governor Thomas O. Moore
Baton Rouge—
Sir,

As I occupy a Quasi-Military position, under the Laws of the State, I deem it proper to acquaint you that I accepted such position when Louisiana was a state in the Union, and when the motto of this seminary was inscribed in marble over the Main Door, "By the liberality of the General Government of the United States, The Union Esto perpetua."

Recent events foreshadow a great change and it becomes all men to choose. If Louisiana withdraw from the Federal Union I prefer to maintain my allegiance to the Old Constitution as long as a fragment of it survives: and my longer stay here would be wrong in every sense of the word.

In that event I beg you will send or appoint some authorized agent to take Charge of the arms and munitions of war belonging to the State, or advise me what disposition to make of them.

And furthermore as President of the Board of Supervisors I beg you to take immediate steps to relieve me as superintendent the moment the State determines to secede, for on no earthly account will I do any act, or think any thought hostile to or in defiance of the old Government of the United States. with great respect yr. obt. servant

W. T. Sherman

Copy (ALS), DLC: William T. Sherman.

TO THOMAS O. MOORE

January 18, 1861

To Govr. Moore.
Private.
My Dear Sir,

I take it for granted you have been expecting for some days the accompanying paper from me.[1] I have repeatedly & again made known to General Graham & Dr. Smith that in the event of a severance of the Relations hitherto existing between the Confederated States of this Union, I would be forced to choose the *Old* Union. It is barely possible that all the states will secede South and North, that new combinations will result, but this process will be one of time and uncertainty. I cannot with my opinions await this subsequent development.

I have never been a politician and therefore undervalue the excited feelings and opinions of present Rulers all over the Land, but I do think if this People cannot execute one form of Government like the present, that a worse one will result.

I will keep the Cadets as quiet as possible. They are nervous, and I think the interest of the State requires them here guarding this Property, and acquiring a Knowledge which will be useful to your state in aftertimes. When I leave, which I now regard as certain, the present Professors could manage well enough, to afford you leisure time to find a Suitable successor to me. You might order Smith to receipt for the arms, and to exercise military command whilst the academic exercises could go on under the Board. In time some Gentleman will turn up better qualified than I am to carry on the Seminary to its ultimate point of success[.] I entertain the Kindest feelings to all, and would leave the State with much regret, only in Great events we must choose one way or the other[.] Truly your friend,

W. T. Sherman

Copy (ALS), DLC: William T. Sherman.
1. See the immediately preceding letter.

TO JOHN SHERMAN

Louisiana State Seminary of Learning
and Military Academy.
Alexandria, Jan. 18, 1861

Dear Brother,

Before receiving yours of the 7th[1] I had addressed a letter to Govr. Moore at Baton Rouge, of which this is a copy—[2]

I regard the Seizure by Govr. Moore of the U.S. arsenal as the worst act yet committed in the present Revolution. I do think every allowance should be made to Southern Politicians for their nervous anxiety about their political power, and the Safety of slaves I think that the Constitution should be liberally construed in their behalf—but I do regard this Civil war as precipitated with undue rapidity.

What to do I know not—of course the Govr. will soon relieve me, for he is a man of action and his nerves are evidently wrought up to war—It is inevitable. All the Legislation now would fall powerless on the South—You Should not alienate such states as Virginia Kentucky, Tennessee & Missouri—

My notion is that this war will ruin all Politicians & that military Leaders will direct the events.

Anderson & Scott already have done more to check the movement, than all Congress. As soon as I leave here and reach Telegraph Stations I will tell you where to look for me.

The mail is ready to Start in and I write in haste. Yrs.

W. T. S.

ALS, DLC: William T. Sherman.
1. Actually JS to WTS, January 6, 1861, DLC: WTS. He urged WTS to resign and said that Winfield Scott agreed with him. If WTS came to Washington, JS added, he could get a good job in the army.
2. Following here was a copy of WTS's first letter to Moore of January 18. See also WTS to Dr. S. A. Smith, January 19, 1861, for his last official letter to the president of the board of the academy. *PM*, 1:185–86.

TO GEORGE MASON GRAHAM

Seminary, Jan. 20. 1861.

My dear Friend,

Yours of yesterday[1] was read with painful interest last night along with Mr. Sanford's[2] two, which I herewith return. Of course now that reason is powerless and the truth cannot be reached through the cloud of mistrust, suspicion, and mutual accusations which envelope us, we are all drifting together no one knows whither.

I was waiting as patiently as a Red headed person could, for the official acts of the convention charged with the destiny of Louisiana, when tidings reached me that Governor Moore had caused the seizure of the Forts and Arsenals, and had driven away with ignominy the small garrison posted among friends for the protection of the dangerous instruments of war. For this I see no justification and felt compelled to announce my determination by letter in the terms I had previously done to Dr. Smith in the presence of Mr. Elgee. Dr. Smith gave me his personal assurance that in no event should I be called on to do any act compromising my national character and preferences. But fearing some unforeseen cause might render him powerless I resolved to move officially and therefore addressed to Gov: Moore a letter of which the subjoined is a copy and at the same time wrote him and Dr. Smith each, other private letters with the view to convey to them the personal reasons for my choice.[3]

Of course they will now make short metre of me and within a week I expect to be homeward bound. I have made all Reports, Returns, and letters to parents and all the books are written up to date. I have asked Dr. Smith to meet me in New Orleans to balance the Bank Account, for I want to leave with clean hands, and they will be clean enough for I have saved but little and can now hardly expect the Legislature will appropriate for the Arsenal.

I have notice that 3300 stand of arms, 70,000 cartridges and 200 Carbine Cartridges and belts are en route for this place. I must as long as I stay be faithful to my trust, and I will take immediate steps for their safe storage, though it will force me to move and use this room as a store-house. I hope however to be relieved in time so that some one else will have the pleasure of receipting for them and accounting for them.

My own opinion is that Lincoln will be installed in office, that Congress will not repeal the Union, that the Revenues will be collected. The consequence is inevitable—War, and ugly war too—I do not think the South will be invaded or plain coercion attempted: but no vessel can be cleared at New Orleans, and no vessel enter without paying duties outside. Commerce will cease unless the South can combine, organize a navy and fight their way, or unless she can form a treaty with our Old Enemy, England. For the northern and eastern cities will never consent to pay duties, and allow New Orleans to be a free port, to send into the Interior goods cheaper than they.

But discussion is useless—The storm is upon us—and we much each to our own ship—I hope I may meet you again but if not accept the assurances of my great affection, respect, and admiration, and my earnest prayer that you and yours may long survive to look back with satisfaction to the time when we started the Seminary in a vain belief that we were serving the cause of our common country. Again Good-bye—Yours,

Sherman

Copy, InND: Sherman Family Papers; docketed "A true Copy, D. F. Boyd."

1. George Mason Graham to WTS, January 19, 1861, DLC: WTS and SFP. Graham announced that he and Sanford would cast their lots with the Confederacy although they thought secession foolish. Graham was so bothered by the tone of Sherman's letter of January 16 that he also sent the enclosures to try to explain the Southern point of view.

2. A member of the Board of Supervisors for the academy.

3. Included in the text of the letter was a copy of Sherman's first to Moore of January 18; he also refers to his second letter to Moore of that date and his to Dr. S. A. Smith of January 19, 1861.

TO ELLEN EWING SHERMAN

Seminary, Jan. 20, 1861

Dearest Ellen,

Here is another Sunday. I have written you often enough of late to keep you in a perfect state of uneasiness, but it does seem that each day brings forth something new—I now have official notice that 3300 muskets, 70,000 cartridges &c. &c. are sent here from Baton Rouge which must be a part of those seized by the State—or otherwise stolen, and I must make provision for their storage. I must move to the new House in order to afford Room for them in my present Quarters[.] But my stay here much longer is impossible—my opinions & feelings are so radically opposed to those in power that this cannot last long—I send you a copy of a letter I wrote to Govr. Moore on the 18th on the receipt of which he will be forced to act. I hate to lose that $500 but I guess it cant be helped. I know all about the forms of Reports, Returns, money accounts &c. &c., and no one here does and I know of no one in the State that Moore can find. Still I think he will feel bound to place the Custody of these arms in the hands of one more faithful to Louisiana than I profess to be. I shall expect a definite answer in a week, when I propose to go to New Orleans and settle the Bank account. I would then ship in some Cincinati Boat, such traps as would not bear Railroad transportation, and then by Rail Road to Cincinati, so that it is not impossible I may be in Lancaster early in February. I must leave here with a clean Record, and this can only be done in the manner I have pointed out to Govr. Moore. He may endeavor to throw obstacles in my way, but I think not. He is too fair a man.

There will be trouble here after I leave as Vallas is incapable of managing American Boys, and he is entitled to the succession unless some one is sent up from Baton Rouge.

As to the future I know you cannot follow a roving commission, and that if we ever expect to live together in any sort of peace it must be now—I am willing to forego my professions if I can control myself, and settle down—but I must have occupation. Your father has written me that he can find moderate employment for me at home, and that he will meet me in February—If he means at the salt wells, so be it, or if not he will sell you the Farm with all its stock & fixtures, we can make out of it a living for ourselves & children, but it will call on us both for our absolute surrender of our past habits. I doubt if either of us are equal to it, but still I am willing to try. I feel no desire to follow an army necessarily engaged in civil war, and as we could start out of debt, it may be we can keep so—Those now in debt will suffer most—or least, for they will likely repudiate all debts. Down here they think they are going to have fine times. New Orleans a free port, whereby she can import Goods without limit or duties, and Sell to the up River Countries. But Boston, New York Philadelphia and Baltimore will never consent that N. Orleans should be a Free Port, and they Subject to Duties. The most probable result will be that New Orleans will be shut off from all trade, and the South having no navy and no Sailors cannot raise a Blockade without assistance from England, and that She will never receive. I have letters from General Graham & others, who have given up all hope of *stemming* the tide. All they now hope for is as peaceable a secession as can be effected. I heard Mr. Clay's speech in 1850 on the Subject of secession, and if he deemed a peaceable secession then as an absurd impossibility—much more so is it now, when the commercial interests of the North are so much more influential.

If I go I think Joe had better say here, he can get employment more congenial than if he returns to Lancaster, and he is in no wise compromised as I am. I have not yet spoken to him distinctly but will in a day or so—He is now at church. You had better write to me till you hear distinctly that I am off or about to Start and Should I go to New Orleans I will telegraph from there. When I once start you may be assured that my movements will be rapid enough. My love to all, Yrs. affectionately

W. T. Sherman

ALS, InND: Sherman Family Papers.

Seminary, Jan. 27, 1861

Dearest Ellen,

Since my last I have three letters from you of latest date 16th inst.[1] The mails have been much disordered by a break on the Mississipi Rail Road. In my last I sent you a copy of a letter written to Govr. Moore, to which I have received no answer[.] He is very busy indeed, Legislature and Convention both in session at Baton Rouge giving him hardly time to think of the Seminary. I would as leave stay here through February as not, because it must be bitter cold with you, whilst here we have pleasant weather, & moreover thereby I will be more likely to receive that money as well as another months pay—I Know that sooner or later I must quit and therefore it is simply a question of time & money—The ordnance of Secession will pass in a day or so, but the Legislature has adjourned till Feb. 4, so that no business can be transacted there for some days. It dont take long to pull down and everybody is striving for the honor of pouring out the deepest insult to Uncle Sam[.] The very men who last 4th July were most patriotic and exhausted their imaginations for pictures of the Glories of our union, are now full of Joy and happiness that this accursed union is wrecked & destroyed.

This rapid popular change almost makes me a monarchist, and raises the question whether the self interest of one man is not a safer criterion than the wild opinions of ignorant men—From all I can read Missouri & Kentucky will go with the crowd south and will be more seriously affected than any other part of the country. It was this belief that made me ask Hugh to hold on to that note, which I fear will endanger the safety of the remaining two which are unpaid.

I have had a long talk with Joe, and I have advised him to stay, because now that a large amount of ordnance has been sent here, he can get good wages, and he will be perfectly Safe here. He thinks so too, and he has letters from his friends that times are very hard in Ohio.

Today Sunday I have been busy receiving muskets, some 154 boxes have been hauled out today, and Joe being at Church I had to attend to it. these are part of those seized by Governor Moore at Baton Rouge[.] I vacated my Rooms in the Seminary Building, and have taken possession of the new House. I sit in the Front Parlor, and have my bed in the Back Parlor, very convenient indeed. The House is an excellent one, and I cannot at times but regret the turn in public Affairs which render it impossible for us to enjoy its use. I do hate to make a new start in life, but it does seem to be my luck. As soon as I get established anywhere some convulsion obliges me to change. Whether to return to the army, to go to the salt wells, or the Farm I cannot now decide. I feel no temptation to take part in a civil war, and I feel unable to work on a farm, and it does seem to me, a bad adventure to attempt a farm without working, for all such experiments that I have seen, have proven failures. As to the Salt works I will wait till I get to Lancaster.

As soon as I hear from Govr. Moore I will let you know when to expect me. I know that he the Governor will feel inclined to get rid of me instanter, but Dr. Smith wants me to stay for a successor, and he has no successor in his mind. If he proposes I should stay till March I will feel disposed to agree to it for pecuniary reasons, but I think the Governor will feel hurt at my letter, and will be disposed to get rid of me. At all events, my position being clearly defined I cannot be complicated by these secession movements. I do feel a little mean at being made partially accessory to the robbing of the Baton Rouge arsenal, by receiving a part of the stolen property.

I have another small check, received on business which I remit to you, $5.47—This is the last, and you must expect no more till I come or till the end of March. Tell your father not to lease to Lynch, for if there be large profits he can have them all. I thought Hugh was to manage them, what is he doing?

Give my Love to all and say to them that I will be at home some time this spring—If we are to go down to the Salt wells what can you do with the White House—Can you find any body to take it off your hands, or do you propose to spend the year there anyhow. I was glad to learn it was the Creed House and not the Old White House farther down the street. Yrs. affectionately,

W. T. Sherman

ALS, InND: Sherman Family Papers.

1. EES to WTS, January 4, 1861, apologized for her large expenditures and sent a detailed accounting of how she had spent money recently. On January 16 she wrote to describe the house she had rented in Lancaster and to urge him to consider running her father's salt-works at Hocking. She reported that Ohioans expected Lincoln to name Salmon P. Chase to the cabinet; JS would then assume Chase's vacated seat in the United States Senate. She felt that JS could always get him a good job in the army. Lizzie was ill, and EES expected WTS to return from Louisiana momentarily. SFP.

TO ELLEN EWING SHERMAN

Seminary, Feb. 1, 1861

Dearest Ellen,

I Suppose you are impatient to hear what next—Last night I got full letters from Baton Rouge.[1] Govr. Moore is in these words, "it is with the deepest regret I acknowledge the receipt of your communication of the 18th inst. (Jan. 23)[.] In the pressure of official business I can now only request you to transfer to Professor Smith the arms, munitions & funds in your hands whenever you conclude to withdraw from the position you have filled with so much distinction. You cannot regret more than I do the necessity which deprives us of your services, and you will bear with you the respect, confidence and admiration of all who have been associated with you.

very truly yr. friend & sevt.

Thos. O. Moore.

Dr. Smith also at Baton Rouge, writes me at length—he says, "I need not tell you it is with no ordinary regret that I view your determination to leave us, for really I believe the success of our Institution now almost opened is jeopardized thereby. I am sure that we will never have a superintendent with whom I shall have more pleasant relations than have existed between you & me. I fully appreciate the motives that have influenced you to give up a position presenting so many advantages to yourself, & sincerely hope that you may in any future enterprise enjoy the Success which your character and abilities merit & deserve. . . . Govr. Moore desires me to express his profound regret that the state is about to lose one whom we all fondly hoped had cast his destinies for weal or woe among us, and that he is sensible that we lose thereby an officer whom it will be difficult if not impossible to replace."

So you see I have at least the good will of my associates. I have called the Board for Feb. 9, and expect to leave here by or before Feb. 20. I Shall delay a while in New Orleans, not long and get to Lancaster by March—If you really desire me to settle in Ohio, you must make some exertions for I cannot abide there long in inactivity and loafing. Apart from the necessity of providing for the future, I cannot change my nature which is fixed for better & worse and it is no use finding fault with it. If we can get possession of some property, with your money still invested so as to bring you some pocket money, well & good—Down Hocking is a sad alternative for our children, and for me who has led an active life, among a class of people no better perhaps than those of Chauncey, yet different in every sense. I have a good letter from Turner in which he infers I cannot stay here, and advises me to come to Saint Louis, but points out no thing definite[2]—He thinks Missouri will not secede, but if she do not they will have a severe contest there, for men who own negros, are blind to all interests other than those of Slavery—Reason has nothing to do in these times of change & Revolution. Politicians start the movement & keep it alive by a process known to themselves and the Poor universal people have nothing to do but follow their lead—It may not be so there, but I am not convinced—I see John takes bold ground. He is right—If the Govt. be a reality, it should defend its flag, property & servants—Anderson should be reinforced if it cost ten thousand lives, and every habitation in Charleston[.] Also the seizure of these arsenals should be resented and the actors made to feel that the U.S. is a reality—But the time is not yet—If this letter reaches you in eight days answer me care of Kennett Bloods Co. (Kennett Blood & Co.) New Orleans—if not—why I'll infer you are all well as usual. I may look in at St. Louis—which is only 60 miles out of the way, to see Turner & Charley.³ Before I leave Ill get my $500. and some 2 mos. pay—in all over $1000—That will be something. Nevertheless I'm going to be as stingy as a miser till I see my way out of the woods, when you may go it again with a looseness—Affectionately

W. T. Sherman

ALS, InND: Sherman Family Papers.

1. Moore to WTS, January 23, 1861; Braxton Bragg to WTS, January 27, 1861; and S. A. Smith to WTS, January 28, 1861; all are in DLC: WTS. Sherman included here a portion of Moore's and Smith's letters.

2. Henry S. Turner to WTS, January 23, 1861, DLC: WTS.

3. Charles Ewing (1835–83) was Ellen's youngest brother and was practicing law in St. Louis.

TO JOHN SHERMAN

Seminary, Feb. 1, 1861

Dear Brother,

I got your Speech last night on the Army Bill,¹ read it with deep interest & have handed it to a friend. I have felt the very thoughts you have spoken—It is war to surround Anderson with Batteries and it is shilly shally for the South to cry—hands off, no coercion: it was war & insult to expel the Garrison at Baton Rouge, and Uncle Sam had better cry *Cave* or assert her power. Fort Sumpter is not material save for the principle—But Key West, and the Tortugas should be held in force, at once by Regulars if possible—if not militia. Quick, they are occupied now, but not in force.

Whilst maintaining the high strong ground you do, I would not advise you to interpose an objection to seeming concessions to the Middle & Moderate States—Virginia, Kentucky, Tennessee and Missouri. Slavery there is local, and even if the world were open to them its extension would involve no principle. If these States feel the extreme South wrong, a seeming concession would make them committed. The Cotton States are gone—I suppose of course their Commerce will be hampered. They want free trade here—to import free, and send their goods up the Rivers free of all charges but freight & insurance— New York Boston, Phila. & Baltimore could not afford to pay duties if New Orleans is a Free port.

But of myself—I sent you a copy of my letter to the Governor—here is his answer.

Baton Rouge, Jan. 23, 1861

Dear Sir,

It is with the deepest regret I acknowledge the receipt of your letter of the 18th inst. In the pressure of official business I can now only request you to transfer to Professor Smith the arms, munitions and funds in your hands whenever you conclude to withdraw from the position you have filled with so much distinction[.] You cannot regret more than I do the necessity which deprives us of your services, and you will bear with you the respect, confidence and admiration of all who have been associated with you. very truly, yr. friend & sevt.

Tho. O. Moore.

This is very handsome, and I do regret this Political Imbroglio—I do think it was brought about by Politicians. The People in the South are evidently unanimous in the opinion that Slavery is endangered by the current of Events, and it is useless to attempt to alter that opinion. As our Government is founded on the Will of the People when that will is fixed—our Govt. is powerless, and the only question is whether to let things slide into General anarchy, or the formation of two or more confederacies, which will be hostile sooner or later. Still I know that some of the best men of Louisiana think this change may be effected peacefully. But even if the Southern States be allowed to part in peace, the first question will be—Revenue—Now if the South have Free trade, how can you collect Revenues in the Eastern cities—Freight from New Orleans to St. Louis, Chicago, Louisville Cincinati & even Pittsburg would be about the same as by Rail from New York & importers at New Orleans having no duties to pay, would undersell the East if they had to pay duties. Therefore if the South make good their confederation and their plan, the Northern Confederacy must do likewise, or Blockade—Then comes the Questions of Foreign Nations. So Look on it on any view I see no result but war, & consequent changes in the Form of Government—I feel no inclination to take part in this Civil Strife because I have not confidence in the military dispositions that may be attempted, unless I were high enough to have a word in the council—I will therefore in the course of February close up my business here, and go north about the 20th inst.—I may stop at St. Louis for a day to see my friends there, but will be in Lancaster before March—If you have the influence I suppose you must, and can use it without indelicacy I would like the Sub Treasurership of St. Louis—I can get testimonials that would Satisfy the most obstinate—Dont represent me as a Republican—but as an American— one who believes that in a few Short years the Inhabitants of the Mississipi & tributaries will *command* this continent.

I expect to be in New Orleans about Feb. 20, and if you have anything for me—drop me a line, care of Kennett Blood & co. New Orleans. I will be there two days to settle accounts. Yrs.

W. T. S.

ALS, DLC: William T. Sherman.

1. JS's speech was in response to one made by George H. Pendleton; both were given on January 18, 1861. John Sherman, *John Sherman's Recollections of Forty Years in the House, Senate and Cabinet*, 2 vols. (Chicago, 1895), 1:215–25.

TO CHARLES EWING

Seminary Sunday, Feb. 3. 1861

Dear Charley,

As soon as I learned that Governor Moore had caused the Forts to be taken, I notified him that as soon as the state seceded he must provide some person to relieve me in my duties & responsibilities here—I have his answer and I am now authorised to transfer to one of the Professors here the arms, munitions and property and to depart so soon as I please—I want to dally out a part of this month for several reasons, one of which is the Severe Cold of February, and another to draw this months pay. I think I might as well look into St. Louis on my way north, and wish you to write me on or before the 20th inst. care of Kennett Blood & Co. New Orleans, and tell me where I will find you in St. Louis—where is your office, and where do you board? I hope Missouri is not going to Secede also—but who knows but the whole fabric of Government will vanish in a mist & dissolve. The fact seems that we really had no Government with force enough to protect itself, and the new one instead of being weaker must be stronger. I dont care about rejoining an army subject to the order and control of Politicians who have not the sense to Govern, and the Spirit to stand by their officers who do act with vigor and Sense.

I must get something to do, and if I can hear of anything in St. Louis I should be most happy—otherwise I suppose I must try farming or the Salt Wells, or some other obscure work for which I am not over qualified—If you see Turner tell him I think I will see him towards the close of February. My best regards to Hunter,[1] affectionately

W. T. Sherman

ALS, DLC: Charles Ewing Family Papers.

1. John Hunter was Charles Ewing's law partner.

TO THOMAS EWING JR.[1]

Dear Tom:

The Secession of this State makes it improper for me to be here, for this is not simply a college, but a Military Station an arsenal, where some of the United States property taken at Baton Rouge is stored. I might also be Called on to do military duty. I have Kept the Governor & others in Authority advised of my opinions & feelings, and that in the event of Secession I must quit— Louisiana has seceded, and a Southern Confederacy will soon be formed, with its President, Congress, cabinet, army & navy all prepared to maintain their independence.

The great struggle will be the middle States and I do hope this Slavery question will not be permitted to array them in hostility, for if they leave [to] the Confederacy, there will be confusion worse confounded.

I will leave here after the middle of February, and think I will go to Saint Louis, where I will look around for a few days and see if any thing offers for me to do—If not then I will go to Lancaster and think what are my best chances. Of Course I want to Know exactly the State of our Common fund, and I would like you to tell me, whether those Leavenworth Lots are worth anything at all. McCook[2] ought to pay that note, to pay taxes.

I suppose Kansas is or has been admitted, but I see your Governor proposes Kansas to set up on her own hook independent of all the world[3]—Go it while you are young. Tell Van Vliet[4] to seize Fort Leavenworth—hoist the Bear flag,[5] and declare himself independent of all Creation. Sell the mules, horses wagons &c. of the late Uncle Sam, and depart for Paris & spend the Proceeds like a Gentleman—That is modern doctrine. Govr. Moore of this state did so with the Public property at Baton Rouge, and has been most liberal with the arms &c. found there within his Jurisdiction, presenting them with his compliments to his Friends & neighbors. I think the People have done as they d—n please so long, that they think their sovereign will is the law—Every state, county, village, family is the Sovereign, and can defy all mankind. Time this farce should cease—if the People are incompetent to Rule, some remedy must be devised. Those who pay the Taxes & Expenses will soon clamor for help and protection.

I suppose you are Chief Justice now of Kansas, that your statutes are the morning papers "and the fundamental constitution" your good will & pleasure.

My opinion is that this Question had gone so far it *must* be met—Secession is Treason—If the will of the People dont conform to the Interest of the Great Whole—it must be made to conform—Louisiana cannot have Free trade to the detriment of the Great Cities East—The state & Local Govts each are so weak they cannot long keep peace along the Mississipi River—but the Status of each State on present issues should be clearly ascertained before Force is resorted to—but in the mean time, army, navy & Police Forces should be well arranged—the Key Forts Monroe, Key West, Tortugas & Ship Island held, and when Legislation is at an end. The principle that the will & pleasure of Local interests must yield to the will interests & pleasure of Great Regions peacefully is possible but forcibly if must—In all this the nigger is a pretext—It is this universal system to which we have all drifted of letting the Local popular will & prejudice override Constitutions & Laws.

Force & Compulsion is as necessary in a Government as in the administration of your Court—what effect would a sentence of Death & imprisonment be without the Scaffold & Penitentiary—or even in civil suits what use would be a Decree in Ejectment without the Sheriff, or marshall with his force to execute—no man surrenders from conviction, but from superior Force, and so with states and communities. They have been taught to regard their will as above law & compulsion, and that is the lesson soon to be taught & learned in America. I intend to lay low to watch events for some time & will seek employment (civil) at St Louis or in Ohio—Affectionately,

W. T. Sherman

ALS, DLC: Thomas Ewing and Family Papers.

1. Thomas Ewing Jr. (1829–96), another of Ellen's brothers, had practiced law with WTS in Leavenworth, Kansas; he was still practicing law there and would be elected the first chief justice of the state's supreme court in 1861.

2. Daniel McCook (1834–64) had been in practice with WTS and Thomas Ewing Jr. in Leavenworth and was still practicing with Ewing at this time. He would serve in the army under Sherman.

3. George M. Beebe had become acting governor of Kansas on January 10, 1861, and had urged that Kansas establish an independent government in light of strife in the United States. Kansas would become a state later that month.

4. Stewart Van Vliet (1815–1901), an army friend of WTS, was stationed at Fort Leavenworth at this time and would become chief quartermaster of the Army of the Potomac in the summer of 1861.

5. The flag used by John Frémont and his men in establishing the short-lived Republic of California in June 1846.

TO ELLEN EWING SHERMAN

Seminary, Feb. 16, 1861 (Sunday)

Dearest Ellen,

I have been busy all day in making up accounts & papers and packing up. I shall leave here on Tuesday and will meet Dr. Smith at New Orleans by Friday, and hope to take the cars by Saturday night for St. Louis. I have two letters from you[1] and one from Minnie since my last, and hope by tomorrows mail to get another which you say Minnie promised to write on my birthday. I am glad to hear you are all so well and that Lizzie is improving I hope spring will restore her hearing, and that Something may be done to sever her from the great misfortune of losing the Sense of hearing which would be a terrible loss. Your many accounts are very full, and all I can hope for is that we may have as much to spend in the next two years without trespassing upon those funds which should be held sacred for after times. I expect nothing at St. Louis and go there merely to See old acquaintances & friends and to look at that little Farm. I will not delay long and will be home before the 4th March. That is I suppose the critical moment—much now depends on the action of that assemblage in Washington of which I am pleased to see your father is a member. Still when opinions so widely vary as they do it is almost impossible to discuss any practicable question. I went up the Bayou last week to visit the Luckitts—Sanfords, Comptons, Grahams and Longs—All however were so full of northern outrages, wrongs, oppressions &c. that twas useless to argue. There seems to be universal regret that I leave, and I received unmistakeable evidences of kindly regard that I cannot but feel some regret at parting—more especially on the indefinite plans and expectations for the future maintenance of my family but as I do so for your sake I know if we come to want you will not deny that I have made every honorable effort to better our condition. If you really wish me to settle down in peace you must bear with my impatience and must not misconstrue my motives or denounce so severely my Religious opinions, or what you believe my want of Religious faith. I dined with the Priest a few days since and he pledged your health in a full glass. All the Ladies express their regret that my departure cuts off all hope of their making your acquaintance. They were prepared to welcome you to this country. But the die is cast and again I must forth, and where to fetch up will depend on the storms of an unknown sea. I think I would feel more at ease anywhere rather than Ohio, but I acknowledge the impossibility and impropriety of moving you away. As I want no delay, if your father is still in Washington, ask him specifically how much he will allow me for one year at the salt wells, to manage all things there according to his wishes—at the end of that time I might bargain for the Lease—but I would not on any account do so, with the imperfect knowledge of the business and resources of the place—My letters to John may have been intercepted. Better let him know I will be in Lancaster by Mch. 4. I will likely write a few lines from Cairo. Yrs. truly

Sherman

ALS, InND: Sherman Family Papers.
1. On January 29, EES wrote to say she was trying to get work for him at the saltworks

and gave an extensive accounting of her expenditures since 1859. Her feelings on Cump's employment were that "you will never be happy in this world unless you go into the army again." She was enraged by Southern attitudes and Buchanan's bungling and weakness: "If Jackson had been in his place the Government would have been strong enough & the rebels weak enough by this time." She was disgusted by Turner's Southern sympathies—"Major Turner was educated & supported by Government for years of his life & in her first emergency he is ready not only to turn his back on her but to turn the knowledge & the arms she has given him against her." She reproached Cump for questioning her loyalty to him because she had made no plans to come south, pointing out that she had moved numerous times in ten years for him as well as enduring "the sickness & pain of bearing & giving birth to five children" and that Cump himself had spoken of the Southern politics and situation so that she had "looked upon your situation there as *temporary*." Two days later she wrote more on general business matters and the health and activities of the children. SFP.

TO DAVID F. BOYD

Feb. 23. 1861. New Orleans.

Dear Mr. Boyd,

I fear from our experience here, the cadets did not have a good time of it last night. It rained here a part of the day and night, and now we are having a sort of Postscript in a heavy shower. I have had a good deal of running about to do to day, because I got here on Thursday after Bank hours and yesterday being a holiday it was closed, and this morning on application I found the Book which I had sent down a week ago by mail only got here this morning; So I did not get it till 2½ P.M. and Dr. Smith wanted to go to Baton Rouge at 5 P.M., so we gave it but a rapid examination, but there being a balance in Bank larger than I claimed Dr. Smith was on the safe side in passing it. I have been with him to the boat, and he is off for Baton Rouge—and I have nought to do but be off for home—I shall to-morrow, Sunday start for St. Louis to reach there Monday evening. Tell St. Ange that I found Madame Lefevre and got the books entered though I was bothered by the Deputy Collector—Still I think he will soon receive the books I made the custom-House oath without seeing the list or invoice of books.

I know you will expect me to tell you some general political news. All here is Secession on the Streets—In doors they are more reasonable and some have said to me that even yet if the North will give guarantees this State would return. More than one have said that leaders were afraid to leave it to a vote of the people. Congress can do nothing—The Peace Conference may report[1]—I don't see what Lincoln or any man can do, when Sections are arrayed against each other and will not believe each other. I still adhere to my old notion that we have to fear anarchy more than a direct conflict on the slavery issue; If any one of the Southern States become dissatisfied with the Tariff policy of the new combination, and I have heard merchants myself talk pretty plainly of the Tariff already imposed on Northern goods, they will secede a second time and so on to the end of the Chapter. I have seen a good deal of Bragg, who goes on quietly but steadily organizing two Regiments of Regulars, and mark my word when a time of Strife does come, he will be prepared. He tells me there is an officer at West Point whose name I now forget, who wants to be your superintendent. But the Governor has advertised for one to apply before April 6, so that no choice will take place till then. In the mean time Dr. Smith has the check-book and can draw for money. I really do hope you may have a clever fellow for your social position is one of isolation and those who are so banished should have respect and even fondness for each other. There is no pleasure or satisfaction in life when one's associate is devoid of feeling, sense, or judgment—with these and a few companions I have never much cared whether my abode was in Wall St., St. Francisco, in the Desert, in Kansas or Ohio. But the truth is I have been socially too much isolated from my children, and now that they are at an age when for good or ill we should be together I must try and allay that feeling of change and venture that has made me a wanderer. If possible I will settle down—fast—and positive—Of a summer eve with my little Minnie and Willy and the rascal Tom I can live over again my Florida life—My ventures in California, and my short sojourn in the pine woods of Louisiana, and I will teach them that there are kind good people everywhere, that a Great God made all the world—that he slighted no part, that to some he assigned the Rock and fir—with clear babbling brooks— but cold and bitter winters—to others the grassy plain and fertile soil—to others the rich alluvium and burning sun to ripen the orange and sugar cane, but everywhere he gave the same firmament, the same gentle moon, and to the inhabitants the same attributes for good and evil. What a beautiful task in theory, which may all explode the first moment of its realization but still one to dream of—And I Know you will believe me sincere when I hope in that little group, wherever it may be, you will some day drop in and try my hospitality. I assure you I know of no gentleman who I would more gladly receive under my roof because I feel you would appreciate what is good in fact, good in intention, and would make allowances for poverty or mismanagement.

If present politicians break up our Country—let us resolve to reestablish it—for the ties "interpartes" ought not to be severed—Good bye Your friend
Sherman

Copy, InND: Sherman Family Papers; docketed "A true copy. D. F. Boyd."

1. The Washington Peace Conference, also known as the "Old Gentlemen's Convention" because of the age of the delegates, had begun meeting in the capital city on February 4 with John Tyler heading the proceedings. On February 15 a committee presented its resolu-

tions for reuniting the country and the conference began debating them. On February 27 they reported their conclusions to the Congress for action, suggesting six constitutional amendments dealing with various aspects of slavery. Congress did not act on any of their suggestions.

TO ELLEN EWING SHERMAN

New Orleans, Feb. 23, 1861

Dearest Ellen,

I enclose for safety Duplicates of Bills on New York the originals of which I keep with me—These Duplicates are not endorsed and cannot be used unless some accident befal me en route. I send them out of precaution. I am here on business & will be busily occupied all day. If I can I will get off tomorrow Sunday morning in the Train & reach St. Louis Tuesday. I will be home about Friday, or Saturday according to the Rail Road time.

Nothing new—all Secession here, & I am "Suspect."

Am quite well, and impatient to be off. Yrs. Ever,

W. T. Sherman

ALS, InND: Sherman Family Papers.

TO ELLEN EWING SHERMAN

On Board the Boat from Columbus Ky. to Cairo
Monday 9 P.M. [Feb. 25, 1861]

Dearest Ellen

I left New Orleans yesterday morning and will be in St. Louis Tomorrow noon. I will not stay there long and will be home by or before Saturday—I want to see Turner & a few others and to look at that Farm—If I can get off Thursday I will, but rather think that Friday will be as soon as I can get off—You may certainly expect me on Saturday—Political matters are certainly as bad as possible, and I see no immediate chances of a favorable change—I fear all the Slave States will secede, for they seem to await Legislation for which there is neither time or inclination. If the Politicians would do the fighting it would be a good thing but when that comes they are the first to run away. I got no letter from you in New Orleans but wrote you ones which you probably received before this—I am quite well and am not at all tired by the trip. I expect to get a sleeping car tonight in which case I shall be fresh in St. Louis.

I will try and take the cars so that I will not stop in Cincinati at all. In St. Louis I will stop at ⟨illegible⟩, where Charley gets his meals. Yrs. in haste

W. T. Sherman

ALS, InND: Sherman Family Papers.

CHAPTER 2

March 9, 1861–July 14, 1861

For all his blunt declarations about the crisis of the Union and his commitment to combat secession, William T. Sherman was slow to act on his beliefs in offering his services to preserve, protect, and defend the United States. Days after Lincoln's inaugural he traveled to Washington at John Sherman's behest to confer with his brother and family members about what he might do. John, soon to be a United States senator, intended to show him off to others. Cump thought he might secure the post of treasurer at St. Louis, despite his ambiguous experience with financial matters in the past. That was impossible: instead, John offered the chief clerkship of the Government Loan Office. This was to be but a temporary position, enabling Sherman to establish residence in Washington, meet people, and exhibit his abilities for advancement. Deeming such a position beneath him, Cump turned it down.

In contemplating whether to seek a position, civil or military, under the new administration, Sherman revealed that at the time he thought highly of himself and not much of most others. Although he was perfectly willing to use John's connections with the incoming treasury secretary, Salmon P. Chase, to ask for a position, he complained when Lincoln used patronage to solidify political alliances and declared that under such circumstances he did not want office. Nor was he impressed by a visit to the new president's office: having come to offer his services in the military, he was chagrined at Lincoln's seeming lack of awareness about the severity of the present crisis. The president did not accept Sherman's offer; brother John led his fuming sibling away from the White House. Roundly damning politicians, Cump announced, "You have got things in a hell of a fix, and you may get out of them as best you can." Instead, he found work as president of a streetcar company in St. Louis—and immediately sought an army commission for the son of the man who had offered him the post, suggesting that he was no stranger to the world of political favors.[1]

As the crisis over the fate of the United States garrison at Fort Sumter, South Carolina, reached its climax, Sherman turned down yet another chance to render service when he declined appointment as the chief clerk of the War Department with the promise of elevation to assistant secretary of war when Congress met. This position should have been more than enough to satisfy any reasonable ambitions Sherman entertained, for, in light of the manifest shortcomings of Secretary of War Simon Cameron, Sherman would have played a major role in preparing the Union war machine—and been in line to replace Cameron. Nevertheless, Sherman turned down the offer. Although he was concerned about his ability to provide for his family, he was also disgusted with the present state of affairs, churlishly telling Montgomery Blair, "I wish the Administration all success in its almost impossible task of governing this distracted and anarchical people."[2]

Days later hostilities commenced in earnest. Refusing to join the rush to enlist, Sherman asserted that in time his qualifications would secure him a suitable commission—although he also caustically commented on the lack of volunteers in St. Louis and elsewhere. Nor did he want to train citizen volunteers, offering comments that would have stung the souls of the men who later cheered him as "Uncle Billy." Eventually he accepted the colonelcy of the newly created Thirteenth United States Infantry. In so doing he could assert that he was assuming command of a regular army unit, although in fact the ranks of the new regiment would be drawn from volunteers.

Although Sherman hoped that he could recruit his regiment in Missouri, he found himself in Washington and its surrounding encampments. He assumed command of a brigade composed of volunteers from New York and Wisconsin and a battery of artillery. If the new recruits did not yet appear to be soldiers, their brigade commander did not look like a leader: his gaunt and disheveled appearance, highlighted by his unruly red hair and bushy, unkempt beard under a straw hat, was a far cry from Napoleon or Winfield Scott. Much had to be done, and there was little time in which to do it, for on July 16, 1861, the Union army under the command of Brigadier General Irvin McDowell commenced marching southward.

During these months Sherman expressed himself freely on the issues of the day, demonstrating that for all his talk about politicians, their major shortcoming in his eyes was that they did not share his priorities or values. He insisted that abolition form no part of the cause of the Union, for otherwise the conflict would "gradually become a War of Extermination a war without End." He had no patience for politicians, displaying no understanding of their concerns or responsibilities. To him the practices of democratic politics demonstrated the shortcomings of the American political system and the people it served—an ironic conclusion in light of his commitment to save that nation from dismemberment. Bad as things were, however, disunion would render them worse; with that in mind, he at last decided to help save the Union.[3]

1. Lloyd Lewis, *Sherman: Fighting Prophet* (1932; reprint, Lincoln, Neb., 1993), 149–50.
2. WTS to Montgomery Blair, April 8, 1861, *PM*, 1:199.
3. WTS to JS, April 22, 1861.

TO JOHN SHERMAN

Lancaster, Sunday, Mch. 9, 61.

Dear Brother,

Mr. Ewing & I got home last night. Theodore Talmadge was in the cars with us, and doubtless reached Columbus yesterday by 2 P.M. He promised to hunt Charles[1] up immediately and tell him I was in Lancaster, and that I would come up to Columbus the instant he telegraphed I could be of any service to you. I will expect such a message tomorrow morning—none came last evening.

We were delayed 2 hours in Turnersville of which I availed myself to See Mary Granger[2] and Doly Reese.[3] I found them well—Mr. Granger had gone to Columbus to befriend you. I also enquired for Mr. Goddard and found that he had also gone on the same errand so that it does seem your friends are wide awake. From items overheard in the Cars I infer that you are very generally preferred, but Wade's[4] strikers fear your Election will damage his prospects two years hence—also the papers say you cannot be spared from your leading Position in the H. R. whereof they think you certainly will be the next Speaker.

All these propositions flattering to yourself, are evident means of opposition to your fair claims and real wishes, but I know you have plenty to represent you in Columbus. Were I to go up I might damage your prospects by my want of appreciation of partizan reasons and combinations. Still if Charles telegraph I will go up, and indeed I think I will make sure by telegraphing him tomorrow morning, to that effect.

I most heartily wish you successful because of the more honorable, dignified & less laborious position of Senator, as contrasted with your present Post.

As to myself, I have revolved all chances in mind, and I will go to Saint Louis anyhow. I will take all the family & household Goods, and establish myself there with the chances. I have written to Gantt[5] who is a member of the Convention, to telegraph me the moment he can, that Missouri will in no event leave the Union. I am almost certain of some break up of our present Confederacy, but to what Extent cannot foresee—and violence must ensue. Still, Missouri is physically bound to the North West, and cannot break off, without sure & certain civil strife within her borders. As soon however as the present Convention declares emphatically that She will remain in the Union, I will move. I see nothing definite to do—but still I cannot remain thus, and am not willing to move my family down to the Salt Wells, where they would grow up in rudeness and without fortune.

I have written to other friends of this my purpose to prepare my way, and have told them of Frank Blair's[6] opposition to my application—I am the only Northern man who has declared fidelity to the Union in opposition to this modern anarchical doctrine of State Secession—and yet this is nothing as compared to local partizans service. If this be the Rule Mr. Lincoln must expect all National men to slide out of his service, and the want of appreciation of fidelity to the Law, as compared with more partizan service will lead to the betrayal of his army & navy already demoralized by shameful neglect and pusillanimity on the part of the General Government. No military man will place his life & honor in jeopardy for the sake of a weak, temporizing & partizan Government. I admit Lincoln has an awful task and if he succeeds in avoiding strife and allaying fears he will be entitled to the admiration of the world—but a time has occurred in all Governments and has now occurred in this when Force must back the Laws, and the longer the postponement the more severe must be the application.

In regard to my affairs all I ask is that Chase should know who & what I am how it happens I am not now at St. Louis, and that I consider the office asked for not as a local office subject to political distribution—but a Branch of his own office of Treasury of the United States. Recent events have shown the necessity of tried and determined Guardians of the public Treasure—with that office I have an easy future, without it a struggle with poverty.

We are all well—I may leave for St. Louis in a week. yr. brother

W. T. Sherman

ALS, DLC: William T. Sherman.

1. Charles Taylor Sherman (1811–79), the eldest of Sherman's siblings, was a lawyer and judge.

2. Mary Reese Granger was the daughter of WTS's sister Mary Elizabeth Sherman Reese.

3. Another of Elizabeth Sherman Reese's daughters.

4. Benjamin F. Wade (1800–1878) was the other U.S. senator from Ohio.

5. Thomas Tasker Gantt of St. Louis had been a law partner of Montgomery Blair and was a Unionist. He would serve on McClellan's staff from 1861 to 1862 before being appointed provost marshal general of Missouri in 1862.

6. Francis Preston Blair Jr. (1821–75) was a U.S. representative from Missouri. Later he would serve under WTS in the Army of the Tennessee.

TO JOHN SHERMAN

> Burnet House, Johnson, Saunders &
> Co. Proprietors.
> Cincinnati, Mch. 21, 1861
> Thursday—

Dear Brother

I am here with all my family & household Goods to embark for St. Louis. The Boat was advertised for today, but will not get off till tomorrow, and I expect to be in St. Louis by Tuesday next.

I was rejoiced to See in this morning's papers, that after a long struggle you got the nomination for Senator, which I suppose amounts to an Election.[1]

That really is an honor, and I congratulate you, for it will now enable you to rise above that little Demagoguery which must I suppose characterize the lower and Popular Branch of the National Legislature. As Senator you represent the whole Govt. and not a Constituency. I Know the modern doctrine of instruction has had a tendency to bring down the Senate in the scale of independence but I hope you will now Kick all platforms & old part precedents to the Devil, and look the Questions that now threaten our national Existence square in the face—and generally aim to be a U.S. Statesman instead of a mere Republican, a mere partizan.

I see the place I aimed at is filled: well I cant help it—the day may come when my services are wanted, and then it may be my turn. I am the only northern man who has been fool enough to suppose his section cared a d——n about the North—The South try to attract People to their section, The North dont care a d——n—and this is a fact you should Know—Davis[2] is securing the very best officers—South & *North*—I know it: and although the vast superiority in numbers of the North, the South is united in the belief—whether true or false that the Political Domination of the North will be fatal to them. On the Slavery Question as much forbearance should be made as possible, but on the Doctrine of Secession, *none* whatever. They are widely different.

If slavery & free labor are inconsistent divide now, at o{nce} and forever— If not then assert the integrity of the Nation and fight for it—The longer it is postponed the worse it will be. Fighting instead of spreading produces quite a different result—Believe me always most affectionately yr. brother

W. T. Sherman

ALS, DLC: William T. Sherman.

1. Chase had resigned his Senate seat on March 7, 1861, to accept the position of secretary of the treasury; JS was elected in his place and took his seat on March 23.

2. Jefferson Davis (1808–89) had been inaugurated provisional president of the Confederacy in February 1861.

TO JOHN SHERMAN

Cincinati, Mch. 22. 61.

Dear Brother,

The Boat *Emma Duncan* on which I have taken passage for St. Louis leaves at 4 P.M. today—I go aboard in about an hour, and before starting I think it proper to write you of one or two things which Keep to yourself, as the source is Confidential—Young Tom Ewing who started last night by R. R. for Kansas told his father that he had asked you to introduce him to Mr. Lincoln, that you put him off, or answered evasively—that he stated his wish to another senator (Fessenden)[1] I think, who promptly took him in his Carriage to the Presdt. and introduced him so flatteringly that the President gave him absolutely the appointment of the three leading appointments for Kansas, viz. Marshal, Indian Agent & some other—Tom Jr. is Chief Justice of Kansas, and will in the Confusion of things in Kansas most likely be selected as the safest man for Senator, and if so will come to Washington with a grudge against you—All the Ewings think you have slighted me—that your mere demand would have secured me anything—that the office of Chief Clerk in the War Dept. was beneath my deserts certainly a shock to my pride, and in general that I have been slighted—This Ellen has let fall since we read of your Election to the Senate.

Now I am satisfied that under the Circumstances I was forced to come away from Louisiana, though I could have Easily got the Governor to release me from any military obligations, other than those of instructing young Cadets and thereby retained a competent salary whereas I am now with an Expensive family actually adrift dependant upon blind chances. My personal friend Turner may succeed in getting me occupation on a Street Railroad but again he may fail, in which event I will try and get a Clerkship in some store.[2] It certainly is humiliating to me, who have filled high posts with honor, credit and success, to be compelled to go begging for mere manual employment, but I will not throw the blame on you for I am well assured if I had Solicited anything definite you would have aided me: but to live with my family was inconsistent with any mere appointment in the army open to Citizens, & therefore it was my choice, not yours, that I cut loose. Now if there be any thing in St. Louis open to your influence I do think you should demand it for me as a means of mere livelihood till I can recover from the loss I have sustained in relinquishing my place South. I confess I Know of none such, & that I would starve and see my family want rather than ask Frank Blair, or any of the Blairs, whom I Know to be a selfish and unscrupulous set of ——. Mr. Ewing is in no condition financially to help me at all, and unless I get employment of Some Kind in four months I will be desperate. I do think the administration is committing a fatal mistake in giving the Cold shoulder to all national men, as compared with mere politicians—It may by so doing, demoralize the army & navy so that when the time does come for action they will incline against your party. New England has succeeded in substituting her local ideas for those of Virginia, and these may be as unpalatable to the Great Centre on which must depend the Future of this Country.

Keep to yourself what I say about the Ewings and reconcile yourself to Tom as you best may, when he returns to Washington. I think he did not make due allowance for the manner you were pressed by others who had equal if not stronger claims on your time, but you had better have him as an ally than enemy. I would like to hear from you when I get to St. Louis.

I heartily congratulate you on your success as Senator, & hope you will honor the place. Yr. brother—

W. T. Sherman

ALS, DLC: William T. Sherman.

1. Republican Senator William Pitt Fessenden (1806–69) of Maine.

2. Henry S. Turner to WTS, February 24, 1861, DLC: WTS, had offered him an appointment as head of a horsecar railway in St. Louis with a $2,000 annual salary.

TO DAVID F. BOYD

Office St. Louis R. R. Co.
St. Louis April 4 1861.

Professor Boyd,
My Dear Friend,

I promised you all to Keep you advised of my whereabouts that we may interchange from time to time the thoughts and feelings of respect and affection which I feel assured still subsist between us.

By the caption of this letter you will see me in a R. R. office of which I am the President with a salary of $2000.

I have my entire family in a good house 226 Locust St., with plenty of Room and a hearty welcome for friends who come to me from the four quarters of the Globe, and I will believe that you, or Smith, or the Doctor, yea Mr. St. Ange, may some summer come up to this Great City, the heart of North America and see me and mine. I acted with energy, went to Washington, satisfied myself that Lincoln was organizing his administration on pure party principles, concluded it was no place for me who profess to love and venerate my whole country and not a mere Fraction—and forthwith to Lancaster, pulled up stakes, to Cincinati, and embarked all hands, with carpets, chairs, beds, and Kitchen utensils, even my household servants and before one month of my vacating my berth in Louisiana, I was living in St. Louis. I see my way ahead for one year, and must trust to the Future, and having an abundance of faith in St. Louis, with its vast fertile surrounding Country I feel no uneasiness—My two eldest girls are in a Catholic School—and this morning I put my boy Willy in a Public School, so that with the exception of some trifling articles of Furniture I am settled. My duties here are clearly within my comprehension and indeed I think I can actually make myself more than useful to the Stockholders by giving personal attention, which heretofore has devolved on hirelings.

In Politics I do not think I change with Country—On the negro question I am satisfied there is and was no cause for a severance of the old Union, but will go further and say that I believe the practice of slavery in the South is the mildest and best regulated system of slavery in the world now or heretofore.

But as there is an incongruity in white and black labor I do think in the New Territories the line of separation should be drawn before rather than after settlement. As to any Guarantees I would favor any approved by Rives,[1] Bell, Crittenden,[2] and such men whose patriotism cannot be questioned. On the question of secession however I am *ultra*—I believe in *coercion* and cannot comprehend how any Government can exist unless it defend its integrity. The Mode and Manner may be regulated by Policy and wisdom, but that any part of a people may carry off a part of the Common Territory without consent or purchase, I cannot understand. Now I Know as well as I can Know any thing uncertain that Louisiana cannot belong to a string of Southern States—She must belong to a system embracing the Valley States—It may be these Valley States may come to Louisiana, but ultimately one way or another the Valley of the Mississipi must be under one system of Government. Else quarrels, troubles, and Confusions worse than war, will be continuous.

My brother John is now senator and quite a man among the Republicans— but he regards me as erratic in politics—He nor politicians generally can understand the feelings and opinions of one who thinks himself above parties and looks upon the petty machinery of party as disgusting. There are great numbers here who think like me—and at the election here a few days ago, the Black Republicans were beaten, because the country expected of Mr. Lincoln a National and not a Party Government. Had the Southern States borne patiently for 4 years they could have had a radical change in 1864 that might have lasted 20 years—whereas now no man is wise enough to even guess at future combinations.

I hope you are all well, that the Seminary continues to prosper—that you have a clever Superintendent and that one day not far distant we may sail under the same flag. My best respects to the Jarreaus and all friends. Yours,

W. T. Sherman

Copy, InND: Sherman Family Papers; docketed "A true Copy. D. F. Boyd."

1. Presumably former U.S. senator William C. Rives (1792–1868) of Virginia.

2. John J. Crittenden (1787–1863) was U.S. senator from Kentucky and the author of the 1860 Crittenden Compromise, which featured guidelines for the territorial expansion of slavery and a constitutional amendment prohibiting Federal interference with slavery.

TO JOHN SHERMAN

Office St. Louis R. R. Co.

St. Louis, Apl. 8, 1861

Dear Brother,

A few days ago, I wrote to you about getting a subordinate commission in the army for Thomas T. Turner son of my particular friend the Major.[1] I again urge it, assuring you I know it is all right, regular & proper—save that it may be doing an injustice to the Class of Cadets to graduate at West Point next June, but the vacancies this year will be ten times as many as that class can fill. You Know I think the administration has made a fatal mistake in appointing to office utterly without regard to qualifications, solely on the basis of service to its Party. Now it should use it honors & offices to attract and attach the vast number of moderate respectable People who can never be partizans, and in this light the appointment of Maj. Turners son would absolutely be a link between the Government and a large wealthy and most respectable family here and in Virginia, the very districts where Policy should be used to invite support. Small as this Boon is I repeat I would be more pleased to hand Maj. Turner a Commission for his son in the Dragoons or Cavalry, than to receive a Brigadier Genls. commission myself.

I have just recd. yours of Apl. 3 from Mansfield.[2] I thought Tom Ewing was unreasonable, Knowing how busy you were at the time in Washington: I assure you I did not share his or Ellens conclusions for I know they exaggerated your influence. They think Lincoln could not say nay if you only breathed a wish— some even have thought I ought to have succeeded Twiggs[3] or Cooper[4]—but an attempt that way would have been an outrage and I would not have dreamed of it.

In the army there is or can be no opening for me, unless in case of a material increase. The only place I would accept would be Inspector General, or Brigadier General. When in Washington, Lancaster & Cincinati, I did feel nervous and anxious as I well might because my family expenses are near $300 a month, and I cannot keep them down, and St. Louis was my only chance: My reputation as a Financier was equal to that in the Army & Frank Blair knew it—The place of Surveyor Genl. too I could have filled but that too was given to a sub editor of a paper, Cuppy who I will venture to say could not adjust a Theodolite,[5] or work up a set of Field notes if his Life depended on it. It does look to me as if our Govt. had Culminated in a condition where some Radical change must occur—but I confess I dont Know what change, or how it is to be accomplished.

Saturday night late I received this despatch. "Will you accept the Chief Clerkship in the War Dept. We will make you assistant secretary when Congress meets—Mr. Blair."[6] This morning I answered by Telegraph "I cannot accept," & by letter, "I came to St. Louis and have accepted a place in this company, have rented a house, & incurred other obligations, so that I am not at liberty to change. I thank you for the Compliment conveyed in your offer: and assure you that I wish the administration all success in its almost impossible task of governing this Distracted & anarchical People."[7]

As to Mr. Bates'[8] supposition that I am well off I will mention to you, that when here as Commissary in 1851 & 2, Mr. Ewing gave Ellen $3000 in property of my choice in Stoddards addition which I have since sold, for $10,000, which I still hold in interest paying notes. Also when I withdrew from California— Mr. Lucas insisted in presenting to Ellen a house & lot he had built for me in San Francisco which also I have sold for $6000 which I still hold in interest paying notes: in 1851, I invested all my means some $7000, in property here and in Illinois: when the Bottom fell out in California I found myself agent for a good deal of money, $136,000, belonging to officers of the army, who had sent it to me: In order to get away from California, I had to make sacrifices to collect, and I conceived myself bound in honor to make good losses as far as my individual property went, so I sold 640 acres in Illinois—3 houses in St. Louis, and about a dozen of lots, all of which I gave away. Some of this went to Bragg, & Myers[9] who are now high in power among our enemies & balance to others whom I will not name. But now I own not a foot in St. Louis and only 40 acres in Illinois valued at say $1000.

My present salary is $2000, but I expect gradually to get into some other channel where I can make additional Salary.

Business here is very depressed from Political causes. I will be prudent & quarrel with no one much less the Blairs. Love to all & believe me most affectionately your Brother

W. T. Sherman

ALS, DLC: William T. Sherman.

1. On April 4, WTS had written his brother, "The best friend I ever had, and the one whom I most esteem is Henry S. Turner of this City." Turner was a friend from West Point and one of his banking partners in California. Turner had gotten WTS his current job with the St. Louis Railroad Company. His son Thomas was twenty-four and had been educated in Europe and the United States and was currently studying law although the promise of a share of his grandmother Hunt's large fortune made him lazy. The Turners sought a commission in the army for Thomas. WTS asked JS to approach Lincoln or Cameron, his secretary of war, directly in this case and bypass Frank Blair. "Turner is no Republican, but he is a Gentleman & Soldier and his son will be an honorable faithful officer." DLC: WTS.

2. On March 22, WTS had written JS that Thomas Ewing Jr. thought that JS had slighted him and not wanted to introduce him to Lincoln. The Ewing family also thought that JS had slighted his brother. While WTS did not share these feelings, he would appreciate it if JS would exert himself to get WTS any St. Louis post he might hear of. On April 3, JS had replied that he was surprised by this news; he had not introduced Tom to Lincoln only because it was not a good time to approach the president. He thought highly of Tom and certainly did not hold a grudge against Thomas Ewing Sr. for the time when the elder Ewing did not make him a district attorney in 1849 because he soon realized that he was too young and inexperienced for the job. JS concluded that WTS had friends in Scott, Montgomery Blair, Cameron, and Chase, and he could expect a job offer soon. DLC: WTS.

3. David E. Twiggs (1790–1862) had been in command of the Department of Texas for

the U.S. Army when he had surrendered his troops to Benjamin McCulloch in February 1861 and had accepted a commission as major general in the C.S. Army.

4. Samuel Cooper (1798–1876), adjutant and inspector general of the C.S. Army, had been adjutant general of the U.S. Army before his resignation in March 1861.

5. A surveyor's instrument for measuring angles.

6. Montgomery Blair to WTS, April 6, 1861, DLC: WTS.

7. WTS to Montgomery Blair, April 8, 1861, *PM*, 1:198.

8. Edward Bates (1793–1869), Lincoln's attorney general, whom JS had reported in his April 3 letter as saying that WTS was rich and ready to enjoy himself.

9. Abraham C. Myers (ca. 1811–89), who had served as chief quartermaster in various U.S. Army departments and with WTS in Charleston in the 1840s, had resigned his U.S. commission on January 28 and would become quartermaster general of the Confederate army.

TO JOHN SHERMAN

Office St. Louis R. R. Co.

St. Louis, April 18, 1861

Dear Brother,

I cannot tell you how glad I was to hear from you the promise of a commission for Turners son.[1] Poor Turner is awfully troubled, full of the warmest feelings and deep convictions he is troubled by Political events.[2] He feels for the South, his Judgment has made him resolve to Stick to and die with Missouri and now Missouri trembles in the Balance. All the Leaders of the State are Virginia, Kentucky and Southern men—the Govr.[3] Lt. Govr.[4] and all leading Politicians. They are alone restrained by habit, and doubt of their true interests: but it is manifest that Missouri will not identify Lincoln with Uncle Sam. Your Party has a platform whether good or bad which is the Rule of action for the Government, and as it is believed to be aggressive to Slavery, will not meet the support of Slave States. If a Great conflict in inevitable, they can only be expected to be neutral. For myself I have taken my Corner. Had Lincoln on his installation to office, made his acts less partizan, I might have been induced to take an active part, but I will not be drawn into such a muddle. In the first place I have not confidence in the head & advisors. I will not act with 3 month volunteers. I will not identify myself with a Partizan Government. I know Mr. Lincoln is President, and entitled to the obedience and support of all loyal subjects; but when the real power is in some obscure evening paper, located no one Knows where, no military man can act with vigor—Look how already our officers have been treated. Even Anderson would be and will be sacrificed by newspapers & the People.

Last night after I was in bed a Gentleman called: I got up & found him a messenger from Frank Blair who wants to see me, he is unwell, or as I believe scared. He is going to Send his family away, & will follow himself—That conforms with my theory, that the Politicians are the first to flee the danger of their own creation. I promised to go up and see him, and will do so in course of the day. I know what he wants. He wants to make use of me. In Washington I was not a citizen of St. Louis & not entitled even to be thought of for any office that would support me, but now I am good enough to be consulted. The first movements of our Govt. will fail, and the Leaders will be cast aside. A second or third set will rise, and amongst them I may be, but at present I will not volunteer as a soldier or anything else. If Congress meet, or if a national convention be called, and the Regular army be put on a footing with the wants of the Country, if I am offered a place that suits me I may accept. But in the present call I will not volunteer.

I have just been up to see Frank Blair[.] He wanted me to undertake to raise a Regiment under the Presidents call,[5] in spite of Governor Jacksons refusal: I told him in substance, that when in Washington I was adrift and met no encouragement for employment, and that I was forced to seek work which I have secured here, and have incurred expense $700 for Rent, $500 for furniture & travelling expenses &c. &c. and that I am in no condition to volunteer for 3 months with the naked chance of permanency: as when the necessity is past I know any foul mouth scamp of a sub editor will be preferred to any amount of professional skill.

The time will come in this country when Professional Knowledge will be appreciated, when men that can be trusted will be wanted, and I will bide my time, I may miss the chance, and if so all right—but I can not & will not mix myself in this present call.[6] You are all right. It is an administration of your choice, as you think it right, and must back it up with power, adequate to its wants and necessities—but I say volunteers & militia never were, and never will be fit for Invasion and whoever tries it will be defeated & dropt by Lincoln like a hot potato.

Minute men are drilling by night and some think will attack the arsenal I think not, at all events till Missouri is out by Act of Convention, and that will take time, and depends on events yet to occur. If an abortive attempt at Invasion be made, it may occur. We are all well Ellen is frightened & wants to go home, but I say no—here we are & here we stay. Yrs.

W. T. S.

ALS, DLC: William T. Sherman.

1. JS wrote WTS on April 9 promising that he would get Thomas Turner a commission and enclosed a copy of his letter to Cameron. JS further verified this in his letters of April 12 and 14. DLC: WTS.

2. Turner had earlier stood as a Constitutional Union candidate for the Missouri Secession Convention. On April 17, Missouri had refused to send its share of militia to the U.S. Army in answer to Lincoln's April 14 call.

3. Claiborne F. Jackson (1806–62) had been elected governor of Missouri; he would be removed from office in June 1861 after the Planters' House Conference.

4. Thomas C. Reynolds (1821–87), a lawyer who had been both a Democrat and a Know-Nothing, would become the Confederate governor of the state and would later flee to Mexico.

5. Upon news of the surrender of Fort Sumter, Lincoln called for the states to raise seventy-five thousand militia troops for three months' service.

6. On April 12, JS had written from Washington that there was "an earnest desire that you go into the War Dept." by men such as Chase who wanted him to accept the proffered post of assistant secretary of war; though JS still thought he should wait for something else, he did urge Cump to think carefully before turning anything down. A position in the army "will at once put [you] into a high position *for life*." DLC: WTS.

TO JOHN SHERMAN

Office St. Louis R. R. Co.

St. Louis, April 22 1861

Dear Brother,

I am this moment in receipt of yours of April 19, from Sandusky.

I know full well the force of what you say. At a moment like this the Country expects every man to do his duty. But every man is not at liberty to do as he pleases. You Know that Mr. Lincoln said to you & me that he did not think he wanted military men. I was then free, uncommitted, and without the means of livelihood, and necessity forced me to seek it here. Ohio has always ignored me. When last fall I sought employment as a Rail Road [agent] I could not get it. Ohio has always preferred strangers, & Foreigners to her Native Born Citizens, and this has always turned me off, when I was really in want. Now she expects me to break a contract for a permanent employment in exchange for a three months service. It may be said that war disturbs all prior engagements. But war existed when I was in Washington. The South had rebelled, had seized Forts, arsenals, and money—had driven out all the faithful servants of our Government and insulted our National flag in a thousand ways. I resented it by a sacrifice, but that sacrifice was not appreciated, so that the present excitement changes not my attitude at all.

I approve fully of Lincolns determination to use all his ordinary and extraordinary powers to defend and maintain the authority with which he is clothed, and the integrity of the nation, and had I not committed myself to another duty, I would most willingly have responded to his Call—But I have engaged my self for one year to this Company, have begun changes involving much money, and which would suffer if I now abandoned it and I shall never abandon any trust which I have voluntarily assumed. I am therefore resolved not to volunteer in Ohio or Missouri and therefore dont suppose I will take part in the present movement. This is spasmodic and chiefly useful to Show the South, that when the time does come, the North is as excitable as themselves, and that Lincoln can command. I hope 500,000 men will respond, although only 75,000 are to be accepted.

But before the Real War does come, Congress must meet, and maybe, the Convention of all the states assembled—and the exact position which each will assume in the coming struggle be clearly ascertained. Kentucky and Tennessee hold the keys of our present Country. If they are hostile, I doubt the power of subjugation: Missouri being out of the way may remain passive and that is all that should be expected. Troops should not leave this State. The population is nearly divided and to weaken the strength of the North, by withdrawing 4 Regts. of Volunteers might prove fatal to this State—Frank Blair whom I have seen twice is rabid, and would not stop till the whole country is convulsed—and slavery abolished everywhere[.] As to Slavery in the abstract, and Slavery in the Territories, I do not particularly take issue—but as to abolishing it in the South or turning loose 4 Millions of Slaves I would have no hand in it. The question of the national integrity and slavery should be Kept distinct—for otherwise it will gradually become a War of Extermination a war without End—if when Congress meets a clearly defined policy be arrived at, a clear end to be accomplished—and then the Force adequate to that end be provided for, then I could & would act with some degree of confidence, not now.

I take it for granted that Washington is safe—that Pickens[1] can beat off all assailants, that Key West, & Tortugas are strong & able to Spare troops for other purposes, that above all Fort Monroe is full of men, provisions & warlike materials, and that the Chesapeake is strongly occupied. Then the first thing will be the avenues of travel. Baltimore must be made to allow the free transit of troops, provisions & materials without question,[2] and the Route from Wheeling to the Relay House kept open—Here there must be some fighting, but a march from Brownsville, or Frostburg would be a good drill, via Hagerstown, Frederick & the Potomac. From present information I apprehend that Virginia will destroy the Road from Harpers Ferry West—& may be the Marylanders will try the Balance, but without an hours delay, that line should swarm with troops, who should take no half way measures. But I should not speculate on matters so distant. Here for some days things looked squally—The people were kept alarmed by all sorts of Reports. The arsenal is held by 600 Regulars. I have been down several times and feel assured that they will defend it well—were St. Louis a mint, this arsenal could soon be carried for it is on the River Bank, with hills to the West & South within easy Range where Batteries could drive every body out of the arsenal enclosure. But the citizens feel an interest to restrain the imprudence of Southerners. It is now generally conceded that no attack will be made on the arsenal unless Frank Blair arouse the indifferent by some Boastful display of his Lager Beer friends. Blair is regarded here as Lincolns Vice Roy, and I doubt the wisdom of the choice. His interest seems to be to keep up angry strife. I look upon every good steadfast Citizen in Saint Louis as worth a soldier in the field. The Governor will call the Legislature, and they will divert money Kept to pay interest on Bonds for arming the State. This will virtually repudiate Missouri Bonds, now down to 47c. Tax payers are in favor of it. But this will open new questions, and may Keep the State neutral, and that is all you should expect. The Indiana & Illinois Levees should be held at Springfield & Cairo in observation & Reserve, and well drilled & practiced in musketry long Range[.] Within a day or so, business has improved here. However much you may differ with me in these conclusions, I want you to give them the benefit of time—affectionately

W. T. Sherman

ALS, DLC: William T. Sherman.

1. Fort Pickens, located next to Pensacola, Florida.

2. On April 19, the Sixth Massachusetts had to switch trains in Baltimore while en route to Washington. They were attacked by a prosecession mob; four soldiers and nine civilians died. Baltimore's mayor claimed that the Federal government had not notified him or the police of the troops' arrival.

TO JOHN SHERMAN

Office St. Louis R. R. Co.

St. Louis, April 25, 1861

Dear Brother,

I think you remember Capt. Van Vliet a classmate of mine and Quarter Master at Fort Leavenworth, since about 1857. He is an old Knickerbocker, from the Highlands of the Hudson and therefore perfectly reliable in these times—though his father has since moved to Milwaukee in Wisconsin. Fred Van Vliet[1] is a fine handsome young fellow, a good Rider, has been to Pikes Peak and across the Plains, and though still a youth has much of that experience which is important for a cavalry officer. I take it in these times an endorsement of a good applicant will not be construed into asking a favor or impertinence, and therefore I send his letter to you, that if you please you may add a word, or simply enclose to the Secretary.[2]

I have as yet heard nothing more of young Turners application[.] If his commission come, his father the Major will be in a tighter place than when living on dead mules, and saddle Skirts at San Bernardino.

Virginias secession influences some six millions of People—no use in arguing about it at all, but all the Virginians, or who trace their linage back, will feel like obeying her dictates & example. As a State she has been proved boastful and we may say overbearing—but on the other hand she by her Governors, and authority has done everything to draw her native born back to their state—Reason may say her course is wrong, and subversive of all Good Government still feeling & prejudice now stronger than Reason will constantly incline her People & descendants to follow her fate. I cannot yet but think that it was a fatal mistake in Mr. Lincoln not to tie to his administration by some kind of link the Border States. Now it is too late, and Sooner or later Kentucky, Tennessee & Arkansas will be in arms against you. It is barely possible that Missouri may yet be neutral. It is pretty nearly determined to divert the half million set aside for the July Interest, for arming the State—All the Banks but one have consented, and the Governor & Legislature are strongly secession. I understand today the orders at the Custom house are to refuse Clearance to Steamboats to Seceding States—All the heavy trade in Groceries & provisions is with the South, and this order at once takes all life from St. Louis. Merchants heretofore for Peace, and even for backing the administration, will now fall off, relax in their exertions and the result will possibly be secession, and thus Free States against Slave. The horrible array so long dreaded. I Know Frank Blair desired this plain square issue[.] It may be that sooner or later it is inevitable—but I cannot bring myself to think so. On the necessity of maintaining a Govt., and that Govt. the old Constitutional one, I have never wavered—but I do recoil from a war, when the negro is the only question.

I am informed that McClellan[3] is appointed to command the Ohio militia, a most excellent appointment—a better officer could not be found—as I conjectured Ohio could not offer any position of trust to a native born. It would have been irregular, maybe unconstitutional, and it in this case is well, for McClellan is theoretically & practically a valuable officer. It relieves me also of a most delicate responsibility, for I would have been in a disagreeable place had Govr. Dennison[4] offered it to me—To decline, my loyalty would be questioned, but now I can well await events, for I suppose Govr. D. has very properly appointed from those actually enrolled in Ohio.

I was in the arsenal yesterday. Besides the 600 regulars, there are 1500 volunteers—not one of whom can speak English—Even the Military commands are in Dutch. Indeed it is a sad spectacle here in the Heart of America, to find that foreigners are the only ones who respond to a Call of our Country.

Mr. Stoddard, Hunter, Ewing & Philemon are all here, but leave today or tomorrow. Love to all, yours affectionately

W. T. Sherman

ALS, DLC: William T. Sherman.

1. Frederick Van Vliet (d. 1891), commissioned a second lieutenant in the Third Cavalry on August 5, 1861, rose to the rank of brevet lieutenant colonel by the war's end.

2. Simon Cameron (1799–1889) was Lincoln's first secretary of war.

3. George B. McClellan (1826–85) started the war as a major general of Ohio volunteers.

4. William Dennison (1815–82) had become governor of Ohio in 1859.

TO THOMAS EWING JR.

Office St. Louis R. R. Co.
St. Louis, April 26 1861

Dear Tom,

After you left us I got your letter from Leavenworth, asking if I could do anything for Luke.[1] You saw enough I think to assure you that there are too many unemployed here now, for others to come. Luke had better stick to Leavenworth till this affair comes to some Crisis.

I know a good many will be displeased with my apparent apathy. I am and always have been an active defender of Law & the Constitution—Twice have I sacrificed myself thereto. In San Francisco to a northern mob, and in Louisiana to a southern Rebellion. I believe now I am a more Zealous friend of Govt. & order, than others who will find fault with me. I did think that war existed against the General Govt. from the date of the first seizure of property—I did resent it as an act of hostility & Treason. I came north prepared to act any part which might be assigned me—I went to Washington & saw the President and heard him say that military men were not wanted. I asked for civil employment here in St. Louis, but it was denied me and when I reached Ohio necessity forced me to seek work, and I found it here. I have undertaken a certain task from which I can not discharge myself, without a breach of Trust. Had Lincoln intimated to me any word of encouragement, I could have waited awhile, but I saw in Washington not a spark of encouragement, & therefore my coming here—

When the call for 75,000 volunteers came the only question was, should I volunteer here or in Ohio. I was not at liberty to go to Ohio, nor had I any assurance that I would there meet with favor—My experience is that no native of Ohio can expect a favor from the State—no man is a prophet in his own Land, and in my case is it specially so, for in Ohio I have received less marks of approval than in any state where I have lived. John thought Dennison would invite me to Ohio, and offer me high service in the volunteers there, but I knew better—McClellan is the Major Genl. a most excellent appointment— and the Brigadiers are to be selected from those in the Regular Militia organizations. Charley says Schleich[2] is to be one, and wrote to him to offer me a place in his Staff—Of Course this would not justify me in asking to be released from an engagement here. If the Country wants my services it wants them in another sphere or not at all—I will not volunteer among the irregular Militia, for I like not the class from which they are exclusively drawn. Therefore I suppose I am out of the present call. If Congress in July should organize an army adequate to the new state of affairs, and I can get a good commission I will accept[3]—but you know the necessities of my Family will not justify me in going it blind.

I think Lincolns call on the country is right. I am glad it is so generally responded to, and I hope the Excitement will not die away until 100,000 good men are enrolled—I suppose no measure of Invasion will be attempted unless the Enemy in Virginia assume so hostile an attitude that it may become necessary to assume the offensive. I hope Missouri and Kentucky will remain neutral—That is all which can be expected, and in this view I think Charley, John Hunter and I can do more here than if we were in Ohio. Your father & Phil are now here. Mr. Hunter left yesterday, and I think all concur in this my opinion—Frank Blair is determined to push things to the bitter end, and if violence occurs here I shall feel disposed to trace it to him. I think all men admit the right & duty of the Govr. to protect the arsenal, and it must be the judge of the means & force necessary: To bring volunteers from another state might create excitement—still I intend to assert that Lincolns Govt. may do *anything at all* to defend the Public Property. Telegraph me 226 Locust Street if any thing *very* important occurs—The General Despatches are unreliable—all well as usual affectionately &c.

W. T. Sherman

ALS, DLC: Thomas Ewing and Family Papers.

1. Luke Clark was an old friend from Lancaster.

2. Newton Schleich was a Democratic leader of the Ohio Senate who was appointed a brigadier general of Ohio state troops by Dennison. He served from April 1, 1861, to September 23, 1862, as colonel of the Sixty-first Ohio Volunteers.

3. On May 3 Lincoln issued a call for 42,034 volunteers to serve for three years.

TO THOMAS EWING JR.

Office St. Louis R. R. Co.

St. Louis, May 1 1861

Dear Tom,

I have just received yrs. of April 24,[1] which you see from your Besieged City was a long time in coming. I left your letter on Mr. McPherson's[2] table, and think he is in possession of it now. I will make it my business to see him. His wife has been ill, at the point of death, but I am informed she is better today.

I wrote you at length a few days since. Your father and Phil went home on

Monday and we are again all alone. About 500 Regulars, and over 3000 volunteers (Germans) are in the arsenal. The Legislature meets tomorrow and we shall soon see the direction to which events point. I expect and that is all I hope that in the Coming Struggle Missouri will remain quiet & neutral, but it is manifest the Secession Element is young, defiant and ready for action, others Conservative.

The Telegraph announces that Washington is well reinforced—that Old Point Comfort full Garrisoned—Pickens with 1000 men enough to defy Bragg, and volunteers offering by the Hundred thousand. Also that Lincoln will accept volunteers till his aggregate force will amount to 150,000—That is no doubt enough to maintain the Status Quo, but for invasion operations will have to be doubled.

At first Politicians will lead this force, till they find their habits and notions are unsuited to war, when maybe a new Class will arise better qualified to meet the ever varying p[h]ases of the Game.

Governor Dennison has an excellent man in McClellan—none better—and if he has time and materials he will make a good Division.

The first events of the war must be in Virginia & Maryland—but the Grand operations of the war will be on the Mississipi, and this will last our time. I watch events as well as I can[.] I know John is utterly angry with me at throwing away such a chance of Military Distinction—He may be right, but I still think that I cannot afford to risk the chances of volunteering. I have no assurance of employment at the end of the three months, and by being here I would surely never have the chance of getting work here again. As to leaving my family to town or country Charity I wont do it—I think the causes of this Rebellion too deepseated, and too virulent to be composed under our present Democratic System of Govt., though I highly approve Lincoln's energetic intentions. Had they occurred earlier it would have prevented much of the mischief now done past all remedy.

Charley & John Hunter are yet with us, sitting cross legged, wishing for some favorable change.

Let me know from you whenever you can—as ever yrs. affectionately

W. T. Sherman

ALS, DLC: Thomas Ewing and Family Papers.

1. Tom spoke of a general fear of a Confederate attack on Washington; expressed doubts about the loyalties of regular army defenders of the city and twenty-three hundred District militia; voiced his belief that the Confederates needed only five thousand troops to take the city; and criticized Lincoln's conduct—"so busy peddling post offices that he could not get time to save the nation." DLC: WTS.

2. Probably William McPherson, a friend of WTS's in St. Louis.

TO SIMON CAMERON

Office St. Louis R. R. Co.

St. Louis, May 8 1861

Hon S. Cameron, Secretary of War.

Dear Sir,

I hold myself now, as always prepared to serve my country in the capacity for which I was trained. I did not, and will not volunteer for three months, because I cannot throw my family on the Cold support of charity, but the three years call of the President would enable an officer to prepare his command and do good service.[1]

I will not volunteer, because rightfully or wrongfully I feel myself unwilling to take a mere private's place and having lived for many years in California and Louisiana, I Know the men among whom I might enlist are not well enough acquainted with me to Elect me to my appropriate place.

Should my services be needed the Records of the War Department will enable you to designate the Station in which I can render best service. Yours truly

W. T. Sherman

ALS (Copy), OHi: Ohio Governors' Papers; another in DLC: Thomas Ewing and Family Papers.

1. Lincoln had issued a call for three-year volunteers and the creation of eight new infantry regiments for the regular army on May 3.

TO WILLIAM DENNISON JR.

Office St. Louis R. R. Co.

St. Louis, May 8 1861

Governor Dennison, Columbus Ohio,

Dear Sir,

I have reason to believe my position in the present disturbed state of our Country is misunderstood in Ohio.

I have never lived in Ohio since a boy, and did not consider it my part to offer my services to you, in the midst of the hurly burly which followed the public announcement of the attack on Fort Sumpter. But in every position I have held, I have manifested my appreciation of the General Government and my conviction that we would be held derelict to our trust, if we failed to transmit our Constitution, unimpaired to future Generations.

I now take the liberty to send you the Copy of a letter I have this day sent to the Secretary of War.[1] In the outset of the Struggle on which we are about to Enter, states may fulfil an important part, but in time all important movements will be controlled by the War Department of the General Government, and it is for this reason I have made my offer direct to the Secretary of War.

I avail myself of this opportunity to express my pleasure at learning you had availed yourself of the services of Maj. General McClellan, than whom no one commands more universally the confidence of his peers, the officers of our army. With respect Yr. obt. Servant

W. T. Sherman

ALS, OHi: Ohio Governors' Papers; copy of WTS to Simon Cameron, May 8, 1861, enclosed.

1. See previous letter.

TO THOMAS EWING JR.

Office St. Louis R. R. Co.

St. Louis, May 11 1861

Dear Tom,

Your two letters of May 6 & 8 are received[1]—Long before you get this you will have received McPherson's letter explaining the cause of his not going per appointment to Washington—His wife was for days dangerously sick but is now better. I have not seen him for some days and think he is up at Jefferson City on business of the Pacific R.R.—at all events he assured me he had in connection with Mr. {Taltt} written you a letter that would fully satisfy you and offered to show me a copy, but since I moved the office of the Company up here to Bremen I see less of the down town folks.

Before receiving your letter I wrote to Governor Dennison and also to the Secretary of War letters, the latter of which I send a copy, the former I did not keep. If we are to have a long & desperate Civil Struggle I suppose I must take part, and if so I prefer service with Regulars. Yesterday I witnessed a scene which has confirmed me more strongly in my opinion that in Civil Strife Militia wont do. You will have heard all sorts of versions from Saint Louis— and I do not profess to be able to add any thing authentic.[2] When I went home to Dinner at 3 P.M.—it was manifest something was on foot—the whole town was pouring out to the west, just beyond the Stoddard property where Gen. Frost[3] was in camp with almost 1000 state militia, under instruction. It was said Certain arms which came up clandestinely from Baton Rouge had been taken to his camp and that Lyons with his Regulars and the U.S. militia were then marching out to take them. I knew well enough that Lyon[4] would not attempt what he could not accomplish, so I staid home quietly to dinner— Hugh Charley & John Hunter were bound to see the battle and would not wait for dinner—After dinner I walked the vacant streets and soon met returning men, saying just what was expected that Frost had surrendered—Taking Willy I started out to meet the returning troops, but kept on till I found myself in Camp—The disarmed volunteers were drawn up on Olin Street with a Column of Regulars & militia ready to escort them as prisoners to the Arsenal. I talked with some of the Regular officers and seeing preparations to march I fell back among a promiscuous crowd of Citizens, men women & children, and soon met Hugh Charley & John Hunter. As a part of the crowd near Olin Street were a parcel of noisy men, occasionally shouting for Jeff Davis—I noticed as the Regulars passed a kind of confused scuffle occurred the Regulars using their bayonets, but after a few moments they resumed their Ranks & followed towards the city: behind them came a Regiment of militia Rosensteins[5] I am told—when they reached the same point a similar scuffle occurred. I heard a couple of shots, then half a dozen and soon a general straggling fire upon the crowd to my front & right—as the fire ran along the Column to the rear, and about abreast of where we stood, I heard balls cutting branches & leaves over our heads, saw Charley down on the ground covering Willy. I prostrated myself crept up & covered Willy, and as soon as the fire slackened I jerked Willy up, and ran for cover. I saw no body shot, & know no ball passed several feet of me, though Charley thinks different—but there were some dozen killed outright and many wounded. The whole resulted from want of discipline. The Crowd was a promiscuous one, comprised of idle spectators, at least two hours after the surrender & disarmament of Frosts men. It was unnecessary, but just what I expected, and I blame myself for being there with a child—Willy was as cool as a cucumber, of course unconscious of our danger—Last night the City was all commotion and is so still. This event will be used at Jefferson City to precipitate secession for it was a direct attack on State authority—Frost being in camp, by orders of the Governor. Of course it is useless to defer this Contest—it is now upon us and must be met—Who is our King? Uncle Sam, or the local State? If we can avoid a general anarchy is all I expect: but of course ultimately the United States must prevail. We are all well. Affectionately

W. T. Sherman

ALS, DLC: Thomas Ewing and Family Papers. Enclosure: autograph copy of WTS to Simon Cameron, May 8, 1861.

1. On May 6, Tom urged Cump to tell his army friends what position he wanted and they would work with Winfield Scott to get it for him. He planned to speak to Irvin McDowell and Scott for WTS. On May 8 he reported that he, along with John and Charles Sherman, had seen Lincoln, who expressed a high opinion of WTS and promised to second any recommended appointment. Cameron promised John later that day that WTS would receive a commission as colonel in the regular army when its size was increased. They thought that this would be better than an appointment as brigadier general of the three-year volunteers but were starting to have doubts after McDowell told them WTS could be a brigadier or even major general of volunteers. He added that WTS had better offer his services soon or all opportunities would be gone. DLC: WTS.

2. Jefferson Davis had sent arms and ammunition to a Confederate encampment in

western St. Louis, at Camp Jackson. Federal troops forced their surrender on May 10 to forestall an attack on the Federal arsenal. A melee ensued when a drunk fired into returning Federal forces; twenty-eight soldiers and civilians were killed. *PM*, 1:200–202.

3. Daniel M. Frost (1823–1900) was a St. Louis businessman, politician, and general of the state militia. Exchanged after his capture, he went on to become a brigadier general in the Confederate army.

4. Nathaniel Lyon (1818–61) was a captain on duty at the St. Louis Arsenal and an ally of Frank Blair. He soon became a brigadier general of U.S. volunteers and was killed at Wilson's Creek in August.

5. Actually this was Osterhaus's regiment of Home Guards.

TO JOHN SHERMAN

Office St. Louis R. R. Co.
St. Louis, May 11, 1861

Hon. John Sherman
Dear Brother,

Very imprudently I was a witness of the firing on the People by the U.S. Militia at Camp Jackson yesterday. You will hear all manner of accounts and as these will be brought to bear on the present Legislature to precipitate events, may be secession I will tell you what I saw. My office is up in Bremen the extreme north of the city. The arsenal is at the extreme south. The State camp was in a pretty grove directly west of the City, bounded by Olive Street & Laclede Avenue. I went to my house on Locust between 11 & 12 at 3 P.M. and saw the whole city in commotion and heard that the U.S. troops were marching from the arsenal to capture the State camp. At home I found Hugh & Charley Ewing & John Hunter so excited they would not wait for dinner, but went out to see the expected Battle. I had no such curiosity and staid to dinner, after which I walked out and soon met a man who told me Gen. Frost had surrendered. I went back home & told Ellen—then took Willy to see the soldiers march back I kept on walking and about 5½ P.M. found myself in the grove, with Soldiers all round standing at rest—I went into the Camp till turned aside by sentinels, and found myself with a promiscuous crowd, men, women & children, inside the Grove, near Olive Street. On that street the disarmed State troops some 800 were in ranks. Soon a heavy column of U.S. Regulars, followed by militia came down Olive, with music & halted abreast of me. I went up and spoke to Some of the officers and fell back to a Knoll where I met Hugh & Charley & John Hunter. Soon the music again started, and as the Regulars got abreast of the Crowd about 60 yards to my front and right I observed them in confusion, using their bayonets to keep the crowd back as I supposed. Still they soon moved on, and as the militia reached the same point a similar confusion began. I heard a couple of shots then half a dozen &

observed the militia were firing on the crowd at that point, but the fire kept creeping to the rear along the flank of the column & hearing balls cutting the leaves of trees over my head I fell down on the grass, and crept up to where Charley Ewing had my boy Willy. I also covered his person—probably a hundred shots passed over the ground, but none near us. As soon as the fire slackened, I picked Willy up, and ran with him till behind the rising ground, and continued at my leisure out of harms way, & went home—I saw no one shot—but some dozen were Killed, among them a woman & little girl. There must have been some provocation at the point where the Regulars charged bayonets, and when the militia began their fire—the rest was irregular & unnecessary—for the crowd, was back in the woods, a fence between them and the street—There was some cheering of the U.S. troops, and some halloos for Jeff Davis.

I hear all of Frosts command who would not take the oath of allegiance to the U.S. are prisoners at the arsenal—I suppose they will be held for the orders of the President—They were mostly composed of young men, who doubtless were secessionist—Frost is a New Yorker, was a graduate of West Point— served some years in the army & married a Miss Graham here, a lady of great wealth & large connections. He was encouraged by order of the Governor, and this brings up the old question of State & U.S. authority we cannot have two Kings—one is enough and of the two the U.S. must prevail, but in all the South, and even here there are plenty who think the State is their King. I think of course that both extremes are determined that Missouri should secede, one from Southern feeling and the other for the satisfaction of beating her. When I got back last evening to my house I found Turner. He gave me a letter for you which I mailed addressed to Mansfield as the More certain method of reaching you. Tom Turner has declined his appointment for reasons the Major gives. I enclose you the copy of a letter I wrote some days since to the Secretary of War—If I must embark in this war I prefer Regulars who can be controlled. I have just received your letter of the 9[1] from Philadelphia—to which point I have already written to you—As ever yours affectionately

W. T. Sherman

ALS, DLC: William T. Sherman.

1. JS to WTS, May 9, 1861, DLC: WTS. JS wrote that he still had not heard whether Thomas Turner had received his commission and wondered whether it had miscarried.

TO DAVID F. BOYD

Office St. Louis R. R. Co.
St. Louis May 13, 1861.

Prof. Boyd, Alexandria.

My dear Friend,

I have been intending for a long while to answer your last very Kind letter.[1] I suppose you still receive papers from New Orleans and Virginia giving tolerably fair versions of the events which are now passing all around us. We are now by Declaration of the Confederate Congress, and by act of our own Constituted authorities, enemies, and I cannot yet realize the fact. I Know that I individually would not do any human being a wrong, take from him a cent, or molest any of his rights or property, and yet I admit fully the fact that Lincoln was bound to call on the country to rally and save our Constitution and Government. Had I responded to his call for volunteers I Know that I would now be a Major General. But my feelings prompted me to forbear and the consequence is my family and friends are almost cold to me, and they feel and say I have failed at the critical moment of my life. It may be I am but a chip on the whirling tide of time destined to be cast on the shore as a worthless weed. But I still think in the hurly-burly of strife, order and system must be generated, and grow and strengthen till our people come out again a Great and purified Nation. Lincoln is of right our President and has the right to initiate the Policy of our Government during his four years, and I believe him sincere, in his repeated declarations that no dismemberment shall ever be thought of. The inevitable result is war and an invasive war. I Know that masses of men are organizing and disciplining to execute the orders of this Government. They are even now occupying the Key points of our country and when prepared they will strike—not in detached columns battling with an excited people, but falling on exposed points: Already is Missouri humbled, I have witnessed it. My personal friends here, many of them Southern, admit that Missouri's fate is sealed. There was a camp of about 1500 young men, who though seemingly assembled by state authority, were yet notoriously disaffected to the Government and were imprudent enough to receive into their camps a quantity of the arms from Baton Rouge, brought up as common merchandise. This justified the Government forces here, Regulars and Militia to surround and capture the whole. For a time intense excitement prevailed but again seeming peace has come. The Governor and State authorities are southern by birth and feeling and may make some spasmodic efforts to move, but they will be instantly overcome. Superior arms and numbers are the elements of war, and must prevail. I cannot yet say if Lincoln will await the action of his Congress in July. I think he will as to any Grand movement. But in the meantime Virginia, Louisiana, and Missouri will be held or threatened. I have no doubt a hundred thousand disciplined men will be in Louisiana by Christmas next. The Mississippi River will be a grand theater of war, but not till the present masses are well disciplined. It is horrible to contemplate but it cannot be avoided. No one now talks of the negro. The integrity of the Union and the relative power of state and General Government are the issues in this war; were it not for the physical geography of the country it might be that People could consent to divide and separate in peace. But the Mississippi is too grand an element to be divided, and all its extent must of necessity be under one government. Excuse these Generalisms—we have said them a thousand times. I was sorry to learn from Dr. Smith that further disaffection had crept into your institution. I fear for the present it will be swept by the Common Storm. Lay[2] was not the man and it is well he has declined. Certainly there must be within reach, some good man to manage so easy a machine—I think that the nucleus should be kept together even on the smallest scale. Joe Miller writes me that the arms have been sent away and therefore his occupation is gone. I will write if he cannot stay to return to his brother in Ohio, and not go to California as he seems to think about—I am still here with this Road and my family living as quietly as possible at 226 Locust Street. No matter what happens I will always consider you my personal friend, and you shall ever be welcome to my roof.

Should I be wrong in my conclusions of this terrible anarchy and should you come to St. Louis I Know you will be pleased with the many objects of interest hereabouts. Give to all the assurance of my kindest remembrance and accept for yourself my best wishes for your health and success in life. Yours,

W. T. Sherman

Copy, InND: Sherman Family Papers; docketed "A true Copy. D. F. Boyd."

1. David F. Boyd to WTS, April 21, 1861, DLC: WTS. Boyd discussed affairs at the academy and results of exams, commented on WTS's successor, and expressed the widespread sentiments about WTS—"We miss you all the time, & no one more than Dr. Smith." He asked WTS what he thought would be the result of Virginia's secession and voiced his own opinion that "this is a suicidal war."

2. George W. Lay of Virginia (d. 1867) was WTS's short-lived successor at the academy. A Mexican War veteran, he had been one of Scott's aides-de-camp until March 3, 1861, and would become a colonel and assistant adjutant general in the Confederate army.

TO THOMAS EWING SR.

Office St. Louis R. R. Co.

St. Louis, May 17 1861

Hon. T. Ewing

Dear Sir,

Yours of May 15 received,[1] and Deeds of Trust, left at store of Kelly & Harding.

I have no Knowledge whatever that I am to be appointed to the Army. I have made up my mind that if the Govt wants me they will ask me. This does not seem to me a time to seek for place. With all the preparations thus far made, the administration is not yet up to the magnitude of the occasion. The entire people of the South are tinctured with the idea that their States are sovereign & superior to the U.S. Even Missouri has taken that position by an almost unanimous vote of her Legislature, and it will take vast power to cover so extensive a Country. I think St. Louis is past the worst, and that whatever Confusion occurs will be along the Missouri & lines of travel. Should I be offered a proper post in the army, I will make the best disposition of my family. Unless I hear on Monday that you have recd. the Dft., I will send Duplicate—yrs. &c.

W. T. S.

ALS, New York: FORBES Magazine Collection.

1. DLC: WTS. Ewing wrote that if WTS received a military appointment, he would expect the Sherman family to return to Lancaster.

TO ROBERT ANDERSON

Office St. Louis R. R. Co.

St. Louis, May 20 1861

Colonel Robert Anderson, Louisville

My Dear Sir,

In common with the millions of your fellow Countrymen, I watched with painful interest, your calm, determined and noble course in the defense of a little Fort, surrounded by batteries worked by the hands of excited men, who were enemies, but should be friends. After having experienced the manifestations of your Country's approval, you may be and doubtless are troubled by the many private commendations thrust upon you, but I think I know you well enough to suppose that you will appreciate this offer of kindness and compliment from one who has had the honor of being your Lieutenant.

When I went to Louisiana I could not believe it the settled purpose of her Politicians to precipitate the danger so long dreaded by our ancestors—Civil

War & Confusion—and therefore I lent myself Zealously to the purpose of building up a college where military discipline was added to insure subordination and attention to study. And the very moment that public acts foreshadowed such a purpose I promptly resigned my post, but took good care to account for every cent of money, and every item of property which had been entrusted to me. I left with the respect and good will of neighbors and associates: and even now, when the South has declared war against us, and is in arms to vindicate that purpose, I for one will endeavor so to demean myself that when the integrity of our Country is demonstrated our enemies and countrymen shall not have reason to add to their embittered feelings, the charge of vindictive Cruelty. Of all People on Earth, the South should deprecate war. They need Peace, profound Peace, and the good will of their neighbors. Without this they cannot enjoy tranquility or even comparative safety. They even now cry out to be let alone, but for myself I cannot see how they can ask to be let alone, after having by violence seized our national arsenals, custom houses, ships, taken Prisoners of War troops and imposed false oaths upon officers who were there for their aid and Protection, and more especially for their fierce Bombardment of you and your Command. But thank God in this last act they met a man equal to the occasion and whose calm vindication of his nations honor, has awakened a Response, that must even startle Davis in his fancied security.

I went to Washington in March but saw there no chance for employment and having now a family of five children I came here, was elected President of this Company, and at the time of the Presidents three months call I was in the act of making changes which required my Personal attention. I could not volunteer, but I have ever done my best to sustain the National Cause—When the President indicated his purpose of increasing the Regular Force I simply notified the Secretary of War that I held myself for the service of the Government, in any capacity they might assign me—I have as yet no response, and really I will not be disappointed if I am allowed to remain here in Peace, to provide for my family. I do not feel like pushing for service when I will be in continual dread that the war may degenerate into an unnatural one—maybe of antagonism to Slavery.

To prevent our People falling into anarchy, to perpetuate our hitherto Common History, to increase a Reverence for our Constitution & laws, and to increase the value and stability of property in our whole land are causes which would command my undivided allegiance, and I will continue to hope, such is the Providential design of this unnatural Conflict, and in it I know you must take a prominent part—If Mrs. Anderson[1] be with you, give her my best

regards, and for yourself personally please accept the assurances of my unbounded respect & admiration. Yours

W. T. Sherman

ALS, DLC: Robert Anderson Papers.

1. Elizabeth Clinch Anderson had been a confidante of WTS since his days at Fort Moultrie.

TO JOHN SHERMAN

Office St. Louis R. R. Co.

St. Louis, May 20, 1861

Dear Brother,

I have now got things on this Road working to a new system which was indispensably necessary from the greatly reduced receipts. I have diminished expenses more than 30 per cent without impairing the efficiency of the work. All the stores and workshops of St. Louis are now idle, and thousands are out of employment. Those enlisted must number near 6000 and are in camp round about the City. One or two excursions have been made to the interior and I understand that Gen. Harney[1] is prepared to come down on the Gover-nor if he attempts to assemble the militia under the Military Bill. I go down to the arsenal, which is one extremity of the Road almost every day, and occa-sionally see Frank Blair in his new Colonels uniform. He is too nervous and full of Politics to be easy long and I have no doubt will be much relieved when the Extra Session calls him to his appropriate place in Washington. Lyon is the best soldier among them, but he is so full of vim that he would be marching upon Jefferson City had he his own way.

The greatest difficulty in the problem now before the country is not to conquer but so conquer as to impress upon the real men of the South a respect for their conquerors. If Memphis be taken, and the army move on south, the vindictive feeling left behind would again close the River, and here in Missouri It would be easy enough to take Jefferson City, Lexington and any other point, but the moment they are left to themselves the people would resume their hatred. It is for this Reason, that I deem Regulars the only species of force that Should be used for invasion. I take it for granted that Virginia will be attacked in great force this summer, and that the great problem of the war—the Mississipi will be reserved for the next winter.

It occurs to me that in advance Ship Island—one of those near Biloxi should be taken now—its unfinished Fort pushed to the height of two tiers, one of embrasures, and one of barbottom, and held by a good Garrison, where Coal, shot & shells might be collected in great quantity, for next winters operations. It would be of inestimable value, as it cannot be bombarded, and cannot be attacked except in boats. I think that it is now held by a few Mississipians, who could not hold it against a Frigate.[2]

Another point—I think Northern men stand a *first* summer at the South, outside of Malaria very well—It is the second and third which tries their strength. I mention these things which you can use in conversation with military men.

McCook[3] was here a few days ago, and said that it was settled in Washington that I was to be offered one of the Regular 3 Battalion Regiments. I think he was mistaken, for the order for these was made May 4,[4] and I have not had a word on the subject,[5] and I infer the President will be forced to confine his appointments to those who volunteered to his first call. I shall continue in my first resolve to mind my private interests so as to become independent of any body, so that I can not be kicked about as heretofore, and if the country needs my services, it can call for them.

I think the President should look for some officers among the majors and captains who have for years been serving on the frontier, far from Washington. There is an old saying that one campaign in Washington is worth more than five in the Field—McDowells[6] promotion as Brigadier will not give satisfaction for the reason his service has been too much in cities, and too little on exposed Frontiers. In the war on which we are now embarking paper soldiers wont do—McClellan is naturally a superior man, and has had the finest opportunities in Mexico, and in Europe. Even his seniors admit his qualifications. Wool[7] is not trustworthy. I would not believe his word. He failed me at a critical moment in California and I would not serve under him, as I would fear he would betray his trust. Yrs. affectionately

W. T. Sherman

ALS, DLC: William T. Sherman.

1. Brigadier General William S. Harney (1800–1889), USA, was in command of the Department of the West with headquarters in St. Louis at this time. A known Southern sympathizer, he would be relieved of his command on May 29.

2. Confederate forces evacuated Ship Island on September 16, 1861; Union forces occupied it the next day.

3. Probably Dan McCook Jr., USA, Tom Ewing Jr. and WTS's former law partner in Leavenworth, who would serve in the Armies of the Ohio and the Cumberland, reaching the rank of brigadier general of volunteers.

4. WTS was mistaken on the date; Lincoln's May 3 call for three-year volunteers had also included raising eight regiments of infantry and one each of artillery and cavalry for the regular army.

5. On May 14, WTS had been commissioned colonel of the Thirteenth U.S. Infantry.

6. Irvin McDowell (1818–85) had been made brigadier general of volunteers a week earlier even though he had never commanded in the field.

7. John E. Wool (1784–1869) had been the officer in command of the U.S. Army post at

San Francisco during the time WTS was trying to prevent Casey's lynching; Wool reneged on a promise to provide WTS and the militia with guns and ammunition. Wool commanded the Department of the East in 1861.

TO JOHN SHERMAN

Office St. Louis R. R. Co.
St. Louis, May 22, 1861

Dear Brother,

I received your Despatch last evening stating I would be appointed Colonel of one of the new 3 Battalion Regiments, this was I suppose in answer to my own despatch to Adjt. General,[1] asking if such were to be the case. The fact is so many persons had written to me and spoken to me, all asserting they had seen or heard I was to have one of the new Regiments, that I thought the letter to me had been misdirected or miscarried.

I took all April to study the affairs of this Company, and on the 1st of May I discharged a large number of useless Employees, and so reduced the working expenses of the Company, that it has assumed a new and more satisfactory condition. It is now so organized that I can leave at short notice without serious detriment to its interest, and I think my course will ensure me employment again if the accidents of service should again cast me adrift—I shall therefore promptly accept the Colonelcy when received, and think I can organize and prepare a Regiment as quick as anybody. I prefer this to a Brigadier in the militia, for I have no political ambition, and have very naturally more confidence in Regulars than militia, not that they are better braver or more patriotic, but because *I know* the People will submit with better grace to them than to militia of any particular locality. For this reason I shall endeavor to get a mixed class of officers and privates. Unless as I suppose will be the case the War Department should restrict the organization & enlistment to particular localities. I take it for granted they are now engaged in the task of preparing such orders & instructions as will ensure uniformity of organization dress & discipline.

McCook told me the purpose was to allow me to appoint my own officers. I dont think I would value such a power, unless it should relieve the War Department of the importunate claims of applicants—Whatever they order I shall enforce, only I should prefer to be put exactly on a line with the other similarly organized troops, perfectly willing to take such officers as the President may appoint. Only as McCook of Leavenworth wants a captaincy I would like to have him—Charley Ewing now 27 years, a long time Lieutenant of a Volunteer Company in Lancaster also wants a captains place.

There are in the old army, on the Frontiers, far from Washington many clever and inteligent officers, familiar with the "common life of a soldier," whose habits are worth half a life of Book study, who ought not to be over-looked, and I should be glad to have a few as majors, for they would be invaluable in the first schooling of new troops.

Jefferson Barracks would be an excellent place for the formation of such a Regiment—and admirably placed for transportation towards Memphis and Little Rock—two of the salient points of attack prior to opening the Mississipi. There are plenty of men here ready to enlist—some old soldiers and men who have been to California and Pikes Peak, both good schools for outdoor life.

You Know that these Colonels will rank in the order of their appoint-ment—if you are behind the Curtain try and get mine as well up as possible—Anderson is fairly entitled to priority.

I think Missouri has subsided into a quiescent state. There will be no attempt to execute the obnoxious & unconstitutional Militia Law[2]—a prompt move on Little Rock from here & Cairo, and recapture of Fort Smith from Kansas would hold Arkansas in check, a movement which could be made simultaneous with that on Richmond—I hope no men or time will be wasted on Norfolk: it is to one side and unimportant.[3] The Capture of Richmond would be fatal to Virginia, and the occupation of Cumberland, Hagerstown & Frederick by the Pennsylvanians, whilst troops threaten Winchester from Washington would make the further occupation of Harpers Ferry useless—But after all the Mississipi is the great problem of this Civil War, will require large forces and good troops. Affectionately your Brother,

W. T. Sherman

ALS, DLC: William T. Sherman.

1. Lorenzo Thomas (1804–75) had succeeded Samuel Cooper in the Adjutant General's Office in March 1861.

2. Missouri had refused to supply troops in answer to the president's call of April 15.

3. Norfolk, Virginia, an important naval port, had been evacuated by U.S. forces on April 20, 1861.

TO THOMAS EWING JR.

Office St. Louis R. R. Co.
St. Louis, May 23 1861

Dear Tom,

I have received your letter of —— inst., which I left at the house. I have answered every one of your letters promptly but I suppose letters are delayed on the way. Before this you must have recd. all. I sent you a copy of my letter to the Sec. of War, which was a simple tender of service in any post of the *Regular Army* he might assign me. I am thankful for the Kind intercession of my friends and frankly say I am not entitled to the Brigadier Genls place. No more was Reeder[1] or McDowell—the former a mere civilian without experience, and the latter a Staff officer too much prone to service in a smooth office chair. When the nations safety may turn on the ability of an officer, the President should at least consult Genl. Scott & military men. There are Colonels, Lt. Cols. and Majors of the Army, who have never seen Washington, but who on the Frontiers have acquired the Experience which made Gen. Taylor have such weight with militia[.] I Know it is no time to criticize, and all should cheerfully confide to the President the fullest powers to manage the Case. John and C. T. Sherman have each telegraphed me that I would be Colonel of one of the new 3 Battalion Regiments—That is as much as I could ask, and I shall accept it, and when ordered shall do my best. I dont object to Blairs opposition to me, nor shall I attempt to conciliate it. I acted in advance of him and when the President Called for Volunteers I could not act without breach of confidence, and it is as much as I can do to manage the Present without laying out the windward anchor for contingencies which I do not understand.

I am satisfied with Mr. Lincolns policy, but I do not like that of the Blairs—I know Frank Blair openly declares war on Slavery. I see him daily, and yesterday had a long talk with him. I say the time is not yet come to destroy Slavery, but it may be to circumscribe it. We have not in America the number of inhabitants to replace the Slaves, Nor have we the national wealth to transport them to other lands. Our constitution has given the owners certain rights which I should be loth to disturb. I declined the Chief Clerkship because I did not want it. You know enough of the social status of a Washington office-holder to appreciate my feelings, when I say I would infinitely prefer to live in St. Louis—I have seen enough of War not to be caught by its first glittering bait, and when I engage in this, it must be with a full consciousness of its real character. I did approve of the Presidents call, and only said it should have been 300 thousand instead of 75. The result conforms to my opinion. I did approve of Lyons attack and said it was inevitable—only I thought the Marshall should have demanded the arms which reached the Camp unlawfully through the Custom House. The firing on the citizens I know was in consequence of the nervousness of new militia—was wrong, but just what every prudent person expected. I have always thought that if it could be avoided Missouri should be held with as little *feeling* as possible because of necessity her People must retain the rights of franchise & property—Wherever I see that Persons miscalculate the state of feeling as the South I endeavor to correct it, because a fatal mistake in war is to underrate the strength, feeling, and resources of an Enemy.

In justice to my family I should stay here where I know I can better educate & provide for them now & hereafter: but being under a species of honorary obligation to tender my military services, I have done so simply, and unreservedly. I would like to know as soon as possible by Telegraph—1st what Regiment I am assigned to—2nd when to be organized—3rd who is to appoint officers, & 4th the time when I must give it my attention.

Tell John & Charles Sherman that I recd. their Dispatches, and hold myself prepared—only I want as much notice as possible to make the necessary arrangements for my family. I suppose I must send them to Lancaster—in which event I must try & sell furniture & sublet my house. Of course I am willing to have McCook & Charley as Captains—but for Majors I would like to have army officers, who have seen service. With these exceptions, I would prefer the appointments to be made and Registered in Washington—A full Regiment could be organized here, on quick notice of good heterogenous materials—Too much Dutch, Irish or Native Americans wont do—a proper mixture gives the most strength.

Ellen is well but anxious to know what is to be done with her—yr. Brother

W. T. Sherman

Col. Schuyler Hamilton[2]—Gen. Scotts Mily. Secretary is a particular friend of mine. See him.

ALS, DLC: Thomas Ewing and Family Papers.

1. Andrew H. Reeder (1807–64), originally from Pennsylvania, had been the territorial governor of Kansas from 1854 to 1855. Charges of speculation and election fraud had marred his administration and brought about his removal. He declined this appointment as a brigadier general.

2. Schuyler Hamilton (1822–1903) was military secretary to Scott.

TO JOHN SHERMAN

Office St. Louis R. R. Co.
St. Louis, May 24, 1861
Friday.

Dear Brother,

I have already written you so much that more would be a bore. Yrs. of the 21 is at hand and I can act with promptness and sufficient vigor when the occasion arises.[1] You all overrate my powers and ability and may place me in a position above my merits, a worse step than below. Really I do not conceive myself qualified for Quarter Master General, or Major General. To attain either station I would prefer a previous schooling with large masses of troops in the field, one which I lost in the Mexican War by going to California. The only possible reason that would induce me to accept high position would be to prevent its falling into incompetent hands. The magnitude of interests at issue now, will admit of no experiments.

After Harney & Price[2] had signed their creed of Peace for Missouri,[3] I was at the arsenal, on business, & meeting Blair & Lyon face to face I asked them frankly what they thought of the arrangement. They answered—We dont like it—then what did I think—if the State authorities were sincere & can control the People I think it a cheap victory. We have enough enemies in this war, to add to their number and when any state has an interest to be quiet—why let them have a loop hole to escape war. My confidence was further strengthened by my knowledge that Gen. Hitchcock[4] an old officer, native of Vermont—direct descendant of old Ethan Allen, & Scotts Chief of Staff from Vera Cruz to Mexico, was Harneys adviser & actual author of the paper. Turner & Robt. Campbell[5] were Prices advisers and all had told me they had ample evidence of the sincerity of Gen. Price & Govr. Jackson, the latter evidently influenced by an apprehension of an attack on Jefferson City and capture of state archives.

Blair asked me to write as much to his Brother Montgomery,[6] especially that I attributed this apparent change of purpose & feeling to the sudden and effective destruction of Camp Jackson. I told Blair I ought not to write to his Brother, as I was not in correspondence with him, and had no reason to believe Montgomery cared to be bored by me, having as I Know his hands full—By Harneys arrangement he is in no wise committed, his forces are at his full command, and in the event of the state authorities avoiding their duty to protect Union men in the Interior he will have just reason to interpose his forces. Perfect peace, quiet and order now prevail here, and the state forces assembled at Jefferson City are I am informed dispersing to their farms, with every prospect of a magnificent crop.

Prior to the assembling of Congress I suppose no real operations will be attempted. Washington should be safe beyond any possible chance, and if diversions would occupy the troops there are half a dozen which could be made, with good effect—Little Rock & Fort Smith Arkansas, Mobile, or Ship Island off Biloxi—But as unity of purpose is indispensable, the plan must originate in Washington, & adhered to. A Bad plan persevered in, is better than a good one, half executed.

I have *now* the affairs of this company so organized—that a Boy could manage it. By doing so I have assured my influence here, so that I could fall back on it.

I want a few days notice of my designated position, that I may make some arrangements. I have written to Elizabeth[7] to See if she will rent her house & furniture to Ellen. She is now living with Henry,[8] and I can pay her rent which will help her much. In that event I could send Ellen to Lancaster, and make arrangements with Mr. Lucas to sublet my present house—I have still my saddle—sword—sash, & some articles of uniform which will come into immediate play—But look out—I want the Regular army and not the 3 year men.

I will merely repeat here a remark made on a former occasion that Jefferson Barracks, 14 miles below St. Louis has Quarters and everything adopted to the organization of a Regiment. Yrs. affectionately

W. T. Sherman

ALS, DLC: William T. Sherman.

1. JS wrote that WTS was to be a brigadier in the regular army, quartermaster general, or colonel of a new regiment and expressed his belief he would have been a major general if he had commanded Missouri troops. DLC: WTS.

2. Sterling "Pap" Price (1809–67), a former governor of Missouri, was in command of the Missouri state troops in 1860 but joined the Confederacy and became a general in the C.S. Army.

3. This pact would lead to Harney's dismissal; he had agreed that Federal troops would leave the Missouri State Guard alone provided that they did nothing active against Federal authority.

4. Ethan Allen Hitchcock (1798–1870) had settled in St. Louis after his retirement from the army in 1855. He rejoined in 1862 as a major general and served mostly on staff duty. His nephew Henry joined Sherman's staff in 1864.

5. Robert Campbell (1804–79) was a St. Louis businessman and trader.

6. Montgomery Blair (1813–83) had been made postmaster general in Lincoln's administration.

7. Mary Elizabeth Sherman Reese (1812–1900), WTS's oldest sister, had married lawyer William J. Reese and settled in Lancaster.

8. Henry Reese, a prosperous lawyer, was Elizabeth's son.

TO THOMAS EWING SR.

Office St. Louis R. R. Co.

St. Louis, May 27 1861

Hon. Thos. Ewing,

Dear Sir,

Yours of —— inst is received. I have traced the property on which the notes of Thompson and Foster are liens, into the hands of Richardson and Mellier Wholesale Druggists on Main Street opposite Virginia Hotel. They complain sadly of the times and rate of exchange. They tell me they have written to you asking that the notes be allowed to new at some agreed rate of interest and ask me to await your reply. The notes are due June 20/23 and therefore we must await the time. I suppose you need the money, and if your answer be that you have counted on it, I will again renew the offer of taking pay in New York Exchange and allow them 5 or even 6 per cent for it. This about splits the loss, for exchange rates between 12 & 15 per cent and is likely to go higher. No body pretends to pay debts, and rents are paid or not according to the ability of Tenants—all work is stopped and merchants complain of sales and collections. But I suppose this is not confined to St. Louis, but is universal. About my going into the army, I only have John Shermans and Toms assurances. I have not a word from the Secretary of War or Adjt. Genl. and I know the Blairs do not like my refusal to accept the Chief Clerkship of the War Dept., or the leadership of the Dutch militia here. I have made a simple plain tender of my individual services and that is all I will do, and I would not feel slighted if they were ignored.

The History of the Revolutionary officers after the war, and the Last Wars disbanded troops gives me a clue to what will be the fate of the hundreds & thousands of those who are now clamorous for Employment.

Still if the General Govt. notify me that my services are needed I will serve and will most likely avail myself of your kind offer to my family. Things always happen un luckily, but Ellen is confident she can make the trip home in June, and therefore I do not wish to incur the expense of the Journey, till I have something definite, till the last moment left for action.

Charley has his head full of the military, and thinks since recent events that his social position here is unpleasant. All the Girls & boys are secessionists, because the richer & more influential classes are of southern origin. But of course all thinking men know that the U.S. will never relinquish her hold on Missouri, and soon this tone of feeling must change—for People must conform to the actual state of facts. My notion is Charley shd. stick to his place here through thick & thin, but as his mind seemed fixed I told him that if left to me I would give him a Captaincy—I think a few hundred miles march through Arkansas, with the scenes attending an invading army will cure him, or put him beyond the reach of cure.

To Conquer Peace I know the intense hatred bred at the South, will make invasion armies necessary in Arkansas, Louisiana & Mississipi, all wooded countries, where a Regular army with its trains of supplies will sustain continued and severe losses.

You will hear before I will, of any appt. for me, and can infer the rest—In the mean time I will try and arrange these notes, as soon as your reply is made to Richardson Mellier & co.

I suppose the Tariff, war, & stoppage of shipments of salt from New Orleans will incur to your advantage in the salt business. Yrs. affectionately,

W. T. Sherman

ALS, DLC: Thomas Ewing and Family Collection.

TO THOMAS EWING SR.

Saint Louis, May 31./61

Dear Sir,

Enclosed is your note paid, due, May 4	1355.58
1 yrs. Int.	135.55
26 ds. Int.—	11.30
Total	1502.43

Thompsons note.	662.50
less 23 ds. Int.	4.25
	658.25

Fosters note	662.50
less 23 ds. Int.	4.25
	658.25
Your Check, Cincinati	179.00
Mine in Gold—	6.93
	1502.43

I endorsed the notes of Foster & Thompson as your agent, after having an interview with Mess. Richardson & Millier, who are the unfortunate owners of the lots on which these notes rest for security. They think it hard to pay in Gold but as gold is demanded of me so I must demand Gold and as these notes now go to Bank, they must pay. At all events your note is retired, and only at an expense to you of $6.93 a mistake in your arithmetic I think. I will be sure to give Ellen an order on you for that amount, should the fortunes of war compel me to put on the Sword.

It may be I feel too little relish for Civil War; and it may be Lincoln is Keen enough to detect it, and has therefore waived all claim to my services. At all events I am yet watching Street Cars, from the Corners of the streets to see that drivers keep their intervals, an inglorious work, but quite as much so as contending with the wild senseless prejudices of People.

With such Generals to lead us as Banks,[1] Reeder, Fremont,[2] & Schleich nothing but good luck, or the mere force of numbers will extricate us from Calamitous results.

Harney is put on a forced leave of absence, and the command devolves on Lyon, a Capt. of Infy.—or Blair Colonel of Militia without commission; or without any one at all—I Know Mr. Lincoln has an Herculean task, but the Safety of this point as a base of operations on Arkansas & Louisiana, ultimately the Command of the Mississipi Valley Strikes me so forcibly, that I hate to see it jeopardized.

Excuse this scrawl. I am writing in Remick & Pollard's office, where I found your note. I have not yet seen Mills. Truly,

W. T. Sherman

ALS, DLC: Thomas Ewing and Family Papers.

1. Nathaniel P. Banks (1816–94), a former member of Congress and governor of Massachusetts, had been named major general of U.S. volunteers on May 16.

2. John C. Frémont (1813–80) had been made a major general on May 14 and given command of the Department of the West with headquarters at St. Louis.

TO THOMAS EWING JR.

Saint Louis, June 3, 1861

Dear Tom,

My last letters from Washington tell me that I am to be one of the Colonels to the New Regiments, but when these appointments are to be made I cannot conjecture. On a mere hypothesis of this kind I do not wish to break up housekeeping here, and send Ellen and all the children to Ohio, for the President may and likely will yield to the pressure of applicants and leave the absent out—For my part I would not come to Washington and ask for a place to be made [by the] President. Still if Ellen is to go to Ohio this summer she ought to leave as soon as possible for she expects to be confined in July. This fact embarrasses me somewhat, and is a reason not pleasant to urge for haste on the part of the appointing power—Capt. or rather Major Williams[1] of the Adjt. Genls. Dept. went East on Saturday & promised to telegraph me if the appointment had been confirmed—I wish you would do the Same, or what amounts to a similar result—telegraph me that the appointment[s] are made, and that my name is omitted. I would feel mean enough to break up house-keeping after so much flourish and at such sacrifice and then be left out.

I really do think it probable that Lincoln will confine his appointments to Such as volunteered at his first Call and his present appointments do so plainly indicate a political bias, that none but Sincere pure republicans should expect anything. The appointment of Pope[,][2] Reeder, Banks, Fremont &c. will afford to Bragg & Davis & Beauregard[3] the liveliest pleasure. The North has so decided an advantage in men for the Ranks, that it is a pity to balance the chances, by a choice of leaders.

I take it that Scott intends by his occupation of Alexandria & semi-circle of heights to make Washington safe from approach—thus to cut off Harpers Ferry from the State, to threaten it, and attack if Johnston[4] shows an opening—also to threaten Norfolk to hold in Check there a large force but to attack & hold Richmond by or before the date fixed for the Southern Congress.[5] These concerted movements can only be made under the orders of one man (Scott I suppose) with inteligent subordinates in charge of the independent

Columns—After all the Mississipi River is the hardest & most important task of the war, & I know of no one Competent unless it be McClellan—But as soon as real war begins, new men, heretofore unheard of will emerge from obscurity, equal to any occasion.

Only I still think it is to be a long war—very long—much longer than any Politician thinks.

If you see John tell him I am still here, ingloriously managing a Street Railroad, and impatient only on Ellens Account—All of us will have enough of war before we are done with it.

We are all well—You had better see to Charley's & Dan McCooks chances for Captaincies. Poor Innocents they are resting under the delusions of some Presidential promise that I will be a Colonel, and will have the appointment of officers. The former may be, the latter impossible under pressure—yrs. affectionately

W. T. Sherman

ALS, DLC: Thomas Ewing and Family Papers.

1. Seth Williams (1822–66) had been serving in the Adjutant General's Department since 1853.

2. John Pope (1822–92) was made a brigadier general of volunteers on June 14 to rank from May 17.

3. Pierre Gustave Toutant Beauregard (1818–93), a prewar friend of WTS, had been made a brigadier general in the Confederate army on March 1, 1861.

4. Joseph Eggleston Johnston (1807–91) had been made a brigadier general in the Confederate army and placed in command at Harpers Ferry in May.

5. The Confederate Congress would convene in Richmond on July 20.

TO ELLEN EWING SHERMAN

Pittsburgh—Sunday
June 8, 61.

Dearest Ellen—

Sunday has caught me here as I expected, only for a longer time. Still I expect to get off at 5 P.M. and be in Washington tomorrow P.M. too late I fear to give you emphatic instructions by Telegraph—but I am fully Conscious of the necessity of the Case and wont delay one minute. The army appointments seem so bad that the papers are rising up indignantly—Still Cameron has his old confidantes to provide for, and Party usage is too strong to be dropt on such short notice. I am afraid they will be playing fast & loose with me, Keeping me dancing attendance on the Secretary, and that I wont stand. This is my second trip, and unless they give me prompt answer I will come back forthwith and consider my patriotic duty fulfilled unless the safety of St. Louis should call all hands to arms.

If on the other hand the Secretary give me a prompt fair answer and assurance that justifies me, I will telegraph you, "Go to Lancaster with all things" or something to that effect—In which event I wish you to send word around to Mr. Lucas—then with as little trouble as you can take Cars for Lancaster—pointing out to some carpenter, say the one we heretofore employed, the articles you particularly want—say your Desk & big chair & bedstead—Then if Mr. Mitchell & Rammelstrong will buy your furniture—viz. Bedstead, dining table, chairs &c. by giving you an order for similar things at Cincinati take it—and let John Yore have the Key, with directions to hold all things "Status quo," till I give emphatic orders.

I see by the papers that Meigs[1] is *not* Quarter Master General, but some Editor of a Sunday school paper—This is more likely—but will so shock what little sense remains, that I would not be surprised if Mr. Cameron would pause & may be offer it to me—if he is determined to go outside the army for his Quarter Mr. Genl. and offers to me I shall of course accept, though it is not a fighting berth—still it calls for extraordinary business energy—next Brigr. Genl. and last Colonel of a new Regt.—In the 1st named case you can remain at Lancaster till next winter, when Washington would be our permanent home—in either of the other cases—you may make yourself quite a fixture in Lancaster, as I doubt whether ever I should be a year in a place.

Now that the war has begun no man can tell when it will end—who would have Supposed Old England Chock full of abolitionists would Side with the southern against their northern descendants—nations like men are governed solely by self interest, and England needs cotton, and the return market for the manufactures consumed in Exchange—Again Corruption seems so to underlie our Govt. that even in this time of trial, cheating in clothes, blankets, flour, bread, every thing is universal—It may be the simple growl of people unaccustomed to the privations of war. Again some 3 or 400,000 people are now neglecting work and looking to war for the means of livelihood—These hereafter will have a say in politics—so that I feel that we are drifting on the high seas, and no one Knows the Port to which we are drifting. The best chance of safety is our old Government, with all its Political chicanery and machinery—and to it we tie our fortunes.

John is with Patterson's Army[2] now supposed to be near Harpers Ferry—Bob {Marcent} is a soldier at Arlington Heights. It may be you will get this Tuesday morning—and I hope you will be able to Start home Wednesday at furthest. Love to all—Yours ever—

W. T. Sherman

ALS, InND: Sherman Family Papers.

1. Montgomery C. Meigs (1816–92) had been made quartermaster general on May 15.
2. Robert Patterson (1792–1881) was major general of Pennsylvania volunteers and would

be put in command of the Military Departments of Pennsylvania, Delaware, Maryland, and the District of Columbia. JS was serving as his volunteer aide.

TO JOHN SHERMAN

Pittsburg, Sunday
June 8, 1861

Dear Brother,

On Wednesday Turner returned to St. Louis, called at my house but I was out & left word he expected me out to his house next morning. Accordingly I took Ellen out Thursday morning, spent the day, and the evening being very stormy we staid all night—on my return to the city Friday I found a despatch from C. T. Sherman, and T. Ewing Jr. from Washington, for me ["]to come on immediately, important,"[1] and after making hasty preparations I started at 6 P.M.—finding myself at Crestline yesterday at 1 P.M., & learning the Fort Wayne cars would not be along till 6 P.M., I hired a buggy—rode to Mansfield, found Cecelia blooming, and in the yard superintending the erection of a {wine} summer house which you had sent from the East—as my stay there was limited she sent for Eliza[2] & Susan[3]—we sat at your house till after 5½ when we rode to McCombs, where I saw Mc[4] & Amelia[5]—with some of the children, at 7 the cars came along, and here I am caught by Sunday—If in luck I will be in Washington tomorrow at 2 P.M.

Turner was much pleased with his interview with you & the President, and the only thing which slackened his Zeal was some sharp words between him and Montgomery Blair about Old General Hitchcock. But on the whole Turner was satisfied from what he saw at Washington that this unhappy war would if possible be confined to the just purpose of maintaining its rightful authority without degenerating into one of angry destruction. He said it was well understood that I was to be a Brig. Genl.—also that the Quarter Master Genls. place lay between me and Meigs—whereas it seems Meigs is not Qr. M. Genl.—but some newspaper man—My God is it possible? I cannot believe it. The rightful man is Sibley[6] or Swords[7] whose names are never mentioned should on my arrival I find the Secretary determined to go outside the Army, and Should he make advances to me, of course I shall accept—In like manner if he tenders me a Brigade I will go ahead my best—or if a Colonelcy—ditto. I still feel that it is wrong to ask for any thing, and prefer they should make their own choice of disposition for me.

You are with Genl. Patterson. There are two A no. 1 men there—Geo. H. Thomas Col. 2nd Cavy.[8]—and Capt. Sykes 3 Inf.[9]—mention my name to both, and say to them that I wish them all success they aspire to, and if in the varying chances of war I should ever be so placed I would name such as them for high places—But Thomas is a Virginian from near Norfolk, and Say what we may he must feel unpleasant at leading an invading army—But if he says he will do it I think he will do it well—He was never brilliant but always Cool, reliable, & steady—maybe a little slow. Sykes has in him some dashing qualities—Shepherd[10] was a Classmate of mine—we never liked him much, but I am told he has made a good soldier. It is now 21 years since we graduated, and they are in their prime.

I will stop at Willards—and will not delay one moment more than necessary—If I find obstacles in my way I can return to St. Louis, resume my work—Only Ellens condition demands almost instantaneous action. As soon as I Know I am to be appointed I am to telegraph her to go to Lancaster. I hope to do so on Tuesday.

If possible I will try and See you in your new Capacity of soldier before I make another distant break.

If you please you may telegraph to Mr. Chase simply that I have come to Washington on Taylors[11] Call—that I cant wait long, and if the administration dont want my services, to say so at once, emphatically. Yrs. affectionately

W. T. Sherman

ALS, DLC: William T. Sherman.

1. Charles T. Sherman and Thomas Ewing Jr. to WTS, June 6, 1861, DLC: WTS.

2. Mary Elizabeth Sherman Reese.

3. Susan Denman Sherman Bartley (1825–76) had married attorney Thomas W. Bartley of Mansfield.

4. Robert McComb (d. 1865), a storekeeper in Mansfield and husband of WTS's sister Amelia.

5. Amelia Sherman McComb (1816–62) was WTS's sister.

6. Caleb Sibley (1806–75) was serving on the frontier at this time and would shortly be captured by Earl Van Dorn in Texas.

7. Thomas Swords (1806–86), a veteran of the Mexican War, would become assistant quartermaster general in August.

8. George H. Thomas (1816–70), a Virginian and classmate of Sherman at West Point, remained loyal to the Union and had been made colonel of the Second U.S. Cavalry in May and would become a brigadier general of volunteers in August.

9. George Sykes (1822–80) was actually a major in the Fourteenth U.S. Infantry, where he had served since 1855.

10. Oliver L. Shepherd (1815–94) had been made lieutenant colonel of the Eighteenth U.S. Infantry on May 14.

11. Presumably Joseph Pannell Taylor.

TO ELLEN EWING SHERMAN

Washington June 12, 61

Dearest Ellen,

I got here Monday night—found C. T. Sherman here, found out he had telegraphed as early as Wednesday, expecting me by Saturday with reference

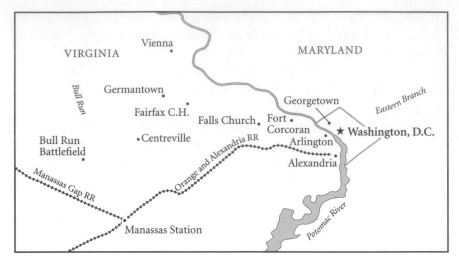

Washington, D.C., and Northeastern Virginia

to the Qr. Mr. Genls. Dept.—We called on Chase that evening & heard from him that the appt. had been conferred on Meigs—I told Mr. Chase that neither Meigs or myself should think of such an office, that Swords in California should have it—he admitted that it was universally admitted that Swords was entitled & qualified, but the want of a Chief Qr. Mr. was so pressing that one must be appointed instanter, though the vacancy has already existed two mos.—I find Washington less of a Camp than I expected, but the same disagreeable crowd, pressing for contracts and sinecure offices. I heard it universally conceded that I should be Colonel at least, and after seeing my name actually on a list in the Adjutant General office I telegraphed you to go to Lancaster, and take all things possible by R. Road—and my special traps along—I am to see the President this morning, and will try and see as much of the actual state of affairs as possible—Already the 1st detachment of Genls. are used up—and so rapacious is American Public opinion that it will eat up a good many worthy men—at this instant the crowd is down on a Genl. Prime[1] for his bungling at Old Point—The fact is when this system of toadyism is encouraged failure will occur—too many cooks, and more than 50,000 patent inventions to Save the Country & catch Jeff Davis—Genl. Scott knows what he is about—he never designed for the 1st 3 mos. to do any thing more than to Secure his key points—open the Roads & prepare materials, but there are so many pushing him that he says he may be beaten, by Genl. Impatience.

Tom will meet you in Lancaster, and I will send word by him of what I am about. I have settled down into the conviction that I will be all summer engaged in raising a Regt. may be in Ohio, or Missouri—and by Fall must take place on some one of the Lines of Operation—But in war all is uncertainty & chance. I shall await with some degree of impatience the news of your safe arrival at Lancaster—As ever

W. T. Sherman

ALS, InND: Sherman Family Papers.

1. Frederick E. Prime (1829–1900), an engineer, had been taken prisoner at Pensacola earlier in 1861 while attempting to reach Fort Pickens. He would later become Grant's chief engineer in the Mississippi campaigns, 1862–63.

TO ELLEN EWING SHERMAN

Washington, June 17, 1861.

Dearest Ellen,

I have recd. yr. two letters & despatch. The order for the new Regiments is still kicked about, altered, and changed—It is printed, and yet amended— Charley is 1st Lieut., and put in my Regiment by my request—Chase had left his name off purposely—but restored it at Toms suggestion. It seems that instead of the Sec. of War or the President or any one person taking charge of this matter every member of the Cabinet has his fling at it, so I fear we will have a sweet set out of which to organize an army. Still actual war will soon make plenty of changes.

Harpers Ferry is abandonned & I propose going up this afternoon & see John—but will return here on Monday by which time I hope the order will be out, and I can then tell what I am to do. I have been all round Washington, Alexandria, Georgetown &c. to See and inspect Forts and troops. Tom will tell you much—since he left I have been to See the Girls at Georgetown, Julia Turner, Coos Patterson, & Miss Whittington who are all well. The number of Girls there is less than 40.

At the Ohio Camp I saw Tom Hunter,[1] and all the Lancaster Boys, also the Mansfield Company—After dark last night they marched across long Bridge, and are now on the Virginia side. There is a chance that Harpers Ferry being abandonned, and Beauregards army reinforced to that extent, they may make a demonstration on Washington at once, but I take it General Scott is fully up to them. Prime is at the Virginia end of Long Bridge building a Fort—I see him often have given him his long lost shirt & received from him many remembrances to you. Barnard[2] is also here, and I was invited to dine there tomorrow, but saw him a while since and told him of my purpose to go to Harpers Ferry to see John Sherman.

Tell Charley that if he wants to See war as a study, that a First Lieutenants place will be as good as Captain, but in any event, I have now not a word to Say on the subject—McDowell is going to try and get me assigned to his Command, & leave the Lieut. Colonel Burbank[3] to recruit the Regiment, but Schuyler Hamilton told me that Genl. Scott thought as I do that each Colonel should raise his own Regiment and identify himself with it. If I go to St. Louis to recruit I will take Lancaster en route, but now that I am in the army—recollect I am but a part of a machine & can only go where bid—Love to all Yrs.

W. T. Sherman

ALS, InND: Sherman Family Papers.

1. Tom Hunter was the brother of John Hunter and member of a Lancaster family close to the Ewings.

2. John G. Barnard (1815–82) was chief engineer of Washington.

3. Sidney Burbank (1807–82), who had previously seen service on the frontier, had been named lieutenant colonel of the Thirteenth U.S. Infantry.

TO JOHN SHERMAN

Washington June 20, 1861

Dear Brother,

At last the order is out and I am Colonel 13 Inf. I have been asking for orders, and am this moment informed for the present, that in as much as Lt. Col. Burbank may enlist my Regiment, and as my personal services here are needed I will forthwith consider myself on duty here. Attached to General Scotts staff, as Inspector General—I did not dream of this, but it really does well accord with my inclinations and peculiar nature.

My duty will be to keep myself advised of the character and kind of men who are in Military Service here near Washington, and to report to General Scott in person—Porter[1] can tell you what these duties will amount to.

Now I will want a good horse you have two, and I suppose dont want more than one—the big Brown—cant you exchange the sorrel for a large fine wagon horse, which here I could exchange for a good Saddle horse and I could pay you his value—or if you have not paid for him yet you had better pay for only the one—I suppose you will soon be here for from Col. Burnside[2] I hear all of Pattersons Army is on the Maryland Side of the Potomac, and no possible movement will be attempted before Congress meets. I will not b[u]y a horse till you write me, but will send for my saddle &c. will stay here at Mr. Wisemanns till you come, and even then can hire another Room, boarding at the Restaurant on I Street. In haste, Your Brother

W. T. Sherman

ALS, DLC: William T. Sherman.

1. Colonel Fitz John Porter (1822–1901) was Patterson's chief of staff.

2. Ambrose E. Burnside (1824–81) was colonel of the First Rhode Island Volunteers.

Washington June 22, 1861

Dear Charley,

I have no facilities for working and have been as it were dancing attendance here in the expectation that immediately that the formalities of appointment were gone through I would go to the Hd. Qrs. of the Regt. wherever it might be, and meet you at Lancaster en route. But all the offices here seem so full of people, so much to do, that I dont feel inclined to join in the Cry of Red tape ism—There are 45,000 men here under arms, 3 mos. men—3 yrs. men—& Regulars of every stripe. To clothe, feed and properly employ these men is some what of a task—Then Pattersons army of about 20,000—Butlers[1] at Old Point of some 20,000—Besides the Missouri & McClellan movements.

Now with all these vast armies I see as yet little done, or attempted nor do I intrude my opinions—or solicit confidence, because I Know it is one of the characteristics of General Scott, slowly but surely to develop his plans, and to execute them about the right time.

Some still think the Confederates design to attack Washington—*I don't* though most assuredly an open, bold attack on our seat of Govt., after so much formal preparation would show to the world the magnitude of their Cause—that Rebellion instead of being put down, has the effrontery not only to threaten but even to attack the Capitol—I think Genl. Scott holds on to me, in the event of quick prompt & decisive movements hereabouts, and I am engaged in satisfying myself of the Geography and actual condition off the forces.

Your appointment has gone out, may be to St. Louis, but you can act on it, that you are a 1st Lieut. 13 Inf.—low down on the List which I could not help—for Chase dont like your family, and only put your name down at the last moment—My opinion was and is still that any Gentleman who has a profession by which he can be certain of a bare livelihood ought to avoid the army. At this particular juncture of course all men are Called on to prevent absolute national ruin & anarchy, and it may be that we will degenerate into mere bands of men, struggling for power & plunder.

Col. Burbank will attend to the Enlistment, and I will join as soon as possible.

You will draw pay monthly after the end of the month from any paymaster; and when on Recruiting service an allowance for fuel & quarters. You had better start out with $100, and that you should pay back within 60 days— Uniform, sash, sword &c. you can get at St. Louis. I will endeavor to find time to write more at length in a few days to you at Jefferson Barracks. Yrs.

W. T. Sherman

P.S. This letter should have been mailed yesterday but I neglected to put it in the office—I was all day yesterday in horseback, to Georgetown and over in Virginia—Was it not for the New forts, and occasional camps it would be hard to realize the fact of war for farmers are quietly making their crops—John Sherman arrived yesterday and will stay till Congress meets. No doubt I will be here that long—In the mean time the Adjt. Genl. assures me he will do all he can to put our Regiment in the process of formation. I have tried to bring in McCook[2] but fear I cannot—John & I will make a renewed effort to make you a Captain but if we cannot do cheerfully the part assigned you—no one can judge what the future has in reserve for us—The Regiment cannot take part in the Virginia Campaigns this Summer. But I know well enough there will be plenty of fighting in the next ten years to satisfy the most greedy hero of war.

ALS, DLC: Charles Ewing Family Papers.

1. Major General Benjamin F. Butler (1818–93), whose commission was owing primarily to his political influence with the Democrats, was in command of the District of Annapolis and had occupied Baltimore on May 13.

2. Dan McCook Jr. would become captain in the First Kansas Infantry on May 31.

TO ELLEN EWING SHERMAN

Fort Corcoran, opposite Geo'town
July 3, 1861, Monday.

Dearest Ellen,

Since my last to you I have received three letters from you, one with the parcel 2 prs. socks & 1 Havelock.[1] For the latter express my thanks to Sis,[2] but tell her I think them a useless contrivance. A Felt hat is better than a Havelock—General Havelock used them in India when he wanted to Shelter the bare neck from the dust, dirt & reflected heat of the naked earth. Here we have trees, green Grass & nothing to guard against but the direct rays of the sun, so the Felt or Straw hat is best—If ladies want to Show their charity and good sense—let them provide good Strong flannel shirts, and knit socks for the coming winter.

On Friday I received orders to report to Gen. McDowell at Arlington—I did so and received orders to relieve Col. Hunter[3] in the Command of this Brigade composed of three Militia Regiments and two companies of Regulars—one of Cavalry & one of artillery—I occupy along with many others a beautiful cottage in full view of Georgetown and Washington City just over the aqueduct—The engineers have erected a Fort named after a New York Colonel, Irish Corcoran,[4] who is most enthusiastic in the cause—and several other little redouts, all designed to protect Georgetown & consequently Washington from an approach this way—This morning I was amazed to see enter my

Room Mr. Hunter and Cecilia & Helen on their way out to the Ohio Camp 4 miles in advance. They have gone out—I took them about, and before they departed John Sherman came over, and he also rode out. I could not go with them. As yet I am simply studying the condition of affairs in anticipation of a forward movement—Of course this depends on affairs with McClellan—Patterson and Butler. When we do move it will be in some force but we Know that Beauregard has long been expecting Such an advance and is as well prepared as he can be. It may be after all that he may retire, but I think he will fight, and it may be it will be in the nature of a Duel—Better Keep even this to yourself—I would not have anything traced back to me—The manner & fact that, nothing is now secret or sacred from the Craving for public news is disgraceful to us as a people—The South manages to Keep their Councils better than we—Beauregard has ceased even to think of attacking—all his dispositions look to defense—even Roads are obstructed to as to prevent his (missing phrase) {w}ay or ones towards (missing phrase) are two or three centers on which he can concentrate before we can reach him. I am now in position ready for service—My saddle has not yet come, and I expect that I must go forward on a common Saddle. I have avoided buying a saddle, or horse by drawing one from the Quarter master, and getting one of John Sherman who had two with General Pattersons Column at Hagerstown—we sent a messenger there & the horses are now in Washington—John & his friend were here this morning on the Horses and I will send over for mine this P.M. I will go over to the City tomorrow and see the Hunters, and if I get time will see the Youngs again. But I cannot give much time to society now—I am glad you are all so well and that Elly is better. I shall await with anxiety for the news of your safe Delivery. I will write often Yrs. as ever

AL (signature clipped), InND: Sherman Family Papers.

1. EES to WTS, June 28, 1861, SFP; this letter also refers to one of June 26. EES said she missed him, sent news of the children, wrote of Lizzie's anxiety about the war and WTS's safety, and sent information about the saddle.

2. Maria Theresa Ewing (b. 1837) was EES's only sister.

3. David Hunter (1802–86) had been named colonel of the Third U.S. Cavalry on May 14.

4. Michael Corcoran (1827–63), an Irish immigrant, had been named colonel of the Sixty-ninth New York in April.

TO ELLEN EWING SHERMAN

Fort Corcoran—opposite Georgetown
Saturday, July 6, 1861

Dearest Ellen,

I have been so busy for some days that really I have no time to write. I now have under my command four Regiments of volunteers, 3 from New York and one from Wisconsin, also two companies of artillery[.][1] We are getting ready to advance from here, but when I know not. Indeed I propose to mind my own show & allow others to do the same. Each of these Regiments has its peculiar troubles all of which are referred to me, and I have to attend their drills. Yesterday I made application for an exchange of Charles Ewing, and Justers A. Boris[.] The former to be Captain & latter 1st Lt.—This Boris, is a young gentleman of 22 years who prefers to be captain instead of 1st Lieutenant and his friend here, a Mr. Cowles of New York & I yesterday made the papers and filed them with the Secretary of War. It is informal for a Lieutenant and Captain to transfer, but I hope this will be done—John sent me Charley's letter, and I sent his acceptance & oath to the adjutant General, and asked him to order Charley to me here, unless his services are needed to recruit. If Charley is ordered here, I will put him on duty as an aid, till I join the Regiment.

My saddle has not come, and of course I give it up as lost—it may be that it was left by Sam Patterson along with your things, and is coming to you by the Ohio River. I need it very much and will try and avoid the purchase of another till I hear something definite about it.

Congress is now sitting. I have read the message, and suppose that we are in for a long war[2]—I wish Congress would drop Texas, New Mexico & Arizona at once and forever, and then Set about the recovery of the Balance—Of course Virginia is the first field of action[.] Then Arkansas, & Louisiana.

I heard that the Kentucky members left the Congress yesterday on the reading of the message—so that I suppose she must also be considered in a hostile state[3]—Maryland & Missouri alone remain of the slave states, and they are ready to rise the moment the army is lessened—Tis strange the deep intense hatred with which the Politicians have imbued the public mind south—the Confederate armies destroy Roads, bridges, fences, farms every thing—take what they want paying in an irredeemable scrip and the people think it all right—whereas if one of our soldiers take a fence rail, or catch a pig, it is an awful act of vandalism. I cannot see the end of all this, but am certain that a heavy contest must occur, to make each respect the other.

I am living in a house of one {Rose} an Englishman, now in Europe—The house is directly opposite Georgetown College, and you must have seen it often—There are two Redoubts built near us occupied by volunteers, and three Regiments are camped about a mile forward—The column with which I expect to move will be under the command of a Connecticut man named Tyler,[4] who was an army officer a long time ago—Schenck[5] will be in the same Column. McDowell will command the whole—and as near as I can Guess there will be in all 10 brigades of about 3000 each.

We will carry but little baggage or provisions and depend upon the country therefor. I expect our Route will be Vienna—Fairfax C. H. Centerville—Manassas Junction, and Fredericksburg—& Aquia Creek.

I go over to Washington but seldom and John occasionally comes to see me here. Moulton[6] was here yesterday, he is a Qr. Master and ordered to report to McClellan.

Of course I am very anxious to hear from and of you, and await with anxiety the result of your present trials. But I have great confidence in the result, and trust that hereafter you will enjoy more peace & tranquility. As ever yrs.

W. T. Sherman

Since I wrote this letter, I have received the saddle, bed—trunk *all right* just in time.

ALS, InND: Sherman Family Papers.

1. WTS's brigade consisted of Battery E, Third U.S. Artillery, and the Thirteenth New York, Sixty-ninth New York, Seventy-ninth New York, and Second Wisconsin volunteer infantry.

2. On July 4, Congress convened for a special session. In his address to them, read on July 5, Lincoln summarized what had happened since March 4 and put all onus for the rebellion on the Southern states while declaring his administration's determination to hold the government's public places and property. War was necessary, and he outlined the means he wished to pursue and asked Congress's cooperation in passing those measures which were beyond the executive's power to enact. He firmly stated his belief that peaceful secession was impossible under the terms of the Constitution.

3. Kentucky remained neutral through early September.

4. Daniel Tyler (1799–1882), USA, who had resigned his earlier army commission in 1834, had been named colonel of the First Connecticut on April 23 and brigadier general of volunteers on May 10.

5. Robert C. Schenck (1809–90), a politician and businessman, had been appointed brigadier general of Ohio volunteers.

6. Charles W. Moulton (d. 1888), USA, an Ohio lawyer and journalist, had married WTS's sister Frances Beecher Sherman in 1855. He was currently a captain and assistant quartermaster of volunteers.

TO MARIA BOYLE EWING SHERMAN

Sunday morning, July 14. 61

My Dear Minnie

I received your good letter the other day, and have got up early this morning, before I have to go out on duty, to write to you.

War is a terrible thing, especially when as now we are fighting people like Mrs. Turner[1] & Mrs. Patterson,[2] and thousands of others whom I used to know as kind good friends: and they thinking they are defending their country, their homes and families against foreign invaders—so my Dear Child dont get in the habit of calling hard names of Rebels, Traitors, but remember how easy it is for People to become deceived and drawn on step by step, till war death and destruction are upon them.

I am now in a pretty cottage, with fine grand walks lined with flowers and box wood—but the fences are down—horses tied to beautiful cedars, tents pitched in among the roses, and every thing trodden down by soldiers from the North. A large Fort is built where the Barn yard was, the Stable is a Guard house, and the Corn Crib full of flour—all round for miles the fences are torn down, and hogs, horses and cattle roam at will through Clover & wheat and Corn fields. No matter how much officers may wish to protect, soldiers will take rail fences for their Camp fires, and it is miraculous how soon a fence disappears, and yet nobody did it—Thus wherever an army goes, there will be destruction of property.

I have under my command two Regiments of New York volunteers here, just by Georgetown, and three Regiments of volunteers, about a mile out, where there is a large field in which to drill them.—We are all daily waiting for orders to march into Virginia, where it is known we may have a Battle at once but I think General Scott dont want a battle here till there has been more fighting where Uncle Boyle is, and at other places. When ready we will move quick. I have a great deal to do. Reports to receive and make—orders to give, and to drill 4000 men is hard work—My voice is now very hoarse—I have Lieut. Piper[3] of the Regular army as adjutant and McQuesten[4] as aid—We have to get along with as few Regulars as possible as these officers are needed elsewhere—Scattered all over the Land. When we march I will have a horse, and a servant named John Hill[5]—two mounted soldiers near me called orderlies, and I will make John lead a pack horse with some blankets & provisions for the party—The soldiers carry each a blanket, pair of socks, and his musket, 40 cartridges, and 3 days provisions in a haversack—Expecting in these three days to come up to the Enemy & fight them. Henry Reese was here yesterday—and Uncle John comes over occasionally—but I am almost entirely among Strangers—Tell Aunt Henrietta that I have been so busy of late that I could not go to See her father & mother, but that I will do so yet, if we dont start tomorrow—Tell her not to be too unhappy, for that I say there are plenty of officers, who feel very Kindly to all the People—We must fight and subdue those in arms against us and our Government, but we mean them no harm—we have not disturbed a single slave—Even the Slaves of Colonel Lee[6] are at Arlington, cultivating the farm and Selling vegetables & milk to Soldiers for their master & mistress who are with the Virginians. This is a strange war. And God Grant it may never be felt near you all——In the quiet of Lancaster I believe you are better off than anywhere else and I am glad you all like it so. You and Lizzy must write often. Let Mamma read this to you——Tell Willy I would like to show him some real soldiers here, but he will see enough of them in his day. Love to all yr. papa,

W. T. Sherman

ALS, OHi: William T. Sherman Papers.

1. Julia Maria Hunt Turner was Henry S. Turner's wife.

2. Probably the wife of WTS's St. Louis friend H. J. Patterson.

3. Lieutenant Alexander Piper (d. 1902), USA, Third Artillery, would serve through the war and reach the rank of colonel in 1863.

4. James F. McQuesten (d. 1864), USA, was a second lieutenant in the Second Dragoons and would transfer to the Second Cavalry in August 1861; he reached the rank of captain before he was killed in September 1864 at Opequan, Virginia.

5. John Hill was WTS's hired black servant.

6. Robert E. Lee (1807–70); his wife's estate was across the Potomac from Washington, D.C., on the grounds of the present-day Arlington Cemetery.

CHAPTER 3

July 15, 1861–December 12, 1861

*I*n July 1861, under a hot summer sun, Union recruits marched south from Washington toward Manassas Junction, Virginia, determined to oust the Confederate Congress in Richmond. Sherman's brigade stumbled forward in ragged fashion, his men resisting orders to remain in ranks. On July 18 the brigade came under fire at Blackburn's Ford as it rushed to the support of a reconnaissance that had met heavy resistance from Confederates posted south of Bull Run. Three days later Sherman led his men into battle once more as part of Irvin McDowell's three-division attack against the Rebel left. Although the original plan called for his brigade to follow up on the success of the initial Union assault, Sherman contributed to the ensuing debacle when he sent up his command in piecemeal fashion, a regiment at a time, in a doomed effort to seize Henry Hill, the key to the Confederate defense. He was amazed when Congressman Owen P. Lovejoy, an abolitionist Republican, offered him the use of a pair of field glasses: when would the politicians (especially the abolitionist ones) leave the fighting to the soldiers? Before long Sherman had to prepare to fend off a counterattack. He hastily ordered his worn regiments to form a square to repulse Confederate cavalry; that done, he brought his command off the field to join the straggle back to Washington.[1]

It had been a rough introduction to battle for both the colonel and his men. Ignoring the fact that he had twice been grazed by bullets (and had a horse shot from under him), Sherman did what he could to rally the retreaters to resist an anticipated enemy pursuit. Soldiers, insisting that their term of service had expired, made plans to go home, only to encounter Sherman's threat to shoot anyone who left. When Abraham Lincoln reviewed the brigade, one officer reported the brigade commander's promise. "Well, if I were you and he threatened to shoot," the president replied in a stage whisper, "I wouldn't trust him, for I believe he would do it."[2]

In August Sherman received word that he had been promoted to brigadier general of volunteers (to rank from May 17). The increased authority brought with it increased burdens. He had to choke off another threatened mutiny by three regiments—persuading him that volunteers were unreliable and that perhaps the North lacked the sustained commitment needed to prevail. He was also losing patience with the political environment around Washington. Fortunately, Major General Robert Anderson—the hero of Fort Sumter—wanted Sherman to serve under him as he organized Union forces north of still-neutral Kentucky. Pleased at the chance both to go west and to escape from Washington, Sherman accepted the offer.[3]

Within a week of Sherman's arrival in Cincinnati on September 1, Kentucky's neutral stance crumbled. Although the Bluegrass State officially declared for the Union, it was a land of divided allegiances, and Confederate forces surged north to stake their claim to it. Sherman, all too aware of his own command's shortcomings, exaggerated both the size and condition of the enemy columns. When Anderson, complaining that he could no longer stand the strain of command, resigned on October 5, Sherman found himself in charge. He had not sought his post: indeed, he had accepted Anderson's offer with the express proviso that he not be elevated to command. Now he did what he could to maintain order while the War Department found a replacement. He ordered his men to leave civilians alone; he returned fugitive slaves who sought refuge in his camps. A reporter noted that he paced the corridors of Louisville's Galt House with such intensity that some observers speculated that he was going insane. He puffed cigar after cigar, each making him even more nervous; drink did not steady his hand. He snapped at reporters (and jailed one). The war was getting to him. Aware that he could not control events, he lost control of himself.[4]

Events began to reach a climax on October 17, when Sherman encountered Secretary of War Simon Cameron and Adjutant General Lorenzo Thomas. Dragging his visitors to the Galt House, he spilled out his troubles and fears, revealed his belief in the vulnerability of the Union position in Kentucky, and jarred his listeners with the declaration that it would take two hundred thousand men to conquer the state. Such numbers were beyond Cameron's comprehension; the secretary and the adjutant general advised Sherman to move forward and wondered about his state of mind. Cameron shared his concerns with a reporter: by month's end they appeared in the *New York Tribune*.[5]

Understandably irritated that confidential conversations had made their way into the public press, Sherman chastised Thomas: "Do not conclude, as before that I exaggerate the facts. They are as stated and the future looks as dark as possible. It would be better if some man [of] sanguine mind was here, for I am forced to order according to my convictions."[6] But the pressures were beginning to get to him. Everywhere he looked he saw disaster looming. "The idea of going down to History with a fame such as threatens me nearly makes me crazy, indeed I may be so now," Sherman told Ellen as November began.[7] Cameron urged him to advance: General in Chief George McClellan inquired about the possibility of a fighting withdrawal. Sherman chose to stay where he was. Meanwhile, the news finally came that Don Carlos Buell would take over Sherman's command. As Sherman waited for Buell's arrival, he panicked at rumors that the Confederates were about to launch an offensive; it was with relief that he greeted Buell. He told Anderson, "I confess I never have seen daylight in the midst of the troubles that now envelope us. I am therefore disqualified to lead, and must follow—You know with what reluctance I entered on my command and have always felt that Somehow or other I would be disgraced by it."[8]

Sherman made his way to Missouri, where he had been assigned to Henry W. Halleck, but his new assignment brought no peace of mind, as he began issuing orders to resist a Rebel offensive that never materialized. Halleck ordered him to St. Louis; Ellen, alarmed by reports that her husband was not quite himself, awaited his arrival. "I am satisfied that General Sherman's physical and mental system is so completely broken by labor and care as to render him for the present entirely unfit for duty," Halleck told McClellan as he sent Sherman home with twenty days of leave. In Lancaster Sherman picked up a copy of the *Cincinnati Commercial* of December 11; it contained a column headed: "General William T. Sherman Insane."[9] It was the sad ending to a troubling year.

1. Lloyd Lewis, *Sherman: Fighting Prophet* (1932; reprint, Lincoln, Neb., 1993), 169–78.

2. Ibid., 178–80.

3. Ibid., 181–82.

4. Ibid., 190–93. Whether Sherman's behavior corresponded to clinical definitions of temporary insanity has long been debated by his biographers. Compare John F. Marszalek, *Sherman: A Soldier's Passion for Order* (New York, 1993), 169, with Michael Fellman, *Citizen Sherman* (New York, 1995), 99. Lacking either the clinical expertise or the opportunity to examine the patient, we prefer to describe what happened rather than to classify it. Clearly Sherman was deeply depressed, easily excitable, and in no condition to exercise command.

5. Lewis, *Sherman*, 193–95.

6. WTS to Lorenzo Thomas, November 6, 1861.

7. WTS to EES, November 1, 1861.

8. WTS to Robert Anderson, November 21, 1861.

9. Lewis, *Sherman*, 199–201.

TO ELLEN EWING SHERMAN

> Rosslyn, opposite Georgetown.
> July 15, 1861.

Dearest Ellen,

Charles Sherman came over yesterday & spent most of the day with me. He brought your two letters of the 11th and I was very glad to hear you were so well and that the little baby was also flourishing.[1] We certainly have a heavy charge in these Six children, and I know not what is in store for them. All I can now do is to fulfil the office to which I am appointed leaving events to develop as they may. After all Congress is not disposed to increase the Regular Army as the President supposed. The ten new Regiments are only for the war, and will be mustered out, six months after the close of hostilities, but who know when hostilities are to cease? I wont bother myself on this point but leave things to their natural development.

I now have my Brigade ready for the March—Mine is the 3rd Brigade, 1st Division[.] Brig. Genl. Tyler commands the Division composed of four Brigades—Keyes's[2] (you remember him in California) Schenck—Sherman and Richardson[3]—In my brigade are—the New York 69, Irish, 1000 strong—the 79 Scots, 900 strong—Quinbys[4] 700 strong, and Wisconsin 2nd Col. Peck[5] 900 strong, and the Battery of Capt. Ayres[6]—used to be Shermans battery 112 men—110 horses and six Guns—We move without baggage—I have Lt. Piper adjt.—McQuesten & Bagley[7] aids—two mounted orderlies and a negro servant John Hill.

4 colums move out against the forces of Beauregard—posted from Fairfax C. H. to Manassas Junction—supposed to be from 30, to 45,000 men—one under Col. Miles[8] starts from below Alexandria—one Col. Heintzelman[9] from Alexandria—one Col. Hunter from Long Bridge—and ones from this point Genl. Tyler—This latter is a West Point graduate, at present Brig. Genl. from Connecticut. I dont know him very well, but he has a fair reputation—McDowell commands the whole—say 40,000 men—The purpose is to drive Beauregard beyond Manassas—break his connection with Richmond, and then to await the further movements of Gen. Patterson and McClellan—I know our plans, but could not explain them to you without maps—It may not produce results but the purpose is to fight no matter the result. We have pretty fair knowledge of the present distribution of Beauregards forces, but he has a Railroad to Richmond from which point he may get reinforcements, and unless Patterson presses Johnston, he too may send forces across from Winchester. Manassas Junction in our possession, Richmond is cut off from the valley of Virginia above Staunton. But with these Grand strategic movements I will try and leave that to the heads, and confine my attention to the mere handling of my Brigade[.]

Keyes Brigade is about 5 miles out—the Ohio[10] 4 miles—mine here, Richardson on the other side—on the first notice we simply close up—and early next morning at Fairfax C. H. where there are 6 or 7 S.C. & Georgia Regts.—Close at hand at Germantown, Flint Hill, Cumberville, Bull Run & Manassas are all occupied & fortified—but we may go round these. I take with me simply valise, & saddle bags—and leave behind my trunks to be sent over to

John Sherman. Letters can take the same course. If we take Manassas, there will be a Railroad from Alexandria to that point, so that letters can be received regularly. Though we momentarily look for orders to cook Rations to be carried along, I still see many things to do, which are not yet done, and General Scott, will allow no risks to be run—He thinks there Should be no game of hazard here. All the Risks should be made from the flanks.

I wrote to Minnie yesterday[11]—Poor Charley will be disappointed sadly— He overrates my influence and that of John Sherman—I have some hopes of the transfer with Boris. I will write again before we start but the telegraph will announce all results before you can hear by mail—as ever &c.

W. T. Sherman

ALS, InND: Sherman Family Papers.

1. Rachel Ewing Sherman (1861–1919) was born on July 5.

2. Erasmus D. Keyes (1810–95), USA, had been Scott's military secretary until April and had then become colonel of the Eleventh U.S. Infantry on May 14 and a brigadier general of volunteers to rank from May 17. He headed the First Brigade in the First Division.

3. Colonel Israel B. Richardson (1815–62), USA, was commanding the Fourth Brigade of the First Division.

4. Isaac F. Quinby (1821–91) was commissioned colonel of the Thirteenth New York, a regiment he had raised, on May 14.

5. Lieutenant Colonel Harry W. Peck, USA, a graduate of West Point.

6. Romeyn B. Ayres (1825–88), USA, had been promoted to captain of the Fifth U.S. Artillery on May 14.

7. Lieutenant Bagley of the Sixty-ninth New York was a volunteer aide who was wounded and taken prisoner during First Bull Run.

8. Colonel Dixon S. Miles; Richardson would later claim Miles was drunk during the Battle of First Bull Run, and a court of inquiry would conclude that he had been drinking but that he could not be court-martialed for the offense.

9. Colonel Samuel P. Heintzelman (1805–80), USA, of the Seventeenth U.S. Infantry.

10. This was Schenck's brigade.

11. WTS to Maria Boyle Ewing Sherman, July 14, 1861, above.

TO ELLEN EWING SHERMAN

Camp opposite Georgetown
July 16, 1861.

Dearest Ellen,

We start forth today at 2 P.M. move forward 10 miles to Vienna, there sleep—and tomorrow morning expect to fight some six or eight thousand of the enemy, at or near Fairfax, Germantown or Centreville—There we may pause for a few days & then on Manassas Junction, Beauregards Hd. Qrs. distant from here about 30 miles. I think we shall make a wide circuit, to come on his Rear.

I am going to mind my own Brigade—not trouble myself about General plans—McDowell commands the whole—Brig. Gen. Tyler our colum of 4 Brigades of about 10, or 11,000 men. I will have 3400—New York 13, 69 & 79th & Wisconsin 2nd with Shermans Battery now commanded by Capt. Ayres.

I take with me a few clothes in the valises & saddle bags—leave my small trunk to follow—have about 50 dollars in money, a Boy named John Hill as servant—have drawn pay to June 30—and you know all else.

I think Beauregard will probably fall back tomorrow on Manassas, and call by R. R. from the neighborhood of Richmond & Lynchburg all the men he can get, and fight us there, in which case we will have our hands full.

Yesterday I went to the convent to bring the Girls over to see a drill—I found India Turner over visiting John Lee—Miss Whittington out in the country—so I brot over Miss Patterson and a Miss Walker of New Orleans—and after drill took them back—I saw Sister Bernard, and another who said she was your drawing teacher—She had a whole parcel of little prayers, and relics to keep me from harm—I told her you had Secured about my neck as it were with a Silk cable a little medal which would be there, and her little relics I would stow away in my holsters.

Whatever fate befals me, I Know you appreciate what good qualities I possess—and will make charitable allowances for defects, and that under you, our children will grow up on the safe side. About the Great Future that Providence that gives color & fragrance to the modest violet will deal justly by all—knowing the Secret motives & impulses of every heart. In the noise, confusion, hustle and {crises} of three thousand volunteers, my tongue and pen may be silent henceforth about you and our children, but I confide them with absolute confidence to you and the large circle of our mutual friends & relations.

I still regard this as but the beginning of a long war, but I hope my judgment therein is wrong, and that the People of the South may yet see the folly of their unjust Rebellion against the most mild & paternal Government ever designed for men—John will in Washington be better able to judge of my whereabouts and you had better send letters to him. As I read them I will tear them up, for every ounce on a march tells.

Tell Willy I have another war sword, which he can add to his present armory—when I come home again—I will gratify his ambition on that score, though truly I do not choose for him or Tommy the military profession. It is too full of blind chances to be worthy of a first rank among callings.

Watch well your investments—that note you left with Turner, as well as your others lest you may be necessitated to fall back on them. Always assure Maj. Turner and Mr. Lucas of the unbounded respect I feel for them. Give your father, mother,[1] sis & all my love. Tell Henrietta it has been an impossibility for me to go over to see her father & mother without neglecting my command which I never do. Good bye—and believe me always most affectionately yrs.

W. T. Sherman

ALS, InND: Sherman Family Papers.
1. Maria Willis Boyle Ewing (1801–64).

TO JOHN SHERMAN

Camp opposite Georgetown,
July 16, 1861.

Dear Brother,

We start forth today—camp tonight at or near Vienna—tomorrow early, we attack the Enemy at or near Fairfax C. H., Germantown, and Centerville— thereabouts we will probably be till about Thursday when movement of the whole force some 35,000 men on Manassas, turning the position by a wide circuit. You may expect to hear of us about Aquia Creek or Fredericksburg (secret absolute)[.]

I leave your saddle & bridle with the Commissary Gray with orders to Send it with my large trunk over to you—I take your saddle bags, along—and will have my small trunk to follow.

If anything befal me, my pay is drawn to embrace June 30—and Ellen has full charge of all other interests. Goodbye, Yr. brother,

W. T. Sherman

(over)

Ellen will write to your care and you can enclose her letters. This will give me a better assurance of receiving them. Send the enclosed to her. Yrs.

W. T. Sherman

ALS, DLC: William T. Sherman.

TO ELLEN EWING SHERMAN

Camp—1 m. West of Centreville
26 from Washington
July 19, 1861

Dearest Ellen,

I wrote to John yesterday, asking him to send you my letter that you might be assured of my safety.[1] Thus far the enemy has retired before us—yesterday our General Tyler made an unauthorized attack on a Battery over Bull Run— they fired Gun for Gun—and on the whole had the best of it—the Genl. finding Centreville a strong place evacuated, followed their tracks to Bull Run which has a valley deeply wooded admitting only of one narrow column. I was sent for and was under fire about half an hour, the Rifled Cannon shot cutting the trees over head and occasionally pitching into the ground. 3 artillerists— 1 Infantry & 3 horses in my Brigade with several wounded—I have not yet learned the full extent of damage—and as it was a Blunder, dont care—I am uneasy at the fact that the Volunteers do pretty much as they please, and on the Slightest provocation bang away—the danger from this desultory firing is greater than from the Enemy as they are always so close whilst the latter keep a respectful distance. We were under orders to march at 2½ A.M.—the Division of Tyler to which my Brigade belongs will advance along a turnpike Road, to a Bridge on Bull Run—This Bridge is gone—and there is a strong Battery on the opposite shore of the River—here I am summoned to a council at 8 P.M. at General McDowell's camp about a mile distant—I am now there, all the Brigade commanders are present and only a few minutes intervene before they all come to this table.

I know tomorrow & next day we shall have had hard work—and I will acquit myself as well as I can—with Regulars I would have no doubts, but these Volunteers are subject to Stampedes[.] Yesterday there was an ugly stampede of 800 Massachusetts men—The Ohio men claim their discharge and so do others of the 3 months men—of them I have the Irish 69th New York which will fight.

I am pretty well, up all night and sleeping a little by day—Prime[,] Barnard, Myers[2] & others of your acquaintance are along—Prime slept in my camp last night.

My best love to all—my faith in you & children is perfect and let what may befal me I feel they are in a fair way to grow up in goodness & usefulness. Goodby for the present yrs. ever

Sherman

ALS, InND: Sherman Family Papers.

1. Presumably WTS to JS, July 19, 1861, following.

2. Probably Frederick Myers (1822–74), who had fought in the Mexican War and on the frontier and was presently organizing Ohio volunteers. He would later join the Quartermaster's Department and rise to lieutenant colonel.

TO JOHN SHERMAN

Camp near Centreville,
July 19. 1861.

Hon. John Sherman
Dear Brother,

I started my Brigade at 2 P.M. the day I wrote you viz. Tuesday the men with 3 days cooked provision in their haversacks. We passed Falls Church in about two hours, took the gravel road a couple of miles then turned left to the village of Vienna, which is hardly entitled to the name. There we camped, and next morning at 5½ started, marched very slowly toward Germantown. The road was obstructed by fallen timber but no signs of an armed opposition we found at Germantown an Earth parapet thrown across the road, but very poor—at or near Germantown we came into the Main Road back of Fairfax C. H. which had been abandoned by about 5000 men. Had we reached their rear in time we might have Caught them—but their Knowledge of the Roads—and extreme ease of obstructing them by simply cutting down trees prevented us reaching the point in time. We followed on to Centreville where also we expected opposition, but it too was evacuated, though the Strongest place I have yet seen to make a stand. This was the point arranged for the Concentration of all the Columns from Alexandria, Geo[']town & Long Bridge. Our Division reached it first, Richardsons Brigade in advance mine next—Gen. Tyler took two 20 pr. Rifled guns, some Dragoons & Richardsons Brigade[1] to follow to discover the line of Retreat—Bulls Run was only 3 miles distant and it was distinctly understood it was not to be attacked by the Route of usual travel, which had been carefully studied and commanded. I went into a large meadow with my four Regts. and soon saw the heads of Miles & Heintzelmans columns showing the details had been well planned. About noon I heard firing in the direction of the Ford at Bulls Run—very irregular and though I knew McDowell did not want it attacked I felt uneasy—The firing was quite sharp at time, and I continued uneasy though my duty was plain to Stand fast—about 2 I got orders to come forward, and about that time I heard heavy musketry firing. In four minutes we were hastening[.] The distance about 2½ miles—the road la[y]ing on the {illegible} or Ridge divide between heavy wooded slopes making a narrow Rocky road—we met too many, far too many straggling soldiers and soon came to the ambulance & Doctors with their appliances at work—I led the head of my column till I came upon our Batteries—that of 2 20 prs.—and Ayers field Battery. I asked Gen. Tyler for orders, and was told to deploy and cover Richardson who was down a Ravine to the left—front was a small house, and Right an open field in which Ayres Battery was unlimbered—the whole comprising a small open farm just where you could look across Bulls Run—It was Known to be fortified, yet the Batteries could not be clearly seen, it was full a mile & half off—the cannonading was quite brisk at the time of my arrival, but the shots mostly passed over us, the Batteries were simply firing at each other. Richardson had previously pushed his Brigade down close to the Run, but was repulsed, his volunteers breaking and not rallying. Then the fighting was very brisk, and our loss heavy. That occurred some twenty minutes before my arrival and it was the dispersed troops we met—After arranging my four Regts. under cover of timber, ready for any movement. I went forward again to the Batteries, and there learned that we were to return. Receiving the order I drew out my Brigade on the Back track and marched to this Camp—Gen. McDowell arrived during the cannonading and I think did not like it—Tyler never intended to attack Bulls Run Ford, but wanted to experiment with Rifled cannon and got a Rowland for his Oliver.[2] We have to cross Bulls run by some Route and attack Manassas. No doubt the enemy is there in all force. We are only about 6 miles off in an air line, but the Country is wooded, and Bulls Run with ugly ragged banks well known to them, and imperfectly to us still lies between. Some manoeuvering must still precede the final attack—The volunteers test my patience by their irregularities Robbing, shooting in direct opposition to orders, and like conduct showing a great want of Discipline—Twill take time to make soldiers of them. Send this to Ellen, to assure her of my safety—day is hot, and we have little shade. Yrs.

W. T. Sherman

ALS, DLC: William T. Sherman.

1. Fourth Brigade, First Division.

2. A reference to *The Song of Roland*, a medieval epic about one of Charlemagne's warriors. The phrase "a Roland for an Oliver" means to strike a blow for a blow and refers to a five-day battle between these two warriors.

TO ELLEN EWING SHERMAN

Fort Corcoran
July 24, 1861

Dearest Ellen,

On my arrival back here carried by the Shameless flight of the armed mob we led into Virginia I tried to stay the crowd, and held them in check to show at least some front to the pursuing force. Yesterday the President & Mr. Seward visited me, and I slipped over for a few minutes last night to see your father. John S. and Tom have seen me and promise to write you—The battle was nothing to the absolute rout that followed and yet exists, with shameless conduct the volunteers continue to flee—a Regiment the N. York 79th Scots were forming to march over to Washington, and I have commanded them to remain. If they go in spite of all I can do there will remain here but one company of artillery 90 Strong and a Wisconsin Regiment. And Beauregard is close at hand—so it seems to be true that the north is after all pure bluster—Washington is in greater danger now than ever.

I will stand by my Post, an illustration of what we all know that when real danger came the Politicians would clear out—The Proud army characterized as the most extraordinary on earth has turned out the most ordinary.

Well as I am sufficiently disgraced now, I suppose soon I can sneak into some quiet corner. I was under heavy fire for hours—brushed on the Knee, & Shoulder—my horse shot through the leg, and was every way exposed and can not imagine how I escaped except to experience the mortification of a Retreat route, Confusion, and now abandonment by Whole Regiments. I am much pressed with business regulating the flight of all save the few to remain on this side [of] the River.

Last night I received several letters from you, and took time to read them, and now trust to Tom & others to tell you of the famous & infamous deeds of Bulls Run.

Courage our people have, but no government.

W. T. Sherman
Col. Comdg.

ALS, InND: Sherman Family Papers.

TO ELLEN EWING SHERMAN

Fort Corcoran July 28, [1861]
Saturday—

Dearest Ellen,

I have already written to you since my return from the Unfortunate defeat at Bulls Run—I had previously conveyed to you the doubts that oppressed my mind on the Score of discipline. Four large columns of poorly disciplined militia left this place—the Long bridge and Alexandria—all concentrating at a place called Centreville 27 miles from Washington. We were the first column to reach Centreville the Enemy abandoning all defenses en route. The first day of our arrival our Commander Genl. Tyler advanced on Bulls Run, about 2½ miles distant, and against orders engaged their Batteries. He sent back to Centreville and I advanced with our Brigade, where we lay for half an hour, amidst descending shots killing a few of our men—The Batteries were full a mile distant and I confess I, nor any person in my Brigade saw an enemy.

Towards evening we returned to Centreville.

That occurred on Thursday. We lay in camp till Saturday night by which the whole army was assembled in and about Centreville. We got orders for march at 2½ Sunday morning. Our column of 3 Brigades—Schenck, Sherman & Keyes—to move straight along a Road to Bulls Run—another of about 10,000 men to make a circuit by the Right (Hunters) and come upon the enemy in front of us—Heintzelmans column of about similar strength also to make a wide circuit to sustain Hunter—We took the road first and about 6 A.M. came in sight of Bull Run—we saw in the grey light of morning men moving about—but no signs of batteries: I rode well down to the Stone Bridge which crosses the Stream, saw plenty of trees cut down—some brush huts such as soldiers use on picket Guard, but none of the Evidences of Strong fortification we had been led to believe. Our business was simply to threaten, and give time for Hunter & Heintzelman to make their circuit. We arranged our troops to this end. Schenck to the left of the Road, & I to the right—Keyes behind in reserve. We had with us two six gun batteries, and a 30 pd. Gun—This was fired several times, but no answer—we shifted positions several times, firing wherever we had reason to suppose there were any troops. About 10 or 11 o.c. we saw the clouds of dust in the direction of Hunters approach. Saw one or more Regiments of the Enemy leave their cover, and move in that direction—soon the firing of musketry, and guns showing the engagement had commenced—early in the morning I saw a flag flying behind some trees. Some of the Soldiers seeing it Called out—Colonel, there's a flag—a flag of truce—a man in the Field with his dog & gun—called out—No it is no flag of truce, but a flag of defiance—I was at the time studying the Ground and paid no attention to him—about 9 oclock I was well down to the River—with some skirmishes and observed two men on horseback ride along a hill, descend, cross the stream and ride out towards us—he had a gun in his hand which he waved over his head, and called out to us, You D——d black abolitionists, come on &c.—I permitted some of the men to fire on him—but no damage was done he remained some time thus waiting the action which had begun on the other side of Bulls Run—we could See nothing, but heard the firing and could judge that Hunters column steadily advanced: about 2 P.M. they came to a stand, the firing was severe and stationary—Gen. Tyler rode up to me and remarked that he might have to Send the N.Y. 69th to the relief of Hunter—a short while after he came up and ordered me with my whole Brigade, some 3400 men to cross over to Hunter. I ordered the movement, led off—found a place where the men could cross, but the Battery could not follow. We crossed the stream, and ascended the Bluff Bank, moving slowly to permit the Ranks to close up—When about half a mile back from the Stream I saw the parties in the fight, and the first danger was that we might be mistaken for Secessionists & fired on—One of my Regiments had on the grey uniform of the Virginia troops—We first fired on some retreating Secessionists, our Lt. Col. Haggerty was killed, and my bugler by my side had his horse shot dead—I moved on and Joined Hunters column. They had had a pretty severe fight—Hunter was wounded, and the unexpected arrival of my brigade seemed a great relief to all. I joined them on a high field with a house—and as we effected the junction the secessionists took to the woods and were *seemingly* retreating and Gen. McDowell who had accompanied Hunter's column ordered me to join in the pursuit—I will not attempt to describe you the scene—their Batteries were on all the high hills overlooking the ground which we had to cross, and they fired with great vigor—our horse batteries pursued from point to point returning the fire, whilst we moved on, with shot shells, and cannister over and all round us. I kept to my horse and head of the Brigade, and moving slowly, came upon their heavy masses of men, behind all kinds of obstacles. They knew the ground perfectly, and at every turn we found new ground, over which they poured their fire. At last we came to a stand, and with my Regiments in succession we crossed a Ridge and were exposed to a very heavy fire, first one Regiment & then another and another were forced back—not by the bayonet but by a musketry & rifle fire, which it seemed impossible to push our men through. After an hour of close contest our men began to fall into confusion. 111 had been killed some 250 wounded and the Soldiers began to fall back in disorder—My horse was shot through the foreleg—my knee was cut round by a ball, and another had hit my Coat collar and did not penetrate an aid Lt. Bagley was missing, and spite of all exertions the confusion increased, and the men would not reform—Similar confusion had already occurred among other Regiments & I saw we were gone. Had they kept their Ranks we were the gainers up to that point—only our field Batteries exposed had been severely cut up, by theirs partially covered. Then for the first time I saw the Carnage of battle—men lying in every conceivable shape, and mangled in a horrible way—but this did not make a particle of impression on me—but horses running about riderless with blood streaming from their nostrils—lying on the ground hitched to guns, gnawing their sides in death—I sat on my horse on the ground where Ricketts Battery[1] had been shattered to fragments, and saw the havoc done. I kept my Regiments under cover as much as possible, till the last moment, when it became necessary to cross boldly a Ridge and attack the enemy by that time gathered in great strength behind all sorts of cover— The Volunteers up to that time had done well, but they were repulsed regiment by Regiment, and I do think it was impossible to stand long in that fire. I did not find fault with them but they fell into disorder—an incessant clamor of tongues, one saying that they were not properly supported, another that they could not tell friend from foe—but I observed the gradual retreat going on and did all I could to stop it. At last it became manifest we were falling back, and as soon as I perceived it, I gave it direction by the way we came, and thus we fell back to Centreville some four miles—we had with our Brigade no wagons, they had not crossed the River. At Centreville came pouring in the confused masses of men, without order or system. Here I supposed we should assemble in some order the confused masses and try to Stem the tide—Indeed I saw but little evidence of being pursued, though once or twice their cavalry interposed themselves between us and our Rear. I had read of retreats before— have seen the noise and confusion of crowds of men at fires and Shipwrecks but nothing like this. It was as disgraceful as words can portray, but I doubt if volunteers from any quarter could do better. Each private thinks for himself—If he wants to go for water, he asks leave of no one. If he thinks right he takes the oats & corn, and even burns the house of his enemy. As we could not prevent these disorders on the way out—I always feared the result—for everywhere we found the People against us—no curse could be greater than invasion by a Volunteer Army. No goths or vandals ever had less respect for the lives & property of friends and foes, and henceforth we ought never to hope for any friends in Virginia—McDowell & all the Generals tried their best to stop these disorders, but for us to say we commanded that army is no such thing—they did as they pleased. Democracy has worked out one result, and the next step is to be seen—Beauregard & Johnston were enabled to effect a Junction, by the failure of Patterson to press the latter, and they had such accurate accounts of our numbers & movements that they had all the men they wanted—We had never more than 18,000 engaged, though Some 10 or 12,000 were within a few miles. After our Retreat here, I did my best to stop the flying masses, and partially succeeded, so that we once more present a front: but Beauregard has committed a sad mistake in not pursuing us promptly. Had he done so, he could have stampeded us again, and gone into Washington. As it is I suppose their plan is to produce Riot in Baltimore, cross over above Leesburg, and come upon Washington through Maryland. Our Rulers think more of who shall get office, than who can save the Country. No body—no one man can save the country. The difficulty is with the masses—our men are not good Soldiers—They brag, but dont perform—complain sadly if they dont get everything they want—and a march of a few miles uses them up. It will take a long time to overcome these things, and what is in store for us in the future I know not. I propose trying to defend this place if Beauregard approaches Washington by this Route, but he has now deferred it Some days and I rather think he will give it up.

The newspapers will tell ten thousand things none of which are true. I have had no time to read them, but I know no one now has the moral courage to tell the truth. Public opinion is a more terrible tyrant than Napoleon—My own hope is now in the Regulars, and if I can escape this Volunteer command I will do so, and stick by my Regular Regiment. Gen. McClellan arrived today with Van Vliet—Stoneman,[2] Benham[3]—Biddle[4]—and many others of my acquaintance. Affecy. &c.

W. T. Sherman

ALS, InND: Sherman Family Papers.

1. James B. Ricketts (1817–87) was captain of the First U.S. Artillery and was wounded and captured.

2. George Stoneman (1822–94) was a major in the First U.S. Cavalry.

3. Henry W. Benham (1813–84) was chief engineer of the Department of the Ohio.

4. Charles J. Biddle (1819–75) was colonel of the Thirteenth Pennsylvania Reserves.

TO ELLEN EWING SHERMAN

Washington Aug. 3, 61

Dearest Ellen,

I sent you a long letter a few days ago, telling you all about Bull's Run. The disaster was serious in its effect on the men, who whether they ought or not to be, are discouraged beyond measure—All the volunteers continue in a bad State, but we must do the best we can with them. It seems Regulars do not enlist, because of the preference always given to volunteers, whose votes are counted even in the Ranks. I doubt if our Democratic form of Government admits of that organization & discipline without which our army is a mob. Congress is doing all that is possible in the way of Laws and appropriations and McClellan is determined to proceed slowly & cautiously[.] I wish we had more Regulars to tie to. We must be the assailants & our enemy is more united in feeling, and can always choose their ground—It was not entrenchments but the natural ground & woods of which they took good advantage, while we in pursuit had to cross open fields and cross the crests of hills which obstructed a view of their forces.

This must continue to be the Case—Beauregard must have suffered much else his sagacity would have forced him to take Washington which he well might—I prefer you should go to housekeeping in Lancaster—Dont come here—I would not permit you to visit my camp—I have as much as I can do to keep my officers & men from living in Washington, and shall not set a bad example—I never expect again to move you from Lancaster. The simple chances of war, provided we adhere to the determination of subduing the South, will of course involve the destruction of all able bodied men of this Generation and go pretty deep into the next. Tis folly to underestimate the task, and you see how far already the nation has miscalculated. The Real war has not yet begun—The worst will be down the Mississipi and in Alabama & Mississipi— provided of course we get that far—already has the war lasted since December last, and we are still on the border, defeated & partly discouraged—I am less so than most people, because I expected it. I will send you what money I can from time to time and you must do the best you can—You write that Harding wants to pay his note due next year what did Turner do with the one you left with him?

Tis said I am to be Brig. Genl.[1] If so I know it not yet—I have closely minded my business which is a bad sign for fame. Love to all—Yrs.

W. T. Sherman

ALS, InND: Sherman Family Papers.
1. WTS was made brigadier general of volunteers on this date, to rank from May 17.

TO ELLEN EWING SHERMAN

Capt. Van Vliet's office
Washington Aug. 3, 1861.

Dearest Ellen,

I came over to see General McClellan on some business and whilst awaiting him have gone and drawn my pay for July $239—I herewith send you $139, and keep $100, for personal expenses—I still am acting as a Brigadier General in command of six Regts. of volunteers called by courtesy Soldiers, but they are all we have got and God only knows the issue—our adversaries have the weakness of slavery in their midst to offset our Democracy, and tis beyond human wisdom to say which is the greater evil. I learn today that the President selected Hunter, Sherman & Buell out of the List for Brigadier Genls. of the Regular army, but Maj. Garesche[1] tells me the List has been changed—that no appointments will now be made in the Regular army, but that a whole Batch of Brigadiers will be made, ranking according to former Commission—This will still keep me where I want in a modest position till time and circumstance show us daylight.

McClellan told me last night he should proceed with great caution endeavoring to advance so as never to make a step backwards. I am now satisfied that the Southern army is not much better than ours—Else Beauregard would certainly have taken Washington—if they could they also from their central position would throw their force on Banks or Rosecrans.[2] In East Virginia all are secessionists and we can gain no authentic information of their movements by spies, it is different I suppose in West Virginia—at all events in invading Virginia from the Chesapeake the Army must be of a size to encounter the whole Southern army. Now that they have been successful Davis can assemble just as many men as he wants, and they are as well armed, dressed and fed as we are. Indeed I never saw such a set of grumblers as our volunteers about their food clothing arms &c. and I shall make a Requisition for two wet nurses per soldier, to nurse them in their helpless pitiful condition.

Oh—but we had a few Regulars, but all our Legislation has so favored the volunteer that no man will enlist in the Regular service. I propose to go on as heretofore, to endeavor to fill my place as well as possible, to meddle as little as possible with my superiors, and to give my opinion only when asked for—My own opinion as you know has been that an advance movement from Washington should never be made—failure on this line is too dangerous—All armies are liable to defeat and this should be risked only on the flanks—thus an attack from Old Point Comfort—Harpers Ferry, or Kanawa would only be disasters. If our Defeat at Bull's Run is not the death of our nation, then it is a miracle.

Had Beauregard followed us up as he should & taken Washington as he might all foreign nations would recognise that as the *de facto* Govt.

I have seen your father twice—also Tom, who stays at {Fants}—The bad consequences of officers leaving their duties on the other side & coming here are so manifest, and I am so prohibiting to others that I set the example of coming over very seldom—Congress will adjourn John says, on Monday—when he too will go home—You may hereafter address me at the Georgetown Post office. I send over there pretty often for marketing—Address me, Col. W. T. S.—Fort Corcoran—Georgetown D.C.—If I am made Brig. Genl.—use Gen. W. T. S.—as above—I know not why I feel no ambition—If we could handle volunteers, so that our plans could be carried out I would launch out—but I know that they will mar any plan and blast the fair fame of anybody—They of course, the People cant do wrong—if defeat arises—then it is misman-agement—masked batteries & such nonsense. McDowell with his wife[3] was at Jeffn. Barracks when we were—Mrs. Van Vliet is now in Connecticut. I am going to form a Brigade of four Regiments—and have two in reserve at Forts Corcoran—Bennett[4] & Haggerty opposite Georgetown—whether I am to go along as now doing as I please I know not—but such seems to be the inten-tion—If I am to be a Volunteer Genl.—I will select my Staff out of the Regi-ments composing the Brigade—as ever yrs.

W. T. Sherman

ALS, InND: Sherman Family Papers.

1. Cuban-born Major Julius P. Garesche (d. 1862) was in the Adjutant General's Office.

2. Brigadier General William S. Rosecrans (1819–98), USA, was commanding a brigade in the Army of Occupation in West Virginia.

3. Helen Burden McDowell (d. 1891).

4. Colonel Bennett commanded the Twenty-ninth New York.

TO ELLEN EWING SHERMAN

[Aug. 12, 1861]

Dearest Ellen,

The incessant wants of 5000 men—all complaining with sick wives & chil-dren & fathers at home—wanting to go to Georgetown & Washington and every wheres where they should not go, growling about clotheing, shoes, beef, pork & everything—Now in an army all these things are regulated by sergeants captains, and colonels. A Brigadier only has to operate through them. An irregularity in a Regiment is checked by a word to the Colonel, but here every woman within 5 miles who has a peach stolen, or Roasting ear carried off comes to me to have a guard stationed to protect her tree, and our soldiers are the most destructive men I have ever known. It may be other volunteers are just as bad—indeed the complaint is universal and I see no alternative but to let it take its course—When in Fairfax County we had a majority of friends now I suppose there is not a man, woman or child but would prefer Jeff Davis or the Czar of Russia to govern them rather than our American Volunteer Army. My only hope now is that a common sense of decency may be inspired into the minds of this soldiery to respect life & property. Officers hardly offer to remonstrate with their men, and all devolves on me. As usual I cannot lie down—go away, without fifty people moving after me—Had I some good Regulars I could tie to them. As it is all the New Brigadiers must manufacture their Brigades out of Raw Material—Napoleon allowed 3 years as a *minimum*. Washington one year—Here it is expected in nine days and Bulls Run is the consequence—I dont believe McClellan will be hurried, and the danger to our country is so imminent that all hands are now conscious that we must build up from the foundation. I go to Washington but seldom—to Georgetown not at all—I sent you money ten days ago, and asked you to Send my letters to Georgetown Post office. None have come yet, and Since John Sherman went I am without letters. A good many little incidents shooting of sentinels & pickets, all the cruel useless attendants of war occur daily, but I no longer apprehend an attack by Beauregards forces, though strange to Say he receives news much more freely than we do. McClellan has notice of large forces coming up from Georgia Alabama and the extreme South. Write to me at Georgetown Post office. tell me what house you have taken, what rent &c.— also if you hear anything about our St. Louis House. There is $500 clear loss. I will write to Minnie the first chance. Tell Willie I have a Real Battle horse which was wounded, and if he & I survive I will bring him home. yrs. ever,

W. T. Sherman

ALS, InND: Sherman Family Papers.

TO MARIA BOYLE EWING SHERMAN

Fort Corcoran Aug. 13, 1861

My Dear Little Minnie,

Since Uncle John has left Washington I do not get any letters. I wrote to your Mama, sending her some money, and asking her to Send her letters to the Georgetown Post office. I have sent over several times but no letters and I fear your Mama did not get my letter. I am still living in a house belonging to an Englishman named Rose, now in England—it is near Fort Corcoran, and there are two other small forts in my District. I have six Regiments of volunteers, and four companies of Regulars. They give me plenty to do, what with Passes, and drills I am kept very busy.

Since our defeat, the volunteers are not so anxious to fight and very many of them have sick families and private business which calls them home, but we wont let them[.] It has been raining very hard, the roads are very muddy and the Streams are all full. This will delay any attack on our position and may prevent it altogether. I have not taken off my clothes for many nights expecting every morning to wake up to a new battle.

Of course we all expect to whip them this time, but no one Knows as Our Volunteers do pretty much as they please, and may run again just as they did at Bull Run—I hope that by this time you are all in a new house, with plenty of yard to play in, and near the school. You must try hard to learn this winter and it may be I can come home for a few days to See you, although I do not promise myself that pleasure. You and Lizzy must write to me often and tell me how the boys behave and how the new baby acts, if she dont behave herself tell her we must trade her off for something more useful.

I am now going to Send my negro boy John over to Georgetown to ask for letters and I hope I may get one as I am beginning to be uneasy lest my own letters do not get to you as regularly as I wish. Tell Mama I Sent her a long letter Yesterday, and that I continue quite well.

Give my love to Lizzie, and to all the children. You are now old enough to be of great assistance to your Mama, and I have no doubt you are very willing. Yr. affectionate Papa

W. T. Sherman

ALS, OHi: William T. Sherman Papers.

TO ELLEN EWING SHERMAN

Washington D.C.

Aug. 17, 1861

Dearest Ellen,

I have not received a word from you for a long time some two weeks. I send regularly to the Georgetown and Washington post offices, but the answer is nothing—I suppose you still send to care of John Sherman, who has gone to Mansfield, and then up Lake Superior, to escape the fatigues of senatorial labors. Wish he had seven volunteer Regiments to provide for, with an enemy in front in hourly expectation of attack. I have not undressed of a night since Bull Run—and the Volunteers will not allow of sleep by day. Two Regiments have mutinied claiming that the U. States has no right to hold their services.[1] Under the influence of a Battery of Artillery and squadron of Regular cavalry the number who refused duty dwindled down to 65 in one Regiment and 35 in another all of whom were marched down to the Navy Yard and placed in *irons* on board a man of war. The remainder of the men & officers of these Regiments are sick of the war and want to go home—McClellan still thinks Beauregard will attack the City. Most assuredly he should do So but it may be he will not.

I was over here a few days ago and met Robert Anderson who sent for me today. It seems he is to organize some kind of a force in Kentucky and Tennessee to Support the General Government and has asked for me.[2] The President agrees to send me as soon as McClellan can spare me, and McClellan will not leave me go until he conceives the City to be out of danger— say one week—then I am to be sent into Kentucky post haste, whether I am to be allowed to stop a day at Lancaster or not I cannot imagine but I suppose not. I will endeavor to stop to see you for a moment, but I know how it will be. McClellan will not relieve me from duty till the latest moment when Anderson will be calling for me in Kentucky—The bluer the times the more closely should one cling to his Country. I do not say I love my country. It does seem to have fallen into degenerate hands, but there are rich lands, and mountains, and streams in America, and occasionally some good People, and I do not know why we should not have a Government. The old Government was as mild as any on Earth and it may be that it is the best—but true it is its administration had become very Corrupt. Even now it is hard to hold her People to their allegiance—but we must have a future, and a Government, and I will not attempt to advise or guide events till I see some end to this muddle. Thus far the Union party has the worst of the fight, and our armies are too Scattered. If they order me to any place I'll go if I can—With Anderson I suppose we will have to go into Kentucky & Tennessee, to organize an army in the face of that prejudice which you complained so much about in Missouri. That prejudice pervades the public mind and it will take years to overcome— In all the Southern States, they have succeeded in impressing the public mind that the North is governed by a mob—(of which unfortunately there is too much truth) and in the South that all is chivalry & Gentility. Out of the Chaos some order in time must arise, but how or when I cannot tell. If I get a chance I will come by way of Lancaster. I take it for granted you write as usual, but I have given up all chance of getting the letters—no doubt the Postmaster sends them on to John Sherman at Lake Superior. I have not heard that you received the money I sent about the 3 instant—I have just sworn in as Brigadier General and therefore suppose I might as well admit the title—If you can get a letter to the Georgetown Post office do so, though I give it up—I also telegraphed you, but no answer. Maybe Lancaster has gone to sleep. Yrs. ever

W. T. Sherman

ALS, InND: Sherman Family Papers.
1. WTS was having trouble with the Sixty-ninth New York and some soldiers in the

Second Wisconsin, who thought that their ninety-day enlistment had expired in spite of a War Department decision to the contrary. The men WTS referred to here were sent to the military prison in Fort Jefferson, Florida.

2. Anderson took command of the Department of the Cumberland on August 15 and requested WTS as his second in command; WTS was sent to him on August 28.

TO ELLEN EWING SHERMAN
Fort Corcoran, Aug. 19, 1861

Dearest Ellen,

I have almost ceased to hope for a letter from you. What accident has thus cut you off I dont know but suppose my letters telling you to address me at Georgetown failed to reach you, and that you still send to the care of John, who left for home a good while ago—Your letters in that case are following him on a pleasure visit up Lake Superior.

Among my Regiments are three, who claim to have been enlisted only for three months, but the Secretary of War has decided they are in for two years— In each of the Regiments there has been a kind of mutiny—not open and decided, but a determination to do no duty. Yesterday Sunday I had two companies of Regular Cavalry and 1 of artillery ready to attack one of these Regiments. For some hours I thought I would have to give an order to fire, but they did not like the artillery and have gone to duty, but I think this is a bad class of men to depend on to fight. They may eat their rations and go on Parade, but when danger comes they will be sure to show the white feather. Still they are now in a State of Subjection. I went over to Washington on this business some days ago, saw the President & Gen. Scott, at the table of the latter I met Robert Anderson for the first time. I only had a few words with him, but on Saturday, he sent for me to meet him at Willards. There I found Senator Johnson,[1] a Mr. Maynard,[2] and two or three other members of Congress from Kentucky and Tennessee. One of them Senator Johnson I think premised by saying, that it was the determination of the Government to send assistance to the Union men of Kentucky & Tennessee, that there were large numbers of them who merely needed arms, money & organization that Anderson was the proper General to organize & lead the movement, but that his health was liable at any moment, to fail him and the President had agreed that he might select any three of the Brigadiers to go with him, that he had at once asked for me, and two others, Burnside and Thomas, which was conceded— that when McClellan heard I was asked for he did not want to spare me, as he thought there remained imminent danger of an attack here—then Anderson said he would prefer to wait a few days till things assumed a more settle shape, say seven to ten days, at the expiration of which time I should be relieved, and ordered to Kentucky. I have said or done nothing one way or other, but in about seven days I will if nothing threatening happen, apply for relief that I may stop at Lancaster to see you, for a day or so. I expect to go to Louisville & thence through East Kentucky & Tennessee, to see myself the State of the Country, and if possible to organize resistance to the Southern Confederacy. It is a matter of great importance and upon it may hang the existence of the present Government.

Most assuredly events have favored the Southern Confederacy, and instead of making friends the administration seems to have lost ground not only in the South and Middle states, but also in the North. The clamors for discharge on every possible frivolous pretext has been a severe blow to the army, and may be to the country—I hear that the new enlistments drag. This every reasonable person must have apprehended from the foolish cry first raised, a mere impulse sure to be followed by reaction.

If I should be permitted to come to Lancaster, I shall expect you to be in a house of your own. I sent you some money about the 3rd inst. but have not heard it was received. About the end of the month I may be able to give you more. I wish I could bring you my war horse, it would be valuable for a buggy & would please Willy, because he was wounded in battle. He was given me by John. Love to all, Yrs. truly

W. T. Sherman

ALS, InND: Sherman Family Papers.

1. Andrew Johnson (1808–75) was U.S. senator from Tennessee; he was the only senator from a seceded state to retain his seat in the United States Senate.

2. Horace Maynard (1814–82) of Tennessee was a U.S. representative.

TO JOHN SHERMAN

Fort Corcoran, Aug. 19, 61

My Dear Brother,

I have not heard from you or any body since you left—my letters I suppose continue to go to you and if you send them to Washington they go to the other Genl. Sherman[1]—at all events since you left I have not recd. a single letter from anybody although I wrote for them to write me at the Georgetown Post office.

I have been here ever since you left hardly taking off my clothes at night— McClellan is so confident that Beauregard will attack that I try to be prepared at all times. Our forts are in pretty good condition, but whether the volunteers can serve the guns or not is to be tested. It does seem to me strange that when all Know that if Beauregard get Washington, the southern Confederacy will be an established fact, that they should leave volunteers to hold the most important point in the world. Out of my seven Regiments, three 3 are in a state of mutiny, and I have been compelled to put about 100 men as prisoners on board a man of war, and yesterday I had my regulars all ready with shotted guns to fire on our own troops, some of whom, not only claim their discharge, but threaten to spike our Guns. They claim to be only 3 months men, whereas the War Department claims their services for three years. Even some of the 3 years men say the President had no right to call for 3 years men and that the subsequent legislation of Congress was *ex post facto*. That is the Patriotism that characterizes the brave & chivalrous volunteers of the North—over 150 officers have resigned, and at least half of them are clamorous for discharge on the most frivolous pretexts, this not in my Brigade alone, but in all the Volunteer Army. You will have to reconstruct the Army & may be the Government for when the colonels are so dependent on the men, when trouble comes, all organization ceases.

A few days since Gen. Robt. Anderson sent for me to meet him at Willards—I found him with Senator Johnson, a Mr. Maynard, and several other members from Kentucky & Tennessee—They told me the President had resolved to send assistance to the Union men of Kentucky & Tennessee—that Anderson being a Kentuckyan to him was given the lead, and that he was allowed to Select three 3 Brigadiers: that he had chosen me first, and Burnside and Thomas next—The president agreed, but McClellan would not spare me till the danger in his front was lessened. It was then agreed to wait a week, when if nothing happens here, I am to be ordered into Kentucky. As I understand we are to go there in person, mingle with the People satisfy ourselves of their purpose to oppose the Southern Confederacy, and then to assist in the organization there of a force adequate to the end in view—that when Kentucky is assured in her allegiance that we then push into East Tennessee. I feel well satisfied that unless Kentucky & Tennessee remain in our Union it is a doubtful question whether the Federal Government can restore the Old Union. If they do there is some hopes. Had more moderate counsel prevailed we should not now be struggling in Missouri, but the Blairs were so emphatic they prevailed and the necessary consequences are at hand and all Kansas, Iowa & Illinois are paralyzed by the force they are compelled to send into Missouri.

If I leave here it will be in a week, and if possible I will stop a day in Lancaster. There is no time to be lost, and I will not spare my individual efforts, though I still feel as one grasping in the dark. Slowly but surely the Public is realizing what I knew all the time the strong vindictive feeling of the whole South. yr. brother,

W. T. Sherman

ALS, DLC: William T. Sherman.

1. Thomas W. Sherman (1813–79), USA, a veteran of the Florida and Mexican Wars, had been named brigadier general of volunteers to rank from May 17.

[Aug. 20–27, 1861]

One a piece of their money which I enclose you as a curiosity to be put among the scraps out of which History is to be made.

If no formidable demonstration be made this week, it is probably next I will be relieved and ordered to report forthwith to Gen. Anderson at Louisville Ky. If possible I will stop at Lancaster for one day, but even that may be impossible. War like a growing monster demands its victims, and must have them—How few realize the stern fact I too well know. Unless we can organize a large strong armed party in Kentucky & Tennessee, there is danger that our old Govt. may disintegrate and new Combinations formed—Our Northern States deal in hyperbolic expressions of patriotism, but allow our armies to be in a large minority at every point of attack. I now think they are deceiving us here and that a large force will fall on Cox[1] in the Kanawha, or Rosecrans at Berkeley—Our army should be in vast masses, not in these insignificant detachments. I think McClellan will bring Banks command here, or near enough for support, and cause Cox & Rosecrans to move towards Kentucky & Tennessee—making that one army—There should be only three, East, Center & West and each should be over 100,000 effective men—But our People wont realize the magnitude of opposition till we are whaled several times a la Bull Run—I hardly know my sphere in Kentucky, but it will be political & military combined. I think Anderson wanted me because he knows I seek not personal fame or Glory, and that I will heartily second his plans and leave him the Fame—Most assuredly does he esteem my motives. Not till I see daylight ahead do I want to lead—but when danger threatens and others slink away I am and will be at my Post.

Give a little attention to Minnie—she does not write well enough (dont tell her so from me) but let her practice. I wish I could bring you my horse—He is a real Battle horse, and would make a good buggy horse—but I must leave him. McClellan wont relieve me this week maybe next—Yrs. ever,

W. T. Sherman

ALS (incomplete), InND: Sherman Family Papers.
1. Brigadier General Jacob D. Cox (1828–1900), USA, commanded the Brigade of the Kanawha in West Virginia.

TO JOHN SHERMAN

Cincinati, Sept. 9, 1861

Dear Brother,

I am still here. General A. went quietly over to Frankfort last Thursday and I hear from him that things are progressing favorably. The time seems to have passed in this country when the voice of the People is considered the voice of God—notwithstanding the large vote for the Union, and the controlling majority in the Legislature there still is a doubt whether that State will go for the Union. If the secessionists had such a majority there is not a shadow of doubt that on the first day of the session an ordinance would have passed, and Kentucky would now be a hostile state, and with a majority of 3 to 1, it hangs in the scale whether the Legislature will do anything decisive. But let them do what they may, the secessionists will not heed the action of the State. They say whatever we promise or Lincoln promises that Sooner or later the war will degenerate into a war of abolitionism, and they fear the consequences.

I think it of vast importance that Ohio, Indiana & Illinois must sooner or later arm every inhabitant and the sooner the better. I hardly apprehend that Beauregard can succeed in getting Washington, but should he it will be worse to us than Manassas, but supposing he falls back, he will first try to overwhelm Rosecrans in Western Virginia and then look to Tennessee. We ought to have here a well appointed army of a hundred thousand men. I dont see where they are to come from, but this is the great center. I still think the Mississipi will be the Grand field of operations. Memphis ought to be taken in all October, even if we have to fortify and hold it a year. I think it of more importance than Richmond. It may be that the Southern Leaders have made such tremendous calls upon their people & resources, that if we remain on the defense they will exhaust themselves, but upon the first manifest symptoms of such a result we should follow it up. Here we have no means of offense, and but little of defense, and if you are full of Zeal you could not do better than to raise your voice to call the young and middle aged men of Ohio to arms. If they cant get muskets, then let them get such arms as can be gathered together or if not that, then let them organize in companies in every township and be ready to collect together and move on short notice—I am amazed to See here and every where such apparent indifference when all know that Rebels threaten their capital and are creeping round us in Missouri & Kansas. If they are united, and we disunited or indifferent they will succeed: I Know this reaction was natural & to be expected, but it is none the less to be deplored. If Anderson is detained at Frankfort, I will attend the State fair at Dayton on Wednesday or Thursday—affectionately

W. T. Sherman

ALS, DLC: William T. Sherman.

TO THOMAS EWING SR.

Louisville—Sunday
Sept. 15, 1861

Hon. Thos. Ewing

Dear Sir

Ellen handed me your letter. I acknowledge the propriety of your rebuke for whatever I may know or think, I may have said it at improper times.

As to Meaghers strictures I have never seen them and I know them to be unwarranted.[1] He is a blathering adventurer without knowledge, attached to the 69. for mischief. He did all he could to avoid marching from Washington, and was the mouthpiece of a few discontented men, who importuned for discharge before we marched to Manassas. I did not see him during the Fight and doubt not he was long in advance of the general retreat—He very early saw I appreciated him and was very shy of me. But the Bulk of the Regiment had full confidence in me and three of its captains appointed to the Regular army applied to be put in my Regiment—after the Fight I had seven Regiments, and I Know all of them were content to serve under me. I was severe, but endeavored to be just, for I know if we could not command our men, we had no business to attempt invasion. Genl. McClellan adopted the very course I began, and the President admitted I was the first to show a decided front after our disaster. I thought it was well all should know that our defeat resulted from our own want of discipline & not from the superiority of our Enemy.

So many people embracing even officers charged the defeat on Gen. McDowell, that I have always thought it should be promptly contradicted by eyewitnesses. Now I know Gen. McD. did all he could—his plans and orders were proper, and the execution of them well managed—but the men did not rally after, not a repulse, but a failure to carry a certain position. The defeat began with the Private soldiers, who would not reform their Ranks or pay any heed to our commands—I saw the colonels commanding, remonstrating and begging—I did so myself, and I heard McDowell plead to them to rest, and make a new effort—but the men kept edging off in masses towards the Rear—now to allow the impression to go down to history that the officers failed, would be an injustice and false—The men must know that if at fault they will be held to account, as well as their officers, but if like Politicians we become afraid of the rank & file of our army, then our nation is at an End.

We are here—without a single musket—The Legislature are ready to pass strong Resolutions for the Union, the Tennesseans are ready to invade the state on the passage of such resolutions, to burn and destroy the several Rail roads, and it is admitted that though the Union Party has a majority of 50,000 yet the secessionists have a majority of fighting men—Fremonts Proclamation[2] and the fact that Missouri and Maryland are worse now than at first, makes our cause a hard one to sustain. We are embarrassed by these facts and only hope to stave off the explosion till arms reach us—we have promise of some as soon as they come from Europe—Strange to say our enemies appear better armed than we. There are 15,000 men distributed among the Home Guards, but I fear they are scattered & lost. If I can get a moment to spare I will write to Ellen—Yrs.

W. T. Sherman

ALS, DLC: Thomas Ewing and Family Papers.

1. Irish-born Captain Thomas Meagher (1823–67) of Company K of the Sixty-ninth New York had just published *The Last Days of the 69th in Virginia*.

2. On August 30, Frémont had established martial law in Missouri and freed the slaves of those resisting the Federal government. Lincoln later rescinded the emancipation edict.

TO ELLEN EWING SHERMAN

Louisville Sept. 18, 1861

Dearest Ellen,

I have not had time to write since I left Cincinati. At Indianapolis I found Gov. Morton[1] willing in a general way to help Kentucky, but all his arms were exhausted and he knew not where to look for more, and Western Virginia was asking for Reinforcements. At Springfield Illinois Govr. Yates[2] was in like manner situated men scattered in Small camps for the benefit of local contractors, without arms and not Knowing how or where they could be got. At St. Louis I found Fremont living in the large house erected by Brant,[3] on Chouteau avenue. He is surrounded by sentinels and I was told it was impossible to get access to him, but I started early, got the Sentinel to carry in my card to the Secretary who turned out to be Isaah C. Woods of California.[4] Of course he hurried out & took me in, and procured me an interview[.] Fremont was very communicative, and the result I have come to is that he has called about him men who will swindle the Government and bring disgrace on us all[.] Think of Woods, Palmer,[5] & Selover[6]—the very men who caused the Vigilance Committee of San Francisco, by local and open corruption being now the advisors of Fremont. I could not discover that he was operating on any distinct plan but was assembling men of all kinds and materials, but whether he can Shape them into an army I dont know. By proclamations and threats which there is no power to execute he has completed what Lyons began in alienating the support of all the moderate men of the city. I saw Mr. Lucas, Patterson and Maj. Turner all for about Half an hour—I think Tom & Willy Turner[7] are in the Enemys ranks though Turner only said he had sent them up the River out of the way of a draft[.] Turner has been offered by Govr.

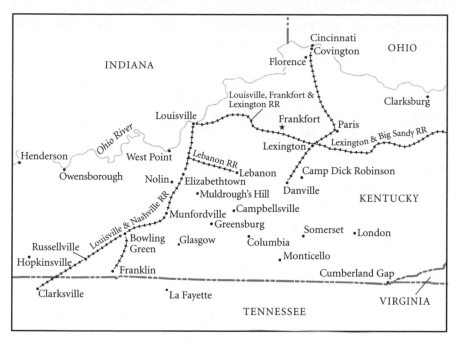

Central Kentucky

Gamble[8] the lead in the State organization but he says he is going to be quiet. He thinks that ultimately the North will hold Missouri and he had better conform, though he would prefer any man to rule rather than their present Government. I must admit that Missouri has had a hard time as between Lyon, Blair & Fremont[.]

At St. Louis I found Charley. He came up from the Barracks with Col. Burbank. They have done little in recruiting only 100 men instead of 2400—unless we can do better than that the South will prevail. They are in a perfect boil—and can get as many men as they want. They are leaving Louisville with arms in their hands and cheered as they go to join the camp on the Tennessee line. The state of Kentucky is ready to Enact a series of Resolutions, denying the right of secession, and giving the Union the whole benefit of her consent—but here wise men admit that although they have a majority of 50,000 voters, it is doubtful which has the most fighting men—and that is now the issue, and all parties are preparing for the contest. They sent us here without arms and without the promise of any. I suppose it could not be helped, but I do think it is wrong for Northern Politicians constantly praising the resources & population of the North when we cannot realize them. I know that every body exaggerates McClellans forces. He at no time has had a force equal to Beauregard—same of Fremont—he is outnumbered in Missouri—same I hear in Western

Virginia, and here we have about 1800 in Indiana opposite here—and about 6000 in a camp beyond Lexington where Thomas has gone to command—Anderson, myself, and the staff officers are here at the Southern hotel Louisville Hotel, receiving letters, and Seeing people who come from every quarter to tell of the state of public feeling—All want the U.S. to guard his house & family, and give him a market for his corn & stock[.]

Prime has gone to Indianapolis to See if the Governor can spare us two or three Regiments now—we expect him back today—We may then make a move that will bring about collision & then no one can tell where it will stop.

The great trouble is that secessionists know they must fight, and the Union People look to the United States as some mythical power with unlimited quantities of men & money—We cannot promise to receive Ohio Companies such as Hunters unless they are armed. We have no arms, and prefer to give such as are promised us to Kentuckyans first—If Hunters company be armed, let him write to me, offering his company, with its strength and condition as to arms & clothing.

I suppose Anderson will keep me near him till we get our men into Shape, but it is too bad the matter has been so long postponed, for winter is near at hand, and I doubt if we can keep volunteers out in the Snow with Tents. Winter operations will be mostly confined to the sea and on the River[.]

I am pretty well. I had a cold which took its usual course, but I am now pretty free from it—I still think you had better get you a strong house, there is no prospect of my ever being in a fixed place as long as the war lasts, and you must be satisfied now that it is to be a long one. yrs.

W. T. Sherman

ALS, InND: Sherman Family Papers.

1. Oliver P. Morton (1823–77) was the governor of Indiana.

2. Richard Yates (1818–73) was the governor of Illinois.

3. Joshua Brant (d. March 1861) had been married to a cousin of Jessie Benton Frémont and was in the construction business.

4. Isaah C. Woods had been the head of the San Francisco bank Adams & Co. and had helped precipitate the run on California financial institutions that led to Sherman's financial ruin there.

5. Joseph C. Palmer (1819–82), a partner in Palmer, Cook, & Co., a California bank, was a prominent financial backer of Frémont. His earlier misappropriations of state and Federal funds in his care had led to his bank's downfall.

6. Abia A. Selover (1823–98), an investor in Frémont's Las Mariposas mines and San Francisco real estate, engaged in profiteering during Frémont's time in St. Louis.

7. In spite of WTS's work to get Tom Turner a Federal commission, he had indeed joined the Confederate army. His brother Wilson Price Turner was a first sergeant in Stuart's Horse Artillery and would be killed at Second Bull Run on August 29, 1862.

8. Hamilton R. Gamble (1798–1864) had been named provisional governor of Missouri earlier in the year following Claiborne Jackson's defection to the Confederates.

TO THOMAS EWING SR.

Muldroughs Hill, Sept. 30, 1861

Hon. Thos. Ewing

Events may transpire which must affect me personally very much of which you are more competent to judge than any other.[1] I never did like to Serve with volunteers, because instead of being governed they govern, and on the principle that the King can do no wrong, so they can do no wrong and any misadventure is charged on the officer. But fate will allow no man a choice and he must perforce drift with the Current of Events. I happened in Louisville when the secessionists cut the Telegraph wire on the Nashville Road, and seized many cars. The report was very indefinite. At the time there were in Louisville only Home Guards to the number of about 1200, composed of young men, such as made up our volunteer companies. There was also a Regiment of so called Kentucky troops across the River from Louisville, with two incomplete Regiments under a Kentucky Lawyer named Rousseau.[2] After consultation Genl. Anderson ordered me to take such of the Home Guards as could be hastily collected together and the men of Rousseau and proceed on the cars as far as possible, posting them so as to protect the road looking to future movements—Muldroughs Hill is a spur laying south of Louisville about 30 miles. The Rolling Fork of Salt River lays against the base of the Hill which is ascended by a steep Grade of 70 feet to the mile to a summit whence the Ground slopes off gradually to the south as far as Green River all closely wooded, save where there are cleared farms. The Road with the exception of two macadam Roads are all bad.

When we reached the Rolling Fork the Bridge spaning it was burned, and we necessarily came to a halt. At first I only sent a strong picket up the Hill, which was afterwards withdrawn by order of Gen. Anderson but knowing that the Kentuckyans would give up if Muldroughs hill were occupied by the Tennesseans I concluded to occupy it, and accordingly came up. I have been here now about ten days. The effect was as I calculated. The Tennesseans fell back of Green River destroying bridges as they went—I have five Regiments all volunteers, and two companies of Regular Recruits. It takes us all we can do to haul up enough provisions for the men from the Junction on the other side of Rolling Fork, and the Country People are perfectly neutral, willing to sell us but at high price and Some Forage—but as to an actual rally nothing like it occurs. The Home Guards which came out have all returned to Louisville, and here we are in a hostile or neutral country, without any retreat, for a retreat down that valley and across Rolling Fork would be an abandonment of the Cause. Ten days have elapsed, time enough for reinforcements from any part of the United States, but few have come, and they are needed to protect the

Railroad, abandonned by the Home Guards. The Volunteers also in compliance with their unbridled will are killing hogs, cattle, burning fence rails, and taking hay and wheat, all calculated to turn the People against us. I do all and promise more to Stop this but it is ineffectual, and I cannot expect to escape the consequences. I have no Regular commissary or Quartermaster and have to resort to all sorts of shifts to provide for the absolute wants of the men, and the nights have been so cold that I have been forced to allow tents and blankets to be hunted up, so that we are in a measure tied to the spot. I have no authentic information of what our Enemy is doing, but I know Buckner[3] and G. W. Smith[4] who command and take it for granted they See at a glance the weakness of my position and Buckner was raised in this neighborhood and knows the ground perfectly. He is supposed to be at Bowling Green 50 miles south—he has a Railroad to Green River only about 25 miles off and has an unlimited quantity of refugee Kentuckyans who have taken up arms, and about 7000 Tennesseans, all armed as well as we.[5] They are all imbued with a bitterness that you cannot comprehend and will jump at the chance to destroy us whom they now regard as northern hordes of Invaders. If the reinforcements designed for us are delayed I cannot foresee the consequences, for the country is all ambush—Woods envelop us, with roads & paths familiar to them and strange to us, and we are tied down.

I have a telegraph from Anderson saying he is compelled to divert some reinforcements coming to us, to another quarter, and so I suppose I must meet the shock with what I have viz. about 5000 volunteers dwindling daily by sickness and causes peculiar to them.

I placed myself in this humiliating position for Political reasons, to enable the People to rally, to support their vote, and the action of their Legislature, but I despair of their apathy. My love to all. Yrs.

W. T. Sherman

ALS, New York: FORBES Magazine Collection.

1. For a coherent account of the events in Kentucky at this time, see *PM*, 1:225–28, and Marszalek, *Sherman*, 158–60. WTS had arrived in Louisville in early September and immediately begun the move to Muldrough's Hill to counter an imagined offensive by Buckner.

2. Lovell H. Rousseau (1818–69), a lawyer and politician active in Kentucky's Union movement, had been commissioned colonel of the Third Kentucky on September 9 and would become a brigadier general of volunteers on October 1.

3. Simon Bolivar Buckner (1823–1914) of Kentucky had been appointed a brigadier general, CSA, under Albert Sidney Johnston earlier that month.

4. Gustavus W. Smith (1822–96) had been appointed a major general in the Confederate army on September 19.

5. In reality, Buckner had only about six thousand men.

Muldrows Hill, 40 miles from
Louisville, Oct. 5, 1861

Dear Brother,

I have received from you two letters in the last of which you tell me you are to raise a volunteer Regiment and asking me the names of some good army officers for Maj. & Lt. Col.[1] The old army is so torn up that I really cannot keep the run of it, and no official Register has been published from which I could make up a list. I doubt much if you can depend on any body except such as you have in your neighborhood.

I'm afraid you are too late to Save Kentucky. The young active element is all secession, the older stay at homes are for Union & Peace. But they will not take part. In the mean time the Southern Confederacy looking forward to this very condition of things has armed, organized, equipped &c. and have the Railroads so disposed that by concentration they can overwhelm any part. There was one camp South & East of Lexington founded by Lt. Nelson U.S. Navy,[2] now commanded by Brig. Gen. Thomas, and an army under Zollicoffer[3] of Tennessee is advancing on it. Gen. Anderson at Louisville Ky. has sent in that direction all the Regiments from Ohio—Here the secessionists secured small trains of Cars & Locomotives, moved them south and broke up the Bridges so that they are safe—We came out here hastily to secure Muldrough Hill a kind of chain which seperates the waters of Salt Creek from Green River—We are at one part of this chain where the Railroad from Louisville to Nashville crosses it, but it is by no means a strong point. I have examined the country all round but every strong defensible position is devoid of water, and our absolute dependence on that element forces me into a position which upon being surrounded by vastly superior forces will be a complete ambush—The People are all unfriendly, Their trade and relations have been with the South, and there their feelings ly, so that when Buckner sees fit he can come up from Green River where he now is with from 8000 to 15,000 men, we have 5000, and the Railroad behind is guarded by three men, but this road can be cut at a hundred different points which would starve us out, or force me to Strike out and live on a country which produces only beef & corn. I have Col. Gibsons Ohio Regt.[4] 3 Indiana Regts. and two of Kentucky, but I must say that these latter were made up in Louisville and over in Indiana and is composed mostly of strangers to Kentucky. It will require near 100,000 men in Kentucky and where they are to come from I dont Know. I may be and hope I am mistaken in my calculation of the Kentuckyans, their Legislature has passed all sorts of Union Resolutions & laws, but the People care very little about Legislatures now. If a soldier steals an apple or potato, there is a howl, and we are styled a

Northern mob, and Should we encounter defeat every tree and fence would be an ambush. If I am reinforced as promised I will advance to a place called Moline, where the ground is better for a desperate fight. Muddy Roads and cold weather will also soon be a strong element of distress, and a few days exposure or deprivation develops wonderful changes. I see they are falling back from Washington I hope McClellan will press forward, and Keep them all engaged—In like manner the Forces in Missouri should be employed without a minutes delay and for that Reason I am sorry to See a change of plan. Fremont was never fit for his post except as a defeated candidate. The English Rule of pensioning such is better than ours of giving them post— Wool is too old and will do nothing. If the Confederates take St. Louis and get Kentucky this winter, you will be far more embarrassed than if Washington had fallen into their possession as whatever nation gets the control of the Ohio, Mississipi & Missouri Rivers will control the continent. This they Know, and for this they will labor. You of the North never fully appreciated the energy of the South. My health is good, but as you perceive I am far from easy about the fate of Kentucky. I hope you will be successful in raising your Regiments, but it will be too late. affectionately

W. T. Sherman

Brig. Genl.

ALS, DLC: William T. Sherman.

1. JS to WTS, September 12 and 28, 1861, DLC: WTS. The first letter spoke of the rapid pace of recruiting in Ohio; JS feared he would not be able to raise his own regiment as conflicts with Dennison would probably deprive him of the power to name his own officers. JS still thought he needed a military position to bolster his political authority and had decided to help Dennison with general recruiting schemes. He discussed events in Kentucky and voiced his belief that the eastern part of the state was unquestionably loyal and that the war in the state would be in the west. He thought Cincinnati was not a logical place for army headquarters and believed that Anderson would give WTS a great deal of responsibility. On the twenty-eighth JS wrote that he was recruiting "two regiments of infantry, one squadron of cavalry, & a battery of artillery" as Dennison had given him the desired latitude in appointments. These troops would be sent to Kentucky.

2. Kentuckian William Nelson (1824–62) had been a midshipman during the Mexican War. Sent by Lincoln to observe the situation in Kentucky and arm the loyal Kentucky Home Guard, he had been made a brigadier general of volunteers on September 16.

3. Brigadier General Felix K. Zollicoffer (1812–62), CSA, a native Tennessean.

4. Lawyer and speechmaker William H. Gibson (1821–94) was colonel of the Forty-ninth Ohio.

Muldro Hill, Oct. 6, 1861

Dearest Ellen,

Here we are still at the Hill. The Reinforcements intended for us have been sent to a camp below Lexington and my force now exceeds but little of four thousand and they new volunteers. I see as yet but little signs of the Kentuckyans acting all the secessionists are armed and flocking to Buckners command which is strong from Green River to Bowling Green. I have sent Prime back to Louisville to see Gen. Anderson and to find out what the plans and design of the Government are—All depend on the People of Kentucky who voted for the Union but wont fight for it. Where is Hugh that he is not wiping out these Southerners[?][1] They swarm at every point from Washington to Leavenworth at Every point superior to us in numbers and equipment, and instead of being wiped out they propose to wipe us out. But enough of this.

As to your situation I can give little help—paymasters do not come here, and I can expect but little of them. You will have to get that note collected in St. Louis, pay to Mr. Lucas the balance of the Rent and use the remainder. I dont know how exchange is, but I suppose you will lose something on that Score.[2]

The weather is now cold and wet[.] If I am much exposed I suppose I will suffer from cold & asthma. At present I am sleeping in a house, but am up all night. I dont like this business because of the anomalous condition of the Inhabitants, who are constantly complaining of little depredations of our soldiers rails burnt, or something of the sort—When the Southern army comes, they will see a different state of things we pay for all things we get, such as hay, corn, beef &c.

We now have a Rumor that one of the naval expeditions has taken New Orleans but I dont believe it. The Confederates too are falling back from Washington, and by this time McClellan should have everything ready to attack & follow up. Affairs too in Missouri appear to be approaching a crisis[.] They should let Fremont fight his fight before destroying him.

I got a letter from Shiras saying through Fremonts influence Isaah C. Woods had been appointed Commissary of Subsistence and ordered to me, because being from California the Supposition was I could control him.[3] I'm afraid our Government is so pulled about by side influences that honesty & Qualifications are no longer the Rule. Woods should not be appointed to an office of Trust, when money is to be handled.

I dont think I ever felt so much a desire to hide myself in some obscure place, to pass the time allotted to us on earth, but I know full well that we cannot if we would avoid the storm that threatens us, and perforce must drift on to the end. What that will be God only Knows. As ever yrs. affectionately

W. T. Sherman

ALS, InND: Sherman Family Papers.

1. Hugh Ewing had been named colonel of the Thirtieth Ohio on August 20 but would not see action until September 1862.

2. EES had written WTS on September 22 about her problems with a note from a Mr. Harding. SFP.

3. Alexander E. Shiras to WTS, September 24, 1861, DLC: WTS. Shiras was more diplomatic than WTS: "He is sent to you because, I believe, he will there be more useful than elsewhere, and will be working under your immediate supervision."

TO ABRAHAM LINCOLN

Recd. Washington Oct. 10th From
Louisville Oct. 10th

To President Lincoln

My own belief is that Confederates will make a more desperate effort join Kentucky than they have for Missouri. Force now here or expected is entirely inadequate[.]

The Kentuckians instead of assisting, call from every quarter for protection against local secessionists. I named T. J. Wood[1] at Govern⟨or⟩ Morton's instance because he is a Kentuckian and has been mustering Officer at Indianap⟨olis.⟩ He should have a Brigade of Indiana Volunteers. Col. R. W. Johnson[2] is now with Col. Jackson's Cava⟨lry⟩ Regiment,[3] in process of formation at Owensbor⟨ough.⟩ Both have good reputation in Regular Army.

McCook has not arrived. All men in Ind. and Ohio are ready to come to Ky., but they ha⟨ve⟩ no arms and we cannot supply them arms c⟨loth⟩ing or anything. Answer.

W. T. Sherman
Brig. Genl.

Telegram, DNA: RG 107, Records of the Office of the Secretary of War, Telegrams Received (Bound); OR, I, 4:300. Text in angle brackets from OR.

1. Thomas J. Wood (1823–1906), who had served on Taylor's staff during the Mexican War and on the frontier, was mustering troops in Indiana as a lieutenant colonel of the First U.S. Cavalry when he was named a brigadier general of volunteers on October 11; he would lead the Second Brigade in McCook's command.

2. Richard W. Johnson (1827–97), USA, who had seen service on the frontier, was a captain in the Fifth U.S. Cavalry when he was promoted brigadier general of volunteers on October 11. He would command the Third Brigade in McCook's division.

3. James S. Jackson (1823–62), a Kentucky lawyer and congressman, had been forced to resign from the army during the Mexican War after killing a fellow officer in a duel. He was colonel of the Third Kentucky Cavalry.

TO ELLEN EWING SHERMAN

Louisville, Oct. 12, 1861

Dearest Ellen,

I have commenced several letters to you but have been compelled to Stop to Some importunate applicant for a pass—I was called from Muldrough Hill by Genl. Anderson, who has gone off sick—his health is tolerable but the anxieties of a command such as this will try the best of constitutions and he gave in. He has gone to Lexington & Frankfort and thence to Cincinati & Washington. I have several letters from you in the last of which you want me to write you a cheerful letter.[1] How any body could be cheerful now I cant tell even Mark Tapley[2] could not be cheerful. Personally I am comfortably enough, but the forbodings of danger against which I have struggled keep me far from being easy. I will not disturb you by these, but I insist on your not moving to Cincinati and since the maker of that note offers to pay in Gold I am glad you have sent it for collection. I will draw some pay tomorrow and will send you some. Col. Swords arrived today, and will be Chief Quarter Master. I am mostly disturbed by the fact that the Kentuckyans do not volunteer and by the fact that I cannot get arms. Troops offer from Michigan & Indiana but no arms and I can['t] get any[.] Some were sent from New York but they are old dutch muskets nearly worn out which our soldiers wont touch. In the meantime the Confederates are gathering behind Green River and I cannot find out their strength, they may fall on my force about 40 miles out and overpower them—I have been begging for some officers, and at Last Brig. Genl. McCook[3] has come and I send him out. I hear the Secretary of War is coming here tonight with Adjt. Genl. Thomas, but I doubt if they can do us any material good.[4] They do not and will not comprehend the situation of affairs until it is too late. Had the Government prepared in time for this crisis we would have had the means now at hand.

I had heard that John was raising a Brigade, but he will encounter the same difficulty about arms, and the materials of war without which men are useless. Those whose business it was never would measure the extent of this war, instead of 10 or 12,000 we should have here 50 or 60,000—I estimated in Washington before I started for 30,000 from Kentucky & 30,000 from other states. They should have been in readiness before a move was made—once being in it is too late to prepare and the small force is liable to be overwhelmed. I have purposely excluded all reporters to conceal the weakness of our forces, yet spies will penetrate as farmers and teamsters and our enemies learn exactly our strength or weakness.

My health is very good though I have headache from smoking too many cigars, and being kept down to a table writing.[5]

Again I say stay in Lancaster dont think of moving to Cincinati[.] You wont be any nearer me, for I dont know where I will be, though I cannot hope to be in Nashville unless the energies of our authorities are aroused to the importance of Kentucky to the Federal Union.

Give my love to all at home and tell Willy that I am very anxious to leave him a name of which he will not be ashamed if the tools are furnished me for the task to which I am assigned. as ever yours

W. T. Sherman

ALS, InND: Sherman Family Papers.

1. Probably EES to WTS, September 29, October 4, 7, and 10, 1861, SFP. Her letter of October 4 assured him of his family's concern for him and their attempts to get him transferred to a different post. Andrew Johnson had been in town to give a speech. On October 7 she wrote that she heard he was to replace Anderson, but she was still worried by the tone of his letters. On October 10, she relayed the news that JS had been authorized by Dennison to raise regiments and was going to send them to him. She closed this letter with "Do write me a cheerful letter that I may have it to refer to when the gloomy ones come."

2. Mark Tapley was a famously good-natured ostler and innkeeper in Charles Dickens's novel *Martin Chuzzlewit*.

3. Alexander M. McCook (1831–1903), the brother of Dan McCook, had been made a brigadier general of volunteers on September 3 and had been assigned to the Army of the Ohio in Kentucky.

4. This would be the meeting at which WTS would present the current state of affairs in Kentucky at their absolute worst and demand that the government send him two hundred thousand men so that he could fulfill his orders. *PM*, 1:228–31.

5. The issue of WTS's health would become increasingly important at this time; many of his superiors soon came to believe that he was having a nervous breakdown.

TO SALMON P. CHASE

Head-Quarters Department
of the Cumberland.
Louisville, Ky. Oct. 14 1861.

Hon. S. P. Chase
Secretary of the Treasury, Washington.
Dear Sir,

I have just received your letter.[1] The Secretary of War and Adjt. General are Known to be in Missouri and I was in expectation of seeing them here, to explain in person my views of matters & things in Kentucky. The line from the mouth of the Tennessee to the Big Sandy is too long for any one person to watch. Our enemies have divided their forces into three (3) columns—Right center & West, on each of which they have seperate Commanders, Zollicoffer, Buckner and A. S. Johnston.[2] For months they were preparing men in Tennessee for the events which they foresaw—They had in Kentucky the assurance of the active help of such men as Magoffin,[3] Breckinridge Preston,[4] Hanson[5] and other enthusiastic leaders, and they know full well that the majority opposed to their designs were passive, inactive farmers.

At present they have at Columbus a well fortified place, with a Gunboat operating on the Mississipi, and Railroad communication south & East.

Buckner had the men who were being drilled all summer at two camps near where the Railroads, from Bowling Green to Nashville & Memphis crossed the Tennessee Line. These were the nucleus of his force with which he advanced on Louisville but our occupation of Muldroughs Hill caused him to fall east of Green River destroying the Railroad as he went.

He has now his forces collected for convenience of subsistence along the Railroad, and we have ours about 9000 men at a point 50 miles in front of Louisville with these Regiments guarding the Rail Road—There we are compelled to Stop and provide transportation for the Railroad is completely destroyed.

At Camp Dick Robinson an assembly about 6000 mixed troops, badly clad, and with limited means of transportation[.] Gen. Thomas reports to me that he was compelled to borrow money of the Bank in Lexington to enable him to provide for their bare clothing and maintenance. Armies are expensive establishments and useless unless well provided, or actuated by a feeling of patriotism or determination that leaves all deprivations—Now on the East there is Known to be a force at Prestonburg of about 2500 which Breckinridge controls, and Zollicoffer with a force in the south east that no doubt has been exaggerated. Now this is the point to which your letter directs my attention. To develop that Union feeling of East Tennessee, of which so much is said and so little Known. Supposing the Tennesseans do rise, can we give them bread— can we give them arms. No. Even the Kentuckyans who apply have to be put off with promises—we have no tents, shoes, blankets, cooking utensils— nothing and winter at hand. We had this promise in Washington of 30,000 muskets and have received about 14,000, of which two thirds are condemned European muskets, that Kentuckyans wont look at, and even an Indiana Regiment will not touch. A Regiment of young strong men now lay in camp opposite Louisville without arms.

I Know nothing of the plans of the Enemy, but I think they are 1st to clear Kentucky of the troops now here, then to threaten Cincinati, and approach Saint Louis from the East.

The Power which controls the Ohio and Mississipi will ultimately control this Continent, and Such men as Davis, Albert Johnston & Buckner have an ambition that is unbounded. They are better prepared to execute this plan than we are to penetrate East Tennessee, and provide for the restoration of the

Union Sentiment that is dominant there. The People of Kentucky would *prefer* the Union but they with of course some notable exceptions do not rise to the occasion and offer to fight for it. Fragments of Regiments are forming all over the State by virtue of appointments from the Secretary of War: and of Genl. Anderson, but without arms they will accept, or clothing cooking utensils & camp equippage I doubt if we can raise here a respectable force. I am sorry I offended the President, but it would be better if all would see things as they are, than as we would they were. With great respect Yrs.

W. T. Sherman

Brig. Genl.

ALS, PHi: Salmon P. Chase Papers.

1. Salmon P. Chase to WTS, September 17, 1861, DLC: WTS. Chase said that the president thought Sherman already had enough troops in Kentucky; McClellan wished to advance and wanted more men, and they were disturbed to discover that Frémont had ordered five regiments to Sherman instead of sending them east where they were needed. He had sent a large shipment of arms to Cincinnati and promised to do what he could to support Sherman because the need to keep Kentucky in the Union was pressing.

2. General Albert Sidney Johnston (1803–62), CSA, was in command of the Western Department at Bowling Green.

3. Beriah Magoffin (1815–85) was the governor of Kentucky who attempted to keep the state neutral.

4. William Preston (1816–87), a Kentucky politician and diplomat, urged his state to join the Confederacy.

5. Roger W. Hanson (1827–63), a Kentucky politician and soldier, favored the state's neutrality and then joined the Confederate army.

TO LORENZO THOMAS

Head-Quarters Dept.
of the Cumberland,
Louisville, Ky. October 22, 1861.

To General L. Thomas
Adjt. Genl. Washington D.C.
Sir:

On my arrival at Camp Dick Robinson, I found General Thomas had stationed a Kentucky regiment at Rock Castle Hill, beyond a river of same name, and had sent an Ohio and an Indiana regiment forward in support. He was embarrassed for transportation but I authorized him to hire teams, and to move his whole force nearer to his advance guard so as to support it as he had information of the approach of Zollicoffer towards London. I have just heard from him that he had sent forward Gen. Schoepf[1] with Colonel Wolford's Cavalry,[2] Colonel Steedman's Ohio regiment[3] and a battery of artillery,[4] followed on a succeeding day by the Tennessee Brigade.[5] He had still two Kentucky regiments,[6] the 38th Ohio and another battery of artillery[7] with which he was to follow yesterday. This force if concentrated should be strong enough for the purpose and at all events, is all he had or I could give him.

I explained to you fully when here, the supposed position of our adversaries, among which was a force in the valley of Big Sandy supposed to be advancing on Paris, Ky. Genl. Nelson at Maysville was instructed to collect all the men he could, and Col. Sill's regiment of Ohio Volunteers,[8] Colonel Harris was already in position at Olympian Springs,[9] and a regiment lay at Lexington which I ordered to his support. This leaves the line of Thomas' operations exposed, but I cannot help it. I explained so fully to yourself and Secretary of War the condition of things that I can add nothing now until further developments. You Know my views, that this great centre of our fields was too weak, far too weak, and I have begged and implored till I dare not say more.

Buckner still is beyond Green river. He sent a detachment of his men, variously estimated from 2000 to 4000 towards Greensburg. Genl. Ward[10] with about one thousand men retreated to Campbellsburg where he called to his assistance some partially formed regiments to the number of about 2000. The enemy did not advance and Genl. Ward was at last dates at Campbellsburg. These officers charged with raising regiments must of necessity be near their homes to collect men and for this reason are out of position; but, at or near Greensburg and Lebanon I desire to assemble as large a force of the Kentucky Volunteers as possible. This organization is necessarily irregular, but the necessity is so great that I must have them and, therefore, have issued to them arms and clothing during the process of formation. This has facilitated their enlistment, but inasmuch as the Legislature provided the means for organizing the Kentucky Volunteers and entrusted their disbursement to a Board of loyal gentlemen, I have endeavoured to cooperate with them to hasten the formation of these corps. The great difficulty is and has been that as volunteers offer we have not arms and clothing to give them. The arms sent us are, as you already Know, European muskets of uncouth pattern which the volunteers will not touch.

Genl. McCook has now three Brigades—Johnson's, Wood's and Rousseau's. Negley's Brigade[11] arrived today and will at once be sent out. The Minnesota regiment[12] has also arrived and will be sent forward. Hazzard's regiment of Indiana troops,[13] I have ordered to the mouth of Salt Creek, an important point on the turnpike road leading to Elizabethtown.

I again repeat that our force here is out of all proportion to the importance of the position. Our defeat would be disastrous to the nation, and to expect of new men who never bore arms to do miracles is not right. I am, with much respect, Yours truly

W. T. Sherman

Brig. Genl. comdg.

Copy (made in January 1862), DLC: William T. Sherman. See L. Thomas to JS, February 1, 1862, in DLC: William T. Sherman (JS had requested the copy made as the Shermans and Ewings readied a defense to the charges that WTS was insane). *OR*, I, 4:315–16.

1. Albin F. Schoepf (1822–86) had been made a brigadier general of volunteers in September and sent to Kentucky.

2. Colonel Frank Wolford commanded the First Kentucky Cavalry.

3. James B. Steedman (1817–83) had been commissioned colonel of the Fourteenth Ohio on September 1.

4. Probably Battery B or C of the First Ohio Artillery.

5. The First Tennessee Infantry.

6. Colonel Speed Fry's Fourth Kentucky and the Tenth or Twelfth Kentucky.

7. Battery B or C of the First Ohio Artillery.

8. Joshua W. Sill (1831–62) had been commissioned colonel of the Thirty-third Ohio on August 27.

9. Colonel Harris commanded the Second Ohio.

10. William T. Ward (1808–78), a brigadier general of volunteers as of September 18, was assigned to Kentucky, his native state.

11. James S. Negley (1826–1901), a brigadier general of volunteers, commanded the Fourth Brigade in McCook's division, soon to be called the Seventh Independent Brigade.

12. The Second Minnesota.

13. The Thirty-seventh Indiana was commanded by Colonel George Washington Hazzard.

TO ELLEN EWING SHERMAN

Head-Quarters Department
of the Cumberland.
Louisville, Ky. Oct. 23, 1861

Dearest Ellen,

I have so much to do, and a dread of danger so hangs around me that I can hardly write to you with any degree of satisfaction. I am doing all I know how, but to be in the midst of people ready to betray is the most unpleasant of all feelings. I have seen the stories.

The two informal receipts I sent you were as I was starting for Camp Dick Robinson. I gave ordnance a Receipt for $10,000 and at some future time must account for it—Keep them sacred till I can attend to it, or should it devolve on you you can remember where the 10,000 are when notified that I am charged with that amount. The money was given to a Quartermaster at Muldroughs Hill and spent there in an informal way, but for the subsistence of the soldiers. I hope Halleck[1] who is a Major General will be sent to relieve me[.] Our troops are more exposed here than in any part of the country. We are weaker and farther from our Base the Ohio River. I must stay here to direct all, but must share the fate of all in case of disaster, for we have no escape. I have been reinforced, but nothing like what it should be. We should have 50,000 men here.

My health is comparatively good. as ever yrs.

W. T. Sherman

ALS, InND: Sherman Family Papers.

1. Henry W. Halleck (1815–72) had been made major general in August and would take Frémont's place in November.

TO JOHN SHERMAN

Head-Quarters Department
of the Cumberland
Louisville, Ky. Oct. 26, 1861

Dear Brother,

I am just in receipt of your letter and am glad the secretary remembered my remark that to accomplish the only purposes for which Kentucky can be used there should be a force here of 200,000 men[1]—my force is ridiculously small, and I hate to augment it by driblets—Look at the fact—we know the South is all armed and prepared, and must have Kentucky, for it they will struggle. They see us undervaluing their force. They have already invaded the state with five times my forces, and are gradually preparing for the onset. I know their leaders, and their designs, and feel that I am to be sacrificed. The western part of the state is now in their possession. They have about 6000 men in the valley of Big Sandy. 6000 or 7000 at Cumberland Gap & ford, and I doubt not at least 35,000 in front of me, with nothing between us but Green River now fordable, and about 23 miles of intervening country. Indiana is devoid of arms, so is Ohio and the North West, and to my crying demand for arms they send me a few hundreds of condemned European muskets whilst the People ask for rifles. We have called on the Kentuckyans to form regiments and they are responding—Slowly to be sure, but when they come for arms, I can only answer I have none, or such as they wont touch. I tell you, and warn you of the danger. So far as my power goes I cannot promise to prevent the enemy reaching the Ohio River at a hundred different points. Our camps are full of their spies, and the People here all prefer their Southern connections. By cutting off these in a measure we turn feeling against us by merchants & farmers. They want to sell their merchandise & produce and all guns south. My forces are hastily raised Regiments imperfectly armed and disciplined thinking themselves in an enemys country they will commit excesses, which begets a feeling of hatred. Again we must pay cash for every thing and I have found but few to give anything except at full price—of us all is expected whilst the other side take as they go and no one expects pay. On a quiet vote they would prefer the old Government, but anything to escape the ravages of war— had 50,000 men been thrown into Kentucky with plenty of arms for the People the game would have been short, but with our half force and no arms to offer the People I cannot help but feel great concern.

I am compelled to distribute them on three weak lines, all dependent on Railroads which may at any moment be interrupted, also on Telegraphs which are daily cut. A reverse to any one of these might be fatal to all—Yet I cannot do otherwise—The forces up Sandy must be driven or threatened from the direction of Paris—Those at Cumberland Gap from Dick Robinson, and those over Green River from here—This is the most important point and most in danger—The Southern army wants it with its mills, foundries shops and all the affairs of a City, besides the control of the River.

I write in haste amid the pressure of business which devolves on me—Yrs.

W. T. Sherman

ALS, DLC: William T. Sherman.

1. Sherman had met with Cameron and Lorenzo Thomas on October 17 in Louisville, when he had apprised them of his views on the emergency in Kentucky and his urgent need for men and matériel to prevent the Confederate capture of Louisville.

TO ELLEN EWING SHERMAN

Head-Quarters Department
of the Cumberland.
Louisville, Ky. Novr. 1, 1861

Dearest Ellen,

The Paymaster has made out my account for October and has given me a check for 361.60 which I enclose to you. God Knows that I think of you and our dear Children all the time, and that I would that we might hide ourselves in some quiet corner of the world.[1] We were so once and then were not content and now I find myself riding a whirlwind unable to guide the Storm. Rumors and Reports pour in on me of the overwhelming force collected in front across Green River. I went to camp to Share its fate, but they did not come and I am here again. I have my forces dependent on Railroads liable to interruption, and of a size that will not compare with our enemies. To advance would be madness and to Stand still folly—more are coming from Indiana and Ohio, but equipped only for travel by Railroads and it takes time to get up wagons and provisions, and the absolute necessities of men are so great that they will break us down—The idea of going down to History with a fame such as threatens me nearly makes me crazy, indeed I may be so now, and the constant application for passes and little things absorbs all my time. I have not written to you enough—I have not laid open to you the secret movings of my mind or heart, but tis true no notice comes to me from the War Department and the materials of war come in driblets just enough to fall into the hands of our enemies if they know how to take advantage of our situation—I cannot order the withdrawal of our present force, nor can I order into Kentucky more troops to share the fate of these till the wagons and means of transportation are provided, and work proceeds slow[.] Winter too is at hand, and the Kentucky volunteers come slowly, and want organization. Prime thinks I give myself unnecessary concern about this, but I know I do not—I am here now but cant say how long I will stay. I was away when your fathers dispatch came, I would like to See him and again I would not, for he would be troubled at my concern, and might not appreciate it. I have not heard from you for some days, but in the quiet of your country you cannot feel as one surrounded by the importunities of contractors and the quiet observation of spies. I am more & more impressed daily with the fact that whatever the Judgment of man may be as to the Status of Kentucky, that She is and ought to remain true to the Union, yet her feelings & interests all point south. The old men revere the Union, they remember its glory and fame, but the young men look the other way, and trade & family feeling *all* point to the South. Thus in trying to carry out my orders of nonintercourse with the South I am esteemed a cold hearted man, and even a lady the other day told me as much, and she seemed relieved to hear me speak as a common mortal with feeling & sympathy. I now hear Buckner has from 25, to 60,000 men, the former number is nearer the truth, and in an open field I would be willing to meet him, but we are 50 miles out and all the road in is lined with secessionists ready to shoot and destroy.[2] The Railroad out is guarded by volunteers who cannot appreciate the true state of the case, and who are off their Guard & might be surprised and taken any night. This thought alone disturbs my sleep, and I cannot rest. Every night I fear this R. R. may be broken and 12,000 men be left to fight their way back before & behind enemies more ruthless than Indians. I have seen Mr. Crittenden, but he lives in the Past. He does not appreciate Young America, which is revolutionary and destructive. He thinks the People of Kentucky will still awaken to their danger. The States of Ohio & Indiana have responded *nobly*, and if the People of Kentucky betray us, let Vengeance blot the Tale. They voted Union—They cut disunion. McCook commands in part of Louisville. Thomas front of Lexington and I here—but I can do but little other than advise. as ever yrs.

W. T. Sherman

ALS, InND: Sherman Family Papers.

1. One week after this letter was written, EES wrote JS that she "was startled and alarmed by the receipt of a dispatch from Capt. Prime in these words—the dispatch was to Father—'*Send Mrs. Sherman & youngest boy down to relieve Gen. Sherman and myself from the pressure of business no occasion for alarm.*' Father was not at home, but Philemon came down with me & we arrived here [Louisville] at three o'clock next morning. Knowing insanity to be in the family & having seen Cump in the seize of it in California, I assure you I was tortured by fears, which have been *only in part* relieved since I got here. Some time ago in writing to me he expressed a hope that Halleck would relieve him of command." WTS had apparently written to McClellan to this effect on November 3 and McClellan had replied on November 5 that he would send Buell to relieve him (DLC: WTS). Ellen continued that "Cump's mind has been wrought up to a morbid state of anxiety which caused him to request McClellan to make the change." She asked JS to come and judge his brother's state of mind and situation for himself. EES to JS, November 10, 1861, DLC: WTS.

2. In truth Buckner's force was much smaller, but Confederate commander Albert S. Johnston had decided to handle his command in such a way as to bluff his Union counterpart as to his total numbers. Moreover, Civil War generals habitually overestimated the size of their opposition.

TO WILLIAM DENNISON JR.

> Head Quarters, Ohio Militia
> ADJUTANT GENERAL'S OFFICE,
> Columbus, ——, 1861.
> Louisville Kty. Nov 6–1861

Governor Dennison

Dear Sir,

You cannot imagine the difficulties under which I have labored without preperation to organize these expeditions and watch them in their progress with no arsenal, with home Guards and Kentucky volunteers in process of formation. The position of things is, that Gen. Nelson is with three Ohio Regiments[1] and two irregular Kentucky Volunteers[2]—he may succeed in dispersing the Prestonburg party,[3] which may cross over and join Zollicoffer[.] In which case Thomas should have immediate assistance. Therefore the necessity of a reserve somewhere between Cincinnati and Thomas' Camp at Loudon[.] In like manner here we may at any moment be in danger, and I would have to judge on the spur of the moment. All these moves take time, and the truth is, adequate preperation has not been made. The requisitions made for ordnance and stores have yet been unfilled. Some Rifled Guns ordered last August are just received boxed up, and no soldiers to manage them. In like manner wagons came in pieces and time is necessary to set them up. Mules are wild and horses distempered, and worst of all no Capts., or Lieutenants to teach the details—Never before was such a body of men thrust headlong into such danger. I will not conceal it from you that there is danger. I pointed it out in advance to the Secretary of War, and wrote to Mr. Chase and the President who paid no attention to any of my warnings or appeals. The people of the country take advantage of all our necessities and demand pay in good gold or Kentucky money for every thing we want besides the rails and damage sustained by their fields and their claims would exhaust any Treasury. Now the Ohio Regiments just arriving come so late, that I have no General to command them. More numbers unsupported and uncommanded will accomplish no result. No one or half dozen men can attend to all the wants of these new raise levies, with all their tents and paraphernalia. I do not think Zollicoffer will press Thomas on his Line, but I do expect Buckner will strike for the Ohio River and may be Louisville. In case he be in the strength reported he has us in his power for there can be no retreat. Rolling Fork of Salt River and the Ohio are impassable to an army, and our proper tactics is to outmuster our enemy, which it seems we cannot do.

Ohio has done well, so has Indiana, but the more remote states seem to hold back, and now at this late time our Regiments are in the heart of a State whose citizens are hostile, and who will turn on us vindictively upon the first reverse.

I hear Gen. Mitchel[4] thinks I have feelings against him. 'Tis not so. Gen. Anderson himself asked that Thomas should be superceded, and Thomas was uneasy on the same score.

Gen. Nelson also complained of interference by Gen. Mitchel, but I never have. If he has so represented he is not fair. You should have some good men ready for any emergency. I am with respect yours

W. T. Sherman
Brig. Gen. Commg.

Lbk, OHi: Visual File Material #2095.

1. Second, Twenty-first, and Thirty-third Ohio.

2. Kentucky regiments of Colonels Marshall and Metcalf.

3. On the previous day, Nelson and his forces occupied Prestonburg, Kentucky, where a group of Kentucky Confederates had been waiting for reinforcements.

4. Brigadier General Ormsby M. Mitchel (1809–62), USA, was assigned to the Department of the Ohio.

TO LORENZO THOMAS

Head-Quarters Dept.
of the Cumberland,
Louisville, Ky. November 6, 1861.

General L. Thomas,
Adjutant General,
Sir:

General McClellan telegraphs me to report to him daily the situation of affairs here. The country is so large that it is impossible to give clear and definite views. Our enemies have a terrible advantage in the fact that in our midst, in our camps, and along our avenues of travel they have active partisans, farmers and business men, who seemingly pursue their usual calling but are in fact spies. They report all our movements and strength whilst we can procure information only by circuitous and unreliable means. I enclose you the copy of an intercepted letter which is but the type of others. Many men from every part of the State are now enrolled under Buckner—have gone to him, whilst ours have to be raised in neighborhoods and cannot be called together except at long notice. These volunteers are being organized under the laws of the State, and the 10th of November is fixed for the time of consolidating them into companies and regiments. Many of these are armed by the United States as Home Guards, and many by General Anderson and myself because of the necessity of being armed to guard their camps against internal enemies. Should we be overwhelmed, they would scatter, and their arms and clothing will go to the enemy furnishing the very material they so much need. We should have here a very large force, sufficient to give confidence to the Union men of the ability to do what should be done—possess ourselves of all the States, but all see and feel we are brought to a stand still and this produces doubt and alarm. With our present force, it would be simple madness to cross Green River and yet, hesitation may be as fatal. In like manner the other columns are in peril, not so much in front as rear, the railroads over which our stores must pass being much exposed. I have the Nashville R. R. guarded by three regiments, yet it is far from being safe and the moment actual hostilities commence these roads will be interrupted and we will be in a dilemma. To meet this in part I have put a cargo of provisions at the mouth of Salt River, guarded by two regiments, all those detachments weaken the main force and endanger the whole. Do not conclude, as before that I exaggerate the facts. They are as stated and the future looks as dark as possible. It would be better if some man [of] sanguine mind was here, for I am forced to order according to my convictions. Yours truly

W. T. Sherman
Brig. Genl. Comdg.

Copy (1862), DLC: William T. Sherman Papers.

Head-Quarters Department
of the Cumberland.
Louisville, Ky. Novr. 21 1861

Genl. R. Anderson
My Dear Genl.,

I enclose you the acct. current of H. D. New {Court} & Bro. in which I see he charges you $500 for commissions—I tried to get him to remit the charge, but he says he was out of the money near a month and interest would have been the same. We find these Louisvillians ready to turn against us on the first turning of the tide. We have now a pretty large force in Kentucky, but the Regiments are hastily assembled and poorly disciplined, and being still in a manner dependant on the Railroad they are scattered. My deep earnest conviction from the secession feeling wherever I went, and from my knowledge of the forces collected round about Kentucky I made my declaration that we should need in this Department a very large force, and the very gingerly way in which they came induced me to think the War Department did not share with me these fears and apprehensions at not only the loss of Kentucky, but the forces sent here—I asked that Halleck or any one else be sent here, and Buell has been here a week, in command and I am ordered to Saint Louis.[1]

I confess I never have seen daylight in the midst of the troubles that now envelope us. I am therefore disqualified to lead, and must follow—You know with what reluctance I entered on my command and have always felt that Somehow or other I would be disgraced by it.

Buell is full of confidence and I sincerely pray he may realize success, though I still think his means utterly inadequate.

Present me with all possible respect to Mrs. Anderson. If we could only sit down once more in peace and quiet I think I would be the most amiable man on earth, but the importuning and fault finding, and abuse have hardened me till I am not myself. With great respect

W. T. Sherman

ALS, DLC: Robert Anderson Papers.

1. On November 13, Buell replaced WTS in Kentucky; WTS was sent west to Halleck at St. Louis.

Head-Quarters Department
of the Cumberland
Louisville, Ky. Novr. 21, 1861

Dear Brother,

Your letter was received yesterday. I know that others than yourself think I take a gloomy view of affairs without cause. I hope to God tis so. All I know is the fact that all over Kentucky the People are allied by birth interest and preference to the South—Their trade points that way, and spite of all efforts letters pass to and fro daily. Applications come by hundreds asking protection which cannot be granted, and all Know the fact that we have not the power to prevent it. Again the men who have come here by Regiments are exposed to not only the chances of war but of interruption to the Railroad, which I have guarded thus far successfully but a child or man with crowbar may destroy it. Now that Buell is in command I might divest myself of all care on this score. We have been out to camp, inspected the troops and he has entered upon his duties and I have delayed him simply to give him information—I have not been instrumental in bringing troops here—and I will give no advice on the Subject.

One soldier less than two hundred thousand will be imperilled the moment the Confederates choose. They have delayed for some purpose of their own, but that they design a simultaneous attack on St. Louis, Louisville and Cincinati I have no doubt. They have the force necessary for a success, and they have the men capable of designing and executing it, Johnston, Buckner & Hardee[1] with subordinates Wilcox[2] Hindman[3] and Tilghman.[4]

I suppose I have been morose and cross—and could I now hide myself in some obscure corner I would do so, for my conviction is that our Govt. is destroyed, and that no human power can restore it—They have sent here old Condemned European muskets, and have sent no arms for Cavalry, and when I bought pistols wherewith to arm some scouts, the accounts have been disallowed at Washington because I had not procured authority beforehand. Troops came from Wisconsin & Minnesota without arms, and receive such as we have here for the first time, and I cannot but look upon it as absolutely sacrificing them. I See no hope for them. In their present raw and undisciplined condition they are helpless, and Some terrible disaster is inevitable—Buell is however imbued with the Same spirit that prevails in Washington that there are plenty of Union People, South, in Tennessee and Kentucky, and does not share with me in my fear of the People among whom we live.

You need not delay in your efforts to raise a Brigade—Every man in Ohio should be armed. Whether they come into Kentucky must be deferred till they are ready. They should at least know how to load, and should not be boys or old men—and should be able to bear exposure. We have a great deal of sickness among our troops mostly of the measles. For myself I will blindly obey my orders and report to Gen. Halleck in Missouri—but till I can see day light ahead I will never allow myself to be in command. affectionately

W. T. Sherman

ALS, DLC: William T. Sherman.
1. Major General William J. Hardee (1815–73), CSA.
2. Brigadier General Cadmus M. Wilcox (1824–90), CSA.
3. Brigadier General Thomas C. Hindman (1828–68), CSA.
4. Brigadier General Lloyd Tilghman (1816–63), CSA.

TO THOMAS EWING SR.

Lancaster Ohio Dec. 12, 1861

Hon. Thos. Ewing
Washington D.C.
Sir,

Among the keenest feelings of my life is that arising from a consciousness that you will be mortified beyond measure at the disgrace which has befallen me—by the announcement in the Cincinati Commercial that I am insane.[1]

In these times tis hard to Say who are sane and who insane, but as I have forborne long I will now to you recount many things which I have heretofore to speak or write of. From the outset of this Civil war I have been unable to See any solution. I could see no chance of reconciliation, and though I Knew that the Superior numbers of the North should prevail, yet I Knew that other elements should enter into the Estimate such as distance, Rivers, mountains &c. &c. and the vast extent of the Southern Territory, the united feelings and interests of its People would make conquest impossible. Still I was willing to follow and always so expressed myself. When Gen. Anderson first spoke to me of Kentucky my answer was to that effect, and in like manner to {Garret} Davis and others I did not want to lead, but to follow.

We had hardly reached Kentucky when the State was invaded, and several of its Key points, Columbus Bowling Green, and Cumberland Ford were secured by our enemy. We on our part held the River, the State & Commercial Capital, but our organized force was comparatively small. When Gen. Anderson insisted on leaving me in command I expressed strong reluctance to assuming it, and only did so from the necessity of the case. I found three bodies of the enemies forces threatening the state and I made the best dispositions against them. Gen. Nelson with 3 Ohio Regiments & some Kentucky militia were sent to the Big Sandy. Gen. Thomas with four Ohio & 1 Indiana two Kentucky & two Tennessee Regiments were to watch and repulse Zollicoffer in the south east. Just before Genl. Thomas moved from his camp I visited him and saw the Tennesseeans, & their leaders. They of course were anxious to push their way into East Tennessee, but the universal opinion was that a force of less than Ten thousand men should not attempt it. We had no arms for the Tennesseeans should they rise, and the road was occupied by 7500 men in two of the strongest natural positions in Kentucky, viz. Cumberland Ford & Cumberland Gap. To have attempted it would have been certain failure. Mr. Maynard of Tennessee and Senator Johnson urged the expedition, but we had not the means to attempt it, and all we could do successfully was to Keep that force from entering the Fertile lands of Kentucky.

The Bulk of the enemys forces were to the South of Green River threatening the Lower Ohio, and the City of Louisville, and to that part of the State I attached most importance and in that direction I established the bulk of the Ohio & Indiana Regts. as they arrived, so disposing of them as to enable us to advance where we had sufficient strength. The Secretary of War & Adjt. Genl. Thomas visited me at Louisville, and there I explained to them fully the situation of affairs.[2] They seemed to favor the East Tennessee scheme which has been and still is the favorite Political move but I thought they were convinced of its secondary importance. The Secretary asked me what amount of force would be necessary and I answered that before we were done we would find that two hundred thousand men would be needed. I reasoned thus. Kentucky has a frontier of near a thousand miles, it is backed by Tennessee, Alabama, Mississipi & has railroad communications with the Entire South, and in Southern Kentucky the Rebels can and will assemble a very large force, for to them is Kentucky of far more importance than Virginia. If we had promptly a good force in Kentucky we might have pressed forward and occupied the whole Country as far as the Cumberland Rim, and made Columbus untenable to them, but the result has been, the War Department had only ordered them up to Novr. 10, about forty thousand men, and the Kentuckyans through their legislation had provided about 15,000 men, in scattered regiments and fragments, whilst the enemy had the active support of the Country and a larger force than ours. I had positive Knowledge of about 2500 men, near Prestonburg, under Williams[3]—7500 under Zollicoffer at Cumberland Gap, 2500 under Stanton[4] near Monticello—8000 under Hardee moving about, 18,000 at Bowling Green strongly intrenched—10,000 at Russellville & Clarksville, and 4500 at Hopkinsville, all of which can be concentrated in a day at Bowling Green—Of course they prefer us to advance further into the Country. Every mile of advance, calls for additional detachments & transportation, and makes defeat more disastrous. I Knew the impatience of the Country for results, but to expect us in Kentucky with troops many of which had come unarmed, to assume the offensive whilst a well organized army lay at Washington was unfair. I may have shown as I certainly did feel great Concern. I had good reports of the assemblage at Bowling Green of our 1500 wagons, and believed that the enemy designed to assume the offensive, and I still believe they only delay because of the great advantage they possess in case our forces cross the Green River. Gen. Thomas' letter was published all over the country[5] and exhibited in strong terms our weakness, and it also gave them my estimate of the force deemed necessary to drive them out of Kentucky, as it was manifest that force could not or would not be sent into Kentucky I was left to wait their movements. I asked to be relieved because I felt that my opinions were not heeded, and that they in Washington believed I overrated the forces of the Rebels. If the Country has 640,000 volunteers, or even 500,000—at least 200,000 of them should be in Kentucky or on the Ohio River, and though I may be mistaken I am still firmly of the opinion that unless that number of armed men, are distributed along that Line, it will fall into the hands of the Rebels. Even now they reach the Ohio River at several points, and the only reason why not at all, is because they have other designs. I gather this from communications of persons who will not be Known, and from the character of their Leaders.

Since Gen. Buell has assumed the command he has been largely reinforced but still not enough to enable him to meet the enemy at all points. I hope he will succeed, but I have great apprehensions, for he underrates an element in this Terrible war that I probably overrate viz. the hostility of the People along the Lines of Railway and Rivers—all People interested in the mule & cattle trade all in steamboats whose trade is south and very many in the Provision business are interested in the Success of the South—and these Classes comprise allmost all Kentucky. They would gladly stand neutral as they term it, they would avoid the perils and losses inseparable from war, but when compelled to act they will aid the cause of their Southern friends. These considerations are all working in Kentucky and I believe that the Southern Leaders are allowing those causes to work for them. I Know full well they have their own troubles, but so intense and bitter is their feeling against us, that they will persevere in their efforts against all ordinary deprivations. There is also another very important point on which I have felt and expressed great solicitude, viz. that drawing troops from Ohio Indiana & Illinois across the Ohio River, without any reserves, would expose those states to inroads in case of accident to our invading army. I find some volunteers scattered about the State, unarmed and of little avail and such too is the case in Indiana and Illinois. I do not blame anybody. This is one of the difficulties under which we labor, but is one reason why our troops should not too hastily push too far into an enemys country. I say enemys, for Kentucky south of Green River is enemys country.

As to Missouri, as soon as I got there I reported to Gen. Halleck who was engaged in organizing his forces—He ordered me in writing to visit the several posts in the Department to inspect & report, but subsequently ordered me to Sedalia with authority to assume Command at my discretion of three Divisions which had been halted at Sedalia Syracuse & Tipton. I found these Divisions in the very camps they had occupied on their march from Springfield to St. Louis. The Camp at Sedalia was very much exposed with poor water and was 28 miles in advance of Tipton too far for support in case of attack or defense. I ordered forward towards Sedalia the Division at Tipton & then both to Sedalia. Gen. Pope no doubt telegraphed to Gen. Halleck, and Gen. Halleck ordered me not to change the disposition of the Force without his orders, and I countermanded the orders. The troops there will be much exposed this winter, and their oxen & mules will surely perish if the winter be severe. I made to Gen. Halleck a written Report, and he informed me he should move their camps to some convenient timbered country, and let them halt themselves.[6] As they are 180 miles from St. Louis and depend on the Railroad for their supplies, I apprehend that the Railroad will be interrupted unless guarded stronger than at present. I simply inspected and made a written Report, which Gen. Halleck has.

There is no doubt my mind is deeply moved by an estimate of strength and purpose on the part of our Enemies much higher than the Government or People believe to be true—I am perfectly willing to leave its solution to Time, and will be much relieved to find I am wholly wrong.

I will stay here till next week and return to St. Louis—but feel certain this paragraph will be widely circulated, and will impair my personal influence for much time to come, if not always.

The cars are about starting and I close merely saying that I have no right to find fault with any member of the administration, unless their want of appreciation of the danger loses the valley of the Ohio. With great respect,

W. T. Sherman

ALS, DLC: William T. Sherman.

1. On December 11, the *Cincinnati Commercial* had published a story bearing the headline, "General William T. Sherman Insane." These rumors had been plaguing WTS since the end of October and had intensified with his departure from Kentucky and his arrival in Missouri, and WTS had agreed to take a twenty-day leave to rest on December 2 after Halleck had reversed Sherman's orders consolidating scattered Federal forces in Jefferson City, Tipton, and Sedalia, Missouri. In spite of military information to the contrary, WTS feared Price's forces would launch a devastating attack on these men.

2. See *PM*, 1:228–31 and 238–42.

3. John S. Williams (1820–98) was colonel of the Fifth Kentucky at this time.

4. Colonel Sidney S. Stanton (ca. 1829–64), a Tennessee lawyer and politician, was leading the Twenty-fifth Tennessee Infantry, CSA.

5. On October 30, 1861, the *New York Times* had printed Lorenzo Thomas's summary of the October 17 meeting between Cameron, Thomas, and Sherman during which WTS demanded two hundred thousand men as necessary to hold Kentucky.

6. WTS to HWH, November 26, 27, and 28, 1861, *OR*, I, 8:379, 381–82, recommended a consolidation of troops in the Missouri Department; although Halleck initially countermanded these orders, he later ordered the very same thing.

TO HENRY W. HALLECK

Lancaster, Ohio, December 12, 1861.

Major-General Halleck,
Saint Louis, Mo.:
Dear Sir:

I believe you will be frank enough to answer me if you deem the steps I took at Sedalia as evidence of a want of mind.

They may have been the result of an excess of caution on my part, but I do think the troops were too much strung out, and should be concentrated, with more men left along to guard the track. The animals, cattle especially, will be much exposed this winter.

I set a much higher measure of danger on the acts of unfriendly inhabitants than most officers do, because I have lived in Missouri and the South, and know that in their individual characters they will do more acts of hostility than Northern farmers or people could bring themselves to perpetrate. In my judgment Price's army in the aggregate is less to be feared than when in scattered bands.

I write to you because a Cincinnati paper, whose reporter I imprisoned in Louisville for visiting our camps after I had forbidden him leave to go, has announced that I am insane, and alleges as a reason that at Sedalia my acts were so mad that subordinate officers refused to obey. I know of no order I gave that was not obeyed, except General Pope's, to advance his division to Sedalia, which order was countermanded by you, and the fact communicated to me.

These newspapers have us in their power, and can destroy us as they please, and this one can destroy my usefulness by depriving me of the confidence of officers and men.

I will be in Saint Louis next week, and will be guided by your commands and judgment.

I am, &c.,
W. T. Sherman,
Brigadier-General.

Printed, *OR*, I, 8:819.

CHAPTER 4

December 18, 1861—May 26, 1862

William T. Sherman was a broken man when he returned to St. Louis in December 1861. "Matters here look gloomy & unnatural," he told Ellen. He saw no end to the war or to his own personal humiliation and imagined himself to be the target of congressional committees eager to find scapegoats for Union failure. He had cast shame upon the family name; "the idea of having brought disgrace on all associated with me is so horrible to contemplate that I cannot really endure it." The idea of suicide crossed his mind. Major General Henry W. Halleck tried to soothe the nerves of his troubled subordinate, but privately even he remarked that Sherman's behavior lent credence to charges of insanity. Although Sherman rejected his father-in-law's advice to institute libel proceedings against the newspapers, he continued to nurse a sense of grievance against those who would expect impossibilities of one man. At the same time he waxed eloquent on what was necessary to secure victory: "As long as we are on Southern ground they have an advantage that we cannot overcome without a complete destruction of all the inhabitants." Railroads were too difficult to guard; the population was hostile; reconciliation seemed counterproductive. He doubted that the North was willing to pay the price to win.[1]

Over the next month Sherman used his correspondence as a way to let off steam and to share his more morbid thoughts. Although he admitted that he was not fit to exercise command in Kentucky, he argued that his replacement Buell was doing no better. He remained convinced that the majority of Southern whites, even in the border states, were secessionist sympathizers. Attempts to foster Unionist sentiment were worthless in the absence of military successes, while the undisciplined behavior of Union soldiers offended civilians. "They commit acts of trespass & violence along the Roads and convert Union men into Enemies," he explained to John Sherman, "so that nothing is gained by the advance of an army, but its effect upon the object arrived at." In a contest of will, he argued, the Confederates would win: "One thing is certain they are in earnest and our people have been actuated by rather the conviction of judgment and reason, which never can compete with the intensity of feeling."[2]

Placed in charge of Benton Barracks by Halleck, Sherman remained depressed about his personal prospects as well as those of the Union cause. "I prefer to follow not to lead," he told John, "as I confess I have not the confidence of a Leader in this war, and would be happy to slide into obscurity." He doubted that he would ever again exercise field command; he continued to contemplate death as a release from the responsibilities of life. There seemed little hope for relief from such gloom.[3]

News from Tennessee changed all that. At the beginning of February, Sherman busied himself with forwarding troops to an expedition up the Tennessee River to Fort Henry, located just south of the Kentucky-Tennessee border. For Sherman, who believed that an invasion of this area offered far brighter prospects than did a drive toward East Tennessee, it seemed a small vindication. Then came news of Fort Henry's capitulation; ten days later Union forces also compelled the surrender of the Confederate garrison at Fort Donelson, located a dozen miles east of Fort Henry on the west bank of the Cumberland River. The Confederate position in Kentucky, already dented in January by a Union victory at Mill Springs, now crumbled, and on February 24 Union soldiers marched into Nashville.

Sherman contributed to the string of Northern triumphs. During the siege of Fort Donelson he had forwarded reinforcements to the Union commander, Brigadier General Ulysses S. Grant. Halleck had assigned Sherman to command at Paducah, Kentucky, to facilitate that process. Although Sherman ranked Grant, he did all he could to help him. Grant expressed his gratitude in words Sherman found as refreshing as they were welcome: "I feel under many obligations to you for the kind tone of your letter, and hope that should an opportunity occur you will win for yourself the promotion, which you are kind enough to say belongs to me. I care nothing for promotion so long as our arms are successful, and no political appointments are made."[4] Unfortunately, Sherman's letter of congratulations has vanished, but he did share his reaction with John: "Grants victory was most extraordinary and brilliant—he was a plain unostentatious man, and a few years ago was of bad habits, but he certainly has done a brilliant act." Nevertheless, Sherman reserved his highest praise for Halleck, judging him "the ablest man by far that has thus far appeared."[5]

At the beginning of March Sherman received a command in the field. He was placed in charge of a division of new recruits that had joined Union forces assembling near Savannah, Tennessee, along the Tennessee River, with an eye toward advancing on the key Confederate railroad junction at Corinth, Mississippi. His first mission was to journey south on the Tennessee to cut the railroad connecting Corinth with Iuka, Mississippi; although he failed in that effort, he spotted a steamboat landing on the river's west bank sufficiently elevated to assure protection from spring floods. By mid-March Grant transferred his command to Pittsburg Landing and began to prepare it for offensive operations. Halleck directed him to await the arrival of Buell's army; once the two columns united, Halleck would assume command and direct the campaign against Corinth.

Sherman threw himself into the work of training his men with a will. He felt renewed: there was less need to write home now that there was more hope for the future. The weather was beautiful; apple and peach orchards were exploding with color. That a large Confederate force was gathering at Corinth caused him little worry. Not that Sherman underestimated the task before the Union army—far from it. "A year of war & devastation here must be followed by starvation," he told his father-in-law. But he now hoped that the North was equal to the task. In the meantime, he drilled his men and laid out his camp around a log cabin known as Shiloh Church. There was no need to erect fortifications: Sherman was confident that the Confederates would not attack, and fortifications might serve to make the men timid. Others, including Grant and Charles F. Smith, agreed. "By God, I want nothing better than to have the Rebels come out and attack us!" declared Smith. "Our men suppose we have come here to fight, and if we begin to spade, it will make them think we fear the enemy."[6]

During the first week of April, Sherman's pickets found themselves in firefights with Confederates south of the main camp. Sherman refused to believe that such skirmishes portended much. Perhaps, as newspaper reporters later claimed, it was because he feared that alarmist reports would mark him as "crazy"; yet the fact was that he simply did not expect an attack. He refused to respond more aggressively to increasing evidence of enemy activity. When one Ohio colonel reported on Saturday, April 5, that he had encountered a large Confederate force on the move, Sherman dismissed it as the conclusion of an untrained eye: "Take your damned regiment back to Ohio. There is no enemy nearer than Corinth." That day he informed Grant, away at Savannah nursing an injured leg and awaiting Buell's arrival, "I do not apprehend anything like an attack upon our position." With this information in hand, Grant informed Halleck, "I have scarsely the faintest idea of an attack, (general one,) being made upon us but will be prepared should such a thing take place."[7]

Grant, Sherman, and the Union army were thus surprised when some forty thousand Confederates under the command of Albert Sidney Johnston attacked on Palm Sunday, April 6. Stories of Union soldiers bayoneted in their tents as they slept went too far in describing what happened, for Sherman's division was in line when the Rebels emerged from the woods, but the truth was bad enough. Sherman, riding forward to check on reports of Confederate activity, turned to see his orderly killed by an initial volley. He hurried back to camp to get his men into line in time to confront the attackers. Scores of Sherman's untried recruits broke at first fire; those who remained, however, gave ground grudgingly. Sherman worked hard to replenish their ammunition and patched holes in his line. One bullet pierced his hand; another nicked his shoulder strap; several of his mounts were killed. Grant, who made his way to the field after hearing the opening guns, visited Sherman but once and left confident that his subordinate would do his job. In midafternoon Sherman pulled his men back to cover the road over which reinforcements would come: at dusk Grant's battered command withstood the final Confederate surge to take the landing itself. It had been a close thing: the valiant effort of Brigadier General Benjamin Prentiss's division to hold what became known as the Hornet's Nest against repeated assaults cost the Confederates time and their commander, who bled to death of a leg wound. Buell's lead divisions and one of Grant's own divisions arrived during the night, making possible a counterattack on the morning of April 7. The following day, Sherman led a halfhearted pursuit down the road to Corinth, only to turn back in the face of spirited Confederate resistance.

Shiloh served to revive Sherman's confidence in himself. Grant, overlooking the fact that his subordinate's analysis of enemy activity had contributed to the initial Confederate success, made clear his indebtedness to Sherman, while Halleck, who arrived days after the battle, claimed that Sherman saved the day on April 6. But it was not long before Sherman found himself forced to defend his newly won laurels, for in the aftermath of the battle, newspapers, taking their cue from many of the soldiers who had run for their lives at the first opportunity, criticized Grant and Sherman for the unpreparedness of the Union camp to resist an attack. This second battle of Shiloh proved as fierce as the first, with newspaper critics holding their ground better than had the Confederates on April 7. Sherman assailed "the Cock & bull story of surprise," attributing such reports to cowards who had scampered rearward, but in refuting the sensational reports that appeared in the papers he asserted that there was no surprise at all. In letter after letter Sherman argued his case and denounced newspaper correspondents and politicians.[8]

In later years it became fashionable to claim that Shiloh and its aftermath solidified the relationship between Grant and Sherman. Surely this was in part because each man refused to point fingers at the other for the shortcomings for which both bore responsibility. Sherman, knowing what it was like to be the target of press attacks, sympathized with Grant as he suffered under criticism. Nevertheless, Sherman's true hero remained Halleck. In May Halleck directed the combined armies of Grant, Buell, and John Pope southward to Corinth. To call the advance deliberate would be an understatement: each night the Federal soldiers prepared their camps to defend against attack. As the month drew to a close, everyone anticipated a battle that might well decide the outcome of the war.

1. WTS to EES, December 17 [18 or 19], 1861; WTS to TESr, December 24, 1861; WTS to JS, December 24, 1861; WTS to EES, January 1, 1862; WTS to JS, January 4, 1862.

2. WTS to JS, January 8, 1862.

3. WTS to JS, January 9, 1862; WTS to EES, January 11, 1862.

4. USG to WTS, February 19, 1862, *PUSG*, 4:248–49.

5. WTS to JS, February 23, 1862.

6. WTS to TESr, April 4, 1862; Lloyd Lewis, *Sherman: Fighting Prophet* (1932; reprint, Lincoln, Neb., 1993), 213.

7. Lewis, *Sherman*, 214, 219; USG to HWH, April 5, 1862, *PUSG*, 5:13–14.

8. WTS to Charles Ewing, April 25, 1862.

TO ELLEN EWING SHERMAN

St. Louis, Dec. 17 [18 or 19], 61[1]

Dearest Ellen,

I arrived here today at noon without interruption—saw Halleck at once and the copy of the letter he wrote me, and which you will see.[2] My movement at Sedalia was premature, the Same that is now going on save that I think Price should be attacked in his camp at Oscala. Pope has been intercepting parties of recruits bound to Prices camp and is on his way back to Sedalia. I cannot see that affairs here are materially changed in my absence. Charley is at the Barracks, and I suppose will be up in a day or so. I will drop him a note, for he complained to Hammond[3] that neither I or you wrote to him.

Matters here look gloomy & unnatural.

Thomas was not on the list, but Mr. Lucas was, but got off, on some representations. He I suppose would not like to be classified as a Secessionist lest it affect the body of his property.

I am not yet assigned a command and hardly know whether to push it, or take it easy, leaving Halleck time to assign me. I will try and be more punctual in my duties to you, who really deserve a better husband than I have been. How I envy the bawling crowd that passes by that care not for the morrow. If I could see any end to this war, save ruin to us all, I could occasionally feel better, but I see no hope at all. You can trust in Providence, and why he has visited us with this terrible judgment is incomprehensible. As soon as I know my destination I will write again. affectionately

W. T. Sherman

ALS, InND: Sherman Family Papers.

1. Sherman misdated this letter; EES to JS, December 17 and 18, 1861, show that he went to St. Louis on December 18; HWH's letter to WTS was dated December 18.

2. HWH to WTS, December 18, 1861, DLC: WTS, was supportive of WTS and expressed HWH's desire to see him return to active duty soon. Earlier, HWH had answered EES's letter to him of December 12, saying, "I perceive that the newspapers, not satisfied with abusing me, have turned upon your husband," and that, with rest, WTS would soon be able to resume his duties. HWH to EES, December 14, 1861, DLC: WTS. Privately, Halleck wrote to his wife the same day that "I enclose a letter just received from Mrs. Sherman. How do you suppose I answered it? I would not say her husband was *not* crazy, for certainly he has acted insane." HWH to Elizabeth Hamilton Halleck, December 14, 1861, MiU-C: James S. Schoff Civil War Collection.

3. Captain John Henry Hammond (1833–90), USA, was on WTS's staff.

TO THOMAS EWING SR.

Head-Quarters, Camp of Instruction,
Benton Barracks, (near St. Louis, Mo.,)
Dec. 24 1861

Hon. T. Ewing
Dear Sir

I yesterday received your letter for which I am thankful.[1] To begin an action for libel would warrant the searching of records and stirring up matters which I cannot properly explain, that I prefer delaying—events must transpire in such succession that mere libel suits will sink into insignificance. I was convinced in Kentucky that I could not guide events, that I either grossly misapprehended them or was unprepared to lead in them. To guide I had not the faith which would inspire success. To continue in such a position would have been unjust to the thousands [of] brave men who [have] confidence in their Leadership. As long as we are on Southern ground they have an advantage that we cannot overcome without a complete destruction of all the inhabitants. Instead of making converts it seems the reverse, a perfect streak of secessionists marks our progress—and all they have to do is to leave us exhaust ourselves. I dont find fault with the administration—they have done their best, all that is possible—same of the President no one doubts his purpose to be national & conservative, but I have desired to keep back, because I cannot see any possible solution for our political troubles. I did not warrant the Publication in the Gazette, on the Contrary I would prefer absolute silence, though that I cannot expect.[2] I also hope the President may avoid the threatened war with England, for we have more enemies now than we can handle.[3] I have been assigned to duty here at Benton Barracks where there is a large body of men but partially armed & equipped, and whom we are preparing for service as fast as possible. Gen. Halleck proposes to keep the army active all winter. There will be much Suffering & Some deaths resulting from it, but I suppose it is unavoidable. Tell Ellen I will write to her tomorrow. With great respect

W. T. Sherman

ALS, DLC: Thomas Ewing and Family Papers.

1. Thomas Ewing Sr. to WTS, December 22, 1861, SFP, advised WTS to sue the news-papers for libel.

2. P. B. Ewing had written to the *Cincinnati Commercial* and *Gazette* on December 12, refuting the charges of insanity and offering two statements of support from Halleck through his adjutant as supporting evidence. John F. Marszalek, *Sherman's Other War: The General and the Civil War Press* (Memphis, 1981), 71 and 91 n. 34.

3. A reference to the *Trent* affair of late 1861, in which an Anglo-American crisis growing out of the seizure of two Confederate diplomats aboard a English mail packet by Captain Charles Wilkes, USN, was defused when the Lincoln administration disavowed the act and freed the diplomats.

TO JOHN SHERMAN

> Head-Quarters, Camp of Instruction,
> Benton Barracks, (near St. Louis, Mo.,)
> Dec. 24, 1861

Dear Brother,

I have received your letter, and assure you that I feel deeply the stain I may have cast on you all, of my name. I did wish and yet have a faint hope that I may keep obscure in this awful war. If we could meet openly on fair ground each with one issue it would be different, but we stand in the nature of invaders—tis not time I admit, but the South has this advantage and they use it, that I fear the result. At all events I have not the faith for a leader. You Know I felt so as to Kentucky and how I was placed so, and had to resort to a pretext to escape. For me personally it would have been better to have remained but I did not want to impress the men who went thither openly & frankly with my apprehensions. I did believe and Still believe a vast majority of the People of Kentucky are Southern Rights or secession, and will manifest their determina-tion in due time. They also have a larger force under arms than the Depart-ment will believe. Why they delay action I dont know—Buell has double my force and yet he can do nothing. As to affairs in Kentucky & my connection with them I feel little concern, but I do fear though the Committee in the House they will fix on me more than my share in the Bull Run disaster. I was with my Brigade until after the fighting was over and then I became separated, and my motive may be misconstrued, and in connection with my leaving the Kentucky Command at a critical moment may overwhelm me. I of course cannot shift the responsibility and must bear it. I would like to have you watch the operations of that committee and give me early notice if they compromise me. In Missouri I find things black enough all my old friends are now against us not openly, but really—We have possession of St. Louis and the Railroads, but the Secessionists have the Country. They have destroyed the North Mis-souri R. R. and will in time the others.[1] These R. Roads are the weakest things in war a single man with a match can destroy a bridge & cut off communication, and no one seems to apprehend the danger by laying in supplies accordingly. Halleck thinks he can catch the perpetrators & punish them as they merit. I hope so—He has placed me in charge of Benton Barracks where there are about 12,000 men, mostly awaiting arms. These will be drilled supplied and Sent forward as the service calls for them. Winter has at last set in and will test the endurance of men & animals.

All I ask & hope for is to be allowed to remain in as much obscurity as possible till we see some issue some hope of ending the war—I hope the administration will avoid if possible the threatened war with England. We have enough in all conscience now in hand. God Knows, I hope you will continue to advance & prosper in lifes Course. affectionately

W. T. Sherman

ALS, DLC: William T. Sherman.

1. The city of St. Louis and all railroads operating in Missouri were placed under martial law on December 26 to prevent further damage.

TO ELLEN EWING SHERMAN

Head-Quarters, Camp of Instruction,
Benton Barracks, (near St. Louis, Mo.,)
Jan. 1, 1862

Dearest Ellen,

Again have I failed to write to you as I promised. Again have I neglected the almost only remaining chain of love & affection that should bind me to earth. I have attempted to write several times but feared to add to the feelings that already bear on you heavily too heavily. Could I live over the past year I think I would do better, but my former associations with the South have rendered me almost crazy as one by one all links of hope were parted. We have seen a Specimen of the Same disorder which prevail elsewhere, a mass of men partly organized and badly disciplined, with their thousand & one wants. But this is nothing to the fact that I am here in a subordinate place whilst others occupy posts that I ought to. I cannot claim them for having so signally failed in Kentucky and here I could not demand a higher place.

Buell I see reports his command a mere mob, and has now to begin to discipline them, in an enemys country, and when everybody is clamorous for action. If I could see the least ray of hope for this combination I would still struggle.

I am about in the same state of health as when at Lancaster but the idea of having brought disgrace on all associated with me is so horrible to contemplate that I cannot really endure it.

I will try & be more punctual in future in writing you my Dearest wife who has been true & noble and generous & comforting always. That She should thus be repaid is too bad—and our Dear Children—may God in his mercy keep them in his mind, and not let them Suffer for my faults. Prices army has again retired south, but I see no end—even of a decline in the secession feeling here. We had men under arms all last night expecting to be called out, but nothing happened. I have not heard from you for some days—in your last you asked me to answer about sending the children to Notre Dame I think you had better keep them near you always, but you know best—Bless you and keep you as their guide till they care for themselves. yrs.

W. T. Sherman

ALS, InND: Sherman Family Papers.

TO JOHN SHERMAN

Head-Quarters, Camp of Instruction,
Benton Barracks, (near St. Louis, Mo.,)
Jan. 4, 1862

Dear Brother,

I am so sensible now of my disgrace from having exaggerated the force of our enemy in Kentucky that I do think I Should have committed suicide were it not for my children. I do not think that I can again be entrusted with a command—Buell remarked to me in Kentucky that I should be Qr. Mr. Genl.—this I do not think though I do believe myself better qualified for a Disbursing Department—Suppose you see McClellan and ask him if I could not serve the Government better in such a capacity than the one I now hold. I do not feel confident at all in Volunteers. Their want of organization, the necessity to flatter them &c. is such that I cannot prosper with them. Telegraph me what you think and would do—affectionately

W. T. Sherman

ALS, DLC: William T. Sherman.

TO JOHN SHERMAN

Benton Barracks, January 8, 1862

Hon. J. Sherman
My Dear Brother,

I am just in receipt of your letter and hasten to answer.

As soon as Anderson left me in Command and the Secretary of War visited Louisiana, I went to Camp Dick Robinson where I found Thomas in command of Two Tennessee Regiments Two Kentucky Regiments and two Ohio—One Indiana, & Ohio Regiment were in advance near Rockcastle River, with

Garrards Kentucky Regt.[1] which I ordered to be reinforced to meet Zollicoffers advance which they did.

The Kentucky & Tennessee Troops were very badly clad & armed, and Thomas was embarrassed by the fact that the clothing contractors in Cincinati & Columbus would not supply the clothing without pay in advance. I then had a full and free conversation with Mr. Maynard—acting Brig. Genl. Carter[2] and a Col. Byrd[3] of the Tennessee Regiment, and the latter was emphatic that less than 10,000 men could not undertake an expedition into East Tennessee. At the time we had no arms at all and Ten thousand men could not be had. The Kentuckyans were enlisting very slowly indeed, and in fact it was not until the 10th of November that they were consolidated. Small fragments scattered all over the State, not enough to hold in check the Secession Sentiment of their localities. At this time the Confederates were gathering in strength South of Green River and their friends boasted they would be in Louisville in a few days at that time we could not have opposed to them 5000 men in front of Louisville and had they taken that place, what would have been the fate of the East Tennessee expedition. All Reinforcements as they came and they came very slowly had to be thrown in front of Louisville. Until Kentucky is safe beyond peradventure it is folly of attempting East Tennessee. To have depended upon a vast uprising then would have been of little avail with our then indifferent supply of arms. I Know how anxious Johnson[,] Maynard and others were to attempt East Tennessee but at no time had I a force at all adequate for such purpose. Nothing would have pleased the Confederates more than to have seen a vast force cross that mountain, dependant on the road behind for supplies. When Thomas was at London he reported the roads so bad that he could not subsist his men there much longer and the Confederate force was withdrawn from the gap and moved towards Somerset[.] I believe that Thomas could have crossed by Cumberland Gap, but he would never have returned. Tis out of the question to carry men so far with such a country behind as Kentucky then was and now is.

Buell when he reached Louisville said that it was all the talk in Washington, the East Tennessee expedition, but the moment he understood the position of affairs he declared it absurd to think of and directed the whole forces over in the direction of Bowling Green.

The occupation of Knoxville today would not materially benefit our cause in Kentucky[.] They draw no troops or supplies from that direction now—at Bowling Green meet two roads for Nashville & Memphis, with the Branch to Columbus, Ky. This is their triangle and it is almost unassailable. They have a common gauge of track, and can run cars indiscriminately on one road or the other, and can assemble the troops at Columbus or Bowling Green at pleasure—This latter point is their Key and I did not at any time have half their force at this one point. Why they did not advance on Louisville has always surprised me, and I am convinced that it was because they prefer to draw on forces further from the River, and from Louisville. Buell has now three or four times my force and he is slow to attack, and I do not blame him. He must be certain before he attacks Bowling Green or passes by it. Their strength in men is no greater than when I was there, but their forts no doubt are. Indeed now his advance must be attended with one in force on either side by Glasgow, and from Henderson or Hopkinsville & Russellville. Neither of these columns should be less than 10,000 men, and he should have 50,000 besides very large support along the Railroad—He cannot feed & maintain so large a force without that Railroad and it will be attacked in his Rear, before he attacks or is attacked.

I am fully conscious that in surrendering that command I confessed my inability to manage it—This is mortifying but true—I think it better that Buell should have it as he has more nerve, but I do think the War Department and McClellan should give him some of his better disciplined troops and more experienced officers, for that command cannot make a retrograde step it must go on, and cannot expect to reach or destroy till it strikes the Mississipi, and then should the River above be closed as now at Columbus he is also gone. These thoughts so bore on me that they broke me down and I am not yet recovered.

As to East Tennessee the proportion of Union men there is not equal to the other element, and any attacking force would be increased in size in less proportion that the opposition for distance is to be considered, and every march forward compels detachments and escorts to wagon trains, and as to their supplying an army sent to their assistance I have not the least faith our experience in Kentucky was quite the reverse. The Union element never aided in that way at all, indeed they would not even for pay have forage into camp least their action would be marked & quoted against them. We had to Send wagons for forage to their farms and pay the highest price, and that Such would have been the case in Tennessee I have not a particle of doubt, but if called on for a reason for the non attempt of an invasion of East Tennessee I would say that until Kentucky is sure & safe it is not proper to advance beyond, unless the Commander has force enough for both purposes. I say I never had enough or anything approximate and the proof is that Buell with a vastly superior force is now only one days march in advance of my advance, and that too without any increase of opposition—I may have urged in improper terms the importance of the Line of the Ohio, which I still esteem of more importance than that of the Potomac. If the Confederates have the Ohio

River, and they now possess it from Henderson to Paducah, and Columbus almost impregnable they will dictate terms to the North West.

It is easy enough for you politicians to Sit and calculate what men should do, but this force in the West has been half armed and increased little by little so that at no one time could we pretend to have superior numbers. Halleck has nominally 8000 in Missouri and Price has maybe only 10,000, but Price has the People of the Country with him and all of Hallecks force is dispersed to guard Railroads not disturbed by armies but by the People, and this is their game, and he cannot help himself and just so it was and is in Kentucky—The secession feeling of the People shows itself in Such a way that you Know it exists and yet you cannot touch it—We all know here that in St. Louis with its 150,000 population, ⅔ are secessionists, and all the famous who stay at home send their sons around with horses & equipments to the war whilst they are quiet Union People—It is this element that is more difficult to handle than the organized armies. I keep very close here, being under a cloud, but I see enough to Satisfy me that the People are against us, some from Southern Connexions and many from self interest—the South holding the River, and the River being the life of the Country. Could we open the navigation of the Mississipi this Class would be loyal enough, but as we cant, they follow the successful party. The southerners have fortified Columbus, Hickman Chalk bluff, and New Madrid so that the Gun boats at Cairo could not even attempt, or if allowed to pass could not return. To carry these Forts a large land force is indispensable, and where is it—Halleck now could not detach from Missouri 10,000 men— and from the garrison of Paducah, Cairo & Birds Point might collect another 10,000, but we know in Columbus alone they have 22,000 men—besides the garrisons of Chalk Bluff & Hickman. I dont believe an expedition down the River will be attempted this winter, and it is for this reason that the wishes of the North, and their habit of self flattery makes them believe that we really have an army of 600,000—Where are they? McClellan has the largest, and he has the advantage of his forts. Kentucky is our weakest point, and Missouri a weak flank. The Confederates fortify, stand fast and public opinion forces us to the attack: The longer Halleck & Buell (and they have as much nerve as any body) pause the more they will hesitate, until Sheer desperation may make them commit rash suicide. All that Halleck can attempt from this quarter is to protect his Railroads, make a dash at Springfield, a diversion about Cairo to help Buell, and defend St. Louis. He will not attempt to descend the Mississippi. I doubt if McClellan will attempt Manassas, and Buell may reach Bowling Green but I doubt it—Why should I then be questioned about taking East Tennessee, when at no time did I have a fourth part of the army of either, and yet had opposed to me armies that had been prepared long in advance and were ready to enter Kentucky before Indiana or Ohio had a Regiment prepared? I may and doubtless have exaggerated the amount of opposition, but why do not others prove that I am mistaken. The South keeps her counsels, has no newspapers to blight every movement by timely notice, but on the contrary to deny every man, and every motive, that does not minister to their enmity. No one will rejoice more than I if Buell prove the fallacy of my judgment, that the Confederates have not the force I estimated. Let him swell his ranks as he may, if Columbus is not at the Same time threatened, when he gets to Bowling Green there will he find a superior force, at home, with two Railroads to bring forward reinforcements & Supplies, whilst he will have to guard his rear by at least ⅓ his whole force. The disadvantage is terrific, and even now I sometimes think a safe line of attack would be from Henderson on Hopkinsville & Russelville, but this would swell his force up to two hundred thousand that I was ridiculed for suggesting. If Kentucky is cleaned of armed, organized Forces, say nothing of its secession population, by an army of less than 200,000 then will I give my head.

At the outset in Kentucky we were forced into the most unmilitary operation—these divergent lines, farther & farther apart every day. Nelson to the East Thomas to the South East and McCook to the S. West. Our opponents had only to let these breaches widen to ensure failure. Twas this realization that made me so urgent for strong forces. Each column should have been self maintaining, and it was to bring them closer together that I ordered Nelson after dispersing the enemy at Prestonburg to Paris or its vicinity and Thomas towards Danville. This movement just preceded Buells' advent to Kentucky and enabled him to mass his forces in part of Lebanon & Louisville within supporting distance. I feel full well that in so doing I have sacrificed myself and this would be nothing if it ultimately result in good to the Government. When at Dick Robinson I met a Mr. Carter⁴ brother of Genl. Carter who was empowered to destroy Bridges in East Tennessee by the highest authority, I did think it proper at the time as the impression was universal that forces would be drawn from Eastern and Northern Virginia over that line of Railroad, but when the Bridges were burned, the Enemy had accumulated such strength at Bowling Green, Clarksville & Hopkinsville that I could not risk the whole state of Kentucky by allowing Thomas to go over the Mountain at the then season of the year October.

Supposing Thomas had advanced with say 10,000 leaving his Detachments to protect Depots he would have been two hundred miles from Nicholasville, when a very inconsiderable force could have advanced from about Johnstown & Somerset, cut off his trains & communication, and he could not have advanced or fallen back, without almost certain destruction. I thought of this as well, and I could not find in my judgment a warrant for it. I also endeavored to procure the best information from East Tennessee, and whilst there appeared no doubt that Union feeling there remained, still it was of that passive Kind that would only have acted on a conviction that the occupation of East Tennessee by the Union forces would be permanent, and that was impossible so long as Kentucky was in that doubtful attitude. The only possible way to hold Kentucky is and was to drive out the organized forces under Johnston, Buckner[,] Polk,[5] Pillow[6] & So on, and I did not have the force, nor is the force now surely adequate. One single repulse and all falls. The secession feeling which pervades the community will lie dormant till such a repulse which God forbid, when they will rise up & commit havoc. The restoration of the Union can only occur after this feeling on the part of the People subsides, and that it will never do unless great success attend our armies. These are composed of good men, good farmers & mechanics, but men not accustomed to restraint, who do pretty much as they please. They commit acts of trespass & violence along the Roads and convert Union men into Enemies, so that nothing is gained by the advance of an army, but its effect upon the object arrived at. In Kentucky several such acts occurred which could not be punished and yet tended to alienate the People: some here in Missouri where there are ten Secessionists where there used to be one. Why this should be so is a mystery when we know that the secessionists are more wanton in their destruction of property & life than our People are, but so it is. Farmers submit tamely to their taking of wagons horses, grain &c., when in our case it would cause a hue & cry.

What distresses me most is that you and Ellen and my children should suffer from my disgrace. Could I alone atone for it there would be some chance of endurance, but I know full well hundreds and thousands who have been my friends will attribute to me the most unworthy motives, and then would adjudge it against my children. They are young, innocent and good, and tis hard they Should suffer for my want of endurance mental & physical[.] It makes me almost crazy to think of them. You can defend yourself by your life & talents, but they are helpless—You must in after years think of them.

Also at Louisville I smoked too many segars & drank somewhat because of the nervous anxiety about matters which seemed to me beyond my control. I ought to have endured and then would have been responsible only for my part, whereas by giving up the command I not only confessed my inability to manage affairs entrusted to me, but placed the burden on other shoulders. Still Buell can and will do far better than I could, and the country gains by the Change.

I have lived so much at the South, and have made my personal friends among them that I no doubt have overrated not only the intensity of their feeling, but their strength, at the Same time doubting that of the North—One thing is certain they are in earnest and our people have been actuated by rather the conviction of judgment and reason, which never can compete with the intensity of feeling.

The Burning of the Bridges in East Tennessee was done under the direction of a Mr. Carter, with Mr. Maynards Knowledge and sanction of the President[.] I approved of it and coincident with the occurrence Thomas' Column was to have entered East Tennessee, but the pressure was so great on Green River and the plan so manifest & feasible to get between Thomas and Lexington whereby his whole command would be endangered that I did not order the movement, especially because at the time Ohio & Indiana were unarmed and Regiments were offering slowly—Before this Ohio troops were ready at Cincinati the season was too far advanced to attempt it—That the men employed on that occasion should have suffered death has been the chief source of my despondency as I may be mainly responsible for it. I did not engage Mr. Carter. He had come from Washington direct for the purpose and communicated to me in Gen. Thomas' quarters—but that after Wildcat it was not followed up was my act, because I thought the risk to that command and to Kentucky was too great—Hardee having made his juncture with Buckner and Pillow having sent reinforcements to Bowling Green from the direction of Clarksville, with the clear purpose of moving on Lexington, a thing we could not then have prevented.

The fact that these men were executed, and the principle being established here also, implicates me and I cannot escape the consequences. In Kentucky it weighed on me so that I felt unequal to the burden, and gave it up. This horrid Civil War has turned human nature wrong side out. Never could I suppose that I would have done any act of such a nature and would not have done so under ordinary circumstances, but the destruction of that Road was universally desired, talked of and written about, till one's mind became familiar to it, and it seemed as a matter of course.

Our enemies also had burned every bridge that lay between Louisville & Bowling Green and used every possible means to obstruct our advance, at Rolling Fork, Bacon Creek and Green River.

AL (incomplete), DLC: William T. Sherman.

1. Theophilus T. Garrard (1812–1902) was colonel of the Seventh Kentucky at the time.

2. Samuel P. Carter (1819–91) was organizing and drilling Tennessee volunteers for the Union.

3. Robert K. Byrd (1822–85), a farmer, politician, and Mexican War veteran, had organized and commanded the First Tennessee Infantry.

4. Rev. William B. Carter had a plan to stop railroad service in Confederate East Ten-

nessee by burning railroad bridges; on the night of November 8, 1861, Unionists following his plans burned nine bridges and ruined five more. When no Federal troops arrived to follow up on their actions, the Confederates stepped in quickly, imposing martial law and rounding up the Unionists and charging them with treason. Several bridge burners were hanged, and others became Confederate prisoners of war. At this time, authorities were beginning to question whether Carter had used the Federal funds given to him to arm and equip the bridge burners or kept them for himself.

5. Major General Leonidas Polk (1806–64), CSA.

6. Gideon J. Pillow (1806–78) was a brigadier general in the Confederate army. At the end of 1861, he had resigned his commission, although he returned to service at the end of January 1862.

TO JOHN SHERMAN

Head-Quarters, Camp of Instruction,
Benton Barracks, (near St. Louis, Mo.,)
Jan. 9, 1862

Dear Brother,

I have received your letter, and will give you what you ask the reasons why I ordered Genl. Thomas to fall back from London towards Danville or Kentucky River. Thomas had his advance in front of London, Schoepfs Brigade at London and he was at Crab Orchard—all the stores for the command had to be hauled from Nicholasville. The country was very barren of Forage, and roads beyond Crab Orchard were very bad. Thomas reported that Gen. Zollicoffer had obstructed the roads into East Tennessee and had moved westward as far as Jacksboro and I knew he would make his appearance in front of Somerset which he did, uniting his force of about 5000 to Stantons of about 2500, giving his a column of 7500 men on a good road leading north to Lexington. It was necessary to move Thomas to check this. Had Zollicoffer alone to have been watched the movement would have been directly to Somerset: but at the same time I had information that Gen. Hardee had left Bowling Green with his Division of 8000 men with a full supply of country wagons to the East, towards Columbia from which point there is a good road to Lexington. I inferred their plan to be as I doubt not it was to join these two columns on the Lexington Road, and therefore Thomas force was required at some point common to the two roads, viz. about Stamford, Danville or the Kentucky River Bridge, where he could act on the defense or offense as the case might be. The Lines of operation from Nicholasville were long & weak and there was at all times danger that a superior force would interpose between Thomas and his Base, and I was satisfied that our Enemies had at Bowling Green enough to send such a force, and we had not enough to make Detachments from the Louisville Line. The fact was our force in Kentucky was ridiculously weak for such an extent of country. My orders to Thomas pointed out the danger of this force getting between him & Lexington and for him to fall back to some point near Danville, and afterwards I notified him of my information that the anticipated movement had been reported from Columbia.

The distance was not great, but it so happened that the weather was very bad and the retrograde was made too rapidly. Of course I do not wish to throw on Thomas any blame but must bear it myself. That this movement on Lexington was contemplated then I am well satisfied, and that some cause interposed, I am also well satisfied. At London Thomas was beyond all reach of succor from Louisville, whereas at Danville I could have reinforced him from Lebanon.

A great deal of feeling always existed about succor to the Union People in East Tennessee, but at no time did I have a force adequate to that expedition[.] The road was long, and Supplies would have had to go along. Thomas wanted in addition to his then command, four Regiments and they could not be spared from the Louisville Line. The moment Buell arrived he expressed his surprise that in Washington they still dwelt on that idea of an expedition into East Tennessee when we were far from safe in Kentucky. The strength of the enemy was along the Railroad from Mumfordsville Green River to Clarksville, and in one body near Bowling Green from 20 to 25,000 men of whom we had full accounts. This force in October collected a large number of wagons & drivers and the intention was to advance on Louisville, the possession of which would have given them the control of the Ohio River. It was on this Line that I grouped our forces, and Buell has done the same. Though he has more than double my command he has not advanced but 23 miles, and I doubt still if he can from the position of Bowling Green. He may pass Bowling Green and get on the Railroad beyond forcing them out, but he cannot advance on Nashville till Bowling Green is broken up. I always attached importance to the local feeling of the Country, it may be more than it merited, but that the People of Kentucky are friendly to the Southern Confederacy I still believe, and upon the least check to our forces there the People will manifest that result by breaking up Railroads and doing all sorts of damage in the rear of the army.

By giving up command in Kentucky I acknowledged my inability to manage the case, and I do think Buell can manage better than I could, and if he succeeds he will deserve all honor, but I do think it is wrong to push him on that Line whilst the army at Washington remains comparatively inert. McClellan has taken all the Regular officers and compels Buell to rely on the Colonels of Regiments. They are all full of Zeal, but if overthrown into Confusion there will be no restoring order. The army in Kentucky should be the largest and best appointed of any in the Field, for it is the Grand Center, and our enemies can assemble there a larger force than at any other point, because at Bowling Green meet two principal Roads, connecting the entire South. All have the same Gauge, and cars run on one or the other at pleasure. This gives them the facility of collecting troops from Columbus, Memphis, Nashville, Georgia and Virginia. They have the River unobstructed up as far as Columbus and therefore are better Supplied than their Virginia army, and before Buell ventures to advance beyond Green River he must be assured of the Safety of Henderson, Louisville & Cincinati the three points from which he draws supplies. If possible coincident with his movement some demonstration should be made on Columbus from which otherwise reinforcements will go just as they did in the Manassas affair. Now Halleck has in Missouri about 80,000 men on paper, and there are not in an organized shape more than 10 or 20,000 opposed to him. Yet the country is full of secessionists and it takes all his command to watch them. This is an element which Politicians have never given full credit to. These local secessionists are really more dangerous than if assembled in one or more bodies, for they could be traced out & found whereas now they are scattered on farms and are very peaceable, but when a Bridge is to be burned they are about. I dont know how this is to be prevented except by moving bodily the Inhabitants of Iowa, & Wisconsin down on the Farms of Missouri, and removing the present population, for imprisonment, as oaths wont change their opinions, and at the first opportunity this will manifest itself. It is far worse in Missouri now than last spring. Many who were then Union men are secessionist now, from interest all their trade being with the South and that is now broken up—I see but little of the People now. I purposely keep close, for my friends now here are all on the other Side. I did then think that they preferred the Union, and such was the case, but now they pretend that the Break in the Country is complete, and when at liberty to choose they choose the South because of the Mississipi River. I cannot but think that even if this Rebellion prevails it will assume new phases, whereby other interests besides Slavery will be experienced, for I notice that many who dont care about Slavery are against us on other grounds such as Mercantile Interests, family connexions &c. I suppose you still think we can actually subjugate the South. Had Kentucky, Tennessee & Missouri been firm & steadfast I would have believed it possible, but now I cannot see how it is to be done, unless the People of the North actually obliterate all in their progress south and fill up by settlement. As long as the present population exists so long will these States be convulsed with Civil War.

I wish I could take another view of this war, but I cannot. It thrusts itself on me from every side, and yet I hope I am mistaken.

With this feeling of course my energy of action is almost paralized, and I fear to open my mouth, or do anything, and if I could slide into a place where I would have only work to do I would do it without pay or compensation, rather than lead large bodies of men to probably imaginary dangers. Halleck has been successful thus far and I hope may continue, but he cannot by mere written papers cope with Price who is in the Field, bothered by no paper or accounts, taking what he can lay his hands on. I think he has orders to move down the River but the moment he moves a man from the Interior to go to Cairo, Price will return. That is his game, and in that way with a comparatively Small force he holds in check five times his number. I have the charge of this camp of instruction—about 12,000 men of all arms, but still deficient in pistols and arms. They are all raw & green and the weather is and has been very bad for drill, and we have a great number of sick from measles & Pneumonia. Indeed sickness is universal in all the Camps[.] That East Tennessee expedition is bound to ruin all who undertake it until Kentucky is absolutely safe. I never would Sanction it in advance of the reduction of Bowling Green and Columbus and anybody who does will sacrifice the whole command, and that too needlessly. No doubt Johnson, Maynard and all are very anxious for it, and that impairs their judgment. When Kentucky is free of Rebels if ever, then the loyal People of East Tennessee can be relieved and not before. The better line to enter Tennessee is by Somerset. I think that Thomas and Buell will agree with me in that, and during my time we had not enough force to stand fast much less advance into Tennessee.

I blame nobody, during this awful civil war—all I say is that an expedition into East Tennessee with my force was impossible. The retreat from London was not designed as a retreat but to Shift the position to another point to meet an expected Contingency which did not happen—If anybody can do better than I can for God's sake let them. I prefer to follow not to lead, as I confess I have not the confidence of a Leader in this war, and would be happy to slide into obscurity. affectionately,

W. T. Sherman

ALS, DLC: William T. Sherman.

TO ELLEN EWING SHERMAN

Benton Barracks, Jan. 11, 1862

Dearest Ellen,

I received your letter of Jan. 8, and could I feel as I used to would feel proud of the allusions.[1] I was very sorry that Elly's eyes are yet sore, and that Lizzy is afflicted as you describe. Poor child, I would not grieve that so innocent a child should Sleep in Calm and innocent death. This world is so convulsed that happiness can be in store for but few, and for ours I feel an intense solicitude. Oh that I could remove the past few months. I know and feel that I stand disgraced by surrendering my command in Kentucky, deservedly so, and I cannot recover from it. It is past hope. Here I can do some service, but not such as was expected of me. Four Regiments are now under orders from here to Cairo, from which point a feint is to be made on Columbus to divert attention from Bowling Green on which Buell is moving in force. I still think his forces are too raw and weak to assail so strong a place, but the pressure on him is so great that he must go on.

Here in Missouri though Price has fallen back towards Arkansas the Secessionists do not feel discouraged for they say reinforcements are coming to him from the South which I believe is so. Another element of discord has also arisen among the German Regiments here, who are so obstinate and dogged that they dictate their own terms. Some of the companies have been disarmed, and many others should be. You know the character of these Germans, and how almost impossible it is to reason with them. Halleck was very much disturbed by this. I inquired for Phil at the Planters house but he was not there. I left word for him to come out here. We have a street Railroad.

I prefer you should not come I will make an effort to get into the Field, but I hardly think they will ever entrust me with a command again. I cannot blame them. My advice is for you to live quietly and as comfortably as you can in Ohio where you are—not to Spend a cent where you can help it and so to manage that in case of accident to me you can live for a few years trusting in that Providence that watches the poor and oppressed. I know I take a gloomy view of things and could not otherwise, but I should stand up to it like a brave man and perish if need be. Feeling thus I could not remain as a leader, and in so doing have committed the fatal mistake for let what come may success or failure, neither but will add to my humiliation. For you I feel most Keenly, and when the figures of Minnie & Lizzie & Willy stand before me I feel as though I should cast myself into the Mississipi. I saw last night a letter your father had written to Halleck about the treatment of Railroad prisoners I know Halleck esteems your father above all other men, and he will be guided by his advice. Some may be hung or shot, and others allowed to go with the news to their comrades, whilst others are held as hostages for the Safety of the Roads. This will be the wisest possible course, but will not stop them. These Rebels are banded together and will destroy the Country and lay it waste rather than See it pass into the possession of the Yankees. Some Bridge Burners have been arrested, tried and convicted, though their Sanction is not public[.] I had a letter from John and I have written to him why I did not order an expedition to East Tennessee. We did not have force enough to attempt it, for the enemy was collecting in too great strength in South Kentucky to justify detaching to the mountains a force large enough to reach Tennessee, nor had we arms to Send them—every thing came so slowly that the Season was passed before means were provided. Still all will fall on me, and I will be held responsible that a brave people did not receive the succor they had reason to expect. affectionately

W. T. Sherman

ALS, InND: Sherman Family Papers.

1. EES to WTS, January 8, 1862, SFP. EES wrote assuring WTS of the family's love for him and pride in his accomplishments: "You *could not* disgrace anyone for you could not do a dishonorable action." Nonetheless, she was afraid that his depression would degenerate into the melancholy that had so affected his uncle Charles Hoyt. She reported on the children's health, expressed her wish to visit him, and added that current public opinion about WTS in Ohio and the East was positive.

TO PHILEMON B. EWING

Head-Quarters, Camp of Instruction,
Benton Barracks, (near St. Louis, Mo.,)
Jan. 20 1862

Dear Phil,

I went to the city today, drew my pay for December, and now send you a check for $300 to be placed to her credit. I have a letter from her, saying she was just starting for Washington. She wants to get me away from St. Louis influence.[1] I have no doubt I have been much biased by my association with Southern people, and that in consequence I have overrated their power. I certainly have not their temper and purpose—There is not power enough in this country to change that. Of course I am fully conscious now of grave errors, but I am not fit for a leader in such a war, and have from the first desired to keep in the background. Our camp is one field of mud, deep & black & drill is impossible—Give my love to Mary and children.[2] Affectionately,

W. T. Sherman

ALS, New York: FORBES Magazine Collection.

1. On January 13, EES wrote WTS that she was leaving soon for Washington with her father. She assured him, "I did not ask you dear Cump to discontinue your visits to the Turner's because they were Secessionists—but *for your own sake*. I am not willing to release you from your promise. . . . You could not go into Mrs. Turner's presence without hearing what I would not listen to or hear, and what no Army officer ought to hear without resenting. It gives your enemies power to injure you & they are on the *qui vive* for any indiscretion or apparent fault. It has already been hinted in the papers that you are more friendly to Secessionists than to Union people." If Turner could see clearly, she continued, he would realize that his invitations endangered WTS's reputation. SFP.

2. Mary Gillespie Ewing was Philemon's wife. Their children at this time were Thomas (b. 1850), Mary Agnes (b. 1851), Eleanor (b. 1853), George (b. 1855), John Gillespie (b. 1858),

Francis Cointet (b. 1859), and Mary Rebecca (b. 1861). Thomas, known as Tommy, was one of Willy Sherman's best friends.

TO ELLEN EWING SHERMAN

Benton Barracks, Jan. 29, 1862

Dearest Ellen,

I received last night your letter from Washington and do feel ashamed that I should have telegraphed to John to prevent your being indiscreet.[1] The idea is absurd—with such a load of indiscretion on my own shoulders that I should caution you against it. Turner is simply indifferent about the angry causes that now inflame the minds of men—Like most army officers his associates were of that class which has tainted us all more or less—I certainly have not the Same character I would have had, had I not lived so much in the South, and experienced so much of their peculiar hospitality—I also wanted to Keep out of the war and Knew the first set would be swept away in the tempest of passion besides in Louisiana I said I would keep in the background, and before I was aware of it I found myself in the prominent position in Kentucky. I ought to have called about me the best men I could find and trust to events, but I was overwhelmed, smoked too much and when Thomas' letter came out I felt so discouraged that I asked relief—It looks to me very different now—Although I would not resume the plan for the world—but being in it I should have staid. The war there has not yet begun. The fight at Somerset was a rare piece of good fortune, and I hope more such will attend us, for without them the People would turn against us.[2] I think I cannot be mistaken in that. But I will not philosophize on these points—I have sent off several Regiments from here lately and would be happy to follow—I have not seen Mr. Lucas, Patterson or Turner for a long time, and it does seem hard—If our side wins of course they are with us, if their side wins then also tis well for us to have old friends—Of course I do not expect to survive the war. I dont expect any of us save the children and would it not be wise for me to leave them at least some friends— Bowman[3] was here yesterday, spent the day and went up to Charleys on business—he was full of his praises of you, yr. father and all—his Regiment is down at Cairo in the mud, and he wants to get away, anywheres, to Kentucky—all want to go to Kentucky and Sure enough there is where all should go. My limit will still be reached before a Blow is struck at Columbus or Bowling Green.

Poor Lizzie. How I would like to lie us down together in that common grave and sleep the long sleep of Eternity—with the manifold ills that might burden me down I would feel safe with her gentle spirit. I should not feel cast down at all were I to hear that poor Lizzie had gone to Heaven, for if she go not there there is no such place. My thoughts fly back to the time when a baby I used to toss her at our place on Stockton and Green Streets—and ever do I recall her look when you came back to California, and frightened Willy by the excess of affection—Scenes long since vanished thus rise up, and all which Little Lizzie leaning dependent on her mother, her nurse or on me, gentle soft and affectionate—Oh but this Damned world is too rude for her. Let her pass gently away and Should it so happen I would ask no greater favor than to sleep by her side. I dont know why it is, but I feel towards her different from our other children—All others seem more of the world, and I somehow or other think they will get along, but Lizzie is different and in my heart I shall grieve but little when I know she is gone, only I hope my time will be measured by hers.

I sent you some money, and caution you again & again about Economy. The time is fast approaching when Govt. will no longer pay for any thing except what cannot be had without money—already is Govt. in debt here 8 millions, and I hear the same all round the Country. What will be done when money & credit are exhausted I know not will our people fight without pay, or can families live without money. Hold on to what you have, and go to the country when money is gone. as ever yours

W. T. Sherman

ALS, InND: Sherman Family Papers.

1. On January 10, EES had written Lincoln to ask him to vindicate her husband. She implied that Lorenzo Thomas was responsible for his downfall. DLC: WTS. She sent a copy of this letter to JS on January 13 and wrote an accompanying letter which expressed her intention to go to Washington to meet with the president. DLC: WTS. On January 22 she wrote to her husband that "we hope and *believe* that things will soon take a turn most *agreeable and advantageous to you.*" SFP. The next day, she wrote WTS again, saying that JS had brought her "the telegraphic dispatch" and said, "I hope you do not fear I will behave ridiculously here. I have not yet done anything myself or seen anyone but John Sherman. Father wished me to wait until he had seen the Sec. of War." She was staying on in the city at her father's request but was very worried about Lizzie's health and was convinced the child would soon die. SFP.

2. The Union victory at Mill Springs near Somerset, Kentucky, on January 19, resulted in the first break in the Confederates' defensive lines across that state.

3. Samuel M. Bowman (1815–85), a California lawyer, was currently a major in the Fourth Illinois Cavalry.

TO JOHN SHERMAN

Head-Quarters, Camp of Instruction,
Benton Barracks, (near St. Louis, Mo.,)
Feb. 3, 1862

Dear Brother,

I was in the city yesterday and learned from General Halleck that a move was on foot to appoint Genl. Hitchcock a Major General, but that Congress being in Session the appointment could not be made without Consent of the Senate.[1] This appointment should be made as soon as possible. Events will force Genl. Halleck to move all his troops very soon and he needs men just like Gen. Hitchcock who can inspire confidence. I should be very glad if you could hasten the confirmation for it would I am sure be acceptable to every body. I telegraphed to the Same effect yesterday, and only write to add to the certainty of your receiving it.

I am still here at the Barracks, doing my best to organize, equip and prepare Regiments for the coming spring. General Curtis[2] is down about Lebanon S. W. towards Springfield and will move against Price at Springfield unless he will again move towards Arkansas. This he will do unless he has great advantages. I go out but little, indeed the details here are enough to occupy ones whole time. I believe an attempt will be made on the Forts on the Tennessee & Cumberland Rivers in cooperation with Buell, who finds with his 120,000 men he still need help. I rather think they will come up to my figures yet. Halleck is expected to Send them from 30, to 50,000 men. Had this been done early & promptly, the Confederates could not have made Bowling Green & Columbus next to impregnable. Until these places are reduced, it will not do to advance far into Tennessee, and I doubt if it will be done. East Tennessee cannot exercise much influence on the final result. West Tennessee is more important, as without the navigation of the Mississipi all commercial interests will lean to the Southern Cause. If the Southern Confederacy can control the navigation of the lower Mississipi, and European nations from the Mouths of the Mississipi, what can Missouri & Kentucky do. These are however questions for the future.

I still feel much depressed by my past errors, but still I do not seek any leading post, on the contrary, prefer any amount of labor & drudgery to attempting to lead when I see no practicable result. Affectionately

W. T. Sherman

ALS, DLC: William T. Sherman.

1. Ethan A. Hitchcock was made a major general of volunteers on February 10. Halleck had urged the promotion in the hopes that Hitchcock would take charge of a planned Union thrust into West Tennessee, superseding Brigadier General Ulysses S. Grant.

2. Brigadier General Samuel R. Curtis (1817–66) was commanding the Southwest District of Missouri.

Head-Quarters, Camp of Instruction,
Benton Barracks, (near St. Louis, Mo.,)
Feb 6 1862

Genl. R. Anderson

I thank you for your very kind letter of Jan. 31.[1] Tell Mrs. Anderson I will bear in mind her request and at some future time hope to comply with her request. I have been here some time aiding all I can by organizing and sending out the Regiments of Volunteers. The number of men here was over 12,000, but is now reduced about one half by detachments to Cairo & Smithland. A large force from that Quarter has gone up the Tennessee & Cumberland to break the Strong line our Enemies have drawn from Columbus to Bowling Green.[2] Large as this Military force now is it seems impossible to get enough to take Columbus, or even to threaten it whilst a dash is made up the Center. Gen. Halleck promises me a command soon. I never did want to play a part in this war but want to do all in my power. It seems to me that there is an irreconciliability between the two Sections that instead of closing is widening, but your faith in the preservation of the Government no doubt remains unshaken. In New York you can hardly realize the sad effects of the war on the Border but here in St. Louis I see the deep & rankling hate the South & southern people bear us all.

Mrs. Sherman is in Ohio I will send her your letter and ask her to write to Mrs. Anderson. She is firm in her devotion to the Cause, and bears toward you the greatest devotion. She has never met Mrs. Anderson but knows of her through your family. May God preserve you for a long life, for only such men as you can cement the broken parts of our once cherished union. I am ever yr. friend

W. T. Sherman

ALS, DLC: Robert Anderson Papers.

1. DLC: WTS. On January 31, Anderson had written that he had received some checks from WTS and that he was glad to hear he was on active duty again. Anderson, however, did not know when he would be able to resume his duties. Mrs. Anderson had requested WTS's photograph and autograph as well as a photograph of Ellen.

2. As WTS wrote, this expedition, under the command of Brigadier General Ulysses S. Grant and Flag Officer Andrew H. Foote, had just forced the surrender of a small Confederate garrison at Fort Henry on the Tennessee River just south of the Kentucky-Tennessee state line.

TO ELLEN EWING SHERMAN

Paducah, Ky. Feb. 17, 1862.

Dearest Ellen,

On Sunday last a week I received a dispatch from Gen. Halleck to prepare to come to the Tennessee or Cumberland—I sent a copy to you at once.[1] On Thursday I received a dispatch to come at once to Paducah and assume command—I started same day telegraphing you at Lancaster. I have just received a dispatch from Phil at Burnet House Cincinati, that you were coming to St. Louis on Friday—My God that you should have gone to the trouble of that trip and your disappointment on arrival—Indeed do I appreciate this mark of affection, and deplore the result. I should have been happy to have seen you, but I took all precautions. I sent you a dispatch the moment I received it, and had to obey Hallecks order was to come immediately, and I came the same day. I got here on Saturday, and am now in command here—we have just heard that Fort Donelson has surrendered with 10,000 prisoners including Sidney Johnston & Buckner—This is by far the most important event of this sad war, and Halleck will doubtless follow it up.[2] A great many wounded have come here and are in our Hospitals. I have about 3000 men here, and there is an apprehension that Beauregard will cross over to this place from Columbus & attack—I do not know but will make all suitable preparations.

I am occupying the house formerly occupied by Gen. Smith.[3] The town is full of secessionists, but they will be sadly annoyed by the surrender of Fort Donelson. Hammond is with me but I have no aids. I must use mounted orderlies. The sick wounded and prisoners are coming down from Fort Donelson and I am very busy.

Write me all about your trip to Saint Louis, and how you fared—It was too bad, but truly & sincerely do I regret that you should have made the trip I did all I could to tell you in time that I should be moved—Ever yours

W. T. Sherman

ALS, InND: Sherman Family Papers.

1. HWH to WTS, February 9, 1862, DLC: WTS. In light of Hitchcock's anticipated appointment and the following assignment of officers, Halleck wanted Sherman to take a column or division on the Tennessee or Cumberland.

2. On February 16, Ulysses S. Grant accepted the unconditional surrender of Fort Donelson, Tennessee, on the Cumberland River. Albert Sidney Johnston was not present. Grant's victory derailed Halleck's plan to place Ethan A. Hitchcock in command of an invading Union column; Hitchcock had declined to take Grant's place during the course of the campaign.

3. Brigadier General Charles F. Smith (1807–62), USA, had commanded the District of Western Kentucky and Missouri until January 31. At the moment he was in charge of one of Grant's divisions, having played a key role in forcing the surrender of the Donelson garrison.

TO ELLEN EWING SHERMAN

Paducah, Feb. 21, 1862

Dearest Ellen,

I have received your letter from St. Louis and I cannot express to you how sorry I am to have caused you that Journey at that time.[1] I wrote you & telegraphed you the moment I received my orders and did all I could to advise you of my movements, but now that you are at home I trust that the fatigue is over and it is forgotten. The News of Grants victory must have electrified the whole country. It certainly was most opportune. More troops are passing into Kentucky—about 10,000 have arrived today—Six Ohio Regiments without arms, and a Division from Green River. Our next move must be against Columbus. I have written to Halleck asking as a special favor that he ordered here the four companies of my Regiment. I think he will do it.

You ask me to pardon you—the idea of your asking my pardon—I ought to get on my Knees and implore your pardon for the anxiety & Shame I have caused you. All I hope for is a chance to recover from the Past—I had a long interview with Buckner today. I used to Know him well and he frankly told me of many things which I wanted to Know—He was restrained from doing what I Knew was his purpose and what he ought to have done, but he was restrained by Sidney Johnston.

We are here in the midst of mud and dirt, rains & thaw. We expect orders every day to move somewheres but no one knows where.

I got your telegraph last night. I had previously written to Halleck asking him to Send the Battalions of four companies to me here at Paducah from Alton. I dont know whether he will. I suppose a large part of the prisoners of war are at Alton and will need Guard.

Give my love to all, and I cant tell now how my thoughts dwell on our dear children & you[.] I am very busy—Affectionately

W. T. Sherman

ALS, InND: Sherman Family Papers.

1. Although this letter was not found, on February 21, after her return to Lancaster, EES wrote her husband about her "inexpressible disappointment" at missing him in St. Louis. She was distraught at the idea he might die without being shriven by a priest. SFP.

TO JOHN SHERMAN

Paducah Ky. Feb. 23, 1862

My Dear Brother,

I have received your letter February 15,[1] and assure you I am completely conscious of my past errors, I have sought obscurity in this ⟨damaged⟩, and fear I have done more, I am now in command here—we ⟨damaged⟩ 8 Ohio Regiments arrived without ⟨damaged⟩, and 2 Indiana & 1 Illinois with arms. I have no doubt all the troops here will soon be armed equipped and put in motion to cause the Confederates to evacuate Columbus. Grants victory was most extraordinary and brilliant—he was a plain unostentatious man, and a few years ago was of bad habits, but he certainly has done a brilliant act—I have seen Buckner & prisoners of war, and learned many things not heretofore Known.

I want to do an act of tardy justice to an excellent officer from Zanesville Ohio by name of Gilbert[2] in Louisville[.] He was Inspector General at Louisville. If you could have him made a Brigadier General it would be a good appointment[.] He was at the Battle of Springfield and received a severe wound from which he is but partially recovered—I wish you would inquire into his antecedents and procure him even the appointment of Brig. Genl.

I have the most unlimited confidence in Halleck—he is the ablest man by far that has thus far appeared—more rapid than McClellan—Dont get at war with McClellan—you mistake him if you underrate him. He must begin to move soon, and I think he will. If he can threaten Richmond and cause Johnston to fall back from Manassas, he will relieve the Capital which is the reason why foreign Govts. talk of acknowledging Southern Independence.

The war is not yet over. I mistrust the Union Sentiment now so much spoken of—I hear of it, but cant find it. Here in Paducah there are only a few who even profess neutrality, it is a regular secession community, and until the navigation of the Mississipi is open it will be so. Halleck understands this perfectly. Columbus must be evacuated before we get south on this Line. I suppose Nashville will be occupied—a day or two—But dont infer that all is gained yet—I have seen the captured men of Fort Donelson and though many of them are tired of war & exposure, none of them but hates the Yankees. Love to Cecilia & Mary.[3] Affectionately yr. brother

W. T. Sherman

ALS, DLC: William T. Sherman.

1. JS had congratulated his brother on his new command and commented on other military and political matters. "McClellan is dead—in the estimation of even military men— He is mixed up with a miserable clique of some traitors, and he has not the ability to resist flatterers." He commented that the widespread Union sentiment in Tennessee and Alabama demonstrated "this rebellion is a political one, managed by 'southern Gentlemen' & not grounded in the universal assent of the People." DLC: WTS.

2. Charles C. Gilbert (1822–1903) was a captain in the First U.S. Infantry when he was wounded at the Battle of Wilson's Creek in August 1861. He acted as inspector general for the Department of the Cumberland and the Army of the Ohio until March 11, 1862, and would become a brigadier general in September 1862.

3. Mary Sherman was JS's adopted daughter.

TO CHARLES EWING

Paducah, February 27, 1862.

Dear Charley,

I have written twice to Gen. Halleck asking him to send the Battalion of 4 Comps. of the 13th Inf. into the Field. I know the mortification you experience at your position and Ellen has written me on the Same subject.[1] Tell Col. Burbank to write to Halleck and recall his promise to him that when he had a Battalion for the Field he would not keep it there. H. has so much to do that he cannot think of Battalions, but contemplates Divisions. I have here twelve (12) Regiments, but a large part are unarmed. We expect arms every moment from St. Louis. They were shipped last Saturday but are not yet come—The un-paralleled success of Grant has deservedly aroused the enthusiasm of the country, and if followed up may prove overwhelming. Columbus is still oc-cupied in force, by General Polk, and Hallecks next move will be to dislodge them not by direct attack but by manoeuvre—He has been so successful thus far that I have great faith in him.

I suppose a force may be sent along the west of the Mississipi on New Madrid, another cross over from the Tennessee to the Rail road—Both if successful will cause the enemy to abandon Columbus. In the mean time it will be necessary to secure Cairo & this place, as they are essential in protect-ing the communications up the Tennessee.

The Mississipi must be possessed in its whole extent before the Rebellion is crushed, for without the trade of the South, the people of the West cannot prosper. You will have your chance. A captain Stands a better chance than a Brigadier. But who can look forward a day.

I fear the great number of prisoners of war will so occupy the attentions of the local volunteers that they cannot be spared to guard those in Alton. Still in the end Halleck will do you justice. Affectionately,

W. T. Sherman

ALS, DLC: Charles Ewing Family Papers.

1. Charles Ewing's battalion of the Thirteenth U.S. Infantry had been assigned to guard the army prison at Alton, Illinois; his family wanted him assigned to the front under WTS's command. EES had apparently telegraphed WTS on the subject on February 20. On the twenty-second she wrote WTS that she was glad he was working for Charley's assignment to his command. She thought that Schuyler Hamilton was responsible for Charley's assign-ment—he "showed a very ugly & unfriendly spirit about it and I will remember him for it." SFP.

TO ELLEN EWING SHERMAN

Paducah, March 6, 1862

Dearest Ellen,

Learning some days past that the Confederates are simply abandoning Columbus I sent a party of cavalry to go as near as prudent and to enter it if possible. Then taking about 900 men in a Steamboat I went down as far as Cairo, & found the Gun boats getting ready to attack Columbus I waited till next morning and accompanied them. We found our cavalry in possession. The place must have been very formidable, but they carried off nearly all their guns, and materiels, burned their huts and some corn and provisions. I placed a Garrison there, staid one day and came back to this my post—Halleck has ordered up the Tennessee, all the troops here except a Small Garrison, and I will go along. I will get off tomorrow if possible. There is a perfect Stream of people passing up and down the Tennessee, but too many sick are constantly passing down—we have a hospital here over a thousand sick, and the Mound City Hospital. I have as yet been unable to see Sister Angela[1] for Mound City is six miles from Cairo and I have never been there time enough to go up. Dr. (illegible) promised to bring her to Paducah, but now that I am going to the Tennessee River I will not be able to See her at all. Our destination is far up the River to a point near Eastport. My February's pay is due and I have some considerable left of January but have to buy two horses. I cannot get a draft and Know not how to Supply you. Maj. McDowell Paymaster[2] is here, and I will try and get him to arrange it for me. He may have some friends in Ohio.

I enclose a sketch I made of Columbus, rough, but it will give your father an idea of the works which are very extensive. The Rebels have dropped down to Island No. 10 just above New Madrid and are preparing to fight there. They are also fortifying on the Tennessee above Savannah and Eastport. The next battle will be at New Madrid, and at some point up the Tennessee. After Columbus was evacuated the Gun boats were expected to go down and attack Island No. 10, but Commodore Foote[3] would not. My love to all Yrs. ever

W. T. Sherman

ALS, InND: Sherman Family Papers.

1. Sister Angela was Eliza Gillespie, Philemon Ewing's sister-in-law and EES's maternal cousin. She was the founder of the American order of the Sisters of the Holy Cross and had founded a girls' academy at Notre Dame in connection with the boys' school there.

2. Major Malcolm McDowell of Ohio had been appointed a paymaster of volunteers on June 1, 1861.

3. Andrew Hull Foote (1806–63) commanded the U.S. western flotilla. He had assisted Grant by moving on Fort Henry; wounded at Donelson, he would eventually give up his command after helping to capture Island Number Ten in April 1862.

Savannah Tennessee.

March 12, 1862.

Dearest Ellen,

Here we are up the Tennessee, near the Line, with about 50 boat loads of soldiers. I have the fifth Division composed mostly of Ohio Soldiers about 9000—but they are raw & Green. Maj. Gen. C. F. Smith is in command and there are Generals Hurlbut,[1] McClernand,[2] Wallace[3] & others. The River is high, navigation good, and weather fine. The object of the expedition is to cut the Line from Memphis to Chattanooga, along which are distributed the Enemy's forces. As I have nothing to do with the plans, I feel perfectly easy, and shall do my best. Hammond is with me but is not well. Lt. Col. Hascall,[4] Maj. Sanger,[5] Lts. McCoy[6] and Taylor[7] are in my staff.

Major McDowell Paymaster is along and I will send you all my pay for February, and he will send it to you from Columbus or Cincinati.

Let what occur that may you may rest assured that the devotion & affection you have exhibited in the past winter has endeared you more than ever, and that if it should so happen that I can regain my position and Self respect and should Peace ever be restored I will labor hard for you and our children.

I am still of opinion that although the blow at Fort Donelson was a terrible one to the Confederates they are still far from being defeated, and being in their own country they have great advantage[.] Yesterday as we came up the River the People gathered on the Shore and manifested pleasure by the waving of handkerchiefs, clapping of hands &c., but I noticed that the young men took little part in their manifestations.

Bragg is at Tuscumbria. Beauregard at Jackson, and there is a force at Eastport and Corinth right ahead. Savannah is a small town on the East bank of the River and is suppposed to be Union in sentiment, but we shall today move further up the River. My love to all & believe me always yrs.

W. T. Sherman

ALS, InND: Sherman Family Papers.

1. Brigadier General Stephen A. Hurlbut (1815–82), USA, a prewar politician, was commanding the Fourth Division of the Army of the Tennessee.

2. Brigadier General John A. McClernand (1812–1900), an Illinois Democrat, was leading the First Division of the Army of the Tennessee.

3. Brigadier General Lewis Wallace (1827–1905), USA, a Mexican War veteran, was commanding the Third Division of the Army of the Tennessee.

4. Milo S. Hascall (1829–1904) was acting as one of WTS's inspector generals and was commanding the Fifteenth Brigade in the Sixth Division of the Army of the Ohio.

5. William D. "Dan" Sanger had been commissioned a major in the Fifth Illinois Infantry

in October 1861. He would become a lieutenant colonel and inspector general the following February.

6. James C. McCoy (d. 1875), a first lieutenant in the Forty-sixth Ohio, would serve on Sherman's staff through the war, rising to the rank of brevet lieutenant colonel of volunteers.

7. John Taylor was also an aide-de-camp.

TO ELLEN EWING SHERMAN

Steamboat Continental
Pittsburg Landing Tenn.,
Mch. 17/18, 1862
Tuesday.

Dearest Ellen,

I wrote you from Savanna Landing sending you a Paymasters certificate for my months pay. I started in command of eleven (11) Regiments, landed at Tylers Landing 18 miles above this and in the midst of a perfect flood attempted to cross over the intervening space of 17 miles to break the Memphis & Charleston Road.[1] The Rain fell in torrents and Streams began to rise, and the Cavalry which led had to turn back for the swollen water. It was very unfortunate, so I had to return the Boats. The Tennessee River rose 15 feet in one day and the Landing was under water. I was compelled to drop down again to this place where there is a high Bluff Landing. Troops are passing in to my command, and again I attempted to make for the Road sending a Cavalry force ahead—Mr. Bowman took part in this movement—The force had only gone 5 miles when in the dark they had a fight with some Secession Cavalry, which retired in disorder. My Infantry force was on the point of starting but as I depended on the Cavalry to travel the 20 miles before daylight which was impossible, I determined to convert my attempt on the Road into a Reconnaissance. This was done, and I have been out two days and have obtained pretty accurate notions of the Roads on which we are to move. Genl. Grant & Smith are at Savannah 19 miles below, and I command here, but as the Force has swollen to 25,000 men, and more are coming I take it for granted that some one else will come to Command. I hear Halleck is coming, may be Grant, and on the whole we are furthest advanced into Secession. In a circuit of many miles I find houses abandonned, the People having fled, because they are told, we take every thing we can lay our hands on, all the pretty girls and leave the Old Ones for the negros. I had an old man who really believed this, and was much assured when I said if he would stay at home & mind his own business I would not permit the Soldiers to disturb him. Upon going to his house, his wife & children had fled to the woods as though we were savages— Our soldiers do in Spite of all efforts burn Rails, steal geese chickens &c. &c.

The Boat is ringing her Bell, and I must ashore to my tent.

I am very tired having ridden for two days, the Enemy under Bragg & Beauregard are to our front from Florence to Corinth with the country full of never-ending cavalry. We may have fights at Purdy and Corinth. My love to all Yrs.

W. T. Sherman

ALS, InND: Sherman Family Papers.
1. See *PM*, 1:255–56.

TO ELLEN EWING SHERMAN

Pittsburg Landing Tenn.
Camp, April 3, 1862.

Dearest Ellen,

I have really neglected writing for some days. I dont Know why, but I daily become more and more disposed to stop writing. There is so much writing that I am sick & tired of it & put it off on Hammond who is sick cross and troublesome. I have plenty of aids but the writing part is not very full. I have been pretty busy, in examining Roads & Rivers. We have now near 60,000 men here, and Bragg has command at Corinth only 18 miles off, with 80 Regiments and more coming. On our part McCook, Thomas & Nelsons Divisions are coming from Nashville and are expected about Monday, this is Thursday, when I Suppose we must advance to attack Corinth or some other point on the Memphis & Charleston Road. The weather is now springlike, apples & peaches in blossom and trees beginning to leave. Bluebirds singing and spring weather upon the hillsides. This part of the Tennessee differs somewhat from that up at Bellefonte. There the Alleghany Mountains still characterized the Country whereas here the hills are lower & rounded covered with oak, hickory & dogwood, not unlike the Hills down Hocking. The people have mostly fled, abandoning their houses, and Such as remain are of a neutral tint not Knowing which side will turn up victors. That enthusiastic love of the Union of which you read in the newspapers is a form of expression easily written, but is not true. The poor farmers certainly do want peace, & protection, but all the wealthier classes hate us Yankees with a pure unadulterated hate. They fear the Gunboats which throw heavy shells and are invulnerable to their rifles & shotguns, and await our coming back from the River.

I have been troubled some days by a Slight diarrhea but am well enough for work. My Division is very raw and needs much instruction. Brigade Commanders are McDowell,[1] Stuart,[2] Hildebrand[3] & Buckland.[4] Genl. Grant commands in chief, and we have a host of other Generals, so that I am content to be in a mixed crowd.

I dont pretend to look ahead far and do not wish to guide events. They are too momentous to be a subject of personal ambition.

We are constantly in the presence of the enemys pickets, but I am satisfied that they will await our coming at Corinth or some point of the Charleston Road. If we dont get away soon the leaves will be out and the whole country an ambush.

Our letters come very irregularly I have nothing from you for more than a week but I know you are all well and happy at home and that is a great source of consolation.[5] My love to all yrs. ever

W. T. Sherman

ALS, InND: Sherman Family Papers.

1. Colonel John A. McDowell of the Sixth Iowa led the First Brigade in Sherman's division.

2. Colonel David Stuart (1816–68) of the Fifty-fifth Illinois led the Second Brigade.

3. Colonel Jesse Hildebrand (d. 1863) of the Fifty-seventh Ohio was in charge of the Third Brigade.

4. Colonel Ralph P. Buckland (1812–92) of the Seventy-second Ohio commanded the Fourth Brigade.

5. Probably EES to WTS, March 17, 1862, a lengthy letter about the children and home and reminiscences of their early lives. SFP.

TO THOMAS EWING SR.

Camp Shiloh, near Pittsburg Tenn.—
April 4, 1862

Hon. Thos. Ewing
Dear Sir,

I was troubled in mind on account of the part, insignificant in fact taken by me in the burning of the Road near Chattanooga. I was at Camp Dick Robinson when Mr. Carter arrived from Washington. At the time I hoped the administration last fall would see the importance of Kentucky as the Centre of the vast Battle field of America, and would order from the East or anywheres an army suited to the occasion. I then expressed a wish that the People of East Tennessee would manifest their declared preference for the Union Cause by organizing with such arms as they could find—We had none to give at the time and should stop the communication between Beauregard in Virginia and Sidney Johnston. Mr. Carter then told me he was authorized to destroy the Railroad, and provided with money by the President himself & with the Knowledge & concurrence of Gen. McClellan[.] I assented to the arrangement, but do not think I promised to cross over into East Tennessee: but thought such events to the rear of Zollicoffer would compel him as it did to retire, and leave that quarter of Kentucky free from his threats.

When I got to Louisville I found the enemy concentrating heavy forces on the Nashville Bowling Green & Paris Line, and had they rapidly approached Lexington they would have checkmated us, and beaten us, just as the unexpected interposition of Grants Army at Donelson defeated Johnston.

I never ordered the advance into East Tennessee by the Gap. Nor should I again. An army thus depending on Kentucky for supply could be beaten by ¼ its numbers, for the Road from Crab Orchard to Knoxville is a common mud Road, where in November 6 mules could hardly haul the empty wagon. Our volunteers will for a few days stand deprivations, but if we bring them to corn & meat, such as the country affords, they will scatter all over the country, and become useless as an army. Buell on his own has adopted that Line, then so popular, and urged with so much Energy by Johnson, Maynard and Etheridge.[1]

The destruction of a Railroad as connected with a Real movement must be justifiable in war, but as an independent thing could not be justified.

I confess the issues involved in this war are so momentous that I shrink from the responsibilities which others seem to court, and much prefer the Subordinate part I now play. I think I see on the part of the People of Tennessee an inclination to Subside into Peace. A year of war & devastation here must be followed by starvation. But in Mississipi, the common people are more bitter than Ever, reckless of consequences. We now hold complete control of the River from Eastport to its mouth—just above Eastport are shoals that the Gunboats will not venture to pass, lest the rapid falling of the River should leave them above: There were Batteries at Eastport. I went up with a small force in cooperation with three Gunboats and found the Batteries abandonned. The Enemy is at Corinth as a Centre with strong detachments along the Rail Road as far east as Tuscumbria: also with strong Cavalry & Infantry pickets towards us, almost to our very Camp. These are mere (illegible) that fall back whenever we show ourselves, designed simply to carry notice back of an advance in force on our part. Of course they must defend with all the power they can, whatever point of this East & west Line of theirs, we select to attack. To fall much further south would take them from their grain supplies.

My Division has 12 Infantry Regime{nts} 8 Cos. of cavalry, and 3 Batteries of artillery nearly all new troops, the last sent from Ohio to Paducah.[2] I keep them pretty well employed and think they are gaining consistency. I have done all the reconnoitering & adventuring thus far, but wh{ere} Glory is to be gained, I suppose McClernand or some newspaper favorite must go ah{ead.} I still think there is no need of has{te} all will get their fill of fighting—as much as they want.

I am always glad to hear my young folks are prospering—of course I have more than faith in Ellens manage{ment} of them, let what will befal me.

Before me are all my Louisiana Boys—Bragg, Beauregard, and the Cadets of the Academy. I hear of them through captured prisoners & deserters—Ever, with profound respect

W. T. Sherman

ALS, New York: FORBES Magazine Collection.

1. Emerson Etheridge (1819–1902) was a U.S. representative for Tennessee in Congress at this time.

2. The First Brigade was the Fortieth Illinois, Sixth Iowa, Forty-sixth Ohio, and the Sixth Indiana Battery; the Second was the Fifty-fifth Illinois, Fifty-fourth Ohio, and Seventy-first Ohio; the Third was the Fifty-third Ohio, Fifty-seventh Ohio, and Seventy-seventh Ohio; the Fourth was the Forty-eighth Ohio, Seventieth Ohio, and Seventy-second Ohio; the cavalry units were the First and Second Battalions of the Fourth Illinois and the additional artillery was Batteries B and E of the First Illinois Artillery.

TO ELLEN EWING SHERMAN

Camp Shiloh, Apl. 11, 1862

Dearest Ellen,

Well we have had a big battle where they Shot real bullets and I am safe, except a buckshot wound in the hand and a bruised shoulder from a spent ball—The first horse I rode was one I captured from the Enemy soon after I got here, a beautiful sorrel race mare that was as fleet as a deer, and very easy in her movements to which I had become much attached—She was first wounded and then shot dead under me. This occurred Sunday when the firing on both sides was terrific and I had no time to save saddle, holsters or valise. I took the horse of my aid McCoy till it was shot, when I took my Doctors horse and that was shot—My Camp was in advance of all others and we caught the first thunder, and they captured all our tents and two horses of mine hitched to the trees near my tent were Killed. So I am completely unhorsed—The first man killed in the Battle was my orderly close by my side a young handsome faithful soldier who carried his Carbine ever ready to defend me his name was Holliday[1] and the Shot that killed him was meant for me. After the Battle was over I had him brought to my camp and buried by a tree Scarred with balls and its top carried off by a Cannon ball. These about embrace all the personal events connected with myself—My troops were very raw and Some Regiments broke at the first fire. Others behaved better, and I managed to keep enough all the time to form a Command and was the first to get back to our front Line. The Battle on Sunday was very severe. They drove back our left flank on the River, but I held the Right flank out about a mile & half, giving room for Reinforcements to come in from Crumps landing to our

North, and for Buells army to land—Beauregard, Bragg Johnston, Breckin-
ridge and all their Big men were here, with their best soldiers and after the
Battle was over I found among the prisoners an old Louisiana Cadet named
Barrow who sent for me and told me all about the others, many of whom were
here and Knew they were fighting me. I gave him a pair of socks, drawers &
Shirt and treated him very kindly. I wont attempt to give an account of the
Battle, but they Say that I accomplished some important results, and Gen.
Grant makes special mention of me in his Report which he shew me.[2] I have
worked hard to Keep down but somehow I am forced into prominence and
might as well submit[.] One thing pleased me well—On Sunday we caught
thunder and were beaten back—Buell arrived very opportunely and came out
to see me—the place of operations was agreed on, and his fresh Kentucky
troops to advance boldly out direct from the Steamboat landing to Shiloh my
Head Qrs.—I was on the Right and to advance when he got abreast of me—
This was done, and I edged to the Road, and reached it about 500 yards from
here, just where the hardest fighting was, and then met the same Kentucky
troops I had at Muldrough hill. They all recognized me and such shouting you
never heard. I asked to pass their Ranks and they gave me the lead[.] I have
since visited their Camps and never before received such marks of favor—
Johns Brigade is also here, indeed we must now have 75,000 men. Figures
begin to approximate my standard—Halleck is coming with reinforcements.
We have been attacked & beaten off our enemy. Now we must attack him. This
would occur at once, but it has been raining so that our Roads are almost impassable. The Enemy expected to crush us before Buell got ⟨here. The scenes
on this⟩ field would ⟨have cured anybody of war. Mangled bodies, dead,
dying, in every conceivable shape, without heads, legs; and horses!⟩ I think we
have buried 2000 since the fight our own & the Enemy, and the wounded fill
houses, tents, steamboats and Every conceivable place. My division had about
8000 men—at least half ran away, and out of the remaining half, I have 302 soldiers 16 officers killed and over 1200 wounded. All I can say this was a Battle,
and you will receive so many graphic accounts that my picture would be
tame[.] I Know you will read all accounts—cut out paragraphs with my name
for Willy's future Study—all Slurs you will hide away, and gradually convince
yourself that I am a soldier as famous as Gen. Greene.[3] I still feel the horrid
nature of this war, and the piles of dead Gentlemen & wounded & maimed
makes me more anxious than ever for some hope of an End but I know such a
thing cannot be for a long long time. Indeed I never expect it or to survive it.
You ask for money—I have none, and now am without horse saddle bridle,
bed, or anything—The Rebels, Breckinridge had my Camp and cleaned me
out. You must learn to live without money, as that is going to be a scarce
commodity—plant a garden & raise your own vegetables—⟨missing text⟩

AL (end of letter is clipped), InND: Sherman Family Papers. Material in angle brackets was taken from the text in *HL*, 220–23.

1. Thomas D. Holliday, Company H of the Second Illinois Cavalry.

2. USG to Captain Nathaniel H. McLean, April 9, 1862, reprinted in *PUSG*, 5:32–36. Grant made special mention of "a gallant & able officer Brig. Genl. W. T. Sherman" and his "great judgment and skill in the management of his men."

3. Nathanael Greene of Revolutionary War fame.

TO ELLEN EWING SHERMAN

Camp Shiloh, Apl. 14, 1862.

Dearest Ellen,

The day before yesterday I heard Halleck had arrived at the River and upon making a short turn through the Camps I found him on board the Continental and Grant on the Tigress. I was there ordered again to try to destroy the Memphis and Charleston Road, a thing I had twice tried and failed. I at once ordered 100 4 Illinois Cavalry under Bowman to be embarked on board the (illegible phrase) and a Brigade of Infantry Fry's[1] on board the (illegible boat name) and the *White Cloud*, and with two Gunboats went up the Tennessee 32 miles to Chickasaw, just the Corner of Alabama, then I disembarked there and sent them on their errand—Bowman reached the Railroad and destroyed the Bridge, and some 500 feet of trestles succeeding perfectly in the undertaking which is very important as it prevents all communication of the enemy with the East. I tried to go up to Florence but the water would not let us pass two shoals above so I returned & Halleck was delighted. This has been with him a chief object. When I got down this morning he handed me the enclosed Copy of one sent last night to Washington[2]—so at last I Stand redeemed from the vile slanders of that Cincinati paper—I am sometimes amused at these newspaper Reporters. They keep shy of me as I have said the first one I catch I will hang as a Spy. I now have the lawful right to have a Court martial, and if I catch one of these Cincinati Newspapers in my camp I will have a Court and they will do just as I tell them. It would afford me a real pleasure to hang one or two—I have seen a paragraph in the Cincinati Commercial about Dr. Hewit.[3] He never drinks, is as moral a man and as intelligent as ever, and all his time is working for the Sick, but because he will not drop his work & listen & babble with a parcel of false humorists who come here from the various (illegible phrase) of our Country he must be stigmatized as a corrupt drunkard. Rebellion is a sin, & of course should be punished but I feel that in these Southerners there are such qualities of Courage, bold daring and manly that though I know they are striving to subvert our Government & bring them into Contempt, Still I feel personal respect for them as individuals, but for these mean contemptible slanderous and false villains who seek reputation by abuse of others—Here called off by a visit of my Kentucky friends who express to me unbounded confidence.

I have just got yours of the 9th my hand is not off[4]—it was a buckshot by a Cavalry man who got a shot at me but was almost instantly killed in return—My shoulder is well and I am as good as ever.

For mercy's sake never speak of McClellan as you write. He ought to have sent me men & officers in Kentucky but did not, but that he had any malice or intention of wrong I dont believe. I committed a fearful mistake in Kentucky and if I recover it will be a wonderful instance. I have made good progress here, and in time can illustrate the motives that influenced me—I knew Mc-Clellan to be a man of talents & having now a well organized & disciplined army, he may by some rapid strokes achieve a name that would enable him to Crush me—Keep your own counsel, and let me work for myself on this Line. Halleck has told me that he had ordered the 4 Cos. of the 13 Inf. here to me, as soon as a certain Battalion could be spared at New Madrid. Charley need not be impatient[.] The southern army was repulsed but not defeated. Their Cavalry hangs about our front now—we must have one more terrible battle—we must attack—My Division is raw—some Regts. behaved bad but I did the best I could with what remained, and all admit I was of good service—I noticed that when we were enveloped and death stared us all in the face my seniors in rank leaned on me—Well I am not in search of honor or fame and only count it for yours & childrens sake.

I think you will have some satisfaction and I know your father will be pleased that I am once more restored to favor. Give him Hallecks letter & tell him I broke the Charleston Road[.] Yrs.

W. T. Sherman

ALS, InND: Sherman Family Papers.

1. James B. Fry (1827–94) was Buell's chief of staff.

2. HWH to Edwin M. Stanton, April 13, 1862, *OR*, I, 10: pt. 1, 98. This brief letter commended WTS on his performance at Shiloh, which "contributed largely to the glorious victory of the 7th," and recommended he be promoted to major general of U.S. volunteers to date April 6.

3. Dr. Henry S. Hewit (1825–73) had entered military service as a brigade surgeon of volunteers and had become medical director of Grant's army at Shiloh and Vicksburg. After a March 31 attack by Whitelaw Reid on Hewit's skill and sobriety, published in the April 4 *Cincinnati Gazette*, Stanton suspended Hewit from duty on April 11. Sherman later wrote a letter endorsing Hewit and his abilities, and he was reinstated in August.

4. On April 9, EES had answered WTS's of April 3. She was worried about his health and went on to discuss McClellan and his alleged connection with the Knights of the Golden Circle at length. "McClellan has been playing into their hands—he is sworn to them under pain of assassination—and he has allowed things to work so as to leave our troops to be killed off by yellow fever when Summer comes on. Men high in authority are watching him

& he will likely be in Fort Warren in Stone's place before long. Stone was a scapegoat for him & he sent Stone to prison to prevent his own treason being discovered. May vengeance fall on him!" Her hasty close to the letter came after she had received the first news of the battle—"Thank our merciful God you are alive but your poor hand has gone—Will you come home." SFP.

TO JOHN SHERMAN

Camp Shiloh near Pittsburg Tenn.
April 16, 1862

Hon. John Sherman
Washington, D.C.
Dear Brother

I send you a copy of a letter written by Genl. Halleck to the Secty. of War, which I think will please you.[1]

My Division is made up mostly of new regiments, some of which behaved well and others badly, but I hope by patience to make it as good as any other Division of the Army.

Since the battle I have been up to Chickasaw from which point I caused the destruction of the Charleston and Memphis Railroad at its crossing over Bear Creek a valuable piece of service. My right hand is temporarily disabled by inflamation from a wound, but with good luck it will be all right in a week. I believe that our hardest fighting is yet to be done, but I have absolute faith in Genls. Halleck, Buell, and Grant. Affectionately Your Brother

W. T. Sherman

Copy, DLC: William T. Sherman.
1. HWH to EMS, April 13, 1862, DLC: WTS. See note 2 in previous letter.

TO WILLIAM T. SHERMAN JR.

Head Quarters Camp Shiloh
April 19, 1862

Dear Willy,

My hand is so sore that I can hardly hold my pen, but I must answer your letter which is a first rate one. Mama has told you all about the Big Battle; we had a hard fight and beat the Rebels back, but they are not afraid and we must have more battles. I have picked up some cannon & musket Balls which I have packed in a box and will send for you & Tom—Some of them have powder in and you must keep them away from fire, else they might burst and kill somebody. Tell mama to paste on them a little paper saying they were picked up near my tent on the Battle field of Shiloh, April 6 & 7, 1862. There is also a spur taken from the Boot of a dead Rebel Captain. These things will remind you of the Battle.

Mama has told me all about the new House which is large and comfortable. I am living in a small tent and have a poor bed and clothes, because the Rebels took my camp and carried off my bed, and some of my clothes. All my horses (3) were killed in the battle and I have now two poor horses I got from the Cavalry Soldiers whose riders were killed.

We have here now a very large army, nearly 100,000 men, and must soon move toward Corinth, where the Rebels are also with a large army, but we have broken their Railroads and they cannot travel as fast as they used to.

I know the newspapers are full of all sorts of stories which your mama will read to you, but the newspaper men are afraid to be where the fighting is and afterward it is all over they are very brave. I wish Uncle Boyle could come here—Uncle Charley will soon be here, and I think he will be under my command.

Mr. Granger, Mary Reese's husband is here.[1] I have seen him. All my old Kentucky Army is here, and among them I have plenty of friends.

I ride a great deal, and have to drill my men ever day. This keeps my hand very sore.

Tell Minnie & Lizzie to write to me and you must always write to me how you get along at school. I want you all to study hard so that when you & Tom are old enough you can let me & Mama rest, if we live that long.

Give my love to Grandpa & Grandma—Uncle Philemon and all the folks at Lancaster. Tell Mama that I will write again as soon as my hand is a little better. Your loving father,

W. T. Sherman

ALS, OHi: William T. Sherman Papers.
1. Moses M. Granger (1831–1913), a lawyer from Zanesville, Ohio, was a captain in the Eighteenth U.S. Infantry.

TO JOHN SHERMAN

Hd. Qrs. Camp Shiloh Tenn.—
April 22, 1862

Dear Brother,

My hand is still very sore, but I am able to write some. The newspapers came back to us with accounts of our Battle of the 6 & 7 inst. as usual made by People who ran away and had to excuse their cowardice by charging bad management on the part of Leaders. I see that we were surprised, that our men were bayonetted in their tents, that officers had not had breakfast &c.— This is all simply false. The attack did not begin till 7¾ A.M. All but the worthless cowards had had breakfast. Not a man was bayonetted in or near his tent. Indeed our Brigade Surgeon Hartshorn[1] has not yet seen a single bayonet wound on a living or dead subject.

The Regiments that profess to have been surprised, lost no officers at all, and the two that first broke in my Division the 53 & 57 Ohio—The 53 lost no officers & only 7 men—and the 57 2 officers & 7 men.

Some of my Ohio Regiments that did fight well lost as many as 49 & 34, but not a bayonet, sword or Knife wound. All cannon or Musket Balls. Three of my Brigades held our original position from 7¾ A.M. when the attack began, till 10 h. 10 m. A.M. when the Enemy had passed my left and got artillery to enfilade my Line when I ordered them to fall back.

We held our 2nd position until 4 P.M.—and then fell back without opposition to the 3rd & last position, more than a mile from the River.

As to Surprise—we had constant skirmishes with the Enemys Cavalry all the week before, and I had Strong Guards out in front of each Brigade, which guards were driven in on the morning of the Battle—but before the Enemy came within cannon Range of my position, Every Regiment was under arms, at posts I had previously assigned them. The Cavalry was saddled, and artillery harnessed up—unlimbered, and commenced firing as soon as we could See any thing to fire at.

On Saturday I had no Cavalry pickets out because I had no Cavalry in my Division. Genl. Grant had made a new assignment of Cavalry & artillery on Friday. The Ohio 5th which had been with me was ordered to Hurlbut, and 8 Cos. of the 4th Ills. Col. Dickey[2] assigned to me did not get into Camp till near Saturday night, and I ordered them under saddle at daylight.

I occupied the right front. McClernand was to my Rear, and on his left in Echelon with me was Prentiss[3]—I watched the Purdy Road & Main Corinth—Prentiss the Ridge Corinth Road.

The Enemy did not carry either of my Roads untill he had driven Prentiss and got in on my left.

During the whole Battle I was the furthest from the River Landing at all times and this story of surprise is an afterthought of the Rascals who ran away & had to Excuse their Cowardice.

Whether we should have been on this or that Side of the Tennessee River is not my business—I did not apprehend an attack from Beauregard, because I thought then & think now he would have done better to have chosen ground as far back from our stores as possible. We are bound to attack him, and had we run out of cartridges, or stores, or got stampeded 20 miles back from the Tennessee the result would be different from now—but we Knew the enemy was in our front, but in what force could not tell, and I was always ready for an attack, and could have held my ground, if my 3rd Brigade had stood firm, and Prentiss held his ground.

I am out of all patience that our People should prefer to believe the horrid stories of butchery—ridiculous in themselves—& got up by cowards to cover their Shame—than the plain natural Reports of the officers who are responsible and who saw what they describe in my Report with all the subordinate reports of Brigadiers & colonels with lists of Killed wounded & missing went to Gen. Grant on the 11th.

The enemy is still in our front & we can get a fight the hour & minute we want it. Halleck, Buell, Grant & all in authority are now here, & responsibility cannot be shifted. The common soldiers & subordinates run away & then want to blame their commanders. This Democracy wont go down with me. Yrs. affectionately

W. T. Sherman

ALS, DLC: William T. Sherman.

1. Dana W. Hartshorn had been appointed surgeon for Ohio volunteers on September 4, 1861.

2. T. Lyle Dickey commanded the Fourth Illinois Cavalry.

3. Brigadier General Benjamin M. Prentiss (1819–1901), USA, was leading the Sixth Division of the Army of the Tennessee at Shiloh when he was captured.

TO ELLEN EWING SHERMAN

Camp before Shiloh Tenn., Apl. 24, 62

Dearest Ellen,

I have written several letters of late to you, to Willy and your mother. Tell Theresa I thank her for hers,[1] but writing is painful to my hand and She must excuse me for a few days. At first the wound gave me no pain, but I rode so much that when it began to inflame it got very sore, and affected my fingers, and they are quite stiff. I had to resort to poultice, but now simple bandage, & in a few days it will be well again. In the small pain I have suffered I can feel for the thousands of poor fellows, with all sorts of terrible wounds such as I have been compelled to witness, but my time has been so absorbed by the Care of the living that I could pay little attention to the dead & wounded, but they have been well cared for. The only difficulty is that hundreds & thousands tired of the war, and satisfied with what they have seen here take advantage of slight wounds and gone home. As usual the noisy clamorous ones—spoiling for a fight have gone home to tell of their terrible deeds, and left others to brave the battles still to be fought. How few know the dangers attending this war—The very men who were most clamorous for fight were the first to run, and leave a few to Stand the brunt of Sunday. I knew this beforehand, and took it so easily that many wondered, thinking me indifferent & nonchalant. I sent a copy of my map to your father, and now enclose the rough notes of my official Report, from which I think you can trace my movements.[2] All the troops south of the main Corinth Road, were forced back to the River. I held my front Line till 10¼ A.M.—fell back to the Line of McClernands camps, & fought there till near 4 P.M., and took up a final position for night, back of McArthurs[3] Hd. Qrs. at all times the furthest out—on Monday advanced almost over the Same ground and reached Shiloh at 4 P.M.—The hue & cry against Grant about surprise is wrong. I was not surprised and I was in advance. Prentiss was not covered by me, and I dont believe he was surprised, although he is now a prisoner cannot be heard—It is outrageous for the cowardly newsmongers thus to defame men whose lives are exposed. The real truth is the private soldiers in battle leave their Ranks, run away and then raise these false issues. The political Leaders do not lay the blame where it belongs. They like the Volunteer officers are afraid of the men, but I will speak the truth and I believe still there are honest men enough to believe me—In the 302 dead, and 1200 wounded of my Division, there was not a bayonet or knife wound, and the story of men being bayonetted in their tents is a pure lie, and even admitting that officers & men had not dressed at 7¾ A.M. I say they deserved it—Reveille is at 5½. They should have dressed then, and if they were too lazy to get up & dress before 7¾ they deserved to be bayonetted, but it is all a lie got up by the cowards who ran to the River & reported we were surprised & all killed. By their false reports they may have prevented succor coming to us earlier than it did.

The enemy treated our wounded well & Kindly. I sent Willy a box of cannon Balls & bullets which he must share with Tom—I would like to see Willys Eyes when he sees the dread missiles. I know the Enemy is still in our Front—They can surprise us tomorrow morning quite as well as they did us that Sunday, but in attacking us they made a mistake—we must attack them on their chosen ground. The next battle will be worse than the last, and of course I dont expect to survive all that follows. This gives me little trouble, but I do feel for the thousands that think another battle will end the war—I hope the war wont end until those who caused the war, the politicians & editors are made to feel it—The Scoundrels take good care of their hides—run up after a fight and back again before there is a chance for another.

Halleck has assured me he gave an order before leaving St. Louis, for the relief of the Battalion of the 13 Inf. to be ordered here. When they come I will get them attached to my Division—I continue to receive marks of great confidence from my old Kentucky associates. I have just come from dinner with some dozen of the Generals at McCooks camp. We must soon move, but the roads are dreadful. Popes army is arrived and disembarked at Hamburg.

I send pay accounts for April. I hope you got the money for the certificate I sent you from Savannah—Ever yours

W. T. Sherman

ALS, InND: Sherman Family Papers.

1. Maria Theresa Ewing to WTS, April 11, 1862, DLC: WTS. She had written to say how glad the family was that he was unharmed and to give news about everyone as Ellen was sick.

2. WTS to John A. Rawlins, April 10, 1862, enclosed.

3. Brigadier General John McArthur (1826–1906), USA, led the Second Brigade of the Second Division of the Army of the Tennessee and succeeded to division command following W. H. L. Wallace's death on April 10.

TO CHARLES EWING

Camp Shiloh. Tenn.—
April 25, 1862

Dear Charley,

Halleck has assured me several times that before he left St. Louis he gave the orders necessary to relieve your Battalion and for it to come here—When it arrives I will ask for it. I have the 5th Division of Grants Corps. The army is still divided into Buells & Grants Corps d armee.[1] Each corps is divided into Divisions, Brigades, Regts. & Battns.—we must have near 150 Regiments here, but somehow in spite of all Efforts these Regiments dwindle down very fast— Since the innocent youth have discovered the southerners will fight & fight hard, they get the diarrhea, bots[2] &c. and go home to brag of their prowess, and leave others to do their fighting & work.

We have had here the same Games that were attempted at Bull Run—Men run away, wont obey their officers, wont listen to the threats, remonstrances, and prayers of their superiors, but after the danger is passed they raise false issues to cover their infamy. I had about 10,000 men on paper—8000 fit for duty, and I am satisfied only about 4000 stood to their Ranks, and they had to do the fighting of 8000. Consequently the loss fell heavy on them. I am determined to speak the truth in these Cases, and if the country wont believe me, I dont care.

As to the Cock & bull story of surprise it is absurd—we had been skirmishing for two days, and on the morning of the Battle, Every Regiment was armed & equipped & in Line of Battle—Every Battery harnessed in position, and cavalry saddled up. Not a knife or bayonet wound among my 1200 wounded and yet the newspapers make out we were surprised & men slaughtered in their beds.

President Lincoln telegraphed to know who was the cause of the surprise & dreadful slaughter at Pittsburg Landing—Halleck answered he thought the Confederate officers and soldiers were to blame, and were the cause of the dreadful slaughter.[3] So I hope old Abe will order Beauregard & Bragg to be court martialled for their cruelty in shooting bullets at us in the indiscriminate manner they did. We have had much rain & Roads are awful. As soon as they dry up a little we must sally forth and have a more bloody battle than that of April 6 & 7. The Confederates are at Corinth with an advance to within 6 miles of us. But of course they will fall back and fight at some chosen spot, maybe about 3 miles this side of Corinth. Corinth is 18 miles from here. The trees are now nearly in full leaf, and bushes will afford good cover for ambush—according to my notion the war will soon begin. As to its being anything like near its close I dont imagine. The Confederates seem to have an army in Virginia enough to hold McClellan & McDowell in check, and in our front they have some of their best troops. I have seen {Connell}, Judge Moore,[4] Granger, and most of the Ohio troops. I hope soon to see you here although I hope you wont be too impatient for fight—you will get your belly full—Your Brother,

W. T. Sherman

ALS, DLC: Charles Ewing Family Papers.

1. Within days Halleck would reorganize his army into three wings and a reserve. Grant was named second in command, while George H. Thomas, Buell, and John Pope commanded the wings.

2. The larvae of the botfly are intestinal parasites.

3. Stanton telegraphed Halleck on April 23 on Lincoln's behalf to ask if Grant or any other general officers were responsible for the high number of casualties at Shiloh; Halleck replied that unfit volunteer officers and "the numbers and bravery of the enemy" were to blame. *OR*, I, 10: pt. 1, 98–99.

4. Lieutenant Colonel Marshall F. Moore (1830–70), USA, an Ohio lawyer and judge, of the Seventeenth Ohio.

TO THOMAS EWING SR.

Let Ellen read this to you. My hand still prevents my writing plain & with care.

Hd. Qrs., 5 Divn.,

Camp Shiloh Tenn., Apl. 27, 62

Hon. Thos. Ewing,

Lancaster Ohio,

Dear Sir,

I had intended to give you an account of country and events preceding the Battle at Shiloh, but my hand has prevented my writing much and somehow I feel more & more a disinclination to write.

I made my official Report with accompanying Sub-Reports & lists of killed & wounded before any other Division Commander, but I have not seen it in print although many others are published. I am too far behind the times in supposing the old method of doing things to be the best, but I find more & more that we have a new Master that newspapers now rule, and one to prosper must ignore the old Government and acknowledge the new Power of the

Press. Their representatives the Reporters are to me the most contemptible race of men that exist, cowardly, cringing hanging round and gathering their material out of the most polluted sources. Thus in our Recent operations here, I can hardly recognize any description, because the Reporters had their stand point on steamboats in the River, and draw their accounts from the cowardly rascals who ran away, and who would not believe that their companions were fighting hard for two days for their camps and lives. They reported that we were surprised, cut up, routed and all that[.] *They* were surprized, astonished routed but not cut up. The Regiments of my Division that profess to have been surprised, were in Line of battle armed, equipped, full of breakfast and warned by me in person that the attack was coming & to be prepared for it. Not a man was killed in his tent, indeed the fugitive Regiments lost in Killed only 7 in an aggregate strength of 600, whereas the Regiments that fought all day lost as high as 50 killed and 200 wounded—If we were surprized, they had time to recover from their surprize as we fought from 7 A.M. till 4 P.M., and all knew it, and yet the surprized did not join us at all.

Even Mr. Lincoln has listened to this tale of surprize and telegraphed to Halleck to know who was to blame for it and the consequent dreadful slaughter of our men—Halleck answered very properly that the Confederate officers & soldiers were the cause of the dreadful slaughter at Pittsburg Landing. I still have faith that there are some honest men left who will in time accept as History the accounts of those who Kept the Front Rank, and not those of the cowards many of whom did not stop at the steamboat landing but kept on they knew not where.

On Sunday we were hard pressed, but not beaten. Many even of our Generals were discouraged, and I noticed on Sunday afternoon they hung round me for orders, which I did not hesitate to give. The position we held on Sunday morning was very strong. Beauregard admits it, and he did not drive back my wings until he had broken our Center.

Whether we should have been at Pittsburg or on the other side of the Tennessee is none of my business. I was ordered to disembark here, and we all knew we were assembling a vast army for aggressive purposes. The President knew it, Halleck knew it, and the whole country knew it, and the attempt to throw blame on Grant is villainous. The fact is if newspapers are to be our Government I confess I would prefer Bragg, Beauregard or anybody as my Ruler, and I will persist in my determination never to be a Leader, responsible to Such a power. I am working hard with my Division composed of Ohio "Boys" who have as much idea of war as so many children. Their officers came for Glory not to fight, but discipline, habit, and example may make something of them—even as they were they did more execution than many troops who are lauded by their Commanders when they know their accounts are not truth. For instance McClernands Division was a mere squad at 5 P.M. Sunday, and he gave it up as a gone day, when I assured him we could and would hold our Ground till night, and night promised strong reinforcements.

Before the Battle all supposed we had enough men here to hold the position against any the Enemy could bring, and it had been resolved to Land Buells forces daily expected for a week before, at Hamburg, a place 6 miles above from which there is a good Road to Corinth but Buell arriving at the critical hour was landed here, & now Popes army is at Hamburg. If a Division of force was wrong before, why not now. You at least can do justice to all parties. I am not in search of Glory or Fame, for I know I can take what position I choose among my Peers. affectionately yr. son,

W. T. Sherman

ALS, DLC: Thomas Ewing and Family Papers.

TO THOMAS EWING SR.

Head Qrs. Camp 2,
Near Monterey Tenn.
May 3, 1862

Hon. T. Ewing
Lancaster, Ohio
Dear Sir,

Yours of April 25 is received, and has of course been read with great Care. I do not think I exposed myself at Shiloh more than was necessary from the shape of the ground and the nature of my men. I had under me no men of either practical or theoretical Knowledge of war, and had to give orders that usually devolve on Colonels, Captains and even Corporals. I had even to instruct Gunners how to cut the *fuses* of their Shells. Therefore at times I had to be in range of artillery that otherwise I would have avoided. I knew all the time the vast importance of time and desperate fighting for each inch of ground. The enemy having the choice of attack could at first have advantage, and they took it boldly & well, and had our men as boldly met them they would not have broken our Front Line. That done however they had to spread, and the equality of force at any point was approximated—then I was able to hold them in check, all we could do and as much as could be expected.

At first their Lines & Columns advanced steadily in spite of cannister & grape—but towards 2 P.M. they approached our Lines with caution, always sending skirmishers in advance of their Lines of Battle[.] Of course I noticed this change of conduct and divined the Cause—Our shots were producing their natural effect, *fear*. Had our men rallied then we could have taken the offensive, but officers sent to the rear could not bring them up, and we had to hold on the best we could. However I suppose in your mind you have grouped the picture about as well as possible, and further explanation is unnecessary.

The experience of that day convinces me that officers should wear their uniform—not epaulettes & chapeaus, but the undress with Shoulder straps, cap with number & letter. In general appearance it does not differ much from the soldiers dress, and the story of picking off officers I discredit. The proportion of officers Killed & wounded was not excessive. I am not conscious that I was a special mark but twice, viz. early Sunday when I rode in advance of my left the weakest point, where my orderly was killed[.] That Shot was meant for me, as also the volley, but I doubt if they Knew who I was except any officer could have judged me to be a General officer from my position with a Staff following—again about 2 P.M. same day when my horse was Killed dead. I was there when grape cannister & shells were flying thick & fast, with bullets from several regiments converging on a spot where the men were down on the ground & aiming true & well.

The undress uniform should be worn that we may recognize each other with Rank & caps without questioning—We are strangers to each other, till the melee brings us in contact. General Halleck will receive from you any suggestion with marked respect, but in this I think he will concede with me that experience demonstrates the necessity of an officers uniform differing in some respects with that of enlisted men. Genl. officers also must be mounted of necessity to rapidly move from point to point, and they must be attended by staff officers to convey legally & officially their orders. Also a change of uniform is a matter of time. Our wardrobes at best are not heavily stocked, & I have been trying without success even to get a pair of shoes from St. Louis.

As to Grand Strategy, I am fully satisfied that Halleck is as competent a theorist as we have—naturally of good strong mind—a head as strongly marked as Websters, and I have known him since 1836, a hard student[.] In our voyage round Cape Horn many a time when others were struggling to Kill time, he was using it in hard study. When the Sea was high, & ship rolling, the Sky darkening so that daylight did not reach his stateroom, he stood on a stool, his book & candle on the upper berth, and a bed Strap round his middle secured to the frame to support him in the wild tossing of the ship. In such a man the country must have confidence. I am willing to repose in his strategy all confidence, and I think the other Generals, not Politicians will do the same. This confidence will secure that concert of action which can alone supply the want of discipline enforced in Europe. If Halleck cannot handle 100,000 men in a campaign no one Can. His combinations thus far have been good &

Successful, and I think they will so continue. He has labored under a serious difficulty. He has been compelled to use *fresh* levies as though they were real soldiers, and this is the Serious

AL (incomplete), Wheaton, Md.: Private Collection of Joseph H. Ewing.

TO JOHN SHERMAN

Camp 8 miles front of Corinth
May 7, 1862

Dear Brother,

I received yours of —— with General Pattersons enclosed.[1] If you have occasion to write to General Patterson say to him that there were many things done and said to be done which seem inconsistent with what I saw & Know— Still I do not attempt to reconcile such inconsistencies.

The scoundrels who fled their Ranks & left about half their number to do their work, have succeeded in establishing the story of surprise, stuck with bayonets & swords in their tents & all that Stuff.

They were surprised, astonished and disgusted at the utter want of respect for life on the part of the Confederates, whom they have been taught to regard as inferior to them—& were surprised to see them approach with banners fluttering, bayonets glistening, and Lines dressed on the Centre. It was a beautiful & dreadful sight, and I was prepared and have freely overlooked the fact that many wilted & fled, but gradually recovering rejoined our Ranks, but those who did not recover their astonishment had to cast about for a legitimate Excuse, & the cheapest one was to accuse their officers, and strange to Say their story is believed before ours who fought two Whole days.

Well you know that nothing of this sort surprises me because I knew it must be when the many govern the few. But in this instance the Scamps will soon learn their mistake—Those who run, & cried surprise cut up &c. expected all who stood to their work to be killed, but all were not killed & enough remain as witnesses after the public are satiated with the horrid stories of men butchered in their tents. Send out an investigating committee and make it complete ridiculous. The proposition made by the Secretary of War that the Chairmen of the two Committees on war should come out & investigate.

Please announce that I commanded the Front Line—that McClernand & Prentiss camped in a Line to my Rear, the Left of this Line extending past my left obliquely forward—that the attack was made on me & Prentiss about the Same time—that the Tale of surprise so far as I am concerned is the pure invention of the Cowards who deserted us & left us struggling for two days, and would *not recover* from their surprise. For two days they hung about the River Bank filling the ears of newspaper Reporters with their tales of horrid Surprise, Regiments *all* cut up—they the only survivors & to our utter amazement we find it settling down as History—Now I assert that Every Regiment of my command 12 was under arms nearly an hour before called into pull trigger—Every battery (3) was harnessed up in position before called on to fire and the cavalry—only 350 in my whole Division was in the Saddle at Daylight & the attack did not begin till the Sun was 2 hours high.

Prentiss was not surprised, for I sent him word an hour before the Enemys Infantry began to appear—and he was not made Prisoner till after 3 P.M.

For my part I am heartily sick of war & especially volunteers, and would not much care if the Committee would come out & make me the scape Goat of the Sins & Cowardice of those fellows who were determined to be surprised in spite of all notice, & staid surprised till danger was all past.

I confess I did not think Beauregard would abandon his Railroads to attack us on our Base when he knew by waiting a short time we would be forced to advance where he would most assuredly have been beaten.

I am now on the Extreme Right and we are in contact with the Enemys Pickets—Some fierce struggle must soon follow—but that the war is ended or fairly begun I do not believe. The taking of New Orleans is most important but it sets free an army to come here to us.[2] If we are defeated here, all that Halleck has gained in the last 8 mos. vanishes as a cloud & Kentucky & Tennessee become worse than ever. I do hope we may succeed, but when so much depends on an issue, it should not be trusted to inferior members. Halleck has raked from every quarter & he cannot get much over 92,000. Beauregard has now the Columbus, Bowling Green, Arkansas—Tuscumbria and New Orleans armies, all well armed, fed & clothed, and under much better discipline than ours. Their numbers run from 90, to 160,000 according to the various accounts. He may abandon Corinth & draw us to Grand Junction, further from our Base—of course we must conquer or die—but the result is not final. My love to Cecelia & all yr. brother

W. T. Sherman

Do get Mr. Lincoln to make Gilbert a Brigadier Genl. unless the title has lost all honor—Ohio has very few officers of any merit.

ALS, DLC: William T. Sherman.

1. JS to WTS not found; Patterson to JS, May 1, 1862, congratulated John on WTS's service at Shiloh and rejoiced that the public and press admitted it as well. He counted himself one of the first to appreciate WTS's abilities and asked JS to send him his thanks for his service to his country. DLC: WTS.

2. Union forces captured New Orleans, Louisiana, on April 25, 1862.

TO JOHN SHERMAN

Hd. Qrs. 5th Divn. May 12. 1862.
Camp before Corinth

My Dear Brother,

I commenced a letter to you some days since but was prevented completing it by the multifarious duties devolving on me. I have since seen the Cincinati Commercial of the 6 & 7 containing your letter and its comments referring to some of the Gazette which I did not see.[1] As you say I do not like newspaper discussions of personal matters. In the first place I deny that I am amenable to the Public much less the Press. I acknowledge full submission to the Laws of Congress & orders of the President but I do hope this war will not end until the army has a chance to prevent the universal slander & howl that arises against officers calculated to impair their usefulness. For my part though silent I have at times felt that I would prefer to be governed by Davis, Beauregard & Bragg, to be thus abused by a set of dirty newspaper scribblers who have the impudence of Satan. They come into camp, poke around among the lazy shirks & pick up their camp Rumors & publish them as facts, and the avidity with which these rumors are devoured by the Public makes even some of our officers bow to them—I will not—They are a pest and Shall not approach me, and I will treat them as spies, which in truth they are.

As to Kentucky you have stated the points strong. I doubtless committed some grave errors, but I surrendered the command purposely. I dont want to lead in this war, because I do not see far enough into the future & am not gifted with that amount of Hope & reliance on Providence which the case calls for in a leader. I find however that in times of danger and trouble all lean on me. During Sunday afternoon April 6, McClernand leaned on me all the time, but since the Battle he has ignored the fact. Every one of my staff heard him despair & despond and I actually gave orders to his troops, but I claim no credit or honor more than has been bestowed on me by Grant, Halleck and all. I was gratified on Monday, when I came in contact with my old Kentucky command. They gathered round me and were evidently pleased to meet me again, officers & men.

I think Mr. Lincoln is a pure minded, honest and good man. I have all faith in him. In Congress & the Cabinet there is too much of old politics, too much of old issues, and too little realization. I think it a great mistake to stop enlistments. There may be enough on paper, but not enough in fact. My aggregate present & absent is 10,452. Present for duty 5298, absent sick 2557—absent wounded 855—The rest are on various detached duties as teamsters and hospital attendants—embracing about 600 sick in camp. About this proportion will run through the whole army. I have not really one thorough soldier in my command—all are green & raw—my Brigadiers are all volunteer colonels, & this devolves on me extra labor & risk—Last evening I had to post my own pickets and come under the fire of enemy pickets, came near being hit, of course being mounted & ahead I & staff always get an undue share of attention.

Another point I must mention. The battle occurred the 6 & 7, on the 8th I pursued and the affair at the fallen timbers was as I reported, 2 companies of Hildebrands Regiment was deployed forward as Skirmishers—the other 8 companies followed in Line. I was in rear of their left near the road, when the enemys cavalry charged they had not to exceed 250 men, Forrests Cavalry—Had Hildebrands Regiment stood & fired as they ought they would have killed half the horses & riders—his Regiment was about 400 strong, and 100 men afoot on good covered ground are enough to receive the charge of 250 broken Cavalry, but they did not stand; but broke to the River. Behind them I had about 200 cavalry ready to assume the charge, when the Infantry fire would as it certainly would have done checked and thrown into confusion the enemys cavalry. The Regiment did break, move to the rear and gather behind the flanks of a Brigade I held in reserve. We afterwards gathered up the muskets on the ground. I only found 3 dead secessionists on the ground, Killed by the Skirmishers in advance. This Regiment itself killed none. Dickey's cavalry was thrown into confusion by the infantry & fell back on the Brigade some two hundred yards to the Rear, rallied & in line charged the cavalry, which drew up in confusion when they discovered our Brigade ready to receive them. In this charge they wounded Col. Forrest, and killed 5 Dragoons, we lost in all 18 killed whom we buried and some 30 wounded. It was not intended to make a real pursuit for we had no artillery and my orders were only to take 1 days rations. I made the Report immediately on reaching Camp that Halleck then just arrived might order a real pursuit if he thought proper—That Report of mine has been published, by whom or what authority I know not.

I made my official report of the Battle of the 6 & 7 on the 11 of April—sent it to Grant & he to Halleck.[2] It has not been published and it is none of my business an officer ought not to publish anything—his Report is to his Government, may contain confidential matter and the War Department alone Should have the discretion to publish or not according to the interest of Government. Some officers have furnished the Press with their Reports. It is very wrong and should be punished. All official Reports should go to the War Dept. and be published there or withheld according to the interest of the Government. A good many have asked for Copies of mine, but I have invariably referred them to Genl. Halleck—I sent my rough draft to Ellen to keep, and have it copied here in my official Letter Book. I have never seen it in print, but have seen allusions to it, such as Genl. Pattersons, but others attribute to me charges against the Ohio troops that I never made. My official report is the truth and I attach no more blame to Regiments & individuals more than they merit. Those Regiments & individuals who retired left a few to do an almost impossible task. Had all stood as McDowells & Bucklands the enemy could not have broken us, but when Prentiss was driven back, I would have been compelled to retire because then they had artillery to our Rear & no troops can stand that. We were not surprised—some were, for they had been taught by Politicians to believe the South would not fight. Certainly I never inculcated any such idea for I have always known & said they would fight & that well. Newspapers and even Genl. Mitchel had published that he never expected to get nearer the Enemy than long range guns, and that they Should leave their Railroads & attack us in our own Chosen Camp seemed improbable. I did not think they would—but so far as sentinels, pickets, Lines &c. are concerned all were prepared, at least all who were willing to do their duty. I have been worried to death by the carelessness of officers and Sentinels, have begged, importuned & cursed to little purpose and I will not be held responsible for the delinquencies of Sentinels fresh from home   with as much idea of war as children. All I know is we had an Entire front covered by pickets, intermediate Guards & grand Guards, and I had all my command in Line of Battle, well selected long before we had seen an Infantry soldier of the enemy. We had been skirmishing with their Cavalry for several days, and we could not get behind them. All we could see was the head of their colum. They might have had a million men. All we could see was Cavalry, and that admirably qualified by familiarity with the country for the purpose of covering an approach—Grant had been expecting Buell a whole week before he arrived— We all knew the enemy was in our front but had to guess at his purpose. Now that it is known all are prophets, but before we were supposed to be a vast aggressive force sent by an intelligent Govt. to invade the South, and for us to have been nervous on the Subject of attack would have indicated weakness— Beauregard then performed the very thing which Johnston should have done in Kentucky last October—My force was divided—he could have interposed his, attacked McCook at Nolin & Thomas at London, and would have defeated us with perfect ease. The Secessionists then would have had Kentucky & Missouri both. Why he did not is a mystery to me, and Buckner told me that Johnston's neglect on that occasion was so galling to him that he made him give a written order not to attempt the manoeuver.

Nor was Prentiss surprised—all his men were drawn up in Line of Battle before the Enemy was seen—in colums of attack. I sent two messengers one near two hours before the Battle, and another when I saw the enemy directing his course towards Prentiss on my left Rear. This aid Maj. Sanger found the Division of Prentiss actually engaged—Prentiss was not made prisoner till after 3 P.M. have been fighting back for over 7 hours. If any of his men were in bed they were lazy scamps that desired to be taken. As to my Division no man was bayonetted or taken in camp—even the sick & wagons had been sent to the rear—all these stories of Surprise were raised by the Fugitives at the River and who *would not* recover from their surprise as long as danger lasted: I am willing to overlook those who fled on Sunday, but there is no pardon for those on Monday who did not & would not join their Regiments. Not a man or officer could plead surprise or ignorance on Monday for all knew where I was and that we were to advance.

We are now encamped 7 miles from Corinth, pickets about 1½ miles in advance. I am on the Extreme Right, McClernand is to my rear, & guards off to the Right—The Roads are again pretty good, and I dont bother myself about the plans & aims of our Generals. I will do all I can with my Division, but regret I have not better disciplined and more reliable men—Too many of the officers are sick of the war, and have gone home on some pretext or other. I am in pretty good health, and keep close to my work. The success of our arms at New Orleans, Norfolk & Williamsburg are extraordinary and may result in Peace sooner than I calculated[3]—all I feel is that though we progress we find plenty of secesh every wheres—Weather begins to be hot[.] Love to Cecilia. Dont be drawn into a newspaper correspondence on my account— The time will come when I can attend to those Cowardly Rascals. yrs

W. T. Sherman

ALS, DLC: William T. Sherman.

1. WTS was confused about the dates of these papers. At this time, the *Commercial* had reversed its position on the insanity charges and supported WTS, while the editorial staff of the *Gazette* continued to question WTS's mental health. The May 5 *Commercial* had published a letter from JS written on April 30 praising WTS's conduct at Shiloh, approving his promotion to major general of volunteers, and pointing out that events in Kentucky had only showed " 'remarkable evidence of [Cump's] foresight and sagacity.' " Quoted in John F. Marszalek, *Sherman: A Soldier's Passion for Order* (New York, 1993), 186. The next day, the *Gazette* had charged that only family connections had saved WTS's career, and the *Commercial* denied these charges on May 7. Marszalek, *Sherman's Other War*, 79–80 and 92 nn. 49 and 50.

2. Actually WTS to John A. Rawlins, April 10, 1862, SFP.

3. Federal troops occupied Norfolk, Virginia, on May 10 after Confederate forces evacuated the city, and the Army of the Potomac took Williamsburg on May 6 after the Battle of Williamsburg on the previous day.

Head Qrs. 5 Divn. Army of the Tenn.
Camp before Corinth, May 16, 1862

Dear Phil,

You Know my opinion of newsmongers and Reporters, and that I scorn
them from the bottom of my soul. Besides endeavoring to injure me in every
way in their power they have attempted to raise the implication that I have
purposely thrown discredit unnecessarily on the Ohio troops. A friend has
shown me a letter from Colonel Rodney Mason of the 71st Ohio[1] now at
Clarksville Tenn., published in a Cincinati paper, in which he says I am surrounded by persons who sneer at the Ohio troops and favor the 55th Illinois at
the expense of the Ohio Regiments which formed a part of the same Brigade.

The history of this matter is this. In February last many Regiments reported to me at Paducah, and were sent forward to Genl. Pope or Grant
according to my orders from Genl. Halleck. Nine Ohio Regiments arrived
without arms. I made every possible effort, & succeeded in procuring arms
just in time to go with them up the Tennessee River. For the purpose of
instruction & discipline it was necessary to organize these Regiments along
with three (3) Illinois Regiments also at Paducah into four Brigades. I assembled all the Colonels together and we fixed their relative Rank according to the
dates of their muster into the service of the United States. The four 4 Senior
Colonels were entitled to the command of these Brigades and I so arrayed
them. Two of the Illinois Colonels, Hicks[2] & Stuart were senior in Rank to all
the Ohio Colonels and I was compelled to give them Brigades; the two other
Brigades were given to Colonels Hildebrand, and Buckland, of the Ohio the
next in order. All present were perfectly content with the arrangement except
Colonel Tom Worthington[3] who being an Old West Point Graduate claimed
that I should put him over others who held superior Commissions a thing I
could not do. Rodney Mason did not pretend that his commission entitled
him to a Brigade and expressed himself perfectly satisfied that I had placed his
Regiment in Stuart's Brigade. Colonel Stuart is of Illinois but is a gentleman
very much esteemed by all under his Command, and is peculiarly sensitive as
to the honor of those entrusted to his Charge—My Brigades remained thus up
to the Battle of Shiloh. On Sunday the 6th April Stuarts Brigade was posted at
a point of vital importance to the Field of Shiloh, viz. at the Ford of Lick
Creek, as it was detached from my other three Brigades which were at the
other extremity of the Front Line. My purpose was when Gen. Prentiss' Division became full, by the arrival of his compliment of troops, to draw back my
2nd Brigade to its proper position on the immediate left of the others, but the
Battle came off before Prentiss Division was strong enough to cover the Left

then occupied by Stuarts Brigade. The day before the Battle I rode with Colonel Stuart to examine his disposition of Guards & pickets and he has in his possession a letter of instructions I wrote him on the preceding Friday, in which I clearly pointed out to him the strong and weak points of his position cautioning him as to his Right the interval between him & Prentiss. Stuarts official Report as well as Masons are in the hands of the proper authorities and I Suppose will be published with mine at the proper time.[4] I did not send them or mine or any to the newspapers because it is positively prohibited. Colonel Mason did not say one word about his dissatisfaction at being placed under an Illinois Colonel, or suffering under the Success of my Staff. Indeed his Brigade being detached on Sunday I made no mention of it, leaving its history to his immediate commander Colonel Stuart, & I must say Col. S. touched his case delicately and softly. On Monday I ordered this Brigade up & it reported to me about 7 A.M.—When the proper time arrived I deployed it forward on the Right of a Battery which I personally directed—I did not see Col. Mason at all. His Regiment was in Line very small in numbers but was in Line & Mason was *not with it*, and Major Sanger of my staff reports to me officially that when he was sent back by me on some duty, he found Col. M. crouching behind a bank of Earth, that he remonstrated with him when Colonel Mason got up, and instead of joining the fragment of his Regiment then steadily advancing under fire, he made direct to the Steamboat Landing. I did not know this fact when I made up my Report, nor can I recal having said one word disrespectful of Col. Mason or of his Regiment then or since. I had not the least instrumentality in detaching his Regiment to Clarksville. The order came from Genl. Grant without my being consulted, and the stories of the Regiment being disgraced, deprived of its colors &c. &c. originated with others & not with me or any member of my staff. Col. Mason was a favorite with us all from his social manners, and you may search in vain in my reports for any unfavorable allusion to him. I knew his Regiment did not stand by their fellows as they Should, and I could not praise them but I spared them censure. He says over his signature that my surroundings sneered at his Regiment and the 54th Ohio (Col. T. Kilby Smith[5]) to elevate the 55th Illinois. I enclose you a letter handed me by Col T. Kilby Smith who was the first to call my attention to this letter of Colonel Mason. Of Course I will leave my official Report stand as my Record of the Battle. Every word of it is true. I may have omitted some details, or even failed to praise where it was due, but certainly I have withheld much censure which should have been bestowed. For two days we were left struggling with half companies & Regiments to do the work, and receive the bullets of whole Companies & Regiments. This was not confined to the Ohio troops, but to all whether of mine Prentiss McClernand or Hurlbuts

Divisions, but it was none of my business to report the conduct of others, but of my own, and I tried to do it truthfully in my Report: but Read Buells Report, Nelsons, every body's, and all concur in the fact that the Landing was crowded with fugitives of all Regiments & corps, that the Roads leading back were thronged by men who reported us all Killed, used up, surprised, bayonetted, every thing horrible. I did not go back to the River to See for myself. I was ever with the foremost and only saw with pain & concern that my Line was contracting in length & thining in depth, but so important was time & stubborn the resistance that I dealt with the present alone, and not with the absent—I have never indulged in fuming against those who on Sunday had not the courage to stand up before that storm of shot and ball but I have indulged in expression and feeling against those who on Monday after reinforcements came, and it was universally Known that we were to advance (who) still hung back, and did not lend us a hand. Among them I am pained to say was Rodney Mason and many far too many of the Ohio 71st Vols.

But when these men turn and say they were surprised after a months preparation for battle, and when they Knew they stood all around & equipped for war for from one to three hours before a shot was fired at them, then I say they are entitled to no delicacy at all from me.

No baser act ever occurred in History than this of trying to throw on Grant, or Prentiss and on me the blame of a surprise, false in fact, and designed to injure us and sustain those who not only exhibited a cowardice & poltroonery that induced Gen. Nelson to ask permission to fire on them as too base to live and as liable to infect other newly arriving troops. Whenever any officer or soldier has shown a disposition to nerve himself to a new effort I have sustained him, and encouraged him: but I will not permit Col. Mason— or anybody over his own signature to accuse me of doing injustice to bodies of men, such as my Ohio Regiments were & are. I have said again & again to them that Sunday's attack on us was not a surprise, but a bold well designed & well executed attack of a brave & inteligent Enemy, that to beat this Enemy we must not only exercise all our bravery & physical strength & power, but also all the skill, strategy and combination Known to the most skilful soldiers. I have even been thought to exaggerate the strength courage and determination of our enemies, and have taken excessive precautions. I did so at Shiloh, knew the ground better than any man there, and availed myself of all the skill I possessed, and though anonomous scribblers may say what they please of me Col. Mason must not shield himself at my expense. As he has wrongfully appealed from the proper tribunal to the Public of Ohio, I wish you to make use of the contents of this to put me right in respect to this matter of surprise and abuse of the Ohio troops. I hold the soldiers harmless, but I do blame those leaders whether of Military or Civil Life who have impressed the men with the belief that all they had to do was to come south and the Secesh would run. They now find themselves mistaken and are "tired of the war". I Knew this in advance and am not disappointed. We must have a terrific battle soon & God Knows I wish the Ohio troops may earn all the honor their friends at home expect of them. I will try & point out the way. As ever yr. affectionate Brother

W. T. Sherman

ALS, DLC: Thomas Ewing and Family Papers.

1. Mason had left the field during the Battle of Shiloh and then begged Grant for another chance. On April 16, Grant sent him to Fort Donelson to relieve Colonel Fouke. Mason later surrendered Clarksville, Tennessee, to Confederate forces and was subsequently cashiered for repeated acts of cowardice; this decision was revoked in 1866 and his status changed to mustered out of service to date from August 22, 1862. *PUSG*, 5:45–46n, 321, 322–23; *OR*, I, 16: pt. 1, 865.

2. Colonel Stephen G. Hicks of the Fortieth Illinois commanded Sherman's First Brigade at Shiloh after McDowell was wounded and was then wounded himself.

3. Colonel Thomas P. Worthington (1807–84) commanded the Forty-sixth Ohio in Sherman's Second Brigade.

4. Stuart's and Mason's official reports are printed in *OR*, I, 10: pt. 1, 257–60 and 261–62. Stuart reported that when he returned to the spot where he had last seen Mason during the fight to give him instructions, his regiment had disappeared; although Mason later told him where he had been, Stuart said he had been there as well and had not seen Mason there (p. 258). Mason expressed his regret that "the regiment did not bear themselves with greater steadiness" and averred that Stuart could vouch for his conduct during the battle (pp. 261–62).

5. Thomas Kilby Smith (1820–87) was the colonel of the Fifty-fourth Ohio in the Second Brigade.

TO ELLEN EWING SHERMAN

Camp on Russells, before Corinth,
May 23, 1862.

Dearest Ellen,

An opportunity occurs by which I can send back word to Pittsburg Landing, and I avail myself of it to tell you I am well and that though we are certainly Skirmishing we have not yet had a pitched Battle.

Our Line is now within 1¼ miles of the Enemys intrenchments, and we only await the arrival of some Regiments from Missouri, from Curtis Army to push on. At this moment our pickets are firing away pretty briskly. All idea of the enemy having abandonned Corinth has vanished and we now expect the enemy to be in great force in our front. My division has much improved and I think we shall hold them better to their places, though Governors & Sanitary Commissions have carried away hundreds and thousands of men, who are at home drawing pay, and leaving us unaided to do their fighting—There are

23,000, absent Sick in Grants Army alone, and as there are three such armies there must be 70,000 men absent sick—Now I know more than half of these men are not sick but have been carried off without leave or permission by Governors who claim to be doing their country service. It is cruel to those who remain behind thus to trifle with a serious matter. This Political demagoguism is being unbearable to army officers and accounts to me for the many instances in History where armies Rebel against their Government. Yesterday Governor Morton was here and wanted to carry off some of his "Indiana boys" but I would not permit it. To be sure sick men are better off at home, but sick men sometimes get well. If left here when they recover, they resume their share of work & duty which is very hard when they go home they are sure to Stay there. If you hear me accused of cruelty to the sick you can explain it. We have elegant physicians here, and plenty of beef, rice, & tea, indeed all that is necessary for the sick, and for examples sake, I will not consent to governors carrying off more, unless they bring back an equal number of well men to replace them. Were they to bring their boats loaded with healthy soldiers, we would willingly exchange sick men for them. I can hear nothing of Charley or Hugh. Write to them for me and Say that I am very busy, but that I would prefer each of us should be on different Lines, to diminish the chances, for the Survivors must take care of the children. If I survive I will take care of theirs and if they survive they must take care of mine.* Tell Phil if he publishes my letters about Lt. Gov. Stanton[1] and Col. Mason I want him to send me copies. I have seen Grant & Hurlbut and they will gladly adopt the quarrel with this Demagogue. On further inquiry I find that Stanton came here with funds & delicacies for the wounded of Shiloh. I have 8 Ohio Regiments in my command & cannot learn that he aided any of them, or relieved their wants.

He came & went away quick, before danger could possibly arise—such are the men who disgrace Ohio, not men like me who stay in the front Rank. Let them be exposed if Ohio wants to be honored & respected beyond her own limits. Love to all, yrs. ever

W. T. Sherman

*This means in plain english that he wants you to live to take care of our children. He has been sincere however in his efforts & hopes to get you down there as you know I have been. Ellen

Of Stone[2] I know nothing—he had with him the Whitings whose brother Henry[3] is high in the Rebel service.[4] Stone is not very strong but very genteel and would naturally associate with southerners & spurn the plain officious Yankees who infest us and bore us beyond endurance. I think the extent of his offending will prove to arise from this fact—as to Balls Bluff, the charge is that he crossed the Potomac with insufficient means of retreat—Had he succeeded this would not have been discovered—But as it turned out, it was a mistake, and a mistake in war is Crime. Knowing as I do the constant pressure on the army to attempt something bold & rash I cannot be critical.

Dr. Hewit is a sober, zealous, and highly educated Surgeon. He was Grants chief and the Sanitary Commission so pressed their humanitary projects on him, criticizing what he did, or what was done under the pressure of events that he lost his temper and committed imprudences. Nothing further I am assured. As to his cruelty to Sick or wounded that is simply absurd. A Surgeon operating with hundreds of wounded waiting their turn often has the appearance of heartlessness, whereas their hearts may be as bleeding as the limbs they are amputating. You see this phase of character in your own limited circle—These Sanitaries flee away when danger is near, are never at hand during the Battle but come days after & criticize the work of their betters. So greedy after victories are our People that newspapers must provide victories to Suit the market. The People are the ultimate cause when Public opinion changes a better condition of things will result & not before.

S.

ALS, DLC: Charles Ewing Papers.

1. Benjamin Stanton (1809–72), a lawyer and former congressman, was lieutenant governor of Ohio. In late April he had published a letter criticizing the conduct of Grant and Prentiss during the Battle of Shiloh in the Bellefontaine, Ohio, newspaper.

2. Charles P. Stone (1824–87), USA, was currently imprisoned under suspicion of treason after his defeat at the Battle of Ball's Bluff.

3. Brigadier General William H. C. Whiting (1824–65), CSA.

4. In her letter to WTS of April 24, EES had reiterated her dislike for McClellan, whom she labeled "a greater traitor than Jeff. Davis," had asked him whether the reports of Hewit's mistreatment of Union wounded were true, and had solicited his views on Stone's imprisonment. SFP.

TO ELLEN EWING SHERMAN

Camp before Corinth May 26, 62

Dearest Ellen,

I received from Washington today the Commission of Major General, but I know not why it gives me far less Emotion than my old commission as 1st Lieut. of artillery.[1] The latter I knew I merited, this I doubt—but its possession completes the chain from cadet up, and will remain among the family archives when you and I repose in Eternity. We still lay before Corinth, behind our trenches, both parties apprehending attack, each preferring to fight behind earth & timber barriers. Halleck told me some days back that he would await the arrival of some reinforcements from Missouri which have reached Hamburg and Should be in Line tomorrow. I am on the extreme Right, the best and largest masses of troops, being on the left—viz. Popes & Buells forces. Thomas' Right wing covers more ground than Buells & Popes combined and consequently I am again on the exposed flank. If the enemy attack us they will attack me first—if in front we are fully prepared, but if on the flank or Rear not so well[.] McClernands Division is in my Rear, but Strung out too long to give much support—We are in easy hearing of the Cars of Corinth whose whistles we hear distinctly all the time—the Branch to the East and north are broken, but the enemy still has open communication with Mobile & Memphis. I dont believe they are hard up for provisions for we find the haversacks of prisoners well stocked with good bread, ham, sugar, Rice &c.

None of us now doubt but that the entire southern army is face to face with us and full of courage & confidence. Our men are also equally full of Confidence and the chances are of one of the most desperate battles of history. So much depends on it, that not a Risk should be run. We should have an army capable of investing Corinth on all sides whereas we simply cover our quarter of the circle, leaving them full liberty to use the other three quarters.

Thus far they have not attacked our trains to the Rear, because I suppose they hold all in hand ready for one attack and make as few detachments as possible.

We hear the Mississipi fleet is up as far as Vicksburg, and that some of the Gunboats have gone to Mobile. The capture of Memphis & Mobile would only give them at Corinth reinforcements of these Garrisons—so it has been with New Orleans. The occupation of that city brought here Lovell[2] with his 20,000 men—we hear of discontent & all that with sickness superadded but I dont believe it. I have daily evidence in the fighting of their pickets of earnest well trained, well clad and well fed Soldiers, our equals in all respects. Still our army is now composed of all the best troops & men in the West and if we cannot conquer here we might as well give it up. One serious loss to us is in the great number of sick. More than 55,000 of our men are "absent sick" of course some of them are really sick, but too many of them are "tired of the war." Well we are better off without them only if we had that number added to our present army of say 100,000 men, we would have equal if not superior numbers to our adversaries. McClellan is I suppose by this time in Richmond. Our Telegraph says 5 miles off—two more miles bring him within cannon Range where a city full of women & children is no longer tenable—Prime has arrived but is at the other end of the army. I have not seen him. Miller of the Galt House[3] & Mrs. Swords wrote by him. I enclose their letters as interesting to you. It does seem to me that these two armies cannot much longer remain thus in presence of each other without collision and the telegraph may at any moment announce to you a great victory or great defeat. I know the intense anxiety felt throughout the Land, and I warrant your father hardly sleeps. For his benefit I make a small sketch of our present position and of the enemy that he may understand the Battle when its history first reaches you. I have now two good Brigadiers—Denver[4] & Morgan L. Smith,[5] who relieve me much of the details & drudgery where I had nothing but inexperienced colonels.

Minnie is now old enough to remember, and even the rest may Keep me in their memory should my career close with this, and I do feel in this fact great consolation. I also feel that let what will befal me you will be taken care of. I suppose you got safely the $200 sent from Louisville by Maj. Judd—Love to all, Yrs. ever

W. T. Sherman

ALS, InND: Sherman Family Papers.

1. WTS was made major general of volunteers on May 1, 1862.

2. Major General Mansfield Lovell (1822–84), CSA, had been in charge of the defenses at New Orleans.

3. Silas P. Miller of Memphis, Tennessee, wrote to WTS on May 19, 1862; DLC: WTS. Miller sent WTS a bottle of whiskey and various foodstuffs and congratulated him on Shiloh.

4. Brigadier General James W. Denver (1817–92), USA, was commanding the Third Brigade of Sherman's division as of May 12.

5. Colonel Morgan L. Smith (1821–74), USA, was in command of the First Brigade of Sherman's division as of May 12.

CHAPTER 5

May 31, 1862–August 25, 1862

C orinth fell at the end of May 1862. Confederate commander Pierre G. T. Beauregard had waited until Halleck was about to launch his long-awaited assault, then pulled out of the city. Instead of winning the battle that decided the fate of the war in the West, Halleck had to be content with gaining control of the railroad junction. Before long, he and his commanders would find themselves beset with the problems of governing an occupied zone populated by citizens still loyal to the Confederate cause. Thus it was with a measure of relief that Halleck accepted the post of general in chief in July 1862, leaving others to wrestle with the local citizenry, refugee blacks, and speculators eager to buy cotton.

Halleck's elevation to the top spot left Grant in charge of the District of West Tennessee. It was not a good time for Sherman's friend. He continued to suffer criticism for what happened at Shiloh. Discouraged by Halleck's treatment of him, he contemplated seeking a transfer elsewhere; if that failed, perhaps he would leave the army altogether. Sherman dissuaded him from taking such a step, reminding him that his luck might change. Like Sherman, Grant had suffered the criticisms of newspaper correspondents. Privately, however, Sherman observed that Grant "has himself thoughtlessly used the press to give him eclat in Illinois." Moreover, Sherman judged his superior "not a brilliant man," although he offered that "he is a good & brave soldier tried for years, is sober, very industrious, and as kind as a child."[1] Halleck remained Sherman's ideal of a commander. His "years of patient study" had made him an expert on the art of war, according to Sherman, who thought highly of the Corinth campaign. "Buell is our best soldier," he told his brother-in-law Philemon Ewing. "Halleck the ablest man—Grant very brave but not brilliant Thomas slow, cool & methodic."[2]

In July Sherman took over as commander of the District of Memphis. He admonished newspaper editors on their papers' contents and reminded civil officials of their obligation to preserve law and order. He was most troubled by the consequences of administration policy concerning slavery. Although he had no problem with using slaves as laborers on fortifications, he shied away from the prospect of emancipation. He believed that he was surrounded by guerrillas waiting for the chance to wreak havoc on his army. He also deplored efforts to trade with the enemy, arguing that it promised to prolong the conflict by providing the Confederates with essential supplies.

Sherman's experiences in Tennessee reinforced his earlier skepticism about the workability of a policy of conciliation toward southern whites. "I am always discouraged when I come in contact with the People They all seem so deeply bitter or indifferent that I see no hope to arise from them." It seemed useless to attempt to persuade them that the Union army was not out to destroy them—although elsewhere Sherman had advocated just such a policy to eradicate resistance. "The People here look on us as invaders come to rob them of home & property and even life," he told his daughter. "We tell them we want nothing they have. We dont want their houses, their farms, their niggers, anything they have, but they dont believe us, and I fear that this universal bitter feeling will cause the very result they profess to dread." Yet four days later he wrote his father-in-law: "As to changing the opinions of the People of the South that is impossible, and they must be killed or dispossessed."[3] In such comments he began to carve out the reasoning that underlay his determination to wage ruthless war against white Southerners so long as they continued to resist the reimposition of the authority of the United States.

As Sherman struggled with secessionists, slaves, and speculators, he continued to lash out at the press. Newspapers on both sides created evil images of the enemy to rouse passion, escalating the conflict, while rendering fickle verdicts on the performance of generals. "The very object of war is to produce results by death & slaughter," he remarked, "but the moment a battle occurs the newspapers make the Leader responsible for the death & misery, whether of victory or defeat." Generals fed reporters stories designed to elevate themselves or disparage rivals.[4] Sherman was equally angry with politicians who continued to criticize Union generalship at Shiloh, especially Ohio's lieutenant governor, Benjamin Stanton, with whom he exchanged several heated letters—until Halleck himself intervened to silence Sherman.

"I am not dependant on the Press in any manner, never having sought popularity," Sherman bragged in late August. "In fact I despise popularity obtained by the usual process of flattery and pusillanimity." Facing a people determined to fight for their independence, generals had to withstand criticism from the press and resign themselves to the consequences of a government-sanctioned policy of trade with the enemy. "Success is demanded & yet the means to attain success are withheld," he declared. It was not yet clear to him whether the North had the will to win the war.[5]

1. WTS to EES, June 6, 1862.
2. WTS to TESr, June 7, 1862; WTS to Philemon B. Ewing, July 13, 1862.

3. WTS to EES, June 27, 1862; WTS to Maria Boyle Ewing Sherman, August 6, 1862; WTS to TESr, August 10, 1862.

4. WTS to EES, June 6, 1862.

5. WTS to W. H. H. Taylor, August 25, 1862.

TO JOHN SHERMAN

[May 31, 1862]

Dear Brother

Of course the Telegraph has announced the evacuation of Corinth—I have sent to Gen. Thomas commanding Right Wing my Report—you ask for a copy—This is wrong as official Reports are the property of the War Dept.—I have sent Ellen the rough draft to keep and have instructed her to make and send you a copy—we have had no Battle and I cannot imagine why Beauregard has declined Battle. I was on the Extreme Right, and yesterday pushed into the town and beyond it, but their army had got off, and I was ordered back to this Camp.

Pope & Buell are in pursuit I understand around by the Left, but you will hear the result long before you can receive my letter.

I send you a copy of my Division order which is public inasmuch as it is issued to my own Command.[1] Its publication would interest nobody, but you Should print it on the supposition that it would interest People. I express the wish that it be not published until Hallecks announcement of the abandonment of Corinth is first made public.

I cannot imagine what turn things will now take, but I do not think Halleck will attempt to pursue far. I think that Beauregard cannot now subsist his army or hold it together long—It must divide to live, and the greatest danger is that they will scatter and constitute Guerilla Bands—The People are as bitter against us as ever, but the Leaders must admit now that they have been defeated. I hope all this army with some exceptions will be marched forthwith to Memphis—a part could be spared for Huntsville Alabama and Nashville—but as to pursuing overland it would be absurd—We want the Mississipi now, in its whole length and a moment should not be lost. I am glad the President has called for more men. He cannot have too many, and the more men, the sooner the work will be done. All is not yet accomplished although certainly large strides have been made—If McClellan succeed at Richmond, and we can take Memphis we could afford to pause and let events work. Banks repulse was certain.[2] Three converging armies whose point was in possession of the enemy was worse Generalship than they tried to force on me in Kentucky, of diverging lines with a superior enemy between—Our People must respect the well established Principles of the art of war, else successful fighting will produce no results. Am glad you are pleased at my Report at Shiloh—It possesses the merit

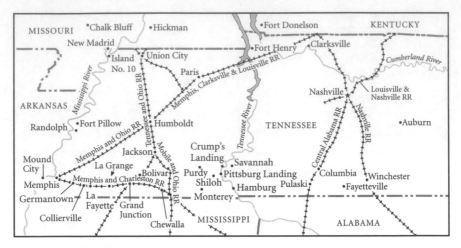

Western Tennessee

of Truth and you may safely rely on it, for I make no points but what I can sustain. Your Speech was timely and proper for you—you could explain whereas I had to repeat actual facts without fear or favor. I will write when more at leisure—The enemys works are very extensive. They must have had 100,000 men. yr brother

W. T. Sherman

ALS, DLC: William T. Sherman.

1. WTS wrote this letter on a printed copy of his Orders No. 30, May 31, 1862, thanking his army for its performance since Shiloh.

2. Stonewall Jackson defeated Nathaniel Banks at the Battle of Winchester on May 25; Banks continued his retreat from the Shenandoah Valley the next day.

TO ULYSSES S. GRANT

Camp at Chewalla June 6th 1862.

Major General Grant
My Dear Sir,

I have just received your note, and am rejoiced at your conclusion to remain.[1]

For yourself you could not be quiet at home for a week, when armies were moving, and rest could not relieve your mind of the gnawing sensation that injustice has been done you.

There is a power in our land, irresponsible, corrupt and malicious—"the press," which has created the intense feelings of hostility that has arrayed the two parts of our country against each other, which must be curbed and brought within the just limits of reason and law, before we can have peace in America.

War cannot cease as long as any flippant fool of an editor may stir up the passions of the multitude, arraign with impunity the motives of the most honorable, and howl on their gang of bloody hounds to hunt down any man who despises their order.

We can deal with armies who have a visible and tangible existence, but it will require tact and skill and courage to clip the wings of this public enemy, and I hope you have sufficiently felt the force of what I say to join in their just punishment before we resign our power and pass into the humble rank of citizens.

The moment you obtained a just celebrity at Donelson, by a stroke of war more rich in consequences than was the battle of Saratoga, envious rivals and malicious men set their pack of hounds at you, to pull you from the pinnacle which you had richly attained.

By patience and silence we can quiet their noise, and in due time make them feel that in defaming others, they have destroyed themselves.

Already is their power of mischief on the wane, and as soon as a few I could name, drop the dirty minions of a corrupt press, they will drop back into the abyss of infamy they deserve.

Of course I only asked for your escort, when I believed you had resolved to leave us, and assure you that I rejoice to learn of your change of purpose.

I wish you would see that the other three companies of the 4th Illinios Cavalry ordered to me are made so by the order.

I instantly relieved Thielemann's Cavalry[2] and sent it to where you assigned it, but the companies ordered to me in their place have not yet come, nor do I hear of them. I would account it a favor if you would remind McClernand of the importance of seeing such orders of transfer obeyed promptly.

I need this Cavalry as I have to picket forward and to the right strongly, and should have in reserve a pretty large cavalry force to send on special scouts. My Cavalry is sadly reduced in strength by sickness, and in even with the addition of the other three companies, I doubt if I shall be able out of the eleven companies of the 4th Illinois Cavalry to get three hundred men in the saddle. I am with great respect Your Obed't. Serv't—

W. T. Sherman
Maj. Gen'l.

Copy, InND: Sherman Family Papers. Addressed in WTS's hand: "To Col. R. N. Scott—/War Records—/Private—Do *not* print/W. T. Sherman/Genl./Oct. 1, 1881."

1. Letter not found. See *PM*, 1:282–84, for an account of Grant's plan to take a thirty-day leave of absence without definite plans to return.

2. Major Christian Thielemann commanded Thielemann's Illinois Battalion of Cavalry.

Camp at Chewalla, 10 miles n. west of
Corinth, on Memphis R.R.
June 6, 1862

Dearest Ellen,

I wrote you after the occupation of Corinth sending you my original Report and orders.[1] I had hardly finished my letter when I got orders to march to dislodge the enemy at Smiths Bridge. I marched through Corinth and four 4 miles this side when dark overtook me with heavy rain. I pushed the Cavalry 3 miles further to Smiths Bridge over the Tuscumbria but there was no enemy to dislodge—The second part of my order was then to cover the work on the Memphis & Charleston R.R.—on the morning of the evacuation the enemy Cavalry by order of Beauregard burned three 3 bridges in a short span 3 miles west of Chewalla Station, and it so happened that 7 trains left Corinth about the same time, and on reaching the Burnt bridge the Conductors finding their way cut off and a return to Corinth dangerous, they burned the Cars, and damaged the Locomotives all they could. This wreck encumbered the Road for a mile in the swamp, very difficult to get at—I took post here and have a thousand men at work with hardly any tools, but we have Cleared away the wrecks and 7 Locomotives and about half a dozen platform Cars, and about 200 pairs of wheels—all the woodwork has been burned up, save the few cars named. Six Locomotives have been sent in to Corinth, and I expect to save the 7th tomorrow though it is now flat on its side in the ditch. My Division is encamped on a high Ridge 10 miles NW of Corinth. Of course I am in camp with it, and Send out details to work at the Burnt Cars and track. I doubt if we can repair the Bridges or make much use of this Road, but the Locomotives can be sent up to Jackson Tenn. and down to Grand Junction. Pope has followed the Enemy south[2] and many stragglers have come in, and from the bulk of testimony I am convinced that much of the Southern army is tired of the War—They certainly at Corinth had all the advantages they can get at any other point, save that we must scatter and then be subject to attack in detail, but after having fairly declined battle I doubt if Beauregard can hold his forces. Such a manoeuvre might succeed in Europe where armies obey orders without question or thought, but not here, where the men are influenced so much by appearances. Certainly the Evacuation of Corinth[3] was successfully accomplished, but the great number of deserters and stragglers shows that its effect on their Ranks has been bad. Yet I doubt not they hold Still a formidable mass against whom we must be guarded—Halleck certainly has displayed great sagacity, more than any leader in this war, and he merits the confidence reposed in him. Your father is a good judge for he Knows the difficult part a man has to play in Our Country where the People Rule. Halleck has dutch blood in him and dont fret at the newspapers, who cannot swerve him from his course. The Correspondents will meet their match in him. A man must be in position to appreciate the arrogance of this new power in the Land, the newspaper clique, and their presumption is only equalled by their cowardice & pusillanimity. This war will have more objects than one to accomplish, and this is one, to make all men North & South obey & revere the Written Law, and despise the mere popular impulse of the hour. There is no man living who better Knows the truth than Your father, and that our Government has gradually been tending to anarchy. This war will instill into our people the conviction that we must obey the Law, not because we like & approve it, but blindly because it is Law. Halleck has been very marked in his attentions to me, promptly yielding to my opinions and suggestions. Sister Angela[4] wrote me of two southern surgeons in her hospital who are pining for home. I wrote to Halleck and he promptly ordered their release. He ordered my 4 companies 13 Inf. to me four 4 weeks ago and when you telegraphed me, I again inquired the Cause of delay, and he reiterated that he had made the order & would enquire the Cause. I doubt if Burbank[5] is as anxious to come as he professes. I have not written to Charley because I have anxiously expected him here—If you learn he is not yet away write him what I say. I owe Hugh a letter also, and wish you to supply the omission. I have very little time to write, always when all else are sleeping. I have been very active, have had to reconnoitre & study ground closely & well. Much depends on this and Halleck has confided this flank to me exclusively & with implicit confidence. My Division is now esteemed one of the best, & although Pope is constantly flourishing in the papers he has made several moves and been compelled to fall back as at Farmington,[6] but I have not lost an inch of ground gained. Thus my Division was in Corinth an hour before Pope got there—There is no Court house on which to display a flag, but beyond Corinth is a large College, and it was the flag of the 54th Ohio of my Division that flew from its steeple first & last. My Provost Marshal first was in possession of the Public property & did not relinquish it till today, when I ordered him to join his Regt. here. These are facts known to thousands and tell who was first in Corinth. It is an empty honor for which I would not contend, but as the Truth develops honest people will detect the attempt at fraudulent claims. I suppose we will still move cautiously till Halleck can divine the purposes of the Enemy, when some of us will move to Memphis. I want to go there. Prime & Hamilton are on the left and we are widely separated—I have not seen Prime yet, & Hamilton but once. Love to All—yrs. ever

Sherman.

2nd Sheet

daylight June 6, 1862

P.S. I got all or nearly all the papers here somehow or other, and have seen most of all the pieces you have clipped out, but I had not seen that of your father from the Louisville Journal signed E.[7]—It is sufficiently complimentary more so than I merit, from such a high source, and the illustration of the fable of the warriors fight with the mud turtles is very strong and like your father. I will get even with the miserable class of corrupt editors yet. They are the chief cause of this unhappy war—they fan the flames of local hatred, and keep alive those prejudices which have forced friends into opposing hostile Ranks. At the North and South each Radical class keeps its votaries filled with the most outrageous lies of the other. In the North the People have been made to believe that those of the South are horrid barbarians, unworthy of christian burials whilst at the South the People have been made to believe that we wanted to steal their negros, rob them of their property pollute their families and to reduce the whites below the level of their own negros. Worse than this at the North, no sooner does an officer rise from the common level, but some rival uses the Press to malign him, destroy his usefulness, and pull him back to obscurity or infamy. Thus it was with me, and now they have nearly succeeded with Grant—He is as brave as any man should be, he has won several victories such as Donelson which ought to entitle him to universal praise, but his Rivals have almost succeeded through the instrumentality of the Press in pulling him down, and many thousands of families will be taught to look to him as the cause of the death of their fathers, husbands & brothers.

The very object of war is to produce results by death & slaughter, but the moment a battle occurs the newspapers make the Leader responsible for the death & misery, whether of victory or defeat. If this be pushed much further officers of modesty & merit will Keep away will draw back into obscurity and leave our armies to be led by fools or rash men, such as Ed Baker. Grant had made up his mind to go home, I tried to dissuade him, but so fixed was he in his purpose that I thought his mind was made up & asked for his escort a Co. of 4th Ills. but last night I got a note from him saying he would stay. His case is a good illustration of my meaning. He is not a brilliant man and has himself thoughtlessly used the press to give him eclat in Illinois, but he is a good & brave soldier tried for years, is sober, very industrious, and as kind as a child. Yet he has been held up as careless, criminal, a drunkard, tyrant and every thing horrible. Very many of our officers Knowing how powerful is public opinion in our Government have kept newspaper correspondents near their persons to praise them in their country papers, but so intense is public curiosity that several times flattery designed for one county has reached others, and been published to the world making their little Heros big fools. It had become so bad, and the evil is not yet eradicated, that no sooner was a battle fought than every colonel & captain was the hero of the fight—Thus at Shiloh for a month all through Illinois & Missouri a newspaper Reader would have supposed McClernand and Lew Wallace were away ahead of my Division, whereas the former was directly behind me, and the other at Cumps Landing. Again at Corinth, you will hear of 500 first men inside the works. Let them scramble for the dead Lions paw. It is a barren honor not worth contending for. If these examples and a few more will convince the Real substantial men of our country that the Press is not even an honest exponent of the claims of men pretending to serve their country, but the base means of building up Spurious fame, and pulling down honest merit, I will feel that I have my full reward in being one of the first to See it and suffer the consequences. I Know that at the time the swarm of newspaper correspondents were besieging our army, and making a proper policy against Spies impossible, that Halleck had official Complaints of several *General* officers against each other, that their rivals by name kept in their camps paid men of the press, to pick up items to write themselves up and their Rivals down. These official papers are still in existence and Halleck can show them as evidence that some high officials appealed to him for protection against this hidden insidious danger. It has more than once led to serious quarrels among our own officers, and both attacks & false praise appearing at home under assumed names, quiet men are disturbed by feeling against probably the wrong author or promoter. What Stranger Evidence was ever produced of the low depth to which our Government had sunk, when newspaper scribblers publish to the world, that spite of Genl. Hallecks order, they might have evaded it, and remained in Camp in false guises near the persons of Generals, colonels, &c. &c.—My Rule is now well understood, and they keep clear of me. If one comes into my camp, I will arrest him as a spy & have him tried by a court marital, & if possible shot or hung. The time has come when the real People will sustain an officer in the exercise of such just & necesssary power, for the Real People can have no desire to bolster up men who resort to such dirty means to acquire a false fame.

Clip out all good articles & paste them in the Scrap book with date &c., and in this way you will Keep a history of passing events. Show this sheet to your father as he will catch my meaning though hastily expressed yrs. ever,

S.

ALS, InND: Sherman Family Papers.

1. WTS to EES, June 2, 1862, SFP, had apparently enclosed these documents, now elsewhere.

2. Pope had pursued Beauregard south of Corinth.

3. Beauregard had evacuated the city on May 30, avoiding confrontation with Federal forces.

4. Angela Gillespie was running the nursing staff at the Union hospital at Mound City.

5. Sidney Burbank was lieutenant colonel of the Thirteenth U.S. Infantry.

6. Federal troops had retreated from Beauregard around Farmington, Mississippi, in May.

7. These clippings apparently included a flattering article on WTS in Kentucky by editor George D. Prentice of the *Louisville Journal*, an editorial from the *Cincinnati Gazette* on Halleck, and Thomas Ewing Sr.'s article praising WTS and Halleck. See EES to WTS, May 29, 1862, SFP.

TO THOMAS EWING SR.

Camp at Chewalla, Tenn.
June 7, 1862.

Hon. T. Ewing
Lancaster Ohio
Dear Sir

I fear you think I have neglected to use my influence to get Charley here, or away from Alton.[1] It was a mere accident of war that the Battalion was sent to Alton. Pope took a lot of prisoners, & Alton was chosen as their Prison. Genl. Halleck naturally cast about for a Guard & thought the Battalion of Regulars then forming would be the very thing & so ordered. As soon as I spoke to him of its demoralizing effect he frankly admitted it and gave me his promise to replace them as soon as he could by some other Detachment. The very first day after his arrival at Pittsburg Landing I reminded him of his promise & received his assurances that he would relieve them by a Detachment of Popes Army then at Island 10. You Know how indelicate it would be for me a Genl. of [a] Division to question the sincerity & truth of my superior in whose word I feel absolute confidence, but when Ellen telegraphed me your solicitude on the same matter I again telegraphed to him and now enclose his answer which is positive and Emphatic. I must and do presume he has given the necessary orders, and cannot imagine why such delay has occurred. The details of a Grand army such as this are vast but I do think Halleck gives them his whole time and thoughts and I cannot push this point further but whenever I go to Head Quarters which is 10 miles off, I will enquire of the proper subordinate how matters stand in this regard. Can I do more. I Know Halleck feels every disposition to oblige me personally. He has manifested it on all occasions, and I still think Charley will have abundant opportunities to display his Zeal & prowess. I did think we would have at Corinth a long, hard and desperate fight in which I feared a terrible slaughter, and in my heart almost rejoiced that Charley was not present to incur the risks of a Captain, but it has resulted otherwise, and I now regret he was not present to learn the lesson which that movement would have taught him.

Still I say he has no reason to despair of a chance for distinction as our Enemy is not yet defeated. He still holds a large army & country, and no one is wise enough to foresee the turn which Events may take.

The first part of Hallecks dispatch to me is in answer to a request I made him to release two Rebel surgeons at Mound City about whom Eliza Gillespie wrote me, to which you see he readily assented.

Please write to Charley and dont let him feel that I have neglected him willingly. Most willingly would I give him all the honors & distinctions in my gift, but the chances of war are so uncertain that I almost dread to have him exposed to them. I dont want him to become enamored of military fame, but to devote his time & talents to his real profession that of the Law. The dignity of that Profession must be enhanced by this war for I contend we are fighting for the supremacy of *Written* Law, as against the Rule of mere party & popular prejudice. Until all the People are willing to refer all questions even of the greatest magnitude to our Courts, instead of to mere Party Cabals, or the dread chances of war there can be no real Peace. Therefore I do feel that all the sacrifices we are now making are to enhance the dignity of the Profession of Law, rather than the influence of the Military class which is too costly to be endured long. I would impr{ess} this on Charley and on all young aspiring Lawyers.

I see and feel that you are deeply interested in the progress of events. At times I have been and am appalled by the magnitude of the danger that envelops us as a People from the Rebellion of the South & tendency to pure democracy & anarchy of the North and therefore will continue to avoid a leading part till I can see daylight ahead—I know & feel that I am fully the equal of any about me except Halleck, who by years of patient study has a{tt}ained a Knowledge of the Laws of War & Peace that I do not pretend to, but I will continue to pla{y} my subordinate part well, looking only for m{y} reward to your respect & approval, and a deeper longer and Keener hope, that Ellen & my Children may in after years look back with pleasure & pride upon the record of my acts & conduct.

Excuse so long a letter on such minor points. With great respect Yours ever,

W. T. Sherman

Photostat of ALS, DLC: Charles Ewing Papers.

1. For an idea of the family pressure WTS was under to effect Charley's transfer, see EES to WTS, April 13, 18, 19, 26, and 29, and May 2 and 9, 1862, SFP.

Camp Chewalla
June 10, 1862

Dearest Ellen,

I have written much of late and have been out in the Sun too much. My head aches terribly and the Dr. says I must not write by candle tonight as tomorrow I must take the Road for Memphis. I have received Phils yours & your fathers letters about mine to Stanton[1] & have modified it so as to be less belligerent & more in accordance with your father's views. The more I think of it the more angry I become that a man high in office should so far abuse his position & opportunities as to injure us who at the least are doing our best. If Stanton can do less bungling why not come here. I will cheerfully surrender my post to him or any one who will bungle less—but he is a Coward & Rascal and I hope my letter will be published and let him digest it. In time Grant will have a word to say. I regret your father does not approve my idea that unless this abuse behind our backs ceases all officers of merit will slide out and let our armies go to the Devil with Politicians to lead. We have plenty Such here who are spoiling for a fight, but take precious care of their hides. This order to Memphis is of my Choice. I think the Mississipi the great artery of America and whatever power holds it, holds the continent. We should not however go much further south till Virginia is possessed by the North. This will in time reduce the war to the limits of the Cotton States proper, where it will be in a shape that can be handled.

Tell Willy & Tom of course to go barefooted all the summer. I will write to him on this important matter soon. Tell Minnie & Lizzie to write me also. I am always glad to hear such good accounts of them. Tell Phil I will answer his and if your father be not at home tell him I have enclosed my Stanton Letter to yr. father but want Phil to have it copied, the copy published in Columbus & Cincinati, and the original sent someday to Stanton. A dirtier trick was never acted than his. He came here with 5000 to relieve the wounded—I had 8 Ohio Regiments with 1000 wounded but I cannot hear any of them were relieved by him.

My head aches awful, so good night & goodbye Ever yrs.

Sherman

ALS, InND: Sherman Family Papers.

1. On June 1, 1862, EES wrote WTS about his letter to Stanton: "I return your letter to Stanton which Father took into his own Hands & desires you to reconsider & write with greater care as he says it is not only for the present time but for future history." Thomas Ewing Sr. had said that WTS should write the letter so that there was nothing that Stanton could attack. EES wanted to see it printed so that "all may know you have flung defiance in the teeth of the base libeller." She added that Tom had written them that Charley's unit

should have been transferred to Elmira, New York, according to orders dated May 1, 1862, and she asked if WTS could check on this. She was certain that there was a conspiracy in the army to hold back those related to WTS. SFP.

TO BENJAMIN STANTON

Camp in the Field near
Chewalla Tennessee
June 10th 1862—

Lieut. Gov. B. Stanton
Columbus Ohio.
Sir;

I am not surprised when anonymous scribblers write and publish falsehoods or make criticisms on matters of which they know nothing, or which they are incapable of comprehending. It is their trade. They live by it. Slander gives point and piquancy to a paragraph and the writer being irresponsible or beneath notice, escapes a merited punishment.

It is different with men in high official station who like you descend to this dirty work. You had an opportunity to learn the truth, for I saw you myself at Shiloh soon after the battle, and know that hundreds would have aided you in your work had you been in search of facts. You never enquired of me concerning the truth of events which you must have known transpired in my sight and hearing, but seem to have preferred the "camp stories" to authentic data then within your reach. A friend by mere accident has shown me a printed slip of newspaper dated April 19th 1862, styled "Extra," published at Bellefontain Ohio, and signed B. Stanton. I am further told, you are the man. If so, and you be the Lieut. Governor of Ohio, I hold that I am your peer as well as Generals Grant, Hurlbut and Prentiss, all of whom you directly charge with conduct on the Field of Shiloh which deserves a Court Martial, whose sentence if you have not become false witness, would be degredation or death.

The accusatory part of your published statement is all false, false in general, false in every particular, and I repeat, you could not have failed to know it false when you published that statement.

To prove what I say, I quote the concluding part of your paper: "Some complaints have been made about the conduct of a few of the new regiments in this battle, including the 54th and 57th. It must be remembered that these are new regiments, that not only have they never seen any service, but that they never received their guns until they arrived on the Tennessee some two or three weeks before the battle. So with Myers Battery, it has been more than six since they had their horses.

Yet these regiments, and this battery were put on the extreme out side of our camp, and were consequently first exposed to the enemy's fire. Add to this that our lines were so carelessly and negligently guarded that the enemy were absolutely on us, and in our very tents before the officers in command were aware of their approach. The wonder therefore is not that these regiments were finally broken and routed, but that they made any stand at all. But the loss sustained by these regiments and especially by Captain Starr's company in the 54th, show that they made a noble and gallant stand, and that their ultimate retreat was not the fault of the men, but of the blundering stupidity and negligence of the General in Command.

There is an intense feeling of indignation against Generals Grant and Prentiss, and the general feeling amongst the most intelligent men with whom I conversed, is that they ought to be court-martialled and shot." Yours &c. signed

B. Stanton."

With Myer's Battery I have nothing to do, as it was in General Hurlbut's Division, who has made his Official report which proves yours untrue, for instead of being kept on the "extreme outside of our Camp," it was at the beginning of the battle more than a mile to the rear of mine and McClernands and Prentiss's Divisions. The 54th, T. Kilby Smith, and 57th Colonel Wm. Mungen, did form a part of my command. No one that I ever heard has questioned the courage and gallantry of the 54th unless it be inferred from your own apology for them, and I know that I speak the mind of the officers of that regiment when I say they scorn to have their merits bolstered up by your loud and impotent conclusion. As to their being on the outer line, it was where they wished to be; and so far from being surprised, they were by my order, under arms at daylight, and it was nearly ten A.M. before the enemy assailed their position. This was so favorable that Colonel Stuart with his small brigade of which the 54th formed a part, held at bay for hours, Hardees whole Division composed of infantry, artillery and Cavalry.

The 57th was posted on the left of Shiloh Meeting House, which I say, and in which Beauregard concurs with me, was the key to the whole position. It was in the very front, the place of honor to which Colonel Mungen, or his men could not object; their front was guarded by themselves and if negligence is charged, it belongs to the regiment itself, and so favorable was the ground that although the regiment lost but two officers and seven men, Colonel Mungen has more than once assured me that he counted fifty dead secessionists on the ground over which he was attacked. As to the enemy being into their very camp before the Officers in command were aware of their approach, it is the most wicked falsehood that was ever attempted to be thrust upon a people already sad and heart-sore at the terrible but necessary casualties of war. That the cowards who deserted their commands in that hour of danger should in their desperate strait to cover up their own infamy, invent such a story was to be expected, but that you should have lent yourself as a willing instrument in perpetuating that falsehood, is a shame from which you can never hope to recover.

The truth is now well understood.

For days we knew the enemy was in our front, but the nature of the ground and his superior strength in cavalry prevented us from breaking through the veil of their approach, to ascertain their true strength and purpose; but as soldiers we were prepared at all times to receive an attack, and even to make one, if circumstances warranted it. On that morning our pickets had been driven in, our main guards were forced back to the small valley in our front. All our regiments of infantry, batteries of Artillery, and squadrons of Cavalry were prepared. I, myself their Commander, was fully prepared, rode along the line of this very regiment and saw it in position in front of their Camp, and looking to a narrow causeway across the small creek by which the enemy was expected and did approach. After passing this regiment I rode into Appler's position[1] and beyond some five hundred yards, when I was fired on and my orderly Holliday killed. After that, I gave some directions about Waterhouse's Battery,[2] and again returned to Shiloh Church in time to witness the attack there.

It is simply ridiculous to talk about a surprise; To be sure very many were astonished and surprised, not so much at the enemy's coming, as at the manner of his coming; and these sought safety at the river, and could not be prevailed on to recover from their "surprise" till the enemy had been driven away by their comrades after two days hard fighting.

I have never made a question of the individual bravery of this or any other regiment, but merely state facts. The regiment still belongs to my command, and has elicited my praise for its improvement and steadiness in the many skirmishes and affairs during our advance on Corinth, and I doubt not the people of Ohio will yet have reason to feel the same pride in this regiment as they now do in many others of that same state of deservedly high repute. As to the intense feeling against General Grant or Prentiss, could any thing be more base than that? Grant just fresh from the victory of Donelson, more rich in fruits than was Saratoga, Yorktown, or any other ever fought on this Continent, is yet held up to the people of Ohio his native state, as one who in the opinion of the intelligent cowards is worthy to be shot; and Prentiss, was absent, and a prisoner, unable to meet your wicked and malicious shaft, also condemned to infamy and death. Shame on You! and I know I tell you an unpleasant truth when I assure you, he nor his men was surprised, butchered in their tents &c., but on the contrary were prepared in time to receive the shock of battle, more terrible than any the annals of American history have heretofore recorded. He met it manfully and well, for hours bore up against the superior hosts, fell back slowly and in order until he met the Reserves under Wallace and Hurlbut, and fought till near four P.M. when he was completely enveloped and made prisoner. Well do I remember the line after line of steady troops displaying the bloody banner of the South, and to me the more familiar Pelican flag of Louisiana, bearing down on Prentiss who was to my left and rear and how though busy enough with my own appropriate point, I felt for his army, and dispatched to him my aid Major Sanger to give him notice. My Aid found him in advance of his Camp, fighting well but the shock was too great, and he was borne back step by step till made prisoner six hours after your supposed informants had sought refuge under the steep banks of the Tennessee.

So much for the history of events you did not behold and yet pretend to comment on.

You came to Shiloh on a mission of mercy, after the danger was over and before a new one arose. You tarried a few days but I Cannot learn from Ohio Colonels how you dispersed your charitable trusts. That is none of my business, but I do know you abused your opportunity and caught up vague, foolish camp rumors from the region of the steam boat landing, instead of seeking for truth where alone you did know it could be found, among the thousands of brave Ohio men who were in my camp, who can and will boast of never having seen the Tennessee River since the day we disembarked.

You then returned to your state, and in an obscure printed paper, circulate libels and falsehoods whose location and distance made it highly improbable that you could ever be held to an account.

You knew that we were in the presence of a fierce, bold and determined enemy, with hundreds of miles of ambush before us, from which a few stray shots would relieve you of your intended victims.

You knew our men were raw and undisciplined and that all our time was taken up in organization, drill and discipline, leaving us no time to meet your malicious slanders, and resent your insults. The hour of reckoning therefore was distant and uncertain. You have had your day, but the retreat of the enemy and a day of comparative rest has given me the leisure to write this for your benefit. Grant and Hurlbut and Prentiss still live and will in due time pay their respects to you. If you have no respect for the honor and reputation of the Generals who lead the Armies of your Country, you should have some regard for the honor and welfare of the country itself.

If your paper could have had its intended effect of destroying the confidence of the Executive, the Army and the people in their Generals, it would have produced absolute and utter disorganization.

It not only placed courage and cowardice, stubbornness and enduring valor and ignominious flight upon the same base, but it also holds up to public favor those who deserted their colors, and teaches them to add insubordination to cowardice.

Such an Army as your military morals would produce could not be commanded by any General who hoped to win reputation or who had reputation to lose.

Our whole force if imbued with your notions, would be driven across the Ohio, and even you would be disturbed in your quiet study where you now in perfect safety write libels against the Generals who organize our Armies, and with them fight and win battles for our Country. I am &c.

W. T. Sherman[3]

Maj. Genl. Comdg.

Copy, InND: Sherman Family Papers. Docketed in Sherman's hand: "Official/To be printed/W.T.S.—" and "It ought to have/been printed, but I/believe I afterwards/withdrew it because/it was too Severe—/but it was literally/true./W.T.S." See note 3.

1. Colonel Jesse J. Appler commanded the Fifty-third Ohio in the Third Brigade. He had been mustered out of service on April 18, 1862, before WTS submitted his name to Grant as an officer who should be court-martialed for his battlefield behavior.

2. Company E of the First Illinois Artillery was attached to the Third Brigade and commanded by Captain Allen C. Waterhouse.

3. Stanton responded with a letter dated June 23, printed in the *Cincinnati Commercial* of June 25, assailing Sherman. WTS replied on July 12, refuting the notion that Federal troops were surprised at Shiloh and questioning the accuracy of Stanton's sources. DLC: WTS and SFP.

TO ELLEN EWING SHERMAN

Moscow Tenn. June 27, 1862

Dearest Ellen,

The weather is intensely hot, and we have been marching, countermarching & Knocking about and have stopped here awhile. We have repaired all the Bridges but the Secesh Cavalry got in on the Road about 18 miles from Memphis, threw off the track the only locomotive we have on that part of the Road. No cars therefore have gone over the track. The secesh must have got about a hundred prisoners mostly men returning from furlough. All my cavalry was out guarding wagon trains and I had none to send in pursuit. The enemy is gathering in considerable force about Holly Springs and we will have to go and attack them. We cannot tell how strong they are and must go it blind[.] McClernands Division will come down from Jackson to Grand Junction. Hurlbut is at Lagrange and I am at Moscow, 40 miles from Memphis. The ground is low & flat and we have to use the water of Wolf Creek. The sun is so hot that many of our men fall down in the Road and have to be hauled in wagons. I dont think one half our force is fit for duty. The enemy has calculated on this and he may win on it.

I have been very sick bilious from terrible head ache, pains & lassitude, for the first time in my life on a march I found myself unable to ride and had to use an ambulance—I attribute my attack to a small military cap I wore. I now have two Straw hats from Memphis.

Has Charley got off yet or not—has he come to Memphis? It is not designed that we go to Memphis but protect this Road. It is going to be a difficult task for there is not a Union man within 50 miles, and the Enemys Cavalry is as thick as thieves down about Cold water, from which they can sally any night and rip up a few Rails. Over goes the next train and we have no trains to Spare.

All the Rolling Stock of these Roads was sent south before we got possession[.] You must not suppose the war is at an end or any thing like it. If McClellan take Richmond which I believe he will it will be another great feat. Still they have a vast country and a determined people. Mrs. Turner would almost be classed as a Union woman here. The women are as much more bitter on the Yankees here, than Mrs. Turner as she is more than you. The men have allowed a few soldiers to burn hundreds and thousands of bales of Cotton and have not dared to raise their hands although it was all they had to buy provisions with for their families. I am always discouraged when I come in contact with the People They all seem so deeply bitter or indifferent that I see no hope to arise from them. Even were they moved by a sense of their own protection I would have some hope of an Union Sentiment, but I see no hope of any here. Though they have lost all the Rivers but Vicksburg they are as still as far from being subdued as they were the first day of the Rebeln. I think I am now free of my illness and with care in a few days will regain my strength.

Dayton[1] is also much better though still on the Sick list. My love to all yrs. ever

W. T. Sherman

ALS, InND: Sherman Family Papers.
1. Captain Lewis Mulford Dayton (d. 1891), USA, an Ohio volunteer officer on WTS's staff, was a favorite of EES.

TO S. S. L'HOMMEDIEU[1]

Camp at Moscow, Tenn. July 7 1862

S. S. L. Hommedieu, Esq.
Cincinnati, Ohio.
Dear Sir

I thank you most kindly for your letter on mine addressed to Lt. Gov. Stanton. Very few know my real opinion of the press. There was a time, that to which you refer, when such men as Gales,[2] Hammond,[3] King,[4] and yourself presided in the Editors sanctum, and scorned to tell a falsehood, or draw an unfair deduction, especially when private character was involved. Then only such as voluntarily placed themselves as candidates for office were dissected; but a change has crept in ever since I have begun to observe facts and draw my own conclusions; and that change has gradually enlarged so that newspapers are used as a private machine. I saw the evil stript bare in California, when adventurers and rascals, with Penitentiary Diplomas, got possession of the Press and openly attempted to black-mail & browbeat Citizens in their private business. I have had newspaper men, of fair standing, demand statistics of a Bank I then controlled with threats of absolutely raising a public clamor unless their wants were satisfied. I then, in California, was brought in close contact with the Press and was amazed at the meaness of men who presumed to criticise the laws and business operations of men engaged in purely private pursuits. I conceived a terrible mistrust of the Press in California because these men are less reserved and the secret operations of the wire pullers are more open to the common man; and when this war broke out and {swarms} of the same genus hung around our camps, publishing items as unlike the truth as possible, writing up this General and down that, my mind was forced to the conclusion that a great change has come over our country since the days of our youth. I went to Kentucky with the clear distinct understanding that I was to play a subordinate part—Gen. Anderson was to lead, I to work. I had then, as now, my reasons and wishes in this, to me, sad but necessary war, to play a subordinate part, and when Anderson left me alone I found myself occupying one of the most important positions on Earth. The South was pretty well prepared—the North not [at] all. Kentucky hung in the Balance, and on her hung the Union. For months I had in front of Louisville less than 6000 men, whilst Buckner and Sidney Johnston from 25, to 40,000 within two days' march of Louisville. It was necessary to conceal our weakness. The Louisville papers published nothing about Army movements, appreciating the good reasons; but the Cincinnati papers published the most minute facts would not desist. One day, when in camp at Muldraugh Hill, one of the New York reporters came to me, and demanded to know the strength of my forces, their position etc., etc. in the most insolent tone and manner. I gave him fifteen minutes to quit camp, or be hung as a Spy—My mistake was in not hanging the insolent scoundrel—and ever since then the whole tribe has let loose on me. Gen. Halleck told me that before he issued his orders about "unauthorised hangers on" he had letters from several General officers, each asking protection against the known newspaper reporters attached to their rivals (Generals) HdQrs. I have myself known of instances of officers keeping such in their employment, to write them up in the newspapers. In the old days of our Army, such a thing would have drawn down the scorn of every officer of the Army, but in these modern corrupt days, it hardly attracts notice. I hope this war will not end, till the highest sense of honor is restored to the Military Profession, and until the Press is made to feel that they cannot libel and violate common decency without punishment. You will observe in the conduct of all our best leaders, such as McClellan and Halleck, a tendency to restrict the Press to its legitimate duty, and this is all I ever ask for. You will also observe in Beauregards, and other official reports, that they derived their chief information of our strength and position from our papers. When papers publicly convey to the enemy the information that enables him to strike a deadly blow, Wherein are editors better than Spies, who are by the laws of War, universally shot? Take our case here—Our chief labor is to keep out spies. Suppose a paper reports my strength—how easy for an enemy to concentrate and fall upon us in superior force. It is this abuse of the Press that I am determined to oppose, and I am really thankful that the Reporters give me a wide berth, for they know I will hang them as spies, if they hang around my camp. I am charged with the lives of my men, and will guard them against the common enemy, as well as more dangerous looking spies. With great respect & in haste

W. T. Sherman

Maj. (damaged)

LS, DLC: William T. Sherman Papers.

1. S. S. L'Hommedieu was an executive with the Cincinnati, Hamilton and Dayton Railroad Company at this time.

2. Joseph Gales (1786–1860) was a co-publisher and editor of the *National Intelligencer*.

3. Charles Hammond (1779–1840) was editor of the *Cincinnati Gazette* from 1825 until his death.

4. Presumably Rufus King (1814–76), currently a brigadier general in the U.S. Army, who had been the proprietor and editor of papers in Albany, New York, and Milwaukee, Wisconsin, before the war.

TO CHARLES EWING

Camp at Moscow, Tenn.—

July 8, 1862.

Dear Charley,

I got your dispatch the other day and confess I was nonplussed. The very first time I saw Halleck after his arrival at Pittsburg Landing I reminded him of his promise to send the 4 Cos. 13 Inf. into the Field. He told me he had made the order at St. Louis before leaving & the time depended on some detachment there with Pope—my camp was never near Halleck, and from the moment we commenced the March towards Corinth we got further & further apart, but every time I saw him I spoke to him on this subject and at last got his word in writing that the detachment *had been* ordered to me. I sent that Telegraphic Dispatch to your Father who with Ellen have written to me some 500 times on this one subject. I have done all a Gentleman should do to his superior officer[.] I could not & cannot believe Halleck would tell me false. I dont understand it at all, but the only solution that I can offer is that the Detail to relieve you is subject to the discretionary authority of Some body Else, who takes his time. Thus when officers are not on the Spot, their orders are to Such a General to relieve such & such a command as soon as practicable—or when such other Detacht. is relieved or some Condition. I will do what I much dislike to do, and rather than which I would rot in Alton or any other prison for Life, but you seem so deeply offended that I will do what I would not do for myself, go behind Halleck and enquire of his adjutant what has been done. If Halleck find it out, of Course my influence with him is gone, for he will detect the fact that for some cause I doubt his word and promise. You are wrong in attributing personal motives to Halleck. The truth is in War the General cares for the men about as much as you care for the horses that Serve you—you use those which are hardiest, and nearest—He dont Know the 13 Inf.—all he Knows is that it is a detachment and by the merest accident got to Alton, and the devil is to get away—But in time you will get away and then for the first time you will begin to question whether you gain by the Choice. As to fighting, that is the exception in a soldiers life—marching, countermarching, dust, thirst, short rations, sickness—wagon mules, and all the complications of life—as to fighting if you live a hundred years you will have plenty of it all the time. Tis folly to talk about this war approaching its end—The Enemy has this day a force in arms superior to ours. Their people embracing Kentucky & Tennessee are more united in feeling than ours. They burn their cotton, their houses anything cheerfully at the order of a Single Southern Dragoon, but if one of our men burns a rail, steals a chicken, robs a Garden, (All our men have turned thieves & pilferers in spite of all efforts to the Contrary) they raise a hue & cry. I have here two Divns. mine & Hurlbut—should be about 20,000 on paper but about 8000 in fact. My Cavalry 16 Companies which should be 1500 men might possibly turn out 300. The Enemy has 1500 cavalry which sweeps round me, takes all my couriers, and attacks every wagon train. I have built all the Bridges to Memphis, yet we are afraid to trust a train of Cars, and haul our provisions by wagon—I have been down to Holly Springs 25 miles south of this, and as long as I stay there the Cavalry keeps back but I was ordered back to the Line of Road and Jacksons Cavalry will be down on the Trains again. When I ask for Cavalry am told I have my complement. The fact is our army is a paper army, is now scattered—The southern army keeps united, and although put to it for Rations I expect them to achieve some brilliant victories this fall. You need not be uneasy. You will get your belly full of fighting—I was in hopes you would content yourself to live and look after Tom, but as you are Determined, "you must die or get crippled." Halleck will want every soldier this fall, and maybe sooner. I dont like these Interior operations—we cannot change the inveterate hatred of these People. We should get the Mississipi and operate from that as a base, and not bother with the Interior except such Key points as Corinth, Grand Junction and Jackson Miss.—Yrs.

W. T. Sherman

ALS, DLC: Charles Ewing Family Papers.

TO PHILEMON B. EWING

Camp 5th Divn. Moscow Tenn.
July 13, 1862

Dear Phil,

I have been railroad & road building ever since Corinth. I first went west 10 miles to Chewalla, where the enemy by the premature burning of a Bridge over Cypress Creek found themselves penned in with seven Locomotives and about sixty cars.[1] These they burned and most effectually destroyed but by the ingenious labor of men found in our ranks the Locomotives were got on the track, patched up and worked back to Corinth where they have been further repaired. Out of the wreck we saved some dozen platform cars more or less burned & damaged and the iron work of the Balance—The R.R. west of Chewalla was found to be badly broken. Some five Bridges of 120 foot span beside an immense amount of trestle work. It was then determined to Send the trains round by Jackson & Humboldt and repair track to Columbus, and I was ordered to Grand Junction to finish the Road into Memphis. I had just got all the Bridges done when the Enemys Cavalry broke in between us & Memphis, run the only locomotive & train off the track, rifled it of the contents sutlers goods, burnt the cars & make prisoners of some 72 of the unarmed men coming out to join their Regiments from furlough. This train was never under my control. I never saw it, it was controlled at Memphis and Wallace was so afraid I would get it and keep it that he would not even let it bring the mail. So when it was lost & Halleck very angry he could not fix it on me. Since this they cannot spare a locomotive from the more important parts of the Railroads under our control and this part of the Road is not {run} I have hauled my stores from Memphis in wagons & have had our trains attacked but successfully defended by the 57 Ohio that I had to pitch into at

Shiloh—I have unduly praised them for this and the Colonel Mungen really a white feather has been blowing a week, but his Lt. Col. Rice[2] is a good Soldier and a promising young man. I have troops at the Junction, Lagrange, here and Lafayette. The Memphis Details extend out to Germantown 15 miles.

I have been twice to Holly Springs to encounter reported troops but found nothing but two Regiments of Cavalry Jacksons & Pinsons 1500 in all, who of course quit on our approach—but who return the moment we retire. They far outnumber us in Cavalry. I have 8 Companies of the 4th Illinois 420 on paper— about 350 in camp, but to Save my life I cannot even get 250 in the Saddle, sick, extraduty, wagoneers, cooks &c. &c. Hurlbut has 3 cos. 5th Ohio with about the same results. His men have pistols & no carbines and are afraid of the southern Cavalry armed with fine Double Barrelled guns. Thus though superior to them in Infantry & Artillery, their superiority to us in Cavalry enable them to hang round us & pick up stragglers and venturesome pillagers of which I confess our army contains too large a proportion. I have sent out various parties to ambush this cavalry, but they Know the country so well and every farmer & planter is in their interest so they get notice as soon as a detachment leaves my camp. There is no union feeling here. Occasionally we find a man that wants Peace, but all say they will never again live under the same Govt. with the Yankees, but they made a wide distinction as to western men.

I have seen my own letter of June 10 in print and also Stantons answer of the 23rd. I think this calls for a rejoinder and I have prepared one. I think you will object to the paragraph which says I meant to insult him.[3] I want that preserved, but you may modify it in any other way & publish—send him written or printed copy as you please. He did not send me manuscript copy & is not therefore entitled to an answer, but if you dont materially change mine send the original to him that he may not have cause to doubt the true author.

Tell Ellen that my last despatch from Halleck intimates extensive changes in which I am to Command Memphis.[4] How soon this change will occur I dont Know, but I dont want her to come down. The Army is no place for a lady and I will have my hands full. McClellans movement was risky & critical but success crowns his merit—why he was not largely reinforced is to me a mystery.[5] The People should Know that this war will consume 300,000 men per year for a long time that they might prepare for it. To allow our armies to run down in the face & country of the Enemy invites defeat & prolongs the strife. We all have to conceal even from ourselves the awful mistake of the war, in not preparing men by drill & organization all last summer fall & winter. It may be the Government could not collect men & armies faster, but I think few comprehended the vast task before us, and dont realize it now till it stares us in the face.

Hallecks first order was to destroy the Memphis & Charleston Road—I attempted it on first arrival at Savannah by landing at Yellow Creek, but the Rains of a Second deluge drowned us out, & made the country impassible—I attempted it a second time and got as far as Pea Ridge, but found the road so picketed that it was foolish to attempt a surprise the only mode laid out for me, but after the Battle, by means of a joint expedition of Gunboats and transports I succeeded in destroying it at Bear Creek Bridge 2½ miles East of Iuka. Mitchel about the same time reached Huntsville & got possession of the Road as far down as Tuscumbria. What he is doing I have no means of Knowing. This army is composed of four distinct Corps d'Armee—That of the Tennessee Genl. Thomas, composed of 5 Divisions (mine has 6000 men & may be a standard of strength)—Army of the Ohio, Buell, about the same—Army of the Mississipi Genl. Pope, about the same—and the Reserve composed of McClernands & Wallace's Divisions. Halleck is still back at Pittsburg Landing—I as the advance of Thomas Right wing am in camp north of Lick Cr. abreast of Monterey. Buell is at Lick Creek about 2 miles to the left read, and Pope is on the Hamburg Road to the left rear. Some of our Division are in Monterey. The Roads were as deep & mud as stiff as you ever saw, but a few days of warm weather has made a marked change, and all the Divisions have large details improving the Roads. Building bridges & causeways—If other Divisions have worked as well as mine, Lick Creek must now have a dozen bridges, and the Side streams from them to form each—An army of 100,000 men with artillery & trains need five or six parallel or Converging Roads. I have 11 Regiments and 5 Batteries of Artillery—Each Regt. has 13 wagons, Each Battery two, beside their own carriages. I think my Division on a Road single track occupies over two miles; do my best to close Ranks & teams. We have in our wing 5 such Divisions so that at the very best we can not get the rear started much before the head of Column reaches Camp. I have therefore in advance prepared two Roads but fear that one will be taken by some of the Rear Divisions. Since commencing this I have received orders to march toward Corinth by my New Road at 7 A.M. tomorrow, and occupy a point 2½ miles from Monterey, or 6½ from Corinth about 3½ miles from the Enemy's lines of Defense. This Line is composed doubtless of rifle ditches or trenches with bushes & trees cut as abattis, somewhat in the form of a semicircle covering the intersections of the two Railroads. According to accounts they have several lines of such work. Their Road east is broken at Bear Creek about the State Line. The Road north is broken near Purdy. With Memphis & the South they still have communication—Their force is estimated at from 100, to 130,000—but of course this is speculation. I dont think they had at Shiloh more than 60,000—of these at least 15,000, and their fresh levies may be some

30,000 more. They evidently have a large force. Deserters who were pressed into service at Memphis, natives in our northern states, who have come into Camp represent their force at 100,000, with trains still pouring in. Last night the trains were running all night. If New Orleans is taken, Beauregard & Bragg both of Louisiana will be desperate, and will fight like Devils, but I am satisfied the Tennesseeans are shaky, but these have mostly gone to enable them to draw other Regiments in their place.

The trees are now in full leaf—oaks of various kinds prevailing—with cottonwood, willow Dogwood, & plum along the watercourses—a good deal of undergrowth, fields few & scattered—people nearly all gone abandoning everything some few cattle & hogs running loose, horses & mules all gone. The destruction of fences & outhouses follows in the wake of each army. To save or protect property appears a work of patience & labor. Corinth is in a hollow or rather level space, with a gentle Ridge north & south, not a place of natural Strength, or importance only as the intersection of two Roads of great length. I prefer them to fight there to Humboldt, or Grand Junction, but you doubtless have as good a geographical idea of the place as I can give without topographical maps and all these we have to construct as we go. Buell is our best soldier. Halleck the ablest man—Grant very brave but not brilliant Thomas slow, cool & methodic. I dont think much of Pope or McClernand— Excuse so long a letter but I Know you will read it. Yrs. affectionately

W. T. Sherman

difference of our army on paper & in fact—thousands (57,000 in Hallecks) are absent without leave and are pursuing their private business at home—4700 were absent from my Division, but is now reduced to 3500. Yours

W. T. Sherman

ALS, Wheaton, Md.: Private Collection of Joseph H. Ewing.

1. For a fuller account of WTS's activities at this time, see PM, 1:284–87.

2. Americus V. Rice (1835–1904) would succeed to the colonelcy of the Fifty-seventh Ohio on May 24, 1863.

3. WTS to Benjamin Stanton, July 12, 1862, DLC: WTS and SFP.

4. HWH to WTS, July 12, 1862, DLC: WTS.

5. WTS accepted at face value McClellan's insistence that the Seven Days Battles (June 25–July 1, 1862) were a Union success because he had shifted his lines of communication and supply from the York to the James River while keeping Robert E. Lee's Army of Northern Virginia from overwhelming him. Sherman also accepted McClellan's complaint that the authorities at Washington had failed to send him sufficient reinforcements. In fact, Mc- Clellan outnumbered Lee, whose campaign put an end to a possible siege of Richmond.

TO PHILEMON B. EWING

Moscow, Tenn. July 14, 1862

Dear Phil,

I received a dispatch from Genl. Halleck this morning on official matters and he adds a paragraph, "dont answer Stantons[.]" The fact is officers should not write for the papers and it might have been better had I not first written. I am very desirous of conforming to Hallecks wishes and therefore write to ask you to withhold from publication the answer of mine sent yesterday. I telegraphed to the Same effect today, but there are some parts that Stanton should see and if you can trust anybody in Columbus say Judge Swayne,[1] or should Mr. Hunter or your father go up, get them to read the letter to Stanton that he may prefer his charges & ask his {consent}, but dont let the letter be copied or pass out of your hands or those of some person equally trustworthy with those I have named.

I should like Govr. Tod, Larz Anderson, Mr. L'Hommedieu, Charles Goddard, Charles & John Sherman and a few in Lancaster to Know of the existence of the Answer till such time as it may be made public—No military officers should write of the events of a Campaign until a year after the Campaign.

I am satisfied Stanton is a Liar and Coward—for he states things by the merest guess, and he Knew I meant to insult him & yet played with the word responsibility. All my Ohio Colonels & officers & Soldiers are indignant at him, because they take the Same view as I do—One of the Colonels, Smith of the 54th for whose Regiment he apologized, after the Regt. & Col. had been highly praised by his Brigadier & myself—wants to go home & whip him. Buckland & Cockerill[2] are very angry with him for coming down & not coming near them. Buckland is a neighbor and has practiced in the same Courts. Cockerill served one term in Congress with him, and they are anxious to pitch in. It might have been better for me to have let them pitch in, but as it has happened, I think there are some points in my answers that Should reach Stanton, Govr. Tod, L'Hommedieu, Anderson & others, that they may see that even in the new points raised Stanton risked every thing on mere assertion & guess—You will observe how wide of the truth he is in Grants case, although he ought to have seen it in the newspapers. For a time Grant did hold a position Like Beauregard, 2nd in Command ready to Succeed Halleck in case of absence, but when the crisis was passed he resumed his old Command. Whilst second in command his duties were nominal and many soldiers thought him in disgrace. Stanton Knowing nothing whatever of the Truth or of Hallecks opinion blurts out the positive assertion—So of the Invitation—he had forgotten it—but there is no doubt on the point, the witnesses I have named remember the details with great clearness—My bed was an old carpet and a blanket—the Same I had in Kentucky which McCook run me about—My silver & plate which Breckinridge captured was the most miscellanious assortment of crockery & tinware you could conceive of, and our mess cook was a very common nigger who run at every alarm. Therefore McCook was laughing at my inviting Stanton to Such a dinner, which impressed it on the memory of those who stood near. He must be a great rascal & liar thus to trifle with the truth. Halleck objects to any further publication on my part and it may be best that the contents should reach him and the parties I have named orally—let no copies get out for they would be used.

I expect to be ordered to Memphis soon. Our wagon trains & foraging trains are all the time attacked & the truth is developing that to Subdue the South there must be the Same process of extermination as with the original Indians. Not a man woman or child but would Shoot us like wild beasts.

I dont {abate one hour} the time and means necessary to Subdue the South. Yr. affectionate Brother

W. T. Sherman

ALS, Wheaton, Md.: Private Collection of Joseph H. Ewing.
1. Associate Supreme Court justice Noah H. Swayne (1804–84).
2. Joseph R. Cockerill (1818–75), an Ohio lawyer, had served in the House of Representatives with Stanton from 1857 to 1859. He was colonel of the Seventieth Ohio Infantry.

TO HENRY W. HALLECK

Moscow, July 16, 1862

General Halleck, Corinth:

I cannot express my heartfelt pain at hearing of your orders and intended departure.[1] You took command in the Valley of the Mississippi at a period of deep gloom, when I felt that our poor country was doomed to a Mexican anarchy, but at once rose order, system, firmness, and success in which there has not been a pause.

I thank you for the kind expression to me, but all I have done has been based on the absolute confidence I had conceived for your knowledge of national law and your comprehensive knowledge of things gathered, God only knows how.

That success will attend you wherever you go I feel no doubt, for you must know more about the East than you did about the West when you arrived at Saint Louis a stranger. And there you will find armies organized and pretty well commanded, instead of the scattered forces you then had. I attach more importance to the West than the East. The one has a magnificent future, but enveloped in doubt. The other is comparatively an old country. The man who at the end of this war holds the military control of the Valley of the Mississippi will be the man. You should not be removed. I fear the consequences.

Personally you will rule wherever you go, but I did hope you would finish up what you had begun, and where your success has attracted the world's notice.

Instead of that calm, sure, steady progress which has dismayed our enemy, I now fear alarms, hesitations, and doubt. You cannot be replaced out here, and it is too great a risk to trust a new man from the East. We are all the losers; you may gain, but I believe you would prefer to finish what you have so well begun. With great respect,

W. T. Sherman,
Major-General

Printed, *OR*, I, 17: pt. 2, 100–101.

1. Halleck had added a note to his orders issued to WTS earlier in the day: "I am ordered to Washington, and leave to-morrow, Thursday. I have done my best to avoid it. I have studied out and can finish the campaign in the West. Don't understand and cannot manage affairs in the East." *OR*, I, 17: pt. 2, 100.

TO E. S. PLUMMER AND OTHER PHYSICIANS

Head Quarters, 5th Divn.
Army of Tenn.
Memphis, July 23d 1862.

Dr. E. S. Plummer & others, physicians
in Memphis, signing to a petition
Gentlemen,

I have this moment received your communication, and assure you that it grieves my heart thus to be the instrument of adding to the seeming cruelty and hardship of this unnatural war.

On my arrival I found my predecessor had issued an order permitting the departure South of all persons subject to the Conscript Law of the Southern Confederacy.[1] Many applications have been made to me to modify the order, but I regarded it as a condition precedent by which I was bound in honor, and therefore I have made no changes or modifications; nor shall I determine what action I shall adopt in relation to persons unfriendly to our cause who remain after the time limited by Gen'l Hovey[2] has expired.

It is now sunset, and all who have not availed themselves of Gen'l Hovey's authority are supposed to be loyal and true men.

I will only say that I cannot allow the personal convenience of even a large class of ladies to influence me in my determination to make Memphis a safe place of operations for an army, and all people who are unfriendly should forthwith prepare to depart in such direction as I may hereafter indicate.

Surgeons are not liable to be made prisoners of War, but they should not reside within the lines of an Army which they regard as hostile. The situation would be too delicate. I am with great respect Your obedient Servt.

W. T. Sherman

Maj. Gen'l

LbkS, DNA: RG 94, Records of the Adjutant General's Office, Generals' Books and Papers, William T. Sherman, Letterbook 2; *OR*, I, 17: pt. 2, 114.

1. The Confederate Senate passed a Conscription Act on April 9 which called up all white males between the ages of eighteen and thirty-five for three years' service, with only a few exceptions. Confederate adjutant general Samuel Cooper had begun strictly enforcing the draft on July 14.

2. Brigadier General Alvin P. Hovey (1821–91), USA.

TO SAMUEL SAWYER

Head Qtrs. Memphis, July 24, 1862

Samuel Sawyer Esqr.

Union Appeal

Dear Sir

It is well I should come to an understanding at once with the Press as well as the People of Memphis which I am ordered to Command, which means control for the interest wellfare and glory of the *whole* government of the United States.

Personalities in a newspaper are wrong and criminal. Thus though you meant to be complimentary in your sketch of my career you make more than a Dozen mistakes of fact, which I need not correct as I dont desire my Biography till I am dead. It is enough for the world to know that I live, and am a Soldier bound to obey the orders of my superiors, the Laws of my country and to venerate its Constitution, that when discretion is given me, I should exercise it and account for it to my Superiors.

I regard your article headed "City Council" "Genl. Sherman and Col. Slack" as highly indiscreet. Of course no person who can jeopardise the safety of Memphis can remain here, much less exercise public authority, but I must take time and be satisfied that injustice be not done.

If the parties named be the men you describe, the fact should not be published to put them on their guard & encourage their escape.

The Evidence should be carefully collected, authenticated and then placed in my hands.

But your statement of facts is entirely qualified in my mind and loses its force by your negligence of very simple facts in your reach as to myself—I had been in the army 6 years in 1846—am not related at all to any member of Lucas Turner & Co.—was associated with them Six years instead of two—am not Col. of the 15th Infantry but 13th. Your correction this morning of the acknowledged error as to Genl. Denver is still erroneous. Genl. Morgan L. Smith did not belong to my command at Shiloh at all—but was transfered to me just befor reaching Corinth.

I mention these facts in kindness to show you how wrong it is to speak of persons.

I will attend to the Judge, Mayor, Boards of Alderman & Policemen all in good time.

Use your influence to reestablish system, order, government—You may rest easy that no military Commander is going to neglect internal safety as well as to guard against external danger, but to do right requires time, and more patience than I usually possess is necessary—If I find the Press of Memphis actuated by high principle and a sole devotion to their Country I will be their best friend, but if I find them personal, abusive, dealing in inuendos and hints at a blind venture, and looking to their selfish aggrandizement & fame, then they had better look out—for I regard such as greater enemies to their country and to mankind than the men who from a mistaken sense of State pride have taken muskets and fight us about as hard as we care about—In haste but in kindness Yours & c.

W. T. Sherman
Maj. Genl.

LbkS, DNA: RG 94, Records of the Adjutant General's Office, Generals' Books and Papers, William T. Sherman, Letterbook 2; OR, I, 17: pt. 2, 116–17.

TO JOHN PARK[1]

Head Qrs. 5th Division
Memphis Ten. July 27, 1862

John Park
Mayor of Memphis
Sirs

Yours of July 24 is before me and has received, as all similar papers ever will, my careful and most respectful consideration. I have the most unbounded respect for the civil law, Courts & authorities and Shall do all in my power to restore them to their proper use viz. the protection of life, liberty & property. Unfortunately at this time civil war prevails in the land and necessarially the Military for the time being must be superior to the Civil Authority but does not therefore destroy it. Civil Courts & Executive Officers should Still exist and perform duties without which Civil or Municipal bodies would soon pass into disrespect, an end to be avoided—I am glad to find in Memphis yourself & municipal authorities not only in existence but in the exercise of your important functions and I shall endeavour to restore one or more civil tribunals for the arbitrament of contracts and punishments of crimes which the Military authority has neither time or inclination to interfere with.

Among these first in importance is the maintainance of order peace & quiet within the jurisdiction of Memphis. To ensure this I will keep a Strong Provost Guard in the City, but will limit their duty to guarding public property, held or claimed by the United States, and for the arrest & confinement of State Prisoners & Soldiers who are disorderly or improperly away from their Regiments. This Guard ought not to arrest citizens for disorder or common crimes—This Should be done by the City Police. I understand that the city police is too weak in numbers to accomplish this perfectly and I therefore recommend that the City Council at once take Steps to increase this force to a number which in their judgment, day & night can enforce your ordinances as to peace quiet & order. So that any change in our Military dispositions will not have a tendency to leave your people unguarded, I am willing to instruct my Provost Guard to assist the Police force when any combination is made too Strong for them to overcome, but the City Police, should be strong enough for any probable contingency. The cost of maintaining this Police force must necessarially fall upon all citizens equitably.

I am not willing nor do I think it good policy for the City Authorities to collect the taxes belonging to the State & Country as you recommend for these would have to be refunded. Better meet the expences at once by a new tax on all interested. Therefore if you on consultation with the proper municipal body will frame a good bill for the increase of your Police force, and for raising the necessary means for their support and maintainance, I will approve it and aid you in the collection of the tax. Of course I cannot Suggest how this tax should be laid, but I think that it should be made uniform on all interests, Real Estate & personal property including money and merchandise.

All who are protected should share the expences in proportion to the interests involved—I am with respect Your Obt. Servt.

W. T. Sherman
Maj. Genl.
comdng.

LbkS, DNA: RG 94, Records of the Adjutant General's Office, Generals' Books and Papers, William T. Sherman, Letterbook 2; *OR*, I, 17: pt. 2, 127.

1. John Park (1812–97), an Irish-born merchant, was mayor of Memphis from 1861 to 1866.

Memphis, July 31, 1862

Dearest Ellen,

When I was back in the country with no means of communicating I fell into the habit of not writing intending to make up when I got here but it is the old game over, a man cant feed his Legs without coming for a pass and no bodys pass will do but the commanding officer. Every nigger has run off, and of course I am supposed to be in immediate possession[.] Miss Nancy raised in her mistress's bosom and nursed like her own children, has run off, and the whole family must rush to Gen. Sherman. Father brother and all gone to fight us, but of course I must neglect all business to catch Miss Nancy—Cases of that kind occur fifty times a day, besides real ones. Now I have got 800 negros at work on the Fort. The Presidents order dont embrace Tennessee & loyal as well as disloyal Slaves are embraced[.][1] My orders are to take all who come in, and we will dispose of them when the Fort is done according to Law and the facts then. My notion is to pay the Kentuckyans niggers for their Stolen horses. As to freeing the negros I dont think the time is come yet—when Negros are liberated either they or masters mush perish. They cannot exist together except in their present relation, and to expect negros to change from Slaves to masters without one of those horrible convulsions which at times Startle the world is absurd. The war this Fall & winter will be very bloody, and the South will get the advantage. They now have the advantage in numbers & position. They are concentrated & we scattered. They were nearly out of Bacon & Salt meat, but the desire of our people to trade has soon supplied this. Cincinati has sent enough salt to supply all the army meat for six months. In like manner the Jews & Speculators have sent in enough Gold to get all the cartridges necessary, so the two wants of the army are supplied, a whole year lost to the War, & some Jews & speculators have made 10 per cent profit—Of course our lives are nothing in the Scales of profit with our commercial People. The Burning of cotton by the People of the South was one act of folly but our buying the refuse of them for Gold & especially shipping salt, which from scarcity has risen to $100 a barrel, is a greater act of folly—I have stopped it instanter on reaching the River, but the thing is going on all round me, by consent of the Boards of Trade of Cincinati, Louisville &c. I am getting tired of this, & of the volunteer service and would escape if I could.

Dayton & Hammond write you all about our Camp & the details of life— tents, mess &c. mosquitos. Our camp is a pleasant one ground enough but contracted. Secesh on both sides and all round. The idea of making them take the oath is absurd. Of course I Know & everybody knows they prefer the South to the North, and that they hope & pray that the Southern Army will in due time destroy us. I go on the theory that all the leading men are secesh, and the laborers & mechanics neutral or tired of war. A good many people have left & many more must or starve for there can be no concession, where the Enemys pickets come within sight—I send out 20 & 25 miles but must send a Regt.—& their cavalry closes in right behind. If a Barrel of salt leave town it is on its way to Holly Springs & the Secesh camp in half an hour. We are in our Enemys country and I act accordingly. The North may fall into Bankruptcy & anarchy first but if they can hold on the war will soon assume a turn to extermination, not of soldiers alone, that is the least part of the trouble, but the People. Maj. Sanger my aide has his second wife—he is about 30 yrs. old, good rider, very cheerful, & my favorite to Hammonds disgust, because he knows something about the military technology a thing Hammond cant learn now[2]—Military language is peculiar & it is too Slow a process to give an order and then to peruse it, and define all its words. Sanger was at West Point about Hughs time but did not graduate. I found him a major of the Ills. 55th & appropriated him.

I have seen John McCracken once he came out to camp which is a mile south & east of the Gayoso House the loafing center of Memphis.[3]

I have received a letter from Charley and in it he copies a telegraphic order from Halleck to the commanding officer of the Battalion 13 Inf. enquiring why a former order had not been obeyed, and then ordering him "to proceed at once via Columbus to Corinth"—Instead of taking this as an order, packing up & Starting

AL (incomplete), InND: Sherman Family Papers.

1. After Lincoln had presented his draft of the Emancipation Proclamation to his cabinet on July 22, the War Department had ordered that Union commanders in rebellious states could use slaves for military labor.

2. On June 14, EES had asked her husband who Sanger was because he had sent a bouquet to Minnie. SFP.

3. On June 20, EES had written to say that Sherman would see McCracken, an old friend from Lancaster, and Sister Angela in Memphis. SFP.

TO MARIA BOYLE EWING SHERMAN

Memphis Tennessee, August 6, 1862

My Dear Minnie,

I received your letter on my arrival here, now two weeks ago, and have been so busily employed in matters that could not interest you that I have hardly had time to think of Dear Mama and the Children that hardly know me.[1] It is only when the selfish crowd is dispersed by night, and the Gentlemen of my staff go to bed, that I can sit & think of you all in quiet Lancaster. Mama says you continue to grow and already are as tall as Aunt Sissy, but sitting here this moonlight night, shining on the dark & flowing Mississipi I think of Minnie now as she was when we carried her a baby down its whole length to New Orleans, than as the tall young lady of our present Home. How I remember leading you about the Boat as we passed the high Bluff, where now lies the Camp of my men, armed & accoutred for war, and where more than a thousand slaves are working on a Fort to take Memphis from its present owners for the new Race of men from the colder & more inhospitable climate of the North. How much better would it be if we could come here in peace and purchase one of the thousands of beautiful cottages that environ the town and live as we never did in Saint Louis, but no you are in Lancaster and I am here the Stern & Cruel tyrant, slave of a Despotic Master, Lincoln. Hundreds of children like yourself are daily taught to curse my name, and each night thousands Kneel in prayer & beseech the almighty to consign me to Perdition. Such is War. The People here look on us as invaders come to rob them of home & property and even life. We tell them we want nothing they have. We dont want their houses, their farms, their niggers, anything they have, but they dont believe us, and I fear that this universal bitter feeling will cause the very result they profess to dread.

I have been forced to turn families out of their houses & homes & force them to go to a strange land, because of their hostility, and I have today been compelled to order soldiers to lay hands on women to force them to leave their homes to go to join their husbands in hostile camps.[2] Think of this and how cruel men become in war, when even your papa has to do such acts. Pray every night that this war may end, not that you want me home but that our whole People may not become Robbers & murderers. It now requires all my energy to prevent our soldiers from robbing & plundering the houses & property of supposed Enemies, but our Enemies are even worse than we, for they Shoot our men if they go outside our Lines, & fire on steamboats as they pass up & down the River. Instead of sitting out on the Guards now as we used to do on the steamboats the passengers lie behind, bales of hay or goods to shelter them from Rifle balls that came from the green bushes which line the shores. Indeed am I thankful that you all are not here, bad enough that I am, but that you are safe & at home keeps me contented. Your mamma & GrandPa think it is a great thing to be a high General. I would in any war but this, but I cannot but look on these People as my old friends. Every day I meet old friends who would now shoot me dead if I were to go outside of Camp and who look on me as a Brutal wretch. I am in hopes Uncle Charley will come here & join my command, for all with me are strangers to you. Maj. Sanger who sent you the Bouquett is nearly as old as I am and has already been married twice. They cant plague you about him. He sent you the flowers because he felt I would be pleased at his remembrance of you. All my staff Know you & Lizzie & Willy & Tom, for I have told them of you all. Poor little Elly & Rachel are not known in foreign parts, but it will not be long before they too are tall young Misses. You must now study hard & help Lizzie. Now is the time to learn to read & write, Geography, arithmetic sewing & music— other things you can always acquire. I want you to write to me often and Lizzie too. Tell Lizzie I know she will beat you in learning Books. When I do get home you will both be able to read to me and tell me all the stories in your Books.—and in time I will drive you out and tell you all about strange countries and about the war. I wrote to Mama yesterday. Give my love to Lizzy, to Willy & Tom & Kiss the babies for their Dear Absent Papa.

W. T. Sherman

ALS, OHi: William T. Sherman Papers.

1. Minnie to WTS, June 27, 1862, SFP.

2. WTS expelled thirty-two men he suspected of being guerrillas or their supporters from Memphis to Confederate lines and forced their families to go with them. John F. Marszalek, *Sherman: A Soldier's Passion for Order* (New York, 1993), 195.

TO THOMAS EWING SR.

Memphis Aug. 10 62

Dear Sir

I enclose a couple of orders made from force of circumstances in advance of specific instructions of the Department[.] As soon as I can submit them through General Grant at Corinth they will reach Washington but this will be some time. I would like to Know if I have guessed right at the Law points. As to the military I am sovereign within my sphere & permit no question.

The Northern People are forced by the Principle of self existence to push their Power and Dominion so as to embrace the lands whose waters flow to the Mississipi. In this they must be despotic. If the Patriotism of our People is unequal to the task of subjugating the whole South still there can be and will be no Peace till a Power exists able & determined to be respected within the limits of our Government. I have always supposed therefore that a large proportion of the People north must move south & possess the Soil.

As to changing the opinions of the People of the South that is impossible, and they must be killed or dispossessed. We have finished the first page of this war in vainly seeking a union sentiment in the South, and our Politicians have substantially committed suicide by mistaking the Extent and power of the Southern People & its Government, and are about Entering on a Second period. Those who sought political advantage by a display of military Zeal have disappeared from the Field of action, and now will begin the real struggle of conquest. Negro property and personal property are fair subjects of conquest, as also the possession of Real Estate during the lives of present owners. In the clause of the Constitution lies a great cause of weakness to our Government, and it may force the North also to Rebel so that the two Rival and warlike powers will stand Equal in the Contest, but for many years we will doubtless cling to the Constitution as a center of strength but sooner or later it too will go to enable that perfect means of conquest without which we cannot repopulate the Country—Already Curtis' Army at Helena has 4000 slaves. I have some 2000—other armies have vast numbers.

These are swelling and by encouraging it and agreeing to protect families I would have here in 30 days—thirty thousand negros—we cant afford to feed such hordes. They must be colonized and that near at hand—we cant afford to Ship them, but must conquer say Arkansas & colonize these negros under some just & fair laws. I do not pretend to See daylight ahead yet but I assume you all mistake[n] who expect to convert the South, to reconcile or subdue them. I can imagine no sure process but the same that began in the colonization of America. affectionately &c.

W. T. Sherman

ALS, Wheaton, Md.: Private Collection of Joseph H. Ewing.

TO ANDREW JOHNSON

Head Qrs. 5th Division
Memphis Tenn., Aug 10, 1862

To his Excellency.
Gov. Andrew Johnson. Nashville
Sir

Your esteemed favor of August 1[1] was handed me yesterday by Mr Smith,[2] Cashier of the Memphis Branch of the Union Bank of Tennessee and I promptly gave him the desired permission to go to Grenada to look up the assets of his Bank, but I know full well that his visit will prove unsuccessful. No officer there would dare give up anything of use or value to them[.] I explained at length my views to Mr Smith of the duties and obligations of himself & associates in the present strait. The Bank has put in circulation notes to the extent of over a million of Dollars and are indebted to their Depositors for funds to a large amount[.]

These liabilities are of a high and honorable character, and the Bank must redeem them. As trustees of this Debt they will be held to a strict account. They must do all that is possible to secure the property and assets of their bank and apply them honestly to the redemption of their Circulation & deposits.

It seems their Bullion or Coin and assets, notes made here & elsewhere, have been Carried away by force & fraud. They deny Complicity. They have not the power to retake their Coin which is therefore lost to them but they can secure the notes. These notes are made payable here and are secured by property in Tennessee. Although the mere pieces of paper are at Grenada the debts are here, and I must insist that the officers of the Bank give public notice that the notes *must be paid* here by the makers, or the securities will be proceeded against.

Again the assets were removed by force & fraud by Beauregard & others who have property here which is liable for their unlawful acts. Out of these the Branch Bank can & must recover the means to redeem their notes & pay back to their Depositors.

They should do so at once lest locks be changed & men pay or pretend to pay their notes elsewhere.

The difficulty only is they fear the power of their Common Enemy and are trembling lest they commit themselves in case our enemy prevails. The Branch Bank here was vacant or not in use. Gen. Grant ordered me to take possession of all vacant buildings and appropriate them to the use of the United States. I could have taken this Building, but have forborne until the Directors have time to assume their ground. They must be true to their trust, declare boldly & openly against the parties who robbed them, and at once begin to realize on assets which, though seemingly removed are still here. Else I have no alternative but to Conclude that they are in Complicity with Our Enemies & treat them as such.

I know that you agree with me in this, that all men must now choose which king[.] This by play is more dangerous than open bold Rebellion. A large amount of the success of our Enemies has resulted from their boldness. They have no hair splitting. We too must imitate & surpass their game & compel all men & Corporations to at once espouse the Cause of their State & National Govts thereby securing full right to protection, or openly to rebel & forfeit their property & their lives. Please say as much to the Presdt of the Bank.[3]

> I am with great respect,
> W. T. Sherman,
> Major-general.

ALS, DLC: Andrew Johnson; *OR*, I, 17: pt. 2, 161–62.

1. Not found.

2. Frederick W. Smith (ca. 1818–fl. 1870) had been an employee of the Bank of Tennessee since 1846. Leroy P. Graf and Ralph W. Haskins, eds., *The Papers of Andrew Johnson* (Knoxville, 1967–), 5:607.

3. Granville C. Torbett was president of the Bank of Tennessee.

Memphis, Aug. 10, 1862

Dearest Ellen,

I have got up at daybreak to get a good chance to write you as I intended yesterday & day before but was interrupted. I selected a camp a little way out on purpose to avoid the crowd of curious women who always flock about to represent absent husbands. There must be about 2000 men in the Southern army from Memphis whose mothers & sisters not only expect us to protect them as long as they the mothers & sisters stay indoors, & sew & write letters to their absent sons, & husbands but actually to hunt up their lost niggers, horses, hogs & ⟨illegible⟩. The fact is we are fast approaching a state of war and if soon we dont awake to the dream we will find ourselves involved in war. Thus far it has been byplay, and whilst the whole South is in deep intense earnest we of the north still try reconciliation, &c. &c. I am putting the screws to some but find more trouble in combatting the North whose merchants & traders think they have a right to make money out of the present state of things and Memphis was on my arrival fast becoming a depot of supplies for the hostile army in the Interior.

If Mr. Lincoln had accepted the fact of war on the Start & raised his army as I then advised of a million of men the South would have seen they had aroused a lion. Whereas by temporizing expedients 1st 75,000—then ten new Regts.—then half a million &c. they find it necessary again & again to increase the call. Well at last I hope the fact is clear to their minds that if the North design to conquer the South, we must begin at Kentucky and reconquer the Country from them as we did from the Indians. It was this conviction then as plainly as now that made me think I was insane. A good many flatterers now want to make me a prophet.

I got the box of clothing your hat box and all are now satisfactory and I am well supplied, and as they arrived the same evening as two other events I will give you the whole story.[1] In the course of the day among other visitors come to my tent came the widow of Shover an Ohio officer of the old 3rd Artillery of my old Florida times. She was a Thornton, relation of those in California and of the Lees of Virginia & resides here to secure a property She inherited of her Grandmother. We take all fugitive slaves here and work them, and she was after a runaway & presumed on my favor which she did not get. Unlike most she did not call me a nigger thief & go away mad, but insisted on my calling to See her so as night closed in finding myself at leisure I had my mare saddled & with an orderly rode to her house on Adams St. staid an hour, & started on my return. The night was bright moonlight & the shadows crossed the Street. My mare was evidently confused on the canter and I walked her a short distance &

again put her to the canter, when she stumbled & finally came to the ground falling on my left Knee. I first thought it seriously injured, but after a short time I mounted & rode to camp. I found all my staff assembled around a beautiful saddle & equipments designed as a present for the one I lost at Shiloh—It is one of Grimsley's best altogether too handsome for war, but I had to accept it. McDowell made the Speech & I replied. I found at the same time your hat box & my clothes¹ So with a jammed Knee I found myself completely equipped & have as yet been unable to sport any of my new finery. My Knee is now much better and unless it be too hot today I will endeavor to ride out to some of our camps, which extend from Fort Pickering around to the rear of the City some 5 miles.

Among other calls yesterday were the Sisters from St. Agnes Academy, the Elder of whom Sister Ann² is well acquainted with you & your mother and asked many questions among which of course did I say my prayers. To that I answered that Bishop Alemany³ had specially exempted me because you were pious enough for half a dozen ordinary families, and had I a medal of course, tied by a rope, and if that broke I believed you would chain it on. They were delighted with your zeal & also that I enabled them to get their supplies at a cheaper rate than they had hitherto done. I promised to call & see them, but doubt if I can find the time. The weather has been intensely hot, but the nights are pleasant our camp is in a good shade so that we feel the heat far less than the dwellers in houses. Spite of my injunctions several families have come to Memphis to See their husbands, but I do not wish you to come. Military camps are no place for ladies and I must be prepared for the field at any moment. I think Halleck designs us to wait till he can push matters further south on that end of the Line. I have not heard from Charley or from Grant about the 4 Cos. of my Regt. I begin to think that Battalion like most of the Military are spoiling for a chance and when it is offered are not so anxious after all. Love to all. yrs. ever

W. T. Sherman

ALS, InND: Sherman Family Papers.

1. On July 7, 1862, EES had sent WTS a box of clothing. On August 1, she also sent her locked hatbox with his suits in it and the key under separate cover. SFP.

2. Sister Ann Hanlon.

3. Joseph Alemany (b. 1814), a Spanish Dominican, had been the first archbishop of San Francisco during the Shermans' time there and was an old friend of the Ewings from his time as a priest in Ohio.

Head Quarters, 5th Division,
Army of the Tenn.
Memphis August 10th 1862.

James Wickersham Esqre.
Memphis, Tenn.
Dear Sir,

Your letter of August 9th, handed to me yesterday in person is before me, accompanied by a copy of a contract made Feby. 6, 1860 by yourself and W. H. Carroll C. Q. M. You claim the possession and rents of the Post Office and Theatre in this City on the ground of clear title and of the contract referred to.

It is entirely out of my province to question your title or examine your contract. The military authorities of the United States hold the possession of the Post Office and Theatre by a title different from any that you hint at in your letter, viz: the title derived from the Laws of War, Memphis was a Military camp in the possession of the Confederate authorities, was captured and is now held by us. War now exists here and only such parts of our Civil System of Jurisprudence can be allowed as are consistent with the laws of War.

Genl. Grant the military superior in this District has ordered that all vacant buildings be taken possession of and rented out in a certain manner, and I have instructed the Quartermaster Captain Fitch[1] to Execute that order, and to enable him to do so in a fair and equitable manner have given him certain instructions under date of August 7th which you refer to and have therefore seen.[2] By perusing them again, you will see you can easily recover possession of your property by proving loyalty. But I infer your desire is to secure your rents without this formality. This to me is simply ridiculous and unworthy a thought. If you be a loyal citizen of the United States tracing your title to property through it, claiming and enjoying its protection, and looking to its tribunals to maintain your rights there can be no difficulty in proving the fact: no particular form is required to prove such loyalty. At present a simple oath of allegiance might be all that is required. On this point I will not even commit myself until you ask for your property on the ground that you are prepared to prove your loyalty. I do not presume you claim the protection of any Foreign Government, and if you are in league with the Confederate Authorities you are in a very unsafe place inside our Military lines. As to the character of your Theatre suffering from being used as a place of exhibition for the Campbell Minstrels, I cannot see it. I have seen such minstrels perform at the St. Charles' Theatre New Orleans, Nible's and Barnum's New York and in the very best theatres of the cities which prescribe the fashions to our Country.

I cannot therefore comply with your request to cause to be restored to you either the possession or rents of the two buildings in question until you comply with Genl. Grant's order to prove your loyalty to the Government of your Birth. I am yr. ob. Sert.

W. T. Sherman
Maj. Genl.

LbkS, DNA: RG 94, Records of the Adjutant General's Office, Generals' Books and Papers, William T. Sherman, Letterbook 4.

1. Captain Henry S. Fitch of Illinois, an assistant quartermaster assigned to Memphis.

2. *OR*, I, 17: pt. 2, 156–57. Sherman had outlined Grant's orders on the question of rents on property owned by Southerners and made it clear that these monies were to be returned to the owners only on evidence of their loyalty, usually an oath of allegiance to the U.S. government.

TO SALMON P. CHASE

Head Qrs. 5th Divn.
Memphis Tenn., Aug. 11, 1862

Hon. S. P. Chase.
Secretary of the Treasury.
Sir,

Your letter of August 2d just received invites my discussion of the Cotton Question.[1]

I will write plain & slow because I Know you have no time to listen to trifles. This is no trifle. When one nation is at war with another, all the People of the one are enemies of the other. Then the Rules are plain and Easy of understanding. Most unfortunately the war in which we are now Engaged, has been complicated with the belief on the one hand that all on the other were *not* Enemies. It would have been better if at the outset this mistake had not been made, and it is wrong longer to be misled by it. The Government of the United States may now safely proceed on the proper Rule that all in the South are Enemies of all in the North; and not only are they unfriendly, but all who can procure arms now bear them as organized Regiments or as Guerillas. There is not a Garrison in Tennessee where a man can go beyond the sight of the flagstaff without being shot or captured. It so happened that these People had cotton and wherever they apprehended our large armies would move, they destroyed that Cotton in the belief that of Course we would seize it and convert it to our use. They did not and could not dream that we would pay money for it. It had been condemned to destruction by their own acknowledged Government, and was therefore lost to their People, and could have been without injustice taken by us and sent away, either as absolute prize of war, or for future compensation. But the Commercial enterprise of the Jews soon discovered that 10 cts. would buy a pound of Cotton behind our Army, that 4 cts.

would take it to Boston where they would receive 30 cents in Gold. The bait was too tempting and It spread like fire; when here they discovered that Salt, Bacon, powder, fire arms, percussion Caps &c. were worth as much as Gold, and Strange to Say this traffic was not only permitted but encouraged. Before we in the Interior could Know it, hundreds yea thousands of barrels of salt & millions of Dollars had been disbursed and I have no doubt that Bragg's army at Tupello and Van Dorn's[2] at Vicksburg received enough salt to make Bacon without which they could not have moved their armies in mass, and that from 10 to 20,000 fresh arms and a due supply of Cartridges have also been got, I am equally satisfied. As soon as I got to Memphis, having seen the effect in the Interior, I ordered (only as to my own command) that Gold Silver & Treasury notes were contraband of war, and Should not go into the Interior, where all are hostile. Tis idle to talk about union men here. Many want Peace, and fear War & its results but all prefer a Southern Independent Government, and are fighting or working for it. Every Gold dollar that goes for cotton goes to the seaboard in exchange for bank notes & Confederate Scrip which will buy goods here, and are taken in ordinary transactions. I therefore required Cotton to be paid for in such notes, by an obligation to pay at the end of the war, or by a deposit of the price in the hands of a Trustee, the U.S. Qr. Master. Under these Rules cotton is being obtained about as fast as by any other process, and yet the Enemy receives no "aid or Comfort". Under the "Gold" Rule, the Country People who had concealed their Cotton from the Burners, openly scorned our Green backs, but now are willing enough to take Tennessee money which will buy their Groceries, and now that the Trade is to be encouraged & Gold paid out, I admit Cotton will be sent in by our open armed enemies who can make better use of this Gold, than they can of their hidden bales.

I may not appreciate the Foreign view of the Question, but my views on that may be ventured. If England ever threatens war because we dont furnish Cotton, tell her plainly if she cant employ & feed her People to Send them here, where they can not only earn an honest living but soon secure independence by moderate labor. We are not bound to furnish her cotton. She has more reason to fight the South for burning that Cotton than us for not shipping it. To aid the South on this ground would be base hypocrisy that the world would detect at once. Let her take her ultimatums and there are enough generous minds in Europe that would Counteract her in the balance. Of Course her Motive is to cripple a Power that rivals her in Commerce & Manufactures, that threatens even to usurp her History. In twenty more years of prosperity it would require a close calculation to determine whether England, her laws & history would claim for a home the Continent of America or the Isle of Britain. Therefore finding us in a death struggle for Existence she would join in the quarrel to destroy both parts. Southern People Know this full well, and they would only accept the alliance of England to get her arms & manufactures in exchange for her Cotton. The Southern Confederacy will accept no other mediation because they Know full well that in Old England her slaves & slavery will receive no more Encouragement than in New England. France certainly does not need our Cotton enough to disturb her equilibrium and her mediation would be entitled to a more respectful consideration than on the part of her present ally. But I feel assured the French will not Encourage Rebellion & Secession as a Political doctrine. Certainly all the German States must be our ardent friends, and in Case of European intervention Could not be kept down.

Were I to receive Englands Call for cotton I would answer, get it where and when you Can.

We are now involved in a Revolution the End of which no man sees, but I do hope & trust the People of the North have at last realized the fact, and that they must lay aside their apathy & desire to make money at the Expense of the lives of their fellow Citizens who are trying to play soldiers. This Cotton order I must believe is the last illustration of the Kind. With great respect, Yrs.

W. T. Sherman

ALS, PHi: Salmon P. Chase Papers; *OR*, III, 2:349.

1. Letter not found. On July 25, Rawlins had issued for USG General Orders No. 64 suspending the trade of cotton for specie. *PUSG*, 5:238–39n. USG had written to Chase on July 31, complaining of the effects of the trade; *PUSG*, 5:255–56. But on August 11, in response to directives from Washington, Grant was forced to reverse himself. WTS also wrote to Lorenzo Thomas in the same vein on August 11: "Gold, silver, and money are as much contraband of war as powder, lead, and guns, because they are convertible terms. Cotton is now procured by Tennessee and Southern bank notes which are inconvertible. If the policy of the Government demands cotton order us to seize and procure it by the usual operations of war, but the spending of gold and money will enable our enemy to arm the horde of people that now swarm the entire South. This cotton order is worse to us than a defeat. The country will swarm with dishonest Jews who will smuggle powder, pistols, percussion-caps, &c., in spite of all the guards and precautions we can give." *OR*, III, 2:350.

2. Major General Earl Van Dorn (1820–63), CSA, was commanding the Army of the West.

TO ULYSSES S. GRANT

Telegraph from Columbus to Corinth
Head Quarters 5th Divisn.
Augt. 11, 1862.

General Grant, Corinth,

Cotton Order of Head Quarters of the Army, encouraging trade in cotton is received and must be respected.[1] But I will move Heaven and Earth for its repeal, as I believe it will be fatal to our success. If we provide our enemy with money we Enable them to buy all they stand in need of. Money is as much contraband of war as powder. All well here.

W. T. Sherman
Maj: General

LbkS, DNA: RG 94, Records of the Adjutant General's Office, Generals' Books and Papers, William T. Sherman, Letterbook 4; *OR*, III, 2:350.

1. See John A. Rawlins to WTS, August 11, 1862, *PUSG*, 5:241n.

TO JOHN SHERMAN

Memphis, Aug. 13, 1862.

My Dear Brother,

I have not written to you for so long a time that I suppose you think I have dropped the correspondence—for six weeks I was marching along the Road from Corinth to Memphis, mending Roads, building Bridges and all sorts of work. At last I got here and found the city contributing Gold, arms, powder Salt, and every thing the enemy wanted. It was a smart trick on their part thus to give up Memphis that the desire of Gain to our northern merchants should supply them with the things needed in war. I stopped this at once, and declared Gold, Silver Treasury notes & Salt as much Contraband of war as Powder lead &c. I have one man under sentence of death for smuggling arms across the Lines and hope Mr. Lincoln will approve it, but the mercenary spirit of our People is too much and my orders are reversed and I am ordered to encourage the trade in Cotton and all orders prohibiting Gold Silver & Notes to be paid for it are annulled by orders from Washington. Grant promptly ratified my order, and all military men here saw at once that the Gold spent for Cotton went to the purchases of arms & munitions of war— but what are the lives of our soldiers to the profits of the merchant?

After a whole year of bungling the Country has at last discovered that we want more men[.] All Knew it last fall as well as now—but it was not popular—now 1,300,000 men are required where 700,000 was deemed absurd before. It will take time to work up these raw recruits, and they will reach us in October when we should be at Jackson Meridian & Vicksburg. Still I must not growl. I have purposely kept back and have no right to Criticize save that I am glad the People have at last found out we are at war, and have a formidable Enemy to combat.

Of course I approve the Confiscation act,[1] and would be willing to revolutionize the Govt. so as to amend that article of the Constitution which forbids the forfeiture of lands to the heirs—My full belief is we must Colonize the Country *de novo* beginning with Kentucky & Tennessee, and Should remove five millions of our people at once south of the Ohio River taking the farms and plantations of Rebels. I deplore the war as much as ever, but if a thing has to be done let the means be adequate.

Dont expect to overrun Such a Country or subdue such a people in our two or five years, it is the task of half a century. Although our army is thus far south we cannot stir from our Garrisons. Our men are Killed or captured within Sight of our lines. I have two Divisions here mine & Hurlbuts—about 13,000 men—am building a strong fort, and think this is to be one of the Depots & bases of operations for future movements. The loss of Halleck is to us almost fatal. We have no one else to replace him. Instead of having one head we have five or six all independent of each other. I expect our Enemies will mass their troops and fall upon our Detachments before the new reinforcements come. I cannot learn that there are any large bodies of men near us here. There are Detachments at Holly Springs & Senatoba the present termini of the Railroads from the South, and all the people of the country are armed as Guerrillas. Curtis is at Helena 80 miles south & Grant at Corinth. Braggs army from Tupelo has moved to Chattanooga & proposes to march on Nashville, Lexington, & Cincinati. They will have about 75,000 men—Buell is near Huntsville with about 30,000, and I suppose Detachments of the new levies are [to] be put in Kentucky from Ohio & Indiana in time. The weather is very hot & Bragg cant move his forces very fast, but I fear he will give trouble. My own opinion is we ought not to venture too much in the interior until the River is safely in our possession, when we could land at any point and Strike inland. To attempt to hold all the South would demand an army too large even to think of. We must colonize & Settle as we go south for in Missouri there is as much strife now as ever. Enemies must be killed or transported to Some other country. I enclose you some of my orders to Show you how I stand on the nigger question[.][2] It is giving us much concern. We can work the men, but what can we do with the women & children. Ellen writes me she is coming to pay you a visit. She wants to come and See me, but I cannot permit it.[3] The camp is no place for women & children. Although all Memphis with its beautiful houses & country Seats are at my disposal I live in tents, ready to move at a moments warning. I have great faith in Halleck but he is the only man yet who has risen to the occasion. {Ohio} ⟨phrase scratched out⟩ {officers} why not try & get some good colonels? Yr. affectionate Brother

W. T. Sherman

ALS, CSmH.

1. The Second Confiscation Act, signed by Lincoln on July 17, allowed military commanders to seize slaves and other property of rebellious citizens when they came under Union control.

2. General Orders Nos. 60 and 67, Headquarters, Fifth Division, Army of the Tennessee,

OR, I, 17: pt. 2, 113, 158–60. Orders No. 60, issued on July 22, 1862, had placed slaves in Memphis at work on Fort Pickering with rations and supplies to be charged against their wages, which, it was implied, would be paid to their owners. No. 67, dated August 8, 1862, was WTS's interpretation of the Confiscation Act. It allowed slaves at Fort Pickering to return to their masters if they wanted to, left the question of wages open, and decreed that no military man could hire a slave as a personal servant.

3. EES to WTS, August 6, 1862 (2), SFP. EES again expressed her desire to come and see Cump if he was not going to get leave and expressed her intention of going to see JS and his wife.

TO GIDEON J. PILLOW

Head Quarters, Memphis, Tennessee
August 14th 1862

Genl. G. J. Pillow, Confederate Army
Oxford, Miss.
Sir,

I have received your letter of August 2d 1862 at the hand of S. P. Walker Esq.[1] It is not proper in War thus to communicate or pass letters, but I am willing to admit the extreme difficulty of applying the harsh rules of war, when but a few days ago all was peace, plenty and free intercourse; and on this ground, not officially, I am willing that you should know the truth of the matter concerning which you inquire. It so happened that Genl. Curtis was here yesterday and I inquired of him the truth concerning the allegations in the first part of your letter touching the seizure and confiscation of your four hundred slaves near Helena, Arkansas, the killing one overseer, the imprisonment of three others, and generally the devastation of your entire estate in that quarter. Genl. Curtis answered, No slave was taken by armed men from your's or any other plantation unless he had proof that such slaves had been used in war against him. No overseer had been killed or none imprisoned, and the damage to plantations was only such as will attend all armies such as marked the progress of yours and Genl A. Sidney's Johnston's columns a year ago in Kentucky.

I understand Gen. Curtis has given letters of manumission to negro applicants, who satisfy him they have been used as property to carry on war.

I grant no such papers, as my opinion is, it is the provision of a Court to pass on the title to all kinds of property: I simply claim that I have a right to the present labor of slaves, who are fugitive, and such labor is regulated and controlled that it may ultimately be paid for to the Master or slave, according to the case. I have no control over Genl. Curtis, who is my superior, but I take it for granted some just and uniform Rule will soon be established by our common superior to all cases alike.

I certainly never have known, nor do I believe it possible that your slaves, or those of any other person have wandered about the streets of Memphis in want and destitution. We have abundance of provisions and no person shall suffer for want here. When we can provide labor it will be done, and thereby they (laborers or slaves) earn their provisions, clothing and necessaries; but wages are always held in reserve to answer the order of the rightful party. The worst you have to apprehend in case you claim the sixty days under the Confiscation law, is that your slaves may become scattered. None are allowed to pass up the River save with written passes, and I understand your negroes are either at your plantation or near Helena. I know of none here.

Genl. Curtis expressed great surprise at your solicitude for these negroes, and at your application, that Genl. Grant and myself would have them restored to you or your agent. He says you had sold them all, or had transferred them by some instrument of writing or record to a gentleman near the plantation who is a loyal citizen of the United States.

I will refer your letter to Genl. Grant with a copy of this,[2] and have already given a copy to Genl. Curtis now at Helena. If Mr. Walker can find any of your negroes here the men will be put to work, but Mr. W. can keep watch of them and of the women; till such time as rules are established for ascertaining and determining the rights and title to such kind of property. At present I know of none of your negroes in or near Memphis. Certainly none are in the negro pen or any cotton shed here. I am &c. Your obt. Serv.

W. T. Sherman
Maj. Gen.

LbkS, DNA: RG 94, Records of the Adjutant General's Office, Generals' Books and Papers, William T. Sherman, Letterbook 4; *OR*, I, 17: pt. 2, 172.

1. Pillow had written to Walker on that date that armed men had taken all his slaves and destroyed his property. *OR*, I, 17: pt. 2, 171–72.

2. See WTS to John A. Rawlins, August 14, 1862, following.

TO JOHN A. RAWLINS[1]

Head Quarters 5th Div.
Army of the Tennesee
Memphis Aug 14, 1862

Major J. A. Rawlins
Asst. Adjt. Genl. Corinth,
Sir,

It has been physically impossible to me personally to give attention to the thousands of things which had to be done here since my arrival, and at the same time keep you fully advised of their progress. All is well now and matters are progressing favourably, and for the sake of history and that the Major General may have a clear insight into our situation, I send a variety of papers, some of which need a word of explanation.

I. Orders no. 61—Abolishes passes on land travel (or the River same as heretofore) and Regulates it confined to five Roads, and on each Road a small guard to inspect each traveller, the wagon, buggy, or carriage. Such guards can better prevent illegal traffic or catch spies than any Provost Marshal who must of necessity delegate his power to make out and sign passes to a clerk.

II. Orders no. 62 defines the posts of my Brigades & defines the duty of their Guards. In that order I threaten incompetent officers with a Board of Examination, which on inspection I find I cannot appoint (Sec 10 act congress Page 521 Army Reg.) I ask the detail of such a Board of five officers composed of say Genl. Hurlbut, Genl. Lauman,[2] Genl. M. L. Smith, Col. D. Stuart, & Col. Buckland. If you have granted leaves of absence to any of these I name, Col. Cockerill, Lieut. Col. Wolcott, Major Flaring, & Maj. Fisher as alternatives.

III. Orders no. 67—About negroes. I found about six hundred negroes employed here, and daily others coming into our works. I had knowledge that a Law had passed Congress, for using the Labor of such negroes, approved by the President and sanctioned by Genl. Halleck. No instruction had come or could come to guide me, and I was forced to lay down certain rules for my own guidance. Masters and mistresses so thronged my tent as to absorb my whole time and necessity compelled me to adopt some clearly defined rules, and I did so. I think them legal and just.

Under the order I must assume to clothe and feed the negroes, but you will observe I make no provisions for any save laboring men. The women and families take refuge here, but I cannot provide for them, but I allow no force or undue persuasions in any case.

IV. Orders no. 70. I had ordered at the Muster of June 30th, that all absentees without authority of Genl. Halleck or myself, should be reported on the Muster Rolls as Deserters. I see in the newspapers that the War Department has adopted the same views, only fixing the date Aug. 18, and to put my troops on a footing with all others I have made this Order. The official notice has not come to me But I see it so universally quoted, that I cannot doubt that such an order is in existence, and I infer that some accident has prevented its receipt in time to prepare the Muster Rolls.

V. Instructions to Capt. Fitch. On the receipt of Genl. Grants telegraphic order, about vacant houses, and the leases of absent Rebels, I gave it to Capt. Fitch Post Quarter Master, with a few instructions. But as he progressed, so many points of Law and policy arose, that he was embarrassed, and called on me for further instructions. I made them in the form of a Letter, which I authorized him to publish, that all the parties might judge for themselves. This has quieted the great mass, but still cases are daily referred to me, of the most delicate nature. One of which I enclose with this, Viz—The letter of Mrs. Lizzie A. Meriwether,[3] whose husband is in the Rebel Service, and who remains under your order permitting such Ladies to remain on taking or making a parole. I venture to risk the opinion that in war the parole of a woman citizen is not good, from them an oath should always be exacted, for the parole is a word of honor which according to the old feudal code, a soldier alone could make, but apart from this, it seems by her own statement her husband deeded this property to her, then Rebelled against his Government and by the fortunes of War, now finds himself under one Government and his wife under another. In either event the property is safe, let which party prevail. Mrs. Meriwether is a Lady and has small children dependant on her in the absence of her husband, but Capt. Fitch under my orders, or rather these printed instructions construes the property to be substantially that of the absent husband and orders the tenants of the property to pay the rents to him. I think in Law and common sense the transfer of property to a wife at such a time and under such circumstances is simply an evasion, and therefore void, but am willing to stretch the Rule as wide as possible to favor distressed women and children, although I fear a single departure from the Rules of severe justice may lead us into many inconsistencies and absurd conclusions.

VI. I finally enclose a copy of a Letter from Genl. Pillow addressed to S. P. Walker of this city, and designed for General Grant and myself, it did not come under a flag of truce but by one of the sent mails, which I have not yet succeeded in breaking up. I also enclose a copy of my answer, which I will hand to Mr. Walker and allow him to send as best he may.[4] I do not consider my answer as strictly official or the matter enquired about, and as to the situation of his private property.

I have published Genl. Grants Order based on the one from the Head Quarters of the Army anulling all restrictions on the purchase of cotton, and payment of Gold therefor.

I cannot see how Genl. Halleck can allow Gold which is universally contraband to pass into possession of our Enemy, but I hope his reasons are as usual based on a far seeing policy. I Shall of course obey the order and facilitate the trade in Cotton and in its shipment, but it runs against the grain. With the exception of small Guerrilla Bands I hear of no Enemy nearer than Holly Springs and Senatobia. Yours,

W. T. Sherman
Maj. Genl. Comdg.

LbkS, DNA: RG 94, Records of the Adjutant General's Office, Generals' Books and Papers, William T. Sherman, Letterbook 4; *OR*, I, 17: pt. 2, 169–71.

1. John A. Rawlins (1831–69) was USG's adjutant general and later chief of staff.

2. Jacob G. Lauman (1813–67) was commanding a brigade of Hurlbut's division.

3. Elizabeth Avery Meriwether, wife of Minor Meriwether, an engineer in the Confederate army. WTS would later send her behind Confederate lines.

4. See WTS to Pillow, August 14, 1862, above.

TO ISAAC F. QUINBY[1]

Head Quarters Memphis
Aug. 15, 1862.

General Quinby
Dear Sir,

Yours of Aug. 13, is received and I am very glad you concur with me in opinion that money is contraband of war quite as much so as guns and powder.

Not only have we to fight but to do all that is possible to deprive them of the means of fighting. Any man in Tennessee can take money and go north and can get his purchases South, or at Havanna. The Small profit on cotton is no offset to the danger which attends sending money South for it, and it is none of our business to supply Europe and England with cotton. Let them get it if they can. Mr. Chase wrote me that this foreign view of the case was what embarrassed the Cabinet. The more we try to please England the more she will bully us. If we take our ground she will begin to back down & not before. I would assist the South in burning cotton and as there is no crop planted let England get her cotton as she may. Your friend

W. T. Sherman
Maj. Genl.

LbkS, DNA: RG 94, Records of the Adjutant General's Office, Generals' Books and Papers, William T. Sherman, Letterbook 4.

1. Isaac F. Quinby (1821–91) was a West Point classmate of Ulysses S. Grant's; at First Manassas he had commanded the Thirteenth New York in Sherman's brigade. Presently he was in command of the District of Mississippi.

TO ULYSSES S. GRANT

Head Quarters 5th Division
Memphis August 17. 1862

Maj. Genl. Grant
Corinth
Dear Sir,

A letter from you of Aug. 4, asking me to write more freely and fully on all matters of public interest did not reach me till yesterday[.][1] I think since the date of that letter you have received from me official Reports & copies of

orders telling almost every thing of interest hereabouts, but I will with pleasure take every occasion to advise you of everything that occurs here.

Your order of arrest of the newspaper Correspondent is executed, and he
will be sent to Alton by the first opportunity.[2] He sends you by mail today a
long appeal, and has asked me to stay proceedings till you can be heard from. I
have informed him I would not do so, that persons writing over false names
were always suspected by honorable men, and that all I could hold out to him
was that you might release him if the dishonest Editor who had substituted his
newspaper name to the protection of another would place himself in prison in
his place. I regard all these newspaper harpies as Spies, and think they could
be punished as such.

I have approved the arrest of the captain and seizure of the Steam Boat
"Salin" for carrying salt down the River without permit & changing it off for
cotton. I will have the captain tried by a military commission for aiding and
abetting the public Enemy by furnishing them salt wherewith to cure bacon, a
contraband article; also for trafficking on the river without License or permit.
I hope the Court will adopt my views and stop this nefarious practice. What
use in carrying on war, whilst our people are supplying arms and the sinews of
war. We have succeeded in seizing a good deal of Confederate clothing, percussion caps &c., some mails &c.

At our last regular Muster I caused all absentees to be reported "Deserted"
whereby they got no pay, but inasmuch as the order for the muster for
tomorrow Aug. 18. is universal I will have the muster tomorrow and all absent
then will be treated as Deserters and I will remit the former penalties as they
are incurred under my orders.

I have sent out several Infantry parties as also cavalry and am certain there
is nothing but Guerrillas between this and Senatobia and Tallahatchee. All the
people are now Guerrillas, and they have a perfect understanding, when a
small body gets out they hastily assemble and attack, but when a large body
move out they scatter and go home. Col. Jackson commands at Senatobia,[3]
Jeff Thompson[4] having been ordered away—Villepigue[5] is at Abbeville Station
18 miles south of Holly Spring. They have guards all along the Rail Road to
Grenada, and Cavalry everywhere. I think their purpose is to hold us and
Curtis here while they mass against you and Buell or New Orleans. Price has
been reported coming here but of this we know nothing. If he comes, he can
and will take care that we know nothing of it till the last moment. I feel certain
that no force save Guerrillas, have thus far passed north towards McClernand.
All the people here were on the "qui vive" for Baton Rouge and Nashville but
there seems to be a lull in their talk. I find them much more resigned and less
presumptous than at first. Your orders about property and mine about "Nig-

gers" make them feel that they can be hurt, and they are about as sensitive about their property as Yankees. I believe in universal Confiscation and colonization. Some Union people have been expelled from Raleigh; I have taken some of the richest Rebels and will compel them to buy and pay for all the land, Horses, cattle and effects as well as damages and let the Union owner deed the property to one or more of them. This they dont like at all. I do not exact the oath universally but assume the grounds that all within our lines are American Citizens and if they do any act or fail in any duty required of them as such then they can and will be punished as "spies."

Instead of furnishing a permanent Provost Guard I give Col. Anthony[6] two good officers to assist him and change the Regiment weekly. All are in tents and have their transportation ready to move. I am also in tents.

I think four thousand men could land opposite Helena, march rapidly to Panola, destroy that bridge, then to Oxford and Abbeville and destroy that thus making the Tallahatchie the Northern limits of their Rail Road, afterwards Grenada, Jackson & Meridian must be attacked, break up absolutely and effectually the Rail Road Bridges, mills, and every thing going to provide their armies and they must feel it. The maintainance of this vast army must soon reduce their strength.

The lines of the Mississipi must be under one command; as it is Curtis and I are perfectly independent of each other. He was here the other day. I know him well, he is very Jealous of interference and will do nothing at anothers suggestion. If you want him to do any thing you must get Halleck to order it. Fort progresses too slow. 1300 negroes at work on it. One instalment of Guns received, balance expected every hour. Weather heretofore unbearably hot but now pretty cool. Yours truly

W. T. Sherman
Maj. Genl.

LbkS, DNA: RG 94, Records of the Adjutant General's Office, Generals' Books and Papers, William T. Sherman, Letterbook 3; *OR*, I, 17: pt. 2, 178–79.

1. Not found.

2. On July 28, the *Chicago Times* had published correspondent Warren P. Isham's erroneous report that thirteen ironclad gunboats had arrived at Mobile Bay for the Confederate navy. He was imprisoned at Alton until November 12, 1862, when USG ordered his release. See USG to WTS, August 8, 1862, *PUSG*, 5:274 and 274–76n.

3. William H. Jackson (1835–1903) was colonel of the Seventh Tennessee and First Mississippi Cavalry.

4. M. Jeff Thompson, CSA, a guerrilla fighter and former mayor of St. Joseph, Missouri, had joined Van Dorn's command in March 1862.

5. Brigadier General John B. Villepigue (1830–62), CSA.

6. Lieutenant Colonel DeWitt Clinton Anthony (1828–91), USA, of the Twenty-third Indiana Volunteers, had been made provost marshal for Memphis on June 24.

TO HENRY W. HALLECK

Memphis, August 18, 1862.
(Via Columbus, Ky., 24th, 1 p.m.
Received 9.10 p.m., 24th.)

Maj. Gen. H. W. Halleck,
General-in-Chief:

Dispatch received.[1] Will religiously carry out any line of policy as to trade the proper authority dictates, and with absolute confidence in its right, as soon as I feel that you are at the helm. I have now a steamer, seized for exchanging salt for cotton without military or customhouse permits. Salt is eminently contraband, because [of] its use in curing meats, without which armies cannot be subsisted. If vigorous war measures are contemplated, I think all commerce should cease. To carry on trade with the interior all our soldiers must be made customhouse spies, as all closed packages may and do contain contraband. We find clothing, percussion-caps, and salt concealed in every conceivable shape, and I doubt not that thousands of pistols reach the interior in this way. All the people of the South are now arming as partisan riders, daring not to be guerrillas.

W. T. Sherman,
Major General.

Printed, *OR*, III, 2:402.

1. Halleck had informed WTS that government policy provided for the purchase of cotton with specie. HWH to WTS, August 14, 1862, *OR*, III, 2:382.

TO ELLEN EWING SHERMAN

Memphis, Aug. 20, 1862

Dearest Ellen,

I have written to you many times very irregularly but cannot help it, of course I must have all the interruptions of thousand and one things that occur about stolen horses niggers &c. &c. but this is all subsiding into comparative peace. The whole male population has gone to the Southern army, and we have a place full of women & run away niggers, not a very interesting set—all the women are secesh. Of course they keep their tongues, but they look the Devil to every one of our cloth. I could expel them all, but dont care to do this till it is adopted as the Uniform policy of the Government. The whole Interior is alive with Guerrillas indeed the entire male population of the South is now armed and even with the new 300,000 men of the north, if ever they do reach us may be too late. I have no doubt the South has an armed force of a million of men with the population at all times ready to give information. Grant is still at Corinth but writes me he has made strong detachments towards Buell. I suppose by this time Bragg has got well into Tennessee and the new levees will have to enter Kentucky at once. Bragg has been drilling his men hard and I fear the raw troops will be unable to Stand him. Buell ought to reach Nashville in time but I can hear nothing of him except through the Cincinati papers. The Boat which came down yesterday was fired in at Island 8, above New Madrid from the Arkansas shore, and last night a boat was burned some 12 miles below this. It was a boat belonging to the Gunboat service which was aground. The River is far from being a safe place for boats. It is only 1000 yards wide and as it falls the boats at places must run close in to Shore. I expect we will be much troubled this fall by this course. All the People are now armed and will avail themselves of every chance to molest the Boats. Indeed I would not be willing to expose you to Such risks. The weather still continues very hot and the roads dusty.

Aug. 21 I commenced yesterday was interrupted and have been busy all day with Governor of Arkansas showing him camps and Forts. I am now to review one of my Brigades, and can only close this to say I am very well and all the better for being worked hard. I get good sleep at night in camp. I would suffocate in a house. I have just got Lizzie's letter and Shall answer it very soon, poor Lizzie I hope the water cure man will make her as large and strong as Minnie. We had a good thunder Shower last night which has laid the dust and cooled the air. I dont think it is much hotter here than in Ohio. I see the Cincinati papers are finding fault with me again. Well thank God I dont owe Cincinati anything & she me. If they want to believe reporters they may.

Eliza Gillespie can tell you whether I take an interest in the Sick or not—I never said I did not want cowards for the Hospital. I said the Sanitary Committee had carried off thousands who were not sick, except of the war, for my part I did not want such to return. Men who run off at Shiloh & escaped in boats to Ohio & remain absent as Deserters will be of no use to us here. This is true & those Deserters should know it, but the real sick receive from me all possible care. I keep my sick with their Regiments, with their comrades and dont send them to Strange Hospitals. Our Surgeons have a very bad way of getting rid of their sick instead of taking care of them in their Regiments, and once in the Genl. Hospitals they rarely return. This course nearly defeated us at Shiloh when 57,000 men were absent from their Regiments *without leave*. McClellan has 70,000 absent from his army. This absence has led to many catastrophes, and you cant pick up a paper without some order of the President & Secretary of war on the Subject.

If the Doctors want to do charity let them come here, where the sick are, and not ask us to Send the sick to them. As to opening the Liquor saloons here, it was done by the city authorities to prevent the sale of whiskey by the smugglers. We have as little drunkenness and as good order here as in any part of the Volunteer army.

Cincinati furnishes more contraband goods than Charleston, and has done more to prolong the war than the State of South Carolina. Not a merchant there but would sell salt bacon, powder & lead, if they can make *money* by it. I have partially stopped this and hence the complaints. I hope Bragg will bring war home to them. The Cause of war is not alone in the nigger, but in the mercenary spirit of our countrymen. yours as usual in haste

W. T. Sherman

ALS, InND: Sherman Family Papers.

TO THE EDITORS OF THE *MEMPHIS BULLETIN* AND *MEMPHIS APPEAL*

Memphis Tenn.
Aug 21, 1862

Editors of Bulletin and Appeal,
Gentlemen,

As the Appeal remarks anonymous publication[s] must not be printed. A man who for any reason with holds his signature for publication has some base motive. The publisher of an anonymous article becomes the author and is liable.

In times like these the Press may be the cause of great good as well as evil. An opportunity for good now exists here. The Confederate authorities have encouraged and sanctioned Guerrillas, issuing commissions and organizing them into Regiments and Brigades, but allowing them to remain at or near home. This enables them to draw in a class that otherwise could not be employed in war, but at the same time it places the People in a very awkward fix. These Guerillas are not Uniformed, they can if pursued disperse and mix up with the people and thereby elude pursuit, but like a few notorious men they involve the whole crowd in the punishment due the few.

If an officer is in pursuit he would be perfectly justified in retaliating on the farmers among whom they mingle. It is not our wish or policy to destroy the farmers or their farms, but of course there is and must be a remedy for all Evils, if the farmers of a neighborhood encourage or even permit in their midst a set of Guerrillas they cannot expect to escape the necessary consequences. It will not do for them to plead simple personal ignorance of a particular transaction they become accessories by their presence and inactivity to prevent murders and distruction of property, besides giving a color of right to our Detachment always in uniform to commit those acts of waste and destruction which will inevitably lead to the entire devastation of the country where the Guerrillas operate. These principles of war and common sense should be made familiar to the people that they may clearly understand how by men in authority or neutrality as they call it, they lay themselves clearly liable to all the risks of war without any of its excitement.

The destruction of the Raleigh Bridge is simply an act of wanton outrage, it merely compels the People who seek the advantages of trade with Memphis, to come by a longer road. We have possession of the Lower Bridges from which we can reach Raleigh and the country beyond. It therefore injures them and does not hurt us at all. The parties who committed the outrage are well known, and their property is liable to the county of Shelby for the damages. In time sooner or later they will have to pay for it. The destruction of the Bridges over Loosahatchee and Big Creek was committed sometime ago to impede the opperations of our forces, but really one of no consequence in military opperations. We can easily reach all parts of that country by Roads subject to our control, so that these acts of mischief only go to the destruction of their own country. I suppose their object is to convince us they are "in earnest," like the burning of their cotton, but the sooner they know that we dont care how much they are in earnest the better.

We are in earnest, or coming so very fast, though late in getting up to the standard of the occasion. These views will give you points for some paragraph. Yours Truly,

W. T. Sherman
Major Genl.

LbkS: DNA, RG 94, Records of the Adjutant General's Office, Generals' Books and Papers, William T. Sherman, Letterbook 4.

TO THOMAS HUNTON[1]

Memphis Tenn. Aug. 24th 1862

Thomas Hunton Esq.
Coahoma, Panolo Co. Miss.
My dear Sir,

I freely admit that when you recall the times when we were schoolfellows, when we were younger than now, you touch me on a tender point, and cause me to deeply regret that even you should style yourself a Rebel.[2] I cannot believe that Tom Hunton the Companion of Gaither,[3] Rankin,[4] and Irvin[5] and many others long since dead, and of Halleck, Ord,[6] Stevens[7] and others still living can of his own free will admit the anarchical principle of secession or be vain enough to suppose the present Politicians can frame a Government better than that of Washington, Hamilton & Jefferson. We cannot realize this but delude ourselves into the belief that by some strange but successful jugglery the managers of our Political Machine have raised up the single issue, North or South, which shall prevail in America? or that you like others have been blown up, and cast into the Mississippi of Secession doubtful if by hard fighting you can reach the shore in safety, or drift out to the Ocean of Death, I know it is no use for us now to discuss this War is on us. We are Enemies, still private friends. In the one Capacity I will do you all the harm I can, yet on the other if here you may have as of old my last Cent, my last shirt and pants. You ask of me your negroes, and I will immediately ascertain if they be under my Military Control and I will moreover see that they are one and all told what is true of all—Boys if you want to go to your master, Go—you are free to choose. You must now think for yourselves, Your master has seceded from his Parent Government and you have seceded from him—both wrong by law—but both exercising an undoubted natural Right to rebel. If your boys want to go, I will enable them to go, but I wont advise, persuade or force them—I confess I have not yet seen the "Confiscation Act," but I enclose you my own orders defining my position. I also cut out of a paper Grants Orders,[8] and I assert that the Action of all our Leading Military Leaders, Halleck, McClellan, Buell, Grant & myself have been more conservative of slavery than the Acts of your own men. The Constitution of the United States is your only legal title to slavery. You have another title, that of possession, & force, but in Law & Logic your title to your Boys lay in the Constitution of the United States. You may say you are for the Constitution of the United States, as it was—You know it is unchanged, not a word not a syllable, and I can lay my hand on that Constitution and swear to it without one twang. But your party have made *another* and have another in force. How can you say that you would have the old, when you have a new. By the new if successful you inherit the Right of Slavery, but the new is not law till your Revolution is successful. Therefore we who contend for the old existing Law, contend that you by your own act take away your own title to all property save what is restricted by *our* constitution, your slaves included. You know I don't want your slaves, but to bring you to reason I think as a Military Man I have a Right and it is good policy to make *you all* feel that you are but men—that you have all the wants & despondencies of other men, and must eat, be clad &c to which end you must have property & labor, and that by Rebelling you risk both. Even without the Confiscation Act, by the simple laws of War we ought to take your effective slaves, I don't say to free them, but to use their labor & deprive you of it; as Belligerents we ought to seek the hostile Army and fight it and not the people—We went to Corinth but Beaureguard declined Battle, since which time many are dispersed as Guerillas. We are not bound to follow them, but rightfully make war by any means that will tend to bring about an end and restore Peace. Your people may say it only exasperates, widens the breach and all that, But the longer the war lasts the more you must be convinced that we are no better & no worse than People who have gone before us, and that we are simply reenacting History, and that one of the modes of bringing People to reason is to touch their Interests pecuniary or property.

We never harbor women or children—we give employment to men, under the enclosed order. I find no negroes Registered as belonging to Hunton, some in the name of McGhee of which the Engineer is now making a list—I see McClellan says that negroes once taken shall never again be restored. I say nothing, my opinion is, we execute not make the Law, be it of Congress or War. But it is manifest that if you wont go into a United States District Court and sue for the recovery of your slave property you can never get it, out of adverse hands. No U.S. Court would allow you to sue for the recovery of a slave under the Fugitive Slave Law, unless you acknowledge allegiance. Believing this honestly, so I must act, though personally I feel strong friendship as ever, for very many in the South. With Great Respect Your friend

W. T. Sherman

Maj. Genl.

LbkS: DNA, RG 94, Records of the Adjutant General's Office, Generals' Books and Papers, William T. Sherman, Letterbook 4.

1. Thomas Hunton (d. 1890), originally from Kentucky, had graduated from West Point in 1839 and declined an appointment as a second lieutenant in the Second Dragoons after his graduation.

2. On August 20, Hunton had written to WTS. He mentioned their school ties and then revealed that several members of General Hovey's command had induced some of his "servants" to join the Federal camp. He thought they would be glad to return to him if they knew that he had come to Mississippi to take active control of his plantation. These slaves, he insisted, would be better off with him; their loss was a serious financial and personal blow to him. He suspected they were in Memphis, and he wanted WTS to return them to him. He was willing to come to Memphis himself to get those willing to return but only if "I can be permitted to return from that place without hindrance and without taking the oath of allegiance to the U.S." He provided WTS with a list of the missing slaves. DLC: WTS.

3. Edgar Basil Gaither (d. 1855), also of Kentucky, graduated from the Military Academy in 1839 and served with the dragoons in the Mexican War.

4. James L. Rankin (d. 1845) of Pennsylvania had accepted a commission in the artillery in 1839 after his graduation from West Point and was killed on duty.

5. William Irvin of Ohio (d. 1852), also of the USMA class of 1839, served in the Mexican War.

6. Major General Edward O. C. Ord (1818–83), USA, was commanding the Second Division of the District of Corinth.

7. Brigadier General Isaac I. Stevens (1818–62), USA, commanded the Second Division of the Department of the South.

8. Presumably General Orders No. 72, issued on August 11, 1862, which authorized army officers to keep those fugitives under their command for either army or private labor. *PUSG,* 5:273–74n.

TO WILLIAM H. H. TAYLOR[1]

Head Quarters 5th Division
Memphis Aug. 25. 1862.

Col. W. H. H. Taylor
President.
Dear Sir:

In compliance with your request I put down a few of the points of our conversation yesterday.

The Cincinnati press has ever taken pains to abuse me personally. I am not dependant on the Press in any manner, never having sought popularity. In fact I despise popularity obtained by the usual process of flattery and pusillanimity. I could easily win the applause of the masses by stooping to practises that would degrade me in my own estimation and that of posterity. I have had many opportunities to take a leading position but have *purposely* declined all, because I do not think that I ought to lead or determine a policy when I do not profess to see clearly the end. In Kentucky I foresaw or thought I foresaw opposition that called for a force that at the time seemed ridiculous or absurd. Time has proved the truth of my representations.

I have been with Genl. Halleck ever since and know that he appreciates my motives and character. Since my arrival here the same game is played.

I admit that the press succeeded in impairing my usefulness. I am not personally injured as I would be most happy if any other would assume my labours & responsibilities and allow me to go to Saint Louis to live in Peace.

But personally I know there can be no *Peace* any where in America till this war is brought to a close, and this is no speedy thing.

There are over six millions of people in the South, every one of whom is a keen, bitter, Enemy. The men are brave and trained to arms. They have educated leaders, as good if not better than ours on the whole they are united, whilst our People & Press appear more determined to ruin our army than that of the Enemy. See the number of leaders already consigned to doom. As soon as any man rises above mediocrity he is made the butt for all the arrows of the envious or disappointed. Success is demanded & yet the means to attain success are withheld. Military men are chained to a Rock; whilst the vultures are turned loose. We must be silent whilst our defamers are allowed the widest liberty & license. We dare not speak the truth unless that Truth be palatable to the crowd. Reputations are not made by the honest soldiers who stand by their colors but by the crowd that flies back to their homes and employ the Press. Our cause is in danger from this alone. It will soon be hard if not impossible to get military men to expose their reputations to such dangers more insidious and sure of destruction than the bullets of our Enemies.

I do say that instead of using our minds to measure the danger in advance we are bungling along having bitter experience as we go. To pull down one man and put up another has been more the work of this war than to destroy the power of the Enemy. Thus any child may see how merchants to make one dollar a barrel on salt furnish our Enemy the means of putting up 2500 lbs of Bacon, Enough for a Regiment for ten days. To make a few dollars on pistols, they supply the Guerrillas with the means of killing our soldiers. "Commerce must follow the flag" sounds well, but in truth commerce supplies our enemy the means to destroy that flag & the Government whose Emblem it is. I have no hesitation in saying that the possession of the Mississipi river by us is an advantage to our Enemy, for by it and the commercial spirit of our people they, the Enemy, get directly or indirectly all the means necessary to carry on the war. This is not a popular Idea but is true.

About the sick. I am held up to the People of Ohio as a monster because I wont let the Sanitary Committee carry off our sick. We take the best care of our sick *here* when they recover they go on duty—If carried away they seldom return. After Pittsburgh you know that 5000 men were carried off without their papers, and poor fellows now hunting their Regiments suffer for want of the evidence which Government *demands* before giving pay, rations & clothing. The parties who carried them away instead of taking the blame to themselves try to throw it off on hard hearted Quarter Masters & commanding officers. They who carried off our men are to blame and not me.

We came near being defeated from this cause and the same probably has led to McClellans failure, for I see he had 70,000 absent without leave who by the muster Rolls were supposed to be before Richmond. This is a monster evil and should be combatted as much as any other Enemy of a distracted country.

I intend to be governed by "Law & the Regularly Constituted Authorities" and not by the Press. If the Press is to Rule and Congress and the President abdicate their Powers, then we can choose what to do. Your Friend,

W. T. Sherman

Maj. Genl.

LbkS: DNA, RG 94, Records of the Adjutant General's Office, Generals' Books and Papers, William T. Sherman, Letterbook 4; *OR*, I, 52: pt. 1, 275–76.
1. William H. H. Taylor of the Fifth Ohio Cavalry.

CHAPTER 6

August 26, 1862–January 25, 1863

*A*s summer turned to fall in 1862, Sherman continued to struggle with the responsibilities of occupation duty. He cared little for the measures adopted by Lincoln and Congress that looked toward emancipation; he growled that to declare blacks free without providing for the consequences was typical of shortsighted politicians who overlooked the practical implications of their policies. "You cannot solve this negro question in a day," he warned his brother in the Senate. To feed and to provide for refugee blacks proved a daunting challenge that sapped time and energy away from the task of subduing the rebellion. Nevertheless, he had little patience for discussions about the constitutionality of emancipation and confiscation. "It is useless to talk about Constitutional means for a condition of things never contemplated by any constitution," he told his stepbrother Philemon. "It is a Revolution where the strongest must prevail."[1]

Even as he questioned the wisdom of emancipation, Sherman offered little sympathy for Southern slaveholders. They deserved to lose their slaves—and more. "I will not go out of my way to protect them or their property," he reminded a newspaper editor. While he did not condone unauthorized acts of pillage or destruction by his soldiers, he did not lose much sleep over them, for in the end white Southerners had brought it all on themselves. When guerrillas and roving bands of Confederates caused trouble, he retaliated, once ordering the burning of Randolph, Tennessee, after learning that unarmed steamers on the Mississippi had come under rifle fire from the Tennessee shore near the town. At one point he went so far as to say that the war would not end until the South "is repeopled by a New Race."[2]

But if Sherman was determined to crush Confederate resistance, he respected the commitment of white Southerners to their cause. In contrast, he mocked the halfhearted way Northerners went about waging war. "The People have long enough deluded themselves with the predictions of Politicians and newspapers & must see things as they are and not as they would they were," he declared.[3] He complained about the impact of desertion and the liberal granting of leaves on the strength of the army. The public, following the lead of newspapers, failed to understand the pressures under which generals operated. Bruised by criticism, he declared that he would never return to Ohio; he persisted in defending himself against his detractors.

Sherman's mind turned back to military operations in the fall of 1862. After fending off Confederate forces at Iuka and Corinth, Grant pushed southward into Mississippi; before long he began contemplating how to take Vicksburg. Sherman jumped at the chance to put aside the frustrations of occupation and return to the main task at hand. Nevertheless, he still had his doubts about his immediate superior, ranking Halleck and McClellan as the Union's top commanders. In December, in compliance with Grant's instructions, Sherman boarded his command on transports and sailed down the Mississippi in an attempt to seize Chickasaw Bluffs, just north of Vicksburg. At the least, he would secure a foothold there; at best, he might actually take the city, especially if Confederate commander John C. Pemberton moved in force to counter a drive by Grant south toward Jackson. When Confederate cavalry raids severed Grant's supply lines, forcing him to withdraw, Pemberton concentrated on Sherman, and the attempt to take Chickasaw Bluffs resulted in a bloody repulse.

It was in the wake of this setback that John A. McClernand arrived at Sherman's headquarters and took command of his men. Several months earlier the politician-general had secured a leave of absence to visit Washington; while there he had laid before Lincoln a scheme whereby he would help raise new regiments in the Old Northwest and then lead them in an independent expedition against Vicksburg. Lincoln had approved the idea with enthusiasm, although the orders authorizing the expedition provided that it would be up to Grant to decide whether he could better employ the new recruits to achieve other objectives—and thus McClernand could exercise independent command only if Grant agreed. It was in part because Grant distrusted McClernand's abilities as a general that he tried to capture Vicksburg before McClernand made his way back to the front. Sherman, who shared Grant's skepticism about McClernand, nevertheless decided to do what he could under the circumstances and advised McClernand to use the force at hand to sail up the Arkansas River and capture Fort Hindman, also known as Arkansas Post. The campaign proved a success, although Grant, who at first thought it McClernand's idea, had criticized it before learning of Sherman's authorship.

Arkansas Post proved a momentary bright spot for Sherman. Disgusted with McClernand, he longed for Grant to take charge. He braced himself for the inevitable deluge of criticism about Chickasaw Bluffs. And though he realized the importance of taking Vicksburg, he knew that it would be "a hard nut to crack."[4]

1. WTS to JS, September 3, 1862; WTS to Philemon B. Ewing, November 2, 1862.
2. WTS to Editor, *Memphis Bulletin*, September 21, 1862; WTS to JS, October 1, 1862.
3. WTS to JS, September 3, 1862.
4. WTS to JS, January 6, 1863.

TO JOHN SHERMAN

Memphis, August 26, 1862

Dear Brother,

Ellen writes me that Elizabeth proposes to remove to Henry Reese's house and vacate the old House and she wants me to secure it for her.[1] I dont exactly like a house with So little ground, but this is not time to choose, for I dont expect to Survive this war. However as long as I do live I can afford to hire a house in Lancaster, but she is liable to be turned off at any moment by the sale of the house she now occupies to an actual purchaser. I of course cannot but laugh at the idea of anybody buying a house in Lancaster now. $50 would be dear for the best house there, but it might so happen that Littles house now occupied by Ellen might be taken for some of his debts & therefore in that view of the case I would like to secure our old House, understanding to buy it at some future time or agreeing to keep the premises in good repair till I leave it. Should I unexpectedly survive the war of course I would not live for any consideration in Ohio. It seems to me that I receive nothing but baseness from that quarter. A Doctor Cook came here to carry off our sick. We had no sick to send, as they were all provided well for in our Regimental Hospitals and the General Hospital equal if not better than any in Cincinati. Beside which I have not the right to let any officer or soldier go without leave of the Secretary of War—and the orders from all superiors from Genl. Grant up to the President positively forbid sending sick soldiers home.

In a rambling communication I expressed a doubt if the Sanitary Committee had done all they claimed. After Bull Run they afforded good excuse for the departure for home of the thousands who left for home. At Shiloh they & others carried off so that our army before Corinth had 57,000 absent without Leave.

In my Division 4600 were at one time absent without Leave, and even yet to 7000 present 2000 are still absent: they were not sick but got off on the plea of sickness some how or other. All sorts of orders have been issued to coax them back threats have been used, & finally the President fixed a date the 11th inst. after which the "absent without leave" were to be treated as Deserters—This was the case to my Knowledge in every Division of the Army of the Tennessee. This Doctor Cook has reported that I did not want the "Cowards back from the Hospital" I never used those words or [any] of similar import, but I did say the class of men whom I have described that were carried off as sick by the Sanitary Boats were not sick, and I dont think if they return they will add to our strength. Any man may get sick and should be and is carefully attended I assert the Sick of my Division have the best possible attention, and that they recover their health and go to duty in half the time as if sent to a General

Hospital. Gradually the practice is coming to my original proposition that none but discharged soldiers should go home, or wounded men. All others Should be in Regimental Hospitals or Hospitals established near at hand where as they convalesce they can join.

Although from the President down to the lowest Brigadier orders & orders to this effect have been issued yet there are hundreds trying to get their sons & brothers home.[2] I know full well the intense desire to get home, but any army will be ruined by this cause alone. McClellan had 70,000 absent from his army.[3] Some were sick, but certainly not over 20,000—with the other 50,000 our Country might have been saved the disgrace of a Retreat from Richmond, for it has resolved itself into that. *At last* all have come to the conclusion that we are at war and great as the draft has been on your population dont suppose you outnumber the South yet—All their people are armed and at war—You hear of vast armies at Richmond at Chattanooga & threatening New Orleans, whilst the whole country is full of Guerilla bands numbering hundreds. All the People are armed. A year ago we could have taken them unprepared, but they have used the year to buy all kinds of arms & munitions of war, & wherever we go we find them well prepared. They seem to have left this quarter—I am glad of the new levies and only regret the loss of the Year—The present operations in Virginia & Kentucky are all important. I enclose you a Photograph taken of my self & staff—Give it to Cecilia—affectionately,

W. T. Sherman

ALS, DLC: William T. Sherman.

1. On August 1, 1862, EES wrote her husband that she wanted him to buy John's and Charles's shares in the house. She reiterated this demand on August 7. SFP.

2. See, for example, General Orders No. 58, District of West Tennessee, August 5, 1862, *PUSG*, 5:280–81.

3. McClellan complained about such absences. See McClellan to Lincoln, July 14, 1862, and McClellan to Lorenzo Thomas, September 28, 1862, Stephen W. Sears, ed., *The Civil War Papers of George B. McClellan, Selected Correspondence, 1860–1865* (New York, 1989), 357–58, 484–85.

TO JOHN SHERMAN

Memphis, Sept. 3, 1862

Dear Brother,

I have your letter and Still think you are wrong in saying that Negros are free & entitled to be treated accordingly by simple declaration of Congress[1]—It requires a Judicial decree in each instance before the officers of our Treasury will give faith to their receipts or recognise any dealings with them—Besides no army could take care of the wants of the host of niggers, women & children that would hang about it freed without the condition attached of earning their food & clothing. I know instead of helping us it would be an incumbrance. Now I have in my orders appropriated the labor of negros as far as will benefit the army.[2] To injure our enemy universal emancipation with the machinery to carry it into Effect would be of course effectual, but by no means conclusive. Not one nigger in ten wants to run off—There are 25,000 in 20 miles of Memphis—all could escape & would receive protection here, but we have only about 2000 of whom full one half are hanging about camps as officers servants. Some plan, some system of labor must be devised in connection with these slaves else the whole scheme fails—It is easy to say "thou shalt not steal" but to stop stealing puzzles the brains of hundreds of men and employs thousands of bailiffs, sheriffs, &c. &c.—so you or congress may command, "Slaves shall be free" but to make them free, and see that they are not converted into thieves, idlers or worse is a difficult problem and will require much machinery to carry out.

Our commissaries must be enduced to feed them, and some provision must be made for the women & children. My order gives employment to say 2000—all men—now that is about ⅛ of the command—extend that proportion to the whole army of 800,000, gives 100,000 slaves, and if we pay $10 a month the estimate can be made—If the women & children are to be provided for, we must allow for the support of say one million. Where are they to get work, who is to feed them, clothe them, & house them. We cannot now give tents to our soldiers, and our wagon trains are now a horrible impediment, and if we are to take along & feed the negros who flee to us for refuge, it will be an impossible task. You cannot solve this negro question in a day.

As to the Law,[3] the 14th Section is positive giving Jurisdiction to the Courts of the United States—The President, nor War Dept. nor Commdg. Genl. has given us minute instructions and the officers on the Frontier have been compelled to act on our own Infant[ry]. I say it is radically wrong that officers should be allowed to make law—we should execute it as it is, and not attempt to construe it. During a war we can take & use all sorts of property but cannot affect titles.

Your Brigade is not here. I think it is with Buell near Chattanooga—the last I saw of these Regiments they were in Garfields Brigade at Shiloh.[4] Still I should be glad if you would come to Memphis on a visit, provided the Southern army do not reach Kentucky or get into Maryland. In either of those events the People of the North must rise en masse, with Such weapons as they can get & repair to the Frontier.

The People have long enough deluded themselves with the predictions of Politicians and newspapers & must see things as they are and not as they would they were.

The People are always right—Of course in the long run, because this year they are one thing, next year another. Do you say the People were right last year in saying acting & believing that 30,000 men were enough to hold Kentucky and carry on an offensive war against the South. The People is a vague expression—Here the People were certainly *not* right, because you are warning against them. People in the aggregate may be wrong. There is such a thing as absolute right & absolute wrong, and People may do wrong as well as right—*Our People* are always Right—but *another* People may be and always are wrong.

If you come to Memphis I will write to Ellen that She may come along. I am opposed to Ladies coming near an army[.] It is not their place, but for a short visit I am willing to waive objection. affectionately yr. brother

W. T. Sherman

ALS, DLC: William T. Sherman.

1. Written in response to WTS's letter of August 13, JS's August 24, 1862, letter to his brother approved his order concerning the employment of blacks, although he added that they should receive pay before the courts adjudicated their status: "You ought to presume their freedom until the contrary is shown & pay them accordingly." The Union, he maintained, would have to befriend blacks in order to defeat the Confederacy, and politicians of all parties were starting to concede this point: "I am prepared for one to meet the broad issue of universal emancipation—If we cant depend upon the loyalty of the white men of the South I would give the land to the blacks or colonize a new set." The only criticism he had heard of his brother's conduct in Memphis was that he was too easy on the Rebels. JS observed that those general officers who agreed with and acted upon the public will were popular and would advance and cited the examples of Butler, Frémont, Mitchel, and Turchin: "We must treat these rebels as bitter enemies to be subdued—conquered—by confiscation, by the employment of their slaves by terror—energy audacity rather than by conciliation." DLC: WTS.

2. On August 11, Grant's headquarters had issued a directive to guide officers in their employment of blacks. See *PUSG*, 5:273–74.

3. WTS is referring to the Second Confiscation Act, which became law July 17, 1862. It declared slaves owned by secessionist masters to be free; the ultimate status of other property owned by secessionists and confiscated by Union authorities would be determined in judicial proceedings.

4. Brigadier General James A. Garfield (1831–81), USA, commanded the Twentieth Brigade of the Sixth Division of the Army of the Ohio at Shiloh.

TO ELLEN EWING SHERMAN

Memphis, Sept. 12, 1862

Dearest Ellen,

I have a few moments of leisure this morning, the Rain keeping away visitors or people in search of negros. Hurlbuts Division is gone to the North East to the vicinity of Jackson Town, and I have sent an expedition out of about 2000 men to the South East to make a division. The enemy has about 4000 Infantry & 12 guns at Holly Springs 50 miles south east of us and the intervening country is full of Guerilla bands that disperse to their farms and reassemble to attack any small party that goes through the neighborhood. In that way all the men of the South are in arms. Breckinridges Division is moving up from Jackson to Holly Springs destined to attack Memphis or to go on to Kentucky. I think the latter is the case. Our First is pretty well advanced. We have 7 Guns mounted and soon will have 23 beside our Field batteries. I have my own Divn. here, about 7000 strong and can hold the Fort against 20,000, but a dash into Memphis would give us trouble as its circuit is extensive and our Line about it extended & weak. In spite of all we can do the People in the Interior smuggle out shoes, salt &c. for which they pay here, and I doubt if any force can overcome the Cupidity of our northern People. If they can make money by any means they will do so. I first forbade any Gold Silver or Treasury notes going into the country. This was overruled at Washington, but yesterday a new order came forbidding Gold & Silver.[1] That is approximating the truth, but we are slow to learn.

The Confederates have now possession of Kentucky and will I suppose get Maryland. Washington will then be of real danger. I think the plan is Kirby Smith[2] will wait in Kentucky till he makes matters there pretty Secure and until Bragg arrives when they will take Cincinati & Invade Ohio. I dont apprehend they will invade the South part of Ohio, but the East part so as to cut off the West & East—I see that the People are aroused, but as soon as Cincinati is safe they will go back home and let the Confederates work out their real plan[.] General Morgan[3] is at Cumberland Gap but I dont see that any effort is being made to go to his relief. All the men of Ohio must become Soldiers. It wont do for them to simply defend Ohio. They must fight for the Union. My predictions of last fall are not much wide of the truth now—The Southern Leaders dont wait till the time comes, they prepare beforehand. The whole of last year has been censured by them in preperation and now they have a larger army, & as well armed as we have. I still dont see the issue of events—but surely we must do more than brag or else the South will carry the war into Africa. I see the People have made a clear sacrifice of Pope & McDowell and are now content with having killed two of their own Generals.[4] This is a Glorious War. With thousands of armed enemies now in the loyal states of Kentucky & Maryland the People are content to kill Pope & McDowell—Well—it may be all right but I would advise a different course—Instead of thinking of us away to the front they think of themselves. I sent one of my Regiments to secure a Battalion of the 13th Infantry[.] They keep both—That was dishonest & unfair, and I have so written to Wright[5] at Cincinati. They see an awful danger at

Cincinati, but dont think of us who are far in the advance. The next time they want one of my Regiments I['ll]ll insist they send me another *first*.

We are all very quiet here, waiting the issue of events in Kentucky & Maryland—but I dont think Kirby Smiths army was designed to invade Ohio, but to catch Morgans command at Cumberland Gap and he would not have attempted the Capture of Lexington & the Blue Grass Region, only he was attacked by those Raw troops whom he easily defeated and followed up— Bragg will probably be in Kentucky by Oct. 1, and Breckinridge will be at Paducah about the Same time.

Buell has a good army enough to move up parallel with Bragg, but I dont think they will come into collision until all reach Kentucky. I dont know what Grants army will do, but I take it I Shall be left here at Memphis on the defensive.

I enclose you a large Daguerrotype pretty rough, but they Say it is a likeness[.]

I will send you a few more, where on that Score you will be content. Tell Phil I have received his letter and will attend to his business—Love to all. yrs.

W. T. Sherman

ALS, InND: Sherman Family Papers.

1. On July 30, WTS had informed John A. Rawlins that he had halted the trade using gold, silver, or treasury notes. Grant soon issued orders in the same spirit. On August 11, Rawlins informed WTS that such restrictions should be lifted. WTS accepted but grumbled to Grant that he would "move Heaven & Earth for its repeal, as I believe it will be fatal to our success. If we provide our enemies with money we enable them to buy, all they stand in need of." See *PUSG*, 5:240–41, 268.

2. Major General Edmund Kirby Smith (1824–93), CSA, was leading the Department of East Tennessee and directing an invasion of Kentucky.

3. Brigadier General George W. Morgan (1820–93), USA, was commanding the Seventh Division of the Army of the Ohio and would be instrumental in driving Confederates out of Cumberland Gap.

4. After the Union defeat at the Battle of Second Bull Run (August 29–30, 1862), both John Pope and Irvin McDowell were transferred from the Army of Virginia to other commands as part of a reorganization that terminated the existence of that army.

5. Major General Horatio G. Wright (1820–99), USA, was commanding the District of Western Kentucky at this time.

TO NEW YORK GENTLEMEN

Hd. Qtrs. Dist. of Memphis
Memphis Aug. [September] 17, 1862

Gentlemen,

I have just received the copy of your letter of September 1, 1862 conveying to me in terms of marked respect an sword of uncommon value, of great beauty in design & magnificently executed.[1] I confess myself overwhelmed by the unexpected honor and feel a just pride in the terms of your letter and especially in contemplating the name of the donors among whom I recognize not only personal friends but merchants whose fame is coextensive with the dominions of our Glorious Flag. The consciousness that my military career is watched with interest by such friends will nerve my arm and impel me to renewed exertions in the struggle yet before us.

I confess that I have sought rather obscurity than prominence in this War, that for a time I was discouraged by a seeming apathy on the part of our People and a want of appreciation of the mighty issue in which our nation had become involved, but this is now dispelled by the manifestations of real Power and strength recently exhibited. The nation is now fully awakened to the magnitude of the work to be done, and I now believe that the just authority of the United States will be respected not only within our proper dominions but all over earth. Even in the past we have no reason to repine. Wars involving far less important principles have in Europe extended through tens of years, and we in this, must allow time to cope with the deep seated prejudices planted by designing demagogues among a whole People, not only have we to grapple with a brave and determined foe, but at every step of our progress we encounter the hate of a deluded people who regard us as Invaders of their soil and sacred rights.

Give the Leaders of your Armies your Confidence & give them time and you will have reason to be proud that our national character shall stand high among the nations of the earth, & our children will inherit the institutions of regulated Freedom transmitted to us, by our Fathers.

We have yet before us, a vast country with obstacles of nature & a people filled with a bitter determined hatred that can be combatted with arms & arms alone. Reason has lost its sway & nothing more is left us but force, but that must be directed with a wise and united purpose. By a close adherence to our constitution and a cheerful obedience to the orders of our constituted authorities we have that simple plain Rule of action which can alone extricate us from our present complications & lead us all to an honorable solution. This shall be my study, and I hope thus to give my feeble aid to our Common purpose, the restoration of our General Government to its rightful power everywhere; where this is established & acknowledged, there our Government can afford to be magnanimous to the people who in an evil hour resorted to arms in search of a Remedy provided by our Fundamental Law.

Thanking you again individually and collectively, for the honor conferred on me, I am with great respect your obt. Servt.

W. T. Sherman
Maj. Genl.
Comdg.

To Messrs. E. D. Morgan & Co., Wm. Scott, Wm. T. Coleman DeWitt Kittle & Co., Ogden Haggerty, Schuckhard & Gibhard Chas. H. Marshall, Weston & Grey, Lockwood & Co., H. A. Hurlbut Sturgis Bennett & Co. Agman & Co., Alfred M. Hoyt, D. N. Burnes and C. K. Garrison of New York City.

LbkS, DNA: RG 94, Records of the Adjutant General's Office, Generals' Books and Papers, William T. Sherman, Letterbook 3.

1. DLC: WTS. The fifteen gentlemen or firms involved sent WTS a ceremonial sword in gratitude for his performance at Shiloh.

TO THE EDITOR OF THE *MEMPHIS BULLETIN*

Hd. Qts. 5th. Division
Memphis Tenn. Sep. 21, 1862

Editor Bulletin
Sir,

Your comments on the recent orders of General's Halleck and McClellan afford the occasion appropriate for me to make public the fact that there is a law of Congress, as old as our Government itself, but reenacted on the 10th of April 1806, and in force ever since. That law reads:

> "All officers & soldiers are to behave themselves orderly in quarters and on their march, and whoever shall commit any waste or spoil, either in walks of trees, parks, warrens, fish ponds, houses & gardens, cornfields, in closes or meadows, or shall maliciously destroy any property whatever belonging to the inhabitants of the United States, unless by order of the then Commander-in-chief of the armies of said United States, shall (besides such penalties as they are liable to by law) be punished according to the nature and degree of the offense, by the judgment of a General or Regimental Court Martial."

Such is the law of Congress, and the orders of the Commander-in-Chief are, that officers or soldiers convicted of straggling and pillaging shall be punished with death. These orders have not come to me officially, but I have seen them in newspapers, and am satisfied that they express the determination of the Commander-in-Chief. Straggling & pillaging have ever been great military crimes, and every officer and soldier in my command knows what stress I have laid upon them, and that so far as in my power lies, I will punish them to the full extent of the law and orders.

The law is one thing, the execution of the law another. God himself has commanded, "Thou shalt not kill," "thou shalt not steal," "thou shalt not Covet the neighbors Goods etc." But will any one say these things are not done now as well as before these laws were announced at Sinai? I admit the law to be, that no officer or soldier of the united States shall commit waste or destruction of cornfields, orchards, potato patches, or any kind of pillage on the property of friend or foe near Memphis, and that I stand prepared to execute the law as far as possible.

No Officer or soldier should enter the home or premises of any peaceable citizen, no matter what their politics, unless on business and no such officer or soldier can force an entrance unless he have a written order from a commanding Officer or Provost Marshal, which written authority must be exhibited if demanded. When property such as forage, building or other materials are needed by the United States a receipt will be given by the Officer taking them, which receipt should be presented to the Quartermaster who will substitute therefor a regular voucher, to be paid according to the circumstances of the case. If the officer refuse to give such receipts, the citizen may fairly infer that the property is wrongfully taken, and he should for his own protection ascertain the name, rank & regiment of the Officer and report him in writing[.] If any soldier commits waste or destruction, the person whose property is thus wasted, must find out the name, company, & regiment of the actual transgressor. In order to punish, there must be a trial and there must be testimony. It is not sufficient that a general accusation be made, that soldiers are doing this or that; I cannot punish my whole command, or a whole battalion, because one or two bad soldiers do wrong. The punishment must reach the perpetrator, and no one can identify him as well as the party who is interested. The State of Tennessee does not hold itself responsible for acts of larceny Committed by her citizens nor does the United States or any other nation. These are individual acts of wrong, and punishment can only be inflicted on the wrongdoers. I know the difficulty of identifying particular soldiers but difficulties do not alter the importance of principles of justice. They should stimulate the parties to increase their efforts to find out the actual perpetrator of the Crime.

Colonels of Regiments & Commanders of Corps are liable to severe punishment for permitting their men to leave their camps to commit waste or destruction, but I know full well that many of the acts attributed to soldiers, are committed by citizens and negroes and are charged to soldiers, because of a desire to find fault with them, but this only reacts upon the Community, and increases the mischief. Whilst every officer would willingly follow up any accusation against any one or more of his men, whose names or discriptions were given, immediately after the discovery of the act he would naturally resent any general charge against his *good* men, for the criminal conduct of a few bad men in his charge.

I have examined into many of the cases of complaint made in this general way, and have felt mortified that our soldiers should do acts which are nothing more or less than stealing, but was powerless without some clue whereby to reach the rightful party. I know that the Great mass of our soldiers would scorn to steal or commit Crime, and I will not therefore entertain vague and general complaints but stand prepared always to follow up any reasonable complaint when the Charge is definite and the names of witnesses furnished.

I know, moreover, in some instances, when our soldiers are Complained of, they have been insulted by sneering remarks about "Yankees," "Northern Barbarians," "Lincoln Hirelings," &c. Such people must seek redress through the civil authorities, for I will not tolerate insults to our country or cause. When people forget their obligations to a Government, that made them respected among the nations of the earth, and speak contemptiously of the flag which is the silent emblem of that country, I will not go out of my way to protect them or their property. I will punish the soldiers for trespass or waste if adjudged by a Court Martial, because they disobey orders, but soldiers are men & citizens as well as soldiers, and should promptly resent any insult to their country come from what quarter it may. I mention this phase because it is too common. Insult to a soldier does not justify pillage, but it takes from the officer the disposition he would otherwise feel to follow up the inquiry and punish the wrong doers.

Again, armies in motion or stationary must commit some waste. Flankers must let down fences & cross fields, & when an attack is contemplated or apprehended a command would naturally clear the Ground of houses, fences & trees. This is not waste but is the natural consequence of war, chargable on those who caused the war. So in fortifying a place, dwelling houses must be taken, materials used, & even wasted & great damage done, which in the End may prove useless. This too is an expense not belonging to us, but to those who made the war, and Generally war is destruction and nothing else.

We must bear this in mind that however peaceful things look, we are really *at war*, and much that looks like waste & destruction is only the removal of objects that obstruct our fire or would afford cover to an enemy.

This class of waste must be distinguished from the wanton waste committed by army stragglers, which is wrong and can be punished by the death penalty, if proper testimony can be produced. Yours &c.

W. T. Sherman
Maj. Genl.
Comdg.

LbkS, DNA: RG 94, Records of the Adjutant General's Office, Generals' Books and Papers, William T. Sherman, Letterbook 4.

Memphis, Sept. 22, 1862

Dear Brother

I write to ask you to use what influence you have in giving to Commander Phelps[1] now & long on duty with the Gun boat fleet in the Mississipi the chief command—when Commodore Davis[2] is relieved to go to Washington.

Phelps is from Ohio, Granger Co.—is in the prime of life, very much esteemed, and has more vim in him than any of the fleet. I think he will naturally succeed to the command, but I would like to have you help him. Things are very quiet here, and mov{ing} along smooth enough—The nigger questions daily arising and the confiscation act are the two great sources of trouble. Are we to free all the negros, men women & children? Whether there be work for them or not? We have no District Court here, and none of the machinery whereby to put in motion the Confiscation act—we take the property of Rebels & use it, but the title remains undisturbed.

You have had a pretty good scare in Ohio, and I regret to see are relaxing back into a condition of peace. Kirby Smiths move on Cincinati was not a part of the plan—he was watching Morgan, and finding a good chance, he turned on that force of green troops at Richmond, and then the Country being open he hurried forward and of course had the chance admitted of it he would have shelled & burned Cincinati, and if you are not wide awake he will do it. Since their repulse in Maryland[3] I doubt if the secesh will cross the Ohio this fall, they will try and hold the line of the Potomac, Ohio, and then make another dash at St. Louis.

Troops are moving up through Arkansas for Missouri. It looks as though they want to swap countries with us. It is about time the North understood the truth, that the entire South, man woman & child is against us, armed & determined. It will call for a million men for several years to put them down. They are more confident than ever—never seem to doubt their independence, but some hope to conquer the North West. My own opinion is there can never be Peace and we must fight it out. I guess you now see how from the very first I argued that you all under Estimated the task. None of you would admit for a moment that after a years fighting, the enemy would still threaten Washington Cincinati and Saint Louis. We ought to hold fast to the Mississipi River, as a great base of operations. I would regard the loss of St. Louis as more fatal to our future success than the capture by them of Harrisburg and Philadelphia.

I have a letter from Ellen that you had given up the trip to Memphis. Your Brigade is with Buell. I dont understand his move but now suppose he will cross Green River and fight north of it—Still I dont see exactly his strategy or tactics. The passage of the enemy north of us, leaving us among a hostile population was a bold & successful movement, and will give them great credit in Europe. You doubtless like most Americans attribute our want of success to bad Generals—I do not—with us you insist the boys—the soldiers govern, they must have this or that or will cry down their leaders in the newspapers so no General can achieve much—They fight or run as they please and of course it is the Generals fault. Until this is cured, you must not look for success—But on the whole things look more favorable now than at any former time, as the numbers engaged on both sides are approaching the occasion.

The war is which Race that of the North or South Shall rule America.

The greatest danger north is Division & anarchy, but I hope the pressure from the South will keep all united, until our armies begin to have some discipline and see how important it is to Success.

Our Fort here is nearly done—I have 20 heavy guns mounted, and about 30 field pieces—7000 Infantry, & 600 cavalry. Some of my Regts. are now in fine drill & discipline & all doing well. We are however tied down till events elsewhere develop. Love to all yrs.

W. T. Sherman

ALS, DLC: William T. Sherman.

1. Seth L. Phelps (1822–1901), USN, was still in the West, on the Red River, in 1864.

2. Commodore Charles H. Davis (1807–77), USN, the flag officer of the Mississippi flotilla, had been made the chief of the Bureau of Navigation in July 1862.

3. After the Battles of South Mountain (September 14) and Antietam (September 17), Robert E. Lee's Army of Northern Virginia retreated south across the Potomac River; George B. McClellan's Army of the Potomac failed to pursue.

TO THOMAS TASKER GANTT

Head Quarters 5th. Division
Memphis Tenn. Sept. 23d. 1862

T. T. Gantt Esq.
Provost Marshal Gen. St. Louis
My Dear Friend

Although the vicissitudes of this War have been wonderful, yet in some respects results have been well. You are Provost Marshal of St. Louis & I command here at Memphis[.] I have no doubt you will bring order out of confusion and I believe in time I can regulate affairs here. I find more real difficulty in contending with the cupidity of northern merchants in search of a good speculation in the way of Cotton or contraband than with the enemy struggling to regain lost Ground. I reached Memphis at a time, when for the first time were let loose two great causes of solid disorder viz. the nigger & confiscation acts. Of course my duty is to obey the law, and orders of my superiors[.] I will cling to this theory because in it I see the only hope of safety.

I will set up no theory of my own but obey blindly the "Laws & orders"; when they are insufficient, then my own judgment comes in. I ignore my allegiance to the press or public opinion. These are too vague & changeable and nothing has more completely exemplified it than the rapid developments of the past two years.

Whether the laws of Congress are right or wrong is none of my business, but the mode of executing them devolves on me somewhat, and I confess it has at times embarrassed me. I hold that I have no power under any possible combinations of circumstances to "free a Negro" or "confiscate any estate." This is a judicial matter not mine; I see by your late Orders that you are of like opinion but in St. Louis you have judicial power, here I have none.[1] There you have a District Court that can declare a Negro "free," or can proceed against the property of a Rebel, condemn & sell it, leaving you merely to execute the decrees or aid the court by getting possession or to supply testimony. Now Gen. Curtis held & John Sherman inclines to that opinion, that when our Enemy has destroyed the Court, rendering the Law inoperative, that the military power may supply the defect, and that Military tribunals may decree the slave free or the property confiscated[.] If such was the intentions of Congress why not so declare it? The Condition of affairs actually existed at the time & yet the law says the District Court of the U.S. shall make all necessary decrees & orders to carry the law into effect. Therefore I contend that the military must not usurp such power, but the execution of the law must remain imperfect until such Court is put into operation here. I do not pretend to distrust titles but under the laws of war, and only with the possession. Thus we take possession of the property, Real & personal, of Rebels and appropriate to the use of Government the Rents & profits, and we permit negroes to take refuge in our lines & allow no force to be used to return them to slavery. If good able bodied hands, we employ them as laborers, teamsters &c. and feed them, but donot say they are free. This is as far as I go. A great many Slaves say 3000 men women & children are here of which we employ on the Fort, as teamsters &c. about 1500; the rest either find employment for themselves or sponge on the others. I foresee much trouble as winter Comes, to the women & children. Does Congress intend to feed & care for all the negroes? Is it not a task too great to be undertaken? Will we not overburden our commissary by attempting so much? These are serious questions and I can get no line or word of advice from Washington. I know they have their hands full there & I am willing to share with them the labor and responsibility, but our action should be uniform throughout the country[.] I would like your views on these points[.][2] I have a Provost Marshal Col. Anthony here a fine officer but I would like your views and we at least can act in concert as to the two cities of

St. Louis and Memphis. I had two Divisions here, but now only one more. No common mind now directs the West, Since Halleck is gone, and we sadly need a common superior out here. Steele[3] at Helena & Grant in West Tenn. act independently of each other. I think you soon will have you hands full as the troops of Holmes & Hindman in Arkansas are moving north towards Mo.

The progress of Bragg in Kentucky[4] is not to my liking but our people & Government deferred too long their preperations for this wholesale movement of the South which all ought to have foreseen[.] I am all the better satisfied that the Game is thus far developed. As Ever Your friend

W. T. Sherman

Maj. Genl.

Comdg.

LbkS, DNA: RG 94, Records of the Adjutant General's Office, Generals' Books and Papers, William T. Sherman, Letterbook 4.

1. Gantt to WTS, October 8, 1862, explained that Gantt had decreed no slaves were to be freed without a specific court order. DLC: WTS.

2. When Gantt replied to this letter on October 8, he was in despair about the growth of Missouri's free black population. The numbers were rising rapidly as Illinois citizens drove them out. Very few had any means of support, but the army was still encouraging them to come, in spite of a state law that forbade their presence and rewarded emigration from Missouri with manumission.

3. Brigadier General Frederick Steele (1819–68), USA, was commanding the Army of Southwest Missouri.

4. Bragg had been moving into Tennessee since early September and had captured a Federal garrison at Mumfordville, Kentucky, on September 17.

TO ELLEN EWING SHERMAN

Memphis Sept. 25, 1862

Dearest Ellen,

I have yours up to Sept. 19.[1] I enclose you a letter I have written to Elizabeth on the matter of the House. Of Course if you want it you must have it, and as our family is even now beginning to Scatter it may suit you as well as any other that you can get. You remember that for years I supplied mother with ready money. I never Kept an account of it as it was freely given. Every time I went home I overhauled her books & accounts paid all bills and left her in funds.

At that time Charles Sherman made his offer to provide house in Mansfield, wood, potatos fruit &c., all of which he got as fees or from his own property, leaving mother the Rest of her house, and what ready money John & I could give. To provide for the very contingencies which have since occurred mother deeded the house to John Sherman in trust for us three, but with the understanding that the property Should be kept for any member of the family that stood in want. Elizabeth has had its use ever since. As she no longer requires it I have the next best right as all our family is provided for well, no exception. I have written to John on the subject but independent of him I would not hesitate to take it if you need it. I have written to Elizabeth to this effect and if you do need it tell her so, and she must not ever think of letting a stranger enter it. If any minister get into it I will see that he quits it instanter.

I wont buy it for it is already ours for use if we need it, and Should I mistake in my belief that this war is to desolate us all, I would not live there. I prefer Missouri, Illinois, California or New York. Lancaster is well enough but not to my taste, unless broken down or crippled, when I could not choose. For yourself & children, as long as I am away, you have a right to it, which John & Charles well can respect. All you have to do if Elizabeth vacate, go take it and Keep it. At all events let no one else a stranger move into it—should this be done, tell the tenant to quit for I will not tolerate such a breach of my rights and pleasure.

I Send you by todays mail another of my public acts—our men do commit some acts of Robbery that disgrace us as a People. I See the same occurs to Halleck & McClellan, and I hope our military leaders may be able to check this tendency to anarchy & misrule. It is one of the dangers to which Civil War exposes us. You must now admit my judgment of men is nearly correct— Halleck leads off as a man of intellect, high education and calm determination. He is the only real Great Man thus far. McClellan is next. All others are mediocre. I can easily be popular if I court favor, but see in this coaxing the people one defect in our system & prefer to be honest. Tom Worthington of the Ohio 46th. has been an Element of disorder in my command for months. I had him tried by a Court Martial & dismissed.[2] He will attack me in the Ohio papers, accusing me of all sorts of tyranny at Shiloh &c. Should he make any serious publications, just publish so much of Hallecks dispatch to me at Moscow, when he was about to take his departure for the East, as will [s]how that I possessed his confidence all the time.[3] Omit such part as refers to the quarrels of McClellan & Stanton, for he would not have that public. I believe now I have the unlimited confidence of my troops, of the Union People here, and of most of the Secesh—Some would hang me as a Negro Stealer &c. &c. but all Know that I stick to the Law, as to the only anchor of safety in the present Confusion.

The Boats coming down are occasionally fired on. I have just sent up a party to destroy the town of Randolph[4]—we cannot reach the real actors, but cannot overlook these acts of outrage. Therefore we punish the neighbors for not preventing them. I send you two more daguerrotypes or cards—Sister Ann asked me for one. I have just sent her two—John two, and you two—so I think my picture will have more circulation than is prudent—In times like this lay low—see Pope, McDowell, Fremont Hunter[5] and all boasters. You remember well what I said of Pope—a humbug, but not half so bad as the fool Editors who a few days since lifted him up, and now drop him *away* down—Yrs. Ever

W. T. Sherman

ALS, InND: Sherman Family Papers.

1. EES to WTS, September 10, 15, and 19, 1862.

2. The court-martial of Worthington for conduct unbecoming an officer in connection with the publication of "Extracts from a diary of the Tennessee expedition, 1862, by T. Worthington, Col. 46th reg't Ohio" was convened on August 12. He was found guilty and sentenced to cashiering, the court concluding that the "diary" had been manufactured after the events it purported to describe in order to make Worthington appear a prophet. The sentence was carried out on October 1, although it would be revoked in 1867 by a special order of the War Department in return for Worthington's resignation to date from November 21, 1862. Joseph H. Ewing, *Sherman at War* (Dayton, Ohio, 1992), 68–69.

3. In that letter, Halleck assured WTS, "I am more than satisfied with everything you have done. You have always had my respect, and recently you have won my highest admiration." Lloyd Lewis, *Sherman: Fighting Prophet* (1932; reprint, Lincoln, Neb., 1993), 242.

4. After the ship *Eugene* was attacked on the Mississippi River near Randolph, Tennessee, Federal troops were dispatched to burn the town in revenge on September 23.

5. Major General David Hunter headed the Department of the South from March 31 to August 22, 1862. On May 9 he had issued an order liberating all slaves in Georgia, Florida, and South Carolina. Although Lincoln annulled the order ten days later, Hunter soon commenced enlisting blacks as soldiers.

TO JOHN A. RAWLINS

Headquarters Fifth Division,
Memphis, September 26, 1862.

Maj. John A. Rawlins,
Corinth, Miss.
Sir:

Nothing of interest here. I hear that Breckinridge with his Kentuckians, some 3,000, have started for Kentucky via Jackson, Chattanooga, and Bragg's route. Also that about 10,000 of the enemy have started for Rienzi to re-enforce Price after the fight at Iuka had been heard from. All these things doubtless reach you direct.

The regular packet Eugene, from Saint Louis, with passengers and stores (not public), landed on Tuesday at the town of Randolph, and came near falling into the possession of a band of guerrillas and was fired into by some 25 to 40 of the band. I immediately sent a regiment up with orders to destroy the place, leaving one house and such others only as might be excepted in case of extraordinary forbearance on part of owner. The regiment has returned and Randolph is gone. It is no use tolerating such acts as firing on steamboats. Punishment must be speedy, sure, and exemplary, and I feel assured this will meet your views. I would not do wanton mischief or destruction, but so exposed are our frail boats, that we must protect them by all the terrors by which we can surround such acts of vandalism as decoying them to the shore and firing on them regardless of the parties on board.

That boat was laden with stores for the very benefit of families some of whose members are in arms against us, and it was an outrage of the greatest magnitude that people there or in connivance with them should fire on an unarmed boat.

The town was of no importance, but the example should be followed up on all similar occasions.[1] I will send full reports as soon as Colonel [Charles C.] Walcutt reports. All well here.

> I am, with great respect, yours,
> W. T. Sherman,
> Major-General, Commanding.

Printed, *OR*, I, 17: pt. 1, 144–45.

1. See Mark Grimsley, *The Hard Hand of War: Union Military Policy toward Southern Civilians, 1861–1865* (New York, 1995), 114–17, for a detailed treatment of this affair.

TO THOMAS C. HINDMAN

> Head Quarters 5th Division
> Memphis Sept. 28th 1862

Major Genl. *T. C. Hindman,*
Comdg. Confederate Forces,
Little Rock Ark.
Sir,

I have just received your two letters of Sept. 24 and 26 at the hands of Capt. Chew of your Staff.[1] Of course being simply the Commander of the U.S. forces here, I have no official knowledge of anything that transpired on White River last summer. I will refer that letter to Genl. Curtis now in St. Louis.[2]

Nor have I any knowledge of the affair of Saul Beauter a citizen of Crittenden Co., nor do I believe one word of it; certainly the men of my command never do such acts as you describe.

As to Lieut. Tolleson he was in the Irvin Block here but escaped last week through the negligence of the guard. Had he remained, he would have been tried, and if convicted of murder, his sentence after approved by the President of the United States, would surely have been executed.

So jealous is our Government of life, that no General of whatever rank can inflict the punishment of death except by sentence of a General Court Martial, and that must be approved by the President of the United States. You know the laws of Congress as well as I do. Now whether the Guerillas or Partizan

Rangers without uniform, without organization except on paper, wandering about the country pillaging friend and foe, firing on unarmed boats filled with women and children, and on small parties of soldiers, always form ambush or where they have every advantage, are entitled to the protection and amenities of civilized warfare is a question which I think you would settle very quickly in the abstract. In practice we will promptly acknowledge the well established rights of war to parties in uniform, but many gentlemen of the South, have beseeched me to protect the people against the acts and inevitable result of this war of ununiformed bands, who when dispersed mingle with the people and draw on them the consequences of their individual acts.

You know full well that it is to the interest of the people of the South, that we should not disperse our troops as Guerillas, but at that game your Guerillas would meet their equal and the world would be shocked by the acts of atrocity resulting from such warfare. We endeavor to act in large masses, and must insist that the troops of the Confederacy who claim the peculiar rights of belligerents, should be known by their dress, so as to be distinguished from the inhabitants. I refer you to the proclamation of your Kirby Smith in Kentucky on this very point.[3]

I will refer your letter to Genl. Curtis at St. Louis with whom I beg you will hereafter confer on all matters under a flag of truce.[4] He commands our forces west of the Mississippi, and I am not aware as yet, that any question has arisen under my Command at Memphis that concerns your Command. The idea of your comments on the failure of your efforts to induce our army to conform to the usages of civilized warfare excites a smile; indeed you should not indulge in such language in official letters. I am &c. Your obed't. servant,

> W. T. Sherman
> Major General
> Comdg.

Copy, DLC: William T. Sherman Papers; *OR*, I, 13:682–83, II, 4:568–69.

1. Hindman's two letters to Sherman dated September 23 and 24 are reprinted in *OR*, II, 4:574–75. The first asked about the whereabouts and well-being of a Lieutenant Tolleson of Captain West Harris's unattached company of cavalry who was captured as a guerrilla; Hindman maintained that Harris's troops had been raised "under proper authority" and that therefore Tolleson was a regular officer. He threatened to execute First Lieutenant Hobbs of the First Wisconsin Cavalry in retaliation. Hindman also inquired into the circumstances surrounding the death of Samuel Berry of Crittenden County, Arkansas (the "Saul Beauter" of Sherman's reply), apparently killed by Federal troops after he had been acquitted of burning his own cotton and sugar to prevent Federal confiscation. If this information was correct, he wanted Sherman to turn over the men responsible. Sherman's failure to do so, he added, would result in the death of Second Lieutenant J. T. Consaul of the First Wisconsin Cavalry. Hindman concluded that he intended to adopt this policy of retaliation in all such future cases. On the twenty-fourth, he asked about the alleged abuse

of one Private Peebles of Captain Richardson's company of the "Provisional Army, C.S." and demanded his exchange for a Federal prisoner.

2. Sherman forwarded the two letters to Curtis on September 29, commenting: "Of course I mentioned incidentally the ridiculous feature of his communication, his claiming the rights of civilized warfare for uniformed cowardly guerrillas firing from ambush on unarmed steamers loaded with women and children and his regret that his efforts to teach us the rules of civilized warfare had proven a failure." *OR*, II, 4:572–73.

3. Kirby Smith had begun conducting raids against civilians he thought to be Union sympathizers.

4. On October 17, WTS forwarded Curtis's two replies of October 10 to Hindman; these letters reiterated WTS's points. DNA: RG 94, Records of the Adjutant General's Office, Generals' Books and Papers, Letterbook 4. Curtis's October 11 cover letter to WTS expressed his suspicion that Hindman used correspondence under flags of truce to get intelligence of troop movements. *OR*, II, 4:615.

TO ELLEN EWING SHERMAN

Memphis Oct. 1, 1862

Dearest Ellen,

A letter of Prime recals to me many things I would forget, how one year ago we occupied Muldro Hill with a Corporals Guard and when by bluster we deterred Buckner from approaching Louisville nearer than Green River &c. &c. and now after one year the Same Enemy is in full possession of all our old Camps because the People of the north with a vanity as blind as the Chinese & ignorance as gross as of the hottentots will not see & Know that Eight millions of men women & Children regard us with a hatred more intense than the Indians ever felt and who are united and determined. After all the newspaper boasts I dont believe any soldiers were raised this summer, though I am three hundred miles in the Enemys Country Ohio calls on us for help. With her three millions of People my small Division must spare a Regiment for their defense. Well if necessary Wright may Keep it, but this illustrates the selfishness of the Country. They dont think of the advance Guard but of the Stay at homes—squirrel hunters &c. I wish to God Kirby Smith had gone into Cincinati, for I suppose now that that city is no longer threatened, nobody will stop to think but everybody go home—There will be a well organized army of 75,000 Rebels in Kentucky this month—they have no newspapers to tell their plans & movements—they Knew the apathy of the northern People who having published a vote of thanks to themselves for the great Courage in going to the rescue of Cincinnati, have now gone home—Well now is the time for them to act, and I would not be astonished any moment to hear of their appearance on the Ohio.

Buell has a good army. I dont know as to Wright, but Bragg has Muldrough Ridge & the Blue Grass country & can defy both, whilst his Guerillas will

Enter the River towns and make steamboating too hazardous. They commenced firing on the Boats at Randolph 60 miles up the River and I Caused the town to be destroyed, all save one house to mark the spot. Hindman at Little Rock threatens to treat us all as Barbarians not entitled to the amenities of Civilized warfare. I was rather amused at Arkansas teaching us civilization—Van Dorn is about 45 miles east of me at Lagrange & Holly Springs with about 13,000 men—Hurlbut is at Bolivar with about 5000 & I have here 7000 effective—Steele at Helena about 12,000 Effective, very many sick. The Confederate Prisoners returned by us to Vicksburg will be up this week when they will have a force near double anything we can muster. I dont apprehend a direct attack on us, but we may move out to attack, and they having the centre & we the circumference the advantage is with them.

I have not heard of Hugh except that he is in command of a Brigade,[1] & Charley[2] & Tom[3] are to be colonels of Regiments—quite a military family. I hope Charley is now satisfied that the [war] wont be over before he has a chance—I had read about the sword, but dont bother myself much about it till I have official notice. Of course such a gewgaw must be for the children not me. I got a letter from another of my cadets a prisoner of war at Annapolis, Cadet Jackson, who told me of all the officers & Cadets, who are in the war— several were killed at Shiloh—they seem yet to regard me as friendly to them. I also got a friendly message from Genl. M. L. Smith in the Confederate Service at Vicksburg.[4] He is a New Yorker but married in Savannah.

I will write to Minnie occasionally, and I want you now to make her write to you regularly & improve her style & handwriting—think she is now near 12 years old—Elly & Rachel seem to be your pride, but somehow I have seen so little of them that I cannot feel for them same as I do those that were with us in California. I have strong hopes that Lizzie notwithstanding her delicate nerves will gain strength & health Soon. I have been inspecting & reviewing two Brigades today, and tonight go down to a club of Union Men in the City. Of these about 600 are organized, but they are very timid & fearful. All are afraid as they Know if the secessionists get to Memphis again they are gone. I sent you $400 by Adams Express of which I have yet no acknowledgment, but suppose it is all right—If you see Eliza Gillespie tell her she did right in leaving our Hospital. Dr. Derby[5] will not let the Sisters have peace. He will persevere till all are gone, and I cannot prevent him. The Doctors now command the Army, for they can through the Sanitary Commission remove or Condemn any officer who does not allow them their own way.

Write me about the House. I dont want Elizabeth to put any family in it— nor do I want you to take it unless you have to {move} as there is not yard Room enough for the children. My love to all yrs. Ever,

W. T. Sherman

ALS, InND: Sherman Family Papers.

1. Hugh commanded a brigade in the Ninth Corps at Antietam.

2. Charley had finally been ordered to WTS's command at Memphis.

3. Tom Ewing had recruited the Eleventh Kansas Cavalry and led them in James Blunt's division of the Army of the Frontier.

4. Brigadier General Martin L. Smith (1819–66), CSA, planned the fortifications at Vicksburg.

5. Surgeon Nelson R. Derby was in charge of the Overton Hospital.

TO JOHN SHERMAN

Memphis Oct. 1, 1862

Dear Brother

I did not expect you would come after the Confederates got possession of Kentucky, for even on the Mississipi the Boats are fired on daily. I have been compelled to burn down one town & resort to retaliation. I understand ⟨Pre⟩ntiss has ordered back from Helena a part of the forces towards S. Louis on the ground that ⟨the⟩ Confederates are again advancing on Missouri. ⟨I⟩ rather think you now agree with me that this ⟨is⟩ no common war, that it was not going to end in a few months or a few years, for after 18 months war the enemy is actually united armed and determined, with powerful forces well handled disciplined & commanded on the Potomac, the Ohio, and Missouri. You must now see that I was right in not seeking prominence at the outstart. I knew & know yet that the northern people have to unlearn all their experience of the past thirty years & be born again before they will see the truth. Newspapers & Politicians have such influence that even you would throw overboard such men as Halleck, McClellan, Wright & others and take up Fremont, Hunter & Cassius Clay[1] because these are radical men—Now in Revolutions extremes must for a time prevail and this war has soon got to that—North vs. South—Free vs. Slave labor—Now put Fremont in my place here. What would he do with refugee negros—would he attempt to feed them in idleness—What could he do with them. They are free, but freedom dont clothe them, feed them & shelter them. I admit these things are beyond my comprehension I dont see where they tend. The President declares negros free, but makes no machinery by which such freedom is assured. I still see no solution of this Great problem except in theory, and am still resolved to keep my subordinate place.

My theory is that without Government there is no property—that we must have a Govt.—that two Rival Govts. cannot exist in Peace here, and that of necessity one must prevail—of the two now struggling for existence the old is the best and can be easiest modelled into the one that will be best adapted to the interests of the People—that of Course the South will not submit until their country is repeopled by a New Race. I think that when we have made one convert during the war we have made the Enemies.

The Presidents proclamation can do no good & but little harm.[2] The South has an united People, and as many men as she can arm, and though our armies pass across & through the land, the war closes in behind and leaves the Same enmity behind. We attempt to occupy places, and the People rise up & make the Detachments prisoners. I know you all recognize in these facts simply that Mason is a coward,[3] Ford an ass, McClellan slow—Buell over-cautious & Wright timid. This may all be so, but the causes lie deeper.

Every body thought I exaggerated the dangers so I have no right to an opinion, but I rather think many now see the character of the war in which we are engaged. I dont see the end or beginning of the end, but suppose we must prevail or perish. I dont believe that two nations can exist within our old limits and therefore that war is on us and we must fight it out. I never dreamed of any thing else. You know I always said the war was inevitable but I felt sure that the Republican party brought it on too Soon, and entirely ignorant of the full extent of the work and also that your leaders gave the Southern Politicians the means of uniting their people on the issues.

Were the work to do over again I know many would be more cautious and less bold in pushing on the War—it reminds me of a strutting boy in Battle, who when the balls were cutting thick & fast, exclaimed that if Old Crittenden would offer his Compromise again he would vote aye.

When any body tells you that I ever doubted your honesty and patriotism tell him he says false. I may have said you were a politician and that we differed widely in the origin of this war, but that being in it we fully agreed that it must be fought out. But you have more faith than I in the People—They are not infallible. People may err as much as men, as individuals and whole communities may err. Can the People of the North be right, and the South too—one of the Peoples must be wrong.

The People of the North are satisfied with killing the leaders, and by making newspaper armies—where are the 600,000 men raised this summer? I have not seen a man of them yet. I fear it is a delusion, but every one of that number will be wanted even to recover Virginia, Tennessee & Missouri.

These states must be secured & populated by the North before this war is even approximated to an end. All well & quiet here—yr. brother,

W. T. Sherman

ALS, DLC: William T. Sherman; material in angle brackets from Rachel Sherman Thorndike, ed., *The Sherman Letters: Correspondence between General Sherman and Senator Sherman from 1837 to 1891* (1894; reprint, New York, 1969), 165.

1. Major General Cassius Marcellus Clay (1810–1903), USA, had refused to fight so long as slavery was protected anywhere in the South by the Federal government.

2. The preliminary Emancipation Proclamation, issued on September 22, 1862.

3. John S. Mason (1824–97) served in McClellan's Peninsular Campaign and would become a brigadier general of volunteers in November.

TO ELLEN EWING SHERMAN

Memphis, Oct. 4, 1862

Dearest Ellen,

I think I must have neglected writing of late for my duties are multifarious though not laborious. As long as we were in tents Candles flickered so much that I did not attempt to write and got in the habit of wasting the evening but now that I am in a house I can put in my evenings. I have got into the habits of your father of rising before day, making my orders, and writing official letters before others are up—breakfast at 7, and after breakfast comes a host of people full of complaints of stolen horses, broken fences, runaway niggers &c. I generally manage to ride around the Lines of our front daily and often on the outskirts of the City to visit the Camps of five Regiments which lay on the five principal roads. I always inspect the Brigade on the outer Lines every Sunday, and those in the Fort every Wednesday, so that my time is taken up fully.

I have lost my parade horse who took sick & died, leaving me without one that suits me—My ordinary riding horse is a small sorrel mare captured at Shiloh but she becomes frantic amid the sound of drums and of arms. I have two others one a bay & other a Black but they are coarse, do not follow the rein as they Should. My fourth is a gray but not suited to my purposes—My horse that died was so used to soldiers that I could ride among guns, drums and men as freely as along a road & I miss him very much. I am well equipped in all other respects—My Division is now in good drill & Grant has written me that when we advance I am to go to Grenada but I dont want to move till events have changed in Kentucky and Virginia. Both those states must be cleaned before we attempt a further advance here—Now that the North has arisen to the Knowledge that we are in a Revolution, that years of hard fighting are necessary I feel more at ease. The People of the South are so much more Zealous in their Cause than our people, have so much more sense that they have every advantage. Their people are willing to sacrifice their wealth & lives to accomplish this purpose whereas our people seem to measure everything by the money they can make. I have more trouble to prevent smuggling and cheating in cotton, than in counteracting the designs of an Enemy. I have never apprehended an attack here, but I Know that the southern Leaders expect to take the Ohio River and get their Batteries above us so as to cut off supplies, but I hope there are now troops enough in Kentucky & Missouri to push back the Enemy as low down as Tennessee by Christmas—I see that Buell is advancing from Louisville, he should have full a hundred thousand men, out of which he could take 60,000 to fight—Detachments to guard the Roads Sick & Stragglers take one half the Army and for these no allowance has ever been made. I think Halleck will Keep McClellan in front of Lee pressing him, whilst he sends another force by James River, or from Norfolk via Petersburg on Richmond—This move if made rapidly would produce great effect. In Kentucky Buell must go straight after Bragg & fight him where & when he will—No manoeuvering or strategy is necessary.

What a sad thing was Nelson's fate. I Knew him well. He was a clever fellow but very overbearing & blustering. Davis on the contrary was a modest bashful quiet but brave man. I cannot justify the act, but do not condemn it.[1] The attempt to remove Buell was wrong.[2] I would rather risk his opinion than of his men—he Knows better what they can do, than they do themselves. I fear that Thomas troops at Nashville are too isolated, but suppose Buell will rapidly interpose his force between Nashville and Lexington near Lebanon. If he have force enough he will leave Garrisons at Louisville & Cincinati, & march his best troops to Lebanon via Bandstown & thence to either Campbellsville or Danville, from which part he should start straight for Lexington or wherever Bragg is—he must expect a terrific Battle[3]—we can do little down here till these events are determined.

I have been to church 3 times—a young lady sings magnificently. I have also done many favors for the Sisters who claim me and are doing an immense amount of praying for me—I invited the school yesterday & one of them gave me a medal & tried hard to extract the promise of repeating its prayers—I told her you had that matter in charge for me. I write to Minnie this evening.

We are all well and things public & private are moving along harmoniously. My love to all. Where is Charley? Yrs. Ever

W. T. Sherman

ALS, InND: Sherman Family Papers.

1. Major General William Nelson was shot and killed by his former subordinate, Brigadier General Jefferson C. Davis, in the lobby of the Galt House in Louisville after Davis provoked a fight.

2. WTS refers to an attempt by the War Department before the Battle of Perryville to replace Buell with George H. Thomas; Buell would be removed as commander of the Army of the Ohio on October 24.

3. Buell and Bragg clashed at Perryville, Kentucky, on October 8.

TO MARIA BOYLE EWING SHERMAN

Head Qrs. Division of Memphis,
Memphis Oct. 4, 1862

My Dear Little Minnie,

Mama has written me that you have gone to School away from home.[1] I know you will be lonely enough away from home, and whenever I have leisure

I will write to you. Although I can tell you little that will interest you except that I am thinking of you all ways and how hard it is that I am seperated from you all this time. You were left at home when we went to California, and again when I went to Louisiana, and now again in the war, but by my Dear Child I am happy that this war does not reach you. In after years you will know all about this war from Books and may remember that I was one of its actors but do not think that I feel in this war like I would if England were the Enemy opposed to us in Battle. I feel that we are fighting our own People many of whom I knew in Earlier years, and with many of whom I was once very intimate.

Sister Angela is now with you, and she must tell you all about Memphis and you can tell her in return what I write. Tell her that the Overton Hospital has now 800 sick soldiers, that I have authorized Dr. Derby to enlarge it by adding another building which stands near the River, that the Doctor makes himself so officious that it is well Sister Angela has gone away, and that I think the other sisters will do the same—I inspected the hospital very closely the two past Sundays and will tomorrow complete the Inspection. I have been to Church three times. There is a Miss McGinn or some name sounding like that who sings beautifully and I rather think I thought more of that than the Sermons. A sweet voice well cultivated is a Gift which God alone can confer, but all ladies can sing and should practice, both to give pleasure to others & health to themselves. Whether you have a good natural voice or not try & sing, just as free and unrestrained as you used to do when we rode in the woods, where you and Lizzie & Willie screamed out your songs Mama brags of little Ellys voice, but I want you to Sing—also to play the Guitar. I also want you to try to acquire a good pronunciation of French and Spanish right away—dont regard these as hard lessons, but try your best for me. I also want you to learn to dance the steps, embracing the waltz, Polka & Schottische—show this to Sister Angela and she will understand my reasons—Utility alone characterizes our American People, but all other people study to pleas others & themselves. God has given the Girls a sweet voice, and grace of motion to please others, and they do him injustice when they neglect these graces—You are now near 12 years old. In three years you will be full grown and now is the time to acquire not only knowledge but form, motion, and habits. I do not mention reading, writing, Geography, history &c. because I know all these are included in all schools and are a matter of course, and I mention the other things because they are neglected in Northern schools—also learn to ride whenever you get a chance and romp & play whenever you can, try and be companionable with all the girls and learn backgammon, checkers or any games you are permitted to learn. My Experience is that young ladies should learn all these things as they fill up time which otherwise would be spent in trifling books.

When you study study hard—learn to apply yourself so that when you are at work you think of nothing else, and when you are done with your books let your mind run free. I have seen a great many young ladies and Know that such are most interesting who are not forward, or bashful—the truth lies between. Modesty is the most beautiful feature in a young girl, but should not degenerate into bashfulness. Think yourself as good as any but never think yourself better than the poorest child of all. If this horrid war should ever end, how happy we could all be in some good home at St. Louis or Leavenworth, or in California—Write to me often, and try and write like Mama—Nobody can write better than she. My Love to Sister Angela and always think of me as your fond father

W. T. Sherman

ALS, OHi: William T. Sherman Papers.
1. EES to WTS, September 19, 1862, SFP.

TO THOMAS C. HINDMAN

Headquarters First Division,
Memphis, October 17, 1862.

Maj. Gen. T. C. Hindman,
Commanding Confederate Forces, Little Rock, Ark.
Sir:

I had the honor to write you on the 28th ultimo in partial answer to your communication of the 23d ultimo, and now inclose you General Curtis' full reply to the matters contained in yours.[1] It should not be that men of enlarged intelligence should make civil war more desperate than it is sure to be made by the acts of a class of soldiers who all their lives have been used to the largest amount of liberty to do their will, good and bad. You know full well that on your side guerrillas or partisan rangers commit acts which you would not sanction, and that small detachments of our men commit acts of individual revenge, leaving no evidence or trace whereby we can fix the responsibility. Instead of yielding to this tendency we ought gradually to improve discipline so that each general in command can trace all acts and then assume the full responsibility. If we allow the passions of our men to get full command then indeed will this war become a reproach to the names of liberty and civilization. No later than yesterday some guerrillas in the State of Arkansas, near Needham's Cutoff, fired 12-pounder howitzer shells at the steamboats Continental and J. H. Dickey, neither of which had on board a single soldier, except a reserve guard, or any Government stores. Both were loaded with goods for the use of the people of West Tennessee, who come to Memphis for the articles they deem necessary for the lives and comfort of their families, as also for the use of the inhabitants of Memphis itself. Now we present the anomalous fact that in Memphis reside the wives and children of hundreds of men who, under (as we think) a misguided belief that we are enemies and invaders, are in arms against us. For my part I am unwilling longer to protect the families and property of men who fire from ambush upon our soldiers whether on the river-banks or the roadside, and I shall gradually compel such families to go forth and seek their husbands and brothers. I will permit them to carry away their household goods and servants, thereby reducing to that extent the necessity for providing for them at our markets. You may style this cruel and barbarous, but I know my heart and have no hesitation in saying to the Southern men, women or children, I will give all the help and assistance I can; that I respect their maternal and legal rights as much as you do, but I will also respect the lives and rights of others who pursue a lawful and common right to navigate the Mississippi River, which is not yours.

We are willing to meet you anywhere and everywhere in manly fight, but to the assassin who fires from the river-bank on an unarmed boat we will not accord the title, name or consideration of an honorable soldier. You may carry word to your guerrillas or rangers that when they fire on any boat they are firing on their Southern people, for such travel on every boat, and if that does not influence them you may trust to our ingenuity to devise a remedy; for every grade of offense there is a remedy. We profess to know what civilized warfare is and has been for hundreds of years and cannot accept your construction of it. If, as you threaten in your letter, you hang an officer, a prisoner in your hands, in retaliation of some act of ours, conjured up by false statements of interested parties, remember that we have hundreds of thousands of men bitter and yearning for revenge. Let us but loose these from the restraints of discipline and no life or property would be safe in the regions where we do hold possession and power. You initiate the game, and my word for it your people will regret it long after you pass from the earth. We are willing to restrict our operations as far as may be to the acts of war controlled by educated and responsible officers, but if you or those who acknowledge your power think otherwise we must accept the issue. My command as you know does not embrace Arkansas, but I will not allow the firing on the boats from the Arkansas shore to go unnoticed.

I am, with great respect,
your obedient servant,
W. T. Sherman,
Major-General, Commanding.

Printed, OR, I, 13:742–43; II, 4:631–32.
1. See WTS to Hindman, September 28, 1862, above.

Memphis Oct. 22. 1862

Miss P. A. Fraser.

Memphis

Dear Lady,

Your petition is received. I will allow fifteen days for the parties interested to send to Holly Springs and Little Rock to ascertain if firing on unarmed boats is to form a part of the warfare against the Government of the United States. If from silence or a positive answer from their commanders, I am led to believe such feindish acts are to be tolerated or allowed it would be weakness & foolish in me to listen to appeals to feelings that are scorned by our Enemies. They must know & feel that not only will we meet them in arms, but that the people shall experience their full measure of the necessary consequences of such barbarity. The Confederate Generals claim the Partizan Rangers as a part of their Army, they cannot then disavow their acts, but all their adherents must suffer the penalty. They shall not live with us in peace. God himself has obliterated whole races from the face of the earth for sins less heinous than such as characterized the attacks on the *Catahola* and *Gladiator*. All I say is if such acts was done by the direct or implied concent of the Confederate Authorities, we are not going to chase through the cane-breaks & swamps, the individuals who did the deeds, but will visit punishment upon the adherents of that cause which employs such agents. We will insist on a positive separation. They cannot live with us. Further than that I have not yet ordered and when the time comes to settle the account we will see which is most cruel, for your partizans to fire Cannon & musket balls through steamboats with women & children on board, set them on fire with women & children sleeping in their berth and shoot down the passengers & engineers with the curses of hell on their tongues, or for us to say, the families of men engaged in such hellish deeds shall not live in peace where the flag of the United States floats.

I know you will say these poor women & children abhor such acts as much as I do and that their husbands & brothers in the Confederate service also would not be concerned in such acts. Then let the Confederate authorities say so, and not employ their tools in such deeds of blood & darkness.

We will now wait and see who are the cruel & heartless men of this War. We will see whether the firing on the *Continental* or *Gladiator* is sanctioned or disapproved and if it was done by the positive command of men Commissioned by the Confederate Governt. You will then appreciate how rapidly civil war corrupts the best feelings of the human heart.

Would to God ladies better acted their mission on earth! that instead of inflaming the minds of their husbands & brothers to lift their hands against the Government of their Birth and stain them in blood, have prayed them to forbear, to exhaust all the remedies afforded them by our glorious Constitution and thereby avoid "horrid war" the last remedy on earth.

Your appeals to me shall ever receive respectful attention but it will be vain in this case if Genl. Holmes does not promptly disavow these acts, for I will not permit the families and adherents of secessionist to live here in peace, whilst their husbands & brothers are aiming the Rifle & Gun at our families on the free Mississippi. Your friend

W. T. Sherman

Maj. Genl.

LbkS, DNA: RG 94, Records of the Adjutant General's Office, Generals' Books and Papers, William T. Sherman, Letterbook 4; *OR*, I, 17: pt. 2, 287–88.

TO PHILEMON B. EWING

Memphis, Nov. 2. 1862

Dear Phil,

I wrote you once or twice whilst Ellen was coming here as I was really alarmed at the length of her trip. This was all accounted for when she arrived having come down the Ohio River in the Same boat which brought the Battalion of Regulars.[1] She & Tommy are regularly enlisted in their Cause, and are dreadfully concerned when the Regulars fall into the tender mercies of my Police Guards or Volunteers. Charley is now safely delivered from the States prison and ought to be content. Ellen viewing things from her stand point will be better able to convey to you an idea of officers than I could. Grant has offered me any command in his Department, but I feel the importance of the main stem of the Mississipi that I prefer it to a large command at Corinth. If all the forces were concentrated we could soon open the Mississipi and then by striking right & left could make our presence so distinctive and offensive as to produce some effect. But as to our attempting to convert the South that seems more & more impossible. The depth & intensity of their hatred to the Yankees, abolitionists &c. can only be understood to me who comes in contact with their families. I am exerting all my power & influence to build up an union party here, but can only draw in the laboring classes, now numbering about 1200 & increasing. The famous too and Small planters are getting tired of having their cotton burned, and their corn consumed by Guerrillas and in some instances force their way in to market. A great deal of smuggling is going on to the Holly Spring Army, but this is mostly managed by union men & Jews instigated by a sense of gain. It is no use shutting our eyes to the fact that the entire South is united against us.

About 6000 Run away negros are here—we employ about 800 on the Fort, some 300 by the Quartermaster and about 1000 as cooks & teamsters. To all these Rations are issued, and the Law allows $10 the month but no provision thus far has been made for the payment of any except the Engineer force. I have sent none to the North. Indeed I think it preferable to keep them here, and if violence must be done, displace the disloyal masters and let the negros have the houses, & cleared land. It is useless to talk about Constitutional means for a condition of things never contemplated by any constitution. It is a Revolution where the strongest must prevail. They must subdue us, or we them. There is no middle Course. If love of money, property or other motive will make Southern people submit to Law, then they Should enjoy property, otherwise all should be taken away. Whenever our Boats are attacked, or our scouts attacked from ambush I order the contiguous property to be destroyed. There is no other way to reach the Case. These Guerrillas are fast degenerating into Robbers, and sooner or later we will be called on to protect the farmers against them. Now I dont pretend to care what they do, as they are a pest to the Country people who have hitherto pretended to Call them defenders of homes & firesides, against the Yankees. They are fast learning that Guerrillas are more to be dreaded than Yankee Armies. A large Confederate army is collecting at Holly Springs 50 miles S.E. of this but whether designed for offensive or defensive operations I cannot tell. I have here my own division about 8000 strong, and can defend the place, but Grant promises me another Brigade of 4 or 5 new Regiments.

At Ellens instance I have written to the Adjutant Genl. at Washington recommending you for appointment as a Judge Advocate with the Rank of Major. I still feel a repugnance to urging people to embrace the military service, though convinced that Sooner or later, every man at the North capable of bearing arms must take part. We must become a Military nation for this war is not a temporary thing, the issues involve the lives of millions & the property of half a continent. In two years we have made hardly any progress, indeed the issue of the war is not yet made up—personal ambition or rather notoriety has not yet given place to a real love of Country. The People of the North seem more intent on building up or pulling down personal reputations than in founding an empire. Ellen will write fully. As ever yrs.,

W. T. Sherman

ALS, Wheaton, Md.: Private Collection of Joseph H. Ewing.
1. The Thirteenth U.S. Infantry.

Hd. Qrts. Dist. of Memphis
Memphis Nov. 6. 1862.

Mrs. Valeria Hurlbut
Memphis
Dear Madam,

Your letter of Oct. —— was duly received. I did not answer it at that time as I had already instructed Col. Anthony Provt. Marshal to suspend the execution of the order expelling certain families from Memphis for fifteen days, to enable them to confer with the Confederate authorities upon the cause of that order, viz. the firing from ambush on our boats carrying passengers & merchandize by bands of guerrillas in the services of our Enemies.

In war it is impossible to hunt up the actual perpetrators of a crime. Those who are banded together in any cause are held responsible for all the acts of their associates. The Confederate Government in resisting what we claim to be the rightful prerogative & authority of our Government by armies in the field, & bands of armed men called Guerrillas or "Partizan Rangers" claims for these latter all the rights of war, which means that the Confederate Government assumes the full responsibility of the acts of these Partizan Rangers. These men have as you know fired on Steamboats navigating the Mississippi River taking the Lives & endangering the safety of peaceful citizens who travel in an accustomed way in no wise engaged in the operations of War. We regard this as inhuman and barbarous and if the Confederate authorities do not disavow them it amounts to a sanction & encouragement of the practice. We must stop this & no measures would be too severe. The absolute destruction of Memphis New Orleans & every city town and hamlet of the South would not be too severe a punishment to a people for attempting to interfere with the navigation of the Mississippi.

I have commenced mildly, by requiring the families of men engaged in this barbarous practice to leave and go to their own people, certainly there Can be no hardship for the wife and Children going to their own husbands and families. They ought to be glad of the opportunity & the measure instead of being severe is very mild.

How would they like it if we were to fire through the houses of their wives and families as they do through the boats carrying our wives and families. If any person will look at this question who feels for our people, he or she will perceive that the measure of retaliation is mild & I do not promise by any means that in future cases I will be so easy.

Misplaced kindness to these Guerrillas, their families and adherents is cruelty to our people. Were you to travel on a boat & have the bullets whistle &

hear the demon yells of these Confederate "Partizans" you would not feel so kindly disposed to those who approve the act.

I have given them time to disavow the attack on the Gladiator; they have not done it. They therefore approve, and I say not only shall the families go away, but all the Confederate allies & adherents shall feel the power of an indignant Government. I am &

W. T. Sherman
Maj. Genl.

LbkS, DNA: RG 94, Records of the Adjutant General's Office, Generals' Books and Papers, William T. Sherman, Letterbook 7; *OR*, I, 17: pt. 2, 860.

TO ULYSSES S. GRANT

Headqrs. Dist. of Memphis,
Memphis Nov. 8. 1862.

Maj. Genl. U. S. Grant
Comd'g. Dept. of W. Tenn. Lagrange
Dear General:

Yours of November 6th from Lagrange,[1] was brought to me by Captain Newell, 3rd Michigan Cavalry, last night, he having ridden by circuitous routes and Reached me without serious opposition yet I fear his return may be hazardous, and I have ordered Col. Grierson, 6th Ills. Cavalry,[2] to escort him back with about 300 select Cavalry and in going and returning to do certain things that will be of advantage to the service. He will show you his instructions. I have not yet received the instructions via Columbus referred to in yours of November 6th but are prepared on short notice to do anything you may require. As yet but one Regiment has reported to me—the 32nd Wisconsin, Col. Howe—a strong regiment of good material, well armed and equipped. By the reduction of transportation under recent orders, I will have enough wagons for double my force and since the incursions of Morgan & Kirby Smith into Kentucky, & Stuart's Raid into Penn.[3] in which they took horses of private owners, we should no longer hesitate to replenish our stock in the country we operate in, giving owners simple receipts to be settled for at the conclusion of hostilities, according to the circumstances of each case.

I deem it good policy now to encourage the non-combatant population to trade with Memphis their cotton and corn for such articles of groceries and clothing as they need for their families and servants. Many of them are justly indignant at their own armies and partizans for burning their cotton by the sales of which alone they can realize the means of purchase of the articles they absolutely need to maintain their suffering families, and I would like some expression of opinion from you on this policy. Of course a part of these supplies will fall into improper hands, but the time must come when the inhabitants must choose their rulers, and even I now do not fear their choice, if protected from their Confederate Armies & Bandits. Some of them of course make loud complaints against our troops for burning rails and stealing potatoes &c., but I tell them plainly these are the inevitable accompaniments of armies, for which those who provoked war & appealed to it, are responsible & not we.

I am satisfied a change of opinion is rapidly growing here which I endeavor to foster & encourage. On Monday next a Union Club will come out in public, will decorate their houses with our flag and have a public procession, speeches &c.; I will attend of course and aid them with every means to produce effect. The advance of your army to Lagrange will have an admirable effect. All my information goes to the belief that the Rebel force at Holly Springs is reduced by detachments to the South, so that it no longer threatens W. Tenn. Some farmers just in, report Holly Springs evacuated, but I am not satisfied on that point. I have out two good men who ought to be back in a day or two, whose report I will get through to you by some safe means. I will keep my force well in hand but will make a demonstration towards Cold Water tomorrow &c., to gain information and withdraw attention from you. I do not believe that there is in Arkansas, a force to justify the armies of Schofield,[4] Steele & Hovey (at Helena) remaining quiet and would advise the latter, to threaten Grenada & the Yazoo, by all means.

I will rapidly organize Brigades & equip all Regiments coming to me, and be prepared to act with promptness the moment I learn the part you design me to play. Cols. McDowell 6th Iowa, Stuart 55th Ills. & Buckland 72nd Ohio, are fully competent to take Brigades and I will so dispose of them, unless you send me Brigadiers duly Commissioned. Cols. Hillyer[5] & Lagow[6] of your staff recently here, will tell you fully of all figures, numbers and facts that I deem imprudent to trust by this route.

I have already ordered one officer of every Ohio Regiment to proceed with dispatch to Columbus, Ohio, to bring back the drafted men for the Ohio Regiments—7 in number.

Health of troops good and everything as well as I could wish.

I will write to Genl. Hovey at Helena, telling him of your movements & asking him to gather all information he can of the Country towards Grenada. Deserters come in constantly, one is just now in from Cold Water, where he was a picket.

He did not know you were at Lagrange, and said he deserted because he did not wish to go further south & heard that Price was to go to Jackson Miss., but he had not been to Holly Springs for 5 Days. I am &c.

W. T. Sherman

Maj. Genl.

I send you our morning papers, one of Mobile, Nov. 3, & Grenada Nov. 5.

Copy, DLC: William T. Sherman Papers; *OR*, I, 17: pt. 2, 860–62.

1. USG to WTS, November 6, 1862, *PUSG*, 6:262–63. Grant told WTS that he was sending sixteen regiments of infantry and several of artillery and cavalry, enough to fill WTS's ranks to two full divisions. He asked that each Ohio regiment send one officer to superintendent recruitment of volunteers in the state.

2. Benjamin H. Grierson (1826–1911) would become a brigadier general of volunteers on June 3, 1863.

3. Major General James Ewell Brown "Jeb" Stuart (1833–64), CSA, led a cavalry raid on Chambersburg, Pennsylvania, from October 9 to 12.

4. Major General John M. Schofield (1831–1906), USA, headed the District of Southwest Missouri.

5. William S. Hillyer (1831–74) had been Grant's aide-de-camp since September 1861.

6. Colonel Clark B. Lagow (1828–67), USA, was one of Grant's staff officers, having been a member of Grant's original regiment, the Twenty-first Illinois.

TO JOHN T. SWAYNE[1]

Head Qrs. District of Memphis,
Memphis Novr. 12. 1862. 11 at night.

Hon. Judge Swayne
Memphis.
Sir,

You Expressed yourself hurt this morning at the Severe terms in which I indulged in Commenting on the Charge you made the Grand Jury. It is now late at night and I am worn out with writing purely official matter and now hastily & candidly wish to convey to you my Serious thoughts.

I concede to you the highest order of Personal character, talents and Education and will not pretend to Argue with you constitutional or Legal Questions. I have Repeatedly asserted and now repeat my belief that you are Honest in your opinions and practice. But must say that in my Judgment you are unintentionally drifting your Country and People to Ruin, misery and death. In the first place I Regret that in Preparing your opinion or charge to the Jury that the main part was Omitted and only that part published to the world which treats of the Sworn duty of the Grand Jury to find Bills under the Enumerated Laws of Tennessee touching Slaves, utterly ignoring the Laws of Congress and the State of war.

Thus take the Statutes you Quote, Nos. 26, 58-9-60-61-63-64, and 82, &c. How can any one of them be executed here without an absolute Relinquishment of all that has been done in this War. Will the United States stultify herself by allowing a criminal court of a country to nullify the acts of the Congress and of Armies raised at the Expense of the blood & Treasure of the Nation? What is the Law of Congress on this Point? "Act No. 160, An act to Suppress insurrection, to Punish Treason & Rebellion, to seize and confiscate the Property of Rebels and for Other Purposes, Sec. 9, and be it further enacted that all Slaves of Persons who Shall after Proclamation giving Sixty days notice be engaged in rebellion against the Government of the United States, or who Shall in any way give aid or comfort thereto, escaping from Such Persons and taking refuge within the Lines of the Army, and all Slaves captured from Such persons, or deserted by them coming under the control of the Government of the United States, and all Slaves of Such Persons found or being in any place occupied by Rebel forces and afterwards occupied by the forces of the United States, Shall be deemed Captives of war, and Shall be forever free of their Servitude, and not again held as Slaves. Sec. 10 x x and no person engaged in the Military or Naval Service of the United States Shall under any Pretence whatever assume to decide on the validity of the claim of any person to the Service or Labor of any other person or surrender up any Such Person to the claimant on pain of being dismissed from the Service."

"Approved July 17, 1862."

Such is the Law of the Congress of the United States which I caused to be published many Successive days in all the newspapers of Memphis as Soon as received, and yet you made no mention of them in your charge to the Jury. Certainly you must admit a State of War, that Memphis was a place held by the Confederate troops in June last, and now in our Military possession, and that during the Pendency of war that I am held by our Government as responsible for all that Occurs in this District, and as much accountable for acts done by persons Subordinate to my Authority as though done by myself. Therefore in charging the Jury you could not but have foreseen it would raise a direct conflict. I admit that in our conversation you contended that your high Sense of the Character of a Judge demanded you should announce the Law, but that in doing So you qualified it by the expression "If in Regard to the Slavery Laws of the State or any of the recited or other Statutory or common Law offences the Jury Should find themselves Physically prevented by the circumstances about them, in other words by the Insufficiency of the Power of the Country from the performance of their high duties as defined by the Law, in that case their failure to perform these duties will be no deriliction on their Part."

Now I hold and so will every reader of your charge infer that the Jury is bound to hear and on their oath find Bills against every Person who has received harbored or Employed a fugitive Slave. No Physical Power will Hinder them from finding Such Bills any more than it did you in making your Charge. On the contrary I would look for Discreet action and a full and comprehensive Laying Down of the Law, to the learned and inteligent Judge rather than the Jury who are bound to receive the Law as he gives it to them to apply to the Cases that may come to their hearing. I say the Grand Jury are bound to indict every man, woman or child in the county of Shelby who has been governed by the laws of the Congress of the United States instead of those of the State of Tennessee late in open Rebellion to the mild and generous Sovereign of the Whole Country. Thus I contend that when your community is already bound down by the afflictions of Stern war, you have insisted from what I deem a too delicate Sense of your official obligation in bringing a direct conflict between The State & national authority. I had in my former conversations with you expressed an earnest desire that while armed Thousands of Strong men were arrayed against each other, ready at any moment to Engage in deadly Struggle that the Common Machinery of Government might be Preserved to Protect the Old, and young feeble & helpless, against the murderous Robbers, thieves and villains that are Sure to take advantage of the complications of war to do their hellish work. I wanted of all things the Criminal court of Shelby County to meet and Punish crime, that class of crime Known all the world over as *Mala in Se*,[2] common to the codes of all civilized People, and Reserve this question of Slavery, this dire Conflict between national and State Authority, to be fought out by the Armies now arrayed for that Purpose.

Personally I have no hostility to Slavery or any of your local laws. I would they had never been disturbed, that Federal and State Authority Had been mutually respected by the Parties to this Strife, but this Event almost convinces me that they are utterly irreconcilable when *Judge Swayne* with the din of Arms in his ears, with bayonets glistening at each Street Corner with Messengers coming & going with the cruel news of the mangling of hundreds & thousands of our Common citizens in deadly strife charging a Grand Jury under the old law of Tennessee as though there was no War & utterly ignoring the Laws made by the Congress of the United States. I wanted and still want you to hold your Court and punish the many malefactors that infect the Country, but you must respect the Laws of our Common Government. I do not want to dictate to you. I appeal to your reason. You cannot administer the laws you quote, but there is plenty you can do, and to make the matter emphatic I have instructed my Provost Marshal & Officers that if the criminal Court of Shelby or any other county attempt by writ or otherwise to enforce those State Laws in {contention} with the plain Laws of the United States, they must treat the Sheriff or Constable as in, "Contempt."

I admit there is a direct issue between the United States & the State of Tennessee in this matter; but a county criminal Court is not the place to adjudicate it. There is a tribunal provided by our fundamental law, our Constitution, viz. the *Supreme Court of the United States*, fit & proper to pass on such momentous issues. Until that tribunal makes its decision, I Shall obey the plain Law of Congress and the order of the *President* of the United States under it, and my army Shall be used to *enforce* it.

I wish I had Seen your charge before it was delivered, as I believe you would have modified it, at all events that you would not have given Such Prominence to the impracticable Statutes you quote. I wish to Repeat that I appreciate the Sense of Duty that actuated you to assert what you believed to be the *only* Law, and I hope you will award to me Similar Zeal when you allow for the Sudden & Stern conclusions to which Military minds Sometimes attain by a rapid intuition or Judgment. I also repeat that I am Still anxious you Should continue your court and Constitutionally and Judiciously Enforce the Law against the many Mischievous Persons that infest your Community. For God's Sake dont let this accursed question of Slavery blind your mind to the thousand other duties and interests that concern you and the People among whom you live.

As you can perceive I throw off these Ideas leaving you to fill up the logical Picture. In my Seeming leaning towards men of your Character, I have risked my reputation and ability for good. Do not force me to conclude the Conflict to be "irreconcilable," as you Surely will, if you or your Grand Jury, or the officers of your court insist on Enforcing the Statutes of Tennessee touching Negroes, at this terrible crisis of our History.[3] With much Respect yr. obt. Servant,

W. T. Sherman

Maj. Genl.

LbkS, DNA: RG 94, Records of the Adjutant General's Office, Generals' Books and Papers, William T. Sherman, Letterbook 7; *OR*, I, 17: pt. 2, 863–65.

1. Lawyer John T. Swayne (ca. 1820–73), a nephew of Ohioan and Supreme Court justice Noah Swayne, presided over Memphis's criminal court during the war.

2. Acts that are universally viewed as morally wrong, regardless of their status under law, such as murder or theft.

3. Swayne responded to this letter on November 14, claiming that it was first and foremost his sworn duty to uphold valid state laws and expressing his belief that by so doing his charges had explicitly avoided conflict with Sherman and the military occupation. Swayne felt that Federal laws were hurtful and urged the greater legitimacy of state laws and assumed that WTS joined with him in feeling that a man's first political loyalties should be to his state. He added that he thought WTS was wrong to worry about these issues although he conceded he could see from where these fears sprang. DLC: WTS.

TO HENRY W. HALLECK

Headquarters District of Memphis,
Memphis, November 17, 1862.

Major-General Halleck, Commander-in-Chief:

General:

Of course I know that officially and privately you have more than your share of work. Though silent I have not been idle this summer. I think Memphis is now the best and most complete base of operations on the Mississippi. The fort is admirable; twenty-eight heavy guns in position with good magazines, shot, shell, and canister piled alongside and men instructed for the guns. My old infantry division now forms a good basis for the new levies, of which fourteen infantry regiments are already come and more *en route*. I shall form them into two divisions of twenty-four infantry regiments, with a reserve of five to be left here to occupy Fort Pickering. My field artillery, nine good batteries, are in good drill, horses in good order, and all well provided with ammunition. I have but one cavalry regiment, ten companies of the Sixth Illinois, and two of Thielemann's; but am advised that three more cavalry regiments will come to me. I am ready to move inland, down the river, or anywhere. At Memphis, troops can be raised, organized, fed, and equipped better than at any place I have ever seen. There is abundance of corn throughout the country, but all else has to come from above.

We have roused, also, the Union element, and our enemies, having burned cotton, taken corn, fodder, and supplies from the country people, have shaken their faith in the secession authorities; so that we have really a substantial beginning of the conversion of the people to our cause.

The new troops come full of the idea of a more vigorous prosecution of the war, meaning destruction and plunder.

I take brick from kilns, lumber from piles, wood, corn, &c., giving brigade quartermaster's receipts, to be settled at the termination of hostilities on proof of loyalty, claims not transferable; but I do not permit any one below the rank of brigadier to presume to take and appropriate private property.

The quartermaster's department here has possession of over 600 houses, some of which are used for public purposes and the balance are rented out, bringing over $12,000 a month income. I mention these facts to interest you in your future plans in this quarter of the world. I expect very soon to move inland to report to General Grant. The enemy is now behind the Tallahatchie, and West Tennessee is free of the enemy, save very small bands of guerrillas, whom the people will soon dispose of rather than feed and submit to. I have learned that the Confederate authorities have adopted a plan of fortification for the mouth of Yazoo, which if completed will embarrass us much. The country between Yazoo and Mississippi is of black vegetable mold, full of streams and bayous, and exceedingly impracticable in wet and wintry weather. With the Yazoo open to us, our land forces could disembark on its east bank on high, fine ground, the same ridge which forms the bluff of Walnut Hills at Vicksburg. If a fort is built on the bluff near mouth of Yazoo (Haines') it would have to be reduced before we could proceed against Jackson and Vicksburg, and would give time for concentration. One or two good iron-clads in Yazoo would prevent the construction of such a fort. I have notified Admiral Porter[1] of this and he may act on such information.

I know your mind and attention are taken up with the East, but feel assured you will so order that a perfect concert of action will result from the ample force now on the Mississippi and its valley under Admiral Porter, Generals Grant and Curtis.

> With great respect,
> your obedient servant,
> W. T. Sherman,
> Major-General, Commanding District.

P.S.—The old navy-yard here was used by the Confederate authorities for founding cannon, constructing gun-carriages, transportation wagons, and all sorts of military stores. Though donated by Congress to the city of Memphis, I think it is fairly liable to confiscation, but I have only taken certain parts of it for necessary workshops, taking accurate inventories of tools and materials. I am making a kind of pontoon train for General Hovey at Helena and another for myself. Indeed, these shops are admirably adapted to Government purposes.

Printed, *OR*, I, 17: pt. 2, 351–52.

1. David Dixon Porter (1813–91), USN, was acting rear admiral of the Mississippi Squadron.

TO F. G. PRATT

> Headquarters District of Memphis,
> Memphis, November 17, 1862.

F. G. Pratt, Esq.,
Memphis, Tenn.:
Dear Sir:

Yours of November 14 has been before me some days. I have thought of the subject-matter, and appreciate what you say, but for the present think best not to tamper with the subject. Money is a thing that cannot be disposed of by an order. Were I to declare that Tennessee money should not be quoted higher than greenbacks, my order would do no good, for any person having cotton to sell has a right to barter it for anything he pleases; thus he might trade it for Tennessee money at 50 cents per pound, and for greenbacks at 52 cents, thereby making the discount. Money will seek its value, and no king or president can fix value by a decree or order. It has been tried a thousand times, always without success; but let money alone and it finds its true value.

The reason why Tennessee money has been above greenbacks was, and is, because that kind of money was in demand for cotton. Now, is it our interest to encourage the bringing in of cotton? If so, must we not let the owner barter it for what he pleases? When we answer these questions in the affirmative, we must let the owner of the cotton sell it as he pleases. Those who own cotton do not insult our Government by preferring Tennessee money to greenbacks. Tennessee money suits their individual purposes better than greenbacks, and it pleases me, as I see they want their money for local home use, and not to send abroad for munitions of war.

Let these things regulate themselves. War, and war alone, can inspire our enemy with respect, and they will have their belly full of that very soon. I rather think they will in time cry, "Hold, enough!" Till then, let Union men feel confident in their real strength, and determination of our Government, and despise the street talk of Jews and secessionists.

Yours,

W. T. Sherman,

Major-General, Commanding.

Printed, *OR*, I, 17: pt. 2, 868.

TO JOSEPH TAGG

Headquarters District of Memphis,

Memphis, November 17, 1862.

Joseph Tagg, Esq.,

President Washington Union Club:

Dear Sir:

The resolutions of November 16 are before me. I heard them read at the time, and the debate on them, but then did not make known what was in progress, nor can I now tell all, but the Union men may rest assured that no insult shall be made to our Government by Judge Swayne or anybody else, and stand unrebuked. Secessionists, when in power, may be tyrants and villains, but we must be men. We must heed the lessons of history and counsels of wise men, who have gone before us. They in rebellion use terror and force; we can afford to do right. They keep up clamors and rumors, boasts and arrogance; we, knowing ourselves to be right, can pursue "the even tenor of our way," calm and conscious of ultimate success.

Now, finding ourselves (the military) in Memphis firmly established, I naturally wanted to see order established among the people of your town. Among all nations, murder, arson, burglary, robbery, and personal violence are deemed crimes against human nature, and there is always a tribunal speedily appointed to try all such cases. These tribunals have no political power, and therefore in war remain unimpaired, and pursue their business, although all the rest of government might be in wreck and confusion. We all know that in Memphis you have a good deal of crime, too much, and some-body must punish it. The military is here to vindicate the right and dignity of the General Government, not to take care of the people. We have enough to do if we mind our own business, so that somebody else must punish murder, &c., among citizens. Finding a criminal court here, I conferred with Judge Swayne, and explained to him that whilst we were determined the flag of our country and the just authority of the Government should be respected all over the world, we wanted the people of Memphis protected against the criminals in their midst, and that he might hold his court.

He has organized it, and appointed his grand jury, and has let off some secession and State's rights nonsense. When a man makes big professions and falls far short in practice, what is the judgment of men? So when a judge makes a magnificent manifesto, and then tries a few pickpockets and loafers, what may we infer? Instead of being a subject of dread and fear, he becomes an object of ridicule. A criminal court is rather a small affair to make trouble among honest men, and this criminal court, what can it do? It may indict criminals that every Union man would like to see punished, but can they hurt any honest man? No; they must punish crime, but dare not attempt to execute any law of Tennessee in opposition to the laws of Congress. Let them attempt to indict a Union man for his opinion, or attempt to punish others for hiring a runaway slave, or let the court attempt the exercise of any foolish or despotic power, and Judge Swayne and that grand jury would learn a lesson in politics that would last them to their dying day. If this court minds its own business, and punishes crime, I will help them; but if they attempt to convert a petty criminal court into a political machine, I will promptly interfere.

Judge Swayne and the grand jury know my opinions, and I think the Union Club will have no reason to fear evil consequences. The Union people are not yet able to compose the necessary courts and machinery of Government. Who are your judges? Who are your lawyers? These you must have, before you can make county courts, district and supreme courts, and it behooves Union men to think of these things, for it is far more easy to destroy than build up a government, and you must be prepared, as the military goes on, to build up your own government. You are not now prepared, but I have no doubt that, by patience, prudence, and forbearance, you will in time be enabled to over-come the secesh, not only in arms, but law. Reason, justice, and all the at-tributes of a good and great Government are on your side of the question.

I am, with respect,
W. T. Sherman,
Major-General.

Printed, *OR*, I, 17: pt. 2, 869–70.

TO JOHN C. PEMBERTON[1]

Head Qrs. District of Memphis.
Memphis, Novr. 18, 1862.

Lieut. Gen. J. C. Pemberton
Comdg. Confederate Forces, Jackson Miss.
Sir,

Your letter of Novr. 12 dated Jackson Miss. is before me. General Grant commands the Department which embraces Memphis and I will send him your letter that he may answer it according to the interests and honor of the Government of the United States.[2]

You recite the more aggravated parts of the story of Mrs. White, concerning the Killing her husband by a party of the 6th Illinois cavalry: but you do not recite the attending circumstances. In the early part of September last the public highway hence to Hernando was infested by a parcel of men who burned the cotton of the People and depredated on their property. A party of the 6th Illinois Cavalry was sent to capture them, but on approach they fled, and only ten prisoners were taken. These were despatched back towards Memphis in charge of a Lieutenant & ten men. As this party was on the Road near Whites, they were fired on from Ambush, the Lieutenant and the Con-federate Soldier at his side were Killed, one or more wounded & the party scattered. As soon as the intelligence reached the Camp of the 6th Illinois Cavalry in Memphis, Capt. Boicourt started to the rescue with a small detach-ment of his men. On the way out they met the dead body of the Lieutenant being brought in punctured by six balls, from which the story was started of barbarous treatment viz. his being shot whilst lying on the ground: they also heard enough to connect the People of the neighborhood with this firing from ambush, and mutilating their dead Lieutenant. The taking of White, the accusation of his being concerned—his resistance, his attempt to escape are all matters asserted and denied, and no one man deplores than I do, that you have torn to pieces the fabric of our Government so that such acts should ever occur, or if they did that they should be promptly punished. Whites house is almost on the Line between Mississipi and Tennessee, but this affair occurred on the Mississipi side of the Line. If the state of Mississipi were in a Condition and Should make due inquiry, and demand the parties for a fair trial there would be some appearance of Law & Justice.

But what shadow of Right you have to inquire into the matter I dont see. White was not a Confederate Soldier, not even a Guerilla and some contend he was a good Union Man. I assert that his Killing was unfortunate, but was the legitimate & logical sequence of the mode of warfare chosen by the Confederate Government by means of Guerillas or Partizan Rangers. Capt. Boicourt has answered for his conduct to the Govt. of the United States, and it may be will to the Civil authorities of Mississipi when Peace is restored to her, but not to the Confederate Government or its officers.

You now hold for retaliation four U.S. soldiers, whose names you say were ascertained by lot. We hold here thirty odd wounded Confederate soldiers left by your companions on the Field at Corinth. They receive Kind treatment at the hands of our surgeons. I expect a Boat load of other Prisoners in a day or so from above en route for Vicksburg to be exchanged according to the solemn cartel made between the two Contracting parties. Under the terms of that Cartel we shall expect at Vicksburg the four men you have named and should they not be at Vicksburg the officer in charge of your Prisoners will have his orders.[3]

Our Armies now occupy many southern states. Even North Mississipi is in our possession. Your Guerillas & Partizan Rangers have done deeds that I know you do not sanction. Do not make this War more vindictive and bloody than it has been and will be in spite of the most moderate counsels. If you think a moment you will admit that Retaliation is not the remedy for such acts as the Killing of White, but the same end will be attained by regulating your Guerillas. This I Know you are doing, and for it you have the thanks of your Southern Rights People who were plundered & abused by them.

General Grant commands this Dept. and you had better await his answer before proceeding to Extremities. All I can now do is to see that the terms for the Exchange of prisoners of War be faithfully executed, by your Exchanging the four men you have in custody for four we will send to Vicksburg. I am with respect yr. obt. Servant

W. T. Sherman
Maj. Genl. Comdg.
District

ALS, CsmH; *OR*, I, 17: pt. 2, 872–73.

1. Lieutenant General John C. Pemberton (1814–81), CSA, in command of the Department of Mississippi, Tennessee, and East Louisiana.

2. Pemberton had written to complain about the brutal killing of a civilian, William H.

White of DeSoto County, Mississippi, by a company of the Sixth Illinois Cavalry, who thought he was responsible for the murder of a Lieutenant Cunningham and the mutilation of his corpse. Pemberton threatened to kill four Union prisoners in retaliation if Boicourt and the others responsible were not punished. *OR*, I, 17: pt. 2, 871–72. WTS sent Pemberton's letter and his response to Rawlins on November 19, 1862, with a cover letter; see following letter. Grant did not respond to Pemberton until December 15, when he received Pemberton's third threat to harm Union prisoners. Grant objected to Pemberton's tone and concluded: "On my part I shall carry on this war humanely and do what I conceive to be my duty regardless of threats and most certainly without making any." *PUSG*, 7:39–40; quote on p. 40.

3. On November 23, WTS instructed the officer who would handle the prisoner exchange to "make specific demand" for the four men named by Pemberton on his arrival in Vicksburg. If these men were not among the Union prisoners, he ordered the officer to draw the names of four Confederate prisoners and hold them for further action. *OR*, I, 17: pt. 2, 873.

TO JOHN A. RAWLINS

Headquarters District of Memphis,
Memphis, November 19, 1862.

Maj. John A. Rawlins,
Assistant Adjutant-General, La Grange.
Sir:

Inclosed is a communication of Lieut. Gen. J. C. Pemberton, Confederate Army, dated Jackson, Miss., November 12, 1862, received by me at the hands of a flag of truce night before last. I replied yesterday and send you herewith a copy. I ought not to have answered, but the time to be consumed in referring it to you would have endangered the safety of the four men enumerated by General Pemberton. It seems he acts on orders from the Government at Richmond, and I thought proper to show him how certain retaliation by them would entail on their own prisoners certain destruction. To enable you to answer fully and conclusively I subjoin a short history of the case.

On the 4th of September last I sent Colonel Grierson with a detachment of the Sixth Illinois Cavalry toward Hernando to break up a rendezvous of guerillas, after accomplishing which his orders were to proceed over to the Pigeon Roost Road and break up certain other parties there forming near Coldwater. He accomplished the first-named purpose, taking ten prisoners, whom he dispatched back toward Memphis with an escort of fifteen of his men commanded by Lieut. Nathaniel B. Cunningham. This party returned along the main road, and when near White's, about three-fourths of a mile south of the State line and distant from Memphis about thirteen miles, the party was fired on from ambush and Lieutenant Cunningham and a Confederate prisoner were killed. The party was scattered, and as soon as intelligence reached the camp of the Sixth Illinois Cavalry Captain Boicourt took a small party of twenty-five men and hastened to the spot. Before reaching White's they met a wagon coming into Memphis with the body of Lieutenant Cunningham, and learned the names of five men of the country who were engaged in the attack on this party.

I subsequently sent Major Stacy, of the Sixth Illinois Cavalry, with 100 men to punish the actors. They met Captain Boicourt near White's and all the mention he made of the killing of White is that "one man was killed while running from the advance guard." Subsequently the mother and wife of Mr. White came to see me, and reported that hearing the firing near their house they went to the road and assisted in burying the dead Confederate, and saw the body of Lieutenant Cunningham taken up by a passing wagon and carried toward Memphis; that soon after Captain Boicourt and party of cavalry came to the house, arrested Mr. White—represented as twenty-three years old, delicate in health and never a guerrilla, but on the contrary peacefully disposed and of Union sentiments; but Captain Boicourt represented that he was concerned in the killing of Cunningham, mutilating his person and stripping it of money and clothing, the sight of which exasperated the men. When White was taken in custody he was taken out through the yard and when near the gate resisted, and finally attempted to escape, when he was killed, partly with blows and shots. The house of White was burned down.

Of course I cannot approve the killing of any citizen on mere suspicion, but the firing from ambush near White's house and the fact that Lieutenant Cunningham was mutilated and stripped of money and clothing were circumstances calculated to inflame the minds of soldiers. The neighborhood, too, was and is infamous, so that I charge the whole on the system of guerrilla warfare adopted, approved and encouraged by the Confederate authorities. Whatever claims the family and friends of White may have on the magnanimity of our Government I would recognize, but would make no concessions to the authorities of that Government which has turned loose bands of men without uniforms—without any marks of a soldier's calling—to do their will. The killing of White was the natural consequence of the shooting of Lieutenant Cunningham, of which General Pemberton makes no mention. White was a citizen, not a Confederate soldier or a partisan. On what rule General Pemberton or his associates propose to retaliate on the persons of four of our soldiers I do not understand. Of course it is not for me to say what we should do should these four men suffer death; but we should demand their exchange promptly under the cartel, and if not acceded to and they carry out their threats, we should make them feel our power and vengeance. Shall I not withhold all their prisoners for exchange until this threat is withdrawn? Strange that these partisans hang, kill and shoot on any and all occasions and yet we are threatened with retaliation for such a case as White's. I await your instructions.

Yours,
W. T. Sherman,
Major-General,
Commanding.

Printed, *OR*, II, 4:729–30.

TO JOHN SHERMAN

Memphis Novr. 24, 1862.

Dear Brother

I am just back from Columbus Ky. where I went to meet Genl. Grant. I start on Wednesday with all the troops that can be spared from Memphis to cooperate with Grant against the enemy now in force behind the Tallahatchee about 60 miles SE of Memphis. Grant may have about 35,000 & I will take about 17,000. Our old Regts. are very small & I am sorry to hear that no Recruits are ready to fill them up. So much clamor was raised about the draft that I really was led to believe there was something in it, but now suppose it was one of those delusions of which the papers are so full. Your letter of the 16th is before me.[1] I could write a good deal on the points that you make, but hardly have time to do them justice. The People have so long been accustomed to think they could accomplish anything by a vote, that they still think so—but now a vote is nothing more than a change, and will produce no effect. The war might have been staved off a few years, or the issue might have been made up more clearly or the first enthusiasm of the Country might have been better taken advantage of, but these are now all past, and fault finding will do no good—We are involved in a war that will try the sincerity of all our professions of endurance courage & patriotism. Leaders will of course be killed off by the scores, thousands will perish by the bullet or sickness, but war must go on—It cant be stopped. The North must rule, or submit to depredation & insult forever more. The war must now be fought out. The President Congress no Earthly Power can now stop it without absolute submission.

As to Finances. The U.S. have a perfect right to drive in the Bank issues of all state Banks and substitute Treasury notes therefor. Of course it will raise a clamor, but what of that. The U.S. has long enough yielded to clamor & local pressure. This is a chief cause of this war. If it is Right it should be done. There are Two thousand millions of Dollars of such notes, & Uncle Sam can well claim half that amount of notes with which to pay soldiers & contractors from whom they go into circulation. Then the Govt. can estimate the maximum amount of taxation the Country can stand, from that amount deduct the current annual expense of Govt. in time of Peace, & the excess forms an interest paying fund from which by simple mathematics you can arrive at the maximum amount of interest paying Bonds can be issued. I should suppose Uncle Sam could use 2000 millions of such Bonds, thus with circulating notes & Bonds the U.S. can so plan for three thousand millions of Dollars, all of which is being expended in the Country. Inasmuch as all the public Debt does not amount to one third this sum I dont see yet why anyone should be alarmed. The Country has said again & again the last man & last dollar of the Country would be given to vindicate the honor & existence of the Genl. Government, and they must be prepared to make good this boast. Again there is another source of Revenue. Being at war we have a right to Seize the property of Rebels. Here at Memphis I have taken 600 houses, whose rents amount to near 150,000 a year which goes to the Govt.—we can & do take corn, mules, horses, wagons and all the materials of transportation & subsistence. The whole army is commanded to do this, and it will act doubly, assist us, and deprive the enemy of revenues. Of course I foresaw all these complications at the outset and was amazed at the apathy of the Country after the South had begun the war by the seizure of arsenals, Forts mints & public property & still more at the contemptible call for 75,000 volunteers when a million was the least that any man who had ever been South would have dreamed of[.] These half way measures at the Start only add labor in the End.

I dont pretend to advise in anything. The only safety in the Country is now in Union, and we must be governed by the President—we have no right to dispute his acts or instructions and must leave him to manage the war in his own way. I was in hopes the newspapers would have been curbed ere this, but they go on making public every movement & act of the army and the only antidote now is that nobody believes them. McClernand is announced as forming a grand army to Sweep the Mississipi when the truth is he is in Springfield Illinois trying to be elected to the U.S. Senate.[2] I believe at this moment we have more men under pay at home than in the Field, and Suppose there is no help for it. If you want to make a Good law make a simple one—No work no Pay No Pay unless on duty at the place where the army is. That would save tens of millions per annum.

I leave here the day after tomorrow for Tchullahoma, to communicate with Grant at Holly Springs. Our joint forces should march near 50,000 men, but sickness and other causes will keep us down to about 40,000. Love to all— Ellen will leave for home at once. yrs. affectionately

W. T. Sherman

ALS, DLC: William T. Sherman.

1. JS to WTS, November 16, 1862, DLC: WTS. JS raised two political concerns: first, what

was the cause and what would be the result of the recent elections, and second, what should be done about depreciated paper money. JS thought that Union parties had lost but Lincoln and his followers had abandoned the Republicans because they did not have enough political organization and people were not pleased with the conduct and results of the war. "No doubt the wanton & unnecessary use of the power to arrest without trial and the ill timed proclamation contributed to the general result." To take care of the money problem, JS suggested that the government would have to use taxes to hinder banks and limit issue of paper money to the government.

2. McClernand had traveled to Washington, D.C., in September to secure Lincoln's permission to raise a force of volunteers from the Midwest with the aim of leading them against Vicksburg—an effort to circumvent Grant's authority.

TO JOHN SHERMAN

College Hill, Miss., Near Oxford,
Dec. 6, 1862

Dear Brother,

I left Memphis Wednesday Nov. 26, with 26 Regts. of Infantry, 10 field batteries & 1 Cavalry Regt. in all about 18,000 men, to cooperate with Grant in attacking the enemy then lying on the South Bank of the Tallahatchee, 18 miles south of Holly Springs and about 70 from Memphis. Their strength estimated from 40 to 50,000 men, under Pemberton, Price, Van Dorn & others. Grant allowed me 4 days to reach Chullahoma. In 3 days I was near Tallaloosa where I communicated with him & next day reached Chullahoma, he advancing to Waterford. Coincident with our movement, an expedition was planned to move from Helena under Genl. Hovey to attack or threaten Grenada about 60 miles to the Rear of the position of the enemy. On approaching the Tallahatchee we found it abandonned although all its fords, ferries and crossing places had been well fortified & obstructed. Grant moved on the Main Road south from Holly Springs and I on his Right about 10 miles, reaching the River at an old town called Wyatt. I had brought boats with me from Memphis with which we soon crossed an infantry & cavalry Regiment, swimming the horses and found two long lines of Entrenchments about 2 miles back from the River where there is a kind of neck. These were however completely abandonned, sending the Cavalry ahead to cooperate with Grant then passing the Rear of the retreating forces we deliberately set to work, built a good bridge, and the day before yesterday I rode forward to Oxford where I found Grant & received his further orders to cross and occupy College Hill, 4 miles to his Right. I have one division Dunns here and two on Hurricane Creek to my rear. We have had two days hard rain & Snow, making the roads very bad. Indeed since the building of the Railroads the mud roads leading north & south are disused, and are washed very badly, the country resembling that about Somerset Ohio.

We find plenty of corn, fodder, cattle hogs sheep &c. so that our enemies have not been starving—Salt is scarce, but they are manufacturing it largely on the Coast, & at wells above Mobile. By our movement we have for the time being cleaned North Mississipi—I doubt if we will proceed much further on this Line, as operations should now proceed against Vicksburg and the Yazoo—I hear nothing from Virginia or Kentucky—we are far ahead of them, and they should push up.

I see much complaint against Butler at New Orleans.[1] I had a similar task in Memphis & succeeded in allaying all opposition without lowering the dignity or pretensions of our National Government. I believe I could do the same in Louisiana. There is a violent antipathy in the South against New England & her men—They do not feel the Same against the West. If they talk of removing Butler I wish you would say to Mr. Stanton that I know the very men in Louisiana who *were* Union men two years ago, and who would I think gradually yield to a firm but just policy. I would undertake it, with enough gun boats & troops to operate up Red River which is Louisiana. That River will now be navigable & Boats could operate up as far as Natchitoches & maybe Shrevesport, cutting off the Texas supplies of cattle of which we find some here. I know that the Southern People prefer a Govt. of their own but as soon as it is demonstrated that there cannot be an independent Southern Confederacy, many then will yield obedience rather than lose their Estates. When in Louisiana I held correspondence with hundreds of families and all will concede to me an honest belief that there can be but one stable Government within the limits of the United States and would I think give me a hold which no other of my Rank exercises. My course in Memphis also held thousands of wavering to their allegiance. I am satisfied here, anywhere, and Still am not ambitious of a leading part, but I do believe I could do good to the Nation & to Louisiana by a command there. It is only in case Govt. intends to remove Butler that I would have you speak to the Secretary. I suppose you hear little of me. I allow no Reporters about—My official Reports go to the proper office, and the enemy shall learn nothing of my forces, plans or purposes through an egotistical & Corrupt Press. It is enough that I am always in the front Line to all—You must have a cold winter as {I} had heavy ice here last night. yrs. affectionately

W. T. Sherman

ALS, DLC: William T. Sherman.

1. In governing New Orleans, Major General Benjamin F. Butler had issued directives calling for harsh treatment of recalcitrant Confederate civilians. These orders—especially one proclaiming that women who mocked soldiers were to be treated as prostitutes plying their trade—sparked controversy and earned Butler his nickname, "the Beast."

TO THE SHERMAN CHILDREN

College Hill. Mississipi.
December 8, 1862.

My Dear Children,

It is now nearly two weeks since I left your mama in Memphis, and mounted my little Mare Dolly to come here as we thought to fight a mighty Battle with the Enemies of our country. I commanded about twenty thousand men, and came to meet General Grant, who had forty thousand men, and with these was thought we would have a terrible Battle in crossing the Talla-hatchie River, which you will find on the map as the main branch of the Yazoo. The weather was fine, and the roads good, so that in four days marching we were at a small town name Tchullahoma, within 10 miles of the Tallahatchie. A part of our plan was for General Hovey to march from the Mississipi River at Helena, towards Grenada, with about 12,000 men, the object of which was to break the Railroads to the south of the Enemy, and this prevent their receiving provisions, stores or more men. The whole proved perfectly success-ful, and as soon as General Grants army and mine approached in front and General Hovey in rear, they abandoned their forts and camps and retreated south faster than we could follow them. Our cavalry however followed them about forty miles and have killed some and taken about 800 prisoners. You are too young yet to understand these things but sometimes battles are won by Strategy instead of fighting and all this was pure strategy.

We must now begin new combinations and I think you will next hear of me at Memphis and going down the Mississippi to Vicksburg. Write to me at Mem-phis which is 75 miles from here but we can march in in five days. You know that I always ride a horse, but the soldiers walk and carry on their back their blankets, and guns and some provisions. It is hard to the new soldiers but the old ones do it easily—Uncle Charley is now also riding a horse, but if we go to Vicksburg he will have to go along with his company which I will always keep with me. I suppose Mama wrote you all about her visit to Memphis and how Tommy was made a Corporal in Uncle Charley's Company, had a uniform made and wore it home looking like a real soldier. He thinks he is a Real soldier with a leave of absence for 7 years till he becomes fourteen when he must join his Company. No body can tell what may happen in the next seven years and therefore Tommy was very prudent in getting a seven years absence.

I wish Willy had a chance to see a large army, because I know he could remember it in after years, but if this war lasts as long as I suppose it will he will have many a chance.

Since I commenced this letter Gen. Grant has sent for me to Oxford to consult on future plans. I will take this letter with me and send it from there.

We are all very friendly here. No jealousy, no trouble. General Grant is a brave good gentleman. The newspapers abuse all such men because they are intent on serving their Country instead of dabbling with newspapers.

Gen. McPherson[1] is also there, a great friend of mine, and you can remember us all then as Ohio Generals. Goodbye, God bless you little children, I know you love me as I do you, and that though far apart and danger surrounding us I know you never sleep without thinking of your Papa. I am proud of you both, and as long as I live you shall want for nothing, but as Minnie says you must study hard & diligently because we expect so much of you, but I want you also to be easy & natural. Study alone will do little without observing others and being pleased with them. Tell Sister Angela I know she watches over you with all care and your mama will see you often. I must go on in the career till Peace is restored to our Country, and until no man will dare again to insult our flag and national honor. Believe me always your loving father

W. T. Sherman

ALS, OHi: William T. Sherman Papers.

1. Major General James Birdseye McPherson (1828–64), USA, was leading the right wing of the Thirteenth Corps.

TO IRVIN MCDOWELL

Head Qrs. Right Wing 13 Army Corps
Memphis, Dec 14, 1862

Maj. Genl. I. McDowell,

I am just in from the Tallahatehec bound down the Mississippi in conjunction with General Grants move inland. I expect to have about 30,000 men, and to operate near Vicksburg and the Yazoo.

I have been amazed to see you even suspected of disloyalty.[1] It is a base and ridiculous charge. At a time when thousands stand aloof, and many true Patriots trembled at the terrible present & future you stepped bravely and boldly forward and assumed a weight & measure of responsibility which entitle you to the thanks of every true Patriot. But in all Revolutions the first Leaders must fall for a time, but I know that your efforts will in due season restore you to your power your influence and the gratitude of all well thinking men. The imputation of intemperance to those who know you excites a smile of contempt. We all know that from your childhood liquor and all stimulants have been your abhorrence. You have not only abstained from all such but even Coffee. Truth will in the end prevail and confound the impudent fools who thus accuse you.

Your brother John A. McDowell has been with me nearly a year commanding one of my Brigades and I left him a few days since at College Hill near

Oxford in command of as good a Brigade as is in our whole army. He is a good kind hearted Gentleman, full of zeal for our cause and I parted with him with feelings of great kindness. I have urged his name for promotion and I hope successfully. We have often talked of you, and through him I have sent you many expressions of my personal regard for your high character as a Patriot and Soldier.

Believing that the ordeal through which you are passing will restore you fully to the confidence of the Government and of our Countrymen. I am as ever Your friend

W. T. Sherman
Maj. Genl.

Typescript, OFH.

1. McDowell's actions at Second Bull Run had been censured and he was investigated for disloyalty, disobedience, and misconduct. He was exonerated but never again took an active part in the war.

TO ELLEN EWING SHERMAN

Memphis Dec. 14, 1862

Dearest Ellen,

Here I am again back from the Tallahatchee charged with the Mississipi expedition. I ought to have 40,000 men, but cannot now count on more than 30,000, but I will go as soon as the boats arrive, the day appointed is the 18th inst., and I will be all ready. As soon as we found the Line of the Tallahatchee abandonned Grant summoned me to Oxford, and we agreed upon a new Plan. The first was perfectly successful & we gained North Mississipi by mind alone. My part is exactly what I would have chose, and I find all enthusiastic & rejoiced that I lead it. I left at College Hill Denvers and Laumans Divisions & brought back Morgan Smiths because I regard it as my best fighting Division. I also brought in the Regulars & my 20 lb. Parrotts. I took Charley from his horse and he footed it manfully 75 miles in 3½ days. He is here in fine feather and delighted with his first bloodless campaign. The Regulars marched fairly and deported themselves well. I keep them and shall keep them near me as a Guard and for special service. Morgan Smiths Division kept a short distance behind the Regulars and reached here next morning. Their old Camp Grounds were occupied by the new arrivals and they now are up near where Mungen Camped.

A. J. Smith commands my 1st Division about	7000
Morgan Smith the 2nd	7000
G. W. Morgan. (Cumberland Gap the 3rd	7000
Total	21,000

I expect 10,000 from Helena, but there may be some slip as Curtis has not yet sent down the necessary orders. I left two of my old Divisions near Oxford Denvers & Laumans. When about to depart I had them in Line, rode along and spoke a few words to each. I had no idea of the attachment which had Sprung up between us. McDowell and Corse,[1] and all my old set almost cried, and the men cheered till my little mare Dolly nearly jumped out of her skin. The day was beautiful and on all our march back the sky was clear and roads perfect.

I received your letter from Cairo, and today the one from home.[2] Elizabeth wrote me that the old house would be ready April 1. I think you had better take it, and when the war is over and I survive it I will make some new combinations. You will be better off at Lancaster than Elsewhere, and your living expenses being light you can better afford to hire teachers for the children. I was glad to hear you had so pleasant a trip and met so many friends by the way and I'm afraid that you are now so imbued with a spirit of travel that you will be wandering all about—Your father & mother are now old and you had better settle down near them. Also your advances are so large on the farm that I suppose you will succeed to it, but I will never live in Ohio. I would today prefer Tennessee or Mississipi or were I called on to Say which state would make most sacrifices in support of their Government I would say Tennessee. Ohio is full of selfishness and conceit. Sneaks & politicians are more honored than brave quiet men. I will not live there but you can till this war ends, and as I Know that it will not be soon I will not think of the future. I was amazed on my return to witness the manifestations of Kindness towards me personally. The Union Club was all alive and I had to make another speech, the burden of which was if we applied the Rule of progress in Memphis in the past four months to the future the war ahead was not such a labor as at first sight would appear. Indeed in Memphis I feel that I have achieved perfect success. Today "I worshipped in Calvary" and Mr. White preached a real good Union sermon. Four months ago he omitted the prayer for Jeff Davis out of naked respect for our presence. The streets are lively, the theatre crowded and really the Town looks prosperous. Cotton comes in freely and trade thrives. I dont believe a real secessionist now wants to recal the past. If I can take Vicksburg and accomplish the same there and finally bring up in Louisiana, I feel that I can make that state admit that "Union is a necessity." This is all my ambition and I hope I will be permitted to stick to the Mississipi—All my military family are well & much pleased at your remembrance of them. Maj. Chase[3] & 13th are well and even the soldiers speak of you as their friend. They ask me how you are, where you are and how is Corporal Tom. I always answer fully. Charley got your letter today, & he & I rejoiced that Hugh is a Brigadier.[4] I will write again before I embark—others will write you of details. Give my love to all and tell me how Tom wears his uniform. He has a large circle of friends here. Write to Scott in New York what you think of the Sword and tell him of things here. I will write again before starting—Yours ever

W. T. Sherman

ALS, InND: Sherman Family Papers.

1. Lieutenant Colonel John M. Corse (1835–93), USA, had been serving on Pope's staff.

2. EES to WTS, November 30, 1862, SFP. EES had just returned to Ohio from her trip to Memphis. She confided to John that WTS "looks thin & worse being more wrinkled than most men of sixty but he was so cheerful & well that I soon ceased to lament those marks of time & care." EES to JS, December 11, 1862, DLC: WTS.

3. Daniel Chase of the Thirteenth U.S. Infantry.

4. Hugh received his promotion on November 29.

TO JOHN SHERMAN

Memphis, Dec. 14, 1862.

Dear Brother,

I am back in Memphis, having been charged by General Grant to organize the forces here and such as may be assigned for Helena and to proceed to Vicksburg and reduce that place and cooperate with Grant whom I left at Oxford Miss. He expected I would have 40,000, but I cannot count on more than 30,000, but expect if steamers arrive according to the design by the 18th to embark for that destination. The move is one of vast importance and if successful will remove the chief obstacles to the navigation of the Mississipi although it will as long as war lasts be a source of Contention. I take it that now Vicksburg is fortified by land & water and that it is a difficult task, but it must be undertaken. Things are not exactly right—Grant commands on the side Curtis on the West, and Admiral Porter on the River. All ought to be under one head, but thus far I meet the heartiest cooperation and I feel certain we will all act in concert.

Our move on the Tallahatchee was well planned and well executed. Though we had no battle yet the Enemy had made every preparation for a determined resistance at the Tallahatchee, but were completely disconcerted by the move on their flank and Rear from Helena which was entirely unexpected. The Country between the Yazoo and Mississipi is all alluvial and a few hours rain renders the roads impassable to artillery, but fortunately the weather was good and all our forces reached their appointed places on time and the result accomplished the object without Battle. The retreat of the Confederate Army was rapid & confused, and the effect was equal to a Victory. Grant now has a well appointed army at Oxford Miss, with which he will move South, as soon as I move in position at Vicksburg. It is very difficult to keep up Communication as his Railroad reaches the Mississipi at Columbus Ky. and the River is lower than it was ever Known at this season, so that navigation is very difficult. The Country is full of Guerilla Bands so that the couriers cannot be relied on across the country 75 miles. I will try and reach Vicksburg by a certain date and will have Grant advised so that though far apart our movements will be in concert. I find things in good Shape here—I have a strong hold on the People here who admit that I am just and Strictly legal in all my acts. Even the Richer classes begin to come in and admit that the war had assumed proportions too great for them to cope with. Now is the time to put forth the whole power of the nation. You cant relax now[.] The North must rule or be ruled. There is no middle course. The whole people of the South are armed and attacking them in their own Country our force should double theirs. These surrenders of Harpers Ferry, Munfordsville and Hartsville illustrate the danger of detach-ments.[1] It is idle to talk about blaming the officers. These were the very loudest in boasting of their prowess, and their destruction dont cure the facts. All the orders wont stop it—Our People are taught insubordination and indepen-dence, and when confused and disordered their commanders are helpless— You dont blame the masses. I do, because I know. Still many are fast becoming soldiers from experience and, as the South flags in Energy—we must increase our efforts. I have some men that I can depend on. I had to leave with Grant two out of my three Divisions, but I find here two other Divisions A. J. Smiths,[2] & G. W. Morgans who seem to be good troops. I hope also to get some good men at Helena, a part of Curtis present force—I will only have one of my old Divisions, Morgan L. Smiths, but will rely much on the enthusiasm attached to this peculiar expedition. I have been in the woods & have seen no newspapers of late, not even the Presidents Message—but I saw the outlines of your speech which is all right.[3] I want you to fan all Bills to Stop the pay of the officers & men who, on the plea of sickness & other excuses keep away from their Regiments—nearly one fourth of the men & officers who draw pay never intend to face danger. This is true, and I see it begins to attract attention. This has been a fruitful source of miscalculation & failure—I saw Henry Sherman[4] today, a fine manly fellow I will watch & support him & in time will ask for him some staff position. I advised him today to remain as now gaining Knowl-edge & Experience which can alone be gained in the Ranks. He is sergeant major. I will see he wants nothing[.] He goes with me to Vicksburg. I have also my own Regt. of Regulars with me. Ellen is back at Lancaster. The Little house is sold and She will want our old house. Elizabeth had rented it to a Preacher and I wrote her that was not fair and She wrote me back most haughtily, talking about Reese having rebuilt it at an expense of 1500 Dolls. She forgets I gave her and Reese $2000 cash on my return from California. I wish you to remind her of that, and that really I have claims as she no longer needs it. I would not live in Ohio—but ask it as a refuge for my family till I am free to hunt a new home, after the war if I survive which of course I do not expect—I will write again before starting

W. T. S.

ALS, DLC: William T. Sherman.

1. Stonewall Jackson's troops had won control of Harpers Ferry on September 15 but evacuated it by September 22; U.S. troops garrisoning Munfordville, Kentucky, had surrendered to Braxton Bragg on September 17, 1862; and John Hunt Morgan had captured the Federal garrison at Hartsville, Tennessee, on December 6, 1862.

2. Andrew J. Smith (1815–97) was commanding the Tenth Division of McPherson's right wing.

3. Lincoln's State of the Union address had been delivered at the opening of the third session of the Thirty-seventh Congress on December 1.

4. Henry S. Sherman (1845–93), later a lawyer, was Charles Taylor Sherman's son and was currently sergeant major of the 120th Ohio Infantry in Morgan's Division. On December 10, he had written to WTS to ask for a staff position if one was available. DLC: WTS.

TO EDWIN M. STANTON[1]

Hd. Qrts. Rt. Wing 13. Army Corps
Memphis Dec. 16. 1862

Hon E. M. Stanton
Secty. of War—Washington D.C.
Sir

Maj. Genl. Hurlbut now in command of Memphis informs me that subsequently to the departure of my command for the Tallahatchie—A letter was received from the War Department addressed to me here requiring an explanation of the reasons why a Mrs. Meriwether was banished the city of Memphis.[2] That letter was sent to me via Oxford Mississippi & cannot overtake me here in time as I expect to depart for the mouth of Yazoo on the 18th. inst.

As I alone am conversant with the facts & reasons why Mrs. Meriwether was forced to leave the city I will report them without awaiting the receipt of the letter herein referred to.

Memphis was captured in June 1862. It was a city of 25,000 inhabitants, from which the enemy had drawn 62 companies of soldiers—The families of the officers & men remained here whilst fathers husbands and brothers went forth armed to fight against the Government of their birth and of their conquerors. Trade at once opened to them the comforts of St. Louis, Louisville and Cincinnati & those officers & men actually had reason to rejoice that their families could remain unmolested in Memphis supplied abundantly & cheaply with all the necessities of life. Indeed the capture of Memphis was an advantage to our Enemy. Here their families lived in comfort & protected whilst they carried on war against us in every form.

They had their armies at Holly Springs only 45 miles distant and their Guerrillas & Partizan Rangers swarmed the Country intercepting supplies, Subduing all reactionary opinion & deriving through their families & servants all information of our movements. We were forced to keep heavy guards to prevent intercourse between city and Country. In September last the enemy began to assail the very boats which were engaged in bringing cheap supplies & their own families. They fired with Guns upon a Packet at Randolph I caused Randolph to be burned. But looking ahead I saw that remedy not the true one—I announced in an order widely circulated and published in our newspapers that if the Enemy attacked our Boats navigating the Mississippi I should proceed to change the population of Memphis. I was unwilling if we were compelled to navigate the river by armed boats prepared to fight to continue to supply the families of men engaged in attacking these very boats. All had public notice that upon every case of firing on unarmed Boats engaged in peaceful traffic the families of ten men know to be in arms against us must quit Memphis—For sometime there was a lull and I had a list of names prepared on which the name of Mrs. Meriwether appeared, her husband being a major in the Confederate Service. Soon after almost on the same day four boats were savagely attacked, viz. the Continental and J. H. Dicky above and the Catahula and Gladiator below, two were fired on by cannon & the others narrowly escaped destruction. On the Gladiator two Citizens were killed & several wounded the boat set on fire and escaped as by a miracle. Out of the list prepared forty names were drawn by lot among them Mrs. Meriwether. She in common with the rest were notified by the Provost Marshal Col. Anthony that pursuant to previous notice, in consequence of the attack on one of the said Boats by Confederate soldiers, of which her husband was a major she must remove to a distance of 25 miles from Memphis—She was permitted to take all her children, household goods, servants, everything moveable she possessed. Not a harsh word was spoken to her or any of them, & she never denied but that her husband was a party to these hellish deeds. It certainly would be an anomaly in war if we should sit tamely by, and allow the husband to war against the very boats carrying supplies to his family—The remedy struck at the Root of the Evil and no boat has been fired on since.

The right to navigate the Mississippi River at all times is so important that I feel assured the Honorable Secretary will justify any and all measures mild and severe that will secure it, and in this believe I will never overlook any attack on any boats engaged in Lawful traffic. I am with great respect your obt. sevt.

W. T. Sherman
Maj. Genl.

LbkS, DNA: RG 94, Records of the Adjutant General's Office, Generals' Books and Papers, William T. Sherman, Letterbook 4.

1. Edwin M. Stanton (1814–69) became secretary of war in 1862.

2. See WTS to John A. Rawlins, August 14, 1862, above.

TO JOHN SHERMAN

Memphis, Dec. 20, 1862

Dear Brother,

I embark today on the Forest Queen and will have 20,000 men in Boats by noon & be off for the Real South. At Helena I will get about 12,000 more—Like much of Our Boasts of the "Myriads of the North West" "sweeping a way to the Gulf" "breaking the Backbone" &c. &c. the Great Mississipi Expedition will be 32,000 men. Vicksburg is well fortified and is within telegraphic & Railroad reach of Meridian, Mobile Camp Moore and Grenada where Pemberton has 30 to 35,000 men. Therefore dont expect me to achieve miracles. Vicksburg is not the only thing to be done. Grant is at Coffeeville with say 40,000 men—he expected me to have the Same but they are not here. We can get the Yazoo can front in any & every direction and can take Vicksburg, clean out the Yazoo, capture or destroy the fleet of enemys Gunboats & transports concealed up above Yazoo City & do many other useful things—Blair is down at Helena, and will doubtless form a part of the Expedition. He will have a chance of catching the elephant by the Tale & get a good lift. Of course the presence of this force acting in concert with Grant must produce good results. Even if we dont open the Mississipi, by the way an event not so important as at first sight until the Great armies of the enemy are defeated—we are progressing. I wish Burnside & Rosecrans were getting along faster, but I suppose they encounter the same troubles we all do[1]—The new levies wander about the Country looking for the Regiments not anxious to find them. At the moment of marching a fearful list of sickness develops and one fourth has to be left behind, measles, mumps & lastly Small Pox develops, but I admit slowly we are getting a better army. I hope you individually will not engage in any efforts to remove individuals like McClellan[.] The President charged with this, has the right and ought to regulate all matters of command. Outside pressure ought not to be resorted to. Burnside of course is a clever man, but he has no confidence in himself and if I mistake not an abiding confidence in McClellan and would lean on him for counsel if present—McClellan will be recalled sooner or later—But leave that to the President. The Great Evil is absenteeism which is real Desertion, & Should be punished with Death. Of course I would have the wounded & Sick well cared for, but the Sick list real & feigned is fearful—More than one half the paper army is not in the enemys Country, and whilst the actual regiments present for duty are in arrears of pay & favor, sick & discharged men are carefully paid & provided for. Unite with others and discriminate in favor of the officers & Soldiers who are with the companies.

The "absent & sick" should receive half pay because of the advantages they receive of fine hospitals or quiet residence at home. The "absent without Leave" should be treated as Deserters, and in no event receive a dollars pay, clothing or any thing else. In course of time we may get an army—Finance is very important but no use of discussing that now—We must fight it out if it devastates the Land and costs every cent of the North. The Law must be vindicated else we are a disgraced & Dishonored Nation. In the outset we might have paused, not now, or for years to come.

The owners of Land, Negros, & other property of the South may show some signs of yielding, but the young & fighting elements not a bit. They are as united & determined as ever.

I dont like to see you favor a Bankrupt Bill no man should ever be discharged for an honest debt, *never.* Better thousands of merchants should perish of want than to stimulate speculation by discharging debtors of their obligations.

My cotton Letter was designed as a good joke to kill a silly proposition to issue shinplasters in Memphis. It succeeded of course, and [I] was amused to see it treated as a serious proposition to make cotton money—I hope all paper money save what is issued by the U.S. will in time disappear from the country. I rise at 3 A.M. to finish up necessary business & as usual write in haste. Ellen will have told or written you of Memphis. I am very popular with the People here & officers here and indeed with all my men—I dont seek popularity with the "sneaks and absentees" or the Dear People—I enclose a copy of some of my orders. The cotton buyers are nuisances & keep alive the idea South that the Yankees would perish without cotton. It would be better to burn all cotton & find a substitute flax, hemp or anything. My personal health is very good— affectionately &c.   W. T. Sherman

ALS, DLC: William T. Sherman.

1. Burnside had just been defeated at Fredericksburg (December 13, 1862); Rosecrans was about to commence a campaign that resulted in the Battle of Stones River (December 31– January 2, 1863).

TO ELLEN EWING SHERMAN

On Board *Forest Queen*
Millikens Bend, Jan. 4, 1863.

Dearest Ellen,

Well we have been to Vicksburg, and it was too much for us, and we have backed out.[1] I suppose the attack on Holly Springs & the Railroad compelled

Grant to fall behind the Tallahatchee & consequently the Confederates were enabled to reinforce Vicksburg. Besides its natural strength had been improved by a vast amount of labor so that it was impossible for me to capture or even to penetrate to the Road from which alone I could expect to take it. For five days we were thundering away and when my main assault failed, and Admiral Porter deemed another requiring the cooperation of his Gunboats "too hazardous" I saw no alternative but to regain my steam boats & the Main River which I did unopposed and unmolested. To reembark a large command in the face of an enterprising & successful enemy is no easy task—but I accomplished it. McClernand has arrived to Supercede me, by order of the President himself. Of course I submit gracefully. The President is charged with maintaining the Government and has a perfect right to choose his agents—my command is to be an army corps, composed of Morgan L. Smiths old command—Poor Morgan now lies wounded badly in the hip on board the "Chancellor" and his Division is commanded by Stuart—and the troops I got at Helena commanded by Fred Steele whom I know well—These are all new & strange to me, but such is Life & Luck. Before I withdrew from the Yazoo I saw McClernand and told him that we had failed to carry the Enemys Line of works before Vicksburg, but I could hold my ground at Yazoo, but it would be useless. He promptly confirmed my judgment that it was best to come out into the Main River at Millikens Bend—We did so day before yesterday and it has rained hard two days and I am satisfied we got out of the Swamp at Chickasaw Bayou in time for now water & mud must be forty feet deep there. Charley was under fire and Grape Canister & Shell—Regulars did well of course, but they or no human beings could have crossed the Bayou & live. People at a distance will ridicule our being unable to pass a narrow Bayou, but no body who was there will. Instead of lying idle I proposed we should come to the Arkansas and attack the Post of Arkansas 50 miles up that River, from which the enemy has attacked the River capturing one of our boats towing two Barges of navy coal, & capturing a mail so I have no doubt some curious Lieutenant has read your letters to me. We must make the River safe behind us before we push too far down. We are now on our way to the Post of Arkansas. McClernand assumed command today, so I will not be care worn again by the duty of looking to Supplies plans &c. I enclose you the rough notes from which my official Report is made our loss is about 1800—say 300 Killed, 400 taken prisoner, and over a thousand wounded.[2] Morgan Smith is among the latter. Capt. Gwin[3] my favorite in the fleet received a mortal wound while Engaging a Battery 7 miles higher up on Yazoo than when we landed. The Boat is in motion & trembles so I cannot write we will rendezvous at Gavins Landing & at the mouth of Arkansas where I will dispatch this & write more. I have made my full reports both to Grant and Halleck some of which will reach the newspapers, but the rough notes I send you will be the Substance of all— Poor Morgan Smith will die I fear—His wound was a partly accidental one, but the ball lodged near his spine and I fear will prove mortal. Gwin is dead— We thus lose two of the best officers in our service. It will in the end cost us at least ten thousand lives to take Vicksburg. I would have pushed the attack to the bitter end but even had we reached the City unassisted we could not have held it if they were at liberty to reinforce from the Interior. Charley & Dayton will write you more details. I am very well and now that my command is limited to my one corps will have less to do, and less area. I certainly envy no one the anxiety of providing for so many people. yrs. ever

Sherman

ALS, InND: Sherman Family Papers.

1. The Battle of Chickasaw Bluffs on December 29 was a crushing defeat for Sherman's expedition at the hands of a smaller Confederate force in Vicksburg. The city's natural and man-made defenses were too strong for a conventional assault; Grant was forced to abandon his march southward when Confederate cavalry sliced his supply line.

2. Enclosed was Sherman's January 1, 1863, draft of his report on events between December 20, 1862, and January 1, 1863, to John A. Rawlins, OR, I, 17: pt. 1, 605–10.

3. Lieutenant Commander William Gwin of the USS Benton had been previously involved in Sherman's operations on the Tennessee River at Shiloh and below. He was mortally wounded on December 27, 1862.

TO JOHN SHERMAN

Steamer Forest Queen,
January 6, 1862. [1863]

Dear Brother,

You will have heard of our attack on Vicksburg and failure to succeed. The place is too Strong, and without the cooperation of a large army coming from the Interior it is impracticable. Innumerable batteries prevent the approach of Gun boats to the city or to the first bluff up the Yazoo, and the only landing between is on an insular space of low boggy ground with innumerable bayous or deep sloughs. I did all that was possible to reach the main Land but was met at every point by Batteries & Rifle pits that we could not pass, and in the absence of Genl. Grants cooperating force I was compelled to reembark my command. My Reports to General Grant a copy of which I send to General Halleck who will let you see it is very full, and more than I could write to you with propriety.[1] Whatever you or the absent may think, not a soldier or officer who was present but will admit I pushed the attack as far as prudence would justify, and that I reembarked my command in the nick of time, for a heavy rain set in which would have swamped us and made it impossible to withdraw artillery & Stores. Up to that time I was acting on the Right Wing of Genl. Grants army, but Gen. McClernand has arrived and we now have a new organization—McClernand commanding the whole, and our present force divided into two commands or Corps d'Armee one of which is commanded by me and one by Morgan of Cumberland Gap. We are now en route for the Arkansas. Up that River about 50 miles the enemy is entrenched, and has sent down to the Mississipi and captured two steamboats carrying to the fleet supplies. Now it is unwise to leave such a force on our rear and flank and inasmuch as Genl. Grant is not prepared to march down to Vicksburg by Land, we can attack this Post of Arkansas and maybe reach Little Rock. Success in this quarter will have a good Effect on the Main River. But in the end Vicksburg must be reduced, and it is going to be a hard nut to crack—It is the strongest place I ever saw, both by nature and art, and so far as we could observe it is defended by a Competent form of artillery Infantry and Cavalry, besides its Rail Road connections with the interior give them great advantage. I wish you would ask Halleck to allow you to See my Report, and as soon as all the Reports of the Division & Brigade commanders reach Washington from Genl. Grant to where they must first go, you will have a complete picture. Of course newspaper men will first flood the country with their stories and what they will be no one can tell, they having their purposes to Serve and not Knowing my orders or plans. My orders from Grant were to leave Memphis by the 18th and I got off the 20th and I was exactly on time to cooperate with Grant. I did not know that he was delayed by the breaking of his Railroad Communications to his Rear. Indeed I supposed him to be advancing south towards the Yazoo River. My entire force was 30,000, and was every man I could raise at Memphis & Helena, and Grant & Halleck were fully advised of my strength & plans. I suppose you are now fully convinced of the stupendous energy of the South, and their ability to prolong this war indefinitely, but I am further satisfied that if it last thirty years we must fight it out, for the moment the North relaxes its energies, the South will assume the offensive, and it is wonderful how well disciplined and provided they have their men—we found everywhere abundant supplies, even on the Yazoo, and all along the River we found cattle & fat ones feeding quietly. The Country everywhere abounds with corn, and the Soldiers though coarsely are well clad. We hear of the manufacture of all sorts of cloth and munitions of war. The River Plantations are mostly abandoned, and all families negros, stock & cotton removed 25 miles back. All corn has been carried in advance to Vicksburg. We find a few old people along the River but all the Young & middle aged have gone to the war. I see no symptoms of a relaxation of their fierce energy, so that I still regard the war as but fairly begun. Young Henry Sherman was under fire, but is well. He is in Lindseys Brigade[2] of Morgans Division. In time I will move for his promotion.

I think I see at the North & in the discussions in the Senate & Cabinet symptoms of that anarchy which I fear more than war.[3] Stand by the Constituted authorities even if it lead to despotism rather than anarchy which will result if popular clamor is to be the Ruling Power. yrs.

Sherman

ALS, DLC: William T. Sherman.

1. WTS to John A. Rawlins, January 3, 1863, *OR*, I, 17: pt. 1, 605–10.

2. Colonel Daniel W. Lindsey was commanding the Second Brigade of the Third Division at Chickasaw Bluffs.

3. Senate Republicans had just failed in an effort to force Lincoln to remodel his cabinet by removing Secretary of State Seward.

TO ELLEN EWING SHERMAN

Post of Arkansas, Jan. 12, 1863.

Dearest Ellen,

We carried the Post of Arkansas yesterday and captured all its stores & Garrison[1]—one Brigadier General Churchill,[2] and three Brigades of soldiers. I cannot tell yet how many. They now stand clustering on the Bank, and will today be put on board of Boats and sent to Cairo. This relieves our Vicksburg trip of all appearance of a reverse as by this move we open the Arkansas and compel all organized masses of the Enemy to pass below the Arkansas River, and it will also secure this flank where we renew our attack on Vicksburg. Charley is all safe. He was under fire four hours and the Regulars behaved well of course. Capt. Smith[3] is wounded in the Knee: it will lay him up some months. As usual my troops had the fighting and did the work, but of course others will claim the merit and Glory. Let them have it. The soldiers Know who studied the ground ahead and directed the movement. It was not a Battle but a clean little "affaire" success perfect. Our loss comparatively light. Yrs. in haste

Sherman

ALS, InND: Sherman Family Papers.

1. The January 11 capture of Arkansas Post by Sherman's and McClernand's forces was designed to free up river traffic on the Mississippi and divert Northern attention from the Federal defeat at Vicksburg the previous month.

2. Brigadier General Thomas J. Churchill (1824–1905), CSA.

3. Captain Charles Campbell Smith (d. 1891) of Indiana had been commissioned a captain in the Thirteenth U.S. Infantry in May 1861.

Napoleon Arkansas, Jan. 16, 186[3]

Hon. Thos. Ewing
Lancaster Ohio
Dear Sir,

We are this moment arrived here from the Post of Arkansas which we captured with all its Garrison and material of war. Gen. McClernand ordered me to bring my corps to this point to await further orders. I send Ellen the rough draft of my report with a sketch which will I think give you as good an idea of the whole thing as any more elaborate description I might attempt.[1] Of course the world will hold me responsible for the failure at Vicksburg and give McClernand credit for the complete success at the Post, and being interested I must not question the verdict. But I feel conscious I have done the best possible and the Soldiers and officers present know who counselled, guided and led them throughout. It was a worry to me to place McClernand in command, but I must not question Mr. Lincolns right to select his own Leaders. To me McClernand is one of the most objectionable because his master is Illinois and personal notoriety, whereas I prefer to serve the whole United States, and to check that gnawing and craving appetite for personal fame and notoriety, which has brought our people into a just contempt with Foreign nations.

We could have gone up to Little Rock, but the Arkansas River is very tortuous, and liable to sudden rises & falls, and it would not do to subject this expedition with its men, materiel and Boats to any mischance, as its purpose and destiny are on the Main River, the Mississipi. The Capture of the Post, with the appearance of the force which has gone up White River under Genl. Gorman[2] will now compel the Confederates to remove their detachments to the south of the Arkansas River, which will have a tranquilizing effect on Missouri and the West. I stole a few moments of leisure to read your pamphlet to Stanton, and enjoyed its wit very much.[3] I regret that I have been the cause of your being drawn into a controversy, but it looks as though you enjoyed it: and that having the Documents well digested in your mind, and Stanton having attempted to change his issues, you have him well hooked, and are playing with him as a skilful angler. I rather suppose he wants to be let alone, and I doubt if again he will attempt to arraign the conduct of officers who are doing their best. Tom Worthington is a dirty puppy. He joined me at Paducah in February 62 with a Regiment, his Rank being 6th among the 12 Regiments which I was called upon to organize into Brigades. All were strangers to me. The Law commands me to respect Rank, and the United States dates the Rank of Colonels of Regiments from the time of their muster into the General Service. Tom was half drunk & noisy all the time, had free admittance into my presence, and he took liberties which no one else would have done, from his Old West Point Standing, and from his acquaintance with all my family. When I arranged the Brigades of course he was not one of the four Commanders. He railed outrageously and I had to be very plain with him. We immediately embarked up the Tennessee and he was all the time out of place, noisy, drunk & insubordinate. At Savannah Tenn. he disembarked a part of his Regiment, drove out a family & put some of his men in a private dwelling against orders—I reproved him for it[.] His Brigadier Hicks put him in arrest there, but I smoothed it over and released him—At the same time Paymaster McDowell and one of Governor Tods[4] aids who {happened} at Savannah preferred written charges against him for Drunkenness & Conduct Unbecoming an officer & Gentleman. These charges too I suppressed and begged him to be more careful. So things went on he criticizing, fault finding and complaining, yet all the time counselling expeditions to Florence, Corinth, Memphis, yea everywhere in utter ignorance of the numbers, strength or designs of the Enemy— He knew I was not in command but that Grant, C. F. Smith, McClernand & Wallace all the time present or near at hand were my superiors, yet he held me responsible for all things that did not run with his mad notions. Every body remarked & expressed surprise at the patience with which I bore with him, and Genl C. F. Smith a splendid soldier & contemporary with Worthington at West Point, half jocularly & half seriously told me that if I again allowed him (Worthington) to escape from his Boat, to come and pester him (Smith) he would hold me officially responsible. Col. McDowell in whose Brigade Worthington was, repeatedly complained of his vagaries, his excentricities & his intemperance & finally said he saw I was determined to shield Worthington from a just responsibility for his Acts. The truth was I did want to shield him for his West Point name the sake of his family & my belief that his own sense of Right would soon make him more respectful to me and his other Superiors. I also knew that his Lieutenant Colonel Walcutt[5] an elegant young fellow was the actual commander of his Regiment and now most worthily commands it as its Colonel. Worthington was wandering about fault finding and criticizing Halleck, Grant and Sherman, "who were all babies when he was a full graduate of West Point." At the Battle of Shiloh he was with his Regmt. for the first four hours and tells himself of performing some inexplicable movement which saved the day. The truth was the day was not saved then or for hours afterward. The tactical movement of a single small Regiment at a time when the enemy had 40,000 hotly engaged and we defending ourselves with less that 25,000 is simply a piece of egotistical nonsense. I know he was not personally present in my front Line after 12 p.m. of April 6, and I did not see him at all on the 7th. After Shiloh he was most active in giving false information to the Press, and he was wandering about making notes but I paid little heed to it—we moved on to Corinth and so in toward Memphis. Worthingtons Regiment was left at a Depot known as Lafayette while I moved to Holly Springs, and when finally I was ordered from Moscow into Memphis, I sent Worthington word to be ready to fall in his place as we passed Lafayette, and when I reached it he was dirty drunk. We marched into Memphis and soon appeared his pamphlet. I saw I had forborn too long, so I ordered charges to be preferred against him and gave him a good court, 13 high impartial officers. He had a long, fair and perfect trial and the Court found him Guilty and Sentenced him to be Cashiered. My understanding of the Law was that this sentence required the approval of the President of the United States and accordingly forwarded the Proceedings to Washington. They came back to me with an endorsement that I had the right to review & carry into effect the Sentence. Of course I approved and he was cashiered. The Governor (Tod) has filled the vacancy by promoting the Lt. Colonel Walcutt, and *now* the 46 Ohio is as good a Regiment as represents that State in the Service. There is not an officer or man in this army that does not know, and who will not admit Worthington was a nuisance and should have been dismissed months before—But you have known him from childhood and can better understand than I can explain, what a nuisance a man like he would be in a Volunteer Army, where discipline at best is hard to approximate. Minding everybody's business but his own, never at his true post, scorning the detailed drudgery of the Camp & March but full of Hannibal and Caesar, Napoleon, Wellington, Jomini[6] & Napier,[7] and utterly ignorant of his own command, its wants, its arms, ammunition, the temper & habits of American Soldiers & character of Roads, & difficulties of ambuscades & Cypress Swamps. He is a good example of that species of critic that now rules the Public Press of our Country. At times I confess I feel sick at heart when I see the tests by which our movements are tried and the People on whom we must depend for resupplying the chasms which war and disease make in our Ranks as we progress. Our Regiments are dwindling down into Corporals Guards, and our Lists of absent "without authority" far exceed "our Present for duty." We are held responsible by our country to do the work [of] tens of thousands when the great majority are back at home technically "sick." My reputation with the foremost "present for duty" has ever been high. The Soldiers on picket and the advance Guard know General Sherman, and I defy any one to bring a witness from this class that I have ever said an unkind word, or done an unkind act to them—I thank you for your well timed remark on this point and I assure you the German Friend has not transported another's Spirit into my carcass,[8] and that to the worthy and deserving I am as gentle as of old—But to the supercilious critic who hangs about my Camp to pick up trophies, who flatters himself by bearing linens & bandages for the maimed and wounded Soldiers, but wines & jellies, and dainties for himself: to the Newspaper Correspondent who searches for items of falsehood & slander and the cowardly slinks who eat their full Ration draw their full clothing & pay, but yet are ever too sick when Battle & danger come, to share in it: and a still larger class who wander from their Ranks, burn the dwellings of peaceful people, plunder & rob, and steal, drawing the fire upon our pickets whilst they sneak to the Rear, and count whole Classes of people into bitter & irreconcilable enemies—Against all such I have been *harsh*, for the Laws of Congress make them all high criminals in War, and I hope the misplaced kindness of our Executive will very soon enable us to follow harsh words by just and harsh treatment. If the People of the U.S. expect armies to be managed like Sunday schools, they the People must be revolutionized for their opinions *must* conform to the result of the Experience of ages. Our enemy is far in advance of us in the discipline of their army, and we here know & feel it.

A very heavy snow storm has reached us here, four inches deep, and it looks wintry & dreary enough on the shores of the Muddy Mississipi with the town of Napoleon absolutely deserted by its People. Plantations & farms all abandonned, and Ruin & desolation written on the face of all things.

I will now leave McClernand to dictate our movements, but we are not strong enough to force the passage at Vicksburg. With great respect, yr son,

W. T. Sherman

ALS, PCarlA.

1. WTS's draft of his January 13 report and map to Colonel Adolph Schwartz, McClernand's assistant adjutant general, was enclosed in his January 16 letter to EES, following.

2. Brigadier General Willis A. Gorman (1816–76) was commanding the District of Arkansas.

3. Probably TESr to Benjamin Stanton, November 1, 1862, which had begun as a private correspondence but was published at the Ewing family's insistence. John F. Marszalek, *Sherman's Other War: The General and the Civil War Press* (Memphis, 1981), 83 and 93 n. 54.

4. David Tod (1805–68) had been elected governor of Ohio in 1861.

5. Charles C. Walcutt (1838–98) had been promoted to colonel on October 16, 1862, and commanded the First Brigade in the First Division of the Sixteenth Corps.

6. Antoine Henri de Jomini (1799–1869) was a well-known expositor of Napoleon's principles of war. His works were highly influential in the minds of some Civil War generals, including Halleck, McClellan, and Beauregard; Sherman also admired him.

7. Presumably British general Sir William Francis Patrick Napier (1785–1869), author of the four-volume work *History of the War in the Peninsula and in the South of France from the Year 1807 to the Year 1814* (1828–40).

8. In his November 1 letter to Stanton, Ewing Sr. had said: "You take great pains to impress the public with the belief that Gen. Sherman is rough and rude and churlish to

officers and men under his command. This cannot be so unless as in the wild story of the German student, he has exchanged souls with someone very unlike himself." Ewing, *Sherman at War*, 85n.

TO ELLEN EWING SHERMAN

Steamer Forest Queen
Napoleon Arks. Jan. 16, 1863

Dearest Ellen,

After levelling the Rifle pits back of the Post of Arkansas and burning long rows of log houses which the Secesh had built for their Winter Quarters I was ordered to bring my Fleet to Helena. A tremendous snow storm prevailed actually blinding the pilots so that we lay till noon before it was safe to Start when the snow slackened up and I make the Signal to Start—fired a Single Gun, and boat after boat dropped down the River. Yesterday my corps rendezvoused here, the town abandonned & looking like desolation covered with snow—Just after noon I noticed five Boats coming down the Mississipi River and as they neared I noticed that the first was the Prima Donna, which I knew did not belong to our fleet, so I sent McCoy to get some newspapers. You can imagine my surprise when he soon returned with Hugh looking as fine as possible as a Brigadier with his morning Report in hand and orders to report to me, as a Brigade in Morgan L. Smiths Division.[1] Charley was soon on hand and a general jubilation. He soon explained how he happened to be sent here, he had the latest newspapers which contained accounts of Rosecrans fight[2]— Gareschis death[3] and the reception of the news of our repulse at Vicksburg, he had also heard of our success at the Post of Arkansas. Today McClernand has come out of the Arkansas, with the rest of the army and the orders are to start back for Vicksburg. The understanding is we are to be reinforced from Memphis, and are to meet Banks[.] Banks has first to reduce Port Hudson and it is important ere that we should be in the vicinity of Vicksburg to threaten that Point whilst Banks is engaged with Port Hudson. Vicksburg is going to be a hard nut to crack, but I think our affair at the Post of Arkansas will help some, it will prevent these fellows pouncing out on every helpless steamboat which passes, and makes them uneasy about Little Rock now open to our Gunboats when the waters rise. There is already a pretty fair stage of water in the Arkansas, but not enough for the larger transports and Gun boats.

As usual I have put in an envelope ready for this the rough notes of my Report the original map I had in leading the attack—the improved sketch made after we had taken the place.[4] A letter I hastily wrote for yr. father which I have not time to review and some other little items which I suppose you will file away for the children. I have nothing from you for a long time and cant imagine where yr. letters have gone. I know you have written but your letters have not come. We are all very well but a good many of the men have diarrhea from the waters of the Yazoo. Our men also have now been on board of Boats a long time and this occasions sickness. Since the snow storm has cleared away the weather is warm, but the ground is very muddy indeed, and as you know there is only a narrow strip along the levee where there is any dry land—from here we will proceed to Millikens Bend, whence we will act against Vicksburg as soon as Banks makes his appearance. I expect Grant will come to command in person—McClernand is unfit and is consumed by an inordinate personal ambition.

I take it for granted that Minnie & Willy are still at St. Marys, and that the rest of the children are at home. If you occupy the old house well, if not hire some other[.] Dont move to Cincinati, the perils of the times are too great to be disregarded. Recollect that you have to encounter discussions, quarrels and strife right at home yet. If we can take Vicksburg it will be a grand stride, but my opinion is that the enemy will struggle for it harder than they have for Richmond: it is really as important and nature has done more for its defense. Nothing could be stronger. To effect a lodgment will cost us ten thousand men, and afterwards comes the taking [of] the City. I have yet seen no troops that can be made to assault. We did not do it at the Post. We merely went through the motions. Charley & Hugh will both write you and I suppose Dayton & Hammond have done likewise. Sanger has gone up with prisoners. Dr. McMillan[5] & Hartshorn been taken by Gen. McClernand, and young Capt. Taylor wants to go home. His mother and Sisters are unprotected. War begins to punish all. You must write to Minnie & Willy for me as really I am too much occupied. My love to all, and believe me ever yours most affectionately

Sherman

ALS, InND: Sherman Family Papers.

1. Hugh Ewing had been assigned the command of the Third Brigade, Second Division, Fifteenth Corps, on January 9.

2. Rosecrans had fought at the Battle of Stones River or Murfreesboro on December 31, 1862–January 2, 1863, and held off Confederate forces. He entered Murfreesboro on January 5.

3. Julius Gareschi, Rosecrans's assistant adjutant general, had his head blown off during the first day's fighting.

4. A copy of WTS to Colonel A. Swartz, January 13, 1863, is enclosed. SFP.

5. Charles McMillan (ca. 1825–90) was a major and surgeon in the Seventy-first New York State Militia.

Hd. Qrts. 15th Army Corps
Str. Forest Queen, Napoleon Ark.
Jan. 17. 1863

Maj. Genl. U. S. Grant
Comdg. Dept. of Tenn.
Dear Genl.—

I take a liberty of writing you direct, semi officially. Official Report will convey to you a pretty clear idea of our success at the Post of Arkansas. I infer from a remark made by Genl. McClernand that you have disapproved the step[1]—If I could believe that Banks had reduced Port Hudson & appeared at Vicksburg during our absence I would feel the force of your disapproval, but I feel so assured that we will again be at Vicksburg before *Banks* is there that I cannot think any bad result of this kind can occur—As long as the Post of Ark. existed on our flank with boats to ship cannon & men to the mouth of Arkansas we would be annoyed beyond measure whilst operating below. The capture of the *Blue Wing*[2] was a mere sample. We were compelled to reduce it—Its importance to the enemy cannot be doubted by any one who has seen their preperation & overheard the assertions of its garrison that it was deemed impenetrable—The fort proper was constructed with great care & its armament as good as it could be made The Post of Arkansas could only have been taken by a strong force both by land & water as we took it, & had we given any previous notice it would have been strongly reinforced. They had huts built for full 10,000 men & with 15,000 they could have held the Levee as far down as the Wotril House & our landing would have been resisted—Could we have followed up the capture of Little Rock would have been easy, but even as it is the Enemy up the Arkansas can be held in check by a single wooden gun boat. I assure you when next at Vicksburg I will feel much less uneasiness about our communications—we leave here tomorrow & will be at Millikens Bend or Young's Point the next day, & if Banks has taken Port Hudson & appeared below Vicksburg we can easily communicate across—but I do not expect he will be there for some time—It may be we can put some guns in position along the shore of the Mississippi at a point where I had my pickets which might occupy the attentions of one set of Batteries—& if the Gun Boats will assail the City in front we might possibly land right under the Guns or we may try Harris Bluff, but as to forcing a passage at any point along the Yazoo from its mouth to Harris's Bluff I doubt it, I wish you would come down & see I only fear McClernand may attempt impossibilities. Again if Banks does come up it maybe the approach from the south may be better but all their old defenses of last year look to the south I saw enough to convince me they have about ten field Batteries—& I should estimate their seige lines at fifty. I saw about thirty—The importance of Vicksburg cannot be overestimated & if possible a large force should some how reach the ridge between Black & Yazoo, so as approach from the Rear.

Please give much attention to the quantity of ammunition & tools, I carried down with me 1200 axes, picks & spades, but spite of all efforts many are lost— we built batte[rie]s at Yazoo & up at the Post & you know how details of our careless men neglect took—we have a good deal of real sickness & still more of that sort which develops on the approach of danger.

Our attack on Vicksburg will surely draw thither the Grenada force so that I think you might safely join us & direct our movements. I am with respect your obt. sevt.

W. T. Sherman
Maj. Genl.

Lbk, DNA: RG 94, Records of the Adjutant General's Office, Generals' Books and Papers, William T. Sherman, Letterbook 5; *OR*, I, 17: pt. 2, 570–71.

1. Grant, believing that the Arkansas Post expedition had been McClernand's idea, initially characterized it as a "wild goose chase" and ordered McClernand back to cooperate with Nathaniel Banks in a possible advance on Vicksburg. USG to HWH, January 11, 1863, and USG to McClernand, same date, *PUSG*, 6:209–11.

2. The *Blue Wing,* loaded with ammunition, had been captured on the Mississippi River below Helena following the action at Chickasaw Bluffs.

TO JOHN SHERMAN

Napoleon Ark. Steamer *Forest Queen*,
Jan. 17, 1863

Dear Brother,

I wrote you after my failure on Vicksburg and that we are going against the Post of Arkansas. We made short work of that capturing the place with all its garrison & materiel. It was stronger and better Supplied than I expected, but our force was adequate and we soon reduced the place. Of course I must be satisfied at being beaten at Vicksburg and leave McClernand to get the credit of this success, though I doubt if there be many in this army who believe he conceived the idea or executed it. I led the colums, gave all orders, and entered the place where he came along and managed the prisoners & captured property.

The Gunboats were handled beautifully and without them we would have had hard work, with them it was easy. Our entire loss will be less than 1000. We took 5000 prisoners, killed & wounded some 500, took 16 Guns, ammunition, corn and wagons mules & all sorts of traps of which you will hear enough[1]—My official Report is in, will go up to Grant at Memphis tomorrow and right on to Washington. Halleck will let you see it, and you can understand the whole thing by a glance at the Maps I send along. But McClernands Reports will precede it and of course will be the accepted History. I have not seen his but I know enough of the gnawing desire for fame & notoriety that consumes him and doubt if my name will appear in his Record save to fill some common place blank.

On the supposition that Banks will have taken Port Hudson & reached Vicksburg we start back for that place tomorrow—Of ourselves we cannot take Vicksburg. With Banks & a fleet below us & a fleet above we may make a desperate attempt, but Vicksburg is as strong as Gibraltar, and is of vital importance to the cause of the South. Of course they will fight desperately for it. We must do the same for all are conscious that the real danger of this war, anarchy among our People begins to dawn—The People of the North mistake widely if they Suppose they can have Peace now by opposing this war. My opinion was this war could have been postponed, or so arranged as to detach from the Cause of the Extreme South the moderates of the Middle States, but now tis too late. Either the Southern Gentlemen must rule America or the Yankee. There is no middle ground and it is surely a bitter pill for any decent man to swallow—Both are wrong, but as in all Revolutions Extremes Control, and now abolitionism or proslaveryism are the only questions present to the Country. Mr. Lincoln intended to insult me and the military profession by putting McClernand over me, and I would have quietly folded up my things and gone to St. Louis only I know in times like these all must submit to insult and infamy if necessary. The very moment I think some other is at hand to take my corps I[']ll slide out. Had he ordered a soldier here I would not have breathed a syllable of complaint, but to put a politician who claims a knowlededge he Knows he does not possess & who envies the earned reputation of every subordinate has but one meaning. Were I to go my old command would be dissolved, and I will not introduce disorder in a Country now on the brink of anarchy. I hope the Politicians will not interfere with Halleck. You have driven off McClellan & is Burnside any better.

Buell is displaced. Is Rosecrans any faster. His victory at Murfreesboro is dearly bought—Let Halleck alone and if things dont go to your liking dont charge it to men but to the condition of things. Human power is limited and you cannot appreciate the difficulty of moulding into an homogenous machine, the discordant elements which go to make up our armies. A thousand dollars a day would not pay me for the trouble of managing a Volunteer Army. I never dreamed of so severe a test of my patriotism as being superceded by McClernand, and if I can keep down my tame spirit & live I will claim a virtue higher than Brutus. I rarely see a newspaper & am far behind the times, indeed am not conscious that a Congress sits though I know it must—Do think of the Army & try and give us the means to maintain discipline, prevent desertion, pillage, & absenteeism. Under the present system of mere threats & no punishment, our armies melt away as snow before the Sun. I doubt if Burnside, Rosecrans, Grant & Curtis now have all combined 300,000 in their front Ranks. This army 30,000 a month ago though reinforced by 2400 men is now down to 24,000, though we have lost only 2500 in Battle—sickness & detachments make a perfect stream to the Rear. Blair has a Brigade in my corps[2] and sees now the practice of war, as contrasted with its theory and could give some useful hints on these points[.] I should like to hear from you—affectionately

W. T. Sherman

ALS, DLC: William T. Sherman.
1. Union casualties were 134 killed, 898 wounded, and 29 missing, a total of 1,061. Confederate commander Thomas Churchill would report only 60 killed and 70 or 80 wounded. Sherman would report that 4,791 prisoners of war had been loaded on transports.
2. First Brigade, Fourth Division.

TO ELLEN EWING SHERMAN
Camp near Vicksburg, Jan. 24, 1863
Dearest Ellen,

Last night a boat came down from Memphis and brought me some letters among them yours of Jan. 14,[1] the only one I have received since leaving Memphis. Hugh had however seen you, and told me you were not quite well though you enjoined him to Say otherwise. I can see from your letter the intense anxiety you have and still feel for us all down here, and catching the guesses and surmises of newspaper correspondents, first you are Kept in a perpetual fever. We on the contrary move along, each step connecting with the last so that we do not feel the pressure of feeling as you do. Indeed my own experience is that when danger is present I feel it less than when it is in the remote future or in the past. I think my past letters which I Know have reached Memphis and must get to you safely will describe so fully all events in which I have taken part that you will have no cause of uneasiness. There are things impossible to man, and I know the taking of Vicksburg by my force was an impossibility: but I was on time, make a sufficient attack, drew there troops from Bragg, Pemberton & even Virginia, relieving those points to that extent. Unable to accomplish the desired result I drew off my forces safely and skilfully and then framed the expedition to the post of Arkansas which resulted exactly as I knew it would—The importance of that attack is not yet appreciated but will be. It should have been followed up, but even as it was it stampeded all Arkansas and Curtis may take Little Rock & Van Dorn at his pleasure. Grant fearing that Banks might reach Vicksburg from below was uneasy and hurried us back and here we are again, but he is not here. Of course McClernand who succeeded me at the time when I drew off from Vicksburg, and commanding during the attack on the Post escapes the popular blame of the former and their praise for the latter—but not a soldier in this army, or officer of the Navy who handles a Gun boat but knows who planned all. It was simply absurd to supercede me by McClernand, but Mr. Lincoln knows I am not ambitious to command, and he Knows McClernand is and must gratify him. He will get his fill before he is done. He sent his Chief of Cavalry Colonel Stewart[2] out on some errand yesterday and he was killed. McClernand is now sick in bed and what is doing is left to me as usual—I know one fact well, that when danger is present, or important steps are necessary Sherman is invariably called for, but in unloading steamboats repairing roads &c. &c. I get provoking, short, curt orders to do thus and so. I think Grant will be down soon and already one Division of about 6000 men have come from Memphis. We have enough men for anything we can do. The trouble is to get on land—to get ashore where we can fight—Vicksburg is very strong & it will be only be a dreadful sacrifice we can get a footing & then the Battle. The original plan was best. Grant to come down by Land—Banks to come up and me to enter Yazoo, but cooperation at such distances and over such long lines is almost an impossibility. We are again landed on the West Bank of the Mississipi and are opening and widening the Ditch which was dug last summer to endeavor to turn the River. But I have not much faith in the Scheme though I will do all I can to help it—Hugh has a Brigade in Morgan L. Smiths Division now commanded by Stuart—he is on the Right at the lower end of the Ditch. Stuarts old Brigade is at the middle of the Ditch or Center, and Giles A. Smiths Brigade[3] in which is the Battalion of Regulars is on the Left or upper end of the Ditch. These three Brigades are working to widen the ditch & deepen it. The River is rising and already the ditch has a foot of water moving through it. I have batteries at each flank and at this moment the one at Hughs end is firing, I suppose at a Rebel Steamboat attempting to go down the River. Steeles Division of my Corps is on the Levee below Hugh. I will get to him this afternoon two Rifles 30 pounders, which will effectually check any boats from coming to or departing from Vicksburg. The town is in full view, and we are within range of their Rifle Guns, but thus far both are sparing of powder as the deep Mississipi intervenes and neither can reach the other. They wont cross over, and we cant, without landing on Yazoo Island, which we attempted once and I doubt if McClernand is anxious to repeat the experiment. I am now in a tent, good bed and Hill is very watchful of all my wants—he is very faithful and will earn whatever Reward you promised him. Charley is very well. I have not seen him today but I sent him the letter you enclosed for him which he will be glad to receive. All the officers & men are well excepting Capt. Wainwright[4] who looks to me like a Kind of indifferent fellow—Major Chase[5] is the worse of all but I cannot order him away, and nothing but a court marital can remove him and there is no time for such things now. In war we must have patience. I suppose the Country is conscious that we have a big job on hand. Rosecrans success is not conclusive—that Battle has to be fought again—In the East they seem to be at a Stand Still—We had a heavy snow Storm up the Arkansas, and last night it rained hard, & mud is without bottom. My love to our Dear Children & believe me ever yours,

W. T. Sherman

ALS, InND: Sherman Family Papers.

1. EES wrote her husband on January 14 saying that she had been sick but was feeling better. She had gotten none of his letters and only newspaper reports about his movements. She was particularly worried about how the Thirteenth U.S. Infantry was faring and told him that Hugh would soon be joining him. SFP.

2. Colonel Warren Stewart of the Fifteenth Illinois Volunteer Cavalry.

3. Colonel Giles A. Smith (1829–76), Morgan L. Smith's brother, led the First Brigade, Second Division of Sherman's Fifteenth Corps, which included the First Battalion of the Thirteenth U.S. Infantry.

4. Captain Samuel A. Wainwright (d. 1899) had received his commission in May 1861.

5. Major Daniel Chase (d. 1877), USA, a Mexican War veteran, was commissioned a major in October 1861 and would receive the rank of brevet colonel for his actions at Arkansas Post.

TO ETHAN A. HITCHCOCK

Hd. Qrts. 15th Army Corps
Genl. *E. A. Hitchcock*   Camp near Vicksburg Jany. 25. 63
Prest. Board for Revising Acts of War &c.
Dear Genl.,

Your circular letter of Dec. 22 reached me last night & as I hear a steamboat will start up river at once I will prepare a hasty reply—I wish I had time to look over the articles of war seriatum & comment on each, but have not time or even the facilities of writing what little I can.

One thing is certain: Times are changed since our present military code was enacted. Then a Law was a command to do or abstain from doing some specific act & I suppose there a common sentiment pervaded the Country & People that the Law was obligatory & must be respected—now Public opinion General or Local is the ruling Power & must be denominated Law, and it will be for you to discover whether you shall frame a just & fair martial order, & effect the military world to conform or whether you will make a code to conform to Public opinion.

Another thing is equally certain, our present "Articles of War" are a dead letter. I believe at this moment of time there are more technical "Deserters" from the Army than actual soldiers present for duty & yet the death Penalty has not yet been enforced in a single case that I know of—Sentinels from the Potomac to the Pacific sit down—lay aside their arms & accoutrements & even go to sleep within sight of a vigilant enterprising Enemy & yet there is no actual remedy.

The Law is good enough, but still the fact glaringly exists that Courts will not inflict adequate punishment or devise a remedy.

Absenteeism in every concievable form exists and all the blows aimed at it in orders, fall harmless—I think I am safe in saying that at no time since this war has begun has one half its proper force been available for Battle. Now these evils result not from want of good & sufficient laws & articles of War but from their non-execution. Can this be remedied? I say no not until our People are born again of Fire & humiliation, until conviction penetrates every breast that our national existence, honor & safety have been & are being imperiled by too much individual liberty & too great a laxity in enforcing Law. Until the nation reaches that stage in the revolution now in progress we must work on with our material as we find it.

1st To assure attendance of Officers & men with their actual Regts. Corps & companies I would suggest

> To a soldier absent without authority, no pay, clothing, or claim of Pension or Bounty (like a hired man)
> To an officer the same
> To a soldier absent sick—pay privilege of hospital if claimed, & pension if sickness arose from exposure in service, no bounty, or pay if he declines to go to a General Hospital. To an absent sick officer, half pay, privilege of hospital at actual cost of subsistence.
> To a wounded soldier or officer full pay bounty & everything with privilege of going home till ordered on some duty becoming the nature of the wound.

A captain to keep a Judgmt. Book in which he or the actual commander of a Company may enter up Judgment against any member of his company, commissioned officer included to the extent of fines for ⅔ of any one months pay.

A Colonel or Commander of a Regt. to keep a Judgmt. Book in which on a hearing a fine may be entered up against any officer or man to the extent of ⅔ of any one months pay, & inflict corporal punishment to the extent of one month labor, confinement, &c.

A Field Officer to receive Judgmts. of Captains & Brigadiers those of Colonels.

Companies, Regiments, Brigades & Divisions in their aggregated both for general acts of trespass plunder & destruction of private & public property not traceable to individuals, or on order of the commanding officer the value of such general damage to be ascertained by a Board of Survey duly appointed & charged pro rata on the muster rolls.

I admit this is a violation of the usual principles of individual responsibility, But government organized companies, Regiment, Brigade & Divisions for the very purpose of control, & yet they are used to cover up some of the grossest outrage that ever disgrace a nation.

Plunder, arson & devastation mark the progress of our armies, & I see no signs of discrimination. On the contrary the highest officers are becoming callous & giving up all efforts to prevent their commission by the futility of all efforts.

Houses are fired under our very feet & though hundreds know why & who did it, yet the comd'g Genl. cannot get a clue. Soldiers in plundering & burning make no discrimination between friends or foe. Even Negroes are plundered of their blankets, chickens, corn meal & their poorest garments—I believe fines may be enforced; every serious punishment not.

Increase ad infinitum the executive power of Captains Colonels Brigadiers & Maj. Generals—Abolish Court Martials save to perpetuate testimony, & though injustice may be done in some instances, yet in the long run, quick, prompt executive action would result—any worthless officer can escape by the dodge of a record Trial, but he could not escape the searching inquiry of a good Colonel or General. No Colonel or General would make a manifestly unjust sentence, but being armed with power he would make his Regt. or Corps obedient prompt & a fit machine to execute. These powers might be subject to reviews of higher authorities & limited to times of War & Rebellion—Colonels & Captains should have the power of promoting from one Grade to a vacancy in the next higher for cause or Choice, limiting his sphere of course to his own command.

I am writing without books of any kind on a board across my knees & I know General Hitchcock will catch my meaning & elaborate it to the proper shape & purpose.

I know that this would involve radical change part for Congress & part for the Dept. of War, but I understand your design to be to compose a whole system consistent in all its parts. I repeat the present articles of war are antiquated and based on the principal of "Fear of pain." If we had tried to breed the present race anew & bring them up in the fear of the Law then "Death or such other punishment as a Court Martial may inflict" would have a restraining influence, but tell one of these volunteers "this poor woman has a safe guard, dont take her corn, she is a good union woman, with a son in the Federal Army" the answer is, "cant help it, train is not up—horse has no corn, must take it"—This occurs daily & no Court Martial will execute the only prescribed penalty, Death—We have sentences of fines of $3 for sleeping on Post, occasionally a few hours of walking a path with a billet of wood or placard—but the trouble is what little discipline there is now in the army arises from pay & advantage & not from fear of punishment, and I doubt our physical ability to change the nature of things during the first volumes of this War. During the subsequent era of the War, sad experience may bring us to the wisdom of our "Predecessors" a direction Young America don't look to for wisdom & stability.

There should be an article of War disqualifying from the future privilege of voting in any national question or holding any office of profit & trust any deserter, or any one discharged on Sug'n's Certificate except in case of wounds or disability incurred in actual services.

Certain national offices should also be reserved for soldiers who have served a full period of three years, such as Marshals of Districts, Keepers of Light-Houses, Ordnance Sergeants & Store keepers, surveyors & all places in the customs except the higher offices, Tax Collectors &c.

Officers & Citizens who make up Companies of old men & boys & should be liable to fine & imprisonment, to make good to Government its losses for such pay, clothing & bounty as have been paid to this class. The records of the War Dept. must show millions paid to men whose names were merely en-rolled to make up a minimum & create a company & Regiment for the benefit of some Captain or Colonel.

Of course we want soldiers but all our calculations have been baffled on promise of numbers which on arrival proved fallacies—so that a regiment of first called 1000 numbers 700 then 500, & now we estimate them at 200 or 300 fighting men & 500 for rations. Brigades now are not equal to Regts., & Divisions are small Brigades.

Far cheaper to the Government to pay $25 or $30 per month to an actual live strong man able to do his work & consuming only one Ration & nothing to the old & feeble, young & sickly, who eat full rations, load down baggage trains, & swell the impediments to the state of absolute "stalling" and some of the most serious mistakes of the War have arisen from Generals having been charged with 20, 50, or 100,000 men which existed only on paper, or as sick to be hauled or left by the Road Side.

Pay the real working soldier twenty five dollars a month & a ration clothing to be charged—The absent without authority nothing & deprive him of ability to vote or hold office & make a mark on him & the sick, his ration and say $10 a month to cover his wants & of course hospital treatment.

Make Murder thieving & all well defined civil crimes, military crimes also & cure a serious defect in our present code, thereby obviating the necessity for Military Commissions, & court martial to limited to specific cases as to times of Peace.

I find I am repeating & I know you have enough to do without reading my hand writing—I still am unambitious of this War, am bandied about as all sorts of fool, ass & crazy by "our special correspondent on the spot" still I find myself always in the advance, & when danger threatens & others despair, they lean on Sherman—I filled my whole part at Vicksburg, was on time, in the manner prescribed by me, and it is absurd to hold me responsible for not taking Vicksburg *alone* but a few weeks & months will show that double & treble my force are requisite & then not sure of success. I planned & executed the move on the Post of Arkansas, but another had arrived at the critical moment & take the honor—I will be rejoiced if Mr. Lincoln shall say, "*Young man we can do without you go home.*" Indeed I would. There is no happiness to me in this mass of selfishness & I believe I serve my country with as pure a feeling as actuates any mortal, though I despise many of the tools that rule & control me. Ever Your friend and Admirer

Sherman

Lbk, DNA: RG 94, Records of the Adjutant General's Office, Generals' Books and Papers, William T. Sherman, Letterbook 5.

CHAPTER 7

January 25, 1863–March 16, 1863

For Sherman, the winter of 1863 proved especially bitter. He grew despondent about the war effort to the point that once more he spoke of resigning his commission, something he always mentioned when he was extremely frustrated. Convinced that the Northern people were not willing to pay the price to win the war, he lashed out at politicians, the press, and the general public. Nor did he have any confidence that Vicksburg would fall. Part of Sherman's lament was rooted in personal frustration. Although the press celebrated the victory at Arkansas Post, McClernand garnered its plaudits. Meanwhile, Sherman continued to suffer criticism for the defeat at Chickasaw Bluffs. Franc B. Wilkie informed readers of the *New York Times* that Sherman's choice of landing sites demonstrated his "madness"; an editorial elaborated, characterizing the action as "the insane attack." These were loaded words to Sherman; another report claimed that Sherman was "confined to his state room perfectly insane."[1]

One account in particular infuriated Sherman. On January 18 the *New York Herald* published Thomas W. Knox's description of the battle. Knox did not restrict his criticisms of Sherman to the battle proper; he also assailed the general's decision to block the sending of newspaper accounts north, claiming that had Sherman acted against the Confederates with the same vigor with which he persecuted reporters, he might have won the battle. Although Ellen warned him that he "might as well attempt to control the whirlwind as the newspaper mania," Sherman sought revenge. He ordered Knox arrested and planned to try him before a court-martial as a spy—a measure far beyond the usual practice followed by other generals of excluding or even arresting reporters they deemed troublesome. It mattered not that Knox had tried to forestall the general by admitting that his account may have been flawed, for he had subsequently told Sherman, "Of course, General Sherman, I had no feeling against you personally, but you are regarded the enemy of our set, and we must in self-defense write you down."[2]

Sherman got his trial, although in pursuing his case he had cause to wonder whether one of his own subordinates, Frank P. Blair of the powerful Blair family, had fed the reporter comments critical of Sherman. Although he was successful in getting the court to drop Sherman's charge that his criticism of officers had aided the enemy, Knox found himself defending his accounts and calling upon other officers (including Blair) to testify about his loyalty and competence. In fact, Sherman's theory of trying Knox as a spy was flawed from the beginning because Knox filed his report *after* the battle and the general could offer no proof that the enemy had learned anything from it. The reporter also argued that his pass from Grant (Sherman's superior) cleared him of charges that he had defied Sherman's orders concerning the transmission of information on military movements through the mails, which in any case applied only to army personnel and people in government employ. These proved less compelling to the court, although its members acquitted the reporter of all charges except one that cited him with violation of War Department directives as well as Sherman's own orders. As punishment Knox was banished outside the lines of Grant's army.[3]

The result did little to placate Sherman, for it did nothing to advance his desire to treat reporters as potential spies, but it did for the moment chill criticism of him in the press. This was little compensation, for as winter came to an end he remained convinced that Vicksburg was unassailable. Both his career and his soldiers seemed mired in the wetlands north and west of that city; in late March he had to rescue an expedition up Steele's Bayou that had become entangled in tree branches and vines—a task that so preoccupied him that his normally active pen remained mostly unused during this period.

1. John F. Marszalek, *Sherman's Other War: The General and the Civil War Press* (Memphis, 1981), 121.
2. Ibid., 123–28.
3. Ibid., 126–38.

TO JOHN SHERMAN

Camp near Vicksburg Jan. 25, 1863

Dear Brother,

I received yours of January 2[1] today and being in camp with some leisure hasten to answer. I shall be glad to meet Genl. Banks on many accounts, because of his known inteligence and high character, and because we have been long expecting him. I was hurried down the River with positive orders to get away from Memphis Dec. 18 to cooperate with Grant to come down by land, and Banks to ascend the River. I was on time and made every effort to carry Vicksburg alone but unsuccessfully. Hearing nothing from Banks or Grant and being superceded by McClernand I proposed we should go to the Arkansas and attack the Post, from which the Enemy threatened our Rear and Line of Communications. We succeeded perfectly there and General Grant came down and met us at Napoleon and hurried us back to Vicksburg on the theory that Banks might be here disappointed at our non appearance—So here we are again but not a word of Banks.

This time instead of landing up to Yazoo we have landed on the Louisiana side and I occupy a neck of low ground enclosed with a high Levee directly in front of Vicksburg—Last summer when Vicksburg was invested by our troops from below a canal was dug across a narrow neck with the purpose of turning the River so as to leave Vicksburg out in the Cold. The River is now rising rapidly and already fills the Canal, which however is a narrow ditch—the water flows across it but thus far it shows no symptom of cutting a channel, but on the contrary threatens to overflow the low ground embraced in the Levee. All my soldiers are busy day and night in throwing up a Levee on the inside of this Canal to prevent the water overflowing us. My Right extends along the Levee below Vicksburg, and I have some Guns below which will prevent the Enemys boats coming up to town. Since I broke the Railroad leading west, most of the necessary supplies to Vicksburg have come from the Red River by water, and we now stop this, but as they hold Port Hudson preventing Banks coming up, and Vicksburg prevents our Boats going down they hold substantially a long reach of the River embracing the mouth of Red River. Last night my extreme Right Brigade Blairs captured a ferry Boat which came in for wood, not suspecting our presence so we have also one boat below Vicksburg—I have not much faith in the Canal. It starts after the Current has been turned and I doubt if the Canal will draw in a volume & depth of water sufficient to cut a new channel and if it do the Enemy will simply shift his Guns to Warrenton a point on the same Range of hills, below the mouth of our Canal—At last we must attack the enemy in his strong position, outnumbering us in every sense, in men in Guns, and holding a position stronger than Gibraltar. It is expecting too much of us to capture the place. The fact is I am beginning to form the same contemptuous opinion of the American People entertained by all the world—Boasting of its superior strength & resources, with your cities and country full of strong healthy young men you send us few in numbers to do the work of ten times our numbers. This Mississipi Expedition is a good illustration of our National Character. For two years the Cry has been the North West will rise as one man and its millions of hardy men will pour down the Mississipi as an avalanche and sweep all before it. After two years boasting the Expedition starts composed of less than thirty thousand men, less than the local population of Vicksburg and adjacent counties. I feel assured at Vicksburg they have double our force. Although Mr. Lincoln intended to glorify McClernand I guess he will have no reason to rejoice. We are of no use here now unless Banks can pass Port Hudson and Grant cannot reinforce us to an Extent of our 18,000 men. If Banks can break through the obstructions at Port Hudson and make his appearance here we ought then to take Vicksburg, but [if] as the Secessionists claim, Port Hudson is too much for him then we will be sucking our thumbs here. We must get on land before we can fight. That was my attempt and the point I chose is the only one between Vicksburg & Haines Bluff—We may attempt the latter and I think it is the softest place, but on this side of the River we do no good whatever, for the Mississipi is an ugly stream to ford at this season of the year.

Unless you enact a Law denying to all citizens between the ages of 18 & 45 who do not enlist and serve three years faithfully, the right of suffrage or to hold office after the war is over you will have trouble. The Army growls a good deal at the apathy of the nation, at home quiet, comfortable and happy yet pushing them forward on all sorts of desperate expeditions. Newspapers cant now turn armies against their leaders. Every officer & soldier knows I pushed the attack on Vicksburg as far as they wanted to venture and if others think different they naturally say, why not come down and try. The early delusions of the War are now passed and I doubt if even Seward would again attempt to put down the Rebellion, break its back bone, clean his way to the sea make commerce follow the flag &c. &c. pretty generalities all in six short months with 75,000 paper soldiers. No, you must now see that to subdue the Rebellion you must obliterate a whole Race, our equals in courage, resources, and determination. Two years have passed and the Rebel flag still haunts our national capitol—our armies enter the vast Rebel territory and the war closes in behind scarcely leaving a furrow mark behind. The utmost we can claim is that our enemy respects our power to do them physical harm more than they did at first, but as to loving us any more it was idle ever to claim it—our armies are devastating the land and it is sad to See the destruction that attends our progress—we cannot help it. Farms disappear, houses are burned & plundered and every living animal killed and eaten. General officers make feeble efforts to stay the disorder but it is idle. Our soldiers are lawless and in time will turn upon their own country. It is possible the small remnants of Regiments that still keep up the name may acquire the habits of soldiers and form a Nucleus around which the Country may cluster in the day of anarchy that must follow. The South abounds in corn, cattle and provisions and their prowess in manufacturing shoes & cloth for their soldiers is wonderful. They are as well supplied as we, and they have an abundance of the best cannon, arms & ammunition. In long Range Cannon they rather excel us, and their Regiments are armed with the very best Enfield Rifles and cartridges put up at Glasgow, Liverpool and their many southern armories, and I still say they have now as large armies in the Field as we—All their people are in the army, and they evince a devotion to their cause more ardent than we—They give up

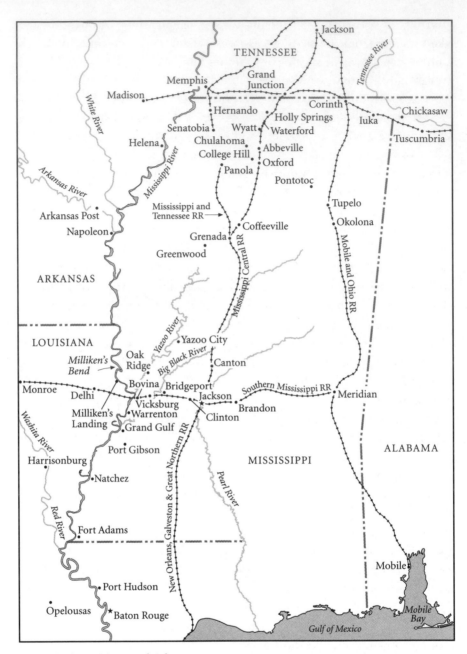

Mississippi, Louisiana, and Arkansas

cheerfully all they have. I still see no end or even the beginning of the End. By detaching Arkansas, & Louisiana from connection with the East we will accomplish a major first result—far more important than the Conquest of Virginia, but the deuce is we pass on & the People rise up behind us more hostile than Ever, and attack our Boats and wagon trains. I will have Henry Sherman put on the staff of some one of my Generals. I will take good care of him. He is a fine young fellow.

You lay low—dont commit yourself too Soon—Let things foment. The early actors & heros of this war will be swept away, and those who study its progress, its developments and divine its course and destiny will be most appreciated— We are in for the war and must fight it out, cost what it may. As to making popularity out of it, it is simply ridiculous and all who attempt it will be swept as chaff before the wind. If you see Mr. Lincoln tell him I appreciate the reproof of ordering McClernand to command me, and that I will count it an honor when he says he can spare my services. yr. affectionate Brother

W. T. Sherman

ALS, DLC: William T. Sherman.

1. From JS, January 2, 1863, DLC: WTS. JS told his brother he was watching his progress with interest because he felt the opening of the Mississippi River was of the utmost importance and would allow the Union to blockade the Confederacy. He praised Banks—"a cool brave, self reliant man" even though he lacked experience—and added that WTS and Banks were the two best officers the Union army had: "I have always believed in you even when you were under a cloud." JS expressed his disgust with the weakness and pusillanimity of those in power in Washington and his doubts about Lincoln's ability but not his sincerity. He thought that Chase, Seward, and Stanton all had ability but were being hindered. JS closed by saying he did not favor the bankruptcy bill and did not know why his brother thought that he did.

TO EDWIN M. STANTON

Head Qtrs. 15th Army Corps.
Camp near Vicksburg Jan. 25th 1863.

Hon. E. M. Stanton
Secretary of War, Washington, D.C.
Sir

A Letter addressed from Memphis Tenn. by a Mrs. Jane Seymore of Buffalo to you on the subject of the conduct of the eight and ninth Missouri Regts. has been referred to me for a report. There was no such regiment as the ninth Missouri at Memphis, and as the eight Missouri has been ordered in to the Field Mrs. Seymore doubtless feels better. The irregularities which offend her Buffalo-sense being removed from her immediate hearing are of little consequence to her or the country *now* I suppose.

Mrs. Seymore has fallen into a common {error} in saying it was useless to complain of a whole Regiment to Brig. Gen. Smith or Maj. Genl. Sherman. We naturally demanded more specific complaint against incendiary acts than a mere vague Suspicions that the 8th Mo. did all iniquitous things, where twenty other Regiments were camped round about Memphis, when Six Thousand vagabonds refugee Negroes were hanging about and the city itself infested by gangs of thieves & incendiaries turned loose upon the world and sheltered in their deeds of darkness by charging them on soldiers—Neither Genl. Morgan L. Smith or myself ever failed to notice a specific complaint against any soldier of our command If accompanied by reasonable proof—but we did and rightfully too resent a mere general charge that every fire originating from careless chimneys, careless arrangment of stovepipes & the designing acts of wicked incindiaries should without even one attempt at proof be charged to the 8th Missouri—That Regiment is one of the bravest & best disciplined in our service & being composed mostly of younger & energetic men from St. Louis, is somewhat famous for its acts of fun, frolic, mischief & even crime, with a perfect skill in evading detection & pursuit.

They are lawless & violent & like all our Volunteer soldiers have for years been taught that the people, the masses, the majority are "king" & can do no wrong. They are no worse than other volunteers, all of whom come to us filled with the popular idea that they must enact war, that they must clean out the Secesh, must waste & not protect their property, must burn waste & destroy— Just such people as Mrs. Seymore have taught this creed, sung this song & urged on our men to these disgraceful acts, & it is such as Morgan L. Smith & W. T. Sherman who have been combatting this foul doctrine, that must ere it is checked, lay our whole country in ashes & ruin—I would delight to have the aid & assistance of even such weak "vassels" as Mrs. Jane Seymour did not the hypocrite stick out in every line of her letter, which I confess I was amazed to find received even the partial consideration of the Hon. Secy. Though our troops in Memphis did acts of which I was ashamed, yet I know that Genl. Smith & I did more to afford substantial protection to Life, liberty & property in Memphis during our sojourn there, than all the Mrs. Seymores of Buffalo multiplied by fifty thousand.

During my administration of affairs in Memphis I know it raised from a condition of death & gloom & darkness to one of life & comparative prosperity. Its streets & stores & hotels & dwellings were sad & deserted as I entered it & when I left it life & business prevailed & over 1400 enrolled union men paraded its streets boldly & openly carrying the Banners of our Country—No citizen Union or secesh will deny but that I acted lawfully, firmly & fairly, & that substantial justice prevailed with even balance—I do feel their testimony better than the hearsay of any Buffalo spinster or would be notoriety. I am with respect yr. obt. sevt.

W. T. Sherman

Maj. Genl.

Lbk, DNA: RG 94, Records of the Adjutant General's Office, Generals' Books and Papers, William T. Sherman, Letterbook 5.

TO ELLEN EWING SHERMAN

Camp before Vicksburg, Jan. 28, 1863

Dearest Ellen,

Today I received by a Mr. Conyer a letter and pair of socks, also a letter of the 22 very late with one from Theresa for Charley. I sent it up to Charleys camp but he came down in the meantime and not having got his letters he started back to his Camp forthwith. He will be glad to hear from home. I suppose we dont make due allowance for the anxiety of all at home and it may be well. Every soldier has his Circle of family & friends and all watch his Career with the same painful solicitude you do ours and cannot look upon war as you will soon be able to do, say Vicksburg will cost us 10,000—Port Hudson 5000, Jackson 30,000 & so on plain mathematical certainties that every military man knew years ago but kept his peace. The Politician think results can be had by breath, but how painfully it begins to come home to the American People that the war which all have striven so hard to bring on and so few to avert is to cost us so many thousands of lives[.] Indeed do I wish I had been killed long since, better that than Struggle with the curses and maledictions of every woman that has a son or brother to die in any army with which I chance to be associated. Of course Sherman is responsible. Seeing so clearly into the future I do think I ought to get away. The presidents placing McClernand here, and the dead Set to ruin me for McClernands personal Glory would afford me a good chance to Slide out and escape the storms and troubles yet in reserve for us. Here we are at Vicksburg on the wrong side of the river trying to turn the Mississipi by a ditch, a pure waste of human labor. Grant has come and Prime is here, and they can figure it out, but the canal wont do—We must carry out the plan fixed up at Oxford—A large army must march down from Oxford to Grenada, and so on to the rear of Vicksburg—and another army must be here to cooperate with the Gunboats at the right time. Had Grant been within 60 miles of Vicksburg or Banks near I could have broken the Line of Chickasaw Bayou, but it was never dreamed by me that I could take the place alone. McClernand or Grant will not undertake it. Not a word of Banks. I doubt if he has left or can leave, or has any orders to leave New Orleans. Therefore here we are to sit in the mud till spring & summer and maybe another year. Soldiers will soon clamor for motion, life—anything rather than Canal digging. The newspapers are after me again. I published an order they must not come along on pain of being treated as spies.[1] I am now determined to test the question. Do they rule on the Comdg. General. If they Rule I quit. I have ordered the arrest of one, shall try him & if possible execute him as a spy.[2] They publish all the data for an enemy, and it was only by absolute secrecy that we could get to the Post of Arkansas without their getting ahead. They did reveal an attempt to attack Hains Bluff—I will never again command an army in America if we must carry along paid spies. I will banish myself to some foreign country first—I Shall notify Mr. Lincoln on this if he attempt to interfere with the Sentence of any court ordered by me. If he wants an army he must conform to the well established Rules of Military nations and not attempt to keep up the open Rules of Peace. The South at the Start did these things and the result has been they move their forces from Virginia to Mississipi and back without a breath Spoken or written.

Hugh is on the Right flank of the Ditch or Canal—his men are very quiet & well behaved—The Regulars are with Morgan Smiths old Brigade and are near the left or north end of the Ditch. I was until noon today in camp, but have just moved into a house—the weather has been frosty and Hammond & the Clerks made so much fuss about Cold hands they could not write that I moved into a house which a lady vacated (Mrs. Groves) and asked me to occupy to Save it from destruction. The fences, barns, corn cribs cotton & everything is gone but the house and she wont recognize it if she ever return. I am just beyond the reach of Rifle Guns from Vicksburg. Our men are working on the Canal, but mostly making levees to prevent the canal overflowing the ground of our camps. If the River rises 8 feet more it will be all over the Country except Levees and we would have to take to trees. There is no high land west of us nearer than Dilki 50 miles west, with these broad deep bayous between Walnut, Tensas, and Macon, so that we may some fine morning be all afloat—The River rose 18 inches for 2 days, then 16, then 8½ and yesterday 5¾. I dont think it will rise more than 1 foot more on this rise and we can stand four (4). I felt much concerned about your being sick, but hope you are now much better[.] Indeed am I rejoiced that our children continue strong and healthy. We have abundant reason to be proud of them. I will write to Minnie & Willy by this mail Yrs. ever

Sherman

ALS, InND: Sherman Family Papers.

1. General Orders No. 8, issued at Memphis (copy in DLC: WTS), decreed that the expedition to Vicksburg was "purely military" and limited to army personnel; only those citizens employed as part of a crew, servants, or nurses to the sick would be allowed south of

Helena; any citizens violating this order could be conscripted immediately or be forced to work as deckhands or in some other menial capacity without wages until the boat returned to Memphis. "Any persons whatever, whether in the service of the United States or Transports, found making reports for publication, which might reach the enemy, giving them information, aid and comfort, will be arrested and treated as spies."

2. For Sherman's efforts to arrest Thomas W. Knox, a correspondent for the *New York Herald*, see WTS to USG, February 3, 1863, below.

TO JOHN SHERMAN

Camp before Vicksburg, Jan. 31, 1863.

Dear Brother,

Several Boats have come down of late and brought newspapers which as I expected put in me all the infamy of our failure at Vicksburg & give McClernand all the merit of our success at the Post of Arkansas. Though ever pushed in the advance I find I am to be arraigned before the Public for the mishaps and mischances of all. I have just read the accounts in the *New York Herald*, whose correspondent Blair carries along for self glorification, and against the experience of the military world. It seems Col. Markland an agent of the Post office Dept.[1] received budgets of correspondence which he sent to my camp in the woods on Yazoo Island. I paid no attention to it but directed it to go back to the mail, never looking at it, indeed I had no time. This is the basis of the newspaper correspondents assault on me. None of my officers complained of want of orders, each had his orders clear and distinct and I send you copies of them to show that such was the case. At the point when the attack was made, Morgans whole Division was present also Steeles, two of my strongest Divisions. Stuarts & half of A. J. Smiths were on the immediate Right crossing at another point. These were the only places where it was practicable to cross the Bayou. There was a perfect concert of action throughout, though it is possible the Correspondents on the Steamboats to the Rear did not have Copies of my orders.

I am not willing to Stoop to the vile practice of keeping this class of Spies about me. They have done infinite mischief in this war, and the enemy by suppressing them has a vast advantage over us. Every movement of ours is revealed before we can act—large bodies cannot be moved like individuals, & intelligence can reach the Enemy faster than Steamboats or legs can carry an army to any point. By means of these correspondents and their Spies in Memphis the Enemy Knows Exactly our forces, its organization and its purposes.

I suppose it is useless to attempt to prevent them, but with our armies thronged by such spies I do not hope for success. It is impossible. We stole a march on them by feigning to land at Millikens Bend, but had they had a chance the Little Rock forces could have reached the Post of Arkansas.

If our Government be of such character that we are to be assailed by this class of men on any and all occasions I for one will no longer serve it. I will take my own time & opportunity and quit. There are now plenty of experienced officers skilled in war, so that the reasons for my reentering the Service no longer exist and I can properly ask retirement. I will wait a reasonable time and then resign.

I believe there is not an officer or soldier in my command but that has confidence in me, but what avails that when a malicious individual hanging about as a spy can accuse me before the world and be believed rather than me. Grant Banks and Sherman were to cooperate. I was the only one on time, and I think I did all that was possible. One movement brought down all of Pembertons forces from the north & Kirby Smiths from the East, Meridian and we then turned and opened the Arkansas. The expedition has achieved more than any other equal number of men in the same time and at less cost of life. We are again here before Banks is heard of. If others can achieve better success let them do it—McClernand is now here, and Grant with increased forces, and yet why not attempt Vicksburg. We are on the opposite side of the River digging a canal which will not divert the Mississipi, and Gen. Grant has to retain the fleet of steamers lest the River continue to rise and drown us out. It is Easy enough to find fault. Let others do better.

Go to the War Dept.—see all official Dispatches & Admiral Porters and see his estimate of men & things. I wish to serve the Cause & Government. Others look to their own Glorification. They will have enough of it, and I am satisfied. I will serve a Government of Law, but not one of mere public opinion, with such tools to manufacture it as infest our armies. I am as ever affectionately

W. T. Sherman

ALS, DLC: William T. Sherman.

1. Colonel Absalom H. Markland of Kentucky, a childhood acquaintance of USG's, was special agent of the Post Office Department for the Southwest.

TO DAVID DIXON PORTER

Hd. Qrts. 15th Army Corps
near Vicksburg Feby. 1, 1863

Admiral D. D. Porter
Comdg. Miss. Squadron
Dear Sir,

The northern press stimulated by parties here, have sown broadcast over our country the most malicious charge and insinuations against me personally in consequence of my failure to reduce Vicksburg. I have some friends that will I know be sadly troubled by these reports. You observed the embar-

kation of my troops, their movement to the point of attack & their reimbarka-
tion. You know whether I took all possible means to gain information &
whether I acted with promptness or otherwise.

For the satisfaction of my Brother John Sherman in the Senate I would
solicit a few lines from you on the matter generally whether to your knowledge I brought my forces in good condition & well supplied to Youngs Point.
Whether I delayed unnecessarily, whether the point of disembarkation was
not the best and only one afforded me & whether I did not meet all difficulties
promptly as they arose.

Whether I did not propose to you the attack on the Post of Arkansas as the
best possible use we could make of time whilst awaiting the arrival of Grant &
Banks & generally whether I acted the part of an intelligent officer or that of
an insane fool. With the utmost confidence in your judgement I will ever
remain Your friend & Servant

W. T. Sherman
Maj. Genl.

Lbk, DNA: RG 94, Records of the Adjutant General's Office, Generals' Books and Papers, William T. Sherman, Letterbook 5; *OR*, I, 17: pt. 2, 882.

TO FRANK P. BLAIR

(private.)
Camp, Near Vicksburg, Feb. 2, 1863

Brig. Gen. F. P. Blair
Dear Sir,

Yours of last Evening handed me in person at your Hd. Qrs. was carefully
perused on my reaching my Room, and I express my satisfaction at the full
and frank answers you have made to my interrogations.[1] Whether under
similar circumstances a next time you will answer in an equally friendly spirit
need not now arrest my thoughts as I do not expect there will be a next time or
if so should I ask you fair plain direct questions again under similar circumstances I believe you will give equally fair and plain answers. I am willing to
admit that I do owe you an explanation of the reason why after your full &
frank disclosures in the presence of Genls. Steele & Stuart I should renew the
subject. I could hardly believe that a white man could be so false as this fellow
Knox. He certainly came down in the Continental, on which for a month you
and Steele had your Head Quarters: he dated his paper then eulogized every
officer, & man of that Division and did not even attempt to approach the
Truth as to any body else, did not Know or care to Know that Burbridge[2]
commanded the Expedition from Millikens Bend, ignored Gen. A. J. Smith or
spoke of him as "frittering away his time" &c. and indeed abused every body

but the officers of the 4th Division. Officers of the other three Divisions could & had come to but one Conclusion that he was in your pay or favor. I now know otherwise, and am glad that your letter enables me to put the fellow where he really belongs as a "spy & infamous dog." I shall show & read your letter to Dr. McMillan, Col. Smith and others that their minds may be disabused on the same point.

At a very early period I took ground that such men were spies. Take this case of Knox. He published in New York the first account of our attempt on Vicksburg, and now to my face tells me if he Knox "cannot get at the Truth he must publish falsehood." In other words a Commander in addition to his already manifold labors must unfold to "every correspondent" (for a distinction would surely be unfair) his orders, plans and the developments. Knox has published his article as coming from a Division Head Quarters. This publication is in Vicksburg and the Commander can tell within 1000 our present Force: but worse yet for our cause Van Dorn now is at Holly Springs en route northward, knows our force, and the chances of Vicksburg as against us, and in full confidence goes on his work of regaining ground we have fought for several times. I do know the day will come when every officer will demand the execution of this Class of Spies, and without further hesitation I declare if I am forced to look to the New York Herald for my Law & Master, instead of the Laws and Constituted Authorities of the United States my military career is ended.

If it be so, that the People of the United States demand and must have news, true if possible but still news—their condition is likened to that of the drunkard whose natural tastes have become so vitiated that nought but Brandy will satisfy—and they must pay the penalty. I for one am no longer willing to tamely to bear their misrepresentations and inferences and shall treat Knox and all others of his type as "Spies and Defamers." I am with respect your friend

W. T. Sherman
Maj. Genl.

ALS, DLC: Blair Family Papers; *OR*, I, 17: pt. 2, 587–88.

1. Frank P. Blair to WTS, February 1, 1863, DLC: WTS. On that day, WTS had written to Frank Blair that Knox had cited him as the authority for all printed reports on the Yazoo affair and asked for Blair's response to this charge even though he had already denied giving Knox the information in front of Steele and Stuart. WTS included a list of twenty-two questions in relation to WTS's commands and movements between leaving Memphis on December 18 and the present time. Lbk, DNA: RG 94, Records of the Adjutant General's Office, Generals' Books and Papers, William T. Sherman, Letterbook 5.

Blair answered all questions in full the same day and expressed his "mortification" at receiving "such a letter from you after the conversation which occurred between yourself

Generals Steele and Stuart and myself" and reiterated that he "made no statement to Mr. Knox at any time which would serve as the foundation of his criticism upon you." All his communications with Knox had been in the presence of Steele and other officers. He concluded by repeating that he had "invariably expressed myself in the Kindest manner towards you, and in a manner entirely becoming in a brother officer engaged in a common object" but that if he received any more letters such as WTS's of February 1, he would "not answer them in the same spirit." He permitted Sherman to make use of the letter, without the restrictions which Sherman, as he pointed out, had placed on his.

2. Brigadier General Stephen G. Burbridge (1831–94), USA, commanded a brigade in the Thirteenth Corps.

TO FRANK P. BLAIR

Head Qrs. 15 Army Corps.
Camp before Vicksburg, Feb. 3, 1863

Brig. Genl. F. P. Blair
Dear Sir,

As it is now proper, I will explain to you certain things which I think you ought to know, to enable you to understand the history of recent events in connection with the attack on Vicksburg.[1]

General Steele never reported to me his belief that Haines Bluff was the true point of attack first to be made. He wrote to Gen. Grant to that effect from Helena, by Col. Grierson who crossed over to General Grant at Oxford after I had taken my departure. But I know it was the general conviction of all military men who studied the maps, that an attack on Vicksburg should be made by way of the Yazoo landing at the first Bluff or hard land above its mouth. This was usually styled Haine's Bluff—but in fact the first high ground touches the Yazoo two or three miles lower down, at Snyders House, and is now known as Dromgoules Bluff, the same on which the enemy has made his Fortifications. I also was of the same impression, and the moment one flat reached the mouth of Yazoo I repaired on board the Flag ship and then met Captain Gwin and many most inteligent Navy officers who had been repeatedly up the Yazoo last summer, fall & winter up to the hour of our arrival.

They described Dromgoules Bluff as very strongly fortified, that not only were heavy guns there in position but earth forts and Rifle pits, and a strong force of Infantry camped immediately behind at "Milldale." The Yazoo also was obstructed by a Raft, and for three miles below by a system of torpedos, one of which had exploded and sunk the "Cairo." Even the Gunboats could not approach Snyders Bluff much less our frail transports. All agreed that a landing of the troops must be made lower down, and there was no difference of opinion but that Johnsons plantation was the best if not only place to debark the troops, even if Haine's Bluff were to be the point of real attack.

From the levee above Chickasaw Bayou where Steele landed all the way up to Snyders is an impracticable swamp, passable at only two points, one near Benson Blakes & the other which Steele attempted and which he pronounces officially as more difficult than the Bridge of Lodi. There is one small Bayou close up to Snyders, another a short distance below, and about a mile below is the large creek called "Skillet Goliah"—and all along the foot of the hills is a swamp and Bayou similar to the one we had so much trouble with. At first the Enemy expected us there, but when we landed at Johnsons they of course changed to the points accessible from Johnson. They were familiar with every foot of ground, and we had to study it under extreme difficulty.

I think that the chances against Snyders were better *after* we had drawn the Enemy to the head of Chickasaw Bayou than before. Moreover in the interim Admiral Porter had constructed a prow to one of the Rams with which to take up or explode in advance the torpedos that filled the Yazoo. The moment he was willing to attack the Batteries at Snyders I was ready to cooperate, and as you say we made prompt & secret preparations for the attack. Genl. Steele was confident, and so was I, and we did not abandon the attempt till the admiral declared it "too hazardous." But an essential feature in the proposed attack on the morning of Jan. 1, 1863 at Snyders was a simultaneous attack at Morgans front and that of A. J. Smith. At great labor we had brought up four 30 lb. Parrott Guns, and had all our Field Batteries placed according to our then more perfect knowledge of the Ground and the Enemys positions. I held all ready to begin the moment I heard you engaged at Snyders, and I contend we at Chickasaw Bayou could and would have held the Infantry force there, leaving the Gun Boats and Steeles forces to fight the Batteries alone at Snyders. It is for this reason that I say the military chances were better on the early morning of January 1st than if we had gone with our Fleet direct up to Haines Bluff on the morning of Dec. 27. We do know the difficulties we encountered, and it may be as is always the case that, we cannot do as well on the ground as we can figure on paper, but in my mind I know I studied night and day to acquire the most accurate information, that I acted in perfect harmony with the naval squadron and that I communicated frankly and fully to all Division Commanders all facts that reached me. I do know that Morgans advance was on the *true Line* of attack that his attack was the signal for all others, that he was full of confidence, that he knew early on the morning of Dec. 29 of the Road by which you returned from the assault, that his entire Division was ordered to carry the Road and up the Hill to the first Summit, that your Brigade and Steeles whole Division was ordered to support Morgan, that the Pontoon Bridge was designed only as Auxiliary so as to enable Morgan to cross a part of his troops by a Route where the Enemy had made no seeming preparations for resistance.

I know that the 2nd Division did commence when Morgan opened fire, and I know it occupied the attention of large masses of the Enemy who otherwise would have encountered Morgan. I know the same of the 1st Division and that the ground to its front was absolutely impassable to any army except skirmishers but still Col. Loudon[2] commanding that Brigade did push his skirmishers through the tangled mass of timber which I have examined personally, and he did occupy the attention of the Batteries and troops in Vicksburg. I have observed an impression that the Road on which A. J. Smith advanced might have been made a Line of attack. I tell you no, and I defy any one who saw it and examined the obstructions placed there by the enemy to say otherwise.

My calculations were that Morgans whole Division supported by Steele could at some considerable loss carry the County Road & first hills at Chickasaw—and then a Gunboat attack on Snyders would be certain of success. We could not have secured a footing at Snyders easier than by way of Chickasaw Bayou.

I may be and am too reckless of Public opinion, but I am not of the opinion of my officers and men. I would not have them think or feel that I am reckless of their safety and honor, or that I neglect to take every possible precaution against danger or fail to study every means to attain success. I am very careful to obey orders and instructions of my superiors because I know the importance of it in large combined operations, and I may expect too much of volunteers who think for themselves and dont feel the implicit confidence of Regulars in the officers. I am fully aware that Genl. Morgan did not carry to the assault all his Division as I expected. I have his official Reports, and all are now in the hands of our Government. I know General Morgans enthusiasm and devotion to the cause and will not question them and rather assume to myself the consequences of failure than throw it off on any generous & brave man or set of men. Failures result from many causes without a necessity for that bitter interpretation that pulls down rather than builds up. As you remark we are all engaged in the same cause which calls for the united action of all, and I think I am in mind as willing to bear and suffer as any one if such forbearance adds one atom to the chances of success in the great national struggle. If at one time I did think you had incautiously dropped expressions which gave a newspaper spy the grounds of accusation against all save those in your Brigade & Division, I now retract that, and assure you of my Confidence & respect. yrs truly,

W. T. Sherman, Maj. Genl.

ALS, DLC: Blair Family Papers; OR, I, 17: pt. 2, 588–90.
1. Blair had answered WTS's letter of February 2 on February 3, expressing his "great

gratification" at its tone and his intention to prove worthy of his commander's trust. DLC: WTS.

2. Colonel D. W. C. Loudon of the Seventy-second Ohio.

TO ULYSSES S. GRANT

Hd. Qrts. 15th Army Corps
Camp near Vicksburg Feby. 3, 1863

Maj. Genl. U. S. Grant
Steamer *Magnolia*
Sir,

There is on board your boat a person named Knox, correspondent of the *New York Herald*, who is here in defiance of my published orders, & who has published in the *New York Herald* information derived within our lines, the publication of which has conveyed to our enemy a knowledge useful to him & dangerous to us—He has eulogised the officers with whom he came in contact & defamed all others, embracing Genls. Smith A. J., Burbridge, Morgan & DeCourcey.[1]

I will prefer charges against him as a Spy, & of publishing infamous & malicious charges against officers in the public service, & ask that you cause his arrest & order a General Court Martial for his trial.[2] I am your obt. Sert.

W. T. Sherman
Maj. Genl.

LbkS, DNA: RG 94, Records of the Adjutant General's Office, Generals' Books and Papers, William T. Sherman, Letterbook 5.

1. Colonel John F. DeCourcey commanded the Third Brigade, Second Division, Fifteenth Corps, at Arkansas Post.

2. Knox was court-martialed, beginning February 5, 1863. On February 18, Knox was found guilty of willfully disobeying both WTS's exclusion order and General Orders No. 67 but was found not guilty of printing news without permission of the commanding general, boarding the *Continental* in spite of General Orders No. 8, and publishing false allegations about various generals. Knox was ordered outside army lines under threat of arrest. For an account of the trial and its aftermath, see Marszalek, *Sherman's Other War*, 126–53.

TO JOHN A. RAWLINS

Head Qtrs. 15th Army Corps
Camp before Vicksburg Feb. 3rd 1863

Col. J. A. Rawlins
A. A. Genl. to Gen. Grant
Sir,

I have the honor to transmit herewith the draft of Charges and Specifications against Knox, also some names of Commissioned Officers of my Division whom I believe fair and impartial judges. The Judge Advocate has acted in that capacity once and is a lawyer and honorable man.[1]

I will be frank to state that I do not care about this man Knox, though the lies and inuendoes that pervade his composition are infamous but I desire to have contemporaneous evidence of facts. I believe the Articles of War will make all who follow an Army into Enemy's country answerable to Martial Law. It should be so and I think is so under Articles 57 and 60.[2] There are parties all over our Country who soon conspire to defeat its armies and destroy its authority. All such are as much enemies as the Southern seceders. At all events an army must have the lawful right to protect itself against spies and false defamers and it can only do so by holding them to account. Under the Articles of War one owing authority to the U.S. is not a spy even if found lurking about our camps but we claim that the Southern People owe allegiance to the U.S. and yet if found lurking about our camps we should most certainly treat them as spies. How much greater the reason for treating as spies men who come into our midst—hear accidental conversations—eaves-drop— and publish to the world nominally for the Public but really for the Enemy.

At all events this trial will test the question can an Army protect itself against this class of men. I am with great respect your obdt. Servt.

W. T. Sherman
Maj. Genl. Comdg.

LbkS, DNA: RG 94, Records of the Adjutant General's Office, Generals' Books and Papers, William T. Sherman, Letterbook 5.

1. Captain C. Van Rensselaer.
2. See WTS to TESr, February 6, 1863, below.

TO DAVID DIXON PORTER

Headquarters Fifteenth Army Corps,
Before Vicksburg, February 4, 1863.

Admiral David D. Porter, Commanding Mississippi Squadron:
Dear Sir:

I thank you most heartily for your kind and considerate letter, February 3, received this day, and am more obliged than you can understand, as it covers many points I had neglected to guard against. Before Vicksburg, my mind was more intent on the enemy intrenched behind those hills than on the spies and intriguers in my own camp and "at home."

The spirit of anarchy seems deep at work at the North, more alarming than the batteries that shell at us from the opposite shore. I am going to have the correspondent of the New York Herald tried by a court-martial as a spy, not that I want the fellow shot, but because I want to establish the principle that such people cannot attend our armies, in violation of orders, and defy us, publishing their garbled statements and defaming officers who are doing their best. You of the Navy can control all who sail under your flag, whilst we are almost compelled to carry along in our midst a class of men who on Government transports usurp the best state-rooms and accommodations of the boats, pick up the drop conversations of officers, and report their limited and tainted observations as the history of events they neither see nor comprehend. This should not be, and must not be. We cannot prosper in military operations if we submit to it, and, as some one must begin the attack. I must assume the ungracious task. I shall always account myself fortunate to be near the officers of the old Navy, and would be most happy if I could think it possible the Navy and the Army of our country could ever again enjoy the high tone of honor and honesty that characterized them in the days of our youth.

With sentiments of profound respect for you and the officers of your fleet, I am, truly, yours,

W. T. Sherman,
Major-General of Volunteers.

Printed, *OR*, I, 17: pt. 2, 889.

TO JOHN SHERMAN

Head Qrs. 15 Army Corps.
Camp before Vicksburg, Feb. 4, 1863.

Dear Brother,

I have hitherto sent you copies of my orders and official instructions to my Division and Brigade Commanders, to show you that from the beginning to the end of our movements since leaving Memphis I kept all advised of the objects of our expedition and the parts each were to perform in the great whole.[1] I assert that never were more clear and distinct duties assigned to each and that the newspaper accusations to the contrary were false and designed to destroy me. I now enclose you a copy of my General orders no. 8 issued at Memphis, a letter of Gen. F. P. Blair,[2] and another of Thos. W. Knox the Correspondent of the New York Herald.[3] I now know the secret of this last tirade against me personally. Of course newspaper correspondents regard me as the enemy of their class. I announced that all such accompanying the expedition were and should be treated as spies. They are spies, because their publications reach the enemy, give them direct and minute information of the composition of our forces, and while invariably they puff up their immediate patrons, they pull down all others. Thus this man Knox, dating his paper upon the Steamer *Continental*, the Head Quarters of Generals Steele and Blair, gives to these General officers and their Division undue praise and libel and abuse all others. This not only plays into the hands of our enemies by sowing dissensions among us, but it encourages discontent among the officers who find themselves abused by men seemingly under the influence of officers high in Command. I caused Knox's communication to be read to him, paragraph by paragraph, and then show him my instructions, my orders made at the time and the official reports of others how wide he was of the Truth, and now I have asked his arrest and trial by Genl. Grant on charges as a spy and informer. The 57 Article of War, which is a Law of Congress, is as follows, "Whoever shall be convicted of holding correspondence with, or giving intelligence to the Enemy, either directly or indirectly shall suffer death &c." I will endeavor to bring in all the facts by means of the evidence of officers who took part in all these Events. My purpose is not to bring Knox to death or other serious punishment, but I do want to establish the principle that citizens shall not [go] against the orders of the competent military superior attend a military expedition, report its proceedings and comment on its officers.[4]

A Regular agent of the Post office Dept. Col. Markland accompanied our expedition for Memphis. After the assault he found in his mail various packages which he suspected were from newspaper correspondents and Sent them to me in my camp at the Bayou. I never looked at them, but my Inspector General Major Sanger did look in some of them, and then returned them to the mail. I never saw a line or word of them and had no time for such things. Several of the Regular correspondents who were about the Steamboats against orders then resolved to destroy me, and their simultaneous false Reports were the consequence.

Of course I knew nothing of it, and took no precautions, but I did promptly send full & minute Reports of every thing, including Lists of killed, wounded & missing to Gen. Grant and he sent the same without delay to the War Dept. The idea of my trying to suppress truthful information is of course absurd. Every Report signed by a responsible officer has gone to the War Dept.

With me the simple question is—Am I willing longer to serve with such influences in existence, influences which if unrestrained will destroy any officer who serves his Government with a single purpose of obeying orders & executing the Law? I answer no. The Government has now an ample supply of Majors & Brigadiers General, and can no longer need me. I am not in search of personal honor or Glory, and Know full well that any newspaper correspondent can blight a reputation based upon a long life of honesty, honor and industry. I must for my childrens sake preserve some of this and shall therefore cast about for a place where I can earn for them the means of existence, and try and transmit to them at least a fair name. This I cannot expect to do in the Service of the United States. Affectionately, yr. Brother,

W. T. Sherman

ALS, DLC: William T. Sherman; notation on top in EES's hand (?): "This is {meant truly} for Col. F. Perceval."

1. See WTS to JS, January 17, 1863, and enclosures. DLC: WTS.

2. Blair to WTS, February 1, 1863, DLC: WTS.

3. Knox to WTS, February 1, 1863, DLC: WTS. Knox sent WTS his account of the Yazoo campaign for him to correct so that the *Herald* could publish it. Knox explained that he did not hear of the existence of General Orders No. 8 until he had arrived at the Yazoo with Federal forces. He had stayed quietly on the boat because he had heard there was an order for his arrest. This isolation had limited his sources, he explained, and had resulted in the bad information he later printed. Upon further examination, he had found that WTS had the best battle plans he had ever seen and their failure was not WTS's fault: "I am fully convinced of your prompt, efficient & judicious management of the troops under your control from its commencement to its close."

4. "Look at Articles of War, 57 and 60. These in my judgment being within the Jurisdiction of a court martial the case of Knox. A military commission is a court unknown to Military Law, but grown out of our military History of the past few years, and their jurisdiction confined to cases not provided for by Law, but to punish, murder, robbery larceny &c. &c. crimes which in ordinary times would be tried by a Civic Court. I want to establish the fact that all citizens whatsoever who follow an army are amenable to Military Law—and think I can establish it." WTS to Hugh Boyle Ewing, February 4, 1863, OHi: William T. Sherman Papers.

TO THOMAS EWING SR.

> Head Qrs. 15 Army Corps.
> Camp before Vicksburg, Feb. 6, 1863.

Hon. Thos. Ewing,

Lancaster Ohio.

Dear Sir,

It is to me the source of infinite pain that I cause my family & friends so much concern and solicitude. Spite of all I can do I am in battle & war pushed forward, catch all the pelts of balls & bullets in front, and then the curses & maledictions of the unthinking herd behind. The Newspapers declare me their inveterate Enemy, and openly say they will write me down. In writing me down are they not writing the Cause and Country down?

The Congress of the United States in 1806 enacted

Art. 55. Whosoever belonging to the armies of the United States in foreign parts shall force a safeguard shall suffer death.

Art. 56. Whosoever shall relieve the Enemy with money, victuals, or shall knowingly harbor or protect an Enemy shall suffer death or such other punishment as shall be ordered by a Court Martial.

Art. 57: Whosoever shall be convicted of holding correspondence with or giving inteligence to the Enemy either directly or indirectly, shall suffer death or such other punishment as shall be ordered by the Sentence of a General Court Martial.

Art. 60. All settlers and retainers to the Camp and all persons whatsoever serving with the armies in the Field though not enlisted soldiers, are to be subject to orders according to the Rules and Discipline of War.

Art. 9. Any officer or soldier who x x x x shall disobey any lawful command of his superior officer shall suffer Death or such other punishment as shall according to the Nature of the offense inflicted on him by the Sentence of a Court Martial.

> *Orders*
> War Department
> Adjt. General Office
> Washington Aug 26, 1861

General Orders
No. 67

By the 57 Article of the Act of Congress entitled an act for Establishing Rules and Articles for the government of the armies of the United States approved April 10, 1806, "holding correspondence with or giving intelligence to the Enemy, either directly or indirectly" is made punishable by death, or such other punishment as shall be ordered by the Sentence of a Court Martial. *Public Safety* requires strict enforcement of this Article. It is therefore ordered that all correspondence and communication verbally or by writing, printing or telegraphing respecting operations of the Army or Military movements on land or water, or respecting the troops camps, arsenals, entrenchments a military affair within the Several Military Districts by which intelligence shall be directly or indirectly given to the Enemy, without the authority and sanction of the General in Command, is and the same are absolutely prohibited, and from and after the date of this order, persons violating the same will be proceeded against under the 57 Article of War. By order,

> L. Thomas
> Adjt. General.

Such is the Law, Such are the orders.

Can any man hesitate what is the Sworn duty of Every officer of the Army of the United States.

Now I know, and every officer knows that no army or detachment moves or can move that is not attended by correspondents of hundreds of newspapers, sometimes with the consent direct or implied of the Commanding officer, and sometimes in direct violation of his orders and in Contempt of his authority. They encumber our transports, occupy state rooms to the exclusion of officers on duty, they eat our provisions, they swell the crowd of hangers on, and increase the impedimenta. They publish without stint position information of movements past & prospective, organizations, names of commanders and accurate information which reaches the enemy with as much regularity as it does our People. They write up one Class of officers and down another, and fan the flames of discord & jealousy. Being in our very midst, catching drop expressions of officers, clerks and orderlies and being keen expert men they detect movements and give notice of them, so that no matter how rapid we move our enemy has notice in advance. To them more than any other cause do I trac{e} the many failures that attend our army an{d} while they cry about blood & slaughter, they are the direct cause of more bloodshed than fifty times their number of armed Rebels. Never had an Enemy a better corps of spies than our army carries along, paid transported and fed by the United States.

The Law, and the command of my lawful Superiors require me to proceed against them under the 57 article of war, and I confess my judgment & experience concur in the Same end. Congress must repeal {i}ts Laws, and the War Dept. annul its orders else I shall not change my actions. If with these Laws & orders, binding me in honor and even with the penalty of death, I am thus to be assailed by an unrestrained Press, I shall no longer serve my Government. Affectionately your son,

W. T. Sherman

I had not the most remote idea that Genl. McClernand was coming until after my orders for the attack were made, and the troops were actually advancing, when I got a few lines from Genl. Grant giving me a copy of Genl. Hallecks dispatch that McClernand was to command one corps, and I another. Of course McClernand being my Senior to command the whole. I could not then have altered my plans if I would, nor was there any occasion for I knew not when he would arrive. He did not arrive at Vicksburg till Jan. 2, 63 my orders were to leave Memphis Dec. 18 and proceed with all dispatch. The truth is fact and falsehood are so commingled in the various productions brought me that the motive is transparent, but the effect is bad, because all soldiers have their little jealousies and feuds, and these sweeping assertions assist to increase them and give them importance. My Old Division that knows me well, openly accuses the Helena Division Steeles of which Frank Blair is the most active man. They openly say he put afloat these stories to enhance his fame and deny all others.

ALS, PCarlA.

Camp before Vicksburg,
February 6, 1863

Dearest Ellen,

1 have written a letter for your father which I want you to See and I have no objection to its going to the Commercial. I cannot show them or anybody else my orders & instructions, but the laws & orders I send your father are public and maybe seen by all. McClernand has not yet made his official Report of the Post of Arkansas affair and holds on to mine. Grant asked me for and I have given him a Duplicate, so that it may reach the War Department as early as possible. I made my Report within two days of the Battle & I dont know when McClernand will make his. Nor can anybody tell what his will be as he is a most deceitful man, taking all possible advantage and having no standard of truth & honor but the public clamor. I appreciate what you say about using the newspapers.[1] This might do if larger interests were not involved, but if these newspapers continue to warp and rule our Government we are sure to be lost—What are the true interests of our Government? Shall the officers of the army obey Laws and orders, or shall they Study the interests of their own persons? The orders of the War Department are that all correspondents shall be proceeded against? But I want your father to read the Laws I have quoted and the orders of the War Department and tell me how I can make terms with these insolent Correspondents. Your last note of that St. Louis property matures this month. You have repeatedly asked what disposition to make of it. I answer hold on we may need it till we can make a new start. The People have got rid of McClellan and now Fitz-John Porter[2]—next Buell and Sumner[3] and Franklin.[4] There is a good supply of Major & Brigadier Generals and this army is well supplied now Grant, McClernand, Prentiss and others so that a better time cannot offer for me to escape the inevitable doom. All hands too are building Canals, one here another at Yazoo Pass, and a third at Providence Lake. The latter is a grand idea, and is the only one in which I feel an interest. Should I conclude to quit I will go to Memphis & then to St. Louis. That is the best harbor to bring up in, but I will not leave without an absolute resignation. I will not accept orders elsewhere. I take it the Secretary to avert the newspaper storm will order me elsewhere. I will not go. If I cannot serve the Government honestly and fairly, I will serve myself & family and let who may be King.

In my report of Arkansas Post I spoke of Kilby Smith in high terms, as high as I could. I did not make a specific recommendation, but you may assure Mrs. Smith that if an opportunity offers I will do so. The truth is he does not know enough tactics and of the art of war. He is recklessly brave, and very courteous, & better qualified than half the apprentices, still I must be exceedingly cautious. Others have similar & equal claims. Besides so many appointments have been made that there are no vacancies. Hugh is not confirmed. If his name has gone to the Senate and not acted on he can hold till the end of the Session, but if it be a rejection he is out of the Service, for he is no longer a colonel. This matter Should be attended to at once. Hugh is in fine health, is here. I have ordered his Brigade this side the swamp as if one canal breaks as it now threatens the Swamp & camps will be four feet under water. The advantage we have here is that we can reach the Levee and our steamboats on this shore. Charley has been staying here in my hd. Qrs. some days and is now at his tent where he has a stove. He has not the diarrhea but the reverse, he looks well. Yorke[5] is sent to Memphis very sick. Dr. Hess too is broken down and sent north sick. I suppose all this sickness will be charged to me and I must bear the (erased phrase). There is nothing that can compensate us for this return for my labor & services. Let us before all my good name is gone seek some quiet place, where at least we can feed our children and prepare them at least for the better future that must be in reserve for this cursed State of things. I know you have been ill, but are now much better, brace yourself up, as we cannot avert the Storm, let us seek a harbor of safety if possible. I will simply choose a favorable slant of wind to make the tack. Ever yrs.

W. T. Sherman

ALS, InND: Sherman Family Papers.

1. On January 28, 1863, EES had written her husband that while everyone seemed to know that the victory at Arkansas Post was due to his military ability, "You must either do as Rosecrans & *every other General in the entire army* but yourself, and treat newspaper reporters with some consideration or you must submit to a constant torrent of abuse & know that your friends at home are forced to hear these things daily & hourly." She continued, "you cannot stand up against newspaper power alone—as you do without being engulphed in abuse & a false public opinion—Instead of resisting why not *use* it." His brother did, she pointed out, and was not someone WTS considered dishonorable. SFP.

2. John Pope held Porter, one of McClellan's close friends, responsible for the Union defeat at Second Manassas (August 29–30, 1862) because Porter failed to launch an attack on the Confederate right on August 29; Porter countered that Pope's orders misapprehended the situation. Relieved of command in November 1862, Porter faced court-martial and was convicted of disobeying orders; he was cashiered on January 21, 1863. For years after the war Porter sought to overturn his conviction and eventually regained his commission as a colonel in the regular army.

3. Major General Edwin V. Sumner (1797–1863), USA, had been relieved at his own request after the Battle of Fredericksburg on December 13, 1862.

4. Major General William B. Franklin (1823–1903), USA, had come under severe criticism for his role in the Union debacle at Fredericksburg.

5. Probably Louis E. Yorke (1832–73), then a captain in the Thirteenth U.S. Infantry. He was made a brevet brigadier general for the Vicksburg siege and his war service.

TO MARIA BOYLE EWING SHERMAN

Camp before Vicksburg,
February 6, 1863

Dear Minnie,

I got your pretty and well written letter of December 26, which was brought down to Memphis by Mother Angela, and Sent to me here. Of Course I have not seen Mother Angela, nor do I expect her for some time, as I must remain here and go with my soldiers wherever war Carries us.

I feel a great deal of pride in hearing such good accounts of you at school, and I see in your letter the proof that you are studying hard and learning fast. Dear little Willy too is writing well, and I have his letter written at the same time when you both were preparing for Christmas which I know you enjoyed so much.

It must be very cold up where you are, for we have ice down here at Vicksburg, where it rarely snows or freezes, but this winter has been unusually severe here and I suppose there has been a great deal of snow and ice at the North.

Uncle Hugh is with me and is very well. So is Uncle Charley here, but he has been Complaining for some time but is not very sick. Luke is very well.

I want to See you very much. Mama writes me a great deal, how tall you are and how good, that you are learning very fast and hold your own in Classes of Older Scholars. This makes me feel very proud of you. Write to me very often by way of Memphis and tell Willy to do the Same. I will write to him very soon. Your affectionate father

W. T. Sherman

ALS, OHi: William T. Sherman Papers.

TO BENJAMIN H. GRIERSON

Hd. Qrts. 15th Army Corps
Before Vicksburg Feby. 9, 1863

Dear Grierson

Yours of Feby. 3, is at hand. I cheerfully & at once send you a letter to the Secy. of War, but cannot promise it will be of any value. I certainly wish your promotion if you want it.[1] Grant speaks in the highest terms of you, so you have the good will of your late & present commanders. You have seen that the newspapers are after me again & the correspondents admit that they must write me down because I am the inveterate enemy of their class. I surely do consider them as much the enemies of the U.S. as the secesh and a great deal more contemptible. The former the secesh openly take arms & declare hostilities, the latter publish all they can to keep the enemy advised of our plans purposes & designs, & also enter our camps as spies sowing sedition & ill feeling. It was & is all nonsense that our troops were demoralized, as usual many get tired of the war when they hear the whistle of the bullits & put it off on any popular excuse. We are now lying on shore digging canals & trying to turn the Mississippi but sooner or later we must get on shore & fight it out. You certainly always will have my respect & good wishes Yr. friend

W. T. S.

Lbk, DNA: RG 94, Records of the Adjutant General's Office, Generals' Books and Papers, William T. Sherman, Letterbook 5.

1. Grierson had been nominated to the rank of brigadier general of volunteers and would receive the promotion on June 3, 1863.

TO JOHN SHERMAN

Camp before Vicksburg, Feb. 12, 1863.

Dear Brother,

I have hitherto sent you original papers or copies to satisfy any one of the falsehood of the attacks against me in the late Vicksburg matter. I had a newspaper Reporter arrested and tried by a court martial but by the rulings of the Court I infer they are of the opinion that to make the accused come within the order of the War Department the fact should be proven that the very substance of the objectionable matter went to the enemy. I have been unable to find the identical matter but in every Southern paper I get I find abundance of evidence to show that Northern papers furnish the Southern Leaders abundant and timely notion of every movement. I send you two to show this fact, in the Vicksburg *Whig* at the bottom of the last Column of the 1st Page you will see that is states positively that a correspondent of one of the Northern Journals wrote *in advance* of the Federal plans in their late move on Vicksburg. Had they received three days notice of our coming to the Post of Arkansas, they could have so reinforced that it would have cost us a Siege, but there we were beyond the province of the Press and succeeded, and so it must ever be. These Newspaper Correspondents hanging about the skirts of our army, retailing scraps of news reveal all plans and are worth a hundred thousand men to the Enemy. I am satisfied the South maintains many a Press at the North, & through them maintains an admirable system of spies in our very camps[.] I may be premature, but the day must come when the army will make short work with this class of enemies. Now they Succeed in intimidating some officers by their vindictive Power, encourage discord by their false praises and abuses, and do more to prevent unity, concord and discipline than any other possible Cause. If they must be tolerated, if the public demands news at the cost of national failure I cant help it, though I am determined as long as I hold a commission I will look to the Law & not the Press for my authority & conduct.

Of course I am at full liberty to judge for myself and as there is an abundance of major and Brigadier Generals *now*, and the Government possesses an *over*supply of military talent & experience any one may retire without compromising his character. As soon as I can hear from St. Louis I will determine what to do.

I have no faith in the canal here, save we may enlarge it to pass supplies for Gun boats below which will enable the latter to keep supplies from Vicksburg via the River, but we in no wise threaten Vicksburg, for the bluffs extend many miles below the outlet of the Canal. The River is Bank full & threatens to overflow our camps—but I have more faith in the efforts above at Yazoo Pass & Lake Providence. The former may admit us to the Yazoo from above, and the latter may open a channel down the Tensas, to Red, and by Atchafalaya below Port Hudson. If Banks had orders to meet me at Vicksburg on Christmas he has been slow of execution, for I cannot hear that he has even left of Port Hudson. At all events we have not heard from him save via New York. Grant is now up at Lake Providence. McClernand & my Corps are here in sight of Vicksburg, but the great Mississipi flows between us. affectionately yr. brother,

W. T. Sherman

P.S. I have read your speech on taxing Banks.[1]

That is right and is designed doubtless to ultimately extinguish their issues, and leave that field of credit open exclusively to Government. I have just seen your move as to drafting—some system must be devised to keep up supplies of men to the army.[2] Of Course Battles cannot be fought without death wounds & prisoners. Next comes death from exposure, change of climate mode of life and natural causes. Still greater than all, desertions and Sickness, which disqualify the soldier for his work. I think at least one half of our army is now absent sick or from some unauthorized cause, and even with the best medical care you may supply estimate that an army of 60,000 will need 300,000 per annum to Keep the Muster Rolls up. New Regiments are false economy and men should come as recruits to Old Regiments, for these have by a process of elimination weeded out the worthless and inefficient officers & non commissioned officers, and 500 men added to our old Regiment are worth more than 1000 in a new Regt. costing less than half as no new officers are needed. Some of our Regiments have less than 300 men for duty and could raise 800 Recruits without a single officer. Tis folly to talk about Peace. The South would grant it, their first demand would be Maryland Kentucky & Missouri, and if acceded to they would be recognized by the Civilized world as the Government of Washington. I know you honestly thought me extravagant at first, but now that you have seen the vindictive spirit and energy of the South you must confess I was not far wrong. Indeed my opportunities for Knowing were better than yours. The North can succeed alone by bulldog perseverance leaving natural causes to assist. Of the final Result no one can tell.

Sherman

ALS, DLC: William T. Sherman.

1. In January, JS had introduced a bill with two measures designed to weaken state banks, which he viewed as unconstitutional and ineffective. The legislation levied a tax of 2 percent per annum on the circulation of all bank bills and a tax of 10 percent per annum on all fractional currency issued by corporations or individuals. John Sherman, *John Sherman's Recollections of Forty Years in the House, Senate and Cabinet*, 2 vols. (Chicago, 1895), 1:285–93.

2. On February 16, the Senate would pass the Conscription Act, the first effective Federal draft, making all able-bodied men between the ages of twenty-nine and forty-five with certain exceptions liable for military service, setting up the framework that would enable the president to set quotas for districts, and allowing draftees to hire substitutes or pay their way out of service.

TO THOMAS EWING SR.

Camp before Vicksburg, Feb. 17, 1863.

Hon. Thomas Ewing
Dear Sir,

Ellen has sent me the enclosed slips from the Cincinnati Commercial.[1] The Editor evidently seems disposed to deal fairly by me, and as I have more leisure than usual now I will illustrate by examples fresh in the memory of all, why I regard newspaper correspondents as spies, & why as a Servant of an enlightened Government I feel bound in honor and in common honesty to shape my official conduct accordingly. A spy is one who furnishes an enemy with knowledge useful to him & dangerous to us. One who bears into a Fortress or Camp a baneful influence that encourages sedition or weakens us. He need not be an enemy, is often a trader woman or Servant. Such characters are by all belligerents punished Summarily & with the extremest penalties, not because they are of themselves filled with the guilty thought & intent that makes the Madman the Burglar the Thief the Felon in civil affairs, but because he or she endangers the safety of an army a nation or the cause for which it is contending. Andre carried no intelligence back to Genl. Clinton but was the mere instrument used to corrupt the fidelity of an Officer holding an important command. Washington admitted the high & pure character of Andre but the safety of the cause demanded his punishment.[2] It is hard to illustrate my point by reference to our past history, but I wish to convey the full idea that a nation & an army must defend its safety & existence by making acts militating against it criminal regardless of the mere interest of the instrument. We find a scout surveying our camp from a distance in noways threatening us but seeking information of the location strength & composition of our forces, we shoot him of course without asking a question. We find a stranger in our camp seeking a stray horse & find afterwards he has been to the enemy: we hang him as a spy because the safety of the army & the cause it fights is too important to be risked by any pretext or chance. Now in these modern times a class of men has been begotten & attend our camps & armies gathering minute information of our strength plans & purposes & publish them so as to reach the enemy in time to serve his purposes. Such publications do not add a man to our strength, in no ways benefit us but are invaluable to the enemy. You know that this class published in advance all the plans of the Manassas movement enabled Johnston to reinforce Beauregard whereby McDowell was defeated & the enemy gained tremendous strength & we lost in comparison. I know the enemy received from the same source some similar notice of our intended attack on Vicksburg & thwarted our well laid scheme. I know that Beauregard at Corinth received from the same source full details of all troops ascending the Tennessee & acted accordingly. I know that it was by absolute reticence only that Halleck succeeded in striking Forts Henry & Donaldson & prevented their reinforcements in time to thwart that most brilliant movement. And it was only by the absence of newspapers that we succeeded in reaching the post of Arkansas before it could be reinforced.

I *know* that the principal northern papers reach the enemy regularly & promptly & I *know* that all the vigilance of our Army cannot prevent it & I know that by this means the enemy can defeat us to the end of time. I could instance other examples but the[se] suffice to illustrate this branch of the subject.

Another view of the case. The Northern Press either make public opinion or reflect it. By gradual steps public opinion instead of being governed governs our country. All bow to it, & even military men who are sworn officers of the Executive Branch of the Government go behind & look to public opinion. The consequence is & has been that officers instead of keeping the Executive Branch advised of all movements events or circumstances that would enable it to act advisedly & with vigor communicate with the public direct through the Press so that the Government authorities are operated on by public opinion formed too often on false or interested information. This has weakened our Executive and has created jealousies mistrust & actual Sedition. Officers find it easier to attain rank known fame and notoriety by the cheap proces of newspapers. This cause has paralized several fine armies & by making the people at home mistrust the ability of Leaders Surgeons & Quarter Masters has even excited the fears of parents so far that many advise their sons & brothers to desert until desertion & mutiny have lost their odious character. I'll undertake to say that the army of the Potomac has not today for battle one half the men whom the U.S. pays as Soldiers & this is partially the case with the army in Tennessee & here. In all armies there must be wide differences of opinion & partial causes of disaffection—*want of pay*, bad clothing dismal camps crowded transports hospitals rudely formed & all the incidents of war. These cannot be entirely avoided & newspapers can easily change them to negligence of commanders & thereby create disaffection. I do not say that the Press intends this but they have done this and are doing it all the time now I know that I made the most minute and careful preperation for the sick & wounded on the Yazoo, plenty of ambulances & men detailed in advance *to remove* the wounded—four (4) of the largest transports prepared & set aside before a shot was fired, & that every wounded man was taken from the field dressed & carefully attended immediately & yet I know that the Press has succeeded in making the very reverse impression & that many good people think there was criminal negligence. The same naked representations were made at Shiloh & I saw hundreds of Physicians come down & when our Surgeons begged & implored their help they preferred to gather up trophies & consume the dainties provided for the wounded & go back & represent the cruelty of the Army Surgeons & boast of their own disinterested humanity. I know this & that they nearly ruined Dr. Hewit one of the hardest working Surgeons in any army. I see similar attempts less successful however against Dr. McMillan not a word of truth not even a pretence of truth but it is a popular & successful theme & they avail themselves of it. What is the consequence? All officers of industry who stand by at all times through storm & sunshine find their reputations blasted & others usually the most lazy & indolent reaping cheap glory & fame through the correspondents of the Press. I say in giving intelligence to the enemy, in sowing discord & discontent in an army these men fulfil all the conditions of spies. Shall we succumb or shall we meet & overcome the evil? I am satisfied they have cost the country hundreds of millions of dollars, & brought our country to the brink of ruin & that unless the nuisance is abated we are lost. Here we are in front of Vicksburg. The attack direct in front would in our frail transports be marked by the sinking of Steamers loaded with troops, a fearful assault against hills fortified with great care by a cunning enemy. Every commander who has looked at it says it cannot be done in front it must be turned. I tried it but newspaper correspondents had sent word in advance & ample preperations were made & reinforcements to double my number had reached Vicksburg.

McClernand was unwilling to attack in front. Grant d[itt]o. Then how turn the position? We cannot ascend the Yazoo to where our men can get a footing. We cannot run our frail transports past the Vicksburg Batteries then we resolve to cut a channel into Yazoo at the old pass near Delta above & into the Tensas by way of Lake Providence. Secrecy & dispatch are the chief elements of success. The forces here are kept to occupy the attention of the enemy two steamers are floated past the Batteries to control the River below & men are drawn secretly from Helena & Memphis to cut the canals & levies & remove all the inhabitants so that the enemy could not have notice till the floods of the Missippi could finish the work of man. But what avail? Known spies accompany each expedition & we now read in the northern papers (the same are in Vicksburg now) that our forces here are unequal to the direct assault but are cutting the two canals above: all our plans revealed & thwarted, the levies are cut & our plans work to a charm but the enemy now knows our purposes & hastens above, fells trees into the narrow head streams, cuts the side levies disperses the waters & defeats our well conceived plans. Who can carry on war thus? It is terrible to contemplate; & I say it that no intelligent officer in this or any American army now in the field but would prefer to have his opponent increased twenty—yea fifty per cent if the internal informers & spies could be excluded from our camps. I know our people are full of anxiety to hear from our armies but every soldier can & does write home, his family can at all times hear of his welfare & if the people could only see as I see the baneful effects of this mischeivous practise they would cry aloud in indignant tones. We may in self defense be compelled to take the law into our own hands for our safety or we may bend to the storm and seek a position where others may take the consequences of this cause. I early foresaw this result & have borne the malignity of the Press but a day will come & that far distant when the Press must surrender some portion of its freedom to save the rest else it too will perish in the general wreck. I think the *Commercial* misjudges my character somewhat. I certainly am not proud or haughty. Every soldier of my command comes into my presence as easy as the highest officer. Their beds & rations are as good as mine & certainly no General officer moves about with as little pomp as I. They see me daily nightly hourly, along the picket line afoot alone or with a Single orderly or officer whilst others have their mighty escorts & retinue. Indeed I am usually laughed at for my simplicity in this respect. Abrupt I am & all military men are. The mind jumps to its conclusions & is emphatic, & I can usually divine the motive of the insidious cotton Speculator camp follower & hypercritical humanity seeker before he discloses his plans & designs & an officer who must attend to the thousand & one wants of thirty thousand men besides the importunities of thousands of mischeivous camp followers must need be abrupt unless the day can be made more than twenty four hours long. A citizen cannot understand that an officer who has to see to the wants and necessities of an army has no time to listen to their usual long perorations & I must confess I have little patience with this class of men. To be sure policy would dictate a different course, & I know I could easily have acheived popularity by yeilding to these outside influences but I could not do what I see other popular officers do furnish transportation at Government expense to newspaper agents & supply them with public horses Seat them at my table to hear conversations of public matter give access to official papers which I am commanded to withhold to the world till my Employer has the benefit of them. I could not do these things & feel that I was an honest man & faithful servant of the Government for my memory still runs back to the time when Peter Hagner was Auditor of the Treasury, & when an officer would not take a Government nail out of a keg on which to hang his coat or feed his horse out of the public crib without charging its cost against his pay. That time is past, but must again return before the United States can regain its lost good name among the nations of the earth.

Again the habit of indiscriminate praise & flattery has done us harm. Let a stranger read our official reports & he would blush at the praise bespattered over who Regiments Divisions and Corps for skirmishes & actions where the dead & wounded mark no Serious conflict. When I praise I mean it & when troops fall into disorder I must notice it but you may read my reports in vain for an instance where troops have kept their ranks & done even moderately well but I have encouraged them to a better future. There is an unwritten history that will come out when the real soldiers come home. At the Post of Arkansas I wanted to storm the rifle pits by a Hurrah! One of my divisions faltered and in reply to my aid "How are things with you"? "Why Damn it my men are only wasting ammunition", I cautioned him to patience. "Be kind & coax along & notify me the moment you think your men are equal to the work"—hundreds heard me & yet this same officer would indulge now in extravagant boa[s]ts. I know that in trouble in danger in emergencies the men know I have patience a keen appreciation of the truth of facts & ground equalled by few and one day they will tell the truth. Many a solitary picket has seen me creeping by night examining ground before I ordered them to cross it & yet other lazy rascals ignorant of the truth would hang behind sleep or crouch around the distant camp fire till danger was passed, & then write "how Sherman with insane rashness had pushed his brave soldiers into the jaws of death.["]

I have departed from my theme. My argument is that newspaper correspondents & camp followers, writing with a purpose & with no data communicate facts useful to an enemy and useless to our cause & calculated to impair the discipline of the army & that the practise must cease We cannot appeal to Patriotism because news are a saleable commodity & the more valuable as it is the more pithy & damaging to our cause I am satisfied the enemy encourages this as the cheapest & most effectual weapon of war either by direct contribution of money or by becoming large purchasers of its numbers. The law gives us the means to stop it & as an army we fail in our duty to the Government to our cause & to ourselves if we do not use them.

To shew how the Press is used I will tell of another recent instance. The Captain of the Gun Boat *New Era*[3] behaved badly, cowardly at Arkansas Post. Admiral Porter, a gallant officer sent him to Cairo in banishment. It was necessary for him to cover up his disgrace. Getting into safety nearly up to the Ohio he pretended he saw an army of 3,000 men near Island No. 10, & he shelled them away at a cost of many thousands of dollars. He alarmed the whole country & wrote his own account but not a man here believes he saw a single Guerilla. This is true of many glorious battles in the newspapers.

Our camp is about flooded & consequent idleness must form my apology for this long letter. If you think proper I have no objection to the Editor of the Commericial seeing this but I confess myself too "haughty" to allow it or anything else of mine to be printed. Affectionately

W. T. Sherman

Copy, PCarlA.

1. In a February 8 letter to her husband, EES sent paragraphs from the *Cincinnati Commercial* of January 24 and February 2 which supported him. The first was a letter from a soldier signed "T. K." and a tribute to WTS's leadership. She suspected that the second clipping, vindicating WTS, had been written from facts supplied by Hurlbut. On February 11, she told WTS that Halstead had told her that a private named Thomas King wrote the letter and that Halstead himself had penned the article of February 2. SFP.

2. WTS here referred to the execution of Major John André for his role in Benedict Arnold's efforts to pass information concerning American defenses at West Point to the British during the Revolutionary War.

3. William C. Hanford.

TO JOHN SHERMAN

Camp before Vicksburg,
February 18, 1863

My Dear Brother,

I have seen your speeches on the subject of absentees, filling up the army with conscripts, and the necessity of standing by the President for the sake of unity of action. So at last I see you and the Country begin to realize what we ought to have known two years ago, that individual opinions however sincere, real & honest are too various to Secure unity of action, and at last that men must forego their individual notions and follow some one Leader, the Legitimate & Constitutional one if possible. Two years of war, costly & bloody have been endured and we have arrived by sad experience at a Result that all the world knew before. If the People of the North will not learn from the experience of the world, but must go on groping in the dark for experience to develop and demonstrate the Truth of established principles of Government, why of course there is no help for it, but as a people we must pay the price.

We have reproached the South for arbitrary conduct in coercing her People—at last we find we must imitate their example—we have denounced their tyranny in filling their armies with conscripts—and now we must follow her example—We have denounced their tyranny in suppressing freedom of speech and the press, and here too in time we must follow her Example. The longer it is deferred the worse it becomes.

Who gave notice of McDowell's movement on Manassas, & enabled Johnston so to reinforce Beauregard that our army was defeated?

The Press.

Who gave notice of the movement on Vicksburg?

The Press.

Who has prevented all secret combinations and movements against our enemy?

The Press.

Who has sown the seeds of hatred so deep, that Reason, Religion and Self interest cannot eradicate them?

The Press.

What is the real moving cause in this Rebellion? Mutual hatred & misrepresentations made by a venal Press.

In the South this powerful machine was at once scotched and used by the Rebel Government, but at the North was allowed to go free. What are the results. After arousing the passions of the people till the two great sections hate each other with a hate hardly parallelled in history, it now begins to Stir up sedition at home, and even to encourage mutiny in our armies. What has paralyzed the Army of the Potomac? Mutual jealousies kept alive by the Press. What has enabled the enemy to combine so as [to] hold Tennessee after we have twice crossed it with victorious armies. What defeats and will continue to defeat our best plans here and elsewhere? The Press.

I cannot pick up a paper but tells of our situation here, in the mud, sickness, and digging a canal in which we have little faith. But our officers attempt secretly to cut two other channels one into Yazoo by an old Pass, and one through Lake Providence into Tensas, Black Red &c., whereby we could turn not only Vicksburg Port Hudson, but also Grand Gulf, Natchez, Ellis Cliff, Fort Adams and all the strategic points on the Main River, and the busy agents of the Press follow up and proclaim to the world the whole thing, and instead of surprising our enemy we find him felling trees & blocking passages that would without this have been in our possession, and all the real effects of surprise are lost. I say with the Press unfettered as now we are defeated to the end of time. Tis folly to say the people must have news. Every soldier can and does write to his family & friends & all have ample opportunities for so doing, and this pretext forms no good reasons why agents of the Press should reveal prematurely all our plans & designs. We cannot prevent it. Clerks of steamboats, correspondents in disguise or openly attend each army & detachment, and presto appears in Memphis & St. Louis minute accounts of our plans & designs. These reach Vicksburg by telegraph from Hernando & Holly Springs before we know of it.

The only two really successful military strokes out here have succeeded because of the absence of newspapers or by throwing them off the trail— Halleck had to make a simulated attack on Columbus to prevent the Press giving notice of his intended move against Forts Henry & Donelson. We succeeded in reaching the Post of Arkansas before the Correspondents could reach their Papers. Now in war it is bad enough to have a bold daring enemy in great strength to our front without having an equally dangerous & treacherous foe within. I know if the People of the United States could see & realize the Truth of this matter they would agree to wait a few days for their accustomed batch of exciting news rather than expose their sons, brothers & friends as they inevitably do to failure and death. Of course I know the President & Congress are powerless in this matter & we must go on till perpetual defeat & disaster point out one of the Chief Causes. Instead of being governed by Reason, our people prefer to grope their way through personal Experience and must pay its cost. I only await a good time to Slide out & let the experiment go on at the expense of others. I have had my share & wish no more. I still have unlimited faith in Halleck & prefer that he should command the whole army than McClellan. Still I would like to have him come West. Affectionately

Sherman

ALS, DLC: William T. Sherman.

TO EDWARD O. C. ORD

Head Qrs. 15 Army Corps,
Camp near Vicksburg Feb. 22. 63

Maj. Gen. E. O. C. Ord,
Cincinati Ohio.
My Dear Friend,

Yours of Feb. 8 is just received.[1] Tell Macfeely[2] if he has not already started to take his time. I have my old Commissary Morton[3] with me, and he is the best in this Army, and he relieves me of all Care and responsibility on this score. When Macfeely joins me I Shall welcome him and will endeavor also to Keep Captain Morton as his assistant.

I wrote you a long letter some time ago addressed to you at Louisville. If you have not received it send to the Post office at Louisville for it as I think I wrote something that I wanted you to Know.

Doubtless you in common with all the world would like to know what we are about here. Others have their troubles, so have we, but probably not more than our share. *Vicksburg is the hardest problem of the War. I would rather undertake Richmond: for there they can get a footing. Here we are on the West bank*; and the River Bank full of water {intervenes}, and we can make no landing on that Side. The canal we are digging here does not Solve the problem, for the lower end of the Canal, although below Vicksburg is not below the Walnut Hills which are fortified for four miles below the outlet of the canal. Our iron clad the Indianola & Ram the Queen of the West ran the Batteries, but the latter was taken by the Enemy up Red River leaving the Indianola alone between Vicksburg & Port Hudson. We know nothing of the operations below at Port Hudson. *Alone we are cutting canals into the head of the Yazoo and Tensas, but these have been discovered by the enemy through the instrumentality of the Newspaper Spies that attend this army, and how the Enemy obstructs as fast as our working parties clear away*—McPhersons Corps is at Lake Providence, Mine and McClernands are here, and Hurlbuts at or near Memphis Jackson & Lagrange. I wish you had a Corps, and I advise you to report to Grant as soon as possible and I think you will get a Command and soon a Corps, unless you prefer the Chances East. I must confess I do not see daylight here yet, though this far we have separated the East from the West. We have had a great deal of rain here, and you Know how it makes the swamps here—we have no ground here even to bury our men save the levee, and the roads are simply quagmires. Men have to back their rations from the Boats to their Camps in the old Cotton fields. Weather has been Cool, but now the signs of spring show themselves in the budding willows & Cottonwood.

Indeed would I be glad to See you, and if you cant do *better come to me and act as my vice Roy*. Like many a disinterested Patriot I would gladly let you do all the work & I would take it easy—Cant you run up to Lancaster, only 5 hours & See Mrs. Sherman and my little children. I assure you of the most hearty welcome. Love to Kelton and all friends. Ever yr. friend

Sherman

ALS, New York: The Gilder Lehrman Collection.

1. DLC: WTS.

2. Lieutenant Colonel Robert Macfeely (1826–1901), USMA 1950, of Pennsylvania had

been assigned to the Fifteenth Corps on January 1 as chief commissary of the Department of the Tennessee.

3. Captain Charles A. Morton, USA, would take Macfeely's place in April when he was assigned to department headquarters.

TO ELLEN EWING SHERMAN

Camp before Vicksburg, Feb. 22, 63

Dearest Ellen,

I have yours of the 4th & 8th[1] Charley is with me and I handed him his letter which I also read, of course I like to read your gossiping letters about the family and never will complain of your laughing heartily at Kinders Charades, or at your excessive vanity about Elly, but I must think the discussion of their future husbands is a little remote, but the truth is it seems but a day since Minnie came to New Orleans a baby, and you went back in the *Tecumseh*, and I am hourly reminded of the event by seeing the self same *Tecumseh* plying about looking rather old and seedy. Also to remind me of the past lies in front of my house the Self same Thos. E. Tutt, the first name that Corporal Tom ever spoke at length fully and distinctly. You know full well however seemingly unmindful of these little things I mark them well & never forget them. As to my exposing myself unnecessarily you need not be concerned. I know better than Charley where danger lies, and where I should be. Soldiers have a right to See & Know that the man who guides them is near enough to See with his own Eyes, and that he cannot see without being seen. At Arkansas Post the ground was nearly level and the Enemy could See me, with officers coming & going & orderlies grouped near. Of course they fired at me, one Rifled 10 p[ounder] repeatedly and when I was grouping the prisoners I recognized the very gun and asked for the Gunner who proved to be a real Paddy and I gave him fits for aiming at me which the fellow did not deny, but we gave them a fair return and the account was squared. I am not at all disappointed in the condition of things in our country. You must recognize much of what I used to say. The North was ignorant & presumptuous and would not believe what I then Knew, and what they begin to See, that we are in for a real war, and that no one can see its end. Many would escape the dilemma but there is no escape. The North must fight it out, or submit to a disgraceful surrender. The South will demand everything and Peace cannot exist with two popular Governments in such close proximity—Now that war exists it will go on spite of parties, politics & the People. The Change of Generals dont change the facts.[2] I will escape if I can, but I know full well go where we may war will follow us further there can be no Peace in this country during our natural lives. Our cause has sustained a heavy loss in the Ram *Queen of the West* up Red River of which I know the papers will be filled.[3] We have one iron Clad below Vicksburg but she may be overpowered by numbers as the *Harriet Lane*⁴ was at Galveston, in which case our boats here may have a Ram threatening our fleet all the time. One Canal has progressed Slowly on account of rain & liquid mud and also both projects are much retarded by the Enemy who learned our purposes from the northern papers. After awhile our people will find they are paying dear for early news of "our army." This early news may delay us a year.

I enclose you a slip from the Memphis Bulletin containing a note of mine to the editors. I see my arrival also announced in Washington.

Hugh is very well and Charley quite recovered—The Regulars get full rations and dont suffer for want of appreciation. They get whisky & Onions as often as they need them. All are as well as may be in the mud. affectionately

W. T. Sherman

ALS, InND: Sherman Family Papers.

1. EES's first letter, of February 4, enclosed one for Charley Ewing full of family gossip; her second letter, February 8, sent an article from the *Cincinnati Commercial*. She also wrote that she was weary of "the trial of staying at home & *quietly enduring*." Her father had written Philemon Ewing from Washington that Cump's standing with Halleck and Stanton was high. She sent the January 24 and February 2 clippings from the *Cincinnati Commercial* and reiterated her belief that he should treat the press differently: "You cannot do anything *unaided* against them & there is *not one* man in power who will unite with you against them. So dear Cump give up the struggle & suffer them to annoy you no longer." SFP.

2. Major General Joseph Hooker (1814–79) had taken command of the Army of the Potomac on January 26.

3. While engaging Confederate batteries on February 4, the *Queen* ran aground and severed her steam pipe. Federal forces had to abandon the ship.

4. The U.S. ship *Harriet Lane* had been captured after her top officers were killed during Magruder's January 1 attack on the Federal-held port of Galveston.

TO JOHN A. RAWLINS

Headquarters Fifteenth Army Corps,
Camp near Vicksburg,
February 23, 1863

Col. John A. Rawlins,
Assistant Adjutant-General, Department of the Tennessee:
Colonel:

General Orders, No. 13, from your headquarters, of date February 19, 1863, involves certain principles that I think should be settled by the highest authority of our Government, and I beg most respectfully their reference, through the Judge Advocate-General, to the Commander-in-Chief.[1]

The findings on the third charge, first specification, are, "the facts proven as stated, but attaches no criminality thereto," viz, that the accused knowingly and willfully disobeyed the lawful command of the proper authority by accompanying the expedition down the Mississippi below Helena. The inference is that a commanding officer has no right to prohibit citizens from accompanying a military expedition, or, if he does, such citizens incur no criminality by disregarding such command. The finding of the first specification, first charge, "Guilty, except the words thereby conveying to the enemy an approximate estimate of its strength, in direct violation of the Fifty-seventh Article of War,' " involves the principle that publication of army organization and strength in a paper having the circulation South and North of the New York Herald does not amount to an indirect conveyance of intelligence to an enemy.

I regard these two points as vital to our success as an army contending against an enemy who has every advantage of us in position and means of intelligence. I do not expect that any court-martial or any officer should do, or attempt to do, an unlawful act, but I do believe the laws of Congress and of war clearly cover both these points, and believing that the true interest of the Government and of our people demand a radical change in this respect, I avail myself of this means to invite their earnest consideration of the issues involved.

If a commanding officer cannot exclude from his camp the very class of men which an enemy would select as spies and informers, and if to prove the conveyance of indirect information to the enemy it be necessary to follow that information from its source to the very armies arrayed against us, whose country thus far our hundreds of thousands of men have been unable to invade, and yet whose newspapers are made up of extracts from these very Northern papers, then it is fruitless to attempt to conceal from them all the data they could need to make successful resistance to our plans, and to attack our detached parties and lines of communication. To this cause may well be attributed the past reverses to our armies and the failure of almost every plan devised by our generals. I believe this cause has lost us millions of money, thousands of lives, and will continue to defeat us to the end of time, unless some remedy be devised.

I am, with great respect,
W. T. Sherman,
Major-General, Commanding.

Printed, *OR*, I, 17: pt. 2, 892–93.

1. On February 19, 1863, Rawlins issued General Orders No. 13, Department of the Tennessee, reporting the results of Knox's court-martial. The court found Knox guilty of several of the specifications with which Sherman charged him but not of the charges of spying or of relaying evidence to the enemy; instead, the court found him guilty of disobeying orders concerning the transmission of dispatches without first gaining Sherman's permission. *OR*, I, 17: pt. 2, 889–92.

Hd. Qrs. 15 Army Corps,
Camp near Vicksburg, Feb. 24, 1863.

Frank J. Bramhall Esq.
No. 48 Franklin St. NY
Dear Sir,

Yours of Feb. 12 1863 is received, and I thank you for the handsome portrait of General Lew Wallace.

I have no photograph of myself, nor can I procure one. I am and have been ahead of the machines for their production.

My autograph will be attached to this. I really cannot recal any events of my Life that would interest the Public, when I am dead I trust some friends will survive me who can record such deeds of mine as will give pleasure & satisfaction to the family I leave behind. Till that event closes my earthly career I prefer to be let alone. Though I have shared the dangers and exposures of several campaigns and Battlefields my memory recals none of those extraordinary acts of Heroism & valor that I see chronicled by others, who from their distance and elevation see far more than we whose eyes are blinded by the Smoke and dust of angry contending Hosts.

Although in your List of "Illustrations of military men" I recognize men with whom I am proud to be associated in Life, and with whom I expect to die, still I am both unable and unwilling to furnish either a Photograph which I have not and cannot obtain without a visit to Vicksburg where I have good reason to know I would not be a welcome visitor.

Should Peace be once more restored to our Distracted Country, through the instrumentality of the Volunteer Army I would then gladly contribute all I have to commemorate the Event and its antecedents but until that Event is complete by a full and just restoration of the authority and Power of our National Government, I must beg to be allowed to keep in as much obscurity as is possible under the circumstances.

With respects and thanks for the kind manner in which you make your proposal I am yr. obt. Servant

W. T. Sherman
Maj. Genl. Vols.

ADfS, DLC: William T. Sherman.

1. Frank J. Bramhall would publish *The Military Souvenir: A Portrait Gallery of Our Military and Naval Heroes* (New York, 1863).

Camp near Vicksburg, Feb. 26, 1863

Dearest Ellen,

I have yours of the 14th inst. and indeed I think all your letters have come somewhat in bunches, but I think all are at hand up to that of the 14th.[1] Of course I will heed your counsels about the newspaper Correspondents but it is hard for me to Know that they are used to spy out and report all our acts of omission & commission to be published at home to prejudice our Cause and advance that of our enemy. It is hard enough to Know that we have a strong well organized and vindictive Enemy in front, and a more dangerous insidious one within our very Camps. These Causes must defeat us, unless the People have resources enough to learn by the Slow and Sad progress of time what they might so much easier learn from Books or the example of our enemy. We look in vain to their newspapers for scraps from which to guess at the disposition of their forces and know and feel all the time that everything we do or attempt to do is paraded in all our newspapers which reach Vicksburg by telegraph from Richmond Va., or Memphis long before we are ourselves advised. I feel also that our Govt. instead of governing the Country is led first by one Class of newspaper, then another and that we are the mere shuttle cocks, flying between. We get all the Knocks & rarely see one grain of Encouragement from "home." I see the eulogies for the brave and heroic acts of men at Springfield Illinois, and Cincinati, and rarely anything but the paid and hired encomiums of some worthless Regiment here that understanding the nature of our People can get cheap representation by writing for the Press and neglecting all their duties here. The further we penetrate, the further we remove from home the less we are esteemed or encouraged. I did not intend to resign unless the Public opinion of the North made it prudent for the President to recal me nominally to Some other command, or unless I detected in my own Corps some symptoms of the natural results of the combined attacks of the Press, in either event, being footloose I would be justified before God & man in making my own choice of vocation. My old troops believe in me, but in this move 1 had a new batch that did not know me, and I had reason to apprehend mistrust on their part, as some of them are Known to me (like Blair), to be mere politicians who come to fight not for the real glory & success of the nation, but for their own individual aggrandizement. Let any accident befal me or any temporary reverse like that at Vicksburg the Same howl will be renewed, because these buzzards of the Press who hang in secret about our camps Know full well that death awaits them whenever I have the power, or when time develops their true character and influence. You in Ohio have one or two papers to conciliate: here we have all. St. Louis, Chicago, New

York, Cincinati, Charleston, Atlanta & Vicksburg—now these are all antagonistic save in one particular in esprit de corps. They stand by each other as a
Profession, but each gathers facts and draws its pictures to suit the home
Market—and really the Southern Correspondents are the most fair. Were I to
judge of public opinion by the tone of the press I would say we were here
regarded as an enemy to the North & rather favorable to the South. Of course
I shall no longer attempt to exclude spies from Camp and allow them to come
& go freely and collect their own budgets. The Ram *Queen of the West* was
captured by the enemy in Red River & yesterday came close up to Vicksburg
with the Rebel Flag flying in defiance. We have an iron boat below, the
Indianola but night before last heavy firing was heard until about 1 o'clock
when it ceased, and this fact being followed by the appearance of the captured
Ram looks bad. I fear the Indianola is gone, and that the Enemy has recovered
the use of the River below Vicksburg. This to us is a bad blow, and may lead to
worse consequences. I at once established a Battery of 20 lb. rifles below the
town and made other dispositions but the Ram has again gone below. I fear
for the Safety of the *Indianola*. If sunk it is not so bad, but if like the *Queen of
the West* she has fallen into the hands of the Enemy it may prove a calamity.
Rain, Rain—water above below and all round. I have been soused under water
by my horse falling in a hole, and got a good ducking yesterday walking where
a horse could not go. No doubt they are chuckling over our helpless situation
in Vicksburg. Accounts from Yazoo, & Providence Lake favorable, but rain,
rain & men cant work indeed hardly a place to Stand, much less lie down—
Hugh is in camp well—Charley is here with me. I saw Luke today, but he was
not drowned out. I made up my Pay accounts for Jan. & Feb. to send you, but
the Paymasters are here and I will send a check—do salt away some money for
I dont like the looks of things at all.

Of course I rejoice to hear such good accounts of Willy, Minnie & all the
children. Tell Tom his friends here always enquire for him and feel a great
interest in him. He will have a chance to fight in this war—Love to all Yrs. ever,

W. T. Sherman

ALS, InND: Sherman Family Papers.
1. EES to WTS, February 10, 1863; February 11, 1863, included more clippings (now lost),
among them an extract from a letter from Thomas Ewing Jr. to his father and the admon-
ishment that Halstead and his correspondents "would only need a kind word to enlist them
strongly as your firm friends." The *Cincinnati Gazette* was still against him because Tom
Worthington's brother-in-law was the editor. She suggested that when reporters disobeyed
his orders, WTS should "submit to them as you would to mosquitos or any other annoying
insect." On February 14, she wrote again about the papers, sympathizing with his frustrations but telling his that his family knew to ignore them and he should learn to do the same:
"But if you abandon your country & her cause when so few are competent & willing to
serve, I shall then indeed be distressed." SFP.

Camp near Vicksburg, Mch. 3, 1863.

Dear Phil,

Yours of Feb. 23 is received. I did not and do not intend to quit the Service unless I find the Press influences the powers above me or those below me. I feel every assurance that my own command feels in me the Same Confidence as before. They have the means to Know & feel the falsehood of the facts reported and the false deductions therefrom. I know that in McDowell's, Sumner's & Franklin's cases the President did allow a clamor to influence him and presumed he would in my case, and Knowing as I well do that reputation can be more easily acquired near home than abroad I made up my mind I would no longer submit to this blind abuse. The army is now well stocked with General Officers most of whom prefer service north of the Ohio where they can criticize and find fault with their fellows near the front and why should not they come and vindicate their persons in the rain & mud of actual warfare instead in cheap newspapers. Our Government has now spent two years of valuable time and near two thousand millions of dollars in arriving at a Conclusion that was plain to any man who had ever been south, and the late Conscription Act is the first sensible move I have yet seen. We have from the start been Compelled to combat superior forces, and to operate in a Country full of national difficulties, whose population was & is deadly hostile, whilst our own People have been more intent in building up and pulling down characters than in defeating the Enemy. If we have ever approached an end to this I will serve with as much Zeal as ever, but if I find that the Same game is to be continued, that men come to the army for political advantage in the hereafter, preventing the truth, distorting facts, and belying all who stand in the way of their fancied glory, I will quit. If Politicians want fame let them win it, if newspapers know best how to manouever & fight, why for godsake let them pitch in. There is fighting enough for them all. If the People prefer to believe Deserters, spies & Such I cant help it, and as they pay the Bill I suppose they have the right to play the game according to their own notions. I will not serve a Cause bolstered up by a set of sneaks and recreants. The army is tongue tied, but if I mistake not the day will come when a man who has not fought his share will be debarred his share in the Government. We all feel that it is wrong for us to have all the risk, dangers, and privations, besides the abuse & misrepresentations and allow these to govern us.

Jeff Davis has his People well in hand—his army is well organized, trained and disciplined, and nothing keeps the war from the well stocked plains & valleys of the North but the armies in the Field, yet our People plot & plan regardless of our opinions or wishes—never think ahead—but wait till the emergency comes and then complain of us. The whole People of the South are armed & enlisted in their Cause and if the North wish to Succeed as succeed they must—they must unite as one man and not underrate the magnitude of their task—all that has hitherto been done is in the way of education, and the War is yet to be fought.

We will not take Vicksburg by any Combinations yet made, but may by means of the Yazoo River reach Land, so as to make Vicksburg untenable. I sent Ellen my map, which is the best extant which will enable you to follow events. The loss of the *Queen of the West* & *Indianola* is a very serious one, as it gives the Enemy again the use of the River below Vicksburg and above Port Hudson, embracing the mouth of Red River.

If I see the least symptom of a want of Confidence in Grant or the President, or in my own Corps, I will of course resign, and really am I tired of the vacillating Policy of our Government & People, & sorry that I ever embarked in a voyage so sure to be disastrous to the first actors.

All have very good health now, and send love to the Folks at home—Ellen writes very often and I write to her almost daily. Affectionately

W. T. Sherman

ALS, DLC: Thomas Ewing and Family Papers.

TO THOMAS EWING SR.

Hd. Qrs. 15 Army Corps.
Camp before Vicksburg, Mch. 7, 63

Hon. T. Ewing
Dear Sir,

Yours of Feb. 20, was not recd. till today. By tomorrow all my camp will be under water and we will be limited to the Levee and such boats as we can obtain. I will therefore for some time be limited in the means of writing and will avail myself of present appliances. I sent Ellen a map compiled from actual movements, angles & intersecting lines, which will show you the difficulties surrounding Vicksburg. To invest it we should have a vastly superior force, and Should be on the same side of the River, but thus far we have not superior forces, or are we on the other Side of the Mississipi. To carry the plan by assault or Regular approaches will be equally costly to life, as the latter involves time & exposure in a strange climate which is as fatal to life as bullets. Our plan thus far was to prepare three 3 Lines of approach: by the Main River: by the Yazoo entering at its head: and by the Tensas and Red Rivers, by which we turn Vicksburg and all the Bluffs which lie on the East bank of the River. The latter is the only one which solves all the problems. We command the Main River to Vicksburg, but have lost it below since the rebels captured the

Queen of the West & the *Indianola*: the Yazoo is a success, and a joint expedition of troops and Gun boats are in, and will be followed by a stronger force at once: the last is progressing but we have not force enough to operate on all at the Same time. Even if we cannot with our present means take Vicksburg we have thus far alienated Arkansas & North Louisiana from the other Rebel parts, and time must influence the inhabitants. If we can succeed in passing boats down the Tensas, the effect will be similar on a larger scale, but none of these conquer the South. This can only be done by meeting them in battle on all occasions and fighting it out—we must make them fear us, that respect may follow.

As you say we have much to fear from Anarchy among our People we have long been drifting that way. I would gladly escape it, and will do so if the President ever manifests the least impatience with me, or if my command is ever shaken by the Press that regard me as their Enemy. I do think the Free Press has done as much to lower our National Character, and pull down our Government as Slavery. It is our course, and this war cannot end, until it is brought within proper restraint & limits. I want to see our Government so strong that no one will dare defy it anywhere or at any time, and it makes little difference whether it be South or North. My own command has always manifested for me the utmost faith & confidence. They know & feel that I have but one simple Rule that they all understand. McClernand is an old politician who looks to self aggrandizement, and is not scrupulous of the means. Grant is brave, honest, & true, but not a Genius. McPherson is a fine soldier & Gentleman. Steele, Logan, & others are good Soldiers, but Blair is a "disturbing Element." I wish he was in Congress or a Bar Room, any where but our Army.

Ellen can tell you of Charley, Hugh & all here for she has a large correspondence. Tom is not with us. Yrs. affectionately

W. T. Sherman

ALS, PCarlA.

TO DAVID TOD

Headqrts. 15th Army Corps
Camp before Vicksburg, March 12, 1863

His Excellency Gov. Tod of Ohio.
Sir,

Your favor of March 1st is received.[1] Young Wallace has gone with his Corps up to Millikens Bend, where I will sent him word, to get the consent of some Colonel of an Infantry Regiment, that he (Wallace) may be promoted in his Regiment.[2]

I feel no solicitude for men so young as Wallace, as knowledge and experience will be gained, which will surely lead to his promotion, and advancement in the end.

I believe you will pardon one, who rarely travels out of his proper sphere to express an earnest hope, that the strengths of our people will not again be wasted, by the organisation of new Regiments whilst we have in the field Skeleton Regiments with Officers, N. C. Officers and men, who only need numbers, to make a magnificent Army.

The President of the United States is now clothed with a power, that should have been conferred just two years ago, and I feel assured, he will use it. He will call for a large mass of men, and they should all be privates, and sent so as to make every Regiment in the field equal to one thousand men. Time has convinced all reasonable men, that war in theory and practice are two distinct things. Many an honest patriot, full of enthusiasm, zeal and thirst for Glory has in practice found himself unequal to the actual requirements of war; and passed to one side, leaving another to his place, and now, after two years Ohio has in the field 126 Regts., whose Officers *now* are qualified, and the men of which would give tone and character to the new recruits. To fill these Regiments, will require 50,000 Recruits, which are so many, as the State could well raise. I therefore hope and pray, that you will use your influence against any more new Regiments, and consolidation of old ones but fill up all the old ones to a full standard. Those, who talk about prompt and speedy peace know not what they say.

The South today is more formidable and arrogant, than she was two years ago, and we lose far more by having an insufficient number of men, than from any other cause. We are forced to invade—we must keep the War South, till they are not only ruined, exhausted, but humbled in pride and spirit. Admitting, that our Armies to the front are equal to the occasion, which I know, is not the case, our lines of communication are ever threatened by their dashes, for which the country, the population and character of the enemy are all perfectly adapted. The whole male population of the South is aimed against us, and we ought to outnumber them, we must outnumber them, if we want to succeed, and the quicker, the better.

Since the first hostile shot, the people of the North has had no option, they must conquer, or be conquered. There can be no midate course. I have never been concerned about the copperhead quabblings, the South spurns and despises this class worse then we do, and would only accept their overtures, to substitute them in their levies—in their cotton and corn fields, for the slaves, who have escaped—I do not pretend, nor have I ever pretended, to foresee [the] end to all this, but I do know, that it is no longer an open question, we *must* fight it out. The moment we relax, down go all our conquests, thus far. I know, my views on this point have ever been regarded as extreme, even verging on to insanity, but for years I had associated with Bragg, Beauregard, and extreme Southern men, and long before others could realize the fact, that Americans would raise their hands against our consecrated government, I was forced to know it, to witness it. Two years will not have been spent in vain, if the North now, by another magnificent upheaving of the real people again fill the ranks of your proven and tried Regiments, and assure them, that through good report, and evil report you will stand by them.

If Ohio will do this, and if the great North will do this, then will our Army feel, that it has a country and a Government worth dying for.

As to the Poltroons, who falter and cry quits, let them dig, and raise the food, this Army needs, but they should never claim a voice in the councils of the nation. With sentiments of great respect I am yours truly

W. T. S.

Major General

Lbk, DNA: RG 94, Records of the Adjutant General's Office, Generals' Books and Papers, William T. Sherman, Letterbook 5; *OR*, III, 3:65–66.

1. Tod to WTS, March 1, 1863, DLC: WTS. Tod had said that voluntary enlistments in Ohio would not be large enough to fill the ranks of state regiments, but if the pending conscription act was passed, he would have no trouble raising men. He also observed that the North's spirit had become more militant.

2. WTS had apparently written to Tod on February 14 recommending a Sergeant Wallace who wished to be transferred to and promoted in another regiment than the one in which he currently served. Tod responded in his letter of March 1 that he would be happy to do what he could but that he needed a letter from the officer of the regiment Wallace wished to join requesting his transfer.

TO ELLEN EWING SHERMAN

Camp before Vicksburg, Mch. 13, 1863

Dearest Ellen,

The trunk of dainties came yesterday.[1] I sent for Charley & Hugh, both of whom are quite well and placed the contents before them, much to their delight. I must confess I could not but laugh at your medicines for Charley, accompanied by a fruit cake that would kill a laboring man. Charley took charge of the can of oysters and savories for Major Chase.

The waters are still rising and Kilby Smith's Brigade is roosting on the Levee with bare standing room. McClernands Corps is at Millikens Bend—and my corps strung along the Levee for four miles. The Levee is about 10 feet wide at top with sloping sides and can hold all the men & may be horses in case of an absolute flood. We have not steamboats enough to float us and if we had there is no dry land to go to. An expedition has entered the Yazoo from above, and when it is heard from we probably will make another dash at Vicksburg, or Drumgoules. I see the whole North is again in agonies about the amount of sickness down here. It is not excessive, not more than Should be expected not more than we had on the Potomac and Tennessee, and our supplies are the best I ever saw. There is a deep laid plan to cripple us, laid by Jeff Davis who is smart and knows our People well. By a few thousands of dollars well invested in newspapers he can defeat any plan or undertaking.

Many really well disposed men have come from St. Louis, Cincinati and Washington and have been amazed at the falsehood of these stories. Only one man of the Regulars has died since we left Memphis. My old Regiments are all in fine health & spirits, some of the new Regiments have passed through the ordeal which afflicts all new troops.

Taylor & McCoy are not yet back, but are hourly expected. Hammond goes to Kentucky in a few days to Seek employment in the Cavalry. I have encouraged him to this as he is not fit for Adjt. Genl. The War Department have not given me any staff and yet have taken from me the right to appoint any. The truth is now as it always was that persons at a distance are neglected, and those near the Seat of power petted. We have made further progress than any army with less means. In Vicksburg we met our match and time must solve the difficulty, but so long as our Camps are full of newspaper spies, revealing each move, exaggerating our troubles & difficulties and giving grounds for discontent, success cannot be expected.

The New Conscript Law is the best act of our Government, and Mr. Lincoln can no longer complain of want of Power—he now is absolute Dictator, and if he dont use the power some one will.

The weather now is very fine, and warm, trees are leafing & blooming. This is against us as the Shores become close ambush from which Guerrillas safely fire on our Boats. McDowell has resigned.[2] Denvers Division will remain at Lagrange and Laumans is assigned to my corps, but where he is I dont know. All the troops between us and Memphis will enter the Yazoo by way of Yazoo Pass. By that route they may reach Yazoo City and then by Land move towards Vicksburg, but this is dividing our forces which is always objectionable in war. I watch with deep interest the Presidents course under the Conscription Law. If he neglect to use all the power thus conferred it will be hard with our army reduced as it is by sickness and desertion.

Give my love to all & believe me ever yours,

W. T. Sherman

ALS, InND: Sherman Family Papers.
1. EES to WTS, March 2, 1863, SFP.
2. Probably Colonel John A. McDowell, a brigade commander in the Fifteenth Corps.

Camp before Vicksburg, Mch. 14, 63.

Dear Brother,

I have your letter of Feb. 20, 63, in which you give me particular fits for saying that I would resign.[1] I took it for granted that Mr. Lincoln would yield to newspaper clamor & hold me responsible for their lies, in which case I had resolved to quit. I see such a deep seated determination to find fault & clamor that I would rather be a miner in California a grazer in Kansas a Railroad employee in St. Louis to holding the highest office under the Government. Of course I was wrong, and as the President has not called on me to answer these Knaves I have done nothing. You in Washington cannot feel the same as we do away down here in mud & mire, a mere skeleton of an army, jum[p]ed on by Coward rascals who stay behind & blackguard us because we do not enact impossibilities.

The Conscript Bill is all even I could ask it is the first real step towards war, and if Mr. Lincoln will now use the power thus conferred ignore popular clamor and do as near what is right as he can we may at last have an army somewhat approximating the vast undertaking which was begun in utter blind wilful ignorance of the difficulties and dangers that we were forced to encounter. Only one thing was omitted, viz. that no one should vote hereafter who did not serve his three years in the war, or contribute largely to its support & maintenance.

The new appointments still smack too much of politics, viz. men are made Major Generals who have been in no battle or but one, whereas others have been neglected who have been steadfast for the first but the Revolution has progressed as fast as any one could expect. Another year of war will bring our People to the point where the South began.

I do not like to write to Stanton or Halleck because it is not my place, but I would be obliged if you would for me. It is vastly important that the new Levies should all come in as privates and be assigned to the old Regiments. Drafted men who have held aloof are not entitled to a share of officers, and now every Regiment has a full proportion of officers, Sergeants & corporals and have moreover the necessary wagons, tents, and armies. It will be a simple process, whereas if an attempt be made to consolidate, half the officers will be thrown out. Regiments or half of them will lose their past history, and will be offended at being assigned to others, it may be rival ones. There is a clause in the Conscription Bill which provides for consolidating old Regiments, and I know Governors of states will urge upon the Department that it will be much easier to raise new Regiments with officers, than to get privates to be assigned to strange officers. Besides the reasons above named I will add another. New

Regiments with inexperienced capts., sergeants and corporals dont know how to take care of themselves and suffer unnecessarily in health. They cant know how to make their camps, how to march, how to cook, how to shelter themselves so that in three months they fall away to mere skeletons. The New Regiments which joined four months ago, have fallen off from 1000 to an average of 300 for duty. Now this same number of men, distributed to old organizations learn quickly from association, and escape in a measure the consequent sickness and death. All considerations should now yield to common sense. Enough sacrifices have been made to popularity. The country knows now that war is not a popularity making machine, but a dread reality that threatens not only the integrity of Government, but the life of every man in the nation, and the safety of every house. Our men have acted so, that the Southern army could not be restrained if it should penetrate the North. We have burned, ravished and destroyed where ever we have gone, and we could not expect them to do less.

We are no nearer taking Vicksburg now that we were three months ago. A pass is made into the Yazoo, by which we may introduce an army as far as yazoo City, but Vicksburg is as far off as ever, *not a blow* has been struck at it since I assaulted Chickasaw. The Canal here is worthless, and the Country is so overflowed that we are roosting on a narrow levee. The Country, the people may find fault. Let them come & do better. The Conscript Bill will give them a good chance. I have been much pleased with your course in Congress, and regret that any thing I have done or may do has given you trouble or concern. I would easily have been popular, as I believe I am with my own command, by courting the newspaper men, but it does go hard to know that our Camps are full of spies, revealing our most secret steps, conveying regularly to the enemy our every act when a thousand dollars wont procure us a word of information from Vicksburg. I know the Press has defeated us, and will continue to do it, and as an honest man I cannot flatter them. I know they will ruin me, but they will ruin the country too. As long as the Press is unlicensed we must be defeated. We deserve it. Knowing the South as I do, I feel it the more keenly when I Know they are laughing at our folly. If the President will now call out six hundred thousand privates, and instruct his District Provost Marshals to imprison any man, editor or spy, who dares to report the movement of a single Regiment, we can then begin to make military combinations, but so long as the system of puffing & prophesying and publishing of the past is maintained I cannot conscientiously attempt anything or advise anything. Napoleon himself would have been defeated with a free press. But I will honestly try to be patient though I Know in this as in other matters time *must* bring about its true result, just as the summer ripens the fruits of the season.

Henry Sherman is well, but has not yet received his Commission. I fear Stuart[2] is left out among the new Brigadiers, also Hugh Ewing, who has an Excellent Brigade.[3] McClernands Corps has moved up to Millikens Bend to keep out of the water and my Corps is alone here at the neck opposite Vicksburg, fighting off the water of the Missississipi which threatens to drown us. Grant is here on board a boat, & Admiral Porter at the Mouth of Yazoo. Affectionately,

W. T. Sherman

ALS, DLC: William T. Sherman.

1. Actually JS to WTS, February 26, 1863. JS had scolded his brother for thinking of resigning, saying that it would harm the family and let down the nation, his men, and his fellow officers. He urged WTS not to be defeated "by a lot of newspaper correspondents—by the thoughtless interference of a fool President & by the jealousies of a few rivals." WTS's resignation, he continued, would show him guilty of just such rashness as his enemies accused him of having. DLC: WTS.

2. David Stuart's November 1862 commission to brigadier general of volunteers was voted down by the Senate on March 13, 1863, apparently because of his involvement in a divorce case in Chicago before the war. Stuart had been named a correspondent, and although he was later proven innocent of the charge of adultery, the story had stuck. EES to WTS, March 26, 1863, SFP. In his *Memoirs*, WTS later remarked that "he had failed in securing a confirmation by the Senate to his nomination as brigadier-general, by reason of some old affair at Chicago." *PM*, 1:341.

3. Ewing's November commission was confirmed.

TO MARIA BOYLE EWING SHERMAN

Camp before Vicksburg, March 15, 1863

Dear Minnie,

Your very good letter of February 25 came to me in a cover from your Mama at Lancaster, and I was much pleased to notice the improvement in your hand writing. It is now very plain and no matter how hurried you may be always write plain so that your words may be easily read. You are old Enough to Know that God creates all things exactly right—he brings you into the world a poor little child helpless and dependant upon the parents who feed you, and clothe you, and educate you so that when in time you become a woman you will be a pride to your parents and a being whom a good husband will love and cherish with a love stronger than you now feel for us. He gives you twenty long years to grow and gain bodily strength, and to learn all the mind can acquire in the fresh springtime of Life. Your Eye learns every day to see things as they are, Your memory learns facts in Geography and history and in science, and your hand learns to sew, to embroider, to paint, to draw and to write, but as you get older your hand will learn no more but will do as it has been taught, therefore now is the time to learn to write plain and well and habit will make it Easy. Your Mama writes very fast and very plain. You Know her letters before you open them and you Know how good you feel that her hand traced the letters.

I am always glad to hear you are happy. I hope you always will be and you will be sure of it, by learning to do as your Teachers tell you. They will provide for you plays and sports, and I will be glad to hear you are happy, singing, dancing, and making merry. God designs all these things to compensate for the troubles and Cares which come fast enough.

So Sister Angela has gone to France. I had not heard she had gone to the North from Memphis. Is she coming back? and when?

There are some sisters of Charity on a boat at the Mouth of the Yazoo who send me Kind messages, they are with Admiral Porter's fleet, and not with my army. One of them sent me a can of preserves she had received from Ohio. They are the best possible nurses for the sick, and as always so clean and neat that it does one good to see them moving about so kindly among the Sick soldiers and Sailors.

Uncle Boyle and Charley are here and I will give them your message. They think of Little Minnie with as much pride as I do. Indeed you are lucky in having so many good relatives and will never want for friends in this world. Luke Clark is a Corporal in Uncle Charley's Company, and is very well.

Tell Granma Redman I remember very well how I used to go to her house, when I was about your age. Give her my best love. Also tell your teachers that if I survive this war and have it in my power I will not forget those who are Kind and good to my Minnie & Willy. Write to me very often and tell Willy to do the same, and tell me all about your studies and Companions. Your loving father,

W. T. Sherman

ALS, OHi: William T. Sherman Papers.

TO STEPHEN A. HURLBUT

Hd. Qrs. 15 Army Corps,
Camp before Vicksburg, Mch. 16, 1863

Genl. S. A. Hurlbut
My Dear Friend

I had always intended to Keep up a communication with you because I regard you as one of the school of men on whom all parties in the End must lean for stability and Security of Government—You cannot imagine my Surprise to read that in the Senate yours and Stuarts nominations were opposed.[1] What are the reasons? they cannot be military or national. Must be local. Who is at the bottom of this? Is it possible while you and Stuart constantly on duty & good duty, and Successful duty, for Say what others may of alternate victory and defeat, we have made more real progress in the war than any other

Column, and yet our most steadfast officers are questioned by the Senate. I Know not the result as yet, and await the news of the final action of the Senate with much concern. In this case as is generally so, we do not hear of adverse influences till it is too late to counter and throw.

Of course I have been foolish to excite the animosity of the newspaper fraternity as a class. I dont think I am very proud, but this class of men are so supercilious that whenever I come in contact with them I feel a natural repugnance which they are smart enough to see.

Since I commenced this letter I have ben {manoeuvred} up to Youngs Point 4 miles above my camp, to Genl. Grants boat. He has been up a Bayou through which he expects he can make a channel into the Yazoo above the Fortifications. He wants me to go up tomorrow to reconnoitre, and I shall go up in a tug tomorrow morning. I cannot mention the exact route. I have always believed the place we started out with the best & only, viz. for the Main Army to march down as though threatening Jackson & Vicksburg, to reach the Yazoo at Yazoo City & then along down to Black River Bridge to the rear of Vicksburg. A smaller force all afloat to act in front the moment the guns of the main attack be heard. Still the country has no reason to be clamorous, as we are far ahead of Rosecrans and Hooker. Col. Johnson is with me as an aid, but the moment I know his Division is going into action I will advise him to join it, for that is what he is after.

I beg to assure you of my respect and affection, and hope you will have patience to bear the buffets of fortune. Like many other wise men, I can give excellent advice though impatient to follow it myself.

I should be glad to hear from you. Mrs. Sherman always sends you messages of regard & esteem. The War is far from being over and in its many phases for the future surely some will favor that class of men who have a pure motive, Love of Country as opposed to others who simply have a personal ambition or Vanity to Subserve. With great respect Yr. friend,

W. T. Sherman
Maj. Genl.

ALS, New York: The Gilder Lehrman Collection.

1. Hurlbut, who had been made a major general of volunteers on September 17, 1862, had had his nomination returned to Lincoln by the Senate because it was dated during a congressional recess. When Lincoln resubmitted his name, the Senate quickly confirmed the appointment on March 13, 1863.

William Tecumseh Sherman and Thomas Ewing Sherman
(Archives of the University of Notre Dame)

Ellen Ewing Sherman and Thomas Ewing Sherman
(Archives of the University of Notre Dame)

William Tecumseh Sherman Jr., "Willy"
(Archives of the University of Notre Dame)

Thomas Ewing Sr. (Archives of the University of Notre Dame)

The four Sherman girls:
Lizzie, Rachel, Elly, and Minnie
(Fairfield Heritage Association)

John Sherman (Library of Congress)

The four Ewing brothers: Hugh, Philemon, Thomas, and Charles, in 1864
(Fairfield Heritage Association)

James B. McPherson (United States Army Military History Institute)

Ulysses S. Grant
(National Archives)

Henry W. Halleck
(Library of Congress)

William T. Sherman, commanding the Military Division of the Mississippi, and his generals: 1. Major General O. O. Howard, 2. Major General John A. Logan, 3. Major General William B. Hazen, 4. Major General William T. Sherman, 5. Major General Jefferson C. Davis, 6. Major General Henry W. Slocum, 7. Major General Joseph A. Mower, and 8. Major General Frank P. Blair (National Archives)

Major General William T. Sherman at Atlanta (Library of Congress)

CHAPTER 8

April 3, 1863–July 4, 1863

*T*he coming of spring in 1863 did not at first brighten William T. Sherman's grim visage. He remained convinced that Grant's efforts to take Vicksburg were doomed to failure; he believed that it was time to pull back to Memphis and attempt once more the plan tried in December 1862. It did not help that Grant rejected this plan on the grounds that such a retrograde movement, however wise it might seem, would be interpreted by the press, public, and politicians as a retreat (and might well cost Grant his command). To Sherman this was simply more evidence of the tyranny of public opinion in a democratic society. So were President Lincoln's efforts on behalf of correspondent Thomas W. Knox, who sought permission to return to cover the Army of the Tennessee for the *New York Herald*. In this instance, however, Sherman derived satisfaction from Grant's decision to leave the final verdict to Sherman, who curtly rejected Knox's application.

At the beginning of April, Grant revealed to Sherman and his other generals yet another plan for capturing Vicksburg. He would march his army south and cross the Mississippi near Grand Gulf, south of Vicksburg; Admiral David D. Porter's gunboats and transports would run Vicksburg's batteries under cover of darkness to ferry Grant's men across the river. Sherman objected strongly and reiterated his preference for a campaign modeled on the endeavor of the previous December. Once more he worried about the impact of politics on military operations. Distrustful of John A. McClernand, who was actively scheming to replace Grant, Sherman sought to pin down his fellow corps commander before the campaign to forestall future criticism. Nor did the arrival of several visitors from Washington quiet his fears; Sherman assumed (correctly) that they had come to investigate Grant's command with an eye toward his possible removal. He cared little for Adjutant General Lorenzo Thomas's efforts to recruit black regiments, openly doubting whether former slaves were capable of becoming good soldiers (much as he had once doubted the quality of volunteers). All the signs that spring pointed to eventual disaster.

When Grant commenced his movement southward, Sherman repeatedly made clear his disapproval. As he consciously tried to distance himself from the operation, his letters may have inadvertently added to the concern felt elsewhere about Grant's fitness for command. Grant, however, appreciating Sherman's willingness to cooperate regardless of his personal assessment of the feasibility of the plan, trusted him to keep an eye on Vicksburg while he kept an eye on McClernand. Needing Sherman to launch a diversionary movement, Grant played on Sherman's mistrust of the press by phrasing his instructions in the form of a request, for reporters might well interpret the feint and withdrawal as another defeat. It worked like a charm: Sherman replied, "We will make as strong a demonstration as possible. The troops will all understand the purpose and will not be hurt by the repulse. The People of the Country must find out the Truth as they best can. It is none of their business. You are engaged in a hazardous enterprize and for good reason wish to divert attention. That is sufficient to me and it shall be done." His men would not be "humbugged." As for the press accounts, "we must scorn them else they will ruin us and our country. They are as much enemies to Good Government as the secesh, and between the two I like the secesh best, because they are a brave open enemy & not a set of sneaking croaking scoundrels."[1]

Nevertheless, Sherman remained a doubter, even after Grant crossed the Mississippi. He wondered how Grant would keep his command supplied, only to learn that Grant planned to live off the land while maintaining a convoy for other supplies—and it worked, as Sherman learned when he caught up with Grant on May 9. In solving this logistical puzzle, Grant opened Sherman's eyes; in beating back the Confederates at Jackson, Champion's Hill, and Big Black River, Grant achieved what Sherman thought impossible. On May 18, as the two men rode over to Chickasaw Bluffs, they came upon the now-deserted fortifications that had thwarted Sherman the previous December. Finally, Sherman turned to Grant. "Until this moment I never thought your expedition a success; I could never see the end clearly until now. But this is a campaign; this is a success if we never take the town."[2]

Success would not be complete until Vicksburg fell. After the Confederates turned back assaults on May 19 and 22, Grant settled down to starve out the defenders with a siege. For the next six weeks, Sherman took the opportunity to vent his frustration about the relative lack of recognition accorded the Army of the Tennessee, the failure of the Lincoln administration to fill up veteran regiments, and the fickle nature of fame. He celebrated Grant's removal of McClernand on June 18 but grumbled several days later when Grant ordered him to take charge of a force that would fend off attempts to lift the siege—thus depriving him of the chance to ride into Vicksburg when it fell on July 4.

1. WTS to USG, April 28, 1863 (two letters), *PUSG*, 8:130–31.
2. Lloyd Lewis, *Sherman: Fighting Prophet* (1932; reprint, Lincoln, Neb., 1993), 277.

TO JOHN SHERMAN

Hd. Qrs. 15 Army Corps
Camp before Vicksburg, Apl. 3, 63

My Dear Brother,

I received your long letter from Mansfield for which I am much obliged[.] You certainly have achieved an envious name in the Senate and I confess I am astonished at your industry and acquirements. I readily understand how in a Revolution of the magnitude that now involves us all, older men should devolve on you & the younger school of men the legislation & experiments necessary to meet a state of facts so different from the Common run of events. The Finance Bill[1] and Conscription Acts of the late Congress in my Judgmt. may keep the management of the affairs of the nation in the hands of the Constitutional Government. Any thing short of them, the war would have drifted out of the Control of President & Congress. Now if Mr. Lincoln will assume the same positive tone that Davis did at the outset he can unite the fighting North against the fighting South, and numerical force systematized will settle the war[.] I know the impatience of the People, but this is one of the lessons of war—People must learn that war is a question of physical force and Carnage. A million of men engaged in peaceful pursuits will be vanquished by a few thousand determined armed men. The Justice of the Cause has nothing to do with it—It is a question of force. Again we are the assailants, and have to overcome not only an equal number of determined men, however wrongfully engaged, but the natural obstacles of a most difficult Country. We get hundreds of most ingenious and honest hints how to take Vicksburg, but the fact is we have not yet got at Vicksburg. We have not got on Shore—no man can wade the Mississipi or the deep sloughs and marshes that surround it, and as to moving our frail Mississipi Boats up to their well handled artillery, it would be simple destruction doing no good. I feel certain that after all, we must recur to the original plan, of the main army marching down by land between the Yazoo and Big Black, whilst a smaller force operates along the river ready to cooperate the moment the main army is engaged inland. The only mistake I made was in not waiting to see the Signs of Grants approach, but to have come to Vicksburg & return would have been as bad as to come to blows as I did. My own opinion is we should fight on all occasions even if we do get worsted—we can stand it longest—We are killing Arkansas & Louisiana—All the lands are overflown and they cannot Cultivate. All the people are moving to Texas with their negroes & cattle—Let them go—Let the back door open, & let them have Texas. Admit an irreconcilability of interest & Character, but assert the absolute Right to the Valley of the Mississipi and leave malcontents go freely to Texas. Once there their pugnacious propensities will be aimed at Mexico. I think immediately the President should call for 500,000 men to fill the Ranks of Existing Regiments. These are now mere skeletons, and should be filled up, when we would have an army of sufficient size, indeed as many as could be handled, but if this be deferred too long, Rosecrans will go tumbling back to the Ohio, our Rear will be threatened East & West, and all the fruits of the past two years lost—The advanced armies are probably large enough, and if equally large Reserves were held to our Rear, there would be no attempt to pass round us. No one doubts that the great mass of People behind us are more determined than ever in their resolve to fight to the last—none more so than the women and children, who simply manifest the real feelings of the men. The Copperheads are easily managed—Disfranchise them. If they wont fight they certainly should have no voice in the Councils of the Nation. Deprive them of their votes & let them sink into mere serfs and they become harmless but useful laborers. As to newspapers & correspondents I am too far committed to change—I cannot show them my instructions. That would be perjury. I cannot confide in them because I dont know any. Their blows come so far as I am concerned from dark & secret sources. I could not guard against them because I never know of their plots till the mischief is done. They are unknown to me, appear in the disguise of sutlers clerks, Cotton thieves and that class of vultures that hang round every army. I never saw or heard of Knox till he had published his falsehoods, and when I did send for him & he admitted how false he had been he Enunciated the Sentiment, that his trade was to collect news, he must furnish reading matter for sale, true if possible otherwise false. Can I or any honest man minister to such a class. If this be so, if our Country is so greedy after news that it must be crammed with false-hood, then is this Revolution right, then we need a master just such as Jeff Davis. The Devil himself would be a better Ruler than People who must be fed on libel & falsehood. Mr Lincoln is President of the U.S. and can command me to go to certain death, and knows I will obey him—he knows that Knox slandered me & that my tongue was tied by a true allegiance to him, and yet tis said he Mr Lincoln has given Knox permission to come to this army & report anew his falsehoods. I dont believe this. It may be so however, but I will tell Mr Lincoln to his face that even he shall not insult me. If Knox comes into my Camp he will never leave it again at liberty. I have soldiers who will obey my orders, and Knox shall go down the Mississipi, floating on a log if he can find one, but he shall not come into my Camp with impunity again.

It is absurd to say these correspondents relieve the anxieties of parents, friends, &c.—Our soldiers write constantly and receive immense numbers of letters. This is right, and if newspapers would report only local matters & discuss matters within their knowledge, parents & families would not be kept half frantic with the accounts of sickness, death, massacre &c of their children & relations. We have had hundreds of visitors from every quarter to Examine our Camps because correspondents represented us as all dying, when the truth is no army was ever better provided for and supplied—We are camped on narrow slips of levee and ground because All Else is under Water. To get on dry ground we must go back to Memphis or Helena.

Notwithstanding the immense amount of abuse of me, I know that all my soldiers are attached to me, and Every officer of whatever Rank who arrives applies for my Corps, because they know I am truthful and will not slaughter them to build up a little personal fame. McClernand is a dirty dog, consumed by a burning desire for personal renown—McPherson is a splendid officer. Grant is honest & does his best. I will do as ordered. I will suggest little, as others talked of my failing to take Vicksburg & I want them to try a hand. I accomplished more in the two weeks I was in command than has been done since, for I claim Arkansas Post—Since McClernand has foolishly laid claim Even to the conception of it, when it is known to many that I had to coax him to allow it to be done. We have been digging canals, and trying to reach the Yazoo by every conceivable channel, but all are unsuccessful, and we stand just where we did. I dont blame Grant or anybody. These are things bordering on the impossible, and to take Vicksburg without the deadly & costly assault is impossible, save by a strong irresistable army moving down inland via Granada. We are doing good—We have isolated Arkansas & north Louisiana from the Confederacy, and their armies have simply wilted away & will be hard to revive unless their arms have immense success against Rosecrans. There is where they will strike, and the quicker Kentucky has the original 200,000 the better.

If I were you, I would make no change in your home or private affairs till you begin to see an End to war. I tell you tis all nonsense about the South being exhausted. I was up to Dan Creek last week, and up Yazoo to sight of Haines Bluff and whilst the northern papers talk about Starvation in Vicksburg I tell you we saw every where cattle, hogs, sheep, poultry and vast cribs of corn. We have Consumed much, and destroyed more, but tis folly to talk of Starvation. Their soldiers are well clad & fat. They are cheerful on their beef & corn bread—Rice & molasses, whilst our men growl over a Ration Such as no Soldier on earth ever before enjoyed. I get deserters & other information daily, and I see not one Symptom of relaxation, on the contrary quite the reverse. The war in Earnest has yet to be fought—Wait therefore before you make changes. Lay low and study events as they develop. As ever yrs. affectionately
W. T. S.

ALS, DLC: William T. Sherman Papers.
1. On March 3, 1863, Lincoln signed the law authorizing the secretary of the treasury to borrow on U.S. credit $300 million in 1863 and $600 million in 1864 for the war effort.

TO THOMAS W. KNOX

Headqrts. 15th Army Corps
Camp before Vicksburg, April 7, 1863

Thos. W. Knox, Esqr.
Corresp. N. Y. Herald
84. Continental
Sir,

Yours of April 6th enclosing copy of President Lincoln's informal decision in your case is received.[1]

I certainly do regret, that Generals McClernand and Thayer[2] regard the disobedience of Orders, emanating from the highest Military source, and the publication of wilful and malicious slanders and libels, against their brother Officers as mere technical offenses, and notwithstanding the Presidents endorsements of that conclusion, I cannot so regard it.

After having enunciated to me the fact, that newspaper correspondents were a fraternity, bound together by a common interest, that must write down all, who stood in their way, and that you had to supply the public demand for news, true if possible, and false, if your interest demanded it, I cannot be privy to a tacit acknowledgment of the principle.

Come with a sword or musket in your hand, prepared to share with us our fate, in sunshine and storm, in prosperity and adversity, in plenty and scarcity, and I will welcome you as a brother and associate. But come as you now do, expecting me to ally the honor and reputation of my country and my fellow Soldiers with you as the representative of the press, which you yourself say, makes so slight a difference between truth and falsehood, and my answer is Never. I am &c.

W. T. Sherman
Maj. Genl. Vols.

Lbk, DNA: RG 94, Records of the Adjutant General's Office, Generals' Books and Papers, William T. Sherman, Letterbook 5; *OR*, I, 17: pt. 2, 894–95.
1. On March 20, Lincoln issued an executive order permitting Knox to return to Grant's headquarters because Thayer, head of his court-martial, and McClernand, among others, thought Knox's offense was technically rather than willfully wrong. Lincoln stipulated, however, that USG could refuse Knox permission to remain and send him away. DLC: WTS. On April 6, USG scolded Knox for coming in violation of WTS's orders and deplored his treatment of WTS in print. He concluded, "Gen. Sherman is one of the ablest soldiers, and finest men in the country. You have attacked him, and been sentenced to expulsion from this Department," and though he wished to accede to Lincoln's order, his feelings for WTS

dictated that "I must decline unless Gen. S. first gives his consent to your remaining." DLC: WTS. That same day Knox wrote WTS, enclosing a copy of Lincoln's order and stating that "Gen. Grant has expressed his willingness to give such approval provided there is no objection from yourself." He expressed regret at the tone of relations between the army and the press and spoke of his desire to return and record the imminent fall of Vicksburg. DLC: WTS. This correspondence is reprinted in *OR*, I, 17: pt. 2, 893–94.

2. Brigadier General John Milton Thayer (1820–1906), USA, led the Third Brigade, First Division, Fifteenth Corps, during the Vicksburg campaign and had been the president of Knox's court-martial.

TO ULYSSES S. GRANT

Headqrts. 15th Army Corps.
Camp near Vicksburg, April 8th, 1863

Major Genl. Grant
Dear Sir,

I received last night the copy of your answer to Mr. Knox's application to return and reside near your Headqrts. I thank you for the manner and substance of that reply. Many regard Knox as unworthy the notice he has received—but I send you his letter to me, and my answer. Observe in his letter to me, sent long before I could have heard the result of his application to you, he makes the assertion, that you had no objection, but rather wanted him back, and only as a matter of form required my assent. He regretted a difference between a portion of the Army and the Press.

The insolence of these fellows is insupportable. I know, they are encouraged, but I know human nature well enough, and that they will be the first to turn against their patrons.

Mr. Lincoln of course fears to incur the enmity of the *Herald*—but he must rule the Herald, or the Herald will rule him, he can take his choice.

I have been foolish and unskilful in drawing on me the shafts of the Press, by opposing Mob-Law in California, I once before drew down the Press—but after the smoke cleared off, and the people saw, where they were drifting to, they admitted, I was right. If the Press be allowed to run riot, and write up and write down at their pleasure, there is an end to constitutional government in America, and Anarchy must result. Even now the real people of our country begin to fear and tremble at it, and look to our armies as the anchor of safety, of order, submission to authority bound together by a real government, and not by the clamor of a demoralized Press and crowd of demagogues. As ever your friend

W. T. Sherman

Lbk, DNA: RG 94, Records of the Adjutant General's Office, Generals' Books and Papers, William T. Sherman, Letterbook 5; *OR*, I, 17: pt. 2, 895.

TO MURAT HALSTEAD[1]

Camp near Vicksburg, April 8th, 1863

Mr. Halstead of Cincinnati

Sir,

As unhappily I am singled out of a great mass of men, who think as I do, but who have either bowed to the storm, or been more lucky in steering their barks clear of the rock of danger, I take the liberty of sending through Mrs. Sherman copies of a short correspondence, which involves a high moral and political principle. The whole will be plain to you at a glance, and I now propose to call your attention to one phase of it, and trace the logical consequences.

Knox a citizen, entitled to all the rights of a citizen of any and every kind, a strong, stalwart man, capable of handling a musket, comes into the camp of a Major General, whom he never saw in person, conversed with, or knew anything about, in open and known violation of his orders; and dating his matter from the Headqrts. of a part of the very Command, publishes a string of falsehoods, abusive of every servant of the government, except a small knob of cunning and knowing ones, "bred in the same litter"—they were heroes, all else were knaves, fools, cowards, everything, and the Major General in Command, with commissions from a cadet all the way up to a Major General, tested by twenty years service in every part of this continent, who has managed all manner of business, without a stain heretofore, is declared by this Youngster and stranger—a mere ass—yea insane. When called on to explain the motive: "of course, Genl. Sherman I had no feeling against you personally, but you are regarded the enemy of our set, and we must in self defence write you down."

When a court Martial banishes him, the President of the United States upon the personal application of this man fortified by "respected persons" sends him back, subject to a condition, not dependant on me. Does Knox exhibit any sign of appreciating the real issue? He *regrets* the unhappy difference between a portion of the Army and himself (the whole "Press") and the sheet, which he represents, will appreciate the fact of my humbling myself to its agent, to my tamely submitting to its insults.

When Mr. Calhoun announced to General Jackson the doctrine of Secession, did he bow to the opinion of that respectable source, and the vast array of people, who he represented; No—he answered: Secession is treason, death. Had he yielded an inch, the storm would than have swept over the country.

Had Mr. Buchanan met the seizure of our mints and arsenals in the same spirit, he would have kept this war within the limits of actual traitors, but by temporizing, he gave the time and opportunity for the organisation of a rebellion, of half the nation.

So in this case. The assertion of the principle, that the "Press" has a right to keep paid agents in our camps, independent of the properly accredited Commanders, appointed by law, would, if successful, destroy any army, and the certain result would be, not only an open, bold and determined rebellion, but dissensions, discord and writing throughout the land, and in our very camps.[2] On this point I may be in error, but for the time being, I am the best judge.

I am no enemy to freedom of thought, freedom of the "Press" and speech, but in all controversies there is a time, when discussion must cease, and action begin. That time has not only come, but has been in plain, palpable existence for two years. No amount of argument will move the rebellious. They have thrown aside the pen and taken the sword. Though slow to realize the fact, though vacillating in preparation and act, the North must do the same, or perish, and become the contempt of all mankind. Persons at a distance, who can look back upon the North see with pain and sorrow the dissensions and vain discussions, which are kept alive by a Free Press. In it they see the exercise of an undoubted right the same that a man has in his own household, to burn his books destroy his furniture, abuse his family, offend his neighbors, and fear lest he continue in the exercise of the same glorious privilege to maintain his right to personal freedom by burning his house with all its contents. All I propose to say is, that Mr. Lincoln and the Press may in the exercise of their glorious prerogative tear our country and armies to tatters, but they shall not insult me with impunity in my own camp. With respect &c.

W. T. Sherman

Lbk, DNA: RG 94, Records of the Adjutant General's Office, Generals' Books and Papers, William T. Sherman, Letterbook 5; *OR*, I, 17: pt. 2, 895–97.

1. Halstead was editor of the *Cincinnati Commercial* and a friend of JS and the Ewings. EES had written to WTS on May 5, 1862, that Halstead recognized his abilities and he should do what he could to enlist the paper's support.

2. Unknown to Sherman, Halstead was advocating Grant's removal, passing on rumors of the general's intoxication to Secretary of the Treasury Salmon P. Chase.

TO JOHN A. RAWLINS

Headquarters Fifteenth Army Corps,
Camp near Vicksburg, April 8, 1863.

Colonel J. A. Rawlins,
Assistant Adjutant-General to General Grant.

Sir: I would most respectfully suggest (for reasons which I will not name)[1] that General Grant call on his corps commanders for their opinions, concise and positive, on the best general plan of a campaign. Unless this be done, there are men who will, in any result falling below the popular standard, claim that *their* advice was unheeded, and that fatal consequence resulted therefrom. My own opinions are

First. That the Army of the Tennessee is now far in advance of the other grand armies of the United States.

Second. That a corps from Missouri should forthwith be moved from St. Louis to the vicinity of Little Rock, Arkansas; supplies collected there while the river is full, and land communication with Memphis opened *via* Des Arc on the White, and Madison on the St. Francis River.

Third. That as much of the Yazoo Pass, Coldwater, and Tallahatchie Rivers, as can be gained and fortified, be held, and the main army be transported thither by land and water; that the road back to Memphis be secured and reopened, and, as soon as the waters subside, Grenada be attacked, and the swamp-road across to Helena be patrolled by cavalry.

Fourth. That the line of the Yalabusha be the base from which to operate against the points where the Mississippi Central crosses Big Black, above Canton; and, lastly, where the Vicksburg & Jackson Railroad crosses the same river (Big Black). The capture of Vicksburg would result.

Fifth. That a minor force be left in this vicinity, not to exceed ten thousand men, with only enough steamboats to float and transport them to any desired point; this force to be held always near enough to act with the gunboats when the main army is know to be near Vicksburg—Haines's Bluff or Yazoo City.

Sixth. I do doubt the capacity of Willow Bayou (which I estimate to be fifty miles long and very tortuous) as a military channel, to supply an army large enough to operate against Jackson, Mississippi, or the Black River Bridge; and such a channel will be very vulnerable to a force coming from the west, which we must expect. Yet this canal will be most useful as the way to convey coals and supplies to a fleet that should navigate the lower reach of the Mississippi between Vicksburg and the Red River.

Seventh. The chief reason for operating *solely* by water was the season of the year and high water in the Tallahatchie and Yalabusha Rivers. The spring is now here, and soon these streams will be no serious obstacle, save in the ambuscades of the forest, and whatever works the enemy may have erected at or near Grenada. North Mississippi is too valuable for us to allow the enemy to hold it and make crops this year.

I make these suggestions, with the request that General Grant will read them and give them, as I know he will, a share of his thoughts. I would prefer that he should not answer this letter, but merely give it as much or a little weight as it deserves. Whatever plan of action he may adopt will receive from me the same zealous cooperation and energetic support as though conceived by myself.[2] I do not believe General Banks will make any serious attack on Port Hudson this spring. I am, etc.,

W. T. Sherman, *Major-General*.

Printed, *PM*, 1:343–44; *OR*, I, 24: pt. 3, 179–80.

1. WTS hoped to show that McClernand was a plotting schemer with no plans beyond how to oust USG and assume his command by forcing him to commit his views to paper before the campaign. *PM*, 1:343–44.

2. At this time USG advocated that his army move southward along the west bank of the Mississippi and cross the river below Vicksburg, preferably at Grand Gulf. Transports and gunboats under the command of Admiral David D. Porter would assist the movement after running the Vicksburg batteries at night. After crossing the Mississippi, Grant anticipated cooperating with Major General Nathaniel Banks in capturing both Port Hudson, Louisiana, and Vicksburg.

TO ELLEN EWING SHERMAN

Camp at Vicksburg. Apl. 10, 1863

Dearest Ellen,

I have yours of April 3rd. I read to Charley what you said of him and he swears vengeance.[1] He will persecute you with letters daily till you Cry, Hold Enough—he says he has perpetrated four distinct epistles in the last month, and why you should not be satisfied he cannot comprehend. I console him with telling him what he know that I write more than semioccasionally and Send you all the old Slips of papers and endorsements laying about loose, and Still you hold out—We agree that you have bottom and in the race of life will hold out against many a nag of more speed. So look out for long & frequent growls from Capt. Charley. I have so much depended on Dayton & Hammond to tell you of mess talk, and on Charley to describe Battles & Skirmishes & awful events that my letters are mostly then fired off against my numerous enemies to the Rear. I was really amused at a circumstance today that may be serious—Grant has been *secretly* working by night to place some 30 pound Rifle Guns as close up to Vicksburg as the water will permit about 2300 yards, and to cover them against the enemies Cross batteries, but today got the Memphis papers of the 7th giving a minute and full account of them and their location. Now he knows as we all do that the Secesh mail leaves Memphis before day, as soon as the morning papers are printed, reach Hernando about 11 A.M. & the telegraph carries to Vicksburg the news in a few minutes. This explains a remark which Maj. Watts of the Confederate Army[2] made to me at parting day before yesterday. We met per appointment on a steamboat just above Vicksburg, and after a long conference relating to exchange of prisoners, Watts who is a very clever man remarked "dont open *those* Batteries tomorrow (last) night for I am to give a party and dont want to be interrupted." Of course the newspaper Correspondents, encouraged by the Political Generals and even President Lincoln, having full swing in this and all camps, report all news secret or otherwise, indeed with a Gossiping world a secret is worth more than common news. Grant was furious, and I believe has ordered the suppression of all the Memphis papers.[3] But that wont do. All persons who dont *have* to fight must be Kept out of camps, else secrecy a great element of military success is an impossibility. I may not, but you will live to See the day when the People of the United Sates will mob the man who thinks otherwise. I am too fast, but There are principles of Government as sure to result from War, as in Law, Religion, or any Moral Science. Some prefer to jump to the Conclusion by Reason, others prefer to follow developments by the Slower and surer road of Experience. In like manner Grant has 3000 men at work daily to clear out Willow Bayou, by which he proposes to move a large part of the army to Carthage and Grand Gulf. Also a secret, but I'll bet my life it is at this moment in all the northern papers and is known through them to the Secesh from Richmond to Vicksburg. Can you feel astonished that I should grow angry at the toleration of such suicidal weakness, that we strong, inteligent men must bend to a silly proclivity for early news, that should advise our enemy days in advance. Look out—we are not going to attack Haines Bluff, or Greenwood—or Vicksburg direct, but are going to come round below Grand Gulf. All the enemy wants is a day or two notice of such an intention and Grand Gulf becomes like a second Vicksburg. But this is a secret remember, and though it is the plan it is not a good plan—We commit a great mistake, but I am not going to advise one way or the other. The Government has here plenty of representatives and they must make the plan and I will fill my part no more, no less.[4]

The only true plan was the one we started with. This Grand Army should be on the Main land, moving south along the Road & Roads from Memphis, Holly Springs, and Corinth, concentrating on Grenada, thence towards Canton where the Central Road crosses Big Black, and then on Vicksburg. The Gunboats and a smaller army should be here, and on the first sign of the presence of the main force inland, we should attack here violently.

This was our plan at Oxford in December last, is my plan now, and Grant knows it is my opinion. I shall communicate it to none else, save you or your father. But he must not write to the War Department as from me, for it (text missing) It is my opinion that we shall never take Vicksburg by operations by River alone.

The armies on the Rappahannock and in Kentucky pause for us at Vicksburg. That is folly. All ought to press at the same instant for the Enemy has the centre or inside track, can concentrate on any one point and return to the others in time. Their position is very strong & they have skill, courage & inteligence enough to avail themselves of all advantages. Their Country is suffering terribly, by the devastations of our armies, and the Escape of their Slaves, but nothing seems to shake their constancy or confidence in ultimate success. Could the North only turn out her strength, fill promptly our thinned ranks, Keep their Counsels, hold their tongues—stop their informal pens and Press, we could make things crack, and either submission or utter horrible Ruin would be their Fate.

It may be however that God in his wisdom wants to take down the conceit of our (people and make them feel they are of the same frail materials of mortality as the other thousand millions of human beings that spin their short) webs and (die all over the earth. In) all former wars, Virtues lost sight of in times of Peace have revived, and to any one who looked, it is unnecessary to say that our Governments, national, state, county and towns had been corrupt, foul and disgraceful. If war will change this it will be cheaply bought—I understand General Thomas is coming here about nigger Regiments.[5] I'll hold my tongue, and if he says nigger to me, Ill show him my moving Reports, ask him to inspect my Brigades or Batteries, or ask him to Sing the Star Spangled Banner and go back whence he comes. When he wants my official opinions again he must ask his questions in writing and take categorical answers.

I suppose my letters are too general and Say too little of personal events. A patent gun firing fifty times a minute on board the admirals Boat whilst we reconnoitered Haines Bluff fired backwards, and the fragments of lead cut my pants badly, and one piece penetrated my leg above the Knee, making an ugly cut but did not need a Doctor—all well now—I was introduced to a General Lee[6] today—a Kansas Jayhawker. He was dressed as a citizen and I did not recognize him, but he asked me if I did not remember travelling once from Leavenworth to Topeka, and Swimming Strange Creek in a coach & four. I recalled him at once as a fellow passenger in one of my stage Rides out to the Farm from Leavenworth, where we performed quite a feat in swimming the River, horses, coach & all afloat, guided by the reins of a skilful driver. He was Colonel of a Kansas Cavalry Regiment famous for its Robbing & plundering propensities.[7] He was made a Brigadier, but Stuart not—To compare the men would be as comparing your father with Squire Embrick. But Stuart was a dangerous immoral man to a Senate that confirmed Dan Sickles[8] and Phil Kearny.[9] Stuart has a tongue & pen & will vindicate himself. He told me so great was his respect for me & you and the exalted character of your father that he would come to see you, and I would not be astonished.

Steele with his Division is still on a (illegible) up at Deer Creek back of Greenville. Blair with Stuarts Division is here but the water contracts our space very much—my third Division is about 5 miles up the shore just where the new Canal is making into Willow Bayou. Buckland is with that Division. The last Flag of Truce brought me from Vicksburg a beautiful Bouquet with compliments of Major Hoadley and Maj. Watts, the Same that wanted me not to fire last night to interrupt his party. The trees are now in full leaf—the black & blue birds sing sweetly and the mockingbird is frantic with Joy—the Rose and violet, the beds of verbina and Mignonette, planted by fair hands now in exile from their homes occupied by the Rude Barbarian, bloom as fair as though Grim war had not torn with violent hands, all the vestiges of what a few short months ago were the homes of people as good as ourselves. You may well pray that a good God in his mercy will spare the home of your youth the tread of an hostile army.

Hugh got to drinking, but I took Steps that have proven effectual and I trust may endure forever. Charley is perfectly well, spite the fruit cake, preserves, horseradish and {yams}[.]

Now if this aint a long letter and a good one I'll follow Charleys terrible threat, if not full of loving kindness for "you and all mankind" think how awkward men are at expressing what is so easy & natural in women—Love to all at home, & to our children always—

Sherman

ALS, InND: Sherman Family Papers. Text in angle brackets is now gone from the manuscript but appears in *HL*, 249.

1. Actually April 2, 1863; "I think Charley ought to have written to me more but if he will not confer that pleasure I cannot help it." She also commented on JS and Elizabeth Sherman Reese. SFP.

2. Major N. Watts was acting for the Confederate army in matters of prisoner exchanges. See, for instance, Watts to WTS, April 6, 1863, DLC: WTS.

3. "Suppress the entire press of Memphis for giving aid and comfort to the enemy by publishing in their columns every move made here by troops and every work commenced," Grant instructed Hurlbut on April 9. He also ordered the arrest of the paper's editor and his deportation to Grant's headquarters. *PUSG*, 8:38–39, 39–40n; quote on p. 38.

4. Sherman here refers to the arrival of War Department representative Charles A. Dana on April 6. Though he bore instructions to investigate the operation of the paymaster department in the western armies, Dana's real mission was to observe and report on Grant—and Grant knew it. Previously medical officers had inquired into the health of Grant's army.

5. On April 8 Adjutant General Lorenzo Thomas had addressed soldiers in James B. McPherson's corps about the administration's policy concerning the raising of black regiments, although it was also rumored that he was to check on Grant.

6. Albert Lindley Lee (1834–1907), a justice on the Kansas Supreme Court, had just been made brigadier general and was McClernand's chief of staff.

7. Seventh Kansas Cavalry.

8. Major General Daniel E. Sickles (1819–1914), USA, commanded the Third Corps, Army of the Potomac. In 1859 he had shot and killed his wife's lover, Francis Scott Key's son.

9. Major General Philip Kearny (1815–62), USA, had commanded a division of the Third Corps, Army of the Potomac, when he rode into Confederate lines and was shot and killed on September 1, 1862. His personal life had come under scrutiny before the war, although he eventually married the woman in question.

Camp before Vicksburg, Apl. 10, 1863

Dear Brother,

I have a letter from Elizabeth and many from Ellen.[1] I see with sorrow the manifestations of a feud that gives me deep pain. I must say that Elizabeth has done much & forgotten much that she ought not *to me.*

Some time last fall Ellen occupied a house owned by "Nick Little" but which had been sold and she was advised the owner might want it on short notice. Inasmuch as Elizabeth had moved to Henrys House, and our old one was in a measure unoccupied she looked to it for shelter, as her fathers house was full by the presence of Hugh Ewings family. She notified Elizabeth of the fact, and yet Elizabeth allowed the family of an Episcopal Minister to occupy it. When notified of it I wrote to her, that I could not stand *that*, for although I never calculated to use the "old house" yet you & Charles & I had taken it with the distinct understanding that it was to be held for the benefit of any member of the family in want. She was very angry at my letter, and wrote me back in harsh terms reminding me that Mr. Reese had in prosperous times spent 1800 dollars on that house, aside sums she had spent in repairing and intimating that she really had a better claim to the House than you or I—I lay no claim to the House at all, only objected to its being rented, when *any* member of our family needed it, as Ellen then feared she would. Elizabeth forgot to mention that on my arrival from California I gave her $500 in Gold for family use in Philadelphia and $2000 in Gold to Mr. Reese & Henry to start a business that promised a livelihood—that Subsequently I gave her means to come to Mansfield and at sundry other times money—of not one cent of all which did I ever *ever* make a memorandum. It was all pure & unalloyed Gift, only accompanied with the regret that it was spent so quick. Well Elizabeth did cause the removal of the family in question and placed the house at Ellens disposal, but she was allowed to retain the Little house longer than She expected and Hugh Ewing has procured a house for his family, leaving Room at her fathers house. She does not want the Old House—Elizabeth writes me again as though in all this She has Sustained a real wrong. I dont care much about these simple details, but out of them & maybe others, there is war between Ellen & Elizabeth. All I pretend is that the Old House should be held for the exclusive use of some member of our family—Better be idle, than rented out—Fanny[2] may need it—Elizabeth may need it. Ellen may need it. Jims[3] or Hoyts[4] Wives may need it. We are in the midst of War and Some one or more of us must perish. I must run 99 Risks out of a hundred. I no more expect to Survive this war, than I do to escape death eventually. But that is not the question. Elizabeth is influencing others against Ellen. Henry has treated her rudely—so have Rose,[5]

Mary[6] and others. I know the love, affection, constancy and confidence she feels to me—I know she has watched & cared for my children with a care that cannot be excelled, and do not wonder that she trembles lest Elizabeth attempt to come between me & her. If Elizabeth were ever to think the thought it would be horrible, but I cannot write to her or answer her letters whilst a feeling exists between her & Ellen. I do not ask a reconciliation. I dont want it. Only let silence exist between them. I in all probability will never see Ohio again—and should unexpectedly Peace set me afloat again, or what is more probable should Mr. Lincoln dispense with the Services of one whose personal services he could not command for one hour were it not for higher motives—I would not return to Ohio—Missouri, Kansas or California are more to my liking. I wish you would write to Elizabeth & tell her not to write to me, that as between her & Ellen my choice is easily made—that twas better none of her children ever spoke a word or did a deed offensive to her—that if she has a Right to the old House I will sign a Blank deed at any time, but would like a simple acknowledgment of the fact that for years I did give to her & Mr. Reese freely, never hoping to be repaid, and generally that it will better enure to her happiness and that of others if she will confine herself to her own sphere.

Henry Sherman has joined his Regiment at Millikens Bend as adjt. (120th Ohio)—Why was Stuart rejected. He was one of the best of the whole lot. Besides for a whole year he has been constantly at the Front when more than half the Major Generals & Brigadiers were clinging to the Ohio & Potomac. His military Record was perfect, and as to that {Burch} case, wherein did that compare with Phil Kearneys or Dan Sickles cases. Blair commands one of my Divisions and dont pretend to know much of the military but keeps well posted in Politics. I am afraid of that class of men. They are so treacherous. My object and Study is to so preserve order, economy, discipline: truth honesty & Honor, that when all else fails the country may safely lean on the army as have been the cases in all civil wars & Revolutions, but Politicians look nearer at hand and study to catch the Breeze at the next change of wind. Mr. Dana[7] is here I suppose to watch us all. He spent a few hours with me yesterday, and I went over with him many of the events of the past year with the maps & Records with which I am well supplied—Indeed all look to me for maps & facts. Dana remarked to one of Grants staff incidentally that he was better pleased with me than he could have possibly expected. In the two days he has been here, he has seen an illustration of the Truth of my Proposition which has drawn on me such volumes of abuse. We have had thousands of men working by night—putting batteries as close up to Vicksburg as possible *secretly*, and in opening a channel by which we may in high water reach the

River 25 miles below Vicksburg. Secrecy *was* essential, but the papers of Memphis announce the whole fact. I know the Memphis Dailies go before daylight each day to Hernando, 25 miles and are telegraphed to Vicksburg by noon of the same day. Indeed the day before yesterday I met some Vicksburg officers who asked that I should come with a flag of Truce to discuss a point as to exchange of Prisoners, and as we parted one a Major Watts asked me not to open our Batteries (the Secret) last night as he was going to have a party and did not want to be disturbed. I say that not an officer or soldier of this or any army but agrees with me that our operations are futile with our camps filled as now by the Reporters, some of whom represent Known hostile sheets— *Memphis Argus, Chicago Times, Cincinati Inquirer* &c. Nothing can prevent this fatal practice, but excluding all men from our camps but men who *must* fight. They at least have a personal interest in what should be revealed and what concealed. I am clean of opinion that the main part of this army should now go to Grenada, leaving a small force here afloat to cooperate with Gunboats. In Kentucky & Tennessee I expect the next battles not here. I dont think Gunboats can take Charleston from the Front—still we must all hammer away and the pluckyest and longest winded will win. I see not the least sign on the part of the army or People of the South of Give-in. affectionately

W. T. Sherman

ALS, DLC: William T. Sherman

1. EES to WTS, August 1 and 7, September 10, 19, and 28, 1862, April 2 and 4, 1863, SFP. For some time EES had been preoccupied with the difficulties of getting hold of the Sherman house in Lancaster for herself and her family; although Elizabeth Sherman Reese was not living in it herself, she was reluctant to let EES have it. Most recently, EES was convinced that JS had sided with Elizabeth Sherman Reese in the matter and had turned against her.

2. Frances Beecher Sherman Moulton.

3. JS and WTS's brother James (1814–64), a Des Moines businessman. His wife was Sophia Connell (d. 1871).

4. Hoyt Sherman (1827–1904), a paymaster in the Union army, was married to Sara Moulton (d. 1887).

5. Elizabeth's daughter.

6. Elizabeth's daughter.

7. Charles A. Dana (1819–97), a journalist, was at this time inspecting Grant's command as a representative of the War Department. Later he would become assistant secretary of war.

TO ELLEN EWING SHERMAN

Camp opposite Vicksburg, Apl. 17, 63.

Dearest Ellen,

I have all your letters up to Apl. 8 inclusive. I think I have anticipated all your propositions. As to writing a good letter to Halsted I doubt if I can without some provoking cause. On business I could make it short enough and to the point, but on any general topic it would depend on the humor, so that if the letter I have written him is not to your liking wait till an occasion offers. I once wrote to Gen. Meigs my opinion of Col. Swords also several times to John. Swords is an honest, strict and conscientious officer. You never hear of fraudulent contracts & charters with him but Halleck thinks he is too close for the times, that he does not rise to the occasion. I remember once up the Tennessee he ordered up from Louisville some steamboats and Halleck thought his aim at economy lost time, which in military matters is awful. Halleck knows Swords as well as I do, and for me to recommend him to notice would be superfluous. I wish you would write to Mrs. Swords, and assure her of the deep friendship I entertain for the Colonel and herself, that I dont claim or wish to pretend to any influence save in my own immediate command, but that if ever it lies in my power to advance Col. Swords interest he may command me. John will also I feel certain advocate his interests, but the Truth is in his Department there is no room for much advancement, and he is now almost famous for having escaped the charges of corruption & fraud that have so lavishly been poured out on the army Quarter Masters. Assure Mrs. Swords of my oft expressed opinion that Col. Swords is one of a Class of Gentlemen I fear that belongs to a Past age, who will serve his Goverment patiently, silently, honestly & well and never complain, but this is no reason why he should be overlooked in the disgraceful scramble for title & power, without the ability to wield it well.

I have never been considered the advocate of McClellan or anybody. I have often said that McClellans reputation as a scholar & soldier were second to none after Mexico. I heard Gen. Persifor F. Smith in 1849, pronounce him better qualified to command than any of our then Generals. I remember once when we were riding along and talking of certain events in Mexico, he named some half dozen young officers who he thought should at once be pushed forward & McClellan was the first in order after Lee. I admit the Right & duty of Mr. Lincoln to slect his own agents and when one displeases him, there can be no accord, and he should set him aside. He is *ex necessitate* to that Extent King & can do no wrong. At all events every body must & should submit with good Grace. But Knowing the very common clay out of which many of our new Generals are made, I have trembled at any shifting of Commanders, until the Army feels assured that a change is necessary. I know Hooker well, and tremble to think of his handling 100,000 men in the presence of Lee. I dont think Lee will attack Hooker in position because he will doubt if it will pay, but Let Hooker once advance or move laterally and I fear the result.

Rosecrans in like manner is obliged to act. Every yard he advances diminishes his strength, and exposes his roads to the incursions of the Southern Guerillas & Cavalry that are bolder and better than ours. Properly he keeps his army massed, and in that shape will fight well, but he must move, and the moment an army moves in this country it draws itself out in a long thin string exposed to all manner of Risk.

Here we have begun a move that is one of the most dangerous in War—Last night our Gunboats, 7 of the largest ran their Blockade and are below Vicksburg. They suffered comparatively little. Three transports followed, one of which was fired and burned to the waters edge. The Silver Wave passed unhurt, and my old Post the Forest Queen, had one shot in her hull, & one through a steam pipe which disabled her. She is below Vicksburg and above Warrenton, and is being repaired.

McClernands Corps has marched along the margin of an intricate Bayou 47 miles to new Carthage and the plan is to take & Hold Grand Gulf, and make it the base of a movement in rear of Vicksburg. I dont like the project for several reasons. The Channel by which provisions, stores ammunition &c. are to be conveyed to Carthage is a narrow crooked bayou with plenty of water now, but in two months will dry up. No boat has yet entered it and though four steam dredges are employed in cutting a Canal into it, I doubt if it can be available in ten days. The road used is pure alluvium, and three hours Rain will make it a quagmire over which a wagon could no more pass than in the channel of the Mississipi.

Now the amount of Provisions, forage, and more Especially coal, used by an army & fleet such as we will have will overtax the Capacity of the Canal.

Again we know the enemy has up the Yazoo some of the finest boats that ever navigated the Mississipi, with plenty of cotton to barricade them and convert them into formidable Rams. Knowing now as they well do that our best iron clads are below Vicksburg and that it is one thing to run down stream and very different up, they can simply swop—They can let us have the reach below Vicksburg and they take the one above, and in that exchange they get decidedly the best of the Bargain. To accomplish such a move successfully we should have at least double their force, whereas we know that our effective force is but little if any superior to theirs. They can now use all the scattered bands in Louisiana to threaten this narrow long canal, and force us to guard it so, that the main army beyond will be unequal to a march inland from Grand Gulf—We could undertake & safely to hold the River and allow the Gun boat fleet to go to Port Hudson and assist in the reduction of that place, so that all could unite against Vicksburg. I have written & explained to Grant all these points but the Clamor is so great he fears to seem to give up the attack on Vicksburg. My opinion is we should now feint on the River and hasten to

Grenada by every available Road, and then move in great force south parallel with the River, leaving the Gunboats and a comparatively small force here. Grant however trembles at the approaching thunders of popular criticism and must risk every thing and it is my duty to back him though the contemplated & partially executed move does not comport with my ideas. I know the Pictorials will give you flaming pictures of the Successful running the Batteries of Vicksburg, but who thinks of their getting back. What will be thought if some ten large cotton freighted Boats come out of Yazoo, and put all our transports to the bottom, and leave us on the narrow margin of a Great and turbid Stream. The fear of public clamor is more degrading to the mind than a just measure of the dangers of Battle with an open fair enemy in equal or even unequal Fight. Hugh and Charley were with me last night at the Picket Station below Vicksburg and saw the cannonading and will describe its appearance better than I could. I cant help but ovelook the present & look ahead. I wish an enemy would commit this mistake with us, but no—they are too cunning.

General Thomas is here raising negro Brigades. I would prefer to have this a white mans war, & provide for the negro after the Storm had passed, but we are in a Revolution and I must not pretend to judge. With my opinions of negros, and my experience, yea prejudice I cannot trust them yet. Time may change this, but I cannot bring myself to trust negros with arms in positions of danger and trust.

I intended to mention in my last that Elizabeth had written me a letter complaining of her treatment about the House—I wrote to John to tell her, that as she had quarrelled with you, and spread her quarrel wrongfully I would not answer, but he might remind her of the fact that on my return from California in 1850, I gave her 600 in Gold & afterwards paid the expenses of the removal of the family to Mansfield—also that I gave Mr. Reese & Henry $2000 to engage in a certain business that failed of course. These sums more than offset any alledged expenses on the House by Mr. Reese in 1838. John understands the whole matter and you need not fear he will be drawn in. He knows too well how true you have been to me in sunshine & Storm, and will never waver in his love & affection—nor will Charles Sherman. I cant believe that Susan or Fanny will—but no matter. We have now our own little Family that we can tie to. Lizzie is as true as the needle to the Pole, and Tom with a Pony will carry us sailing high above the efforts of envious or mischievous Relations. Two Sheets are enough so good night, Dearest Ellen and believe me that my sleeping & waking thoughts are with you more than my mere words told here Ever yours

W. T. Sherman

ALS, InND: Sherman Family Papers.

Camp before Vicksburg, April 23, 1863

Dearest Ellen,

Last night another Batch of transports were prepared to run Vicksburg Batteries. In order to afford assistance to the unfortunate I crossed over through the Submerged Swamp with 8 yawls, and was in the Mississipi about 4 miles below Vicksburg and three above Warrenton. The first boat to arrive was the *Tigress* a fast sidewheel boat, which was riddled with shot & reported struck in the hull. She rounded to, tied to the Bank & sunk a wreck. All hands saved. The next was the *"Empire City"* also crippled but afloat—then the *Cheeseman* that was partially disabled—then the *Anglo-Saxon*, and *Moderator*, both of which were so disabled that they drifted down stream catching the Warrenton Batteries as they passed—the *Horizon* was the sixth & last—passed down about daylight. The *Cheeseman* took the *Empire City* in tow & went down just after day, catching thunder from the Warrenton Batteries. Five of the Six boats succeeded in getting by, all bound for Carthage, where they are designed to carry troops to Grand Gulf or some other point across the Mississipi. This is a desperate and terrible thing, floating by terrific Batteries without the power of replying. Two men were mortally wounded, and many lacerated & torn, but we Could not ascertain the full extent of damage for we were trying to hurry them past the Lower or Warrenton Batteries before daylight. The only way to go to Carthage is by a Bayou Road, from Millikens Bend, and over that narrow Road our army is to pass below Vicksburg, and by means of these boats pass over to the east side of the Mississipi. I look upon the Whole thing as one of the most hazardous & desperate moves of this or any war. A narrow difficult Road, liable by a shower to become a quagmire. A canal is being dug on whose success the coal for steamers, provisions for men—and forage for animals must all be transported. McClernands corps has moved down—McPhersons will follow and mine come last—I dont object to this for I have no faith in the whole plan.

Politicians and all sorts of influence are brought to bear on Grant to do something. Hooker remains status quo—Rosecrans is also at a deadlock & we who are now six hundred miles [ahead] of any are being pushed to a most perillous & hazardous enterprise.

I did think our Government would learn something by experience if not by reason—An order is received today from Washington to consolidate the Old Regiments. All Regts. below 500 embracing all the old Regiments which have been depleted by death & all sorts of causes are to be reduced to Battalions of 5 Companies—in each Regt. the Col. & Major & 1 asst. surgeon to be mustered out, and all the officers, sergeants & Corporals of 5 companies to be discharged—This will soon take all my colonels—Kilby Smith, Giles Smith, & hundreds of our best captains, Lieutenants and sergeants & corporals. Instead of drafting & filling up with privates—One half of the officers are to be discharged and the privates squeezed into Battalions. If the worst enemy of the United States were to devise a plan to break down our army a better one could not be attempted, two years have been spent in educating colonels, captains, sergeants & corporals, and now they are to be driven out of service at the very beginning of the Campaign, in order that Governors may have a due proportion of officers for the drafted men. I do regard this as one of the fatal mistakes of this war—It is worse than a defeat. It is the absolute giving up of the Chief advantage of two years work. I dont know if you understand it, but believe you do. The order is positive and must be executed. It is now too late to help it, but I have postponed its execution for a few days to see if Grant wont suspend its operation till this move is made. All the old Politician Colonels have been weeded out by the process of the war, and now that we begin to have some officers who do know something they must be discharged Because the Regiments have dwindled below one half the Legal Standard—We all know the President was empowered to do this but took it for granted that he would fill up the Ranks by a draft, & leave as the sinews of the men who are now ready to drill & instruct them as soldiers. Last fall the same thing was done, that is New Regiments were received instead of filling up the old ones, and the consequence was these new Regiments have filled our Hospitals & depots, and now again the same thing is to be repeated. It may be the whole war will be turned over to the negros, and I begin to believe they will do as well as Lincoln and his advisors. I cant imagine what Halleck is about. We have Thomas, and Dana both here from Washington, no doubt impressing on Grant the necessity of achieving something brilliant. It is the same old Bull Run Mania. But why should other armies lay passive and ours be pushed to destruction.

Prime is here, and agrees with me, but we must drift on with events, we are excellent friends. Indeed I am on the best of terms with everybody, but I avoid McClernand, because I know he is envious & jealous of every body who stands in his way. He knows I appreciate him truly and therefore he would ruin me if he could. He knows he shew the white feather at Shiloh, that he hung round me like a whipped cur, that his troops reported to me for orders in his presence. Then danger made him complaisant, but when that was past and his self arose, he hated me the more for what I knew—The Same thing was repeated at Arkansas post—he was helplessly ignorant, but when we had the enemy bowed then he was the Hero. He is a true type of an American Modern Hero. He should not seek fame in the Field, but at Springfield Illinois by means of the press & newspapers. He now has the lead—Admiral Porter is there, and he is already calling for Gods sake send down some one—he calls for me—Grant has gone himself—went this morning. I know they have got their fleet in a tight place, Vicksburg above & Port Hudson below, and how are they to get out. One or other of the Gates must be stormed & carried or else none. I tremble for the result Of Course it is possible to land at Grand Gulf & move inland, but I doubt the Capacity of any channel at our Command equal to the conveyance of the supplies for this army. This army should not all be here. The great part should be at or near Grenada, moving south by Land.

I want Charley & Hugh to describe these brilliant scenes of cannonading, but Charley says you sent his letter of the Deer Creek expedition to Mr. Stanton, he wont trust you any more as a confidante. What does Stanton care for the fine drawn pictures of a young Capt. of Regulars? I have no doubt you will have the mortification of seeing me abused for the passage of the Fleet below Vicksburg & attempt to reach Jackson via Grand Gulf, though the truth is I opposed the movement at {*incipio*}. The best use that we could put present affairs to would be to go down & help Banks who it seems instead of bagging Port Hudson is drawing in his Lines to New Orleans. What think you now of the Grand attack on Charleston. I accomplished far more at Vicksburg alone, and yet the world is amazed at the mighty promises of Hunter & Dupont[1]—If Lincoln do not very soon resort to the draft—and dont stop discharging our armies, Davis will walk over the track on the summers campaign without opposition. Weather is getting hot here—and I have no cotton socks or Mosquito (illegible). Dayton has gone home sick—he has been drooping for some weeks. He will see you of course—Tell him I will march for Carthage via Millikens Bend in about 4 days, but where to fetch up dont know. He may have to join us via New Orleans, for I take it for granted the enemy will swop Rivers with us. We take the lower reach & they the upper. For we leave no Guard above Vicksburg except the Sick and Niggers to be manufactured into Soldiers.

We are all very well—I had the bones to ache, indicating ague, but it went no further. Hugh & Charley are very well—both write you occasionally—As ever yours

W. T. Sherman

ALS, InND: Sherman Family Papers.

1. Rear Admiral Samuel Francis Du Pont (1803–65), USN, was directing operations against Charleston, South Carolina. On April 7, 1863, his fleet of ironclads failed to take the city; Lincoln pressed for the admiral to remain inside the harbor bar. David Hunter would be replaced as head of the Department of the South on June 12 by Quincy A. Gillmore.

TO JOHN SHERMAN

Head Qrs. 15 Army Corps,

Camp before Vicksburg, Apl. 23, 1863

Dear Brother,

I had noticed in the Conscript act the Clauses which empowered the President to consolidate the 10 companies of a Regt. into 5 when the aggregate was below one half the Maximum standard, and to reduce the officers accordingly. Had I dreamed that this was going to be made universal I would have written you, and begged you for the love of our ruined country to implore Lincoln to spare us this last & fatal blow. Two years of costly war have enabled the North to realize the fact that by organized & disciplined armies alone can she hope to restore the old or found a new empire. We had succeeded in making the skeleton of armies, eliminating out of the crude materials that first came forth the worthless material and had just begun to have some good young colonels, and Congress had passed the Conscript Bill which would have enabled the President to fill up these Skeleton Regiments full of privates who save for their fellows, and with experienced officers would soon make an army capable of marching & being handled & directed. But to my amazement comes the order to muster out the colonels & majors & asst. Surgeons, and to make up Battalions of five companies, dismissing one half the captains, Lieutenants, sergeants & corporals. This is a far worse defeat than Manassas. Mr. Wade in his Report to condemn McClellan gave a positive assurance to the army that henceforth instead of fighting with diminishing Ranks we should hereafter feel assured that the gaps made by the Bullet, by disease, desertions &c. should be promptly filled, whereas only such parts of the Conscript Law as tends to weaken us are enforced viz. 5 per cent for furlough & 50 p.c. of officers & n.c. officers discharged to consolidate Regiments.

Even Blair is amazed at this—he protests the order cannot be executed and we should appeal to Mr. Lincoln, who he still insists has no desire to destroy the army. But the order is positive and I cant see how we can hesitate. When the aggregate is below 500 we *must* discharge the Col. & Maj. & asst. surgeon and half the company offcs. and N.C. offcs. Grant started today down to Carthage and I have written to him which may stave it off for a few days, but I tremble at the loss of so many young and good officers who have been hard at work two years, and now that they begin to see how to take care of soldiers must be turned out. It will absolutely cripple my best troops, and we are actually moving on one of the most hazardous & desperate enterprises that any army ever undertook—one fleet of Gunboats now is below Vicksburg and we have at considerable loss & sacrifice passed down 7 transports. The whole army is in the act of passing below Vicksburg along a narrow crooked bayou, that may be dry before we have time to accomplish half the undertaking. All the army with its materiel, with provisions forage & ammunition has to be passed down this bayou to Carthage & thence crossed over to Grand Gulf, where we are sixty miles by land from the Railroad which now feeds Vicksburg. Grant seems to be pushed to extremity by pressure from without. Thomas is here with his project of making Black Regiments, & Dana is here. I have seen a good deal of the latter and feel assured he knows many things he never did before. He has gone to Carthage also I will march with my corps to the Same destination as soon as assured that the Road is clear, but I know the narrow Road & still unfinished Canal are unequal to the tax imposed on them and I have no faith in the Scheme.

If not too late do for mercys sake exhaust your influence to stop this Consolidation of Regiments. Fill all the Regiments with conscripts, and if the army is then too large disband the Regiments that prefer to serve north of the Potomac & the Ohio. Keep the war South at all hazards—If this consolidation Law is literally enforced and no new draft is made, this campaign is over, and the outside world will have a perfect right to say our Government is afraid of its own People.[1]

The weather is becoming hot here, and soon marching will be attended with the risk of sunstroke & fever. The enemy counts on our exhausting ourselves without their taking the trouble to shoot us. Affectionately yrs.,

W. T. Sherman.

ALS, DLC: William T. Sherman.
1. See WTS to USG, June 2, 1863, below.

TO JOHN SHERMAN

Head Qrs. 15 Army Corps:
Camp before Vicksburg, Apl. 26 1863

My Dear Brother,

Tomorrow I start with my Corps to bring up the Rear of the Movement against Grand Gulf, & may be Jackson Miss. I feel in its success less Confidence than any similar undertaking of the War, but it is my duty to cooperate with Zeal and I shall endeavor to do it. Grant is pushed on by Clamors from the rear—the Same old damned Cowardly herd, who disgrace our nation lay back in Ohio & remote places & raise the hue & cry and we must disregard all Sense and wisdom & common prudence to realize impossibilities. Our Army here in the Mississipi has accomplished more than all the other Armies of the Country have achieved more results, more actual success & yet must be hounded on by Newspaper Clamor. We have completely parallyzed Arkansas—and North Louisiana—The Trans-Mississipi is alienated from the central

Govt. at Richmond, and the Great Empire of the West is now Subject to our Military dictation. Yet does the country appreciate this fact? No—They have their mind on Vicksburg alone—they lay down impossible plans for its reduction and publish every movement however minute & then cry aloud failure, failure till even our armies begin to mistrust success. Has not Fredericksburg—Vicksburg, Charleston Port Hudson and hundreds of other examples taught Our People that these are Stern facts to be over come not by Clamor, but by hard fighting & combination? But you know I have no faith in our Government as a War Machine and that I am bound to lay low and let the Revolution work. But as to our Campaign here. The plan agreed on at Oxford in Decr. last was the plain true & proper one, viz. The Main Army under Grant was to march down parallel with the Mississipi to Grenada, & on towards Vicksburg—Banks & the Gunboat fleet was to move against Port Hudson, whilst I with 30,000 men & the Porter fleet was to move against Vicksburg—The Mishap at Holly Springs turned Grant back and I was left alone to cope with the most formidable natural & artificial fort in this County. All that is past—Grant came down by River and his entire army about 70,000 is now near here, but the whole country is under water save little ribands of alluvial ground along the Main Mississipi or parallel Bayous—My proposition was one month ago to fall back upon our original plan, modified by the fact that Yazoo River could be entered by its head and could be used as far down as Greenwood, which is the mouth of Yalobusha—If our Gunboats could have passed that point a real Substantial advantage would have been gained, for it would have enabled the army to pass the Yalobusha, whereas now, it is a serious obstacle like the Rappahannock and will have to be fought for. Still I hold our Main Army should now be aiming for Grenada—that place once in our hands, & the Railroads back to Memphis put in order, we would have a good open country all the way to the rear of Vicksburg. As this army moved South parallel to the Yazoo, Greenwood, Yazoo City & other points now held by the enemy would be relinquished, and the City of Vicksburg could be fully invested. But I dont know why, Grant has resolved on another move.

McClernands Corps has marched from Millikens Bend along a narrow road to Carthage. McPhersons has followed, and I start tomorrow. 60,000 men will thus be on a single Road, narrow, crooked & liable to become a quagmire on the occurrence of a single Rain. We hope to carry 10 days rations with us. 7 Iron Clad Gunboats, and 7 transports have run the Vicksburg Batteries. With these we can reach Grand Gulf below the Mouth of Black River, whence there is a Road to Raymond 65 miles & Jackson—The destruction of this Road isolates Vicksburg—Now if we can sustain the army it may do, but I know the Materiels of food, forage & ammunition cannot be conveyed over that Single precarious Road. Grant has been opening a canal from the Mississipi to Willow Bayou 3 miles, & Willow Bayou Roundaway, & Bayou Vidal form a connected channel, for 47 miles terminating at Carthage, but it is crooked, narrow, and full of trees. Large working parties are Employed in removing these, but at best it is only calculated that it can be used by scows drawn by small steamtugs. It is not even contemplated that the Smallest transports can navigate it. The Canal itself is far from being done. I went through it yesterday in a small Boat & estimate it will take one month to give it 8 feet water with the present stage, but the water in the River is now falling rapidly. We count on another rise in June from the Missouri, but these Rises are accidental & may or not come. The great difficulty will be to Support an army operating from Grand Gulf. The Enemy should and will of course attack our Line. We leave behind only a few Common Gunboats and the Sick. Now there are in the Yazoo plenty of fine boats with which they can emerge from the Yazoo and possess themselves of our Depot at Millikens Bend, the effect of which will be that Grant will be forced to return to reestablish his communications, or else cut loose from the upper River and turn towards New Orleans.

Between the two choices open to him I far prefer Grenada. One is sure and natural the other is difficult and hazardous in the Extreme.

There is no national or Political reason why this Army should be forced to undertake unnecessary hazards. It is far in advance of Hooker, Rosecrans or Curtis. We have done far more than either of these armies, but have encountered more calumny & abuse than all. General Thomas & Dana are with Grant, a kind of spy on his movements.

Thomas made a speech to my command about the Negros. I followed & Know the men look to me, more than anybody on Earth. Blair also spoke to his Division. I of Course always tell the Soldiers we are likened to a Sheriff, that must execute the Writ of the Court & not go into an inquiry into the merits of the case. I expressed a hope if the Government did make use of negros as armed men, they Should be used for some side purpose & not be brigaded with our white men. Long before Congress acted on this matter I employed cooks & teamsters for my Regiments, but Experience has even changed this—The companies prefer now to be rid of negros—they desert the moment danger threatens—As soon as we began our march to the Tallahatchee from Memphis, the Negros quit leaving their Teams standing in the Roads and details of soldiers had to be sent back to bring up the wagons. At Shiloh all our negro servants fled, and Some of them were picked up by boats 40 miles down the River. I wont trust niggers to fight yet, but dont object to the Government taking them from the Enemy, & making such use of them as experience may suggest.

The order consolidating our old Regiments is fatal to the army. It takes 78 of the best men in each Regiment out. If Lincoln desires to defeat our armies he could not have hit upon a better plan. In like manner I infer the draft will not be enforced, or if so that it will be completed with Bounties & a promise of a full share of officers. If this be so, no one will ever look for further success during this administration.

In the hurry of packing up today I wrote this letter, and tonight received a letter from Grant at Carthage countermanding my march and explaining the difficulties that already surround him.[1] He calls on me to make a Road where there is not a foot of dry ground for five miles, indeed on a swamp in which I passed night before last in a large yawl. But I can aid him and have sent a messenger to him that I will make a wagon Road back 3 miles to Willow Bayou[2]—one which can be navigated by barges to Richmond & then in larger boats to Carthage. But even this will not be enough—He cannot support his army & the fleet at Carthage or Grand Gulf, with the Vicksburg & Warrenton Batteries behind him. It was just this way with Porter. He went up Dan Creek without even advising with me. When he got there jammed in the willows & trees he appealed to me to come to his aid. By an energy which could not be exceeded I got up to him just in time to Save his fleet, and yet I have read in a New York paper that had I got to Rolling Fork two days sooner the admiral would have succeeded in his design of reaching Yazoo—The fact was that he was in Deer Creek, before a Soldier of my command knew of the proposed expedition. I have no doubt also that in this case I will be the Scape Goat, though I have opposed this move on Grand Gulf from the beginning—Our Iron Clad fleet is below Vicksburg—and 7 transports & innumerable barges. The iron clads may get back but none else. They are in a fatal trap. They must escape below Port Hudson or be burned. They cannot operate against Vicksburg any better below than above the City. Vicksburg can alone be taken by a powerful army moving inland in cooperation with the Gunboat & a floating force in the River, the plan we made at Oxford in December last is but Clamor, newspaper clamor unnerves & unmans every American and makes him helpless. I would not hesitate an hour, but would put things back to when we started. I say we are further from taking Vicksburg today than we were the day I was repulsed.

The Gunboat fleet is in a false position[.] They only want enough boats in that reach to cut off communication with Red River. Banks is afraid even to attempt Port Hudson, & from all I can hear is more likely to be caged up in New Orleans than to assist us against Vicksburg. Gunboats of themselves can do nothing, in cooperation with a land force they can occupy the heavy batteries whilst Infantry & land force approach from the rear—500 Gun boats could not take Vicksburg. They might silence the shore batteries, but could not touch a man on & behind the Hills. Porter knows this & Grant knows it, but they must play to the popular clamor. Our time here is wasted, and the quicker we get back on the Grenada Road, the Sooner will there be a prospect of success. If a large part of the army does not get into North Mississipi they will make & gather crops there. I dont believe in the Starvation cry, for wherever we penetrate the Land we find plenty of Cattle & Corn. I have met many Vicksburg officers & soldiers under flags of truce, they arc fat, healthy and as well clad as we. Do urge Mr. Lincoln to fill up the Regiments full, & stop this consolidation if not too late. With the old Regiments full we would have armies as large as we can handle & feed, but if consolidated in the manner proposed, this years campaign is lost before a step is taken. My health is good—Gen. Thomas pronounced my troops the best he had seen—I dont oppose negro arming, further than I have no confidence in them & dont want them mixed up with our white soldiers. I would rather see them armed & colonized in Florida & North Arkansas. Give my love to all & believe me always most affectionately yr. Brother

W. T. Sherman

ALS, DLC: William T. Sherman.

1. USG to WTS, April 24, 1863, *PUSG*, 8:117–18. USG had made a reconnaissance trip to Grand Gulf with Porter and thought that it would fall soon. Declining water levels in the bayous had made any hope of water transport dim at best, and he ordered WTS to "watch that matter and should the water fall sufficiently make the necessary roads for this purpose" (p. 117).

2. WTS to USG, April 26, 1863, *PUSG*, 8:118n.

TO MARIA BOYLE EWING SHERMAN

Camp before Vicksburg, Apl. 26. 63

Dearest Minnie,

We are on the point of moving our army south of Vicksburg. We have not yet captured that city and I dont Know that we can, but we are gradually extending beyond it. Tomorrow I move with my army up to Millikens Bend, whence we march along a Road on the West of the Mississipi to a point on it at Carthage where we again take Boats and Cross over to the east Bank.[1] I expect we will have some hard fighting but we dont Know. I am in very good health, and our soldiers are generally very well, though if we pass the Summer here in these swamps I expect a good deal of sickness.

The Spring is about a month earlier here than where you are. The trees are all now in full leaf, and the flowers in bright bloom. The Rose, the honeysuckle, the verbenia, and lilac are all in full bloom, and I wish I could send you some, but suppose it will not be long till you have them bright and beautiful in the Gardens at Notre Dame. It will not be long now till you go home. You will all be most happy there together. Mama is now living with Granpa, and you will be all together. Uncle Charley sent to Tommy a pony for him to ride and I have written to Mama to get you and Willy a horse that you also may take plenty of exercise. I want you to learn to ride & Swim this summer. Dont fail to try. The time will come when everything you now learn will be the source of pleasure or use. When I do come home I will want you to read to me, to ride with me on horseback and enjoy with me the rambles through the hills and country that I know you will enjoy. Everybody tells me how you have grown, and I can easily imagine you now as tall as your mother, for your aunt Reese, & Julia[2] long since dead were as tall at 14 as when grown women. You will be like them tall & full grown at 14 and will then be considered a young lady. I hope to See you again before then, although I cannot yet see a chance to come home. Willy & Tom & Lizzie are all growing fast, and I ought to See you from time to time lest you forget me but I Know that although I am away you think of me all the time. Write to me often, and I will try at some future time to write you more regularly, but as you must understand, my time is much taken up with my necessary duties.

Give my love to Willy, to Tommy Ewing, and to his Sisters, also to your Teachers. Ever yr. affectionate father,

W. T. Sherman

ALS, OHi: William T. Sherman Papers.

1. WTS was beginning a feint on Haines' Bluff designed to distract the Confederates from USG's advance against Grand Gulf.

2. WTS's sister Julia Ann Sherman Willock (1818–42).

TO ELLEN EWING SHERMAN

Head Qrs. 15 Army Corps,
before Vicksburg, Apl. 29, 1863

Dearest Ellen,

I got your letter from Cincinati[1] and am glad I did not misjudge you in Supposing you had too much sense to come down here on a wild goose errand—Mrs. Grant came down & poor Grant had to make so many & such antic apologies that even his wife must have been mortified—it will be quoted as one of the many pieces of evidence that he did nothing at Vicksburg & meant to do nothing, for I see in the horizon the first faint clouds that threaten Grants fair fame and history. Well though I would rather See you than any one on earth, I say honestly & truly you did right not to come— indeed it would have been wrong to come—I will escape from the popular pen in which a supposed virtue & patriotism caught me along with others as soon as decency will permit & it may be in some safe place we may enjoy peace & each others society whilst the factions of a Demagoguism tears our Dear People to pieces. The Noises & clamor have produced their fruits. Even Grant is cowed & afraid of the newspapers—He is down at Carthage, the Fleet is below Vicksburg, and I was on the point of following when the order was countermanded—then I got an order that he would like to have a feint made on Haines Bluff provided I did not fear the People might style it a Repulse—I wrote him to make his plans founded on as much good Sense as possible & let the People mind their own business. He had ordered me to attack Vicksburg, & I had done so—Now to divert attention from his movement against Grand Gulf he wants another demonstration up Yazoo—Of course I will make it and let the People find out when they can if it be a Repulse or no—I suppose we must ask the People in the Press—or some half dozen little whippersnappers who represent the Press, but are in fact spies in our Camp too lazy, idle, & cowardly to be soldiers these must be consulted before I can make a simulated attack on Haines Bluff in aid to Grant & Porter that I know are in a tight place at Grand Gulf—Therefore prepare yourself for another blast against Sherman blundering & being repulsed at Haines whilst McClernand charges gallantly ashore and Carries Grand Gulf. But when they take Grand Gulf they have the Elephant by the tail. I say the whole plan is hazardous in the Extreme but I will do all I can to aid Grant. Should as the papers now intimate Grant be relieved & McClernand left in command, you may expect to hear of me at St. Louis, for I will not serve under McClernand, he is the impersonation of my Demon Spirit, not a shade of respect for truth, when falsehood is easier manufactured & fitted to his purpose—an overtowering ambition and utter ignorance of the first principles of war. I have in my possession his orders to do "certain things" which he would be ashamed of now—he knows I saw him cow[er] at Shiloh— he knows he blundered in ignorance at the Post & came to me—beseechingly Sherman what shall we do now? and yet no sooner is the tempest past, and the pen in hand—his star is to be brightened and none so used to abuse—none so patient under it as Sherman—and therefore Glory at Shermans expense—The day will come when they will know that Sherman has about as much feeling as is proper, and though he may bottle it up when it does come out somebody will feel it—indeed McClernand was at the bottom of all the stories of mis-management, of want of medicines, supplies &c.—fault finding during the period he was not in command. My own opinion is that this whole plan of attack on Vicksburg will fail must fail, and the fault will be on us all of course, but Grant will be the front—his recall leaves McClernand next—I could sim-ply get a leave & Stay away—You keep easy at home and . . . ⟨I start in an hour to make the demonstration up the Yazoo. I shall have ten regiments of infantry, two ironclads, the *Mohawk* and *De Kalb*, and a parcel of mosquitoes. I don't expect a fight, but a devil of noise to make believe and attract any troops in motion from Vicksburg towards Grand Gulf back. I think Grant will make a safe lodgment at Grand Gulf, but the real trouble is and will be the maintenance of the army there. If the capture of Holly Springs made him leave the Tallahatchie, how much more precarious is his position now below Vicksburg with every pound of provision, forage and ammunition to float past the seven miles of batteries at Vicksburg or be hauled thirty-seven miles along a narrow boggy road. I will be up Yazoo about three days. . . . I am not concerned about the Cincinnati *Gazette*. The correspondent's insinuations against Grant and myself about cotton are ridiculous. Grant is honest as old Zack Taylor, and I am a cotton-burner. I have even forbidden all dealing in cotton and not an officer of my command ever owned a bale. As to myself, I would burn every parcel of it as the bone of contention and apple of discord. Now that Mr. Chase has undertaken to manage cotton as well as finance I wish him a good time with it. . . .)

AL (incomplete), InND: Sherman Family Papers; text in angle brackets from *HL*, 257–58.

1. EES to WTS, April 19, 1863, SFP. She wrote that she had been advised by Burnside not to come down because of the danger from guerrillas.

TO ELLEN EWING SHERMAN

Millikens Bend, May 2, 1863.

Dearest Ellen,

As I wrote you on Wednesday I went up Yazoo with 2 iron clad boats, four or five mosquitos or small stern wheel Gunboats and ten transports carrying a part of Blair's Division for the purpose of making a simulated attack on Haines Bluff to divert attention from Grants movements on Grand Gulf. The first night we spent at our old Battle ground of Chickasaw Bayou and next morning moved up in Sight of the Batteries on Drumgoulds Hill. We battered away all morning and the enemy gave us back as much as we sent. The leading Gun boat got 53 shots in her, but her men being in Iron casemates were not hurt. A wooden boat had a shot through the Engine Room. I was in the *Blackhawk* which was a wooden boat with two thirty pound Rifles on the Bow. We kept up a brisk cannonade for about 5 hours, and then hauled out of Range. I then disembarked the men in full view and made all the usual demonstrations of attack, and remained so till night, when the men were recalled. Next morning we made renewed examinations and I had just given orders for a new Cannonade when a messenger came up from Grant saying they had had hard work at Grand Gulf and were compelled to run below, but that he would land at Bayou Pierre and turn back on Vicksburg, ordering me to come with two of my Divisions to Perkins' Plantation about 40 miles down the River. I sent down orders for Tuttles[1] and Steeles Divisions to march at once, and yesterday afternoon we renewed the Cannonade & kept it up till night when we ran down to our camp, and moved up to Millikens Bend— Steeles and Tuttles Divisions have gone out, and I start tomorrow to overtake & pass them. I have nothing positive from below. Blairs Division remains here, this leaves both Hugh & Charley here, and I do think it is well as the movement below is extra hazardous, and the labor of sustaining them is going to be terrible. The new canal is dug the River having fallen very much. I got yours of April 24, after your return from your visit to Cincinati, and Charley got two of date Apl. 20th both of which I read & delivered. Hugh is all right and keeps very steady since I fetched him up. I wrote him a note and asked him after he read it to destroy it and say not a word of its contents which were plain and to the point. I think he will keep all right unless something occurs to disturb his Peace of mind.

The idea of accusing me of complicity in Cotton Speculation is so absurd that no one but laughs at it and would at me for noticing it. I send you an express receipt for $871 my pay for March & April which is better than cotton if you will only salt away a little of it. We cant make much out of newspapers when Juries will decide that Lies are more readable & palateable to the People than the uninteresting details confirmed by Truth. Slander is the Rule, unless one pays for truth as the advertisement. Before this war is over all this will be remedied. If our People dont learn more honesty & propriety Jeff Davis with his armed warriors will rule as with a rod of iron, and I dont know a People that merit a despotism more than we do. Hugh & Charley will write you all about things. You will miss Daytons letters. I will be out of the line of letters for some time and you will have to guess pretty liberally. I should like very much to see Minnie & Willy now—I dreamed that Willy crept into my bed and lay up softly to me, and I cannot explain my disappointment at waking in my narrow cot and discovered the illusion—I saw him as plainly as possible.

Two of my friends have died recently in Colonel Hildebrand, and Bishop Otey of Memphis.[2] You remember the latter, a stately elegant gentleman and a good christian, though somewhat secesh. Still in Principles he was an Union man, though all his associations in life were Southern. From this time forth all armies must be active, and it may be this Campaign may foreshadow the end, but order & system cannot result till one or other of the parties is defeated—I have your fathers letter. It is too late. Stuart is gone. He will not again accept service till he has had time to cover his mortification at the result of his last venture. Nothing but pure patriotism would induce him to submit his name to the U.S. Senate. I think Grant will take Grand Gulf, but that is not Vicksburg yet.[3] My love to all, Affectionately

W. T. Sherman

ALS, InND: Sherman Family Papers.

1. James Madison Tuttle (1823–92), a brigadier general, was leading Sherman's Third Division.

2. James Hervey Otey (1800–1863), the Episcopal bishop of Tennessee since 1834, was a Unionist who had refused to attend the general convention of his church from the seceding states since 1861.

3. Grant's victory at Port Gibson, Mississippi, on May 1 resulted in the evacuation of Grand Gulf by the Confederates on May 3.

TO ELLEN EWING SHERMAN

Camp opposite Grand Gulf, Miss.
May 6, 1863.

Dearest Ellen,

I have sent back orders for my 2nd Division[.] This will bring Hugh & Charley forward, the distance here is 63 miles here we cross over to Grand Gulf by means of steamboats and Grant is waiting for me 18 miles out. I dont know what his move will be. I did not favor this move, and now shall advise a rapid march up the East of Black, break the Rail road good, and then cross over to the Yazoo reuniting our communications with the River above. There we could operate against Vicksburg unless Vicksburg should fall before. We hear that Banks is approaching Alexandria from the South, Porter has gone there from here with 3 fine gunboats. I have no doubt they will reach Alexandria, and that the chances are they may reach Shreveport. Opposition of a serious character on the West of the Mississipi is very slight down here. We only hear of small parties of cavalry out about the Tensas, but none of them come near our Route of march.

Steeles Division is up and Tuttles close behind but Blairs will not be up for three days. It will take up two days to get across here and another to reach Hawkin's Ferry, where Grant now is. I dont know if he will wait for me or push on. Weather is fine, and Roads very good. Along Lake St. Joseph where we now are the Planters never dreamed of our Coming. They had planted vast fields of corn & vegetables, and we find old corn, and some beef cattle. It is folly to suppose the enemy to be suffering for food—They have plenty of Beef and corn. We will have trouble in getting supplies and must learn to live on corn & beef ourselves. I am in good health and every thing thus far moves well, but I am not one who suppose we can take Vicksburg by stratagem, but shall be agreeably surprised if we do. We have found some magnificent plantations most horribly plundered. Dr. Allen T. Bowies[1] Plantation is the first I ever Saw. The house was a palace and furnished as fine as any in New York[.] Magnificent portraits one of Mrs. Reverdy Johnson[.][2] Bowie is 1st cousin to Dr. Bowie[3] of San Francisco & Brother I think to Mrs. Reverdy Johnson. All Rosewood furniture, pier glasses, splendid bedsteads were all smashed, books of the most valuable kind strewn on the floor & about the yard, and every possible indignity offered the palace. It is done of course by the cursed stragglers who wont fight, but hang behind and disgrace our Cause & Country. Dr. Bowie had fled, leaving everything on the approach of our troops. Of course devastation marked the whole path of the army, and I know all the principal officers detest the infamous practice as much as I do. Of course I expect & do take corn, bacon, horses, mules and everything to support an army, and dont object much to the using fences for firewood, but this universal burning and wanton destruction of private property is not justifiable in war. I thought of saving Mrs. Johnsons portrait, as I fear the house & contents will be burned by the stragglers from my corps, but we are moving in the wrong direction to save anything.

I have just received yours of Apl. 25, and was glad to hear you were safe back at home. I would like to know when the children are expected home, when their vacation is. How does the little Pony do[.] Does Tom claim it all or is it joint stock.[4]

I dont know when I will next write but it will be from the east side of the River near Vicksburg. If we can reach the Yazoo we will succeed sooner or later. Grant is calling for me very impatiently and I will probably push out to him with my advance Guard tomorrow.[5] Love to all yrs.

Sherman

ALS, InND: Sherman Family Papers.

1. Allen T. Bowie (1813–72) was a prominent doctor and Natchez planter. Educated in Baltimore and Ohio, he moved to Mississippi in 1837 and settled on a plantation on Lake Joseph in Tensas Parish.

2. Reverdy Johnson (1796–1876), a U.S. senator from Maryland, was married to Bowie's sister, Mary Mackall Bowie.

3. Alexander J. Bowie, a naval surgeon and onetime San Francisco alderman.

4. EES to WTS, April 19, 1863, reported the safe arrival of a pony for Tommy from his father. SFP.

5. On May 3, USG ordered WTS to collect a wagon train, send it to Grand Gulf, and fill it with rations: "It's unnecessary for me to remind you of the overwhelming importance of celerity in your movements. . . . The road to Vicksburg is open; all we want know are men, ammunition and hard bread—we can subsist our horses on the country, and obtain considerable supplies for our troops." Abandoning plans to unite with Banks, USG now proposed to advance northeast, threatening both Vicksburg and Jackson, Mississippi. A second letter on May 4 urged WTS to "make all possible dispatch to Grand Gulf." PUSG, 8:151–52, 158–59.

15 Army Corps, Hankinsons Ferry

18 miles from Grand Gulf, May 9, 1863

Dearest Ellen,

One week after hammering away at Haines Bluff I got here and overtook Grants army, having marched 83 miles, & crossed the Mississipi—we are short of wagons and provisions, but in this starving country we find an abundance of corn, hogs, cattle sheep and Poultry.[1] Men who came in advance have drawn but 2 days rations in 10, and are fat. Tomorrow I march to Big Sandy 9 miles. Next day to Auburn 15 miles and we will then be within striking distance of the Railroad running east from Vicksburg. The enemy must come out to fight us soon as we will be in their rear. The army is in good condition and if they fight us we will have a desperate one. Grant was delighted to See me and everything works well.

Hughs Brigade was left at Millikens Bend, and Blair is following with the two other Brigades. I expect Blair to be at Grand Gulf tonight. There is great trouble in crossing wagons. All the Boats that run the Batteries are more or less damaged & work slow except the *Forest Queen* is a good Boat & a good captain.[2] My party are all in good health. Hill keeps me as near tucked in as an infant and must have a powerful Hope of Reward. I never saw as faithful a fellow. I let him ride Dolly. I rode Dolly over to See Grant today, and she is Keen as a Ram. All the army is moving. I remain to break a Bridge here at noon tomorrow & then follow, towards Raymond & Jackson. It was *Maj.* Grierson who made the famous Raid from Lagrange to Baton Rouge. You Remember him at Memphis. I find that Regt. 6th Ills. down at the heels & brought it out. I hope Grierson will be rewarded, as the feint was a daring & successful one. I fear Poor Charley will have a long & dusty march, but when he catches up, I will see he is all right. The marches are not long, & the worst is the dust.

Magnolias in full bloom, and strawberries ripe.

Love to all. Express waits Goodbye. Yrs. Ever

Sherman

ALS, InND: Sherman Family Papers.

1. Earlier on May 9, WTS had warned USG that traffic jams would make it difficult to maintain a convoy of wagons back to Grand Gulf: "It is useless to push out men out here till their supplies are regulated, unless you intend to live on the Country." USG replied the same day: "I do not calculate upon the possibility of supplying the Army with full rations from Grand Gulf. . . . What I do expect however is to get up what rations of hard bread, coffee & salt we can and make the country furnish the balance." *PUSG*, 8:178–79, 183–84.

2. Captain C. Dan Conway.

TO ELLEN EWING SHERMAN

On Walnut Hills, above Vicksburg,
May 19, 1863.

Dearest Ellen,

We made a full circuit, entered Jackson first, destroyed an immense quantity of Railroad & Confederate property, and then pushed for this Point which secures the Yazoo & leaves [us] to take Vicksburg. We assaulted yesterday but it is very strong. We estimate its present Garrison at 15,000 or 20,000 and Johnston is hovering about with reinforcements. We had a heavy fight yesterday. Regulars suffered much—Capt. Washington[1] killed, 5 officers wounded—Charley in the hand. He saved the colors. He is now in the midst of shells and shot. Hugh is also under fire, had a hard time yesterday. We reached the very parapet, but did not enter the works. We are now encircling the town. I am on the Right. McPherson Center & McClernand Left. We are all in good health & spirits at this moment, & having reached & secured the Yazoo will soon have plenty to eat. I must again go to the Front amid the Shot & shells which follow me but somehow thus far have spared me. Charleys wound is in the hand, slight, & he now commands the Battalion. Keep easy & trust to Luck[.] This is a death struggle & will be terrible. Thus far success has crowned our Efforts and we are on high ground, on a level with the enemy, but they are fortified and we must attack, quicker the better. Grant is off to the Left with McClernand, who *did not* press his attack as he should. Bang, pop, go the Guns & muskets & I must to the Front. I have slept on the ground the last two nights to Hills disgust, and he hangs around me like a shadow with a canteen. He is very faithful, but came up to me yesterday under fire with great reluctance. Yrs. faithfully

W. T. Sherman

ALS, InND: Sherman Family Papers.

1. Captain Edward C. Washington commanded the Thirteenth U.S. Infantry. He died of his wounds while a prisoner in enemy hands.

TO ELLEN EWING SHERMAN

Hd. Qrs. 15 Army Corps.
Walnut Hills, May 25, 1863

Dearest Ellen,

Whilst the men are making Roads and ditches to enable us to get close up to the enemys parapet without crossing within full view and fatal effect their well prepared forts and trenches I have availed myself of the favorable opportunity to pitch a tent and get out writing materials to write up. I have made a preliminary Report in advance of the Sub Reports that should first be made that an outline of our movements may be made to Washington. As it is copied in the Book, I send you my personal draft also a map,[1] that will enable you and your father to trace our Course. Devastation & Ruin lay behind us and a Garrison of some 15 or 20,000 men are cooped up in Vicksburg with about 5 or 6000 people women & children. The Forts are well built to command the Roads, and the hills and valleys are so abrupt and covered with fallen trees, standing trunks and Canebrake that we are in a measure confined to the Roads. We have made two distinct assaults all along the Line, but the heads of Colums are swept away as Chaff thrown from the hand on a windy day. We are now hard at work with roads and trenches, taking all possible advantage of the Shape of ground. We must work smartly as Joe Johnston is collecting the shattered forces, those we beat at Jackson and Champion Hill, and may get reinforcements from Bragg & Charleston and come pouncing down on our Rear. The enemy in Vicksburg must expect aid from that quarter, else they would not fight with such desperation. Vicksburg is not only of importance to them, but now is a Subject of Pride and its loss will be fatal to their power out west. Grants movement was the most hazardous, but thus far the most successful of the war. He is entitled to all the Credit, for I would not have advised it. We have now perfect Communication with our supplies, plenty of provisions, tools, and ammunition and if vast reinforcements do not come from the outside Vicksburg is ours as sure as fate.

I suppose you have all been in intense anxiety. Charley was very conspicuous in the 1st assault, and brought off the Colors of the Battalion which are now in front of my tent the Staff ¼ cut away by a ball that took with it a part of his finger. Luke is all safe. Washington killed & taken inside of Vicksburg. We brought off nearly all our dead & all the wounded, and the enemy called from their pits warning the burial parties not to come closer as they would take care of those left—our pickets are up so close that they can hardly show their heads without drawing hundreds of shots. In like manner we can hardly show a hand without the whirr of a minnie Ball. Our artillery is all well placed and must do havoc in the Town. We have over a hundred Cannon which pour a constant fire over their parapets, the Balls going right towards their court house & depot.

In about 3 days our approaches will be so close that another assault will be made, but the enemy like beavers are digging as hard as we. Hughs Brigade lies forward against the face of a hill within 150 yards of one of the Main forts that I want to approach, mine & blow up, before trying another Charge. I have a nice camp and Grant is near me. McPherson is a noble fellow, but McClernand a dirty dog.

Our present position is high & healthy, and we are all in good health &

spirits—Charley is in Command of his Battalion & is camped near me as a Head Quarters Guard. As soon as we take Vicksburg I will name Charley in terms of as much praise as you can want Love to all Yrs. Ever

W. T. Sherman

ALS, InND: Sherman Family Papers.
1. Map enclosed along with WTS's draft of his report to Rawlins, May 24, 1863, on events of the past month. SFP.

TO JOHN SHERMAN

Hd. Qrs. 15 Army Corps,
Walnut Hills Vicksburg, May 29, 1863

My Dear Brother,

I received a few days since your most acceptable letter of May 7, which met me here.[1] You will now have a fair understanding of the whole move thus far. The move by way of Grand Gulf, to Secure a foothold on these hills wherefrom to assail Vicksburg appeared to me too Risky at the time and General Grant is entitled to all the merit of its completion and execution. In our Route we consumed the fruits of the Country, broke up the important Rail Road communications, whipped the enemy wherever encountered, and secured the Yazoo as a Base the object for which we have contended so long and so patiently. I do assert that none of the Great Armies of our Country has labored so hard, so Zealously & faithfully as this, and none less afflicted with the petty jealousies that disgrace us as a People. We are all perfectly harmonious save McClernand and he is so envious and selfish that he cannot harmonize with any where he does not command. Blair and I are on the very best of terms, and had you heard the cheers of my old Division as I rode down among them on Black River you would have been satisfied that the Soldiers know the intense interest I take in them. Indeed I have never served under anybody or had any one serve under me faithfully that did not want to renew the relation. We have Vicksburg closely invested and its fate is sealed unless the enemy raises a large force from Carolina & Tennessee and assails us from without. In that event we must catch them at the crossing of Black and fight them desperately. The place is very well fortified and is defended by 20,000 brave troops we have assaulted at five distinct points two distinct times and failed to cross the parapet. Our loss was heavy and we are now approaching with pick and shovel. If we did not apprehend an attempt on our Rear we could wait patiently the Slow process of besiegers, but as this danger is great we may try and assault again. In the mean-time we are daily pouring into the city a perfect stream of shot & shells, and our sharpshooters are close up and fire at any head that is rash enough to show itself above ground. I could (damaged—

half of last sheet is cut off) I arrived at last winter, draw on supplies from the very point I then Selected, and cross Chickasaw at my Battle Field. The correctness of every step I then took is now verified by actual possession. I pity Hooker & Mr. Lincoln.[2] I fear that we are approaching that stage of Revolution when no man of principle will accept command under our Government. I suppose Halleck will have to take command of the Potomac Army. Rosecrans has not made a move. I fear too he will go to Seed. In the meantime our army from Battle and the usual Casualties of war may fall below the strength necessary to accomplish what has been so well begun. (damaged—half of last sheet is cut off)

AL (incomplete), DLC: William T. Sherman

1. JS to WTS, May 7, 1863, DLC: WTS. In reply to his brother's letter of April 10, JS responded that he did not know why Stuart was rejected by the Senate as he had not been present at the vote and debate, but he promised to help Stuart as much as possible. He also supported EES in her dispute with Elizabeth Sherman Reese, expressing disdain for the latter. He acknowledged the truth of WTS's predictions about the war: "You certainly have been sagacious in your anticipation of military events. Charleston is not taken, the war is prolonged—and but little chance of its ending until we have a new *deal* or new President."

2. WTS here refers to Hooker's defeat at Chancellorsville during the first week of May 1863.

TO ULYSSES S. GRANT

Hd. Qrts. 15th. Army Corps
Walnut Hill, Miss. June 2d. 1863.

Maj. Genl. U. S. Grant, Present.
Dear General:

I would most respectfully suggest that you use your personal influence with President Lincoln to accomplish a result on which it may be, the Ultimate Peace and Security of our Country depends. I mean to his use of the draft to fill up our old Regiments. I see by the Public Journals that a draft is to be made and that 100,000 men are to be assigned to fill up the Old Regiments and 2,000,000 to be organized as New troops. I do not believe that Mr. Lincoln or any man would at this Critical period of our History repeat the fatal mistakes of last year. Taking this Army as a fair example of the whole, what is the Case? The Regiments do not average 300 men, nor did they exceed that strength last fall; when the new Regiments joined us in November and December their Rolls contained about Nine hundred names, whereas now their Ranks are even thinner than the older Organizations. All who deal with troops in fact instead of theory, know that the knowledge of the little details of Camp Life is absolutely necessary to keep men alive. New Regiments for want of this knowledge have measles, mumps, Diarrhea and the whole Catalogue of Infantile diseases, whereas the same number of men distributed among the older Regiments would learn from the Sergeants, and Corporals, and Privates the art of taking care of themselves which would actually save their lives and preserve their health against the host of diseases that invariably attack the New Reg'ts. Also Recruits distributed among older Companies catch up, from close and intimate contact, a knowledge of drill, the care and use of arms, and all the instructions which otherwise it would take months to impart. The economy too should recommend the course of distributing *All* the Recruits as Privates to the old Regiments; but these reasons appear to me so plain that it is ridiculous for one to point them out to you, or even to suggest them to an intelligent Civilian. I am assured by many that the President does actually desire to support & sustain the Army, and that he desires to know the wishes and opinions of the officers who serve in the woods instead of the "Salon." If so you would be listened to. It will take at least 600 good Recruits per Regiment to fill up the present army to the proper standard. Taking one thousand as the number of Regiments in actual existence this would require 600,000 recruits. It may be, the industrial interests of the Country will not authorize such a call, but how much greater the economy, to make an Army, and fight out this War at once? See how your success is checked by the want of prompt and adequate enforcements, to guard against a new enemy, gathering to our rear. Could your Regts. be filled up to even the standard of 700 men for duty, you would be content to finish quick and well the work, so well begun.

If a draft be made, and the men be organized into new Regiments, instead of filling up the old, the President may satisfy a few aspiring men, but will prolong the war for years and allow the old Regiments to die of natural exhaustion.

I have several Regiments, who have lost honestly in battle and by disease more than half their original men, and the wreck, or remainder, with Colonel, Lt. Col. Major ten captains &c. &c. and a mere squad of men reminds us of the Army of Mexico, All Officers, and no men.

It would be an outrage, to consolidate these old, tired and veteran Regiments, and bring in the new, and comparatively worthless bodies; but fill up our present ranks, and there is not an Officer or man of this Army, but would feel renewed hope and courage to meet the struggles before us.

I regard this matter as more important, than any other that could possibly arrest the attention of President Lincoln and it is for this reason, that I ask you to urge it upon him at the auspicious time.[1] If adopted, it would be more important, than the conquest of Vicksburg, and Richmond together, as it would be a victory of common sense over the popular fallacies, that have ruled and almost ruined our Country. With great Respect &c.

W. T. Sherman

Maj. Genl.

Lbk, DNA: RG 94, Records of the Adjutant General's Office, Generals' Books and Papers, William T. Sherman, Letterbook 5; *OR*, III, 3:386–88.

1. Grant forwarded this letter to the president on June 19, 1863, with a letter endorsing WTS's position: "Taken in an economic point of view, one drafted man in an old regiment is worth three in a new one." *PUSG*, 8:395. Halleck replied on July 14 that the War Department had already decided to raise new regiments. *PUSG*, 8:397n.

TO ELLEN EWING SHERMAN

Walnut Hills, June 2, 1863

Dearest Ellen,

Since our arrival here I have written you several short letters and one telegraph dispatch simply telling you of our safety[1]—I suppose by this time you have heard enough of our march and safe arrival on the Yazoo whereby we reestablished our communications supplying the great danger of this round about movement. We were compelled to feel and assault Vicksburg as it was the only way to measure the amount of opposition to be apprehended. We now Know that it is strongly fortified on all sides and that the Garrison is determined to defend it to the last. We could Simply invest the place and allow famine and artillery to finish the work but we Know that desperate efforts will be made to relieve the place. Joe Johnston, one of the most enterprising of all their Generals is assembling from every quarter an army at Jackson & Canton and he will soon be coming down between the Yazoo & Black. Of Course Grant is doing all he can to provide against every contingency. He sent to Banks, but Banks is investing Port Hudson & asks for reinforcement from us. All the men that can be spared from West Tennessee will be called here, and I trust Rosecrans will not allow any of Bragg's army to be detached against us, but we hear he is planting Gardens and it may be he will wait to gather a crop. The weather is now very hot and we are digging Roads and approaches so that it tells on our men, but they work cheerfully and I have approaches and parallels within 80 yards of the Enemys Line. Daily we open a Cannonade and make the dirt fly, but the Rebels lay close in their pits and holes and we cannot tell what execution is done. I pity the poor families in Vicksburg women & children are living in caves and holes underground whilst our shot & shells tear through their houses overhead—daily & nightly conflagrations occur but still we cannot see the mischief done. We can see the Court House and Steeples of Churches, also houses on the hills back of town, but the City lies on the face of the Hill towards the River, and that is hidden from view by the shape of ground. The hills are covered with trees and are very precipitous affording us good Camps I have mine close up on a spur where we live very comfortably. I go out every morning and supervise the progress of work, and direct the fire of the Guns. The enemys sharp shooters have come very near hitting me several times, but thus far I have escaped unhurt. Pitzman my engineer was shot in the hip and is gone north. Hugh & Charley are well the latter hurt in the finger only as I wrote you. He has also written you as he says a fearfully long letter and has told you doubtless much that would not occur to me.

Mr. Yeatman of St. Louis[2] was here today and I took him all through the trenches[.] He is an excellent Gentleman, President of the Sanitary Commission, and we have made such arrangements that my men get a full share of the vegetables and other articles supplied by that association. We work in perfect harmony, and he is always delighted with his visits to my camps and men. Our camps have been visited by Governors & civilians but the great crowd of curiosity seekers are not allowed to come up the Yazoo[.] Some Ladies have come as far as the Chickasaw which is now an admirable Base of supplies. All the points of my winter movement loom up in their real importance, and I am surprised to find how perfectly I comprehended the whole topography of the place with such limited means of Knowledge. Every body now admits that I accomplished there all that was possible. The Northern papers bring back accounts of our late movements very much exaggerated, but still approximating the truth. I did not go to Haines Bluff at all, because the moment I reached the ground in its rear I was master of it, pushed on to the very gates of Vicksburg and Sent cavalry back to Haines to pick up the points of the strategic movement[.] Grant is now deservedly the hero. He is entitled to all the Credit of the movement which was risky & hazardous in the Extreme and succeeded because of its hazard. He is now belabored with praise by those who a month ago accused him of all the vices in the Calendar, and who next week will turn against him if so blows the popular breeze.

Vox populi—vox humbug. We are in good fighting trim, and I expect still some hard Knocks. The South will not give up Vicksburg without the most desperate struggle. In about three days we ought to be able to make another assault, carrying our men well up to the enemys ditch under cover.

I got the shirts & socks by Hammond—I needed them. Tell Dayton to remain till he is well enough to be of service. A sick man cannot be of much use here. Hammonds return settles Sanger—of course he will not now return, and I may appoint Charley Inspector General with the Rank of Lieut. Colonel, unless he should succeed to the command of the Battalion.[3] We have heard nothing positive of Capt. Washington whom we suppose to be wounded in the Hospitals of Vicksburg, poor fellow pursued by our Shot & Shells.

Tell Minnie & Willie I will write them soon. Love to Lizzie & all. I am rejoiced to hear your mother is so much better. Yrs. ever,

W. T. Sherman

ALS, InND: Sherman Family Papers.

1. WTS to EES, May 25, 1863, SFP.

2. James E. Yeatman (1818–1901), a St. Louis banker and businessman, was president of the Western Sanitary Commission.

3. Charley received the post of inspector general on June 22.

TO ELLEN EWING SHERMAN

Walnut Hills, June 11, 1863

Dearest Ellen,

We have now been before the very gates of Vicksburg for over 3 weeks and I have heard from you but once and that a short letter of introduction brought me by Mr. Carrier Priest.[1] What is the matter, or rather what is the matter with the mail carriers all others get their letters and I get none. I have to go to Hugh & Charley for news. By Mr. Carrier also I got letters from Willy and Minnie. I feel sure you are all well and nothing particular has happened but I miss your letters very much.

I dont believe I can give you an idea of matters here. You will read so much about Vicksburg and the People now gathered about it that you will get bewildered, and I will wait till maps become more abundant. I miss Pitzman very much. I feel his loss just as I did that of Morgan L. Smith at Chickasaw, both wounded in the hip, reconnoitering. So far as Vicksburg is concerned the Same great features exist. The deep washes and ravines with trees filled makes a net work of entangled abattis all round the city and if we had a Million of men we would be compelled to approach it by the narrow heads of colums which approach the concealed trenches & casemates of a concealed and brave and desperate enemy. We cannot carry our men across this continuous parapet without incurring fearful loss. We have been working making Roads & paths around Spurs, up hollows until I now have on my front of over two miles three distinct ways by which I can get close up to the ditch, but still each has a narrow front and any man who puts his head above ground has his head Shot off. All day and night continues the sharp crash of the Rifle and deep sound of mortars & cannon hurling shot & shells at the doomed city. I think we have shot 20,000 cannon Balls, and many millions of musket Balls into Vicksburg, but of course the great mass of them bury into the earth and do little harm. We fire 100 shot to their one, but they being scarce of ammunition take better care not to waste it. I rode away round to McClernands Lines the day before yesterday, and found that he was digging his ditches & parallels further back from the enemy than where I began the first day. My works are further advanced than any other but still it will take some time to dig them out. The truth is, we trust to the Starvation. Accounts vary widely—some deserters say they have plenty to eat, and others say they are down to pea bread and poor beef. I can see horses and mules gently grazing within their Lines and therefore do not count on Starvation yet—All their soldiers are in the trenches & none know anything but what occurs close to them. Food is cooked by negros back in the hollows in rooms cut out of the hills & carried to them by night. The People, women & children, have also cut houses under ground out of the peculiar earth, where they live in comparative safety from our shells & shot. Still I know great exertion must have been done, & Vicksburg at this moment must be a horrid place yet the People have been wrought up to Such a pitch of enthusiasm that I have not yet met one but would prefer all to perish rather than give up. They feel doomed but rely on Joe Johnston. Of him we know but little save we hear of a force at Yazoo City at Canton, Jackson and Clinton. We have received some reinforcements which are at Haines Bluff—Weather has been intensely hot, but yesterday it rained in torrents in the midst of which rode to my pickets to the rear, viz. 7½ miles back on the Ridge Road and above Chickasaw Creek in the Valley a Yazoo City Road. No steamboat has come down for two days and I fear Price has reached the River at some point[2] but I take it for granted this will be attended to. We are well camped & comfortably provided, and can afford to let Time work for us.

We are all well—Yrs. ever

W. T. Sherman

ALS, InND: Sherman Family Papers.

1. EES to WTS, May 25, 1863, introduced Carrier as a priest assigned to Hugh's brigade.

2. Price had not blocked the Mississippi; he was apparently trying to reach other Confederate troops at this time. *PUSG*, 8:327n and 345n.

TO JOHN T. SWAYNE

Hd. Qrs. 15th. Army Corps.
Camp on Walnut Hills, June 11, 1863

Judge Swayne, Memphis
Dear Sir,

As you can readily understand, I have about as much local business, as should engage the attention of one man, desirous of following the great revolution, which is sweeping as with whirlwind speed to destruction or Safety, I enclose you a letter, I have hastily written to General Hurlbut, which is as Specific as I ought to write.[1] The General is a Southerner born and educated Lawyer, as well as Politician and it looks like an absurdity in one, who professes nothing of the kind to suggest to him any course of policy founded in a state of facts, of which I must be ignorant. If God himself smote Sodom and Gomorra, for departing from the law, and setting up their blind prejudice instead, surely I could not plead forbearance on the part of the U.S. if the people of Memphis are known to be conspiring against our law and safety.

But on the other hand, if the people of Memphis are acting in good faith, I will plead for them, that they be dealt with fairly honestly and even with kindness.

I fear me, that politicians and news mongers have so stirred up the vile passions of our People, and so poisoned their minds, that a government founded on public opinion, will for years to come be too unstable to curb these passions, and restrain the excesses, to which they lead, and that the U.S. Government assume the strong and dictatorial form, which alone can protect life and property.

The value of theoretical political notions, must I fear yield to that of more substantial interest. The sooner the people of the South discover this truth, and act upon it, the more will they save from the wrack of matter, that now threatens their universal ruin.

They may display heroic courage, they may elicit the admiration of the world, by the display of military genius, but they cannot stay the hand of destruction, that is now setting adrift their Slaves, occupying with fruitless muskets their adult whites, consuming and wasting their fields and improvements, destroying their roads, bridges, and the labor and fruits of near a century of undisturbed prosperity.

Men of extreme opinion and action cannot reason together and calm this tumult. It is the task allotted to such as you, and the time will come, and that soon, that even you, if you fail to act will be swept aside, helpless as a wisp of straw in the gale of wind.

Instead of appealing to Genl. Hurlbut to assist you, to escape a dangerous remote contingency, I say: think—act. Take your part and see, that some power is raised in America, that can stay the hand of strife, and substitute the rule of justice and mercy for that of force, violence and destruction.

If such men as you sit idle now, you are barred in all future Tribunals to plead for mercy and forbearance. What is a court without Power and a Sheriff? What is a Government, without Power and an Executive? Restore to our old Government its wonted power, and soon will cease this strife, and the Rights, you once prized, but now fast sinking into insignificance amidst new issues, will return and assume their natural weight.

But prolong the strife, and you may safely burn your library and turn your thoughts to some more lucrative trade than the Law.

I believe, you will receive from me in good part thoughts so crude, and it may be unreasonable. I surely wish you well. With Respect

W. T. Sherman

Maj. Genl.

Lbk, DNA: RG 94, Records of the Adjutant General's Office, Generals' Books and Papers, William T. Sherman, Letterbook 5.

1. WTS to Stephen Hurlbut, June 12, 1863, DNA: RG 94, Records of the Adjutant General's Office, Generals' Books and Papers, William T. Sherman, Letterbook 5. WTS urged some restraint in the application of General Orders No. 65, particularly in the case of someone such as Swayne. "My idea is this: We have acknowledged the Belligerent 'Rights of the South,' by flags of truce, exchanging Prisoners, and other interchanges of courtesy. When we capture a place held by them, and establish there actual military Rule, all the people are bound to take notice and depart unless they implicitly accept the conditions attached to them as living within a military camp. If after notice, or a reasonable time to quit, they still remain, and hold communication with an enemy outside, give him encouragement, aid or comfort, they become spies and should suffer death; or if they conspire together within the place, they should be tried for sedition and punished, and indeed in all things be held subject to military Law. I never have, nor do I think, I will exact of any one a 'naked oath'—I have always doubted its efficiency and policy but admit, the problem, we are now solving is one of such mighty character, as to surpass my understanding, and therefore I stand ready to learn by hard experience, as it develops results."

TO MARIA BOYLE EWING SHERMAN

Camp on the Walnut Hills,

Vicksburg, Miss. June 13, 1863

Dear Little Minnie,

I received your letter by the Revd. Mr. Carrier and was glad to hear from him such good accounts of you and Willy. The time is now near at hand when you will have an examination and go home. I Suppose you will be very glad once more to see home, and I only regret we cannot all be together. But we are here on the high hills, fighting daily with the Garrison of Vicksburg which are surrounded and must soon be destroyed or surrendered unless a very large Southern army Comes to their aid.

We also have a very large army, and it is daily increasing by the arrival of troops from the North. I need not tell you how many but our camps extend for fourteen miles. I suppose you hear a good deal about it but it is impossible that you should yet Comprehend the Complicated operations of war, which even few men can—and God Grant that you may never see a hostile army.

Our Camps used to be on the low, level and sickly banks of the River, but we have fought our way to the top. I have a good tent, plenty to eat and drink and you would be surprised to See how Comfortable we all are. Night & day our soldiers are digging Roads leading up to the Enemys forts, and I daily ride about to See how the work progresses. All the time the heavy roar of Cannons and the Sharp Crack of rifles tells that we are near our enemy, and that at any moment a Battle may happen.

A good many of our soldiers have been Killed or wounded, and I suppose before we get Vicksburg more will be, but I hope still to escape and to See you all grow up good & happy. Mama wrote me that She would take Lizzy up to See you at the Examination. I wish I could be along, but when our Country is at war it is the duty of all men to help fight it out.

Tell Willy I will write to him in a day or so, and that I have gathered some cane fishing poles which grow here in what is called cane-brakes, which I will send for him & Tom to catch fish with in the reservoir. He will value them because I sent them and because they come from the Battle fields where so many men have fallen and where for months war has raged in all its fury. It may be some time before we conquer but I think we shall do so at last.

Give my love to Sister Angela, & to Willy, Tommy, Agnes & Elly, and write to me as often as you can, because you can now write all you feel. I can hardly realize that you are so large, but time passes faster than I think. Yr. affectionate father,

W. T. Sherman

ALS, OHi: William T. Sherman Papers.

TO THOMAS EWING SR.

Head Qrs. 15 Army Corps.
Camp, Walnut Hills, Miss., June 14, 1863

Hon. T. Ewing
Lancaster Ohio.
Dear Sir,

I see by a Northern paper that the Hon. Thos. O. Moore, Governor of Louisiana has fallen prisoner into our hands.[1] It occurs to me he may be made the instrument of much good to our cause.

The Election for President occurred in Novr. 1860—Lincolns Election became known in Decr. and the agitation in the South followed. Some time that winter the Legislature was in Session at Baton Rouge and the ordinance of secession passed, Governor Moore taking an active part, but even before the State seceded in form and whilst the state was still represented in Congress Governor Moore in person caused the Seizure of Forts Jackson and St. Philip then unoccupied, as also of Forts Pike and Wood. Each of these Forts held public property, with ordnance Sergeants left to take care of them.

Some time in January 1861, Governor Moore ordered about 500 of the Uniformed Militia of the City of New Orleans to Baton Rouge where the U.S.

had an arsenal containing much valuable property, including near 40,000 stand of arms assorted. Major J. A. Haskin 1st Artillery with a small company of Regulars garrisoned the place. One morning without notice he found himself surrounded by the militia described under the Serving Command of Col. now General Bragg, and Governor Moore was present. An unconditional surrender was demanded. Major Haskins at first proposed to defend his post to the last extremity; but General Bragg had Such influence with Haskins, that he convinced him of the utter absurdity of a defense against such odds, and after much preliminary negotiation, the little Garrison surrendered, was marched to a Steamboat & went up to St. Louis, leaving in Governor Moores possession that valuable arsenal with all its contents. The whole matter was paraded in great detail in the New Orleans Journals, and Governor Moores friends justified the act on the ground that he had telegraphic notice from Benjamin & Slidell still holding seats in the U.S. Senate that Reinforcements were on the way to Maj. Haskin. The arms in the arsenal were scattered, over 4,000 were sent to me at Alexandria for storage & guard by the Corps of Cadets I then commanded. It was this act that I pronounced High Treason, and as you Know I quit the State.

There is now a Cartel or agreement for the Exchange of Prisoners of War, and of other citizens, which may compel us to exchange Moore for some other citizen, but as they have none of like Rank or Station a point could easily be made. Moore could be indicted in New Orleans in the U.S. Dist. Ct. if in existence, and certain great questions might be made and sent up to the Supreme Court, whose decision would Still be greatly respected by thousands at the Extreme South and millions in the Middle or Border States. The Constitutional Right of Secession is actually believed in by many. State Sovereignty was the old Democratic Doctrine South & North, and is held as Law by the best Judges of the South.

Of Course Governor Moore if arraigned for trial on an indictment for Treason would set up his acting in subordination to the authority of the State which I think he can do, and the Supreme Court of the U.S. could then decide absolutely and authoritatively this question which in my judgment has given such perfect unanimity to the People of the South in their War Policy. Though Late, still I know that a decision of the Supreme Court of the U.S. on these great issues would be respected in Tennessee, Louisiana and even Mississipi. If the Inhabitants of the South, believing as they do, maintain their present political Faith, War must be eternal, or extermination take place. I have yet to See the first honest Convert. There remains yet thousands of witnesses to the overt acts of Govr. Moore, who is an able, acute & wealthy Planter. With great respect &c.

W. T. Sherman, Maj. Genl.

ALS, PCarlA.

1. This was a false rumor. Moore had moved the state's capital to Opelousas after the fall of New Orleans.

TO DAVID DIXON PORTER

Head Qrs. 15 Army Corps.
Camp Walnut Hills, June 14, 1863

Dear Admiral,

I owe you a letter our siege is settling down into a chronic state, but I feel certain that Time is working favorably to us. We have as you Know received reinforcements and they are composed of good troops. I feel no concern about Johnston though assured public feeling at the South will force him to make a desperate attack ⟨damaged⟩ he has ⟨illegible⟩. We must commit {no} mistake. I think their men have fought so much behind parapets that we can whip them in the open field and therefore we must manage not to be too much divided, and to catch Johnston {the} moment he offers Battle. The Garrison of {Vic}ksburg will soon feel the effects of pestilence. I see acres of hospital tents and the yellow flag denotes nearly all the hospitals. I can See dead animals lying unburied, but I am free to admit their men stand to their places like heros. My "Sap" is up to their Main Ditch and I have two Side parallels quite close up. The place you visited near the scarred oak tree is now a large "Place d'Armes" and I have Six guns in its left flank. I wish we had a better Supply of 30 pr. Parrott amunition as it is a favorite Gun and spite of all orders my Gunners will fire it too often. Capt. Selfridge[1] is doing good work, and his guns make a mark when they do hit. I have been down to that flank less than usu⟨al⟩ of late having looked more to the country[.] I am going up to Haines Bluff tonight and will return tomorrow, making a circuit to the Right. General Parke[2] has gone to Haines. I commend him to you as a young officer of great promise and one whose acquaintance if not already made will afford you pleasure. I deem our army here at this time extremely fortunate in Securing him, he has with him 5 Brigades of Burnsides Old Corps the 9th about 8000 men. General Ord is also expected here & will command Herrons[3] & Laumans Divisions, so we will have one of the best appointed Armies on the continent, and if Joe Johnston whips us he will achieve wonders. He cant do it. We have Vicksburg now in our grasp and it must & Shall not escape us.

I have read the Black Hawk Chronicle and will always read it with pleasure emanating from such a quarter. In return I send you the *Vicksburg Daily Citizen* of reduced dimensions. I Know you will read it and though you will pity the poor victims of your bombs, you will not feel hurt at being charged with purposely firing at yellow flags. They stream from nearly every house top. I hope you will keep up the Shelling to the maximum capacity day &

night whilst we dig our trenches. The web is closing in fast and we will secure our victim unless some superhuman effort from without relax our grasp.

I wish you would ride up again. The Roads are now good, dust is laid, and the weather more bearable.

I hope our Guard may waylay that party of officers on their return. Should you see anything requiring a guard of soldiers along the Mississipi near the Cincinati telegraph or rather signal direct to Colonel Woods[4] who commands that Brigade and he will attend to it immediately. It will seem more than the hour it takes to get a message from the Station to my Hd. Qrs. & back to Woods, besides I am so often out in the trenches.

Present me kindly to Capt. Breese,[5] and tell him I want to see him very much. I dont want to get on board a Boat, till it be at Vicksburg Wharf. With great respect your friend,

W. T. Sherman
Maj. Genl.

ALS, PPRF.

1. Thomas O. Selfridge Jr. had been made a lieutenant commander on February 21, 1863, to rank from July 16, 1862. He commanded naval guns on shore during the siege of Vicksburg.

2. Major General John G. Parke (1827–1900), USA, commanded the Ninth Corps at Vicksburg.

3. Major General Francis Jay Herron (1837–1902), USA, commanded a division in the Thirteenth Corps.

4. Charles Robert Woods (1827–85), later a brigadier general, commanded the Second Brigade in Sherman's First Division.

5. Captain K. Randolph Breese, USN.

TO JOHN A. RAWLINS

Headquarters Fifteenth Army Corps,
Camp on Walnut Hills, June, 17, 1863.

Lieut. Col. John A. Rawlins,
Assistant Adjutant-General, Department of the Tennessee:
Sir:

On my return last evening from an inspection of the new works at Snyder's Bluff, General Blair, who commands the Second Division of my corps, called my attention to the inclosed publication in the Memphis Evening Bulletin of June 13, instant, entitled "Congratulatory Order of General McClernand," with a request that I should notice it, lest the statements of fact and inference contained therein might receive credence from an excited public. It certainly gives me no pleasure or satisfaction to notice such a catalogue of nonsense— such an effusion of vain-glory and hypocrisy; nor can I believe General Mc-Clernand ever published such an order officially to his corps. I know too well that the brave and intelligent soldiers and officers who compose that corps will not be humbugged by such stuff.[1]

If the order be a genuine production and not a forgery, it is manifestly addressed not to an army, but to a constituency in Illinois, far distant from the scene of the events attempted to be described, who might innocently be induced to think General McClernand the sagacious leader and bold hero he so complacently paints himself; but it is barely possible the order is a genuine one, and was actually read to the regiments of the Thirteenth Army Corps, in which case a copy must have been sent to your office for the information of the commanding general.

I beg to call his attention to the requirements of General Orders, No. 151, of 1862, which actually forbids the publication of all official letters and reports, and requires the name of the writer to be laid before the President of the United States for dismissal. The document under question is not technically a letter or report, and though styled an order, is not an order. It orders nothing, but is in the nature of an address to soldiers, manifestly designed for publication for ulterior political purposes. It perverts the truth to the ends of flattery and self-glorification, and contains many untruths, among which is one of monstrous falsehood. It substantially accuses General McPherson and myself with disobeying the orders of General Grant in not assaulting on May 19 and 29, and allowing on the latter day the enemy to mass his forces against the Thirteenth Army Corps alone. General McPherson is fully able to answer for himself, and for the Fifteenth Army Corps 1 answer that on May 19 and 22 it attacked furiously, at three distinct points, the enemy's works, at the very hour and minute fixed in General Grant's written orders; that on both days we planted our colors on the exterior slope and kept them there till nightfall; that from the first hour of investment of Vicksburg until now my corps has at all times been far in advance of General McClernand's; that the general-in-chief, by personal inspection, knows this truth; that tens of thousands of living witnesses beheld and participated in the attack; that General Grant visited me during both assaults and saw for himself, and is far better qualified to judge whether his orders were obeyed than General McClernand, who was nearly 3 miles off; that General McClernand never saw my lines; that he then knew, and still knows, nothing about them, and that from his position he had no means of knowing what occurred on this front. Not only were the assaults made at the time and place and in the manner prescribed in General Grant's written orders, but about 3 p.m., five hours after the assault on the 22d began, when my storming party lay against the exterior slope of the bastion on my front, and Blair's whole division was deployed close up to the parapet, ready to spring to the assault, and all my field artillery were in good position for the work, General Grant showed me a note from General McClernand, that moment handed him by an orderly, to the effect that he had carried three of the enemy's forts, and that the flag of the Union waved over the stronghold of Vicksburg, asking that the enemy should be pressed at all points lest he should concentrate on him. Not dreaming that a major-general would at such a critical moment make a mere buncombe communication, I instantly ordered Giles A. Smith's and Mower's brigades to renew the assault under cover of Blair's division and the artillery, deployed as before described, and sent an aide to General Steele, about a mile to my right, to convey the same mischievous message, whereby we lost, needlessly, many of our best officers and men.

I would never have revealed so unwelcome a truth had General McClernand, in his process of self-flattery, confined himself to facts in the reach of his own observation, and not gone out of the way to charge others for results which he seems not to comprehend. In cases of repulse and failure, congratulatory addresses by subordinate commanders are not common, and are only resorted to by weak and vain men to shift the burden of responsibility from their own to the shoulders of others. I never make a practice of speaking or writing of others, but during our assault of the 19th several of my brigade commanders were under the impression that McClernand's corps did not even attempt an assault.

In the congratulatory order I remark great silence on the subject. Merely to satisfy inquiring parties, I should like to know if McClernand's corps did or did not assault at 2 p.m. of May 19, as ordered. I do not believe it did, and I think General McClernand responsible.

With these remarks I leave the matter where it properly belongs, in the hands of the commanding general, who knows his plans and orders, sees with an eye single to success and his country's honor, and not from the narrow and contracted circle of a subordinate commander, who exaggerates the importance of the events that fall under his immediate notice, and is filled with an itching desire for "fame not earned."[2]

> With great respect,
> your obedient servant,
> W. T. Sherman,
> Major-General, Commanding.

Printed, *OR*, I, 24: pt. 1, 162–63.

1. WTS refers to McClernand's General Orders No. 72, issued May 30, 1863, which appeared in several newspapers within weeks. *OR*, I, 24: pt. 1, 159–61.

2. McClernand's order had not only slighted the contributions of the corps commanded by Sherman and James B. McPherson, it had also implied that both corps failed to support the Thirteenth Corps during the May 22 assault at Vicksburg. McPherson joined Sherman in protesting the order; Grant, after further investigation, decided to relieve McClernand of command on June 18. See *OR*, I, 24: pt. 3, 159–64.

TO WILLIAM T. SHERMAN JR.

Head Qrs., 15 Army Corps.

Camp on Walnut Hills, June 21, 1863

Dear Willy,

I got your letter by the Revd. Mr. Carrier Priest, who came here from Smith Bend, and told me all about you and Minnie, Tommy Ewing and Elly. Of course I was very glad to hear from you by one who had come straight from you. Mama tells me that She will be at your Examination on the 28th and that as soon as it is over she will take you all home to Lancaster. Indeed would I like to meet you all there but you are old enough now to know that I must be here with the army which is besieging the City of Vicksburg. We have had many Battles, and yesterday we again fired nearly twenty thousand Cannon Balls into the City. Vicksburg is on a high hill overlooking the Mississipi River, with Batteries so constructed that any Boat which approaches will be shot into and sunk. On the high ground back of the City is a Fort about 8 miles long and the trees are cut down, and ground cleared so that the Enemy can shoot our men if they come within the range of their muskets whilst they are concealed by a wall of dirt piled up on their front. Some day you will be able to understand this. We first tried to run fast over this ground and to climb inside their wall, but they killed so many of our men that the rest stopped and got behind a hill. Since that time we are digging ditches so that men can wash in them, without being seen and fired at. These ditches can only be dug at night, but I have one finished right up to the Enemys wall, and we are working night and day to make many others so that when we next attack we expect to get inside Vicksburg, where we must have another great Battle. Maybe their provisions will give out, for no person can get out or in Vicksburg without our consent, and if they have nothing to eat, they will starve or give up.

I have five horses. My little mare Dolly is a roan mare and can run very fast—Abner is a large bay horse very strong and is generally ridden by my orderly Boyer. Sam is the horse I generally ride when there is fighting. He is not afraid of shot & shells, or the Sound of Muskets & Cannon, but Dolly is— she is a little Coward—Then I have two other horses without particular names, a sorrel & bay—I have a black boy who used to be a slave that I hire to take care of my horses, his name is Carter, and he and the horses are as fat as they can be. He takes good care of the horses and Sleeps with them. We have no stables but all lie out doors. I sleep in a tent and my staff officers are near me, and the 13th Regulars are camped close by. A sentinel walks before my tent day & night and the Flag of the 13th riddled with balls the Same that Uncle Charley carried in the Battle of May 19, is before my tent. I wish you could see it for a minute, but it is not right for children to be here, as the danger is too great. There is more or less fighting all the time and bullets are whistling in every direction.

My army is on the North front of Vicksburg, about two miles long, and I ride along it every day, but to go up near have to get off and go on foot through the ditches, with bullets clipping only a few inches above our heads, all the time, but we now understand the points of danger. The ground is very broken, the hills steep, and hollows dark and filled with cane brake, the same kind the boys use for fishing. It occurred to me you would like to have a fishing pole from the Battle Field, so I had about a dozen cut and put up nicely and sent to Lancaster for you. Give one to Tom Sherman—one to Tommy Ewing, and the rest distribute among your friends and tell them that they were gathered close up to Vicksburg, right on a Battle Field on which thousands have already been killed, and thousands more will be. Every cane has vibrated to the sound of near fifty thousand cannon balls fired with intent to kill, and it may be that more than one poor fellow has crawled to the Shadow of their leaves to die. Each cane is therefore a precious memento. I felt you would prefer them to any book or toy bought with money.

You must continue to write to me, and tell me everything—how tall in feet & inches—how heavy—can you ride, swim—how many feet & inches you jump. Everything. Of me you will always hear much that is bad, and much that is good—The world is full of good and bad men and they have their reasons to praise or blame others, but you and my children will feel and know that I am always good to them, for they are growing up to fill stations higher and better than any I now fill and must be prepared. My love to Sister Angela and Your Teachers—Yr. affectionate Father,

W. T. Sherman

ALS, InND: Sherman Family Papers.

TO ELLEN EWING SHERMAN

Camp on Bear Creek,
20 miles N.W. of Vicksburg.
June 27, 1863.

Dearest Ellen,

I am out here studying a most complicated Geography and preparing for Joe Johnston if he comes to the relief of Vicksburg. As usual I have to leave my old companions & troops in the trenches of Vicksburg, and deal with strange men, but I find all willing & enthusiastic. Although the weather is intensely hot, I have ridden a great deal, and think I know pretty well the weak and strong points of this extended Line of Circumvallation, and if Johnston comes I think he will have a pretty hard task to reach Vicksburg, although from the broken nature of the country he may feign at many points and attack but on one. Black River the real Line is now so low it can be forded at almost any point and I prefer to fight him at the Ridges along which all the Roads lead. Of these there are several some of which I have blocked with fallen trees and others left open for our own purposes, and which will be open to him if he crosses over—Our accounts of his strength & purposes are (erased) as the (erased) of fact of deserters & spies (erased) are. I (erased) to be governed by what I suppose he will do, under the pressure of opinion that must be brought to bear on him to relieve a brave & beleaguered Garrison. I suppose he made large calculations on obstructing the River at some point above us, and it seems the Boats coming down & going up receive shots at various points along the River, but thus far reinforcements and supplies have reached us without serious check. My Line extends from the Railroad Bridge on Black River, around to Haines Bluff, both of which are entrenched. I have some works at intermediate points, but if Johnston crosses the fight will be mostly by detachments along the narrow Ridges with which the country abounds, and along which alone Roads can be made.

The siege of Vicksburg progresses. From my camp I hear the booming of cannon, telling of continued battering. My trenches had connected with the main ditch before I left, and had I remained I think by this time we should have made a push for the Bastion in my front. I hear every day, that things remain status quo. I left Charley at Head Qrs. to continue his inspections and Hugh in command of his Brigade which is on the main approach. He say he writes often to his wife and to you all. (sentence erased) I have (remainder of sentence erased)—He is very stubborn & opinionated, but has his Brigade in good order, which is the only test to which I refer in official & military matters. I must not favor him or Charley unfairly, as it would do them no good & me much harm. You will feel sure that each has as much of my thoughts and affections as can be spared for the thousands subject to my orders & care. My military family numbers by the tens of thousands and all must know that they enjoy a part of my thoughts and attention. With officers & soldiers I know how to deal but am willing to admit ignorance as to the People who make opinion according to their contracted Knowledge & biassed prejudices, but I know the time is coming when the opinion of men "not in arms at the countrys crisis, when her calamities call for every man capable of bearing arms" will be light as to that of men who first, last & all the time were in the war. I enclose a slip which came to me by accident, describing our Leaders here. Were I to erase the names you would not recognize one, although the narrative meant to be fair & impartial.

I meet daily incidents which would interest you but these you will have to draw out on cross examination when we meet—I find here a Mrs. Klein only child of Mrs. Day of New Orleans & niece of Tom Bartley[1] (phrase erased) and will continue to befriend them. They have a son in the Confederate Army now in Vicksburg, a lad some 18 years of age. The day I approached Vicksburg, my advance Guard caught a Confederate soldier and a negro, servant to George Klein, carrying a letter to the father at his Country refuge near here. Of course the negro was sent north and the letter read. It contained much useful information, and among other things he described the loss of the Battery of Guns at Champion Hill in which he used the Expression, "We lost our Guns, but they will do the Yankees no good, for we broke up the carriages and hid the Guns in a Ravine" so this boy of Ohio birth is not very loyal, though he was with John Sherman during his Electioneering Canvas which resulted in Lincolns Election. Mr. Klein father continually exclaims, "they cant hold out much longer—their provisions must be out &c." but the enemy in Vicksburg in my judgment shows no abatement of vigorous resistance or short food— with every house in sight of our lines marked with the Hospital Flag—Orange Yellow. We cant show a hand or cap above our rifle pits without attracting a volley. But of course there must be an end to all things & I think if Johnston do not make a mighty effort to relieve Vicksburg in a week they will cave in.

I would at this moment be in the saddle, but have sent a Brigade down to Black River to examine a certain Ford where one of our Pickets was fired on last night by Cavalry. I rather think two of our patrols came together & mistook. Nobody was hurt but I must watch closely, as I know Joe Johnston will give me little time to combine after he moves. He may approach from the North North East or East, all of which routes I am watching closely, but it will be necessary to draw from two quarters to reinforce one, and it will be exceedingly difficult to judge from signs the Real point from the Feints. Their cavalry is so much better than ours, that in all quick movements they have a decided advantage.

As I am now on my second sheet, and as I am listening for signs of action at a Ford in the bottom 3 miles off, I might as well go on and punish you with a surfeit after the manner of your affectionate son & uncle, and bosom friend, Lt. Col. Charley Ewing. My Head Qrs. here are in a tent by the Road side, where one forks down to Bear Creek & the other goes along down to Black River direct. I have with me the invariable Hill who still puts me on a damned allowance of segars & whiskey & insists on blacking my boots & brushing my clothes in & out of season. Boyer my orderly is also here, with my horses Dolly, Abner, Sam and a new one recently presented me by General Steele called Duke. Dolly carries me when I explore—Sam & Duke when I expect to be shot at[.] Yesterday morning with Dolly, Boyer, McCoy & Hill aids and a small escort I started on a circuit visiting outposts & pickets—At a Mrs. Fox's I found as is the case of all farms here a bevy of women waiting patiently the fate of husbands & sons penned up in Vicksburg—one of them a Mrs. Eggleston, whose pretty children I noticed asked me if I were the Genl. Sherman of New Orleans—of course not—She asked because a Mrs. Wilkinson[2] was a great friend of his—What Mrs. Wilkinson? a Mrs. Wilkinson of New Orleans. Where was she? spending the day at another Mrs. Fox, Parson Fox about a mile further on—As my route lay that way I rode up the yard of Parson Fox. A company of Iowa men lay in the shade on picket, and about a dozen ladies sat on the broad balcony. I rode up close saluted the ladies & inquired for Mrs. Wilkinson a small old lady answered—I asked if she were of Plaquemine Parish—Yes—Where was her husband the General?[3] Killed on the Plains of Manassas, fighting for his Country," with a paroxism of tears at tearing open the old wound, and all the women looking at me as though I had slain him with my own hand—I knew him well, he was a direct descendant of the General Wilkinson[4] of the old wars, and was once a client of your father, I think in the famous Land case of Penrose St. Louis. He had a son at Alexandria[5] about whom we corresponded a good deal. When I left Louisiana I regarded him as an Union man and had forgotten that he was killed at Manassas at the first Battle—After the old lady had cooled down a little I inquired for the Son. He is in Vicksburg, and the mother has got this near to watch his fate. Do, oh do General Sherman spare my son, in one breath and in another, that Lincoln was a tyrant and we only Murderers, Robbers, plunderers and defilers of the houses and altars of an innocent & outraged People. She and all the women were real secesh, bitter as gall & yet Oh do General Sherman protect my son. The scene set all the women crying, and Dolly & I concluded to go into the more genial atmosphere out in the Fields & Woods. I doubt if History affords a parallel of the deep & bitter enmity of the women of the South. No one who sees them & hears them but must feel the intensity of their hate. Not a man is seen—nothing but women, with houses plundered, fields open to the cattle & horses, pickets lounging on every porch, and desolation sown broadcast—Servants all gone and women & children bred in luxury, beautiful & accomplished begging with one breath for the soldiers Ration and in another praying that the Almighty or Joe Johnston will come & kill us, the despoilers of their houses and all that is sacred—Why cannot they look back to the day & the hour when I a stranger in Louisiana begged & implored them to pause in their course, that secession was death, was everything fatal, and that their seizure of the public arsenals was an insult that the most abject nation must resent or pass down to future ages an object of pity & scorn. Vicksburg contains many of my old pupils & friends. Should it fall into our hands I will treat them with kindness, but they have sowed the wind & must reap the whirlwind. Until they lay down their arms, and submit to the rightful authority of their Government, they must not appeal to me for mercy or favors—The weather is very hot, though the nights are cool—wild plums abounded, have ripened and are gone. Blackberries are now as abundant as ever an army could ask, and are most excellent—Apples & peaches & figs are ripening, and of all these there will be an abundance even for our host. Corn too is in silk & tassel and soon Roasting ears will give our soldiers an additional tendency to sickness—advice, orders & remonstrance are all idle[.] Soldiers are like children, and eat, eat all the time. Water is very poor & scarce on the hills but is found in moving brooks down in the chasms and hollows of Clear & Bear Creeks near which all my Camps are—I have written Minnie & Willy & sent the latter some fishing poles from the "Battle Field"—Tell Tom & Lizzy they must write me also. Tell them all that actually I have hardly time to write to you and I get tired of writing more than I used to—Love to all yrs. ever

Sherman

ALS, InND: Sherman Family Papers.

1. Thomas Wells Bartley (d. 1885), an Ohio politician, had married WTS's sister Susan Denman Sherman (1825–76) in 1848.

2. Presumably Mrs. Mary F. Wilkinson (b. ca. 1821), for whom WTS would later give a letter of introduction to USG that would enable her to get inside Vicksburg to see her son on July 3, before the surrender of the city. *PM*, 1:358; *PUSG*, 8:460n.

3. Presumably Robert A. Wilkinson (ca. 1815–61), a planter born in Mississippi.

4. James Wilkinson (1757–1825), the controversial general who fought in the Revolution and on the young nation's frontier.

5. Probably Robert A. Wilkinson Jr. (b. ca. 1845).

TO JOHN SHERMAN

Camp on Bear Creek
20 mi. N.W. of Vicksburg
[ca. June 27, 1863]

Dear Brother,

Your letter from Washington came to me out here yesterday. I am here in observation of the movements of Johnston who has a pretty large force which he is gathering near Canton & Brownsville and preparing to relieve Vicksburg. Our accounts coming from spies, deserters & informers vary much for indeed not one man in the militia can ride through armies and give an approximate estimate of numbers. I prefer to judge from general facts and principles. All know the importance of Vicksburg and that honor & every obligation of life will impel Johnston whose ability no one questions to come to the relief of the beleaguered Garrison.

Vicksburg is now girt about by land and water with a force adequate to the end in view.

The country back of it is singularly broken—Black River is behind varying from 12 to 20 miles of the Bluffs that run along the Yazoo & Mississipi making the site of Vicksburg. This space is a General Ridge whose line is followed by a Road known as the Benton or Ridge Road. From this ridge flow right & left innumerable smaller spans with their laterals, with deep chasms & valleys between—Roads follow the Ridges which as a general Rule are cleared, & cultivated in corn & fruits, whilst the valleys are filled with dense timber bushes & canebrake. Black River can be crossed almost anywhere, but the roads following their lateral spans are very defensible. I have the general supervision & command of all the forces looking to Johnston. Osterhaus[1] is at the point of the River due east of Vicksburg where it is crossed by the old R. R. Bridge partially burned and a floating Bridge. A strong Garrison is also en-trenched at Haines Bluff in Yazoo. Some of the Roads leading from fords & ferries are obstructed by fallen trees, and the others are watched by cavalry & Infantry. I hold the greater part in hand ready to assemble at certain centers according to the threatened points. Thus far the enemy has made no demon-stration, but I know he will, because he should. I only came out five days ago, prior to which I was pushing the attack on the North Front of Vicksburg.[2] At some future time maps & diagrams will make all this familiar and it suffices now that I explain that the Enemy chose of course the most favorable ground for their Redoubts & Lines and prepared the ground outside so that assaults whether in Line or Column had to pass over ground most exposed to us and favorable to their deliberate fire. We were bound to assault as we did, as the Chances of war were in favor at the earliest moment that we should measure strength to ascertain the exact situation of affairs, since those events we have been hard at work making approaches & parallels which you know are sunken Roads obliquely towards the Enemy & parallel, whereon to move and assem-ble troops covered by Earth. At the time of my leaving my main approach was in the Enemys ditch at a Salient—and I had two other approaches within 60 yards of the Curtains right & left. In my absence Steele will supervize the work—most of it is done at night by men inexperienced in Such work, and when you know the bulk of this work is done within pistol shot of an enemy lying in comparative safety behind prepared Breastworks you will say we have not been idle. Similar approaches are all round the city. My part is near 3 miles. The whole line must be 8 or 9 miles.

Grant has at last rid himself of McClernand, who was a vain, newspaper publishing, ambitious, designing demagogue.[3] He has had luck from Donelson to Vicksburg and only those along know how little he was an actor or thinker in these matters. His riddance was a relief to the whole army.

Mr. & Mrs. Klein & 4 children happen to be staying at a Mr. Markhams near where I now am. I have been able to see them and they are grateful but Klein must lose the bulk of his property which consists mostly of a mill & houses in Vicksburg—More than 50,000 shots have gone into that town and say what they may, they must have done havoc & damage—the increased numbers of hospital flags tell a better tale than their boasts—we must give them credit for courage & obstinacy. New York or Cincinati, or St. Louis would have surrendered to Such battering. Mr. Klein wonders how they hold out his son George is in Vicksburg, a soldier & clerk in Genl. Martin L. Smiths office. (Smith is a N. Yorker at West Point with me). The day I was marching on Vburg my advance captured a negro boy carrying a letter from George Klein to his Father. At the time I did not think of the parties, but since I have seen Mr. Klein the subject was raised & the truth apparent. George wrote of several things but among others speaking of the loss of the Battery to which he belonged—(Cowans) he said they had lost the Guns, but would do the Yankees no good, for they had broken up the carriages and concealed the Guns in a Ravine—so I doubt *his* loyalty, though Mr. Klein says he is a strong friend of yours.

Henry Sherman is coming out well, has got over his homesickness & has tasted blood & war. Of course I am too careful to express opinions of Events which must happen in due course of time, but I do think it a shame that Mr. Lincoln has so long delayed his draft, that now he must compromise 3 years men for 6 months volunteers, to repel invasion. Why not rise to the occasion at once. Every man in the South capable of carrying a musket is now in arms against us. Yrs. affectionately

W. T. Sherman

ALS, DLC: William T. Sherman.

1. Brigadier General Peter J. Osterhaus (1823–1917), USA, commanded a division in the Thirteenth Corps.

2. On June 22 USG ordered WTS to take charge of a makeshift force gathering to resist a possible attempt by Joseph E. Johnston to relieve the besieged Vicksburg garrison. The date of this order and of WTS's letter to EES suggest that the above letter was written June 27 or 28. *PUSG*, 8:408.

3. Grant ordered McClernand's removal from command of the Thirteenth Corps on June 18 after receiving evidence that McClernand had allowed newspapers to publish a congratulatory order to his men on the assault of May 22 in violation of War Department guidelines. The order slighted the performance of Sherman and McPherson's men.

TO ULYSSES S. GRANT

July 3 1863
By Telegraph from Paokes

to Gen. Grant

I am this momos m {moment in} & have your despatch[.][1] telegraph me the moment you have Vicksburg in possession, & I will secure all the crossings of Black River & move on Jackson or Canton as you may advise[.] I want my own corps & Ords with Parke in reserve train small all of which will be arranged [when] I know for certain that you are in absolute possession[.] If you are in Vicksburg Glory Hallelujah the best fourth of July since 1776[.] Of course we must not rest idle only dont let us brag too soon[.] I will order my troops at once to occupy the forks of Big Black & await with anxiety your further answer

W. T. Sherman
Maj. Genl.

Telegram, DNA: RG 94, Records of the War Records Office, Military Command Correspondence Relating to "Official Records," Department of the Tennessee, Letters, Telegrams and Reports; *OR*, I, 24: pt. 3, 461.

1. USG to WTS, July 3, 1863, *PUSG*, 8:461. Grant explained that Pemberton was asking him about the terms for surrendering the Vicksburg garrison. As Sherman had suggested, Steele and Ord would move into Vicksburg; meanwhile, he directed Sherman to pursue and destroy Johnston.

TO ULYSSES S. GRANT

Camp on Bear Creek
July 4, 1863.

Major-General Grant:
My Dear General:

The telegraph has just announced to me that Vicksburg is ours;[1] its garrison will march out, stack arms, and return within their lines as prisoners of war, and that you will occupy the city only with such troops as you have designated in orders. I can hardly contain myself. Surely will I not punish any soldier for being "unco happy" this most glorious anniversary of the birth of a nation, whose sire and father was a Washington. Did I not know the honesty, modesty, and purity of your nature, I would be tempted to follow the examples of my standard enemies of the press in indulging in wanton flattery; but as a man and soldier, and ardent friend of yours, I warn you against the incense of flattery that will fill our land from one extreme to the other. Be natural and yourself, and this glittering flattery will be as the passing breeze of the sea on a warm summer day. To me the delicacy with which you have treated a brave but deluded enemy is more eloquent than the most gorgeous oratory of an Everett.[2] This is a day of jubilee, a day of rejoicing to the faithful, and I would like to hear the shout of my old and patient troops; but I must be a Gradgrind[3]—I must have facts, knock, and must go on. Already are my orders out to give one big huzza and sling the knapsack for new fields. Tuttle will march at once to Messinger', Parke to Birdsong, and I will shift my headquarters to Fox's. McArthur will clear the road of obstructions made against the coming of the unseen Johnston, and as soon as Ord and Steele's columns are out, I will push ahead. I want maps, but of course the first thing is to clear the Big Black River and get up on the high ground beyond, when we move according to developments. I did want rest, but I ask nothing until the Mississippi River is ours, and Sunday and 4th of July are nothing to Americans till the river of our greatness is free as God made it. Though in the background, as I ever wish to be in civil war, I feel that I have labored some to secure this glorious result. I am, with respect, your friend,

W. T. Sherman

Printed, *OR*, I, 24: pt. 3, 472.

1. USG to WTS, July 4, 1863, *PUSG*, 8:476, announced, "Propositions have been sent in for the surrender of Vicksburg. Pemberton's reply is momentarily expected If he does not surrender now, he will be compelled to by his men within two days no doubt."

2. Edward Everett (1794–1865) of Massachusetts was a famous orator and politician.

3. Thomas Gradgrind, a retired merchant, was a main character in Charles Dickens's 1854 novel, *Hard Times*, who emphasized the importance of facts over imagination and personified much of what Dickens saw as bad in the current education system.

July 5, 1863–December 30, 1863

*V*icksburg's capitulation offered no respite for Sherman, who carried out his assignment to drive Joseph Johnston's Confederates away from Jackson by mid-month. He viewed the victory with some ambivalence. Justly proud of the accomplishments of the Army of the Tennessee, he was now willing to concede that Grant had more ability than he had once suspected; moreover, he now acknowledged that Grant possessed the temperament needed to succeed as a general. He was quick to note, however, that not all newspapers lauded the achievement with the same vigor they had used to assail Grant, Sherman, and their men and wondered how long it would be before Grant's laurels withered. Again he questioned the wisdom and stability of democratic institutions, preferring to stand behind the law—although the laws he praised were crafted by the institutions and people he so often questioned.

Sherman also was of several minds about the best way to crush Confederate resistance. At times he favored harsh measures, going so far as to speak of executing some Confederate leaders and relocating populations. Here and there, however, he began to discuss the need to pulverize the will to resist by a show of overwhelming power relentlessly applied. When Halleck asked him to offer his views on reconstruction, Sherman jumped at the opportunity, producing an extensive analysis of Southern white society and institutions that revealed much about his own thinking. He would be ready for peace when the time came; for now, it was "time for us to pile on our blows thick and fast." As he looked forward to future campaigns, Sherman continued to fight past battles. He asked Lew Wallace to stop complaining about Grant's dismal evaluation of Wallace's performance at Shiloh; he warned a member of Don Carlos Buell's staff that Buell's search for vindication was counterproductive.

Tragedy struck the Sherman family in the fall of 1863. In September the general welcomed the arrival of Ellen and the children; in the weeks that followed he noticed an improvement in his offsprings' health. That proved cruelly deceptive; Willy, his eldest son, contracted typhoid and died on October 3. "This is the only death I have ever had in my own family," he told Grant, "and falling as it has so suddenly and unexpectedly on the one I most prised on earth had affected me more than any other misfortune could." Although he tried to escape his grief by throwing himself into his work, he could not shake his sorrow.[1]

Events in late 1863 compelled Sherman to contain his mourning. In October Grant assumed command of the Military Division of the Mississippi; his primary task was to repel Confederate efforts to take back East Tennessee. Immediately he called for Sherman to assist him by marching to Chattanooga with part of the Army of the Tennessee—now Sherman's army. Sherman made his way to Chattanooga by mid-November, but in the battle that followed he did not distinguish himself. Overlooking this, Grant dispatched him to relieve Ambrose Burnside's beleaguered force at Knoxville, although by the time Sherman arrived the threat had ended. The victories allowed him to take a well-deserved leave, and as the year drew to a close he made his way back to Lancaster.

1. WTS to USG, October 4, 1863, *PUSG*, 9:274–75. Michael Fellman, *Citizen Sherman* (New York, 1995), 199–212, contains an excellent discussion of how WTS mourned the loss of his son.

TO ELLEN EWING SHERMAN

Camp near Black River,
20 miles east of Vicksburg,
July 5, 63

Dearest Ellen,

You will have heard all about the capitulation of Vicksburg on the 4th of July, and I Suppose duly appreciate it. It is the event of the war thus far. Davis placed it in the scale of Richmond, and pledged his honor that it should be held even if he had to abandon Tennessee. But it was of no use, and we are now in full possession. I am out and have not gone in to See, as even before its surrender Grant was disposing to send me forth to meet Johnston who is and has been since June 15 collecting a force about Jackson to raise the siege. I will have Ords corps, the 13th (McClernands) Shermans 15th and Parkes 9th. All were to have been out last night but Vicksburg & the 4th of July were too much for one day and they are not yet come. I expect them hourly. I am busy making 3 bridges to cross Black River and Shall converge on Bolton and Clinton and if not held back by Johnston shall enter Jackson, and then finish what was so well begun last month and break up all the Railroads & bridges in the Interior so that it will be impossible for armies to assemble again to threaten the River.

The capture of Vicksburg is to me the first gleam of daylight in this war—It was strong by nature, and had been strengthened by immense labor & stores— Grant telegraphs me 27,000 prisoners, 128 Field Guns and 100 siege pieces—

add to these, 13 Guns, & 5000 Prisoners at Arkansas Post, 18 Guns & 250 prisoners at Jackson, 5 Guns & 2000 prisoners at Port Gibson—10 heavy Guns at Grand Gulf, 60 field Guns & 3500 prisoners at Champion Hill, and 14 heavy Guns at Haines Bluff, beside the immense amounts of ammunition, shot shells, horses, wagons &c. make the most extraordinary fruits of our six months campaign. Here is Glory enough for all the Heros of the West, but I content myself with Knowing & feeling that our enemy is weakened so much, and more yet by failing to hold a point deemed by them as essential to their empire in the South West. We have ravaged the Land, and have sent away half a million of negros so that this country is paralyzed and cannot recover its lost strength in twenty years.

Had the Eastern armies done half as much war would be substantially entered upon. But I read of Washington, Baltimore & Philadelphia being threatened & Rosecrans sitting idly by, writing for personal favor in the newspapers, and our Government at Washington chiefly engaged in pulling down its leaders. Hooker now consigned to retirement.[1] Well I thank God, we are far from Washington and that we have in Grant not a Great man or a hero—but a good, plain sensible kindhearted fellow. Here are Grant, & Sherman & McPherson, three sons of Ohio, have achieved more actual success than all else combined and I have yet to see the first kindly notice of us in the State, but on the contrary a system of abuse designed & calculated to destroy us with the People & the Army: but the army of the Tennessee, those who follow their colors & do not skulk behind in the North, at the Hospitals & depots far to the Rear, Know who think & act, and if Life is spared us our Countrymen will realize the Truth. I shall go on through heat & dust till the Mississipi is clear, till the large armies of the enemy in this quarter seek a more secure base, and then I will renew my hopes of getting a quiet hour when we can grow up among our children & prepare them for the dangers which may environ their later life. I did hope Grant would have given me Vicksburg and let some one else follow up the enemy inland, but I never suggest anything to myself personal, and only what I deem necessary to fulfil the purposes of war. I know that the capture of Vicksburg will make an impression the world over, and expect loud acclamations in the North West, but I heed more its effects on Louisiana & Arkansas. If Banks succeed as he now must at Port Hudson, and the army in Missouri push to Little Rock, the Region west of the Mississipi will cease to be the Theater of war save to the Bands of Robbers created by war who now prefer to live by pillage than honest labor. Rosecrans army & this could also, acting in concert, drive all opposing masses into the recesses of Georgia & Alabama, leaving the Atlantic slopes the great Theater of War.

I wish Halleck would put a Guard on the White House to keep out the

Committees of preachers Grannies & Dutchmen that absorb Lincolns time & thoughts, fill up our thinned Ranks with conscripts, and then handle these vast armies with the Single thought of success regardless of who shall get the personal credit and Glory.

I am pleased to hear from you that occasionally you receive Kindness from men out of regard to me. I know full well there must be a large class of honest people north who are sick of the wrangling of officers for power and notoriety and are sick of the silly flattery piled by interested parties on their favorites. McClernand the only sample of that List with us played himself out, and there is not an officer or soldier here but rejoices he is gone away. With an intense selfishness and lust of notoriety he could not let his mind get beyond the limits of his vision and therefore all was brilliant about him and dark & suspicious beyond. My style is the reverse. I am somewhat blind to what occurs near me, but have a clear perception of things & events remote. Grant possesses the happy medium and it is for this reason I admire him. I have a much quicker perception of things than he, but he balances the present & remote so evenly that results follow in natural course. I would not have risked the passing the Batteries at Vicksburg & trusting to the long route by Grand Gulf & Jackson to reach what we both knew were the key points to Vicksburg, but I would have aimed to reach the same points by Grenada—But both arrived at the same points and though both of us Knew little of the actual ground, it is wonderful how well they have realized our military calculations.

As we sat in Oxford last November we saw in the future what we now realize and like the architect who sees developed the beautiful vision of his Brain, we feel an intense satisfaction at the realization of our military plans. Thank God no president was near to thwart our plans, and that the short sighted Public could not drive us from our object till the plan was fully realized.

Well the campaign of Vicksburg is ended, and I am either to begin anew or simply make complete the natural sequences of a finished Job. I regard my movement as the latter, though you and others may be distressed at the guesses of our newspaper correspondent on the Spot (Cairo) and made to believe I am marching on Mobile, or Chattanooga or Atlanta. The weather is intensely hot, and dust terrible I may have to march far & long, but unless Johnston fight at Clinton or Jackson I will not expect more than affairs of Cavalry till my return.

Dayton brought me the clothes, but the truth is I never undress now except semioccasionally to put on clean under clothes. For near two months I have slept in my clothes ready to jump to the saddle, for I have been close upon an enemy since we crossed the Mississipi near two months ago. I have just written to Brooks Bros. New York to send me two Coats & two pants—Sweat & dust have made my clothes shabby, and the bushes have made me ragged below the Knee. Hill takes admirable care of things and I can always get clean drawers, socks & shirts by asking for them. Indeed I distress him sometimes by wearing shirts & socks too long. Still we manage to get along most admirably. He is the most faithful fellow I ever saw—and my nigger Carter keeps my horses seat fat. So I am well off—Hammond is with me as cranky as ever, but as long as he can find buttermilk he lives. He has found some secesh relations and at this moment has gone to {Bovina} to See a cousin, a handsome widow? whose husband is in Vicksburg. Oh the wail of these secesh Girls when Vicksburg surrendered. They cried and tore their hair, but I told them they had better not—they would survive the humiliating thought and eat whatever bread with as much relish as they ever did the corn dodgers of Aunt Dinah—now Gone to the Land of Linkum. It is hard to see as I do here an old preacher Mr. Fox, 40 years resident on this spot, with 17 children born to him lawfully & 11 still alive—carrying wood and milking cows. Two months ago he had a dozen house servants & 40 field hands, but now all gone, fences open & corn eaten up—garden pillaged by soldiers, house gutted of all furniture &c., indeed desolation, and he & his family compelled to appeal to us for the Soldier's Ration. This you will say is the judgment of God, but stiff necked he dont see it.

Yesterday I expected to cross Black River today but the troops have not come out from the siege, but I hope to cross Black tomorrow and see who are behind the saucy pickets that sit their horses so jauntily in the Cornfield beyond.

Charley has written you, we are all well—Love to all the folks. Yrs. Ever
W. T. Sherman

ALS, InND: Sherman Family Papers.
1. George G. Meade had replaced Joseph Hooker as commander of the Army of the Potomac on June 28.

TO ELLEN EWING SHERMAN

Army before Jackson Miss.
July 15, 1863.

Dearest Ellen,

I send a courier in today to Vicksburg and avail myself of the Chance to write you a few lines, & to enclose a few papers that may form a part of your Family Record,[1] that I fear will swell to the dimensions of another trunk in case we put on our travelling boots again to Seek a new House. We are investing Jackson with the Rebel army of Johnston inside—the town is surrounded by Rifle trenches on three Sides, its fourth resting on Pearl River, a stream hard to pass, but they have a couple bridges, but the Railroad Bridge destroyed by us in May last is not reconstructed. At this time I will now speak more definitely of the army within or without. Weather is hot—water scarce and our hauling is from Black River Bridge 30 miles towards Vicksburg. General Grant remains at Vicksburg, and leaves me to manage this Interior army. I did want Rest indeed mind & body have been on a stretch ever since you left me at Memphis, or rather since I left you. Not an hour sleeping or waking but all my thoughts and energies have been absorbed in the one idea to open the Mississipi River to the Free Navigation of the Commerce of our Country. It is now magnificently accomplished, and here I would seek repose, but no—it has been ever thus, when desperate schemes are in contemplation, or pursuit after Battle Sherman is called for. He dont mind abuse, has no political aspirations, and moves with celerity—Therefore I am the man for any and every emergency. The soldiers complain that they were not allowed even to See Vicksburg the goal of all their hopes, but they saw me start without a murmur, and have sense enough to know if any man living had a Right to enter Vicksburg I am the man. I enclose you a letter from Admiral Porter—I hope in a few days Johnston will come out and fight us or run. I dont care much which.

Hugh is very well, commands his Brigade close up to the town. Charley is now Lieut. Colonel, is in my Camp but is complaining, not seriously however. Ord is here, and many of your old acquaintances.

The news from the Potomac & Richmond appear so favorable that I some-times begin to think the Secesh will have to give in and submit.[2] Indeed at this moment their Country is suffering the Scourge of War, and Peace or destruc-tion seems their fate. This is a beautiful country, handsome dwellings and plantations, but the negros are gone, houses vacant fields of corn open to the cattle, and our army has consumed or is consuming all the cattle hogs, sheep chickens turkies and vegetables Everything.

The People are flying east, into Alabama and Georgia. I want to hear from you after you hear of the fall of Vicksburg. I have bet you will get tight on the occasion, a la fashion of Green Street California—Well I confess a saint would be justified in sinning on such a Fourth of July as we have just passed through. After we get through here and get back to the River some months must pass to rest, reorganize our troops and pass the summer heats. If so I will consent to you coming down with all the Children[.] I might come up to Memphis to meet you, and spend a month, but Everybody wants a furlough and I cannot ask for one. I am pledged to a 30 years war without asking anything and only two years are passed. I fear the People now instead of filling up our Ranks will fall into the delusion that war is over. They must not commit so fatal a mistake, but must fill our army and enable us to finish what is so well begun. Recent successes are due to combinations, and partly to accident—nothing Should be left to accident.

Tell your father that both Hugh and Charley stuck close to their duties and earn their honors without my aid. I give them no advantage not due their rank, same of Henry Sherman, whom I require to serve as close as if he were anybodys son.

I suppose you are all at home now, and happy as possible. I hope Willy got the fishing Rods, and Lizzy the bouquet of flowers from Black River. I have nothing to send from here.

Love to all. Yrs. ever

W. T. Sherman

ALS, InND: Sherman Family Papers.

1. ADfS of WTS to USG, July 14, 1863, reporting on military activities in the past few days. SFP.

2. WTS here refers to the Union victory at Gettysburg, July 1–3, 1863, and to operations in southeast Virginia that proved less rewarding than he had anticipated.

TO DAVID DIXON PORTER

Hd. Qr. Army in the Field
Jackson, Miss. July 19, 1863.

Admiral D. D. Porter, Comdg. Miss. Fleet.

Dear Admiral—

Your kind and considerate Letter reached me at Clinton, as we were trudging along in heat and dust after Johnston, that had been troubling us about Vicksburg during our eventful siege. We must admit, these Rebels outtravel us, and Johnston took refuge in the fortified Town of Jackson. My heads of columns reached the place on the 9th, but the forts and lines were too respectable to venture the assault, and I began a miniature Vicksburg.[1] The enemy was about 30,000 strong, with plenty of Artillery, which he used pretty freely. Some rifled 32s of too heavy metal for our Field guns, but we got close up and made the invariable sap, succeeding in disabling one of the 32s knocking off a trunnion, and breaking up the carriage. We expended on the Town as much of our ammunition, as was prudent to expend, and a train with a re-supply reached me the very night, he concluded to quit. We had a good deal of picket work, in all which we succeeded, driving the enemy behind his earth works, but we made no assault—indeed—I never meditated one—but I was gradually gaining round by the flank, when he departed in the night. Having numerous bridges across Pearl River—now very low—and a Rail Road in full operation to the Rear—he succeeded in carrying off most of his Material and men. Had the Pearl been a Missisippi, with a Patrol of Gunboats, I might have accomplished your wish in bagging the Whole. As it is, we did considerable execution, have 500 prisoners, are still pursuing and breaking Rail Roads, so that the good folks of Jackson, will not soon again hear the favorite Locomotive whistle.

The enemy burned nearly all the handsome dwellings, round about the Town, because they gave us shelter, or to light up the ground, to prevent night attacks. He also set fire to a chief block of Stores in which were Commissary supplies, and our men in spite of guards have widened the Circle of fire so that Jackson, once the pride and boast of Missisippi is now a ruined Town. State House, Governors Mansion and some fine dwellings, well within the lines of entrenchments, remain untouched. I have been, and am yet employed in breaking up the Rail Road, 40 miles North and Sixty South; also ten miles East. My ten miles break west of last May is still untouched, so that Jackson ceases to be a place for the enemy to collect Stores and men, from which to threaten our Great River.

The weather is awful hot, dust stifling, and were I to pursue Eastward, I would ruin my Command, and on a review I think I have fulfilled all, that could have been reasonably expected, and be driving Johnston out of the valley of the Missisippi, we make that complete, which otherwise would not have been.

I hope soon to meet you, and that we may both live long to navigate that noble channel, whose safety has absorbed our waking and sleeping thoughts so long. I trust we may sit in the shade of the awning, as the Steamers ply their course—not fearing the howling shell at each bend of the River, or the more fatal bullett of the guerilla at each thicket.

Last night at the Governors Mansion in Jackson we had a beautiful supper and union of the Generals of the Army, and I assure you, "the Army and the Navy *forever*" was sung with a full and hearty chorus. To me it will ever be a source of pride, that real harmony has always characterized our intercourse, and let what may arise, I will ever call upon Admiral Porter with the same confidence, as I have in the past. Present my kindest remembrances to Capt. Breese, to Capt. Walker,[2] McLeod, Bache[3] and all the gallant gentlemen, you have called about you, and please say to Captain Selfridge,[4] I regret exceedingly, that I was called off so suddenly, as not even to say good-bye to him. Most sincerely and truly your friend

W. T. Sherman

Maj. General.

Lbk, DNA: RG 94, Records of the Adjutant General's Office, Generals' Books and Papers, William T. Sherman, Letterbook 6; *OR*, I, 24: pt. 3, 531–32.

1. Johnston had evacuated Jackson in the face of WTS's superior forces on July 16.

2. John G. Walker (b. 1835), USN, was the captain of the *Baron de Kalb* in the Mississippi Squadron and had commanded the land battery during the siege of Vicksburg.

3. Lieutenant Commander George M. Bache, USN, was commanding the timberclad *Lexington*.

4. Lieutenant Commander Thomas O. Selfridge, USN, had commanded the naval guns placed on shore during the siege of Vicksburg and the tinclad *Manitou*.

TO JOHN SHERMAN

> Head Qrs. Army in the Field
> Jackson Miss. July 19, 1863

My Dear Brother,

The fall of Vicksburg & consequent capitulation of Port Hudson, the opening the navigation of the Mississipi and now the driving out of this Great Valley the only strong army that threatened us complete as pretty a page in the history of war & of our country as even you could ask my name to be identified with. The share I have personally borne in all these events is one of which you may take pride for me. You know I have avoided notoriety and the Press my standard enemy may strip me of all popular applause, but not a Soldier of the Army of the Tennessee but knows the part I have borne in this Grand drama, and the day will come when that army will speak in a voice that cannot be drowned by the carpings of that crass crowd of sycophants and hirelings known as newspaper correspondents. In the events resulting thus, the guiding minds and hands were Grants, Shermans & McPhersons, all natives of Ohio, and we have yet to See the first honest impulse of thanks or appreciation of our native state. Others who support a toady press, and Support near their persons at the public expense agents of the Press, receive votes of thanks and public honors, whilst we performing our parts well receive nought but the buffets of Fortune and the slanders of the multitude. Grant now is the Hero whom all worship, but tomorrow should fortune frown the very sycophants so loud in his praise would renew the old stereotyped story of the careless drunkard & fool. The People of Ohio may be good, may be wise, but I dont see it.

When our army lay round about Vicksburg digging trenches and slowly creeping on the doomed City, rumor from every quarter told that General Johnston, the Same that opposed Patterson at Winchester two years ago, was gathering a vast army to relieve Vicksburg, that Jeff Davis had said must be held at all hazards. Grant was uneasy and—{as usual} Sherman was called from {his} trenches and ordered to see to it—I gathered strange troops together and by July 4 was prepared to resist at Black River the crossing of any force however large. Johnston was to cross July 5. We faced each other. On the 4th Vicksburg capitulated and as soon as my corps & the 13th could reach

Black I crossed & chased Johnston into his entrenchments here at Jackson. I would not assault as it would have cost us too much, but I gradually threatened his flank & rear and he has cleared out leaving us in undisputed possession. The weather is terribly hot & the dust stifling. He has the advantage of a Railroad to help his tired troops and were I to pursue to Meridian 88 miles it would kill my men more than bullets. I let the enemy move, pursuing him only to ensure a good Start. I have sent North and destroyed Railroads, locomotives cars &c. at Canton, and a large Bridge 12 miles beyond, and I have cavalry doing destruction 60 miles south to Brookham, and four thousand men are working to destroy Railroads here. Jackson will never again be a point where our enemy can assemble and threaten us on the River. As soon as my Detachments are In, I will return to Black River. Our men & officers, must have rest—Five months in trenches working day & night—in the heat & dust of the Roads all are exhausted and need Rest. We have done our share and are entitled to Rest. I could fill pages of details that would interest you, but as you can well understand my time is all taken up with requisitions, estimates, details & orders that no man can manage but the Commander, but as soon as I finish up the work, I will move my Corps back of Black river & rest a couple months. I would like to hear from you, and now that the River is open you might come down and See Vicksburg, and I can point out to you the Spots of Interest. I think I will let Ellen & all the children come down on a short visit. I hope the Army of the Potomac will finish Lee—Morgan should not escape from Indiana.[1] Love to all. yr. brother

W. T. Sherman

ALS, DLC: William T. Sherman.

1. Brigadier General John Hunt Morgan (1825–64), CSA, had led his fourth cavalry raid into Kentucky, Ohio, and Indiana, beginning on July 2, and was badly defeated before he surrendered and was taken prisoner on July 26 at New Lisbon. He would later escape and rejoin the Confederate army.

TO PHILEMON B. EWING

Camp on Black River,
18 miles East of VBurg July 28. 63

Dear Phil,

On the theory that Ellen and all the children are now coming down the Mississipi I propose to deposit with you for general information in our rather large family circle a description of our Location. Between the Yazoo and Black Rivers is a ridge of ground about 150 feet above Mississipi high water of a sandy clay soil which has washed in chasms & valleys of the most complicated shape. The west slopes are peculiarly steep & gutter-like—whilst the spires &

valleys decline with Easier grade to the East. Nevertheless the soil is rich in the Extreme and the country was covered with a dense growth of forest trees and the sharp ravines and valleys filled with cane (fishing Rods). The Railroad from Vicksburg East crosses the Ridge by heavy grades and deep cuts and crosses Black River 12 miles due east of Vicksburg. That Bridge was destroyed but a floating Bridge has been made by us, and has been used in Crossing the army on several occasions. That part of the R. Road is also in good order and has 5 locomotives and plenty of cars found in Vicksburg after the siege. We use these cars to carry our stores to Black River which is our Depot. Our Division is there. Hugh now commands a Division at a Bridge which I built at a post 6 miles north & east of the Rail Road Known as Messengers.

Another Division watches & guards another ford & ferry about 3 miles further up.

The 4th Division of my Corps occupies a central position a little in rear, and my Head Qrs. are in front of this Reserve and is about 4½ miles north by east of the Railroad Bridge. I keep the Battalion of Regulars near me as a Guard. We are camped in a beautiful oak grove, with large abandoned fields to the front, as handsome a place as you would wish to See. We live in tents of course and have all our mess arrangements complete, with our horses close at hand perfectly independent of all the world. Grant offered to send my {Corps} to Natchez but as he left it to my option I preferred to stay here for good reasons. This Land is stripped of niggers, and Every thing, whereas the Country about Natchez is comparatively untouched. Were we to go to Natchez it would be one endless strife about run away Negros, plundering and pillaging soldiers and I am sick and tired of it. I have had my share of this trouble and am willing others should try it—Our men are now all Expert thieves, sparing nothing not even the clothes of women, children & Negros. Nothing is left between Vicksburg & Jackson so I can have peace here—Nearly all the officers & many of the men have gone on furlough, to enjoy the pleasing applause of friends north, but I remain to prepare for new labors as soon as the heats of summer will admit of motion. I have a healthy camp & have no fears of yellow or other fevers. All I ask is for the U.S. to give me 10,000 Recruits and I will have my corps ready for Mobile & Atlanta by October. One last campaign surely must satisfy all reasonable minds, and I must say that the Revolution is progressing as fast as is healthy. We have not only to combat open Rebellion, but inherent anarchy. I want to have the satisfaction to dispose of one mob, a city mob, like that in New York[1] when I will feel that I have travelled the full circle and then be most happy to slide out & let younger & more ambitious men finish the job. Were your mother in better health I would expect yr. father down for in Vicksburg he would see much of deep interest—but I suppose he cannot leave now. Hugh is in good condition and Charley seems well pleased at his new Rank & office. We have all had good luck in dodging bullets of which we have heard a goodly quantity.

I was in hopes Morgan would pay Lancaster a visit in his course and give Charley (illegible) a call, but I suppose he had wasted his fire before he got that far—Our last accounts are that with a fragment he passed through Nelsonville.

Give all the assurances of my best love, and if your Boy Tom remembers me tell him I often think of him. I have no doubt he will be a famous scholar. As ever yrs. affectionately

W. T. Sherman

ALS, Wheaton, Md.: Private Collection of Joseph H. Ewing.
1. WTS is referring to the antidraft riots in New York City in mid-July 1863.

TO JOHN SHERMAN

Head Qrs. 15 Army Corps.
Camp, 18 m. e. of Vicksburg,
July 28, 1863.

Dear Brother,

Since my return from Jackson, I have been very busy—every General officer but two has gone on furlough and every body wants to go. We have been on the Jump since last November, have lost heavily and done good Service and I cannot say no as we have a prospect of a couple months Rest. I need 10,000 recruits and must have them. Grant offers to send my Corps to Natchez, but I prefer to stay out here in the woods. I have a splendid camp, & would be glad if you would come down. I expect Ellen and all the children down—You will see much to interest you in Vicksburg. Being in Camp I can accomodate all Creation, for all you want is a Ration & a blanket—The Rail Road comes within 4 miles of my tent, and I have its exclusive use, & a telegraph at my elbow. If you come down you will find your name a passport but should that fail you, see Genl. Grant or McPherson in Vicksburg and they will put you through. I dont think there is any danger on the River now, unless it be on the Ohio, which you can avoid by taking cars to Cairo. Vicksburg is worth seeing, and a glance will tell you more than reams of paper why it took us six months to take the place.

I am camped near Big Black 4½ miles N.E. of where the Rail Road crosses it. My Depot of supplies is at the crossing. Colonel J. Condit Smith[1] is my Quarter Master and should you reach that point before I am advised by telegraph apply to him and he will send you to my camp.

I have four (4) Divisions here, much reduced, but still a good stock to graft on. In the riots of New York I recognize the 2nd stage of this war, but I trust our Govt. will deal with them summarily. The War has progressed as fast & as successfully as should be. To cure all the ills the Revolution must be perfect. Yrs. truly,

W. T. Sherman

ALS, DLC: William T. Sherman
1. John Condit Smith (d. 1883), USA, was a lieutenant colonel of volunteers.

TO CHARLES ANDERSON[1]

[ca. August 1863]

Hon. Charles Anderson,
Dear Sir,

I have not read a Speech in two years, but accidentally finding one of yours published in a Cincinati paper of July 30, I read it all the other night.

You make some good points—War existed before Sumpter was fired on— The seizure of our Forts & arsenals by armed bodies led by Governors & Commissioned officers preceded the attack on Sumpter. It was the seizure of the Forts & mails of Louisiana, more especially the arsenal at Baton Rouge with its small Garrison by a force of vols. led by Govr. Moore & Col. (now Genl.) Bragg, then my most intimate friends, that made me declare it "high Treason," and I quit the state, before as in your case malignant men had wrought up public feeling to a maddened State. Were every negro freed & every male in the South capable of bearing arms Killed outright by the U.S. the insult to our nation would not be more than avenged for the Studied insults in those cases.

The talk of Peace by Vallandigham[2] & men of his school is the veriest nonsense. They are cowards and try to cover up their Cowardice by a plea of Peace. I have seen such men in battle, when bursting shells & hissing bullets made things uncomfortable they would discover suddenly that they were sick, or had left something back in Camp.

Thank God the Southern men sunk as they are in crime are yet too proud to admit Vallandigham as an associate. They are willing to use him as a Stink pot, but not as an associate. Today I declare I have more sympathy with the misled but brave man who shoots at my heart when I come within the range of his gun, than of the miscreant, who tries to deceive a People by calling his Cowardice patriotism—Take the bold ground—Disfranchise all who will not help their Country, yea fight for it in this its hour of trial, and all true & brave & worthy Americans will cry aloud Amen.

I am no voter, but I have some 20 lb. Rifles that have more sense than 4/10 of the voters of Ohio and if you want them say so. They can throw 20 pounds of metal right to the mark, and all the time for the honor & glory of Uncle Sam, and for the regeneration of Poor Ohio consequently for Brough[3] & Anderson.

W. T. Sherman

Maj. Gen.

ALS, CSmH. Letter written on a circular copy of Sherman to the officers and soldiers of the Fifteenth Army Corps, July 27, 1863, a recapitulation of the seven-month campaign leading to the capture of Vicksburg. Filed as dated between October 14 and 31, 1863.

1. Charles Anderson (1814–95), brother of Robert Anderson, had been in Texas at the start of the war and had tried to escape but was arrested and confined by Confederate authorities. He escaped to Dayton, went to England on a special diplomatic mission at Lincoln's request, and then became commanding colonel of the Ninety-third Ohio Volunteer Infantry, which position he resigned after being wounded. He would be elected lieutenant governor of Ohio in the coming elections and would become governor after Brough's death in August 1865.

2. Clement Laird Vallandigham (1820–71), an Ohio politician, was running for the governorship of Ohio as an opponent of Lincoln and the war. He had been banished to the Confederacy by Lincoln on May 25 and Jefferson Davis had sent him to Canada. He was nominated for the governor's chair on June 1 and defeated on October 13.

3. John Brough (1811–65) would defeat Vallandigham for the governorship of Ohio.

TO DAVID STUART

Hd.Qrs. 15th Army Corps

Camp on Black River, August 1, 1863.

General David Stuart, Chicago

Dear Stuart,

I had expected you would write to me from time to time, keeping me advised of your whereabouts, plans and purposes. I have heard of you from Sawyer, but not from yourself. At last I have a little promise of leisure, and avail myself of it, to remind the absent, that we still live and retain them in kindly remembrance. I know, that you are satisfied, that your separation from my Command cost me no little feeling; and even yet I never see the 55th Ill. or my old Second Division, without being reminded of you.

From among the mass of events, painted by that busy mischievous class, the Press I doubt not, you have kept the run of our movements, somewhat excentric, but always producing good results. How few in this world can look back to causes, and trace their true bearings—when Vicksburg fell, how many appreciated the fact, that it resulted from the labor and plans laid in Oxford, last November. I only regret, that those who started with me, had not remained to the end.

But in a revolution, such as now sweeps us along, with resistless force we hardly have time to philisophize, but must go on to the end.

The capture of Vicksburg, the opening the Missisippi and driving out of the valley all the main armies, that threatened it, are the only real events of the War thus far, that look to a conclusion. In the East, and in Kentucky and Missouri they have fought battles and manouvered fast armies, but no great results have been achieved. Here we have achieved a real conclusion. I know, there must be in our country minds, that see all this, and that will appreciate it.

McPhersons Corps occupies Vicksburg, now a gnarled, cut up fortified town, full of foul smells, and full I fear of the seeds of pestilence. Grant offered to send me to Natchez, but I preferred to halt out here on Black River for the summer. We have beautiful camps, and I should delight to have you, or your friends come down to see us. Ords Corps, the 13th will probably go to Natchez and have the bore that I avoid, by remaining here—of the pillage and plunder, of a district, heretofore not much visited by our troops. Here the country is cleared out and all the mischief done.

I have four Divisions:

1st Steeles, now commanded by Genl. Dennis,[1] at the point, 12 miles East of Vicksburg, where the R. R. Bridge crosses Black River.

2d Your old Division, 4 miles North East at Fox's, in reserve, commanded by Genl. Lightburn[2] (Blair & everybody on leave.)

3d Tuttles, about 4 miles still further North, on Bear Creek, Watching a Ford across Black River, known as Birdsongs.

4th Ewing's, in front of the Second, guarding a good bridge, I made as Messengers; This Division came from Memphis, composed in part of the Troops, I left at College Hill, viz. the 6th Iowa, the 40th Ill.—Hicks—53d & 70th Ohio and some 8 other Regiments.

My own Hd. Qrs. is in a beautiful grove of oaks, in front of the 2d Division, with my Regulars near me. I never saw better camps. All are delighted—many wanted to go to Natchez, but now they begin to appreciate my reasons, and feel a relief, that we are here to rest and recruit. Our Regiments are much reduced and we have granted furlough to 5 p. ct. of the men, and nearly all officers. I will have to consolidate some Regiments, and hope drafted men will be sent us for others. If I can make my corps 25,000 strong by September, I will be ready for the Alabama.

I am rejoiced at Morgan's fate, but more especially at the promptness, with which the rioters were put down. You remember, how I feared anarchy at home. Extreme Democracy is anarchy; not in a party sense, but in the sense of proper language. I certainly will favor any species of despotism, rather then the wild, terrible despotism of mobs, vigilance committees or any species of irresponsible crowds.

Should you "take on" to Soldiering again, come to me, and I will make a place for you, or should you or any of your friends come as visitors, you will not be classed as "irresponsible hangers on."

The newspapers give me a wide berth, knowing full well, that if power should ever settle into my hands, their number and unbridled license would cease very promptly. With respects to your wife and daughters, I remain you friend

W. T. Sherman

Lbk, DNA: RG 94, Records of the Adjutant General's Office, Generals' Books and Papers, William T. Sherman, Letterbook 6.

1. Elias S. Dennis (1812–94) was a brigadier general who led the First Division, Fifteenth Corps, from July 28 to September 1.

2. Brigadier General Joseph Andrew Jackson Lightburn (1824–1901), USA, commanded the Second Brigade, Second Division, Fifteenth Corps, and led the division from July 26 to September 10.

TO EDWARD O. C. ORD

Head Qrs. 15 A. C.
Camp on Black River, Aug. 3, 1863

Dear Ord,

Some of our vandals got in the home of Jn. Davis a chest which on Examination contains about 4 bushels of letters & papers of all kinds. I have overhauled a good many and among others have found the real Boomerang letter in which I know you feel a deep interest.[1] I therefore enclose it to you and beg you will promise not to tell on me that I abstracted papers so valuable. I found a few other papers from Professors Mahan[2] & Bartlett[3] which I have also enclosed to them, but the Box would take me a week even to assort much less to read over so I will screw up seal and send to the War Department when they have a dept. to overhaul assort & dispose of.

Jeff would make a fuss if he could see me reading his cherished correspondence—most of which is stale enough but still enough left to show how matters were shaping in 1860, 61.

All your Reports have been duly received about the Jackson matter and have been duly forwarded—I will surely help you to advance any officer of your corps that you think should be so advanced. Hurry of Course.

I do not treat this Jackson movement as a separate matter. It was simply a postscript to the Vicksburg affair. Had we quietly entered Vicksburg the South would have raised the old story of Gun boats &c. afraid to leave the River. But we did leave the River, and we did beat Johnston at his own Game. He can only boast of beating us at a Retreat—well, Let him have that Glory—You know & I know that it would have been folly for us with our Men in their then condition to have followed him into Alabama, when we know he had run to his rear all his heavy stuff, retaining of course his cavalry and best troops as Rear Guard.

We must not ask any Glory, but we justly claim that we did right in chasing an hostile army away off from the Mississipi. He was about Lauderdale Springs the last I heard—Jackson came back to Brandon with part of his cavalry, a small detachment came into Jackson and out as far as Clinton, but I have in my hands papers with a long string of names, asking us both to stay away—"The People are tired of the War—they want a Ration, a wagon &c." the old Seminole story.

You will have a hard time in Natchez—Our Country here is all plundered— You have that to go through yet. I have a magnificent camp, and think it will be healthy. Yrs. truly,

W. T. Sherman

Maj. Gen.

ALS, PCarlA: William T. Sherman Papers.

1. Ord had written a very proslavery letter to Davis, probably in 1849. As he replied to Sherman, "There is no doubt about it, I was in 49 & until 54, a pro slavery man, and I am not quite such a radical now as to think we can turn all these black people loose among the whites, any more than we could so many tame Indians, with advantage to either race." Ord to WTS, August 14, 1863, DLC: WTS.

2. Dennis Hart Mahan (ca. 1802–71) was professor of military science and civil engineering and the science of war at West Point.

3. William J. C. Bartlett taught physics and astronomy at the Military Academy.

TO JESSE REED AND W. B. ANDERSON

Black River, August 3, 1863.

Messrs. Jesse Reed, W. B. Anderson,

Hinds County Committee:

Gentlemen:

Yours of August 1 is received. I withdrew from Jackson purposely to avoid the destruction to private property, always incident to the occupation of an army. You have seen enough of armies to know that they are so intent on overcoming their opponents that the poor people receive very little consideration at their hands. I do not believe we will again have occasion to visit Hinds County, and the people who have wives and children to feed and protect should, as soon as possible, begin to reorganize a government capable of protecting them against the bands of scouts and guerrillas that infest the land, who can do no good, and may do you infinite mischief.

I am satisfied General [W. H.] Jackson, C.S. Army,[1] will restrict the operations of his scouts, and I will do the same with ours, and in that way I hope and trust the citizens may have enough leisure to study their real interests, which must lead them to the conclusion that war was not the remedy for grievances, or supposed grievances, for which our forefathers provided the

Supreme Court of the United States to arbitrate and remove. You may safely count on all United States officers in authority to encourage the return of the people of Mississippi to the peace and prosperity that they enjoyed under the Union.

With great respect,

W. T. Sherman.

Printed, *OR*, I, 24: pt. 3, 571–72.

1. Brigadier General William H. "Red" Jackson was commanding the Confederate cavalry in Mississippi.

TO JOHN SHERMAN

Head Qrs. 15 Army Corps,

Camp on Big Black, 18 m. from

Vicksburg—August 3, 1863

Dear Brother,

Yours of July 18. did not come till today just after Henry Sherman had started for home.[1] On a letter from his father he has resigned. He was in receipt of $115. a month—was adjt. of a Regiment—stood well with all his officers, and Ord the new Commander of his Corps is my oldest friend and would have done everything for him. I therefore think Charles has done wrong. Henry is young, and as war must be familiar to us for years he should have left him to work out his fortune. Say what he may the boy will be restless. He will not study. Rest to him will be irksome and when again he seeks his old place he will find it filled.

Col. Spiegel[2] caught the fragment of one of our defective shells at Jackson which sent him home. So you will have plenty of eye witnesses of our position and need no description from me. I have halted my Corps on the West side of Black and have gone into camp deliberately to allow 5 percent of the men and a large proportion of officers go on furlough—We have been on the jump for 7 months and the reaction after Such stress of mind and body calls for Rest. Of course there is no Rest for me, but I saw from the sluggishness of the men that they wanted Rest, and I have asked to stay here 2 months. No enemy is near—we have cleared the Valley, and have a right to Some relaxation. I could have gone to Natchez, but I am sick and tired of the plundering & pilfering that marks our progress. This country is cleaned out and at Natchez, we would have the same to go through. Ord will go to Natchez McPherson & Grant are in Vicksburg and I am out in the country. We have lovely camps, plenty of grass, water and shade trees, and here I fear not yellow fever or any epidemic. A Railroad comes within 4½ miles of my Head Qrs., and we have plenty of horses & wagons to keep our supplies up to the maximum. I have written to

Ellen she may come down, and you can the Same. I can give you a tent & bed—plenty to eat, a horse to ride, and four Divisions of soldiers with Eleven Ohio Regiments. Here you could See all the havoc of war, and may see the germ of Military Rule, on which the Great democracy of America may yet have to call to save what little of Constitutional freedom is left to our People. You and I may differ in our premises, but will agree in our conclusions. A Government resting immediately on the caprices of a People is too unstable to last. The Will of the People is the *Ultimate* appeal, but the Constitution, Laws of Congress Regulations of the Executive Depts. subject to the decisions of the Supreme Court are the Law, which all must obey, without stopping to enquire why. All *must* obey. Government, that is the executive having no discretion but to execute the Law must be to that extent despotic. If this be our Government it is the "best on Earth"—but if the People of localities can bias & twist the Law or execution of it to Suit their local prejudices that our Govt. is the worst on Earth[.] If you look back only two years you will see the application. There are about 7 millions of men in this country, all thinking themselves sovereign & qualified to govern. Some 34 Governors of States who feel like petty kings, and about ten thousand Editors who presume to dictate to Generals, Presidents and Cabinets. I treat all these as nothing, but when a case arises I simply ask—what is the Law. Supposing the pilot of a ship should steer his vessel according to the opinion of every fellow who watched the clouds above or currents below where would his ship land. No the Pilot has before him a little needle, he watches that and he never errs. So if we make that our simple code, The Law of the Land must & shall be executed no matter what the consequence, we cannot err. Hundreds & thousands may honestly differ as to what the Law should be but it is rarely the case, but all men of ordinary understanding can tell what the Law is. We have for years been drifting towards an unadulterated democracy or demagogism, and its signs were manifest in most Laws and Vigilance Committees all over our Country, and states & towns and more squads of men took upon themselves to set aside the constitution and Laws of Congress & substitute therefore their own opinions. I saw it and tried to resist it in California, but always the General Govt. yielded to the pressure. I say that our Govt. judged by its conduct as a whole paved the way for the Rebellion. The South that lived on slavery saw the U.S. yield to abolition pressure at the North, to pro slavery pressure at the South, to the miners of California, the rowdies of Baltimore to the People everywheres, they paved the way to this Rebellion. The People of the South were assured that so far from resisting an attempt to set up an independent Government of homogenous interests the U.S. would give in and yield. They appealed to precedents and proved it, and I confess I had seen so much of it that I doubted whether our Government would not yield to the pressure & die a natural death. But I confess my agreeable surprise[.] Though full of corruption & base materials our country is a majestic one, full of natural wealth and good people. They have risen, not in full majority, but in enough to give all hopes of vitality. Our progress has been as rapid as any philosopher could ask. The resources of the Land in money, in men, in provisions, in forage and in inteligence has surprised us all, and we have had as much success as could be hoped for.

The Mississipi is now ours not by concession but by Right, by the Right of manly power. We dare and defy any Enemy to attack it.

Slavery as a Power is crippled dead—it cannot dictate terms to our Government, but some will be a petitioner for mercy.

No great interest in our Land has risen superior to Government, and I deem it fortunate that no man has risen to dictate terms to all. Better as it is. Lincoln is but the last of the Old School Presidents, the index (mathematically) of our Stage of our national existence. Seward is a humbug—Chase an able man—Put a woman, a child, a block of wood as president anybody that feels & admits he is a mere enabler and our Govt. will move on four years better than if a Genius filled the place. Our Govt. should become a machine, self Regulating, independent of the man.

There are features of stability in the English Govt. we should study, when the Industrial classes & Property have just so much influence in Govt. as to be felt after years of conviction, but an execution that rarely meddles with the Congress.

As to the Press of America it is a shame and a reproach to a civilized People. When a man is too lazy to work, & too cowardly to steal he turns Editor & manufactures public opinion, and blackmails for a living. I begin to feel a higher opinion of myself that I am their butt—I shall begin to Suspect myself of being in a decline when a compliment appears in type. I know in what estimation I am held by my Peers, those who have been with me all the time, and they are competent to judge, from privates to Maj. Genls.—I see a move to bringing Grant & myself East—No they dont. We flatter ourselves we have too much sense to approach Washington on foot. We will be in Mobile in Octr. and Georgia by Christmas if required, but I would see Lee in Washington before I would go east of the Allegheny.[3]

I see much of the People here—men of heretofore high repute. The fall of Vicksburg has had a powerful effect. They are subjugated. I even am amazed at the effect. We are actually feeding the People.

Banks was at Vicksburg day before yesterday but I did not know it till too late—Grant & wife visited me in camp yesterday. I have the handsomest camp I ever saw, and should really be glad to have visitors come down.

I dont think a shot will be fired at a Boat till Jeff Davis can call his friends about him and agree upon the next campaign. I want recruits & conscripts & will be all ready in October. as ever yr. brother

W. T. Sherman

ALS, DLC: William T. Sherman.

1. JS to WTS, July 18, 1863, DLC: WTS. In this lengthy letter, JS had commented on "how completely the tone of the press has changed in regard to you. . . . Popular opinion is so changeable that it is worthless. . . . I have often thought that one branch of education was neglected at West Point—and that is the power to use popular masses of men." He discussed Lincoln and his performance at length. "Poor Lincoln after suffering all the pains of martyrdom will leave the executive chair with the reputation of an honest clown." JS criticized his use of presidential power to enforce conscription and declared that emancipation "is one of those acts of folly which a weak man only could commit. I consider slavery as doomed by the logic of current military movements," so the Emancipation Proclamation would only give enemies fuel for their propaganda. The presidential election next fall looked ominous: "The war has done a great deal to shake that implicit obedience to *law* which has been the great conservative element of our government, but the Administration has done a great deal more." He still believed in the Republican party and blamed the administration's problems on the advice of "an old school of politicians who never belonged to the Republican party." Most men in the North were loyal to the Union but "hate niggers." In the Ohio gubernatorial race, he hated Vallandigham and thought that Brough would win.

2. Presumably Colonel Marcus M. Spiegel of the 120th Ohio Infantry.

3. After Gettysburg President Lincoln and some of his advisers expressed dissatisfaction that George G. Meade did not attack Lee's army at Williamsport, Maryland. Under these circumstances, they entertained thoughts of transferring Grant, Sherman, or both to the East.

TO JOHN A. RAWLINS

Camp on Big Black River,
August 4, 1863.

Lieut. Col. John A. Rawlins,
Asst. Adjt. Gen., Dept. of the Tennessee, Vicksburg, Miss.:
Sir:

I have the honor herewith to transmit for the action of the general-in-chief the proceedings of a general court martial in the case of Private [James O] Tebow, Sergeant [Henry] Blanck, and Captain [William B.] Keeler, of Company A, Thirty-fifth Iowa. These constitute one case, all involving the burning of a cotton-gin during our march from Jackson back to our camps on Big Black.

The amount of burning, stealing, and plundering done by our army makes me ashamed of it. I would quit the service if I could, because I fear that we are drifting to the worst sort of vandalism. I have endeavored to repress this class of crime, but you know how difficult it is to fix the guilt among the great mass of all army. In this case I caught the man in the act. He is acquitted because his superior officer ordered it. The superior officer is acquitted because, I suppose, he had not set the fire with his own hands, and thus you and I and every commander must go through the war justly chargeable with crimes at which we blush.

I should have executed the soldier on the spot, and would have been justified, but he pleaded his superior orders, and now a volunteer court-martial, tainted with the technicalities of our old civil courts, absolves the officer on the old pleas, good when all men were held responsible alone for the acts done by their own hands. I believe there is a remedy; General Grant can stamp the act as a crime, and can pronounce the officer unworthy a commission in the Army of the United States. This will in a measure relieve our General Government of the obloquy attached to such acts of vandalism, and this would form a good occasion for a general order announcing to all that our province is to maintain good law, and not to break it. The burning of this building in no way aided our military plans. No enemy was within 50 miles. A major riding behind his regiment is not the man to know the policy of the General Government of the United States. I have issued orders again and again on this subject, but our commands change so often that time is not afforded to prohibit all sorts of misdemeanors to each new command, nor is it necessary. This major had no reason to presume that he, in the presence of his regimental, brigade, and division commanders, should judge of the policy of the Government, and I was close at hand and he knew it. He knew that he had no right to order this burning, or, if ignorant, he is Unworthy a commission.

I ask that he be dismissed summarily and in disgrace. Not that I would visit upon him undeserved punishment, but that the United States authorities should wash their hands of the obloquy attached to such wanton acts of destruction.

I am, &c.,
W. T. Sherman.

Printed, *OR*, I, 24: pt. 3, 574–75.

TO PHILEMON B. EWING

Camp on Big Black, Aug. 5, 1863.

Dear Phil,

I have letters to July 26 from Ellen.[1] She had not then got leave to come to Vicksburg, but she must have got Gen. Grants letter written at my request about the time I entered Jackson and it became demonstrated that we were to be idle a month or so here.[2] I still presume Ellen to be on her way here, and have made every preparation in the way of transportation, subsistence tents &c.—If she will cry war, she must {convert} over to Hard tack & Canvas, but the truth is we have one of the most beautiful camps I ever saw, and we are all as comfortable more than we could be in Ohio. As Ellen has named her Castle in Air, "Hawthorne Cottage" I have named my place, "Polliwoggle Retreat," in honor of a horse pond, very convenient to our Camp and full of songster frogs.

Charley went home a few days ago and may be with you now. Tell him we are in status quo—I am sending a thousand Cavalry up to Grenada with orders to work up to Memphis or Grand Junction a fine lot of cars & Locomotives we have cut off from the Southern Roads by the destruction of the Mississipi Central, & the Great Southern Road. Two years hence the destruction of these Roads will be more appreciated than now—Our Enemy can no longer run parallel with the River to counteract our plots. One or two minor blows at Harrisonburg & Monroe on the Washita and the capture of Little Rock from Missouri which should have been made last winter, and the Valley of the Mississipi with a hundred miles on each side will be substantially in our military control.

Looking to the Past year I feel some what amazed to find how truly we have acted on the real strategic points—*Entre nous* Luck has favored us, and considerable mismanagement on the part of our Enemy, but on the whole our whole campaign will bear examination.

As a nation however we must not commit the Fatal blunder of Supposing the war over. Our Enemy has a large force in the Field. An army that would even in Europe alarm Crowned heads—if we slumber, the tide will again turn against us. Our Ranks are very thin. I conceal from myself the fact even that some Regiments have less than 100 men. We have not yet established a discipline that in Europe would be called respectable—Officers & men yet do as they please, have no more fear of the Law in their minds than militia. The Southern troops are better disciplined, and we must be careful. If we Can hold the Mississipi with a firm stiff hand time will work for us.

The Capture of Morgans entire command is creditable to Ohio, but the State should not let her Regiments in the Field dwindle down to tens instead of hundreds. There is no danger of either Grant or Sherman being ordered to the East. For my part I would not go—I rather think it would be a good thing if Lee could hold Philadelphia, Baltimore and Washington with a good firm hand for a few years. It would teach them some sense. At all events I want to stick by the Mississipi and go with it as spite of Democrats, or Whigs or Know Nothings it will run down stream in spite of them altogether.

I heard of yours & Charleys marches to Columbus and appreciate the patriotism but deplore the fact that after two years full notice Ohio should allow a squad of Cavalry to make the almost entire transit of the State. It is all for the best and it may be in good time.

I shall expect Ellen here in about six days and Charley back by the 25—I am really rejoiced that your mother is better. Hugh cannot possibly come, he is now a Division Commander & cannot leave consistent with duty.[3] He will write fully and I hope your mother will live long and see them all back, safe, and covered with the honor of faithful soldiers. As ever yours,

W. T. Sherman

I am decidedly opposed to Ellens building a House in Ohio. I shall put her on a d——d allowance. Of course convert her Leavenworth property into any thing but Taxes (illegible)

W. T. S.

ALS, Wheaton, Md.: Private Collection of Joseph H. Ewing.

1. EES to WTS, July 1, 8, 18, and 26, 1863. The last expressed her eagerness to see him. SFP.

2. Letter not found. On July 22, WTS had asked USG in a telegram to write to Ellen to say that she should come to Vicksburg if he thought the chances were good for a summer respite. *PUSG*, 9:66–67n.

3. Hugh was commanding the Fourth Division, Fifteenth Corps, as of July 28.

TO THOMAS EWING SR.

Head Qrs. 15 Army Corps.
Camp on Big Black, Aug. 13, 1863

Hon. T. Ewing
Lancaster, Ohio
Dear Sir,

I owe you a letter but as for the present all danger is past. I need not reply to the subject matter of your last further than that many suppose I run more risks than I should actually do. I can better judge of where balls are likely to strike than a mere looker on. The fact that I have thus far substantially escaped proves either this or good luck.

I expected Ellen & the children before this, but they are not yet come. I am well prepared to receive them in my camp which is in reality one of the best possible. It combines comfort, retirement, safety and beauty, but Charley is with you now, and will have described all you want to know. I have no apprehensions on the Score of health and the present condition of my command satisfies me on this score. It is no hotter here than with you, only the warm seasons are more prolonged.

Hugh is with me. Commands my 4th Division but he too wants to go home as soon as a General Officer comes back to command the Division. I would prefer he should remain as thereby I think he could retain command of a fine

Division of four Brigades, but he is bent on going home. He is wrong in finding fault at the non-receipt of pay. He can at any time draw pay from the date of his acceptance and his claims for the time back to the date when he actually entered on duty can be adjusted by the 3rd Auditor or Comptroller of the Treasury. A Commission is a contract of service and the Ruling has always been that pay begins only after actual acceptance. The mistake was in vacating his commission as Colonel 30th *Ohio*, till he had received and *accepted* his Commission as Brigadier Genl., *U.S.A.* two separate & distinct services. I have no doubt you as Secretary of the Treasury have made this very decision, but in the present complicated state of affairs, I doubt not that the comptroller would decide that a actual performance of duty would constitute a virtual acceptance.

I now enclose you a short dispatch just received, which will I know give you real pleasure. The Commission as Brig. Genl. in the Regular Army is a high honor, and to have it date July 4, places my name next to Grants as an actor in the most complete Act of the war this far. This is founded on no mere popular claim, no side influence, no management on my part. I have not lifted a finger to produce this result. All the chief actors in the Drama accord me the place. Grant makes no concealment, & McPherson concedes it gracefully and cheerfully. We know each other, we have consulted together from the moment I parted with them at Oxford last November till now, and each knows the part the other has borne. I am at home in the Field, in the Camp and in the Counsel of none but Soldiers are, but with such men as Cameron, and mere Political trimmers I am lost and of no account. With this estimate of myself I shall keep as far from Washington as the limits of our Territory will admit and I beg that my Friends will allow me to play my own Game of Life. My children & children's children will now associate my name with their Country's History. With such a reflection I may justly lay low, and seek as much retirement as comports with my native inclination.

I read John's speeches, and think too he is coming round all right. I have placed both Hugh & Charley in positions to which they can lay claim by actual service and not favor, so that I hope I have made some amends for deep anxiety which I know I have caused you at times.

Give to Mrs. Ewing the assurances of my unfailing affection & earnest wish that her health may still be restored to her. I would be obliged if you would show this dispatch to Mr. Hunter whose good opinion I would like to preserve always. Yr. son

W. T. Sherman

two seperate & ⟨illegible⟩

ALS, DLC: Thomas Ewing Family Papers.

TO ULYSSES S. GRANT

Head Qrs. 15th Army Corps
Camp on Big Black, August 15. 1863

Maj. General U. S. Grant
Comd'g Dept. of the Tenn.
Vicksburg, Miss.
Dear General—

I had the satisfaction to receive last night the appointment as Brigadier General in the Regular Army, with a letter from General Halleck, very friendly and complimentary in its terms.[1] I know, that I owe this to your favor, and beg to acknowledge it, and add, that I value the Commission far less, than the fact, that this will associate my name with yours and McPhersons in opening the Missisippi, an achievement, the importance of which cannot be over estimated.

I beg to assure you of my deep personal attachment and to express the hope, that the chances of War will leave me to serve near and under you, till the dawn of that Peace, for which we are contending with the only purpose, that it be honorable and lasting. With great Respect

W. T. Sherman
Major General Vols.

Lbk, DNA: RG 94, Records of the Adjutant General's Office, Generals' Books and Papers, William T. Sherman, Letterbook 6; *OR*, I, 30: pt. 3, 31.

1. HWH to WTS, August 4, 1863, DLC: WTS. For similar letters of appreciation, see WTS to HWH and James B. McPherson, August 15, 1863, DNA: RG 94, Records of the Adjutant General's Office, Generals' Books and Papers, William T. Sherman, Letterbook 6.

TO THOMAS EWING SR.

Head Qrs. 15 Army Corps.
Camp on Big Black, Aug. 20. 63.

Hon. T. Ewing
Lancaster, Ohio
Dear Sir,

I enclose you a couple of papers that will I think afford you more satisfaction than they have me though I confess to feel some pride that I have linked my name with Grants in achieving one of the Stupendous works of this war.

There are many able Generals and men than Grant, myself, and McPherson, but we have been smart enough to direct our efforts to the critical "Line of operations"—the "strategic directrix" of the North American Continent.

When read please put them away among Ellens archives. She will write fully and will doubtless catch more points of interest than would naturally suggest themselves to me. Yrs. truly,

W. T. Sherman

M. G.

ALS, DLC: Thomas Ewing and Family Papers.

TO JAMES W. TUTTLE

Hd. Qrs. 15th Army Corps
Camp on Big Black, August 20, 1863

General J. W. Tuttle
Keokuk, Iowa
Dear General,

The receipt yesterday of a letter, you wrote me at Duckport, last April, when I was up at Haines Bluff, reminds me to write you a few words.[1]

General Buckland got here a few days after you left, and things move on quietly and well. So many Officers and men are still on furlough, that all we can attempt, is to keep our men in good health, and ready for the fall Campaign.

I see, you are nominated as a candidate for Governor of Iowa. Permit me to advise you to accept it. You will I think pardon my frankness, when I say, that I regard you as a fine, honest and fearless man, but your body has received some shock, that makes it painful for you to move about rapidly, and to that extent impairs your usefulness as a Soldier, who must have impulse, activity and a body, that delights in violent exercise.[2]

I believe, you will make a good State Governor and that you could be a most excellent link in the chain of change or revolution, through which we are now passing.

Our country has always been, and it may be, always will be divided into two great parties, one in power, claiming everything allowed by the constitution and Laws, and the other denying them.

Every Government, whether democratic, republican or monarchical or despotic, must to a certain extent be alike. Each must have power enough to defend its existence. Now it has heretofore happened that all our people were so satisfied with our Government, that a comparatively small executive force could keep down all open enemies; but this is changed, and now it needs all the people to be organised and even armed to keep the Government from being overwhelmed by open Rebellion. We all know and feel, that if the loyal people of our Country from force of habit will still keep up their party organisations, and divide into two, nearly equal parts, that they may be defeated by a minority of the whole—or in other words—if the people of the

North still insist on dividing into Republicans and Democrats, that the people of the South, though in vast minority, may still prevail, and acquire a certain Kind of independence; the result of which would be, as you know, an eternal Border War.

The War is not yet over—much has been done, but you know enough of the character of the South—to see, that the young hot-bloods have lost their negros, their lands and their boasted powers, on which they built their dreams of power and conquest, and they cannot settle back in peace.

The farmers and mechanics of the South now would vote for Peace, but the young-bloods, who have the control, wont let them. Instead of being divided ourselves, we should unite, and sow dissension among our enemies.

As long as they have hopes of division among us, they will be united as one man, but let us show them, that Democrats and Whigs and Republicans and Knownothings, and whatever party our People in their exuberance of freedom may choose to divide themselves—will drop all their seeming differences, when the life and integrity of the nation are threatened, and any quantity of disaffection and differences will display themselves South. To have peace and prosperity in the valley of the Missisippi, we *must* prevail, and we now have the cards to win—if we don't relax our efforts, and drop back into a state of security and lethargy.

We must now pile on our elements of strength—ranks should be filled to the maximum, and as soon as the sun goes a little further South, our Armies should be seen at Natchitoches, Little Rock, Mobile, Montgomery and Chattanoga at the same time. This we cannot do with equal forces—you have seen how great results are accomplished in War by the mere display of Force. It is more honorable to produce results by an exhibition of Power, than by slaying thousands. Still, we have not yet killed enough, we must make this War so fatal and horrible, that a Century will pass, before new demagogues and traitors will dare to resort to violence and war, to achieve their ends.

I hope, that you will be a candidate, and that you will take the bold ground, that the people of Iowa must drop all their intestine differences, till the integrity and manhood of the United States are established beyond hope of disturbance by any of the enemies of Social Order and National fame that have assailed us from every quarter. Your friend

W. T. Sherman
Major General

Lbk, DNA: RG 94, Records of the Adjutant General's Office, Generals' Books and Papers, William T. Sherman, Letterbook 6.

1. On April 30/May 1, 1863, Tuttle had written to WTS congratulating him and expressing his eagerness to join him. "I am *ready* for *anything*, if you want me up there I can be ready in

a very few minutes." DLC: WTS. On April 3, Tuttle received command of the Third Division, Fifteenth Corps.

2. Tuttle would lose this election and was defeated again the following year in a bid for Congress. He would not resign from the service until June 1864.

TO LEW WALLACE

Head Qrs. 15 Army Corps.
Camp on Big Black Miss., Aug. 27, 1863.

Maj. Genl. Lew Wallace
Crawfordsville, Indiana,
Dear General,

I was much gratified at the receipt of your letter of Aug. 16, and accept the tender you make of congratulations at the success which has marked our recent Campaign. I assure you that I regret exceedingly that General Grant had not carried with him throughout his entire campaign the Generals with which he opened it, and Donelson was as important a beginning as the Capture of Vicksburg the End of the one Great Design. General Grant is now up the River and when he returns I will endeavor to convey to him your proper expressions of confidence without in the least compromising your delicate sense of honor. I have reasons to Know that the General esteems you as possessing as large a share of high soldierly qualities as would satisfy the ambition of most men, and that he would readily aid you to regain the high position you held in the Estimation of the Country. If I can aid you it will afford me real pleasure.

We have all made mistakes and Should be generous to each other. Some men possess one quality, others another, but all can be made to Subserve a great whole. General Grant possesses in an eminent degree that peculiar & high attribute of using various men to produce a Common result, and now that his Character is well established we can easily subordinate ourselves to him with the absolute assurance of serving the Common Cause of our Country. For my part I would be glad that every General officer should have an appropriate command, and that all should learn from one short military Career that we can only gain a permanent fame by subordinating ourselves, and our peculiar notions to that of the Common Commander. I will not say that you have not always done this, but I do think that if I am you I would not press an inquiry into the old matter of the Crumps Landing and Shiloh march but leave that till War is over.[1] Subsequent Events may sweep that into the forgotten of the Past. I would advise that as soon as possible you regain the command of a Division, identify yourself with it, keep as quiet as possible and trust to opportunity for a becoming sequel to the brilliant beginning you had. I think I appreciate the feelings of Gentlemen such as you and many others of our General officers, but I do say that in war there can be but one solid foundation for a lasting Fame. A single occasion can give a meteor like Reputation, but real enduring fame can only result from long patient hard labor, study, courage and actual experience which can only be gained by continuous service with armies in the Field. I do not think Genl. Grant or any officer has any unkind feelings towards you. Some one or more may have been envious of your early & brilliant career, but as I know, you must be ambitious of more lasting and Real fame. I feel that with the advice of unselfish friends that end is still within your Reach. There are some of our Generals (necessarily chosen in haste by a distracted Government) that are concerned by a growing desire for Fame & notoriety who are miserable if any one achieves a little more than they, but I know you are not of that class. I believe you have a proper desire to be appreciated, but probably have been a little impatient at the slow process, but now that the Public mind is toned down to a pitch that will admit of waiting for the natural developments of Time I think you too would be willing to fall into our Slower School. I have been more frank than you probably expected, but I assure you that I will gladly serve you in the best way I know how, and that is in giving you very honest, unselfish advice. Avoid all controversies, bear patiently temporary reverses, get into the Current events as quick as possible, and hold your horses for the last home stretch.

The War is not yet over. The South still has a large army, and though we have made large inroads yet her People have an ugly, keen and desperate Spirit, and we must not presume too much. For all real hard working, and self sacrificing soldiers there is still a Larger Future. If these my ideas approximate your convictions it will afford me great satisfaction to assist you in regaining your true place among the Young and conspicuous Generals of this war—with respect your friend,

W. T. Sherman
M. G.

ALS, InHi: Lew Wallace Collection, M292.

1. Grant was critical of Wallace's performance at Shiloh, especially the failure of his division to arrive on the field of battle on April 6; Wallace contended that his delay was not due to any negligence on his part. In July 1863, Wallace had written to Stanton to challenge Grant's assessment of his role at Shiloh and asked for a court of inquiry. He then apparently wrote to WTS to ask for a command under him. After receiving this reply of WTS's, Wallace withdrew his request for a court of inquiry and told Stanton that he was ready for and would accept any active duty. WTS did intercede with USG on Wallace's behalf; on August 27 he wrote to Rawlins, asking if he thought it a good idea to hold out any hope to Wallace since he had expressed great respect for USG: "At Shiloh he was laggard, but has he no good qualities which, with proper cultivation, might save his honor and be of use to the service?" OR, I, 30: pt. 3, 183–84. USG was not receptive, and on October 9, WTS reported to Wallace that although he had forwarded the August 16 letter to USG via McPherson, during "a full

and frank conversation," USG had told him "that So many new & young men had commands of Divisions & Brigades that it would be unjust to deprive them." WTS was forced to share this conclusion but once again urged Wallace to keep seeking active duty. WTS to Lew Wallace, October 9, 1863, InHi: Lew Wallace Papers, M292. See also Robert E. Morsberger and Katharine M. Morsberger, *Lew Wallace: Militant Romantic* (New York, 1980), 129–30.

TO JAMES B. McPHERSON

Headquarters Fifteenth Army Corps,
Camp on Big Black, September 1, 1863.

Maj. Gen. J. B. McPherson,
Commanding Seventeenth Army Corps, Vicksburg:
Dear General:

Yours of August 31 is received. I will strengthen my picket (now two regiments) at Oak Ridge by two more regiments and a battery to-morrow, and will order a picket of four companies to be sent to the valley road east of Haynes' Bluff. Our telegraph at this moment is interrupted, and as soon as it operates I will dispatch to you the same assurance.

The negroes at Blake's plantation have been for some time a nuisance. I think it would be advisable for you to send up and bring them all into Vicksburg, the available men to work on the forts and the women and children to be sent to Island No. 10. It is represented to me that there is an officer there who does not attempt to control or restrain them, for they wander all about the country doing no good, but infinite mischief. The negroes naturally cluster about the old negro inmates of abandoned plantations and put on the majestic air of soldiers. I have had occasion to punish some of these already.

I have read with pain the narrative of James Pearce, Thomas H. Hill, and others, of Deer Creek. When citizens represent to you that General Sherman sends negroes out to kill and plunder you may safely assure them that it is not only false, but the very reverse of my practice. On the contrary, I have done more than most persons to restrain the violence and passion of the negro. But I do say, and have said to these very planters, both before they would have war and since, that by breaking up the only earthly power that could restrain the negroes—by openly rebelling against the Government of the United States—they prepared the way for those very acts against which they now appeal to us to shield them.

I know the parties named and have been on their plantations, and with the exception of Mr. Fore, who is simply one who acts either way, the others were extreme secessionists—rebels. The Hills were notoriously so. We cannot undertake to guard them in their isolated swamps, and all we are bound to do in the name and cause of humanity is to invite them into our lines for personal safety and to leave their property to revert to a state of nature for the use of alligators and negroes. This is not our act, but the natural immediate, and necessary result of their own conduct.

It is in this very Deer Creek country that are nursed and harbored the banditti who fired on our boats at Greenville Point, and of all the people of this region they, least of all, are entitled to the generous protection of any government, because they profess not to have done this with their own hands. They claim to be non-combatants, but I was there on Hill's and Fore's plantations last winter and know they were not our friends. They fled from us, gave us no information, but, on the contrary, aided Ferguson in his efforts to entrap the gunboats. I deplore the calamity that has now overtaken them, but repeat it is the natural fruit of their own conduct.

With great respect,
W. T. Sherman,
Major-General, Commanding.

Printed, *OR*, I, 30: pt. 3, 277.

TO JOHN M. WRIGHT[1]

Head Qrs. 15th Army Corps
Camp on Big Black, Miss.
Septbr. 2. 1863

Major J. M. Wright—A.A.G.
Louisville, Ky.
My Dear Friend—

Yours of August 25th is received. I am here guarding the Line of Black River, and drilling my Corps after a short rest made necessary by the preceding seven 7 months of continual labor. I have none of the Books or Memoranda of dates, that would enable me to speak with precision of Events or the state of facts in Kentucky at the time, General Buell relieved me, nor am I willing yet to give my full ideas of the political and military state of affairs at that exact time; though always willing to say, that I then regarded the task, on which he entered a most difficult and delicate one.

I feel towards General Buell great personal and official respect and will do all I can, to secure to him the respect of his Fellow Soldiers and Fellow men, and with this remark I take the liberty to add, that I do not believe General Buell as a Soldier or Citizen will be benefitted by a Publication, which will be regarded as a mere personal matter. The time for history is, after the end is attained. That end may yet be far off in the future, and when War is over, and people settle down to the Arts of Peace, they will regard all questions according to the new state of affairs. I fear the northern people are again settling back into one of their periodical states of apathy, on the supposition, that War is over, whereas we all know and feel; that the Leaders of the South are buckling on their armor and preparing for a new, and it may be, a more successful display of desparate physical energy.

General Buells friends may well, and very properly collect and collate all facts, illustrating his important part of the Great Whole, but to segregate his administration and connect it with the former and subsequent periods of the War may raise personal controversies, that will further embarass him and impair his future usefulness. The Record of the Court, which sat so long in Cincinnati in his Case,[2] and his own answer, which I and all his friends have read with satisfaction are full and comprehensive, but even then the claim set up, that he saved Grants Army at Shiloh has raised a prejudice against him, in the minds of many worthy Officers, who have gone on and strengthened their fame, so that, if a controversy should arise, Buell would get the worst of it. I advise Buell and all men to stop writing but to join the Army in the field in any capacity, for we need the actual Service of every man in the Military Service. There should be no idlers now. When War is over, we may have a Century, in which to scramble for personal fame. Current events are still too absorbing for any patriot to stop to discuss the Past. Let us all go on to secure the object of the War, save the Ship of State, before we undertake to explain, how it was done, or who did it. To us, with an angry, embittered enemy in front and all round us it looks childish, foolish, yea criminal for sensible men to be away off to the Rear, sitting in security, torturing their brains and writing on reams of foolscap to fill a gap, which the future Historian will dispose of by a very short, and may be an unimportant chapter, or even paragraph.

I would like General Buell to know, what I say. I am his friend, have been always, and always hope to be; and my advice is for him to stop writing, but to join some one of our armies, as a Commander if possible, or as a Subordinate otherwise. Like in a Race, the end is all, that is remembered by the Great World. Those, who are out at the end will never be able to magnify the importance of intermediate actions, no matter how brilliant and important. Assuring you of my personal Respect I am truly your friend

W. T. Sherman
Maj. Genl.

Lbk, DNA: RG 94, Records of the Adjutant General's Office, Generals' Books and Papers, William T. Sherman, Letterbook 6; *OR*, I, 30: pt. 3, 294–95.

1. Wright had been made assistant adjutant general on June 30, 1862, and would resign on January 16, 1864.

2. From November 23, 1862, to May 10, 1863, Buell had been under investigation by a military commission concerning his command and battles in Tennessee and Kentucky. The report was never published. From May 10, 1863, to June 1, 1864, he was waiting orders to return to service but was mustered out because he refused two commands under Canby and

Sherman. See also WTS to James B. Fry, April 11, 1864, for Buell's desire to take Schofield's place as commander of the Department of the Ohio.

TO FREDERICK A. P. BARNARD[1]

Head Qrs. 15th Army Corps
Camp on Big Black Miss.,
Septbr. 4th 1863

F. A. P. Barnard, Esqr.
Coast Survey Office, Washington, D.C.
Dear Sir—

I really feel under obligations to you for the moral support contained in yours of August 18th which I have delayed answering until I could answer more fully your inquiries.

In both our visits to Jackson I met Judge Yerger, Dr. Poindexter and many others and *Judge Sharkey*. The enemies line of parapet ran across the rear of Judge Sharkey's lot, and as it is situated near the Clinton Road, we peppered it pretty thick with musket and cannon shots. The house is damaged but still habitable. The shrubbery is in the main ruined, and fences all gone—The Judge is in good health, but "subjugated." I like him very much, and our intercourse was hearty, cordial and friendly in the highest degree. He has been in here once and General Grant and myself united in extending to him every possible favor. I have seen many Confederate Officers of Rank and intelligence, conversing with them in the most unreserved manner, and all admit, that Judge Sharkey, though seemingly yielding to the Southern Revolution was, is and must be a Union man. They dare not persecute him, and he has intellect enough to steer his own course. Financially he is ruined but in health of body and mind, he is as you left him. Marshall has never manifested himself to us. His house in Vicksburg, and his plantation out about 5 miles are abandoned and deserted. He and family are gone away, and it has never been in our power to discriminiate as to him. He may have got his Slaves and personal property away, but I think not. I remember only a few days after we started on our Grand Gulf Tour, to have sent in to him jointly with a man named Miller, his Brother in Law, a Sum of Confederate money, about ($5000) but since we have reached and possessed the country, his name has not turned up. A couple of Kentucky Officers came in yesterday with a flag of Truce and I inquired of them his whereabouts, and their impression, though obscure was that he and family were out near Meridian. I shall bear in mind what you have said, and it shall influence me favorably towards him, should we meet.

Bishop Green's[2] house, furniture, Library and manuscripts were all on the

Clinton Road, about two hundred yards from the Chief salient of Joe John-ston's trenches. In pushing forward our lines, they embraced the house, which was of Brick, and therefore convertible into a strong Block house—Library, Pictures, furniture and "Barrels of Sermons," all fell a prey to our "Barbarian Host," and before we left, the flames finished the destruction. This last was done without Orders and wrongfully but I dont know, but that it is better, the flames should obliterate the traces of destruction to the Sanctum of a learned and pious Gentleman. To me, the ravages of War are bitter. I have labored hard to stay them, and can now only repeat, what in Clinton I said emphat-ically to a Confederate Officer, as we stood looking at a burning Block of Buildings, set fire to by one of our unruly Soldiers "Sir—we are not responsi-ble for that work—you did it—you and your associates applied the Torch to the only earthly power, that could restrain the wicked, and you are clearly re-sponsbible for the natural and unnecessary consequences of your own acts"— "I disclaim all responsibility and say that Jeff Davis and adherents set fire to that building."

Bishop Green therefore is without house and home, and is now staying I am told with (also completely ruined) old Joe Davis[3] at Lauderdale Springs, near Meridian.

During our first visit many of my Staff saw Bishop Green and gave him Guards, protection and kindness, the last time he was gone, and his house was desolated and burned. Personally I have not met him.

Jacob Thompson[4] was Lieut. Col. of Cavalry up with Pembertons Army on the Tallahatchie, and fled South last November, when we moved on Oxford— His family remained in Oxford and many Gentlemen called to see his wife, among them General Denver of my Command. I did not—being very busy. He was on Pemberton's Staff, was made Prisoner, and went out with Pember-ton. Whether he has gone to gather up the wreck of his vast estate, *all* desolate, or whether he is at Montgomery, sharing the fate of his Chief, I know not. I inquired about him of the flag of Truce yesterday, and they Knew nothing definite. He is one of the Political Criminals, endowed with intellect, wealth, power and experience. He chose War, and for him I have no mercy. He should drink of the cup of poisoned venom to its bitterest dregs.

I can hear nought of General Clark,[5] who came up under flag of Truce to me and thence into Vicksburg about March last from Baton Rouge. His wound had ceased to be dangerous, but I understood, he was crippled for life. I take it, he is lying perdu in Some village of Mississippi, "out of the {Brig}." You have interested me in the fate Hillgard. I can hear nothing of him. I have made diligent inquiries, but it is not likely, one of his type would attract the attention of a Secesh Officer, or common farmer, the classes, with whom I come in contact. Yesterday Capt. Bullock of Brig. General Cosby's[6] Staff, who came in with a flag of Truce, said he had a faint recollection of some one in Jackson, at our last occupation, who was deemed "Suspect" and sent to the Interior. All Alabama & Georgia is filled with this class of men, who not being fitted for War are useless and an incumbrance to the Ruling Powers of the South.

How they procure food & clothing is to me a mystery. We find all Classes flush of money, but money will procure nothing. Such as have Corn & Bacon know too well the value of them in relation to Confederate money, unless the offer to purchase is backed by a square of Cavalry. I will bear Hillgards name in my memory, but should rumor or authentic intelligence reach me, you shall Know, and you may rest assured, if he fall within my Lines, he shall have safe conduct and assistance if necessary.

I have cast me eyes over your Letter again and think I have covered all your points of inquiry as far as my Knowledge goes, and having reached a Second Sheet, for which I apologize, as well as my handwriting, habituated for Copy by a better Clerk, I will indulge in a little more, because I have leisure, and presume you have patience.

Mississippi as a flank of the Mississippi River is vastly important to us. I regard this now as a Revolution and that we must control this Continent of North America, not by the absolute occupation of all its parts, but by the physical control of its great River. First in importance is the Mississippi, Second the Lakes and St. Lawrence and Last—the coast of the Pacific. The race of men, who are under Providence to control America, were to have the Power to command all these. All else will follow. If our present System of Government prove equal to the task it must be perpetuated, if not it must be modified and strengthen till it is. If the People, who own the land in Mississippi will gradually lower their pretensions, so as to live in harmony with the Great Whole, I would protect, maintain and defend them, spite of past errors and crimes. But if they are so imbued with notions adverse and hostile to the interests of the nation—they should be sent off or killed. If they submit to the Courts of Civil Law, well—but if they must have War, we must accept the issue, and make War terrific. There cannot be two Ruling or antagonistic powers in America (North). There must be but one and whether Democratic, Republican or Despotic as to its internal relations, it must be despotic as to its external. All who set up their vague, crude notions in opposition ot the national interest and will, must be swept away. In my personal intercourse with our armed enemies, or the People of these hostile Districts I treat Slavery, State Rights and all questions growing out of them as trifles, hardly worthy [of] attention, but assert the broad Doctrine, that all men must obey the Law, and not dare to stop and discuss it. Some say, this is worse than Slavery, but I say—No—The proudest and most chivalric races on earth have bowed in meekness to the Sovereign, who in our case is a myth, represented by the Law, duly enacted and declared.

I tell them, the time is not far distant, if not actually present when they will hail as a Savior a Power, that can shield them and their families and necessary Provisions to sustain life from the Demon of Secession, Anarchy and Discord, which they have so foolishly and wickedly let loose upon our hitherto *too* free and *too* ungoverned Country. I believe the old Constitution to contain the elements of this Power and therfore willingly and cheerfully go on to maintain and defend it against all antagonistic influences from without and within. Strange as it may seem I say, that in time the South will hail our Armies as its deliverers from Anarchy and absolute destruction. I am always glad to hear from you, and beg you present me kindly to your wife[7] and brother.[8]

W. T. Sherman

Major General

Lbk, DNA: RG 94, Records of the Adjutant General's Office, Generals' Books and Papers, William T. Sherman, Letterbook 6.

1. Frederick A. P. Barnard (1809–89), a mathematician and astronomer, had been president of the University of Mississippi from 1856 to 1861. When the war broke out he stayed on to take care of pressing obligations and then escaped from the Confederacy through Norfolk, Virginia. At this time he was in charge of publishing charts and maps for the U.S. Coastal Survey and would become the president of Columbia College in 1864.

2. William Mercer Green (1798–1887) was appointed the first Episcopalian bishop of the diocese of Mississippi in 1849 and was stationed in Jackson.

3. Joseph Davis (1784–1870), a former lawyer, was Jefferson Davis's oldest brother and a planter near Vicksburg.

4. Lieutenant Colonel Jacob Thompson (1810–85), CSA, had been a member of Congress and Buchanan's secretary of the interior. He was Pemberton's inspector general, had been taken prisoner and released at Vicksburg, and would go on to cooperate with secret organizations in the western United States to undermine the Union's war effort. He would be closely associated with the Knights of the Golden Circle and Clement Vallandigham of Ohio.

5. General Charles Clark (1811–77), CSA, had been wounded at Shiloh and again in July 1862 at Baton Rouge. At this time he was in New Orleans behind Federal lines and would leave the city upon his exchange on October 31, 1863. He resigned his commission at this time and became governor of the state of Mississippi later in the year.

6. George Blake Cosby (1830–1909) was a brigadier general in the Confederate army.

7. Margaret McMurray of Ohio.

8. Brigadier General John G. Barnard.

TO JAMES B. MCPHERSON

Headquarters Fifteenth Army Corps,
Camp on Big Black, September 4, 1863.

Maj. Gen. J. B. McPherson,
Commanding Seventeenth Army Corps, Vicksburg:
Dear General:

Yours of yesterday is received. I can as well picket the point above Haynes Bluff as not, and you need not send any men there, as it will simply add to our joint sick-list, and I think that flank is well covered by my brigade (Buckland's) at Oak Ridge Post-Office, with a picket of four companies down on the Valley road above the bluff.

A batch of negroes have collected at Roach's plantation on the Valley road, near the Bald Ground Creek. I authorized General Corse, when in command at Oak Ridge—and will renew to General Buckland the same instructions—to organize the males of that gang into a kind of outlying picket, giving them a few mills to grind the corn which abounds there, and giving them a little bacon, &c. There are about 100 negroes fit for service enrolled under the command of the venerable George Washington, who, mounted on a sprained horse, with his hat plumed with the ostrich feather, his full belly girt with a stout belt, from which hangs a terrible cleaver, and followed by his trusty orderly on foot, makes an army on your flank that ought to give you every assurance of safety from that exposed quarter.

Should, however, the secesh be rash enough to gobble up that picket, I still think we could survive the loss, for behind them is Buckland's picket of four companies. If you have a regiment of negroes, it might be advisable to post them in the intrenched position at Snyder's gill, with orders to remove to some floating scow—for transfer to you—the heavy, ordnance that did lie where the carriages burned by Admiral Porter's orders left them. These guns are useless to us at that place, and should any awkward accident ever put our enemy in possession again of Snyder's Bluff, they might soon be put in position to our detriment.

I review my four divisions on Tuesday, Wednesday, Thursday, and Friday of each week; will have leisure on Saturday, Sunday, and Monday. I propose on Sunday, if all is quiet, to drive my children and Mrs. Sherman in by land to our old camp of investment north of Vicksburg, that they may see a place in which they naturally feel an interest. I may camp about your headquarters, if you are not appalled by the sight of so much non-combatant material, on Sunday night, and return by the Hall's Ferry road on Monday, thus making the circuit. I can then see you and talk over matters.

I wish you would restrict the provost-marshal in giving passes out of our lines. Individuals may want to go and come back. I allow no person the privilege of going and returning; they should elect to stay out or in; we are liable to a system of spies otherwise. Let the people of Mississippi expel the dragoons if they want the favor of trade or intercourse with us, As long as their country is traversed by these bands we have no interest in them. I tell all I see that we don t care what they do. If they befriend us we will favor them, but if they are inert they must bear the burdens of two hostile armies. They cannot expel us, but they can our enemy, and that is their only hope of peace.

As ever, your friend,
W. T. Sherman,
Major-General.

Printed, *OR*, I, 30: pt. 3, 336–37.

TO H. W. HILL

Camp on Big Black Septbr. 7. 1863

H. W. Hill, Esqr.
Chairman of Meeting of Citizens of Warren County Miss.
Sir—

The communication addressed to General Grant, myself and other Officers in the nature of a Petition is received.[1] I think it proper and right, that the Property holding classes of Warren County, and indeed of the whole State of Mississippi should meet in their capacity as Citizens to talk over matters, so that they may take any steps, they deem to their interest; and if such meetings be open and with the Knowledge of the nearest Military Commander, I will protect them whilst so engaged.

Your Preamble, however, starts out with a mistake. I do not think any Nation ever undertook to feed, supply and provide for the future of the inhabitants of an insurgent District. We have done so here and in other instances in this War, but my Reading has discovered no parallel cases. If you know of any, I will thank you for a Copy of the History, which records them. I know it is the purpose of the controlling Generals of this War, to conduct it on the most humane principles of either ancient or modern times, and according to them I contend, that after the firing on our Steamboats, navigating our own Rivers, after the long and desperate resistance to our Armies at Vicksburg, on the Yazoo, and in Mississippi generally, we are justified in treating all the inhabitants as combatants and would be perfectly justifiable in transporting you all beyond the Seas, if the United States deemed it to her interest. But our purpose is not to change the population of this Country but to compel all the inhabitants to acknowledge and submit to the common Laws of the land. When all, or a part of the inhabitants acknowledge the just Rights of the U.S., the War as to them ceases. But I will reply to your questions in the order you put them.

1st The duty of the Government to protect and the inhabitants to assist is reciprocal. The People of Warren County have not assisted the U.S. much as yet, and are therefore not entitled to {undue} protection. What future protection they receive will depend on their own conduct.

2d The negroes, former Slaves by inheritance or purchase, that now fill the Country have been turned loose upon the world by their former owners, who by rebelling against the only earthly power, that ensured them the rightful possession of such property have practically freed them. They are a poor, ignorant class of human Beings, that appeal to all for a full measure of forbearance.

The task of providing for them at present, devolves on the U.S. because ex necessitate the U.S. succeeds by Act of War to the former, lost title of the Master. This task is a most difficult one, and needs time for development and execution. The white inhabitants of the Country must needs be patient, and allow time for the work.

In due season the negroes at Roaches' and Blakes' will be hired, employed by the Government or removed to Camps where they can be conveniently fed, but in the mean time no one must molest them or interfere with the agents of the U.S. entrusted with this difficult and delicate task. If any of them are armed it is for self defence, and if they mistake their just relation to the Government, or the people, we will soon impress on them the Truth.

3d Your 3d inquiry is embraced in the above. I don't know, that any fixed and determined plan is matured—but some just and proper provisions will be made for the negro population of this State.

4th Congress alone can appropriate public money—We cannot hire Servants for the people, who have lost their Slaves, nor can we detail negros for such purposes. You must do as we do, hire your Servants and pay them. If they dont earn their hire, discharge them and employ others. Many have already done this and are satisfied with the results.

5th I advise all Citizens to stay at home—gradually put their houses and contiguous grounds in order and cast about for some employment or make preparations on a moderate Scale to resume their former business and employment. I cannot advise any one to think of planting on a large Scale for it is manifest, no one can see far enough in the future to say, who will reap what you sow. You must first make a Government, before you can have property. There is no such thing as property without government. Of course we think that our Government (which is still yours) is the best and easiest put in full operation here. You are still citizens of the United States and of the State of Mississippi. You have only to begin and form one precinct, then another—

soon your County will have such organisation, that the Military authorities would respect it. The example of one County would infect another, and that another in a compound ratio, and it would not be long, till the whole State would have such strength by association, that with the assistance of the United States you could defy any insurgent force. The moment the State can hold an open, fair election, and send Senators and Members to Congress, I doubt not, they would be received, and then Mississippi would again be as much a part of our Government as Indiana and Kentucky now are equal to them in all respects and could soon have Courts, Laws and all the Machinery of Civil Government. Until that is done it is idle talk about little annoyances, such as you refer to at Deer Creek and Roaches'. As long as the War lasts, these troubles will exist, and in truth the longer the War is protracted, the more better will be the feeling, and the poor people will have to bear it, for they cannot help themselves.

General Grant can give you now no permanent assurances or guarantees, nor can I, nor can anybody. Of necessity in War the Commander on the spot is the judge, and may take your house, your fields, your everything, and turn you all out, helpless to starve. It may be wrong, but that don't alter the case. In War you can't help yourselves, and the only possible remedy is, to stop war.

I know this is no easy task, but it is well for you, to look the fact square in the face, and let your thoughts and acts tend to the great solution. Those who led the People into War promised all manner of good things to you, and where are their promises? A Child may fire a City, but it takes a host of strong men to extinguish it. So a Demagogue may fire the minds of a whole people, but it will take a host like yourselves to imbue the flames of anger thus begotten. The task is a mammoth one, but still you will in after years be held recreant, if you do not lend your humbled assistance. I know that hundreds and thousands of good Southern men now admit their error in appealing to War—and are engaged in the worthy effort to stop it, before all is lost. Look around you and see the wreck. Let your minds contemplate the whole South in like chaos and disorder, and what a picture? Those who die by the bullet are lucky, compared to those poor fathers and wives and children, who see their all taken and themselves left to perish, or linger out their few years in ruined poverty. Our duty is not to build up, it is rather to destroy both the Rebel Army and whatever of wealth or property it has founded its boasted strength upon. Therefore don't look to any Army to help you—ask for yourselves. Study your real duties to yourselves and families, and if you remain inert, or passively friendly to the Power, that threatens our national existence, you must reap the full consequences; but if like true men you come out boldly and plainly and assert, that the Government of the United States is the only Power on earth,

which can insure to the inhabitants of America that protection to Life, property and fame which alone can make life tolerable, you will then have some
reason to ask of us protection and assistance; otherwise *Not*.

General Grant is absent; I doubt if he will have time to notice your petition,
as he deals with a larger Sphere[2]—and I have only reduced these points to
writing that your people may have something to think about, and divert your
minds from the questions of Cotton, Niggers and petty depredations, in
which the engines of all order and all Government have buried up the real
issues of this War. I am &c.

W. T. Sherman
Maj. Genl. Comdg.

Lbk, DNA: RG 94, Records of the Adjutant General's Office, Generals' Books and Papers,
William T. Sherman, Letterbook 6; *OR*, I, 30: pt. 3, 401–4.

1. H. W. Hill, Chairman, and J. W. Rice, Secretary, Resolutions from a meeting of the
citizens of Oak Ridge and Milldale precincts, September 4, 1863, *OR*, I, 30: pt. 3, 733–35. The
citizens requested supplies from the military authorities and that they be protected from
"armed negroes" and other ruffians. They further asked that Sherman's men send "suitable
negroes" to serve those in need. They also demanded to know how the authorities would
ensure their well-being.

2. USG would concern himself with their fears; he forwarded Hill's petition with another
one to HWH on September 19, 1863, urging a more moderate policy toward civilians in
conquered territory. *PUSG*, 9:221–24; *OR*, I, 30: pt. 3, 732–35.

TO JOHN SHERMAN

Head Qrs. 15 Army Corps,
Camp on Big Black, Sept. 9, 1863
Wednesday

Dear Brother,

I went into Vicksburg on Sunday (17 miles) taking Ellen & the children to
see the Fortifications of the Place and all the points of interest, including
Chickasaw. They gathered pockets full of bullets and fragments of iron shot &
shells, but soon so overloaded themselves that like children they disgorged
and got back empty pocketed. We got back yesterday. All well satisfied with
our Camp on Big Black. I have two large Hospital tents for Ellen & myself and
two common wall tents for the children and you would be surprised to see
how well they get along. All are well and really have improved in health down
here. Minnie though only in her 13th year has nearly her growth and is really a
beautiful woman. It makes me feel old to See her and the others growing so
fast, but as long as I like I can maintain them in proper state. I am perfectly
satisfied that I acted wisely in staying south and Grant and McPherson the
Same. So many of our Generals have gone north partly for personal reasons,
and partly to receive the ovations of a public that our army has been com-

pelled to lay quiet. To be sure the heat and drought would have made marches impossible, but the absence of so many officers and men makes our poor Regiments look so small that I feel discouraged. I now read that there is no enlistment and that the Govt. is afraid to make a draft, & that consequently till new reverses occur we have no hopes of filling our Ranks—Some of the Ohio Regiments could not march out of Camp with 100 men fit for duty and yet they Say that Ohio's quota is full; if this be so they are on duty at the North & not here. I have letters from Blair and all my Division commanders who say the People appreciate the Services of the Army of the Tennessee, but this will avail us little if instead of taking the open Field this winter we are compelled to rest on the defensive. Three or four thousand of the enemys Cavalry swoop round through the interior of Mississipi and I cannot stop it for I only have 800 cavalry which has but recently returned from the Successful expedition to Grenada & Memphis, and it would be folly to chase Cavalry with Infantry[.] I have frequent communications with the Confederate Army by flags of Truce, and with the citizens of the Interior. The former seem confident yet of their ultimate independence, but of course calculate on anarchy north & European complications. The Citizens are helpless. Their negros are gone, and they cant tell which power will prevail and fear to commit themselves by adhering to Either party. Their condition is to be pitied and yet as long as their sons, horses and materiel are arrayed against us in the Confederate Armies they have no right to expect us to protect them much against our own men, but our soldiers were fast degenerating into robbers and I have checked it not so much on account of the poor people here, as for our own sake. On the discipline of our armies must be built the future Government of this Country. Dont talk or think about reconstruction. It is not going to result from any law or Plan, but out of the Stern necessities of the people. Agitators & theorists have got us into this scrape, and only practical men and Fighting men can extricate us. I would be willing that Vallandigham should be elected as it would be the *reductio ad absurdum*. Of course he will not be allowed to govern Ohio, with its Railroads Rivers and Lines of communication. The armies in the Field would demand that these be held by a safe & trusty agent. Though as a nation we are making slow progress, in War we are plunging along fast enough in the lessons of Politics & Statesmanship.

The affair at Lawrence will develop a new antagonism.[1] Jim Lane[2] will attempt to wipe out the Frontier settlements of Missouri. Their impulse is right, because those people are responsible, without their last convention that Body could not have reached in secrecy the plan of its destruction. Still no Government should allow any local People to take their own vengeance in their own way even if right—for then all Govt. would Cease. The U.S. may rightfully do, what a local People may not. No matter how brutal a murder, you cannot punish the murderer. That is reserved to the State.

Grant is expected up from New Orleans today[3] but I dont think any active campaign will begin here for some time. I will expect you in October and if everything favors I may go with you to New Orleans. I have purposely kept out of Louisiana save in transition, till the day of reconstruction is reached. It is not yet. affectionately

W. T. Sherman

ALS, DLC: William T. Sherman.

1. On August 21, 450 Confederate guerrillas, many from Missouri, stormed the Kansas town, stole property, burned buildings, and killed all the men and boys they could find.

2. James Henry Lane (1814–66), former leader of the Kansas militia, was a U.S. senator who supported Lincoln and his policies.

3. Grant had gone to New Orleans on September 2 to consult with Banks on his proposed campaigns for the winter and to review his troops. He had suffered a serious leg injury when his horse fell on his left side.

TO JAMES B. McPHERSON

September 10, 1863.

General McPherson,
Vicksburg:

The enemy can ford Big Black anywhere above Birdsong's. They are burning cotton and destroying property, and I don't think it is any of our business to protect those people. They deserve little help at our hands. Indeed the rebels are serving our cause in making the people of Mississippi hate their rule. I want the people to feel that their rebel authorities care but little for them.

I can make them evacuate that country by marching on Canton, but don't see why I should march our infantry this hot weather to help a parcel of people who are not our friends or even allies. When these people act as friends and offer to help. I will respond.

W. T. Sherman,
Major-General.

Printed, *OR*, I, 30: pt. 3, 504.

TO DENNIS HART MAHAN

Head Qrs. 15th Army Corps
Camp on Big Black, Septr. 16, 1863

Professor D. H. Mahan, West Point
Dear Sir,

Yours of August 28th is received.[1] I assure you, Generals Grant, McPherson, Steele, Sherman and indeed all Graduates in this army feel the deepest interest in our Alma Mater; we see and feel and daily acknowledge the truth and force of much, that was taught us there, which then we could not appreciate, and our social bonds are so strong, that we have at times to moderate our expressions, lest they generate a feeling among our associates, less favored than ourselves. I am now some twenty miles from McPherson, and General Grant is down the River, and Steele at Little Rock, but though space separates us, the utmost harmony has always existed between us, and as we are far removed from contaminating Politics; I fear not harmony will continue to prevail, till the great problem of Nationality is solved by the Law of Force.

Your high commendation of our recent campaign of Vicksburg is so handsome, and coming from so high a source, I will send it to General Grant, for whom I entertain not only a respect but an affection. I know he will feel in it a gleam of satisfaction and pleasure, second only to that, which he experienced, when you signed his Diploma and turned him loose upon the mystery of a world, vain with the beliefs, that his education was done, whereas it was only begun. I am not surprised, that you and his Professors should feel grandly disappointed in him—He possesses many traits of character, that should form a subject of encouragement to others, who are coming after us in this world's Grand Drama. Even now if arrayed before a just Tribunal of learned men, he might not be rated high in any one branch of knowledge or character, nor would he ever claim superiority over any contestant for honor, save in purity of motive and character, that any honest mind may claim with the most gifted, that God starts in the race of life. He does his Best and leaves the result to the Laws of nature. He can easily see the honest agents that surround him, he can listen to the emanations of their minds and memory, he can well balance chances and select the course that appears itself to his mind; and then he goes on, with almost the confidence of a child, conscious of his own motives and fearless of results. He is fortunate in the Physique of his Army and can sit like a driver with a team of Spirited horses, that obey the gentlest rein.

I surely will respond to your Confidential Circular, and will do all I can in War and Peace to reconcile the elements of our Country[2]—so discordant, that they have not only torn asunder the ties that bound families together by natural affinities, but of our own old Army Circle, that once seemed the very Siamese Twins of Society. The time is hardly yet. We must manifest the Physical Power of a Great Country we must demand as a Physical Right the obedience of the subjects of our Government and the respect of the world, and then we can be as gentle as a Franklin or Washington.

Men must tremble if they offend our insulted nationality and then we may soothe them as corrected children.

West Point can perform a part in each stage of the mighty game. She has and may continue to teach subordination and combinations, and in the sequel can demonstrate how the most gallant, high spirited man can be the proud Soldier, yet humble and obedient citizens. This has been her mission, and may continue to be, and for one I will endeavor so to enlarge its sphere, that instead of sending forth its annual tens, it may contribute to our country its hundreds of emissaries.

I would enlarge it to the full capacity of 1000 cadets, and that too now, at once. Our Volunteer Army could send you annually 200 worthy youths, tried in the school of experience.

I would that our army had in some one at West Point a sort of Father Confessor, to whom we could confide our crude notions, to be by him tried in the crucible of truth and justice, instead of the dirty boiling cauldron of the Public Press, that taints and defiles every thought and feeling, however worthy. If such could be found, I know many Officers would make him the recipient of thoughts that are felt to be too sacred to be imparted to a mere worldly mind or Press.

I beg to assure you and your associates of my profound personal Respect.

W. T. Sherman
Maj. Genl. Vols.

Lbk, DNA: RG 94, Records of the Adjutant General's Office, Generals' Books and Papers, William T. Sherman, Letterbook 6.

1. Mahan to WTS, August 28, 1863, DLC: WTS. Mahan thanked WTS for returning some of his letters that his men had found on Jefferson Davis's plantation. "I am glad of this occasion to say to you how proud I feel of you all in the West. Duty has been nobly done, and, so far as I hear, with little or none of the dirty bickering that have done our graduates so much mischief elsewhere. Please say this from me to Grant; and that he has grandly disappointed me, and won my hearty admiration for his skill and indomitable determination not to fail."

2. Mahan had mentioned his plans for a "*confidential circular*" to his old pupils, asking them to join in an association to work together for the Union. He thought that quarrels among them should be arbitrated in private by mutual friends. He had done what he could to defend his graduates in print until they started going after each other. He asked Sherman's opinion on the matter and asked him to gauge the level of support for such an enterprise among the USMA graduates.

TO HENRY W. HALLECK
private and confidential

Head Qrs. 15 Army Corps.
Camp on Big Black Miss. Sept. 17. 63

Maj. Genl. Halleck, Comdr. in Chief, Washington, D.C.
Dear General,

I have received your letter of Aug. 29, and with pleasure confide to you fully my thoughts on the important matter you suggest, with absolute confidence that you will use what is valuable, and reject the useless or superfluous.[1]

That part of the Continent of North America Known as Louisiana, Mississipi, and Arkansas is in my judgment the Key to the Whole Interior. The valley of the Mississipi is America, and although Railroads have changed the scenery of intercommunication, yet the water channels still mark the Lines of fertile land, and afford carriage to the heavy products of it. The inhabitants of the country on the Monongehela, the Illinois, the Minnesota, the Yellowstone and Osage are as directly concerned in the security of the Lower Mississipi as are those who dwell on its very banks in Louisiana, and now that the nation has recovered its possessions, this Generation of men would make a fearful mistake if we again commit its charge to a People liable to mistake their title, and assert as was recently done that because they dwelt by sufferance on the Banks of this mighty stream they had a right to control its navigation. I would deem it very unwise at this time, or for years to come, to revive the State Governments of Louisiana &c. or to institute in this Quarter any Civil Government in which the local People have much to say. They had a Government, and so mild & paternal that they gradually forgot they had any at all, save what they themselves controlled; they asserted an absolute right to seize public monies, Forts, arms, and even to Shut up the national avenues of travel & commerce. They chose War. They ignored & denied all the obligations of the Solemn Contract of Government and appealed to force.

We accepted the issue, and now they begin to realize that War is a two edged sword, and it may be that many of the Inhabitants cry for Peace. I know them well, and the very impulses of their nature, and to deal with the Inhabitants of that part of the South which borders the Great River, we must recognise the classes into which they have naturally divided themselves.

1st The Large Planters, owning Lands, slaves and all kinds of personal property. These are on the whole the ruling Class. They are educated, wealthy, and easily approached. In some districts they are bitter as gall, and have given up, slaves, plantations & all, serving in the armies of the Confederacy, whereas in others they are conservative. None dare admit a friendship to us, though they Say freely that they were opposed to disunion and war. I *know* we can manage this class, but only by *action*. Argument is exhausted, and words have not their usual meaning. Nothing but the Logic of events touches their understanding, but of late this has worked a wonderful change. If our Country were like Europe, crowded with people, I would say it would be easier to replace this population than to reconstruct it subordinate to the Policy of the Nation, but as this is not the case it is better to allow them with individual exceptions gradually to recover their plantations to hire any species of labor and adapt themselves to the new order of things. Still their friendship and assistance to reconstruct order out of the present Ruin cannot be depended on. They watch the operations of our Armies, and hope still for a Southern Confederacy that will restore to them the slaves and privileges which they feel are otherwise lost forever. In my judgment we have two more battles to win before we should even bother our minds with the idea of restoring civil order, viz. one near Meridian in November, and one near Shreveport in February and March where Red River is navigable by our Gunboats. When these are done, then & not till then will the Planters of Louisiana, Arkansas & Mississipi submit. Slavery is already gone, and to cultivate the Land, negro or other labor must be hired. This of itself is a vast revolution and time must be afforded to allow men to adjust their minds and habits to the new order of things. A civil Government of the Representative type would suit this class far less than a pure Military Rule, one readily adapting itself to actual occurrences, and able to enforce its laws & orders promptly and emphatically.

2nd. The smaller farmers, mechanics, merchants and laborers:

This class will probably number ¾ of the whole, have in fact no real interest in the establishment of a Southern Confederacy, and have been led or driven into war, on the false theory that they were to be benefitted somehow, they Knew not how. They are essentially tired of the War, & would slink back home if they could. These are the real Tiers-etat of the South and are hardly worthy a thought for they swerve to & fro according to events they do not comprehend or attempt to shape. When the time for reconstruction comes, they will want the old political system, of caucuses, Legislatures &c. something to amuse them, and make them believe they are achieving wonders, but in all things they will follow blindly the lead of the Planter. The Southern Politicians who understand this class use them as the French do their masses. Seemingly consulting their prejudices they make their orders and enforce them. We should do the same.

3rd. The Union men of the South. I must confess I have little respect for this class. They allowed a clamorous set of demagogues to muzzle & drive them as a pack of curs. Afraid of shadows, they submit tamely to squads of dragoons and permit them without a murmur to burn their cotton, take their horses, corn and everything; and when we reach them, they are full of complaints, if our men take a few fence rails for firewood, or corn to feed our horses. They give us no assistance or information, and are loudest in their complaints at the smallest excess of our Soldiers. Their sons, horses arms and everything useful are in the army against us, and they stay at home claiming all the exemptions of peaceful citizens. I account them as nothing in this Great Game.

4th. The young Bloods of the South, sons of Planters, Lawyers about Town, good billiard players & sportsmen. Men who never did work, or never will.

War suits them: and the rascals are brave, fine riders, bold to rashness, and dangerous subjects in every sense. They care not a "sous" for niggers, land or anything. They hate Yankees "per se" and don't bother their brains about the Past, present or Future. As long as they have a good horse, plenty of Forage and an open Country they are happy. This is a larger class than most men suppose, and are the most dangerous set of men which this war has turned loose upon the world. They are splendid riders, shots, and utterly reckless. Stuart, John Morgan, Forrest,[2] and Jackson are the types & leaders of this class. They must all be killed, or employed by us before we can hope for Peace. They have no property or future & therefore cannot be influenced by anything except personal considerations. I have two Brigades of these fellows to my Front, commanded by Cosby of the old army and Whitfield of Texas,[3] Stephen D. Lee[4] in command of the whole. I have frequent interviews with the officers, and a good understanding; and am inclined to think when the resources of their country are exhausted we must employ them. They are the best Cavalry in the world, but it will tax Mr. Chase's Genius of Finance to supply them with horses. At present horses cost them nothing for they take where they find, and dont bother their brains, who is to pay for them. Same of the corn fields which have, as they believe been cultivated by a good natured people for their special benefit. We propose to share with them the free use of these cornfields planted by willing hands that will never gather them.

Now, that I have sketched the People who inhabit the District of Country under consideration, I will proceed to discuss the Future. A Civil Government for any part of it would be simply ridiculous. The People would not regard it, and even the Military Commanders of the antagonistic party would treat it lightly. Governors would be simply petitioners for military assistance to protect supposed friendly interests, and Military Commanders would refuse to disperse & weaken their armies for military reasons. Jealousies would arise between the two conflicting powers, and instead of contributing to the end we all have in view, would actually defer it. Therefore I contend that the interest of the United States, and of the real parties concerned, demand the continuance of the simple military Rule till long after *all* the organized armies of the South are dispersed, conquered and subjugated. All this Region is represented in the Army of Virginia, Charleston, Mobile and Chattanooga. They have sons & relations in each and naturally interested in their fate. Though we hold military possession of the Key Points of this country, still they contend & naturally that should Lee succeed in Virginia, or Bragg at Chattanooga, that a change would occur here also. We cannot for this reason attempt to reconstruct parts of the South as we conquer it, till all idea of the establishment of a Southern Confederacy is abandonned. We should avail ourselves of the lull here, to secure the Geographical points that give us advantage in future military movements, and Should treat the idea of Civil Government as one in which we as a nation have a Minor or subordinate interest. The opportunity is good to impress on the population the Truth that they are more interested in Civil Government than we are, and that to enjoy the protection of Laws, they must not be passive observers of events, but must aid and Sustain the constituted authorities in enforcing the Laws: they must not only submit themselves, but pay their taxes, and render personal services when called on.

It seems to me in contemplating the past two years history, all the people of our country north, south, east & west have been undergoing a Salutary Political Schooling, learning lessons which might have been taught by the History of other People; but we had all become so wise in our own conceit that we would only learn by actual experience of our own.

The people even of small & unimportant localities north as well as south, had reasoned themselves into the belief that their opinions were superior to the aggregated interest of the whole nation. Half our territorial nation rebelled on a doctrine of secession that they themselves now scorn, and a real numerical majority actually believed, that a little state was endowed with such sovereignty, that it could defeat the Policy of the Great Whole. I think the present war has exploded that notion, and were this war to cease now, the experience gained though dear would be worth the expense.

Another Great & important natural Truth is still in contest and can only be solved by War. Numerical majorities by vote is our Great Arbiter. Heretofore all have submitted to it in questions left open, but numerical majorities are not necessarily physical majorities. The South though numerically inferior, contend they can whip the Northern superiority of numbers, and therefore by natural Law are not bound to submit. This issue is the only real one, and in my judgement all else should be deferred to it. War alone can decide it, and it is the only question left to us as a People.

Can we whip the South? If we can, our numerical majority has both the natural and constitutional right to govern. If we cannot whip them they contend for the natural right to Select their own Government, and they have the argument. Our Armies must prevail over theirs, our officers, marshals and courts must penetrate into the innermost recesses of their Land before we have the natural right to demand their submission. I would banish all minor questions, and assert the broad doctrine that as a nation the United States has the Right and also the Physical Power to penetrate to every part of the National domain, and that we will do it—that we will do it in our own time and in our own way, that it makes no difference whether it be in one year, or two, or ten or twenty: that we will remove & destroy every obstacle, if need be take every life, every acre of land, every particle of property, every thing that to us seems proper, that we will not cease till the end is attained, that all who do not aid are enemies, and we will not account to them for our acts. If the People of the South oppose they do so at their peril, and if they stand by mere lookers on the domestic tragedy, they have no right to immunity, protection or share in the final Result.

I even believe and contend further, that in the North every member of the Nation is bound by both natural & constitutional Law to "maintain and defend the Government against all its opposers whomsoever." If they fail to do it, they are derelict, and can be punished, or deprived of all advantage arising from the labors of those who do—If any man north or south withholds his share of taxes, or physical assistance in this crisis of our History, he could and should be deprived of all voice in the future Elections of this country and might be banished or reduced to the condition of a Denizen of the Land.

War is upon us. None can deny it. It is not the act of the Government of the United States but of a Faction. The Government was forced to accept the issue or submit to a degradation fatal & disgraceful to all the Inhabitants. In accepting war it should be pure & simple as applied to the Belligerents. I would Keep it so, till all traces of war are effaced, till those who appealed to it are sick & tired of it, and come to the emblem of our Nation and Sue for Peace. I would not coax them, or even meet them half way, but make them so sick of war that Generations would pass before they would again appeal to it.

I know what I say, when I repeat that the insurgents of the South sneer at all overtures looking to their interest. They Scorn the alliance with Copperheads: they tell me to my face that they respect Grant, McPherson and our brave associates who fight manfully & well for a principle, but despise the Copperheads & sneaks, who profess friendship for the South, and opposition to the War, as mere covers to their Knavery & poltroonery.

God knows that I deplored this fratricidal war as much as any man living, but it is upon us a physical fact; and there is only one honorable issue from it. We must fight it out, army against army, and man against man, and I know and you Know, and civilians begin to realize the fact, that reconciliation and reconstruction will be easier through and by means of strong, well equipped & organised armies than through any species of conventions that can be framed. The issues are made & all discussion is out of place and ridiculous.

The Section of 30 pounder Parrott Rifles now drilling before my tent is a more convincing argument than the largest Democratic or Union meeting the State of New York could assemble at Albany: and a simple order of the War Department to draft enough men to fill our Skeleton Regiments would be more convincing as to our national perpetuity, than an humble pardon to Jeff Davis and all his misled host.

The only Government now needed or deserved by the States of Louisiana, Arkansas and Mississipi now exists in Grants Army. It needs simply enough privates to fill its Ranks, all else will follow in due season. This army has its well defined code of Laws and Practice, and can adapt itself to the wants and necessities of a city, the country, the Rivers, the Sea, indeed to all parts of this Land. It better subserves the interest and Policy of the General Government and the People prefer it to any weak or servile combination, that would at once from force of habit revive & perpetuate local prejudices and passions. The People of this country have forfeited all Right to a voice in the Councils of the Nation. They Know it and feel it, and in after years they will be the better citizens from the dear bought experience of the present Crisis. Let them learn now, and learn it well that good citizens must obey as well as command. Obedience to law, absolute yea even abject is the lesson that this war under Providence will teach the Free & enlightened American Citizen. As a Nation we will be the better for it.

I never have apprehended Foreign Interference in our family quarrel. Of course Governments founded on a different & it may be antagonistic principle with ours, would naturally feel a pleasure at our complications: but in the end England & France will join with us in jubilation in the triumph of a Constitutional Government over Faction: even now the English manifest this. I do not profess to understand Napoleons design in Mexico, but I do not see that his taking military possession of Mexico concerns us. We have as much territory as we want. The Mexicans have failed in self Government and it was a question to what nation she would fall a prey. That is solved, and I dont see that we are damaged. We have the finest part of the North American Continent, all we can people & take care of, and if we can suppress rebellion in our Land and compose the strife generated by it, we will have people, resources & wealth which if well combined can defy interference from any and every quarter. I therefore hope the Government of the U.S. will continue as heretofore in collecting in well organized armies the physical strength of the nation, apply it as heretofore in asserting the national authority, persevering without relaxation to the end. This whether near or far off is not for us to say, but fortunately we have no choice. We *must* succeed. No other choice is left us but degradation.

The South must be ruled or will rule. We must conquer them or ourselves be conquered. There is no middle course.

They ask and will have nothing else, and all this talk of compromise is bosh, for we know they would even now scorn and despise the offer.

I wish this war could have been deferred for twenty years, till the superabundant population of the North could flow in and replace the losses sustained by War, but this could not be, and we are forced to take things as they arise.

All therefore I can now venture to advise is the pushing the draft to its maximum, fill the present Regiments to as large a standard as possible, and push this War, "pure and simple."

Great attention should be paid to the discipline of our armies, for on them will be founded the future stability of our Government. The Cost of the War is of course to be considered, but finances will adjust themselves to the actual state of affairs, and even if we would, we could not change the cost. Indeed, the larger the cost now, the less will it be in the end, for the End must be attained somehow regardless of cost of Life and Treasure, and is merely a question of Time. Excuse so long a letter. With great respect your friend & servant

W. T. Sherman
Maj. Genl.

ALS, DLC: Edwin M. Stanton Papers; *OR*, I, 30: pt. 3, 694–700.
1. On August 29, HWH had solicited WTS's views on reconstruction. *PM*, 1:363.
2. Nathan Bedford Forrest (1821–77), the Confederate cavalry commander.
3. John W. Whitfield (1818–79) was a brigadier general under Forrest's command.
4. Stephen Dill Lee (1833–1908) was also a brigadier general in the Confederate cavalry.

TO JOHN A. RAWLINS

Head Qrs. 15th Army Corps
Camp on Big Black Sept. 17, 63

Brig. Genl. J. A. Rawlins, A.A.A.G., Vicksburg.

Dear General—

I enclose for your perusal and for you to read to General Grant such parts as you may deem interesting to him a letter received by me from Professor Mahan and General Halleck with my answer. After you have read my answer to General Halleck I beg you to enclose it to its address, and return me the others.

I think Professor Mahans very marked economium upon the campaign of Vicksburg is so flattering to General Grant, that you may offer to let him keep the letter if he values such testimonials. I have never written a word to General Halleck since my Report last Decbr. after the affair at Chickasaw except a short letter a few days ago, thanking him for the kind manner of his transmitting me the appointment of Brigadier General. I know, that in Washington I am incomprehensible, Because at the outset of the War I would not go it blind and headlong into a War, unprepared and with an utter ignorance of its extent and purpose—I was construed unsound, and now that I insist on War pure and simple with no admixture of civil compromises I am again supposed vindictive. You remember what Polonius spoke to his son Laertes, (Hamlet)

"Beware a quarrel, but being in, bear it, that thy oppressor may beware of thee." What is true of the single man is equally true of a Nation. Our leaders seemed at first to thirst for the quarrel willing, even anxious to array against us all possible elements of opposition, and now being in, they would hasten to quit, long before the oppressor has received that lesson, which he needs.

I would make this War as severe as possible and make no Symptoms of tire, till the South begs for mercy—Indeed, I know and you know, that the end would be reached quicker by such course, than by any seeming yielding on our part. I don't want our Government to be bothered by patching up local Governments, by trying to reconcile any class of men. The South has done its worst and now is the time for us to pile on our blows thick and fast.

Instead of postponing the Draft till after the elections, we ought now to have our Ranks full of drafted men; but at best if they come at all they will reach us, when we should be in motion.

I think Halleck would like to have the honest, candid opinion of each of us, viz. Grant, McPherson and Sherman. I have given mine, and would prefer of course, that they should coincide with the others.

Still no matter what my opinion, I can easily adapt my conduct to the plans of others, and am only too happy, when I find theirs better than mine.

If no trouble, please show Hallecks letter to McPherson, and ask him to write also—I know his Regiments are like mine, mere squads, and need filling up. Yours truly

W. T. Sherman
Maj. Genl.

Lbk, DNA: RG 94, Records of the Adjutant General's Office, Generals' Books and Papers, William T. Sherman, Letterbook 6.

TO CHARLES C. SMITH

Gayoso House, Memphis, Tenn.,
October 4, Midnight. [1863]

Captain C. C. Smith,
Comd'g. Bat. 13th Regulars.
My Dear Friend:

I cannot sleep to-night till I record an expression of the deep feelings of my heart to you, and to the Officers and Soldiers of the Battalion, for their kind behaviour to my poor child.[1] I realize that you all feel for my family the attachment of kindred; and I assure you all of full reciprocity. Consistent with a sense of duty to my profession and office, I could not leave my post, and sent for my family to come to me in that fatal climate, and in that sickly period of the year, and behold the result! The child who bore my name, and in whose future I reposed with more confidence than I did in my own plans of life, now floats a mere corpse, seeking a grave in a distant land, with a weeping mother, brother, and sisters clustered about him. But, for myself I can ask no sympathy. On, on, I must go till I meet a soldier's fate, or see my country rise superior to all factions, till its flag is adored and respected by ourselves and all the Powers of Earth.

But, my poor WILLY was, or thought he was, a Sergeant of the 13th. I have seen his eye brighten and his heart beat as he beheld the Battalion under arms, and asked me if they were not real soldiers. Child as he was, he had the enthusiasm, the pure love of truth, honor, and love of country, which should animate all soldiers. God only knows why he should die thus young. He is dead, but will not be forgotten till those who knew him in life have followed him to that same mysterious end.

Please convey to the Battalion my heartfelt thanks, and assure each and all, that if in after years they call on me or mine, and mention that they were of the 13th Regulars, when poor WILLY was a Sergeant, they will have a key to the affections of my family that will open all it has, that we will share with them our last blanket, our last crust. YOUR FRIEND,

W. T. SHERMAN

MAJOR GENERAL

Printed letter, Millbury, Mass.: Private Collection of Frederic S. Cauldwell; also in SFP.

1. Willy Sherman died of typhoid fever on October 3, 1863, at the Gayoso House. He contracted the disease while returning from Mississippi to Memphis en route to Ohio.

TO ELLEN EWING SHERMAN

Gayoso, Memphis Oct. 6 [1863]

7 A.M.

Dearest Ellen,

I have got up early this morning to Steal a short period in which to write to you but I can hardly trust myself. Sleeping—waking—everywheres I see Poor Little Willy. His face & form are as deeply imprinted on my memory as were deepseated the hopes I had in his Future. Why oh Why should that child be taken from us? leaving us full of trembling & reproaches. Though I know we did all human beings could do to arrest the ebbing tide of Life, still I will always deplore my want of judgment in taking my family to so fatal a climate at so critical period of the year—You Know why—I know why but to it must be traced the loss of that child on whose future I had based all the Ambition I ever had. If human sympathy could avail us aught, I Know & feel we have it—I see it in every eye and in every act—Poor {Malmbury}, an old scarred Soldier, whom the world would Style unfeeling, wept like a babe as he came to See me yesterday, and not a word was spoken of Poor Willy.

My Judgment teaches me that the bitter pang that has nearly killed us will gradually heal, and leave Willy's memory as a more tender link between us, and our other children, who are all we could ask—each seems to have a distinct character and disposition, but all are good and loving to us—I follow you in my mind and almost estimated the hour when all Lancaster would be shrouded in gloom to think that Willy Sherman was coming back a corpse. Dear as may be to you the Valley of Hocking, no purer, noble boy ever will again gladden it.

I am in the large Room occupied by the children. Hugh is with me—The Staff & officer is in camp in a Grove near the Convent—Gen. Corse is up, but his Division is still on the River. I hope to get all out to Corinth by next Sunday & move them to Tuscumbria by Land. Write to me here say till Oct. 15, after that according to what you hear—Look out for me about Huntsville Alabama, or Athens about the 15 or 20th inst.

Coolbaugh[1] got back from Canton on Wednesday, found Joe Johnston, Stephen J. Lee, Jackson Cosby &c. all at Canton with a large force of cavalry, 7000. Some important movement on hand—yet they were stampeded by the move I made the day we left camp.

My command will be much smaller than the world thinks, but I do not even name the fact to those about me.

Our country Should blush to allow our thinned Regiments to go on till nothing is left. But I will go on to the End but feel the Chief Stay to my faltering Heart is now gone.

But I must not dwell so much on it. I will try and make Poor Willys memory the cure for the defects which have sullied my character[.] always yours

W. T. Sherman

ALS, InND: Sherman Family Papers.

1. George Coolbaugh had acted as a railroad agent for McPherson at Corinth and then as an aide on his staff. Rumors that he had indulged in cotton speculation while in Union employ threatened to scuttle McPherson's nomination to brigadier general, USA, in early 1864.

TO ELLEN EWING SHERMAN

Memphis, Oct. 8, 1863

Dearest Ellen,

I am yet here but expect to go out to Corinth tomorrow—The River is lower than ever before, and Corses Division which left on Wednesday & Thursday after us is not yet in. I hope I may hear of you before I start. In my mind I have followed you step by step and suppose you arrived at home

Wednesday noon. Though I can never efface from memory, nor do I wish to the scenes of affliction through which we have passed—now that is so, I feel satisfied that it is past. We did all we could for Poor Willy—In life & death, and it may be that he has escaped a long life of anxiety and pain mental & bodily. From every quarter I experience a measure of sympathy that is delicate & proper among other things I wrote a note to Capt. Smith commanding the Battalion asking him to thank all for their kindness to Willy. Of course I did not design my letter for publication but the Capt. had it printed and gave each man a copy. I enclose you some printed copies, and each of our children must retain a Copy forever that we may long after others have forgotten the little events of our sojourn on Big Black, our children may help some old soldier that drifts where they may happen to be.

I opened a letter from Theresa to you yesterday telling you your father was quite ill. I hope he had recovered much before he heard of Poor Willy as I believe he will feel it as much as we. Hugh is with me and is quite uneasy and we hope to hear more today, but I really expect little till Charley comes and tells me the last details of this Sad event of our Life. Dr. Plummer has been in and was amazed to hear of Willy's death, but said at one time Poor Minnie frightened him. I explained to him exactly how she was when she started up River, and he said that was quite as well as he had expected. Her languid and enervated state he said was natural but that travel and her accustomed food & mode of Life would Soon restore her.

I send you some Photographs you can select the one that pleases you most and order any number[.] The Daguerrotypist will Send them to you on an order by express—offer to pay, and I know not whether he will accept or not— I dont like Daguerrotypes because they are all too harsh, but People will have them & I suppose I am foolish in refusing them. To have my likeness hawked about is to me no satisfaction. I know I have the esteem & respect of all the good people of my acquaintance and I am amazed at the expressions of confidence & respect which meet me every wheres about Memphis. Citizens of all shades of opinion want me here because they Say they know I am honest.

Oh! that Poor Willy could have lived to take all that was good of me in name character & standing, and learn to avoid all that is captious, excentric or wrong, but I do not forget that we have other children worthy of my deepest Love. I would not have one different from what they are. Give them all my deep Love, and I will write to each and all before I start if I can steal time and seclusion[.] Yours always

W. T. Sherman

ALS, InND: Sherman Family Papers.

Headquarters Fifteenth Army Corps,
Memphis, October 10, 1863.

Major-General Halleck,
Commander-in-Chief, Washington:
Dear General:

I start out early-in the morning to take the head of my corps, now stretched out as far as Bear Creek. A heavy force of the enemy's cavalry hovers to the south and is going to bother us, not in reaching Athens, but in making this road a safe line of supply.

I have just received your letter of October 1, and assure you of my hearty concurrence in all you say. It has been to us all a source of pleasure to know that such perfect cordiality, social and official, existed among the generals on this line. One noted exception alone, who is disposed of. I hear of jealousies elsewhere and am astonished, as the war is not yet over, and a feeling of common safety and interest should make all harmonize, if not the higher sense of patriotism and duty. Neither McClellan nor Buell ever had a shadow of cause of ill feeling to an administration or commander-in-chief who lavished on them all that man could ask. I know you had for both great personal friendship and manifested it on many occasions, and they mistake you, and are ungrateful, if they attribute to you what thinking men in all times will attribute to their failure to appreciate the situation of the army and the country.

This war might end sooner than it will, but it may be the good of the future requires our people to pass through all the phases of revolution before they are again permitted to enjoy the luxury of peace and safety. When that time comes I believe we will be a better people, and the very ones who provoked war so thoughtlessly will be cured.

I have your telegram saying the President had read my letter and thought it should be published. I have no copy by me, but if I can recall it I think it won't bear publication. Would it not impair my usefulness here? A great many people here and in Louisiana are influenced by men of my shade of opinion. They are full-blooded Southrons, were never disunionists, but were carried into rebellion by the tempest of feeling which their politicians knew so well how to beget and guide. As long as a doubtful contest for supremacy exists between the two races they cannot control their choice; but as soon as we demonstrate equal courage, equal skill, superior resources, and superior tenacity of purpose, they will gradually relax and finally submit to men who profess, like myself, to fight for but one single purpose, viz, to sustain a

Government capable of vindicating its just and rightful authority, independent of niggers, cotton, money, or any earthly interest.

Might not the publication of 'my letter, even without my signature, impair my usefulness with the South? Still if you or Judge Holt, or General Hitchcock, or Reverdy Johnson, or Mr. Ewing would take my letter and mold it in such shape as not to compromise me, so as to serve any good purpose, I give my full consent to its use, or indeed to use anything I have. If I covet any public reputation it is as a silent actor. I dislike to see my name in print.

Thanking you always for many favors, I am, always your sincere friend,

W. T. Sherman.

Printed, *OR*, I, 30: pt. 4, 234–35.

TO ELLEN EWING SHERMAN

Memphis, Oct. 10, 1863.

Dearest Ellen,

I still feel out of heart to write. The moment I begin to think of you & the children, Poor Willy appears before me as plain as life. I can see him now stumbling over the Sand hills on Harrison Street San Francisco, at the table in Leavenworth, running to meet me with open arms at Black River & last, moaning in death in this Hotel. I hardly know how to feel, at times I cannot realize the truth So dreamlike, and yet I Know we can never see his bright honest face again. I dont think years if reserved to me can efface that memory yet we know that others have sustained a loss to them as precious. But the world moves on. I see ladies & children playing in the Room where Willy died, and it seems sacrilege. I know you are now at home, and I pray that Minnie has gradually recovered her health & Strength, and I hope all our Children will regain their full health. Why should I ever have taken them to that dread Climate? It nearly kills me to think of it. Why was I not killed at Vicksburg and left Willy to grow up to care for you? God Knows I exhausted human foresight, and human love for that boy and will pardon any error of Judgment that carried him to death.

I have experienced more sympathy than I could reasonably expect. I have seen the Sisters who witnessed with us the last pulsation of that precious body. I have done all I can to manifest my appreciation of the universal kindness manifested to him and to us. Would that I could Subside into Some quiet corner & live out in Peace my life[.] But how can I. As well might

AL (incomplete), InND: Sherman Family Papers.

TO MARY ELIZABETH HOYT SHERMAN

[ca. October 10, 1863]

Dear Lizzie,

Learn by heart what your Papa told the Soldiers who used to call Willy their brother. I do believe Soldiers have stronger feelings than other men, and I Know that every one of the Regulars would have died, if they could have saved Willy.

We must all now love each other the more that Willy watches us from Heaven. Yr. loving Father,

W. T. Sherman

ALS, Millbury, Mass.: Private Collection of Frederic S. Cauldwell. Written on the verso of a printed copy of WTS to Captain C. C. Smith, October 4, 1863.

TO THOMAS EWING SHERMAN

[ca. October 10, 1863]

Dear Tommy,

You are now our only Boy, and must take Poor Willy's place, to take care of your Sisters, and to fill my Place when I too am gone. I have promised that whenever you meet a Soldier who knew Willy that you will give him half you have. Give him all if in want, and work hard to gain knowledge & health which will when you are a man, insure you all you need in this world. Your loving father

W. T. Sherman

ALS, InND: Sherman Family Papers. Written on the verso of a printed copy of WTS to Captain C. C. Smith, October 4, 1863.

TO DAVID DIXON PORTER

Hd. Qrs. 15th Army Corps
Corinth, Miss. Octbr. 14, 1863

Admiral D. D. Porter or C. O. U.S. Navy, Cairo

Dear Admiral,

I suppose you Know, that I am moving my Corps to the Tennessee and further, according to circumstances. The Rail Road out of Memphis is now in running order out to Bear Creek, and we may repair it to Tuscumbria, but as a source of supply it is too precarious to depend on. As I came out on Sunday with my little Battalion of Regulars, I happened at Colliersville, 24 miles out from Memphis, just as General Chalmers[1] with about 2500 rebel Cavalry demanded its surrender.

The place was held by Col. Anthony and six companies of the 66th Indiana—I got my men off the cars in time, and we beat off Genl. Chalmers.

This illustrates the danger to the Rear, and I only refer to it to show, that I must look to a less precarious chance this moment, and the season is far enough advanced for us to count on the Tennessee. I will be personally and officially obliged, if you will allow one of your light draft boats to watch that river and ascend it at the earliest possible moment to Eastport to communicate with me. The moment, the stage of waters permit, I would prefer to draw my supplies that way, and I can have the means to haul out from there.

I have no doubt, the Rebels have every man, that is in the Southern Confederacy now armed against us, and the most desperate struggle of the War must be expected. A large proportion of their men are "forced," still we know the vindictive feelings that animate their whole People, and should not be blinded by any false theories.

You have almost finished your Job, and can and will doubtless with infinite pleasure help us, who must live, whilst we penetrate the very bowels of their land.

I lost recently my little boy by sickness incurred during his visit to my Camp on Big Black. He was my Pride & Hope of Life, and his loss takes from me the great incentive to excel, and now I must work on purely and exclusively for love of country and Professional Pride.

To you I can always unfold my thoughts as one worthy and capable of appreciating the feelings of a Soldier & Gentleman. With great Respect—

W. T. Sherman
Major General

Lbk, DNA: RG 94, Records of the Adjutant General's Office, Generals' Books and Papers, William T. Sherman, Letterbook 6; reprinted in part in *OR*, I, 30: pt. 4, 356–57.

1. James R. Chalmers (1831–98), CSA, commanded the District of Missouri and Eastern Arkansas.

TO ELLEN EWING SHERMAN

Corinth Miss. Oct. 14, 1863.

Dearest Ellen,

I was much relieved at the receipt of your two letters from Cairo & Cincinati, both of which came out last night.[1] I shew your message to Dr. Roler,[2] who was afflicted to tears. Poor Doctor although I have poured out my feelings of gratitude to him he seems to fear we may have a lingering thought that he failed somehow in saving Poor Willy. Your loving message may have dispelled the thought, & I shall never fail to manifest to him my heartfelt thanks for the unsleeping care he took of the Boy. I believe hundreds would have freely died could they have saved his Life. I know I would, & occasionally indulge the wish that some of those bullets that searched for my life at Vicksburg had been successful, that it might have removed the necessity for that fatal visit. I paid Dr. Brown $15 for his consultation visit, but Dr. Roler advised me not to offer anything to Hurlbuts physician as that was a professional courtesy which would have offended by a mere offer of compensation.

Col. Cockrill[3] of the Gayoso would take nothing from me. Last year I saved his House from being appropriated as a hospital and he never tires of doing me kindness[.] I would be pleased to know that you had written to him acknowledging his kindness at that critical moment. I know he would appreciate it beyond measure. Phoebe and Mrs. Hurlbut called, and everybody in Memphis manifested for me a respect and affection that I never experienced north. I am told when the Report went into Memphis that my train was surely captured at Collinsville the utmost excitement prevailed at Memphis, and a manifest joy displayed when they heard the truth, that we are not only safe, but that we had Saved Colliersville and the Railroad—At Lagrange east of Colliersville Gen. Sweeny[4] the one army officer you may remember at St. Louis Arsenal, hearing that I was captured started south with his whole force determined to rescue Gen. Sherman. As soon as I learned the fact I sent a courier to overtake him, advising him of my safety, but advising him to push on and drive Chalmers far to the South. He is still out. I have this moment received a Dispatch from Gen. Grant at Memphis[5]—He is en route to Cairo to communicate by telegraph with Washington. I know there is a project to give him Command of the Great Center, the Same idea I foreshadowed in my days of depression and insult—I advise him by all means to assent, to go to Nashville and Command Burnside on the Left Rosecrans Center & Sherman Left. That will be an army, and if our Ranks were full I would have hopes of Great & decisive results. I have stood by Grant in his days of sorrow. Not six miles from here he sat in his tent almost weeping at the accumulated charges against him by such villains as Stanton of Ohio, Wade & others. He had made up his mind to leave for good—I begged him, and he yielded. I could See his good points & his weak points better than I could my own, and he now feels that I stood by him in his days of dejection and he is my sworn friend. Corinth brings back to me the memory of those events & bids me heed my own counsels to others. Oh that Poor Willy could live to reap the fruits of whatever is good in me, and avoid the evil. If it so be that he can see our hearts from above he will read in mine a love for him such as would not taint the purest heaven that you ever dreamed of. God spare us the children that are left us: and if I am pardoned for exposing them wrongfully I will never again. I wrote you from Colliersville a short note, and Suppose the rumor which first reached Memphis was corrected before a boat left for the North so that you were not disturbed by false rumors, and will be pleased to know that the Regulars again saved a threatened Garrison, and a part of the Railroad vital to our present enterprise. I will endeavor to Send you a list of the poor fellows that lie buried there, as also those who were sent back wounded to Memphis. These soldiers look to you, and it was only yesterday that Smith issued a barrel of whiskey and Said that was the last of your present at Memphis. You think I dont manifest enough regard for the Battalion—You dont know soldiers as I do—they dont want any puffing & flattery, they Know what I think & feel when danger is near or present, and they have the most implicit faith in my Knowledge & judgment. It was only yesterday that one of them spoke of a Brevet. I asked him if he had ever had occasion to speak to Genl. Grant, announcing himself as one of the 13th. He said he had and Grant said—well that is Shermans pet & he treated him with more attention & respect than if he had been a volunteer General. All the volunteers, officers and men treat these Regulars with a respect that makes them feel the true pride of soldiers. When Quarter Masters want stores properly guarded, or Paymasters want an escort, they ask for my Regulars and would rather have a corporals Guard of them than a Company of Volunteers[.] Dont the Regulars know & appreciate this—When I wrote Capt. Smith a short note of thanks for their kindness to Willy, each one wanted a copy to Send home, and he had it printed. Soldiers have a language conveyed not by words, signs or emotion, but they understand Each other.

Now that I know you are all home again I feel more at ease. Minnie will I feel sure react as soon as she has her accustomed food, & Lizzies symptoms you describe seem more to result from cold than miasma—and as you do not name Tom I infer he is quite well.

Hugh and I were uneasy at a letter Sis wrote you thinking you still at Vicksburg, but you mention your father had been ill but was much better. Hugh is here, but staying down at the Tishamingo Hotel he has not been up this morning, but I will send for him and Show him what you write. I expect to leave here for Iuka in two days, and will as soon as possible push on to Tuscumbria & Athens, from which place I will put myself in communication with Nashville & Chattanooga. I expect Charley up in a day or so. He has lost his two Swords and I suppose I must present him a new one, but I cant do it now as they are beyond my reach. I will defer it to a more suitable period.

I left "Sam" with Capt. Lewis Qr. Mr. at Memphis to be sent to Cincinati & Lancaster as soon as the Ohio River Rises—Dolly was captured from me at Colliersville, and I have the Satisfaction to know She will break the neck of the first Guerilla that fires a pistol from her back. Daytons little sorrel was killed— "Henry" the horse I lent Henry Sherman but now used by Dayton has a bullet in his left hind leg will recover. Charleys little brown mare picked up at Vicksburg has an ugly wound in the hind hip. Duke, Abner, George & Smith (Boyers) are all right. So I am well provided.

I expect to ride from this point but will use the Railroad for supplies.

Give my love to Minnie and tell her she must be prudent & careful. I do wish her education should keep pace with her too rapid development. Lizzie too Should be allowed to read & write much. Tell Tom for me, that he must remember that he is our only boy and that he too must be good & learn so as to take care of you and all the rest, a heavy burden for so young a boy. This is an additional reason why you should not expend a cent in building houses. Get along any how—bear with temporary inconvenience & trouble lest worse befal you. If I am killed you will have but a small pension, and if I live I will never see Ohio if I can avoid it. Yrs. ever

W. T. Sherman

ALS, InND: Sherman Family Papers.

1. EES to WTS, two undated letters of October 1863, SFP.

2. Edwin O. F. Roler; in her second letter, EES asked her husband to "Thank good dear Doctor Roler for me." SFP.

3. Sterling M. Cockrill.

4. Brigadier General Thomas William Sweeny (1820–92), USA, was commanding the Second Division, Sixteenth Corps.

5. USG to WTS, October 14, 1863, *PUSG*, 9:281.

TO JOHN M. WRIGHT

Hd. Qrs. 15th Army Corps
Corinth, Octbr. 14, 1863

Major J. M. Wright, A.A.G., Louisville, Ky.

Sir—

Yours of Septbr. 18th overtook me here. I have no time to reexamine my Letter of the 2d of Septbr. which was written with a desire to serve General Buell. I do say, that any one who makes any publication whatever during the existence of the War will do General Buell greater wrong, than his worst enemy could desire. No matter what the motive and purpose of a writer may be, the world makes its own construction of Motive. No one can misconstrue your kind intent, but having been a member of General Buell's Staff, your publication of a history will be construed as his act, for all Know, that you could not do such a thing, without consulting him. Therefore, independent of the contents of the volume, whether confined to facts, witnessed by the narrator, or explaining results, it will complicate the General, and therefore do him a disservice.

If the War were over and the time come for History I would gladly give you any assistance in my power, but now that we are still daily grappling with a bitter enemy, I must repeat that it does excite us painfully to see publications treating of past events as though they were critical.

It was not and is not my purpose to rebuke you or any one not subject to my authority, or to discourage young Officers who seek to improve their time and advance the cause of their Profession and military Literature, nor to cast disrespect on General Buell. But you asked me to assist in doing, what I believe and know would injure Genl. Buell more than you can realize. I know, that Genl. Buell is one of the coolest, most methodic and patient men living. I feel assured in his Letter Book and Orders is the best History of his campaign, that every step taken was well considered, and record made of it. There is, where the Historian will look for his facts, and already an official body has elicited in the form of evidence every material fact of the events, you propose to reduce to an historical treatise.

I repeat my warning, if you persist in carrying out your plan, you are bound to advise Genl. Buell, and if he assents, he will repent it forever. If in warning you against so fatal a mistake I impair my hitherto reputation for magnanimity I don't see it. On the contrary were I to fail in warning you of the danger in which you are about to involve your friend, I would have just reason to reproach myself always.

The conception is wrong and no matter how delicate and truthful the execution, such a publication as you foreshadow will involve Genl. Buell in a controversy injurious to his well earned reputation.

You know I am no newspaper favorite. I never see my name in Print without a feeling of contamination and I will undertake to forego half my Salary if the newspapers will ignore my name.

I do repeat, now is the time for work and I know that every Soldier and officer should be employed night & day. The present affords ample scope for every hand, and I never think without effect of such men as Buell and Mc-Clellan and other first rate Soldiers being unemployed, when there is so much to be done. I never said, Buell was thus unemployed of his own choice and I believe I express the feelings of his heart, when I say, he would rather have a Division this day, than be out.

As to my expressing disrespect for him, he knows better. He knows I always esteemed him as one of the best, if not the best, practical Soldier of our Army. I disagree with you in toto in your conclusions, and if you write a history of the Army of the Ohio now, before the War is *all* over, mark my words for it, you will regret it forever. I am &c.

W. T. Sherman
Maj. Genl.

Lbk, DNA: RG 94, Records of the Adjutant General's Office, Generals' Books and Papers, William T. Sherman, Letterbook 6; *OR*, I, 30: pt. 4, 357–58.

TO PHILEMON B. EWING

Dear Phil

Your kind letter of condolence by Charley reached me in due season, and was most grateful, though without a word or scratch of pen I would have known the deep pang it gave all who knew him & loved him as he deserved. Somehow by the accidents of life that have buffeted me about, this boy seemed to me more a part of myself than any other human being, and though all my children at times seem to fill some necessary part of our Existence, Willy was to me the one I looked to inherit all I could learn on Earth. Yet Ellen & I did for him all that mortals could, and though at times a feeling of reproach creeps over me for want of judgment or proper feeling in calling for my family to go to that Country in that dread season, yet again it was the only lull I could foresee in the long bloody future before me. Now I would recall the act, but it is too late. It was wonderful the avidity with which he gathered all the details of my army, every division, Brigade, Regiment, battery, everything belonging to my corps because as well Known to him as to me, and he seemed to inherit an instinct I have of going across the country direct to the object regardless of beaten roads or paths. Alone & with the full confidence of a man, seemingly without fear would he ride everywhere, & engage in manly conversation with anybody. It may be his nervous organization was too sensitive for the intense excitement he endured at Big Black though we were all seemingly at the utmost rest—but his mind followed every scout or picket that came to my tent for orders or to make reports. But a few days before his fatal illness, we sat at our Mess table in the Bungalow, when I spoke of a ship beating to windward, he asked me the direct question, How can the wind blow a ship toward itself? a question that not one educated man in a thousand can explain. I had to tell him that it resulted from Mechanical Laws that would require a great deal of study for him to comprehend. But I must not dwell on this topic. I feel in my heart that we all loved & Cherished him in Life as he deserved, and that in his Death we are the losers.

Grant has been ordered to command the Armies of the Ohio, the Cumberland and the Tennessee.[1] So after two long years of almost discordant war, the Govt. has arrived at the very conclusion I made at the outset. We have one vast Field of Battle extending from the Atlantic to the Plains. As in all armies the proper natural subdivision is Right center, Left & Reserve. Now as I understand the Game Grant has the center, Meade the Left & Schofield the Right all facing South. The Reserve is still in the Militia & People. Better and more economical in the End to organize the Reserve at once, and the draft mercilessly enforced in the quickest & best mode. Grant in shaping his force for convenient handling naturally makes a similar subdivision of his Army. I have his Right—Rosecrans his Center & Burnside his Left. It may be he can hold Hooker in reserve, though I now believe him to be with Rosecrans near Stevenson—Grant dont like Rosecrans—He found great fault with him here at Iuka a year ago, and though he is disposed to yield to any body who will make some show of sacrifice I doubt if Rosecrans will take it Kindly.[2] Rosecrans may be Grants superior in intellect, but not in sagacity, purity of Character and singleness of purpose. Rosecrans is selfish & vainglorious. Grant not a bit so. He would never appropriate the just fame of another. He & I have been *always* perfect friends. I confide to him my innermost thoughts and when we think differently, which we have on many minor occasions each respects the motive of the other. I would rather serve under Grant than Rosecrans, for in an extended country like this any one of us may be worsted, Grant would stand by his friend, but Rosecrans would sacrifice his brother if he stood in the way of his popular renown. Grant has felt in his own person the wrong that may be done by popular Clamor, and he appreciates it at its worth. He cannot make a speech of five sentences and he writes easily, naturally & without strain, therefore he may escape the trap that our Countrymen lay for all successful military men.

Your Ohio Elections are now over, and I see the Result is the occasion of universal Joy.[3] It may be all right but it sounds to me like the tingling of empty bells. When war is upon us to have such shouts of victory over a Non Combatant Enemy. A million of idle votes north wont kill a secesh. The only vote that now tells is the cannon & the musket. But it may be the Election & the Kindred ones in Iowa and Pennsylvania are steps in the right direction, tending to avert the Civil war which should exist in the north to cap the Climax of our Democratic institutions.

Since Poor Willy's death I have felt more than ever my natural desire to slide out into obscurity. The Constant wear & tear of mind & body will make me old & feeble before my time, & yet the moment I cast about to See how I could get away it seems impossible for all naturally & by habit come to me for orders & instructions. Without being aware of it, I seem to possess a knowledge of men & things, of Rivers, Roads, capacity of trains wagons &c. that no one near me even professes to have, and yet I See Buell & McClellan & Porter & Others of greater Rank & more fame hugging fine hotels and summer resorts.

I ought to give some of my thoughts to Ellens pecuniary matters. I think I have supplied

AL (incomplete), Wheaton, Md.: Private Collection of Joseph H. Ewing.

1. USG was ordered to take command of the Military Division of the Mississippi on October 17; he assumed command the next day.

2. In fact, the orders announcing USG's appointment as commander of the Military Division of the Mississippi also directed Rosecrans to turn over the Army of the Cumberland to George H. Thomas—a decision made by USG.

3. Brough defeated Vallandigham for the governorship in the state elections earlier in October.

TO ELLEN EWING SHERMAN

Iuka, Miss. Oct. 24, 1863

Dearest Ellen,

I have yours of Oct. 16 & 17.[1] I have had a pretty bad cold for the past two days and am delayed here by bad breaks on the Railroad ahead. The Tennessee is also swollen, and I expect all sorts of trouble in getting over, useless Boats are sent up the Tennessee. We have had Some fighting ahead with the Enemys Cavalry, a pretty formidable body sent ahead from Mississipi, the Same Division that was in my front at Big Black and all of Wheelers Cavalry that escaped from Tennessee, but I can engage their attention and thus divert their minds from the Roads which Supply Rosecrans Army. Grant I suppose now is at Nashville, and will by his presence unite the army more in feeling than it seems hitherto to have been. He is so unpretending & honest that a man must be base who will not yield to him. The only possible danger is that Some may claim his Successes hitherto have been the result of accident, but there too I hope they will find themselves mistaken. I have Telegraphic notice from Memphis that he has assumed Command of the armies of the Cumberland, Ohio and Tennessee, & that I am to command the latter. My desire has always been to have a distinct compact command as a Corps, but spite of my efforts I am pushed into Complicated plans that others aspire to and which I wish they had. But with Grant I will undertake anything in reason.

I had an impression that you had taken home all my letter Books, but I found my three last here. They contain all my principal letters during the whole River Campaign, Some of which may be vital to us in after years. I have sent them to you, and now enclose Adams & Cos. receipt. Take care of these books & let no one but the most confidential look at them. Some of the copying is bad, but the Sense can always be arrived at. I also send you a list of the killed, wounded & missing among the Regulars. They have a hard time of it, and The dirty newspapers make up all sorts of accounts giving credit to Regiments that were fifty miles off, whereas the chief fighting done was by the Regulars. I lost not a thing but Dolly perfectly naked, and I have already captured another Dolly quite as good.

I see your thoughts as mine dwell with poor Willy in his grave. I do not, and you should not reproach yourself a moment for any neglect of him. He knew & felt every moment of his life our deep earnest love for him—The day he came on board the *Atlantic* I think I observed that usual suppressed feeling of pride at having secured that gone. I know I joked him about it and think he received it in his usual manner, & yet at that moment he must have felt the seeds of that disorder which proved so fatal. He did not know it then, and we could not so quickly detect the Symptoms. Minnie had so recently passed the dangerous point that it was hardly possible we could be alarmed by the simple Diarrhea that troubled him. Could we have foreknown we might have provided against the fatal Cause, but this passes the bounds of human Knowledge. God Knows and he knows that either of us, and hundreds of others would have died to save him.

I have written a short letter to Mrs. C. E. Smith Yellow Springs, & now enclose you letters from Alfred Hoyt & Rose.

Three (3) of my Divisions are east of Bear Creek and one near here. Hugh & Charley are here quite well.

Give my love to all. Tell Minnie & Lizzie to write to me. Letters to Memphis will find their way out[.] Ever yours,

W. T. Sherman

ALS, InND: Sherman Family Papers.
1. EES to WTS, October 16 and 17, 1863, SFP.

TO JOHN SHERMAN

HdQrs. Iuka, Oct. 24, 1863

Dear Brother,

I have not written you much of late because I know you to be busy about the Election, and also acted on the Supposition that I would See you about this time. The Election has resulted as you wished for, quite as successfully, and you have reason to be satisfied on that Score.[1] Now make People who vote realize their vote is idle boasting if they dont back it by fighting. If we only had the 300,000 recruits now that the Presidt. has called for next January we would be in condition, but while the Secesh have been conscripting everywhere up to the very Ohio river and almost inside our Military Posts, our Regiments have been melting away from the usual causes. My Corps 15th has now 52 Rgts. Inf. 12 batteries & 1 Cavalry Regt. & some little detachments with an aggregate present for duty 15,595. Of Course the enemy estimates my Corps at 25,000 and I must act accordingly. The reduction of our Ranks has a most depressing effect on the best officers, viz. the Captains & Colonels who fret at seeing their ranks so thin. I think Jeff Davis understands Human Nature better than our Politicians for he made the Universal Draft Popular with the Army of course & the People by putting it on the Ground that it was mean for an able bodied man to Stand back and see the Decimated armies overwhelmed. But I believe you always favored the Draft prompt & quick. It has become a Necessity.

Grant is ordered to Nashville to Command the Grand Army of the Center. Rosecrans Center Sherman Right Wing, Burnside Left—Rosecrans will squirm at this as he & Grant did not agree at all over here last Year. Rosey is ambitious & notoriety seeking, & Grant is the very reverse. Grant encourages his Juniors & takes pleasure in supporting them but I am told that Rosecrans is jealous of the reputation of all his Subordinates. I know that Grant was much displeased with Rosecrans here last Fall, and I apprehend this may lead to complications. Of course I will have nothing to do with such personalities—Grant is an honest plain Sensible well meaning officer and I like that style of man better than Rosecrans—the former tries to have genteel folks near him, whereas Rosecrans is surrounded by Detectives & newspaper sneaks. I dont know but that in the End I will be best off—Newspaper men are afraid of me, and I hope before the war is much older we will be allowed to conscript every citizen of good Physique found about our Camps, on the ground that he has fled to escape the draft. Such an order would have an admirable effect.

I have been delayed here some days on my estimate by the very bad break in the Railroad & my orders are to carry the Railroad forward to Tuscumbia. I expect soon to communicate with Nashville. But I have little Cavalry, whereas the enemy to my front has all of the Cavalry of the South West—I expect every hour a dash on some of my Road Guards.

Two light draft Gunboats is now up at Eastport 8 miles from here and I have sent down for the officer to ride up to See me.

Both you & Cecilia can feel for me the death of Willy—Somehow he was more to me than the other children because he was with me in California and was so wrapt up in me down here. He was utterly fearless, and would ride with me on all reviews, & anywhere I went. He seemed to be in fine health till the very hour we embarked at Vicksburg. Minnie had been quite ill and our thoughts were of her, till attracted to Willy, but really before I was aware of it the Doctor foresaw the danger. Nothing seemed to check the disorder Diarrhea & congestion of the bowels. I miss the child in my thoughts because I had in his future the best hopes. Tom the younger is more violent & headstrong, but not so patient & persistent. I would like to hear from you. I suppose you have given up the New Orleans trip. Love to all, yrs. affectionately

W. T. Sherman

ALS, DLC: William T. Sherman.

1. On October 18, JS had written his brother with his condolences on Willy's death. He had also discussed his pleasure at the Republican triumph in the Ohio elections and his dismay that the draft had not been enforced. DLC: WTS.

TO EDITORS OF THE *MEMPHIS BULLETIN*

Hd. Qrs. Dept. of the Tenn.

Iuka Miss. Octbr. 27. 1863.

Editors of Memphis *Bulletin*

I don't think you can conceive the mortification, a Soldier feels at the nauseating accounts given to the Public as History. That affair at Collierville should have been described in three words "Chalmers tried to take Collierville and didn't"[1]—but ridiculous, nonsensical descriptions have followed each other so fast, that you ought to be ashamed to print Collierville.

Now I am again in authority over you and you must heed my advice. Freedom of speech and freedom of the Press, precious relics of former History, must not be construed too largely. You must print nothing, that prejudices Government or excites envy hatred and malice in a community. Persons in Office or out of Office must not be flattered or abused. Don't publish an account of any skirmish, battle or movement of an Army unless the name of the writer is given in full and printed.

I wish you success, but my first duty is to maintain "Order and Harmony[.]" Yours

W. T. Sherman

Lbk, DNA: RG 94, Records of the Adjutant General's Office, Generals' Books and Papers, William T. Sherman, Letterbook 7; *OR*, I, 31: pt. 1, 765.

1. For Chalmers's attack on Collierville, Tennessee, on October 11, and Sherman's participation, see WTS to David Dixon Porter, October 14, 1863, and to EES, October 14, 1863, above; *PM*, 1:351–53.

TO ELLEN EWING SHERMAN

Hd. Qrs. Iuka Oct. 28, 1863

Dearest Ellen,

I have all your letters up to Oct. 21, and have signed the Power of Attorney & now enclose it. I again reiterate that we did on earth all we could for Poor Willy and he knew how we loved him. Now that he is past all pain & sorrow his Memory must be a strange link in the chain of fammily love that binds us all together. I myself did not realize the hopes & pride I had in him till made manifest by his loss.

I have been delayed here longer than I supposed but my orders were to repair Road as I came, and not approach the Flank of Rosecrans without the means of supply, the roads to his Rear being far overtaxed already. I sent Blair forward to Tuscumbria with Osterhaus & Morgan L. Smiths Division to clear out the cavalry that Swarmed to our front, and I have sent Hughs Division to Florence to cross the River at Eastport where there are two Gunboats. I expect henceforth to draw my supplies from the Tennessee which is now in better boating order than any of the western Rivers. I now command the Dept. and army of the Tennessee, embracing the Corps 15, 16 & 17, Sherman, Hurlbut and McPherson, but as I push east, I will devolve on Corps Commanders large powers made necessary by my being difficult of access. I take to Athens with me my Old Corps 15, and about 8000 of Hurlbuts command, leaving McPherson at Vicksburg and Hurlbut at Memphis. I will establish at Florence a kind of Depot. Address your letters "via Cairo," and I will order our mails to come up the Tennessee. The Tennessee is now up and if Bragg wished he could not come across. Whether Grant will assume the offensive I know not & cannot tell till I get within reach.

Weather is now beautiful. We have had some rain, giving us elegant water, and the roads have dried up so that everything is favorable to us. The enemys cavalry hangs round me and I have not the Cavalry to push them back, but I fulfil our great purpose of clearing Rosecrans flanks & rear.

The Change in the Commands is radical. I dont pretend to understand all the secrets of Rosecrans position. I know that He & Grant had sharp words & feelings over at Corinth & hear a year ago, and that Grant does not like him, besides Rosecrans has all along had a set of flunkeys about him, pouring out the oil of flattery that was sickening to all true men. In my judgment there is no surer index of weakness & meanness than the Common disposition to exaggerate little Skirmishes into Grand Battles. I have ordered the Press in Memphis to dry up, & never again publish Such stuff as followed the Colliersville matter. The way to stop the Missouri Imbroglio is to suppress the Missouri *Republican* & *Democrat*.[1] Take them away and Peace, quiet & order would reign there. I have a notion to make the newspapers in Memphis publish every Sunday the Chapters in Pickwick giving the History of the Great Election & newspaper controversy of "Eatanswill."[2]

I have heretofore written and now repeat that I left "Sam" at Memphis with Capt. Lewis to be sent to Lancaster for you. I am told he was about being sent up in the Lady Jackson to Cincinati. Capt. Lewis understands the business and you will surely receive the horse and will have a Bill of about $25 to pay. Of course you will see that he is taken good care of. I have also sent you a list of the killed & wounded of Regulars at Colliersville, and by express my three (3) letter Books which contain all my official letters at Memphis and during the Vicksburg Campaign. These are now complete, and I now enter on a new series.

Capt. Pitzman is here on a visit quite recovered of his wound, but is a candidate for Surveyor of St. Louis County. I of course approve his being a candidate and he is here to get the vote of the Missouri Regts.

Sawyer is here also on a visit, but returns to Illinois. His father wants to come to serve as a volunteer aid for the winter.

Hammond is still about at Vicksburg and Sawyer goes with me. I must leave with the Corps the Corps Staff—but we will be together all the time. I will keep the Regulars near me. They are in fine order and the Band ditto. The latter has lost one musician and several of their instruments were taken out of the cars. I have just heard from Blair at Tuscumbria and I shall move in person to Florence as soon as I have concluded certain other preliminary arrangements. I am very glad to Know that Tom & Minnie are doing so well. I fear little they will have the wonted health. Give all my love and believe me ever yrs.,

W. T. Sherman

ALS, InND: Sherman Family Papers.

1. WTS here refers to the split between rival groups of Missouri Republicans over issues of slavery and reconstruction.

2. This episode of *The Pickwick Papers* was one of Dickens's commentaries on the corruption and folly of contemporary politics.

TO JAMES B. BINGHAM[1]

Hd. Qrs. Dept. of the Tenn.
Fayetteville Tenn. Novbr. 9, 63

J. B. Bingham, Esqr.
Editor "Memphis Bulletin."
Dear Sir—

Yours of Octbr. 30th overtook me here, as I paused for my column to close up. I admit I find it difficult to define clearly my wishes as to the conduct of the Press in this Department.

The insatiable desire for "news" startling & poignant is so great, that an Editor, catering to the taste of the public, must prepare his food accordingly. I believe in Freedom as near absolute, as is consistent with safety. I believe in free thought, free speech and free Press—but the moment we think we see that each of these freedoms must be limited, else in bad hands they generate discord, confusion and War; resulting in Military Rule, Despotism and *no* freedom at all, thus forming a circle of events, which the history of every old nation has exemplified.

You or any fair man, looking back on the history of our own country for the past forty years must admit, that the Press has gradually intensified the feelings of mutual jealousy and hatred between the North and the South till war not only resulted, but was bound to result. You see yet the Press of each Section, instead of healing the gap, is vigorously widening it. Now, this country *must be* united, by the silken bonds of a generous and kindly union if possible; or by the harsh, steel bands of a Despot otherwise. Of course we all prefer the former. In that event the Press will have freedom regulated by Statute Law, in the other, their freedom will be one sided as in France, a freedom to praise and sustain the Government, but death to oppose.

If all men were good, we would need no Law or restraint, but unfortunately, some will steal and murder, and commit all sorts of crime and therefore punishment and pain must be resorted to. So if the Editors were filled with a desire to do right they would allay rather than arouse the passions of men they would publish the Truth alone, and would slander nobody; but unfortunately some editors have an object to serve, to pull down one man or interest, to elevate another and so on. Now you know, and every Editor is conscious when he does right, but he may have some motive to serve, that biasses his judgment, therefore even in peaceful times, I would make every Publisher liable in money for the Truth of every thing he prints. I would not allow him to publish anonymous precis and throw off by saying, the author was so & so. I would make the Editor responsible 1st—that all, he publishes is true, 2d—that the publication was necessary to the Public good. Even if true, I would make him liable as in slander and libel, and in times of War and Insurrection, I would restrict them altogether, for the reasons, that in Wars & Insurrection which suspend the functions of the Courts and Civil Offices, the executive of a nation by his Army and Navy must control all the Physique and Morale of the Nation, to restore such Peace and quiet, as will enable the courts to resume their sway.

In my Department I contend, that subordinate to the Powers above, I have a right to use every man, every influence, every moral, intellectual and physical power, within my limits to restore quiet, order, Peace and finally produce the restoration of the Civil Power when "*eo instante*" this Civil Government having regained its vitality, resumes its wonted control. These ideas are very general and not very specific but they give you the Key to my conduct.

If a man disturbs the Peace, I will kill or remove him, if he does anything wrong and there is no Civil Power in existence, the Military Power does exist and must act, for we must have some Law. "Nature abhors Anarchy"—As of a man so of a combination, or the Press, or anything. All must act in concert to stop War, strife anarchy. When these are done, Peace restored, Civil Courts & Law respected, then you and all are free again. yours

W. T. Sherman Maj. Genl.

Lbk, DNA: RG 94, Records of the Adjutant General's Office, Generals' Books and Papers, William T. Sherman, Letterbook 7; *OR*, I, 31: pt. 3, 97–98.

1. James B. Bingham (ca. 1830–fl. 1881) purchased the *Memphis Bulletin* in May 1861 and edited it during the Federal occupation of the city.

TO JAMES E. YEATMAN

Head Qrs. Army of the Tenn.
Fayetteville Tenn. Novbr. 9, 1863

Jas. E. Yeatman, Esqr.
St. Louis Mo.
My Dear Sir,

I received your letter, asking me to send you back a pass to come forward to Iuka. Of course you had no means of knowing the changes then contemplated and will be disappointed to find me away from here with the "Army" of the Tennessee whilst the "Department" remains behind.

If all men had the pure charity and manliness that you have always displayed, and if all Soldiers have the plain singleness of purpose, which I profess, how delightful would be the relations of life.

I enclose you a paper, which you may keep and only exhibit when necessary, as I would not like to be asked for a similar paper by too many in this selfish world.

I acknowledge fully that your Commission has done a world of good and have enacted "charity" in that quiet and unostentatious manner that must command the love of all—and your agents have always acted with that subordination to authority, which is the result of "Union"—the Union, that we strive for—With great respect your friend,

W. T. Sherman
Maj. Genl. Comdg.

Lbk, DNA: RG 94, Records of the Adjutant General's Office, Generals' Books and Papers, William T. Sherman, Letterbook 7.

TO ELLEN EWING SHERMAN

Bridgeport, Novr. 17, 1863.

Dearest Ellen,

I got here four days ago, and went up to Chattanooga to See Genl. Grant. I got back last night and find many letters, all of which I must answer now as tomorrow I move back to Chattanooga with the 15th Army corps. Hugh has already started, another Division is moving, and all will be off by tomorrow.

The enemy still invests Chattanooga in force and we must drive them back. Great difficulty has existed to Supply Chattanooga and I cannot now explain it and I hate to take my troops & horses & mules up into that mountain Gorge, where our men will be half starved and horses totally So. I have all your letters up to the 12th[1] two from Minnie and one from Lizzie. I will answer all at length as soon as I can. We are all well. I regret that you have to go to Washington, and I wish your father would remain at home. If he be afflicted as you say he ought to remain tranquil and give up all business. I know it would be hard thus for him to remain, but I only wish he would do so. I approve highly Theresa's hurrying at once, tell her so. When parties are agreed the Sooner they consummate the marriage the better for all concerned. Give her and Col. Steele[2] my best love. I hope & trust your mother & father may live many years yet in quiet.

We cannot expect any rest, and it is for this reason I so prefer you to be at Lancaster. The next year is going to be the hardest of the war. I see no signs of relaxation on the part of the South. Every man is now in their army, and ours is fearfully small from detachments & Sick. I will have my hands full, and must do my best. Logan[3] will command the 15th Corps and Hurlbut & McPherson the others.

I am very busy.

Love to all, yrs.

W. T. Sherman

ALS, InND: Sherman Family Papers.

1. These letters focused on Thomas Ewing Sr.'s activities; EES to WTS, October 23 and November 9 and 10, 1863, SFP.

2. Colonel Clement F. Steele had joined the service at the outbreak of the war and had met Ellen's sister in 1862 when he was in Lancaster on recruiting duty. He had been wounded in the attack on Fort Wagner and was invalided out of the service in the summer of 1863. He and Theresa were married on November 24, and he took over the management of the Ewing family saltworks at Chauncey.

3. Major General John Alexander Logan (1826–86), USA, a lawyer and politician, commanded the Fifteenth Corps as of December 11, 1863.

TO JAMES B. McPHERSON

Hd. Qrs. Army of the Tenn.
Bridgeport, Novbr. 18, 1863.

Maj. Genl. Jas. B. McPherson, Comd'g. Vicksburg.

General—

I enclose for your action a paper, purporting to be a Petition of certain Citizens of Tensas Parish to organize a Police force to restrain excesses on the part of the negroes. The statement of facts in the paper varies so widely from that made by General Hawkins,[1] to whom it has been referred, that I can not consent to the prayer of the Petitioners.

My theory and practice on the negro question are simple and easily understood.

The Masters by rebelling have freed the negro and have taken from themselves the Courts and Machinery by which any real Law could be enforced in their country. By themselves, sons, friends and relations firing upon us, the

Army of the U.S. in the execution of our lawful office, they have engendered a suspicion, that prevent us trusting them with arms. They must bear the terrible infliction, which has overtaken them, and blame the authors of the rebellion and not the U.S.

The U.S. has its hands full, and must first assert its authority and maintain it as against the Armies of the Confederacy, and then it will have time to give some attention to these negroes who have been turned loose by the Planters and former owners.

At present there is no law, regulating contracts of labor and no Courts to interpret such Laws or alleged infraction.

The Army is not the Tribunal, even to discuss such trivial matters. It is merely to suppress *all* disorders on the part of all, White, Indian and negro, but not to judge of contracts of labor or of any kind.

The white men, who want Laws and contracts to be enforced, and civil order, must go to work to establish a Government—and being the judge, I as a Military Commander say, that the only evidence of their sincerity, which I will entertain, is their enlistment in one of our organized Regiments of Soldiers, whose first duty it is, to destroy the rebel armies and then to build up the civil Govt. which will regulate all manner of contracts, such as are embraced in the Petition.

You as Military Commander in that region and each subordinate in his sphere will suppress all riots disorders and irregularities, that disturb the peace but need not bother yourselves about the rights or wrongs growing out of differences between Masters and Servants, the employer and employed. That is none of our business, I am &c.

W. T. Sherman
Maj. General Comdg.

Lbk, DNA: RG 94, Records of the Adjutant General's Office, Generals' Books and Papers, William T. Sherman, Letterbook 7.

1. Brigadier General John P. Hawkins (1830–1914), USA, was commanding a brigade of black troops in the District of Northeastern Louisiana.

TO JOHN A. LOGAN

Hd. Qrs. Dept. of the Tennessee
Nashville, Decbr. 21, 1863

Logan, John A. Maj. Genl.
Comdg. 15th A. C., Bridgeport.
Dear General—

I got here last night, stay over to day and go to Louisville to morrow. I have seen Genl. Grant, and General Dodge is also here. I think I can see the drift of events for a short time ahead and you should know them. I will go home for

Christmas (the first for more than 20 years) but on the 2d of January will start for Cairo and in concert with Admiral Porter must do something to check the boldness of our enemy in attacking Boats on the Mississippi. To secure the safety of the navigation of the Mississippi, I would slay Millions. On that point I am not only insane, but mad. Fortunately, the Great West is with me there. I think I see one or two quick blows, that will astonish the natives of the South and will convince them, that though to stand behind a big cottonwood and shoot at a passing Boat is good sport and safe that it may still reach and kill their friends and families, hundreds of miles off. For every bullett, shot at a Steamboat I would shoot a thousand 30 pdr. Parrotts into even helpless Towns on Red, Washita, Yazoo, or wherever a Boat can float or Soldier march.

Well—I think in all January and part of February I can do something in this Line. In the mean time Dodge will go on in concert with the Contractor in putting the Nashville and Decatur Road in order, you will have to take that from Stevenson to Decatur, so timing your work, that you will be done as soon as he.

We will then have a triangle of R. R.—Nashville the apex and the base along the Tennessee. You are to repair and hold this base; gather forage and supplies and be ready for the next great move. A part of this contemplates crossing the Tennessee, for which you have 70 Pontoons. Let Jenney[1] have a Saw-mill and get out balks and chesses for that length of bridge. Keep the Boats well guarded in any creek above Guntersville, as near as possible to one of your Divisions. Keep your Corps stationed by Divisions, and if Detachments are called for, let them go out from the nearest Division.

General Grant tells me, he has already ordered a Brigade to Huntsville— send a whole Division and instead of Keeping the corps between Paint Rock and Stevenson, let it stretch down to Huntsville or even Athens, but so arranged, that concentration is easy. The enemy however, cannot cross the Tennessee, save in squads.

Grant may want you some time to feign on Rome, if so, the proper way will be to cross at Guntersville a Division, very lightly equipped to move out on the old Huntsville and Rome Road towards the Coosa, near Gaylesville, but of this you can judge as soon as you see the country. I would like my Head Quarters, Army in the field, at Huntsville, with 13th Regulars and 3d U.S. Cavalry as Hd. Qrs. Guard.

Remember, the 5th Ohio Cavalry belongs to you. I left it temporarily on Hiwassee with orders to join you as soon as Col. Longs[2] Brigade was reenforced, but unless you watch them, the Regt. will be gobbled.

If weather continues good, I advise you to slip the corps down to their positions as soon as possible, for we are liable to have rain and very bad roads in winter.

Athens, Huntsville, Paint Rock and Larkinsville would be a good distribution for the four Divisions, with outposts forward on the Tennessee at fords and ferries. Your friend

W. T. Sherman
Maj. General

Lbk, DNA: RG 94, Records of the Adjutant General's Office, Generals' Books and Papers, William T. Sherman, Letterbook 7; *OR*, I, 31: pt. 3, 459–60.

1. William LeBaron Jenney (1832–1907) was Sherman's chief engineer.

2. Colonel Eli Long (1837–1903), USA, commanded the Second Brigade, Second Division, of the cavalry of the Army of the Cumberland.

TO JOHN SHERMAN

Lancaster Dec. 29, 1863

Dear Brother,

As soon as I got here I telegraphed to Charles, not knowing where you were, and shortly after got your dispatch from Mansfield telling me you would be there till Monday and asking if we could not meet. As I only can stay here two more days I could not attempt Mansfield and had to leave it to you whether to come to Lancaster or not. I hear you have gone on to New York and therefore I must go off without seeing you. I have been off the Line of communication since leaving Memphis save a few hours at Bridgeport during which I had hardly time to put my official signature to papers demanding my hand. I have made a Report of our movements up to the return to Bridgeport and enclose it with this a copy which I brought here and which you may keep,[1] only of course under the confidence of absolute secresy till the War Dept. thinks proper to make the original public. In this I was right, am right, and time will sanction my adherence to the Rule. In civil office the incumbent comes so immediately from the People that he naturally looks to the People as the Govt. but we sworn officers of the military Govt. look to the Constituted Authorities, and to them alone. I have no doubt Mr. Lincoln would sleep easier of nights if all officers civil & military would be as tenacious as I have been on this point.

I suppose you will read this Report and I invite attention to the part referring to the Assault on Tunnel Hill. I know that Grant in his Report will dwell on this same part. I was provoked that Meigs, looking at us from Chattanooga should report me repulsed, and that Mr. Stanton should publish his letter as senior official.[2] Meigs apologized to me for using Thomas name instead of mine throughout which he charged to a copyist but made no amends for the Repulse.[3] The whole philosophy of the Battle was that I should get by a dash a position on the Extremity of Missionary Ridge from which the enemy would be forced to drive me, or allow his Depot at Chickamauga

Station to be in danger. I expected Bragg to attack me at daylight, but he did not and to bring matters to a crisis quick, as time was precious for the Sake of Burnside in East Tennessee Grant ordered me to assume the offensive. My Report contains the rest—again after the Battle, Granger[4] was ordered to push for Knoxville, but his movements were so slow that Grant impatient called on me, and my move was the most rapid of the war & perfectly successful. I could have gone on after Longstreet,[5] but Burnside Ranked me and it was his business not mine. So I reenforced him all he asked & returned.

The 15th Corps now Logans & Dodges Divn. of the 16th Corps are now at work on the Railroad from Nashville to Decatur, & from Decatur to Stevenson thus making a triangle of Railroad which it is Estimated will relieve the great difficulty of supplies which has parallized the Army of the Cumberland. This will take 5 weeks. I leave my Hd. Qrs. at Huntsville and go in person down the Mississipi to strike some lateral blows to punish the country for allowing Guerillas to attack the Boats. I go on Friday to Cincinati, and then to Cairo where with Adml. Porter I will concert measures to produce the result. I expect to send an Expedition up the Yazoo, and go myself with another up Red River, levying a contribution to make good losses to Boats, & punish for death & wounds inflicted. I think we can make People feel that they must actively prevent Guerillas from Carrying out their threat, that though we have the River it will do us no good. My address will be Memphis for a month, and Huntsville after. We can hardly fashion out the next campaign but it looks as though we would have to move from the Tennessee River. I would prefer to take Mobile & the Alabama, as well as the Chattahoochee, & move east from Montgomery and Columbus Miss.

I wish you would introduce a Bill into Congress increasing the number of Cadets on this Basis—one from each congressional district *per annum*. In districts not represented vest the appointment in the Sec. of War out of Boys not over 18 in the Armies in the Field, to be selected in any manner that may be prescribed by Law, or by the Regulations of the President.

This would hold out to young fellows the prospect of getting a cadetship. Last summer we were called on to recommend candidates, and I was amazed to find so many worthy applicants. All who came forward for examination preferred West Point to a commission. The great want of the Army is good Subordinate officers. The army is a good school, but West Point is better. It is useless to deny that a special preliminary education is necessary to the military officer, and the cheapest school is now at West Point susceptible of infinite increase. The mode I point out is simple & just & simply multiplies the cadets by four, and as states come back, with representation they recover their proper proportion of Cadets. Whilst in rebellion, the armies of invasion or occupation are fairly entitled to their Share. The Cost of Increase will hardly exceed the annual expense of a Regiment and will give us two hundred good officers per annum. It is unwise in Congress to legislate on the Supposition that the war must soon end. Better look to the worst and if peace should come it will be easy enough to curtail. If you are willing to take the initiative in this, send for General J. G. Barnard U.S. Engineers and Show him what I have written and he can frame a Bill. Or if he be absent see General Hitchcock, General Cullum[6] or Colonel James A. Hardie[7] in the Adjt. Genls. office.

Barnard is most industrious and could give you all statistics, but either of the others would do the same.

I think the Presidents Proclamation[8] unwise knowing the temper of the South I know that it but protracts the war by seeming to court Peace. It to them looks like weakness. I tell them that as they cool off, we warm to the work, that we are just getting ready for the war, and I know the effect is better than to coax them to come back into the Union. The organization of a Civil Govt. but complicates the Game. All the Southern States will need a pure military Govt. for years after resistance has ceased. You have noticed the debate in Richmond on the Presidents Proclamation. That is a true exhibit of the Feeling South. Dont fall into the error that the masses think different. Of course property holding classes south deplore the devastation that marks the progress of their own and our armies, but the South is no longer consulted. The army of the Confederacy is the South, and they Still hope to worry us out. The moment we relax they gain strength & confidence. We must hammer away and show strict persistence, such bottom that even that Slender hope will fail them. Even after that, will remain a large body of armed men that never did or will work, and war to them is both a necessity & pleasure.

Dont allow yourself to be drawn into a league against Halleck. He has more capacity than any man in our army. Grant has qualities that Halleck does not possess but not such as would qualify him to command the whole army. The war has not yet developed Hallecks equal as a General in Chief.

Of course no man could make an army so near Washington as the Army of the Potomac. Unless you can manage to bring over Lee & his army, you must needs wait till we reenlist & recruit our Army of the Mississipi and Swing round by Georgia & the Carolinas. This will take more than a year.

I still am opposed to *all* Bounties. The Draft pure & simple—annual—to fill vacancies in the Ranks. Pay of men in the Front increased to 25, 30 or even 40 a month and that of men at Depots, Hospitals and to the rear diminished to a bare maintenance—if not less—$400 Bounty is an absurd commentary when ⅔ draw bounty, remain absent from their ranks, & are discharged for disability without hearing a shot. Deal with the Army as you would if you were hiring men for Special work. Those who do the work pay high—those who are sick, unfortunate or shirking pay little or nothing—Same of officers from the Major General to Lieutenant—The President *must* make vacancies for the rising officers, the "*Creations*" of the War. I am willing to quit if a Younger & better man can be found for my place, indeed I may anyhow as soon as I feel I have done my share.

I would like to have met you, but I could not possibly spare time, and you had doubtless cut out your work before you heard of my coming. Love to Cecilia & all yr. brother,

W. T. Sherman

ALS, DLC: William T. Sherman.

1. WTS to John A. Rawlins, December 19, 1863, *OR*, I, 31: pt. 2, 568–83.

2. Montgomery C. Meigs to Edwin M. Stanton, November 26, 1863, was published in the *New York Tribune* on November 30. Having viewed the Battle of Chattanooga from a vantage point atop Orchard Knob, Meigs told Stanton that on November 24 WTS had launched an assault on Bragg's right on a peak next to the one on which WTS and his troops were entrenched. "The assault was gallantly made, reached the edge of the crest, held its ground for what seemed to me an hour, but was then bloodily repulsed by reserves." DLC: WTS.

3. Meigs to WTS, December 6, 1863, DLC: WTS. Meigs sent WTS a copy of his original letter so that Sherman would know that he had tried to give him credit; a copyist had inadvertently written Thomas's name for WTS's. DLC: WTS.

4. Robert S. Granger (1816–94), USA, was commanding the post at Nashville.

5. Lieutenant General James Longstreet (1821–1904), CSA, had been sent to support Bragg in the West in September 1863.

6. George W. Cullum (1809–92), USA, was Halleck's chief of staff.

7. James A. Hardie (1823–76), USA, was assistant adjutant general.

8. On December 8, Lincoln had published his Proclamation of Amnesty and Reconstruction, pardoning rebellious Southerners if they took an oath of loyalty to the United States, with the exceptions of high-ranking military officers, those who resigned commissions in the United States military forces to join the Confederate service, members of the Confederate government, and those Southerners who had not treated black or white soldiers lawfully as prisoners of war. If 10 percent of the citizens of a rebellious state who had voted in 1860 met the criteria and voted in a new state government, it would be recognized as legitimate by Lincoln. Slavery, however, would have to be prohibited.

TO JOHN SHERMAN

Lancaster, Dec. 30, 1863

Dear Brother,

Susan arrived this evening and brought me your letter of the 28. I should like to have seen you, but I have written you a long letter telling you all you want to Know from me.

Ellen wants me to write to you about a picture of Father[1] which she has received from Brady of New York.[2] It bears no one feature of father and is not recognized by Mr. Ewing, Reese or anybody. I have a faint memory of his face and know the picture is not at all a likeness, but I do see that it is an Enlargement of a small miniature that Mother[3] had. I wish you would write to Ellen whether you want her to pay for this & how much. If you ordered the miniature copied & enlarged it must be paid for, but if Brady made the picture at a venture he has lost, for it is no likeness. We will of course bear our proportion of the cost—You had better pay the Bill and let Ellen know her share. Ellen says she has forgotten what you told her at Cincinati about it, but thinks you said the cost would be 48 Dollars.

I have been importuned from many quarters for my likeness, Autographs, & Biography. I have managed to fend off all parties & hope to do So till the End of the War. I dont want to rise or be notorious for the reason that a mere slip or accident may let me fall, and I dont care about falling so far as most of the temporary heros of the War. The Real men of the War will be determined by the closing scenes, and then the army will determine the questions. Newspaper puffs and Self written Biographies will then be ridiculous caricatures. Already has time marked this progress & indicated this conclusion.

If parties apply to you for materials in my behalf, give the most brief & general items and leave the result to the close of the war, or of my Career. As well might a Judge or Senator seek for fame outside their sphere of action as an officer of the Army. We must all be judged by One Press, stand or fall by their verdict. I know I Stand very high with the Army & feel no concern on the Score. Today I can do more with Admiral Porter or the Generals out west than any General Officers out west except Grant, and with him I am as a second self. We are personal and official friends. On this score you can see Dana, who was with me at Knoxville. I would on no account come East and will so far as I can control it hold fast to the Mississipi.

My Hd. Qrs. are at Huntsville Ala., but for the next month you can address me at Memphis. I will be there or below it may be as far as Red River.

Tell Mr. Lincoln he ought to clear the Docket of Generals, to make room for the rising Generation of young Colonels whom he must advance. From thence must come the Successful Generals of the War. The old ones must slide out. By manufacturing commands for Old Generals as in Curtis case,[4] he ties up the army which should be in moving masses to the Front. Affectionately &c.

W. T. Sherman

ALS, DLC: William T. Sherman.

1. Charles Sherman (d. 1829).

2. Mathew Brady (1823–96), known for his innovative battlefield photographs, ran a respected portrait studio in New York City.

3. Mary Hoyt Sherman (d. 1852).

4. Samuel Curtis had been assigned to the Department of Kansas in May 1863.

CHAPTER 10

January 6, 1864–May 4, 1864

*I*n 1864 William T. Sherman finally got another chance to exercise independent command. By now the ghosts that had plagued him since 1861 were gone (although he did not forget them). Under Grant's tutelage he had learned much about what it really took to be a good general. Although Sherman would retain a residual fondness for Henry W. Halleck, he came to understand that Grant, not Halleck, was the Union's true military genius.

In February Sherman embarked on a campaign to destroy the railroads and strip the countryside in central Mississippi. With a select force of approximately twenty thousand soldiers, mostly infantry regiments, he advanced eastward from Vicksburg, tearing up railways as he went before reaching Meridian. The result severely damaged the Confederate rail net and hampered the enemy's ability to draw supplies from the area, reducing the threat of a substantial enemy counteroffensive in this area during 1864. "Of course I must fight when the time comes," he told his daughter Minnie, "but whenever a result can be accomplished without Battle I prefer it."[1] The campaign was not without its memories, for as Sherman crossed the Big Black, where he had once pitched his headquarters tent, his memories of Willy became so strong that he could almost see his son running toward him. The Meridian Campaign also served as a preview of what was to come later that year in Georgia.

No sooner had Sherman returned to Vicksburg than he learned that Grant was headed east to assume the position of general in chief with the rank of lieutenant general. Grant generously attributed the contributions of his subordinates to his success; in turn, Sherman revealed how important Grant's example and unwavering belief in ultimate victory had been in building up his own confidence. "My only points of doubt were as to your knowledge of grand strategy, and books of science and history," he admitted, thus suggesting the origins of his reverence toward Halleck; "but I confess your common-sense seems to have supplied all this."[2] So long as Grant kept himself apart from the political intrigues of Washington, Sherman believed he would triumph.

Elevated to replace Grant as head of the Military Division of the Mississippi, Sherman knew he would play a major role in the coming spring campaign. His assignment was expressed simply by Grant: "You I propose to move against Johnston's Army, to break it up and to get into the interior of the enemy's country as far as you can, inflicting all the damage you can against their War resources." How Sherman went about this was up to him.[3] Politics, however, was never far from both men's minds, for the Lincoln administration insisted that Nathaniel P. Banks be allowed to conduct an expedition up the Red River, thus delaying the use of his men to capture Mobile, Alabama. That Banks retained one of Sherman's corps was bad enough; that the president had reassigned John A. McClernand to command it was almost too much. It was no surprise to Sherman to learn that Banks's drive resulted in a fiasco in April, although he still regretted that he could not get his corps back in time for the spring offensive.

Otherwise, however, Sherman was in good humor. Not only did he appreciate the advantages that would accrue to the Union cause from Grant's efforts to coordinate the movements of his armies, but he also realized that his friend had taken upon himself the task of defeating Robert E. Lee and the Army of Northern Virginia. Grant understood the psychological as well as military importance of this confrontation, although he himself thought the decisive blow could be struck in Georgia against Joseph E. Johnston's Army of Tennessee. Sherman would have about one hundred thousand men in all to accomplish that task.

In the winter of 1864 Sherman pondered anew about the roots of the war and how best to wage it. With tongue in cheek he admitted that there was a right of secession—so long as those who seceded moved elsewhere. Many Southern whites, he believed, would someday accept the restoration of the Union; however, he recommended that the most bitter rebels "be killed or sent away."[4] He justified the destruction of enemy property and his views on the treatment of Confederate civilians, endeavoring to show with historical examples that his actions were well within the accepted rules of war and adding that he would treat generously all those who returned to the fold. Although he now accepted the destruction of slavery as warranted by circumstances, he had no interest in mobilizing black men for combat, believing them incapable of serving well. In his eyes the enlistment of blacks offered lazy Northern whites yet another way to avoid enlistment, leaving them at home in the position of armchair generals and critics. Nor was he surprised by reports that Confederate soldiers under the command of Nathan Bedford Forrest had butchered a black and white Federal garrison at Fort Pillow, Tennessee. "I feel certain the war will soon become barbarous," he observed, "but it is inevitable."[5] For now, it was enough to prepare for the spring campaign.

1. WTS to Maria Boyle Ewing Sherman, January 19, 1864.
2. WTS to USG, March 10, 1864.

3. USG to WTS, April 4, 1864, *PUSG*, 10:252.
4. WTS to JS, January 28, 1864.
5. WTS to JS, April 22, 1864.

TO MARIA BOYLE EWING SHERMAN
U.S. Gunboat "Juliet"
Near Cairo January 6, 1864

My Dear Minnie,

I am now on board the pleasant little Gunboat Juliet, in the Ohio River, approaching Cairo, having been to Paducah to examine that Post. I shall delay a few hours at Cairo and pass down to Columbus, and down to Memphis. It is all we can do to get along for the ice, which is fast closing up the River, but the ice rarely if ever closes the Mississipi below Cairo.

I cannot tell you how bad I felt to leave you alone at that School in Cincinati but it is so important you should now be studying that I could not help it. I hope the next day you got out to Mount Notre Dame, and that you met there not only Kind Sisters, but congenial Companions. While I want you to learn all a young lady should Know I am equally anxious that you should be associated with agreeable pleasant People. Though but a Child in Years you know how we love you, how for years in California, in Kansas, Louisiana and on the Battle field my little Minnie has been the object of almost adoration. Oh, how I have hoped that Some chance would allow me to get you all together in some home where we could travel along our Earthly journey together. Already Willy is gone from us, and you are growing into woman-hood, before I have had the time to Know you, but I feel assured that you will in some way remember me and make my later years compensation for our long separation. There is nothing I have or can obtain that you shall not have by asking if for your good, and in return you must tell me every thing that happens to you or interests you, no matter what, tell me, and you need not fear. I want you to be acquainted with all whom you naturally meet, but reserve your friendship for such as you specially admire, or who are likely to be your associates in after life. I know Girls will think of their beaus. I dont want you to be an exception, on the contrary, but marriage should not be even thought of or promised until after sixteen. Indeed 18 or 20 are better, but all I will ever ask you is always to be frank and candid in this as well as all other Subjects to your Mama & me. We are the best friends you will ever have in this world, and sensible as we are, we will never impose on you any unreasonable restraints or conditions. I would rather think of Minnie as a little child creeping up to me for protection, but I know She is no longer a Child and only ask her to retain that affection & confidence of childhood, which is the most beautiful & loving feature of women of any life or station. I want you to Know

Mrs. Col. Swords, and the favorites of Mr. L'Hommedieu and Larz Anderson as they may come to See you or may send for you at some vacation[.] Write to me as often as you can, and to Mama & Lizzie quite as often. Never forget or neglect Lizzie who will be to you as a companion long after I am gone, & it may be forgotten.

You may not hear from me or of me for some weeks, but you Know that I think of you always, and that I will write when I can. Many friends have already enquired for you, and more will down at Vicksburg, and all will be made happy to Know that you are recovered from the sickness of last Summer. Yr. affectionate father,

W. T. Sherman

ALS, OHi: William T. Sherman Papers.

TO ELLEN EWING SHERMAN

Memphis, Jan. 11, 1864

Dearest Ellen,

I only got here yesterday, four days floating down the Arctic Ice, think of Ice floating by New Orleans but it must be so. All the way from Cairo here the River was one mass of floating Ice and navigation above is closed by ice, and even below it is very bad. I find all things here as I expected. Only Forrest is below, joined to the Same Brigade that used to hover on my front at Big Black. It is exceedingly difficult to deal with these Mounted Devils and I am sure all we can do is to make the Country feel that the People must pay for these wandering Arabs. I will run down to Vicksburg, and back to Memphis and be ready to start on some expedition by the 20th. I may strike for Meridian and Selma. I wrote you from the Gunboat *Juliet*, telling you that I left Minnie in Cincinati with orders to Send her out to the College, Mount Notre Dame.[1] Phil will also tell you all about it. I would feel much better Could I have gone out, but the day was bitter cold, and we were employed all day. I ought to be well schooled now at parting but really I felt bad to leave Minnie alone in that dark house, Almost as bad as when Lizzie clung to me as for life in the School at Mrs. Kings Old House. I confess myself amazed at the calm & easy manner of Minnie at all times, unabashed, almost too much so for her years, and yet she seems loving and kind. To me she acts somewhat like Willie with that Simple confidence that is very captivating. She will make a beautiful woman, and we cannot be too careful of her in her next three years. I must be away, and you have your hands full, but I saw that even in Cincinati you & I have friends that will watch her with parental Care. I wrote to Mrs. Swords, and She will be like a hen with a Single Chicken. I would not be surprised if she were to make herself Minnies confidante. Tell Tommie I will draw him a good picture one of these days. Today my pen has been going for ten hours, and I have signed the death warrant of several soldiers, two negros & one Guerilla, all for murder & hard crimes. People here have Crowded about all day and seem disappointed I am not coming here to Stay, but I will make some salutary changes. I will put Buckland in Command.[2] I Know him to be sober, industrious and honest.

Hurlbut will Command the District but I will take him with me down to Vicksburg and out to Meridian.[3]

I came down in a Gunboat *Juliet*—small but very comfortable, have been very well, but now am hoarse, but no sore throat or other ailment—a great many have inquired after you most kindly, Colonel Cockrill, General Hurlbut, Valeria—& Mrs. Williamson. The latter is unwell, but sent her little daughter & son to call and insist on my coming out, fear I cant go.

This cold weather will try our troops up the Tennessee. You need not fear I will let Condit Smith, Sanger or anybody put any cause of difference between Charley & me—No danger. I dont object to your having strong dislikes & expressing them to me, but I do object to your stooping to noticing any man with whom you may be as a stranger, or putting any one between me & you. Leave me to play my game of life and I honestly believe you will be satisfied. I am now past forty & according to natural Law cant change and you must take me "for worse." Yrs. Ever

W. T. Sherman

ALS, InND: Sherman Family Papers.
1. WTS to EES, January 5, 1864, SFP.
2. Ralph Buckland would command the District of Memphis from January 25 through June.
3. Hurlbut would command the Sixteenth Corps through April.

TO ELLEN EWING SHERMAN

On Board Silver Cloud,
Jan. 19, 1864.

Dearest Ellen,

I am now returning from Vicksburg to Memphis, and will be there tomorrow, and by the 25–6th inst. I expect to embark again for Vicksburg with Genl. Hurlbut and a large part of his command to march inland for Meridian & Demopolis. If I can keep it from the enemy I will succeed, otherwise may be checkmated but we must in war risk a good deal. The boat shakes so I can hardly write but you are so familiar with my scrawl that you can get my meaning if you can make out one word of three. I found Vicksburg as we left it—McPherson at Mrs. Edwards, two of the Girls at home, a third in the Country. Coolbaugh has gone to Mexico via New Orleans[1]—No body is at our old Camp, but a Brigade is at the Railroad Bridge and another at the Creek where you remember we found a wagon upset and had to go round—Where the newspapers represented 30,000 negro Soldiers, and Gen. Thomas represented 6000, I found 2100. This ridiculous exaggeration in the end will kill Thomas as it should. He ought to know that the Truth will manifest itself. I had ordered Genl. Hawkins who commands the negros to have 4000 ready on my arrival, and he was mortified & feared I would blame him. There are some Negro troops at Port Hudson, at Natchez and Vicksburg but their aggregate will fall far short of public expectation, and if the Government depends on them and relaxes its efforts to procure white men we may lose the coming year. We have not Seen a Guerilla on the River, and from all accounts Boats run to & from New Orleans with little Risk, as we went down the River was full of floating ice, but it is now clear, but we expect to meet some before we reach Memphis. The severity of the winter down here was as great as with you. At Memphis the Ponds froze 5 inches thick and at Vicksburg, ice formed in patches in the house. It is expected that the floating ice reached the Gulf of Mexico, which will be an extraordinary phenomenon. At Vicksburg they had no coal & all the wood was green so that People shivered around the dull fires. Now the Sun is bright & warm, and we hope the worst is past. February is usually a pleasant month South and I hope to have good weather for my trip.

I suppose the newspapers carried to you the fact that the People of Memphis offered me a public Demonstration and that I accepted—I must soon endure the affliction and will be as careful as possible. If I can yet avoid it without discourtesy I will but suppose I must submit. In what form it will appear I yet dont know but I will be called on to Speak, & must be careful, as I know full well there is a clique who would be happy to catch me tripping—I do believe I can do more on the Mississipi that any Genl. officer in the Service except Grant. Admiral Porter & myself are most friendly—he has given me a Gunboat, and I am now on board of one. I enclose you a slip from the Memphis Bulletin which is a little strong but I would like to have it reprinted in California. If you write to Mr. & Mrs. Casserly[2] I wish you would enclose it & say that I am desirous my California friends should see I am doing good Service—I see that John Sherman has given "Mack"[3] access to papers I have sent him & he is publishing them "without my consent." Well so be it.

I hope your mother & father continue as well as when I left—I have as yet only the letter written by you the day after I left, but at Memphis shall receive more. Write me at Memphis till 15th February. yrs. ever

W. T. Sherman

ALS, InND: Sherman Family Papers.
1. George Coolbaugh had apparently been sent with the Federal troops dispatched to

protect and remove the U.S. consul at Matamoros, Mexico, where two Mexican factions were fighting.

2. Eugene Casserly (1820–83), an Irish-born journalist and lawyer in California, would be U.S. senator from the state from 1869 to 1873.

3. Joseph B. McCullagh of the *Cincinnati Commercial*, who the previous year had passed stories about Grant's drinking to editor Murat Halstead.

TO MARIA BOYLE EWING SHERMAN

Steamboat Silver Cloud—
January 19, 1864

Dearest Minnie,

I am now returning to Memphis from Vicksburg where I found Gen. McPherson and all the Gentlemen we used to meet there except Col. Cool-baugh who has gone to Mexico. All enquired very kindly for you and were delighted to know that you had recovered from your illness. I shall be in Memphis for about six days & then again for Vicksburg and hope to find there on arrival tomorrow a letter from you telling me of your first feelings on reaching the School. I wish I could have gone out with you, but you know it was impossible. I wrote you from Memphis and fear I gave you too much advice. I would have you perfectly natural, and almost feel sorry that time will so soon change you from the loving little child to a woman, but we cant help it and all I hope & pray for is that you may be to us the same good loving child you have ever been. You can hardly know how we love you, and what we would do to make you happy, but you must learn as other children do, so that when you become a woman you will feel easy among your equals. Dont be impatient to become a young lady for that time will come fast enough and dont hesitate to call me Papa, or anything that Seems to you natural. I would rather a million times that you should be happy than that I should become honored & famous. I have many kind friends in New York, in California, in Missouri and all over our Country as well as Ohio—and it gives me more pleasure to think that in after years when I am dead and almost forgotten that Some of these kind friends will remember My Minnie and Lizzie and other children who must live long after me. The War is not yet over, and I do not see its end. Many of us must die by it yet, and it may be my fate, but I feel certain Our Cause will prevail so that my children will reap the fruits of my labor. Were it not for this I would not feel the Same interest in Success—People wonder why I dont try to get more fame, but my Dear Minnie will remember that before she was born I lived much in South Carolina and afterwards in Louisiana, and that in every Battle I am fighting some of the very families in whose houses I used to spend some happy days. Of course I must fight when the time comes, but whenever a result can be accomplished without Battle I prefer it.

The Cold Nights that we felt at Morrowtown, and when we nestled so lovingly together in Cincinati froze the Rivers so that the ice was floating down the River all the way to Vicksburg, a thing that rarely occurs, but now it is warm and the Sun shines bright as with you in May, the ice has disappeared and the Mississipi River is in good order—we are at this moment stopping at the mouth of White River and soon will be in motion, the boat will tremble so that one cannot write, therefore I must close, asking you to write to me at Memphis till February 10. Tell me everything in your own way and Know that any little thing that attracts your notice will be dear to me. I have just written to Mama, and will also to Lizzie before we reach Memphis. Your loving father

W. T. Sherman

ALS, OHi: William T. Sherman Papers.

TO JOHN A. LOGAN

Hd. Qrs. Dept. of the Tenn.
Near Memphis, Jan. 20, 1864

Genl. Jno. A. Logan.
Comdg. 15 Army Corps, via Nashville
Dear Genl.,

I have been to Vicksburg, and am now near Memphis on my return. McPherson and all his command are in fair condition, his new Forts being nearly done. At Memphis I propose to start the Cavalry down from Lagrange to Pontotoc and Meridian, whilst I with some of Hurlbuts Infantry & Mc-Phersons command move on the Same point from Vicksburg. I judge this move will have an effect on Joe Johnston in front of Chattanooga as well as doing us a real service here in cutting off the Railroad connection between Mississippi and Alabama. Bishop Polk[1] commands down here, with some good cavalry and Long's Infantry. He will annoy us doubtless but will hardly offer us pitched Battle.

I want to be at Meridian by Feb. 8–10, and must be busy in the mean time. I trust to you to keep things moving on that Line. The Railroads should be pushed to completion as rapidly as possible. I will join you in all February via Nashville or I may come across by Savannah.

The Winter has been very severe. Ice ran in heavy masses below Vicksburg, but we have now had some warm Rain & weather and the ice has disappeared, but the River is at least 20 feet lower than it was this time last year.

The River has been little molested by the Guerillas who find it dont pay, and as the waters rise they know we will go up Yazoo & Red Rivers and punish the Interior for their rascality. On this trip I have not seen or heard of a Guerilla and the Merchant Boats pass up and down with little fear. Abundance of wood has been gathered, and swarms of adventurers are crowding Vicksburg to hire Abandonned Plantations. The negro soldier idea is nearly exhausted and the *popular* idea is now to convert them into laborers for the benefit of the hungry Plantation Contractors. Well I am willing the Philanthropists should take the job off our hands and I tell them to go ahead, but I will not divert troops from Military duties to guard local interests. I should like to hear from you privately as well as publicly.

McPherson has reenlisted about 12,000 of his Corps. I should like to hear a similar account of the old 15th—my love to all. Yr. friend

W. T. Sherman

ALS, DLC: John A. Logan Papers.
1. Lieutenant General Leonidas Polk (1806–64), CSA.

TO ULYSSES S. GRANT

Head Qrs. Dept. of the Tenn.
Memphis, Jan. 24, 1864

Maj. Genl. U. S. Grant
Comdg. Div. of the Miss.
Dear General,

I have received at the hands of Colonel Duff[1] your letter of the 15th inst.[2] with copies of yours to Genl. Halleck[3] and those of General Halleck to you[4] and Genl. Steele.[5] All these concur in their general plan, & my acts thus far are perfectly in concordance.

The 16th Corps had become so domiciled at Memphis & along the Railroad that it is like pulling teeth to get them Started, but I think these Divisions, Veatchs[6] Tuttles & A. J. Smiths will be embarked to day & tomorrow for the south. The Cavalry under Genl. Wm. Sooy Smith[7] should also be ready tomorrow the day appointed, when I will start the former in the Boats already collected here for Vicksburg, and the latter by land in light order for Pantator, Okallora, Meridian &c. As soon as the Cavalry is off I will hasten for Vicksburg and with the Infantry & a sufficient form of artillery *double* teamed will start for Black River, Jackson, Brandon and Meridian. I will use all caution and feel no doubt unless Johnston has caught wind of our movement and brought an additional force from Georgia which I do not believe. I have good scouts out & will know everything in time. I believe that W. Sooy Smith will have a form of Cavalry superior to that of Forrest & Stephen Lee which is all that can meet him, and Genl. Polk cannot have at Canton, Brandon & Meridian a force to meet me.

Admiral Porter is hourly looked for, and I will confer with him. I will ask him to send a squadron of light draft Gunboats up the Yazoo & may send

Hawkins up as far as Greenwood with orders if the opportunity offers to strike Grenada another blow. This would make a division, confuse the enemy, and demonstrate the value to us as a military channel of the Yazoo.

It may be that Forrest will let Smith pass down & make a dash for Memphis. I leave Genl. Buckland in command here with about 3200 men. These with the Fort will assure the Safety of the place, but in addition Genl. Veatch under my orders has enrolled three Regiments of Citizens to whom I will issue arms, partial clothing & ammunition, and have ordered the Quarter Master to Set aside for their use as armories Cotton sheds which will make excellent Citadels or Block houses.

The Mayor & citizens offered me a dinner & I had to accept—I recall your experience and as the affair comes off tonight I will try to be cautious in any remarks I will be forced to make. I pity you when you will have to go back to the States for you will not be allowed to eat or sleep for the Curious intrusion of the Dear People. Red River is still low, but should it rise by the time we get back from Meridian I will be tempted to help against Shreveport. Steele could move direct by land to Archadelphia & Fulton. Banks could regain Opelousas & Alexandria, the Admiral & I could pass directly up the River to Shreveport. This would be a connection movement, but a little risky if Dick Taylor, Price & Magruder should unite, but the latter is supposed to be off in Texas, and the two latter dont seem to pull together. I will send you a Messenger the moment I can after I reach Meridian. My supposition is that you will want Wm. Sooy Smith with his cavalry back to Pulaski by March, and will keep that in mind as soon as he can be spared. I am much troubled by the promises we have made the veterans for the furlough. All want the furlough at once. I doubt if 35 days will see any of them back once at home they will be beyond our reach and control. Yours truly,

W. T. Sherman
Maj. Genl.

ALS, NjP: Alexander DeCoppet Collection; *OR*, I, 32: pt. 2, 201–2.

1. Lieutenant Colonel William L. Duff (1822–94) was one of USG's staff officers who had joined the army in 1862 in the Second Illinois Artillery.

2. DLC: WTS; *PUSG*, 10:19.

3. USG to HWH, January 15, 1864, *PUSG*, 10:14–17. USG gave HWH a report on current conditions, including WTS's whereabouts and instructions.

4. HWH to USG, January 8, 1864, *PUSG*, 10:17–18n. Halleck had placed Steele and his army under USG's command. HWH wanted to give USG military control in the West while relieving him from tedious tasks. He also discussed Banks's activities in Texas.

5. HWH to Frederick Steele, *OR*, I, 32: pt. 2, 42–43.

6. Brigadier General James Clifford Veatch (1819–95), USA, was reassigned on this day from the Fifth Division, District of Memphis, Sixteenth Corps, to the Fourth Division, Sixteenth Corps.

7. Brigadier General William Sooy Smith (1830–1916), USA, was chief of cavalry for the Army of the Tennessee and Military Division of Mississippi.

TO JAMES B. BINGHAM

Hd. Qrs. Dept. of the Tenn.
Memphis, January 26th, 1864

J. B. Bingham Esq.
Memphis, Tenn.
Dear Sir,

Yours of the 25th is before me. I have hardly time to do justice to the subject you present, and can only answer your questions in very general terms.

1st. Gov. Andy Johnson should send you an official copy of the order of the Sec. of War to feed and clothe his recruits while they are being collected.[1] It would need no order for me to make issues to men who are enlisted under the General Law; but these State troops are for local defense and are subject to Gov. Johnson's orders and not mine. If the troops were subject to my orders for duty, I could clothe and feed them and promise to keep them for home or local defense; but in this case they would not expect pay, bounties, &c.

I would encourage all loyal men in East Tennessee to organize and arm to protect themselves and their families.

2nd. I do not think Tennessee will gain time by a premature State organization[.] What the people want is protection in their homes, and this cannot be promised them till the Armies of Lee & Joe Johnston are defeated & scattered; and until we can turn our attention to the small bands that now infest the Interior. These intimidate the Courts, Sheriffs, Constables &c., the only officers who can bring protection to life and property. State organizations would determine political questions, but would be powerless against the Armies of the South, that would pay them little or no respect.

3rd. Slavery is already dead in Tenn. The moment a negro cannot be bought and sold, or when he can run off without danger of recapture, the question is settled. Conventions cannot revive Slavery. It should be treated as a Minor Question. If a convention is called in Tenn., it should be without regard to Slavery, or any other single question for when assembled the members would naturally discuss any and all questions, and no doubt would waste more sound on the histories of Greece & Rome, than on the commonplace business before it.

4th. I will not, unless ordered, imitate Genl. Banks example in any part of this Department. I will encourage the people to organize for self defense in their own way, and let order come out of chaos in a natural manner. I think if the Military Authorities will confine their attention to Military matters, that civilians will in due season attend to the rest. I am &c.

W. T. Sherman.

Major General

LS, DLC: William T. Sherman Papers.

1. Bingham, who was raising Union militia guards for duty in Tennessee, would have difficulty in getting Andrew Johnson to send him this document; see Bingham to Johnson, February 11, 1864, and February 16, 1864, Leroy P. Graf and Ralph W. Haskins, eds., *The Papers of Andrew Johnson* (Knoxville, 1967–), 6:613, 625–26. Although the Union commander in Memphis was supposed to provide for these recruits, Hurlbut and Veatch had been putting obstacles in Bingham's way. Bingham to Johnson, April 23, 1864, ibid., 681. In fact, Johnson may never have sent Bingham the relevant order.

TO ELLEN EWING SHERMAN

On Board Gun boat *Juliet*,

Mouth of White River, Jan. 28, 1864

Dearest Ellen,

It was my intention to have written you again at Memphis before starting but time slipped along so fast that I had to start at the appointed time without fulfilling my purpose. I wrote you on Monday and Sent you a check for $250 all I could Spare, and I will receive no more till I get back from this expedition. Knocking about so much my expenses are heavy, and I am in debt to Dayton. I sent you a paper about the banquet which was really a fine affair, the hall of the Gayoso was crammed and the utmost harmony prevailed. Every thing passed off well my remarks as reported by the *Argus* were about right. The Bulletin got mere incoherent points. I cannot speak consecutively, but it seems that what I do say is vehemently applauded[.] The point which may be wrongly conceived was this. As the South resorted to war, we accepted it, and as they fought for slaves and States Rights they could not blame us if they lost both as the result of the war—and again that they the South prided themselves on high grounds of honor I was willing to take issue there adopting their own Rules, or those of the most fashionable clubs of Paris, London, New Orleans and Paris. If a member goes into an election he must abide the result or be blackballed or put in Coventry. Now as the Southern People went into the Presidential Election they as honorable men were bound to abide the result. I also described the mode & manner of seizure of the Garrison & arsenal at Baton Rouge & pronounced that a breach of soldierly honor, and the firing on boats from behind a cotton wood tree. People at the North may not feel the weight of these points but I know the South so well that I know what I said will be gall & wormwood to Some but it will make others think. I was at Memphis Tuesday & part of Wednesday the Festival was on Monday & Several real old Southerners met me and confessed their cause would be recorded in History as I put it. I was not aware of the hold I had on the People till I was there this time. Hurlbut did not mingle with them & was difficult of access, and everytime I went into a theatre or public assemblage there was a storm of applause. I endeavored to avoid it as much as possible, but it was always so good natured that I could not repel it. If I succeed in my present blow I would not be surprised if Mississipi would be as Tennessee, but I do not allow myself to be deceived. The Old Regime is not yet dead, and they will fight for their old privileges yet—so many of our old Regiments are going on furlough that we will be short handed. If we had our Ranks full I know we could take Mobile & the Alabama River in 30 days and before summer could secure all of Red River also—leaving the grand Battle to come off in East Tennessee or Georgia in June. We could hold fast all we have & let the South wriggle but our best plan is activity—I have had my share but cannot avoid the future. Surely if we do succeed as we have in the past I ought to be allowed rest—If I could be sure of employment in California I would go this spring but I fear that my motives would be misconstrued. Beside you are so situated that you and the children are dependent on my Salary & before I could get a start at something else you would suffer—but again I am now on the wave of popularity and the next plunge is away down, down. I know it well and would avoid it, but how is the question. I am about to march 200 miles straight into danger with a comparatively small force and that composed of troops in a manner strange to me, but my calculations are all right and now for the Execution[.] I expect to leave Vicksburg in a very few days, and will cut loose all communications so you will not hear from me save through the Southern papers till I am back to the Mississipi. You of course will be patient and will appreciate my motives in case of accident, for surely I could ask rest and an opportunity for some one Else, say McPherson, but there are double reasons I will never order my command where I am not willing to go, and besides it was politic to break up the force at Memphis which was too large to lie idle & Hurlbut would not reduce it. I had to bring him away & make a radical change—He ranks McPherson and we have not confidence enough in his steadiness to put him on this expedition—he is too easily stampeded by rumors. I have a better sense of chances. I run two chances, 1st In case the Enemy has learned my plans or has guessed them he may send to Meridian a superior force—or bad Roads may prevent my moving with the celerity which will command success—would that I had the 15th Corps that would march in Sunshine or storm to fulfil my plans without asking what they were. I almost wish I had been left with that Specific command, but confess I prefer service near the Old Mississipi which enables us to Supply ourselves so bountifully. I hear but little from Huntsville, but suppose all our folks are comfortable there.

I sent Maj. Taylor, Fitch & MacFeely back to Huntsville from Memphis & have with me only my aids and Quarter Master. I dont want any non combatant mouths along to feed, and am determined this time not to have a tribe of leeches along to consume our food—not a tent Shall be carried or any baggage save on our horses. The wagons & packs shall carry ammunition & food along. I will set the example myself. Experience has taught me if one tent is carried any quantity of trash will load down the wagons. If I had ten more Regiments I would be tempted to try Mobile, but as it is if I break at Meridian & Demopolis I will cut off one of the most fruitful corn supplies of the Enemy and will give Mississipi a chance to rest. The State is now full of conscripts gangs carrying to their armies the unwilling, the old & young. We will take all provisions and God help the Starving families. I warned them last year against this last visitation, and now it is at hand. I will write to Tommy, and will send him some photographs in lieu of the picture which I promised to draw him. Indeed I have no time and want Tommy to feel that I do not neglect him. I admit my heart was too much wrapped up in Willy, that I was too partial to him—he was so near me, and so confiding and Seemed to reflect the better parts of my nature that I dreamed that he would be so much better & yet like myself—I know Tommy has more intellect and all the Elements of a fine boy and I will love him & cherish him as well. You think I Slight Lizzie for Minnie. I do not feel so at all. I am uneasy lest Minnie should mature an awkward, uneducated girl, and therefore dwelt on her case more. Lizzie is different, much gentler and will develop slower and more gradually—The truth is I fear I shall see less of them in after years than I have in the past, but promise to do by all as near right as I can. I feel the full load of care and anxiety you bear—mourning for Willy, fearing for the future and oppressed with intense anxiety for parents. I believe you can bear all, and that you will for our sake.[1] Just think of me with 50,000 lives in my hands, with all the anxieties of their families. This load is heavier than even you imagine—I will write again. as ever

W. T. Sherman

ALS, InND: Sherman Family Papers.
1. EES was preoccupied by family cares; see EES to WTS, January 20 and 21, 1864, SFP.

TO JOHN SHERMAN

On Board *Juliet*, bound for
Vicksburg in a fog,
Friday, Jan. 28, 1864

Dear Brother,

I wrote you from Lancaster, & it may be since but I forget—Some things have transpired since that you would like to know and I now have more leisure than I can hope to have after arrival at Vicksburg. I have organized a cavalry force to Swoop down from Memphis towards Mobile, and have gathered together out of my garrisons a very pretty force of 20,000 men which I shall command in person and move from Vicksburg, due East in connection with the Cavalry named, to reach Meridian & break up the Rail Road connections there. This will have the effect to disconnect Mississipi from the Eastern Southern states, and without this single remaining link they cannot keep any army of importance west of the Alabama River. Our armies are now at the lowest point, and So many are going home as reenlisted veterans that I will have a less force than should attempt it. It seems my luck to have to make the initiation and to come in at desperate times, but thus far having done a full share of the real achievements of this war I need not fear accidents. I observe the Cincinati paper would now fawn on me, but I despise them. I prefer rather the respect of such men as Mr. Ewing, Henry Stanbery,[1] Mr. S. S. L'Hommedieu, Larz Anderson and Such men, than the adulation of all the *Commercials* and *Gazettes* of all Ohio, and this I am assured of. You who attach more importance to popular fame would be delighted to See in what estimation I am held by the People of Memphis Tennessee and all along this mighty River. I could not decline an offer of a public dinner in Memphis but I dreaded it more than I did the assault on Vicksburg. I had to Speak & sent you the Report that best suited me, viz. that in the *Argus*—The report of the *Bulletin* which may reach the Northern press is disjointed & not so correct. Indeed I cannot speak from notes, or keep myself strictly to the points, but tis said that the effect of my crude speeches is good. My manner is earnest and language emphatic, but sometimes what I say in jest is taken for earnest. I think the organizations of Civil Government down here is premature. I enclose you a copy of a letter I wrote to J. B. Bingham of Memphis, who is a right hand man to Governor Johnson of Tennessee, giving my views on this point, which I think will stand the test of Reason and of Time. We are committed to the Right of Revolution. A People distinct & separate as our Colonies were, who have separate interests and the ability to maintain them have a natural Right to a Separate Government provided they have the power to enforce it. The People of the South have asserted this Right—We admit it, but make issue on their ability to maintain a separate Political existence. The test is war. During this test Laws are silent, argument fruitless and arms can alone decide. We have accepted the war have maintained it & profess ability to maintain it, and until war produces a result, a solution, or cessation, all other questions should be waived. As a war measure we can introduce discordant elements into the enemys counsels. We may do anything that weakens them & strengthens us, but it seems to me idle to attempt permanent political organizations until war ceases. Now if Cannon on this River, a civil Govt. in Arkansas, Tennessee, and Louisiana will strengthen us & weaken the enemy in War, it is right, but I doubt it. These state governments revive old political jealousies, hatreds, & enmities that in a state of pure war would die out. That is my stand, & moreover I know that for us to assume that slavery is killed, not by a predetermined act of ours but as the natural logical & legal consequence of the acts of its self constituted admirers we gain strength & the enemy loses it. I think it is the true doctrine for the time being. The South have made the interests of Slavery the issue of the War. If they lose the war they lose Slavery. Instead of our being abolitionist it is thereby proven that they are the abolitionists. I always assert that we were bound by our Constitutional compact to restore fugitive slaves, but as they broke the Constitution the compact as to them was void, and we were released—also that the question of Slavery in the National Territories was an open one, not clear, and the South were bound to abide the decision of a National Congress & a National Court. But they preferred war, & cannot in after years complain if by war they lose that chance. In like manner I admit the right of secession. Men may expatriate themselves. They may go away, but they cannot carry with them the ground which is tied down. In this ground we have some right—all they do not possess with ability to carry beyond our jurisdiction. Therefore if the People of the South are unwilling to live in the same land with us, let them go, even to Madagascar and if they cannot pay their passage we might help them, as an act of grace. They allege they cannot abide us. I Know that is the feeling of some, but the masses can. I have associated with rebels & have seen our soldiers do it under flags of truce, and during lulls in war, but I do admit that Some of them are so embittered that all would be benefitted by an eternal separation. They cannot kill us all, but we may them. They must be killed or sent away. I would like to see the tide of emigration from down this way, and I would like to see the abandoned plantations pass into new hands, even that of negros, rather than to speculators with Contract negros whom they treat as Slaves. Still even this must be a slow & gradual change. All of Tennessee & Arkansas are suited to free labor. There is no doubt—and much of Mississipi and Louisiana & Texas. I would like to See a bona fide population coming this way to hold cultivate & defend the Territory we acquire by conquest. The Mississipi is now substantially clear, occasionally a band of Guerillas come to the bank & fire at a boat but as a Rule boats pass up & down free. Freights are moderate & no boat seems afraid of the risks. Some boats engaged in hunting up the Cotton hid away in swamps get peppered, but it is a risk run voluntarily & covered by the price they get for the Cotton when found. The Mississipi is a Substantial Conquest—We should next get the Red River, then the Alabama, & last push into Georgia. In the mean time that Army of the Potomac which seems more intent on getting fame in the newspapers than in providing results might achieve something. Of course no soldier would expect an army so near Washington to do anything but it might at least prevent Lee from detaching against Grant. Butler at Norfolk[2] & Foote in Richmond[3] are doing us good service. They will worry Jeff Davis to death, but should Jeff's power pass to Lee, we would lose by the change. Gillmore[4] at Charleston is making valuable experiments in artillery & Banks in Louisiana reproducing effective political combinations. In Grants army along the Tennessee the country alone can look for real valuable results. After my present move I will hasten round to Huntsville to command the army I left there to repair Railroads & prepare for the coming Campaign. You may write me at Memphis & Vicksburg till Feb. 20 I do not think Grant will move forward till in March or April. The only effect of my present move is to widen our influence in the Mississipi Valley. Give my love to Cecilia and any friends who may be near you. Yr. affectionate Brother,

W. T. Sherman

ALS, DLC: William T. Sherman.

1. Henry Stanbery (1803–81), an Ohio politician, lawyer, and former state attorney general, had been Ewing Sr.'s law partner and would become Andrew Johnson's attorney general in 1866 and his chief counsel during the impeachment trial.

2. Major General Benjamin F. Butler had taken command of the Department of Virginia and North Carolina (later known as the Army of the James) in late 1863.

3. Henry Stuart Foote (1804–80), a Confederate congressman from Mississippi and former U.S. senator and state governor. A longtime opponent of Jefferson Davis, he had recently leveled critical attacks on the Confederate president's military and civil policy.

4. Brigadier General Quincy A. Gillmore (1825–88), USA, commanded the Tenth Corps and Department of the South at Charleston.

TO MARIA BOYLE EWING SHERMAN

On board the Juliet, near Vicksburg,
Friday night, Jan. 28, 1864

My Dearest Minnie,

I am again approaching the old Town of Vicksburg that we all remember so well, and after my arrival & it may be a month after I will have so little time to write that I must now tell you again how much I think about you, and how anxious I am that you should improve the few years that remain to you of Childhood. Time passes so fast to me, and my life is such a turmoil that it is only in the quiet of night that I can think of my dear Children that Seem to me dearer and dearer as they are farther away. I got your short letter at Memphis but hope to hear again from you that you are better acquainted with your school companions and less homesick. The Cold Winter will soon be over and you will have the green grass and bright flowers of spring which will make your Country School more cheerful & homelike. Mama too will come down to See you, and she thinks I also may come to Cincinati to See you, but I cannot promise it for I see too much work for me to think of Coming to Ohio for a long time, probably not as long as you are at school. I judge that this year of the war will be the most important of all, and I must be busy. I have a most important office, more than fifty thousand men are at my command and you Know that they are scattered from Huntsville to Natchez. I have not seen Uncle Charley or Boyle since I saw you they are at Huntsville and I am away down the Mississipi, but if things turn out as I calculate I will go there in about a month. In a few days I will go out to the Big Black where we were so happy last summer, when you and Willy used to ride with me, but instead of riding for pleasure I must go on where there is danger & battle. I have escaped death thus far, and it may be will again, but I always am prepared for anything. If I should be killed or wounded I Know that my Sweet Minnie will think of me always.

Tell the Sisters who teach you that you are the child of one who is fighting that they may have a country and Peace, and that I expect them to be to you both as father & mother. I Know they will. Write to me as often as you can, that I may note your progress. Yr. affectionate father,

W. T. Sherman

ALS, OHi: William T. Sherman

TO ROSWELL M. SAWYER[1]

Head Qrs. Dept. of the Tenn.
Vicksburg, Jan. 31-1864.

Major R. M. Sawyer
A. A. G. Army of the Tenn., Huntsville, Alabama
Dear Sawyer,

In my former letters I have answered all your questions save one, and that relates to the treatment of inhabitants known or suspected to be hostile or "Secesh." This is in truth the most difficult business of our Army as it advances & occupies the Southern Country. It is almost impossible to lay down Rules and I invariably leave this whole subject to the local commander, but am willing to give them the benefit of my acquired Knowledge and experience.

In Europe whence we derive our principles of war Wars are between Kings or Rulers through hired Armies and not between Peoples. These remain as it were neutral and sell their produce to whatever Army is in possession. Napoleon when at War with Prussia, Austria and Russia bought forage & provisions of the Inhabitants and consequently had an interest to protect the farms and factories which ministered to his wants. In like manner the Allied Armies in

France could buy of the French Habitants, whatever they needed, the produce of the soil or manufactures of the Country. Therefore the General Rule was & is that War is confined to the Armies engaged, and should not visit the houses of families or private Interests. But in other examples a different Rule obtained the Sanction of Historical Authority. I will only instance one when in the reign of William and Mary the English Army occupied Ireland then in a state of revolt. The inhabitants were actualy driven into foreign lands and were dispossessed of their property and a new population introduced. To this day a large part of the North of Ireland is held by the descendants of the Scotch emigrants sent there by Williams order & an Act of Parliament. The War which now prevails in our land is essentially a war of Races. The Southern People entered into a clear Compact of Government with us of the North, but still maintained through State organizations a species of seperate existence with seperate interests, history and prejudices. These latter became stronger and stronger till at last they have led to war, and have developed the fruits of the bitterest Kind. We of the North are beyond all question Right in our Cause but we are not bound to ignore the fact that the people of the South have prejudices which form a part of their nature, and which they cannot throw off without an effort of reason, or by the slower process of natural change. The question then arises Should we treat as absolute enemies all in the South who differ from us in opinion or prejudice, Kill or banish them, or should we give them time to think and gradually change their conduct, so as to conform to the new order of things which is slowly & gradually creeping into their country?

When men take up Arms to resist a Rightful Authority we are compelled to use like force, because all reason and argument cease when arms are resorted to. When the provisions, forage, horses, mules, wagons, &c. are used by our enemy it is clearly our duty & Right to take them also; because otherwise they might be used against us. In like manner all houses left vacant by an inimical people are clearly our Right, and such as are needed as Storehouses, Hospitals & Quarters. But the question arises as to dwellings used by women, children & non-combatants. So long as non-combatants remain in their houses & Keep to their accustomed peaceful business, their opinions and prejudices can in no wise influence the War & therefore should not be noticed; but if any one comes out into the public streets & creates disorder he or she should be punished, restrained or banished, Either to the rear or front as the officer in Command adjudges. If the People or any of them Keep up a correspondence with parties in hostility they are spies & can be punished according to Law with death or minor punishment. These are well established principles of War & the People of the South having appealed to *War* are barred from appealing for protection to our Constitution which they have practically and publicly defied. They have appealed to War and must abide *its* Rules & Laws. The United States as a belligerent party, claiming Rights in the soil as the ultimate Sovereign, has a right to change the population—and it may be & is both politic and just we should do so in certain districts; When the Inhabitants persist too long in hostility, it may be both politic and right we should banish them and appropriate their lands to a more loyal and useful population. No man could deny but that the United States would be benefited by dispossessing a single prejudiced, hard headed and disloyal planter and substituting in his place a dozen or more patient industrious good families, even if they were of foreign birth. I think it does good to present this view of the case to many Southern Gentlemen, who grew Rich and wealthy, not by virtue *alone* of their personal industry and skill, but in great part by reason of the protection and impetus to prosperity given by our hitherto moderate & magnanimous Government. It is all idle nonsense for these Southern planters to say that they made the South, that they own it, and that they can do as they please, even to break up our Government & shut up the natural avenues of trade, intercourse and Commerce. We Know and they Know if they are inteligent beings, that as compared with the whole World, they are but as 5 millions to one thousand millions—that they did not create the land, that the only title to its use & usufruct is the deed of the U.S. and that if they appeal to War they hold their all by a very insecure tenure. For my part I believe that this War is the result of false Political Doctrine for which we are all as a people more or less responsible, and I would give all a chance to reflect & when in error to recant. I know that Slave owners, finding themselves in possession of a species of property in opposition to the growing sentiment of the whole Civilized World, conceived their property to be in danger and foolishly appealed to War, and that by skilled political handling they involved with themselves the whole South on this Result of error & prejudice. I believe that some of the Rich & slave holding are prejudiced to an extent that nothing but death & ruin will ever extinguish, but I hope that as the poorer & industrial classes of the South realize their relative weakness, and their dependence upon the fruits of the earth & good will of their fellow men, they will not only discover the error of their ways & repent of their hasty action, but bless those who persistently have maintained a Constitutional Government strong enough to sustain itself, protect its citizens, and promise peaceful homes to millions yet unborn.

In this belief, whilst I assert for our Govt. the highest Military prerogatives, I am willing to bear in patience the political nonsense of Slave Rights, State Rights uncontrolled freedom of conscience, License of the press and such other trash which have deluded the Southern People and carried them into War, Anarchy, & blood shed, and the perpetration of some of the foulest Crimes that have disgraced any time or any people.

I would advise the Commanding officer at Huntsville and such other towns as are occupied by our troops to assemble the Inhabitants & explain to them these plain, selfevident propositions & tell them that it is for them *now* to say whether they and their children shall inherit the beautiful lands which by the accidents of nature have fallen to their share.

The Government of the United States has in North Alabama any and all the rights of Sovereignty which they choose to enforce in War, to take their lives, their homes, their lands, their every thing, because they cannot deny that War does exist by their acts, and War is simply Power unrestrained by Constitution or Compact. If they want Eternal War, well & good. We must accept the issue & will be forced to dispossess them and put our own people who at a simple notice, would come to North Alabama & accept the elegant houses & Plantations now there.

If the People of Huntsville think differently, let them persist in this War three years longer and then they will not be consulted.

Three years ago by a little reflection and patience they could have had a hundred years of Peace & Prosperity, but they *preferred* War. Last year they could have saved their Slaves but now it is too late, all the Powers of Earth cannot restore to them their slaves any more than their dead Grandfathers. Next year in all probability their lands will be taken, for in War we can take them & rightfully too, and in another year they may beg in vain for their lives, for sooner or later there must be an end to strife.

A People who will persevere in a War beyond a certain limit ought to Know the consequences. Many, Many People with less pertinacity than the South has already shown have been wiped out of national Existence.

My own belief, is that even now the non-slaveholding classes of the South are alienating from their associates in War. Already I hear Crimination & recrimination. Those who have property left should take warning in time.

Since I have come down here I have seen many Southern Planters, who now hire their own negroes & acknowledge that they were mistaken and knew not the earthquake they were to make by appealing to secession. They thought that the Politicians had prepared the way, and that they could part the states of this Union in Peace. They now see that we are bound together as one nation by indissoluble ties, and that any interest or any fraction of the people that set themselves up in antagonism to the Nation must perish.

Whilst I would not remit one jot or tittle of our Nations Rights in Peace or War, I do make allowances for past political errors and prejudices.

Our National Congress and the Supreme Court are the proper arenas on which to discuss conflicting opinions & not the Battle field.

You may not hear from me again for some time and if you think it will do any good, Call some of the better people of Huntsville together & explain to them my view. You may even read to them this letter & let them use it, so as to prepare them for my coming.

To those who submit to the Rightful Laws & authority of their State & National Government promise all gentleness and forbearance, but to the petulant and persistant secessionist, why death or banishment is a mercy, and the quicker he or she is disposed of the better. Satan & the rebellious saints of Heaven, were allowed a continuance of existence in Hell, merely to swell their just punishment.

To such as would rebel against a Government so mild and just as ours was in Peace, a punishment equal would not be unjust.

We are progressing well in this quarter, but I have not changed my opinion that although we may soon make certain the existence of the Power of our National Government yet years must pass before ruffianism, murder & Robbery will cease to afflict this region of our country. Your friend,

W. T. Sherman
Maj. Genl. Comdg.

LS, with emendations in WTS's hand, DLC: William T. Sherman; *OR*, I, 32: pt. 2, 278–81.
1. Major Roswell M. Sawyer (d. 1866) was assistant adjutant general of volunteers.

TO ELLEN EWING SHERMAN

Jackson Miss.
Feb. 7, 1864

Dearest Ellen,

I am here again and a new burning has been inflicted on this afflicted town. We had some pretty Skirmishes on our way out and we handled the enemys cavalry rather roughly. No Infantry has yet been encountered, but I expect them on our way east. Weather is beautiful & roads good—all of us in fine condition. I am on the point of sending a Courier back and avail myself of the opportunity to send you this surprise message and the assurance of my unfailing love. yrs. ever

W. T. Sherman

ALS, InND: Sherman Family Papers.

TO ULYSSES S. GRANT
[private and confidential]

Near Memphis, March 10, 1864

General Grant
Dear General:

I have your more than kind and characteristic letter of the 4th, and will send a copy of it to General McPherson at once.[1]

You do yourself injustice and us too much honor in assigning to us so large a share of the merits which have led to your high advancement. I know you approve the friendship I have ever professed to you, and will permit me to continue as heretofore to manifest it on all proper occasions.

You are now Washington's legitimate successor, and occupy a position of almost dangerous elevation; but if you can continue as heretofore to be yourself, simple, honest, and unpretending, you will enjoy through life the respect and love of friends, and the homage of millions of human beings who will award to you a large share for securing to them and their descendants a government of law and stability.

I repeat, you do General McPherson and myself too much honor. At Belmont you manifested your traits, neither of us being near; at Donelson also you illustrated your whole character. I was not near, and General McPherson in too subordinate a capacity to influence you.

Until you had won Donelson, I confess I was almost cowed by the terrible array of anarchical elements that present themselves at every point; but that victory admitted the ray of light which I have followed ever since.

I believe you are as brave, patriotic, and just, as the great prototype Washington; as unselfish, kind-hearted, and honest, as a man should be; but the chief characteristic in your nature is the simple faith in success you have always manifested, which I can liken to nothing else than the faith a Christian has in his Saviour.

This faith gave you victory at Shiloh and Vicksburg. Also, when you have completed your best preparations, you go into battle without hesitation, as at Chattanooga—no doubts, no reserve; and I tell you that it was this that made us act with confidence. I knew wherever I was that you thought of me, and if I got in a tight place you would come—if alive.

My only points of doubt were as to your knowledge of grand strategy, and of books of science and history; but I confess your common-sense seems to have supplied all this.

Now as to the future. Do not stay in Washington. Halleck is better qualified than you are to stand the buffets of intrigue and policy. Come out West; take to yourself the whole Mississippi Valley; let us make it dead-sure, and I tell you the Atlantic slope and pacific shores will follow its destiny as sure as the limbs of a tree live or die with the main trunk! We have done much; still much remains to be done. Time and time's influences are all with us; we could almost afford to sit still and let these influences work. Even in the seceded States your word *now* would go further than a President's proclamation, or an act of Congress.

For God's sake and for your country's sake, come out of Washington! I foretold to General Halleck, before he left Corinth, the inevitable result to him, and I now exhort you to come out West. Here lies the seat of the coming empire; and from the West, when our task is done, we will make short work of Charleston and Richmond, and the impoverished coast of the Atlantic. Your sincere friend,

W. T. Sherman

Printed, *PM*, 1:427–28; copy, DLC: WTS; *OR*, I, 32: pt. 3, 49.

1. On March 4, USG had written to WTS that he was probably to receive the rank of lieutenant general in the U.S. Army. He had been summoned to Washington. He went on to say that "no one feels more than me how much of this success is due to the energy, skill, and harmonious putting forth of that energy and skill, of those it has been my good fortune to have occupying a subordinate position under me.... What I want is to express my thanks to you and McPherson as *the men* to whom, above all others, I feel indebted for whatever I have had of success." *PUSG*, 10:186–87.

TO ELLEN EWING SHERMAN

Steamboat Westmoreland—
approaching Memphis, Mch. 10, 1864

Dearest Ellen,

Again I am approaching you. I have done all I undertook & am now en route for Huntsville, but must stop it may be a week at Memphis to complete certain matters made necessary by Genl. Grants orders received yesterday when I expect to come to Cairo, and Louisville and Huntsville.[1] I do not think I can come to Cincinati, for too much rests with me now, and however disposed I must go on for the Spring Campaign which I judge will be the most Sanguinary of all. I have all your letters up to the 26 of February.[2] I was prepared to hear of your mothers death, and feel that it is a mercy to her & us all that she is now beyond bodily pain, and when during a long and good life she would wish to be. Indeed have we been afflicted this year. Had I or Hugh or Charley been killed it would have been natural & Expected but whilst we have been permitted to look death in the face daily, till it is a familiar thing, without hardly a scratch, Death has taken your mother, and our almost too loved boy, also Father Lange[3] who was almost as of the Family. I had been so much seperated from Willy, he had lived more in my thoughts than real person that I yet can dream of him as alive. I can recal him at any moment, and it seemed to me a dream as a few days since I crossed Black River at Messengers, saw the ruins of our old Camp, and rode over that familiar Road to the Railroad where but a few months ago, Willy ran to me his whole heart beaming in his face—all came back as a flash, and I could hardly realize that I should never see him again. On reflection I agree with you that his name must remain sacred to us forever[.] He must remain to our memories as though living, and his name must not be taken by any one. Though dead he is still our Willy and we can love him as God only knows how we loved him. I know that he felt at all times of his life that we loved him better than we did ourselves and I feel no sense of reproach for so doing. Tommy felt slighted then, but as he grows he too will recal the memory of his brave & manly brother. Oh that he now could take his map and trace the course in life of his father as he labors to secure to his children a home and a Government that will stand the Shocks of human passion and the worlds ambition. I have just received from Genl. Grant a letter in which he gives me & McPherson credit for having won for him his present high position. I have just answered it and as we approach Memphis will dispatch to him a special Courier with my answer, and full Reports of all my doings down here. As usual as soon as I have time to record these papers I will send them to you as the Custodian of all family Records. I have no doubt you were amused at the thousand & one stories about my Meridian trip. It certainly baffled the Sharp ones of the Press and stampeded all Alabama, but in fact was a pleasant excursion. Weather was beautiful, roads good & plenty to eat. What fighting wc had was all on one side. Our aggregate Loss is 21 killed, 68 wounded, and 81 missing = 170 all told. but in a day or two I will send you my Report which will be clear & explicit. I have sent 10,000 men up Red River under Genl. A. J. Smith with Admiral Porter to cooperate with Genl. Banks. They are to be gone only 30 days when they come round to me at Huntsville. I want to make up my army to 40,000 men, so when we cross the Tennessee look out.

Grant in command—Thomas the Center Schofield the Left & Sherman Right, if we cant whip Joe Johnston we will Know the reason why. Banks in the mean time to come out of Red River & swing against Mobile. If we had been smart he could have walked into Mobile when I was at Meridian. I am down on Wm. Sooy Smith. He could have come to me, I know it, and had he, I would have captured Polks Army, but the Enemy had too much Cavalry for me to attempt it with men afoot. As it was I scared the Bishop out of his senses, he made a clean run and I could not get within a days march of him. He had Railroads to help him, but these are now *gone*. Had I tolerated a Corps of newspaper men how could I have made that march a secret? Am I not right? And does not the world *now* see it? As you Know & have scolded me for it, my mind looks to remote effects and I cant help it—You have told me often I was not listening to you, but afterwards found out I heard all & was making the application. So in all moments my mind jumps to the next thing, not the present—It might be better were it otherwise, but the best results in life come from each one acting his national Character. Hugh is wrong again.[4] He has Command of a Division that will make him a Major General if he holds on, but if he gives up that Division for a command in Louisville or elsewhere he is gone helplessly. I know it and you may tell him so. I have recommended *no one* for Major General, and do not intend to now, because there are *no* vacancies and the War Dept. do not desire to be pressed on the point. If the list be cleared and I am notified I will make my names, and Hugh knows I will be honest at any and all events. That I lean against him is not so. I have twelve Brigadiers Commanding Divisions and you Know how the friends & family of each naturally and properly exaggerate the claim of their member, but I shall judge from my own Stand Point. I have done well by Charley & by Hugh— Instead of feeling against me, they Should let me accomplish results in my own way. They do me injustice if they act otherwise. You Know I will give them if in want the last dollar or shirt I have, but I will not ask the U.S. to bestow on them office & Reward till as compared with others in the Same Race they win it fairly and manfully. What would you think were I to use my office to favor Hoyt or Moulton, or Henry Reese? But I will not discuss it. Let me act my own game and even you will be satisfied—I want you of course always to tell me everything no matter what its bearing, but dont allow yourself to be drawn into Conclusions unfavorable to me, for better or worse we must glide down the hill of life together & for Godssake and Willys sake let it be in harmony.

The boat shakes so I can hardly write, but you are a better scholar than I and must decypher my letters. You will expect a letter from me by this mail, and I expect to Send off a Bearer the moment we reach Memphis. I could tell you many things of interest but will recall them in my subsequent letters. At New Orleans I was entertained by General Banks, and other families. I was there but two days, one of which I was 8 hours at table, breakfasting out & dining out. I saw Storm who is married again to a Creole Blonde. Mrs. Banks[5] was there and is a smart Yankee woman—I saw Mr. & Mrs. Day but for a few minutes. I drove to their house on Magazine Street above where we used to live, but as F. W. Sherman with his one leg was waiting for me in the carriage I could only exchange words. They are both old and broken, but appeared better than I expected.

On my way down I picked up at Natchez a prisoner of war Professor Boyd, my favorite among the officers of the Academy at Alexandria. I never saw a man evince more gratitude. He clung to me till I came away. Stone promised to be Kind to him, and to exchange him the first opportunity. He told me all about the People up the River and said they talked about me a great deal, some with marked respect and others with bitter hatred.

Smith now commands a Battery on James River below Richmond—Clark is at Alexandria an ordnance officer, Louisa Boyce is with him. Judge Boyce is on the Plantation and so is Maj. Graham—the latter is cross, and dont harmonize with any of the mixed elements of society—Many of the Negros are gone, and the present trip up Red River will clean out the Balance. Boyd tells me the motto over the door of the Seminary is chisselled out—Your remember it in my letter of Resignation—"By the liberality of the General Govt. of the U.S. The Union, Esto perpetua[.]" The fools. Though obliterated it lives in the memory of thousands and it may be will be restored in a few days. I wanted to go up Red River, but as Banks was to command it in person I thought best not to go. Grant wanted me to command, but I reported my reason as before stated. Banks ranks Grant and myself.[6] But now Grant will be Lt. General and will command all he pleases. Of course I can get any thing I want but as soon as the Spring Campaign is over I want to come here and look after the Mississipi. Like the Story in Gil Blas—"Here lies my Soul." Though Willy died here, his pure & brave Spirit will hover over this the Grand Artery of America. I want to live out here & die here also, and dont care if my grave be like De Soto's in its muddy waters.

I suppose I must undergo a new infliction of the Memphisites—Mrs. Shover—Phebe and Valeria. I dont want to swear, but I think you would pardon it if I would indulge a little on this score. Valeria has another baby and wants me to Stand for it. Poor woman, her brother committed suicide on a similar event, and to ensure the consummation of her mission I think I will advise her to follow her brothers example.

Well Ellen in truth I wanted to write you a good long letter, but this will be to you no pleasure but the boat trembles so I cannot write. Ill promise better in a day or two at Memphis—write me care of Genl. Reid[7] Cairo. I sent you $1000 or thousand dollars from Vicksburg about Feb. 28, which I hope reached you safely. You are therefore flush. You had better stay quiet in your fathers house though it must be sad enough now. Still do as you think best. I cannot promise anything better as long as War lasts, and I see no end yet. My love to all—your distribution of Mrs. Kleins presents are all Right—she merely asked me the name of the *Youngest* child & marked the things accordingly. Yours Ever

W. T. Sherman

ALS, InND: Sherman Family Papers.

1. USG to WTS, March 4, 1864, *PUSG*, 10:190–91.

2. EES to WTS, January 29–30, February 2, 8, 16, and 17, 1864; her letter of February 26 broke the news of her mother's death. She also believed that their new baby should not be named for Willy; that name should remain sacred. SFP.

3. Lange had been the Ewings' priest in Lancaster at St. Mary's; he had died on February 9. EES to WTS, February 16, 1864, SFP.

4. On February 16, EES had written her husband that Hugh had decided to accept USG's offer of the command of the District of Louisville since he could never get promotion under WTS because of their family relationship. He didn't want to serve under Logan, "a man inferior to himself." "At the same time he is cut off by your fastidious views from all prospect of honourable promotion." Her father thought that his drinking should not be held against him "when Grant has been in the same condition quite as often." She reiterated these points in her letter of the twenty-sixth, adding that Hugh might resign if he did not receive the Louisville post. SFP.

5. Mary Palmer Banks.

6. Actually, Grant ranked Banks as a result of his promotion to major general in the regular army after Vicksburg.

7. Brigadier General Hugh Thompson Reid (1811–74), USA, commanded the District of Cairo until March 19.

TO ELLEN EWING SHERMAN

Memphis, March 12, 1864

Dearest Ellen,

I wrote you a long letter from on board the *Westmoreland* on my way up from Vicksburg, which I sent up to Cairo by General Butterfield Bearer of dispatches. I then told you that I was en route for Huntsville, but was compelled to Stop at Memphis and send back orders to Genl. McPherson at Vicksburg, and await the answers before resuming my journey. I sent a steamer back the day before yesterday and expect to hear by return of it in six days when I propose to start for Cairo Louisville & Huntsville. I expect to be at Cairo on the 20, Louisville 21. Write me at latter place Care of Silas Miller at the Galt House. I Shall not stop any where but hurry to Huntsville as I know an immense amount of business awaits me there. I Enclose you the letter from Grant, which you can show to Phil, and then put it away as one of the family Records which I fear is swelling to an inconvenient Size—Dayton has not copied my official Report in the Book, but so soon as he has it too Shall be sent you. Of all the expeditions sent out this Spring mine has been best conducted & most Successful, simply because of the secresy and expedition with which it was planned and executed. Had the Enemy been informed of these in advance by our Prying Correspondents I might have shared the Fate of Seymour.[1] He did not go 40 miles from his Base, whereas I went 182 miles. I have written Grant a long letter & begged him to adhere to his Resolution not to stay at Washington. He would not stand the intrigues of politicians a week. He now occupies a dazzling height and it will require more courage to withstand the pressure than a dozen battles. I wonder if you Kept a certain dispatch Halleck made me from Corinth in June 1862 and my answer from Moscow.[2] I foretold to Halleck his loss, and the fact that the man who won the Mississipi would be *the* man. I wish you would hunt it up. I Know I saw it among your papers, and show it to Phil to satisfy him however extravagant my early assertions may have seemed how they are verified by time. I feel that whilst my mind naturally slights the events actually transpiring in my presence, it sees as clear as any one's the results to be evolved by Time. Now Halleck has more Booklearning & Knowledge of men than Grant, and is therefore better qualified for his present Post, whereas the latter by his honesty, simplicity, candor & reliance on friends is better suited to act with soldiers. I would rather occupy my present relations to the military world than any other command & therefore must serve out this Campaign which is to be the Test—All that has gone before is mere Skirmishing—The War now begins and with heavy well disciplined masses the issue must be settled in hard fought Battles. I think we can whip them in Alabama and it may be Georgia, but the Devils seem to have a determination that cannot but be admired—No amount of poverty or adversity seems to shake their faith—niggers gone—wealth & luxury gone, money worthless, starvation in view within a period of two or three years, are Causes enough to make the bravest tremble, yet I see no signs of let up—Some few deserters—plenty tired of war, but the masses determined to fight it out. I will take McPherson & two Divisions of 5000 each from the River to add to my Army at Huntsville, but they are not available till they get the furlough of 30 days. I will write more frequent now to make up. Yrs. Ever

W. T. Sherman

ALS, InND: Sherman Family Papers.

1. Brigadier General Truman Seymour (1824–91), USA, had been surprised and defeated at the Battle of Olustee or Ocean Pond on February 20.

2. HWH to WTS, July 16, 1862, announced his orders to go to Washington and expressed his high esteem for WTS: "I am more than satisfied with everything you have done. You have always had my respect, but recently you have won my highest admiration." *OR*, I, 17: pt. 2, 100. WTS replied the same day that he would miss Halleck too, particularly as "the man who at the end of this war holds the military control of the valley of the Mississippi will be the man," and he doubted whether any other commander could do the job that Halleck had. *OR*, I, 17: pt. 2, 100–101.

TO JOHN SHERMAN

Head-Quarters Military Division
of the Mississippi,
Nashville, Tenn., Mch. 24, 1864

Dear Brother,

I went to Cincinati with Grant to see Ellen. I staid but 2 days, and am now here. I go to Decatur, Huntsville & Chattanooga, to be gone a week and then return here. I will have plenty to do. I am bored for Photographs &c. I send you the only one I have which you can have duplicated, & let the operator sell to the Curious. Give Grant all the support you can. If he can escape the toils of the schemers he may do some good. He will fight, and the Army of the Potomac will have all the fighting they want. He will expect your friendship— We are close friends. His simplicity and modesty are natural & not affected.

Whatever part is assigned me I will attempt cost what it may in life & Treasure. My love to Cecilia yr. brother,

W. T. Sherman

ALS, DLC: William T. Sherman.

TO MASON BRAYMAN[1]

Hdqrs. Military Division
of the Mississippi,
Nashville, April 2, 1864.

General Brayman, Cairo:

Read my dispatches to Veatch and Hurlbut.[2] Forrest will try and carry off plunder. If Hicks could defeat him at Paducah, surely Columbus must not only be safe, but should invite his attack.

If you can collect a couple thousand men of returning veteran regiments, you can go out to Union City and prevent his delaying in that neighborhood; but it would be idle for you to follow him. I depend on Hurlbut and Veatch to catch him or his plunder at the Hatchie.

I observe an article in an Evansville paper that looks as though you had communicated my instructions to private parties for publication. If this be so, it is a high military offense for which you must account. You are an officer of the United States and in no manner of ways accountable to an irresponsible press. I am to judge whether Veatch's command can do better service up the Tennessee behind Forrest, or chasing him about Union City.

If my dispatches to you reach the public and the enemy again you will regret it all the days of your life.

W. T. Sherman
Major-General.

Printed, *OR*, I, 32: pt. 3, 230–31.

1. Brigadier General Mason Brayman (1813–95), USA, a former newspaperman and lawyer, was commanding the District of Cairo.

2. *OR*, I, 32: pt. 3, 230.

Cypher.

Cypher telegraph—

Nashville April 2, 1864

Lt. Genl. U. S. Grant

Washington D.C.

After a *full* consultation with all my Army Commanders I have settled down to the following Conclusions to which I would like to have the Presidents Consent before I make orders.

1st. Army of the Ohio. Three Divisions of Infantry to be styled the 23rd Corps. Maj. Gen. Schofield in Command. One Division of Cavalry, Maj. Genl. Stoneman, to push Longstreets forces well out of the Valley, then fall back breaking Railroad to Knoxville & to hold Knoxville & London & be ready by May 1. with 12,000 men to act as the Left of the Grand Army.

2nd. Gen. Thomas to organize his Army into three Corps. The 11th and 12th to be United under Maj. Genl. Hooker to be composed of four Divisions. The Corps to take a new title, viz., one of the Series now vacant. Genl. Slocum[1] to be transferred East, or assigned to Some local Command on the Mississipi.

The 4th Corps Grangers, to remain unchanged, save to place Genl. Howard[2] in Command.

The 14th Corps to remain the Same. Genl. Palmer[3] is not equal to such a Command, and all parties are willing that Genl. Buell or any tried Soldier should be assigned.

Thomas to guard the Lines of communication, and have by May 1. a Command of 45,000 men for active service, to constitute the Center.

3rd. Gen. McPherson to draw from the Mississipi the Divisions of Crocker[4] & Leggett[5] now en route, mostly of veterans on furlough, and of A. J. Smith now up Red River, but due on the 10th inst. out of that Expedition, and to organize a force of 30,000 men to operate from Larkinville or Guntersville as the Right of the Grant Army. His Corps to be commanded by Logan, Frank Blair and Dodge. Hurlbut will not resign and I know no better disposition of him than to leave him at Memphis.

I propose to put Newton[6] when he comes at Vicksburg.

With these changes this army will be a unit in all respects, and I can suggest no better. I ask the President to consent and ask what title I shall give the New Corps of Hooker, in place of this 11th and 12th consolidated. The lowest number of the Army Corps now vacant will be most appropriate.[7]

I will from the Cavalry of the Dept. of the Ohio reorganize under Stoneman[8] at or near Camp Nelson, and the Cavalry of Thomas at least one Good Division under Garrard[9] at Columbia.

W. T. Sherman

Maj. Genl.

ADfS, MiU-C: James S. Schoff Civil War Collection; *OR*, I, 32: pt. 3, 221.

1. Major General Henry W. Slocum (1827–1924), USA, would assume command at the post of Vicksburg.

2. Major General Oliver O. Howard (1830–1909) took command on April 10.

3. Major General John M. Palmer (1817–1900), USA, would not be relieved of the command of the Fourteenth Corps until August.

4. Brigadier General Marcellus M. Crocker (1830–65), USA, was commanding the Fourth Division, Seventeenth Corps.

5. Brigadier General Mortimer D. Leggett (1821–96), USA, commanded the Third Division, Seventeenth Corps.

6. Brigadier General John Newton (1822–95), USA, would command the Second Division, Army of the Cumberland, through the Atlanta Campaign.

7. The new organization was designated the Twentieth Corps.

8. Major General George Stoneman was appointed head of the cavalry division of the Twenty-third Corps on April 10.

9. Brigadier General Kenner Garrard (1827–79), USA, was leading the Second Division, Cavalry Corps, Army of the Cumberland.

TO JOHN SHERMAN

Head-Quarters Military Division
of the Mississippi,
Nashville, Tenn., April 5, 1864

Dear Brother,

I have your letter of —— March, and as I have pretty well cleaned my table of current business will answer, though you must know all I can say on the points of your last. I wish you would See my Meridian Report as it will show how completely I fulfilled all my programme. Had the cavalry joined me I could have done more, but Still I had limited myself to one month & that at a time when otherwise those troops would have been idle. Ten thousand of those men have cleaned Red River up as far as Natchitoches & opened the way for Banks & Steele to reach Shreveport—Smith will go on with Banks, but Smith will at the end of 30 days (all the time I could spare him) return to Vicksburg and thence make another move that will be misunderstood till it is accomplished. However much I dislike war for its pains & turmoils I do hope it wont Cease till our People learn to leave to Congress, to the Armies, & to the Courts their appropriate business. The idea that the People through the instrumentality of the Press should supervise these matters which from their nature must be confidential is what brought on us the contempt of all Civilized Peoples. I have no doubt but the Result will be arrived at though at a costly expense, and in a bungling manner. Congress has been much at fault by allowing its action to be controlled by this public clamor, and the Senate cannot wipe its skirts of all blame, as by the very theory of our Government it was designed as a check to sudden popular pressure. I am willing to admit that the People ultimately have a Right to control but you know, and all know that the People, the property holding classes, and laborious classes have not been the People of our Country, a parcel of Scamps about the County Court Houses have been the People of the United States and have operated on the Government under the name of the whole People. I also fear the Financial difficulty, but not to the Extent you do. We have no choice. We must fight out this War. Reason is silent & impotent and men in arms listen to nothing but force. The South must govern us, or we them. There can be no division, and finances must adjust themselves to facts. Though economy should be enforced strictly still the war should be carried on without reference to Cost. You have no choice. If possible the public debt should not exceed our ability to pay interest and more, but now we must war if we have to appropriate by violence not only the resources of the South, but of the North too. You cannot put forth too much of an army this year, it may be the Crisis of the War. It will be real economy, for if Congress dont provide, the army will, and then Congress would drift behind in the Revolution and would sink into Contempt.

Too much stress has been laid on the Negro. It is used as a touch Stone, a test. It should not be, but treated as any other minor question. The Negro question will solve itself. The Government of the United States is the Issue. Shall it stand or fall? If it stands it can in Some way control Negros as well as whites, but if it fall another combination will grow up that will govern all discordant Elements with an iron hand for the world will go on.

We are gradually shaping things for a Grand Campaign. We have a well organized force to our front, and a disorganized element in our midst. The interest of every man in America is to Sustain our armies that have organisation & strength for if all else fails you must fall back on it. Grant is as good a Leader as we can find he has honesty, simplicity of character, singleness of purpose, and no hope or claim to usurp civil Power. His character more than his Genius will reconcile Armies and attach the People. Let him alone, dont disgust him by flattery or importunity. Let him alone. He wants no help. If you are not satisfied with him, where is there a better? He has personal knowledge now of all the Country, measures his difficulties, and is preparing to encounter them. If bothered hampered or embarassed, he would drop you all in disgust, and let you slide into Anarchy. You can hardly understand the intense disgust we have for the sickly sycophantic meddling of newspaper men, of sanitary & religious humbugs, who on a pretense of charity would usurp our Roads, our cars, our officers our very authority. I hope the day is past and that by universal assent the armies will be let alone to work out its destiny in which the whole Country has so vital an interest.

Let us manage the Whites & Niggers and all the Physical resources of the country & apply them when most needed. Let us accomplish great results, leaving small ones to conform in due season. The war is not yet over by a d——d sight, and when it is will be time enough for the fools to scramble for the forms of ending it by prayers, by nigger sympathy and other usual influences and the Storm of events, as the odors of a blossom have on the tempests of the wind.

I have in hand three armies here and one in Arkansas. All are in harmony, and all are willing to go & come at my bidding. I am also in perfect harmony with the civil authorities. I know their province and my own. I believe also our enemies have more respect for me than they do for Congress, so that I will be ready with the Spring. But I see with regret causes still at work north which should not be. States quarreling about Quotas, when we see their Regiments here dwindling to mere squads, absentees by the hundreds of thousands and all efforts to get men, who have drawn large bounties and are drawing larger pay still lounging at a safe distance. Yet I hope that by the voluntary consent of the men themselves we will have enough.

As our enemy fills his Ranks by Conscription, ours dwindle by sickness & furloughs. I am laboring hard to get all on the Rolls into position and Still harder to get forward the stores on which they must feed as we advance. All the Country thro which we have marched is cleaned of all subsistence & forage & everything must be sent forward by cars & wagons. It is estimated that there are now the carcasses of 30,000 animals in the valley of the Tennessee. Not one cavalry soldier in ten has a horse, and on a recent visit to Schofield out of 41,000 men he should have, I find but 7000 in Line of Battle but the furloughed men are returning and I will see that by May 1, I have on the Tennessee one of the best armies in the world. You must look for causes of the apparent incongruities not in the Army, but among our People.

I will be here about two weeks and then to the Front. Let me hear from you. I care no more for the squabbles about the Presidency, than I do for the causes of the Schleswig Holstein difficulty & Grant cares still less.[1] Therefore bore him as little as possible on such matters. In all else you will find him pleasant enough. He will necessarily be in Washington till matters are arranged from the Potomac to Orleans. I saw Banks. He thinks ideas are Stronger than the passions of men. He will find out before he is done. Love to all Your brother,

W. T. Sherman

ALS, DLC: William T. Sherman.

1. WTS's reference to Schleswig-Holstein concerns the invasion of Denmark by Prussia on February 1 and the resulting war between the two powers (with Austria as a Prussian ally) over these provinces. During the winter of 1863 some War Democrats and various Republican dissident groups sounded out the possibility of Grant as a presidential candidate in 1864, although the general did his best to dampen their enthusiasm. There were also occasional mentions of Sherman as a candidate, mainly in editorial columns.

TO JOSEPH HOLT[1]

Nashville, Tenn., April 6, 1864.

Col. Joseph Holt, Judge-Advocate-General, Washington:

Sir:

I wrote you from Memphis some time ago asking your specific instructions as to the power of a commander of an army in the field to approve and execute the sentence of death. I have not yet time nor the means to examine the question, but the law of Congress approved December 24, 1861, on page 490 of the volume Military Laws, 1776–1863, gives division and even brigade commanders power to order general courts-martial and to approve and execute sentences, save in cases of death and dismissal of a commissioned officer, which requires the approval of the general commanding the army in the field. I have always construed that as final, and to substitute the said commander in place of the President of the United States in the cases enumerated in the Sixty-third and Eighty-ninth Articles of the old Articles of War.

The question arises daily, and I expect to execute a good many spies and guerrillas under that law without bothering the President. Too many spies and villains escape us in the time consumed by trial, review, and remission to Washington, and we all know that it is very hard for the President to hang spies, even after conviction, when a troop of friends follow the sentence with earnest and *ex parte* appeals.

Spies and guerrillas, murderers under the assumed title of Confederate soldiers, deserters on leave, should be hung quick, of course after a trial, for the number of escapes made easy by the changes on guard during the long time consumed by trial and reference have made that class of men bold and dangerous, and our own scouts an detachments have so little faith in the punishment of known desperadoes that a habit is growing of "losing prisoners in the swamp," the meaning of which you know. This horrible attendant of war originated in the practice of our enemies, and I have seen it chuckled over in their public journals; but our own men are quick to learn, and unless a legal punishment can be devised you will soon be relieved of all such cases. I believe that the veriest demon should have a hearing and trial, but punishment should be prompt, yea speedy, or it loses its efficacy.

I believe the laws I have quoted give the commander of an army in the field lawful power to try by court-martial, approve and execute the sentence, and I believe the law to be right and humane to society. If wrong I should be corrected at once. Forty or fifty executions now would in the next twelve months save a thousand lives.

> Very respectfully,
> your obedient servant,
> W. T. Sherman,
> Major-general.

Printed, *OR*, II, 7:18–19.

1. Brigadier General Joseph Holt (1807–94), a Kentucky lawyer and politician, had been named judge advocate general in September 1862.

TO JAMES B. FRY[1]

> Hdqrs. Military Division
> of the Mississippi,
> Nashville, Tenn., April 10, 1864.

Col. James B. Fry, Washington, D.C.:

Dear Colonel:

Yours of April 5 received. I have, by letter and telegraph, stated my entire willingness to have General Buell assigned to duty with me, and I indicated two commands for him, either of which would be highly honorable, but I don't think it would be just for me to advise Schofield to be displaced as commander of the Department of the Ohio. He enjoys the confidence of General Grant and of his command, and were I to give preference to General Buell I would do an act of injustice by adding what little weight I possess to that of a clamor raised because General Schofield did not allow himself to be used by a political faction.

General Buell's true interest is to be on duty, and then rise to his proper station by the ordinary progress of events.

If General Buell's friends put in circulation the reports that gained publicity that he was to supersede Schofield for the purpose of producing that result, I would be compelled, as an honest man, to counteract it; but I think I know the general too well to believe he would resort to such measures to injure a brother officer, who, though younger than himself, seems to have devoted his best energies and services to the common cause.

The damned newspaper mongrels seem determined to sow dissensions wherever their influence is felt. With great respect,

> W. T. Sherman,
> Major-General.

Printed, *OR*, I, 32: pt. 3, 319–20.

1. Provost Marshal General James B. Fry had been Buell's chief of staff for a year from November 1861 to October 1862 and thereafter remained a devoted adherent of his former commander.

TO ULYSSES S. GRANT
Private & Confidential

> Head-Quarters, Military Division
> of the Mississippi,
> Nashville, Tenn., April 10 1864

Lt. General U. S. Grant
Comdr. in Chief
Washington D.C.
Dear General,

Your two letters of April 4 are now before me, and afford me infinite satisfaction.[1] That we are now all to act on a Common plan, Converging on a Common Center looks like Enlightened War. Like yourself you take the biggest load and from me you shall have thorough and hearty cooperation. I will not let side issues draw me off from your main plan in which I am to Knock Joe Johnston, and do as much damage to the resources of the Enemy as possible.

I have heretofore written to Genl. Rawlins and Col. Babcock of your staff somewhat of the method in which I propose to act. I have seen all my army, corps and Division Commanders and have signified only to the former, viz. Schofield, Thomas and McPherson, our general plans, which I inferred from the purport of our conversation here and at Cincinati.

First I am pushing stores to the Front with all possible despatch, and am completing the organization according to the orders from Washington which are ample & perfectly satisfactory. I did not wish to displace Palmer, but asked George Thomas to tell me in all frankness exactly what he wanted. All he asked is granted and all he said was that Palmer *felt* unequal to So large a Command and would be willing to take a Division provided Buell or some tried & experienced soldier were given the Corps. But on the whole Thomas is now well content with his Command, so are Schofield & McPherson. It will take us all of April to get in our furloughed veterans, to bring up A. J. Smiths command, and to collect provisions and cattle to the Line of the Tennessee. Each of the three armies will guard by detachments of its own their Rear Communications. At the signal to be given, by you, Schofield will leave a select Garrison at Knoxville & Loudon and with 12,000 men drop down to Hiwassee & march on Johnstons Right by the Old Federal Road. Stoneman now in Kentucky organizing the Cavalry forces of the Army of the Ohio, will operate with Schofield on his left front, it may be pushing a select body of about 2000 Cavalry by Ducktown on Elijay & towards Athens.

Thomas will aim to have 45,000 men of all arms and move straight on Johnston wherever he may be, fighting him cautiously, persistently and to the best of advantage. He will have two Divisions of Cavalry to take advantage of any offering.

McPherson will have nine Divisions of the Army of the Tennessee if A. J. Smith get in—in which case he will have full 30,000 of the best men in America. He will cross the Tennessee at Decatur and Whitesburg march towards Rome and feel for Thomas. If Johnston fall behind the Coosa, then McPherson push for Rome, and if Johnston then fall behind the Chattahoochie as I believe he will, then McPherson will cross and join with Thomas. McPherson has no cavalry, but I have taken one of Thomas' Divisions, viz. Garrards, 6000 strong, which I now have at Columbia mounting Equipping and preparing. I design this Division to operate on McPherson's Right Rear or Front according as the Enemy appears. But the moment I detect Johnston falling behind the Chattahoochee I propose to cast off the Effective part of this Cavalry Division after crossing Coosa, straight for Opelika, West Point, Columbus or Wetumpka, to break up the Road between Montgomery and Georgia. If Garrard can do this work good he can return to the main army, but should a superior force interpose, then he will seek safety at Pensacola, and join Banks, or after Rest act against any force that he can find on the East of Mobile, till such time as he can reach me.

Should Johnston fall behind Chattahoochee I would feign to the Right but pass to the Left and act on Atlanta or on its Eastern communications according to developed facts. This is about as far ahead as I feel disposed to look, but I would ever bear in mind that Johnston is at all times to be kept so busy that he cannot in any event send any part of his command against you or Banks. If Banks can at the Same time carry Mobile and open up the Alabama River he will in a measure solve the most difficult part of my problem, *Provisions*. But in that I must venture. Georgia has a million of Inhabitants. If they can live we should not starve. If the enemy interrupt my communications I will be absolved from all obligations to Subsist on our own resources, but feel perfectly justified in taking whatever & whereever I can find. I will inspire my command if successful with my feeling that Beef & Salt are all that is absolutely necessary to Life, & parched Corn fed General Jacksons Army once, on that very ground. As Ever your friend & Servant

W. T. Sherman
Maj. Genl.

ALS, PHi: Gratz Collection; *OR*, I, 32: pt. 3, 312–14.

1. The first letter of April 4, 1865, in *PUSG*, 10:251–53, confided Grant's plans for the coming campaign: "It is my design, if the enemy keep quiet and allow me to take the initiative in the Spring Campaign to work all parts of the Army to-gether, and, somewhat towards a common center. For your information I now write you my programme as at present determined upon" (p. 251). Sherman was to attack and destroy Johnston's army and march into the interior of the enemy's country, "inflicting all the damage you can against their War resources" (p. 252). Grant told him to do it however he wished but to submit the plan of operation to him as soon as possible. The second letter of April 4, in *PUSG*, 10:254–55, offered but minor alterations to the command changes WTS had suggested in his April 2 letter.

TO JOHN SHERMAN

Head-Quarters, Military Division
of the Mississippi,
Nashville, Tenn., Apl. 11, 1864

Dear Brother,

Of course I have enough to do but more to think about.[1] We have now been two years & more at War and have reached a period where we should consider the War as fairly begun. Dont you delude yourself that it is even approaching an end. For a shrewd people we have less sense even than the Mexicans, paying fabulous bounties for a parcel of boys & old men, and swelling our Muster Rolls, but adding nothing to our real fighting Strength. Instead of enlarging we are all cutting down our organizations. I will have the fragments of some Corps on the Tennessee, but over 30,000 animals have died and it is going to be a terrible job to replace them and to accumulate to the Front the necessary food for mules & men in time, but though assured that the country for a long distance into Georgia & Alabama is stripped as it is on this side, yet at the right time I shall go ahead and if necessary feed on anything. I will not be behind hand when the Grand beginning is announced. I can tell you nothing more. I hope Grant will be equally retentive, he ought not to trust even Mr. Lincoln, and as to a member of Congress I hope Grant will make it a death penalty for one to go south of the Potomac. I expect soon to have a new howl against me. The pressure to go in our cars to the front was so great & the difficulty of getting to Chattanooga so momentous, that I ordered absolutely no citizen, private freight or anything but freight purely military, till the wants of the troops were supplied.[2] I make the Soldiers march & yet am bored to death by men & women to go to Chattanooga & Knoxville. Of course I deny all. Even Mrs. {Linet}, sister to Moulton, who wanted to see her husband—A parcel of preachers came with a positive demand under some promise of the Sec. of War, they were denied and persisted in a written application. I endorsed "Certainly not. The Road is wanted purely for military freight. 200 pounds of powder or oats are worth more to the U.S. than that amount of bottled piety." Every Regt. has its chaplain and there is no necessity at all for these wandering preachers who are a positive nuisance. I am told they meditate vengeance.

It will require the conjoined energies of the whole nation to meet the Shock this spring, and it may be the end will be made certain, but still the long, persistent struggle with half a million of men far more desperate than our old Indians is yet to come. We can beat them on the Sanitary Commission question but when it comes to Stubbornness, intensity of earnestness and Zeal for the Cause the South beats us all to pieces. There is no doubt we have to repeople the Country and the Sooner we set about it the better. Some device must be made to deed houses and lands captured of the enemy. The whole population of Iowa & Wisconsin should be transferred at once to West Kentucky, Tennessee & Mississippi, and a few hundred thousand settlers should be pushed into south Tennessee. I enclose you a letter of instructions I made to my adjutant Sawyer, who remained at my Hd. Qrs. Huntsville when I went to Meridian.[3] I would not object to have this letter printed as it is something new and is true. Sawyer tells me it had a powerful effect on the People of Huntsville. As the letter is equally applicable to large districts still to be gone over, its publication would do no harm, except to turn the Richmond Press against me, as the Prince of Barbarians Yrs. in haste,

W. T. Sherman

ALS, DLC: William T. Sherman.

1. On March 26, JS had written his brother from Washington to warn him that all his movements would now be under scrutiny and that he should avoid distraction whenever possible. He also wrote about seeing USG ("he is subjected to the dangerous process of being lionized") and expressed his belief that all was well in the army and that it was "wonderfully filled up." DLC: WTS.

2. General Orders No. 6, Headquarters, Military Division of the Mississippi, April 6, 1864, OR, I, 32: pt. 3, 279–80.

3. WTS to Roswell M. Sawyer, January 31, 1864, above.

TO LORENZO THOMAS

Hdqrs. Military Division
of the Mississippi,
Nashville, Tenn., April 12, 1864.

General Lorenzo Thomas,
Adjutant-General U.S. Army, Vicksburg, Miss.:
Dear General:

Yours of March 30, from Natchez, is received, and I take pleasure in answering. I confess I fear to enunciate any plan that can reconcile all objections, but am willing to say that I will use all my official power and influence to carry out yours or that of the War Department. My objections to the plantation scheme are purely military. The Mississippi is a long, weak line, easily approached from the rear. Plantations of, say, three whites and fifty blacks to a mile of river can be broken at any point by a guerrilla band of 100 with perfect impunity. You and I know the temper of the whites in the South.

I heard a young lady in Canton, educated at Philadelphia, who was a communicant of a Christian church, thank her God that her negroes, who had attempted to escape into our lines at Big Black, had been overtaken by Ross' Texas brigade and killed. She thanked God, and did so in religious sincerity. Now, a stranger to the sentiment of the South would consider this unnatural, but it is not only natural but universal. All the people of the South, old and young, rich and poor, educated and ignorant, unite in this, that they will kill as vipers the whites who attempt to free their slaves, and also the "ungrateful slaves" who attempt to change their character from slave to free.

Therefore, in making this change, which I regard as a decree of nature, we have to combat not only with organized resistance of the Confederate forces, but the entire people of the South. Now, I would prefer much to colonize the negroes on lands clearly forfeited to us by treason, and for the Government to buy or extinguish the claims of other and loyal people in the districts chosen. I look upon the lands bordering the Mississippi, Steele's Bayou, Deer Creek, Sunflower, Bogue Phalia, Yazoo, &c., in that rich alluvial region lying between Memphis and Vicksburg, of which Haines' Bluff, Yazoo City, and Grenada are the key points, as the very country in which we might collect the negroes, and where they will find more good land already cleared than in any district I know of, and it would enable the negro at once to be useful.

If, however, the Government prefer the "lessee" system, then I shall favor the occupation by a black brigade of Harrisonburg, and cover as well as may be the Mississippi country lying between the Washita and Yazoo. General Slocum will soon come down, and we believe he will co-operate with you with his whole heart. Of course the possession of Vicksburg is a *sine qua non*. We don't want the task of taking it again; but if he can spare troops he will be instructed, in connection with Natchez, to hold Harrisonburg, with one or more gun-boats up the Washita and Tensas.

Steele is ordered to hold the line of Red River, but I must have Smith's command, which I loaned for but thirty days, and I have reason to know that Banks must swing over against Mobile, so Steele will have only his Arkansas command, and that may be insufficient; of this we cannot judge until we know what is already done. If Shreveport be taken before these orders reach Steele, he may hold that point; otherwise, all he should attempt would be Alexandria, in connection with the gun-boats.

We have sure enough a big job on hand, and the only way is to go on trusting to consequences following naturally grand results. Lee and Johnston must be whipped, and it should not be deferred an hour beyond the first possible practicable moment.

I necessarily write in some haste, but you will catch the drift of my argument.

> With respect, your friend and servant,
> W. T. Sherman,
> Major-General, Commanding.

Printed, *OR*, III, 4:225–26.

TO THOMAS EWING JR.

> Head-Quarters, Military Division
> of the Mississippi.
> Nashville, Tenn., Apl. 18, 1864

Dear Tom,

I got your letter enclosing Miss Baileys appreciation for a lock of my hair. Her first letter was referred to my redheaded orderly Hill, whose modesty was so shocked that his face outrivalled in brilliancy his brick top—Miss Baileys 2nd letter I answered sending autograph and describing my hair as red, bristly & horrid—I think She is satisfied to leave my locks out of the cluster of flowers to be made up out of the hairs of the Great men of the day. Such nonsense is repulsive to me, and I cant stop to notice Such things.

I am intent on Collecting from all the corners the vast army I have on paper, and by May 1st I hope to have a host as vast & terrible as Alaric led into Rome's doomed Empire. I am waiting for the men I sent up Red River which were loaned to Banks for one month, and which Should now be coming back. I hope they took Shreveport, as the expedition will not be complete till that Stronghold is ours.

Grant is now the Chief & I abstain from any action west of the Mississipi further than is imposed on me by orders. I have given it as my opinion that all the Department west of the Mississipi should be united under one mind. It should be done as my thoughts and interests will naturally be drawn to the objects to my immediate front, and may lead me to Slight other & quite as important interests[.]

My opinion is Grant will unite everything East and go straight on Lee. I will do the Same against Johnston[.] If we can defeat these two armies, the Smaller ones will gradually disband leaving us to deal only with scattered bands, which however mischievous to neighborhoods can in no wise influence the great course of the war. Forrests whole movement was intended to divert our attention from this concentration, which Johnston has surely detected.

Hugh is at Mumfordsville commanding the District of West Kentucky, and Charley is Lt. Col. of the 15th Corps at Huntsville. I suppose both want to be with me, but my staff is now less than even before, because I deal only with the heads of these large armies, which have a complete organization. Affectionately,

W. T. Sherman

ALS, DLC: Thomas Ewing and Family Papers.

TO CHARLES A. DANA

> Head-Quarters Military Division
> of the Mississippi,
> Nashville, Tenn., Apr. 21 1864

C. A. Dana Esq.
Asst. Sec. of War, Washington
My Dear Friend

It may be Parliamentary, but is not military for me to write you; but I feel assured anything I may write, will only have the force of a casual conversation, such as we have indulged in by the Camp fire, or as we jogged along by the Road. The text of my letter is one you gave a Philadelphia Gentleman who is going up to East Tennessee to hunt up his Brother Quakers and administer the Bounties of his own & his fellow citizens charity. Now who would stand in the way of one so kindly & charitably disposed? Surely not I. But other questions present themselves—We have been working hard with tens of thousands of men, and at a cost of millions of dollars to make Railroads to carry to the Line of the Tennessee enough provisions & material of war to enable us to push on our Physical Force to the next step in the war. I have found on personal inspection that hitherto the Railroads have barely been able to feed one man, but that mules have died by the thousand, that arms and ammunition had lain in the depot for two weeks for want of cars, that no accumulation at all of clothing & stores had been or could be made at Chattanooga, and that it took four sets of cars & locomotives to accomodate the Passes given by Military Commanders, that gradually the wants of citizens & charities were actually consuming the real resources of a Road designed exclusively for army purposes. You have been on the spot & can understand my argument. At least one hundred Citizens daily presented good claims to go forwards women to attend sick children, parents in Search of the bodies of sons slain in battle, Sanitary Committees sent by states & corporations to look after the personal wants of their constituents, ministers & friends to minister to the Christian wants of their flocks, men who had fled, anxious to go back to look after lost families &c. &c. and move still the Tons of goods which they all bore on their merciful errands. None but such as you, who have been present & seen the tens hundreds & thousands of such cases can measure them in the aggregate & segregate the exceptions.

I had no time to hesitate, for but a short month was left me to prepare, and I must be ready to put in motion near one hundred thousand men to move when nought remains to Save life. I figured up the mathematics & saw that I must have daily 145 car loads of essentials for 30 days to enable me to fill the requirement, only 75 daily was all the Roads were doing. Now I have got it up to 136. Troops march—cattle go by the roads. Sanitary & Sutlers stores limited and all is done that human energy can accomplish. Yet come these pressing claims of charity, by men & women who cannot grasp the Great Problem. My usual answer is, Show me that your presence at the front is more valuable than 200 pounds of powder, bread or oats, and it is generally conclusive. I have given your Mr. Savery a Pass on Your letter, and it takes 200 pounds of bread from our Soldiers, or the Same of oats from our patient mules, but I could not promise to feed the suffering Quakers at the expense of our Army. I have ordered all who cannot procure food at the Front to be allowed transportation back in our empty cars, but I cannot undertake to transport the food needed by the Worthy East Tennesseeans or any of them. In Peace there is a beautiful harmony in all the departments of Life—they all fit together like the Chinese puzzle: but in war all is ajar. Nothing fits and it is the struggle between the Stronger & Weaker, and the latter however it may appear to the better feelings of our nation must kick the beam. To make war we must & will harden our hearts.

Therefore when Preachers clamor, & the Sanitaries Wail dont give in, but Know that war, like the thunderbolt follows its laws, and turns not aside even if the beautiful, the virtuous and charitable stand in its path.

When the day & the hour comes I'll strike Joe Johnston be the result what it may, but in the time allotted to me for preparation I must & will be selfish in making those preperations which I know to be necessary[.] Your friend,

W. T. Sherman
Maj. Genl.

ALS, DLC: Charles A. Dana Papers.

TO PHILEMON B. EWING

Head-Quarters, Military Division
of the Mississippi,
Nashville, Tenn., Apl. 21, 1864

Dear Phil,

I have your letter and am gratified to Know that you at least feel the embarrasment natural at finding Hugh dissatisfied. He applied for some of his

Division Staff to be sent him to Mumfordsville Capt. Comyn,[1] and it affording me the opportunity I invited him to come down. He did so the day before yesterday & remained with me all day yesterday. He told me all about his trouble with Logan, which was as usual a difficulty with one of Logans staff who had meddled with his business. It is difficult to define clearly in what cases a General may delegate powers to another, but I do not doubt Hugh was right in the abstract though the case hardly warrants the feeling he expresses. We must deal with men as we find them and it is not Logans fault that he was a Citizen only three years ago, and looks at all questions from another view than a professional soldier. I am so anxious to have at least harmony prevail, that I was not sorry to have him say that on the whole he would content himself with his present Command, though it is an inferior one. He simply commands the Road Guards from here to Louisville, which is not at all threatened & may not be as our stores are here and forward of this. He passed the time very pleasantly, and left me last night about midnight, and by this hour is at Mumfordsville on Green River. We called to see Mrs. Flanner who lives here with her son Gen. Granger, who however now is absent on recruiting business in Ohio.

Charley is still with Logan. He too wants to come away, but you must remember the Law, which gives him the Specific Rank of Lt. Col. when acting as Inspector General. I need less staff now than before, & the Law provides none but aids and such of the General Army Staff as I draw near me. I have far less of detailed work now than before.

All furloughs, discharges, transfers and returns which so load down a Division or Corps Commander, do not come to me. I merely distribute the armies & give General Instructions. My whole thoughts now are on concentrating in the Tennessee, and in getting forward the supplies that will enable me at the right time to move against Joe Johnston, entrenched in the Mountain Gaps of Georgia. So many men went on furlough, and it is like drawing teeth to get them back, but next month for better or worse. I am sorry to see the People settling down to the belief that this year will end the war. That is impossible. Full 300,000 of the bravest men of this world must be killed or banished in the South, before they will think of Peace, and in killing them we must lose an equal or greater number, for we must be the attacking party. Still we as a nation have no alternative or choice. It must be done whether we want or not. We must rule them or they will us. Forrests move indicates the animus, and yet our People will persevere in carrying on farms, plantations & commerce, in the very thick of war, though we all know that it but serves to provide our enemy. I am very anxious that Ellen shd. keep her finances smooth & simple, and think well of her conversion of any money she receives into County Bonds.

I will now soon go to Chattanooga and not come back again. Things are working as smooth as I could expect, and I will have by May 1. my armies well in hand and a pretty fair supply of edibles to the Front. I have only accomplished this by the strictest measures of prohibition of all business else. affectionately

W. T. Sherman

ALS, Atlanta, Ga.: Private Collection of C. Parke Day.

1. Captain John Comyn was the commissary of subsistence for the Second Division, Fifteenth Corps.

TO ELLEN EWING SHERMAN

Head-Quarters Military Division
of the Mississippi,
Nashville, Tenn., Apl. 22, 1864

Dearest Ellen,

I suppose you saw Luke Clark,[1] and have received letters of me very irregularly. I have all of yours which come promptly but I fear mine come less regularly. I dont feel that I have too much to do, yet the days slip along very fast, and the time is approaching when I must to the Front, and then lookout. It seems that Banks got a whaling up Red River.[2] He was to have left New Orleans Mch. 5, but did not till the 25, and he left my troops go up to Alexandria & above without keeping his appointment, the consequence is that he is behind time.

The accounts from there are not full, but he has double the force necessary to whip Kirby Smith, but he has got his men scattered & Smith has got his united. Well he must fight his way out the best way he can. Hurlbut is ruined by his apathy & fear to go out of Memphis to fight Forrest. He seems to have set down on the Defensive, when he had plenty of men who by marching out fifty miles could have made Forrest quit that Country long before he did. The mischief done was however to the Negros & People of West Tennessee, rather than to us. Hurlbut is timid and there is no use in denying it. He is now at Cairo and Washburn[3] goes to Memphis. All this results from Smiths failing to meet me at Meridian. Hugh at my invitation came to See me a few days ago. He is pleasantly Situated at Mumfordsville with his family, but so far as the War goes he might as well be in Ohio, but he can come in when War's havoc makes vacancies. He has a feeling against Logan, and one of the greatest troubles of this war results from the intestine troubles in our own Camps, so rather than Encourage him to resume his Old Division he will stay where he is. Cockerill[4] and Loomis[5] have resigned, and it seems men are more intent on their own personal claims to advancement than the interest of the Country.

The President cannot satisfy all claimants and I do not envy him the task of deciding among the thousands of applicants whose Claims are highly endorsed.[6] I have on three several occasions named Col. Cockerill and twice Col. Loomis, yet I would not accuse Mr. Lincoln of improper preferences for others. We must submit to him or Jeff Davis—No other choice is left us. I am quite well, and ride out when I can. I will have riding enough to do. ever yrs.

W. T. Sherman

ALS, InND: Sherman Family Papers.

1. Clark was an old Ohio friend of the Shermans serving with WTS's forces.

2. In early April, Banks's army had been defeated at Mansfield and Pleasant Hill, Louisiana, and he had begun drawing his troops back down the river on April 10; this retreat would continue through the month.

3. Major General Cadwallader C. Washburn (1818–82), USA, was commanding the District of Western Tennessee.

4. Cockerill had resigned on April 13 after holding various western commands.

5. Colonel Cyrus O. Loomis (1818–72) of the First Michigan Light Artillery.

6. In March and April, EES had been asking about Hugh's status with regard to possible promotion. On March 26 she had asked what had been done with Hugh and expressed her hope that WTS could persuade him "to return to the field." She did agree with her husband in an April 9 letter "that Boyle made a great mistake in leaving his Division & taking the position he has" and that her family concurred. Yet she still thought that WTS had slighted his family socially and that he had hurt Hugh's feelings. She reiterated that Hugh was in error in accepting the Kentucky post on April 15. With regard to Cockerill's promotion, she asked her husband in an April 7 letter if Dan McCook's promotion had galled Cockerill. SFP.

TO JOHN SHERMAN

Head-Quarters Military Division
of the Mississippi,
Nashville, Tenn., Apl. 22, 1864

Dear Brother,

I got yours of Apl. 17 is received.[1] I understand exactly the force of your letters of introduction to me. You may further explain to each that my mind is so positively made up that men who come to the front for purposes of trade & civil business are out of their place and I invariably advise them to go north of the Ohio. The men who hang round our armies to make money out of the soldiers are like vultures and are entitled to little consideration. Such as want to buy cotton and Stolen horses are little better than public enemies for they play into the hands of the enemy. Our Sanitary Dept. is now so systematyzed that there is no use of any one male or female going south of Nashville. We here have a depot of Sanitary Supplies and forward them as fast as we can get means of hauling. Every person who goes south of Nashville loads our cars to the extent of 200 pounds and takes that much from our men, or mules, and besides they eat bread & meat which we need there. You can have no idea of the crowds of men & women who come here on seeming errands of charity, but they might as well stay at home for they simply aggravate the trouble. We cannot feed our army & animals much less the suffering and patriotic Tennesseeans. I enclose my last orders and you may be sure I will enforce them.[2] I know the pressure brought to bear on the Secretary of War, and officials, but I must and will give preference to the Army proper, over the wants of others however meritorious. We cannot carry on War & Peace at the Same time.

As to Negros, whatever the proper authorities resolve on I must do. I think the negro question is run into the ground. Negros should be allowed to make some provision for their families and to pass through a preparatory state before being called on for war. Of course Forrest & all southerners will kill them and their white officers.[3] We all knew that, and should not expose small detachments—We were using them in moderation and in connection with whites as fast as the demands of service justified, but it was made a Policy, and all had to bend to it—then it became the means by which Massachusetts and other states could dodge their share. They raised the cry that a negro man was as good to stop a Rebel bullet as a white man. But is it the only use you can put a soldier to to stop a bullet? I thought a soldier was to be an active machine, a fighter. Dirt or cotton will stop a bullet better than a mans body. We ought not to engraft a doubtful element in an army *now*, it is too critical a period. Our own soldiers have prejudices and these are aroused by the foolish squabbles of Governors to show they have given their quotas. Every man in the United States must fight irrespective of quotas and those who dont or wont fight must drift into the character of a woman non combatant or mere denizen of the Land. Of course some must work & raise corn, and why not use in a great measure the negro labor we have Captured, instead of scattering it and dissipating it in a poor quality of soldiery and in raising cotton. Of course all the Leasehold plantations on the River will be cleaned out, for no army can protect them. Their establishment is merely calculated to scatter along a weak line, what if compressed would be self protection. I take it for granted that Forrest & bands of that Kind will supply themselves bountifully out of the mules & horses which lessees have got seemingly for that very purpose. A limited quantity of negro troops can be used, but it will be years before any General officer would use them in open Battle, and even in Fortifications they must form the moiety. If in the service they must be protected. I feel certain the war will soon become barbarous, but it is inevitable. Prisoners should not be exchanged, but the war should be with desperation, the sooner the better. Yr. brother,

W. T. Sherman

ALS, DLC: William T. Sherman.

1. On April 17, JS answered his brother's letter of April 11: "Your letter to Maj. Sawyer is entirely correct but just now I do not think it best to publish it." WTS's friends in Washington agreed with his assessment of affairs. JS went on to say that he tried to avoid sending letters of introduction and told his brother to ignore those he did receive. He did hope, however, that WTS would do what he could to help those in his command who had been JS's political allies. DLC: WTS.

2. General Orders No. 8, Headquarters, Military Division of the Mississippi, April 19, 1864, prohibited civilian use of army provisions. *OR,* I, 32: pt. 3, 420.

3. Nathan Bedford Forrest's cavalry captured Fort Pillow, Tennessee, on April 12, 1864, overwhelming the Federals with approximately three times their numbers. Virtually all Union soldiers were killed, wounded, or captured; most of the black soldiers were killed, and testimony from survivors indicated that Confederates killed them in cold blood after their surrender.

TO EDWIN M. STANTON

> Head-Quarters Military Division
> of the Mississippi.
> Nashville, Tenn., Apl. 23 1864

Hon. E. M. Stanton,
Sec. of War, Washington
Sir,

Pursuant to your orders, two officers are now engaged in making affadavits & collecting testimony as to the Fort Pillow affair. They are ordered to Send you direct a copy of their Report, and on to me. I know well the animus of the Southern Soldiery, and the truth is they cannot be restrained[.] The effect will be of course to make the negros desperate and when in time they commit horrid acts of retaliation we will be relieved of the responsibility. Thus far negros have been comparatively well behaved and have not committed the horrid excesses and barbarities which the Southern People so much dreaded.

I send you herewith my latest newspaper from Atlanta of the 18th and 19th inst. In them you will find articles of interest and their own accounts of the Fort Pillow affair. The enemy will contend that a place taken by assault is not Entitled to quarter, but this Rule would have justified us in any indiscriminate slaughter at Arkansas Post—Fort De Russy & other places taken by assault.

I doubt the wisdom of any fixed Rule by our Government, but let Soldiers affected make their Rules as we progress. We will use their own logic against them, as we have from the beginning of the war. The Southern Army, which is the Southern People cares no more for our Clamor than the idle wind, but they will heed the Slaughter that will follow as the natural consequence of their own inhuman acts. I am with respect Your Servant

> W. T. Sherman
> Maj. Genl. Comdg.

ALS, DLC: Edwin M. Stanton Papers.

TO THOMAS EWING SHERMAN

Headquarters, Military Division
of the Mississippi
Nashville, Tenn., April 25 1864

My Dear Tommy,

Captain Poe[1] of the Engineer Corps has put up in a Box some Photographic pictures of Chattanooga and Knoxville which he sends to day to Mama by Express. When they come you can claim them to be put away for you. They are of course very accurate for they are painted by the picture itself which you will understand when you get old Enough to Study Chemistry.

I suppose you saw Luke and he told you all about the Regulars who are now here, but I must go to the Front in a day or two and will lose their services. I cannot tell when I will come back, as we must have some more hard Battles.

Whatever may now happen to me you are old enough to remember me, and will take my place[.] Dont study too hard as it may make you weak and Sick. Play at all sorts of games, and learn to ride your pony this summer. Get Some of the boys to break it for you. Also as soon as you are old Enough you can learn to Swim, to hunt and to fish. All these things are as necessary as to read and write.

I am going to Chattanooga and from there into Georgia. I can hardly tell, and you could hardly understand the great things now transpiring, but whatever I do, is for you, and our Country. We must have peace, and that can only be had by Battle.

Give my best love to Mama and Lizzie—dont let Elly and Rachel forget me. And be as you always have been a good boy. Yr. father,

W. T. Sherman

ALS, InND: Sherman Family Papers.
1. Captain Orlando M. Poe (1832–95), USA, who had earlier had an appointment of brigadier general, was Sherman's chief engineer at this time.

TO THOMAS EWING SR.

Head-Quarters Military Division
of the Mississippi.
Nashville, Tenn., Apr. 27 1864.

Hon. Thos. Ewing
Washington D.C.
Dear Sir,

I am in receipt of yours of April 21, & have but a moment to answer.

I see you have fallen into two errors. I had not the selection of Genl. Wm.

Sooy Smith. General Grant selected him after a long personal and official association. If the failure to meet me at Meridian be personal as to General Wm. Sooy Smith it is not *mine*.

At Chattanooga Grant was with Thomas in person—he held back Thomas' troops till Hooker got into position—we were delayed by Chattanooga Creek impassable that day without a Bridge to construct which took *time*, 4 hours. If we were to dispose of such men as Thomas summarily who would take his place? We are not masters as Napoleon was. He could make & unmake on the Spot. We must take the tools provided us, and in the order prescribed by Rank of which the Law judges.

We cannot be judged by the Rules of war in Europe, where a sovereign is master, whereas our master is "public clamor," a hard thing to control. We have to fight with ideal armies, & with such men & officers as chance gives us. Our real fighting force is not ⅓ of our paper force, and the paper force is half what the Public supposes and by which standard we are judged.

The Real Power that controls us is a swarm of men who are trying to make money, who exalt those who minister to their schemes and pull down those who thwart them or make them subordinate to war. The Plantation lessees, & cotton thieves can reverse any policy that our Generals may devise and disperse our troops in weak bodies to cover their selfish plans. We are required to respect the Policy of the Government, which is to encourage common trade and the gathering of dishonest wealth. These things cannot change, till the whole character of our People is changed by the sad calamities of war, and self acquired experience. We will not heed the examples of Other People.

I have tried to buffet the storm, but must subside to Powers that no man can control. I am with affection yr. son

W. T. Sherman

ALS, DLC: Thomas Ewing and Family Papers.

TO ELLEN EWING SHERMAN

Nashville, Apl. 27, 64

Dearest Ellen,

I wrote you a long letter yesterday sending you a check for $300.[1] Last night I got yours of the 23rd,[2] one from Minnie same date and one from your father, all of which I answer today for tomorrow I start for Chattanooga and at once prepare for the coming campaign. I will have 20,000 less men than I calculated for the Red River disaster, and two Divisions of McPherson, whose furlough wont expire. These furloughs have as I feared impaired if not lost us this campaign. When men get home they forget their comrades here, and though Governors are very patriotic in offers of troops their acts fall far short of their promises. Our armies are now weaker than at any former period of the war. My old corps has dwindled away to 10,000 though we had promises that all the Regiments would come with two or three hundred Recruits each—but the recruits seem to have pocketed the money and like selfish men staid at home.

I will begin with Schofield 12,000 Infantry & 5000 cavalry. Thomas 40,000 Infantry & 5000 cavalry, and McPherson 20,000 Infantry and 5000 cavalry combined it is a big army, and a good one, and it will take a strong opposition to Stop us once in motion.

Dalton will be our first Point—Kingston next, then Alatoona and then Atlanta. All the attacks of the enemy on Paducah, Fort Pillow and in North Carolina are to draw us off from our Concentration. As soon as we move they will attempt to cut in behind & cut our Roads and fight us in front, so we are forced to detach men, to guard our Railroads all the way from Louisville to Chattanooga.

I send you parcels of photographs which I trust are the last I will have to endure for a long time. I will leave Genl. Webster[3] & Maj. Sawyer here, and take with me McCoy, Dayton Audenreid,[4] and some chiefs of artillery subsistence eng[inee]rs &c. but my staff will be comparatively small.

I expect to be at Chattanooga till May 5 and then on. Address your letters to Nashville. yrs. ever

W. T. Sherman

ALS, InND: Sherman Family Papers.

1. WTS to EES, April 26, 1864, SFP.

2. In this letter, EES sent her husband family news and commented on the opening of a new campaign. SFP.

3. Brigadier General Joseph D. Webster (1811–76), USA, was Sherman's chief of staff at this time.

4. Joseph C. Audenreid (d. 1880) had been Sherman's aide since 1863 and USG's before then.

TO MARIA BOYLE EWING SHERMAN

Head-Quarters Military Division
of the Mississippi,
Nashville, Tenn., May 1 1864

Dearest Minnie,

This is Sunday, May 1st. and a beautiful day it is. I have just come from a long ride over my Old Battle field of November 25th which is on a high Ridge about four or five miles from Chattanooga. The leaves are now coming out, and the young flowers have begun to bloom. I have gathered a few which I send you in token of my love, and to tell you I gathered them on the very spot where many a brave man died for you, and such as you. I have made up a

Similar Bouquet for Lizzie, which I will send her in a letter today, so that both of you will have a present of flowers to commemorate this night opening of Spring.

You can keep this Bouquet in some of your Books, and though it may fade away entirely it will in after years remind you of this year whose history for good or evil is most important and may either raise our Countrys fame to the highest Standard or sink it to that of Mexico.

Lizzie has written me a very good letter showing great progress. I think by next year if we all live, she will be willing and anxious to be with you. She is so much more timid than you, so much more afraid of strangers that I am anxious she should be with you at school. Write to me when you Can, and letters sent to Nashville will find me somewheres, as our mails will come via Nashville.

Give my best respects to your teachers and the Girls that you like & believe me always yr. affectionate father,

W. T. Sherman

ALS, OHi: William T. Sherman.

TO ELLEN EWING SHERMAN

> Head-Quarters Military Division
> of the Mississippi,
> Chattanooga, Tenn., May 4, 1864

Dearest Ellen,

I received today the enclosed paper, which I explain in the way I did the last, these three lots were a part of that trade, and I suppose we had made a Deed to Tom, and instead of taking a deed back which would have cost some dollars to record we took this paper, the effect of which is simply Tom may have sold, or can sell these lots, but is bound to account to you for the money. Your Leavenworth agent can see whether Tom has sold them. If so he is indebted to you the proceeds of sale, but if unsold you can claim a deed from him to you for them. Tear off your note to me, and send your Irish Lawyer the part in Toms handwriting and he can either procure of Tom the Money or the Deed. I am willing to concede to you more closeness in money matters than me. An Irish Yankee is the closest sort of one but if you can get rid of your Leavenworth Estate & not call on me for Cash to pay the balance I will be content. The Illinois Farm is hid, and I want you to lay low about it for if it were discovered that I had ever been fool enough to buy land my Credit would be gone. Yet the immense cost of this war will strip all things of value that cannot be transported abroad. This is the real reason of the increased cost of every thing for your money is only half the value of Gold, and in the south, it takes about sixteen of paper to make one. At the Same rate three more years would extinguish all values. But I have no time to talk or think of such things now. We are now moving[.] Thomas whole army is at Ringgold—Schofield is on his left near Red Clay, and McPherson is here, and moves out tomorrow. I will go to Ringgold tomorrow and will then be within Four miles of the enemy. We may have some of the most desperate fighting of the war, but it cannot be avoided deferred or modified[.] I will as heretofore do my best and trust to the troops. All my dispositions thus far are good.

I have written to you and all the children. I sent Minnie & Lizzie Bouquets collected on our Battle Field of last November, and if any ill fate attend me in this, they will remember me by that. The weather is beautiful, and the Army is in fine condition. I did expect to have back more of the furloughed veterans, but it takes more time for them to assemble from their homes than we military minds calculate.

Banks too instead of being near Mobile, where he would assist me, will be cooped up at Grand {Ecosse}. Poor Stone is again I see the Scape Goat. It was not his fault, but the fault of our People, who will insist on such heavy trains of wagons, and not providing against danger unless seen—Had I marched that Carelessly in Mississipi I should have met the same, but the enemy saw that they could not get at me without paying for it—Banks had more men than I did, four times as much cavalry, and did not need many wagons as he was at all times near his Boats. You saw that my part of the army did its share. Indeed they seem to have been the only true part of that army. Mower is one of my young pets. Charley has not yet reported to me. Tomorrow I will be off & may not write for some time, but the telegraph will announce the result of our first Stops. My love to the Children, & let what fate befal us, believe me always true to you & mindful of your true affection, ever yrs.,

W. T. Sherman

ALS, InND: Sherman Family Papers.

CHAPTER 11

May 20, 1864–September 4, 1864

On May 7, 1864, Sherman commenced his advance into Georgia. Under him were three armies: the Army of the Ohio, led by John M. Schofield; the Army of the Cumberland, headed by George H. Thomas; and Sherman's old Army of the Tennessee, now commanded by James B. McPherson. Opposing him were some sixty thousand Confederates of Joseph E. Johnston's Army of Tennessee. Over the next six weeks Sherman used Schofield and McPherson to outflank Johnston, forcing him to abandon a series of prepared positions and pull back ever closer to Atlanta. Sherman failed to bring his foe to battle, although he just missed scoring a major triumph at the outset of the campaign, when McPherson failed to cut off Johnston's line of retreat at Snake Creek Gap near Resaca.[1]

In letter after letter Sherman kept his wife and brother John up to date on his progress—although he said virtually nothing in his letters home about the Battle of Kenesaw Mountain on June 27, where he threw his men forward in a fruitless frontal assault against Johnston's fortifications. By July he could see the city in the distance. At the same time he became anxious about Ellen's health, for he had heard nothing from his pregnant wife. It came as some relief that both mother and child—a son, Charles—were fine. No sooner had that news come than he had to fend off a series of attacks launched by Johnston's replacement, John Bell Hood, which did nothing to shake Sherman's tightening grip on Atlanta.

Victory in July did not come without its costs. One of the most grievous was the death of James B. McPherson on July 22. Nothing except Willy's death so moved Sherman during the war. As McPherson's lifeless body lay nearby, Sherman struggled to hold back his tears as he issued orders to stop the Confederate attack. That evening, he mused: "I expected something to happen to Grant and me; either the Rebels or the newspapers would kill us both, and I looked to McPherson as the man to follow us and finish the war."[2] Sherman wrestled with the notion that he had somehow been responsible for the death of his eldest son; although he did not feel so about McPherson, he knew that he had intervened to prevent McPherson from marrying Emily Hoffman of Baltimore. Surely his letter to her after McPherson's death was one of the most difficult he ever wrote.

For a man who claimed he did not care about what others said about him, Sherman kept a careful eye on early efforts to record the history of the war, including his own career. Once more he refought Shiloh; once more he presented his version of what happened to him in 1861. But the best way for him to establish his own place in the history of the war was by triumphing in Georgia. At the end of August he decided to sever the city's supply lines by advancing on Jonesboro; when Hood responded, he left Atlanta vulnerable. Realizing his mistake, he decided it was better to lose the city and save the army. It was thus with great satisfaction that Sherman announced on September 3, "So Atlanta is ours, & fairly won."[3]

1. The definitive account of these operations is Albert Castel, *Decision in the West: The Atlanta Campaign of 1864* (Lawrence, Kans., 1994).

2. John F. Marszalek, *Sherman: A Soldier's Passion for Order* (New York, 1993), 277–78.

3. WTS to HWH, September 3, 1864.

TO ELLEN EWING SHERMAN

Kingston Geo. May 20, 64

Dearest Ellen,

I have no doubt you will complain of neglect on my part, but you have sense enough to see that my every minute has been taken. According to appointment with Genl. Grant I got everything as far ready as possible on the 5th and Started from Chattanooga on the 6th. Troops had to be marched & collected from all parts of the country without attracting attention, and I got McPherson up to Chattanooga and on Johnstons flanks before he suspected anything more than a detacht. of Thomas command.[1]

Dalton lies in a valley, but the road passes through a gap which was a most formidable place. I drew Johnstons attention to it whilst I moved the army round through a Gap thirty miles further south and appeared on his rear & flank. He hastily evacuated Dalton and succeeded in getting into Resacca, 18 miles, where he had prepared a strong position[.] This we attacked at all points getting closer & closer, whilst I got a bridge across the Oostenaula, and again threatened his Rear. Again he started & we chased him fighting all the way to Cassville, & today the army is pushing him across the Etowah. Having a Railroad, & familiar with all the byeways he has got off but at a cost of about 6000 men—we have a thousand prisoners, have killed & wounded 5000 and have ourselves lost less than 4000. We have had no time to count noses. The Enemy buried the Railroad bridge at Oostenaula but we have repaired it and now have the telegraph cars to the very Rear of our army. The whole movement has been rapid, skilful & successful, but will be measured by subsequent events. Difficulties increase as we go, for I have to drop men to guard our

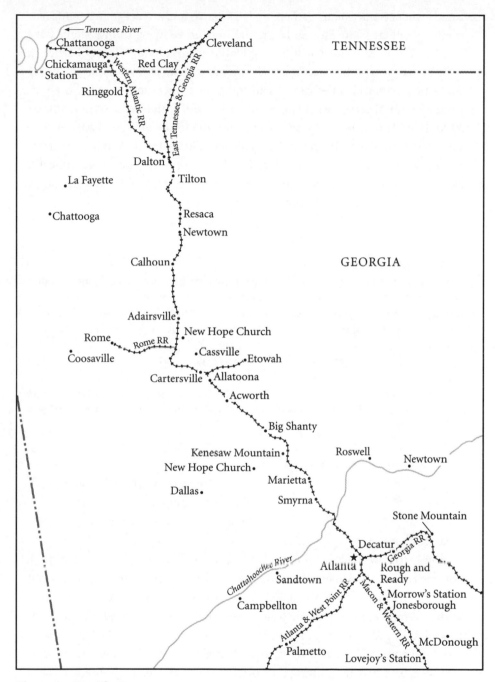

Chattanooga to Atlanta

Roads whereas our enemy gathers up his Guards and collects other reinforcements. I will cross the Etowah & Chattahoochee, & swing round Atlanta. If I can break up that nest it will be a splendid achievement. Grants Battles in Virginia are fearful but necessary.[2] Immense slaughter is necessary to prove that our northern armies can & will fight. That once impressed will be an immense moral power. Banks utter failure is awful as that force should now be at Mobile.[3] It may be that Cavalry can straighten out matters. Banks was so intent on Civil Govt. that he underrated the military features of his Territory. All attempts at Civil Govt. in the midst of war are folly. I am in good health and See no reason to apprehend any reverse, though I shall be duly cautious, as we have a large army skilfully commanded at my feet. Love to all

W. T. Sherman

M. G.

ALS, InND: Sherman Family Papers.

1. Sherman's troops had forced Johnston's army out of its fortified positions at Dalton and then Resaca, Georgia; only McPherson's hesitation at Snake Creek Gap on May 8 prevented Federal troops from scoring a major victory. They then forced Johnston to keep retreating until he reached a position south of the Etowah River on May 19 and dug in at Cassville.

2. In the Wilderness (May 5–7) and at Spotsylvania Court House (May 8–21) Grant had battled Lee's Army of Northern Virginia, both sides suffering severe casualties.

3. Intended to establish a Federal presence in Texas to counteract the French presence in Mexico and gain control of rich agricultural land and cotton, Banks's Red River Campaign of March–May 1864 proved a disaster.

TO ELLEN EWING SHERMAN

Head-Quarters, Military Division
of the Mississippi,
Kingston, Geo., May 22, 1864

Dearest Ellen,

Tomorrow we start again for Atlanta. I would like to go back & give you a connected narrative of events but I know it would take more time than I can devote to it, and I suppose you will have curiosity enough to read every thing with Sherman at the top of the page. I believe the world now admits my right to maintain public silence and recognizes it as a Military Power. The officers and Soldiers also have realized that by bringing up McPhersons Army with secresy & dispatch and putting it through Snake Creek Gap unobserved that I saved them the terrible door of death that Johnston had prepared for them in the Buzzard Roost. We were forced to attack at Resaca and there too by catching the Strong and weak points I enabled the army to fight at as little disadvantage as possible, and following up quick & strong we gave Johnston no time to fortify though every pass was barricaded all the way down. I think we inflicted more loss on the enemy than we sustained ourselves, and up to this time we have taken 15 Guns, 2500 prisoners and a large lot of property. Of course being compelled to guard our Communications our strength is diminished as we advance and that of the Enemy increases. I have no doubt we must have a terrific Battle at some point near the Chattahoochee. The Main Roads however cross the Etowah 13 miles from here and for six miles lay among hills that afford Strong positions. These I must avoid, and Shall move due south to Dallas, & thence to Marietta & the Chattahoochee Bridge. You will no doubt recognize this very country as the one I was in twenty years ago, and to which I took such a fancy. Yesterday I rode my Lines and passed quite close to Col. Tumlins[1] place, the same where the Big Mounds are where I stopped in going from Marietta to Bellefonte & back. I will probably pass by those Same big mounds tomorrow[.] The weather is oppressively hot, & roads dusty. I do hope we will have rain as it is choking to Soldiers & mules. Our large trains make a fearful dust.

I will put up a map to you by this mail by which you can trace our progress. Thomas is my center & has about 45,000 men, McPherson my Right 25,000, and Schofield my Left 15,000, in all 85,000 men, a vast army to feed, and to move. I cant move about as I did with 15 or 20,000 men. I think I have the best army in the country, and if I cant take Atlanta and Stir up Georgia considerably I am mistaken. Our greatest danger is from Cavalry, in which Arm of Service the Enemy is superior to us in quantity & quality, Cutting our wagons or Railroads. I have on hand however Enough for twenty days, and in that time I ought to determine a good deal. You will no doubt have full accounts of the fighting—at Rocky Face I made one display to attract attention away from McPherson—at Resaca, we had Several pretty Sharp fights—One Hooker pressing down from the North—another the 15th Corps dashing for position closer to the Enemys flank and holding it against repeated night assaults, and Sweenys Division holding the Pontoon Bridge at Lays Ferry—all well & handsomely done. In pursuit I tried hard to strike in behind Johnston with my Cavalry but they did not accomplish it, but we did force the Enemy to abandon the Line of the Coosa & Etowah, which was the 1st Step in the Game. The next is to force him behind the Chattahoochee & last to take Atlanta & disturb the peace of the Inhabitants of Central Georgia and prevent Reinforcements going to Lee. If that Banks force could only go to Mobile now, there would not be a shadow of doubt of full success[.] yrs. ever

W. T. Sherman

ALS, InND: Sherman Family Papers.
1. Colonel Lewis Tumlin, with whom WTS had stayed in 1844 and had become friends. *PM*, 1:31–32.

TO JOHN SHERMAN

Head-Quarters, Military Division
of the Mississippi,
Kingston, Geo., May 26, 1864

Dear Brother,

I have daily telegraphed to Genl. Halleck our progress, and have no doubt you have kept pace with our movement. Johnston had chosen Dalton as his place of Battle, but he had made all the Roads to it so difficult that I resolved to turn it, so I passed my army through a pass 20 miles South of Dalton and forced him to Battle at Resaca. That too was very strong, but we beat him at all points and as I had got a bridge across the Oostenaula below him and was gradually getting to his Rear he again abandoned his position on the right and I have been pushing my forces after him as fast as possible yet his knowledge of the country and the advantage of a good Railroad to his Rear enabled him to escape me, but I have now full possession of all the Rich country of the Etowah. We occupy Rome Kingston and Cassville. I have repaired the Railroads to these points and now have ordered the essential supplies forward to replenish our wagons, where I will make for Atlanta 59 miles from here, and about 50 miles from the advance. Johnston has halted across the Etowah at a place called Allatoona where the Railroad and common Road passes through a span of the mountains making one of those formidable passes, which give an army on the defensive so much advantage but I propose to cross the Etowah here, and to go for Marietta via Dallas. Look at your map and you will see the move. We expect to cross the Etowah on the 23, when we will move straight on fighting when opposed. Of course our labors & difficulties increase as we progress, whereas our enemy gains strength by picking up his Road Guards & Detachments—The failure of Banks doubles my labors as we counted on that Red River force partly here, & partly at Mobile, whereas the enemy now has before me all the army from that quarter. I hope Banks is now satisfied that the civil part of his office was not of more importance than the military. I repeat all efforts to form civil Govts. till all the armies of the South are beaten are absurd and actually embarrass us. *They* are a nuisance. Put forth the whole strength of the nation now, and if we cant whip the South, we must bow our necks in patient submission. A Division of our Territory by the old Lines is impossible. Grant surely is fighting hard enough, and I think this army will make its mark. Yr. brother,

W. T. Sherman

ALS, DLC: William T. Sherman.

TO EMILY HOFFMAN[1]

Head-Quarters Military Division
of the Mississippi,
Acworth, Geo. June 9 1864

My Dear Young Lady,

I hardly feel that I should apologise for intrusion, for I can claim an old acquaintance with your Brother and Sister in California,[2] and feel almost that I know you through them, and others of your honored family. It has come to my Knowledge that you are affianced to another close friend and associate of mine Maj. Genl. McPherson, and I fear that weighing mighty matters of state but lightly in the Balance of Love, you feel that he gives too much of his time to his Country and too little to you.[3]

His rise in his profession has been rapid steady and well earned, not a link unbroken, not a thing omitted. Each step in his progress however has imposed on him fresh duties that as a man and a Soldier and still more as a Patriot he could not avoid. I did hope as we returned from Meridian, when his Corps the 17th was Entitled to go home on furlough, that he too could Steal a month to obey the promptings of his heart, to hasten to Baltimore and I so instructed but by the Changes incident to General Grants Elevation McPherson succeeded to the Command of a seperate Army and Department, and could not leave.

There is no rest for us in this war till you and all can look about you and feel there is Peace & Safety in the Land. God purifies the atmosphere with tempests and Storms which fall alike upon the just and unjust, and in like manner he appeases the jarring Elements of political discord, by wars and famine. Heretofore as a nation we have escaped his wrath, but now with the vehemence of an hundred years accumulation we are in the Storm, and would you have us shrink? Would you have us to leave our posts at the Rudder of the Ship in the Midst of the Angry Sea of War? What would you think in a California Steamer if the Captain, who regardless of the hundreds of human beings consigned to his Care, would leave his deck, to dally with his loved one below? But I will not discuss so plain a point with one who bears the honored name of Hoffman, rather tell you of him whose every action I Know fills your waking and Sleeping thoughts, him so young but so prominent, whose cause is among the Gallant & brave, who fight not for oppression and wrong but that the Government bequeathed to us by Your ancestors Shall not perish in ignominy and insult: but which shall survive in honor & glory, with a power to protect the weak, and Shelter the helpless from the terrible disasters of a fratricidal war. I Know that at the outset of this war many of the Class with whom you associate, were wont to Style us the barbarian hosts of the North, not unlike the hordes that followed Alaric from the Woods of Northern

Europe to desolate the fair fields of the degenerate Romans. There may be a parallel but not a fair one. The People of the South were bound to us by a Solemn Compact which they have broken, and they taunted us with cowardice and poltroonery, which had we borne with submission, we would have passed down to history as a craven and Coward Race. I doubt Even now if Our Brothers of the South would if free again to Choose make so base an issue but now we go further. We of the North have Rights in the South, in its Ruins & vacant Lands, the Right to Come & go when we please and these Rights as a Brave people we cannot & will not surrender on Compulsion[.]

I know McPherson well, as a young brave, handsome & noble soldier, actuated by motives as pure as those of Washington, and I know that in bearing my testimony to his high & noble Character I will not offend the Girl he loves. Be patient and I Know that when the happy day comes for him to Stand by your side as one Being identical in heart & human Existence you will regard him with a high respect & honor that will convert Simple love into Something sublime & beautiful[.] Yrs. with respect

W. T. Sherman

ALS, New York: Private Collection of Walter Lord.

1. Emily Hoffman (ca. 1834–91), daughter of Samuel Hoffman, a prominent Baltimore merchant and venture capitalist, was engaged to James McPherson, whom she had met in California in 1859.

2. Louis McLane Jr., the son and namesake of the politician and diplomat, had married Emily's sister Sophie and had become a banker in California. A former military man, he was set up in business in California by his father-in-law, and he became the head of Wells, Fargo & Co.'s Pacific Coast express business in 1855, an original incorporator of the Bank of California, and the manager of the Nevada Bank of San Francisco.

3. McPherson had left Vicksburg on March 26 for a twenty-day furlough during which he intended to marry Hoffman, whom he had not seen for nearly three years. Both he and his fiancée were bitterly disappointed when, upon reaching Cairo, McPherson was greeted by two telegrams announcing his promotion to the command of the Army of the Tennessee and ordering his immediate return to Huntsville, Alabama, to help WTS in planning the Atlanta Campaign.

TO ELLEN EWING SHERMAN

Head-Quarters Military Division
of the Mississippi,
Acworth Geo., June 9, 1864

Dearest Ellen,

I dont know that you can find this place on your map, but it is on the Main Road from Chattanooga into Georgia, 7 miles in front of Alatoona, 12 from Marietta & 30 from Atlanta. The army lies about this place extending east north & south. We are replenishing our wagons with ammunition, forage and provisions. The Railroad to our Rear is all in good order except the bridge across Etowah burned by the Enemy, which will soon be done. I am forced to move with due deliberation to give time for other combinations from Memphis & New Orleans on Mobile &c. But we will soon move forward to the Chattahoochee 11 miles beyond Marietta. Johnston may fight us at the Ridge of hills just this Side of Marietta, but I think I can dislodge him and this will leave the Great Battle on or near the Chattahoochee the passage of which he must dispute[.] He has a strong well disciplined army but I think we can whip him on any thing like fair terms, so I will not run but headed against any works prepared for us.[1] He thinks he checked us at Dallas. I went there to avoid the Alatoona Pass, and as soon as I had drawn his Army there I Slipped my Cavalry into Alatoona Pass & moved the main army in its front a perfect success. I never designed to attack his hastily prepared works at Dallas and New Hope Church, and as soon as he saw I was making for the Railroad around his Right flank he abandoned his works and we occupied them for a moment and moved by the best Roads to our present position. We have captured several of their mails and it is wonderful to See how the soldiers talk of driving me back to the Ohio, and their returning to their Loving families in Tennessee and Kentucky. I fear they Count without their host, as they will have an awful reckoning if they attempt to pass over or around this army. The paucity of news from this army at this time in northern papers is most satisfactory to me. My Circular was exactly right—every officer & soldier should Keep his friends & family advised of his own adventures & situation whilst the busy & mischievous Scribblers for newspapers are discountenanced.[2] I Know my course is right and meets the unqualified approval of all good soldiers— The Press is angry at my term, the "cheap" flattery of the Press. We all Know that Genls. and aspirants bribe these fellows by the loan of Govt. horses and other conveniences *not* at their individual Cost, but at the Cost of the U.S. and in return receive the cheap flattery of the Press. The Press caused the war—the Press gives it point and bitterness, and as long as the Press, both North & South is allowed to fan the flames of discord & hostility so long must the war last—The Southern Press is just the Same, and as long as People look to the Press for Truth & counsel so long will war & anarchy prevail. The Liberty of the Press like that of Individuals must be restrained to just limits consistent with the good of the whole, and every fool must not be allowed to print & publish falsehood & slander as he pleases.

Blair is up, and many detachments have come forward so my army today is stronger than when I first sallied from Chattanooga.

I have received no letters from you of late and Suppose you think it unsafe—only one mail has been captured by the Enemy and that an unimportant one. I got the Short telegraph of yesterday saying all were well. I feel anxious to hear from you more often, but Know you are all in a safe & bountiful Country. All my staff are well & have not been harmed—Col. Taylor was wounded as he accompanied me on a tour of the Lines. He is here, but will go home as soon as the Railroad is done. Maj. Giesy[3] was killed at Dallas & Rise wounded. No others of yr. acquaintance hurt. But of course the Real Battle is not yet fought—when it does come I will take good care to have it a big & decisive one. Yrs. Ever

W. T. Sherman

ALS, InND: Sherman Family Papers.

1. On June 5, WTS told Halleck: "I expect the Enemy to fight us at Kenesaw Mountain near Marietta, but I will not run head on his fortifications. An examination of his abandoned Line here show an immense Line of works, all of which I have turned with less loss to ourselves than we have inflicted on him." WTS to HWH, June 5, 1864, Lbk, DNA: RG 94, Records of the Adjutant General's Office, Generals' Books and Papers, William T. Sherman, Letterbook 10.

2. Circular, May 20, 1864, Headquarters, Military Division of the Mississippi, read:

"Inasmuch as an impression is afloat that the Comd'g General has prohibited the mails to and from the army, he takes this method of assuring all, officers and men, that on the contrary he encourages them by all his influence and authority to keep up the most unreserved correspondence with their families and friends wherever they may be. Army Corps and Division Commanders should perfect their arrangements to receive and transmit all mails and all chaplains Staff Officers and Captains of Companies should assist the soldiers in communicating with their families.

"What the Commanding General does discourage is the maintenance of that class of men who will not take a musket and fight, but follow the army to pick up news for sale, speculating in a species of information which is dangerous to the army and to our cause and who are more used to bolster up idle and worthless officers, than to notice the hard working and meritorious, whose modesty is generally equal to their courage and who scorn to seek the cheap flatter of the Press." Copy of original, MiU-C: James S. Schoff Civil War Collection.

3. Presumably Major Henry H. Giesy of the Forty-sixth Ohio Volunteers, a friend of the family who had been with Sherman since 1862.

TO JOHN SHERMAN

Head-Quarters, Military Division
of the Mississippi,
Acworth, Geo., June 9, 1864

Dear Brother,

It is out of all reason to expect me to write much and I know you do not expect it. Were I to attempt narration it would swell to unreasonable lengths, and even in my communications to the War Dept. I must confine myself almost to generalities. Suffice it to say that General Grant & I had a perfect understanding and all things are now as near our calculations as possible save

& except that the Red River failure has clipped from the General Plan our main feature, a simultaneous attack on Mobile from New Orleans. But the Red River Expedition is out and I have substituted a smaller force of my own subject to my own orders, in line of the larger one contemplated made up by General Banks. You no doubt have been mortified by Banks failure. I warned him again & again about going above Alexandria if he found less than 12 feet water on the Falls, as also that the whole Philosophy of the expedition like mine to Meridian was to do quick what was done, so in thirty days to be out of Red River ready to swing against Mobile. I gave him ten thousand of my best men under Smith & Mower, and put them at Alexandria the very day appointed, and when the thirty days were out I had a General officer Corse on the Spot ready to lead them to their new destination Banks failed, because he construed the repulse of his advance Guard into a defeat and began a retrograde, whereas had he advanced after his Battle at Mansfield the fight of the day before however costly would have been his victory. A. J. Smith begged alone with his command to hold the ground, and Banks knew the Gun boats escorting his transports were at Conshetta Chute higher up, so his nearest road to water and provisions was ahead & not back to Grand Ecoss. But in the night he ordered his command to fall back. Then began his troubles, though the cause existed before—The truth is Banks is not a soldier—he is too intent on reconstruction, when he ought to have sense enough to See that all the elements of society in the South are too disturbed, too tinctured by old feelings & prejudices to admit of Government in which the People have a voice. Years, it may be tens of years must elapse before the People of the South can have a voice in a Government that they now hate with a hate you can hardly measure. But of myself—I concentrated my army skilfully & well, and at one blow started Johnston from his very strong position at Dalton, and had McPherson fallen on Resaca with the violence I had ordered Johnstons army would have retreated eastward leaving all his artillery & wagons. Since that time I have had no alternative but to press his Rear. The possession of a Railroad & good wagon Roads enabled him to retreat fast and in good order. Whilst the mountainous (text missing) country prevented me getting round on his flanks—I am now South of the last mountain pass, and the next difficulty is the Chattahoochee—My long and single Line of Railroad to my rear, of limited capacity is the deliberate part of my game, as also the fact that all of Georgia except the cleared bottoms is densely wooded with few Roads, and at any point an enterprising enemy can in a few hours with axes & spades make across our path formidable works, whilst his sharpshooters, spies & scouts in the guise of peacable farmers can hang round us and kill our wagoneers, messengers & couriers. It is a Big Indian War, still thus far I have won from strong positions, advanced a hundred miles & am in possession of a large wheat growing Region and all the Iron mines and works of Georgia. Johnstons army is still at my front and can fight or fall back as he pleases. The future is uncertain but I will do all that is possible. as ever yr. brother

AL, signature clipped, DLC: William T. Sherman.

TO ELLEN EWING SHERMAN

Headquarters Military Division
of the Mississippi,
In the Field, Big Shanty Geo.
June 12, 1864

Dearest Ellen,

I have received Phils dispatch announcing the birth to us of another son, it took me somewhat by surprise but was not altogether unexpected.[1] Well, I am glad you are over the terrible labor and hope that it is the last you will have to endure. Of course I am pleased to Know the Sex of the child, as he must succeed to the place left vacant by Willy, though I fear we will never again be able to lavish on any one the love we bore for him. Still we hardly Know ourselves or what is in store for us. I agree with you that we should retain Willys name vacant for his memory, and that though dead to the world he yet lives fresh in our memories. Whatever name you give this child will be acceptable to me. Charles is a common family name would do, but I will suggest none that you may name him as you choose only that it be simple and common. I received within the past few days a great number of letters some three or four from you all in a heap, but all were short, and those for Charley were delivered. I have not named to Charley the birth of the Child and dont Know as I will till he finds it out, and I am now so used to conceal my thoughts that no one can suspect my Knowledge till I reveal it. You say that pending the important events now transpiring you Cannot write. I feel so too. That it should have devolved on me to guide one of the two great armies on which may depend the fate of our People for the next hundred years I somewhat regret. Yet you Know I have been drawn into it by a slow & gradual process which I could not avoid. Grant was forced into his position and I likewise.[2] I think thus far I have played my game well. Had my plans been executed with the vim I contemplated I should have forced Johnston to fight the decisive Battle in the Oostenaula Valley between Dalton & Resaca, but McPherson was a little overcautious, and we cannot move vast armies of this size with the rapidity of thought or of smaller bodies. For the past ten days our movements have been vastly retarded by Rains. It has rained hard all the time and today harder than ever, a steady Cold rain. I am in an old house with a fire burning which is not uncomfortable. Johnston has 60,000 Infantry, 15,000 Cavalry and a good deal of militia. We must have a terrific Battle, and he wants to choose & fortify his ground. He also aims to break my Roads to the Rear. I wish we could make an accumulation of stores some where near but the Railroad is taxed to its utmost to supply our daily wants.

The Country is stripped of cattle, horses, hogs, and grain, but there are large fine fields of growing oats, wheat and corn, which our horses & mules devour as we advance—Thus far we have been well supplied, and I hope it will continue, though I expect to hear every day of Forrest breaking into Tennessee from some quarter. Jno. Morgan is in Kentucky but I attach little importance to him or his Raid, as we dont draw anything from Kentucky, and there are plenty of troops there to capture & destroy him. Forrest is a more dangerous man. I am in hopes that an expedition sent out from Memphis on Tupelo, about the 1st of June will give him full employment. I have also ordered A. J. Smith with the force he brought out of Red River to move against Mobile by way of diversion. Johnston is now between me and Marietta. As soon as these Clouds and Storms clear away I will study his position and determine to assault his Line or turn it and force him back of the Chattahoochee. As long as I press him close and prevent his sending anything to Lee I fulfill my part of the Grand Plan. In the mean time Grant will give Lee all the fighting he wants until he is sick of the word. Every man in America should now be aroused, and all who will not help should be put in petticoats & deprived of the Right to vote in the affairs of the after nation. I will telegraph you on all important occasions—Hoping you will soon be well & contented, I am as ever yrs.,

W. T. Sherman

ALS, InND: Sherman Family Papers.

1. Charles Celestine Sherman was born on June 11.

2. By early June Grant had worked his way to within a dozen miles of Richmond; he suffered a severe setback at Cold Harbor on June 3, 1864. As Sherman wrote, Grant was about to implement his plan to cross the James River and strike at Petersburg, Virginia.

TO HENRY COPPÉE[1]

Hd. Qrs. Mil. Div. Miss.
In the Field Near Kenesaw Geo.
June 13th 1864.

Prof. Henry Coppée
Philadelphia
Dear Sir:

In the June number of the *United Service Magazine* I find a brief sketch of Lieut. Genl. U. S. Grant, in which I see you are likely to perpetuate an error, which Genl. Grant may not deem of sufficient importance to correct.[2]

To Genl. Buell's very noble, able and gallant conduct you attribute the disasters of April 6th at Pittsburg Landing being retrieved, and made the victory of the following day.[3] Like General Taylor is said in his late days to have doubted whether he was at the Battle of Buena Vista at all, on account of the many things having transpired there according to the historians which he did not see, so I begin to doubt whether I was at the Battle of Pittsburg Landing of modern description. But I was at the Battles of April 6 & 7 1862. Genl. Grant visited my Division in person about 10 A.M. when the battle raged fiercest—I was there on the Right, after some general conversation he remarked that I was doing right in stubbornly opposing the progress of the enemy, and in answer to my inquiry as to cartriges told me he had anticipated their want and made orders accordingly—He then said his presence was more needed over at the Left. About 2 P.M. of the 6th the enemy materially slackened his attack on me, and about four P.M. I deliberately made a new Line behind McArthur's drill field, placing Batteries on chosen ground and repelled easily a Cavalry attack, and watched the cautious approach of the Enemy's Infantry that never dislodged us there. I selected that Line in advance of a Bridge across Snake Creek, by which we had all day been expecting the approach of Lew Wallace's Division from Crump's Landing—About 5 P.M., before the Sun set Genl. Grant came again to me and after hearing my report of matters explained to me the situation of affairs on the Left which were not as favorable. Still the Enemy had failed to reach the Landing of the Boats. We agreed that the enemy had expended the Furors of his attack, and we estimated our loss, and approximated our then strength including Lew Wallace's fresh Division expected each minute, and he then ordered me to get all things ready and at daylight the next day to assume the offensive. That was before Genl. Buell had arrived, but he was Known to be near at hand. Genl. Buell's troops took no essential part in the first days fight and Grants Army though collected together hastily, green as Militia, some Regiments arriving without cartriges even, and nearly all hearing the dread sound of Battle for the first time had successfully withstood and repelled the first days terrific onset of a superior Enemy, well Commanded and well handled. I Know I had orders from Gen. Grant to assume the offensive before I Knew Genl. Buell was on the west side of the Tennessee. I think Genl. Buell, Col. Fry and others of Genl. Buells Staff rode up to where I was about sunset, about the time Genl. Grant was leaving me. Genl. Buell asked me many questions and got of me a small map which I had made for my own use, and told me that by daylight he could have 18,000 fresh men which I Knew would settle the matter. I understood Grants forces were to advance on the right of the Corinth Road, and Buells on the Left, and accordingly at daylight I advanced my Division, by the flank the resistance being trivial, up to the very spot where the day before the battle had been most severe, and then waited till near noon, for Buell's troops to get up abreast—when the entire Line advanced, and recovered all the ground we had ever held—I Know that with the exception of one or two severe struggles the fighting of April 7th was easy as compared with that of April 6th. I never was disposed, nor am I now to question anything done by Genl. Buell and his Army and Know that approaching our Field of Battle from the Rear, he encountered that sickening crowd of laggards and fugitives that excited his contempt and that of his Army, who never gave full credit to those in the Front Line, who did fight hard, and who had at 4 P.M. checked the enemy and were preparing the next day to assume the offensive. I remember the fact the better from Genl. Grants anecdote of his Donelson Battle which he told me then for the first time, that at a certain period of the Battle he saw that either side was ready to give way, if the other showed a bold front, and he determined to do that very thing, to advance on the enemy, when as he prognosticated the Enemy Surrendered. At 4 P.M. of April 6th he thought the appearances the same, and he judged with Lew Wallace's fresh Division, and such of our startled troops as had recovered their equilibrium we would be justified in dropping the defensive and assuming the offensive in the morning, and I repeat I received such orders before I knew Genl. Buell's troops were at the River. I admit that I was glad Buell was there, because I Knew his troops were older than ours and better systematized and drilled, and his arrival made that certain which before was uncertain. I have heard this question much discoursed and must say that the officers of Buell's Army dwelt too much on the Stampede of some of our Raw troops and gave us too little credit for the fact that for one whole day, weakened as we were by the absence of Buell's Army long expected, of Lew Wallace's Division only four miles off, and of the fugitives from our Ranks, we had beaten off our assailants for the time. At the same time our Army of the Tennessee have indulged in severe criticisms at the slow approach of that Army which Knew the danger that threatened us from the concentrated armies of Johnston, Beauregard, and Bragg that lay at Corinth. In a war like this where opportunities for personal prowess are as plenty as blackberries, to those who seek them at the Front, all such criminations should be frowned down, and were it not for the Military Character of your Journal I would not venture to offer a correction to a very popular Error.

I will also avail myself of this occasion to correct another very common mistake in attributing to Genl. Grant the selection of that Battlefield. It was chosen by that veteran soldier Maj. Genl. Charles F. Smith who ordered my Division to disembark there and strike for the Charleston Rail Road. This order was subsequently modified by his ordering Hurlbuts Division to disembark there and mine higher up the Tennessee to the mouth of Yellow Creek, to strike the Railroad at Burnsville. But flood prevented our reaching the Railroad, when Gen. Smith ordered me in person also to disembark at Pittsburg Landing, and take post well out so as to make plenty of room with Snake and Lick Creeks the flanks of a camp for the Grand Army of Invasion. It was Genl. Smith who selected that Field of Battle and it was well chosen—on any other we surely would have been overwhelmed, as both Lick and Snake Creeks forced the Enemy to confine his attack to a direct Front attack for which new troops are better qualified than where the flanks are exposed to a real or chimerical danger, even the Divisions of that Army were arranged in that camp by Genl. Smiths order, my Division forming as it were the outlying Picket, whilst McClernand and Prentiss were the Real Line of battle, with W. H. L. Wallace[4] in support of the Right wing and Hurlbut of the Left—Lew Wallaces Division being detached. All those subordinate dispositions were made by the order of Genl. Smith before Genl. Grant succeeded him to the Command of all the forces up the Tennessee, Head Qrs. Savannah. If there was any error in putting that Army on the west side of the Tennessee, exposed to the superior force of the enemy also assembling at Corinth, the mistake was not Genl. Grants. But there was no mistake. It was necessary that a combat firm and bitter to test the manhood of the two armies, should come off, and that was as good a place as any. It was not then a question of military skill and strategy but of courage and pluck, and I am convinced that every life lost that day to us was necessary, for otherwise at Corinth at Memphis & at Vicksburg we would have found harder resistance, had we not shown our enemies that rude and untutored as we then were we would fight, as well as they.

Excuse so long a letter which is very unusual from me, but of course my life is liable to cease at any moment and I happen to be a witness to certain truths which are now begining to pass out of memory, and from what is called History.

I also take great pleasure in adding that nearly all the new troops that at Shiloh drew from me official censure have more than redeemed their good name, among them that very Regt. which first broke, the 53rd Ohio, Col. Appler. Under another leader Col. Jones,[5] it has shared every campaign and expedition of mine since, is with me now, and can march and bivouac and fight as well as the best Regiment in this or any army. Its reputation now is equal to that of any from the state of Ohio. I am with respect Yours truly,

W. T. Sherman
Maj. Genl.

Lbk, DNA: RG 94, Records of the Adjutant General's Office, Generals' Books and Papers, William T. Sherman, Letterbook 10; *OR*, I, 52: pt. 1, 559–61.

1. Henry Coppée (1821–95), a West Point graduate and Mexican War veteran, had taught ethics and English at the Military Academy and was a professor at the University of Pennsylvania at this time.

2. Henry Coppée, "Lieutenant-General Grant," *United States Service Magazine* 1 (June 1864): 561–64.

3. Ibid., 563.

4. William H. L. Wallace (1821–62) commanded the Second Division of the Army of the Tennessee at Shiloh; he was mortally wounded during the battle.

5. Colonel Wells S. Jones (1830–1914), an Ohio physician and politician, became colonel of the regiment on May 21, 1862, and went on to command the Second Brigade, Second Division, and then the Third Brigade, Fourth Division, Fifteenth Corps.

TO HENRY COPPÉE

> Headquarters Military Division
> of the Mississippi,
> In the Field, near Kenesaw, Geo.
> June 13, 1864.

Prof. Henry Coppée
Philadelphia.
Dear Sir,

I see in the Fly leaf of the June number of your Military Magazine you propose to give a Biography of myself, from a brother officer, who has had every facility to make it accurate.[1] I cannot recal ever having given any data to a Brother officer or any other person, but on the contrary have stubbornly & it may be wrongfully withheld such data preferring the after Judgment of mankind to contemporaneous flattery or otherwise. But I see that I am forced by Events into a most Conspicuous place, which God Knows I wish were better filled, and that I cannot prevent that curiosity which exists among our People to Know something of military Leaders whose records have heretofore been short and unimportant.

I merely, therefore, will give you a few brief data whereby to test the paper which you possess and pronounce very interesting—I was born Feb. 8, 1820, at Lancaster Ohio, the sixth child of Charles R. and Mary Sherman both natives of Connecticut, but who migrated to Ohio in 1811. My father was Judge of the Supreme Court of Ohio at the time of his death at Lebanon, Ohio, in 1829. I went to West Point in 1836, graduated no. 6 in the Class of 1840, and was commissioned 2nd Lt. 3rd Artillery—served in Florida the winters of 1840 & 1841 in companies A & G; with the latter was ordered to Mobile in March 1841, and soon after the company was sent to Fort Moultrie and remained there untill 1846—was sent on Recruiting service to Pittsburg & in July same year was transferred to Company F, Capt. Tompkins and sent to California in the U.S. Steamship *Lexington*, reached Monterey Cal. Jan. 1847, and Served there with the company and afterwards as General Mason's Adjutant Genl. until after the war, when on the arrival of Gen. Persifor F. Smith was taken as his Adjt. Genl. to San Francisco. I remained on his Staff till January 1850, when I was ordered to Washington City with despatches. Was appointed a Commissary of Subsistence that year & stationed at St. Louis till Oct. 1851, when I was ordered to New Orleans. That winter Certain parties at St. Louis offered me very fair terms to go to San Francisco to manage a Bank and my army pay being inadequate to my support I got a leave of absence, went to San Francisco—returned & resigned. Moved my family to California where we resided till 1857, when the interest of my partners called me to New York & finally to a discontinuance of the business. I first went to Leavenworth & engaged in business but soon after was named Superintendent of the Louisiana Military Academy. I went to Alexandria, organized the Institution, & put it in successful operation, but the seed of this unnatural war began to bear fruits—the State seceded, in January 1861, and the national arsenal was taken possession of by State troops—the arms were scattered, and some sent to me to guard. I then saw that war & anarchy were upon us and determined to leave. My letter of resignation was public. I have no copy, but Mrs. W. T. Sherman Lancaster Ohio, has a copy, and to Show my status there it should enter into any Biography of mine to Show how I viewed matters there from that Stand point. Giving my employers thirty days to replace me and no successor being appointed I turned over all business to the proper officers, went to Baton Rouge and New Orleans, settled carefully all Cash accounts which I had with the State, and left the South I think with the respect and affection of all with whom I had been associated.

Reaching my family in Ohio, I was invited by my brother John Sherman to go to Washington which I did, but confess I was sadly disappointed to find as I thought the little appreciation of the terrible future that awaited us. I declined all offers of assistance and anxious to earn an honest living for my family I reverted to my old Banking friends who had always offered to help me. I promptly received an office of moderate Salary, the Presidency of a Street Railroad—moved my family there and resolved to keep aloof from the complications of events that seemed to bode no good. I was in that capacity in St. Louis in May and June, declining an offer made me in the Militia by Hon. Frank P. Blair, and subsequently of a post in Washington as Assistant Secretary of War. Whatever others may think I do honestly believe that the Politicians of that day did not make up the issue for War fairly. I know that the People of the South did not expect *war*—They had been Cajolled into the belief that the excitement of the day was of the Same nature and Kind which had every four years agitated the People, and that it would gradually subside, somehow, they

Knew not why. Slave owners of course had an interest. They did believe their property was unsafe in the hands of an administration composed as they thought of Abolitionists. Still large Masses were as much attached to our Past history & National unity as we profess to be, and it did seem to me that instead of going to work to make up a Clear, single issue, so plain that all who wanted to fight would know Exactly what the fight was about, that all, on both sides were determined so to obscure the issue that there was no Alternative but to array two angry People, one against the other. My opinion was, that we must be united, and that no better common bond could be chosen than the Constitution, yet, if War must come, issue or no issue, I was clear that Every Citizen should support the National Govt., because right or wrong the Government must be sustained, Else Anarchy, (which nature abhors) would be inevitable. The idea of two seperate Governments with so ragged a Boundary as divided the Slave & free states was and is an impossibility. With such a Boundary Endless War would be the Rule and Peace the Exception. Yet I say it did appear to me, that the active busy politicians & mischief makers did seem resolved on War, without any clear well defined issue made up, which you & I, simple soldiers could understand. This was the reason why at first I kept out. But Sumpter was attacked and although war had begun with the Seizure of the United States arsenals and the insult to the flag universally taken as the National Emblem, this act was the first that Seemed to arouse the feelings of the North. I suppose through the instrumentality of my brother John, my name was put down as Colonel of the 13th U.S. *Regulars*, and I was so Confirmed. I was then not at liberty to decline military service, and on reporting for duty was sent by Genl. McDowell to command a Brigade of Volunteers at Fort Corcoran. I took that Brigade to Bull Run & came back with the Crowd, and think on the whole it was the best lesson a vain & conceited Crowd ever got. Up to that time no one seemed to measure the danger, the necessity for prolonged preperation, and infinite outlay of money. The Fighting force of some Eight Million of Inhabitants, united by an intense Zeal and hatred, could not be encountered in their own country without more trouble than most of our men supposed; and it was manifest that our Statesmen, instead of grasping the Subject, preferred to approach it through their own vain conceptions of what they supposed or rather wished to be the Case. When it became necessary to Enlarge the Field to the West, Genl. Robt. Anderson was ordered to Kentucky & asked me to go with him. I was willing provided I could take an humble seat in the background. I was unwilling to risk myself as a Leader, and when his health failed him and he was compelled to leave me there in command, he knew, the President knew, and all knew with what reluctance I was forced into a position of prominence. From the first conception of the idea I opposed it and it may be I resorted to improper reasons to avoid a prominent post, for which I was so disinclined, and wherein a Leader should be in perfect accord with superior powers. None of my views or thoughts were in accord with the Secretary of War, and I insisted it may be wrongfully & in bad taste to be replaced by some one better qualified and more at ease. This is all I need Say now. Subsequent Events are of official Record. I now think we must and will have a United Government, one that can *govern* & not *be* governed by schisms, faction or caprice, one of Power to command what is Right & punish what is wrong. Until that result is attained, there can be no Peace, no safety, no honor, no property in our hitherto peaceful Land, and until then all who are able & deserve to live and share the fruits of such a Government *must* fight for it. I am, &c.,

W. T. Sherman M. G.

ALS, PHi: Gratz Collection; *OR*, I, 52: pt. 1, 561–64.

1. Samuel M. Bowman would write "Major General William T. Sherman," which appeared in the *United States Service Magazine* 2 (August 1864): 113–24 and 2 (September 1864): 240–55.

TO ULYSSES S. GRANT

Headquarters, Military Division
of the Mississippi,
In the Field, June 18, 1864.

Dear General,

I have no doubt you want me to write you occasionally letters not purely official, but which will admit of a little more latitude than such documents possess. I have daily sent to Halleck, telegraphs which I asked him to repeat to you and which he says he has done. You therefore Know where we are and what we have done. If our movement has been slower than you calculated I can explain the reasons though I know you believe me too Earnest and impatient to be behind time.

My first movement against Johnston was really fine, and now I believe I would have disposed of him at one blow if McPherson had crushed Resacca as he might have done, for then it was garrisoned only by a small Brigade, but Mc was a little over Cautious lest Johnston still at Dalton might move against him alone, but the truth was I got all of McPhersons Army 23,000, 18 miles to Johnstons Rear before he knew they had left Huntsville. With that Single exception McPherson has done very well. Schofield also does as well as I could ask with his small force. Our Cavalry is dwindling away, we cannot get full forage and have to graize so that the Cavalry is always unable to attempt anything. Garrard is over Cautious and I think Stoneman is lazy. The former has 4500, & the latter about 2500. Each has had fine chances of Cutting in but was easily checked by the appearance of an Enemy.

My Chief source of trouble is with the Army of the Cumberland which is dreadfully slow. A fresh furrow in a ploughed field will stop the whole column, and all begin to intrench. I have again and again tried to impress on Thomas that we must assail & not defend. We are the offensive, & yet it seems the whole Army of the Cumberland is so habituated to be on the defensive that from its commander down to the lowest private I cannot get it out of their heads. I came out without tents and ordered all to do likewise yet Thomas has a Head Quarter Camp in the Style of Halleck at Corinth. Every aid, & orderly with a wall tent and a Baggage train big enough for a Division. He promised to send it all back but the truth is every body there is allowed to do as he pleases, and they still think and act as though the Railroad and all its facilities are theirs. This Slowness has cost me the loss of two splendid opportunities which never recur in War. At Dallas there was a delay of four hours to get ready to advance, when we first met Johnstons head of Column, and that four hours enabled him to throw up works to cover the head of his column and he extended the work about as fast as we deployed. Also here, I broke one of his Lines, and had we followed it up as I ordered at daylight there was nothing between us & the Railroad back of Marietta. I ordered Thomas to move at daylight and when I got to the point at half past nine I found Stanley & Wood quarrelling which should *not* lead. I'm afraid I swore, and said what I should not, but I got them started, but instead of reaching the Atlanta Road back of Marietta which is Johnstons centre, we only got to a creek in the south of it by night, and now a heavy Rain stops us, and gives time to fortify a new Line. Still I have all the high and commanding ground but the *one* peak near Marietta which I can traverse

We have had an immense quantity of Rain, from June 2nd to 14th and now it is raining as though it had no intention ever to stop.

The enemys cavalry sweeps all round us and is now to my rear somewhere. The wires are broken very often but I have strong guards along the Road which make prompt repairs. Thus far our supplies of food have been good, and forage moderate, and we have fo[u]nd growing wheat, rye oats &c.

You may go on with the full assurance that I will continue to press Johnston as fast as I can overcome the natural obstacles and inspire motion into a large ponderous and slow (by habit) army. Of course it cannot keep up with my thoughts & wishes but no impulse can be given it that I will not guide. As Ever your friend,

W. T. Sherman

ALS, CsmH; *OR*, I, 38: pt. 4, 507–8.

TO JAMES B. STEEDMAN

> Hdqrs. Military Division
> of the Mississippi,
> In the Field, Big Shanty, June 23, 1864.

Maj. Gen. J. B. Steedman,
Commanding District of the Etowah, Chattanooga:
General:

As the question may arise, and you have a right to the support of my authority, I now decide that the use of the torpedo is justifiable in war in advance of an army, so as to make his advance up a river or over a road more dangerous and difficult. But after the adversary has gained the country by fair warlike means, then the case entirely changes. The use of torpedoes in blowing up our cars and the road after they are in our possession, is simply malicious. It cannot alter the great problem, but simply makes trouble. Now, if torpedoes are found in the possession of an enemy to our rear, you may cause them to be put on the ground and tested by wagonloads of prisoners, or, if need be, citizens implicated in their use. In like manner, if a torpedo is suspected on any part of the road, order the point to be tested by a car-load of prisoners, or citizens implicated, drawn by a long rope. Of course an enemy cannot complain of his own traps.

> I am, &c.,
> W. T. Sherman,
> Major-General, Commanding.

Printed, *OR*, I, 38: pt. 4, 579.

TO ELLEN EWING SHERMAN

> Headquarters, Military Division
> of the Mississippi,
> In the Field, near Marietta Geo.,
> June 26, 1864

Dearest Ellen,

Phils dispatch of the 11 is my last from Lancaster. I have a letter which you must have written just before the birth of our Child.[1] I am anxious to hear more in detail. I have written but little because my thoughts & mind have been so intent on other matters. Johnston has fallen back several times abandoning long lines of intrenchments, but he still occupies a good position with Kenesaw Mountain as the apex of his triangle embracing Marietta. His wings fell back four miles one day and I thought he had gone but not so.

We have worked our way forward untill we are in close contact, constant skirmishing & picket firing—He is afraid to come at us, and we have been cautious about dashing against his breastworks, that are so difficult to understand in this hilly & wooded Country. My Lines are ten miles long, and every change necessitating a larger amount of work. Still we are now all ready and I *must* attack direct or turn the position. Both will be attended with loss and difficulty but one or the other must be attempted. This is Sunday and I will write up all my letters and tomorrow will pitch in at some one or more points.

I am now 105 miles from Chattanooga, and all our provisions have to come over that single road—which is almost daily broken somewhere—but thus far our supplies have been ample. We have devoured the land and our animals eat up the wheat & corn fields close—All the People retire before us, and desolation is behind. To realize what war is one should follow our tracks. I am very anxious to hear from you and the youngster. I suppose Tom feels the pride of having a younger brother to rule over and control—May the child grow up and possess the courage, confidence and Kindness of heart of our poor Willy. I would gladly surrender all the honors & fame of this life if I could see him once more in his loving confidence & faith in us, but we must now think of the living & prepare them for our exodus, which may be near at hand.

Though not conscious of danger at this moment I Know the country swarms with thousands who would shoot me, & thank their God, they had slain a monster, and yet I have been more kindly disposed to the People of the South than any general officer of the whole army. Yrs. Ever

W. T. Sherman
M. G.

ALS, InND: Sherman Family Papers.

1. On June 9, EES had written her husband: "It never occurs to me that you may be anxious to hear from us." She still thought she had nearly two weeks until the child would be born. SFP.

TO LORENZO THOMAS

Headquarters Military Division
of the Mississippi,
Near Kenesaw Mountain, June 26, 1864.

General Lorenzo Thomas,
Louisville, Ky.:

I was gratified at the receipt of your dispatch from Chattanooga. I would have answered sooner if our telegraph had not been broken so often of late. As I wrote you, I know all the people have left North Georgia for the regions of the Flint and Appalachicola with their negroes.

The regiments of blacks now in Chattanooga and Tennessee will absorb all the recruits we can get, but if you raise new regiments they could be well employed about Clarksville, Bowling Green, and on the Tennessee River, say at the terminus of the Northwestern Railroad. My preference is to make this radical change with natural slowness. If negroes are taken as soldiers by undue influence or force and compelled to leave their women in the uncertainty of their new condition, they cannot be relied on; but if they can put their families in some safe place and then earn money as soldiers or laborers, the transition will be more easy and the effect more permanent.

What my order contemplated was the eagerness of recruiting captains and lieutenants to make up their quota in order to be commissioned.

They would use a species of force or undue influence and break up our gangs of laborers as necessary as soldiers. We find gangs of negro laborers well organized on the Mississippi at Nashville and along the railroads most useful, and I have used them with great success as pioneer companies attached to divisions, and I think it would be well if a law would sanction such an organization—say of 100 to each division of 4,000 men.

The first step in the liberation of the negro from bondage will be to get him and family to a place of safety, then to afford him the means of providing for his family, for their instincts are very strong, then gradually use a proportion—greater and greater each year—as sailors and soldiers. There will be no great difficulty in our absorbing the four million of slaves in this great industrious country of ours, and being lost to their masters the cause of war is gone, for this great money interest then ceases to be an element in our politics and civil economy. If you divert too large a proportion of the able-bodied into the ranks, you will leave too large a class of black paupers on our hands; the great mass of our soldiery must be of the white race, and the black troops should for some years be used with caution and with due regard to the prejudice of the races. As was to be expected, in some instances they have done well, in others badly, but on the whole the experiment is worthy a fair trial, and all I ask is that it be not forced beyond the laws of natural development.

In Maryland, Missouri, and Kentucky it may be wisely used to secure their freedom with the consent of owners.

W. T. Sherman,
Major-General, Commanding.

Printed, *OR*, III, 4:454–55.

TO HENRY W. HALLECK

Near Kenesaw, Ga., June 27, 1864, 8 p.m.
(Received 1.35 a.m. 28th.)

Maj. Gen. H. W. Halleck,
Washington, D.C.

Pursuant to my orders of the 24th, a diversion was made on each flank of the enemy, especially on the Sandtown road, and at 8 a.m. General McPherson attacked at the southwest end of Kenesaw, and General Thomas at a point about a mile farther south. At the same, time the skirmishers and artillery along the whole line kept up a sharp fire. Neither attack succeeded, though both columns reached the enemy's works, which are very strong. General McPherson reports his loss about 500, and General Thomas about 2,000; the loss particularly heavy in general and field officers. General Harker is reported mortally wounded, also Col. Dan. McCook, commanding a brigade; Colonel Rice, Fifty-seventh Ohio, very seriously. Colonel Barnhill, Fortieth Illinois, and Captain Augustin, Fifty-fifth Illinois, are killed. The facility with which defensive works of timber and earth are constructed gives the party on the defensive great advantage. I cannot well turn the position of the enemy without abandoning my railroad, and we are already so far from our supplies that it is as much as the road can do to feed and supply the army. There are no supplies of any kind here. I can press Johnston and keep him from re-enforcing Lee, but to assault him in position will cost us more lives than we can spare. McPherson took to-day 100 prisoners, and Thomas about as many, but I do not suppose we inflicted heavy loss on the enemy, as he kept close behind his parapets.

W. T. Sherman,
Major-general.

Printed, *OR*, I, 38: pt. 4, 607.

TO ELLEN EWING SHERMAN

Head-Quarters, Military Division
of the Mississippi,
In the Field, near Marietta
June 30, 1864.

Dearest Ellen,

I got Mary Ewings letter, also that of Susan Stambaugh telling me of your serious illness after the birth of the new baby, but I had got Phil's dispatch saying you had been very sick but were much better and on the mend. I have no doubt your anxiety on many accounts has caused your illness but now having a new object of interest I hope your interest will revive & restore you rapidly to health. It is enough to make the whole world start at the awful amount of death & destruction that now stalks abroad. Daily for the past two months has the work progressed and I see no signs of a remission til one or both and all the armies are destroyed when I suppose the balance of the People will tear each other up, as Grant says reenacting the Story of the Kilkenny cats.[1] I begin to regard the death & mangling of a couple thousand men as a small affair, a kind of morning dash—and it may be well that we become so hardened. Each day is killed or wounded some valuable officers and men, the bullets coming from a concealed foe.[2] I suppose the people are impatient why I dont push or move rapidly to Atlanta but those who are here are satisfied with the progress. It is as much as our Railroad can do to Supply us bread meat & corn, and I cannot leave the Railroad to Swing on Johnstons flank or rear without giving him the Railroad which I cannot do without having a good supply on hand. I am moving heaven and earth to accomplish this, in which event I shall leave the Railroad & move to the Chattahoochee, threatening to cross which will I think force him to do that very thing when I will swing round on the road again. In that Event we may be all ready and attempt to hold both Road & river, but my opinion is he has not force enough to do both. In that Event you will be without news of us for ten days. I think we can whip his army in fair battle, but behind the hills and trunks our loss of life & limb on the first assault would reduce us too much, in other words at this distance from home we cannot afford the losses of such terrible assaults as Grant has made[.] I have only one source of supply, Grant had several in Succession. One of my chief objects was to prevent Joe Johnston from detaching against Grant till he got below Richmond & that I have done. I have no idea of besieging Atlanta, but may cross the Chattahoochee & circle round Atlanta breaking up its Roads. As you begin to get well I fear you will begin to fret again about changing your abode. If you are not comfortable at home try and rent some house, not the Small one of Martins you bespoke, but get Martin or Phil to find some other, & live as quietly & comfortably as possible. The worst of the war is not yet begun, the civil strife at the North has to come yet, and the tendency to Anarchy to be cured. Look at matters in Kentucky & Missouri and down the Mississipi & Arkansas where Shallow People have been taught to believe the war is over & you will see troubles enough to convince you I was right in my view of the case from the first. Stay as quietly as you can at Lancaster till Grant & I have our downfall, or are disposed of & then if we can do better, will be time enough to change. In such a quiet place as Lancaster you can hardly realize the truth that is so plain & palpable to me.

I hardly think Johnston will give us a chance to fight a decisive Battle, unless at such a disadvantage that I ought not to accept, and he is so situated that when threatened or pressed too hard he draws off leaving us a barren victory. He will thus act all summer unless he gives a great advantage in position or succeeds in breaking our Roads.

My love to all the children & folks and believe me always Yrs.

W. T. Sherman

ALS, InND: Sherman Family Papers.

1. Grant once added that the Union cat had the longer tail. In Irish folklore, the Kilkenny cats fought until only their tails were left.

2. WTS does not mention that on June 27 he had suffered a serious setback at Kenesaw Mountain.

TO MARIA BOYLE EWING SHERMAN

Head-Quarters, Military Division
of the Mississippi,
In the Field, Near Marietta Geo.
June 30 1864.

Dear Minnie,

I ought to write to you more often, but you are old enough to understand that I have not the time at my disposal to do all I should like. My army is very large, scattered over a vast extent, and I have so much riding to do, that when night comes I feel too tired to write much[.] I have hardly had time to write to Mama who has been quite sick, but is now getting well. She has sent me your letter of June 12 by which I see your examination comes off on the 7th of July, so that you will be almost starting for home when you get this—You will find there a new Brother to take Willy's place, but I fear we all loved Willy too much to let another supply his place. I ought to have written to you more about your studies. You seemed to fear you could not succeed at Music and Drawing. I think you will although it is no Cause of anxiety as they are merely accomplishments very well in themselves but not necessary to a good Education. Your Mama was and is a very good musician, and when I was at West Point I used to draw pretty well, indeed I stood at the head of my Class in Drawing—but no matter, try your best at all things and Excel in those for which you have a liking or natural facility. I observe a marked improvement in your hand writing, that is very important there is no accomplishment so agreeable in a lady as to write well and easily, always study to write plain so that whosoever gets your letter may read it easily. I am no example at this but you have already seen that those can give the best advice who set the worst examples, for we realize best our own defeats. I have not heard from Lizzie for a long time, but I suppose she is so busy during her mamas sickness in taking care of the little Children that She has no time to write to me. I fear Lizzie is destined to be a Stay at home, whilst you and I will be gad abouts. I will keep my promise to you, if you stay another year at your present school to take you myself to New York, and give you a year at the best Seminary I can find there. I ought not to make many promises for I daily see too many officers buried by the road side, or carried to the rear maimed and mangled to count on much of a future but if I do come out of this war safe I will try to See more of my family and Children. For three years constantly have I been in danger, and it may be that in the next I may be spared as in the Past—Write to me more frequently. Do your best at school, and always feel that though I may not write often I always think of you. Yr. father,

W. T. Sherman

ALS, OHi: William T. Sherman.

TO HENRY W. HALLECK
Cypher   Hd. Qrts. Mil. Div. of the Miss.
                                              In the Field Near Chattahoochee
                                              July 7 64

Genl. Halleck
Washington D.C.

Genl. Garrard reports to me that he is in possession of Roswell where [there] were several valuable cotton & wool factories in full operation also paper mills all of which by my order he destroyed by fire. They had been for years engaged exclusively at work for the confederate Govt. & the owner of the woolen factory displayed the French Flag but as he failed also to show the United States Flag, Genl. Garrard burned it also. The main cotton Factory was valued at a million of U.S. Dollars. The cloth on hand is reserved for use of U.S. Hospitals & I have ordered Genl. Garrard to arrest for treason all owners & employees foreign & native & send them under guard to Marietta whence I will send them North. Being exempt from conscription they are as much governed by the Rules of War as if in the Ranks. The women can find employment in Indiana. This whole region was devoted to manufactories but I will destroy every one of them.[1] Johnston is manouvering against my Right & I will try & pass the Chattahoochee by my Left. Ask Mr. Stanton not to publish the substance of my despatches for they reach Richmond in a day & are telegraphed at once to Atlanta.

The Atlanta papers contain later news from Washington than I get from Nashville. Absolute silence in Military matters is the only safe rule—Let our public learn patience & common sense.

W. T. Sherman
Maj. Genl. Comdg.

Lbk, DNA: RG 94, Records of the Adjutant General's Office, Generals' Books and Papers, William T. Sherman, Letterbook 11; *OR*, I, 38: pt. 5, 73.

1. Sherman told Garrard, "I had no idea that the Factories at Roswell remained in operation but supposed the machinery had all been removed. Their utter destruction is right & meets my entire approval & to make the matter complete you will arrest the owners & employees & send them under guard charged with Treason, to Marietta, & I will see as to any man in America hoisting the French Flag & then devoting his labor & capital to supplying armies in open hostility to our Government & claiming the benefit of his Neutral Flag. Should you under the impulse of anger natural at contemplating such perfidy, hang the wretch I approve the act beforehand." He added, "I repeat my orders that you arrest all people male & female connected with those factorys no matter what the clamor & let them foot it under guard to Marietta, whence I will send them by cars to the North. Destroy & make the same disposition of all mills save small flouring mills manifestly for local use—but all saw mills & factories dispose of effectually, & useful laborers, excused by reason of their skill as manufacturers, from conscription are as much prisoners as if armed. The poor women will make a howl. Let them take along their children & clothing providing they have the means of hauling or you can spare them. We will retain them until they can reach a country where they can live in Peace & Security." WTS to Garrard, July 7, 1864, Lbk, DNA: RG 94, Records of the Adjutant General's Office, Generals' Books and Papers, William T. Sherman, Letterbook 11.

TO ELLEN EWING SHERMAN

> Head-Quarters, Military Division
> of the Mississippi,
> In the Field, near Chattahoochee,
> July 9, 1864.

Dearest Ellen,

It is now more than two months since I left Chattanooga and I think during all this time I have but one letter from you. I fear you have been more ill than I had supposed but I hope that it in no manner resulted from uneasiness about me. I have been very well all the time but necessarily so employed that I could not write much. All my letters partake more of the Dispatch kind than any thing else & I have settled down so that I dislike to write a regular letter. Charley & Dayton have often written and I have no doubt you have followed us in our tedious and dangerous journey. We are now on the Chattahoochee in plain view of the City of Atlanta 9 miles off. The enemy and the Chattahoochee lies between us, and intense heat prevails, but I think I shall succeed, at all events you Know I never turn back. I see by the papers that too much stress was laid on the repulse of June 27. I was forced to make the effort, and it should have succeeded, but the officers & men have been so used to my avoiding excessive danger and forcing back the Enemy by strategy that they hate to assault, but to assault is sometimes necessary, for its effect on the

Enemy. Had that assault succeeded I would have then fought Johnston with the advantage on my side instead of his having all the benefit of forts, ground, creeks &c. As it was I did not give him rest, but forced him across the Chatta-hoochee which was the first great object. I have already got Schofield and Garrard across the River, and therefore can cross the Army when I choose. I sent to Genl. Webster my pay accounts for May, & after paying some small accounts he was to send a check for the Balance to you. He writes me he has done so. I want you to write to Professor Albert E. Church,[1] U.S. Mil. Acad. West Point & ask him what is my assessment towards the National Monu-ment, that is being erected there in Memory of the West Point Graduates that have fallen in this war[.] It is about $27.—when the exact figure is thus ascertained send him a check. Also subscribe for the United States Service Magazine of which Professor H. Coppée of Philadelphia is Editor. It is a monthly magazine and will be good authority—I see he proposes to publish in the Aug. number a sketch of my life compiled by authority of a friend of mine. I wrote to Coppée to know what friend & he answered, Bowman. I dont know what data Bowman has, but of course I know he will deal in more Eulogy & generalisms than I would prefer, but cannot avoid it. I wish the letter of resignation I made in Louisiana embraced in any sketch of me, and I remem-ber you said you had a Copy. If you have it still make a copy & send it to Bowman if you Know where he is, or to Professor Coppée who will see to it. If you cannot attend to these matters get Phil or some one else to do it for you. The distant booming of cannon, & sharp rattle of musketry is now so familiar that it feels unnatural unless they are constant. The army is very large and extends from Roswell factory at the north (around to) Sandtown, but my centre is directly in front of Atlanta. I will have to manoeuvre some here-abouts to drive the Enemy and to gain time to accumulate Stores by Rail to enable me to operate beyond Reach of the Railroad. Thus far our supplies have been ample and the country is high, mountainous, with splendid water & considerable forage in the nature of fields of growing wheat, oats & corn, but we sweep across it leaving it as bare as a desert. The People all flee before us. The task of feeding this vast host is a more difficult one than to fight. I hope by this time you are well, and that the youngster is beginning to develop so you can make a guess what he is to be. I should like to have your opinion of him though it will be a prejudiced one. I should like Minnie and Lizzie & Tom to write more frequently, they must not expect me to write letters for theirs—they must understand my present family is numbered by hundreds of thou-sands all of whom look to me to provide for their wants. I shall not attempt an official account of this camp again until it approaches completion. Give my love to your father and all the young folks. Yrs. Ever

AL (signature clipped), InND: Sherman Family Papers; words in angle brackets from *HL*, 301.

1. Church was a professor in mathematics at West Point.

TO HUGH B. EWING

Head-Quarters, Military Division
of the Mississippi,
In the Field, near Chattahoochee,
July 13, 1864.

Dear Hugh,

I received yours of June 30, a few days ago, and assure you of my thanks at its kindly tone. I feel uneasy about matters at home. I cannot hear, a full month is now past since my last dispatch saying that Ellen was better, but had been quite ill. I have written as often as I could, and telegraphed several times without eliciting a reply. I should not thus be kept uneasy whilst charged with so high responsibilities. Much of this campaign has been strategy. I have brought this army to the Banks of the Chattahoochee 130 miles from Chattanooga, and no part of it has been a day without ample supplies of food, ammunition, clothing and all that is essential we have defeated Johnston entrenched at Dalton Resacca, Cassville, Alatoona, Dallas Kennesaw, Surgeons Camp & the Chattahoochee, All natural features and strengthened by the labor of large masses of negros & militia as also by the Army of Johnston well commanded & in good discipline. I have had a superior force of course, but this has been fully neutralized by artificial works and the necessity of my guarding against real & supposed Danger to my Rear. I have also secured already without the loss of a man thru good crossings of the Chattahoochee though the River had been regarded for years as a natural barrier and all points defended in advance by Earthworks & guarded by militia. I only await the Return of some Cavalry sent down the Chattahoochee to cross the whole army & advance against Atlanta in plain view only 9 miles distant but as a siege cannot be attempted at this distance from my Base, I will make a circuit and operate against its communications. Weather is very hot, but the country is mountainous well watered & healthy.

I ought probably in justice to the subject pay more attention to the Record as we progress, but I want to attain the Result: before Entering on the official narrative so that thus far I have merely made daily telegrams short & not descriptive, but I hope ere long to make such a Report as will make the Campaign take its place side by side with the one of Knoxville, & indeed of some of the Old World. Officers & men evince the utmost Confidence, only they prefer Strategy to fighting, whereas they must go hand in hand. Give my love to Henrietta & if you ever hear from home tell me some news, probably they account me dead & disposed of. Charley is well, though he did have a severe cholera morbus a few nights since from indulging the rare luxury of sanitary onions. Yr. affectionate Brother,

W. T. Sherman

M.G.

ALS, OHi: William T. Sherman Papers.

TO PHILEMON B. EWING

Head-Quarters, Military Division
of the Mississipi,
In the Field, near Chattahoochee,
July 13, 1864.

Dear Phil,

I really feel very uneasy about Ellen. She never before neglected to write as now. It is more than two months since she has written, and it is nearly if not quite a month since your last telegraph announced she was much better. I was very thankful to Mary Ewing and to Susan Stambaugh for their letters and I wish you to thank them for me. Still so much time has since elapsed that I feel more uneasy than ever. Our mails are pretty regular, and the telegraph is to my tent. I hear from all parts of the world daily, but can get nothing from Lancaster. If Ellen be really too unwell to write I wish you would see that some one tells me the truth for I really have enough care & responsibility here without the uneasiness naturally resulting from absolute silence at home.[1]

As to this campaign I have now driven my adversary wholly across the Chattahoochee and have three Corps across ready to be followed by my whole army, when certain necessary preliminaries are complete. Atlanta is in full sight 9 miles off. I have brought one hundred thousand men from Chattanooga 120 miles and driven a well commanded & well organized army of 60,000, from the fortified positions at Dalton, Resacca, Cassville, Alatoona, Kenesaw, Smyrna and the Chattahoochee, taking his only Nitre country—his vast Iron works, & beds of ore, and lastly the most extensive cotton & woollen manufactories of Georgia. We had sixty days of continual combat, with several pretty smart battles interspersed. I dont believe there are ten men in the United States other than those here who appreciate & measure the vast labor of mind & body consumed in accomplishing these results and I may be at fault for discouraging flattering descriptions however I prefer at the end, or rather at some pause in the Grand drama to paint a connected whole rather than scatter it piecemeal to satisfy the greedy curiosity of a gaping public. I think in crossing the Chattahoochee as I have, without the loss of a man, I have achieved really a creditable deed. Thomas told me he dreaded it more than any one thing ahead and when he learned that I had Schofield across, fortified and with two pontoon bridges laid, only 3 miles above where Johnston lay entrenched on this bank, he could not believe it, and Johnston himself the moment he found it out, evacuated the permanent defenses of the Chattahoochee & burned all his bridges five in number. I now have McPherson across at Roswell with a good bridge on the old pins—Schofield at the mouth of Soape Creek with two pontoon bridges—and Howard at Powers Ferry with two pontoon bridges. I have also accumulated provisions that will last the army till the 1st of August in Marietta & Allatoona Pass, both fortified positions. I only await the return of some cavalry sent down along the Chattahoochee, to pass the River & move against Atlanta. If I can take Atlanta without too large a sacrifice I may then allow my friends to claim for me the Rank of a General, for I have given daily direction to 200,000 men on distant fields with a full hundred thousand under my own eye.

Professor H. Coppée of Philadelphia is about to publish a sketch of my life in the August number of the U.S. Service Magazine, the composition of Bowmans. I have heretofore escaped this infliction but cannot escape this, and have asked him to make it as short as possible & to introduce into it my letter of resignation when in Louisiana. Ellen has the only copy I know of, and I wish you would see that Coppée gets a copy in time.

My health is good. I live out of doors under a tent fly, have good rations & ride a good deal. Indeed my Lines are always over ten miles long, and at this moment full twenty, but my office labors are not great as the details fall upon army commanders.

Give my best love to Mary and all the children[.] Tell Tom if I survive the war & save any war horses I will give one to him. My special respect to your father who I fear watches me with undue apprehension & solicitude. yrs.

W. T. Sherman

ALS, Atlanta, Ga.: Private Collection of C. Parke Day.

1. On July 20, Ewing answered this letter, apologizing for keeping WTS in suspense. EES's recovery had been so rapid after the first telegrams that he had quite forgotten that she had been ill and that he should be keeping his brother-in-law informed. He had helped Bowman with material, including WTS's letter of resignation from the Louisiana State Seminary. He also commented that while few appreciated the strategy behind WTS's maneuvers, many appreciated that he was "a prudent, vigilant & able general." Joseph H. Ewing, *Sherman at War* (Dayton, Ohio, 1992), 134–35.

TO HENRY W. HALLECK

Cypher.   Hd. Qrs. Mil. Div. of the Miss.
                                           In the Field near Chattahoochie River
                                           July 13th/64

Genl. Halleck
Washington, D.C.

All is well. I have now accumulated Stores at Allatoona and Marietta both fortified and Garrisoned points. Have also three points at which to cross the Chattahoochie in my possession, and only await Genl. Stonemans return from a trip down the river to cross the army in force and move on Atlanta. Stoneman is now out two days, and had orders to be back on the 4th or 5th day at farthest. Rousseau should reach Opelika about the 17th of July.[1]

Before Regulations are made for the States to send recruiting officers into the Rebel States, I must express my opinion that it is the height of folly. I cannot permit it here. I will not have a set of fellows here hanging about on any such pretences. We have no means to transport and feed them. The Sanitaries and Christian Commission are enough to eradicate all traces of Christianity from our minds; much less a set of unscrupulous State agents in search of recruits. All these dodges are make shifts that render us ridiculous in our own estimation. I must protect my army, and I say beforehand, I have no means to transport Recruiting Parties South of Nashville, or to feed them, if they come here, in spite of me.[2]

                                           W. T. Sherman
                                           Major Genl. Comdg.

Lbk, DNA: RG 94, Records of the Adjutant General's Office, Generals' Books and Papers, William T. Sherman, Letterbook 11; *OR*, I, 38: pt. 5, 137. The letter is dated July 14 in *OR*.

1. Lovell H. Rousseau, commanding the District of Nashville in the Army of the Cumberland, had left Decatur, Alabama, with twenty-five hundred cavalry to destroy railroad lines between Montgomery, Alabama, and Columbus, Georgia. On July 17, he reached the railroad junction near Opelika and then returned to Marietta on July 22.

2. The following day, WTS wrote to HWH on the same subject: "If State Recruiting Agents must come into the limits of my command under the Law, I have the honor to request that the Commanding officers or Adjutants of Regiments be constituted such agents, and that States be entitled to a credit for Recruits they may enlist, who are accepted and mustered in by the Regular mustering officer of their Division and Corps. This will obviate the difficulty I apprehend from Civilian agents." *OR*, I, 38: pt. 5, 136.

On July 18, 1864, Lincoln wrote WTS in response to WTS's protests against Northern states opening recruiting stations near his army. Pointing out that such recruiting was authorized by law, the president added that he hoped that many blacks would be recruited, "which, unlike white recruits, help us where they come from, as well as where they go to." He asked for WTS's "hearty co-operation." *CWAL*, 7:449–50; quote on p. 450.

TO ELLEN EWING SHERMAN

> Head-Quarters, Military Division
> of the Mississippi,
> In the Field, Chattahoochee,
> July 13, 1864.

Dearest Ellen,

I have not written as often as you should expect in the midst of the incessant war in which I have been engaged for the past two months. I have not heard a word from you since the birth of our son and only two short telegrams from Phil. I have telegraphed since & elicited no reply. Charley does not hear from Lancaster either, but today heard from Sis at Chauncey and she said you were doing well at last accounts. Still I supposed you must be dangerously ill, or that your letters miscarried, but today Ellen Lynchs letter came addressed in your hand & postmarked July 6. You should write occasionally or make Lizzie write or Minnie who must now be at home, or get some one for I should not be kept uneasy about you, when my mind is kept on such a stretch by the circumstances that surround me. I believe I have conducted this campaign as skilfully as possible, and when understood in all its details it will attract the notice of Military Judges. Still much remains and I may be all the year. I do not pretend to See the End of this War, though I am far down in the very heart of the Enemys Country. You will hear less of us hereafter. I have asked Mr. Stanton not to publish my daily dispatches because they give a clue to the Enemy and I prefer silence. It is an Element of Power. I wrote a long letter to Phil which will explain our position. In a few days I will cross the Chattahoochee, and then will come the Real Struggle. I know we will whip Johnston in anything like a fair fight, but being on the defensive he can take great advantage of Forts, field works and the nature of the ground which naturally favors him. But we have overcome all obstacles thus far, and trust we can continue to do so, though it involves time. My army is as strong as the day we left Chattanooga and full of confidence. Weather is very hot, but we have plenty of water and the Country is mountainous and healthy. I am in very good condition, and my horses are all well, which is important. Give my love to all the folks and have Minnie, Lizzie & Tom write to me. Describe the young one. Yrs. Ever

> W. T. Sherman

ALS, InND: Sherman Family Papers.

TO GEORGE H. THOMAS

Headquarters, Military Division
of the Mississippi,
In the Field July 20, 1864 8 P.M.

Genl. Thomas,

Dear Genl.

I have just recd. Gen. Stonemans letter with your Endorsement. We have seen enough today to convince us that all of Stonemans information is incorrect. Some thing more than Militia remains at Atlanta and they are not demoralized. They have fought hard and persistently all day and this heavy musketry fire still continues with Howard and Schofield. I do not hear McPhersons guns now; I will send him your letter but fear his answer will be that he has all the Rebels on his flank. I think he is already impressed with the importance of pushing hard on that flank.

If we cannot break in, we must move by the Right flank and interpose between the River and Atlanta, and operate against the Roads south.

If you can advance your whole Line say to within three miles of Atlanta I can throw a {force} around your Rear to East Point. If you see a good Chance to strike in that quarter you may call for Stoneman's & McCooks men and let them come across by (illegible) and march down this Bank.

My own opinion is that in the morning you will find the forts on the Chattahoochee abandonned, and think you will have no difficulty in pushing your Line up close to Atlanta. At all Events try it. I will send yours & Stonemans letters to McPherson but think the opportunity of operating on that flank if it did exist is now past. Yours truly,

W. T. Sherman
Maj. Genl.

ALS, MiU-C: James S. Schoff Civil War Collection; *OR*, I, 38: pt. 5, 195.

TO LORENZO THOMAS

Headquarters, Military Division
of the Mississippi,
In the Field, Near Atlanta Ga.
July [23][1] 1864.

To Genl. L. Thomas
Adjt. Genl. U.S. Army

General,

It is my painful duty to report that Brig. Genl. James B. McPherson, U.S. Army, Major Genl. of Vols. and Commander of the Army of the Tennessee in the Field was killed by a musket shot from ambuscade about noon of yesterday. At the time of this fatal shot he was on horseback placing his troops in position near the City of Atlanta and was passing by a crossroad from a moving column towards the flank of troops that had already been established on the Line. He had quitted me but a few moments before and was on his way to see in person to the execution of my orders. About the time of this sad event the Enemy had sallied from his Entrenchments around Atlanta, and had by a circuit got to the Left and Rear of this very line, and had begun an attack which resulted in serious battle; so that Genl. McPherson fell in Battle, booted and spured as the Gallant Knight and Gentleman should wish. Not his the loss, But the country and the Army will mourn his death, and cherish his memory at that of one who though comparatively young, had risen by his merit and ability to the command of one of the best Armies, which the nation had called into existence to vindicate its honor and integrity.

History tells us of but few who so blended the grace and gentleness of the friend, with the dignity courage, faith and manliness of the soldier. His public enemies, even the men who directed the fatal shot, never spoke or wrote of him, without expressions of marked respect, those whom he commanded loved him even to idolatry, and I his associate and Commander fail in words adequate to express my opinion of his great worth. I feel assured that every Patriot in America on hearing this sad news will feel a sense of personal loss, and the country generally will realize that we have lost not only an able military Leader, but a man who had he survived was qualified to heal the National Strife, which has been raised by designing and ambitious men.

His body has been sent north in charge of Major Willard, Captains Steele and Gile his personal Staff. I am with great respect

W. T. Sherman
Major General Comdg.

LS, OHi: William T. Sherman Papers; *OR*, I, 38: pt. 5, 241.
1. This copy was mistakenly dated July 24.

TO ELLEN EWING SHERMAN

Head-Quarters, Military Division
of the Mississippi,
In the Field near Atlanta Geo.
July 26, 1864.

Dearest Ellen,

I got your long letter[1] and one from Minnie last night and telegraphed you in general terms that we are all well—We have Atlanta close aboard as the Sailors say but it is a hard nut to handle. These fellows fight like Devils & Indians combined, and it calls for all my cunning & Strength.

Instead of Attacking the Forts, which are really unassailable, I must gradually destroy the Roads which make Atlanta a place worth having. This is have partially done. Two out of three are broken and we are now manoeuvering for the third.

I lost my Right bower[2] in McPherson—but of course it is expected for with all the natural advantages of bushes, cover of all Kinds we must all be killed. I mean the Genl. officers. McPherson was riding within his Lines behind his wing of the Army, but the enemy had got round the flank & crept up one of those hollows with bushes that concealed them completely. It has been thus all the way from Chattanooga, and if Beauregard can induce Davis to adopt the Indian policy of ambuscade which he urged two years ago, but which Jeff thought rather derogatory to the high pretenses of his Cause to Courage & manliness, every officer will be killed, for the whole country is a forest, so that an Enemy can waylay every path and Road, & could not be found.

Poor Mac, he was killed dead instantly. I think I shall prefer Howard to Succeed him[.][3] Charley is quite well—goes today to inspect some cavalry that must start tomorrow on a Raid—Corse is relieved from my Staff & given a Divn. in Dodges command.[4] Charley ought to keep you advised of these things, the truth is I have other things to think of—Yrs. ever,

W. T. S.

P.S. You have fallen into an Error about McPherson. He was not out of his place or exposing himself nearer than I and Every General does daily—he was to the Rear of his Line, riding by a Road he had passed twice that morning. The thing was an accident that resulted from the blind character of the Country we are in, dense woods fill all the ravines & hollow, and which little cleared ground there is is on the Ridge levels, or the alluvium of Creek bottoms. The hills are all Chestnut ridges with quartz and granite boulders & gravel. You Cant find an hundred acres of land clear ground between here & Chattanooga, and not a day passes but what every Genl. officer may be shot as McPherson was. That you may understand I make a small diagram—

ALS, InND: Sherman Family Papers; diagram enclosed.

1. EES's eight-page letter of July 20 related mostly family news. SFP.

2. Bower, as used here, is an archaic term for "anchor."

3. Howard would succeed to the command of the Army of the Tennessee on July 27.

4. Corse had been WTS's inspector general and on this day took command of the Second Division, Sixteenth Corps.

Cypher.   H'd Qrts. Mil. Div. of the Miss.
                                           In the field Near Atlanta July 27th 64

Genl. Halleck
Washington D.C.

My two Cavalry Expeditions are off to make a wide circuit[1] & reach the Macon Road well to the South East of Atlanta, & the Army of the Tennessee is shifted to the extreme Right reaching well towards the Railroads, so that I think tomorrow must develop something. The Cavalry will have to fight the Enemys Cavalry & we can hold the Infantry & artillery to Atlanta & force them to extend & choose between Atlanta & East Point. I dont think the Enemy can hold both. All are well pleased with Genl. Howards appointment but Genls. Logan & Hooker.[2] The former thought he ought to have been allowed the Command of the Army in the Field until the end of the campaign; but I explained to him that a permanent Dept. Comdr. had to be appointed at once, as discharges, furloughs & much detailed business could alone be done by a Department Commander. Genl. Hooker is offended because he thinks he is entitled to the Command. I must be honest & say he is not qualified or suited to it. He talks of quitting. If Genl. Thomas recommends I shall not object.[3] He is not indispensable to our success. He is welcome to my place if the President awards it, but I cannot name him to so important a command as the Army of the Tennessee.

All is well. The Enemy today offered no serious opposition to the charges of today & our skirmishing & artillery was just enough to make things interesting.

                              W. T. Sherman
                              Maj. Genl. Comdg.

Lbk, DNA: RG 94, Records of the Adjutant General's Office, Generals' Books and Papers, William T. Sherman, Letterbook 11; OR, I, 38: pt. 5, 271–72.

1. The only remaining railroad from Atlanta was that leading south to Macon, and WTS believed that its destruction would guarantee the surrender of Atlanta. On July 26, he sent Stoneman with his and Garrard's cavalry division from Decatur to a point on the railroad between Jonesboro and Griffin. He also authorized him to raid Macon and free Union prisoners at Andersonville. Brigadier General Edward M. McCook (1833–1909), a Kansas lawyer and politician, was commanding the First Division of the Cavalry Corps of the Army of the Cumberland and was ordered to take his and Rousseau's divisions to the same point from the Chattahoochee River below Sandtown.

2. On this date WTS had named Howard to lead the Army of the Tennessee. Logan had been commanding the army since McPherson's death. See WTS to Logan, July 27, 1864, below.

3. Hooker would leave his command the following day.

Headquarters, Military Division
of the Mississippi,
In the Field, Near Atlanta Geo.,
July 27, 1864.

To his Excellency,
President Lincoln, Washington
Sir,

Your Dispatch of yesterday is received.[1] I beg you will not regard me as fault finding, for I assert that I have been well sustained in every respect during my Entire Service. I did not suppose my dispatches would go outside the offices at the War Dept. I did not suppose you were troubled with such things. Hovey and Osterhaus are both worthy men, and had they been promoted on the eve of the Vicksburgh campaign it would have been natural & well accepted but I do think you will admit that their promotion coming to us when they had gone to the Rear, the one offended, because I could not unite in the same Division five Infantry and five Cavalry Regiments, and the other for temporary sickness, you can see how ambitious aspirants for military Fame regard these things. They come to me, and point them out as evidences that I am wrong in encouraging them in a silent patient discharge of duty. I assure you that every General of my army has spoken of it, and referred to it as evidence that promotion results from importunity and not from actual services. I have refrained from recommending any thus far in the Campaign, and I think we should reach some stage in the game before stopping to balance accounts or writing History[.] I assure you that I do think you have conscientiously acted throughout the war, with marked skill, in the matter of military appointments and that as few mistakes have been made as could be expected. I will furnish all my army and Division Commanders with a copy of your dispatch that they may feel reassured. With great respect,

W. T. Sherman
Maj. Genl.

ALS, DLC: Robert Todd Lincoln Collection of Abraham Lincoln Papers; *OR*, I, 38: pt. 5, 271.

1. Lincoln to WTS, July 26, 1864, *CWAL*, 7:463. Hovey's and Osterhaus's appointments as brevet major generals of volunteers on July 4 and 23 had caused WTS to write to Inspector General James Hardie on July 25 "that it is an act of injustice to officers who stand by their posts in the day of danger to neglect them and advance such as Hovey and Osterhaus, who left us in the midst of bullets to go to the rear in search of personal advancement. If the rear be the post of honor, then we had all better change front on Washington." Ibid., 463–64n. Lincoln's reply assured WTS that they had thought Hovey had nonetheless deserved the honor and had not known of Osterhaus's departure. He had been promoted partly, Lincoln

confided, because of his nationality. He asked WTS "to believe we do not act in a spirit of disregarding merit" and thanked him for his current military efforts. Ibid., 463.

TO JOHN A. LOGAN

Headquarters, Military Division
of the Mississippi,
In the Field, near Atlanta, July 27, 1864

Gen. Jno. A. Logan
Dear Genl.

Take a good rest. I know you are worn out with mental & physical work. No one could have a higher appreciation of the responsibility then devolved on you so unexpectedly and the noble manner in which you met it. I fear you will feel disappointed at not succeeding permanently to the command of the Army & Dept. I assure you in giving preference to Gen. Howard I will not fail to give you every credit for having done so well. You have Command of a good Corps, a command that I would prefer to the more complicated one of a Dept., and if you will be patient it will come to you soon Enough. Be assured of my Entire Confidence[.] After you have rested come down to Davis position and then thence to the new position of your Corps. Assume command of it and things will move along harmoniously & well. If I can do anything to mark my full sense of the honourable manner in which you acted in the Battle & since, name it to me frankly and I will do it. Gen. Howard & I will go off to the Right to Survey the New Field and prepare the way for the troops. Yr. friend,

W. T. Sherman
Maj. Genl.

ALS, DLC: John A. Logan Papers.

TO ELLEN EWING SHERMAN

Head-Quarters, Military Division
of the Mississippi,
In the Field, near Atlanta July 29, 1864.

Dearest Ellen,

Since crossing Chattahoochee I have been too busy to write—we have had three (3) pretty hard battles, the Enemy attacked my center as we were fairly across the Peachtree Creek, and got badly beaten. Next as we closed in on Atlanta he struck our extreme Left, and the fighting was desperate, he drove back a part of the Left, but the men fought hard and when night closed our losses amounted to 3500 and we found nearly 3000 Dead Rebels, making the usual allowance the enemy must have sustained a loss of 10,000. Yesterday I shifted the Army of the Tennessee to my Extreme Right, and in getting into position it was again attacked & repulsed the attack. The fight was mostly with the 15th Corps. Logan commands it McPhersons death was a great loss to me. I depended much on him[.] In casting about for a Successor I preferred Howard, who is a man of mind and intellect. He is very honest, sincere & moral Even to piety but brave having lost an arm already. But he was a junior Major General to Hooker who took offense and has gone away. I dont regret it—he is envious, imperious, and braggart. Self prevailed with him and Knowing him intimately I honestly preferred Howard—Yesterdays work justified my choice for Howards dispositions and manner Elicited the shouts of my old Corps, and he at once stepped into the Shoes of McPherson and myself. I have now Thomas, Schofield & Howard, all tried & approved soldiers. We are gradually drawing our lines close up to Atlanta, fortifying our front against their bold sallies, and I now have all the Cavalry out against the Roads between Atlanta & Macon. I am glad I beat Johnston for he had the most exalted reputation with our Old Army as a strategist. Hood[1] is a new man and a fighter and must be watched Closer, as he is reckless of the lives of his Men. It is wonderful with what faith they adhere to the belief that they whip us on all occasions though we have them now almost penned up in Atlanta. If no reinforcements come I think I will cut them off from all communication with the rest of the Confederacy. Bowman has sent me the proof sheets of the August No. of the U.S. Service Magazine. The sketch is strong, but contains enough original material to give it the coloring of truth.

I enclose you a letter for you, which seems to be from the mother of your "Norah." I also repeat that I prefer that Minnie should return to that School at Cincinati, & Lizzie go along if willing. I prefer you should stay at Lancaster at whatever sacrifice of feeling or personal convenience till we can see daylight ahead in this war. But if you will go, better to Cincinati than Notre Dame. There you have no better medical attendance than you will find within reach of Lancaster. I dont pretend to See a week ahead, and if I get killed which is not improbable at any moment, you will of course be compelled to live at Lancaster. Yesterday a solid Canister Shot passed me Close & killed an orderlys horse (Charleys orderly) close behind me, in fact I daily pass death in the most familiar shape and you should base your calculations on that event. I got Minnie's letter. It is plainly and well written and I feel satisfied she has made good progress at her new School, and do not wish her to change. I have cut out of a magazine two rough woodcuts of Grant & myself which approximate likenesses. Keep them as samples. Charley & I are both well and my staff remains unchanged except I have given Corse to Dodge to command one of his

Divisions. Give my love to all the children & the folks Generally—Poor Jim.[2] He was a good fellow, but John Barleycorn was too much for him. Yrs. Ever

W. T. Sherman

ALS, InND: Sherman Family Papers.

1. Lieutenant General John Bell Hood (1831–79), CSA, had succeeded to the command of the Army of Tennessee on July 18.

2. WTS's brother James Sherman (b. 1814) had died of complications arising from his alcoholism in Cincinnati on July 10.

TO JOHN A. SPOONER

Head Qtrs. Milt. Div. of the Miss.
In the Field near Atlanta Ga.
July 30" 1864.

Jno. A. Spooner Esq.
Agent for the Commonwealth of Massachusetts
Nashville
Sir.

Yours from Chattanooga of July 28th is received, notifying me of your appointment by your State as Lieut. Col. and Provost Marshall for Georgia, Alabama and Mississippi, under the act of Congress approved July 4th 1864 to recruit volunteers to be credited the Quotas of the States respectively. On applying to Genl. Webster at Nashville he will grant you a pass through our lines, to these States, and as I have had considerable experience in those States would suggest recruiting Depots to be established at Macon and Columbus, Mississippi—Selma, Montgomery and Mobile, Alabama and Columbus, Milledgeville and Savannah Georgia. I do not see that the Law restricts you to Black recruits, but you are at liberty I suppose to collect white Recruits also. It is [a] waste of time and money to open rondevouz in North West Georgia, for I assure you I have not seen an able bodied man black or white fit for a soldier, who was not in this Army or the one opposite it.

You speak of the impression going about that I am opposed to the organization of Colored Regiments. My opinions are usually very positive and there is no reason why you should not know them. Though entertaining profound reverence for our Congress, I do doubt their wisdom in the passage of this Law. 1st because Civillian Agents about an army are a nuisance. 2nd The duty of citizens to fight for their country is too sacred an one to be peddled off by buying up the refuse of other States. 3rd. It is unjust to the Soldiers and Volunteers who are fighting as those who compose this army are doing to place them on a *par* with the class of recruits you are after. 4th The negro is in a transition state and is not the equal of the white man. 5th He is liberated from his Bondage by act of war and the armies in the Field are entitled to al his assistance in labor and fighting *in addition* to the proper quota of the States. 6th This bidding and bartering for Recruits white and black has delayed the reinforcements of our armies at this time when such reinforcements could have enabled us to make our successes permanent. 7th The Law is an experiment which pending war is unwise and unsafe and has delayed the universal draft which I firmly believe will become necessary to overcome the wide spread resistance offered us, and I also believe the universal draft will be wise and benificent for under the Providence of God it will seperate the Sheep from the Goats and demonstrate what citizens will fight for their country and what will only talk.

No one shall infer from this that I am not the Friend of the negro as well as the white race. I contend that the Treason and Rebellion of the Master *freed* the slave; and I and the armies I have commanded have conducted to safe points more negroes than those of any other General officer in the army, but I prefer some negroes as pioneers, teamsters, cooks, and servants, others gradually to experiment in the art of the Soldier, beginning with the duties of local garrison such as we had at Memphis, Vicksburg, Natchez—Nashville and Chattanooga: but I would not draw on the Poor race for too large a proportion of its active athletic young men, for some must remain to seek new homes, and provide for the old and young, the feeble and helpless.

These are some of my peculiar notions, but I assure you they are shared by a large proportion of our fighting men. You may show this to the agents of the other States in the same business with yourself. I am &c.

W. T. Sherman

Major Genl. Comdg.

Lbk, DNA: RG 94, Records of the Adjutant General's Office, Generals' Books and Papers, William T. Sherman, Letterbook 11; *OR*, I, 38: pt. 5, 305–6.

TO JOHN SHERMAN

Headquarters, Military Division
of the Mississippi,
In the Field, Near Atlanta, July 31, 1864

Dear Brother,

I received your long letter of the 24[1] last night and before starting out this morning will answer. I dont want Hugh to engage in the cotton business. At first the speculators made large profits by buying cotton of niggers, overseers & thieves, but that is now all over and the competition is so great that though that means we have lost all we gained in our Mississipi campaign but the naked River, and the Guerillas render it almost a barren conquest. The only orders I give as to cotton is to burn it as the chief cash resource of the South.

Even with what is left to them at present prices they are richer in money than you of the North, and as Mr. Chase encouraged the trade in cotton he supplied the armies of the South better than they were enabled to do, through the blockade. In my Meridian trip I found the enemys camps well stocked with Shoes clothing & ammunition of Cincinati and Philadelphia manufacture. This greed after gain encourages the South to believe what our army already knows that our People are so avaricious that they would sell our lives for a small profit. I dont want Hugh to engage in it, it is a dirty business—until he is drafted let him cultivate potatoes & vegetables to feed his family, Same of Moulton. Of course before we can make our conquests permanent we have to populate the South *de novo*. Dont understand me as opposed to the progress of the War, on the contrary since the first day of it we have had no choice only our govt. had no sense and kept on with temporary expedients instead of resorting to the universal compulsory draft, with terms of enlistment adequate to the End. We no sooner get an army than it dissolves away. I have seen with sorrow some of my best Regts. march to the Rear—time out. Whilst mine dwindles thus that of the enemy constantly grows and may in the End overreach me. I dont believe you can appreciate the disgust felt by the real men of the army for the recent Law of Congress allowing states to Send agents into the Rebellious states to enlist the refuse and negros with high bounties, to be credited them on the draft—our soldiers do not feel complimented that Such stuff shall go into the count as par with them.

You speak of the drift of popular sentiment that Grant & Sherman would now be good candidates. Fortunately we are not candidates for before the election is over "Mack" or some other "Skunks" would write us down, in the Method of Sim Tappertit.[2]

Since we crossed Chattahoochee Hood attacked my center & got whipped—July 20th—on the 22nd he shortened his lines drew inside of Atlanta well fortified and then his whole available force against my left, where a real hand fight ensued, but there again he got the worst of it—on the 27th I was extending my Lines and attack by the Right & he repeated the same manoeuver and got dreadfully whipped—In Each of these battles we killed as many as our entire casualties. My aggregate losses will not foot up 5000, whereas on the 20th we buried near 700 Rebels—on the 22nd 3200, and the 27, 642, making 4700 dead, and the wounded at the rate of 6 to 12 makes this loss over 20,000—we have taken near 3000 prisoners, and 21 Battle flags, but in the Rush of the 22nd we lost McPherson and 10 cannon. I do not think Hood will attack me again. Atlanta is too Strong for an assault and I must manoeuver on its communications. Weather dreadfully hot. I am sorry you sold yr. house, but you can get another, dont change your residence "during the War." If I survive this campaign in life or Reputation I will seek some rest and retirement, and let the Rising Generals step in for a term of three years, when I will be ready to come in afresh. Love to all yrs. affectionately,

W. T. Sherman

ALS, DLC: William T. Sherman; misplaced as July 31, 1863.

1. On the twenty-fourth, JS had written to his brother with the news of James Sherman's death. He also asked Cump's opinion on Hugh's desire to become a cotton broker and his attempt to enlist JS's help to that end. JS also remarked on the widely held view that the fate of the Union rested now on WTS and USG and that anarchy would be the result of disunion. He went on to mention the "absolute indifference" in the capital toward the presidential election and Lincoln. Democrats could easily win if they "would select some one who was for prosecuting the war until an honorable peace was attained." He went on to comment, "The conviction is general that Lincoln has not the energy dignity or character to either conduct the war or to make Peace . . . a popular ticket would be Grant and Sherman." DLC: WTS.

2. Sim Tappertit of Dickens's novel *Barnaby Rudge* was a locksmith's apprentice and leader of anti-Catholic riots in eighteenth-century London.

TO ELLEN EWING SHERMAN

Headquarters, Military Division
of the Mississippi,
In the Field, Near Atlanta Geo.,
Aug. 2, 1864.

Dearest Ellen,

I got a letter from you last night[1] and one for Charley, and was glad to hear you were getting along so well, and that the baby exhibits signs of healthy life. I have for some days been occupying a good house on the Buckhead Road about 4 miles north of Atlanta but am going to move in the morning nearer to the Right to be nearer where I expect the next battle. You have heard doubtless full accounts of the Battles of the 20, 22 & 28, in all which the Enemy attacked a part of our Lines in force but was always repulsed with heavy loss. But I fear we have sustained a reverse in some Cavalry that I sent round by the Rear to break the Macon Road. It was commanded by McCook[2] a cousin of Dans[.] They reached the Railroad & broke it also burned a large number of the Baggage wagons belonging to the Enemy and were on their way back when they were beset by heavy forces of Cavalry about New Macon and I fear were overpowered and a great part killed or Captured. Some 500 have got in and give composed accounts but time enough has elapsed for the party to be back, and I hear nothing further of them. Somehow or other we cannot get Cavalry. The enemy takes all the horses of the Country and we have to buy and our People wont sell. Stoneman is also out with a cavalry force attempting to reach our prisoners confined at Andersonville, but since McCooks misfortune I also have fears for his safety.[3] I am now moving so as to get possession of the Railroad out of Atlanta to the South. We already have possession of those on the north & east, where it will be difficult for Hood to maintain his army in Atlanta. This army is much reduced in strength by deaths sickness and Expiration of service. It looks hard to see Regiments march away when their time is up. On the other side they have every body old & young and for indefinite periods. I have to leave also along the Railroad a large force to guard the supplies, so that I doubt if our army much exceeds that of Hood. No Recruits are coming for the draft is not till September and then I suppose it will consist mostly of niggers & bought recruits that must be kept well to the Rear. I sometimes think our People do not deserve to succeed in War. They are so apathetic[.]

McPherson was shot dead. I had his body brought to me, and sent it back to the Railroad. He was shot high up in the breast with a bullet, & must have fallen from his horse dead. Howard who succeeds him is a fine gentleman and a good officer. Hooker got mad because he was not appointed to the command and has gone north. This ought to damn him, showing that he is selfish & not patriotic. He was not suited to the Command. I expect we will have a hard fight for the Railroad about the day after tomorrow, and must be more heavy on us as we must attack. I am always glad when the enemy attacks for the advantage then is with us. Now our Line is as strong as theirs, but being on the Outer Circle is longer. I see that Grant has sprung his mines at Petersburg and hope he will succeed in taking that town, as it will be a constant threat to Richmond but Richmond itself can only be taken by regular siege.[4] Atlanta is on high ground and the woods extend up to the forts which look strong and encircle the whole town. Most of the People are gone & it is now simply a big Fort. I have been a little sick today but feel better—weather very hot—love to all yrs. ever

W. T. Sherman

ALS, InND: Sherman Family Papers.

1. EES's letter to WTS of July 25 with a July 26 postscript expressed her sorrow at McPherson's death and included a warm description of Charley Sherman. SFP.

2. Brigadier General Edward Moody McCook (1833–1909), USA, a Kansas lawyer, politician, and former secret agent, would later command the First Division, Cavalry Corps, Military Division of the Mississippi. After reaching the railroad on July 29 and demolishing track, rolling stock, and supplies, McCook was surrounded by enemy cavalry at Newman on July 30. Although he and his brigades escaped, it was at the cost of five hundred men, his pack train, two guns, and a large number of horses. He did, however, destroy a large number of Hood's supply wagons.

3. WTS's fears were well founded. Stoneman had first sent Garrard on a diversionary

feint which led to his being attacked and forced north away from Stoneman by Wheeler. Wheeler then surrounded Stoneman at Macon and captured him along with seven hundred men on July 30.

4. Grant's effort to force a breakthrough at Petersburg by digging a mine under Confederate fortifications backfired at the Battle of the Crater on July 30.

TO EMILY HOFFMAN

> Headquarters, Military Division
> of the Mississippi,
> In the Field, Near Atlanta Geo.
> August 5, 1864

Miss Emily Hoffman,
Baltimore.
My Dear Young Lady,

A letter from your Mother to General Barry[1] on my Staff reminds me that I owe you heartfelt sympathy and a sacred duty of recording the fame of one of our Country's brightest & most glorious Characters. I yield to none on Earth but yourself the right to excel me in lamentations for our Dead Hero. Better the Bride of McPherson dead, than the wife of the richest Merchant of Baltimore. Why oh! Why should deaths darts reach the young and brilliant instead of older men who could better have been spared. Nothing that I can record will Elevate him in your minds Memory, but I could tell you many things that would form a bright halo about his image. We were more closely associated than any men in this Life. I knew him before you did, when he was a Lieutenant of Engineers in New York we occupied rooms in the Same house. Again we met at St. Louis almost at the outset of this Unnatural war, and from that day to this we have been closely associated. I see him now, So handsome, so smiling, on his fine black horse, booted & spurred, with his easy seat, the impersonation of the Gallant Knight. We were at Shiloh together, at Corinth—at Oxford—at Jackson, at Vicksburg, at Meridian, and on this campaign. He had left me but a few minutes to place some of his troops approaching their position, and went through the woods by the same road he had Come, and must have Encountered the Skirmish Line of the Rebel Hardees Corps, which had made a Circuit around the flank of Blairs troops. Though always active and attending in person amidst danger to his appropriate duties on this occasion he was not exposing himself. He rode over ground he had twice passed that same day, over which hundreds had also passed, by a narrow wood road to the Rear of his Established Line.

He had not been gone from me half an hour before Col. Clark[2] of his staff rode up to me and reported that McPherson was dead or a prisoner in the hands of the Enemy. He described that he had Entered this road but a short distance in the woods some Sixty yards ahead of his Staff & orderlies when a loud volley of muskets was heard and in an instant after his fine black horse came out with two wounds, riderless. Very shortly thereafter other members of his staff came to me with his body in an ambulance[.] We Carried it into a house, and laid it on a large table, and examined the body. A single bullet wound, high up in the Right breast, was all that disfigured his person. All Else was as he left me, save his watch & purse were gone. At this time the Battle was raging hot & fierce quite near us and lest it should become necessary to burn the house in which we were I directed his personal Staff to Convey the body to Marietta & thence north to his family. I think he could not have lived three minutes after the fatal Shot, and fell from his horse within ten yards of the path or road along which he was riding. I think others will give you more detailed accounts of the attending circumstances. I Enclose you a copy of my official letter announcing his death.[3]

The lives of a thousand men such as Davis and Yancey[4] and Toombs,[5] and Floyd,[6] and Buckner, and Greeley,[7] and Lovejoy[8] would not atone for that of McPherson. But so it is in this world Some men by falsehood and agitation raise the Storm which falls upon the honorable, and young who become involved in its Circles.

Though the Cannon booms now, and the angry rattle of musketry tells me that I also will likely pay the same penalty yet while Life lasts I will delight in the memory of that bright particular star which has gone before to prepare the way for us more hardened Sinners who must struggle on to the End. with affection & respect,

W. T. Sherman

ALS, New York: Private Collection of Walter Lord.

1. Brigadier General William F. Barry (1818–79), USA, was Sherman's chief of artillery.

2. Lieutenant Colonel William T. Clark (1831–1905), USA, was McPherson's adjutant general and later a brigade commander in the Fifteenth Corps during the Campaign of the Carolinas.

3. WTS to Lorenzo Thomas, July 23, 1864, above.

4. William Lowndes Yancey (1814–63) of Alabama was a Confederate senator at the time of his death.

5. Politician Robert A. Toombs (1810–85), a former United States senator and Confederate secretary of state, was a division adjutant and inspector general of the Georgia militia.

6. Lawyer and politician John B. Floyd (1806–63) of Arkansas had been one of Buchanan's secretaries of war. He had been a brigadier general in the CSA and was major general of the Virginia State Line at the time of his death.

7. Horace Greeley (1811–72) was the influential editor of the *New York Tribune*.

8. Abolitionist Owen Lovejoy (1811–64) had served in Congress as a Republican from 1857 until his death and had been a close political associate of Lincoln's.

TO ULYSSES S. GRANT

From Near Atlanta 8 P.M.
Aug. 7th [1864]

Lieut. Gen. Grant

I was gratified to learn you were satisfied with my progress[.][1]

Get the War Department to send us recruits daily as they are made for we can teach them more war in our camp in one day than they can get at a rendezvous in a month, also tell the President that he must not make the least concession in the matter of the September draft. It is right and popular with the army and the army is worth considering.

I am glad you have given Gen. Sheridan[2] the command of the forces to defend Washington; he will worry Early[3] to death[.] Let us give these southern fellows all the fighting they want and when they are tired we can tell them we are just warming to the work[.] Any signs of a let up on our part is sure to be falsely construed and for this reason I always remind them that the siege of Troy lasted six years and Atlanta is a more valuable town than Troy[.]

We must manifest the character of dogged courage & perseverance of our race.

Dont stay in Washington longer than is necessary to give impulse to events and get out of it. It is the centre of *intrigue*[.] I would like to have *Mower* made a Major General, he is a real fighter[.][4]

W. T. Sherman
Maj. Gen.

Telegram Received, DNA: RG 108, Records of the Headquarters of the Army, Letters Received, AUS 1864, M151; *OR*, I, 38: pt. 5, 408.

1. USG to WTS, August 7, 1864, *PUSG*, 11:381. USG expressed his pleasure with WTS's progress and told him that Sheridan was in command in the Shenandoah Valley.

2. Major General Philip H. Sheridan (1831–88), USA, was named to the command of the Middle Military Division on August 6. This would lead to his successful Shenandoah Valley Campaign, and he did indeed eventually demolish Early's army.

3. Major General Jubal A. Early (1816–94) commanded Confederate forces in the Shenandoah Valley in the summer and fall of 1864.

4. Mower (1827–70) received the rank of major general of volunteers on August 12.

TO ELLEN EWING SHERMAN

Headquarters, Military Division
of the Mississippi,
In the Field near Atlanta, Aug. 9, 1864.

Dearest Ellen,

I got your note of Aug. 4 today enclosing one for Charley which I have handed him. Tell Mrs. Hunter & Mrs. Griesy it is idle to attempt the exchange of Dr. Griesy. I have already lost Stoneman & near 2000 Cavalry in attempting to rescue the Prisoners at Macon. I get one hundred letters a day almost asking me to effect the exchange or release of these Prisoners. It is not in my power. The whole matter of Exchanges is in the hands of Col. Hoffman[1] Commissioner at Washington. I am capturing & sending north hundreds of prisoners daily and have not intercourse with the Enemy. I have not exchanged a single message, not even a flag of truce. I assented to the Enemy sending a partial Flag to bury some dead, on a particular spot, but did not suspend the fire at any other. I have cannonaded Atlanta pretty heavily today, and our Lines are extended full ten miles, but still the enemy is beyond. They have either a larger force than we estimate or their Lines are well concealed by their Forts. They occupy a high Ridge and we are on densely wooded hill sides & slopes. To assault their position would cost more lives than we can Spare, and to turn the position I would have to cut loose from our Base, which is rather a risky business in a country devoid of all manner of supplies.

I drew two months pay & send you it nearly all. I will not preach Economy any more, only will say that next months pay is due to Hill, & my servants here whom I have not paid for a long while. Though I eat nothing but rations my mess costs me $50 or $60 a month. I have given my consent to your moving to South Bend only take the whole family[.] There is no chance of my even getting north again & therefore you can choose a house utterly regardless of my movements. I regard the war as hardly begun, & see no chance of escaping unless in the Revolution of this Fall & Winter new Favorites arise. The People of the North always have slackened their efforts to reinforce our army when reinforcements are needed, & then break out when it is too late. I suppose such will be the case this year. The whole South is now armed & the whole North should be, Every man that can carry a musket.

I have not yet seen Young Wagenhals,[2] indeed the Cavalry is so far out on the flanks that I rarely see it. Ever yrs.,

W. T. Sherman

ALS, InND: Sherman Family Papers.

1. Colonel William Hoffman (1807–84), USA, of the Third U.S. Infantry had been commissary general of prisoners at Washington since August 1862.

2. Apparently the son of a prominent Lancaster physician. EES to WTS, July 20, 1864, SFP.

TO DANIEL MARTIN

Headquarters, Military Division
of the Mississippi,
In the Field Near Atlanta, Georgia,
August 10th, 1864

Daniel Martin, Sand Mountain.

My Dear Friend:

When in Larkinsville last winter, I enquired after you, and could get no positive answer. I wish you had sent me your letter of January 22d, which I have just received, for I could have made you feel at ease at once.[1] Indeed, do I well remember our old times about Bellefonte, and the ride we took to the corn mills, and the little farm where I admired the handsome colt and tried to buy it. Time has worn on, and you are now an old man, in want, and suffering, and I also, no longer young, but leading a hostile army on the very road I came when I left Bellefonte, and, at the moment, pouring into Atlanta the dread missiles of war, seeking the lives of its people. And yet, I am the same William Tecumseh Sherman you knew in 1844, with as warm a heart as ever, and anxious that peace and plenty shall prevail in this land, and, to prove it, I defy Jeff Davis, or General Lee, or General Hood to make the sacrifice for peace that I will, personally or officially.

I will today lay down my power and my honor—already won—will strip myself naked, and my wife and child stark naked in the world as we came, and begin life anew, if the people of the South will but cease the war, elect their members of Congress and let them settle, by argument and reason, the question growing out of slavery, instead of trying to divide our country into two angry halves, to quarrel and fight to the end of time. Our country cannot divide by an east and west line, and must be one, and if we must fight, let us fight it out now, and not bequeath it to our children. I was never a politician, but resigned from the army and lived in California till 1857, when I came back with my wife and three children, who wanted to be near home—Mr. Ewing's, not Mr. Corwin's—but I had the old army so ground in my composition that civil pursuits were too tame and I accepted an offer as president of the Louisiana Military Academy. Therefore, at the time of Lincoln's election I was at Alexandria, on Red River.

I saw, and you must have seen, that the southern politicians wanted to bring about secession—separation. They could have elected Mr. Douglas but they so managed that Lincoln's election was made certain, and after they had accomplished this, was it honest or fair for them to allege it as a cause of war? Did not Mr. Breckinridge as Vice President, in his seat declare Mr. Lincoln the lawfully elected President of the United States? Was it ever pretended the President was our Government? Don't you know that Congress makes laws, the supreme court judges them, and the President only executes them? Don't you know that Mr. Lincoln of himself could not take away your rights? Now, I was in Louisiana, and while the planters and mechanics and industrious people were happy and prosperous, the politicians and busybodies were scheming and plotting, and got the Legislature to pass an ordinance of secession, which was submitted to the people, who voted against it, yet the politicians voted the State out, proceeded to take possession of the United States mint, the forts, the arsenal—and tore down our flag and insulted it. That, too, before Mr. Lincoln had got to Washington. I saw these things, and begged Bragg and Beauregard, and Governor Moore, and a host of other friends to beware. In that was high treason. But they answered, "The North was made up of mean manufacturers, of traders, of farmers, who would not fight." The people of the North NEVER dreamed of interfering with the slaves or property of the South. They simply voted, AS THEY HAD A RIGHT TO DO, and they could not understand why the people of the South should begin to take possession of the United States forts and arsenals till our Government had done something wrong—something oppressive. The South BEGAN the war. You know it. I, and millions of others living at the South, know it—but the people of the North were as innocent of it as your little grandchild. Even after forts had been taken, public arms stolen from our arsenals and distributed among the angry militia, the brave and honest freemen of the great North could not realize the fact, and did not until Beauregard began to fire upon a garrison of United States troops, in a fort built by the common treasury of the WHOLE country. Then as by a mighty upheaval, the people rose and began to think of war, and not until then.

I resigned my post in Louisiana in March, 1861, because of the public act on the part of the State in seizing the United States arsei..' at Baton Rouge, and went to St. Louis, where I received lucrative employment, hoping that some change would yet avert the war. But it came, and I, and all of military education, had to choose. I repeat, that then, as now, I had as much love for the honest people of the South as any man living. Had they remained true to the country, I would have resisted, even with arms, any attack upon their rights— even their slave rights. But when, as a people, they tore down our flag, and spit upon it, and called us cowards, and dared us to the contest, then I took up arms to maintain the integrity of our country, and punish the men who challenged us to the conflict. Is this not a true picture? Suppose the North had patiently submitted, what would have been the verdict of history and the world? Nothing else but that the North was craven and cowardly. Will you say the North is craven and cowardly now?

Cruel and inhuman as this war has been, and may still continue to be, it was forced upon us. We had no choice and we have no choice yet. We must go on, even to the end of time, even if it result in sinking a million of lives and desolating the whole land, leaving a desert behind. We must maintain the integrity of our country. And the day will come when the little grandchild you love so well, will bless us who fought, that the United States of America should not sink into infamy and worse than Mexican Monarchy, who care no more for you, or such as you, than they care for Hottentots. I have never underrated the magnitude of this war, for I know the size of the South, and the difficulty of operating in it. But, I also know the northern races have, ever since the war began, had more patience and perseverance than the southern races. And so it will be now, we will persevere until the end. All mankind shall recognize in us a brave and stubborn race, not to be deterred by the magnitude of the danger. Only three years have passed, and that is but a minute in a nation's life, and see where we are. Where are the haughty planters of Louisiana, who compared our hard-working, intelligent whites of the North with their negroes?

The defeats we have sustained have hardly made a pause in our course, and the vaunted braves of Tennessee, Mississippi, Louisiana, Missouri, etc., instead of walking rough-shod over the freemen of the North, are engaged in stealing horses and robbing poor old people for a living, while our armies now tread in every southern state, and your biggest armies in Virginia and Georgia lie behind forts, and dare not come out and fight us cowards of the North, who have come five hundred miles into their country to accept the challenge.

But, my dear friend, I have bored you too much. My handwriting is not plain, but you have time to study it out, and, as you can understand, I have a great deal of writing to do, and it must be done in a hurry. Think of what I have written. Talk it over with your neighbors, and ask yourselves if, in your trials and tribulations, you have suffered more from the Union soldiery than you would had you built your barn where the lightning was sure to burn or tear it down. Their course has provoked the punishment of an indignant God and Government. I care not a straw for niggers. The moment the master rebels, the negro is free, of course, for he is a slave only by law, and the law broken, he is free. I commanded in all Tennessee, Kentucky, Mississippi, Alabama and Georgia. The paper I endorse will be of service to you. Love to Mrs. Martin.

W. T. SHERMAN,
Major-General

Printed, Grenville M. Dodge, *Personal Recollections of President Abraham Lincoln, General Ulysses S. Grant and General William T. Sherman* (1914; reprint, Denver, 1965), 169–72. Letter also reprinted in the *New York Times*, September 7, 1865.

1. Daniel Martin to WTS, January 22 and July 24, 1864, DLC: WTS. In his first, Martin reported that he was "now liveing in verry destitute circumstances in a log-cabin in the woods." He had heard good reports of WTS's conduct in Memphis and hoped that he could help Martin reclaim his slaves, who had run off. Martin had been a Union man until Lincoln's election, and events had forced him into neutrality. In his July letter he reiterated that he was destitute and needed help and enclosed the January letter, which he had been too shy to send before. Martin wanted to bring corn and hogs across the Tennessee River and asked if WTS could get him the necessary permit and expressed his willingness to take an oath as a noncombatant.

TO THOMAS EWING SR.

> Head-Quarters, Military Division
> of the Mississippi,
> In the Field, near Atlanta Ga.,
> Aug. 11, 1864.

Hon. Thos. Ewing,
Lancaster Ohio
Dear Sir,

I can well understand the keen feelings of apprehension that agitate you, as you sit with mind intent on the fate of a vast machine, like the one I am proud to guide, whose life & success depend on the single thread of Rails that for near five hundred miles lays within an hostile or semi hostile country. I assure you that to the Extent of my ability, nothing has been left undone that could be foreseen, and for 100 days not a man or horse has been without ample food, or a musket or gun without adequate ammunition. I esteem this a triumph greater than any success that has attended me in Battle or in Strategy, but it has not been the result of blind chance at this moment I have abundant supplies for twenty days, and I keep a Construction Party in Chattanooga that can in ten days repair any break that can be made to my Rear. I keep a large depot of supplies at Chattanooga & Allatoona, two mountain fortresses which no cavalry force of the enemy can reach, and in our wagons generally manage to have from 10 to 20 days supply.

I could not have done this without forethought beginning with the hour I reached Nashville. I found thousands of citizens actually feeding on our stores on the plea of starvation, and other citizens by paying freights were allowed to carry goods, wares, & merchandize to all the towns from Nashville to Chattanooga, also crowds of idlers, Sanitary agents, Christian commissioners & all sorts of Curiosity hunters loading down our cars. It was the Gordian knot and I cut it. People may starve, and go without but an army cannot & do its work— A howl was raised, but the President and Secretary of War backed me, and now all recognize the wisdom & humanity of the thing. Rosecrans had his army starving at Chattanooga, and I have brought an army double its size 138 miles from there, and all agree that they were never better fed, clothed & supplied. I think you may rest easy on that Score. My only apprehension arises from the fact that the times of the 3 year men is expiring all the time & daily Regiments are leaving for home, diminishing my fighting force by its best material, and the draft has been so long deferred, and the foolish law allowing niggers and the refuse of the South to be brought up and substituted on paper (for they never come to the Front) will delay my reinforcements until my army on the offensive, so far from its base, will fall below my opponents, who increases, as I lose. I rather think today Hoods army is larger than mine, and he is strongly fortified. I have no faith in the People of the North—They ever lose their interest when they Should act—they think by finding fault with an officer they clean their shirts of their own sins of misfeasance. I have fought right through the mountain fastnesses of Georgia to the Line of the Chatta-hoochee, which was my task while Banks took Mobile & advanced to Mont-gomery, but his Red River expedition kept that back & let me to meet the whole South, but the good news has just come that Farraguts Fleet is in Mobile Bay, and has captured the Rebel fleet there,[1] also that Fort Gaines which guards the best Entrance to the Bay has surrendered,[2] and some pris-oners we took this morning say it was the talk in their camp that the Yankees had the City of Mobile.[3] So all is coming round well, only we should not relax our Energies or be deluded by any false hope of a speedy end to this war, which we did not begin, but which we must fight to the End, be it when it may. I have made no professional mistakes but one, in consenting that Stoneman should make the premature attempt to reach our prisoners of war at Macon & Anderson & release them. Stoneman begged for it & I consented, my judg-ment being warped by our Feelings for 20,000 poor men penned up like cattle—All well. Yrs. with great affection,

W. T. Sherman

ALS, DLC: Thomas Ewing and Family Papers.

1. Admiral David G. Farragut (1801–70) and his fleet captured the port of Mobile and the ironclad ram *Tennessee* on August 5.

2. Fort Gaines was surrendered by Colonel D. C. Anderson, CSA, on August 8.

3. The city of Mobile itself would not be captured until April 12, 1865.

TO SCHUYLER COLFAX[1]

Headquarters, Military Division
of the Mississippi,
In the Field Before Atlanta,
Aug. 12, 1864

Schuyler Colfax Esq.
South Bend, Indiana
My Dear Sir,

John Sherman has sent me your letter of Aug. 2[2] in which you intimate a wish that certain nine Regiments of Indiana troops should be ordered when they can be furloughed so as to vote in the Fall elections.

Of course it is impossible. I have not now troops enough to do what the case admits of without extra hazard, and to send away a single man would be an act of injustice to the remainder. I think you need not be concerned about the soldiers' vote. They will vote, it may not be in the coming election, but you may rest assured the day will come when the Soldiers will vote, and the only doubt is if they will permit the Stay at homes to vote at all.

I hope you will be elected, but I do think the conscript Law is the only one that is wanted for the next few years, and if the President uses it freely he can checkmate the copperheads, who are not in favor of being governed by Jeff Davis, but are afraid to go to the war. Their motives are transparent. Jeff Davis despises them more than you do and if he prevails in this war he will deal with copperheads with infinitely more severity than he will with men who fight for their country & for Principle. I am &c.

W. T. Sherman

ADfS, DLC: William T. Sherman.

1. Indiana congressman Schuyler Colfax (1823–25) had been elected Speaker in December 1863.

2. Colfax to JS, August 2, 1864, DLC: WTS. Colfax wrote that since Indiana soldiers could vote only in their townships, they needed to be furloughed after mid-September to return to vote in the October congressional elections. He asked JS to intercede with his brother to release those Indiana regiments in his district if it was possible. JS forwarded his request to his brother on August 6, asking him to help Colfax if he could. DLC: WTS.

TO JOHN SHERMAN

Headquarters, Military Division
of the Mississippi,
In the Field near Atlanta, Aug. 12, 1864.

Dear Brother,

I have received yours of Aug. 6, enclosing one from Schuyler Colfax. I have answered it and send you copy of his answer.

Of course I cannot spare these Regiments, and if I would it would be an outrageous breach of public Law, to use an Army to facilitate Elections. Why Congress itself is not half as important now as this army and the Last Congress cannot be worsted. If that Congress did nothing else it piled on insult to us, by allowing state agents to go round buying up niggers & refugees to take the place of the very best blood & muscle in the Land—Had I a vote I would not give it to one of you. I dont think you meant to insult us but how else can it be construed. The three years men are now marching to the Rear, leaving me weaker & weaker every day & I can see the Macon cars piling in reinforcements to my front, and I cannot expect any till next spring because Congress must give the Cowardly state authorities time to buy up vagabonds to *avoid the draft*, the very thing every soldier has wanted for the past three years, the very thing to kill Copperheadism and all the other Sham Elements of opposition to the war.

Jeff Davis had the same opposition to contend with and he saw it in the light of an Army man—He made the Conscription universal & he is now the most Popular man now in the South. Had he yielded to the Clamors of the outsiders he would have gave up after the fall of Vicksburg. I have met a great many southern officers & citizens & know they entertain the most sovereign contempt for the Copperheads, but of course they chuckle over the effect of their opposition for it tends to sustain them in their theory that the South should remain united until the North breaks up in Anarchy.

I was in hopes I could remain unpopular, but I see even the newspapers begin to pick out good points in my character. This is the certain presage of a downfall—well it is inevitable and I will try and do my best and trust to Future, with a strong brave army, strongly entrenched to my Front, enemys Cavalry hovering all round—my communications through a semihostile country, for over four hundred miles, and our own Country afraid to act, afraid of internal causes. The fall of the Mobile Forts is good news, and if it can be followed up by the occupation of the City & Alabama Ri{ver} as high up as Montgomery, it will have an excellent bearing on this Campaign. Affectionately yr. Brother,

W. T. Sherman

M. G.

ALS, DLC: William T. Sherman Papers.

> Hdqrs. Military Division
> of the Mississippi,
> In the Field, near Atlanta,
> August 14, 1864.

Hon. James Guthrie,
Louisville:
My Dear Sir:

I regret exceedingly the arrest of many gentlemen and persons in Kentucky, and still more that they should give causes of arrest. I cannot in person inquire into these matters, but must leave them to the officer who is commissioned and held responsible by Government for the peace and safety of Kentucky. It does appear to me when our national integrity is threatened and the very fundamental principles of all government endangered that minor issues should not be made by Judge Bullitt and others. We cannot all substitute our individual opinions, however honest, as the test of authority. As citizens and individuals we should waive and abate our private notions of right and policy to those of the duly appointed agents of the Government, certain that if they be in error the time will be short when the real principles will manifest themselves and be recognized. In your career how often have you not believed our Congress had adopted a wrong policy and how short the time now seems to you when the error rectified itself or you were willing to admit yourself wrong. I notice in Kentucky a disposition to cry against the tyranny and oppression of our Government. Now, were it not for war you know tyranny could not exist in our Government; therefore any acts of late partaking of that aspect are the result of war; and who made this war? Already we find our selves drifting toward new issues, and are beginning to forget the strong facts of the beginning. You know and I know that long before the North, or the Federal Government, dreamed of war the South had seized the U.S. arsenals, forts, mints, and custom-houses, and had made prisoners of war of the garrisons sent at their urgent demand to protect them "against Indians, Mexicans, and negroes." I know this of my own knowledge, because when the garrison of Baton Rouge was sent to the Rio Grande to assist in protecting that frontier against the guerrilla Cortina, who had cause of offense against the Texan people, Governor Moore made strong complaints and demanded a new garrison for Baton Rouge, alleging as a reason that it was not prudent to have so much material of war in a parish where there were 20,000 slaves and less than 5,000 whites, and very shortly after this he and Bragg, backed by the militia of New Orleans, made "prisoners of war" of that very garrison, sent there at their own request. You also remember well who first burned the bridges of your railroad, who forced Union men to give up their slaves to work on the rebel forts at Bowling Green, who took wagons and horses and burned houses of persons differing with them honestly in opinion, when I would not let our men burn fence rails for fire or gather fruit or vegetables though hungry, and these were the property of outspoken rebels. We at that time were restrained, tied by a deep-seated reverence for law and property. The rebels first introduced terror as a part of their system, and forced contributions to diminish their wagon trains and thereby increase the mobility and efficiency of their columns. When General Buell had to move at a snail's pace with his vast wagon trains, Bragg moved rapidly, living on the country. No military mind could endure this long, and we are forced in self-defense to imitate their example. To me this whole matter seems simple. We must, to live and prosper, be governed by law, and as near that which we inherited as possible. Our hitherto political and private differences were settled by debate, or vote, or decree of a court. We are still willing to return to that system, but our adversaries say no, and appeal to war. They dared us to war, and you remember how tauntingly they defied us to the contest. We have accepted the issue and it must be fought out. You might as well reason with a thunder-storm. War is the remedy our enemies have chose. Other simple remedies were within their choice. You know it and they know it, but they wanted war, and I say let us give them all they want; not a word of argument, not a sign of let up, no cave in till we are whipped or they are. Those side issues of niggers, State rights, conciliation, outrages, cruelty, barbarity, bankruptcy, subjugation, &c., are all idle and nonsensical. The only principle in this war is, which party can whip. It is as simple as a schoolboy's fight, and when one or the other party gives in, we will be the better friends. I confess to-day I have more respect for some of the open enemies than I have for the canting sneaks to my rear, and though they call me pretty hard names I believe the feeling is reciprocated. I hope the question will soon resolve itself into "Shall we have a government that must be obeyed, and will you fight for it?" and if the answer be affirmative they are friends, if in the negative or doubtful, then they are enemies or mere denizens of the land, stript of the right of suffrage, debarred from speaking or writing, yea even from marrying, for I would stop the breed. If the people of our country had at any stage of existence of this war risen to the full occasion, instead of being put off with sickly expedients, we would long since had peace, and the longer we remain blind to it the longer will be the war, the more of the insidious, mean little side issues that harass you in Kentucky and the fearful load of debt that somebody must pay.

I surely wish you all in Kentucky well. I want to push the main rebel army far from you, and to root out that other class, who, under the plea of being soldiers, are regarded by us all as common vagabonds and thieves. Joe Johnston would never sanction such dogs as call themselves guerrillas in Kentucky, nor would Lee or Bragg, or any other man who thinks he is fighting to establish a new and independent government better suited to their interests and honor. I will, therefore, sustain General Burbridge[2] if satisfied he is not influenced by mere personal motives, and nothing has occurred to evince anything of the kind. Bullitt and the rest must therefore spend some years abroad and take time to study and reflect on the great theory of self-government which began with old Adam and has made precious little progress since. I should like Governor Bramlette[3] and the real thinking men of Kentucky to know the kindly feelings I entertain toward them, and how earnest is my wish to insure to them tranquillity and peace. With respect,

W. T. Sherman
Major-General, Commanding.

Printed, *OR*, I, 39: pt. 2, 247–49.

1. James Guthrie (1792–1869) had been Franklin Pierce's secretary of the treasury and a pro-Union member of the 1861 peace convention. An ally of Sherman's during his time in Kentucky, he was currently the president of a Louisville railroad and would become a United States senator from 1865 until his death.

2. Stephen G. Burbridge was commanding the District of Kentucky.

3. Thomas E. Bramlette (1817–75) had been elected governor of Kentucky in 1863 and declined a nomination to be brigadier general.

TO HENRY W. HALLECK

Cypher   H'd Qrts. Mil. Div. of the Miss.
By courier to Atlanta.   In the Field Near Lovejoys Station
                                         26 miles South of Atlanta Sept. 3d 1864.

Maj. Genl. Halleck
Washington D.C.

As already reported the Army drew from about Atlanta, & on the 30th had made a good break of the West Point Railroad & reached a good position from which to strike the Macon Railroad—The Right Genl. Howard near Jonesboro, the Left Genl. Schofield near Rough & Ready & center Genl. Thomas at Conche.

Genl. Howard found the Enemy in force at Jonesboro & entrenched his troops, the salient within half a mile of the Railroad. The Enemy attacked him at 3 P.M. & was easily repulsed leaving his dead & wounded. Finding strong opposition on the Right I advanced the Left & center rapidly to the Railroad made a good Lodgement & broke it all the way from Rough & Ready down to Howards Left near Jonesboro & by the same movement I interposed my whole Army between Atlanta & the part of the Enemy entrenched in &

around Jonesboro. We made a general attack on the Enemy at Jonesboro on the 1st of September, the 14th Corps Genl. Jeff C. Davis carrying the works handsomely with ten (10) Guns & about a thousand prisoners. In the night the Enemy retreated south & we have followed him to another of his well chosen & hastily constructed Lines near Lovejoys. Hood at Atlanta finding me on his Road, the only one that could supply him, & between him & a considerable part of his Army, blew up his Magazines in Atlanta & left in the night time when the 20th Corps Genl. Slocum took possession of the place; so Atlanta is ours, & fairly won.

I shall not push much further on this Raid, but in a day or so will move to Atlanta & give my men some rest. Since the 5th of May we have been in one constant battle or skirmish & need rest. Our losses will not exceed 1200 & we have possession of over 300 Rebel dead—250 wounded & over 1500 well prisoners.

W. T. Sherman
Maj. Genl. Comdg.

Lbk, DNA: RG 94, Records of the Adjutant General's Office, Generals' Books and Papers, William T. Sherman, Letterbook 12; *OR*, I, 38: pt. 5, 777.

TO ELLEN EWING SHERMAN

Headquarters, Military Division
of the Mississippi,
In the Field 26 miles South of Atlanta,
Sept. 3, 1864.

Dearest Ellen,

My movement has been perfectly successful, and the Corps I left at the Bridge are now in Atlanta which was abandonned by the Enemy the moment I made a good lodgment on the Macon Road. We have had severe fighting at Jonesboro, where we beat Hardees corps bad. We now confront the Rebel Army and we are studying their position. I am very well. You doubtless hear of us through the papers oftener than I can write.

We are in a country rich in corn and our supplies are ample. Yrs. ever

W. T. Sherman

ALS, InND: Sherman Family Papers.

TO HENRY W. HALLECK

Cypher.   H'd Qrts. Mil. Div. of the Miss.
                                           In the Field Near Lovejoys Ga.
                                           Sept. 4th 64.

General Halleck
Washington

The 20th Corps now occupies Atlanta & the Chattahoochee bridges. The main Army is now here, grouped below Jonesboro. The Enemy hold a Line facing us with front well covered by parapets, & flanks by Walnut Creek on the Right & a confluent of Flint River on his Left. His position is too strong to attack in front & to turn it would carry me too far from our base at this time. Besides there is no commensurate object, as there is no valueable point to his Rear till we reach Macon 103 miles from Atlanta.

We are not prepared for that & I will gradually fall back & occupy Atlanta which was & is our grand objective point already secure.

For the future I propose that of the drafted men I receive my due share, say 50,000. That an equal or greater number go to Genl. Canby who should now proceed with all energy to get Montgomery & the Reach of the Alabama River above Selma—that when I Know he can move on Columbus Georgia, I move on Lagrange & West Point, keeping to the east of the Chattahoochee—that we form a junction repair Roads to Montgomery & open up the Apalachicola & Chattahoochee Rivers to Columbus & move from it as a base straight on Macon. This campaign can be made in the winter, & we can safely rely on the Corn of the Flint & Chattahoochee to supply forage.

If the Tensas Channel of the Alabama River can be used, Genl. Gardner[1] with his Rebel Garrison could continue to hold Mobile for our use when we want it.

I propose to remove all the Inhabitants of Atlanta, sending those committed to our cause to the Rear & the Rebel families to the front. I will allow no trade, manufactories or any citizens there at all, so that we will have the entire use of Railroad back as also such corn & forage as may be reached by our troops.

If the people raise a howl against my barbarity & cruelty, I will answer that War is War & not popularity seeking. If they want Peace, they & their relations must stop War.

                                           W. T. Sherman
                                           Maj. Genl. Comdg.

Lbk, DNA: RG 94, Records of the Adjutant General's Office, Generals' Books and Papers, William T. Sherman, Letterbook 12; *OR*, I, 38: pt. 5, 794.
    1. General Franklin Gardner (1823–73), CSA.

Hdqrs. Military Division
of the Mississippi,
In the Field, near Lovejoy's,
twenty-six miles south of Atlanta,
September 4, 1864.

General Halleck:

My Dear Friend:

I owe you a private letter, and believe one at this time will be acceptable to you. I appreciate your position and the delicate responsibilities that devolve on you, but believe you will master and surmount them all. I confess I owe you all I now enjoy of fame, for I had allowed myself in 1861 to sink into a perfect "slough of despond," and do believe if I could I would have run away and hid from the dangers and complications that surrounded us. You alone seemed to be confident, and opened to us the first avenue of success and hope, and you gradually put me in the way of recovering from what might have proved an ignoble end. When Grant spoke of my promotion as a major-general of the regular army, I asked him to decline in my name till this campaign tested us. Even when my commission came, which you were kind enough to send, I doubted its wisdom, but now that I have taken Atlanta as much by strategy as by force, I suppose the military world will approve it.

Through the official bulletins you are better acquainted with all the steps of our progress than any other man in the country, but I will try and point out to you more clearly the recent achievement. By the rapid falling off of my command, by expiration of service, I found myself reduced in number, close up against Atlanta, which was so protected by earth-works that I dared not assault. Fortunately Hood detached 6,000 of his best cavalry to our rear, and I quickly sent my cavalry to break the Macon road, over which his provisions and supplies came. I knew my cavalry was the superior to his, but he managed skillfully to send a brigade of infantry, which, in connection with his cavalry, about 4,000, managed so to occupy mine that though Kilpatrick reached the road he could work but little. The damage was soon repaired, and nothing was left me but to raise the siege, and move with my army. I moved one corps by night back to the bridge, which had been intrenched, using mostly old rebel works, then withdrawing from the left I got my whole army over on the West Point road, from Red Oak to Fairburn, with the loss of but one man. There I spent one day and broke twelve miles of that road good. I then moved rapidly so that my right flank was within half a mile of the Macon road at Jones-borough, and the left two miles and a half from Rough and Ready. Hood had first sent Lee's corps to Jonesborough and Hardee's to Rough and Ready, but the Army of the Tennessee (my right) approached Jonesborough so rapidly that Hardee's corps was shifted at night also to that flank. Seeing his mistake I ordered Howard rapidly to intrench and hold his position, "threatening," and threw the balance of my army on the road from Rough and Ready to within four miles of Jonesborough. The moment that was done, I ordered Thomas and Schofield to rapidly break up that road, and without rest to turn on Jonesborough and crush that part. My plan was partially, but not thoroughly, executed. Hardee assaulted Howard, but made no progress; left his dead, about 400, and wounded in our hands, and fell behind his own works. I expected Thomas to be ready by 11 A.M., but it was near 4 when he got in; but one corps, Davis', charged down and captured the flank with 10 guns and many prisoners, but for some reason Stanley and Schofield were slow, and night came to Hardee's relief, and he escaped to the south. Hood finding me twenty miles below him on his only railroad, and Hardee defeated, was forced to abandon Atlanta, and retreated eastward, and by a circuit has got his men below me on the line to Macon. I ought to have reaped larger fruits of victory. A part of my army is too slow, but I feel my part was skillful and well executed. Though I ought to have taken 10,000 of Hardee's men, and all his prisoners, 10 guns on the field and 14 in Atlanta, 7 trains of cars captured and burned, many stragglers fleeing in disorder, and the town of Atlanta, which, after all, was the prize I fought for.

The army is in magnificent heart, and I could go on, but it would not be prudent. Wheeler is still somewhere to my rear, and every mile costs me detachments which I can illy spare. This country is so easily fortified that an enemy can stop an army every few miles. All the roads run on ridges, so that a hundred yards of parapet, with abatis, closes it, and gives the wings time to extend as fast as we can reconnoiter and cut roads. Our men will charge the parapet without fear, but they cannot the abatis and entanglements, which catch them at close range. I stay here a few days for effect, and then will fall back and occupy Atlanta, giving my command some rest. They need it. The untold labor they have done is herculean, and if ever you pass our route you will say honestly that we have achieved success by industry and courage. I hope the administration will be satisfied, for I have studied hard to serve it faithfully.

I hope anything I may have said or done will not be construed unfriendly to Mr. Lincoln or Stanton. That negro letter of mine I never designed for publication, but I am honest in my belief that it is not fair to our men to count negroes as equals.[1] Cannot we at this day drop theories, and be reasonable men? Let us capture negroes, of course, and use them to the best advantage. My quartermaster now could give employment to 3,200, and relieve that number of soldiers who are now used to unload and dispatch trains, whereas those recruiting agents take them back to Nashville, where, so far as my experience goes, they disappear. When I call for expeditions at distant points, the answer invariably comes that they have not sufficient troops. All count the negroes out. On the Mississippi, where Thomas talked about 100,000 negro troops, I find I cannot draw away a white soldier, because they are indispensable to the safety of the river. I am willing to use them as far as possible, but object to fighting with "paper" men. Occasionally an exception occurs, which simply deceives. We want the best young white men of the land, and they should be inspired with the pride of freemen to fight for their country. If Mr. Lincoln or Stanton could walk through the camps of this army and hear the soldiers talk they would hear new ideas. I have had the question put to me often: "Is not a negro as good as a white man to stop a bullet?" Yes, and a sandbag is better; but can a negro do our skirmishing and picket duty? Can they improvise roads, bridges, sorties, flank movements, &c., like the white man? I say no. Soldiers must and do many things without orders from their own sense, as in sentinels. Negroes are not equal to this. I have gone steadily, firmly, and confidently along, and I could not have done it with black troops, but with my old troops I have never felt a waver of doubt, and that very confidence begets success. I hope to God the draft will be made to-morrow; that you will keep up my army to its standard, 100,000 men; that you will give Canby an equal number; give Grant 200,000, and the balance keep on our communications, and I pledge you to take Macon and Savannah before spring, or leave my bones. My army is now in the very condition to be supplied with recruits. We have good corporals and sergeants, and some good lieutenants and captains, and those are far more important than good generals. They all seem to have implicit confidence in me. They observe success at points remote, as in this case of Atlanta, and they naturally say that the old man knows what he is about. They think I know where every road and by-path is in Georgia, and one soldier swore that I was born on Kenesaw Mountain. George Thomas, you know, is slow, but as true as steel; Schofield is also slow and leaves too much to others; Howard is a Christian, elegant gentleman, and conscientious soldier. In him I made no mistake. Hooker was a fool. Had he staid a couple of weeks he could have marched into Atlanta and claimed all the honors. I therefore think I have the army on which you may safely build. Grant has the perseverance of a scotch terrier. Let him alone, and he will overcome Lee by untiring and unceasing efforts. The Mobile column is the one that needs a head, and no time should be wasted on the city. The river, Montgomery, and Columbus, Ga., are the strategic points. The latter has a double line by Montgomery and the Appalachicola River. It will not be safe to push this line farther until that is done, but stores and supplies may be accumulated here, and the country behind Chattahoochee purged a little more.

To-morrow is the day for the draft, and I feel far more interested in it than any event that ever transpired. I do think it has been wrong to keep our old troops so constantly under fire. Some of those old regiments that we had at Shiloh and Corinth have been with me ever since, and some of them have lost 70 per cent, in battle. It looks hard to put those brigades, now numbering less than 800 men, into battle. They feel discouraged, whereas if we could have a steady influx of recruits the living would soon forget the dead. The wounded and sick are lost to us, for once at a hospital they become worthless. It has been very bad economy to kill off our best men and pay full wages and bounties to the drift and substitutes. While all at the rear are paid regularly, I have here regiments that have not been paid for eight months, because the paymaster could not come to them. The draft judiciously used will be popular, and will take as many opponents of the war as advocates, whereas now our political equilibrium at the North seems disturbed by the absence of the fighting element, whereas the voting population is made up of sneaks, exempts, and cowards. Any nation would perish under such a system if protracted.

I have not heard yet of the Chicago nominations, but appearances are that McClellan will be nominated. The phases of "Democracy" are strange indeed. Some fool seems to have used my name. If forced to choose between the penitentiary and the White House for four years, like old Professor Molinard, I would say the penitentiary, thank you, sir. If any committee would approach me for political preferment, I doubt if I could have patience or prudence enough to preserve a decent restraint on myself, but would insult the nation in my reply.

If we can only carry our people past this fall, we may escape the greatest danger that ever threatened a civilized people. We as soldiers best fulfill our parts by minding our own business, and I will try to do that.

I wish you would thank the President and Secretary for the constant support they have given me, and accept from me my personal assurance that I have always felt buoyed up by the knowledge that you were there. Your sincere friend,

W. T. Sherman

Printed, *OR*, I, 38: pt. 5, 791–94.

1. WTS to John Spooner, July 30, 1864, was first reprinted in the August 18, 1864, *Chicago Tribune* and soon appeared in other papers both north and south. See John F. Marszalek, *Sherman's Other War: The General and the Civil War Press* (Memphis, 1981), 168–69.

CHAPTER 12

September 7, 1864–November 12, 1864

S herman's capture of Atlanta proved as important politically as it was militarily—perhaps more so. Coming ten days after Abraham Lincoln had expressed grave doubts about the possibility of his reelection, it did much to firm up eroding support for the president and countered Democratic charges that the war effort was a failure. Northerners, embracing Napoleonic concepts of what constituted a victory, saw the occupation of the city as a major triumph. Such a political triumph contained military consequences, for Lincoln's reelection would assure the continuance of Grant as general in chief with Sherman as his top lieutenant providing full support to fight the war through to the end.

Sherman took great pride in his accomplishment, frequently setting it in the context of military history, but he had not satisfied Grant's original directive instructing him to "break up" the Army of Tennessee. In evacuating Atlanta, Hood guaranteed that he would be around to fight another day. During the rest of September and all of October, Hood repeatedly threatened Sherman's supply line between Chattanooga and Atlanta. Although Sherman successfully fended off these attacks, he was unable to bring Hood to bay; before long he realized that Atlanta was becoming an albatross around his neck. In these circumstances he began to ponder more seriously an idea Grant and he had previously discussed—cutting loose from Atlanta and marching across the Confederate heartland, his army living off the land as they destroyed the Confederates' ability and will to persist in their struggle for independence.

That Sherman was willing to war once more against Confederates' psyches as well as armies became evident in several exchanges with Confederate leaders during this period. Soon after occupying Atlanta, he ordered its residents to evacuate. Hood protested, claiming that it was a barbaric measure. Sherman dismissed his argument, pointing out that in the past Confederate military decisions had placed civilians in harm's way and that the displacement of civilian populations in war zones was nothing new. The exchange soon became public, and Northerners applauded their new hero. "What do you think of Sherman's letter to Hood!" exclaimed Charles F. Adams Jr. to his brother Henry. "What a 'buster' that man is! No wonder they said in the early days of the war that he was either a drunkard or a crazy man. How he does finish up poor Hood!"[1] That Sherman was open to other ways of achieving victory became evident when he entertained the possibility that Georgia's governor, Joseph E. Brown, would withdraw his state from the Confederacy. In that case, Sherman stated, he would keep to the roads, discipline his men, and pay for what they seized or damaged. So long as Confederate resistance persisted, however, he would bring all the force he could to crush it: if Southern whites wanted to put a stop to the war all they had to do was to submit to the restoration of the Union. As he explained to Halleck, "This war differs from European wars in this particular; we are not only fighting hostile armies, but a hostile people, and must make old and young, rich and poor, feel the hard hand of war."[2]

Sherman's vision continued to exclude emancipation and black equality. Although he would not coerce black slaves into accompanying white families as they evacuated Atlanta, neither did he insist upon their emancipation. He continued to speak in disparaging terms about black soldiers, and defended what he came to call "my Negro letter" (see WTS to John A. Spooner, July 30, 1864, above), which highlighted his view that recruiting blacks enabled Northern whites to avoid military service, confirming his belief that they were not as committed as their Confederate counterparts to achieving victory.

Throughout September and October Sherman shared his evolving thoughts on his next step with Grant and others. His correspondence traces how he pressed and finally convinced Grant to approve the operation, overcoming Grant's concern about Hood by promising to leave a sufficient force under George H. Thomas to keep an eye on the combative Confederate. Grant decided, however, that Sherman would not commence his campaign until after the presidential election, for the commanding general did not want to offer the Confederates a chance to undo much of what Sherman and Philip H. Sheridan had done in September and October. Moreover, in the emphasis usually accorded to the supposed destructiveness of Sherman's March to the Sea, it is easy to forget that Sherman's prime targets were the hearts, minds, and souls of Confederate civilians, not their bodies or possessions—although he had no problem with destroying property as a way to shake the will of its owner. As he explained to George H. Thomas, "I propose to demonstrate the vulnerability of the South and make its inhabitants feel that war & individual Ruin are synonimous terms."[3]

One reading Sherman's letters to Grant justifying his plan might conclude that he embarked on the March to the Sea brimming with confidence. Yet just under the surface he wondered whether he was up to the task, admitting that Grant's "unmeasured faith" in him was discomforting.[4] When he left Atlanta on November 15, he knew that he had placed at risk all his accomplishments to date on the outcome of his march from Georgia to the sea.

1. Charles F. Adams Jr. to Henry Adams, September 23, 1864, in Worthington C. Ford., ed., *A Cycle of Adams Letters, 1861–1865* (Boston, 1920), 2:198.

2. James M. Merrill, *William Tecumseh Sherman* (Chicago, 1971), 266.

3. WTS to George H. Thomas, October 2, 1864.

4. WTS to Philemon B. Ewing, November 10, [1864].

TO JOHN BELL HOOD

Head Qtrs. Milt. Div. of Miss.
In the Field Atlanta Ga. Sep 7th 1864

General Hood
Comdg. Confederate Army
General.

I have deemed it to the interest of the United States that the citizens now residing in Atlanta should remove, those who prefer it to go South and the rest north. For the latter I can provide food and transportation to points of their election in Tennessee, Kentucky or further north. For the former I can provide transportation by cars as far as Rough and Ready and also wagons; but that their removal may be made with as little discomfort as possible, it will be necessary for you to help the families from Rough and Ready to the cars at Lovejoys. If you consent, I will undertake to remove all families in Atlanta who prefer to go South, to Rough and Ready, with all their moveable effects, viz., clothing, Trunks, reasonable furniture, bedding &c. with their servants, white and black, with the proviso, that no force shall be used towards the blacks one way or the other. If they want to go with their masters or mistresses they may do so otherwise they will be sent away, unless they be men, when they may be employed by our Quartermaster. Atlanta is no place for families or noncombatants, and I have no desire to send them north if you will assist in conveying them South. If this proposition meets your views I will consent to a truce in the neighborhood of Rough and Ready, stipulating that any wagons, horses, or animals or persons sent there for the purposes herein stated, shall in no manner be harmed or molested; you in your turn agreeing that any cars, wagons, carriages, persons or animals sent to the same point shall not be interfered with. Each of us might send a Guard of say 100 men to maintain order, and limit the truce to say two days after a certain time appointed.

I have authorized the mayor to choose two citizens to convey to you this letter, and such documents as the mayor may forward in explanation and shall await your reply. I have the honor to be Your Obdt. Servt.

W. T. Sherman
Major Genl. Comdg.

By Messrs. Ball & Crew.

Lbk, DNA: RG 94, Records of the Adjutant General's Office, Generals' Books and Papers, William T. Sherman, Letterbook 12; *OR*, I, 38: pt. 5, 822.

Hdqrs. Military Division
of the Mississippi,
In the Field, Atlanta, Ga.,
September 10, 1864—8 p.m.
(Received 11.50 a.m. 11th.)

General Grant,
City Point:

I have your dispatch of to-day. My command needs some rest and pay. Our roads are also broken back near Nashville, and Wheeler is not yet disposed of; still, I am perfectly alive to the importance of pushing our advantage to the utmost. I do not think we can afford to operate farther, dependent on the railroad; it takes so many men to guard it, and even then it is nightly broken by the enemy's cavalry that swarm about us. Macon is distant 103 miles, and Augusta 175 miles. If I could be sure of finding provisions and ammunition at Augusta or Columbus, Ga., I can march to Milledgeville and compel Hood to give up Augusta or Macon and could then turn on the other. The country will afford forage and many supplies, but not enough in any one place to admit of a delay. In scattering for forage we lose a great many men picked up by the enemy's cavalry. If you can manage to take the Savannah River as high as Augusta, or the Chattahoochee as far up as Columbus, I can sweep the whole State of Georgia. Otherwise I would risk our whole army by going too far from Atlanta.

W. T. Sherman,
Major-General.

Printed, *OR*, I, 39: pt. 2, 355–56.

TO JOHN BELL HOOD

Letter.

Head Quarters Milt. Divn.
of the Miss.
In the Field Atlanta Ga. Sept. 10th 1864.

Genl. J. B. Hood
Comdg. Army of Tennessee
Confederate Army
General.

I have the honor to acknowledge the receipt of your letter of this date[1] at the hands of Messrs. Ball and Crew, consenting to the arrangements I had proposed to facilitate the removal South of the People of Atlanta who prefer to go in that direction. I enclose you a copy of my orders which will I am satisfied accomplish my purpose perfectly.

You style the measures proposed "unprecedented" and appeal to the dark history of war for a parallel as an act of "studied and ungenerous cruelty." It is not unprecedented, for General Johnston himself very wisely and properly removed the families all the way from Dalton down, and I see no reason why Atlanta should be excepted. Nor is it necessary to appeal to the dark History of war when recent and modern examples are so handy. You yourself burned dwelling houses along your parapet, and I have seen to day fifty houses that you have rendered uninhabitable because they stood in the way of your Forts and men. You defended Atlanta on a line so close to town that every cannon Shot, and many musket shots from our Line of investment that overshot their mark went into the habitations of women and children. Genl. Hardee did the same at Jonesboro, and Genl. Johnston did the same last Summer at Jackson, Mississippi. I have not accused you of heartless cruelty but merely instance those cases of very recent occurrence, and could go on and enumerate hundreds of others and challenge any fair man to judge which of us has the heart of pity for the families of a "brave People."

I say that it is a kindness to these families of Atlanta to remove them now at once from scenes that women and children should not be exposed to, and the "brave People" should scorn to commit their wives and children to the rude barbarians who thus as you say violate the Laws of War, as illustrated in the pages of its dark History.

In the name of common sense I ask you not to appeal to a just God in such a sacreligious manner. You who in the midst of Peace and prosperity have plunged a nation into War, dark and cruel War, who dared and badgered us to Battle, insulted our Flag, seized our arsenals and forts that were left in the honorable custody of a Peaceful Ordnance Sergeant, seized and made "prisoners of War" the very Garrisons sent to protect your people against negroes and Indians long before any overt act was committed by the to you hateful Lincoln Government, tried to force Kentucky and Missouri into Rebellion, spite of themselves, falsified the vote of Louisiana, turned loose your Privateers to plunder unarmed ships, Expelled Union families by the thousands, burned their houses and declared by an act of your Congress the confiscation of all debts due northern men for goods had and received—talk thus to the marines but not to me who have seen these things and who will this day make as much sacrifice for the peace and honor of the South, as the best born Southerner among you. If we must be Enemies let us be men, and fight it out as we propose to do, and not deal in such hypocritical appeals to God and humanity. God will judge us in due time, and he will pronounce whether it be more humane to fight with a town full of women, and their families of a brave

People at our back or to remove them in time to places of safety among their own friends and People. I am very Respectfully Your Obdt. Servt.

By Flag of Truce.   W. T. Sherman
Lt. Col. Warner[2] in charge.   Major Genl. Comdg.

Lbk, DNA: RG 94, Records of the Adjutant General's Office, Generals' Books and Papers, William T. Sherman, Letterbook 12.

1. Hood to WTS, September 9, 1864, *PM*, 2:119. Hood retorted in reply to WTS's proposals of September 7 that "I do not consider that I have any alternative in this matter." He further commented that "the unprecedented measure you propose transcends, in studied and ingenious cruelty, all acts ever before brought to my attention in the dark history of war." He concluded, "In the name of God and humanity, I protest, believing that you will find that you are expelling from their homes and firesides the wives and children of a brave people."

2. Colonel Willard Warner (1826–1906), USA, of the 180th Ohio was Sherman's inspector general during the Atlanta Campaign and was later a U.S. senator from Alabama.

TO JAMES M. CALHOUN ET AL.

Headquarters, Military Division
of the Mississippi,
In the Field, Atlanta Sept. 12 1864.

James M. Calhoun, Mayor, E. E. Rawson, and S. C. Wells, representing City Council of Atlanta.

Gentlemen,

I have your letter of the 11th in the nature of a Petition to revoke my orders removing all the inhabitants from Atlanta.[1] I have read it carefully and give full credit to your statements of the distress that will be occasioned by it, and yet shall not revoke my orders, simply because my orders are not designed to meet the humanities of the case, but to prepare for the future struggles in which millions yea hundreds of millions of Good People outside of Atlanta have a deep interest. We must have *Peace*, not only at Atlanta, but in All America. To secure this we must stop the war that now desolates our once Happy and Favored country. To stop war we must defeat the Rebel Armies, that are arrayed against the Laws and Constitution which all must respect and obey. To defeat those armies we must prepare the way to reach them in their recesses provided with the arms and instruments which enable us to accomplish our purpose. Now, I know the vindictive nature of our enemy, and that we may have many years of military operations from this Quarter, and therefore deem it wise and prudent to prepare in time. The use of Atlanta for warlike purposes is inconsistent with its character as a home for families. There will be no manufactures, commerce, or agriculture here for the maintenance of families and Sooner or later want will compel the Inhabitants to go. Why not go *now*, when all the arrangements are completed for the transfer instead of waiting till the plunging shot of contending armies will renew the scenes of the past month? Of course I do not apprehend any such thing at this moment, but you do not suppose this army will be here till the war is over. I cannot discuss this subject with you fairly, because I cannot impart to you what I propose to do, but I assert that my military plans make it necessary for the Inhabitants to go away, and I can only renew my offer of services to make their exodus in any direction as easy and comfortable as possible. You cannot qualify war in harsher terms than I will. War is cruelty, and you cannot refine it: and those who brought war into our Country deserve all the curses and maledictions a people can pour out. I know I had no hand in making this war, and I know I will make more sacrifices today than any of you to Secure Peace. But you cannot have Peace and a Division of our Country. If the United States submits to a Division now it will not stop, but will go on till we reap the Fate of Mexico, which is Eternal War. The United States does and must assert its authority wherever it once had power, if it relaxes one bit to pressure it is gone, and I know that Such is the National Feeling. This Feeling assumes various shapes, but always comes back to that of *Union*. Once admit the Union, once more acknowledge the Authority of the National Government, and instead of devoting your houses, and Streets and Roads to the dread uses of War. I & this army become at once your protectors & supporters, shielding you from danger let it come from what quarter it may. I know that a few individuals cannot resist a torrent of error and passion such as swept the South into rebellion, but you can part out, so that we may know those who desire a Government, and those who insist on war & its desolation.

You might as well appeal against the thunder storm as against these terrible hardships of war. They are inevitable and the only way the People of Atlanta can hope once more to live in peace & quiet at home is to Stop the war, which can alone be done by admitting that it began in Error and is perpetuated in pride. We don't want your negros or your horses, or your houses or your Lands, or any thing you have, but we do want and will have a just obedience to the Laws of the United States. That we will have and if it involves the destruction of your improvements we cannot help it. You have heretofore read public sentiment in your newspapers that live by falsehood & excitement and the quicker you seek for truth in other quarters the better for you.

I repeat then that by the original compact of Government the United States had certain Rights in Georgia which have never been relinquished, and never will be: that the South began the war by seizing Forts, Arsenals Mints Custom Houses &c. &c. long before Mr. Lincoln was installed, & before the South had one jot or tittle of provocation. I myself have seen in Missouri, Kentucky Tennessee and Mississipi hundreds and thousands of women & children fleeing from your armies & desperadoes, hungry and with bleeding feet. In Memphis Vicksburg and Mississipi we fed thousands upon thousands of the families of Rebel Soldiers left on our hands and whom we could not see starve. Now that war comes home to you you feel very different. You deprecate its horrors, but did not feel them when you sent car-loads of soldiers and ammunition, moulded shells & shot to carry on war into Kentucky & Tennessee, & desolate the homes of hundreds & thousands of good People who only asked to live in Peace at their old homes, and under the Government of their inheritance. But these comparisons are idle. I want peace, and believe it ⟨can⟩ now only be reached through union and war, and I will ever conduct war partly with a view to perfect & early success.

But my dear sirs when that Peace do come you may call on me for anything—Then will I share with you the last cracker, and watch with you to shield your homes & families against danger from every quarter.

Now you must go, & take with you the old & feeble, feed & nurse them, & build for them in more quiet places proper ⟨ha⟩bitations, to shield them against the ⟨wea⟩ther till the mad passions of men ⟨coo⟩l down, and allow the Union and ⟨pe⟩ace once more settle over your old homes at Atlanta[.] Yrs., in haste,

W. T. Sherman

ALS, MH. Material in angle brackets taken from *PM*, 2:125–27.

1. Calhoun et al. to WTS, September 11, 1864, MH. As "the only legal organ of the people" of Atlanta, they asked WTS to "reconsider the order requiring them to leave Atlanta." Convinced the move would cause "consequences appalling and heartrending," they cited the cases of pregnant women, mothers with young children, invalids, those with no place to go and no money to get there, and those who wished to leave the railroad line before the point where Hood would pick up their belongings. In addition, the countryside to the south was already crowded with refugees.

TO JOHN BELL HOOD

Headquarters, Military Division
of the Mississippi,
In the Field, Atlanta Sept. 12 1864.

Genl. J. B. Hood,
Comdg. Dept. of Tenn., Confederate Army
General,

I have yours of today.[1] You asked to Exchange Prisoners, and I consented as far as those which remained in my hands here and this side of Chattanooga. These I will exchange in the manner I have stated and not otherwise. As you Cannot know those of our men whose terms have expired I authorized Col. Warner to say I would receive any number taken of this army between certain dates, say the last two thousand or in any other single period: but as a matter of business I offered terms that could not be misunderstood.

You have not answered my proposition as to the "men captured in Atlanta who are soldiers of the Confederate Army detailed on Extra duty," in the shops.

I think I understand the Laws of Civilized nations and "the Customs of War", but if at a loss at any time I Know where to Seek information to refresh my memory. If you will give our prisoners at Anderson, a little more Elbow Room, and liberty to make out of the abundant timber shelters for themselves, as also a fair allowance of food to enable them to live in health, they will ask nothing more till such time as we will provide for them. I am with respect yr. obt. Servant

W. T. Sherman
Maj. Genl.
Comdg.

ALS, New York: The Gilder Lehrman Collection; *OR*, II, 7:808.

1. John Bell Hood to WTS, September 11, 1864, objected to the terms of prisoner exchange set by WTS. By refusing to exchange the approximately eighteen hundred Confederates he had on hand for any prisoners save those who had unexpired terms of service with his army, WTS had, Hood asserted, doomed most of the prisoners in Andersonville as well as those men whose enlistments had expired while in captivity. *OR*, II, 7:799. On September 9, WTS had written to Hood, asking that only men who could immediately take up active duty with his army be traded for the prisoners he had, but he added that he had one thousand prisoners from various armies and details captured at Atlanta whom he was willing to exchange for an equal number of prisoners from Andersonville. *OR*, II, 7:791–92.

TO JOHN BELL HOOD

Headquarters Military Division
of the Mississippi,
In the Field, Atlanta, Georgia,
September 14, 1864.

General J. B. Hood, commanding Army of the Tennessee, Confederate Army.
General:

Yours of September 12th is received,[1] and has been carefully perused. I agree with you that this discussion by two soldiers is out of place, and profitless; but you must admit that you began the controversy by characterizing an official act of mine in unfair and improper terms. I reiterate my former answer, and to the only new matter contained in your rejoinder add: We have no "negro allies" in this army; not a single negro soldier left Chattanooga with this army or is with it now. There are a few guarding Chattanooga, which General Steedman[2] sent at one time to drive Wheeler out of Dalton.

I was not bound by the laws of war to give notice of the shelling of Atlanta, a "fortified town, with magazines, arsenals, founderies, and public stores;" you were bound to take notice. See the books.

This is the conclusion of our correspondence, which I did not begin, and terminate with satisfaction. I am, with respect, your obedient servant,

W. T. Sherman,
Major-General commanding.

Printed, *PM*, 2:127–28.

1. *PM*, 2:121–24. Angered by the tone of WTS's September 10 letter, Hood had fired off a lengthy reply. He denied that Johnston had removed any families and that he and Hardee had committed any such acts as WTS had described at Jonesboro or Atlanta, respectively. He argued that WTS was to blame for the destruction of civilian life and property in Atlanta because he had not given notice "of your purpose to shell the town, which is usual in war among civilized nations" (p. 121). He accused WTS's artillery of deliberately firing over his works and into private homes. He said that it was not a soldier's place to discuss the origins of the war and then went on to do just that "to repel any unjust conclusion which might be drawn from my silence" (p. 122). He was angry that WTS had accused him of hypocrisy and sacrilege and stated his belief that the Union army had come to subjugate Southern whites and "make negroes your allies, and desire to place over us an inferior race, which we have raised from barbarism to its present position, which is the highest ever attained by that race, in any country, in all time" (p. 123). He concluded that "we will fight you to the death! Better die a thousand deaths than submit to live under you or your Government and your negro allies!" (p. 124).

2. Major General James B. Steedman would be in charge of the District of Etowah until the end of the war.

TO THOMAS EWING SR.

Headquarters, Military Division
of the Mississippi,
In the Field, Atlanta Ga. Sept. 15, 1864.

Hon. Thos. Ewing
Lancaster, Ohio
Dear Sir,

I have just closed my official Report of the Campaign of Atlanta.[1] I cannot say it is as satisfactory as the work itself for any description seems meager to us who for four months have been intent on one thing which once attained seems a matter of course. The Grand Outlines contemplated these Grand Armies moving on Richmond, Atlanta & Montgomery Alabama, & Mine alone has yet reached its goal, So that in fact I am now at a loss, for the "next." But soon that will be discussed and I will be off again. I can well understand the deep interest with which apart from personal considerations you have watched my progress, and with what real pleasure you have seen doubt and difficulty vanish before actual facts.

You have often Said that Napoleon had no subordinate to whom he was willing to entrust an hundred thousand men & yet have lived to See the little redheaded urchin not only handle an hundred thousand men, smoothly & easily, but fight them in masses of tens and fifty thousands at a distance of hundreds of miles from his arsenals and sources of supply. I feel in this less active pleasure than I know you do, and I only hope that I may be equally successful in telling the tale simply and well so that the reader may follow as through the mazes of forest and mountain that lay in our Path. If I fail to do this I can only promise to Send the War Dept. the data which will enable some one there with more leisure and patience to make a narrative truthful, yet full of almost dramatic interest.

I have been able to write but little to Ellen of late, but as soon as my Report is copied in my Books, I will according to my custom send it to Ellen who will read it to you, So that on your Maps you may trace out our devious course to this the Grand Objective. I receive floods of letters from all sorts of People but my universal answer is that I am a soldier & have only one opinion and one idea, a common country & an inteligent submission to its Laws and con- stituted authorities. My Negro letter got to the Newspapers through the very man who I thought would be the last to publish it, for it was penned in haste & with some irony against a class that have done more to hurt our army than an Equal number of Enemies—men who by pay & money have filled up our Muster Rolls with names, impoverished our Treasury by high & useless boun- ties & brought us no men, but on the contrary cut off the only valuable source of supply through a fair & square "draft."—I hear of Quotas being filled but not a man comes from the "Quota" to the Army. This is true and a burning shame to an army that has now been fighting near three years, till the Regi- ments Ohio Re{quests} too have less than 100 men for duty. Excuse this long letter, which Ellen may read to you, when you have nothing more interesting. Yrs. affectionately,

W. T. Sherman

ALS, DLC: Thomas Ewing and Family Papers.
1. WTS to HWH, September 15, 1864, *OR*, I, 38: pt. 1, 61–84.

TO EUGENE CASSERLY

[September 17, 1864]

Dear Casserly,

I can hardly treat seriously of property in San Francisco—but do get rid of that lot, and though Gold is something hard to get in this country I will buy and get enough to pay the balance due on that lot. I know that Capt. Welch meant to do Lizzie a kindness in giving that lot—still I never intended to commit the folly of paying taxes, but Ellen tells me Mr. Moss has done so, and he must be reimbursed. Let it be sold if you can make title Pay over the proceeds to Mr. Moss and the balance to repay Mr. Moss in full I will deposit for him with Schuchardt & Gebhard New York. I can handle an hundred thousand men in battle, and take the "City of the Sun", but am afraid to manage a lot in the Swamp of San Francisco, with your taxes and street assessments, and Greenbacks at 256.—but in taking Atlanta we brought Gold down to 220, so now is the time for me to reimburse Mr. Moss for his advances on account of that unfortunate piece of property—I have made a short truce with General Hood at a place called Rough & Ready 12 miles out, where I deliver the People of Atlanta and he transports them beyond the break I made in his Road, which made him quit Atlanta in a hurry. I got a letter from Calhoun Penham[1] who is an officer on some Rebel Genl. staff. He is a pretty "chivalry"—These fellows have a way of leaving us to take care of their families, but when I took Atlanta I ordered them all to quit and a big howl is raised against my Barbarity—Butler is the Beast—Sherman the Brute & Grant the Butcher. This is somewhat on the order of the school bully who if he cant whip you, can call you hard names or make mouths as you listen. I think I will make a Record of this campaign that will compare well with that of the European Models. I made two moves that I would like to demonstrate to you at home with the maps but which I cannot now essay—the passage of the Chattahoochee, and the raising the siege & striking Hoods communications before he suspected my movement. Give my love to Mrs. C. to Dr. Bowie, Mr. Moss and others of my acquaintance if they still remember me. Yr. friend

W. T. Sherman

ALS, NjP: Andre deCoppet Collection.

1. Penham to WTS, undated, appears at the end of 1864 in DLC: WTS. Penham asked WTS to tell his sister Mrs. George D. Prentice of Louisville, Kentucky, that he was fine; so was her son when he last saw him.

TO EDWARD EVERETT

Headquarters, Military Division
of the Mississippi,
Atlanta Geo. Sept. 17, 1864.

Hon. Edward Everett,
Boston Mass.
Dear Sir,

The Hon. Sec. of War has been kind enough to enclose me a Copy of the Boston *Advertiser* which contains your letter addressed to a Public meeting called to celebrate the recent successes to our arms, in which you associate my name honorably with those of Admiral Farragut, and Lt. Genl. Grant. So high a Compliment, coming from one who looks deep into the Causes of Events, and who foreshadows the judgment of History to which all men must submit, is one which even I must appreciate. I thank you for such a mark of your esteem, and can only promise to use the physical Force entrusted to my care to the end that our Nations honor and Power may stand vindicated, and may serve as the buckler and shield of safety to the thousands of millions of human beings that must succeed us in the Favored Region of Earth, committed to our Custody.

In your letter I was more than pleased to see revived Mr. Websters Magnificent Simile, comparing our political system with that of the Grand Universe, when each little Planet or asteroid if Kept to its place remains in perfect harmony, having an influence upon the whole proportionate to its mass but no more: but if rudely withdrawn the Equilibrium is destroyed, and wreck & chaos sure to follow.[1] How true was his prediction and plain and palpable the only remedy.

Mr. Stephens[2] to whom you also refer with the predictions made by him of the consequences of Secession, is now living "perdu" in this state, witnessing all the Sad Calamities which he foresaw, but Could not prevent. I am told by Citizens that he is universally regarded as an Union Man, and has not been permitted to Exercise any influence or power in a Govt. in which he is nominally second in Station. All these things are elements in the Great Problem, that will be worked out in Time, and it were Sacrilegious in us to pronounce the sacrifices made as useless. Good will come out of their incongruities and complications and our Government will be strengthened that it may fulfil its destiny in a more eminent degree.

I feel the more confidence since men like you heed the passing storm and guide it to its logical end, whilst we mere artizans mould the unsteady Elements of a democratic mass, into a well ordered army, and impress on it a love of country, a Reverence for its Laws & Civil Authorities, and a Courage that will sustain it in these wild struggles of Maddened Strife.

Permit me to subscribe myself as your Friend and humble servant,

W. T. Sherman

Maj. Genl.

ALS, MHi: Edward Everett Papers.

1. This simile is from Daniel Webster's famous March 7, 1850, speech, "The Constitution and the Union." Reprinted in Charles M. Wiltse and Alan R. Berolzheimer, eds., *The Papers of Daniel Webster*, series 4, *Speeches and Formal Writings*, vol. 2, *1834–1852* (Hanover, N.H., 1988), 515–51; the particular reference appears on pages 546–47. Webster concluded that a disruption of the federal system "must produce war, and such a war as I will not describe."

2. Alexander Stephens (1812–83), a Georgian, was vice president of the Confederacy.

TO THOMAS EWING JR.

Atlanta Sept. 17 [1864]

Dear Tom,

Charley has shown me yr. letter of Aug. 30, in which you foreshadow for me great things in case I take Atlanta—Atlanta is "took," but I only see harder work before me. As to being a rival of Lincoln or McClellan or any aspirants to such honor, I think I have too much sense to trouble myself about it. The People of the U.S. have too much sense to make me their President. Men old & young and women too would be organized & armed and you would have the d——st fight ever read of. Xerxes armies would be Corporal Guards to mine, and the Old & best Govt. of the World would expire in a Grand Raid. But to be serious I have taken Atlanta steadily & purposely and have reason to believe separate and apart from its intrinsic value, it has illustrated what we may & can do (damaged phrase) see where I am, {but} like {a}ll the operations of our Government just {as} I reach our Goal, from which vital {b}lows might be inflicted my Army {v}anishes from purely American causes. Every General Officer wants to go home {&} glorify, and half my men's times are out and Lincoln is trembling about the draft. In other words do what we may, we lose its natural effect by want of national traits of weakness—The idea of the enervated & delicate South, beating us in the Northern virtues of persever-ance & bottom, but that is the real danger. You have called to Missouri one of my Divisions A. J. Smiths to head off Price, when I'll bet that there are loafers Enough about St. Louis today to make four such Divisions. If a Census were to ask me honestly a question about the Presidency, I would answer, Grant {a}nd I can manage your Armies, but (damaged phrase) a manner as Jeff Davis or Lou{is} Napoleon.[1]

Atlanta is a very important place and Hood has fortified it beautifully to our very hands: but the fortifications even have too much ground. I have expell{ed} the People, and will contract the Lines to a comparatively small circle embracing the vital points and of course do not expect to be idle long.

Tell Rosecrans to raise the hue & cry, go down & clean out Shelby & Price, and not take my troops to defend Missouri. It is ridiculous & absurd. If Missouri cant at this day keep Price out, then Price ought to capture you all, and send you as Slaves down to take the places of the freed negros. What is the Free State of Arkansas doing? And the reorganised State of Louisiana? that they do not stand as a shield against the frightened people of Missouri.

I am almost tired of playing war (damaged word) an abdication in {favor} of some of (damaged word) more persistent and plucky Lieutenants. I now comprehend why Cromwell scattered (damaged and illegible) House, and Napoleon sent the {C}ouncil of Five Hundred back to their wives.

I am no fit subject for a Democratic {or} Republican Candidate for any office.

Charley is well, and we are all enjoy{ing} Rest—for the first time in five months {without} the luxury of cannon & musket shots—breakfast dinner & supper.

Minnie & Lizzie are now at school up in Indiana and Ellen really contemplates spending much of her time with them, but years are so fleet that both the misses will be independent & off on their own voyage of Life before Ellen is fairly awake to the fact that they have begun the school. Yrs. in haste as usual

{W. T. Sherman}

ALS, DLC: Thomas Ewing and Family Papers. Margins of letter badly singed.

1. Louis Napoleon (1808–73), who as Napoleon III served as emperor of France.

TO ABRAHAM LINCOLN

Atlanta Ga.

6 p.m. Sept. 17" 1864

A. Lincoln

President U.S.—

I will keep the Department fully advised of all developments as connected with the subject in which you feel so interested[1]—A Mr. Wright,[2] former member of Congress from Rome Ga. and a Mr. King of Marietta are now going between Gov. Brown[3] and myself—I have said that some of the people of Georgia are now engaged in rebellion began in error and perpetuated in pride; but that Georgia can now save herself from the devastation of War preparing for her only by withdrawing her quota out of the Confederate Army, and aiding me to repel Hood from the border of the State; in which even instead of desolating the land, as we progress. I will keep our men to the high roads and commons, and pay for the corn and meat we need and take—I am fully conscious of the delicate nature of such assertions, but it would be a magnificent stroke of policy, if I could without wasting a foot of ground or of principle arouse the latent enmity to Jeff Davis, of Georgia.

The people do not hesitate to say, that Mr. Stephens was, and is, a Union man at heart, and they feel that Jeff Davis will not trust him, or let him have a share in his Government.

W. T. Sherman

Maj. Genl.

Telegram, DLC: Robert T. Lincoln Collection of Abraham Lincoln Papers; *OR*, I, 39: pt. 2, 395–96.

1. On September 15, WTS has written to Halleck that Georgia governor Joseph E. Brown had disbanded the state militia to gather crops and said that Alexander Stephens and Brown

wanted to visit him, intimating a desire on the state's part to surrender separately from the Confederacy. *PM*, 2:138–39. On September 17, Lincoln telegraphed WTS that he was extremely interested in this report. *CWAL*, 8:9. Brown ultimately felt unable to take such a drastic step and never met with Sherman.

2. Augustus R. Wright (1813–91) had served in the U.S. Congress from 1857 to 1859.

3. Joseph E. Brown (1821–95) had been governor of the state since 1857.

TO ELLEN EWING SHERMAN

Headquarters, Military Division
of the Mississippi.
Atlanta Geo. Sept. 17, 1864.

Dearest Ellen,

I have many letters from you of late some of which seem by an unexplained cause to have laid at Nashville or Chattanooga, but I think the Series is complete up to and including your visit to the School at South Bend.[1] I got last night also Minnies letter which you seem to have carried to Lancaster & mailed from there. I have telegraphed you & written short hasty letters to you, to yr. father & Tommy and cannot add much if any thing of interest not involved in my original Telegraph[.] Atlanta is ours & fairly won. I have had some sharp correspondence with Hood about expelling the poor families of a brave People, which correspondence in due time will become public, and I take the ground that Atlanta is a conquered place and I propose to use it purely for our own military purposes which are inconsistent with its habitation by the families of a Brave People—I am shipping them *all* and by next Wednesday the Town will be a real Military town with no woman boring me every order I give. Hood no doubt thought he would make Capital out of the barbarity &c. but I rather think he will change his mind before he is done. I beat him on the Strategy and fighting, and if my troops had only been as smart as my old Tennessee Army I could have bagged all of Hardees Corps at Jonesboro. Still on the whole the Campaign is the best, cleanest and most satisfactory of this war. I have received the most fulsome praise of all from the President down, but I fear the world will jump to the weary conclusion that because I am in Atlanta the work is done. Far from it, we must *kill* these three hundred thousand I have told you of so often, and the further they run the harder for us to get them.

I will Send you the rough notes of my Report as soon as copied in my letter Book, and you can read it to your father who will be more interested than you.

Do you remember when I was at Belfonte in 1844 I boarded with a man named Martin. Some months ago he found out I was the same & wrote me asking me to enable him to gather his corn and Some hogs, of course I did So & wrote him very kindly.[2] I Send you his answer, it is a gem in its way. I send you a letter from a Mrs. Biddle also as a sample of the many that come to me, and I really have not time to answer—I already write so hastily & badly that no one but my regular clerks can make it out. Dayton does much of my writing but the truth is I can write a dozen letters before he can one. I find it about as quick work to write as to tell what to write & modify & correct after.

Hill's time was out July 19, but he staid {with me till} the day before yesterday when he went to Illinois, to see his brother who has charge of some cows calves, mares and colts. I paid him up, and had a grand settlement, paying him in full $292. He was honest & faithful to the last. I have two negros to take care of my horses, one a boy who now makes up my bed, blacks my shoes and swipes out the Room under the mastery of a very good orderly who Succeeded Boyer, So that the machinery of my household works smooth as possible—we occupy a fine house, that of Judge Lyons, and have a good mess. I enclose you a letter to mail to Mr. Casserly, asking him to Sell that lot. I told Hill to write to you when he got home, and you would Send him a Deed to a Lot in Leavenworth, but I gave him to understand I would not be responsible for the Consequences.[3] He promised to come back to me before the Winter Campaign and I think he will. He turned over to his successor a minute account of Shirts with orders on all points. Love to all yrs. ever,

AL (signature clipped), InND: Sherman Family Papers.

1. EES to WTS, August 16 (two letters), 22, 24, 26, 27, and 30, and September 1 and 4, 1864. SFP.

2. Daniel Martin to WTS, January 22 and July 24, 1864, DLC: WTS. See WTS to Martin, August 10, 1864, above.

3. EES to WTS, August 16, 1864, mentioned their joint concern that Hill would not be able to pay taxes on the lot.

TO JOHN SHERMAN

Headquarters, Military Division
of the Mississippi,
Atlanta Sept. 17, 1864.

Dear Brother,

I have your letter of the 5th[1] and would have replied at an earlier date but I knew you would hear all you wanted to know from the public sheets—I have now finished my official Report of Atlanta and am devoting myself to the collating of the addenda or appendix which are the statistics. I did not mean to be severe on your friend Colfax, but it is to me incomprehensible that any one would wish to withdraw nine Regiments from my army actually engaged in Battle, before a strongly fortified town, and to put our already overtaxed Country the Expense of transporting them six hundred miles to vote for a member of Congress. The mere thought is more severe than any commentary I could make.

As to the negro letter I never dreamed it would be printed & made public, and cannot now imagine why the person to whom it was addressed Should give it notoriety. I know of course that the nigger like all other popular questions would follow the national law & swings from one extreme to the other till it settle down to something like Right, but it was hard to force us to wait so long. I believe the United States are now paying 60,000 negro soldiers many of whom are subject to my command, but we never Count them anything in our Estimates for the Field. I tried when I went to Meridian to make up a force of 4000 but failed for General Hawkins though nominally in command of our 20,000 could not raise but 2100 and did not feel disposed to risk them.

I am glad that at last the draft is to be enforced. That is the only legitimate source of supply, and we have a Right to ask the Govt. to use it to replace our natural and necessary losses. We are all in good condition here and await the next Great Combination, which will carry me deeper & deeper into the heart of Georgia. Give my love to all & believe me Affectionately

W. T. Sherman

ALS, DLC: William T. Sherman.

1. The letter's date was actually September 4. JS had sent his congratulations on the fall of Atlanta to his brother and then chided him for his sharp response to Colfax. He revealed that Schenck and Garfield were the ones in the House who had forced the black enlistment issue; these "Army men" insisted it be retained during a committee of conference. He bemoaned the nomination of McClellan as it would mean a closer fight in the presidential election. "I have no reason either to respect or like Lincoln yet. I believe his election necessary to prevent Disunion and support him with all my might. I know he dislikes me & I believe in his mind has no friendship for you. . . . We are not likely ever to have a President with less dignity & energy—or business capacity than Lincoln—He is however better than so timid & unready a man as McClellan." DLC: WTS.

TO T. S. BELL[1]

Headquarters, Military Division
of the Mississippi,
Atlanta Sept. 18, 1864.

Dr. T. S. Bell, Louisville
My Dear Sir,

Gen. Whitaker[2] has handed me your kind letter of Sept. 12,[3] with the parcel of newspapers with the Sept. no. of the U.S. Service Magazine. I have read the resolutions at the Court House Meeting and fear you have piled up the praise a little too high. I fear Elevation as a fall would be the harder, but if the Draft ordered for tomorrow be made thoroughly it does seem that with present advantages we should make big strides to that end, for which I know the loudest Peace men of the land do not yearn with more solicitude than you and I. I have met many confederates who want Peace, on the terms of Vallandigham of Southern independence, and have asked them fairly if they Could have the impudence to ask us to give up Memphis, and Vicksburg, and New Orleans, and the Forts of the Seashore, and Louisville and Nashville and Chattanooga and Atlanta and hundreds of other places that we have paid for with human lives, and the uniform answer is that Southern Independence without these points would be a mere sham, but not one *dared* to ask us to give up these places as it would be an insult to Common decency and Common sense. No; we must have a Country Embracing all these & more too, and the only question is who is to govern it. We offer them a fair share, but not the weight of the feather more than they are entitled to. When this only question of sovereignty is settled by war, and nothing else can settle it, all Else is Easy, and may be dispatched by congresses, committees, caucuses or any other of the devices of civilians. I am always glad to hear of the Steadfastness of our Kentucky Friends, and that they are not led astray by false issues. If our Country is not good & great enough to command universal love & veneration let us make it so, instead of pulling it to pieces which would make us the despised and hated of all People. Dont fear that I shall falter in my energies, for you Know that I began war with my fellow Countrymen with pain & Sorrow, but when it Could not be avoided, I began in Earnest, and have only warmed to the work. Months & years are as nothing in the Past, and we must not measure a Cause by Time. The end we seek will justify a century of labor and toil and when the Enemies of our Country, be they at home or abroad see that we can and will persevere to the End, they will shrink from the encounter, and like Beelzebub of old go forth and Seek congenial space Elsewhere, to work out their devilish anarchy.

I will gladly help Colonel Barry,[4] who is young and sure of advancement if he perseveres as he has so well begun, and your little Nephew Harper[5] must come and See me and for his Mothers and your sake I will cheerfully notice and encourage him. I have a big family and it takes nearly all my time to feed & clothe *them*. With great respect,

W. T. Sherman
Maj. Genl.

ALS, CSmH.

1. Bell wrote for the *Union Press.*

2. Brigadier General Walter C. Whitaker (1823–87), USA, had commanded a brigade in Stanley's Division of the Fourth Corps during the Atlanta Campaign.

3. DLC: WTS. Bell had sent news of the public rejoicing in Louisville on September 9 when they heard the news of Atlanta's capture. He agreed with WTS on the need for a draft to fill up army ranks.

4. Colonel Henry W. Barry (1840–75), USA, of the Eighth U.S. Colored Heavy Artillery, the first black regiment in Kentucky. He would later serve in Congress as a representative from Mississippi from 1870 until his death.

5. James Harper of Kentucky's commissary or quartermaster service.

TO MARIA BOYLE EWING SHERMAN

Headquarters, Military Division
of the Mississippi,
Atlanta Sept. 18, 1864

Dear Minnie,

I have your letter from Notre Dame telling me you are again at your studies and that Lizzie is with you. I am very glad of it and you can always steal a little time to tell me all about your present studies. I have much to occupy my time as even you can understand, and neither you or Lizzie must expect me to be even on the score of Letters. You will hear so much about Atlanta and the Battles that I need not speak of them to you, but I hope some day we will all sit round the Fire when I can tell you all many stories about the Battles. Atlanta is a town which once had 20,000 people, with large foundries and work shops, but these are all gone and nothing remains but the dwelling houses, which are empty. There is a Depot as large as that at Indianapolis or Cincinati with some large locomotive buildings. My Engineer officer Capt. Poe has just brought me some daguerreotypes of the Locomotive House and of the track when the Rebels burned up seven trains of cars on leaving. I send them to you for they are very pretty pictures, and after awhile I will send you more. Give one to Lizzie and keep one yourself.

Tell Sister Angela, that it is hard to have you away off in the North part of Indiana where there is no chance of my ever seeing you till you are out of school, for it is off away from all Roads, that I can have any chance to travel. But time slips along very fast and your few years of school will soon be over and by that time the war may be over and we may then have a home.

Give my love to Agnes and Elly & to Cousin Tom. I suppose the latter is almost a young Gent. Tell Lizzie I will Soon write to her also. Yr. loving father,

W. T. Sherman

ALS, OHi: William T. Sherman Papers.

TO ULYSSES S. GRANT

Hdqrs. Military Division
of the Mississippi,
Atlanta, Ga., September 20, 1864.

Lieut. Gen. U. S. Grant,
Commanding Armies of the United States, City Point, Va.:
General:

I have the honor to acknowledge at the hands of Lieutenant-Colonel Porter,[1] of your staff, your letter of September 12,[2] and accept with thanks the
honorable and kindly mention of the services of this army in the great cause
in which we are all engaged. I send by Colonel Porter all official reports which
are completed, and will, in a few days, submit a list of names which I deem
worthy of promotion. I think we owe it to the President to save him the
invidious task of election among a vast number of worthy aspirants, and have
ordered my army commanders to prepare their lists with great care and to
express their preferences based upon claims of actual capacity and services
rendered. These I will consolidate and submit in such a form that if mistakes
are committed they will at least be sanctioned by the best contemporaneous
evidence of merit, for I know that vacancies do not exist equal in number to
that of the officers that really deserve promotion. As to the future, I am
pleased to know your army is being steadily reenforced by a good class of men,
and I hope it will go on until you have a force that is numerically double that
of your antagonist, so that with one part you can watch him and with the
other you can push out boldly from your left flank, occupy the South Shore
[Side] Railroad, compel him to attack your position, or accept battle on your
own terms. We ought to ask our country for the largest possible armies that
can be raised, as so important a thing as the "self-existence of a great nation"
should not be left to the fickle chances of war. Now that Mobile is shut out to
the commerce of our enemy it calls for no further effort on our part, unless
the capture of the city can be followed up by the occupation of the whole
Alabama River and the railroad across to Columbus, Ga., when that place
would at once become a magnificent auxiliary to my farther progress into
Georgia, but until General Canby is much reenforced, and until he can more
thoroughly subdue the scattered armies west of the Mississippi, I suppose that
much cannot be attempted as against the Alabama River and Columbus, Ga.

The utter destruction of Wilmington, N.C., is of importance only in connection with the necessity of cutting off all foreign trade to our enemy, and if
Farragut can get across the bar, and the move can be made quick, I suppose it
will succeed. From my knowledge of the mouth of Cape Fear, I anticipate
more difficulty in getting the heavy ships across the bar than in reaching the

town of Wilmington, but of course the soundings of the channel are well known at Washington as well as the draft of his iron-clads, so that it must be demonstrated as feasible or else it would not be attempted. If successful, I suppose that Fort Caswell will be occupied and the fleet at once sent to the Savannah River. Then the reduction of the city is the only question. If once in our possession, and the river open to us, I would not hesitate to cross the State of Georgia with 60,000 men, hauling some stores and depending on the country for the balance. Where a million of people live my army won't starve; but, as you know, in a country like Georgia, with few roads and innumerable streams, an inferior force could so delay an army and harass it that it would not be a formidable object, but if the enemy knew that we had our boats on the Savannah I could rapidly move to Milledgeville, where there is abundance of corn and meat, and would so threaten Macon and Augusta that he would give up Macon for Augusta; then I would move to interpose between Augusta and Savannah, and force him to give me Augusta, with the only powder mills and factories remaining in the South, or let us have the Savannah River. Either horn of the dilemma would be worth a battle. I would prefer his holding Augusta as the probabilities are; for then, with the Savannah River in our possession the taking of Augusta would be a mere matter of time. This campaign could be made in winter. But the more I study the game the more am I convinced that it would be wrong for me to penetrate much farther into Georgia without an objective beyond. It would not be productive of much good. I can start east and make a circuit south and back, doing vast damage to the State, but resulting in no permanent good; but by mere threatening to do so I hold a rod over the Georgians who are not overloyal to the South. I will therefore give my opinion that your army and Canby's should be re-enforced to the maximum; that after you get Wilmington, you strike for Savannah and the river; that General Canby be instructed to hold the Mississippi River and send a force to get Columbus, Ga., either by the way of the Alabama or the Appalachicola, and that I keep Hood employed, and put my army in fine order for a march on Augusta, Columbia, and Charleston, to be ready as soon as Wilmington is sealed as to commerce, and the city of Savannah is in our possession. I think it will be found that the movements of Price and Shelby west of the Mississippi are mere diversions. They cannot hope to enter Missouri save as raiders, and the truth is Rosecrans should be ashamed to take my troops for such a purpose. If you will secure Wilmington and the City of Savannah from your center, and let Canby have the Mississippi River and west of it, I will send a force to the Alabama and Appalachicola, provided you give me 100,000 of the drafted men to fill up my old regiments, and if you will fix a day to be in Savannah, I will insure our possession of Macon and a point on the river below Augusta.

The possession of the Savannah River is more than fatal to the possibility of a Southern independence; they may stand the fall of Richmond, but not of all Georgia. I will have a long talk with Colonel Porter and tell him everything that may occur to me of interest to you. In the mean time know that I admire your dogged perseverance and pluck more than ever. If you can whip Lee and I can march to the Atlantic I think Uncle Abe will give us a twenty days' leave of absence to see the young folks. Ever, yours,

W. T. Sherman
Major-General

Printed, *OR*, I, 39: pt. 2, 411–13.

1. Lieutenant Colonel Horace Porter (1837–1921) had joined Grant's staff as an aide-de-camp in April 1864.

2. *PUSG*, 12:154–55. The letter read in part: "I feel you have accomplished the most gigantic undertaking given to any General in this War and with a skill and ability that will be acknowledged in history as unsurpassed if not unequalled" (p. 155).

TO PHILEMON B. EWING

Headquarters, Military Division
of the Mississippi,
Atlanta Sept. 23, 1864.

Dear Phil

I have yours about young {Lobenthal} and have referred it to General Thomas in whose army he is with an endorsement that will result in his release if it can be done without too much favoritism. I will in time notify you of the result.

I continue to receive commendations as to the Campaign of Atlanta from sources too high to be undervalued—I suppose I must assume the real title of a General & carry it as I best may. The capture of Atlanta and its Line of Railroads gives me a fine opening for another still more decisive move in war, but we must have Our Regiments filled up. War is costly in life, but it is thrust on us and we must meet it in all its magnitude. The last dollar & the last man, must not be a mere boast but if necessary must be a reality. I would Still prefer that others Should lead, but if events force me into the position I must go on. Now even if any ill fate befals me I trust the country will take care of my family. So Smoothly and harmoniously have things worked on this Line, and Such results have been achieved by unseen roads, that the soldiers & officers will follow me into any enterprise however hazardous. Just enough doubt & uncertainty hung over us just before we took Atlanta that all {give} to remind the larger Share in the result. I think my official Report which I sent to Ellen by Col. Moore will interest your father much, and after you have decyphered it I want you to read it to him carefully, for I think it unfolds the story truthfully and clearly.

I Should like to See you all but it cannot be. I must stay and Share the fortunes of my comrades. Yrs. affectionately

W. T. Sherman

ALS, Atlanta, Ga.: Private Collection of C. Parke Day.

TO THOMAS EWING SR.

Headquarters, Military Division
of the Mississippi,
Atlanta, Geo. Sept. 23, 1864.

Hon. T. Ewing,
Lancaster, Ohio,
Dear Sir,

I have yours of Sept. 10, telling me that the Citizens of Lancaster have invested $1700 in the purchase of a horse & equipment for me, and asking me what I prefer should be done with them. Of course I feel much gratified at this mark of honor and kindness on the part of my old Townsmen and feel sure the horse at such a price will be no common one but rather too valuable to risk in these war times. I have with me one very valuable horse "Dick" presented me at Louisville that Suits my style of riding exactly, and I also have some six others of various kinds that do very well for the march and for the Knocking about among our Lines, trains of wagons & camps, so that I really do not need another at this time. Still I apprehend in the future as in the Past, I will lose some of these, and therefore deem it prudent to hold any surplus in "reserve." Nashville is our Depot, or Louisville, but even Lancaster would be preferable now, for I could order forward the horse in the Spring, which is as soon as I will likely need a new horse of such quality. The probabilities are that the Course of war will take me this winter far from here even, and therefore I prefer the horse should be Kept at Lancaster provided he can be Kept in full vigor by constant practice. The horse to be [pre]sented to me should be a free, bold, walker, trotter and canter, especially the former. He should "take" a leap anything in reason, such as a fence, gully, or log. Should be well bitted to the curb, and not afraid of anything. Thus far I have had but four 4 such, three of which are dead and one was killed under me, the fourth I still have in fine order.

If you will communicate these facts to the Committee I feel assured they will with pleasure conform to my wishes, but if you think it more graceful to bring him to the Front, send him to Col. J. L. Davidson, Nashville. I am with respect &c.

W. T. Sherman
Maj. Genl.

ALS, MiU-C: Clinton H. Haskell Collection.

TO ABRAHAM LINCOLN

Atlanta Ga.
11.30 A.M. Sep. 28. [1864]

His Excellency
The President of the U.S.

I have positive knowledge that Jeff Davis made a speech at Macon on the 22nd" which I mailed to Genl. Halleck yesterday[.][1] It was bitter against Johnston & Gov. Brown. The militia is on furlough. Brown is at Milledgeville trying to get a legislature to meet next month but he is afraid to act unless in concert with other Governors.

Judge Wright of Rome has been here and Messrs. Hill[2] and Nelson[3] former members of our Congress are also here now and will go to meet Wright at Rome and then go back to Madison and Milledgeville. Great efforts are being made to re-enforce Hood's army and to break up my Railroads, and I should have at once a good reserve force at Nashville. It would have a bad Effect if I were to be forced to send back any material part of my army to guard roads so as to weaken me to an extent that I could not act offensively if the occasion calls for it.

W. T. Sherman
Major General Commanding

Telegram, DLC: Robert Todd Lincoln Collection of Abraham Lincoln Papers; *OR*, I, 39: pt. 2, 501.

1. Davis had spoken unexpectedly at a refugee relief meeting in Macon. He said that WTS could not maintain his long communication lines and his advance would falter.

2. Joshua Hill (1812–91) had served in the House of Representatives from 1857 to 1861 and would later serve in the Senate from 1871 to 1873.

3. Thomas A. R. Nelson (1812–73), a Tennessee lawyer, was a former member of the House of Representatives. He had been arrested by Confederate scouts when traveling to Washington, D.C., for the opening of the Thirty-seventh Congress. He was sent to Richmond and paroled and would be a member of Andrew Johnson's defense counsel during his impeachment.

TO WILLIAM M. McPHERSON[1]

[ca. Sept. 15–30, 1864]

Wm. M. McPherson, Esq.

St. Louis

Dear Sir,

Yr. kind note of Aug. 24 from Rochester N.Y. reached me here and I am really thankful for the warm terms in which you write, and I know you will not feel the less kindly when you Know we are *inside* Atlanta. I dont see why we cant have some sense about negros, as well as about horses mules, iron, copper &c.—but Say nigger in the U.S. and from Sumner[2] to Abby Kelley[3] the whole country goes Crazy[.] I never thought my negro letter would get into the papers, but since it takes I lay low—I like niggers *well enough* as niggers, but when fools & idiots try & make niggers better than ourselves I have an opinion.

We are also ruining our Country financially in this Bounty & substitute business. It only amounts to *Spending* money, it dont make a single soldier. Fools think they can beg off and will spend their money on some worthless substitute who shirks and is of no use & after Spending all his money, will have to serve *besides*[.] Well the Thing will work out its natural Solution.

W. T. Sherman
Maj. Genl.

ALS, CSmH. Written on a printed copy of Sherman's Special Field Orders No. 68, thanking his army for their conduct during the Atlanta Campaign.

1. William M. McPherson (b. ca. 1812) was a wealthy citizen of St. Louis.

2. Charles Sumner (1811–74), Republican senator from Massachusetts and well-known abolitionist.

3. Abby Kelley (1811–73) was a prominent abolitionist and reformer.

TO ULYSSES S. GRANT

Atlanta 1 P.M.
Oct. 1st 1864

Lt. Gen. Grant

City Point

Hood is evidently on the west side of Chattahoochie below Sweetwater. If he try to get on my road this side of the Etowah I shall attack him, but if he go over to the Selma and Talladega road, why would it not do for me to leave Tennessee to the force which Thomas has, and the reserves soon to come to Nashville, and for me to destroy Atlanta, and then march across Georgia to Savannah or Charleston, breaking roads and doing irreparable damage? We cannot remain on the defensive[.]

W. T. Sherman
Maj. Genl.

Telegram, DNA: RG 107, Records of the Office of the Secretary of War, Telegrams Collected (Bound); *OR*, I, 39: pt. 3, 3.

TO ELLEN EWING SHERMAN

Headquarters, Military Division
of the Mississippi.
Atlanta Oct. 1, 1864.

Dearest Ellen,

We are all well. Forrest is threatening our Road in Tennessee, but I think ample steps are in progress to meet & defeat him. Should he temporarily disturb our Roads we are well prepared, with accumulated supplies here, and our Repair parties are so distributed that breaks can be speedily repaired.[1] Should Hoods main Army attempt Our Rear, I think we can make him suffer. Georgia is now open to me, and steps are being perfected at other & distinct points that will increase the value of my position here.

The telegraph brings me word that Grant is not idle about Richmond. I know his perseverance and have no apprehensions that in the end he will worry Lee out. Sheridans success up the Valley of the Shenandoah, will again threaten Lees line of supply which is by Gordonsville & Lynchburg, also that same Road is being attacked at a point further west from another quarter. I am in advance of all the other Columns and therefore should not be in a hurry, but if the Enemy is restless I may go ahead. Our men are now well clad & fed, well rested and ready to go wherever I lead.

The People of the South have made a big howl at my moving the families of Atlanta but I would have been a silly fool to take a town at such cost, and left it in the occupation of a helpless and hectic People. The War dept. has simply been silent, has not committed itself one way or other so that the whole measure rests on me, but I am used to Such things. Some of the correspondence between Hood & myself has been published, and the whole has been sent to Washington, where at some day it also will be published and I think Gen. Hood will have no reason to glorify. I have letters of thanks from the Mayor of Atlanta and Col. [Clare][2] who was the Confederate officer appointed to receive the families & transport them to the South. Instead of robbing them not an article was taken away, not even their negro servants who were willing to go along, and we even brought their provisions which I know to have been Confederate stores distributed to the People at the last moment, and were really our captured property.

Charley tells me he writes to you often but I think he means to do so and wants you to take the will for the deed. I sent you a few days ago some photographs, one of which Duke was very fine. He stood like a gentleman for his portrait, and I like it better than any I ever had taken.

I have two large groups of all my staff, which I will send you if an opportunity offers. They are very fair. I have not heard from you for some time, but of course you have got ere this the bundles I send by Col. Moore.[3] They will prove interesting and will answer for Reading a long time. I want to See the Critiques of the English Military Press on my campaign. They seem to study the principles and really are the only persons that caught the true Spirit of the Chattanooga and Knoxville Campaign. As to the Cincinati papers, and Catholic Telegraph I have the most profound contempt. Their praise or censure is alike puerile. If they would confine their observations to street nuisances and religious picnics they would better fill their offices. They have no more Knowledge or appreciation of Military men or measures than the children of a Sunday School. If you get a chance let Bishop Purcell[4] convey to his brother[5] this my opinion. I hope Master Charley is again well, and that the rest of our flock are progressing well. yrs. ever,

W. T. Sherman

ALS, InND: Sherman Family Papers.

1. Several days earlier WTS had remarked, "I take it for granted Forrest will cut our Road, but I think we can prevent his making a serious lodgment. His Cavalry will travel a hundred miles in less time than ours will ten." WTS to HWH, September 29, 1864, DNA: RG 94, Records of the Adjutant General's Office, Generals' Books and Papers, William T. Sherman, Letterbook 13.

2. Sherman left the officer's name blank in the original document; Clare was on Hood's staff. *PM*, 2:129.

3. Marshall F. Moore was colonel of the Sixty-ninth Ohio and would receive the brevet rank of brigadier general for his role at Jonesboro.

4. Archbishop John B. Purcell of Cincinnati was an outspoken Unionist.

5. Father Edward Purcell, also of Cincinnati.

TO GEORGE H. THOMAS

Headquarters, Military Division
of the Mississippi,
In the Field, Summerville Geo.
Oct. 2, 1864 4 AM

Maj. Gen. Thomas
Comdg. Dept. of the Cumberland,
General,

I think I have thought on the whole Field of the Future, and being now authorized to act I want all things bent to the following General plan of action for the next three months.

Out of the forces now here, and at Atlanta I propose to organize an efficient army of 60, to 65,000 men, with which I propose to destroy Macon, Augusta, and it may be Savannah and Charleston, but I will always Keep open the alternates of the Mouth of Apalachicola and Mobile. By this I propose to demonstrate the vulnerability of the South and make its inhabitants feel that war & individual Ruin are synonimous terms. To pursue Hood is folly, for he can twist & turn like a fox and wear out any army in pursuit. To continue to occupy long lines of Railroad simply exposes our small detachments to be picked up in detail and forces me to make countermarches to protect Lines of Communication. I know I am right in this and Shall proceed to its maturity.

As to details. I propose to take Howard & his army, Schofield & his, and two of your Corps, viz. Davis and Slocums. I propose to remain along the Coovee watching Hood till all my preperations are made, viz. till I have repaired the Railroad, sent back all supplies men & material and Stript for the work. Then I will send Stanley with the 4th Corps across by Wills Valley and Caperton to Stevenson to report to you. If you send me 5 or 6000 new conscripts I may also send back one of Slocums or Davis Divisions, but I prefer to maintain organizations. I want you to retain command in Tennessee, and before starting I will give you delegated authority over Kentucky and Mississipi Alabama &c. whereby there will be unity of action behind me. I will want you to hold Chattanooga and Decatur in force, and on the occasion of my departure of which you shall have ample notice to watch Hood close. I think he will follow me, at least with his Cavalry in which Event I want you to push south from Decatur and the head of the Tennessee for Columbus Miss. and Selma—not absolutely to reach these points but to divert or pursue according to the state of facts. If however Hood moves on you, you must act defensively on the Line of the Tennessee. I will ask and you may also urge that at the same time Canby act vigorously up the Alabama River. I do not fear that the Southern Army will again make a lodgment on the Mississipi, for past events demonstrate how rapidly armies can be raised in the North West on that question and how easily handled & supplied. The only hope of a southern success is in the remote regions difficult of access. We now have a good entering wedge, and Should drive it home. It will take some time to complete these details and I hope to hear from you fully in the meantime. We must preserve a *large* amount of secrecy, and I may actually change the ultimate point of arrival, but not the main object. I am &c.

W. T. Sherman
Maj. Genl.

ALS, MiU-C: James S. Schoff Civil War Collection; *OR*, I, 39: pt. 3, 377–78 (dated October 20).

TO ULYSSES S. GRANT

Allatoona 7.30 p.m.
Oct. 9th 1864

Lt. Gen. Grant
City Point

It will be a physical impossibility to protect this road now that Hood, Forrest, Wheeler and the whole batch of Devils are turned loose without home or habitation. I think Hoods movements indicate a direction to the end of the Selma and Talladega road to Blue Mountain about sixty miles south west of Rome from which he will threaten Kingston, Bridgeport and Decatur and I propose we break up the road from Chattanooga and strike out with wagons for Milledgeville Millen and Savannah.

Until we can repopulate Georgia it is useless to occupy it, but the utter destruction of its roads, houses, and people will cripple their military resources. By attempting to hold the roads we will lose a thousand men monthly and will gain no result. I can make the march and make Georgia howl. We have over 8000 cattle and 3,000,000 pounds of bread but no corn, but we can forage in the interior of the state[.][1]

W. T. Sherman
M. Genl.

Telegram, DNA: RG 107, Records of the Office of the Secretary of War, Telegrams Collected (Bound); *OR*, I, 39: pt. 3, 162.

1. See WTS to USG, October 11, 1864, n. 1.

TO GEORGE H. THOMAS

Cipher

Head Quarters Mil. Div.
of the Miss.
In the Field Allatoona, Oct. 9th 1864.

Maj. Genl. Thomas.
Nashville.

I came up here to relieve our Road. 20th Corps at Atlanta. Hood reached our Road and broke it up between Big Shanty and Acworth and attacked Allatoona but was repulsed. We have plenty of bread and meat but forage scarcer. I want to destroy all the Road below Chattanooga including Atlanta and make for the Seacoast. We cannot defend this long line of Road.

Replace all the Guards on the Road down as far as Chattanooga and have a Reserve force for the defense of Tennessee and bring back your Divisions of Newton and Morgan.

We can have the Road repaired in a week and have plenty of grub in the meantime, but I expect Hood will make a break at Kingston Rome or some other point soon.

Sorry that Forrest escaped—I doubt the necessity of repairing the Road about Elk River and Athens, and suggest that you wait before giving orders for repairs.

W. T. Sherman

Maj. Genl. Comdg.

Lbk, DNA: RG 94, Records of the Adjutant General's Office, Generals' Books and Papers, William T. Sherman, Letterbook 13; *OR*, I, 39: pt. 3, 169–70.

TO ULYSSES S. GRANT

Cartersville Ga. 12 m. Oct. 10, 1864

Lieut. Genl. U. S. Grant,

City Point,

Dispatch about Wilson just rec'd.[1]

Hood is now crossing Coosa twelve miles below Rome bound west.

If he passes over to the Mobile and Ohio road had I not better execute the plan of my letter sent by Col. Porter,[2] and leave Thomas with troops now in Tennessee to defend the State? He will have an ample force when the reinforcements ordered reach Nashville.

W. T. Sherman

Maj. Genl. Cmdg.

Telegram, DNA: RG 107, Records of the Office of the Secretary of War, Telegrams Collected (Bound); *OR*, I, 39: pt. 3, 174.

1. USG telegraphed WTS on October 4 that General James H. Wilson was being sent to him as the "good Cavalry officer" he had requested on September 23. *PUSG*, 12:194–95n; WTS to USG, September 23, 1864, *PUSG*, 12:194n.

2. WTS to USG, September 20, 1864, above.

TO ULYSSES S. GRANT

Kingston Ga. 11 A.M. Oct. 11. 1864

Lieut. Gen. U. S. Grant

City Point Va"

Hood moved his army from Palmetto Station across by Dallas and Cedartown and is now on the Coosa south of Rome. He threw one Corps on my road at Ackworth and I was forced to follow. I hold Atlanta with the 20th Corps and have strong detachments along my line. These reduce my active force to a comparatively small army. We cannot remain here on the defensive. With 25,000 men and the bold Cavalry he has he can constantly break my road. I would infinitely prefer to make a wreck of the roads and of the country from Chattanooga to Atlanta, including the latter City, Send back my wounded and worthless and with my effective army move through Georgia smashing things to the sea.

Hood may turn into Tennessee and Kentucky but I believe he will be forced to follow me.

Instead of being on the defensive I would be on the offensive, instead of guessing at what he means to do he would have to guess at my plans. The difference in war is full twenty five per cent.

I can make Savannah, Charleston, or the mouth of Chattahoochie. Answer quick as I know we will not have the telegraph long.[1]

> W. T. Sherman
> Major General
> Commanding

Telegram, DNA: RG 107, Records of the Office of the Secretary of War, Telegrams Collected (Bound); *OR*, I, 39: pt. 3, 202.

1. USG replied that same day that he thought Hood would invade Middle Tennessee and should be stopped: "If you were to cut loose I do not believe you would meet Hood's Army but would be bushwhacked by all the old men, little boys and such railroad guards as are still left at home." He concluded, however, that "I must trust to your own judgment." *PUSG*, 12:289–90. WTS's comment about the telegraph proved correct: he never received Grant's reply. See Horace Porter, *Campaigning with Grant* (New York, 1897), 318.

TO JOHN SHERMAN

> Headquarters, Military Division
> of the Mississippi,
> Kingston, Geo., Oct. 11, 1864.

My Dear Brother,

Hood swung over against my Road & broke it this side of Marietta and forced me to come out of Atlanta to drive him off. He sheered off to the West and is now below Rome. I have taken position here where I can watch him. I still hold Atlanta in strength and have so many detachments guarding the Railroad that Hood thinks he may venture to fight me. He certainly surpasses me in the quantity and quality of cavalry which hangs all round & breaks the railroad & telegraph line every night—You can imagine what a task I have 138 miles of Rail road and my force falling off very fast. I hear some new Regiments am now arriving at Nashville & they may strengthen my Line so that I may go ahead, but Mobile or Savannah should be taken before I venture further. I am far beyond all other Columns.

I got your letter about my being for McClellan. I never said so, or thought So, or gave any one the right to think so. I almost despair of a popular Government, but if we must be so inflicted I suppose Lincoln is the best choice, but I am not a voter. Even if I am north I could not vote. I am not a citizen of any state unless it be Louisiana, & that has no vote—It is a ridiculous farce to be voting at all. No man should now vote unless he has a musket at his shoulder. It is an insult to the human Race, that when I am down here I have to turn back to protect my Road—that after 3 years Price is back in Missouri and that The Enemys Guerillas are yet almost in Sight of the Capital[1] & that too when political Conventions number tens of thousands. I wish to vote was to {enlist} and then we would have less voters and more soldiers. If the Country wont guard my communications after I have fought over this ground so help me God I will deny my country and go to Some other Land. I get an awful big mail now from strangers who feel an intense interest in me, all at once, and anxious to Know how I propose to vote. I generally refer them to Louis Napoleon who can pick out some Dutch Prison good enough for us. I am very busy, nearly all my Commanders went home after we got Atlanta leaving me alone in this time of trouble. Yrs. affectionately,

W. T. Sherman

ALS, DLC: William T. Sherman

1. Price invaded Missouri on September 19; he was forced from the state by the end of October.

TO JOHN M. SCHOFIELD

Head Quarters, Mil. Div. of the Miss.
In the Field, Ships Gap Ga.
October 17th 1864.

Genl.

Your dispatch is received.[1] Hood is not at Deer-Head Cove. We occupy Ships Gap and Lafayette.

Hood is moving South via Summersville, Alpine and Gadsden. If he enters Tennessee it will be to the Left of Huntsville, but I think he has given up all such idea.

I want the Road repaired to Atlanta, the Sick and Wounded sent north of the Tennessee, my army recomposed, and I will make the interior of Georgia feel the weight of War. It is folly for me to be moving our armies on the reports of scouts and citizens. We must maintain the offensive. Your first move on Trenton and Valley-Head was right, the move to defend Caperton's Ferry is wrong. Notify Gen. Thomas of these my views. We must follow Hood till he is beyond reach of mischief, and then assume the offensive.

[W. T. Sherman]
Maj. Gen. Comdg.

Telegram, DNA: RG 393, Military Division of the Mississippi, Telegrams Sent in the Field, Old Volume 25; *OR*, I, 39: pt. 2, 335.

1. Schofield to Sherman, October 17, 1864, forwarded to Sherman a copy of a dispatch from Thomas dated October 16 that contained the news that Hood and his men were at Deer Head's Cove. *OR*, I, 39: pt. 3, 313, 335.

TO GEORGE H. THOMAS

Hdqrs. Military Division
of the Mississippi,
In the Field, Ship's Gap, Ga.,
October 17, 1864—12 m.

General Thomas,
Nashville:

Hood won't dare go into Tennessee. I hope he will. We now occupy Ship's Gap and La Fayette, and Hood is retreating toward Alpine and Gadsden. I am moving General Garrard to-day to Dirt Town, and will move General Corse out to Coosaville, and with the main army move on Summerville. If Hood wants to go into Tennessee west of Huntsville let him go, and then we can all turn on him and he cannot escape. The gun-boats can break any bridge he may attempt above Decatur. If he attempts to cross let him do so in part, and then let a gun-boat break through his bridge. I will follow him to Gadsden, and then want my whole army united for the grand move into Georgia.

W. T. Sherman,
Major-General, Commanding.

Printed, *OR*, I, 39: pt. 3, 333.

TO HENRY W. HALLECK

Hdqrs. Military Division
of the Mississippi,
In the Field, Summerville, Ga.,
October 19, 1864.

Maj. Gen. H. W. Halleck,
Washington, D.C.:
General:

At some more leisure time I will record the facts relating to Hood's attack on my communications.[1] He has partially succeeded from the superior mobility of his columns, moving without food or wagons. I now have him turned back and am pursuing him till he will not dare turn up Will's Valley without having me at his rear and the Tennessee at his front. My opinion is he will go to Blue Mountain, the terminus of the Selma and Talladega road, where he and Beauregard will concoct more mischief. We must not be on the defensive, and I now consider myself authorized to execute my plan to destroy the railroad from Chattanooga to Atlanta, including the latter city (modified by General Grant from Dalton, &c.), strike out into the heart of Georgia, and make for Charleston, Savannah, or the mouth of the Appalachicola. General Grant prefers the middle one, Savannah, and I understand you to prefer Selma and the Alabama. I must have alternates, else, being confined to one route, the enemy might so oppose that delay and want would trouble me, but, having alternates, I can take so eccentric a course that no general can guess at my objective. Therefore, when you hear I am off have lookouts at Morris Island, S.C., Ossabaw Sound, Ga., Pensacola and Mobile Bays. I will turn up somewhere, and believe I can take Macon and Milledgeville, Augusta and Savannah, Ga., and wind up with closing the neck back of Charleston so that they will starve out. This movement is not purely military or strategic, but it will illustrate the vulnerability of the South. They don't know what war means, but when the rich planters of the Oconee and Savannah see their fences and corn and hogs and sheep vanish before their eyes they will have something more than a mean opinion of the "Yanks." Even now our poor mules laugh at the fine corn-fields, and our soldiers riot on chestnuts, sweet potatoes, pigs, chickens, &c. The poor people come to me and beg as for their lives, but my answer is, "Your friends have broken our railroads, which supplied us bountifully, and you cannot suppose our soldiers will suffer when there is abundance within reach." It will take ten days to finish up our road, during which I will eat out this flank and along down the Coosa, and then will rapidly put into execution the plan. In the mean time I ask that you give to General Thomas all the troops you can spare of the new levies, that he may hold the line of the Tennessee during my absence of, say, ninety days. I am, &c.,

W. T. Sherman,
Major-General.

Printed, *OR*, I, 39: pt. 3, 357–58.
1. Hood had broken the Western and Atlantic Railroad on October 2 and had briefly gained control of the Chattanooga-to-Atlanta railroad but was now headed for Alabama.

TO ELLEN EWING SHERMAN

Headquarters, Military Division
of the Mississippi,
In the Field, Sommerville Geo.
Oct. 19, 1864.

Dearest Ellen,

I owe you several letters but our mails have been so much interrupted that I could not write save in cypher, for a private letter of mine written with however much caution would contain much our enemy should not know. I have yours of the 11th.[1] The monument should not be changed from the original design of the Donors. You might order a hood or shelter of White Pine of the design of the Artist but if superadded of marble it would so change the original that the contributors would construe it into a reflection upon their design, in other words they would infer "theirs" imperfect to the Extent of the addition. Hood is afraid to fight me in open ground & therefore he tries to break up the Railroad which supplies my Army. First Forrest got across the Tennessee but never reached the Chattanooga Road—Next Hood with 3 Corps about 40,000 men, swung round by Dallas & broke the road at Big Shanty to Kenesaw. He stole a march on me of one day, and his men disencumbered of baggage move faster than we can. I have labored hard to cut down wagons, but spite of all I can do officers do not second me. All the Campaign I slept without a tent, and yet Doctors & teamsters & Clerks & Staff officers on one pretext or another got tents & baggage, and now we can hardly move. I[']ll Stop this or dispense with Doctors, clerks & Staff officers as "useless in War"—Hood got up as far as the Tunnel before I could head him off, but at Resaca I broke through the Gap and he at once commenced to move south, and is now beyond my reach. He may now try to enter Tennessee by way of Decatur. I shall make proper dispositions and if seconded can keep him south, but I cannot get any body to move as quick as they Should, save some of my old favorites. Corse saved Alatoona, by obeying promptly a message sent him by signals over the head of Hoods army. Mower is also coming to me, and *when I move south* I shall have some *smart* columns. I am not going to Stand on the defensive and you will soon hear of me on a bigger Road than that to Meridian, unless things take a turn not anticipated. You will have to get used to being without letters from me for some years, as it will be impossible to keep up mails much further. As to Charley being a Brig. General it is simple folly to think of it till he Commands a Regiment and a Brigade in Battle. I will give a Recommendation to no one unless he has fulfilled the above conditions. You know that I did not want him to have a staff position but recommended he should Seek the command of a Regt. & work his way up, but he *would* come on my staff spite of my advice and now I cannot do a wrong act because he is my brother. You Know that. There has been too much of this during the war, and the consequence is ⅔ of the Brigadiers are at home. But he need not be uneasy. The war will last all his life and he will have ample chances to become Lt. Genl. if he has the industry. Charley is careless you Know—He often tells me he has just written you, or is just going to, and yet you say he never writes. I do not say this is characteristic, but You Know enough of soldiering that one must be sleepless & tireless and most exact. As to Judge Moore he has gained the good will of all his superiors. Thomas has a high opinion of him, and at Jonesboro he commanded the Brigade of Regulars, and they prefer him to many of the Regular officers. He goes home too much, a fatal defect to me, but he is in the Army of the Cumberland, and Each

AL (incomplete), InND: Sherman Family Papers.

1. EES's letter of October 11–12 dealt with the Thirteenth U.S. Infantry's plans to erect a monument to Willy on his grave and her desire to add a canopy to it. SFP.

TO ELLEN EWING SHERMAN

> Headquarters, Military Division
> of the Mississippi,
> In the Field, Gaylesville Ala.
> Oct. 21, 1864.

Dearest Ellen,

I enclose a Bill of Brooks Bro. showing me in debt $12. This I honestly believe is the only debt I have in the world so pay it off. I have some money in my pocket, and have two months pay nearly due, so I can promise you $1000, before I take my final departure for the Pine Woods. Since I have become famous for taking Atlanta and writing imprudent letters I get the most wonderful medley that you Can conceive of from all parts of the world. Some are amusing but all breath the utmost respect, and cannot be disregarded. Some I toss in the camp fire—and Some I answer but usually in a very hasty imperfect manner, but it seems that my letters now even are sought after like hot cakes. As long as I am not a candidate I hope none will be published as sample of literary composition. You can read my letters & guess at the meaning, but judging from my Copy clerks, some readers would make an awful jumble of my letters, written usually in the small hours of the night, by a single candle on a box. Actually one man wrote that it was seriously contemplated once to put me up for President. That was cruel & unkind. You remember when the Solemn Committee waited on me at San Francisco to tender the Regular Democratic Nomination for Treasurer my answer was that I was ineligible because I had not graduated at the "Penitentiary[.]" If a similar committee Should be rash enough to venture the other nomination I fear I should proceed to personal violence, for I would receive a sentence to be hung and damned with infinitely more composure than to be the Executive of this Nation. I send you a few letters that may interest you as samples.

Hood escaped south down the Valley of the Chattooga to Gadsden and is en route for Blue Mountain 10 miles south of Jacksonville the End of the Selma Road, where he hopes to threaten my Road & Tennessee to keep me out of Georgia. Maybe he will & maybe he wont. If a reasonable member of the drafted now reach me I think he wont.

This Army is now ready to march to Mobile, Savannah or Charleston, and I am practising them in the art of foraging and they take to it like Ducks to water. They like pigs sheep, chickens, calves and Sweet potatoes better than

Rations. We wont starve in Georgia. Our mules are doing better on the corn fields than on the bagged corn brought by the Railroads.

Love to all.

In haste as usual—Charley reiterates he writes all the time. Yrs. Ever
W. T. Sherman

ALS, InND: Sherman Family Papers.

TO JOSEPH P. THOMPSON[1]

Headquarters, Military Division
of the Mississippi,
Gaylesville, Ala. Oct. 21, 1864.

Rev. Jos. P. Thompson
Dear Sir

I have received your letter of Oct. 3d and acknowledge the hit, but as you have wit and sense I can with safety devote to you a part of my usual nights labor. When the Soldier sleeps the General is watchful, and such are my habits and if as you say you spent some time in my camp, I beg you to bear testimony to a fact never noticed that in my camps the soldier sleeps quietly and undisturbed by Long Rolls & False alarms.

This is not accident but a truth for which I feel sure all soldiers will give me credit, and as you say, I am not the heartless Boor I am often represented. I rarely see my children, but were you to behold them watching for my expected coming, and rush to me with eyes all love, you would not say that I was heartless. Again when the final day of reckoning comes I will risk a comparison with men professing more, for examples of acts of charity where the Left hand knoweth not what the Right hand gives, but when my mind is intent on a purpose it is jealous of all clogs & obstructions.

How many of our plans have been defeated, how many lives lost because our columns have been clogged with useless baggage & civilians? Go to our Camps and towns, as you say you have done & see if the commander thinks of destroying an Enemy or is engaged in answering complaints of women, cotton and trade speculators or citizens who study to use the cover of an army to buy cheap commodities and answer on your conscience if I am not right as a Rule to declare Citizens about an army a "nuisance." The Rule is right and is proved by the exceptions. Let every thought of the mind, every feeling of the heart, every movement of a human muscle all be directed to one sole object, Successful War and consequent Peace, and you have the ideal I aim at. But all ideals are dreams but they form the directions of Real Results and the closer they can be followed the better.

But as I said, I see you have wit and sense and I will trust you to do this noble army justice. Who can know the daily toils, the dangers the hopes and fears of this vast army? I know them and all here know them and the time will come when they will return to their homes and be the living witnesses of the acts of their Fellows and leaders. For my reward I trust to them and still more in my confidence that God will not permit this fair land and this Brave People to subside into the anarchy and despotism that Jeff Davis has cut out for them.

I have this faith as clear & distinct as you see the sacrifice of Gods own Son in your mental vision to secure to us an immortal Reward. I have read the Editorials but not the sermon, but shall read it too, and in the mean time You may assure your congregation that this army fights that they may sleep in peace and enjoy the protection of a civilized government. yours

W. T. Sherman
Maj. Genl.

Copy, MiU-C: James S. Schoff Civil War Collection.

1. Thompson (1819–79) was a popular New York City clergyman, an army chaplain, and an antislavery activist.

TO EDWIN M. STANTON

Headquarters, Military Division
of the Mississippi,
In the Field, Gaylesville, Ala.
Oct. 25, 1864

Hon. E. M. Stanton
Sec. of War, Washington D.C.
Sir,

I do not wish to be considered as in any way adverse to the organization of negro Regiments further than as to its Effects on the White Race. I do wish the Fine Race of men that Peoples our Northern States should rule & determine the future destiny of America: but if they prefer trade and gain, and leave to bought substitutes & negros the fighting, (the actual conflict,) of course the question is Settled, for those who hold swords & muskets at the end of this war (which has but fairly begun) will have something to say. If negros are to fight, they too will not be content with sliding back into the status of slave, or Free Negro either. I much prefer to keep negros, yet for some time to come, in a subordinate State, for our prejudices, yours as well as mine are not yet schooled for absolute Equality. Jeff Davis has succeeded perfectly in inspiring his People with the truth, that liberty and Government are worth fighting for—that pay, and passions are silly nothings compared to the prize fought for.

Now I would aim to inspire our People also with this same idea, that it is *not* right to pay $1000 for some fellow who will run away to do his fighting, or some poor negro who is thinking of the day of Justice, but that Every young and middle aged man should be proud of the Chance to fight for the Stability of his country, without profit and without price and I would like to see all trade, commerce & manufactures *absolutely* cease till this fight is over: and I have no hesitation or concealment in saying that there is not & should not be the remotest chance of Peace again on this continent, till all this is realized: save the Peace which would result from the base & cowardly submittal to Jeff Davis terms. I would use Negros as Surplus, but not spare a single white man, not one. Any white man who dont or wont fight *now* should be killed, vanished or de-nationalized, and then we would discriminate among the noisy patriots and see who really should vote.

If the Negros fight and the whites dont of course the negros will govern. They wont ask you or me for the privilege but will simply take it, and probably revise the relation hitherto existing, and they would do right.

If however the Government have determined to push the policy to the End it is both my duty and pleasure to assist, and in that Event I should like to have Col. Bowman now comdg. the Dist. of Wilmington Delaware to organize & equip such as may fall into the custody of the Army I command. I am with respect yr. obt. servant

W. T. Sherman
Maj. Genl.
Comdg.

ALS, DLC: Edwin M. Stanton Papers; *OR*, I, 39: pt. 3, 428–29.

TO ELLEN EWING SHERMAN

Headquarters, Military Division
of the Mississippi,
In the Field, Gaylesville Ala.
Oct. 27, 1864.

Dearest Ellen,

I have just received your letter of the 16th[1] and as I have more leisure at this moment than I will likely again for a long time I will write at length. I have written not often but certainly as often as possible consistent with my manifold duties and the fear of my letters unless in cypher falling into wrong hands. Hood has swung over towards Decatur and may and probably will attempt to enter Tennessee about Huntsville, but I think there are troops enough in Tennessee, but we are expected to defend so many points that our difficulties grow exactly in proportion to our advance and the Rebels gain proportionally[.] I expect very soon now to attempt another feat in which I think I will succeed but it is hazardous and you will not hear from me for months. The War Dept. will Know my whereabouts and the Rebels and you will be able to guess. Charley went to Nashville to have his teeth fixed. I told him he would be left behind but He knew he would get back in time. I think not and suppose I understand the chances better. He is always provoked when I after each letter tell him you say he does not write to you. He uses even strong language and seems offended. One thing is certain he says he writes very often. I know he gets all your letters for I hand them to him. As to his being Brig. Genl. he must first be Colonel of a Regt. & then must Command it in battle. This will take time and all chance of promotion was & is cut off by his accepting a Staff place. I told him so at the time & a hundred times since, and I am not going to commit the folly of recommending for a General one who has not demonstrated his fitness—Mr. Lincoln says he used to be very careless about such appointments but now it is very different. There are many colonels who have commanded Brigades for 3 years, and done it well who are not promoted what would they say of me who would recommend a brother in Law, that had not even had a Regiment. As to Dayton he has not resigned. I have no vacancies on my staff, and had I would be disposed to leave them, for every staff officer must have a wagon & tent. I can get along with a fly & blanket, but the moment there is a Staff spite of all I can do, tents & wagons multiply. I am about to order the abolishment of all Head Quarters except that of the Doctors and Teamsters. Hood can march all round me and laugh, whilst I drag along with a wagon train. This wagon train in the end will defeat me. Soldiers get along well enough, but we are bow down with Generals Head Qrs. and staff. I have been making some sweeping reforms but yet there is wide Room for improvement. I might be a hundred miles further on my journey were it not for the excess of wagons and artillery, but I am sending it back. The break in our Railroad will be done tonight and if the Rebels let it alone for a few days I will get back the worthless & sick & baggage, and then cut loose. However I expect next to hear of Hood between this and Nashville.

You ask my opinion of McClellan. I have been much amused at similar inquiries of John & others in answer to a news paragraph that I pledged 99 votes of the hundred to McClellan. Of course this is the invention of some Rumor. I never said such thing. I will vote for nobody because I am not entitled to vote. Of the two, with the inferences to be drawn at home & abroad I would prefer Lincoln, though I Know that McClellan Vallandigham or even Jeff Davis if President of the U.S. would prosecute the war, and no one with more vigor than the latter. But at the time the howl was raised against Mc-Clellan I knew it was in a measure unjust, for he was charged with delinquencies that the American People are chargeable for. Thus how unjust to blame me for any misfortune now when all the Authorities & People are conspiring to break up the army till the Election is over. Our Armies vanish before our eyes and it is useless to complain because the Election is more important than war. Our armies are merely paper armies. I have 40,000 Cavalry on paper but less than 5000 in fact. A like measure runs through the whole, and So it was with McClellan. He had to fight partly with figures. Still I admit he never manifested the Simple courage & manliness of Grant, and he had too much Staff too many toadies, and looked too much to No. 1. When I was in Kentucky he would not heed my counsels, and never wrote me once, but since I have gained some notoriety at Atlanta and the papers announced as usually falsely, that I was for him, he has written me twice and that has depreciated him more in my estimation than all else.[2] He cannot be elected—Mr. Lincoln will be, but I hope it will be done quick that voters, may come to their Regiments and not give the Rebs the advantage they Know so well to take. I believe McClellan to be an honest man as to money, of good habits, discreet, and of far more than average inteligence and therefore I never have joined in the hue & cry against him. In Revolutions men fall & rise. Long before this war is over much as you hear me praised now you may hear me cursed & insulted. Read History, Read Coriolanus[3] and you will see the true measure of popular applause. Grant Sheridan & I are now the popular favorites but neither of us will survive this war. Some other must rise greater than Either of us & he has not yet manifested himself.

Some of my best officers are those whom I favored at Big Black. Corse, Mower, (illegible) Wood, Warner &c. Corse saved us Allatoona—and Mower saved Banks command up Red River. Still they are not great leaders but rather Soldiers in training. I hardly look for any real developments of military talents on our side for two years yet. Congress instead of providing an army has legislated it out of existence. In twelve months we will have no army and Jeff will walk on the track without an opponent, unless some one rises this winter. The old men have gone out, and the officers disgusted at new ones coming in over their heads have retired. We are now getting one year men, who will be discharged before they Know how to post a guard, so that I see more trouble ahead than Ever. I am satisfied the People of the United States would rise to the occasion if they were only told the truth, but everybody tells them the Rebels are played out, starved out—tired of the War &c. when if they were just to think they would see Guerillas in Sight of Washington, Louisville and St. Louis today. When we concentrate our energies to any one point as Vicksburg, Mobile or Atlanta we can take it, but the trouble is the country at large. We should as a People declare that we would have Peace and Submission to authority if we had to devastate every acre, and Should proceed to do it. A merciless Conscription should fill our Ranks, and we Should {mark} out our

Lines and go ahead leaving nothing behind, not one colum but six eight or ten. We can now live on the Corn of the South, some salt & beef on the hoof, but it discourages our men to be compelled to turn back to attend to what others in our Rear should. I would make every man north a Soldier till the War is over, and then he might go home & not before. I think at the rate we are now going it will take more than my 30 years, so you can begin to School even the younger Charley.

I am glad to hear such good accounts of the Children. I have not heard from Minnie or Lizzie for some time, but have no doubt they are progressing well. As to Tom he will need much of your attention for he is solitary and will need boys company. As to Elly & Rachel the Pony team, they will gather shells & flowers for many years yet and still be children. Master Charley must now begin to assume the human form and to manifest some of his future self. I would like to See him as a curiosity but have not the remotest Chance this year.

I cannot tell much of things hereabout. Hill is not with me, his successor and a couple of black boys fill my household as well as I expect—my horses are all well groomed and come at my bidding. We have about the Same old mess out of doors, and I Sleep on the ground with a Comfort, pillow pair of blankets & spread. It has been Cold and I have no winter socks or flannels. Those you sent from Cincinati have not come. I have telegraphed for some out of my trunk at Nashville, but have pretty much made up my mind to get along with what I have. Our Railroad is broken so often and the difficulties of the trip so great that I think somebody else gets my consignments. I suppose I will have to appeal to the Sanitary or Christian Commission—Paymasters are afraid to come down, and the Army has not been paid for *ten* months. This is a long letter and not much in it, but there is not much here that can interest you.

The town of Gaylesville that was, is now among the Past, and is converted into Soldiers huts soon to be abandoned. We have foraged close, and Guerillas & Armies wont follow this Road. That was one object of my coming. Yrs. ever,

W. T. Sherman

ALS, InND: Sherman Family Papers.

1. EES to WTS, October 16, 1864, SFP. EES had asked her husband if he could get Charley promoted to brigadier general now that he was WTS's inspector general. She asked his opinion of McClellan because it would look suspicious if she couldn't give people her husband's opinion of him. She had heard that Dayton had resigned and wanted Mrs. Miner's son appointed in his place. She was moving into the old Sherman place at last, and she and Elizabeth had patched up their relationship.

2. McClellan to WTS, September 26, 1864, DLC: WTS. He had sent congratulations on the "remarkable campaign." Having been concerned about the safety of WTS's long lines of communication, he particularly admired how WTS had circumvented the difficulty. He also sent condolences on the loss of McPherson. His other letter to WTS was not found.

WTS replied to McClellan on October 11. While thanking him for his good wishes, WTS clearly expressed his belief that "I think I understand the purpose of the South properly and that the best way to deal with them is to meet them fair & square on any issue—we must fight them. Cut into them—not talk [to] them, and pursue till they cry enough. If we relax one bit we could never hold up our head again. They would ride us roughshod." DLC: George B. McClellan Papers (the exchange is reprinted in Stephen W. Sears, ed., *The Civil War Papers of George B. McClellan, Selected Correspondence, 1860–1865* [New York, 1989], 604). Sherman's assessment of McClellan's motives was probably correct; the next day, McClellan wrote to a political ally in New York on the developments in his campaign to win public support for the presidency and then added that he had written to several prominent political figures and WTS. McClellan to Samuel L. M. Barlow, September 27, 1864, ibid., 605–6. He would later confide to this colleague that he thought "Sherman will come to grief" on the March to the Sea. Ibid., 626.

3. A reference to Shakespeare's play in which the title character, a popular hero, loathes the public that idolizes him; eventually, he is accused by an envious rival of betraying his country.

TO GEORGE H. THOMAS

Rome, Ga., October 29, 1864.

Major-General Thomas:

We have reconnoitered well down to Gadsden and Jacksonville. Hood took with him all his infantry, but left a good deal of cavalry. He started for Bridgeport and Guntersville, but my movements have thrown him clear across to the Mobile and Ohio Railroad. If he does not attack Decatur to-day he will not at all, but he will go to Tuscumbia and depend on the Mobile road. Now, I want you to be all ready for him if he enters Tennessee. He will work as fast as possible, for winter is coming, but he cannot haul supplies and will be dependent on the country.[1] I have sent Stanley back. Give him as many conscripts as possible and use him as the nucleus. I will also send Schofield back, who will relieve you of all that Knoxville branch, but if necessary break up all minor posts and get about Columbia as big an army as you can and go at him. You may hold all the cavalry and new troops except the men actually assigned to the corps with me. I would like Dalton held, but leave that to you, Chattanooga, of course, and Decatur in connection with the boats. If to make up a force adequate, it be necessary, abandon Huntsville and that line and the Huntsville and Decatur road, except as far as it facilitates an army operating toward Florence. Already the papers in Georgia begin to howl at being abandoned, and will howl still more before they are done. Get, if you can, A. J. Smith's and Mower's divisions, belonging to my army, from Missouri, and let them come to you via Clifton. Get the gun-boats to fill the Tennessee River, and that will bother him much. If you could make a good lodgment at Eastport Hood could not use the Corinth and Decatur road, for there are only seven miles of good road from East-port to Iuka. General Schofield has not got in yet, but I will push him right on to Resaca. I will give you notice when I start. All preparations are now progressing, but I want to know Hood's movements, and how well you are prepared before I start.

W. T. Sherman,

Major-General.

Printed, *OR*, I, 39: pt. 3, 498.

1. The same day Sherman informed Thomas: "I hear that the enemy has passed to the west of Decatur, and, therefore, will cross about Florence. I don't see how Beauregard can support his army; but Jeff. Davis is desperate, and his men will undertake anything possible. . . . With Decatur held and a good gun-boat three up at the head of navigation, the enemy will be bold to enter Tennessee; but we must expect anything." *OR*, I, 39: pt. 3, 499.

TO ULYSSES S. GRANT

Rome, Ga., November 1, 1864—9 a.m.

Lieut. Gen. U. S. Grant,

Comdg. Armies of the United States, City Point, Va.:

As you foresaw, and as Jeff. Davis threatened, the enemy is now in the full tide of execution of his grand plan to destroy my communications and defeat this army. His infantry, about 30,000, with Wheeler's and Roddey's cavalry, from 7,000 to 10,000, are, now in the neighborhood of Tuscumbia and Florence, and the water being low is able to cross at will. Forrest seems to be scattered from Eastport to Jackson, Paris, and the lower Tennessee and General Thomas reports the capture by him of a gun-boat and five transports. General Thomas has near Athens and Pulaski Stanley's corps, about 15,000 strong, and Schofield's corps, 10,000, *en route* by rail, and has at least 20,000 to 25,000 men, with new regiments and conscripts arriving all the time; also Rosecrans promises the two divisions of Smith and Mower, belonging to me, but I doubt if they can reach Tennessee in less than ten days. If I were to let go Atlanta and North Georgia and make for Hood, he would, as he did here, retreat to the southwest, leaving his militia, now assembling at Macon and Griffin, to occupy our conquests, and the work of last summer would be lost. I have retained about 50,000 good troops, and have sent back full 25,000, and having instructed General Thomas to hold defensively Nashville, Chattanooga, and Decatur, all' strongly fortified and provisioned for a long siege, I will destroy all the railroads of Georgia and do as much substantial damage as is possible, reaching the sea-coast near one of the points hitherto indicated, trusting that General Thomas, with his present troops and the influx of new troops promised, will be able in a very few days to assume the offensive. Hood's cavalry may do a good deal of damage, and I have sent Wilson back with all dismounted cavalry, retaining only about 4,500. This is the best I can do, and shall, therefore, when I can get to Atlanta the necessary stores, move as soon as possible.

W. T. Sherman,
Major-General.

Printed, *OR*, I, 39: pt. 3, 576–77.

TO ULYSSES S. GRANT

Rome Ga. 12 30 P.M. Nov. 2nd 1864

Lt. Gen. U. S. Grant
City Point Va.

Your despatch recd.[1] If I could hope to overhaul Hood I would turn against him with my whole force. Then he retreats to the South-West drawing me as a decoy from Georgia which is his chief object. If he ventures North of the Tenn. I may turn in that direction and endeavor to get between him and his line of retreat, but thus far he has not gone above the Tenn[.] Thomas will have a force strong enough to prevent his reaching any country in which we have an interest and he has orders if Hood turns to follow me, to push for Selma[.] No single army can catch him and I am convinced the best results will follow from thwarting Jeff Davis cherished plan of making me leave Georgia[.][2] Thus far I have confined my efforts to thwart his plans and reduced my baggage so that I can pick up and start in any direction, but would regard a pursuit of Hood as useless: Still if he attempts to invade Middle Tenn. I will hold Decatur and be prepared to move in that direction, but unless I let go Atlanta my force will not be equal to his[.]

W. T. Sherman
Maj. Genl.

Telegram, DNA: RG 107, Records of the Office of the Secretary of War, Telegrams Collected (Bound); *OR*, I, 39: pt. 3, 594–95.

1. USG to WTS, November 1, 1864, *PUSG*, 12:370–71. He asked whether WTS should "entirely settle [Hood] before starting on your proposed campaign?" Hood could go off in the opposite direction from WTS—"If you can see the chance for destroying Hood's Army, attend to that first & make your other move secondary." USG later explained that this exchange was sparked by some last-minute hesitation on the part of Lincoln and Stanton, which he believed was inspired by his chief of staff, John A. Rawlins, who stopped off in Washington on his way to Missouri to reiterate his belief that WTS should first defeat Hood before setting out on his march. To soothe their concerns, USG went through the motions of a last exchange with WTS. Mark Twain, *Autobiography*, 2 vols. (New York, 1924), 2:145. Elsewhere, however, Grant's own words reveal that he also might have entertained some last-moment doubts and needed reassurance from Sherman. See Ulysses S. Grant, *Personal Memoirs of U. S. Grant*, 2 vols. (Hartford, Conn., 1885–86), 2:376, 357, 359. Rawlins's friends later protested Grant's characterization of Rawlins's position (see, for example, Sylvanus Cadwallader, *Three Years with Grant* [1955; reprint, Lincoln, Neb., 1996], 254–55). In fact,

however, USG had sent Rawlins west to arrange for reinforcements to be sent to Tennessee to keep an eye on Hood; Rawlins first went to Washington, and his opposition to Sherman's plan was well known at headquarters. Porter, *Campaigning with Grant*, 314–16, 318.

2. See WTS to Lincoln, September 28, 1864, above.

TO ULYSSES S. GRANT

Kingston via Louisville 6 P.M.
Nov. 2d 1864.

Lt. Gen. Grant
City Point

If I turn back the whole effect of my campaign will be lost. By my movements I have thrown Beauregard well to the west and Genl. Thomas will have ample time and sufficient troops to hold him until reenforcements reach him from Mo. and recruits—We have now ample supplies at Chattanooga and Atlanta to stand a months interruption to our communications and I dont believe the Confederate army can reach our line save by cavalry raids and Wilson will have cavalry enough to checkmate that—I am clear of opinion that the best results will follow me in my contemplated movements through Georgia[.]

W. T. Sherman
Maj. Genl.

Telegram, DNA: RG 107, Records of the Office of the Secretary of War, Telegrams Collected (Bound); *OR*, I, 39: pt. 3, 595.

TO ULYSSES S. GRANT

Kingston Ga. 9 30 P.M. Nov 2d. 1864.

Lt. Gen. Grant
City Point

Despatch of 11.30 A.M. received:[1] I will go on and complete my arrangements and in a few days notify you of the day of my departure[.]

Gen. Thomas reports today that his cavalry reconnoitred within three miles of Florence yesterday and found Beauregard entrenching—I have ordered him to hold Nashville Chattanooga & Decatur all well supplied for a siege. All the rest of his army to assemble around Pulaski and to pursue Beauregard cautiously and carefully—At the same time for A. J. Smith and all reenforcements to get up to enable him to assume a bold offensive and to enable Wilson to get a good mount of Cavalry.

I think Jeff Davis will change his tune when he finds me advancing into the heart of Georgia instead of retreating and I think it will have an immediate effect on your operations at Richmond[.]

W. T. Sherman
Maj. Genl.

Telegram, DNA: RG 107, Records of the Office of the Secretary of War, Telegrams Collected (Bound); *OR*, I, 39: pt. 3, 595.

1. USG to WTS, November 2, 1864, 11:30 A.M., *PUSG*, 12:373. USG had changed his mind and now thought Thomas should take care of Hood. Sherman might have to give up too much of what he had gained to follow Hood. "I say then go on as you propose" (p. 373).

TO ULYSSES S. GRANT

Head Quarters Mil. Div. of the Miss.,

In the Field Kingston Ga., Nov. 6" 1864.

Lieut. Genl. U. S. Grant

Commander-in-Chief, City Point Va.

Dear General

I have heretofore telegraphed and written you pretty fully, but I still have some thoughts in my busy brain that should be confided to you as a Key to future developments.

The taking of Atlanta broke upon Jeff Davis so suddenly as to disturb the equilibrium of his usually well-balanced temper, so that at Augusta, Macon Montgomery and Columbia (S.C.) he let out some of his thoughts which otherwise he would have Kept to himself.[1] As he is not only the President of the Southern Confederacy, but also its commander in chief we are bound to attach more importance to his words than we would to those of a mere civil magistrate.

The whole burden of his song consisted in the statement that Shermans communications must be broken and his Army destroyed. Now it is a well settled principle that if we can prevent his succeeding in his threat, we defeat him, and derive all the moral advantages of a victory.

Thus far, Hood and Beauregard conjointly, have utterly failed to interrupt my supplies or communications with my base. My railroad and telegraph are now in good order, from Atlanta back to the Ohio River. His losses at Allatoona, Resacca, Ships Gap and Decatur exceed in number (his losses in men) ours at the Block-houses at Big Shanty, Allatoona Creek and Dalton, and the rapidity of his flight from Dalton to Gadsden, takes from him all the merit or advantage claimed for his skillful and rapid lodgement made on my Railroad. The only question in my mind is whether I ought not to have dogged him far over into Mississippi, trusting to some happy accident to bring him to bay and to battle. But I then thought that by so doing I would play into his hands by being drawn or decoyed too far away from our original line of advance. Besides I had left at Atlanta a Corps and railroad guards back to Chattanooga, which might have fallen an easy prey to his superior Cavalry. I felt compelled to what is usually a mistake in war—divide my forces—send a part back into Tennessee, retaining the ballance here. As I have heretofore informed you I sent Stanley back directly from Balesville and Schofield from Rome; both of whom have reached their destination, and thus far Hood who had brought up at Florence, is farther from my communications than when he started, and I have in Tennessee a force numerically greater than his; well commanded and well organized, so I feel no uneasiness on the score of Hood reaching my main communications. My last accounts from General Thomas, are to 9.30 last night; when Hoods Army was about Florence in great distress about provisions, as he well must be. But that devil Forrest was down about Johnsonville, and was making havoc among the Gunboats and Transports, but Schofields troops were arriving at Johnsonville, and a fleet of Gunboats reported coming up from below able to repair that trouble. But you Know that that line of supplies was only opened for Summers use, when the Cumberland could not be depended upon. We now have abundant supplies at Atlanta, Chattanooga and Nashville with the Louisville and Nashville R. Road, and the Cumberland River unmolested, so that I regard Davis threat to get his Army on my rear or on my communications as a miserable failure. Now as to the second branch of my proposition. I admit that the first object should be the destruction of that Army, and if Beauregard moves his Infantry and Artillery up into that pocket about Jackson and Paris, I will feel strongly tempted to move Thomas directly against him and myself more rapidly by Decatur on Purdy to cut off his retreat. But this would involve the abandonment of Atlanta and a retrograde movement which would be very doubtful of expediency or success, for as a matter of course Beauregard who watches me with his Cavalry and his friendly Citizens would have timely notice and would slip out and escape to regain what we have carried at so much cost. I am more than satisfied that Beauregard has not the men to attack fortifications, or meet me in battle: and it would be a great achievement for him to make me abandon Atlanta by mere threats and manoeuvres.

These are the reasons which have determined my former movements. I have employed the last ten days in running to the rear the sick and wounded and worthless, and all the vast amount of Stores accumulated by our Army in the advance—aiming to organize this branch of my Army into four well commanded Corps, encumbered by only one Gun to a thousand men, and provisions and ammunition which can be loaded up in our mule teams so that we can pick up and start on the shortest notice. I reckon that by the 10″ instant this end will be reached, and by that date I also will have the troops all paid, the Presidential election over and out of our way, and I hope the early storms of November now prevailing, will also give us the chance of a long period of fine healthy weather for campaigning. Then the question presents itself—"What shall be done?" On the supposition always that Thomas can hold the line of the Tennessee, and very shortly to be able to assume the offensive as against Beauregard, I propose to act in such a manner against the material resources of the South as utterly to Negative Davis' boasted threat and promises of protection. If we can march a well appointed Army right through his territory, it is a demonstration to the World, foreign and domestic, that we have a power which Davis cannot resist. This may not be war, but rather Statesmanship, nevertheless, it is overwhelming to my mind that there are thousands of people abroad and in the South who will reason thus—"If the North can march an Army right through the South, it is proof positive that the North can prevail in this contest," leaving only open the question of its willingness to use that power. Now Mr. Lincolns election which is assured, coupled with the conclusion thus reached makes a complete logical whole.

Even without a battle, the result operating upon the minds of sensible men, would produce fruits more than compensating for the expense, trouble and risk.

Admitting this reasoning to be good, that such a movement *per se* be right, still there may be reasons why one route would be better than another. There are three from Atlanta South East, South and South West all open, with no serious enemy to oppose at present.

The first would carry me across the only East and West Railroad remaining in the Confederacy, which would be destroyed and thereby sever the communications between the Armies of Lee and Beauregard. Incidentally I might destroy the enemys Depots at Macon and Augusta, and reach the Sea shore at Charleston or Savannah, from either of which points I could reinforce our Armies in Virginia. The second, and easiest route would be due South, following substantially the Valley of Flint River, which is very fertile and well supplied, and fetching up on the navigable waters of the Apalachicola, destroying *en-route* the same Railroad taking up the Prisoners of War still at Andersonville, and destroying about four hundred Thousand (400,000) Bales of Cotton near Albany and Fort Gaines. This however would leave the Army in a bad position for future movements.

The third down the Chatthoochee to Opelika and Montgomery, thence to Pensacola or Tensas Bayou in communication with Fort Morgan. This latter route would enable me at once to cooperate with Genl. Canby in the reduction of Mobile and occupation of the line of the Alabama.

In my judgement the first would have a material effect upon your Campaign in Virginia—the second would be the safest of execution, but the third would more properly fall within the sphere of my own command, and have a direct bearing upon my own enemy Beauregard. If therefore I should start before I hear further from you or before further developments turn my course, you may take it for granted that I have moved *via* Griffin to Barnsville, that I break up the road between Columbus and Macon *good* and then if I feint on Columbus, will move *via* Macon and Millan to Savannah, or if I feint on Macon you may take it for granted I have shot off towards Opelika, Montgomery, and Mobile Bay or Pensacola. I will not attempt to send Couriers back, but will trust to the Richmond papers to Keep you well advised. I will give you notice by telegraph of the exact time of my departure.

General Steedman is here to clear the Railroad back to Chattanooga, and I will see that the road is broken completely between the Etowah and Chattahoochee including their bridges; and that Atlanta itself is utterly destroyed. I am with respect

W. T. Sherman
Maj. Genl.

Lbk, DNA: RG 393, Records of the Military Division of the Mississippi, Letters Sent in the Field; *OR*, I, 39: pt. 3, 658–61.

1. See WTS to Lincoln, September 28, 1864, above. Davis's speaking tour was designed to bolster Confederate morale in Georgia in the aftermath of the fall of Atlanta. One historian has observed that in his remarks the Confederate president "let his enthusiasm lead him to commit some rather severe breaches of military secrecy," offering Grant and Sherman some insight on future Confederate military operations. See Steven E. Woodworth, *Jefferson Davis and His Generals: The Failure of Confederate Command in the West* (Lawrence, Kans., 1990), 293.

TO PHILIP H. SHERIDAN

Headquarters Military Division
of the Mississippi,
In the Field, Kingston, Ga.,
November 6, 1864.

Maj. Gen. Philip H. Sheridan,
Commanding Middle Division:
Dear General:

I have been wanting to write to you for some days, but have been troubled by an acute pain in my shoulder resulting from recent exposure. I wish to assure you of the intense interest I feel in your personal and official success. If I have not caused the burning of as much gunpowder as our mutual friend Grant in your honor, I can assure you that our army down in Georgia have expended an equal amount of yelling and noisy demonstration at your success. I notice particularly the prominent fact that you in person turned the tide in the recent battle of Cedar Creek. You have youth and vigor, and this single event has given you a hold upon an army that gives you a future better than older men can hope for. I am satisfied, and have been all the time, that the problem of this war consists in the awful fact that the present class of men who rule the South must be killed outright rather than in the conquest of territory, so that hard, bull-dog fighting, and a great deal of it, yet remains to be done, and it matters little whether it be done close to the borders, where you are, or farther in the interior, where I happen to be; therefore, I shall expect you on any and all occasions to make bloody results. I beg to assure you of my warm personal attachment and respect.

I am, with respect, your friend,
W. T. Sherman,
Major-general.

Printed, *OR*, I, 43: pt. 2, 552–53.

TO JOHN E. SMITH

Hdqrs. Military Division
of the Mississippi,
In the Field, Kingston, Ga.,
November 8, 1864.

Brig. Gen. John E. Smith,
Cartersville, Ga.:

Arrest some six or eight citizens known or supposed to be hostile. Let one or two go free to carry word to the guerrilla band that you give them forty-eight hours' notice that unless all the men of ours picked up by them in the past two days are returned, Kingston, Cassville, and Cartersville will be burned, as also the houses of the parties arrested. I suppose the band of guerrillas is known to you; and you can know where to strike.

W. T. Sherman,
Major-General.

Printed, *OR*, I, 39: pt. 3, 703.

TO MARIA BOYLE EWING SHERMAN AND MARY ELIZABETH SHERMAN

Headquarters, Military Division
of the Mississippi.
In the Field, Kingston Geo.,
Novr. 9, 1864

Dear Minnie and Lizzie

I got Uncle Charley to write you a letter today because my arm pains me so much if I attempt to write on a table. I have caught Cold in it by sleeping on the ground. I hate to confess to Rheumatism or Neuralgia, but it is one or the other, but by putting a book on my Knee I can write with less pain. I did not get your letters sent by the Priest Father {Crory} till tonight and I was so glad to hear you were not homesick, but so very happy at school that I determined to write you a short letter although every motion of my hand was as painful as a toothache.

It is now raining but as soon as the storm clears up I am going to make another campaign that I hope will prove as successful as that of Atlanta and after it is over I will try to come & see you. I want to See you very much, indeed I cannot Say how much, and then I can tell you all about the things of which you hear so much but Can Know so little. War is something about which you should not concern yourself and I am now fighting that you may live in peace. I am not fighting for myself but for you and the little children, who have more to live than us older People. But if I do lose my life I Know there will be some people still living who will take care of you. Mama tells me the baby is quite sick, and she is afraid he will not get well. I hope that he will live long and take poor Willy's place in our Love. Mama also tells me how smart Elly & Rachel are, but I am like Lizzie and wonder why they aint smart when we are at home. You may not hear of me for some time but I will turn up if alive. Give my love to Sister Angela, to Aunt Mary & all our little Cousins, and believe me always thinking of you, no matter how great the danger. Yr. father,

W. T. Sherman

ALS, OHi: William T. Sherman Papers.

TO CHARLES A. DANA

Kingston, Ga., November 10, 1864—
8.30 p.m.
(Received 11th.)

Hon. C. A. Dana,
Assistant Secretary of War:

If indiscreet newspaper men publish information too near the truth, counteract its effect by publishing other paragraphs calculated to mislead the enemy—such as "Sherman's army has been much reinforced, especially in the cavalry, and he will soon move by several columns in circuit, so as to catch Hood's army;" "Sherman's destination is not Charleston, but Selma, where he will meet an army from the Gulf," &c.

W. T. Sherman,
Major-General.

Printed, *OR*, I, 39: pt. 3, 727.

TO PHILEMON B. EWING

                              Head-Quarters Military Division
                              of the Mississippi,
                              In the Field Kingston Geo.
                              Novr. 10, [1864]

Dear Phil,

I got yours enclosing Mrs. Goddards letter. I answered the latter through one of my staff in the most polite terms possible, complimenting all parties but declining the Services of the Italian Major on the Score that it is impracticable for him to reach me. The real truth is however I have positive objections to a large staff, especially to Foreign officers who require too much *nursing*. We got yesterday the *Commercial* of the 4th containing your fathers speech. Apart from the natural partiality for everything emanating from him, I regard this Speech as the only one that reduces to plain terms many vague thoughts I have long entertained & expressed though rudely of Course, and confirms me in the belief that we are not fighting Davis alone, but all the elements of Anarchy, which have organized resistance to an attempted civilized and compact Government. I do honestly believe I crave Peace as much as any man living, and that in feeling and prejudice I have if anything leaned to the South, still in adherence to Principle I have steered my Course as straight as the currents of events would permit. If spite of my efforts at mediocrity, and subordination, if my name must go to History, I prefer it should not as the enemy to the South, or any mere system of labor which however objectionable has cleared the Forest & Canebrake and developed a wealth otherwise latent, but against mobs, vigilance Committees and all the other phases of sedition and anarchy which have threatened and still endanger the Country which our Children must inherit.

I always Knew you would share with me any honors naturally falling to my share. I believe they exalt me as little as possible, but when I have manifested ability I Simply ask it to be appreciated by military men, and I observe with satisfaction that my course attracts much attention in Europe, where unhindered by local prejudices they realize actual facts better than our own People do. I run more risks than any of our Generals and must take the consequences. To command as I have done a large army smoothly & successfully forces me to accept the name of General with all its attendant responsibilities and I only hope I may come out as well at the end as now. I feel more troubled by the unmeasured faith Grant has in me—He never speaks of himself but always says that Sherman is the man—I fear this, and would much rather occupy a lower seat.

Ellens arrangements for the winter seem the best possible. I have sent her a check for 1100 Dollars, which must Suffice her till I am disposed of, or out of the woods. Even with the Past to my credit the world owes her & my children an honorable maintainance.

Be assured of my continued affection & remembrance of all the family. Yrs.
W. T. Sherman

ALS, Atlanta, Ga.: Private Collection of C. Parke Day.

TO THOMAS EWING SHERMAN

Head-Quarters Military Division
of the Mississippi,
In the Field Kingston Geo.
Novr. 10, 1864

Dear Tommy,

I have not had a letter from you for a long time, but Mama writes me often and tells me how good a boy you are, and how you like to go to the farm in the time of gathering grapes and apples. That is right, get your share of fruit now, and be careful not to eat too many at any one time. Do you remember the time you and Willy & I gathered the Chestnuts on that tree by the Rock, and afterwards the walnuts in the tiller wagon. In a short time you will be able to drive Old Sara in a wagon & gather your own walnuts & hickory nuts. I well remember our taking Willy out by Mount Pleasant where we gathered a bag of hickory nuts and poor little fellow, not as big as you now are, he was so happy and so proud to carry his own bag of hickory nuts. People write to me that I am now a Great General, and if I were to come home they would gather round me in crowds & play music and all such things. That is what the People call fame & Glory, but I tell you that I would rather come home quietly and have you & Willy meet me at the cars than to hear the Shouts of the People. Willy will never meet us again in this world and you and I must take care of the family as long as I live and then will be your turn. So you see you have a good deal to do. You have much to learn, but while your body is growing up strong as a man you will have time to learn all I know & more too. Mama tells me that the baby is very sick but I hope he is now well and that he too will grow up and help you, but let what happen always remember that on you now rests the care of our family. Minnie & Lizzie will soon be young ladies, will marry and change their names, but you will always be a Sherman and must represent the family.

Mama will soon go to St. Marys. I dont know much about that School, but I dont care much about the School you can learn in any school if you want to, and if you dont want to learn, the School wont do much good—as it depends more on you than the Schoolmaster, and I know in time you will be ambitious to learn as fast as other boys of your age. I want you also to learn to ride, so if I come home you can go along, when I want to ride on horseback. The girls can ride in carriages but boys & men are better on a saddle. I am told you are all very fond of the baby, and am glad of it. I have not seen him yet, and expect he will be a big fellow before I do. Yr. loving father,

W. T. Sherman

ALS, InNd: Sherman Family Papers.

TO HENRY W. HALLECK

Kingston, Ga., November 11 1864,
midnight.
(Received 5.30 a.m. 12th.)

Major-General Halleck,
Chief of Staff:

My arrangements are now all complete, and the railroad cars are being sent to the rear. Last night we burned all foundries, mills, and shops of every kind in Rome, and to-morrow I leave Kingston with the rear guard for Atlanta, which I. propose to dispose of in a similar manner, and to start on the 16th on the projected grand raid. All appearances still indicate that Beauregard has got back to his old hole at Corinth, and I hope he will enjoy it. My army prefers to enjoy the fresh sweet-potato fields of the Ocmulgee. I have balanced all the figures well, and am satisfied that General Thomas has in Tennessee a force sufficient for all probabilities, and I have urged him the moment Beauregard turns south to cross the Tennessee at Decatur and push straight for Selma. To-morrow our wires will be broken, and this is probably my last dispatch. I would like to have General Foster to break the Savannah and Charleston road about Pocotaligo about December 1 All other preparations are to my entire satisfaction.

W. T. Sherman,
Major-general.

Printed, *OR*, I, 39: pt. 3, 740.

TO GEORGE H. THOMAS

Kingston, November 11, 1864—
12 midnight.

Maj. Gen. George H. Thomas:

Dispatch of to-night received. All right. I can hardly believe that Beauregard would attempt to work against Nashville from Corinth as a base at this stage of the war, but all information seems to point that way. If he does you will whip him out of his boots, but I rather think you will find commotion in his camp in a day or two. Last night we burned Rome, and in two or more days will burn Atlanta, and he must discover that I am not retreating, but on the contrary fighting for the very heart of Georgia. About a division of cavalry made its appearance this morning south of the Coosa, opposite Rome, and fired on the rear guard as it withdrew. Also, two days ago some of Iverson's cavalry, about 800, approached Atlanta from the direction of Decatur with section of guns, and swept around toward White Hall, and disappeared in the direction of Rough and Ready. These also seem to indicate that Beauregard expects me to retreat. I hear of about 1,500 infantry down at Carrollton, and also some infantry at Jonesborough, but what number 1 cannot estimate. Those are all the enemy I know to be in this neighborhood, though a rumor is that Breckinridge has arrived with some from Western Virginia. To-morrow I begin the move-merit laid down in my Special Field Orders, No. 115, and shall keep things moving thereafter. By to-morrow morning all trains will be at or north of Kingston, and you can have the exclusive use of all the roll-ing-stock. By using detachments of recruits and dismounted cavalry in your fortifications you will have Generals Schofield and Stanley and General A. J. Smith, strengthened by eight or ten new regiments and all of Wilson's cavalry. You could safely invite Beauregard across the Tennessee River and prevent his ever returning. I still believe, however, that public clamor will force him to turn and follow me, in which event you should cross at Decatur and move directly toward Selma as far as you can transport supplies. The probabilities are that the wires will be broken to-morrow and that all communication will cease between us, but I have directed the main wire to be left, and will use it if possible, and wish you to do the same. You may act, however, on the certainty that I sally from Atlanta on the 16th instant with about 60,000, well provisioned, but expecting to live chiefly on the country.

W. T. Sherman,
Major-General.

Printed, *OR*, I, 39: pt. 3, 746–47.

TO ELLEN EWING SHERMAN

Headquarters, Military Division
of the Mississippi,
In the Field Kingston, Geo.,
Novr. 12, 1864

Mrs. W. T. Sherman
Lancaster, Ohio

We start today. My arm is quite well. The box of clothing came last night. I have all your letters too including Novr. 3.

Write no more till you hear of me. Good bye.

W. T. Sherman

ALS, NjP: Andre deCoppet Collection.

CHAPTER 13

December 13, 1864–February 24, 1865

From mid-November to early December there was not a word from Sherman or his army. Abraham Lincoln, anxious about the fate of some sixty thousand soldiers and their commander, tried to conceal his concern, telling one crowd, "We all know where he went in at, but I can't tell where he will come out at." Grant, his faith in Sherman complete, was far less concerned. Following his lieutenant's progress in the Southern press, he readied supplies to be sent to Savannah and arranged for the delivery of the army's mail.[1] Toward the end of the second week in December reports filtered northward that Sherman was outside Savannah, having arrived on December 10. Eleven days later his men occupied the evacuated city, although once more the Yankees failed to cut off the retreat of the Rebel garrison. Sherman offered the city to the president as a Christmas gift.

Although much would be made in later years about what Sherman's men did—and didn't—do on their excursion through Georgia, Sherman did little more than to report his success in foraging and stripping the land of resources. Only dimly aware of the progress of John Bell Hood's counterstroke into Tennessee, he was relieved when he learned that John M. Schofield at Franklin and George H. Thomas at Nashville had achieved what he had failed to do—put Hood's army out of commission. The result vindicated his decision to set forth on his march; however, had Schofield and Thomas failed, it would have seriously dampened the celebration of victory at Christmastide 1864.

Some tempers still flare when the topic of discussion concerns what exactly happened on the March to the Sea. It is clear that some of the more passionate and vivid accounts of the destruction wrought by Union soldiers are the product of heated and bitter imaginations. Property, not people, remained the primary target of their destructiveness; incidents of rape (at least against white women) were both rare and summarily punished. And the Yankees were not alone in terrorizing the countryside, for Confederate cavalry, deserters from both sides, and bands of blacks and whites contributed their share to the chaos. Finally, as Sherman himself observed, "Sweeping around generally through Georgia for the purpose of inflicting damage would not be good generalship." Rather, what he aimed to do was to intimidate and terrorize

Southern whites in order to crack their will to persist in their quest for independence. It was psychological warfare, and it worked. One sign of his success is the durability of the myth that his men destroyed all that was before them. Nor did he have any patience with those who protested. "These people made war upon us, defied and dared us to come south to their country, where they boasted they would kill us and do all manner of horrible things," he later remarked. "We accepted their challenge, and now for them to whine and complain of the natural and necessary results is beneath contempt."[2]

Accounts of Sherman's march that emphasize its destructiveness overlook his occupation of Savannah. Its population acquiesced in defeat; able to retain possession of the city as a future base of operations, Sherman left it alone. He sought to curry the favor of its white residents as a way to win back their allegiance to the Union, but he was firm when he felt it proper, especially when merchants and agents tried to lay claim to the cotton he had captured when he occupied the city. Again his position on emancipation and black enlistment drew fire from antislavery advocates, including Chief Justice Salmon P. Chase; when Secretary of War Edwin M. Stanton visited Sherman in January 1865, he asked a delegation of blacks to discuss how they felt about the general. Ten days later, on January 16, Sherman issued Special Field Order No. 15, setting aside an area extending thirty miles inland from Charleston south to the St. Johns River in Florida for black refugees. Others saw in this proposal a chance for blacks to gain control of their own land; Sherman later asserted that it was a temporary measure, designed in part to deter blacks from interfering with his operations.

Sherman understandably gloried in his military achievements, offering comparisons to past operations in military history, and boasted that everyone, including Grant, now leaned on him. Not even the news that his youngest son, Charles, had died, had much effect on his spirits, for he had never seen the child—although the death brought back memories of Willy once more. Sherman was wise enough to discourage talk of his own elevation to the rank of lieutenant general, even though Grant would have retained his position as general in chief. Instead, he devoted his energies to mapping out his next move, convincing Grant that it would be far better for him to march northward through the Carolinas than to transport his command by water to Richmond. On the face of it, Sherman's argument made sense, especially after Grant discovered that he lacked sufficient transportation for a transfer by water, but it is also evident that Sherman was eager to bring the war home to South Carolina. Even Georgians prodded him to pay their neighbors a visit. As Sherman later observed, "My aim then was, to whip the rebels, to humble their pride, to follow them to their inmost recesses, and make them fear and dread us."[3]

At the end of January Sherman commenced his march into South Carolina. Once more, as his columns plunged into the interior of the Palmetto State, his correspondent's pen fell still. Thus it would not be until March that family and friends would hear him comment on what would become perhaps the most controversial issue connected with his campaigns—the burning of Columbia, the state capital. There is little doubt that South Carolina held a special place in the general's heart. "You need not be so careful there about private property as we have been," he advised Army of Georgia commander Henry W. Slocum. "The more of it you destroy the better it will be. The people of South Carolina should be made to feel the war, for they brought it on and are responsible more than anyone else for our presence here. Now is the time to punish them." He did not order Columbia to be burned; indeed, fires had broken out in the city before Sherman's men occupied it, for in his haste to withdraw, Wade Hampton had ordered his men to set fire to bales of cotton rather than to let them fall into the hands of the Yankees: these unwatched fires were at the root of what followed. While some Union soldiers rejoiced in the result and helped spread the blaze, Sherman took steps to contain it, although he did not regret the result, resting content with placing responsibility for what happened squarely on Hampton's shoulders. By the end of the month he was on his way to North Carolina, with the end of the war coming into sight.[4]

1. Lincoln, "Response to a Serenade," December 6, 1864, *CWAL*, 8:154; USG to WTS, December 3, 1864, DLC: WTS.

2. Michael Fellman, *Citizen Sherman* (New York, 1995), and John F. Marszalek, *Sherman: A Soldier's Passion for Order* (New York, 1993), offer evaluations of the march; see also Mark Grimsley, *The Hard Hand of War: Union Military Policy toward Southern Civilians, 1861–1865* (New York, 1995), chaps. 8 and 9; Lee Kennett, *Marching through Georgia: The Story of Soldiers and Civilians during Sherman's Campaign* (New York, 1995); and Brooks D. Simpson, introduction to Henry Hitchcock, *Marching with Sherman* (1927; reprint, Lincoln, Neb., 1995).

3. *PM*, 2:249.

4. See in particular Marion B. Lucas, *Sherman and the Burning of Columbia* (College Station, Tex., 1976), and Charles Royster, *The Destructive War: William Tecumseh Sherman, Stonewall Jackson, and the Americans* (New York, 1991); Marszalek, *Sherman*, 320.

TO HENRY W. HALLECK

On Board Dandelion,
Ossabaw Sound—
Dec. 13: 11:50 P.M. 1864

Genl. H. W. Halleck,
Washington.

Today, at 5 P.M. Genl. Hazen's[1] Division of the 15th Corps carried Fort McAllister by assault capturing its entire Garrison and stores. This opened to us the Ossabaw Sound, and I pulled down to this Gunboat to communicate with the Fleet. Before opening communication, we had completely destroyed all the Railroads leading into Savannah and invested the city. The Left is on the Savannah River, 3 miles above the city and Right on the Ogeechee, at King's Bridge. Were it not for the swamps, we could march into the city; but as it is I would have to assault at one or two places, over narrow causeways, leading to much loss; whereas in a day or two with my communications restored, and the Batteries in position within short Range of the city I will demand its surrender.

The army is in splendid order, and equal to any thing. Weather has been fine and supplies abundant. Our march was most agreeable, and we were not at all molested by Guerillas. We reached Savannah three days ago, but, owing to Fort McAllister, we could not communicate, but now we have McAllister we can go ahead. We have already captured two boats in the Savannah River, and prevented their Gunboats from coming down, and if Gen. Foster[2] will prevent the escape of the Garrison of Savannah and its people by land across South Carolina, we will capture all. I estimate the population at 25,000, and the Garrison at 15,000. Genl. Hardee commands. We have on hand plenty of meat, salt and potatoes. All we need is bread and I have sent to Port Royal for that. We have not lost a wagon on the trip but have gathered in a large supply of negros, mules, horses, &c. and our teams are in far better condition than when we started. My first duty will be to clear the army of surplus negros, mules and horses, and suppose Genl. Saxton[3] can relieve me of these.

I am writing on board a dispatch boat down Ossabaw at midnight, and have to go back to where I left my horse, 8 miles up in a Row boat, and thence 15 miles over to our Lines by daylight so that I hope this will be accepted as an excuse for this informal letter, but I know you are anxious to hear of our safety and good condition. Full and detailed Reports of the events of the past month will be prepared at a more leisure moment and in the meantime I can only say that I hope by Christmas to be in possession of Savannah, and by the New Year to be ready to resume our Journey to Raleigh. The whole army is crazy to be turned loose in Carolina; and with the experience of the past 30 days, I judge that a month's Sojourn in South Carolina would make her less bellicose. The Editors in Georgia profess to be indignant at the horrible barbarities of Sherman's army, but I Know the people dont want our visit repeated. We have utterly destroyed over 200 miles of Railroad, and consumed stores & provisions that were essential to Lee's & Hood's armies. A similar destruction of Roads & Resources hence to Raleigh would compel General Lee to come out of his entrenched Camp. I hope Genl. Thomas has held Hood. My last accounts are of the fight at Franklin,[4] but Rebel papers state that Decatur Alabama has been evacuated. This I regret though it is not essential to the

Future. If Hood is making any real progress, I would not hesitate to march hence, after taking Savannah for Montgomery which would bring him out of Tennessee, but it seems to me that winter is a bad time for him. I will try & see Admiral Dahlgren[5] and Genl. Foster before demanding the Surrender of Savannah, which I do not propose to make till my batteries are able to open. The quick work made with McAllister, and the opening communication with our fleet, and consequent independence for supplies, dissipates all their boasted threats to head me off and Starve the army. Their efforts thus far have been puerile, and I regard Savannah as already gained. Yrs. Truly

W. T. Sherman
Maj. Genl.

ALS, DLC: Edwin M. Stanton; *OR*, I, 44:701–2.

1. Brigadier General William B. Hazen (1830–87), USA, was commanding the Second Division, Fifteenth Corps.

2. Major General John G. Foster (1823–74), USA, was commanding the Department of the South.

3. Brigadier General Rufus Saxton Jr. (1824–1908), USA, commanded the District of Beaufort, South.

4. Schofield had defeated Hood's forces at Franklin, Tennessee, on November 30.

5. Admiral John A. Dahlgren (1809–70), USN, was commanding the South Atlantic Blockading Squadron.

TO ULYSSES S. GRANT

Headquarters, Military Division
of the Mississippi,
In the Field, Near Savannah Ga.
Dec. 16" 1864

Lieut. Genl. U. S. Grant
Commander in Chief, City Point, Virginia.
General,

I received, day before yesterday, at the hands of Lieut. Dunn,[1] your letter of Dec. 3d[2] and last night at the hands of Col. Babcock,[3] that of Dec. 6th.[4] I had previously made you a hasty scrawl from the tug-boat "Dandelion" in Ogeechee River, advising you that the Army had reached the sea coast, destroying all rail-roads across the State of Georgia, and investing closely the City of Savannah, and had made connection with the fleet. Since writing that note I have in person met and conferred with Genl. Foster and Admiral Dahlgren, and made all the arrangements which I deemed essential to reducing the city of Savannah to our possession. But, since the receipt of yours of the 6th I have initiated measures looking principally to coming to you with 50.000 or 60.000 Infantry and incidentally to take Savannah, if time will allow. At the time we carried Fort McAllister by assault so handsomely—with its 22 guns and entire garrison, I was hardly aware of its importance: but since passing down the river with Genl. Foster and up with Admiral Dahlgren, I realize how admirably adapted are Ossabaw Sound and Ogeechee river to supply an Army operating against Savannah—Sea-going vessels can easily come to Kings Bridge, a point on Ogeechee River 14½ miles West of Savannah—from which point we have roads leading to all our camps. The country is low and sandy and cut up with marshes which in wet weather will be very bad, but we have been so favored with weather that they are all now comparatively good, and heavy details are constantly employed in double corduroying the marshes, so that I have no fears even of a bad spell of weather. Fortunately also, by liberal and judicious foraging, we reached the sea coast abundantly supplied with forage and provisions, needing nothing on our arrival except bread: of this we started from Atlanta provided with from eight (8) to twenty (20) days supply per Corps and some of the troops only had one (1) days issue of bread during the trip of thirty days: and yet they did not want—for sweet potatoes were very abundant, as well as corn meal, and our soldiers took to them naturally. We started with about 5.000 head of cattle and arrived with over 10,000—of course consuming mostly turkeys, chickens, sheep, hogs and the cattle of the country. As to our mules and horses we left Atlanta with about 2,500 wagons, many of which were drawn by mules which had not recovered from the Chattanooga starvation, all of which were replaced, the poor mules shot, and our transportation now is in superb condition—I have no doubt the State of Georgia has lost, by our operations, 15,000 first rate mules. As to horses, Kilpatrick[5] collected all his remounts, and it looks to me in riding along our column, as though every officer had three or four horses and each regiment seems to be followed by at least fifty negroes and foot-sore soldiers, riding on horses and mules. The custom was for each Brigade to send out daily a foraging party of about fifty men, on foot, who invariably returned mounted, with several wagons loaded with poultry, potatoes, &c., and as the army is composed of about forty Brigades, you can estimate approximately the quantity of horses collected. Great numbers of these were shot by my orders, because of the disorganizing effect on our Infantry of having too many idlers mounted. Genl. Easton[6] is now engaged in collecting statistics in this line, but I know the Government will never receive full accounts of our captures—although the result arrived at was fully attained—viz.: to deprive our enemy of them. All these animals I will have sent to Port Royal, or collected behind Fort McAllister, to be used by Genl. Saxton in his farming operations, or by the Quarter Masters Department after they are systematically accounted for. Whilst Genl. Easton is collecting transportation for my troops to James river, I will throw to Port Royal Island all our means of transportation I can, and collect the balance near Fort McAllister, covered by the Ogeechee River and intrenchments to be erected and for which Capt. Poe my chief Engineer is now reconnoitering the ground—but in the mean time, will act as I have begun, as though Savannah City were my objective, namely, the troops will continue to invest Savannah closely, making attacks and feints whenever we have firm ground to stand upon and I will place some 30 lb. Parrots, which I have got from Genl. Foster, in position, near enough to reach the centre of the city, and then will demand its surrender, otherwise, I will bombard the city but not risk the lives of my men by assaults across the narrow causeways by which alone I can now reach it. If I had time, Savannah with all its defendant fortifications, is already in our possession, for we hold all its avenues of supply. The enemy has made two desperate efforts to get boats from above to the city, in both of which he has been foiled—Genl. Slocum whose Left flank rests on the river—capturing and burning the first boat, and on the second instance driving back two gunboats and capturing the steamer "Resolute" with seven Naval officers and a crew of 25 seamen. Genl. Slocum occupies Argyle Island, and the upper end of Hutchinson Island, and has a Brigade on the South Carolina shore opposite, and he is very urgent to pass one of his Corps over to that shore—But in view of the change of plan made necessary by your order of the 6th I will maintain things in *Status quo* till I have got all my transportation to the rear & out of the way and until I have Sea transportation for the troops you require at James River, which I will accompany and command in person. Of course I will leave Kilpatrick with his cavalry—Say 5,300— and it may be a Division of the 15th Corps, but before determining this I must see Genl. Foster, and may arrange to shift his force, (now about the Charleston R. R. at the head of Broad River) to the Ogeechee, where, in co-operation with Kilpatricks Cavalry he can better threaten the State of Georgia than from the direction of Port Royal. Besides I would much prefer not to detach from my regular Corps any of its Veteran Divisions, and would even prefer that other less valuable troops should be sent to reinforce Foster from some other quarter. My four Corps full of experience and full of ardor coming to you *en-masse*, equal to 60,000 fighting men, will be a reinforcement that Lee cannot disregard. Indeed, with my present command I had expected, upon reducing Savannah, instantly to march to Columbia S.C. thence to Raleigh, and thence to report to you. But this would consume, it may be, six weeks time after the fall of Savannah—whereas, by Sea, I can probably reach you with my men and arms before the middle of January. I myself am somewhat astonished at the attitude of things in Tennessee—I purposely delayed at Kingston until Genl. Thomas assured me that he was *all ready*; and my last despatch from him, of the 12th November, was full of confidence: in which he promised me that he would "ruin Hood" if he dared to advance from Florence, urging me to go ahead and give myself no concern about Hoods' army in Tennessee—Why he did not turn on Hood at Franklin after checking and discomfiting him; surpasses my understanding. Indeed I do not approve of his evacuating Decatur, but think he should have assumed the offensive against Hood from Pulaski in the direction of Waynesburgh. I know full well that Gen. Thomas is slow in mind and in action: but he is judicious and brave, and the troops have great confidence in him—I still hope that he will out-manoeuvre & destroy Hood. As to matters in the South-east, I think Hardee in Savannah has good artillerists, some 5000 or 6000 good Infantry, and it may be a mongrel mass of 8,000 or 10,000 Militia and fragments. In all our marching thro' Georgia he has not forced me to use anything but a skirmish line, though at several points he had erected fortifications and tried to alarm us by bombastic threats. In Savannah he has taken refuge in a line constructed behind swamps & overflowed rice-fields, extending from a point on the Savannah River about three miles above the city, around by a branch of the Little Ogeechee—which stream is impassable from its Salt marshes and boggy swamps, crossed only by narrow causeways or common corduroy roads—There must be 25,000 citizens men, women, and children, in Savannah, that must also be fed; and how he is to feed them beyond a few days, I cannot imagine, as I know that his requisitions for corn on the interior counties were not filled, and we are in possession of the rice fields and mills which could alone be of service to him in this neighborhood. He can draw nothing from South Carolina, save from a small corner down in the South East, and that by a disused wagon road. I could easily get possession of this but hardly deem it worth the risk of making a detachment which would be in danger by its isolation from the main army—Our whole Army is in fine condition as to health, and the weather is splendid. For that reason alone I feel a personal dislike to turning North-ward. I will keep Lt. Dunn here until I know the result of my demand for the surrender of Savannah, but whether successful or not, shall not delay my execution of your orders of the 6th, which will depend alone upon the time it will require to obtain transportation by sea—I am with respect &c. Your Obt. Servant

> W. T. Sherman
> Major General, U.S.A.

LS, DLC: Edwin M. Stanton Papers; *OR*, I, 44:726–28. Grant endorsed this letter on December 20, "Respectfully forwarded to the Secretary of War, for his information."

1. First Lieutenant William M. Dunn Jr. of the Eighty-third Indiana Volunteer Infantry was one of USG's staff officers.

2. USG to WTS, December 3, 1864, *PUSG*, 13:56–57. He suggested holding Savannah "to get controll of the only two through routes, from East to West, possessed by the enemy

before the fall of Atlanta." Holding Savannah or Augusta would achieve this end. He reported Thomas's falling back to Nashville.

3. Lieutenant Colonel Orville E. Babcock (1835–84), USA, was an aide-de-camp on USG's staff.

4. USG to WTS, December 6, 1864, *PUSG*, 13:72–73. Grant had changed his mind and now thought it more important to destroy Lee than to control communications, which should take a while to reestablish in any event. He suggested that WTS establish a base on the coast with sufficient force to harass the interior and keep militia occupied. WTS and the rest of his men should join USG by water at once.

5. Major General Hugh Judson Kilpatrick (1836–81), USA, commanded the Third Division of the Cavalry Corps, Military Division of the Mississippi.

6. Brigadier General Langdon C. Easton (1814–84), USA, was chief quartermaster of the Military Division of the Mississippi.

TO ELLEN EWING SHERMAN

Headquarters, Military Division
of the Mississippi,
In the Field, near Savannah,
Dec. 16, 1864

Dearest Ellen,

I have no doubt you have heard of my safe arrival on the Coast. The fact is I never doubted the fact, but these southern Blatherscytes have been bragging of all manner of things but have done nothing. We came right along living on turkeys, chickens pigs &c. bringing along our wagons to be loaded as we started with bread &c. I suppose Jeff Davis will now have to feed the People of Georgia, instead of collecting provisions of them to feed his armies. We have destroyed nearly 200 miles of Railroad and are not yet done. As I approached Savannah I found every river & outlet fortified. The Ogeechee River emptying into Ossabaw Sound was best adapted to our use, but it was guarded by Fort McAlister, which has defied the Navy for 2 years. I ordered Howard to carry it with our Division. The detail fell on the 2nd Division of the 15th Corps and it was the handsomest thing I have seen in this war. The Division is the same I commanded at Shiloh in which Buckland, Hildebrand, Cockerill & others were, and Cockerill's Regt. was about the 1st to reach the interior and now its Garrison, but Cockerill is not in service now. As soon as we got the Fort I pulled down the Bay & opened Communication. General Foster & Admiral Dahlgren received me, manned the yards & cheered, the highest honor at sea. They had become really nervous as to our safety and were delighted at all I told them of our early success. I can now starve out Savannah unless Events call my army to Virginia. I would prefer to march through Columbia & Raleigh but the time would be too long, & we may go by sea. I have letters from Grant of the 3rd & 6th. I never saw a more confident army. The soldiers think I know everything and that they can do anything. The strength of Savannah lies in its swamps which can only be crossed by narrow causeways all of which are swept by heavy artillery. I came near being hit the 1st day, in approaching too near to reconnoiter. A negros head was shot off close by me. The weather is and has been all we could have asked[.] It is now warm & pleasant, and the Live oaks are sublime, Japonicas in blossom in the open air, and the orange is but slightly touched by the Frost. I expect Rain soon and have heavy details at work corduroying the Roads, in anticipation of such an event. I have some heavy guns coming from Port Royal, and as soon as they come I shall demand the surrender of Savannah, but will not assault, as a few days will starve out its Garrison about 15,000, and its People 25,000. I do not apprehend any army to attempt to relieve Savannah, except Lees, and if he gives up Richmond it will be the best piece of strategy ever made, to make him let go there. We have lived Sumptuously, turkeys, chickens and sweet potatos all the way, but the poor women & children will starve. All I could tell them was, if Jeff Davis expects to found an empire on the ruins of the South, he ought to afford to feed the People. Charley promises to write fully—Dayton says he wrote yesterday, and the newspapers & mischief mongers will give you gorgeous details of our march across Georgia. It was just 30 days from Atlanta till I was sitting with the Admiral in a Sea Steamer at sea. Grants letter of the 3rd proposed to bring you down to see me, but his of the 6th looked to my coming to James River. Await Events and trust to Fortune. I'll turn up when & where you least expect me. I Should like to hear how you all are, but suppose of course you are at South Bend. Write me, care of Adjt. Genl. Washington D.C.—Love to all yrs. ever

Sherman

ALS, InND: Sherman Family Papers.

TO WILLIAM J. HARDEE

Headquarters, Military Division
of the Mississippi,
In the Field, Near Savannah Ga.
Dec. 17" 1864

Genl. William J. Hardee
Comdg. Confederate Forces in Savannah,
General,

You have doubtless observed from your station at Rosedew that seagoing vessels now come through Ossabaw Sound and up Ogeechee to the rear of my Army giving me abundant supplies of all kinds, and more especially heavy ordnance necessary to the reduction of Savannah. I have already received guns that can cast heavy and destructive shot as far as the heart of your city: also I have for some days held and controlled every avenue by which the people and garrison of Savannah can be supplied, and I am therefore justified in demanding the Surrender of the City of Savannah and its dependent forts; and shall await a reasonable time, your answer, before opening with heavy ordnance.[1] Should you entertain the proposition I am prepared to grant liberal terms to the inhabitants and garrison; but should I be forced to resort to assault, or the slower and surer process of Starvation, I shall then feel justified in resorting to the harshest measures, and shall make little effort to restrain my Army, burning to avenge a great National wrong they attach to Savannah and to large Cities which have been so prominent in dragging our Country into civil war. I enclose you a copy of Genl. Hoods demand for the surrender of the town of Resacca,[2] to be used by you for what it is worth—I have the honor to be Your Obedt. Servant

W. T. Sherman
Major General

Copy, DNA: RG 108, Records of the Headquarters of the Army, Letters Received, enclosure accompanying AUS 1864, M243; OR, I, 44:737.

1. Hardee's reply, also dated December 17, is printed in PM, 2:211–12. He refused to surrender because WTS's men were at least four miles from the heart of the city and he was still "in free and constant communication with [his] department." He concluded that "with respect to the threats conveyed in the closing paragraphs of your letter (of what may be expected in case your demand is not complied with), I have to say that I have hitherto conducted the military operations intrusted to my direction in strict accordance with the rules of civilized warfare, and I should deeply regret the adoption of any course by you that may force me to deviate from them in future."

2. John Bell Hood to WTS, October 12, 1864, demanded the immediate and unconditional surrender of the post and threatened to take no prisoners if he took Resaca by assault. DLC: WTS.

TO ULYSSES S. GRANT

Headquarters, Military Division
of the Mississippi,
In the Field, Near Savannah, Ga.
Dec. 18" 1864
(8. P.M.)

Lieut. Genl. U. S. Grant
City Point—Va.
General:

I wrote you at length by Col. Babcock on the 16th" inst. As I therein explained my purpose, yesterday I made a demand on Genl. Hardee for the surrender of the City of Savannah, and to-day received his answer, refusing: copies of both are herewith enclosed. You will notice that I claim that my lines are within easy cannon range of the heart of Savannah: but General Hardee claims we are four and a half miles distant—But I myself have been to the intersection of the Charleston and Georgia Central Railroads, and the three mile post is but a few yards beyond, within the line of our pickets. The enemy has no pickets outside of his fortified line, which is a full quarter of a mile within the three (3) mile post; and I have the evidence of Mr. R. R. Cuyler, President of the Georgia Central Railroad, who was a prisoner in our hands, that the mile-posts are measured from the Exchange, which is but two squares back from the river. But by tomorrow morning I will have six 30 pounder Parrots in position, and Gen. Hardee will learn whether I am right or not— From the left of our line, which is on the Savannah River, the spires can be plainly seen: but the country is so densely wooded with pine and live oak, and lies so flat, that we can see nothing from any other portion of our lines. Genl. Slocum feels confident that he can make a successful assault at one or two points in front of the 20th″ Corps, and one or two points in front of Genl. Davis (14th″) Corps. But all of Genl. Howards troops—the right wing—lie behind the Little Ogeechee, and I doubt if it can be passed by troops in the face of an enemy—Still we can make strong feints, and if I can get a sufficient number of boats, I shall make a cooperative demonstration up Vernon River, or Warsaw Sound—I should like very much indeed to take Savannah, before coming to you—but as I wrote to you before, I will do nothing rash or hasty, and will embark for the James River as soon as Genl. Easton, who is gone to Port Royal for that purpose, reports to me that he has an approximate number of vessels for the transportation of the contemplated force—I fear even this will cost more delay than you anticipate, for already the movement of our Transports and the Gun-boats has required more time than I had expected— We have had dense fogs, and there are more mud-banks in the Ogeechee than were reported; and there are no pilots whatever—Admiral Dahlgren promised to have the channel buoyed and staked, but it is not done yet. We find only Six (6) feet water up to King's Bridge at low tide, about ten (10) up to the rice-mill, and Sixteen to Fort McAllister—All these points may be used by us, and we have a good strong bridge across Ogeechee at Kings, by which our wagons can go to Fort McAllister, to which point I am sending the wagons (not absolutely necessary for daily use)—the negroes, prisoners of war, sick &c., en-route for Port Royal. In relation to Savannah, you will remark that Genl. Hardee refers to his still being in communication with his War Department—This language he thought would deceive me, but I am confirmed in the belief that the route to which he refers, namely, the Union plank-road, on the South Carolina shore, is inadequate to feed his Army and the people of Savannah, for Genl. Foster assures me that he has his force on that very road near the head of

Broad river, and that his guns command the Railroad, so that cars no longer run between Charleston and Savannah—We hold this end of the Charleston Rail-road, and have destroyed it from the three (3) mile post, back to the Bridge—about twelve (12) miles. In anticipation of leaving this country, I am continuing the destruction of their Railroads, and at this moment have two Divisions and the Cavalry at work breaking up the Gulf Railroad from the Ogeechee to the Altamaha, so that even if I do not take Savannah, I will leave it in a bad way. But I still hope that events will give me time to take Savannah, even if I have to assault with some loss. I am satisfied that unless we take it, the Gunboats never will: for they can make no impression upon the batteries which guard every approach from the Sea—And I have a faint belief that when Col. Babcock reaches you, you will delay operations long enough to enable me to succeed. With Savannah in our possession, at some future time, if not now, we can punish South Carolina as she deserves, and as thousands of people in Georgia hoped we would do. I do sincerely believe that the whole United States, North and South, would rejoice to have this Army turned loose on South Carolina, to devastate that State in the manner we have done in Georgia: and it would have a direct and immediate bearing on your campaign in Virginia—I have the honor to be, Your Obedient Servant,

W. T. Sherman
Major General U.S.A.

LS, DNA: RG 108, Records of the Headquarters of the Army, Letters Received, AUS 1864, M243; *OR*, I, 44:741–43.

TO ULYSSES S. GRANT

Hdqrs. Military Division
of the Mississippi,
In the Field, Savannah, Ga.,
December 22, 1864.

Lieut. Gen. U. S. Grant,
Commanding Armies of the United States, City Point, Va.
Dear General:

I take great satisfaction in reporting that we are in possession of Savannah and all its forts. At first I proposed to extend across the river above the city from Slocum's left, but the enemy had a gun-boat and ram heavily armed that would have made the step extra hazardous; also the submerged rice fields on the northeast bank were impracticable. I then went to Hilton Head to arrange with General Foster to re-enforce his movement from Broad River, but before I had completed the move Hardee got his garrison across and off on the Union plank road. Our troops entered at daylight yesterday, took about 800 prisoners, over 100 guns (some of the heaviest caliber), and a perfect string of forts from Savannah around to McAllister, also 12,000 bales of cotton, 190 cars, 13 locomotives, 3 steam-boats, and an immense supply of shells, shot, and all kinds of ammunition. There is a complete arsenal here, and much valuable machinery. The citizens mostly remain, and the city is very quiet. The river below is much obstructed, but I parted with Admiral Dahlgren yesterday at 4 p.m., and he will at once get about removing them and opening a way. The enemy blew up an iron-clad (Savannah), a good ram, and three tenders, small steamers. As yet we have made but a partial inventory, but the above falls far short of our conquests. I have not a particle of doubt but that we have secured 150 fine guns, with plenty of ammunition. I have now completed my first step, and should like to go on to you, via Columbia and Raleigh, but will prepare to embark as soon as vessels come. Colonel Babcock will have told you all, and you know better than anybody else how much better troops arrive by a land march than when carried by transports. I will turn over to Foster Savannah and all its outposts, with, say, one division of infantry, Kilpatrick's cavalry, and plenty of artillery. Hardee has, of course, moved into South Carolina, but I do not believe his Georgia troops, militia and fancy companies, will work in South Carolina. His force is reported by citizens at from 15,000 to 20,000. The capture of Savannah, with the incidental use of the river, gives us a magnificent position in this quarter; and if you can hold Lee, and if Thomas can continue as he did on the 18th, I could go on and smash South Carolina all to pieces, and also break up roads as far as the Roanoke. But, as I before remarked, I will now look to coming to you as soon as transportation comes. We are all well and confident as ever.

Yours, truly,
W. T. Sherman,
Major-General, U.S. Army.

Printed, *OR*, I, 44:6–7.

TO ABRAHAM LINCOLN

Savannah Ga. Dec. 22, 1864
Via Ft. Monroe Va. Dec. 22.

His Excellency
Prest. Lincoln.

I beg to present you as a Christmas gift the City of Savannah with 150 heavy guns & plenty of ammunition & also about 25,000 bales of cotton.

W. T. Sherman
Major Genl.

Telegram, DLC: Robert T. Lincoln Collection of Abraham Lincoln Papers; *OR*, 44:783.

Headquarters, Military Division
of the Mississippi,
Savannah, Ga. Dec. 24 1864

Lieut. Genl. U. S. Grant
City Point, Va.
General:

Your letter of Decr. 18th[1] is just received. I feel very much gratified at receiving the handsome commendation you pay my army. I will in General Orders convey to the officers and men the substance of your note.[2] I am also gratified that you have modified your former orders, as I feared that the transportation of them by sea would very much disturb the unity and morale of my army, now so perfect.

The occupation of Savannah, which I have heretofore reported, completes the first part of our game, and fulfils a great part of your instructions: and I am now engaged in dismantling the rebel forts which bear upon the sea and channels, and transferring the heavy ordnance and ammunition to Fort Pulaski, where they can be more easily guarded than if left in the city.

The rebel inner lines, with some modifications, are well adapted to our purposes, and with slight modifications can be held by a comparatively small Force: and in about ten days I expect to be ready to sally forth again. I feel no doubt whatever as to our future plans. I have thought them over so long and so well, that they appear as clear as daylight. I left Augusta untouched on purpose: because now the enemy will be in doubt as to my objective point after crossing the Savannah River, whether it be Augusta or Charleston, and will naturally divide his forces. I will then move either in Branchville or Columbia, on any curved line that gives us the best supplies, breaking up in my course as much Railroad as possible. Then, ignoring Charleston and Augusta both, occupy Columbia and Camden: pausing there long enough to observe the effect, I would strike for the Charleston and Wilmington R. Road, somewhere between the Santee and the Cape Fear River, and if possible, communicate with the fleet under Admiral Dahlgren, whom I find a most agreeable gentleman, in every way accommodating himself to our wishes and plans. Then I would favor Wilmington, in the belief that Porter and Butler will fail in their present undertaking. Charleston is now a more desolated wreck, and is hardly worth the time it would Take to starve it out. Still I am aware that historically and politically much importance is attached to the place, and it may be that apart from its military importance, both you and the Administration would prefer I should give it more attention, and it would be well for you to give me some general idea on that subject, as otherwise I would treat it, as I have expressed, as a point of little importance after all its Railroads leaving into the interior are destroyed or occupied by us. But on the hypothesis of ignoring Charleston and Taking Wilmington I would then favor a movement direct on Raleigh. The game is then up with Lee, unless he comes out of Richmond, avoids you, and fights me: in which event, I should reckon on your being on his heels.

Now that Hood is used up by Thomas,[3] I feel disposed to bring the matter to an issue just as quick as possible. I feel confident that I can break up the whole R. Rd. system of South Carolina and N. Carolina, and be on the Roanoke, either at Raleigh or Weldon, by the time the Spring fairly opens. And if you feel confident that you can whip Lee outside of his entrenchments, I feel equally confident that I can handle him in the open country. One reason why I would ignore Charleston is this: that I believe they will reduce the garrison to a small force, with plenty of provisions, and I know that the Neck, back of Charleston, can be made impregnable to assault, and we will hardly have time for siege operations. I will have to leave in Savannah a garrison, and if Thomas can spare them, would like to have all detachments, convalescents, &c., belonging to these four Corps, sent forward at once. I don't want to cripple Thomas, because I regard his operations as all-important, and I have ordered him to pursue Hood down into Alabama, trusting to the country for supplies.

I reviewed one of my Corps today, and shall continue to review the whole army. I don't like To boast, but believe this army has a confidence in itself that makes it almost irresistible. I wish you would run down and see us: it would have a good effect, and would show to both armies that they were acting on a common plan. The weather is now cool and pleasant, and the general health very good. your true Friend

W. T. Sherman

Maj. Genl.

LS (salutation also in WTS's hand), DNA: RG 108, Records of the Headquarters of the Army, Letters Received, AUS 1864, M245; *OR*, I, 44:797–98.

1. USG to WTS, December 18, 1864, *PUSG*, 13:129–30. "I congratulate You, and the brave officers and men under your command, on the successful termination of your most brilliant campaign. When apprehensions for your safety were expressed by the President I assured him with the Army you had, and you in command of it, there was no danger but you would *strike* bottom on Salt Water some place." He did not think that any other living commander could have done it and complained of Thomas's slowness. He had changed his mind about Sherman's joining him as it would take too long to get his men to Virginia by water and thought that he could do more good where he was.

2. Special Field Orders No. 6, January 8, 1865, *PM*, 2:219–20.

3. On December 15–16, 1864, Thomas defeated Hood in the Battle of Nashville.

TO HENRY W. HALLECK

Headquarters Military Division
of the Mississippi,
In the Field, Savannah, Ga.,
December 24, 1864.

Maj. Gen. H. W. Halleck,
Chief of Staff, Washington City, D.C.;
General:

I had the pleasure to receive your two letters of the 16th and 18th instant to-day, and I feel more than usually flattered by the high encomiums you have passed on our recent campaign, which is now complete by the occupation of Savannah. I am also very glad that General Grant has changed his mind about embarking my troops for James River, leaving me free to make the broad swath you describe through South and North Carolina, and still more grati-fied at the news from Thomas in Tennessee, because it fulfills my plan, which contemplated his being fully able to dispose of Hood in case he ventured north of the Tennessee River; so I think, on the whole, I can chuckle over Jeff. Davis' disappointment in not turning nay Atlanta campaign into a Moscow disaster. I have just finished a long letter to General Grant, and have explained to him that we are engaged in shifting our base from the Ogeechee over to the Savannah River, dismantling all the forts made by the enemy to bear upon the salt-water channels, and transferring the heavy ordnance, &c., to Fort Pulaski and Hilton Head, and in remodelling the enemy's interior lines to suit our fu-ture plans and purposes. I have also laid down the programme of a campaign which I can make this winter, and put me in the spring on the Roanoke, in direct communication with him on the James River. In general terms, my plan is to turn over to General Foster the city of Savannah, and to sally forth, with my army resupplied, cross the Savannah, feign on Charleston and Augusta, but strike between, breaking *en route* the Charleston and Augusta Railroad, also a large part of that front Branchville and Camden toward North Carolina, and then rapidly moving to some point of the railroad from Charleston to Wilmington, between the Santee and Cape Fear Rivers; then, communicating with the fleet in the neighborhood of Georgetown, I would turn upon Wil-mington or Charleston according to the importance of either. I rather prefer Wilmington, as a live place, over Charleston, which is dead and unimportant when its railroad communications are broken. I take it for granted the present movement on Wilmington will fail, because I know that gun-boats cannot take a fort, and Butler has not the force or the ability to take it. If I should determine to take Charleston I would turn across the country, which I have hunted over many a time, from Santee to Mount Pleasant, throwing one wing on the peninsula between Ashley and Cooper. After accomplishing one or other of these ends I would make a bee-line for Raleigh, or Weldon, when Lee would be forced to come out of Richmond or acknowledge himself beaten. He would, I think, by the use of the Danville railroad, throw himself rapidly between me and Grant, leaving Richmond in the hands of the latter. This would not alarm me, for I have an army which I think can maneuver, and I would force him to attack me at a disadvantage, always under the supposition that Grant would be on his heels; and if the worst came to the worst I could fight my way down to Albemarle Sound or New Berne.

I think the time has come now when we should attempt the boldest moves, and my experience is that they are easier of execution than more timid ones, because the enemy is disconcerted by them—as for instance, my recent campaign. I also doubt the wisdom of concentration beyond a certain point, as the roads of this country limit the amount of men that can be brought to bear in any one battle; and I don't believe any one general can handle more than 60,000 men in battle. I think my campaign of the last month, as well as every step I take from this point northward, is as much a direct attack upon Lee's army as though I were operating within the mound of his artillery. I am very anxious that Thomas should follow up his successes to the very uttermost point. My orders to him before I left Kingston were, after beating Hood, to follow him as far as Columbus, Miss., or Selma, Ala., both of which lie in districts of country which I know to be rich in corn and meat. I attach more importance to these deep incisions into the enemy's country, because this war differs from European wars in this particular. We are not only fighting hostile armies, but a hostile people, and must make old and young, rich and poor, feel the hard hand of war, as well as their organized armies. I know that this recent movement of mine through Georgia has had a wonderful effect in this respect. Thousands who had been deceived by their lying papers into the belief that we were being whipped all the time, realized the truth, and have no appetite for a repetition of the same experience. To be sure, Jeff. Davis has his people under a pretty good state of discipline, but I think faith in him is much shaken in Georgia; and I think before we are done, South Carolina will not be quite so tempestuous. I will bear in mind your hint as to Charleston, and don't think salt will be necessary. When I move the Fifteenth Corps will be on the right of the Right Wing, and their position will bring them, naturally, into Charleston first; and if you have watched the history of that corps you will have remarked that they generally do their work up pretty well. The truth is the whole army is burning with an insatiable desire to wreak vengeance upon South Carolina. I almost tremble at her fate, but feel that she deserves all that seems in store for her. Many and many a person in Georgia asked me why we did not go to

South Carolina, and when I answered that I was *en route* for that State the invariable reply was, Well, if you will make those people feel the severities of war, we will pardon you for your desolation of Georgia." I look upon Columbia as quite as bad as Charleston, and I doubt if we shall spare the public buildings there, as we did at Milledgeville. I have been so busy lately that I have not yet made my official report, and think I had better wait until I get my subordinate reports before attempting it, as I am anxious to explain clearly, not only the reasons for every step, but the amount of execution done, and this I cannot do until I get the subordinate reports; for we marched the whole distance in tour or more columns, and, of course, I could only be present with one, and generally that one engaged in destroying railroads. This work of destruction was performed better than usual, because I had an engineer regiment provided with claws to twist the bars after being heated. Such bars can never be used again, and the only way in which a railroad line can be reconstructed across Georgia will be to make a new road from Fairburn Station, twenty-four miles southwest of Atlanta, to Madison, a distance of 100 miles; and before that can be done I propose to be on the road from Augusta to Charleston, which is a continuation of the same. I felt somewhat disappointed at Hardee's escape from me, but really am not to blame. I moved as quick as possible to close up the "Union Causeway," but intervening obstacles were such that before I could get my troops on the road Hardee had slipped out. Still, I know that the men that were in Savannah will be lost, in a measure, to Jeff. Davis; for the Georgia troops, under G. W. Smith, declared they would not fight in South Carolina, and have gone north *en route* for Augusta, and I have reason to believe the North Carolina troops have gone to Wilmington— in other words, they are scattered. I have reason to believe that Beauregard was present in Savannah at the time of its evacuation, and I think he and Hardee are now in Charleston, doubtless making preparations for what they know will be my next step.

Please say to the President that I received his kind message through Colonel Markland, and feel thankful for his high favor. If I disappoint him in the future, it shall not be from want of zeal or love to the cause. Of you I expect a full and frank criticism of my plans for the future, which may enable me to correct errors before it is too late. I do not wish to be rash, but want to give my rebel friends no chance to accuse us of want of enterprise or courage.

Assuring you of my high personal respect, I remain, as ever, your friend,

W. T. Sherman,
Major-General.[1]

Printed, *OR*, I, 44:798–800.
1. This letter was endorsed by Grant, who noted that Sherman had asked that Grant read

the letter before it was sent on to Halleck, "as it contained one or two points which his letter addressed to me does not contain." *OR*, I, 44:800.

TO ELLEN EWING SHERMAN

> Headquarters, Military Division
> of the Mississippi,
> In the Field, Savannah Dec. 25, 1864

Dearest Ellen,

This is Christmas Day and I hope truly & really that you and the Little ones may enjoy it, in the full Knowledge that I am all safe after our long march—I am at this moment in an elegant chamber of the house of a Gentleman named Green. The house is elegant & splendidly furnished with pictures & Statuary—my bed Room has a bath & dressing Room attached which look out of proportion to my poor baggage. My clothing is good yet and I can even afford a white Shirt. It would amuse you to See the negros, they flock to me old & young they pray & shout—and mix up my name with that of Moses, & Simon, and other scriptural ones as well as Abram Linkum the Great Messiah of "Dis Jubilee[.]" There are many fine families in this City, but when I ask for old & familiar names, it marks the Sad havoc of war. The Goodwins, Teffts, Cuylers, Habershams, Laws, &c. &c. all gone or in poverty and yet the girls remain, bright and haughty, and proud as ever. There seems no end but utter annihilation that will satisfy their hate of the "sneaking yankee" and "ruthless invader"—They no longer Call my army "Cowardly yanks" but have tried to arouse the Sympathy of the civilized world by stories of the cruel barbarities of my Army. The next stop in the progress will be "for gods sake Spare us," we must surrender"—When that end is reached we begin to See daylight, but although I have come right through the heart of Georgia, they talk as defiantly as ever. I think Thomas' whipping at Nashville, coupled my march will take Some conceit out of them.

I have no doubt you hear enough about "Sherman" and are sick of the name, and the interest the public takes in my whereabouts leaves me no subject to write about. Charley & Dayton promise to write details[.] All I can do is to make hasty scrawls assuring you of my health and Eternal affection

> W. T. Sherman

ALS, InND: Sherman Family Papers.

TO MARIA BOYLE EWING SHERMAN

Headquarters, Military Division
of the Mississippi,
Savannah, Dec. 25, 1864

Dear Minnie,

A happy Christmas I hope this will prove to you, and Lizzie and all for you will probably Know by this time that we have Captured Savannah, and that we are all well—We are enjoying ourselves, in an elegant house, and will have a real Christmas Dinner, turkey and all. I have no doubt you read the papers and Know all you want to Know and that you will be content to know that Uncle Charley & I are well.

Tell Mama if she is at South Bend that I have written to her twice at Lancaster, as I have not yet heard whether She has actually moved up to Notre Dame. I have not even heard if the baby got well of the Cold with which he was suffering at the time I left Atlanta.

I suppose it is now bitter Cold with you, it is cold here but not near so much so as with you. The trees are green here, but Still the air is frosty. I expect to be here a Couple of weeks, and then again will be off. Write to me right off at Savannah, via New York, and tell Lizzie to do the Same for I cannot Count on mails long. Give my love to all your Cousins and believe me your affectionate Father

W. T. Sherman

ALS, OHi: William T. Sherman

TO GEORGE H. THOMAS

Headquarters, Military Division
of the Mississippi,
In the Field, Savannah Ga. Dec. 25 1864

Maj. Genl. Geo. H. Thomas
Comdg. Dept. of the Cumberland, Nashville, Tenn.
Dear General:

I have heard of all your operations up to about the 17th,[1] and I do not believe your own wife[2] was more happy at the result than I was. Had any misfortune fallen you I should have reproached myself for taking away so large a proportion of the army and leaving you too weak to cope with Hood. But as events have turned out my judgment has been sustained: but I am none the less thankful to you, and to Schofield, and to all, for the very complete manner in which you have used up Hood. I only hope you will go on and pursue your advantage to the very uttermost. And if you can get far down into

Alabama, don't hesitate to do so, for my own experience is that you can fine plenty of forage and provisions along down the valleys of The Tombigbee and Black Warrior.

Here I am now in a magnificent house, close by the old barracks around which cluster so many of our old memories of Rankin, and Ridgely,[3] and Fraser[4] and others. But the old families that we used to know are nearly all gone or dead. I will not stay here long however, but push Northwards as the season advances.

The old live oaks are as beautiful as ever, and whilst you are freezing to death in Tennessee we are basking in a warm sun, and I fear I did you personal injustice in leaving you behind whilst I made my winter excursion. But next time I will stay at home and let you go it.

Davis and Slocum are very well, and their troops are in fine condition. They will doubtless write you fully, and I will avail myself of the first leisure to tell you all matters of interest that I know you would like to hear. Truly your friend,

W. T. Sherman
Maj. Genl.

LS, CSmH.

1. On December 23, Sherman wrote Joseph D. Webster, in part: "I have also from the War Department a copy of General Thomas' dispatch, giving account of the attack on Hood on the 15th, which was successful, but not complete. I await further accounts with anxiety, as Thomas' complete success is necessary to vindicate my plans for this campaign; and I have no doubt that my calculations that Thomas had in hand (including A. J. Smith's troops) a force large enough to whip Hood in a fair fight was correct. I approve of Thomas' allowing Hood to come north far enough to enable him to concentrate his own men, though I would have preferred that Hood should have been checked about Columbia. Still, if Thomas followed up his success of the 15th and gave Hood a good whaling, and is at this moment following him closely, the whole campaign in my division, will be even more perfect than the Atlanta campaign; for at this end of the line I have realized all I had reason to hope for, except in the release of our prisoners, which was simply an impossibility." Continuing the letter the next day, he reported that he had just learned that Thomas had overwhelmed Hood on December 16. *OR*, I, 44:787–93.

2. Frances Lucretia Kellogg of Troy, New York.

3. Randolph Ridgely (d. 1846), USA, had served as a lieutenant in the Third Artillery and as a rear adjutant.

4. William D. Fraser (d. 1856) had been a captain in the Second Engineers.

TO P. J. STANFIELD, A. J. PAGETT, AND OTHERS

Headquarters Military Division
of the Mississippi,
In the Field, Savannah,
December 28, 1864.

Messrs. P. J. Stanfield, A. J. Pagett, and others,
Of Liberty and Tattnall Counties, Ga.:

Gentlemen:

I have a copy of the resolutions adopted by you.[1] They are surely strong enough and patriotic enough. I will aid you all possible, and do all in my power to encourage you and defend you in your course. I do think we have been at war long enough for truth to reveal itself. We are fellow-countrymen and bound by every principle of honor and honesty to maintain and defend the Union given us by Washington, and that is all I aim at, and the moment Georgia resumes her place in the Union and sends Representatives to Congress she is at once at peace, and all the laws both national and State are revived. If you will stay at home quietly, and call back your sons and neighbors to resume their peaceful pursuits, I will promise you ammunition to protect yourselves and property. If rebel soldiers do any of you violence I will retaliate, and if you will bring your produce to Savannah I will cause it to be protected *in transitu*, and allow it to be sold in market to the highest bidder, and our commissary will buy your cattle, hogs, sheep, &c. It would be well to form a league, and adopt some common certificate, so that our officers and soldiers may distinguish between you and open rebels. I will be glad to confer with any of your people, and will do all that is fair to encourage you to recover the peace and prosperity you enjoyed before the war.

I am, with respect, &c.,
W. T. Sherman,
Major-General.

Printed, *OR*, I, 44:827.

1. P. J. Stanfield, A. J. Pagett, Asa Barnett, J. E. Beasly, and John S. Long had adopted resolutions declaring that they had either resisted conscription or had always been loyal to the Union and pledged to support Sherman's army. *OR*, I, 44:827–28.

TO THOMAS EWING SR.

Headquarters, Military Division
of the Mississippi,
Savannah, Geo. Dec. 31 1864.

Hon. T. Ewing
Washington, D.C.
Dear Sir,

I have received yrs. of the 18, and by Christmas day you must have heard
that my army had possession of Savannah and all its Forts which have heretofore defied the Navy and the Expeditions hitherto sent against it. I ought to
have caught its garrison but the Swampy ground prevented me reaching the
Causeway on the South Carolina Shore but if Hardee had given me two more
days I would have closed that also. As it was however, his men only escaped
and with Savannah I got all the Guns Stores and Gunboats which made it
formidable. Of course I feel a just pride in the satisfaction you express, and
would rather please and gratify you than all the world beside. I know full well
that I enjoy the unlimited confidence of the President and Commander in
Chief, and better Still of my own Army. They will march to certain death if I
order it, because they know & feel that night & day I labor to the end that not a
life shall be lost in vain. I always ignore secondary objects and strike at
principals with a foreknowledge that the former follow the latter. Nor are my
combinations extra hazardous or bold. Every movement I have made in this
war has been based on sound military principles, and the result proves the
assertion. At Atlanta I was not to be decoyed from the fruits of my summers
work, by Hood's chaseing to the left, but I sent my oldest Lieutenant in whom
I had confidence (Thomas) to Tennessee, and gave him a liberal part of my
volunteers and *all my recruits* which I knew would enable him to cope with
Hood defensively, as also hold the vital parts of former conquests; there again
has my judgment been verified by Events. Nor was I rash in cutting loose from
a Base and relying on the Country for forage & provisions. I had wagons
enough loaded with essentials and beef cattle enough to feed us for more than
a month, and had the census statistics showing the produce of Every County
through which I designed to pass. No military expedition was ever based on
sounder or surer data.

Besides my army has by time & attention acquired too much personal
experience and adhesion to disintegrate by foraging or its incident disorganizing tendency. I have just reviewed my *four* Corps and challenge competition
for soldierly bearing & behavior. No City was ever occupied with less disorder,
or more system than this of Savannah, and it is a subject of universal Comment that though an army of 60,000 men lay camped around it, women &

children of an hostile People walk its Streets with as much security as they do in Philadelphia. I attach much importance to these little matters, as it is all important our armies should not be tainted by that Spirit of anarchy that threatened the Stability of our Government, but on the contrary that when war does End we may safely rest the fabric of Govt. if necessary on the strong and safe base of a well disciplined army of Citizens. My official reports will reach the Department in due season and will I trust give you as much personal satisfaction as those hitherto. Charley is well & will answer yr. letter. Tom did very well in Missouri[1] and I hope he may have more opportunities. Yr. affectionate Son,

W. T. Sherman

ALS, DLC: Thomas Ewing and Family Papers.

1. Thomas Ewing Jr. had checked Confederate progress in Missouri at Fort Davidson at the Battle of Pilot Knob on September 27 and 28.

TO ULYSSES S. GRANT

Headquarters, Military Division
of the Mississippi,
Savannah, Geo. Dec. 31 1864 3 P.M.

Dear General,

A mail leaves at 5 P.M. for Hilton Head and New York. I have written a short official letter to Genl. Halleck amounting to nothing simply because I suppose you want to hear from me at every opportunity. I have already reviewed my 4 corps and wind up in a day or two with Kilpatricks Cavalry which I Keep out about 9 miles. There is no doubt of it, but this army is in fine condition, and impatient to go ahead. I would like to have Foster reinforce, if possible, so that I will not have to leave him a Division to hold Savannah. I will have all the heavy work done, such as moving the captured artillery to Hilton Head where it can be more safely guarded, and building the redoubts in the New Line for the defense of Savannah. This will be close in for we dont care if the Enemy does shell the town. 5000 men will be plenty and white troops will be best as the People are dreadfully alarmed lest we garrison the place with Negros. Now no matter what the negro soldiers are you Know that people have prejudices which must be regarded. Prejudice like Religion cannot be discussed. As soon as I can accumulate enough provisions & forage to fill my wages I will be ready for S. Carolina, and if you want me to take Charleston I think I can do it for I know the place well. I was stationed there from 42 to 46, and used to hunt a good deal all along the Cooper River. The direction to approach Charleston is from the North West, down the peninsula between Ashley & Cooper, as also that ending on the Bay at Mount Pleasant. You had better notify Genl. Meigs to send at once enough provisions for 60,000 men and 40,000 horses & mules for 60 days, instead of the daily allowance for you Know I must work on the *surplus* & not on the daily receipts. We have pretty well eaten up all the Rice & Rice Straw for 50 miles. By making a wide circuit by Barnwell, Orangeburg, Columbia and Santee, I can reach the neighborhood of Georgetown and get a *re* supply. I do not issue Rations to the people, but order the mayor to look to the People, and have given him the rough Rice to be sold & exchanged into flour & meat. Thus the expense will fall on the holders of this Rough Rice, which I treat as Prize of war, inasmuch as Hardee refused to surrender & thereby escaped with his Garrison. I take it for granted that we will have to fight in South Carolina, though I believe G. W. Smith[1] with his Georgia Militia has returned to Georgia, by way of Augusta saying he would be d——d if *he* would fight for South Carolina. The People here seem to be well content as they have reason to be for our troops have behaved magnificently[.] You would think it Sunday, so quiet is every thing in the City day & night. All recognize in my army a different body of men than they have ever seen before. I hope you will push Thomas up. Keep him going south anywhere. Let him make a track down into Alabama, or if you think better he can again come to Chattanooga and as far down as the Etowah, to which point I preserved the iron rails ready to be used again. I am fully aware of your friendly feelings towards me, and you may always depend on me as your steadfast supporter. Your wish is Law & Gospel to me and such is the feeling that pervades my army. I have an idea you will come to see me before I start[.] yrs. in haste,

W. T. Sherman M. G.

ALS, DNA: RG 108, Records of the Headquarters of the Army, Letters Received, AUS 1864, M253; *OR*, I, 44:841.

1. General Gustavus W. Smith had commanded the Georgia militia and the First Division attached to the Confederate Army of Tennessee. On December 30 he was assigned to assist in the defense of South Carolina, Georgia, and Florida.

TO ELLEN EWING SHERMAN

Headquarters, Military Division
of the Mississippi,
Savannah, Geo., Dec. 31, 1864

Dearest Ellen,

The Steamer *Fulton* arrived at Hilton Head yesterday, bring N.Y. mails to Dec. 24. I got a letter from yr. father at Washington, Hugh in Kentucky and John Sherman all alluding to the death of our baby,[1] but I got nothing from you or the girls at school. I also found in the N.Y. *Herald* of the 22nd a full obituary and notice of funeral ceremonies from which I see you are up at

South Bend. I have written you twice to Lancaster, and to Minnie at Notre Dame so you will know that I am safe again for a few days, and the northern papers seem so full of speculations about me and my army that I suppose you are sick of seeing the name. The last letter I got from you at Kingston made me fear for our baby, but I had hoped that the little fellow would weather the ailment, but it seems he too, is lost to us, and gone to join Willy. I cannot say that I grieve for him as I did Willy, for he was but a mere ideal, whereas Willy was incorporated with us, and Seemed to be designed to perpetuate our Memories. But amid the Scenes of death and desolation through which I daily pass I cannot but become callous to death. It is so common, so familiar that it no longer impresses me as of old—You on the Contrary surrounded alone by life & youth cannot take things so philosophically but are stayed by the Religious faith of a better and higher life elsewhere[.] I should like to have seen the baby of which all spoke so well, but I seem doomed to pass my life away so that even my children will be strangers. I did hope for some rest but all lean on me so, Grant, the President, the Army, and even the world now looks to me to strike hard & decisive blows that I cannot draw out quietly as I would and Seek rest. After having participated in severing the Confederacy down the Mississipi I have again cut it in twain, and have planned & executed a Campaign which Judges pronounce will be famous among the Grand deeds of the world. I can hardly realize it for really it was easy, but like one who has walked a narrow plank I look back and wonder if I really did it: but here I am in the proud City of Savannah, with an elegant mansion at my command, surrounded by a confident, brave & victorious army that looks to me as its head— Negros & whites flock to me and gaze at me as some wonderful being, and letters from Great men pour in with words of flattery & praise, but still I do more than ever crave for peace & quiet, and would gladly drop all these and gather you and my little ones in some quiet place where I could be at ease. People here talk as though the war was drawing to a close, but I know better. There remains yet a large class of Southern men who will not have Peace, and they Still have the power to do much mischief. Thomas success in Tennessee inures to my advantage as his operations there are a part of my *plan*. I know you have written to me, and I shall expect a big budget by the Next N.Y. steamer.

It will not be long before I sally forth again on another dangerous & important Quixotic venture. Love to all Yrs. Ever

Sherman

ALS, InND: Sherman Family Papers.
1. Charles C. Sherman had died December 4.

TO JOHN SHERMAN

Headquarters, Military Division
of the Mississippi,
Savannah, Geo., Dec. 31, 1864

Dear Brother,

Yours of Dec. 18. is at hand.[1] A mail leaves today at 5 P.M. and I have much to do. Mr. Chase has always been most Kind to me and I have always acknowledged it. His ability is unquestioned and I doubt not he will attain the highest celebrity as Chief Justice.[2] In like manner Mr. Stanton has always treated me with the utmost consideration and I have endeavored always to assure him of my entire satisfaction, but as you can well understand my time is so occupied that I am unable to keep up a correspondence other than what is essential. But I would be glad if you would say to Mr. Chase & Stanton that I am fully sensible of the friendship & appreciate it. I receive vast numbers of letters from distinguished men, awarding me a measure of praise higher than the case calls for, but looking back I surely have done my full share in this war, and would like to slide out quietly and See more of my family which is growing up almost strangers to me. I have now lost Willy and the baby without ever seeing him and were it not for Genl. Grants unmeasured confidence in me, I should insist on a little rest and leisure. As it is I must go on. Such success has attended me that every officer & man with me thinks he would be lost unless I am at hand. I hear the Soldiers talk as I ride by—There goes the old man. All's Right—not a waver, doubt or hesitation when I order, and men march to certain death without a murmur if I call on them because they Know I value their lives as much as my own. I do not feel any older, and have no gray hairs yet—My health is good, and Save a little Rheumatism in my Right arm during the last march I have not been indisposed a day and even then I rode daily my march. I got Mr. Mahan's note,[3] write him that he was right in his estimate of me. I saw my way from Atlanta to the Sea Coast as plain before starting as I do now after it is over. I have a Singular Capacity for knowledge of *Roads* the resources of a Country, and the Capacity of my Command. I wrote Charles Sherman a letter you will see, and in time you will have enough official details of this Campaign to Satisfy you. I do not fear want of appreciation but on the contrary that an exaggerated faith will be generated in my ability that no man can fulfill. Better promise little & fulfil much than the reverse. I think you will now admit I was right in my appreciation of the Press & of the war generally was as near right as that of any.

You have reason to be proud of yr. position in the Senate, and I have no doubt your tact & experience will enable you to hold your own. About your locating at Cincinati I hardly know what to Say. The moment you feel assured the Financial condition of the Country will justify the purchase of Real Estate subject to taxation you could venture on the step—I cannot do anything looking to permanency till the war is ended. Thomas success in Tennessee, which was part of *my Plan* will go far to assure the *Safety* of the Ohio valley. Love to all. Yrs. affectionately

Sherman W. T.

ALS, DLC: William T. Sherman.

1. DLC: WTS. After congratulating his brother on the success of his March to the Sea, JS had expressed his concern that Thomas Ewing Sr. had poisoned WTS's mind against Chase and explained his loyalties: "Chase has always been friendly to me and Mr. Ewing has not." JS went on to say that he was living next door to Stanton, who shared WTS's dispatches with him. "By the way he is your fast friend & was when you had fewer."

2. Abraham Lincoln appointed Chase to succeed the late Roger B. Taney as chief justice.

3. Dennis H. Mahan to JS, December 19, 1864, DLC: WTS. He congratulated JS on his brother's success and said that he had never doubted it would come: "General Sherman had made war too long and showed too much good sense to make any mistake in an affair either as to his own resources or that of the enemy."

TO ELLEN EWING SHERMAN

Headquarters, Military Division
of the Mississippi,
Savannah, Geo. Jan. 2, 1865

Dearest Ellen,

I am about to Send a Steamer to Genl. Grant with dispatches and propose to send Charley if I can find him, but as usual he is out of the way and cannot be found. I have written you and the children several times, and the newspapers keep you well advised of my whereabouts. I am now in a magnificent mansion living like a Gentleman, but Soon will be off for South Carolina and then look out for Breakers. You may count on me being here till the 15. I have not yet had one word from you since you Knew of my having reached the Coast and only Know of the death of our little boy, by the New York papers of Dec. 22, but was in a measure prepared for it by your letter received at Kingston. I suppose you felt his loss far more than I do because I never saw him, but all the children seemed to be so attached to him that you may be so grieved at his death you Cannot write to me. I Know by the Same source that you are now at South Bend in Mr. Colfax house[.] It must be very cold up there—It is really cold here, though the Sun shines warm and the trees have green leaves, of course no snow, but ice formed in the Gutters and on the ponds. General Barnard got here last night from Genl. Grant with dispatches which I have answered,[1] and the clerks are copying my letters and as soon as finished I will send a flat steamer to Port Royal, whence a sea steamer will go to City Point, and thence this letter will be sent you. I enclose a check for $800. I drew pay for Novr. & Decr. & Kept 300 & send you the balance. It is good for you that I Keep in the woods where my expenses are small and you get the lions share of pay. I see that the State of Ohio talks of making me a present of a home &c.—for myself I would accept nothing but for you & the children I would be willing—especially if such a present were accompanied as in Farraguts place, with Bonds enough to give interest to pay taxes. My pay would not enable me to pay taxes ⟨on property.⟩ I have received from ⟨high sources⟩ highest praises and yesterday New Years was toasted &c. with allusions to Hannibal, Caesar &c. &c., but in reply I turned all into a good joke by saying that Hannibal & Caesar were small potatos as they had never read the New York *Herald*, or had a photograph taken. But of course I feel a just pride in the Confidence of my army, and the singular friendship of Genl. Grant, who is almost childlike in his love for me. It does seem that Time has brought out all my old Friends, Grant, Thomas, Sheridan &c[.] All sorts of People send me Presents, and I hope they dont slight you or the Girls. I want little in that way, but I think you can Stand a good deal. Thus far success has crowned my boldest Conceptions and I am going to try others quite as Quixotic. It may be that Spite of my fears I may come out all Right—Love to all. Yrs. Ever

AL (signature clipped), InND: Sherman Family Papers. Text in angle brackets is from *HL*, 323.

1. USG to WTS, December 27, 1865, *PM*, 2:237–38. Grant expressed his pleasure that WTS thought he could march north through the South to join him. In addition to Savannah, he thought they needed an entrenched camp between Savannah and Charleston. He gave WTS permission to embark on a march through the Carolinas as soon as possible. On January 2, WTS answered to say that he did not have much to add since his lengthy letter of December 24 and that he would send the Seventeenth Corps to entrench on the railroad lines at Pocataligo. *PM*, 2:237–38.

TO EDWIN M. STANTON

> Headquarters Military Division
> of the Mississippi,
> In the Field, Savannah, Ga.,
> Jan'y 2d 1865.

Hon. Edwin M. Stanton
Secretary of War, Washington City D.C.
Sir:

I have just received from Lieut. Gen. Grant a copy of that part of your telegram to him of 26th December,[1] relating to cotton, a copy of which has been immediately furnished to General Easton, my Chief Quartermaster, who will be strictly governed by it.

I had already been approached by all the consuls and half the people of

Savannah on this cotton question and my invariable answer has been that all the cotton in Savannah was prize of war, and belonged to the United States, and nobody should recover one bale of it with my consent. And that as cotton has been one of the chief causes of the war, it should help to pay its expenses: that all cotton became tainted with treason from the hour the first act of hostility was committed against the United States, some time in December, 1860,—and that no bill of sale subsequent to that date could convey title. My orders were that an officer of the Q. M. Department, U.S. Army might furnish the holder, agent or attorney, a mere certificate of the fact of seizure, with description of the bales, marks, &c.—the cotton then to be turned over to the Agent of the Treasury Department to be shipped to New York for sale. But since the receipt of your dispatch I have ordered Gen. Easton to make the consignment himself to the Quartermaster at New York, where you can dispose of it at pleasure. I do not think the Treasury Department ought to bother itself with the prizes or capture of war.

Mr. Barclay, former Consul at New York, representing Mr. Molyneux, formerly Consul here but absent since a long time, called on me in person with reference to cotton claimed by English subjects. He seemed amazed when I told him I should pay no respect to consular certificates; and that in no event would I treat an English subject with more favor than one of our own deluded citizens—and that for my part, I was unwilling to fight for cotton for the benefit of Englishmen openly engaged in smuggling arms and munitions of war to kill us. That on the contrary, it would afford me great satisfaction to conduct my Army to Nassau and wipe out that nest of pirates.[2] I explained to him, however, that I was not a diplomatic agent of the General Government of the United States, but that my opinion, so frankly expressed, was that of a soldier, which it would be well for him to heed. It appeared also, that he owned a plantation on the line of investment of Savannah, which of course is destroyed, and for which he expected me to give him some certificate entitling him to indemnification, which I declined emphatically.

I have adopted in Savannah rules concerning property, severe but just: founded upon the laws of Nations, and the practice of civilized Governments: and am clearly of opinion that we should claim all the belligerent rights over conquered countries that the people may realize the truth that war is no childs play. I embrace in this a copy of a letter dated December 31st 1864, in answer to one from Solomon Cohen, a rich lawyer, to Gen. Blair, his personal friend, as follows:

"General:
Your note of this date, endorsing Mr. Cohen's is received: and I answer frankly, through you, his inquiries.

First: No one can practice law as an attorney in the United States, without acknowledging the supremacy of our Government. If I am not in error, an attorney is as much an officer of the court as the Clerk: and it would be a novel thing in a Government to have a court to administer law, that denied the supremacy of the Government itself.

Second: No one will be allowed the privileges of a merchant, or rather, to trade is a privilege that no one should seek of the Government, without in like manner acknowledging its supremacy.

Third: If Mr. Cohen remains in Savannah as a denizen, his property, real and personal, will not be disturbed unless its temporary use be necessary for the military authorities of the city. The title to property will not be disturbed in any event until adjudicated by the Courts of the United States.

Fourth: If Mr. Cohen leaves Savannah under my Special order No. 143,[3] it is a public acknowledgment that he adheres to the enemies of the United States, and all his property becomes forfeited to the United States: but as a matter of favor he will be allowed to carry with him clothing and furniture for the use of himself, his family and servants, and will be transported within the enemy's lines at our cost, but not by way of Port Royal.

These rules will apply to all parties, and from them no exceptions will be made.

I am &c."

This letter was in answer to specific inquiries: it is clear and specific, and covers all the points. And should I leave before my orders are executed, I will endeavor to impress upon my successor, Gen. Foster, their wisdom and propriety.

I hope the course I have taken in these matters will meet your approbation, and that the President will not refund to parties claiming cotton or other property, without the strongest evidence of loyalty and friendship in the part of the claimant, or unless some other positive end is to be gained. I am with great respect, Your obedient Servant

W. T. Sherman Maj. Genl.

Copy, DLC: Edwin M. Stanton Papers; *OR*, I, 47: pt. 2, 5–6.

1. Stanton to USG, December 26, 1864, 1:00 P.M., *PUSG*, 13:164n. "I hope you will give immediate instructions to seize and hold the cotton. . . . It ought not to be be [*sic*] turned over to any Treasury agent but held by Military authority until a special order of the Department is given for the transfer." All claims of title by British and other private claimants were to be ignored.

2. Confederate blockade runners operated from Nassau in the Bahamas.

3. Printed in *PM*, 2:233–34. This order, dated December 26, 1864, laid out the rules pursuant to Savannah's military occupation, stating that "during war, the military is superior to civil authority, and, where interests clash, the civil must give way." The mayor should

notify all citizens that they must "remain within our lines, and conduct themselves as good citizens [of the United States], or depart in peace."

TO ELLEN EWING SHERMAN

Headquarters, Military Division
of the Mississippi,
In the Field, Savannah, Jan. 5 1865

Dearest Ellen,

I have written several times to you and to the Children. Yesterday I got your letter of Dec. 23, and realize the deep pain and anguish through which you have passed in the pain and sickness of the little baby I never saw. All spoke of him as so bright and fair that I had hoped he would be spared to us to fill the great void in our hearts left by Willy, but it is otherwise decreed and we must submit. I have seen death in Such quantity and in Such forms that it no longer startles me, but with you it is different and tis well that like the Spaniards you realize the fact that our little baby has passed from the troubles of life to a better existence[.] I sent Charley off a few days ago to carry to Genl. Grant & to Washington some important dispatches, but told him he must not go farther than Washington as by the time he returns I will be off again on another Raid. It is pretty hard on me that I am compelled to make these blows which are necessarily trying to *me*, but it seems devolved on me and cannot be avoided. If the honors prof[f]ered and tendered me from all quarters are of any value they will accrue to you & the children. John writes that I am in every body's mouth and that even he is Known as my brother, and that all the Shermans are now feted as relations of me. Surely you and my Children will not be overlooked by those who profess to honor me. I do think that in the Several Grand Epochs of this war my name will bear a prominent part, and not least among them will be the determination I took at Atlanta to destroy that place & march on this City, whilst Thomas my Lieutenant should dispose of Hood. The idea, the execution and Strategy are all good and will in time be understood. I dont Know that you comprehend the magnitude of the thing, but you can see the importance attached to it in England, where the Critics stand ready to turn against any American General who makes a mistake or fails in its execution. In my case they had time to commit themselves to the conclusion that if I succeeded I would be a great General, but if I failed I would be set down a fool. My success is already assured so that I will be forced to sustain the title. I am told that were I to go north I would be feted and petted, but as I have no intention of going you must sustain the honors of the family. I know exactly what amount of merit attaches to my own conduct, and what will survive the clamor of time. The quiet preperation I made before the Atlanta Campaign, the rapid movement on Resaca, the crossing the Chattahoochee without loss in the face of a skilful General with a good army—the movement on Jonesboro, whereby Atlanta fell, and the resolution I made to divide my army, with one part to take Savannah and the other to meet Hood in Tennessee are all clearly mine, and will survive us both in History. I dont know that you can understand the merit of the latter, but it will stamp me in years to come, and will be more appreciated in Europe than in America. I warrant your father will find parallel in the history of the Greeks & Persians, but none on our Continent. For his sake I am glad of the success that has attended me and I Know he will feel more pride in my success than you or I do. Oh! that Willy was living, how his Eyes would brighten and his bosom swell with honest pride if he could hear & understand these things. I may be mistaken but I dont think Tommy so entirely identifies himself in my fortunes. He is a fine manly boy, and it may be as he develops he will realize our fondest expectations, but I Cannot but think that he takes less interest in me than Willy showed from the hour of his birth. It may be I gave the latter more of my personal attention at the time when the mind began to develop. You will doubtless read all the details of our march & Stay in Savannah in the Papers whose spies infest our Camps spite of all I can do, but I could tell you thousands of little incidents which would more interest you. The women here are as at Memphis disposed to usurp my time more from Curiosity than business. They had been told of my burning & killing till they expected the veriest monster but their eyes were opened when Hardee G. W. Smith & McLaws,[1] the three Chief officers of the Rebel Army fled across the Savannah River consigning their families to my special care. There are some very elegant people here, whom I Knew in Better days and who do not seem ashamed to call on the Vandal Chief. They regard us just as the Romans did the Goths and the parallel is not unjust. Many of my stalwart men with red beards and huge frames look like Giants, and it is wonderful how smoothly all things move for they all seem to feel implicit faith in me not because I am strong or bold but because They think I Know every thing. It seems impossible for us to go anywheres without being where I have been before. My former life from 1840 to 1846 seems providential and every bit of Knowledge then acquired is returned tenfold. Should it so happen that I should approach Charleston over that very ground where I used to hunt with Jim Poyas, and Mr. Quash, and ride by moonlight to Save daytime it would be even more strange than here where I was only a visitor. Col. Kilburn[2] arrived here from Louisville yesterday, and begged me to remember him to you. I continue to receive letters most flattering from all my old friends and Enclose you two, one from General Hitchcock & one from Professor Mahan[3]—such men do not flatter and are judges of what they write. I See by the papers that the movement to give us a

farm originates with Mr. Hunter, Talmadge and Brazen and their paper pre-
cedes the taking of Savannah—"{Salwannas} where the wars is"—Tell Minnie
& Lizzie that I will write them again before starting out, and I will send
Tommy some papers that he will value, as parts of the history of the Campaign. My Report is nearly done, but will be General, short and uninteresting.
I hope you are as comfortable as you expected. I Sent you a check for $800
from here & $1100 from Atlanta which you should acknowledge[.] yrs.

W. T. Sherman

ALS, InND: Sherman Family Papers.

1. Major General Lafayette McLaws (1821–97), CSA, had commanded the District of
Georgia and the defense of Savannah. For WTS's treatment of the families of Confederate
generals, see *PM*, 2:235–36.

2. Charles Lawrence Kilburn (1819–99) was chief commissary of the Department of the
South.

3. E. A. Hitchcock to WTS, December 26, 1864; Hitchcock had sent his congratulations
and added, "You have long since justified your early opinions of the true character of the
war." DLC: WTS. D. H. Mahan to JS, December 19, 1864, cited above.

TO ABRAHAM LINCOLN

Hdqrs. Military Division
of the Mississippi,
In the Field, Savannah, January 6, 1865.

His Excellency President Lincoln,
Washington:
Dear Sir:

I am gratified at the receipt of your letter of Dec 26,[1] at the hand of General
Logan, Especially to observe that you appreciate the division I made of my
army, and that each part was duly proportioned to its work. The motto,
"Nothing ventured, nothing won" which you refer to is most appropriate, and
should I venture too much and happen to lose I shall bespeak your charitable
inference. I am ready for the Great Next as soon as I can complete certain
preliminaries, and learn of Genl Grant his and your preferences of intermediate "objectives."

With great respect, your servant,
W. T. Sherman,
Major-General.

Telegram, DLC: Robert T. Lincoln Collection of Abraham Lincoln Papers; *OR*, I, 47: pt.
2, 18–19.

1. Lincoln had written Sherman about his anxiety at the beginning of the March to the
Sea, "but feeling you were the better judge, and remembering that 'nothing risked, nothing
gained' I did not interfere. . . . In showing to the world that your army could be divided,
putting the stronger part to an important new service, and yet leaving enough to vanquish

the old opposing force of the whole—Hood's army—it brings those who sat in darkness, to see a great light. But what next? I suppose it will be safer if I leave Gen. Grant and yourself to decide." *CWAL*, 8:181–82.

TO SALMON P. CHASE

Headquarters Military Division
of the Mississippi,
In the Field, Savannah Jan. 11 1865

Hon. S. P. Chase.
Washington D.C.
My Dear Sir,

I feel very much flattered by the notice you take of me, and none the less because you overhaul me in the Negro question.[1] I mean no unkindness to the Negro in the mere words of my hasty despatch announcing my arrival on the Coast.[2] The only real failures in a military sense, I have sustained in my military administration have been the expedition of Wm. Sooy Smith and Sturgis, both resulting from their encumbering their columns with refugees. (negros)[3] If you can understand the nature of a military column in an enemys country, with its long train of wagons you will see at once that a crowd of negros, men women and children, old & young, are a dangerous impediment.

On approaching Savannah I had at least 20,000 negros, clogging my roads, and eating up our subsistence. Instead of finding abundance here I found nothing and had to depend on my wagons till I opened a way for vessels and even to this day my men have been on short rations and my horses are failing. The same number of white refugees would have been a military weakness. Now you Know that military success is what the nation wants, and it is risked by the crowds of helpless negros that flock after our armies. My negro constituents of Georgia would resent the idea of my being inimical to them, they regard me as a second Moses or Aaron. I treat them as free, and have as much trouble to protect them against the avaricious recruiting agents of New England States as against their former masters. You can hardly realize this, but it is true. I have conducted to freedom & asylum hundreds of thousands and have aided them to obtain employment and houses. Every negro who is fit for a soldier and is willing I invariably allow to join a Negro Regiment, but I do oppose and rightfully too, the *forcing* of negros as soldiers. You cannot Know the acts and devices to which base white men resort to secure negro soldiers, not to aid us to fight, but to get bounties for their own pockets, and to diminish their quotas at home. Mr. Secretary Stanton is now here and will bear testimony to the truth of what I say. Our Quartermaster and commissary can give employment to every negro (able bodied) whom we obtain, and he protests against my parting with them for other purposes, as it forces him to use my veteran white troops to unload vessels, and do work for which he prefers the negro. If the President prefers to minister to the one idea of negro Equality, rather than military success; which as a major involves the minor, he should remove me, for I am so constituted that I cannot honestly sacrifice the security and Success of my army to any minor cause.

Of course I have nothing to do with the Status of the Negro after war. That for the law making power, but if my opinion were consulted I would Say that the negro should be a free race, but not put on an equality with the whites. My Knowledge of them is practical, and the effect of equality is illustrated in the character of the Mixed race in Mexico and South America. Indeed it appears to me that the right of suffrage in our Country should be rather abridged than enlarged.

But these are all matters subordinate to the issues of this war, which can alone be determined by war, and it depends on good armies, of the best possible material and best disciplined, and these points engross my entire thoughts. with sincere respect & esteem

W. T. Sherman
Maj. Genl.

ALS, PHi: Salmon P. Chase Papers.

1. Chase to WTS, January 2, 1865, DLC: WTS. Chase had reprimanded WTS for his language about blacks. "You are understood to be opposed to their employment as Soldiers, and to regard them as a set of pariahs, almost without rights." Particular attention had been paid to WTS's remarks about the need to get rid of surplus negroes, mules, and so on, all lumped together, in his first communication with Halleck after reaching the coast. "I do remember the regret I felt that an expression classing men with cattle found place in a paper, which cannot fail to be historical." Chase stated that blacks had natural rights, and he thought that they needed to vote to secure their freedom. He asked Sherman to reconsider his position on freedmen and think more carefully about what he said: "Your example, for good or evil, will be followed by officers of lower character & less discretion."

2. See WTS to HWH, December 13, 1864, above.

3. Smith had been driven back to Memphis by Forrest during his moves between that city and Meridian in January 1864, and Sturgis had failed to destroy Forrest and his men in a June 1864 campaign out of Memphis.

TO HENRY W. HALLECK

Hdqrs. Military Division
of the Mississippi,
In the Field, Savannah, January 12, 1865.

Major-General Halleck:

My Dear Friend:

I received yours of January 1 about the "negro."[1] Since Mr. Stanton got here we have talked over all matters freely, and I deeply regret that I am threatened with that curse to all peace and comfort—popularity; but I trust to bad luck enough in the future to cure that, for I know enough of "the people" to feel that a single mistake made by some of my subordinates will tumble down my fame into infamy.

But the nigger? Why, in God's name, can't sensible men let him alone? When the people of the South tried to rule us through the negro, and became insolent, we cast them down, and on that question we are strong and unanimous. Neither cotton, the negro, nor any single interest or class should govern us.

But I fear, if you be right that that power behind the throne is growing, somebody must meet it or we are again involved in war with another class of fanatics. Mr. Lincoln has boldly and well met the one attack, now let him meet the other.

If it be insisted that I shall so conduct my operations that the negro alone is consulted, of course I will be defeated, and then where will be Sambo?

Don't military success imply the safety of Sambo and *vice versa*? Of course that cock-and-bull story of my turning back negroes that Wheeler might kill them is all humbug. I turned nobody back. Jeff. C. Davis did at Ebenezer Creek forbid certain plantation slaves—old men, women, and children—to follow his column; but they would come along and he took up his pontoon bridge, not because he wanted to leave them, but because he wanted his bridge.

He and Slocum both tell me that they don't believe Wheeler killed one of them. Slocum's column (30,000) reports 17,000 negroes. Now, with 1,200 wagons and the necessary impedimenta of an army, overloaded with two-thirds negroes, five-sixths of whom are helpless, and a large proportion of them babies and small children, had I encountered an enemy of respectable strength defeat would have been certain.

Tell the President that in such an event defeat would have cost him ten thousand times the effort to overcome that it now will to meet this new and growing pressure.

I know the fact that all natural emotions swing as the pendulum. These southrons pulled Sambo's pendulum so far over that the danger is it will on its return jump off its pivot. There are certain people who will find fault, and they can always get the pretext; but, thank God, I am not running for an office, and am not concerned because the rising generation will believe that I burned 500 niggers at one pop in Atlanta, or any such nonsense. I profess to be the best kind of a friend to Sambo, and think that on such a question Sambo should be consulted.

They gather round me in crowds, and I can't find out whether I am Moses or Aaron, or which of the prophets; but surely I am rated as one of the congregation, and it is hard to tell in what sense I am most appreciated by Sambo—in saving him from his master, or the new master that threatens him with a new species of slavery. I mean State recruiting agents. Poor negro—Lo, the poor Indian! Of course, sensible men understand such humbug, but some power must be invested in our Government to check these wild oscillations of public opinion.

The South deserves all she has got for her injustice to the negro, but that is no reason why we should go to the other extreme.

I do and will do the best I can for negroes, and feel sure that the problem is solving itself slowly and naturally. It needs nothing more than our fostering care. I thank you for the kind hint and will heed it so far as mere appearances go, but, not being dependent on votes, I can afford to act, as far as my influence goes, as a fly wheel instead of a mainspring.

With respect, &c., yours,

W. T. Sherman.

Printed, *OR*, I, 47: pt. 2, 36–37.

1. In his letter Halleck warned Sherman that the general's reputation for racial prejudice against blacks was damaging his image and influence. *OR*, 1, 47: pt. 2, 4–5.

TO ELLEN EWING SHERMAN

Headquarters, Military Division

of the Mississippi,

In the Field, Savannah Geo. Jan. 15 1865

Dearest Ellen,

I have all your letters up to the 4th as also yours to Charley which I have read in his absence, so that I am now well advised of all matters.[1] It may be some days yet before I dive again beneath the Surface to turn up again in Some mysterious place. I have a clear perception of the move, but take it for granted that Lee will not let me walk over the track without making me sustain some loss. Of course my course will be north. I will fcignt on Augusta & Charleston, avoid both and make for Columbia, Fayetteville and Newbern N.C. Dont breathe for the walls have ears and foreknowledge published by some mischievous fool might cost many lives. We have lived long enough for men to thank me for Keeping my own counsels, and Keeping away from Armies those pests of newspapermen. If I have attained any fame it is pure & unalloyed by the taint of parasitic flattery and the result is to you and the children more agreeable, for it will go to yours & their benefit more than all the Surface flattery of all the Newspaper men of the country. Mr. Stanton has been here and is cured of that Negro nonsense which arises not from a love of the negro but a desire to dodge Service. Mr. Chase & others have written to me to modify my opinions but you Know I cannot for if I attempt the part of hypocrite it could break out at each Sentence. I want soldiers made of the best bone & muscle in the land and wont attempt military feats with doubtful materials. I have said that Slavery is dead and the Negro free and want him treated as free & not hunted & badgered to make a soldier of when his family is left back on the Plantations. I am right & wont Change[.] The papers of the 11th are just in and I see Butler is out[2]—that is another of the incubi of the Army. We want & must have professional soldiers, young & vigorous. Mr. Stanton was delighted at my men and the tone which pervades the army.[3] He enjoyed a good Story which is true told of one of my old 15 corps men. After we reached the Coast we were out of bread, and it took Some days for us to get boats up—A foraging party was out and got a boat & pulled down the Ogeechee to Ossabaw & met a steamer coming up—They haild her & got answer that it was the *Nemeha*, and had Major General Foster on board. The Soldier answered Oh H— l, we've got 27 Major Generals up at Camp, what we want is hard tack. The soldiers manifest to me the most thorough affection, and a wonderful Confidence. They havent found out yet where I have *not* been. Every place we go, they hear I lived there once, and the usual Exclamation is—The "Old Man" must be "omnipresent" as well as omnipotent—I was telling some officers the other day if events should carry us to Charleston I would have advantage because I Knew the ground &c. &c. They laughed heartily at my innocence for they Knew I had been everywhere. But really my long sojourn in this quarter of the world from 1840 to 1846 was & is providential to me.

I have read most of the current discourses about me, those you sent including, but take most interest in the London Spectator, the same that reviewed my Knoxville Campaign[.] He is surely a critic, for he catches the real points well. The *Times* utterly overstates the case, and the Dublin papers are too fulsome. Our American papers are Shallow. They dont look below the Surface. I receive letters from all the Great Men, so full of real respect that I cannot disregard them, yet I dread the Elevation to which they have got me. A single mistake or accident my pile, though well founded would tremble, but I base my hopes of fair fame on the opinion of my own army, & my associates[.] I know nothing as yet of the project to present us a farm or house. I would personally prefer land cleared & improved as property but wont think of it till asked, or I will say nothing if you conduct the whole matter as I cannot expect ever to have a local habitation. I would rather have such a property settled on the children, or entailed on the survivor of the name. For myself individually I Should hardly accept—I Sent you a check for 1100 from Atlanta and 800 since my arrival here. I can hardly expect any more for two months as I will surely be off in the course of this week, and you will hear of me only through Richmond for two months. You have got used to it now and will not be concerned though I think the chances of getting killed on this trip about even. If South Carolina lets me pass across without desperate fighting her fame is gone forever. Charley is still absent north, but I look for him hourly. He should not go beyond Washington, or be there more than one day. He will have written & telegraphed you. No doubt you will see several persons who have seen me here, and the newspapers complete the picture. Savannah would be an agreable place to me less burdened with the cares of armies, women, cotton negros and all the disturbing Elements of this war. I would not be surprised if I would involve our Govt. with England. I have taken all the Cotton as prize of war 30,000 bales, equal to 13 millions of dollars, much of which is claimed by English merchants. I disregard their Consular Certificates on the ground that this cotton has been notoriously employed to buy cartridges & arms, and practical Ships, and was collected here for that very purpose. Our own merchants are equally Culpable, they buy cotton in advance and take the chances of capture, and then clamor. I am glad Tommy is now fairly established at School. I will risk his being a Priest—Of course I should regret such a choice and ask that no influence be let to produce that result—Let him have a fair manly Education, and his own instincts will lead him right—I dont care how strict he may be in Religion, but dont want him a Priest, but he is too young for even the thought. As to myself dont distress yourself, I am as good as the average and must take my chances, and exposed as I have been and Still am, you may rest assured I have given death a fair study, and fear it but little. I fear somewhat your mind will settle into the "Religio Melancholia," which be assured is not of divine inspiration, but rather a morbid state not natural or healthful

AL (incomplete), InND: Sherman Family Papers.

1. EES to WTS, December 29 and 30, 1864, and January 3 and 4, 1865, SFP, apprised her husband of family matters, such as getting their children settled at school.

2. USG had sent Butler back to Massachusetts to await further orders after his failure to take Fort Fisher in December.

3. Stanton visited Sherman at Savannah in early January 1865, in part because of complaints about Sherman's treatment of blacks.

TO JOHN SHERMAN

Headquarters, Military Division
of the Mississippi,
In the Field, Savannah, Geo.
Jan. 19, 1865

Dear Brother,

I got your letter about Mr. Rees who arrived today and Mr. Hoyt not yet come.[1] I send you some of my orders touching trade and other matters in this Dept. I cannot of myself take control of this matter as it involves details that would take up too much of my time. My troops are already in motion and I will soon be off again without a real Base or line of Communication, leaving others here and on this coast to execute plans & a policy that I am forced to initiate. I am afraid that my acts & merits have exalted me too high. Charley Ewing tells me that the talk was to make or create an office for me. You may say to Senators that I would much prefer that if my name is confused with an act of Congress it do not pass, or rather that no such Bill be offered or discussed.[2] I dont want Promotion, but on the Contrary I want rest, as soon as I can ask for it decently. The Law cannot confer military fame nor can it make my right to command greater than it now is. I have all the Power that can possibly be exercised Acts of Special Legislation never do good. When the War is over there will be time enough for honors and Pensions, but now every possible pretext for jealousy and envy should be avoided. Repeal that mischievous act of sending agents to get recruits, abolish all bounties, enforce the draft honestly and fairly, and make service an honor instead of onerous. Try and arrange that Recruits come in by instalments, and organize no new Regmts. Then raise plenty of money and leave Grant alone. We will work as fast as we can and attempt any thing that is possible. I never saw Gen. Butler but cannot deny that I look on his downfall as the addition of 20,000 men to Grant's Army. The trouble with such men is they wont fight themselves, but keep their commands out—Terrys success[3] simply fulfils Grants calculation, and stamps Butlers pretension about shedding blood uselessly as poltroonery & Knavery. I have been delayed here longer than I calculated by the new arrival of vessels with forage, delayed by foul weather. Give my love to Cecilia and the Girls Affectionately,

W. T. Sherman

ALS, DLC: William T. Sherman.

1. JS had written on January 11 introducing David Rees, an Ohio legislator who had helped engineer JS's election to the U.S. Senate, and Samuel Hoyt, a relation who worked for the firm of Jesse Hoyt & Co. in New York City. He also urged his brother to accept the house offered to him by the state of Ohio as thanks for his war services for the security of his family. DLC: WTS.

2. After the successful March to the Sea, a bill had been introduced into Congress to create another lieutenant generalship for WTS and to split control of the army between him and USG. Lloyd Lewis, *Sherman: Fighting Prophet* (1932; reprint, Lincoln, Neb., 1993), 472.

3. Major General Alfred H. Terry (1827–90), USA, captured Fort Fisher and closed the last open Confederate port, Wilmington, in January, after Grant ordered him to assault the post in the wake of Butler's abortive expedition.

TO EDWIN M. STANTON

Headquarters, Military Division
of the Mississippi,
In the Field, Savannah, Ga.
Jan'y 19th 1865

Hon. Edwin M. Stanton
Secretary of War, Washington, D.C.
Sir,

When you left Savannah a few days ago you forgot the map which Gen. Geary[1] had prepared for you, showing the route by which this division entered the city of Savannah, bring[ing] the first troops to occupy that city. I now send it to you.

I avail myself of the opportunity also to enclose you copies of all my official orders touching trade and intercourse with the people of Georgia, as well as for the establishment of the negro settlements.[2]

Delegations of the people of Georgia continue to come in, and I am satisfied that with a little judicious handling and by a little respect being paid to their prejudices, we can create a schism in Jeff Davis' dominions. All that I have conversed with realize the truth that Slavery as an institution is defunct: and the only questions that remain are what disposition shall be made of the negroes themselves. I confess myself unable to offer a complete solution for these questions, and prefer to leave it to the slower operation of time. We have given an initiative, and can afford to wait the working of the experiment.

As to trade matters, I also think that it is to our interest to keep the people somewhat dependent upon the articles of commerce to which they have been hitherto accustomed. General Grover[3] is now here and will, I think, be able to manage this matter judiciously and may gradually relax, and invite cotton to come in in larger quantities. But at first we should manifest no undue anxiety on that score for the rebels would at once make use of it as a power against us. We should assume a tone of perfect contempt, for cotton and everything else in comparison with the great object of the war—the restoration of the Union with all its rights and power. If the rebels burn cotton as a war measure, they simply play into our hands by taking away the only product of value they now have to exchange in foreign parts for warships and munitions. By such a course also they alienate the feelings of the large class of small farmers that look to their little parcels of cotton to exchange for food and clothing for their families. I hope the Government will not manifest too much anxiety to obtain cotton in large quantities, and especially that the President will not endorse the contracts for the purchase of large quantities of cotton. Several contracts, involving from six to ten thousand bales, indorsed by Mr. Lincoln, have been shown me, but were not in such a form as to amount to an order for me to facilitate their execution.

As to Treasury trade agents, and agents to take charge of confiscated and abandoned property, whose salaries depend upon their fees, I can only say that as a general rule they are mischievous and disturbing elements to a military government. And it is almost impossible for us to study the law and regulations so as to understand fully their powers and duties. I rather think the Quartermaster's Department of the Army could better fulfill all their duties and accomplish all that is aimed at by the law. Yet on this subject I will leave Gen. Foster and Gen. Grover to do the best they can. I am with great respect, your obedient servant

W. T. Sherman

Maj. Gen. Comdg.

LS, DLC: Edwin M. Stanton Papers; *OR*, I, 47: pt. 2, 87–88.

1. Major General John W. Geary (1819–73), USA, commanded the Second Division, Twentieth Corps.

2. WTS was referring to his controversial Special Field Orders No. 15, January 16, 1865, setting the Sea Islands aside for black habitation. *PM*, 2:250–52. For "trade and intercourse with the people of Georgia," see Special Field Order No. 143, December 26, 1864, *PM*, 2:233–34.

3. Brigadier General Cuvier Grover (1828–85), USA, had recently taken command of Grover's Division, District of Savannah, and would command the District of Savannah after mid-February.

TO CAROLINE CARSON[1]

Jan. 20 1865

Savannah Geo.

Mrs. Caroline Carson,

151. e. 15th St. New York.

Dear Madam,

I have your valued favor of Jan. 8, and answer your that I remember well your home on Cooper, with your two pretty children, and the well ordered plantation of Col. Carson, still better the family of your venerated father,[2] your mother, Sue[3] and Dan and the sweet Miss Carrie North. To any of these would I gladly extend any favor official or personal in my power. Already is the advance of my army at Pocataligo and other masses are marching into position and I merely delay here to give them time when I too will enter Carolina, not as they say with a heart bent on desolation and destruction, but to vindicate the just power of the Government which received terrible insults at the hands of the People of that State. Gladly will I try to temper the harsh acts of war, with mercy towards those who by falsehood and treachery have been led step by step from the generous practice of hospitality to deeds of crime & violence. If I hear of your mother & Sister, or of your boy I will be sure to put them where they will be at least safe from personal danger, and I would account it a most fortunate event if your boy should fall into my hands.[4] I will see that no harm befalls him, but that he will go where you can reach him. There is not an officer in my army but knows that Mr. Petigru stood almost alone a Rock against which the waves of Treason beat in vain, but swept all that was near and dear to him into mire.

I cannot promise you that I will go to Charleston or Summerville, because I am making Grand War, when lesser objects must be left to follow Greater Results, but I pledge you that my study is to accomplish Peace and honor at as small a cost to life and property as possible. I know this end will be attained, but how & when are still in the future. I grieve to hear you are not well, doubtless more sick at heart than in body, but cheer up, for the day will surely come, when the name of Petigru will be a passport everywhere and when the sweet persimmons and roses of your old home will welcome back their mistress. I thank you for the expressions of confidence in me, and repeat that you do me but justice in thinking that I am not the scourge and monster that the Southern Press represents me, but that I will take infinitely more delight in curing the wounds made by war, than in inflicting them. Carolina herself tormented us with posturing and cowardice, and forced us to the Contest. Let her admit her error, and we will soon make all sunshine and happiness, where Gloom and misery reign Supreme. I will bear in mind the name & Regt. of your son James, and need no memorandum of Sue or your mother[.] I think the former will recall me as one of her standard beaux on Sullivan's Island, & if need be will seek me out, for she cannot be so estranged as to suppose me different from what I was. With sincere respect, your friend & servant

W. T. Sherman

ALS, DLC: James L. Petigru Papers.

1. Caroline Petigru Carson (b. 1819–fl. 1885), a portrait painter and miniaturist, had married William A. Carson in 1840 and had moved to New York City in 1860 because of her Unionist sympathies. During the 1880s she would spend time in Rome.

2. James Louis Petigru, a noted Charleston lawyer and Unionist.

3. Susan Petigru King (1824–75) was an author and a widow; her husband, a lawyer, had been killed in action in 1862. She would later write to WTS herself for protection of her property in South Carolina. King to WTS, May 10, 1865, DLC: WTS.

4. On January 31, Carson replied to this letter. "I shall preserve your letter as a treasure on account of its noble expressions," she declared. South Carolina, she was sure, would get what it deserved from Sherman's men. She reiterated that her son James Carson had not been a willing recruit; he was taken from school against his wishes. As he was a minor and she his legal guardian, she wanted him returned. DLC: WTS. On March 24, WTS replied that he had not found James but that a neighbor of hers in South Carolina had reported that he was an officer in Hardee's Signal Corps. WTS left word with this neighbor that if she saw him she was to tell him the WTS would protect him and send him north or abroad if he wished to desert. DLC: James L. Petigru Papers.

TO ULYSSES S. GRANT

> Headquarters, Military Division
> of the Mississippi,
> In the Field, Savannah Geo.,
> January 21, 1865

General U. S. Grant,
City Point Va.
General,

In fulfilment of my projet General Howard moved the 17th Corps Genl. Blair from Thunderbolt, to Beaufort SC, and on the 14th by a Rapid movement secured the Port Royal Ferry, and moved against Pocataligo which he gained on the 15th the day appointed. By that course we secured the use of the Ground in South Carolina up the SalkeeHatchee (Saltketchee) and Gen. Slocum was ordered in like manner to get his wing up about Robertville by way of the Savannah River and the Union Causeway. The transfer of men, animals & wagons by steamers is a very slow process, and on the 19th Genl. Slocum had only two Divisions of the 20th at Purysburg and Hardeeville, with open Communications with Howard. Jno. E. Smith crossed by the Union Causeway on which Slocum had put ten days hard work, but the hard rains had raised the Savannah River so that the whole country was under water and the Corduroy Road on the Union Causeway was carried away, cutting off our Brigade of Jno. E. Smith, one Division of the 15th Corps (Corses) and all of the 14 Corps Genl. Davis. All were ordered to move up the West Bank of the Savannah, to Cross at Sisters Ferry but the Rains have so flooded the Country that we have been brought to a Stand Still, but I will persevere and get the army as soon as possible up to the Line from Sisters Ferry to Pocat=ligo, whence we will have terra firma to work on. Our supplies have come daily, that is we have never had four 4 days forage ahead, but I will depend on enough Coming to get me out to the neighborhood of Barnwell, where we will find some.

Gen. Grovers Division now occupies Savannah which I had re-fortified, and I have turned over everything to Genl. Foster so that nothing now hinders me but water. I rather think the heavy Rains in January, will give us good weather in February and March. You Cannot do much in Virginia till April & May, and when I am at Goldsboro, and move against Raleigh, Lee will be forced to divide his Command, or give up Richmond.

I am rejoiced that Terry took Fisher because it silences Butler, who was to you a dangerous man. His address to his troops on being relieved,[1] was a direct mean & malicious attack on you, and I admire the patience & skill by which you relieved yourself & the Country of him. If you want some new and Fresh men able to handle large armies I will offer you Charles R. Woods, Hazen and Mower, all good and Capable officers for an army of any size. Of Course I prefer to have them myself, but would give them up if you can do better by them. As soon as possible if I were in your place I would break up the Dept. of the James, make the Richmond Army one, then when I get to Goldsboro, you will have a force to watch Lee, and I can be directed to gradually close in, cutting all communications. In the mean time Thomas army should not be reduced too much, but he should hold Chattanooga, Decatur & Eastport, collect supplies, and in all February and March move on Tuscaloosa, Selma, Montgomery, and back to Rome Georgia, where he could be met from Chattanooga. I take it for granted that Beauregard will bring as fast as he Can such part of Hoods Army as Can be moved over to Augusta, to hit me in flank as I swing round Charleston. To cover the withdrawal Forrest will be left in Mississipi and west Tennessee to divert attention by threatening the Boats on the Mississipi and Tennessee River. These should be disregarded, and Thomas should break through the Shell, expose the Trick and prevent the planting of Corn this Spring in Middle Alabama. The People of Georgia, like those of Mississipi are worn out with Care, but they are so afraid of their own People, that they fear to organize for positive resistance. Their notions of "honor" & "fair play" are that by Abandoning the Cause now they would be Construed as "mean" for leaving their Comrades in the Scrape. I have met the overtures of the People frankly & given them the best advice I know how. I enclose copies of orders issued for the guidance of Gen. Foster & other officers on this Coast. These orders were made in conference with the Sec. of War.

I have been told that congress meditates a bill to make another Lt. Genl. for me.[2] I have written to John to stop it if it is designed for me. It would be mischievous, for there are enough rascals who would try to sow differences, whereas you & I now are in perfect understanding. I would rather have you in Command than *anybody* for you are fair, honest, and have at heart the Same purpose that Should animate all. I should Emphatically decline any Commission Calculated to bring us into rivalry, and I ask you to advise all your friends in Congress to this Effect, Especially Mr. Washburn. I doubt if men in Congress fully realize that you and I are honest in our professions of want of ambition. I know I feel none and today will gladly surrender my position and influence to any other who is better able to wield the power. The flurry attending my recent success will soon blow over, and give place to new developments. I Enclose a letter of General instructions to Gen. Thomas[3] which I beg you to revise and Endorse or modify. I am truly yours,

W. T. Sherman
Maj. Genl.

ALS, CSmH; *OR*, I, 47: pt. 2, 102–4.

1. Butler's farewell to the soldiers of the Army of the James, published on January 8, asserted that he had been removed because of his reluctance to sacrifice needlessly the lives of his men, a pointed reference to Grant's high casualty rates. *OR*, I, 46: pt. 2, 120.

2. WTS to JS, January 19, 1865. USG responded to WTS on February 1 that "I have received your very kind letter in which you say you would decline, or are opposed, to promotion. No one would be more pleased at your advancement than I, and if you should be placed in my position and I put subordinate it would not change our personal relations in the least. I wo[uld] make the same exertions to support you that you have ever done to support me, and would do all in my power to make our cause win." *PUSG*, 13:350.

3. Presumably WTS to Thomas, January 21, 1865, below.

TO THOMAS EWING SHERMAN

Headquarters, Military Division
of the Mississippi,
In the Field, Savannah Geo.,
January 21, 186[5]

Dear Tommy,

I suppose Mama has told you all about my army travelling across Georgia and coming out on the ocean at the beautiful City of Savannah. You will find it in your Geography, but can hardly understand the importance of it till you are larger and older. I expect soon to march again to danger & battle but hope the good luck of the Past will stick by me, and that one of these days, we will all have a home where we can live together and then I will tell you all about my travels and battles. You will be told that I am a great General and the boys will expect you to be the same, but you need not mind them[.] When I was a boy I was not as smart as you, and you can take your own time learning as fast as you please and when you get old Enough can choose for yourself whether to be a Soldier or Lawyer, Doctor or Farmer. Mama tells me the People are going to give us a farm or house in Cincinati. If it be a farm you will have to be a farmer for the Girls cannot take care of a farm, but I suppose Mama will pick a house, which will do for us all, and then you can choose a profession. I dont want you to be a Soldier or a Priest but a good useful Man—We are all very sorry that Poor little Charley is lost to us, but we must submit for death does not consult our Wishes.

Mama tells me that you have had a sore throat but that you would be well in a day or so, and back at School which you like very much. I cannot expect to come to See you till next summer and even then I may not but I will come to See you all as soon as I can. I send you some photographs which are not good but the best I have. One of these days I will send you some more maps and papers to keep as Mementos of the War. Give my love to Tommy Ewing and all the children. Yr. father,

W. T. Sherman
Maj. Gen.

ALS, InND: Sherman Family Papers.

TO GEORGE H. THOMAS

Headquarters, Military Division
of the Mississippi,
In the Field, Savannah Geo.,
January 21, 1865

Maj. Genl. Geo. H. Thomas
Comdg. Army in the Field, N. Alabama
via Nashville.
General,

Before I again dive into the Interior and disappear from view I must give you in general terms such instructions as fall within my province as Commander of the Divn.

I take it for granted that you now reoccupy in strength the Line of the Tennessee, from Chattanooga to Eastport. I suppose Hood to be down about Tuscaloosa & Selma and that Forrest is again scattered to get horses & men, and to divert attention (paper damaged) You should have a small cavalry force of say 2000 men to operate from Knoxville through the Mountain Pass along the French Broad into North Carolina, to keep up the belief that it is to be followed by a considerable force of Infantry. Stoneman could do this, whilst Gillem[1] merely watches up the Holston.

At Chattanooga should be held a good reserve of provisions & forage, and in addition to its garrison a small force that could at short notice relay the Rail road to Resacca, prepared to throw provisions down to Rome on the Coosa. You remember I left the Railroad track from Resacca to Kingston & Rome with such a view. Then with an army of 25,000 Infantry & all the cavalry you can get under Wilson, you should move from Decatur and Eastport to Some point of concentration about Columbus Miss., and thence march to Tuscaloosa and Selma, destroying fences, gathering horses, mules, (wagons to be burned,) and doing all the damage possible, burning up Selma, that is the Navy Yards the Rail road back towards the Tombee, and all Iron foundries, mills & factories. If no considerable army opposes you, you might reach Montgomery and deal with it in like manner, and then at leisure work back along the Selma & Rome Road, via Talladega, & Blue Mountains to the Valley of Chatooga, to Rome, or Lafayette. I believe such a Raid perfectly practicable and easy, and that it will have an excellent effect. It is nonsense to Suppose that the People of the South are enraged or united by such movements. They reason very differently. They see in them the Sure and inevitable destruction of all their property, they realize that the Confederate armies cannot protect them, and they see in the repetition of such raids the inevitable result of starvation & misery. You should not go south of Selma & Montgomery because south of that Line the Country is barren & unproductive. I would like to have Forrest hunted down & Killed, but doubt if we can do that yet. Whilst you are thus employed I expect to pass through the center of South & North Carolina, and I suppose Canby will also Keep all his forces active & busy. I have already secured Pocataligo & Grahamville, from which I have fine roads into the Interior. We are all well. yrs. truly

W. T. Sherman
Maj. Gen. Comdg.

ALS, MH; *OR*, I, 45: pt. 2, 621–22.
1. Brigadier General Alvan C. Gillem (1830–75), USA, was commanding the Fourth Division, Cavalry Corps, Army of the Cumberland.

TO JOHN SHERMAN

Headquarters, Military Division
of the Mississippi,
In the Field, Savannah, Geo.
Jan. 22, 1865

Dear Brother,

I have often read of votes of Thanks by Congress to me & my army, but have never received official notice of any.[1] I dont know whether it is customary for the Clerk of Either branch to send notice of such Resolutions, or that one is left simply to find out as he best may. Will you enquire and if I should have copies of the Resolutions get them and send them to Ellen for deposit to the use of my children.

I start today for the advance of my army at Pocataligo, but we have had such storms & rains that the whole country is under water, but I will be off as soon as possible. No one is more alive to the importance of time than I am.

I wrote you that I deem it unwise to make another Lt. Genl. or to create the Rank of General. Let the Law Stand as now. I will accept no commission that would tend to create a rivalry with Grant. I want him to hold what he has earned, and got. I have all the Rank I want, and on the score of pay, as long as I can keep out in the woods my family can live on my pay, about $550 a month. I dont save anything for Ellens expenses have been and are heavy—Mine are comparatively light. If you ever hear anybody use my name in connection with a Political office tell them you know me well enough to assure them that I would be offended by such association. I would rather be an engineer of a Rail road, than President of the U.S. or any political office. In military titles I have now the Maximum, and it makes no difference whether that be Maj. Genl. or Marshal. It means the same thing I have commanded one hundred thousand men in battle, and on the march, successfully and without confusion, and that is enough for reputation. Next I want rest & Peace and they can only be had through war. You will hear of me but not from me for some time.

AL (closing and signature clipped), DLC: William T. Sherman.

1. On January 10, 1865, Congress voted its thanks to WTS and his command for operations in Georgia.

TO HENRY W. HALLECK

Head-Quarters, Military Division
of the Mississippi,
In the Field, Pocataligo, S.C.
Jan. 27 1865.

Maj. Genl. H. W. Halleck,
Chief of Staff, Washington D.C.
General,

We had heavy and continuous rains up to and including the 24th inst. causing all the Rivers the Savannah included to overflow their banks, and making the Roads simply impassable. I came up to this point on the 25th and with the troops here, 17th Corps have been demonstrating against the Salke hatchee but that Stream is out of its banks and we cannot cross. I only aim to drive the Enemy over towards Edisto a little further from our flank when I move against the Charleston and Augusta road. I have in person reconnoitered the ground from Salketchee Bridge back to Coosawhatchee and find the Country very low and intersected by creeks and points of salt marsh, making Roads very bad, but I am pushing to get the Right wing here, and have official notice from Gen. Slocum that he and the 20th Corps Genl. Williams on this side the Savannah or {Perrysburg}, and on the 25th the 14th Corps Genl. Davis would resume his march from Cherokee Hill 10 miles out of

Savannah where he was Caught by the rain storm, so that I expect to hear of the Left wing and cavalry reaching {Sitter} ferry tomorrow, a Gunboat, and fleet of transports will attend the left wing up the Savannah River, and Gen. Slocum is ordered to replenish his wagons, rendezvous at Robertville & report his readiness to me. I expect on Monday or Tuesday next viz. Feb. 1st to be all ready when I will move rapidly up towards Barnwell, and wheel to the Right on the Railroad at Midway leaving Branchville to the Right, after destroying that road, I will move on Orangeburg and So on to Columbia, avoiding any works the enemy may construct in my path and forcing him to fight me in open ground if he risk battle.

I will use Hatch's Division of Fosters Command (4000) to cover my movement by posting it between this and Salkehatchee bridge. You will note that our position is now nearer Branchville than from Charleston. I get a few deserters & have made some prisoners who report Cavalry only between me and Barnwell, and Infantry between me and Charleston. Of Course I shall Keep up the delusion of an attack on Charleston *always*, and have instructed Gen. Foster to watch the harbor Close from Morris Isd. and when he hears of my being on the Rail road near Branchville to make a landing at Bulls Bay and occupy the Georgetown Road 24 miles east of Charleston. Admiral Dahlgren will also keep up the demonstration on Charleston. My Chief difficulties will be to Supply my army but on this point I must risk a good deal, based upon the idea that where other People live we can, Even if they have to starve or move away.

Weather is now Cold & clear. I will write again. I am with respect &c.

W. T. Sherman
Maj. Gen. Comdg.

ALS, CsmH; *OR*, I, 47: pt. 2, 135–36.

TO PHILEMON B. EWING

Head-Quarters, Military Division
of the Mississippi,
In the Field, Pocataligo S.C.
Jan. 29 1865.

Dear Phil,

I have been wanting to write you for a month but have let days & weeks pass by and now find myself on the Edge of civilization about to cut loose to attempt another of those Grand Schemes of War that make me stand out as a Grand Innovator. Of course I know better that I have done nothing wonderful or new, but only incur risks proportioned to the ability to provide for them. The Dutch & Greek navigators clung to the Land, but others struck out across the ocean depending on the Compass, and now who clings to the land is deemed the less safe Sailor. So in War, who clings to a base or defends it is less at Ease than one who makes his army strong and dont dissipate it by detachments. But let the world draw its own conclusions I know my Enemy and think I have made him feel Effects of war, that he did not expect, and he now Sees how the Power of the United States can reach him in his innermost recesses. I have gained thus far more Earthly fame than is Convenient, for it imposes labors & responsibilities that have to be met, and these I would avoid if possible. Grant & I by preserving our Common relation of friends have been enabled to act in unison & harmony and anything tending to disturb that harmony would damage the Common interest and detract from our Common honors. I hear of a Bill to create a new office of Lt. General, for me. I have written to John not to allow it, but to say in Committee I would not accept as it might cause a rivalry not with us individually, but on the part of mischievous friends. Again it is proposed to make the Rank of General for Grant & me for Lt. General. This too I oppose we began the war with our present system and should not alter now. My Rank is now Enough for legal purposes, and additional Rank would confer no title. I am now a General in Command of an Army as large as possible, indeed my Command now runs from the Mississipi to the Atlantic and in fact I command wherever I go and no one disputes and it is impossible to confer more. I prefer to let things remain as now and have so urged upon John who will doubtless make Known my preference. Indeed the fact that Such perfect harmony Exists between me and all Commanders gives me as much influence in the military world as I could ask.

The movement in Ohio militated by Mr. Hunter, Talmadge & Brazen seems to need form and I observe in some paper that a meeting was held at Columbus in which it took form & shape, to give me an hundred thousand dollars, and to consult me as to its disposal before being committed. I of course cannot deny that I have at times been uneasy lest some shot would leave Ellen & the children dependent on the world—but this if successful supplies that defect. Then it wont make much difference if I do occasionally go where bullets are thicker than comfortable. I would much prefer the investment to remain in the form of interest paying Bonds, and the nearer the investment takes the Shape of such an investment the nearer will it Conform to my wishes. A farm which is a Comfortable thing to a farmer is an Elephant to a wanderer. A house in Cincinati to one of my habits would also be of doubtful propriety for I cannot imagine any contingency of life that would Keep me in Cincinati longer than a day: so that the house would only be acceptable as a place of refuge to my family in case of my being out of the way,

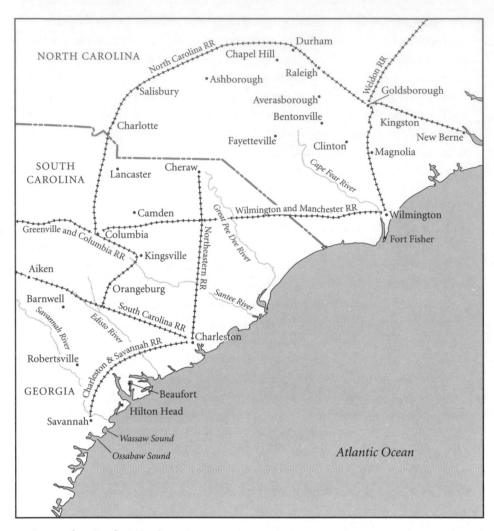

Savannah to Durham Station

and personally of the two I would prefer a farm as something tangible that might by judicious management pay its own taxes. But on the whole Bonds of the United States or of the State of Ohio would be more appropriate and acceptable. If the contributions be confined to Ohio, then her Bonds would be appropriate, if they be of various states then the Bonds of the U.S. In a few days I will again be cut off from Communication and it is for this reason that I write to you, that Mr. Hunter and the others who have so Kindly interested themselves Should know my wishes. Were I alone in the World or had I in former years secured a competence I would not accept Even this tribute, but I admit that Ellen calls for so much money that at times I have nothing ahead.

My wants are few and my pay ample, but money now has little comparative value—my pay now is less than I paid a negro Porter in one California Bank, viz. $300 Gold per mo.—my pay is about $550 in Greenbacks. If however the Contributors insist on land or fixtures, then a Country Seat near Cincinati would most fulfil the conditions, but it should be all finished, one on which some retired merchant had spent a fortune in hopes to Secure peace after a life of bustle and probably secured an Early death. I remember Several Such places near Cincinati. I could if free Settle down anywhere, but it is not likely I will be consulted, for no sooner is one war over before I have another, for I have actually been at war since 1840.

I am at this moment at a Plantation home near Pocataligo around which I am assembling men & materiel of war for the invasion of South Carolina where I spent so many years. The rice fields look familiar, the River Forest, and rows of live oaks, but the People are all gone, Negros & whites and desolation is supreme. I know that at Some point I will meet a desperate Set, who look upon me as a renegade, one who has enjoyed their hospitality and now threatens them with fire & sword. Their devotion is wonderful, Men of immense Estates of incomes of 30 to 50,000 dollars have given up all and now Serve as Common Soldiers in the Ranks. Why cannot we inspire our people with the Same ardor, Whereas they Seem men intent on getting negros & vagabonds to take the place of Soldiers.

I have no doubt Hugh is offended with me. He wrote me for a command in this Army. I offered him a Division at Nashville but he declined & now to give him place I would have to remove some General who has stood by his command through both the Atlanta & Savannah Campaigns. I foresaw it at Nashville & told him so but he knew better & now I cannot remedy it. A man might as well sit on the banks of the Mississipi and complain he did not get down the River faster, a man in War must go with Events. If he steps to one side for a moment he is drifted into an Eddy and can never recover the chance. In the Same way Charley should not hope for a General Commission unless he gets a Regiment & takes the time necessary. It is now too late to expect those accidents by which Genls. were made at the beginning of the War. Actual Experience in Command on the Field of Battle is the only proper title to promotion. It is pitiful now to See the Brigadiers kicked about in search of a command. I will not displace one of my faithful officers for another who has a senior commission. Congress should rectify the whole matter by expunging the list and commissioning only such as Exercise the Command. I am told that at Cincinati, New York Washington you Encounter more Generals than you do in my Camp. I have been writing by twilight and got off the Lines, but will dress up now that Candles are lighted. I cant do anything more for Charley unless you can get him a Commission as Colonel of an Ohio Regiment. As to Hugh I have written to General Thomas if possible to give him a Division, but we are all burdened down with Generals, and as fast as a vacancy happens by death or resignation some one is on the ground ready & prepared for the Command, and it is impossible to hold vacancies for the absent. I think Hugh made his Choice last fall and should content himself as he best may. It is only by being just to all present, and preferring only the Zealous officer that I maintain such a hold on my Army. I never absent myself an hour, and cannot overlook it in others. George Thomas has not been absent since the War began, & Slocum and Howard who command my wings have not been away an hour since the war began some when carried home wounded. These are the men that can be relied on. Blair has been away, but he has a "Corps" which is a Specialty—not vacated by absence.

My Right wing is now here, draws its supplies from the head of Port Royal. My left Wing is over on the Savannah River near Sisters Ferry. I expect to be all ready by the 30th when I will again cut loose and penetrate the State trusting to our Strong Arms to cut our way out. I have pretty clearly marched out in my mind my course which does not touch Charleston, but it will force that place to extremity and the Enemy may give it up, but it makes little difference, as it does us little harm now, and is not worth the time of a seige. You may not hear from me for a month and then on the N. Carolina Coast. Keep this to yourself, and breath not a syllable, for it is only by keeping my own Counsels that I have succeeded.

I still threaten the newspaper men with instant death as Spies and they give me a wide berth. They manage to go along, but not in that dictatorial way they used to. They are meek & humble enough save on paper.

Weather has been very bad, swelling all the Streams and Swamps but now it is fair and beautiful. Give my love to Mary to Aunt Sissy and all at home. affectionately yr. brother,

W. T. Sherman

Assure Mr. Hunter, Mr. Talmadge & Brazen that I am more than thankful for the extraordinary interest they have manifested in me. Also to Martin & Doughterty the Same.

ALS, Atlanta, Ga.: Private Collection of C. Parke Day.

Headquarters, Military Division
of the Mississippi,
In the Field, Pocataligo S.C.
Jan. 29 1865.

Lt. Genl. U. S. Grant,
City Point, Va.
Dear General,

Capt. Hudson[1] has this moment arrived with your letter of Jan. 21,[2] which I have read with interest. The capture of Fort Fisher has a most important bearing on my campaign and I rejoice in it for many reasons, because of its intrinsic importance and because it gives me another point of security on the sea board. I hope General Terry will follow it up by the capture of Wilmington although I did not look for it from Admiral Porters dispatch to me. I rejoiced that Terry was not a West Pointer, that he belonged to your army, and that he had the Same troops with which Butler feared to make the attempt—Porter is in high glee.

Admiral Dahlgren, whose fleet is reinforced by some more iron clads wants to make an assault a-la-Fisher on Ft. Moultrie but I withold my consent for the reason that the capture of all Sullivans Island is not conclusive as to Charleston. The capture of all of James Island would be, but all pronounce that impossible at this time. Therefore I am moving as hitherto designed for the Railroad west of Branchville, then swing across to Orangeburg, which will interpose my army between Charleston and the Interior. Contemporaneous with this Foster will demonstrate up the Edisto, and afterwards make a lodgment at Bulls Bay, and occupy the common Road which leads from Mount Pleasant towards Georgetown. When I get to Columbia I think I shall move straight for Goldsboro via Fayetteville. By this circuit I cut all Roads and devastate the land; and the forces along the Coast commanded by Foster will follow my movement taking anything the enemy lets go, or so occupies his attention that he cannot detach all his forces against me. I feel sure of getting Wilmington & may be Charleston: and being at Goldsboro, with its railroads finished back to Morehead City & Wilmington, I can easily take Raleigh, where it seems that Lee must come out of his trenches or allow his army to be absolutely invested. If Schofield comes to Beaufort he should be packed out to Kingston on the Neuse, & may be Goldsboro, or rather a point on the Wilmington Road south of Goldsboro. It is not necessary to storm Goldsboro, because it is in a desolate region of no importance in itself; and if its Garrison is forced to draw supplies from its north it will be eating up the Same stores on which Lee depends for his command. I have no doubt Hood will bring his army to Augusta, and Canby and Thomas should penetrate Alabama as far as possible, to keep employed at least a part of Hoods army: or what would accomplish the same thing Thomas might reoccupy the Railroads from Chattanooga forward to the Etowah, viz. Rome, Kingston & Allatoona thereby threatening Georgia. I know that the Georgia troops are disaffected. At Savannah I met delegations from the several counties to the South West, that manifested a decidedly hostile spirit to the Confederate Cause. I nursed it along as far as possible and instructed Grover to Keep it up.

My Left Wing must now be at Sisters Ferry crossing the Savannah River to the East bank Slocum has orders to be at Robertville tomorrow prepared to move on Barnwell. Howard is here all ready to Start for the Augusta Railroad at Midway. We find the enemy on the east side of the Salkiehatchee and Cavalry in our front, but all give ground on our approach, and seem to be merely watching us. If I start on Tuesday, on one week I will be near Orangeburg, having broken up the Augusta Road from the Edisto westward twenty or twenty-five miles. I will be sure that every Rail is twisted. Should I encounter too much opposition near Orangeburg then I will for a time neglect that Branch, and rapidly move on Columbia and fill up the triangle formed by the Congaree & Wateree, tributaries of the Santee, breaking up that great center of the Carolina Roads. Up to that point I feel full confidence, but from there I may have to manoeuvre some, and will be guided by the questions of weather and supplies. You remember I had fine weather all February for my Meridian trip, and my memory of the weather at Charleston is that February is usually a fine month. Before the March storms come, I Should be within striking distance of the Coast. The months of April & May will be the best for operations from Goldsboro, to Raleigh and the Roanoke. You may rest assured that I will Keep my troops well in hand, and if I get worsted will aim to make the enemy pay so dearly that you will have less to do. I know this trip is necessary to the war. *It must be made* sooner or later, and I am on time and in the right position for it. My army is large enough for the purpose, and I ask no reinforcement but simply wish the utmost activity at all other points, so that Concentration against me may not be universal. I expect Davis will move Heaven & Earth to catch me, for Success to my Columns is fatal to his dream of empire. Richmond is not more vital to his Cause than Columbia and the heart of South Carolina.

If Thomas will not move on Selma, order him to occupy Rome, Kingston and Allatoona, and again threaten Georgia in the direction of Athens. I think the Poor White trash of the South are falling out of their Ranks by sickness, desertion and every other available means; but there is a large class of vindictive southerns who will fight to the last. The Squabbles in Richmond, the howls in Charleston, and the disintegration elsewhere, are all good omens to us, but we must not relax one iota, but on the Contrary pile up our efforts.

I would ere this have been off, but we had terrific Rains which caught me in motion, and nearly drowned some of my Colums in the Rice fields of the savannah, swept away our Causeway which had been carefully corduroyed, and made the Swamps here about mere lakes of slimy mud, but the weather is now good and I have my army on terra firma. Supplies too came for a long time by daily driblets instead of in bulk, but this is now all remedied, and I hope to Start on Tuesday. I will issue instructions to Foster, based on the reinforcement of North Carolina, and if Schofield come you had better relieve Foster who cannot take the Field & needs an operation on his leg, and let Schofield take Command, with Head Qrs. at Beaufort N.C. & orders to secure if possible Goldsboro, with railroad connections back to Beaufort & Wilmington. If Lee lets us get that position he is gave up. I will start with my Atlanta Army about 60,000, supplied as before and depending on the Country for all in excess of 30 days. I will have less Cattle on the hoof, but I hear of hogs, cows & calves in Barnwell & the Columbia Districts. Even here we found some forage. Of course the Enemy will carry off & destroy Some forage, but I will burn their houses where the People burn forage, and they will get tired of that.

I must risk Hood & trust to you to hold Lee, or be on his heels if he comes south. I can observe that the Enemy has some respect for my men, for they gave up Pocataligo quick, when they heard that the attacking force belonged to me. I will try and keep up that feeling which is a real Power. With respect Your friend,

W. T. Sherman
Maj. Gen. Comdg.

I leave my chief Qr. mr. & commissary behind to follow coastwise.

ALS, PPRF; *OR*, I, 47: pt. 2, 154–56.

1. Captain Peter T. Hudson of USG's staff.

2. USG to WTS, January 21, 1865, *PUSG*, 13:291–93. USG announced that he had ordered Schofield to join USG as Thomas was proving too slow and would not be done by spring. Thomas was to be ordered to move on Selma if he could; Canby to "act offensively from the Sea coast to the interior towards Montgomery & Selma." If Thomas's men did not move from the north, some of his men should be sent to supplement Canby's. Fort Fisher had been captured; Wilmington was rumored to be, too. Schofield would go there if the rumor was true, to New Bern otherwise to cooperate with WTS. Sixteen thousand men from Lee's army had been sent south. All Federal troops would be subject to WTS's orders as he came into contact with them.

TO OLIVER O. HOWARD

> Hdqrs. Military Division
> of the Mississippi,
> In the Field, Rocky Mount,
> February 23, 1865—10 a.m.

Major-General Howard,
Commanding Right Wing:
General:

I have just been down to the bridge. It will take all of to-day and to-morrow to get this wing across and out. You may go ahead, but keep communication with me. I expect Kilpatrick here this p.m. and will send him well to the left. He reports that two of his foraging parties were murdered by the enemy after capture and labeled, "Death to all foragers." Now it is clearly our war right to subsist our army on the enemy. Napoleon always did it, but could avail himself of the civil powers he found in existence to collect forage and provisions by regular impressments. We cannot do that here, and I contend if the enemy fails to defend his country we may rightfully appropriate what we want. If our foragers act under mine, yours, or other proper orders they must be protected. I have ordered Kilpatrick to select of his prisoners man for man, shoot them, and leave them by the roadside labeled, so that our enemy will see that for every man he executes he takes the life of one of his own. I want the foragers, however, to be kept within reasonable bounds for the sake of discipline. I will not protect them when they enter dwellings and commit wanton waste, such as woman's apparel, jewelry, and such things as are not needed by our armor; but they may destroy cotton or tobacco, because these are assumed by the rebel Government to belong to it, and are used as a valuable source of revenue. Nor will I consent to our enemy taking the lives of our men on their judgment. They have lost all title to property, and can lose nothing not already forfeited; but we should punish for a departure from our orders, and if the people resist our foragers I will not deem it wrong, but the Confederate army must not be supposed the champion of any people. I lay down these general rules and wish you to be governed by them. If any of your foragers are murdered, take life for life, leaving a record of each case,

> I am, with respect,
> W. T. Sherman,
> Major-General, Commanding.

Printed, *OR*, I, 47: pt. 2, 537.

TO HUGH JUDSON KILPATRICK

> Hdqrs. Military Division
> of the Mississippi,
> In the Field, Rocky Mount, S.C.,
> February 23, 1865.

Major-General Kilpatrick,
Commanding Cavalry:
General:

Yours of last night is received and your dispositions of matters are all right. The bridge is laid and troops are crossing. I am anxious to get the wagons across and up on high ground before the rain comes. I wish you would keep your cavalry on roads to the north of the direct one by Gladden's Grove, as that will be needed all day for infantry and wagons. You shall have the bridge as fast as your brigades come. I regret the matter you report, that eighteen of your men have been murdered after surrender, and marked that the enemy intended to kill all foragers. It leaves no alternative; you must retaliate man for man and mark them in like manner. Let it be done at once. We have a perfect war right to the products of the country we overrun, and may collect them by foragers or otherwise. Let the whole people know that the war is now against them, because their armies flee before us and do not defend their country or its frontier as they should. It is petty nonsense for Wheeler and Beauregard and such vain heroes to talk of our warring against women and children. If they claim to be men they should defend their women and children and prevent us reaching their homes. Instead of maintaining their armies let them turn their attention to their families, or we will follow them to the death. They should know that we will use the produce of the country as we please. I want the foragers to be regulated and systematized so as not to degenerate into common robbers, but foragers, as such, to collect corn, bacon, beef, and such other products as we need, are as much entitled to our protection as our skirmishers and flankers. You will, therefore, at once shoot and leave by the roadside an equal number of their prisoners, and append a label to their bodies stating that man for man shall be killed for every one of our men they kill. If our foragers commit excesses punish them yourself, but never let an enemy judge between our men and the law. For my part I want the people of the South to realize the fact that they shall not dictate laws of war or peace to us. If there is to be any dictation we want our full share.

> Yours, truly,
> W. T. Sherman,
> Major-General, Commanding.

Printed, *OR*, I, 47: pt. 2, 543–44.

TO WADE HAMPTON[1]

Headquarters, Military Division
of the Mississippi
In the Field Feb. 24—1865

Lt. Genl. Wade Hampton
Comdg. Cavalry forces C.S.A.
General,

It is officially reported to me that our foraging parties are murdered after capture and labelled "Death to all Foragers." One instance of a Lieut. and seven men near Chesterville and another of twenty "near a Ravine 80 rods from the main Road" about 8 miles from Fosterville[.]

I have ordered a similar number of prisoners in our hands to be disposed of in like manner.

I hold about 1000 of prisoners captured in various ways, and can stand it as long as you; but I hardly think these murders are committed with your Knowledge, and would suggest that you give notice to the People at large, that every life taken by them simply results in the death of one of your confederates.

Of course you cannot question my right to "forage on the country." It is a war right as old as history. The manner of exercising it varies with circumstances, and if the civil authorities will supply my Requisitions I will forbid all foraging. But I find no civil authorities who can respond to calls for Forage or provisions, and therefore must collect directly of the People. I have no doubt this is the occasion of much misbehavior on the part of our men, but I cannot permit an enemy to judge or punish with wholesale murder.

Personally I regret the bitter feelings engendered by this war: but they were to be expected, and I simply allege that those who struck the first blow, and made war inevitable, ought not in fairness to reproach us for the natural consequences—I merely assert our War Right to Forage, and my resolve to protect my foragers to the extent of life for Life.[2] I am with respect, Yr. obedt. servt.

W. T. Sherman
Maj. Genl. U. S. A.

Copy, CsmH; *OR*, I, 47: pt. 2, 546.

1. Lieutenant General Wade Hampton (1818–1902), CSA, commanded a cavalry corps ordered to cover Johnston's retreat through South Carolina.

2. Hampton's reply, dated February 27, said that he would shoot two Federal soldiers for every Confederate WTS killed. He denied that his men had murdered anyone but admitted issuing an order to shoot any soldier caught burning a private dwelling. *OR*, I, 47: pt. 2, 597–98.

CHAPTER 14

March 12, 1865–April 9, 1865

"**S**outh Carolina has had a visit from the West that will cure her of her pride and boasting," Sherman declared as his army made its way into North Carolina in March 1865.[1] Once in the Tar Heel State, however, Sherman directed his men to restrain themselves. He did so because he was aware that a good number of North Carolinians were either Unionists or susceptible to abandoning the Confederate cause; in such a case the olive branch might prove more effective than the sword in drawing these people back to the Union. The signs of Confederate collapse were multiplying each day, and Sherman no longer predicted that the conflict would drag on.

In anticipation of Sherman's advance, Grant ordered an amphibious assault against Fort Fisher, North Carolina, which protected Wilmington, the last major Confederate port. After Benjamin F. Butler botched an initial effort in December 1864, a second operation, directed by Alfred F. Terry, captured the fort in January. Convinced that George H. Thomas would not exploit his victory at Nashville, Grant decided to send for John M. Schofield and the Twenty-third Corps to travel by rail and sea to assist in taking Wilmington (a task accomplished on February 22) before moving inland to link up with Sherman. On March 19 Joseph E. Johnston, who had been restored to command in February, attempted to check Sherman's progress at Bentonville. Two days later, he withdrew after a pitched struggle, leaving Sherman free to link up with Schofield's column at Goldsboro on March 23.

Sherman anticipated that he might well have to help Grant in compelling Robert E. Lee to surrender; it was with this thought in mind that on March 26 he headed north to Grant's headquarters at City Point. There he encountered not only the general in chief but also President Lincoln. After discussing strategy with Grant on March 27, the following day Sherman joined Grant, Lincoln, and Admiral David D. Porter aboard the president's steamer, the *River Queen*, in a wide-ranging discussion of how best to terminate the war and establish the foundations for a lasting peace. Sherman and Lincoln did most of the talking; the president made clear his preference for generous terms and a lenient postwar settlement, although he did not dictate instructions. Sherman, who had once expressed a great deal of skepticism about Lincoln, was profoundly impressed by the president. Returning to his army at the end of the month, he looked forward to resuming operations on April 10.

1. WTS to EES, March 12, 1865.

TO ULYSSES S. GRANT

> Headquarters, Military Division
> of the Mississippi,
> In the Field, Fayetteville N.C.,
> March 12, 1865

Lt. Gen. U. S. Grant
Comdg. U.S. Army, City Point.
Dear General,

We reached this place yesterday at noon. Hardee as usual retreating across the Cape Fear burning his Bridge, but our pontoons will be up today, and with as little delay as possible I will be after him towards Goldsboro. A tug has just come up from Wilmington and before I get off from her I hope to get up from Wilmington some shoes & stockings, some sugar coffee & flour. We are abundantly supplied with all else, having in a measure lived off the Country. The Army is in Splendid health, condition and Spirit although we have had foul weather and roads that would have stopped travel, to almost any other body of men I ever read of.

Our march was substantially what I designed, straight on Columbia feigning on Branchville & Augusta. We destroyed in passing the Railroad from the Edisto nearly up to Aiken. Again from Orangeburg to the Congaree. Again from Columbia down to Kingsville and the Watersee, and up towards Charlotte as far as the Chester Line. Thence I turned east on Cheraw, and thence to Fayetteville. At Columbia we destroyed immense arsenals & Railroad establishments, among which were 43 cannon. At Cheraw we found also machinery & material of war from Charleston among which 25 guns, and 3600 barrels of Gun powder. And here we find about 20 guns, and a magnificent U.S. arsenal.

We cannot afford to leave detachments, and I Shall therefore destroy this valuable arsenal for the Enemy shall not have its use, and the United States Should never again confide such valuable property to a People who have betrayed a trust.

I could leave here tomorrow but want to clean my columns of the vast crowd of refugees and negros that encumber me. Some I will send down the River in boats & the balance will send to Wilmington by land under small escort as soon as we are across Cape Fear River.

I hope you have not been uneasy about us, and that the fruits of this march will be appreciated. It had to be made, not only to secure the valuable depots by the way, but its incidents in the necessary fall of Charleston, Georgetown and Wilmington. If I can now add Goldsboro, without too much cost, I will be in position to aid you materially in the Spring Campaign. Joe Johnston may try to interpose between me here and Schofield about Newbern, but I think he will not try that but concentrate his scattered armies at Raleigh, and I will go straight at him as soon as I get my men reclothed and our wagons reloaded. Keep everybody busy, and let Stoneman push towards Greensburg or Charlotte from Knoxville. Even a feint in that quarter will be most important. The Railroad from Charlotte to Danville is all that is left to the Enemy, and it wont do for me to go there on account of the "Red Clay" hills that are impassable to wheels in wet weather. I expect to make a junction with Schofield in ten days. Yrs. truly,[1]

W. T. Sherman Maj. Genl.

ALS, DNA: RG 108, Records of the Headquarters of the Army, Letters Received, AUS 1865, M57; *OR*, I, 47: pt. 2, 794–95.

1. USG replied on March 16 (*PUSG*, 14:172–75), commenting on Butler's failure to capture Fort Fisher, labeling George H. Thomas as "slow beyond excuse," and discussing troop movements, Sheridan, and Lee's present situation.

TO ELLEN EWING SHERMAN

Headquarters, Military Division
of the Mississippi,
In the Field, Fayetteville N.C.
Sunday March 12, 1865

Dearest Ellen,

We reached this place yesterday in good health and condition—we have had bad roads and weather but made good progress, and have achieved all I aimed to accomplish. Our Main Columns came through Columbia & Cheraw S.C. We have had no general battle, and only skirmishes on the Skirts of the army. The Enemy gave ground wherever I moved in force. The importance of this march exceeds that from Atlanta to Savannah. South Carolina has had a visit from the West that will cure her of her pride and boasting. I sent Couriers to Wilmington and a tug boat got up this morning and I will start her back at 6 P.M. with dispatches for Grant, the Sec. of War, and all my subordinate Commanders. I do not intend to go to the Sea Shore, but will move on. I have no doubt you have all been uneasy on our account, but barring bad weather & mud we have had no trouble. I fear the People along our Road will have nothing left wherewith to Support an hostile army, but as I told them their sons & brothers had better Stay at home to take Care of the females instead of running about the Country playing soldiers. The same brags and boasts are Kept up, but when I reach the path where the lion crouched I find him slinking away. My army is in the Same condition as before, and seem to possess abiding confidence in its officers[.] It would amuse you to hear their comments on me as I ride along the ranks—but I hope you will hear the jokes & fun of war at a fitter time for amusement. Now it is too Serious. I think we are bringing matters to an issue. Johnston is restored to the Supreme Command[1] and will unite the forces hitherto Scattered and fight me about Raleigh or Goldsboro. Lee may reinforce him from Richmond, but if he attempts that Grant will pitch in. I can whip Joe Johnston unless his men fight better than they have since I left Savannah. As I rode into Columbia crowds gathered round me, composed of refugees & many officers who had Escaped their prison Guards, and hid themselves. One of them handed me the enclosed which is so handsomely got up that I deem it worthy of preservation. I want Lizzie to keep it. The versification is good and I am told the music to which the Prisoners set and Sung it is equally so. I have never heard it sung, as the officers who composed the Glee Club in their prison at Columbia were not of the number who did escape. The author did escape and he is the one I have appointed to carry my dispatches down to Wilmington tonight.[2]

I expect to stay here a few days in hopes to receive some bread & shoes for Wilmington. The River is now high and easily navigated, and had I time I should have no trouble in getting supplies up, but time is so important that I must "Forward." Charley is very well and Should write you but I doubt if he will. He ought to Know that I have not time on occasions like this.

It is now 2 P.M. and I have written ten letters of 4 pages each—orders and instructions to my commanders on the sea board. Give my best love to the the young folk. You will next hear from me at Newbern North Carolina. yrs. ever,

W. T. Sherman
Maj. Genl.

ALS, InND: Sherman Family Papers.

1. On February 22, 1865, at the request of Robert E. Lee, Jefferson Davis approved his request to restore Johnston to command over both the Department of South Carolina, Georgia, and Florida and the Department of Tennessee and Georgia.

2. Captain Samuel H. M. Byers (1838–1933) of the Fifth Iowa Infantry had written "Sherman's March to the Sea" and now began his long relationship with WTS.

Headquarters, Military Division
of the Mississippi,
In the Field, Fayetteville N.C.
Sunday March 12, 1865

Hon. E. M. Stanton
Sec. of War
Dear Sir,

I Know you will be pleased to hear that my army has reached this point and have opened communication with Wilmington. A Tug boat came up this morning and will start back at 6 P.M. I have written to General Grant a letter the Substance of which he will doubtless communicate and it must suffice for me to tell you what I know will give you pleasure that I have done all I proposed, and the fruits seem to me ample for the time employed. Charleston Georgetown and Wilmington are incidents, whilst the utter demolition of the Railroad System of South Carolina, and the utter destruction of the enemys arsenals at Columbia, Cheraw and Fayetteville are the Principals of the movement. These points were regarded as inaccessible to us, and now no place in the Confederacy is safe against the Army of the West. Let Lee hold on to Richmond, and we will destroy his Country, and then of what use is Richmond. He must come out, and fight us on open ground, and for that we must ever be ready. Let him stick behind his parapets and he will perish.

I remember well what you asked of me, and think I am on the right road though a long one. My army is as united and cheerful as ever, and as full of confidence in themselves and their leaders as ever. It is utterly impossible for me to enumerate what we have done but I enclose a slip just handed me which is but partial. At Columbia & Cheraw we destroyed nearly all the Gunpowder & cartridges the Confederacy had in this part of the country.

This arsenal is in fine order and much enlarged. I cannot leave a detachment to hold it, and therfore shall burn it, blow it up with Gunpowder, and then with rams Knock down its walls. I take it for granted the United States will never again trust Carolina with an arsenal to appropriate at her pleasure.

Hoping that Good fortune may still attend my army I remain your servant
W. T. Sherman
Maj. Genl.

ALS, DLC: Edwin M. Stanton Papers; *OR*, I, 47: pt. 2, 793–94.

TO ALFRED H. TERRY

Head Qrs. Mil. Div. of the Miss.
In the Field Fayetteville, N.C.,
March 12th 1865

Maj. Genl. Terry
Comdg. U.S. Forces, Wilmington
General:

I have just received your message by the Tug which left Wilmington at 2 P.M. yesterday and arrived here without trouble.[1] The scout who brought me your cipher message started back last night with my answers which are superceded by the fact of your opening the river.[2] Genl. Howard just reports that he has secured one of the Enemy's Steamboats below the City and Genl. Slocum will try and secure two known to be above: and we will load them with refugees white & black that have clung to our skirts, impeded our movements, and consumed our food.

We have swept the country well from Savannah here, and my men and animals are in fine condition. Had it not been for the foul weather I would have caught Hardee at Cheraw or here—but at Columbia, Cheraw and here we got immense Stores and have destroyed machinery, guns, ammunition and property of inestimable value to our Enemy. At all points he has fled from us, "Standing not on the order of his going." The people of South Carolina instead of feeding Lee's Army, will now call on Lee to feed them.

I want you to send me all the shoes, stockings, drawers, sugar, coffee and flour you can spare, finish the loads with oats or corn. Have the boats escorted, and let them run at nights at any risk.

We must not lose time for Joe Johnston to concentrate at Goldsboro. We cannot prevent his concentrating, at Raleigh, but he shall have no rest. I want General Schofield to go on with his Railroad from Newbern as far as he can, and you do the same from Wilmington. If we can get the roads to and secure Goldsboro by April 10" it will be soon enough, but every day now is worth a million of dollars. I can whip Joe Johnston provided he dont catch one of my Corps in flank, and I will see that my army marched hence to Goldsboro in compact form. I must rid my army of from 20 to 30,000 useless mouths, as many to go down Cape Fear as possible and balance will go in the vehicles and captured horses, via Clinton to Wilmington.

I thank you for the energetic action that has marked your course, and shall be most happy to meet you. I am truly your friend,

W. T. Sherman
Maj. Genl: Comdg.

Lbk, DNA: RG 94, Records of the Adjutant General's Office, Generals' Books Papers, William T. Sherman, Letterbook 15; *OR*, I, 47: pt. 2, 803.

1. Terry to WTS, March 11, 1865, *OR*, I, 47: pt. 2, 790, discussed the Rebels' obstruction of the river and his moves to clear it.

2. WTS to Terry, March 11, 1865, *OR*, I, 47: pt. 2, 790.

TO ULYSSES S. GRANT

Hdqrs. Military Division
of the Mississippi,
In the Field, Goldsborough, N.C.,
March 23, 1865.

Lieut. Gen. U. S. Grant,
Commanding Armies of the United States, City-Point, Va.:
General:

On reaching Goldsborough this morning I found Lieutenant Dunn waiting for me with your letter of March 16 and dispatch of 17th.[1] I wrote you fully from Bentonville [Cox's Bridge] yesterday, and since reaching Goldsborough have learned that my letter was sent punctually down to New Berne, whence it will be dispatched to you. I am very glad to hear that Sheridan did such good service between Richmond and Lynchburg, and hope he will keep the ball moving. I know these raids and dashes disconcert our enemy and discourage him. Slocum's two corps—Fourteenth and Twentieth—are now coming in, and I will dispose them north of Goldsborough, between the Weldon road and Little River. Howard today is marching south of the Neuse, and to-morrow will come in and occupy ground north of Goldsborough, and extending from the Weldon railroad to that leading to Kinston. I have ordered all the provisional divisions made up of troops belonging to other corps to be broken up and the men to join their proper regiments and organizations, and have ordered Schofield to guard the railroads back to New Berne and Wilmington, and make up a movable column equal to 25,000 men with which to take the field. He will be my center as in the Atlanta campaign. I don't think I want any more troops other than absentees and recruits to fill up the present regiments, but that I can make up an army of 80,000 men by April 10. I will put Kilpatrick out at Mount Olive Station, on the Wilmington road, and then allow the army some rest. We have sent all our empty wagons under escort, with the proper staff officers, to bring up clothing and provisions. As long as we move we can gather food and forage, but the moment we stop trouble begins. I feel sadly disappointed that our railroads are not done. I don't like to say that there has been any neglect until I make inquiries, but it does seem to me the repairs should have been made and the road properly stocked. I can only hear of one locomotive besides the four old ones on the New Berne road and two damaged locomotives found by Terry on the Wilmington road. I left Easton and Beckwith purposely to make arrangements in anticipation of my arrival, and I have heard from neither, though I suppose them both to be at Morehead City. At all events we have now made a junction of all the armies, and if we can maintain them will in a short time be in position to march against Raleigh, or Gaston, or Weldon, or even Richmond, as you may determine. If I get the troops all well placed, and the supplies working well, I might run up to see you for a day or two before diving again into the bowels of the country. I will make in a very short time accurate reports of our operations for the past two months.

Yours truly,

W. T. Sherman,

Major-General, Commanding.

Printed, *OR*, I, 47: pt. 2, 969.

1. On March 16, Grant wrote Sherman: "I have never felt any uneasiness for your safety but I have felt great anxiety to know just how you were progressing. I knew, or thought I did, that with the magnificent Army with you, you would come out safely some place." *PUSG*, 14:172–75.

TO ELLEN EWING SHERMAN

Headquarters, Military Division
of the Mississippi,
In the Field, Goldsboro, N.C.,
March 23, 1865

Dearest Ellen,

I wrote you from Fayetteville. On our way there the enemy struck on Left flank and I turned on him and after three days manoeuvering & fighting defeated him and drove him off towards Raleigh. The fight was ncar Bentonville, 20 miles from here on the South side of the Neuse in the direction of Smithfield. I got here today and all the army will be in by tomorrow. Thus have I brought the army from Savannah in good order, beaten the enemy wherever he attempted to oppose our progress, and made junction with Schofield & Terry from Newbern & Wilmington on the 21st, one day later than I had appointed before leaving Savannah. It is far more difficult and important than the Savannah march. Besides the immediate results we have forced the Rebels to abandon the whole sea coast. I almost fear the consequences of the Reputeign this will give me among military men. I have received one letter from you[1] and one from Minnie, also a vast package from everybody. I now have a Staff officer Maj. Hitchcock[2] to answer them. I only have time to make general orders, and to write special letters. I must be more careful as I find silly people to claim my acquaintance publish my letters as extracts. You Know how hurriedly I always write and that I might be falsely placed by such things. I will be here some weeks. I should See Grant before assuming the offensive and think he will come down. I could have time to run to Washington, but prefer to Stay with my troops. It gives me great power with them to Share the days & nights. I always encamp and am now in a shaky fly, open, with houses all round occupied by Rebels or staff officers. Soldiers have a wonderful idea of my Knowledge and attach much of our continued success to it, and I really do think they would miss me, if I were to go away for even a week. I notice that you propose to take part in a sanitary fair at Chicago.[3] I dont much approve of ladies selling things at a table. So far as superintending the management of such things I dont object, but it merely looks unbecoming for a lady to Stand behind a table to sell things. Still do as you please. I have nothing that would engross the profits. My Saddle bags, a few old traps &c. I would collect plenty of trophies but have always refrained and think it best I should. Others do collect trophies & send home but I prefer not to do it. I have no doubt that you will be sufficiently gratified to know that I have eminently succeeded in this last venture, and will trust to luck that in the next still more hazardous I will be again favored. I dont believe anything has tended more to break the pride of the South, than my steady persistent progress. My army is dirty ragged & Saucy. I have promised them rest, clothing & food, but the Railroads have not been completed as I expected and I fear we may be troubled thereby. I am just informed that the telegraph Line is finished from the Sea to this place, so our Lines of Communication will be shortened. Strange to Say we are all in fine health & condition, only a little blackened by the pine smoke of our Camp fires. I would like to march this army through New York just as it appears today, with its wagons, pack mules, cattle niggers and bummers, and I think they would make a more attractive show than your fair. Give my love to Maj. Taylor if you see him, and if this finds you at Chicago, you will find many who claim me as an acquaintance. I am glad to hear the Children thrive so well I wish you would consult some Eminent physician about Lizzies cars. It may be some simple operation may be of life long service to her. I will write when more at leisure I am now writing whilst a letter for Grant is being copied to go off by a special Courier. yrs. ever,

W. T. S.

ALS, InND: Sherman Family Papers.

1. Probably EES to WTS, March 7–8, 1865, SFP.

2. Major Henry Hitchcock (1829–1902), USA, joined Sherman's staff before the March to the Sea.

3. EES had received an invitation from the Sanitary Commission in December to help organize a fair for the relief of soldiers and their families, with the profits to be split between the commission and the Chicago Soldiers' Home. She went to Chicago in mid-February, and the fair's planning committee told her all she had to do was lend her name and approval to the project. She asked her husband to send any item he thought might be of value, to be

sold. In mid-late March she attended another planning meeting. The fair did not take place until June, and WTS would open it. See also EES to WTS, February 15 and March 7–8, 1865. SFP.

TO ULYSSES S. GRANT

Headquarters, Military Division
of the Mississippi,
In the Field, Goldsboro, N.C.,
March 24, 1865

Lt. Genl. U. S. Grant,
City Point, Va.
General,

I have Kept Lt. Dunn over today that I might report further. All the Army is now in save the Cavalry which I have posted at Mt. Olive Station south of the Neuse, and Gen. Terry's command which tomorrow will move from Cox's ferry to Faisons Depot also on the Wilmington Road. I send you a copy of my orders of this morning the operation of which will I think soon complete our Roads. The telegraph is now done to Morehead City & by it I learn that Stores have been sent to Kingston in boats, and our wagons are there loading with rations and clothing. By using the Neuse as high up as Kingston and hauling from there 26 miles, and by equipping the two Roads to Morehead City and Wilmington I feel certain I can not only feed & equip the army, but in a short time fill our wagons for another start. I feel certain from the character of the fighting that we have got Johnstons army afraid of us. He himself acts with timidity & caution. His cavalry alone manifests spirit, but limits its operations to our struggles & foraging parties. My marching columns of Infantry dont pay the Cavalry any attention but walk right through it.

I think I see pretty clearly how in one more move we can checkmate Lee, forcing him to unite Johnston with him in the defense of Richmond, or by leaving Richmond to abandon the cause. I feel certain if he leaves Richmond Virginia leaves the Confederacy. I will study my maps a little more before giving my clear views. I want all possible information of the Roanoke, as to navigability, how far up, and with what draft.

We find the country here sandy, dry, and with good roads, and more corn & forage than I expected. The families remain but I will gradually push them all out to Raleigh or Wilmington—We will need every house in the Town. Lt. Dunn can tell you of many things of which I need not write. Truly yrs.,

W. T. Sherman
Maj. Genl.

ALS, DNA: RG 108, Records of the Headquarters of the Army, Letters Received, AUS 1865, M71; OR, I, 47: pt. 3, 3–4.

TO FREDERICK F. LOW[1]

> Hdqrs. Military Division
> of the Mississippi,
> In the Field, Goldsborough, NC.,
> March 24, 1865.

To His Excellency Frederick F. Low,
Governor of California:

Dear Sir:

It gave me great pleasure on my arrival here yesterday to receive your letter of January 2, and I shall convey to the army the thanks of the people of California by the very language in which you have so well expressed them.[2] I do not believe a body of men ever existed who were inspired by nobler Impulses or a holier cause than they who compose this army, and yet I know that each Individual of it will feel a new pride when he is assured that far off on the golden coast of the Pacific, hundreds of thousands of our fellow-citizens have hailed our progress through this land whose inhabitants had well-nigh brought our Government to ruin and infamy. I think when the tidings reach you of our more recent march from Savannah to Goldsborough you will find it a fit sequel to the Atlanta campaign, and we shall spare no efforts to make it also the precursor of yet another, which we pray may be final. Accept my personal thanks, and know that it was in California we learned the art of making long journeys with safety, to endure privations with cheerfulness, and to thrive under the most adverse circumstances, and these have enabled us to make strides in war which may seem gigantic to the uninitiated. I bid you all to be of good cheer, for there are plenty of brave men still left who are determined that the sun, as he daily reviews our continent from the Chesapeake to San Francisco Bay, shall see a united people, and not a bundle of quarreling factions.

> I am, with great respect,
> your friend and servant,
> W. T. Sherman,
> Major-General, U.S. Army.

Printed, *OR*, I, 47: pt. 3, 6.

1. Frederick F. Low (1828–94) had been a banker in California during WTS's time there. He had been elected governor in 1863 and would serve until 1867. He was later U.S. minister to China from 1869 to 1873, when he returned to banking.

2. DLC: WTS. Low expressed admiration for the March to the Sea and WTS's army and happiness for WTS's success.

TO WILLIAM M. McPHERSON

Headquarters, Military Division
of the Mississippi,
In the Field, Goldsboro N.C.,
March 24, 1865

Wm. M. McPherson Esq.
St. Louis Mo.
Dear Sir,

On reaching Goldsboro yesterday I found many letters & among them yours of January 27.[1] One of later date I think reached me at Fayetteville a fortnight since. I thank you Kindly for your friendly expressions. As my opinions of the various questions which arise in the progress of events are formed for my own use, and not designed to please the people, or self con-stituted representatives of the People, I am utterly indifferent whether they please or displease. I am a better judge of what is right & proper touching the negro with whom I deal hourly, than Ben Butler, Sumner[,] Giddings,[2] or any mere theorist dealing with the hypothetical negro of their own creation. If I risk my life & health in the vindication of a Cause I claim to prove my sincerity by a more honest test than all the mouthings of the noisiest preacher or demagogue. I believe the honest, working People of the United States agree with me, to fight to maintain the Government according to the form be-queathed to us, and not to carry out any pet speciality. When the just powers of the President Congress & Supreme Court are recognized by all the People of our Country reason & argument may resume their sway, and Settle the thousand little questions that always have and always will agitate human Councils—but of what use is Congress? or Laws when the Marshal & Sheriff cant go & enforce his writs? Then the sword steps in, and Commands the Peace. When peace is restored, and men find it to their interest to submit to Law *whether right or wrong*, then the machinery resumes its motion, and generally all interests are reconciled. I have always thought we mixed up too many little side issues in this war. We should make a single plain issue & fight it out. The Extreme Radicals North & South have long since dodged, *shirked* the dangers of this war & left the moderates to blow each others brains out. I again repeat I make up my opinions from facts & reasoning, and not to suit any body but myself. If People dont like my opinions, it makes little difference as I dont solicit their opinions or votes. But a man who preaches and thunders offensive opinions, and when the storm raises sneaks out and lets others in to catch the blows is a villain ten thousand times worse than a murderer, and I Know many such who are Coiled away in fancied security, but the day will come when they will be dragged out & made to taste the cup they have drugged—We have no time for this now—The Constitution & Laws of the U.S. must be obeyed implicitly, from the Lakes to the Gulf, & from the Atlantic to the Pacific.

I see my name occasionally alluded to in connection with some popular office. You may tell *all* that I would rather serve 4 years in the Singsing Penitentiary than in Washington & believe I could come out a better man. If that aint emphatic enough use strong expressions and I will endorse them. Let those who love niggers better than whites follow me, and we will see who loves his Country best—a nigger as such is a most excellent fellow, but he is not fit to marry, to associate, or vote with me, or mine. Your friend,

W. T. Sherman
Maj. Genl.

ALS, CSmH.

1. DLC: WTS. McPherson had reported on events in Washington before his return to St. Louis. He hoped that JS would prevent Benjamin F. Butler from becoming secretary of war. "You will see that I assume that you will view Butler's appointment in the same light that I should for as our views are so identical on the nigger question I *Guess* we shall think alike about Butler." He also referred to a recent *New York Tribune* dispatch painting WTS as "an ultra abolitionist" and expressed his disbelief at that idea. He had traveled with Cameron, who had tried to explain his differences with WTS about the number of troops needed in Kentucky in 1861 by saying that he thought that WTS had wanted two hundred thousand men for Louisville alone.

2. Abolitionist Joshua Reed Giddings (1795–1864).

TO MARIA BOYLE EWING SHERMAN

Headquarters, Military Division
of the Mississippi
In the Field, Goldsboro N.C.,
March 24, 1865

My Dear Minnie,

I got here from the Battlefield at Bentonville 20 miles north west of this place yesterday, but all the army did not get in until today. We have been marching for two months in a low swampy country, with very bad roads, and had to bridge many large Rivers so that we had a hard time beside the fighting which seemed the easiest part.

Take your Geography and look at South Carolina. We started from Savannah—crossed the River and occupied the Country from Robertsville to Pocataligo. We then marched up towards Barnwell, crossed the Salkehatchie, and got on the Railroad from Midway nearly up to Aiken—then we marched to Columbia, crossing the Edisto, the Saluda and Broad Rivers—then to Winnsboro and turned east to Cheraw crossing the Catawba. At Cheraw we crossed the Peedee & marched through Lancaster to Fayetteville N.C. Then we crossed Cape Fear River and marched up about 20 miles near Averysboro where we had a pretty smart battle: then towards Goldsboro, and at Bentonville we had a real battle which we won of course. Here we have two Railroads one going down to Wilmington and one to Newbern. Ships come to these places & have in them clothing food and horse feed. It will take us some days to get the Railroad fixed up so as to bring us what we need, so that we may be here some time. No doubt the newspapers will publish many letters which you will read telling you all about our adventures. You may not understand how we took Charleston & Wilmington without going near them, but these cities are on the sea shore where the Country is poor, and all the People had to eat came from the interior by Railroad. Now when my army was in the Interior we broke up the Railroads and eat up the provisions so the Rebel army had to leave or starve. I knew this beforehand, and had small arms on ships ready to take possession when they left. Our soldiers have been fighting for Charleston nearly four years, but they did not go about it right. So you see what power is knowledge. I took Charleston fortified with our 400 Guns, without fighting at all. I got a great many letters some of which I answer and some of which majors Dayton & Hitchcock answer for me. It is now nearly midnight and I have written nearly thirty long letters, but have a great many more to write. I got your letter of January 3rd & Mamas of Feb. 15, but suppose there are more mails down at Newbern. We have sent wagons for them while I expect more letters from you, You & Lizzie must write more frequently now, for I suppose hereafter I will be nearer the Sea, and will not again be so far from our ships so that I will be able to write & receive letters more frequently. I am in good health & so is Uncle Charley. Uncle Hugh is down at Newbern & will come up as soon as the Railroads are finished. I sent Lizzie a pretty piece of poetry from Fayetteville & now send you a picture which some man in New York sent me. It is a good picture but you can tell better than I if it be a good likeness. Give my love to Lizzie, to Tommy, to Sister Angela, Aunt Mary your Cousins and all that enquire of me. Yr. father

W. T. Sherman

ALS, OHi: William T. Sherman Papers.

Head-Quarters, Military Division
of the Mississippi,
In the Field, Goldsboro, N.C.,
March 25, 1865.

Commodore T. Turner
U.S. Navy, Philadelphia
Delancy Place 2006.
My Dear Friend,

I received you Kind letter of January 22.[2] on Coming into this Port, after a two months land voyage. I was glad to hear from you, as it gives me the Chance of saying that I felt for Henry Turner a friendship as pure & perfect as I am capable of, and have received so many marks of his Esteem that the loss of his notice & friendship has been to me the Source of much pain. I fear he believes all the absurd stories people tell of me. I Know and believe I have bent less to the Storm of passion which has swept across our poor Country than any General of the Army. Still though I have repeatedly Sent parcels, or letters, or messages to yr. brother I have not received a word, scrap of paper or Kindly message to cheer me in my dark & Stormy Career. The Envelope to which you refer must have contained one of many papers or notes by which I have tried to Elicit a word or scrap of recognition. I Know the bitter grief that Consumes his heart & that of Mrs. Turner at the fate of her two boys,[3] but you Know that Jeff Davis and his {nayminders} are the murderers of the thousands of handsome, brave & manly youths who have swept to death by the war they Evoked for their mad, suicidal and ambitious ends. I wash my hands clean, and proclaim aloud that this day I am a better southern man, a truer friend to the People of the South, and will make more sacrifices than Jeff Davis, Robt. Lee, Joe Johnston or the other So Called Leaders who hunt down with hounds the young men of the South, to volunteer in their armies. This day ¾ of the People of the South want Peace and Union, but their voice is silenced by the Clamors of the devils who have been carefully schooled in the belief that all is base and inferior that does not spring from Certain families south of the Potomac. But the day of vengeance is coming, and you will live to See Jeff Davis, Slidell, Benjamin, Magrath,[4] Memminger[5] & other villains "not of real American stock" who have played on the blind prejudices of the South for their aggrandizement. I say you will hear them Call on us to Shelter them from the storm they themselves have raised. I feel the Same personal friendships as Ever—am not conscious of having done anything wonderful, further than to persevere in what I deemed the only way to Suppress mutiny & Sedition in our Grand Camp. I would like your brother Henry to Know that I feel uneasy at his long

& seeming studied Silence. If I have offended him I would like to Know how & when.[6] The greater the friendship the greater the jealousy. Yrs. in haste,

W. T. Sherman M. G.

ALS, PHi: Society Collection.

1. Thomas Turner (1808–83), a brother of Henry S. Turner of Virginia, had reached the rank of commodore in the United States Navy in December 1862 and had commanded the *New Ironsides* in her attack on Charleston Harbor. At this time he was on ordnance duty in Philadelphia.

2. DLC: WTS. Turner had sent his congratulations on the March to the Sea and passed on a message from his brother Henry, now living in Philadelphia. A letter in WTS's handwriting addressed to him at St. Louis had apparently been lost in forwarding and Henry Turner was upset by the loss and wanted WTS to know why he had not answered it.

3. Wilson P. Turner (ca. 1844–62), a first sergeant in Stuart's Horse Artillery, CSA, had been killed at the Second Battle of Manassas. Thomas Turner, the son for whom WTS had gotten a Federal commission, had apparently been killed as well.

4. Andrew G. Magrath (1813–93), a judge and politician, had been elected governor of South Carolina in December 1864.

5. Christopher G. Memminger (1803–88) was CSA secretary of the treasury from February 1861 to July 1864.

6. Elizabeth Blair Lee said of Henry Turner's political views that "[he is] for the saving of his property & is on the fence generally getting down occasionally first on one side & then the other." Virginia Jeans Laas, ed., *Wartime Washington: The Civil War Letters of Elizabeth Blair Lee* (Urbana, 1991), 191. Turner wrote WTS on April 5, "I hardly know how to express the feeling which the perusal of this letter has elicited. . . . It is true I have not written to you for a long time: full two years I believe: nor have I in this interval recd. one scratch of pen from you." He had thought this silence entirely natural and had not resented it. While he was not in sympathy with WTS's current actions, he was "gratified" by his success, which gave him some hope for the ultimate outcome of the war. He thought that WTS would prove to be the truest friend of Southerners and had not believed any of the stories told about him. DLC: WTS.

TO ELLEN EWING SHERMAN

Headquarters, Military Division
of the Mississippi,
On Board Steamer Russia at Sea
Sunday Mch. 26, 65

Dearest Ellen,

The Railroad was finished yesterday into Goldsboro and I came down to Newbern & Morehead City and am now in a fleet Blockade Runner on my way to meet Genl. Grant at City Point to confer on some points when I shall forthwith go back to Goldsboro and get ready for another Campaign.[1] There is no doubt we have got the Rebels in a tight place and must not let them have time to make new plans. They abandonned all their cities to get near Enough to Whip me but did not succeed. They may unite Johnston & Lee, when if they make the further mistake of holding on to Richmond, I can easily take Raleigh and the Roanoke, when Richmond will be of little use to them. If Lee lets go of Richmond the People of Virginia will give up. I regard my two moves from Atlanta to Savannah & Savannah to Goldsboro as great blows as if we had fought a dozen successful Battles. At Bentonville Johnston attempted to prevent my making a junction with Schofield, but he failed and I drove him off the field with my own army without the help of a man from Schofield. Also got all my armies at Goldsboro the 21st of March only one day from the time appointed. I will now concoct with Grant another move. I have all the army I want and can take one hundred thousand if I want them.

I met Hugh at Newbern for a minute last night. He is ordered to report to Schofield. He told me Tom had resigned and Charley succeeded to his place. I brought only McCoy with me as I shall return to Goldsboro, after a few hours conference with Grant.

The ship is pitching a good deal, we are just off Hatteras, and I cannot write more. Love to the children & believe me always yrs.

W. T. Sherman

ALS, InND: Sherman Family Papers.

1. WTS arrived at City Point on March 27; he met with USG and Lincoln that day and planned strategy with USG. The next day, WTS, USG, Lincoln, and David Dixon Porter met to map out the last days of the war, and Lincoln gave his opinion that they should give lenient surrender terms to avoid a guerrilla war. WTS returned to North Carolina that night.

TO ELLEN EWING SHERMAN

Goldsboro N.C. Mch. 31, 1865

Dearest Ellen,

I made a hasty visit to City Point to see Genl. Grant, to confer with him on points of importance and am back before Joe Johnston or the newspapers found out the fact. I was at City Point 20 hours, telegraphed to you, but did not get an answer[.] The truth is I have hardly time nowadays to write letters, and I know you will make due allowances for the newspapers tell such wonderful tales of "Mr. Shermans Company" that you can trace my whereabouts and almost find out what I get for breakfast but in the many Biographical sketches you will hardly recognize me. I dont recognize myself. I now get bushels of letters and dont read one in five but let them go to my aids.

As soon as I get the machinery of supply working smooth I will make my official Report of the last campaign and then be off for Virginia. Of course if in the meantime Grant has not disposed of Lee I must try him. Grants army was in motion when I left and a day or so will develop Lee's Strategy that we can make a guess at the future.

John Sherman came with me here and will return tomorrow and I will ask him to write you from Washington. He spoke about investing a part of the Ohio Contribution in a homestead for you and seemed to talk as though you wanted it.[1] I dont Know yet that the Ohio Subscription has amounted to any thing more than a brag, but if it realize $100,000 I think we can invest the whole in U.S. or State Bonds and use the funds you now have say 15,000 in a house, but you Know how rapidly we change. What today would seem most desirable tomorrow would be a burden. Until the war is over and determines my fate I think you had better get along as you best may, and there will be time Enough to think of a homestead. Like an old Sailor I often dream of a home, a fixture, but of course I Know enough of mankind & womankind to conclude that a single accident would put me in motion again. Still if you want a home in Cincinati I shall not object. If I live I shall redeem my promise to Minnie to Send her, and Lizzie too to the best school I can find in New York next year. We now have a regular mail via Fortress Monroe, the Norfolk Canal, Newbern & Goldsboro, but by the time you find it out we shall be off again, but you had better write me via Fortress Monroe. I expect to Start April 10. Give my love to the Children. Yrs. Ever

W. T. Sherman

ALS, InND: Sherman Family Papers.

1. The state of Ohio would present WTS with at least $10,000 in bonds after the war. John F. Marszalek, *Sherman: A Soldier's Passion for Order* (New York, 1993), 361.

TO EDWIN M. STANTON

Headquarters, Military Division
of the Mississippi,
In the Field, Goldsboro N.C.,
March 31, 1865

Hon. E. M. Stanton
Sec. of War
Dear Sir,

I had the honor & satisfaction to receive your letter and telegram of welcome when at City Point & Old Point Comfort.[1] I am again back at my post, possessed of the wishes and Plans of the General in Chief, and think in due time I can play my part in the Coming Campaign. All things are working well, and I have troops enough to accomplish the part assigned me, and only await the loading our wagons, patching up and mending made necessary by the wear & tear of the past winter. Feeling as I do the responsibilities that rest on me, I shall spare no labor of body or mind to deserve the success and consequent blessings that you so heartily call down on me. Others must tell you of the continued harmony & confidence that pervade this army, to which qualities the Country owes more than to any mere ability I possess.

Your son is now here and will return to Washington with John Sherman. With great respect

W. T. Sherman
Maj. Gen.

ALS, DLC: Edwin M. Stanton Papers; OR, I, 47: pt. 3, 65.

1. Stanton to WTS, OR, I, 47: pt. 3, 42. Stanton had sent him an unusually warm message, commending him to God's care.

TO GEORGE F. GRANGER[1]

Head-Quarters Military Division
of the Mississippi,
In the Field Goldsboro, Apl. 3. 1865

Col. Granger, "V"

Tell S. L. Fremont[2] that I am the same person he knew in the Old Army but that he is not.[3] Tell him I dont want to See a man who Knew better but in the hour of trouble abandonned the Country that had nurtured him. I shall appropriate to the use of the U.S. every particle of property pertaining to the Railroad which is forfeited a thousand times for treason. Tell S. L. Fremont I will give him a Pass to Nassau or to a Foreign Port but if he remains in our lines he is simply tolerated and must Keep close indoors. Let him return to Wilmington and not meddle with the Road or anything pertaining to it.

Sherman M.G.

ALS, CSmH.

1. Colonel George F. Granger (1837–83), USA, commanded the Third Brigade, Second Division, Tenth Corps, under Terry's command.

2. Sewall L. Fremont (d. 1886), who had graduated from West Point in 1840 as Sewall L. Fish, had served in the artillery and the quartermaster department of the U.S. Army before his resignation in 1854. He served as a colonel of artillery in the Confederate army from 1861 to 1865.

3. Fremont had written to WTS on February 20 from his offices at the Wilmington and Weldon Rail Road Company, asking WTS to protect his "civil rights" on the strength of their old friendship. He also hoped that WTS would protect his railroad, as WTS's men would probably want to use it. He assured WTS that he had been a Union man until North Carolina's secession and had not been actively engaged in the war.

Headquarters, Military Division
of the Mississippi,
In the Field, Goldsboro N.C.,
April 5, 1865

Maj. Genl. Robert Anderson
Charleston S.C.
Dear General,

I see in the papers that an order has been made by the War Dept. that on the 14th instant you are to raise the same flag over Sumpter which you were compelled to lower from years ago, and that I am supposed to be Present.[1] I will be there in thought but not in person, and I am glad that it falls to the lot of one so pure and noble to represent our country in a drama so solemn so majestic and so just. It looks as a Retribution decreed by Heaven itself. I doubt if we could have fashioned Events ourselves, we could have produced a better conclusion. Four years of bitter war have tested our Manhood, and dissipated the rude boasting of a class of men of which nothing but Horrid war could have purged our Country. But alas many of them have escaped punishment as yet, and have involved thousands & millions of innocents. But the End is not yet. The brain that first conceived the thought must burst in anguish, the heart that pulsated with hellish joy must cease to beat, and the hand that pulled the first lanyard must be palsied, before the wicked act that began in Charleston on the 13th of April 1861 is avenged. But Mine not thine is Vengeance saith the Lord, and we poor sinners must let Him work out the drama to its Close.

I have not been in Charleston since we parted then, captain & Lieutenant in the spring of 1846: but I can see it in imagination almost as clearly as you behold it with your Eyes: and though I may be far away, you may think of me as standing by your side, ready to aid you with labor to achieve the End I know you Strive to attain, Not to pull down the Sacred fabric of our Government, but to improve it, and to strengthen it, so that the good and the brave will seek the shelter of its Flag, and the Evil & treacherous shall fly to other Lands. Your Lieutenant

W. T. Sherman Maj. Genl.

ALS, DLC: Robert B. Anderson Papers; OR, I, 47: pt. 3, 107–8.
1. General Orders No. 50, War Department, Adjutant General's Office, March 27, 1865; printed in PM, 2:319–20.

TO JOHN A. DAHLGREN

Headquarters, Military Division
of the Mississippi,
In the Field, Goldsboro N.C.
April 5, 1865

Admiral Dahlgren, Washington D.C.

Dear Admiral

I was in hopes when we reached a Port I would find you, but the winds & {wane} of fortune carried me beyond your jurisdiction and landed me in Admiral Porters Dominions. I first found the Gunboat {Eden} in Cape Fear River, and Since have found Capt. Macomb in Pimlico Sound as well as the Admiral himself at City Point. But I hear you are relieved at your own request and gone home. I Should have much liked to have seen you and talked over the Symptoms which Our Patient Charleston exhibited as I touched her vital chords with my {blunt Army}. You see I was right in not wasting time on Fort Moultrie, and had Adml. Porter waited [a] couple months I could have taken Wilmington Fort Fisher and all without a blow. There was no power Save Lee & Johnston combined that could prevent me reaching Fayetteville N.C. Over there no Enemy could remain down in the Right of Cape Fear River. I told Admiral Porter that he had stolen my thunder, But on the whole we all have reason to be satisfied. No longer does a little dirty flag defy us on Salt Water. The majesty of our Govt. is beginning to be felt, and {Guerillas} will pause when they think of Charleston ere they dare raise their hands in anger against the Emblem of our Nationality.

I cannot even go to Charleston to weep over its Ruins—where many a happy day of my early life was spent—nor do I feel inclined to go, but its lesson will stand long after you & I are gone, Eloquent in its Sadness.

I trust your health is better, and that you soon may realize another hope which I Know you Cherish, to go to that other proud but doomed city, and remove thence all that is left to earth of your son Ulric.[1] May we meet soon in Peace. Your friend,

W. T. Sherman Maj. Genl.

ALS, New York: The Gilder Lehrman Collection.

1. Colonel Ulric Dahlgren (1842–64), USA, was killed on March 2, 1864, while leading a cavalry raid on Richmond. Angered by Confederate authorities' ill treatment of the corpse, the Union underground of Richmond, led in part by notorious spy Elizabeth Van Lew, spirited his corpse from an unmarked grave in the Oakwood Cemetery to the farm of Robert Orrocks, where it would remain until after the war.

TO THOMAS EWING SR.

Headquarters, Military Division
of the Mississippi,
In the Field, Goldsboro N.C.,
April 5, 1865

Hon. T. Ewing
Washington D.C.
Dear Sir,

I send a messenger tonight for Washington with my Report map &c. I also send him to Ellen to carry her some letters, the MS. of my Report with maps I have used on the Campaign for her to preserve among the family archives.[1] The Sergeant takes to Ellen from his Regiment 13 Iowa Inf. the Rebel flag that was over the State House Columbia S.C. as a contribution to the Fair of which it seems she is a patroness. She wrote to me for trophies. Of course I can have no trophies, nor strictly speaking should any officer or Soldier appropriate any {capture}. But as Flags have been taken by hundreds, and the War Dept. dont want them I generally let the Captors take them or send them to their Sweethearts. The Col. of this Regt. sends the flag to Ellen for the Fair, and I cannot well say nay, but if you think there is any impropriety in Ellens touching it as a trophy, telegraph her, and the flag can quietly go to Iowa, or come back to the Garret in the War office. It might be proper to inquire of Mr. Stanton the only person who would be likely to notice the fact. I think Mr. Lincoln would say amen, if I had rolled & appropriated the contents of a Bank. I have been the means of saving to the Treasury Twenty millions in cotton and nearly as much in food & forage for my army and yet I have not money enough to get a pair of shoes. There is no paymaster about. I have to draw on Halleck to pay the Sergeants way from Washington out to South Bend. I advise this person to enquire for you that you will likely Know if Ellen be at Chicago or South Bend. Charley has now a Brigade & must work out his destiny[.][2] It is impossible for Schofield to give Hugh a Division. The Division he was assigned to was composed of fragments belonging to this army & the moment they come together the Division was absolved & ceased to exist. I think Schofield contemplates giving Hugh a command up the Chowac, which will probably be my next Base[.] I would like to have you Read my Report, which goes to Halleck, the original notes to Ellen. I think you will be satisfied with the manner in which I dispose of Charleston, as also of the burning of Columbia. I am preparing to go butt end, at Joe Johnston towards Raleigh, but shall trust to manoeuvre which wins better than rough fighting. My army now is 30,000 stronger than when I left Atlanta and even more in Morale. I certainly have maintained the army in wonderful health and Strength. It has never been so hungry or tired but that it could have fought a battle at night. I have also had a full share of luck in making combinations on arrival. This at Goldsboro, surpasses that at Savannah. Still the struggle is to come and I feel ready & willing to meet it and Shall not postpone it an hour[.] affectionately, yr. son

W. T. Sherman

ALS, DLC: Thomas Ewing and Family Papers.

1. WTS to EES, third letter of April 5, 1865, includes his draft of WTS to HWH, April 5, 1865. SFP.

2. Charley had been given the First Brigade in the Third Division, Seventeenth Corps, under Leggett's command.

TO MICHAEL HAHN[1]

Hdqrs. Military Division
of the Mississippi,
In the Field, Goldsborough, N.C.,
April 5, 1865.

His Excellency Michael Hahn,
Governor of Louisiana, New Orleans:
Dear Sir:

I had the honor to receive your letter of March 3 inclosing the engrossed copy of the resolutions of the Legislature of Louisiana approved March 3, 1865.[2] I will publish them in general orders to the army, and think that it will be a source of pride for the officers and men to see the deep interest that is felt in them by the constituted authorities of your favored State. I thank you kindly for recalling to me the events that attended me at Alexandria at the outset of this war. No man not actually present at the South can comprehend the toils and snares laid by old, wily, and mischievous traitors to ensnare the young and credulous. Truth was perverted, prejudices kindled into a wild passion, and a false pride begotten, calculated to mislead the youth, and even old men, into a belief that the whole fabric of our Government was weak and tottering, and was about to fall with a crash that would ruin all who clung to its fortunes. I cannot pretend to superior wisdom, but in the retirement of the pine woods of Rapides Parish my day dreams still rested on the high seas, in California, on the broad plains of Kansas, the majestic valley of the Mississippi, and the Atlantic slope with its busy, industrious people, where I had roved in former days, everywhere realizing the fact that our General Government was kind and paternal, and that its faults (if any) arose from an excess of leniency and forbearance, and I could not be made to believe that it should yield the destiny of our future to the guidance of the few discontented demagogues of the South, or its conceited cotton planters and negro owners. I am willing to say, however, that I regarded the Constitution as a bargain. That we of the North should respect slave property without going into its abstracts, merits, or defects, and had the Southern people abided by the common laws and tribunals, would have fought to maintain such property, but the moment they ignored the compact and appealed to war we were no longer bound in law or honor to respect that obnoxious species of property. As soon as war is over I believe that good men can readjust the affairs of the country so that slaves will never again be bought and sold, and yet the labor of all be directed again to the development of the vast agricultural wealth that lies in the future fields of the South. Accept my hearty thanks for considering me still a citizen of Louisiana, and I beg you to foster and encourage all its native population to adapt their thoughts and feeling to the new order of things, which will soon efface the dread ravages of war, and make Louisiana the safe guardian of the outlet of the mightiest river on earth.

> With great respect,
> your friend and servant,
> W. T. Sherman,
> Major-General

Printed, *OR*, I, 47: pt. 3, 101–2.

1. Michael Hahn (1830–86), a German-born Louisiana lawyer, was a committed Unionist and abolitionist. He represented the state in Congress after the Federal government took it over and was inaugurated as governor in March 1864.

2. DLC: WTS. Hahn's letter, conveying fulsome praise, enclosed a joint resolution passed unanimously by both houses of the legislature, thanking WTS for all he was doing to bring the war to a successful close.

TO ELLEN EWING SHERMAN

> Headquarters, Military Division
> of the Mississippi,
> In the Field, Goldsboro N.C.,
> April 5, 1865

Dearest Ellen,

I have now finished my Report, & answered all letters that called for my personal action. These are being copied and sent by a courier tomorrow and then "What Next" as old Lincoln says.[1] That next is also thought over and it again takes me into danger and trouble, but you must now be so used to it that you can hardly care. I have no late letters from you, none since you wrote to Chicago, but you too are becoming a public character and the busy newspapers follow you. I see that the public authorities & citizens of Chicago paid you a public visit with speeches & music & that Bishop Duggan[2] responded for you. If these give you pleasure I am glad of it for I would rather that you and the children should be benefitted by any fame I may achieve than that it Should Enure to me personally. Of Course as a General my case will be scrutinized very closely by men abroad as well as here and my reputation will rather depend on their judgment than on any mere temporary applause. I have been trying to get some pay to send you, for I suppose you are "short", but the Paymasters cannot catch up, and in a few days I will be off again. I have pay due since Jan. 1.—and yet was unable the other day to buy a pair of shoes which I need—I have those big boots you sent me from Cincinati but the weather is getting warmer and they are too close & heavy—They stood me a good turn however on the last march when for weeks we were up to our eyes in mud & water. When we got here the Army was ragged & hard up, but already our new clothing is issued and I will challenge the world to Exhibit a finer looking set of men—Brawny, strong, swarthy, a contrast to the weak & sickly fellows that Came to me in Kentucky three years ago. It is a great truth that men exposed to the Elements dont "Catch Cold" and I have not heard a man cough or sneeze for three months, but were these Same men to go into houses in a month the Doctor would have half of them. Now the Doctors have no employment. I myself am very well *though* in a house for the time being and to have the convenience of a table & chair to write, also to prevent the flaring of the candle which makes writing in a tent almost impossible. I write as usual very fast & can Keep half a dozen clerks busy in copying. Hitchcock (nephew of the Genl.) writes private letters not needing my personal attention such as autographs & locks of hair. Dayton the military orders, but I must of Course keep up correspondence with War Dept., Gen. Grant, my army commanders, Govrs. of States &c. and you should be satisfied even if my letters are hasty & ill digested. You can almost trace my progress through the world by the newspapers. Charley now has a Brigade in Leggetts Division, Blairs Corps. I have given him the best advice, which amounts to a close & personal attention to all details and to work out his own destiny. Hugh is at Newbern waiting orders. Schofield has no Division vacant, and may have to Send him up to the *Chewan* likely to be our *next* base. It is utterly impossible for me now to amend the fatal mistake he made in quarrelling with Logan & giving up his Division in North Alabama. I offered to restore him before we started from Nashville but he emphatically declined in Spite of my earnest advice, and now I cannot & will not displace a Junior who has worked and fought as my Division Commanders have done from Chattanooga to this place. I want you to be of my mind on this point because I fear that Hugh thinks I can & will not give him a Division. Tis not so without a breach of decency. A Cry would properly go up if I were now to displace Wood, or Hazen, or Corse, or any of my 13 Division Commanders to give position to Hugh. Had he come with me from Nashville he would long since have been a Major General, with a command & history of which he would have been proud. Whereas now he is one of those Senior Brigadier Generals that any Commanders perfectly dread. They will not accept a Brigade, the legitimate command of a Brig. Genl. but insist on a Division which is the legitimate command of a Maj. Genl. All the young Maj. Genls. now with me are younger men than Hugh, but the Services & Battles of the last year have carried them over him, not from any fault of his, but as a just reward for their own zeal & labor. Charley has now a Brigade and if he too is not too impatient to be commander in chief may in due season be a Major Genl. also. In war as in Peace men must carve out their own destiny, office age & Rank are not conclusive.

I got a long letter from Bowman last night[3]—he is resolved to write up my Campaigns, and is anxious for the most authoritative records. These are contained in my Letter & order Books. You have some up to the time of my leaving Atlanta, Webster has those for Atlanta to Savannah, and I have here the Balance[.] I would much prefer he would wait the end of the war, but he wants to make money out of the job, and I do not object, for he says that others less capable will do the thing, and make a botch of it—He can get access to my official Reports at Washington as also those of my subordinate Reports—but the letters I daily write give the gradual unfolding of plans & events, better than Reports made with more formality after the events are past. The last march from Savannah to Goldsboro, with its legitimate fruits the capture of Charleston, Georgetown and Wilmington is by far the most important in conception & execution of any act of my life. You can safely trust the fame of our children on this one campaign ignoring the past & regardless of the Future. The Country owes you & my children an honorable maintanance and now let what befal me personally I believe you & they are as well provided for as if I had laid by lands & money. Yet I would be willing to know that Something more definite were concluded—I hear nothing of that Ohio Scheme and fear like most such things it too has melted into a general resolve without execution. John Sherman says no and wanted me to consent to buying for you in Cincinati a homestead. I dont object but think money invested in bonds the interest of which would be paid you for daily expenses would be a more wise provision than houses that call for taxes, repairs and expenses of maintenance. You ought to have 20,000 of your own money, and if possible get it also into Shape to pay you interest. If your father needs it of course you can say nothing, but rightfully it ought not be loaned to him but to some one with whom you could deal in a business like way. If you meet John this summer you might let him look over the papers & advise you. He has a good business mind.

I continue to receive the highest compliments from all quarters, and have been singularly fortunate in escaping the envy & jealousy of rivals. Indeed officers from every quarter want to join my "Great Army." Grant is the same enthusiastic friend. Mr. Lincoln at City Point was lavish in his good wishes and Since Mr. Stanton visited me at Savannah he too has become the warmest possible friend. Of course I could not venture north, and it accords both with my pleasure and interest to Keep close with my army proper. Officers & Soldiers have in my foresight & Knowledge a child like confidence that is really most agreeable—Whilst wading through mud & water, & heaving at mired wagons the Soldiers did not indulge in a single growl but always said & felt that the Old Man would bring them out all right, and no sooner had we reached the Cape Fear River at Fayetteville than a little squeaking tug came puffing up the River with news, and we had hardly spread out in the Camps about Goldsboro than the Locomotive & train came thundering along from the Sea 96 miles distant loaded with shoes, & pants, & clothing as well as food. So remarkable and happy a coincidence which of course I had arranged from Savannah, made the woods resound with a yell that must have reached Raleigh. Some of our officers who escaped from the enemy say that these two Coincidences made the Rebel officers swear that I was the Devil himself a compliment that you can appreciate. But enough of this vanity, save & except always when it redounds to your advantage & pleasure. My wants are few & easily gained, but if this Fame which fills the world contributes to your happiness & pleasure enjoy it as much as possible. Oh, that Willy could hear & see—his proud little heart would swell to overflowing and it may be that tis better he should not be agitated with such thoughts. The girls are less thoughtful and Tommy is more calmly constituted. I see you had him with you at Chicago. I fear his thoughts will be drawn too much away from the books, for which he must gain the Knowledge on which to base his Future much more valuable than the Short Remnants left to us.

I have written to Minnie & Lizzie and will also to Tommy before I start[.] I may also write again to you short letters, but this is offered as the starting point of the next.

The army is now well clad & fed—our wagons are loading and on the 10th I will haul out towards Raleigh. I need not tell you my plans but they are good, and I do not see but the next move and one more will determine the Fate of this war. Not conclude it—but assure the fact that the United States have not ceased to be a nation. If we can force Lee to let go Richmond, and can whip him in open fight, I think I can come home & rest and leave others to follow up the fragments.

John Sherman came with me from Old Point only staid one day & can tell or write you much more than I can because he would notice what would interest. Charley says he writes you often, but I doubt it. We are all in good health—weather fine & Spring fairly opened—Trees leafing & fruit trees in blossom. Roads sand & good—Love to all yrs. ever

W. T. Sherman

ALS, InND: Sherman Family Papers.

1. WTS here refers to Abraham Lincoln's response to WTS's message announcing the surrender of Savannah: "But what next? I suppose it will be safer if I leave Gen. Grant and yourself to decide." Lincoln to WTS, December 26, 1864, *CWAL*, 8:181–82.

2. Bishop James Duggan of Chicago.

3. Bowman to WTS, March 30, 1865, DLC: WTS. He thanked WTS for his of March 24, especially as he was so busy. "Well you are a great man and a great hero, and however disagreeable it may be you may as well make up your mind to it and submit with whatever grace you can to all the penalties." He reported that articles on his Atlanta and Savannah campaigns were scheduled for the April and May issues of the *U.S. Service Magazine* and jokingly complained that "you make history faster than any one man can write it." Bowman had decided to resign from the army and work on a book on WTS's campaigns, one which he hoped would become the basic source. He also urged WTS to consider political office after the war: "Don't try to struggle with destiny."

TO ELLEN EWING SHERMAN

Headquarters Military Division
of the Mississippi,
In the Field Goldsboro N.C.,
Apl. 5, 1865

Dearest Ellen,

I send Sergeant Wm. A. Rose, 13 Iowa Infantry as Mail messenger to Washington with a furlough to go to his home in Iowa. He brings you as a trophy for the Fair the Rebel Flag which was captured at Columbia S.C. which you can dispose of for the benefit of the Fair. I have no trophies. It would not be right for me to have any, and it is of doubtful right for any Regt. to appropriate Articles captured, but Rebel flags are not recognized and I generally let the captors hold them. You can present this and it may be some person may attach to it a value that will contribute more to the Soldiers than to have the Rag stuck away in the garret of the War Dept. If we could remain in communication any time I think the officers here would overwhelm you with trophies. I prefer you should not use any thing from me for sale simply because it is not right. Let others do that.

I also send you a Raleigh paper of April 1, which some fellow may pay you $5 for as a curiosity & Keepsake. I put my name on it. Yrs.

W. T. S.

ALS, InND: Sherman Family Papers.

TO JOHN SHERMAN

Headquarters, Military Division
of the Mississippi,
In the Field, Goldsboro NC,
April 5, 1865

Hon. John Sherman
Washington DC.
Dear Brother,

The Bearer of this Sergeant Rose carries to Washington my Report and Despatches. He has some papers for Ellen, and I dont know whether she be at South Bend or Chicago. Will you ascertain by telegraph and let her know the Sergeant is coming. He takes to her the Rebel flag that was over the State House Columbia S.C. as a contribution to the Fair at Chicago.

The sergeant is represented as a brave good Soldier, and he can tell you any thing of which you wish to enquire. All has gone well since you left us. Railroads work well and our supplies are well up, and we shall march next Monday Apl. 10. The next two months will demonstrate whether we can manouever Lee out of Richmond and whip him in open Battle.[1] Yr. brother,

W. T. Sherman

ALS, DLC: William T. Sherman.

1. In fact, Grant had already forced Lee to evacuate Richmond and Petersburg on April 2–3, 1865.

TO ELLEN EWING SHERMAN

Headquarters, Military Division
of the Mississippi,
In the Field, Goldsboro N.C.,
April 6, 1865

Dearest Ellen,

I sent you last night a long letter and Some Documents in which you will be interested. I also sent by a Sergeant Rose who promised to go to you at South Bend or Chicago the Rebel flag which was over the State House at Columbia S.C. to be sold for the benefit of the Fair. I now send you a seal taken by some soldier off some public Document which I have no doubt was one of the Old

Indian Treaties made by the Proprietors of the Colony of Georgia in the Old Colonial Times. Gen. Blair sends you this. I have mentioned incidentally to Some of our General officers that you were interested in the Fair and had we time or were we not so absorbed in the preperations for a march I could obtain many things that though of little value would be prized at Chicago, such as the Autographs of the Leading Generals of this Army. You can safely label this seal—Official Seal of the Colony of Georgia at the time of General Oglethorpe—taken at Milledgeville by a Soldier of Shermans Army November 1864. Yrs. Ever

W. T. Sherman

ALS, MiU-C: Clinton H. Haskell Collection.

TO ULYSSES S. GRANT

Headquarters, Military Division
of the Mississippi,
In the Field, Goldsboro N.C.,
April 8, Saturday. [1865]

Lt. Genl. U. S. Grant
City Point Va.
General,

I have just received your letter of the 5th[1] from Wilsons Station and although I have written you several letters lately will repeat.

On Monday at daylight all my army will move straight on Joe Johnston, supposed to be between me and Raleigh, and I will follow him wherever he may go. If he retreats on Danville to make junction with Lee, I will do the Same though I may take a course round him bending towards Greensboro, for the purpose of turning him north. I will bear in mind your plain and unmistakeable point that the Rebel Armies are now the strategic points to strike at—I will follow Johnston presuming that you are after Lee or all that you have left to him and if they come together, we will also.

I think I will be at Raleigh on Thursday the 13, and shall pursue Johnston towards Greensboro, unless it be manifest that he has gone towards Danville. I shall encourage him to come to Bay, or to move towards Danville, as I dont want to race all the way back through South Carolina and Georgia. It is to our interest to let Lee & Johnston come together just as a billiard player would {nurse} the balls when he has them in a nice place.

I am delighted and amazed at the result of your move to the South of Petersburg, and Lee has lost in one day the Reputation of three years, and you have established a Reputation for perseverance and pluck that would make

Wellington jump out of his Coffin. I wish you could have waited a few days, or that I could have been here a week sooner, but it is not too late yet, and you may rely with absolute certainty that I will be after Johnston with about 80,000 men provided for 20 full days, which will last me 40—and I will leave a small force here at Goldsboro, & repair the Railroad up to Raleigh. If you have a spare division, you might send it to Schofield to help him hold this Line of Railroad out from Morehead City to Goldsboro, but I will not hesitate to let go Railroad and everything if I can get at Joe Johnston in an open field. If Sheridan dont run his horses off their legs, and you can spare him for a week or so, let him fall down for me, and I think he can make a big haul of horses. Tell him I make him a free gift of all the blooded stock of North Carolina including Wade Hampton whose pedigree and stud are of high repute.

Dont fail to have Stoneman break through the mountains of west North Carolina, he will find plenty of Union men who will aid him to reach either your army or mine; and Canby should if he takes Mobile, get up the Alabama River about *Selma* from which place he can catch all fragments passing towards Texas. I have an idea that he can get up the Alabama River, even if he do not take Mobile. I have a Report from Wilson who will I think break up all Railroad Lines in Alabama. Yours truly,

W. T. Sherman
Maj. Gen. Comdg.

ALS, DNA: RG 108, Records of the Headquarters of the Army, Letters Received, AUS 1865, M256; *OR*, I, 47: pt. 3, 128–29.

1. USG to WTS, April 5, 1865, *PM*, 2:343. USG reported that Lee appeared to be heading toward Danville, Virginia. "If you can possibly do so, push on from where you are, and let us see if we cannot finish the job with Lee's and Johnston's armies." Confederate armies were the only strategic points left at which to strike.

TO PHILEMON B. EWING

Head-Quarters Military Division
of the Mississippi,
In the Field, Goldsboro, N.C.
Apl. 9 1865.

Dear Phil,

I must be off again tomorrow to look after Joe Johnston. Grant has made good work at Richmond, and I hope between us we can prevent Davis from making any new combinations. Dont conclude yet that the war is over for there is a class of men who can no more adapt themselves to the new order of things than Cherokee Indians. They must die, or remove to Some other Country. All who have property, families or expect to live a civilized life may if they get a chance to act, Submit and go to work to save what little of property is left there, but the young men, who have been taught to regard us with abhorrence will continue to fight to the last. If we could so manage that this class Could {pull out} we could Soon Kill them, but they are a dominant class and manage by appeals to the pride or fears of the many to control others of less determined character. Yet of course we cannot begin to think of these fragments till the main armies of the Confederacy cease to have existence. I can whip Joe Johnston if I can bring him to bay, but he may retreat so far that I cannot follow him. I may therefore manoeuver some to get him where he can not escape. Grant at my last advises had reached Burkesville, with Lee still to his north. He may pen him in Lynchburg and cut off all chances of supply. I can hardly expect to do the Same by Joe Johnston who has a more open country still, in my progress through the Country I necessarily make such havoc that the farmers & People are getting very tired. They expected we would confine ourselves to public stores, but I take all food, sometimes leaving with a family a small supply enough to last them till the male part can come home & procure more. This gives the men an occupation different from fighting us at a distant point. My March through Georgia and South Carolina, besides its specific fruits actually produced a marked Effect on Lees Army, because fathers & sons in his Ranks felt a natural Solicitude about children or relations in the regions through which I had passed with Such relentless Effect. I begin to hope that Lesser armies will soon be needed and that I can leave Junior Generals finish up what we have done. I have heard but little of Ellen or of any of my folks since my arrival[.] Their letters must have got on the wrong track—it may be went by steam for N. York to Savannah—we have little communication with Savannah—but our Mails come from Old Point Comfort through the Dismal Swamp canal, Albemarle & Pamlico Sounds to Newbern & then here by Rail— I will Keep up the Railroad & telegraph as far as Raleigh, but if I go beyond will again cast loose, & live on the Country or the Contents of our wagons. Charley is now with his Brigade and has a chance of carving out his own fame. Hugh was here, but has I think gone to Grant—Schofield could not give him a Division without displacing some worthy incumbent, which would not be fair. There is only one way to Succeed in war and that is to stick close & persevere. My army now is in Splendid heart & condition and if we Encounter Johnston I am confident of the result. Give my regards to all the neighbors and it may be I will drift back to see you all once more. I am not yet absent as long as I was in California, but have had rather a more Exciting time. affectionately,

W. T. Sherman

ALS, DLC: Thomas Ewing and Family Papers.

Headquarters Military Division
of the Mississippi,
In the Field, Goldsboro, N.C.
Apl. 9, 1865.

Dearest Ellen,

I have written you very often since I have been here, but have received very few letters from you, and those of old date. I also telegraphed you from City Point. John Sherman came back with me, and you must have heard all you wanted to Know of me & Goldsboro. I wanted to Send you some money having pay due me from January 1, but Paymasters Cant Keep up with this Army, and now we must be off again. Tomorrow we move straight against Joe Johnston wherever he may be. Grants magnificent victories about Petersburg, and his rapid pursuit of Lees army makes it unnecessary for me to move further north and I expect my course will be to Raleigh and Greensboro. I will fix up the Railroad to Raleigh, but then Shall cast off as my custom has been and depend on the Contents of our wagons and on the resources of the Country. Poor North Carolina will have a hard time for we sweep the Country like a swarm of locusts. Thousands of People may perish, but they now realize that war means something else than vainglory & boasting. If Peace ever falls to their lot they will never again invite war. But there is a class of young men who will never live at Peace. Long after Lees & Johnstons Armies are beaten & scattered they will band together as Highwaymen and Keep the Country in a fever, begetting a Guerilla War—It may be that the Govt. may give us who have now been working 4 years a rest and let younger men follow up the sequel. I feel confident we can whip Joe Johnston quick if he stops but he may travel back towards Georgia and I dont want to follow him again on that long Road. I wish Grant had been a few days later or I a few days sooner but on the whole our Campaigns have been good. The weather now seems settled and if I have good Roads think I can travel pretty fast. The sun is warm, the leaves are all coming out, and flowers are in bloom, about as you will have it a month hence. The Entire Army has new clothing and with Soap & water have (made a wonderful) change in our appearance. The fellows who passed in review before me with smoke black faces, dirty & ragged, many with feet bare or wrapped in cloth, now strut about as proud as young chicken cocks, with their clean faces and bright blue clothes. All are ready to plunge again into the labor and toil and uncertainty of war. You doubtless have heard all you can Stand of these matters.

My health is good—I have enough horses though Duke is still lame. I leave Gen. Webster Col. Sawyer & Hd. Qrs. at Newbern—& take with me the Same staff. I cannot tell where I will fetch up. That will depend on Joe Johnston but you will be able to trace me by the newspapers—write via Fortress Monroe, where I will have a Post office Agent to forward letters—I send to Tommy today a hundred dollars, and now enclose you $200, which is all I can raise and I got it of the Qr. Master. I think however you will not suffer, but as a Rule dont borrow—tis more honest to Steal. yrs. ever

AL (signature clipped), InND: Sherman Family Papers; material in angle brackets written above the verso of the clipped signature.

TO THOMAS EWING SHERMAN

> Head-Quarters Military Division
> of the Mississippi,
> In the Field, Goldsboro N.C.
> Apl. 9 1865.

Dear Tommy,

I have been very busy since our arrival, and must start again for Battle tomorrow. I have written to Mama, Minnie, & Lizzie, and now write to you to say that I hope some time this summer to be able to come and see you. The great Battles at Richmond are very important and may bring Peace to our Country when we will all be able to come home but as long as the war lasts you Know that we have to fight the Rebels. I will have a good deal to tell you when you are older for I have travelled all the way from the Mississipi since we were in our Camp at the Big Black. I have with me the same soldiers except the Regulars that I left at Nashville. I did intend to send and bring them here, but there is not time for as I said tomorrow I move for Raleigh and Greensboro.

Mama always tells me what a fine manly boy you are growing to be and I am very proud of you. I have in my pocket at all times a photograph of Mama, of you, Elly & Rachel. I have none of Minnie or Lizzy, but I remember all as plainly as if I had seen you yesterday. The last I heard of you and Mama was in the newspapers at Chicago. Mama was receiving the mayor and citizens at Bishop Duggans and Tommy Sherman was on the Steps with a flag.

That flag you know is the Emblem of our Country and is what we are fighting for. I have seen that flag in many battles and on our long march through Georgia and South Carolina, so that it is more than Country to me. It will recal as long as I live many scenes of which I will tell you when we have a house all together. No doubt you are now learning fast, and I want you to write to me by way of Fortress Monroe. We will have a Regular Mail from there up to our army in the Interior of North Carolina. Uncle Charley is now a Genl. and has his own soldiers and his own Camp. He used to be with me, but now he is in his own camp, and with his own soldiers. He ought to write home often but I fear he does not. Give my Love to Minnie & Lizzy and to your cousin Tommy Ewing and the girls. Tell Sister Angela that I think I have done a good deal of good and that She will do all that any person can for my children. Indeed you will find plenty of friends, for all Know I am off at the wars, fighting that you may have Peace.

I enclose in this an hundred Dolls. which you can give to Mama or Minnie to pay to the Academy for your Board and schooling. I will send more as soon as I get time to See the Paymaster, but we travel so fast and so far in the Country that paymasters dont come where we are[.] Your loving father,

W. T. Sherman

ALS, InND: Sherman Family Papers.

CHAPTER 15

April 12, 1865–May 30, 1865

S herman had just embarked on an offensive against what remained of Joseph E. Johnston's army when news arrived on April 12 of Lee's surrender to Grant. It seemed obvious now that the war was drawing to a close; two days later Sherman received word from Johnston that the Confederate commander wanted to suspend hostilities and commence negotiations "to terminate the existing war." Sherman agreed to the proposition, notifying Grant and others that he would offer Johnston the same terms Grant gave to Lee "and be careful not to complicate any points of civil policy."[1]

Sherman did not long hold to his pledge, and the result embroiled him in a major controversy just when it seemed that he would finally be able to rejoice in the triumph of the Union. Although Johnston's original letter suggested that peace negotiations would be left to the civil authorities, when he met with Sherman on April 18 at Durham Station, North Carolina, he was prepared to engage in such negotiations himself. With him was Confederate secretary of war John C. Breckinridge; when Sherman pondered the propriety of sitting down with a civil official, Breckinridge quickly claimed that he was present in his status as a major general, although in fact Johnston hoped he would help persuade Jefferson Davis to accept the terms to be hammered out that afternoon.

In the next several hours Sherman's self-confidence and belief that soldiers were better equipped than politicians to settle the conflict got the better of him. The man who claimed that he would not "complicate any points of civil policy" proceeded to do just that; in so doing he usurped the authority of his military and civil superiors in an effort to take his own turn as a politician making peace. Then and later he offered a series of justifications for acting as he did. He feared that Johnston's army might well break up into bands of roving guerrillas; he dismissed charges that the terms made no mention of slavery, for he believed the peculiar institution doomed. The former possibility had also concerned Grant, who nevertheless at Appomattox avoided the pitfalls Sherman stumbled into at Durham Station; in the case of the latter, it would have been better to realize that a military convention could not address the issues of slavery and emancipation (Grant had not done so on April 9). Indeed, much of what Sherman claimed he sought to achieve he could well have gained without stumbling into the quagmire of controversy that resulted when the terms of the Sherman-Johnston convention were transmitted northward.

It may have been the news of Lincoln's assassination that led Sherman down this path. It excited his imagination with the specter of guerrilla warfare and terrorism as few acts could; moreover, Sherman somehow believed that in his way he was carrying out what he believed to be the president's intentions when he assented to various parts of the agreement, especially those concerning the continued operation of civil governments and a general amnesty. Grant himself had crossed the line in assuring that Lee and his men would not be disturbed by Federal authorities so long as they abided by the law, but Lincoln had sanctioned that. For the very circumstances that may have propelled Sherman to act as he did also rendered the acceptance of the agreement he made highly unlikely—and, indeed, contributed to the backlash it inspired. Nevertheless, one can conclude that in all likelihood Lincoln would also have rejected the agreement, for it would have impaired his own freedom of action and violated some of his assumptions about how best to restore civil authority in the South.[2]

If in the end one is hard-pressed to defend Sherman's action, however, it is equally difficult to justify how many Northerners, including Secretary of War Edwin M. Stanton, responded to them. It took Grant only one reading of the text of the agreement to deem it unsatisfactory, and he promptly passed it on to the new president, Andrew Johnson, and Stanton with the advice that the cabinet should meet immediately. Just that day Lincoln's coffin had left Washington for its long ride back to Springfield; perhaps exhaustion after days of mourning contributed to what happened at the meeting, for Grant had to defend his friend from wild charges that Sherman had committed treason. The general in chief thought it best to deliver the news of the rejection of the terms to Sherman personally, in part so that he could oversee the negotiation of a new surrender agreement based on the Appomattox terms. Even as he prepared to leave Washington, however, he still could not believe how Stanton and others had characterized Sherman's motives: "It is infamous—infamous! After four years of such service as Sherman has done—that he should be used like this!"[3]

At first Sherman accepted the news of the rejection of the terms calmly, although he continued to justify his actions and complained that no one had informed him of a letter from Stanton to Grant, written before the *River Queen* conference, that enjoined the general not to enter into negotiations on matters of civil policy (in fact, Lincoln had composed the text of this directive). His defensiveness gave way to outrage, however, when he learned that Stanton had released a series of documents bearing on the agreement to the

New York Times, fueling rumors that the general was a traitor, insane, or both. It was almost too much for him to bear, for it seemed as if two of his traditional foes—politicians and the press—had joined together to assail him precisely at his greatest moment. No doubt Sherman was right to feel anger and contempt, for Stanton's action was both unnecessary and unwarranted. So was the response of Henry Halleck, who had assumed command in Virginia, to instructions that the initial armistice would be voided, for in speculating that the suspension of hostilities might enable Confederate civil officials to escape, carrying with them the Confederate treasury, Halleck let slip nightmares better kept to himself. It was no way for a man who had assured Sherman of his friendship to act, and it severed a bond that Sherman had once treasured.

Thus it was with a mixture of pride and bitterness, joy and anger that Sherman accompanied the majority of his army north to Washington in May 1865. He declined to meet Halleck at Richmond and ordered his men not to pass in review before his former friend. He saved his most intense fury for Stanton, despite Grant's efforts to mediate between the two men. "I am not much of a Talker," he assured John A. Logan, "but if ever my tongue is loose & free, I think I can and will say some things that will make an impression resembling a bomb shell of the largest pattern"—just what Grant feared.[4] Oddly enough, however, when he testified before the Joint Committee on the Conduct of the War on May 22—as good a forum as any—he pulled his punches, although remaining critical of Stanton and Halleck.

In the end, the controversy fizzled out, as the North celebrated victory. On May 23 and 24, Washington's Pennsylvania Avenue provided the stage for a grand review of the Army of the Potomac (minus Phil Sheridan and the Sixth Corps), the Army of the Tennessee (the Fifteenth and Seventeenth Corps), and the Army of Georgia (the Fourteenth and Twentieth Corps). Meade led the procession on the first day, while Sherman rode at the head of his columns on the second. The hero of Atlanta gained a measure of revenge when he ignored Stanton's outstretched hand; he took more pride in the soldierly bearing of his rough-hewn veterans. He betrayed his impatience after the ceremonies concluded, becoming so exasperated at the crowd that blocked his way home that he finally popped: "Damn you, get out of the way, damn you!"[5]

As May drew to a close it was time for Sherman to bid his men farewell. Peacetime military responsibilities awaited him; he shuddered as he contemplated associating with politicians and wondered how they would fumble the process of making peace and defining what exactly military victory had wrought. One thing was for sure: the war had made him. No longer did he have to worry about obscurity; despite his expressions of concern about money, never again did he have to contemplate poverty. He had gained fame and reputation too precious to barter away, and he would always remember with fondness his wartime friends and his men. Much yet waited him, but, for better and for worse, William T. Sherman had left his mark on his nation.

1. Joseph E. Johnston to WTS, April 13, 1865, *PM*, 2:346–47. WTS to USG, April 15, 1865.

2. For the Grant-Lee agreement and reaction to it, see Brooks D. Simpson, *Let Us Have Peace: Ulysses S. Grant and the Politics of War and Reconstruction, 1861–1868* (Chapel Hill, 1991), 84–97.

3. Ibid., 97.

4. WTS to John A. Logan, May 12, 1865.

5. Lloyd Lewis, *Sherman: Fighting Prophet* (1932; reprint, Lincoln, Neb., 1993), 577.

TO ULYSSES S. GRANT

Head-Quarters Military Division
of the Mississippi,
In the Field, Smithfield N.C.,
April 12, 1865—5 A.M.

Lt. Gen. U. S. Grant,
Comdg. Armies of the U.S.
Virginia
General,

I have this moment received your telegram announcing the Surrender of Lee's Army.[1] I hardly Know how to express my feelings, but you can imagine them. The terms you have given Lee are magnanimous and liberal. Should Johnston follow Lee's example I shall of course grant the Same. He is retreating before me on Raleigh, and I shall be there tomorrow. Roads are heavy, but under the inspiration of the news from you we can march 25 miles a day. I am now 27 m. from Raleigh but some of my army is 8 miles behind. If Johnston retreats South I will follow him to ensure the scattering his force, and capture of the locomotives & cars at Charlotte: but I take it he will surrender at Raleigh. Kilpatrick's cavalry is 10 m. to the South and west of me viz. on Middle Creek and I have sent Maj. Audenreid with orders to make for the South & West of Raleigh to impede the Enemy if he goes beyond Raleigh. All the Infantry is pointed straight for Raleigh by five different Roads. The Railroad is being repaired from Goldsboro to Raleigh, but I will not aim to carry it further. I shall expect to hear of Sheridan in case Johnston do not surrender at Raleigh. With a little more cavalry I would be sure to capture the whole army.
yrs. truly

W. T. Sherman
Maj. Gen. Comdg.

ALS, DNA: RG 108, Records of the Headquarters of the Army, Letters Received, AUS 1865, M259, *OR*, I, 47: pt. 3, 177.

1. USG to WTS, April 9, 1865, DLC: WTS. On April 12, WTS issued Special Field Orders No. 54, announcing Lee's surrender: "A little more labor, a little more toil on our part, the great race is won, and our Government stands regenerated after four long years of war." *PM*, 2:344.

TO ULYSSES S. GRANT

Raleigh, N.C., April 13, 1865.
(Received 7 p.m. 15th.)

Lieut. Gen. U. S. Grant,
City Point, Va.:

We entered Raleigh this morning. Johnston has retreated westward. I shall move to Asheville and Salisbury or Charlotte. I hope Sheridan is coming this way with his cavalry. If I can bring Johnston to a stand I will soon fix him. The people here had not heard of the surrender of Lee, and hardly credit it. All well.[1]

W. T. Sherman,
Major-general.

Printed, *OR*, I, 47: pt. 3, 191.
1. Grant forwarded this dispatch to Sheridan. *OR*, I, 47: pt. 3, 191.

TO HUGH JUDSON KILPATRICK

Head-Quarters Military Division
of the Mississippi,
In the Field, Raleigh, Apl. 14 1865.

Maj. Gen. Kilpatrick
Comdg. Cavalry
General,

I sent you orders today, but now enclose a copy.[1] You will see I am to put my army where if Johnston tries to pass out by Charlotte I can strike him in flank, but if he remains, at Greensboro, I shall capture the whole.

All I expect of you is to keep up a delusion, viz. that we are following him via the university and Hillsboro, until I get my Infantry heads of Columns across the Haw River, where I want you to cross also and fall out towards Greensboro, till I get to Ashboro when if he remain at Greensboro, I can approach him from the South, and force him to Battle, to surrender or disperse. You will perceive that we save a couple of days by cutting across the Bend in the direction of Saulsbury. I am very anxious to prevent his escape towards Georgia. If he does go to Georgia we can capture all the Rolling stock and vast amounts of property on the Road for Saulsbury back to Greensboro. The Governor[2] asks me to Suspend hostilities and to confer with him. I am willing to confer with him, but not to Suspend hostilities. I will not suspend hostilities till Johnstons army is captured or scattered. Howard tomorrow will have one Corps at Jones Station and one at Morrisons Station. Next day all move by seperate Roads for Ashboro. My Army is very large and cannot run as fast as Johnstons who has the Assistance of the Railroad. I am in hopes that Sheridan will come down, when he with the aid of your Cavalry can get ahead of him and hold him until we get up where we can make short work of him.

The People here manifest more signs of Subjugation than I have yet seen, but Jeff Davis has more lives than a cat and we must not trust him. If you reach the University do not disturb its library buildings or specific property. Yours truly,

W. T. Sherman

Maj. Genl. Comdg.

ALS, CsmH; *OR*, I, 47: pt. 3, 215.

1. Special Field Orders No. 55, Headquarters, Military Division of the Mississippi, April 14, 1865, gave the plans for troop movements designed to cut off and surround the remaining Confederate army. *PM*, 2:345–46.

2. Zebulon B. Vance (1830–94), who became governor of North Carolina in 1863, had just won reelection.

TO JOSEPH E. JOHNSTON

Hd. Qrs. M. D. M. in the field,

Raleigh 14th Apl. 1865

Gen J E Johnston

Comdg. C.A.

Genl.

I have this moment received your Communication of this date.[1] I am fully empowered to arrange with you any terms for the suspension of further hostilities between the armies commanded by you & those commanded by myself & will be willing to Confer with you to that End I will limit the advance of my main Column tomorrow to Mechanicsburg & the Cavalry to the university & expect that you will also maintain the present position of your forces until each has notice of a failure to agree—That a basis of action may be had I undertake to abide by the same terms & conditions as were made by Gen. Grant & Lee at Appomatox C. H. of the ninth (9th) inst. relative to our two armies & further move to obtain from Gen. Grant an order to suspend the movements of any troops from the direction of Virginia—Genl. Stoneman is under my command & my orders will suspend any devastation or destruction Contemplated by him I will add that I really desire to save the people of North Carolina the damage they would sustain by the march through Central or Western parts of the state—I am with respect your obdt. servt.

W. T. Sherman

Maj. Genl. Comdg.

Telegram, DNA: RG 107, Telegrams Sent by the Field Office of the Military Telegraph and Collected by the Office of the Secretary of War, 1865: Sherman, William T.; *OR*, I, 47: pt. 3, 207.

1. On April 13, Johnston had written WTS: "The results of the recent campaign in Virginia have changed the relative military condition of the belligerents. I am, therefore, induced to address you in this form the inquiry whether, to stop the further effusion of blood and devastation of property, you are willing to make a temporary suspension of active operations, and to communicate to Lieutenant-General Grant, commanding the armies of the United States, the request that he will take like action in regard to other armies, the object being to permit the civil authorities to enter into the needful arrangements to terminate the existing war." *PM*, 2:346–47.

TO ULYSSES S. GRANT

Raleigh N.C. April 15" 1865, 9:30 A.M.

Lieut. Gen., or copy to sec'y of war

I send copies of a correspondence begun with Johnston which I think will be followed by terms of capitulation. I will accept the same terms as Genl. Grant gave Lee and be careful not to complicate any points of civil policy.

If any cavalry have started towards me caution them that they may be prepared to find all works done. It is now raining in torrents and I shall await Johnstons reply here and will propose to meet him at Chapel Hill.

I have invited Governor Vance to return to Raleigh with the civil officers of his staff.

I have seen ex Governor Graham,[1] Mr. Badger,[2] Moore Holden and others all of whom agree that the war is over and that the states of the south must resume their allegiance, subject to the constitution & laws of Congress and that the military power of the South must submit to the national arms. This great fact once admitted all the details are easily arranged.

W. T. Sherman
Maj. Gen.

Telegram, DLC: Ulysses S. Grant Papers; *OR*, I, 47: pt. 3, 221.

1. William A. Graham (1804–75), former state legislator, U.S. senator, governor of North Carolina, U.S. secretary of the navy, and a Whig candidate for vice president in 1852, was a member of the Confederate Senate.

2. George E. Badger (1795–1866) had been secretary of the navy for six months in Taylor's cabinet with Thomas Ewing Sr.

TO JOSEPH D. WEBSTER

Headquarters, Military Division
of the Mississippi,
In the Field, Raleigh,
Apl. 17, 7 PM. [1865]

Gen. Webster,

Newbern

I have returned from a point 27 miles up the Railroad where I had a long interview with Genl. Johnston with a full & frank interchange of opinions. He evidently seeks to make terms for Jeff Davis and his Cabinet[.] He wanted to consult again with Mr. Breckinridge at Greensboro, and I have agreed to meet him at noon tomorrow at the same place. We lose nothing in time as by agreement both armies stand still, and the roads are drying up, so that if I am forced to pursue, will be able to make better Speed. There is great danger that the Confederate armies will dissolve and fill the whole land with robbers and assassins, and I think this is one of the difficulties that Johnston labors under. The assassination of Mr. Lincoln[1] shows one of the Elements in the Rebel army, which will be almost as difficult to deal with as the main armies. Communicate Substance of this to Genl. Grant, and also that if Sheridan is marching down this way to feel for me, before striking the Enemy. I dont want Johnstons army to break up in fragments.

W. T. Sherman
Maj. Genl. Comdg.

ALS, CsmH; *OR*, I, 47: pt. 3, 237.

1. On April 14, 1865, John Wilkes Booth shot Abraham Lincoln in Washington, D.C. The president died the next morning.

TO ULYSSES S. GRANT

Headquarters, Military Division
of the Mississippi,
In the Field, Raleigh N.C.,
April 18, 1865.

Lt. Genl. U. S. Grant, or Maj. Gen. Halleck,

Washington D.C.

General,

I enclose herewith a copy of an agreement made this day between Gen. Joseph E. Johnston and myself which if approved by the President of the United States will produce Peace from the Potomac and the Rio Grande[.] Mr. Breckinridge was present at our conference in his capacity as Major General, and satisfied me of the ability of General Johnston to carry out to the full extent the terms of this agreement, and if you will get the President to simply endorse the copy, and commission me to carry out the terms I will follow them to the conclusion.

You will observe that it is an absolute submission of the Enemy to the lawful authority of the United States, and disperses his armies absolutely, and the point to which I attach most importance is that the dispersion and disbandment of these armies is done in Such a manner as to prevent their breaking up into Guerilla Bands. On the other hand we can retain just as much of an army as we please. I agreed to the mode and manner of the surrender of arms set forth, as it gives the States the means of repressing Guerrillas which we could not expect them to do if we stript them of all arms.

Both Generals Johnston & Breckinridge admitted that Slavery was dead and I could not insist on embracing it in such a paper, because it can be made with the states in detail. I know that all the men of substance south sincerely want Peace and I do not believe they will resort to war again during this century. I have no doubt that they will in the future be perfectly subordinate to the Laws of the United States.

The moment my action in this matter is approved, I can spare five Corps and will ask for orders to leave Gen. Schofield here with the 10th Corps and to march myself with the 14, 15, 17 20 and 23d Corps, via Banksville, and Gordonsville to Frederick or Hagerstown there to be paid and mustered out. The question of Finance is now the chief one and every soldier & officer not needed should be got home at work. I would like to be able to begin the march north by May 1. I urge on the part of the President speedy action as it is important to get the Confederate Armies to their homes as well as our own. I am with great respect yr. obt. Servant

William T. Sherman
Maj. Gen. Comdg.
(Copy)

Memorandum or basis of agreement, made this 18th day of April, A.D. 1865, near Durham's Station in the State of North Carolina, by and between General Joseph E. Johnston, commanding the Confederate army, and Major General William T. Sherman, commanding the Army of the United States in North Carolina, both present:

First: The contending armies now in the field to maintain the "*status quo,*" until notice is given by the commanding General of any one to its opponent, and reasonable time, say forty-eight hours, allowed.

Second: The Confederate armies now in existence to be disbanded and conducted to their several State capitals, then to deposit their arms and public property in the State Arsenal: and each officer and man to execute and file an agreement to cease from acts of war, and to abide the action of both State and Federal authority. The number of arms and munitions of war to be reported to the Chief of Ordnance at Washington City, subject to the future action of the Congress of the United States, and in the meantime to be used solely to maintain peace and order within the borders of the States respectively.

Third: The recognition by the Executive of the United States of the several State Governments, on their officers and Legislatures taking the oaths prescribed by the Constitution of the United States: and where conflicting State Governments have resulted from the war, the legitimacy of all shall be submitted to the Supreme Court of the United States.

Fourth: The re-establishment of all the Federal Courts in the several States, with powers as defined by the Constitution and laws of Congress.

Fifth: The people and inhabitants of all the States to be guaranteed, so far as the Executive can, their political rights and franchises, as well as their rights of person and property as defined by the Constitution of the United States and of the States respectively.

Sixth: The Executive authority of the Government of the United States not to disturb any of the people by reason of the late war, so long as they live in peace and quiet, abstain from acts of armed hostility, and obey the laws in existence at the place of their residence.

Seventh: In general terms, the war to cease: a general amnesty so far as the Executive of the United States can command, on condition of the disbandment of the Confederate armies, the distribution of the arms, and the resumption of peaceful pursuits by the officers and men hitherto composing said armies.

Not being fully empowered by our respective principals to fulfil these terms, we individually and officially pledge ourselves to promptly obtain the necessary authority and to carry out the above programme.

(signed) W. T. Sherman   (signed) J. E. Johnston
  Maj. Genl. Com'd'g   General Comg.
  Army U.S. in N.C.   C.S. Army in N.C.

compared with the original in my possession and hereby certified.
    W. T. Sherman
    Maj. Gen. Comdg.

ALS, DNA: RG 94, Records of the Adjutant General's Office, Records of the Record and Pension Office, Document File, No. 520059. The agreement between Johnston and Sherman is a copy endorsed in Sherman's hand. *OR*, I, 47: pt. 3, 243–45.

TO HENRY W. HALLECK

Headquarters, Military Division
of the Mississippi,
In the Field, Raleigh, N.C.,
April 18, 1865

Genl. H. W. Halleck,
Chief of Staff, Washington, D.C.
Genl.,

I received your dispatch describing the man Clark detailed to assassinate me.[1] He had better be in a hurry or he will be too late.

The news of Lincolns death produced a most intense effect on our troops. At first I feared it would lead to excesses, but now it has softened down and can easily be guided. None evinced more feeling than General Johnston, who admitted that the act was calculated to stain his cause with a dark hue, and he contended that the loss was most serious to the People of the South, who had begun to realize that Mr. Lincoln was the best friend the South had. I cannot believe that even Mr. Davis was privy to the diabolical plot, but think it the emanation of a set of young men of the South who are very devils. I want to throw upon the South the care of this class of men who will soon be as obnoxious to their industrial classes as to us. Had I pushed Johnstons army to an extremity these would have dispersed and would have done important mischief. Johnston informed me that Stoneman had been at Salisbury and was now about Statesville. I have sent him orders to come to me. Genl. Johnston also informed me that Wilson was at Columbus, Ga. and he wanted me to arrest his progress. I leave that to you. {Indeed} if the President sanctions my agreement with Johnston, our interest is to cease all destruction.

Please give all orders necessary according to the views the Executive may take, and influence him if possible not to vary the terms at all, for I have considered everything, and believe that the Confederate Armies once dispersed, we can adjust all else fairly and well. I am yours &c.

W. T. Sherman
Maj. Gen. Comdg.

Copy, DLC: Edwin M. Stanton Papers; *OR*, I, 47: pt. 3, 245.
1. See HWH to WTS, April 15, 1865, *OR*, I, 47: pt. 3, 220–21.

TO ELLEN EWING SHERMAN

Headquarters, Military Division
of the Mississippi,
In the Field, Raleigh N. C., Apl. 18, 1865

Dearest Ellen,

I have just got back from a long interview with Genl. Johnston and Breck-inridge Sec. of War to the Confederacy, in which we arranged terms for the disbandment of *all* the Confederate Armies from this to the Rio Grande, the Submission to the National authority &c., which I send at once to Washington for ratification when this cruel war will be over. I can hardly realize it, but I can see no slip. The terms are all on our side. If approved I can soon complete the details, leave Schofield here and march my army for the Potomac there to be mustered out and paid. If I accomplish this I surely think I will be entitled to a months leave to come and See you. The assassination of Mr. Lincoln is most unfortunate but we ride a whirlwind and must take events as they arise. I have notice that I was embraced in the programme but the fellow who was to do the job did not appear, and if he is not in a hurry he will be too late.[1] I dont fear an assassin, though I would prefer for the name of the thing to get my quietus in a more honest way in open manly fight.

I got yours & Tommys photograph and will Keep them. I dont think Tommys is as good as one I already had—I have those of Elly & Rachel but none of Minnie & Lizzie.

I now expect a week of Comparative leisure till my messenger returns from Washington,[2] and I will try and write more at length.

I have sent you some trophies and may send you more. Yrs. ever

W. T. Sherman

ALS, InND: Sherman Family Papers.

1. When Stanton telegraphed the news of Lincoln's assassination to WTS on April 17, he intimated that leaders in Washington feared that a like fate was planned for USG and other military leaders. *PM*, 2:347–48.

2. Major Henry Hitchcock carried the dispatches to Washington.

TO SEWALL L. FREMONT

Hdqrs. Military Division
of the Mississippi,
In the Field, Raleigh, N.C.,
April 21, 1865.

S. L. Fremont, Esq,
Wilmington, N.C.:
Sir:

I have before me your letter addressed to General Hawley,[1] inclosing a paper signed by John Dawson, Edward Kiddon, and others testifying to your feelings of loyalty and attachment to the Government of the United States.[2] Of course I am gratified to know the truth as to one for whom I entertained friendship dated far back in other and better days. I will be frank and honest with you. Simple passive submission to events by a man in the prime of life is not all that is due to society in times of revolution. Had the Northern men residing at the South spoken out manfully and truly at the outset the active secessionists could not have carried the masses of men as they did. It may not be that the war could have been avoided, but the rebellion would not have assumed the mammoth proportions it did. The idea of war to perpetuate slavery in the year 1861 was an insult to the intelligence of the age. As long as the South abided by the conditions of our fundamental contract of government, the Constitution, all law-abiding citizens were bound to respect the property in slaves, whether they approved it or not, but when the South violated that compact openly, publicly, and violently, it was absurd to suppose we were bound to respect that kind of property or any kind of property. I do have a feeling allied to abhorrence toward Northern men resident South, for their silence or acquiescence was one of the causes of the war assuming the magnitude it did, and in consequence we mourn the loss of such men as John F. Reynolds, McPherson, and thousands of noble gentlemen, any one of whom was worth all the slaves of the South and half of the white population thrown in. The result is nearly accomplished, and is what you might have foreseen, and in a measure prevented—desolation from the Ohio to the Gulf, and mourning in every household. I am not made of stone, and cannot help indulging in a feeling toward the Union men South who failed at the proper time to meet the storm and check it before it gained full headway. I have a right to speak thus, because I was South in 1861 and saw myself such men as Duncan,[3] Bush Johnson,[4] and others join in the popular sneer at Yankees when they knew better. For them I have not a particle of sympathy, and for the other classes of Northern men who were coerced or wheedled into acquiescence or neutrality, all I can say is that I will not sit in judgment on them: but I shall never confide in their courage, manliness, or virtue.

I am, with respect,
W. T. Sherman,
Major-General.

Printed, *OR*, I, 47: pt. 3, 271–72.

1. Brigadier General Joseph R. Hawley (1826–1905), a newspaperman and Republican operative, was commanding the District of Wilmington, N.C., at this time.

2. See also WTS to George F. Granger, April 3, 1865.

3. General Johnson Kelly Duncan (1827–62), CSA, had left the army in 1855 to become a government servant in New Orleans. He died of typhoid fever while serving in Knoxville in late 1862.

4. General Bushrod Rust Johnson (1817–80), CSA, graduated from West Point with WTS and served in the army before resigning in 1847 to take up a career in military education. During the war he saw action in both the eastern and western theaters.

TO JOSEPH E. JOHNSTON

Headquarters, Military Division
of the Mississippi,
In the Field, Apl. 21 1865, Raleigh N.C.

Genl. J. E. Johnston
Comdg. Confederate Army—
General,

I send you a letter for Genl. Wilson which if sent by telegraph and Courier will check his career.[1] He may mistrust the telegraph and therfore better Send the original, for he cannot mistake my handwriting with which he is familiar. He seems to have his blood up, and will be hard to hold. If he can buy any fodder & rations down about Fort Valley it will obviate the necessity of his going up to Rome or Dalton. It is reported to me from Cairo that Mobile is in our possession, but it is not minute or official.[2]

Gen. Baker[3] sent in to me wanting to surrender his Command, on the theory that the whole Confederate Army was surrendered. I explained to him or his staff officer the exact truth and left him to act as he thought proper. He seems to have disbanded his men—deposited a few arms about 20 miles from here, and himself awaits your action. I will not hold him, his men or arms subject to any condition other than the final one we may agree on.

I shall look for Major Hitchcock back from Washington on Monday, and Shall promptly notify you of the result. By the action of Genl. Weitzel in relation to the Virginia Legislature,[4] I feel certain we will have no trouble on the score of recognizing *existing* State Govts. It may be the Lawyers will want us to define more minutely what is meant by the Guarantee of Rights of

Person & property. It may be construed into a compact for us to undo the past as to the Rights of Slaves, and "Leases of Plantations" on the Mississipi, of "Vacant & Abandonned" Plantations. I wish you would talk to the best man you have on these Points, and if possible Let us in the final Convention make these points so clear as to leave no room for angry controversy.

I believe if the South would simply & publicly declare what we all feel that Slavery is dead, that you would inaugurate an Era of Peace & prosperity that would soon efface the ravages of the past four years of war. Negros would remain in the South and afford you abundance of cheap labor, which otherwise will be driven away: and it will save the country the senseless discussions which have Kept us all in hot water for fifty years. Although strictly speaking this is no subject of a military convention, yet I am honestly convinced that our simple declaration of a Result, will be accepted as good Law everywhere. Of course I have not a single word from Washington on this or any other point of our agreement, but I know the effect of such a step by us will be universally accepted. I am with great respect Yr. obt. servant

W. T. Sherman
Maj. Genl. U.S. Army.

ALS, MiU-C: James S. Schoff Civil War Collection; *OR*, I, 47: pt. 3, 265–66.

1. WTS to James H. Wilson, April 21, 1865, advised him of the truce with Johnston and commanded him to release two Confederate generals captured at Macon and observe the truce unless Confederates broke it. MiU-C: James S. Schoff Civil War Collection.

2. Federal attacks against the forts surrounding Mobile on April 8 and 9 forced CSA general Dabney H. Maury to evacuate the city on April 11; the next day it was occupied by Union forces.

3. Brigadier General Laurence S. Baker (1830–1907), CSA, commanded a brigade at Bentonville.

4. Major General Godfrey Weitzel (1835–84), USA, had entered Richmond on April 3 in command of the Twenty-fifth Corps; Lincoln met with him there on April 6. In a letter of the same date, Lincoln authorized him to allow the members of the state legislature to meet, albeit only to "take measures to withdraw the Virginia troops, and other support from resistance to the General government" in return for which confiscated property would be restored (*CWAL*, 8:389). Lincoln had written to John A. Campbell, former U.S. Supreme Court justice and assistant secretary of war for the Confederacy, outlining these terms (Lincoln to Campbell, April 5, 1865, *CWAL*, 8:386–87). Lincoln telegraphed Weitzel twice on April 12, first asking him what response there had been to the offer and second withdrawing it in light of a letter Campbell had written to Weitzel on April 7 which implied that Lincoln had "called the insurgent Legislature of Virginia together, as the rightful Legislature of the State, to settle all differences with the United Sates," not merely to withdraw state troops and resources from the support of the Confederate war effort. Furthermore, he concluded, Lee's surrender at Appomattox had rendered the issue moot (*CWAL*, 8:406–7; quote on p. 406; Campbell's letter of April 7 is 407–8n).

Headquarters, Military Division
of the Mississippi,
In the Field, Raleigh N.C. Apl. 22, 1865

Dearest Ellen,

I wrote you a hasty letter by Maj. Hitchcock and promised to write more at length as soon as matters settled away somewhat—I am now living in the Palace and the Army lies round about the City on beautiful rolling hills of clear ground with plenty of water, and a budding spring[.] We await a reply from Washington which finishes all the war by one process or forces us to push the fragments of the Confederate Army to the wall. Hitchcock should be back the day after tomorrow & then I will Know. I can start in pursuit of Johnston who is about Greensboro, on short notice, but I would prefer not to follow him back to Georgia. A pursuing army cannot travel as fast as a fleeing one in its own Country. Your letters have come to me in driblets—and mine will miss you as all from Goldsboro were directed to South Bend. I sent you there the Columbia Flag and a Revolutionary Seal for your fair[.] I have the Circulars and have sent them out to parties to collect trophies for you, but it is embarassing for me to engage in the business as trophies of all Kinds belong to Govt. and I ought not to be privy to their conversion. Others do it I Know, but it shows the rapid decline in honesty of our People. Pillow in the Mexican War tried to Send home as trophies a brass Gun & other things, such as swords and Lances, and it was paraded all over the Land as evidence of his dishonesty.[1] I feel certain soldiers & Junior officers will send any quantity of things picked up in our recent march obtained by questionable means. When you go to Chicago, better Stop at some good Hotel or Mr. Shermans,[2] who is not a relative but is a worthy & wealthy man. Dont go near those Tribune men. They are as mean sneaks as possible. They would report your conversations, and pick your pockets of my letters and publish them if it would contribute to their temporary advantage. Chicago is doubtless a city destined to attain large properties & great wealth more so than Cincinati, but it is too Cold for us. Our next Move will probably be down the Mississipi. If the war closes with the terms I have made I expect to make a hasty visit to Charleston and Savannah, and then come up to about Frederick or Hagerstown Md. to receive my army which will probably march there. I would have a magnificent pageant, before all are mustered & discharged. Meade could take the Atlantic Slope, I the Mississipi and Halleck the Pacific, Thomas & Sheridan would have the Prairies & Texas. The present armies should all be mustered out and the Regular army increased to 100,000 men & these would suffice to maintain & enforce order at the South. There is great danger of the Confederate armies breaking up into Guerillas and that is what I most fear. Such men as Wade Hampton, Forrest, Wirt Adams[3] &c. never will work and their negros are all gone their plantations destroyed, &c. I will be glad if I can open a way for them abroad. Davis, Breckinridge &c. will go abroad or get killed in pursuit—my terms do not embrace them but applies solely to the Confederate Armies. All not in Regular Muster Rolls, will be outlaws. The people of Raleigh are quiet & submissive enough, and also the North Carolinians are subjugated, but the young men *after* they get over the efforts of recent disasters and wake up to the realization that nothing is left them but to work will be sure to stir up trouble, but I hope that we can soon fix them off—Raleigh is a very old city with a large stone Capitol and Governors Mansion called the Palace, now occupied by me & staff—They are distant abt. half a mile apart with a street connecting somewhat in the nature of Washington. This street is the business street and some very handsome houses and Gardens make up the town. It is full of fine people who were secesh but now are willing to encourage the visits of handsome young men—I find here the family of Mr. Badger who was with your father in Taylors Cabinet[.] He is paralyzed so as to be hardly able to walk & sits all day, he has his mind and is glad to have visitors. I have called twice. Though a moderate man he voted to go out and actually drafted one of the Resolutions of Secession. His wife must be much younger than he and is a lively interesting lady chock full of Washington. She was *dying* for some news, and Harpers Magazine. I could tell you much that might interest you, but will now merely say that if Mr. Johnson will ratify the terms I will leave Schofield here to complete the business—will start 5 corps for the Potomac, to march, and in person will go to Charleston & Savannah to give some necessary orders, and then go to the Potomac to receive the troops as they arrive. I may bring you and the children there to See the last final Grand Review of my army before disbanding it. That is the dream, and is possible. It will take all May to march & June to muster out & pay so that the 4th of July may witness a perfect Peace. My new Sphere will I suppose be down the Mississipi—How would Memphis suit you as a home. The Mississipi Valley is my hobby, and if I remain in the Army, there is the place Grant will put me. Memphis or Nashville. But I am counting the chickens before they are hatched and must wait to See this thing out—When the war ends our labors begin for we must organize the Permanent army for the future.

I have this moment received Mr. Casserlys letter,[4] also Minnies most excellent letter of April 6. I suppose there must be a poetic aspect to the wanderings of my army away down in Dixie, from the way Mr. Casserly writes. If I have leisure I will write him. What did Lizzies Lot bring? Did it pay last years taxes? What about that Sherman testimonial—was it all brag? Love to all yrs. ever

W. T. Sherman

ALS, InND: Sherman Family Papers.

1. In 1847 after the Battle of Chapultepec, several soldiers placed the barrels of two Mexican howitzers in General Gideon Pillow's baggage wagon. Pillow denied that he had authorized the act, but a skeptical Winfield Scott believed otherwise, sparking a controversy.

2. Francis C. Sherman (1805–70), the father of General Francis Trowbridge Sherman, was a Chicago businessman and politician. He had opened one of the city's first hotels, served on the boards of utilities and banks, and was currently the city's mayor. Elected to office as a War Democrat in 1862, he had earlier served in the same position from 1841 to 1842, as well as serving in the state legislature and at the state constitutional convention. His current term would expire in 1865.

3. Brigadier General Wirt Adams (1819–88), CSA, had joined Forrest's men earlier in 1865.

4. Presumably Casserly to WTS, February 2, 1865, DLC: WTS. The second of two letters of this date (the first deals strictly with business matters), it expressed Casserly's interest in WTS's progress and his impatience to hear about the general's next move.

TO DAVID L. SWAIN[1]

Hdqrs. Military Division
of the Mississippi,
In the Field, Raleigh, N.C.,
April 22, 1865.

Hon. D. L. Swain,
Chapel Hill, N.C.:
My Dear Sir:

Yours of April 19 was laid before me yesterday, and I am pleased that you recognize in General Atkins a fair representation of our army. The moment war ceases, and I think that time is at hand, all seizures of horses and private property will cease on our part, and it may be we will be able to spare some animals for the use of-the farmers of your neighborhood. There now exists a species of truce, but we must stand prepared for action; but I believe that in a very few days a definite and general peace will be arranged, when I will make orders that will be in accordance with the new state of affairs. I do believe I fairly represent the feelings of my countrymen, that we prefer peace to war, but if war is forced upon us we must meet it, but if peace be possible we will accept it and be the friends of the farmers and working classes of North Carolina, as well as actual patrons of churches, colleges, asylums, and all institutions of learning and charity. Accept the assurances of my respect and high esteem. I have read the volume sent me and find it interesting.

I am, truly, yours,
W. T. Sherman,
Major-General, Commanding.

Printed, *OR*, I, 47: pt. 3, 279–80.

1. David L. Swain (1801–68) was president of the University of North Carolina and a former governor of North Carolina.

TO JOSEPH E. JOHNSTON

Head-Quarters Military Division
of the Mississippi,
In the Field, Raleigh,
Apl. 23. 1865. 7 A.M.

General Jos. E. Johnston.
Comdg. Confederate Army, Greensboro.
General,

Your communication of 2.30 P.M. of yesterday is received. My Line of Communication with Genl. Wilson is not secure enough for me to confuse him by a change in mere words. Of Course the *status quo* is mutual, but I leave him to apply it to his case according to his surroundings. I would not instruct him to undo all done by him between the actual date of our agreement and the time the Knowledge reached him. I beg therefore to leave him free to apply the Rule to his own case. Indeed I have almost exceeded the bounds of prudence in checking him without the means of direct Communication, and only did so in my absolute faith in your personal character.

I Enclose a despatch for Wilson in cypher which translated simply advises him to Keep his command well together and to act according to the best of his ability, doing as little harm to the Country as possible, until he Knows hostilities are resumed. I am with respect

W. T. Sherman
Maj. Genl. U.S.A.

ALS, MH.

TO JOSEPH E. JOHNSTON AND WILLIAM J. HARDEE

Unofficial.

Hdqrs. Military Div.
of the Mississippi,
In the Field, Raleigh, N.C.,
April 23, 1865.

Generals Johnston and Hardee:

I send bundle of papers for you jointly. These are the latest. Telegraphic dispatches are here to the 19th. Young Fred. Seward is alive, having been subjected to the trepan, and may possibly recover. There appears no doubt the murder of Mr. Lincoln was done by Booth, and the attempt on Mr. Seward by Surratt, who is in custody.[1] All will sooner or later be caught. The feeling

North on this subject is more intense than anything that ever occurred before. General Ord, at Richmond, has recalled the permission given for the Virginia Legislature,[2] and I fear much the assassination of the President will give such a bias to the popular mind which, in connection with the desire of our politicians, may thwart our purpose of recognizing "existing local governments." But it does seem to me there must be good sense enough left on this continent to give order and shape to the now disjointed elements of government. I believe this assassination of Mr. Lincoln will do the cause of the South more harm than any event of the war, both at home and abroad, and I doubt if the Confederate military authorities had any more complicity with it than I had. I am thus frank with you and have asserted as much to the War Department. But I dare not say as much for Mr. Davis or some of the civil functionaries, for it seems the plot was fixed for March 4, but delayed, awaiting some instructions from Richmond. You will find in the newspapers I send you all the information I have on this point. Major Hitchcock should be back to morrow, and if any delay occurs It will result from the changed feeling about Washington arising from this new and unforeseen complication.

I am, yours,

W. T. Sherman.

Printed, *OR*, I, 47: pt. 3, 287.

1. Actually, Lewis Paine assaulted the Sewards; John Surratt, although one of Booth's conspirators in other matters, was not part of the assassination attempt of April 14 and was not arrested until 1866, when he was discovered serving in the papal guard at the Vatican.

2. WTS here refers to Lincoln's idea of having the members of the Virginia legislature meet to withdraw Virginia from the Confederacy—an idea that was dropped by Lincoln in the aftermath of Lee's surrender, when it became apparent that the president's idea verged on recognizing the legitimacy of a Confederate state government.

TO JOSEPH E. JOHNSTON

Raleigh April 23rd/65 8 P.M.

General Jos. E. Johnston
C.S.A.

Maj. Hitchcock reports his arrival at Morehead City with dispatches from Washington & will be here in the morning.

Please be in readiness to resume negotiations when the contents of Dispatches are Known. Very Resp'y

W. T. Sherman
Maj. Genl. U.S.A.

Telegram, MH; *OR*, I, 47: pt. 3, 287.

TO JOSEPH E. JOHNSTON

Raleigh April 24th" 1865 6 A.M.

Genl. Johnston,

You will take notice that the truce or suspension of Hostilities agreed to between us will cease in forty Eight (48) hours after this is received at your lines under first of the Articles of our Agreement[.]

W. T. Sherman
Maj. Genl.

Telegram, MH. Noted "Recd. at 11h. A.M. April 24th 1865." *OR*, I, 47: pt. 3, 293.

TO JOSEPH E. JOHNSTON

Raleigh Apr. 24th 1865

Genl. Johnston
Comdg. Confederate Armies

I have replies from Washington to my Communications of April Eighteenth (18th)[.] I am Instructed to limit my operations to your Immediate Command not to attempt civil negotiations[.]

I therefore demand the surrender of your army on the same terms as were given Genl. Lee at Appomatox of April ninth (9th) Inst. purely and simply[.]

W. T. Sherman
Maj. Genl.

Telegram, MH; *OR*, I, 47: pt. 3, 294.

TO ULYSSES S. GRANT

Headquarters, Military Division
of the Mississippi,
In the Field, Raleigh N.C., April 25 1865

Lt. Genl. U. S. Grant,
Present,
General,

I had the honor to receive your letter of April 21,[1] with enclosures yesterday and was well pleased that you came along, as you must have observed that I held the military control so as to adapt it to any phase the case might assume.[2]

It is but just that I should record the fact that I made my terms with General Johnston under the influence of the liberal terms you extended to the Army of Genl. Lee at Appomatox C. H. on the 9th and the seeming policy of our Government as evinced by the call of the Virginia Legislature and Governor back to Richmond under yours and President Lincolns very eyes. It now appears that this last act was done without consultation with you or any Knowledge of Mr. Lincoln, but rather in opposition to a previous policy well considered.

I have not the least desire to interfere in the Civil Policy of our Government, but would shun it as something not to my liking, but occasions do arise where a prompt seizure of results is forced on military commanders not in immediate communication with the proper Authority. It is probable that the terms signed by Genl. Johnston & myself were not clear enough on the point, well understood between us, that our negotiations did not apply to any parties outside the officers and men of the Confederate armies, which would have been easily remedied.

No surrender of an army not actually at the mercy of an antagonist, was ever made without "terms," and these always define the military status of the surrendered. Thus you stipulated that the officers and men of Lee's army should not be molested at their homes so long as they obeyed the Laws at the place of their residence.

I do not wish to discuss the points involved in our recognition of the State Governments in actual existence, but merely state my Conclusions to await the solution of the future. Such action on our part in no manner recognizes for a moment the So called Confederate Government or makes us liable for its debts or acts.

The Laws and acts done by the several States during the Period of Rebellion, are void because done without the oath prescribed by the Constitution of the U.S. which is a "condition precedent[.]" We have a Right to use any sort of machinery to produce military results, and it is the commonest thing for military commanders to use the Civil Government in actual existence as a means to an End. I do believe we could and can use the present state Governments lawfully, constitutionally and as the very last possible means to produce the object desired, viz. entire and complete submission to the Lawful authority of the U.S. As to punishment for past crimes, that is for the Judiciary and can in no manner of way be disturbed by our acts, and so far as I can I will use my influence that Rebels shall suffer all the personal punishment prescribed by Law, as also the civil liabilities arising from their past acts. What we now want is the mere forms of Law by which common men may regain the positions of industry so long disturbed by the war.

I now apprehend that the Rebel Armies will disperse; and instead of dealing with six or seven states, we will have to deal with numberless bands of desperados headed by such men as Mosby, Forrest, Red Jackson, & others who Know not, and care not for danger or its consequences. I am with great respect yr. obt. Servant

W. T. Sherman
Maj. Genl.

ALS, PPRF; *OR*, I, 47: pt. 3, 302–3.
1. *PUSG*, 14:424–25. USG informed his friend that, after carefully reading the terms of

agreement between WTS and Johnston before submitting it to the president, he "felt satisfied that it could not possibly be approved" (p. 424). Convinced of the importance of the issues that the document addressed, USG had immediately notified Stanton of its receipt and suggested that the president and the entire cabinet meet to discuss it. The result of this meeting was that the entire negotiations between WTS and Johnston were disapproved with the exception of the surrender of Johnston's army. He enclosed a copy of a letter he had received from Stanton, written on March 3, 1865, which had outlined Lincoln's thoughts on military surrenders—"you are not to decide, discuss, or confer upon any political question." Only the president would decide these matters. *PM*, 2:359–60. Johnson had decided to continue this policy. That Lincoln's meeting with Grant and Sherman aboard the *River Queen* in late March may have modified these orders (for Grant's terms to Lee at Appomattox, which Lincoln subsequently approved, touched on the political question of whether the surrendered Confederates were subject to trial for treason) did not concern either Johnson or Stanton.

2. USG had been sent by Stanton and Johnson; "The President desires that you proceed immediately to the headquarters of Major-General Sherman, and direct operations against the enemy." Stanton to USG, April 21, 1865, *PM*, 2:359.

TO EDWIN M. STANTON

Headquarters, Military Division
of the Mississippi,
In the Field, Raleigh N.C., Apl. 25 1865

Hon. E. M. Stanton
Sec. of War Washington
Dear Sir,

I have been furnished a copy of your letter of April 21, to Genl. Grant—signifying your disapproval of the terms on which Gen. Johnston proposed to disarm and disperse the Insurgents on condition of amnesty &c. I admit my folly in embracing in a Military convention any Civil matters, but unfortunately Such is the Nature of our situation that they Seem inextricably united and I understood from you at Savannah that the Financial State of the Country demanded Military Success and would warrant a little bending to Policy. When I had my conference with General Johnston I had the public Examples before me, of General Grants terms to Lees Army and General Weitzels invitation to the Virginia Legislature to assemble. I still believe the Govt. of the U.S. has made a mistake, but that is none of my business: Mine is a difficult task and I had flattered myself that by four years patient, unremitting, and successful labor I deserved no reminder such as is contained in the last paragraph of your letter to General Grant. You may assure the President that I heed his suggestion. I am truly,

W. T. Sherman

ALS, DLC: Edwin M. Stanton Papers; *OR*, I, 47: pt. 3, 302.

Terms of a Military Convention entered into this twenty-sixth (26th) day of April 1865, at Bennett's House, near Durhams Station, N.C. between General Joseph E. Johnston, Comdg. the Confederate Army and Maj. Genl. W. T. Sherman, comdg. the United States Army in North Carolina.[1]

All acts of war on the part of the troops under General Johnstons command to cease from this date.

All arms and public property to be deposited at Greensboro, and delivered to an ordnance officer of the United States Army.

Rolls of all the officers and men to be made in duplicate, one copy to be retained by the commander of the troops, and the other to be given to an officer to be designated by General Sherman.

Each officer and man to give his individual obligation in writing not to take up arms against the Government of the United States until properly released from this obligation. The side arms of officers and their private horses and baggage to be retained by them.

This being done, all the officers and men will be permitted to return to their homes, not to be disturbed by the United States authorities so long as they observe their obligation and the laws in force where they may reside.

W. T. Sherman,   J. E. Johnston,
Maj Genl,   General, Comg C.S. Forces in N.C.
Comdg U.S. Forces in N Cara
Approved,
U. S. Grant,
Lt. Genl.
Raleigh, N.C., Apl 26, 65

ADS, DLC: William T. Sherman; *OR*, I, 47: pt. 3, 313.
1. What follows is closely modeled on the terms Grant offered Lee on April 9, 1865, although Grant was not present at the meeting between Sherman and Johnston.

TO JOSEPH E. JOHNSTON

Hdqrs. Military Division
of the Mississippi,
In the Field, Raleigh, N.C.,
April 27, 1865.

General Johnston,
Commanding Confederate Armies, &c., Greensborough:
General:

I herewith inclose you copies of my Field Orders, Nos. 65 and 66, which give General Schofield full and ample power to carry into effect our convention, and

I hope at your personal interview with General Schofield you satisfied your mind of his ability and kind disposition toward the inhabitants of North Carolina. In addition to the points made at our interview of yesterday, I have further instructed General Schofield to facilitate what you and I and all good men desire, the return to their homes of the officers and men composing your army, to let you have of his stores ten days' rations for 25,000 men. We have abundance of provisions at Morehead City, and if you send trains here they may go down with our trains and return to Greensborough with the rations specified. Colonel Wright did intend to send his construction train up to-day, but did not get up his carpenters in time. The train with square timber and carpenters will go up in the morning, and I think by the morning of the 29th your trains can run down on the road and fall in with ours of the 30th. I can hardly estimate how many animals fit for farm purposes will be "loaned" to the farmers, but enough, I hope, to insure a crop. I can hardly commit myself how far commerce will be free, but I think the cotton still in the country and the crude turpentine will make money with which to procure supplies. General Schofield in a few days will be able to arrange all such matters. I wish you would send the inclosed parcel for General Wilson, as it contains the orders "65" and "66," and instructions to release all his prisoners on the conditions of our convention. Now that war is over, I am as willing to risk my person and reputation as heretofore to heal the wounds made by the past war, and I think my feeling is shared by the whole army. I also think a similar feeling actuates the mass of your army, but there are some unthinking young men, who have no sense or experience, that unless controlled may embroil their neighbors. If we are forced to deal with them, it must be with severity, but I hope they will be managed by the people of the South.

I am, with respect,
your obedient servant,
W. T. Sherman,
Major-General, U.S. Army.

Printed, *OR*, I, 47: pt. 3, 320.

TO ULYSSES S. GRANT

Headquarters, Military Division
of the Mississippi,
In the Field, Raleigh N.C., April 28 1865

Lt. Genl. U. S. Grant
Genl. in Chief Washington D.C.
General,

Since you left me yesterday I have seen the *New York Times* of the 24, containing a Budget of military news authenticated by the signature of the

Secretary of War, which is grouped in such a way as to give very erroneous impressions.[1] It Embraces a Copy of the basis of agreement between myself & Gen. Johnston of April 18 with commentaries which it will be time enough to discuss two or three years hence, after the Government has experimented a little more in the machinery by which Power reaches the Scattered People of the vast area of Country Known as the South; but in the meantime I do think that my Rank, if not past services, entitled me at least to the respect of Keeping secret what was Known to none but the Cabinet, until further inquiry could have been made instead of giving publicity to documents I never saw, and drawing inferences wide of the Truth. I never saw or had furnished me a copy of President Lincolns dispatch to you of the 3rd of March[2] until after the agreement nor did Mr. Stanton or any human being ever convey to me its substance or anything like it. But on the contrary I had seen Gen. Weitzels invitation to the Virginia Legislature made in Mr. Lincoln's very presence and had failed to discover any other official hint of a Plan of reconstruction, or any ideas calculated to allay the fears of the People of the South, after the destruction of their armies and civil authorities would leave them without any Government at all. We should not drive a People into anarchy, and it is simply impossible for our Military Power to reach all the recesses of their unhappy country. I confess I did not wish to break Gen. Johnstons army into bands of armed men, roving about without purpose, and capable only of infinite mischief. But you say on your arrival that I had my army so disposed, that his escape was only possible in a disorganized shape: and as you did not choose to direct military operations in this quarter, I infer you were satisfied with the military situation. At all events the instant I learned what was proper enough, the disapproval of the President, I acted in such a manner as to compel the Surrender of Gen. Johnstons whole army on the Same terms you prescribed to Genl. Lees Army when you had it surrounded and in your absolute Power.

Mr. Stanton in stating that my orders to General Stoneman were likely to result in the escape of "Mr. Davis to Mexico or Europe" is in deep error. Stoneman was not at Salisbury then, but had gone back to "Statesville"— Davis was supposed to be between us and therefore Stoneman was beyond him. By turning towards me he was approaching Davis, and had he joined me as ordered I would have had a mounted force greatly needed for that and other purposes. But even now I dont Know that Mr. Stanton wants Davis caught, and as my official papers deemed sacred are hastily published to the world it will be imprudent for me to State what has been done in that respect.

As the Editor of the *Times* has (it may be) logically and fairly drawn from this singular document the conclusion that I am insubordinate I can only deny the intention. I have never in my life questioned or disobeyed an order, though many and many a time have I risked my life, my health and reputation in obeying orders or even hints to execute plans and purposes not to my liking. It is not fair to withhold from me plans and Policy, if any there be, and expect me to guess at them. For facts and events appear quite different from different stand Points. For four years I have been in camp dealing with soldiers, and I can assure you that the conclusion at which the Cabinet arrived with such singular unanimity differs from mine. I conferred freely with the best officers in this army as to the points involved in this controversy and strange to Say they were singularly unanimous in the other conclusion, and they will learn with pain and amazement that I am deemed insubordinate & wanting in common sense that I, who in the complications of last year worked day and night, summer and winter for the Cause and the administration ⟨cut the Gordian Knot in which our state affairs seemed entangled,⟩ and who have brought an army of seventy thousand men in magnificent condition across a country deemed impossible, and placed it just where it was wanted almost on the day appointed have brought discredit on our Government. I do not wish to boast of this but I do say that it entitled me to the courtesy of being consulted before publishing to the world a proposition rightfully submitted to higher authority for proper adjudication, and then accompanied by other statements which invited the Press to be let loose upon me. It is true that non-combatants, men who sleep in comfort & security whilst we watch on the distant Lines are better able to judge than we poor soldiers, who rarely see a newspaper, hardly can hear from our families, or stop long enough to get our Pay. I envy not the task of reconstruction, and am delighted that the Secretary has relieved me of it. As you did not undertake to assume the management of the affairs of this army I infer that on personal inspection your mind arrived at a different conclusion from that of the Secretary of War. I will therefore go on and execute your orders to their conclusion, and when done will with intense satisfaction leave to the Civil authorities the execution of the task of which they Seem to me so jealous. But as an honest man and soldier I invite them to follow my path, for they may see some things, and hear some things that may disturb their Philosiphy. With sincere respect,

William T. Sherman
Maj. Genl. Comdg.

P.S. As Mr. Stantons singular paper has been published, I demand that this also be made public, though I am in no manner responsible to the Press, but to the Law, and my proper Superiors.

William T. Sherman
Maj. Genl. Comdg.

ALS, DNA: RG 94, Records of the Adjutant General's Office, Letters Received, M-1055-1865; OR, I, 47: pt. 3, 334–35. Material in angle brackets was deleted by WTS.

1. The *Times* of this date printed several documents which are reprinted in *PM*, 2:364–65, including WTS's and Johnston's surrender terms of April 18, Stanton's ten reasons for rejecting them, a report on the cabinet meeting of April 21 at which they were rejected, and Stanton to USG, March 3, 1865. Stanton also expressed concern that the moving of Stoneman's troops would allow Jefferson Davis and a large amount of Confederate gold to escape to Mexico.

2. On March 2, 1865, Lee asked USG to meet with him under the terms of a military convention; USG forwarded the request to Washington and asked for instructions (USG to Stanton, March 3, 1865, *PUSG*, 14:90). In reply, a dispatch written by Lincoln but signed by Stanton stated that the president "wishes you to have no conference with General Lee unless it be for the capitulation of Gen. Lee's army. . . . He instructs me to say that you are not to decide, discuss, or confer upon any political question." Stanton to USG, March 3, 1865, *PUSG*, 14:91n.

TO ELLEN EWING SHERMAN

Headquarters Military Division
of the Mississippi,
In the Field, Raleigh Apl. 28, 1865.

Dearest Ellen,

The capitulation of Johnstons army at Greensboro completes my campaign. I leave Schofield to do the work, and have ordered the 15 & 17th 14th & 20th Corps to march to Richmond. I will go tonight to Wilmington & Charleston & Savannah to make some orders and instructions when I will go by sea to Richmond to meet my army. Thence it will march to *Alexandria* (& Washington) where I will move my Head Qrs. to in anticipation of mustering out the Army. It may be that while the army is on the march from Richmond to Alexandria I can run out to Lancaster to See you all. This will be about the 15 & 20th of May, and if I could take all the family to Alexandria to witness the final success attending "Shermans" army it would be a prize in the memory to our Children that would somewhat compensate for the expense & loss of time. I may be a little ahead but think that the present volunteer army must be mustered out and a new Regular Army made, & the quicker the better before new complications arise.

The *mass* of the People South will never trouble us again. They have suffered terrifically, and I now feel disposed to befriend them. Of course not the leaders and lawyers, but the Armies who have fought & manifested their sincerity though misled by risking their persons. But the rascals who by falsehood & misrepresentation Kept up the war, they are infamous. It will be difficult for anyone to tread a straight path amid these new complications, but I will do my best.

I perceive the Politicians are determined to drive the Confederates into Guerilla bands, a thing more to be feared than open organized war. They may fight it out—I wont. We could settle the war in three weeks by giving shape to the present disordered elements, but they may play out their game. Yours in haste

W. T. Sherman

ALS, InND: Sherman Family Papers.

TO JOHN A. RAWLINS

Goldsboro, Apl. 29—3 A.M. [1865]

Genl. Rawlins

Dear Genl.,

I worked all day at Raleigh, and am now here, en route to Charleston, where I will instruct Gillmore to send a garrison to Augusta, to open communications with Wilson at Macon. I wish you would have the enclosed letter copied carefully, and send a copy to Mr. Stanton, and say to him I want it published.[1] The tone of all the papers of the 24th is taken up from the compilation of the War Department of the 22d, which is untrue, unfair, and unkind to me, and I will say undeserved. There has been at no time any trouble about Joe Johnstons army. It fell and became powerless when Lee was defeated; but its dispersion, when the country was already full of Lee's men, would have made North Carolina a Pandemonium. I desired to avoid that condition of things. The South is broken and ruined, and appeals to our pity. To ride the people down with persecutions and military exactions would be like slashing away at the crew of a sinking ship. I will fight as long as the enemy shows fight, but when he gives up and asks quarter, I cannot go further. This state of things appeals to our better nature, and it was an outrage to torture my forbearance into the shape the Secretary has done. He has either misconceived the whole case, or he is not the man I supposed him. If he wants to hunt down Jeff. Davis or the politicians who have instigated civil war, let him use sheriffs, bailiffs, and catch thieves, and not hint that I should march heavy columns of infantry hundreds of miles on a fool's errand. The idea of Jeff. Davis running about the country with tons of gold is ridiculous. I doubt not he is a beggar, and who will say that if we catch him, he will be punished? The very men who now howl the loudest will be the first to intercede. But all this is beneath the dignity of the occasion, and I, for one, will not stoop to it. We must, if possible, save our country from anarchy.

I doubt not efforts will be made to sow dissension between Grant and myself, on a false supposition that we have political aspirations, or, after Killing me off by libels, he will next be assailed. I can keep away from Washington, and I confide in his good sense to save him from the influences that will surround him there.

I have no hesitation in pronouncing Mr. Stanton's compilation of April 22 a gross outrage on me, which I will resent in time. He Knew I had never seen or heard of that despatch to Genl. Grant[2] till he sent it to me a few days ago, by Gen. Grant himself, and the deduction from Stoneman's orders is exactly the reverse of the fact and truth, as an inspection of the map will show. Davis was supposed to be cached somewhere about Greensboro, and Stoneman was at Statesville, to the west of Greensboro, and I could not communicate with him, because Johnston had more cavalry than I. By getting him to me at Chapel Hill, I would have had superior cavalry, and, on the renewal of hostilities, I could have broken up Hampton, Butler,[3] and Wheeler, and pursued Davis. But even Grant would not say that we had any interest to hunt up Davis. Look at the hunt after Booth, with a hundred thousand dollars reward, at your very capital, and in a friendly country. What would be the chances after Davis, with all the Carolinas, and Georgia to hide in?

I will be with Gillmore for four or five days. He will be reinforced by two brigades from here, and can occupy Augusta and Orangeburg. I can then return to Moorhead City, whence I can learn how Schofield progresses at Greensboro, when I will go to Petersburg to meet my matching columns, which ought to reach Richmond about May 12–14. Thence I will report for orders.

If the Northern papers take up, as they will, the lead Stanton has given, I will be obliged if you will send a copy of my letter to Gen. Grant and this to John Sherman, who will vindicate me. I cannot neglect current business and events. If, however, Gen. Grant thinks I have been outwitted by Joe Johnston, or that I have made undue concession to the rebels to save them from anarchy and us the *needless* expense of military occupation, I will take good care not to embarrass him. Believe me truly your friend,

W. T. Sherman

Copy, DLC: Edwin M. Stanton Papers. Copies of endorsements show that Grant forwarded it to Stanton for his information, and Stanton gave his permission for Sherman to publish it. *OR*, I, 47: pt. 3, 345–46.

1. Probably WTS to USG, April 28, 1865, as endorsements on the letter show that it was forwarded to Stanton by Grant to get his permission to publish it.

2. Presumably Stanton's March 3, 1865, letter to USG, which Lincoln composed.

3. Major General Matthew C. Butler (1836–1909), CSA, was with Johnston.

TO GEORGE H. THOMAS

Headquarters, Military Division
of the Mississippi,
In the Field, Savannah River, Geo.,
May 2 1865

Maj. Gen. Geo. H. Thomas.
Comdg. Dept. of the Cumberland.
General.

Capt. Hosea[1] is here en route for Nashville from Genl. Wilson now at Macon. He got possession of that place just as he learned of the Suspension of hostilities that proceeded the final surrender of Genl. Johnstons army at Greensboro. I have sent orders to Wilson to parole his prisoners there on the same terms as presented to Johnston & Lee, and to return to the neighborhood of Decatur Alabama and thence report to you or me. I came to Savannah from Raleigh to send stores up to Augusta by Boat for Wilson & to take steps to occupy Augusta. I will have much to tell you at some future time of the details of my negotiations with Johnston, which have been misconstrued by the People at the North, but I can afford to let them settle down before telling all the truth. At my first interview with Johnston he admitted the Confederate Cause was lost, and that it would be murder for him to allow any more conflict, but he asked me to help him all I could to prevent his Army and People breaking up into Guerilla Bands. I deemed that so desirable that I did make terms subject to the approval of the President which may be deemed too liberal. But the more I reflect the more satisfied I am that by dealing with the People of the South magnanimously we will restore ⅘ of them at once to the Condition of good Citizens leaving us only to deal with the remainder. But my terms were not approved and Johnstons present surrender only applies to the troops in his present command viz. East of Chattahoochee.

The Boat is in motion & I write with great difficulty and will wait a more convenient season to give you fuller details. Truly your friend

W. T. Sherman
Maj. Gen. Comdg.

ALS, CSmH.
1. Captain Louis M. Hosea, a staff officer who served with James H. Wilson.

Headquarters, Military Division
of the Mississippi,
Morehead City, May 5 1865.

Genl. Schofield
Raleigh.

Your Despatch of today is just received,[1] and I feel deeply the embarrassment that is sure to result from the indefinite action of our Government. It seems to fail us entirely at this crisis, for I doubt if any one at Washington appreciates the true situation of affairs south. Their minds are so absorbed with the horrid deformities of a few assassins & southern Politicians that they overlook the wants and necessities of the great masses. You have seen how Stanton & Halleck turned on me because I simply submitted a skeleton or basis. Any thing positive would be infinitely better than the present doubting halting, nothing to do policy of our poor bewildered government. After Stantons perfidious course towards me officially, I can never confer with him again, and therefore am compelled to leave you to approach him as you best can. Now that all danger is past, and our former Enemy simply asks some practicable escape from the terrible vicissitudes of his position it is wonderful how brave and vindictive former non-combatants have become. It makes me sick to contemplate the fact, but I am powerless for good, and must let Events drift as they best may. If left alone I Know you Could guide the state of North Carolina into a path of Peace Loyalty and Security in three months; and Could place every negro in the state in a way to earn an honest livelihood with his freedom secure, but I doubt whether those who are so slow to come to the fight will permit you to act. Whatever you may do I will back you with my influence which however cannot amount to much in the present attitude of affairs. With sincere respect Yr. friend & servant

W. T. Sherman
Maj. Gen. Comdg.

By telegraph from Morehead City & original by Mail.W. T. S.

ADfS, CSmH. Two telegraph copies dated May 6, 1865, are also in CsmH. *OR*, I, 47: pt. 3, 405–6.

1. Schofield to WTS, May 5, 1865, *PM*, 2:371. Schofield had asked if he could open North Carolina to trade at once. He expressed the belief that the government should immediately let it be known what its ideas were for reestablishing political order. He also inquired as to what was to be done with the freedmen and asked if he was to assume permanent command in the area: "If I am to govern this state, it is important for me to know it at once."

Hdqrs. Military Division
of the Mississippi,
Steamer Russia, Beaufort Harbor,
May 6, 1865—6 a.m.

Hon. S. P. Chase,
Chief Justice United States, Steamer Wayanda:
Dear Sir:

On reaching this ship late last night I found your valued letter, with the printed sheet, which I have also read, but not yet fully matured.[1] I am not yet prepared to receive the negro on terms of political equality for the reasons that it will arouse passions and prejudices at the North, which superadded to the causes yet dormant at the South, might rekindle the war whose fires are now dying out, and by skillful management might be kept down. As you must observe, I prefer to work with known facts than to reason ahead to remote conclusions that by slower and natural laws may be reached without shock. By way of illustration, we are now weather bound; is it not better to lay quiet at anchor till these white-cap breakers look less angry and the southwest wind shifts? I think all old sailors will answer yes, whilst we, impatient to reach our goal, are tempted to dash through, at risk of life and property. I am willing to admit that the conclusions you reach by pure mental process may be all correct, but don't you think it better first to get the ship of state in some order, that it may be handled and guided? Now at the South all is pure anarchy. The military power of the United States cannot reach the people who are spread over a vast surface of country. We can control the local State capitals, and it may be slowly shape political thoughts, but we cannot combat existing ideas with force. I say honestly that the assertion openly of your ideas as a fixed policy of our Government, to be backed by physical power, will produce new war, and one which from its desultory character will be more bloody and destructive than the last.

Our own armed soldiers have prejudices that, right or wrong, should be consulted, and I am rejoiced that you, upon whom devolves so much, are aiming to see facts and persons with your own eye. I believe you will do me the credit of believing that I am as honest, sincere, true, and brave as the average of our kind, and I say that to give all loyal negroes the same political status as white "voters" will revive the war and spread its field of operations. Why not, therefore, trust to the slower and not less sure means of statesmanship? Why not imitate the example of England in allowing causes to work out their gradual solution instead of imitating the French, whose political revolutions have been bloody and have actually retarded the development of political freedom? I think the changes necessary in the future can be made faster and more certain by means of our Constitution than by any plan outside of it. If, now, we go outside of the Constitution for a means of change, we rather justify the rebels in their late attempt, whereas now, as General Schofield tells us, the people of the South are ready and willing to make the necessary changes without shock or violence. I, who have felt the past war as bitterly and keenly as any man could, confess myself "afraid" of a new war, and a new war is bound to result from the action you suggest of giving to the enfranchised negroes so large a share in the delicate task of putting the Southern States in practical working relations with the General Government.

With great respect,

W. T. Sherman,

Major-general.

Printed, *OR*, I, 47: pt. 3, 410–11.

1. The chief justice was in North Carolina on a fact-finding tour concerning Reconstruction, although his avowed agenda was to convince President Johnson to make black suffrage part of Reconstruction policy. Chase informed WTS that his own views on freedmen and Reconstruction had evolved through careful consideration: "my trouble in attempting reorganization without the loyal blacks proved quite as much from the apprehension that it will work more practical evil than it will avoid, as from any abstract theory." He urged WTS to think more on this topic. Chase to WTS, May 5, 1865, DLC: WTS.

TO SALMON P. CHASE

Head-Quarters Military Division
of the Mississippi,
On Board the steamer *Russia*
Beaufort Har. N.C. May 6 1865.

Hon. S. P. Chase

On Board *Wayanda*

Dear Sir,

Your note with the letter of Instructions of the Secretary of War to Govr. Shepley[1] of Louisiana is received and I thank you for the perusal.[2] I approve in my mind every word of those Instructions for it is a well established Principle & Practice that *During War* the Conqueror of a Country may use the local government & authorities already in existence, or create new ones subordinate to his use. That is not the question now, for war has ceased and the question is to adapt legal Governments to constitutional Communities which fully admit their subordination to the national authority. I have had abundant opportunities to Know these People both before the war, during its existence and since their public acknowledgment of submission. I have no fear of them armed or disarmed, and believe that by one single stroke of the pen nine tenths of them can be restored to full relations to our Government so as to pay taxes, live in Peace, and in war I would not hesitate to mingle with them and lead them to battle against a national foe. But we must deal with them with frankness and candor, and not with doubt, hesitancy and prevarication. The nine tenths would from motives of self interest restrain the other mischievous tenth, or compel them to migrate to Mexico, or some other country cursed with anarchy & civil war.

I return you the paper as you request and send you a copy of an order I make to my troops to counteract the effect of the insult so wantonly and unjustly, and so publicly inflicted on me by the Secretary of War.[3] Of course this will soon lead to the closing my military career and I assure you that I can have no aspirations to civil favors, but would shun them with disgust. Indeed I have not yet thought whither I will cast my fortunes, but probably to some foreign land, if in my judgment events are drifting us further into another civil or anarchical war.

That you may study the chances of changing the tone & character of a People by military occupation and military Governors I invite your attention to the occupation of Spain by Napoleons best armies from about 1806 to the close of his career. With great respect your friend,

W. T. Sherman
Maj. Genl.

P.S. I feel additional confidence in the ability of the United States to rule the late Rebel States by and through even their existing state authorities by reason of the facts, that we now have possession of all forts arms and strategic Points—we have a vast political majority which cannot be lost unless by seeming acts of oppression a reaction is created in their support. Their resources are all gone and their confidence in their leaders is turned to hate. With moderation & courage on our part Jeff Davis, Toombs, Cobb,[4] Benjamin Slidell and other Political leaders will receive less mercy at the hands of their country men, than ours. Where is the single act of severity shown to a Political Prisoner in our hands? To this hour the War Dept. has sent me no orders to hunt for, arrest, or capture Jeff Davis, but on the contrary as near as I know their wishes it is that he escape provided it be "unbeknown" to them. But the Tribunal before which all conflicts must come at last, the Supreme Court, before whose decrees I and all soldiers of my school bend with the veneration of Religion, is now surely safe to us on the "Oxford questions" which led to our war and now threatens another. In it I hope is the "anchor of Safety"— Again with respect & affection

W. T. Sherman

ALS, NHi: War 1861–5, Box 7: S# 99; *OR*, I, 47: pt. 3, 411–12.

1. Major General George F. Shepley (1819–78), USA, currently chief of staff for Weitzel, had been the military governor of Louisiana in 1862 and 1863.

2. Chase had written a second letter in which he discussed Andrew Johnson's views on Reconstruction and reiterated his faith in WTS. He added that he was glad to have finally heard WTS's side of the controversy surrounding Johnston's first surrender. Chase to WTS, May 5, 1865, DLC: WTS.

3. Special Field Orders No. 69, Headquarters, Military Division of the Mississippi, May 6, 1865, reads: "The General commanding announces to the Armies under his command that a most foul attempt has been made on his fair fame, whilst he was in a remote land, laboring with the single purpose to secure the safety and success of the Armies entrusted to his care. The matter is purely personal and in no manner reflects on your reputation and he commands all officers and men to restrain their feelings when they come in Contact with their Comrades in Virginia, for he feels assured, that the acts done when fully understood will excite in their minds as much disgust as he knows it will in yours. The parties who instigated this base *attempt* are yet unknown, but will be discovered and properly punished. They are men of influence, for they have used tools, that could not be controlled by {commoner} assassins and Slanderers. They used the Press the common resort of libellers, when the General was too far away to Check or counteract its influence. They made use of the gossiping official Bulletins of our secretary of war, with their garbled statements and false contexts: and last and worst they made use of a brother officer who had reasons & motives that Should have made him stand above such vile purposes. Maj. Gen. Halleck, who as long as our Enemy stood in bold & armed array sat in full security in his Easy chair at Washington, was suddenly seized with a Newborn Zeal and Energy, when that Enemy has become (by no agency of his,) defeated, disheartened & submissive. He publicly disregarded Truce of which he was properly advised, and turned his victorious legions to 'head off' and destroy an enemy that was halted, at our mercy, and in the act of surrendering its arms to us and worse still he advised subordinate Generals operating on distant lines, and in the fulfilment of a Common Plan, to disobey his orders without notifying the General, or giving him the means of Counteracting such disorganizing and baneful measures, all of which was withheld from him but paraded before the Northern Public in direct violation of the Army Regulations, of the orders of the War Department and his own reiterated emphatic commands, when in authority, as well as Common decency itself. But thanks to our noble and honest Commanding officer, Lt. Genl. Grant, after coming in person to Raleigh, and seeing and hearing for himself was enabled to return to the North in time to prevent the Enactment of a scheme that might have turned one of the most successful results of the war, into an act of Perfidy that would have stood forever as a foul stain on our National Honor.

Whilst our Armies will fight an armed Enemy at any and all times, and follow him across mountain & plains, through swamps and defiles, let it be proclaimed far and wide that we scorn to Strike or insult a Fallen Foe. By order of Maj. Gen. W. T. Sherman." ADfS in MiU-C: James S. Schoff Civil War Collection.

4. Howell Cobb (1815–68), a former Georgia governor and secretary of the treasury, had been active in Georgia's secession movement and then served as a general in the Confederate army.

TO HENRY W. HALLECK
cypher

By Telegraph Morehead City—
Beaufort Harbor N.C. May 7th 1865

To Maj. Gen. Halleck 7th
Richmond

After your dispatch to Mr. Stanton of Apl. 26[1] I cannot have any friendly intercourse with you. I will come to City Point tomorrow, and march with my troops and I prefer we should not meet.

W. T. Sherman
Maj. Genl.

ALS, CsmH; *OR*, I, 47: pt. 3, 435 (dated May 8, and with dateline of Fort Monroe; in *PM*, 2:374, WTS confirms the latter date, although the dateline of the above dispatch suggests that WTS had composed the letter before his arrival at City Point on the evening of the eighth).

1. HWH to Stanton, April 26, 1865, *PM*, 2:372. HWH told Stanton that Meade, Sheridan, and Wright had been instructed to disregard "any truce or orders of General Sherman respecting hostilities" and had been instructed "to push forward, regardless of orders from any one except from General Grant." He countermanded orders suspending movements of the Sixth Corps because WTS had reached a new agreement with Johnston and had ordered that all commanders on the Mississippi be on the lookout for Davis and his cabinet and six to thirteen million dollars worth of specie.

TO ELLEN EWING SHERMAN

Headquarters Military Division
of the Mississippi,
At sea Steamer *Russia*
Monday May 8, 1865

Dearest Ellen,

We are now approaching Cape Henry and by 9 oclock tonight will be at Old Point, where I expect to Stop an hour or so to communicate with Grant and then go on up to City Point & Petersburg to meet my army. I have been to Savannah, Charleston and Wilmington on business connected with past affairs and now I am free to join my army proper. I have seen the New York papers of April 24 & 28 but dont mind them much for it is manifest that Some deviltry is on foot—The telegram of Halleck endorsed by Stanton[1] is the worst, but its falsity and baseness puts them at my mercy, and in a few days look out for breakers. This cause may delay me east a few days and I will likely accompany my army up to Washington. At all Event from this time forth I can hear from you and write to you. My latest letter is April 11, received at Raleigh. I want you to go right along, attend the Fair, and I will join you wherever you may be as soon as I can leave. We will probably all spend the Summer together at Lancaster.

At Savannah, Charleston, Wilmington, and Morehead City Officers, soldiers, sailors and citizens paid me every sort of honored respect especially my old soldiers, more especially when they heard they were down on me at Washington. Now that war is over how brave and fierce have become the men that Thousand dollar bounties, patriotism the appeals of Generals and others would not bring out. How terribly energetic all at once Halleck became to break my truce—cut off "Johnstons Retreat" when he Knew Johnston was halted anxious to surrender and was only making excuses to keep his own men from Scattering, a thing I did not want, and a reason I reported to Halleck & Stanton before my "Memorandum" went to Washington. Worst of all his advice that my subordinates Thomas Wilson & Stoneman should not obey my orders[.] Under my orders, those Generals have done all they ever did in their lives, and it sounds funny to us to have Halleck *better* my plans & orders. But of all this hereafter. Go along as comfortably as you can. I am not dead yet by a long sight and these matters give me new life for I see the *Cause*. A Breach must be made between Grant & Sherman, or certain cliques in Washington who have a nice thing are gone up. I am glad Grant came to Raleigh for he saw at a glance the whole thing and went away more than satisfied. But heaven & earth will be moved to Kill us. Lincolns assassination was not plotted in Richmond, but nearer his Elbow. Washington is as corrupt as Hell, made so by the looseness and extravagance of war. I will avoid it as a pest house. Go to the Fair and I will probably join you at Chicago, we can take the Children home, spend a quiet summer and get ready for the next war that is brewing in another quarter. The Gates of the *Press* cant prevail with my old army against me, and in them I put my Faith. ever yours,

W. T. Sherman

The ship vibrates with the Engine & rough sea.

ALS, InND: Sherman Family Papers.

1. Stanton to John A. Dix, April 27, 1865, *PM*, 2:371–72, was sent with a copy of HWH to Stanton, April 26, 1865.

TO ULYSSES S. GRANT
private and confidential.

> Headquarters, Military Division
> of the Mississippi,
> In the Field, Camp opposite Richmond
> May 10, 1865

Lt. Gen. U. S. Grant
Washington, D.C.
Dear Genl.

I march tomorrow at the head of my army through Richmond for Alexandria, in pursuance of the orders this day received by telegraph from you. I have received no other telegram or letter from you since you left me at Raleigh. I send by Gen. Howard who goes to Washington in pursuance of a telegram dated 7th but received only today my official Report of events from my last official Report up to this date.[1]

I do think a great outrage has been enacted against me, by Mr. Stanton and General Halleck. I care nought for Public opinion, that will regulate itself, but to maintain my own self respect and command our brave men I must resent a public insult.

On arrival at Old Point I met a despatch from Genl. Halleck inviting me to his house in Richmond. I declined most positively and assigned as a reason the insult to me in his Telegram to Secretary Stanton of Apl. 26. I came here via Petersburg, and have gone under Canvas. Halleck had arranged to review my Army in passing through Richmond. I forbade it. Yesterday I received a letter of which a copy is enclosed.[2] I answered that I could not reconcile its friendly substance with the public insult contained in his despatch & notified him I should march through Richmond and asked him to Keep out of sight lest he should be insulted. My officers and men feel this insult as Keenly as I do. I was in hopes to hear something from you before I got here to guide me, & telegraphed with that view from Morehead city, but I have not a word from you and have acted thus far on my own responsibility. I will treat Mr. Stanton with like scorn & contempt unless you have reasons otherwise, for I regard my military career as ended, save & except so far as necessary to put my Army into your hands. Mr. Stanton can give me no orders of himself. He may in the name of the President & those Shall be obeyed to the letter, but I deny his right to Command an Army. Your orders and wishes shall be to me the Law, but I ask you to vindicate my name from the insult Conveyed in Mr. Stantons despatch to Gen. Dix[3] of Apl. 27 published in all the newspapers of the Land. If you do not I will. No man shall insult me with impunity, even if I am an officer of the Army. Subordination to Authority is one thing, to insult Another.

No amount of retraction or pusillanimous excusing will do. Mr. Stanton must publicly confess himself a common libeller or—but I wont threaten. I will not enter Washington except on yours or the President's emphatic orders, but I do wish to stay with my army, till it ceases to exist, or till it is broken up and scattered to other duty. Then I wish to go for a time to my family and make arrangements for the Future. Your private and official wishes when conveyed to me shall be sacred, but there can be no relations between Mr. Stanton & me. He seeks your life and reputation as well as mine. Beware, but you are Cool, and have been most skilful in managing such People, and I have faith you will penetrate his designs—He wants the *vast* patronage of the Military Governorships of the South, and the votes of the Free Negro *loyal* Citizens for political Capital, and whoever stands in his way must die. Read Halleck's letter and See how pitiful he is become. Keep *above* such influences, or you will also be a victim—See in my case how soon all past services are ignored & forgotten.

Excuse this letter. Burn it, but heed my friendly Counsel. The lust for Power in Political Minds is the strongest passion of Life, and impels Ambitious men (Richard III) to deeds of Infamy. Ever your friend,

W. T. Sherman

ALS, CSmH.

1. WTS to John A. Rawlins, May 9, 1865, *OR*, I, 47: pt. 1, 29–40.

2. HWH to WTS, May 9, 1865, DLC: WTS. See WTS to HWH, May 10, 1865, n. 1.

3. Major General John A. Dix (1798–1879), USA, commander of the Department of the East.

TO HENRY W. HALLECK

Headquarters, Military Division
of the Mississippi,
In the Field, Manchester, Va.
May 10, 1865

Genl. H. W. Halleck, U.S. Army
Richmond, Va.
General

I received your cypher despatch last Evening[1] and have revolved it in my mind all night in connection with *that* telegraphic message of Apl. 26 to Secretary Stanton and by him rushed with such indecent haste before an excited public. I cannot possibly reconcile the friendly expressions of the former with the deadly malignity of the latter, and cannot consent to the renewal of a friendship I had prized so highly, till I can see deeper into the diabolical plot than I now do. When you advised me of the Assassin Clark being on my track, I little dreamed he would turn up in the direction and guise he did. But thank God I have become so blase to the dangers to life and reputation by the many vicissitudes of this "cruel war" (which some people are resolved shall never be over) that nothing surprises me.

I will march my Army through Richmond quietly and in good order without attracting attention, and I beg you to keep slightly perdu, for if noticed by some of my old command I cannot undertake to maintain a model behavior, for their feelings have become aroused by what the world adjudges an insult to at least an honest commander. If loss of life or violence result from this you must attribute it to the true cause, a public insult to a Brother officer when he was far away on public service, perfectly innocent of the malignant purpose and design. I am etc.

W. T. Sherman
Maj. Gen. Comdg.

Copy, DLC: William T. Sherman, docketed "a true copy, Elizabeth Halleck." Also a copy by L. M. Dayton. *OR*, I, 47: pt. 3, 454–55.

1. HWH to WTS, May 9, 1865, DLC: WTS. HWH wrote, "You have not had during this war, nor have you now a warmer friend & admirer than myself." He apologized for his language in his April 26 letter to Stanton if it offended him and insisted that his motives had been pure. He concluded, "It is my wish to regard, and receive you as a personal friend."

TO ELLEN EWING SHERMAN

Headquarters, Military Division
of the Mississippi,
In the Field, Camp opposite Richmond,
May 10, 1865

Dearest Ellen,

I wrote you on arrival from Savannah at Old Point. I got here yesterday and found my army all in, have seen Charley who is very well. We march tomorrow for Alexandria, whither I have sent my office papers. We will march slowly & leisurely and should reach Alexandria in ten or twelve days. I may have chance to write you mean time. I want you to go on attend your Fair, and say little of me, save that I regard my presence with my army so important that I will not leave it till it is discharged or sent on new duties. I shall surely spend the summer with you, preferably at Lancaster, but will come to Chicago or wherever you may be when I can leave with propriety. This army has stood by me in public and private dangers and I must maintain my hold on it, till it ceases to exist. All the officers & men have been to See me in camp today and they received with shouts my public denial of a Review for Halleck. He had ordered Stonemans Wing to pass him in review today. I forbade it. Tomorrow

I march through Richmond with Colors flying & drums beating as a matter of Right & not by Hallecks favor and no notice will be take of him personally or officially. I dare him to oppose my march—He will think twice before he again undertakes to Stand between me and my subordinates. Unless Grant interposes from his yielding & good nature I shall get some equally good opportunity to insult Stanton. They will find that Sherman who was not scared by the Crags of Lookout, the Barriers of Kenesaw, and long and trackless forests of the South is not (to be intimidated by the howlings of a set of sneaks who were hid away as long as danger was rampant, but now shriek with very courage. I will take a Regiment of my old Division & clear them all out—) Stanton wants to Kill me becau(se I do not) favor the Scheme of declaring the negro of the South *Now Free*, to be loyal voters whereby Politicians may manufacture just so much more pliable Electionary material. The Negros dont want to vote. They want to work & enjoy property, and they are *no* friends of the negro who seek to complicate him with new prejudices. As to the People of the South they are subjugated, but of course do not love us any more than the Irish or Scotch love the English, but that is no reason why we should assume all the expenses of their State Govts. Our power is now so firmly established that we need not fear again their internal disturbances. I have papers and statistics which I will show your father in time. I showed some to Charley (to-day and he perfectly agreed with me; so do all my officers. . . .) We cannot kill disarmed men all this Clamor after Jeff Davis, Thompson and others is all bosh—any young man with a musket is now a more dangerous object than Jeff Davis—He is old, infirm, a fugitive hunted by his own People, and none so poor as do him Reverence. It will be well in June before I can expect to leave my army. Dont attempt to come to Alexandria for I will be in a common tent, and overwhelmed with papers & business. Ord, Merritt,[1] Crook[2] and all the Big men of Hallecks army have been to See me, and share with me the disgust occasioned by their base betrayal of my confidence. Love to all. Yrs. as ever,

W. T. Sherman

ALS, InND: Sherman Family Papers. The first and third sets of bracketed material are written in Rachel Sherman Thorndike's hand—she had torn off the upper portion of the second sheet, noting that "I have torn this out because of personal (not public) reasons." The second set of bracketed material comes from *HL*, 353.

1. Major General Wesley Merritt (1834–1910), USA, commanded a division in the Cavalry Corps of the Army of the Potomac.

2. Major General George Crook (1829–90), USA, also commanded a division in the Cavalry Corps of the Army of the Potomac.

TO JOHN A. LOGAN

Headquarters, Military Division
of the Mississippi,
In the Field, Hanover C H.
May 12, 1865 (noon)

Maj. Gen. Jno. A. Logan
Comd. Right Wing,
Dear General,

It was my purpose to join your Column here, and travel with it via Fredericksburg, but I feel anxious to See the ground about Spottsylvania C. H. and Chancellorsville and may accompany Slocum that far, and swing across to you at Fredericksburg. Slocum leaves your Road six miles north of Hanover C. H. and then takes the Road off to the Left by Chilesburg, and will not again come into your Road at all, and you will not see him till you reach Alexandria. I have official notice that Genl. Meade leaves his pontoon Bridge for your use, across the Rappahannock at the Mouth of Deep Creek which I understand to be a couple of miles below the town of Fredericksburg. The heavy Cold Rain of last night has improved the atmosphere very much, but leaves the Road bad, and if other Rains come about the time you reach Fredericksburg you had better Keep the Roads (of which I am told there are several) most to the Left, but dont cross the Manassas Rail Road, for in that case you would run into Slocums Columns. The distance to Alexandria by your Roads from Richmond is 125 miles. Take 10 full days and lay by one or two days to bathe & clean up. In any event dont rush your men, but let them arrive at Alexandria fresh and (illegible). I believe you will be more at Ease on the Road than lying idle in Camps about Alexandria. There is no reason or necessity for haste. I suppose you will have sent one Corps by Mechanicsville, and will bring the others by this Road which seems to be considered the Main Fredericksburg and Alexandria Road. I wanted to see you before starting after seeing Howards orders, but had no chance as I had [been] appointed to ride at the head of the Whole Army, and I did want to leave Richmond to my Rear. The manner of your welcome was a part of a Grand Game to insult us, *us* who had marched a thousand miles through a hostile country in midwinter to help *them*. We did help them, and what has been our Reward? Your men denied admission into the City, when Halleck had invited all citizens, (Rebels of course) to come and go *without* Passes. If the American People sanction this Kind of courtesy to Old & tried troops, where is the honor satisfaction and Glory of serving them in constancy and Faith? If such be the welcome the East pays to the West, we can let them make war, and fight it out themselves. I know where is a Land & People that will not treat us thus, the *West*, the Valley of the Mississipi the heart & soul, and future Strength of America, and I for one will go *there*.

I am not much of a Talker, but if ever my tongue is loose & free, I think I can and will say some things that will make an impression resembling a bomb shell of the largest pattern.

Chew the cud of "bitter fancy" as you ride along, and when events draw to a conclusion, we can step in the Ring. Men who are now so fierce and who would have the Army of the Potomac violate my truce, and attack our Enemy disheartened discomfited & surrendered will sooner or later find foes face to face of different metal. Though "my voice is still for Peace," I am not for such a Peace, as makes me subject to insult by former friends, now perfidious enemies. with respect your friend,

W. T. Sherman
Maj. Genl.

ALS, DLC: John A. Logan Papers; *OR*, I, 47: pt. 3, 477–78.

TO OLIVER O. HOWARD

Hdqrs. Military Division
of the Mississippi,
In the Field, Dumfries, Va.,
May 17, 1865—9 p.m.

General O. O. Howard,
Washington, D.C.:
Dear General:

Your letter of May 12, inclosing General Orders, War Department, No. 91, of May 12, reached me here on arrival at camp about dark.[1] Colonel Strong is camped just behind me, General Logan about two miles back, and the Fifteenth Corps at Aquia Creek, eight miles back. Copies of Orders, No. 91, are being made and will be sent back to them. I hardly know whether to congratulate you or not, but of one thing you may rest assured, that you possess my entire confidence, and I cannot imagine that matters that may involve the future of 4,000,000 of souls could be put in more charitable and more conscientious hands. So far as man can do, I believe you will, but I fear you have Hercules' task. God has limited the power of man, and though in the kindness of your heart you would alleviate all the ills of humanity it is not in your power, nor is it in your power to fulfill one-tenth part of the expectations of those who framed the bureau for the freedmen, refugees, and abandoned estates. It is simply impracticable. Yet you can and will do all the good one man may, and that is all you are called on as a man and Christian to do, and to that extent count on me as a friend and fellow soldier for counsel and assistance. I believe the negro is free by act of master and by the laws of war, now ratified by actual consent and power. The demand for his labor and his ability to acquire and work land will enable the negro to work out that amount of freedom and political consequence to which he is or may be entitled by natural right, and the acquiescence of his fellow men (white). But I fear that parties will agitate for the negro's right of suffrage and equal political status, not that he asks it or wants it, but merely to manufacture that number of available votes for politicians to work on.

If that be attempted we arouse a new and dangerous element, prejudice, which, right or wrong, does exist, and should be consulted. There is a strong prejudice of race which over our whole country exists. The negro is denied a vote in all the Northern States save two or three: and then qualified by conditions not attached to the white race and by the Constitution of the United States. To States is left the right to fix the qualification of voters. The United States cannot make negroes vote in the South any more than they can in the North without revolution, and as we have just emerged from one attempted revolution it would be wrong to begin another. I believe the negro is free constitutionally, and if the United States will simply guarantee that freedom and allow the negro to hire his own labor, the transition will be comparatively easy, but if we attempt to force the negro on the South as a voter, "a loyal citizen," we begin a new revolution in which the Northwest may take a different side from what we did when we were fighting to vindicate our Constitution. I am more than usually sensitive on this point because I have realized in our country that one class of men makes war and leaves another to fight it out. I am tired of fighting, and if the "theorists" of New England impose this new condition on us I dread the result. The country is now deeply in debt, the South is exhausted and can contribute little or nothing toward its payment no matter how severe the laws of taxation be made, and the sale of her lands and plantations will not realize one tenth part of the money required to pay the troops that will be needed to enforce the sales and maintain possession to the purchasers. I know the people of the South even better than you do, and you at least cannot doubt the sincerity of my opinion. I do believe the people of the South realize the fact that their former slaves are free, and if allowed reasonable time, and are not harassed by "confiscation" and political complication, will very soon adapt their condition and interest to their new state of facts. Many of them will sell or lease on easy terms part of their land to their former slaves and gradually the same political state of things will result as now exists in Maryland, Kentucky, and Missouri. The West will not submit to the taxation necessary to maintain separate colonies of negroes, or the armies needed to enforce the rights of negroes dwelling in the Southern states in a condition antagonistic to the feelings and prejudices of the people, the result of which will be internal war, and the final extermination of the white or black majority. But I confess I am not familiar with the laws of Congress which originated your bureau, and repeat my entire confidence in your pure and exalted character. As to Mr. Stanton I expect nothing. My orders announcing to the troops the terms of our convention (first, at Durham's Station) was addressed to the troops and not to the world. Mr. Stanton's official bulletin published to the world conveyed false information, for it contained matter that he knew I did not possess, and he thereby stimulated a public attack on my motives. But what reason did my "order" give for his scrutiny and indorsing Halleck's order to violate my truce, attack an enemy in the act of surrendering, when he knew General Grant was present (April 27), and orders to my juniors to disobey my orders. I don't yet understand his motives and don't care. I did succeed in doing, spite of him, all the good my office demanded within the limits of Johnston's command, and could as easily have extended them over the whole South. Stanton's eight reasons against my terms are all bad and he knows it. His assertion that he could have made as good terms any time in the past four years is simply untrue, and you know it, and as a lawyer he knows that my terms did not make us liable for the rebel debt, or in any manner recognize the Southern Confederacy any more than the Dix-Hill cartel, or any of the many "terms" hitherto made between army commanders. But I will not bother you with such matters. Stanton's and Halleck's conduct to me was an insult, and I shall resent it as such, when I choose. We will all be near Alexandria on Friday, and I know you will call to see us. Don't let the foul airs of Washington poison your thoughts toward your old comrades in arms.

Truly, your friend,
W. T. Sherman,
Major-general.

Printed, *OR*, I, 47: pt. 3, 515–16.
1. The order in question assigned Howard to head the Bureau of Freedmen, Refugees, and Abandoned Lands.

TO JOHN A. RAWLINS

Head-Quarters Military Division
of the Mississippi,
Camp near Alexandria May 19 1865.

Genl. Jno. A. Rawlins
Chief of Staff, Washington D.C.
General,

I have the honor to report my arrival at Camp near the Washington Road, three miles north of Alexandria. All my army should be in camp near by today. The 15th Corps the last to leave Richmond camped last night at the

Ocoqua. I have seen the order for the review in the papers, but Col. Sawyer says it is not here in official form. I am old fashioned and prefer to see orders through some other channel but if that be the new fashion so be it I will be all ready by Wednesday though in the rough. Troops have not been paid for 8 & 10 months, and clothing may be bad, but a better set of legs & arms cannot be displayed on this Continent.

Send me all orders and letters you may have for me, and let some one newspaper know that the Vandal Sherman is encamped near the canal bridge half way between the Long Bridge & Alexandria to the West of the Road, where his friends if any can find him. Though in disgrace he is untamed and unconquered. As ever your friend,

W. T. Sherman
Maj. Genl.

ALS, CsmH; *OR*, I, 47: pt. 3, 531.

TO THEODORE S. BOWERS[1]

Head Qrs. Mily. Divn. of the Miss.
Washington D.C. May 26, 1865

Col. T. S. Bowers
Asst. Adjt. General, Washington D.C.
Colonel,

I had the honor to receive your letter of March [May] 25. last evening and I hasten to answer.[2] I wish to precede it by renewing the assurance of my entire confidence and respect for the President and Lt. General Grant, and that in all matters I will be most willing to Shape my official and private conduct to suit their wishes. The past is beyond my control, and the matters embraced in the official Report to which you refer are finished. It is but just the reasons that activated me right or wrong should stand of Record, but in all future cases should any arise I will respect the decision of General Grant though I think it wrong. Supposing a Guard has prisoners in charge, and officers of another Command should aim to rescue or Kill them, is it not clear the Guard must defend the Prisoners? Same of a Safe Guard. So Jealous is the Military Law to protect and maintain *Good Faith* when pledged that the Law adjudges Death and no alternative punishment to one who violates a safe guard in foreign parts see Article of War No. 55. For murder, arson, treason and the highest military crimes, the punishment prescribed by Law is death or some minor punishment, but for the violation of a "Safe Guard" Death and Death alone is the prescribed penalty. I instance this to illustrate how in military stipulations to an enemy our Government commands & enforces "Good faith." In discussing this matter I would like to refer to many writers on Military Law, but am willing to take Halleck as the Text. See his Chapter No. 27.[3] In the very first article he prefaces that *Good Faith* should always be observed between Enemies in war, because when our Faith has been pledged to him, so far as the promise extends he ceases to be an Enemy. He then defines the meaning of *Compacts* & *Conventions* and says they are made sometimes for a general or a partial suspension of hostilities for the "surrender of an Army &c. They may be *special*, limited to particular places, or to particular forces but of course can only bind the Armies subject to the General who makes the Truce and co extensive only, with the Extent of his Command.

This is all I ever claimed and clearly covers the whole case[.] All of North Carolina was in my immediate command, with General Schofield its Department Commander & his army present with me. I never asked the Truce to have effect beyond my own *territorial* Command. General Halleck himself in his orders No. 1 defines his own limits clearly enough viz. "such part of North Carolina as was *not* occupied by the command of Maj. Genl. Sherman." He could not pursue & cut of[f] Johnstons retreat towards Saulsbury & Charlotte without invading my command, and so patent was his purpose to *defy* and *violate* my Truce that Mr. Stantons publication of the fact, not even yet recalled, modified or explained was headed "*Shermans Truce Disregarded*" that the whole world drew but one inference. It admits of no other. I never claimed that the Truce bound Genl. Halleck or Canby within the Sphere of *their* respective commands as defined by themselves. It was a *partial truce* of very short duration, clearly within my limits and Right, justified by events; and as in the case of prisoners in my custody, the violation of a safe guard given by me in my own Territorial limits[.] I was bound to maintain *Good Faith*. I prefer not to change my Report; but again repeat that in all future cases I am willing to be governed by the interpretation of Gen. Grant, although I again invite his attention to the limits of my command, and those of Gen. Halleck at the time, and the pointed phraseology of Gen. Hallecks despatch to Mr. Stanton wherein he reports that he had ordered his Generals to pay no heed to *my orders* within the clearly defined area of my Command. I am &c.

W. T. Sherman

Maj. Genl. U. S. Army Comdg.

ADfS, CsmH; *OR*, I, 47: pt. 3, 576–77 (dated May 27).

1. Theodore S. Bowers (1832–66) was an assistant adjutant general on USG's staff.

2. Bowers to WTS, May 25, 1865, DLC: WTS. Grant had asked Bowers to tell WTS that in his report his reference to keeping a truce at the expense of many lives was misleading; a commander could be responsible only for his own men. The enemy general was responsible for treating with all armies who opposed him. He asked if WTS wished to change the report.

3. HWH, *Elements of Military Art and Science*, 2d ed. (New York, 1861).

TO ULYSSES S. GRANT

> Hdqrs. Military Division
> of the Mississippi,
> In the Field, Camp near
> Finley Hospital,
> Washington, May 28, 1865—7 a.m.

[General Grant:]

Dear General:

I got your letter late last evening,[1] and hastened down to see General Augur,[2] but he was not in, when I saw his officer of the day and provost-marshal, and asked them as a favor to me to arrest and imprison any officer or man belonging to my command who transgressed any orders, rules, or regulations of the place, more especially for acts of drunkenness, noise, or rowdyism. I also went around to your office, but you were not there, but I saw Colonel Bowers, and told him what I had done. I was on the streets until midnight, and assure you I never saw more order and quiet prevailing. I had also, during yesterday, ridden all through the camps and observed no signs of riot and drunkenness, and believe I may assure you that there is no danger whatever that the men we know so well, and have trusted so often, will be guilty of any acts of public impropriety. The affair at Willard's Hotel was a small affair, arising from a heated discussion between a few officers in liquor, late at night, and unobserved save by the few who were up late. I will see that no officers presume to misbehave because of the unfortunate difference between the Secretary of War and myself. Of that difference I can only say that every officer and man regarded the Secretary's budget in the papers of April 24, the telegram of General Halleck indorsed by himself in those of the 28th, and the perfect storm of accusation which followed, and which he took no pains to correct, as a personal insult to me. I have not yet seen a man, soldier or civilian, but takes the same view of it, and I could not maintain my authority over troops if I tamely submitted to personal insult, but it is none the less wrong for officers to adopt the quarrel, and I will take strong measures to prevent it. I hope the good men of the command will have a few days in which to visit the Capitol and public grounds, to satisfy the natural curiosity, and then if the presence of so large a body of men so near Washington is deemed unpleasant I would suggest that the armies be dissolved, and all matters of discharge be imposed on the corps commanders, who have the lawful power in the premises, and during the period of pay and discharge and consolidation, these corps might be scattered, say one to Bladensburg (Twentieth), one to Relay House (Fourteenth), one to Monocacy (Fifteenth), and one to Frederick (Seventeenth). I would much prefer this to sending them back to the south bank of the Potomac, where they are crowded in with other troops, and have only choice of inferior ground for camps. I thank you for leaving the matter of orders to my management, and I will put myself and command perfectly on an understanding with General Augur and his garrison, and assure you that nothing offensive shall occur of any importance. Such little things as a tipsy soldier occasionally cannot be helped, but even that shall be punished according to "local orders."

With great respect,
W. T. Sherman,
Major-General, Commanding.

Printed, *OR*, I, 47: pt. 3, 581–82.

1. USG to WTS, May 27, 1865, *OR*, 47: pt. 3, 576. WTS's men had apparently been getting drunk and threatening Stanton for insulting their leader. One particularly rowdy group of officers drinking at Willard's Hotel on the evening of May 26 took turns jumping on the counter and leading the crowd in choruses of three groans for Stanton.

2. Major General Christopher Columbus Augur (1821–98) was commanding the Twenty-second Corps and the Department of Washington.

TO ULYSSES S. GRANT

Head-Quarters, Military Division
of the Mississippi,
In the Field, May 28, 1865.

Lt. Genl. U. S. Grant,
Commander in Chief, Washington D.C.
Dear General,

As I am today making my arrangements to go west, preparatory to assuming my proper duties, I think it proper to state a few points on which there is misapprehension in the mind of strangers.

I am not a politician, never voted but once in my Life, and never read a Political Platform. If spared I never will read a Political Platform or hold any Civil office whatsoever. I venerate the Constitution of the United States, think it as near perfection as possible, and recent Events have demonstrated that it vests Government with all the Power necessary for self vindication and for the protection to life & property of the Inhabitants. To accuse me of giving aid and Comfort to Copperheads is an insult. I do not believe in the sincerity of any able bodied man who has not fought in this war, much less in the Copperheads who opposed the war or threw obstacles in the way of its successful prosecution.

My opinions on all matters are very strong but if I am possessed properly of the views and orders of my superiors, I make them my study and conform my Conduct to them as though they were my own. The President has only to tell me what he wants done, and I will do it.

I was hurt, outraged and insulted at Mr. Stanton's public arraignment of my motives and actions, at his endorsing Gen. Hallecks insulting & offensive dispatch, and his studied silence when the Press accused me of all sorts of base motives, even of selling myself to Jeff Davis for Gold, of sheltering Criminals and entertaining ambitious views at the expense of my Country. I respect his office, but cannot him personally, till he undoes the injustice of the Past. I think I have soldierly instincts and feelings, but if this action of mine at all incommodes the President or endangers public harmony all you have to do is to say so, and leave me time to seek civil employment, and I will make room. I will serve the President of the United States not only with fidelity but with Zeal. The Government of the United States and its Constituted authorities must be sustained & perpetuated, not for our own good alone, but for that of rising, and coming Generations.

I would like Mr. Johnson to read this letter and to believe me that the newspaper gossip of my having Presidential aspirations is absurd, and offensive to me, and I would check it if I knew how.[1] As ever your ardent friend, and Servant,

> W. T. Sherman
> Maj. Genl.

ALS, CsmH; *OR*, I, 47: pt. 3, 582–83.

1. This letter is endorsed by USG: "Respectfully forwarded/to the President of the/ United States with the/request that this letter/be returned after reading/U.S. Grant/Lt. Gen./ May 28th/65." Endorsed as returned to Grant the same day by Johnson's military secretary.

TO JOHN M. SCHOFIELD

> Head-Quarters, Military Division
> of the Mississippi,
> In the Field, Camp near Washington,
> D.C. May 28. 1865.

Maj. Genl. Schofield,
Comdg. Dept. N. Carolina, Raleigh.
Dear Schofield,

Col. Wherry[1] has waited for me some days till I could find leisure to write you fully, but even now I feel pressed and cannot promise to tell you all I would. The army reached Alexandria May 19, and we met an order for the Grand Review. It came off in magnificent style, and Wherry can tell you all about it Stanton offered to shake hands with me in the presence of the President but I declined, and passed him to Shake hands with Grant. I have been before the War Committee & gave a minute account of all matters connected with the convention which will soon be published in full—Halleck tries to throw off on Stanton and Stanton on Halleck, and many men want me to be patient under this infliction for the sake of patriotism but I will not—the matter being more than official, a personal insult, and I have resented it, and Shall continue to do so[.] No man, I dont care who he is shall insult me publicly or arraign my motives. Mr. Johnson has been more than Kind to me, and the howl against me is narrowed down to Halleck & Stanton, and I have partially resented both. I have watched your Course & approve highly—Maintain Peace & good order, and let Law and harmony grow up naturally. I would have preferred to leap more directly to the result, but the same end may be obtained by the Slower process you adopt. I cannot yet learn that the executive has clearly laid down any policy, but I have reason to believe Mr. Johnson is not going as far as Mr. Chase in imposing Negro votes on the Southern or any States. I never heard a negro ask for that and I think it would be his ruin. I believe it would result in riots & violence at all the Polls north & south. Besides it is not the Province even of our Congress, much less the Executive to impose conditions on the voters in "organized states." That is clearly reserved to them. So strong has become the national Govt. by reason of our successful war, that I laugh at the fears of those who dread that Rebels may regain some political power in the Several states. Supposing they do, it is but local & can in no way endanger the whole Country. If northern Politicians are going to divide again into two parties nearly equal, & enable the minority of the South to throw its weight into one or the other scale to govern both it is *our fault*, not theirs. I believe the whole idea of giving votes to the negros, is to create just that many votes to be used by others for political uses, because I believe the negro dont want to vote *now*, when he is mixed up with the whites in nearly equal proportion, making strife dangerous.

I think I See already signs that events are sweeping all to the very conclusion I jumped to in my Terms, but I have refrained from discussing them till in after times it will be demonstrated that that was the only constitutional mode, whether popular or not. The People of this Country are subject to the Constitution, and Even they Cannot disregard it without Revolution, the very thing we have been fighting against.

I am to go west in a few days to resume command of the Divn. of the Mississipi embracing all west of the Alleghenies & east of the Mississipi all Grant waits for is Kirby Smiths action, and I know he will not fight. In that event I will go to Cincinati or Louisville. I go in a day or so to Chicago to attend the Fair, & thence home to Lancaster Ohio, where I should be delighted to hear from you. I esteem you as one of the best Military Minds of our Country and hope you will attain the highest honors. I read your letter on the Subject of Chases proposition and I endorse your action perfectly, and think

Grant does also. You may give to General Cox the assurance of my high esteem and I commend to you Col. Willard Warner whom you will remember as once on my staff. My best regards to all as ever your friend,

W. T. Sherman
Maj. Genl.

ALS, CSmH; *OR*, I, 47: pt. 3, 585–86.

1. Lieutenant Colonel William M. Wherry (1836–1918), USA, was aide-de-camp to Schofield.

SPECIAL FIELD ORDER NO. 76
[May 30, 1865]

The General commanding announces to the Armies of the Tennessee & Georgia that the time has come for us to part. Our work is done, and armed Enemies no longer defy us. Some of you will go to your homes & others will be retained in service till further orders.

And now that we are about to Seperate, to mingle with the civil world, it becomes a pleasing duty to recall to mind the situation of national affairs, where but little more than a year ago we were gathered about the towering cliffs of Lookout Mountain and all the future was wrapped in doubt and uncertainty. Three armies had come together from distant fields with seperate histories, yet bound by one common cause, the Union of our Country and the perpetuation of the Govt. of our inheritance. There is no need to recal to your memories the Tunnel Hill with the Rocky Far Mountain & Buzzard Roost Gap with the ugly Forts of Dalton behind, but we were in earnest and paused not for danger & difficulty, but dashed through *Snake Creek* Gap and fell on *Resacca*, then on to the Etowah, to Dalton, Kennesaw and the heat of summer found us on the banks of the Chattahoochee far from home and dependent on a single Road for supplies. Again we were not to be held back by any obstacle and crossed over and fought four hard battles for the possession of the citadel of Atlanta. That was the Crisis of our History as doubt still clouded our Future, but we solved the problem, and destroyed Atlanta struck boldly across the State of Georgia, severed all the main arteries of life to our Enemy, and Christmas found us at Savannah. Waiting there only long enough to fill our wagons, we again began a march which for peril, labor, and results will compare with any ever made by an organized army. The floods of the Savannah, the Swamps of the Combahee and Edisto, the "High hills" and rocks of the Santee, the flat quagmires of the Peedee & Cape Fear Rivers were all passed in midwinter, with its floods and rains and in the face of an accumulating enemy: and after the battles of Averysboro and Bentonville we once more came out of *the Wilderness* to meet our friends at Goldsboro. Even then we paused only long enough to get new clothing to reload our wagons and again pushed on to Raleigh and beyond until we met our enemy suing for Peace instead of war, and offering to Submit to the injured Laws of his and our Country. As long as that enemy was defiant nor mountains, nor Rivers, nor swamps, nor hunger, nor cold had checked us, but when he who had fought us hard & persistently offered submission, your General thought it wrong to pursue him further, and negotiations followed which resulted as you all know in his *surrender*. How far the operations of this army have contributed to the final overthrow of the Confederacy and the Peace which now dawns on us must be judged by others not by us, but that you have done all that men could do has been admitted by those in authority, and we have a right to join in the universal Joy that fills our land—the War is over, and our Government stands vindicated before the world by the joint action of the Volunteer Armies of the United States. To such as remain in the military service your General now only reminds you that success in the Past was due to hard work & Discipline, and that the same work & discipline are equally important in the Future. To Such as go home he will only say that our favored Country is so Grand, so extensive, so diversified in climate soil, and productions that every man may find a home & occupation suited to his tastes, and no one should yield to the natural impatience sure to result from our past life of excitement & adventure. You will be invited to seek new adventure abroad, but do not yield to the temptation for it will lead only to death or disappointment. Your Genl. now bids you all farewell, with the full belief that as in war, you have been good soldiers so in Peace you will make good citizens and if unfortunately *new war* should arise in our country, "Shermans army" will be the first to buckle on its old arms and come forth to defend & maintain the Government of our inheritance & choice.

By order of W. T. Sherman
Maj. Genl.

ADfS, CsmH; *OR*, I, 47: pt. 1, 44–46.

Chronological List of Letters

CHAPTER ONE
To Ellen Ewing Sherman
   November 3, 1860
To Ellen Ewing Sherman
   November 10, 1860
To Ellen Ewing Sherman
   November 23, 1860
To Ellen Ewing Sherman
   November 26, 1860
To Ellen Ewing Sherman
   November 29, 1860
To Thomas Ewing Sr.
   December 1, 1860
To John Sherman
   December 1, 1860
To John Sherman
   December 9, 1860
To Maria Boyle Ewing Sherman
   December 15, 1860
To Hugh B. Ewing
   December 18, 1860
To Ellen Ewing Sherman
   December 18, 1860
To John Sherman
   December 18, 1860
To Ellen Ewing Sherman
   December 23, 1860
To George Mason Graham
   [December 25,] 1860
To John Sherman
   December 29, 1860
To George Mason Graham
   January 5, 1861
To Ellen Ewing Sherman
   January 5, 1861
To Thomas Ewing Sr.
   January 8, 1861
To Ellen Ewing Sherman
   January 8, 1861
To Hugh B. Ewing
   January 12, 1861

To George Mason Graham
   January 16, 1861
To Ellen Ewing Sherman
   [January 16, 1861]
To John Sherman
   January 16, 1861
To Thomas O. Moore
   January 18, 1861
To Thomas O. Moore
   January 18, 1861
To John Sherman
   January 18, 1861
To George Mason Graham
   January 20, 1861
To Ellen Ewing Sherman
   January 20, 1861
To Ellen Ewing Sherman
   January 27, 1861
To Ellen Ewing Sherman
   February 1, 1861
To John Sherman
   February 1, 1861
To Charles Ewing
   February 3, 1861
To Thomas Ewing Jr.
   February 3, 1861
To Ellen Ewing Sherman
   February 16, 1861
To David F. Boyd
   February 23, 1861
To Ellen Ewing Sherman
   February 23, 1861
To Ellen Ewing Sherman
   [February 25, 1861]

CHAPTER TWO
To John Sherman
   March 9, 1861
To John Sherman
   March 21, 1861
To John Sherman
   March 22, 1861

To David F. Boyd
April 4, 1861
To John Sherman
April 8, 1861
To John Sherman
April 18, 1861
To John Sherman
April 22, 1861
To John Sherman
April 25, 1861
To Thomas Ewing Jr.
April 26, 1861
To Thomas Ewing Jr.
May 1, 1861
To Simon Cameron
May 8, 1861
To William Dennison Jr.
May 8, 1861
To Thomas Ewing Jr.
May 11, 1861
To John Sherman
May 11, 1861
To David F. Boyd
May 13, 1861
To Thomas Ewing Sr.
May 17, 1861
To Robert Anderson
May 20, 1861
To John Sherman
May 20, 1861
To John Sherman
May 22, 1861
To Thomas Ewing Jr.
May 23, 1861
To John Sherman
May 24, 1861
To Thomas Ewing Sr.
May 27, 1861
To Thomas Ewing Sr.
May 31, 1861
To Thomas Ewing Jr.
June 3, 1861
To Ellen Ewing Sherman
June 8, 1861
To John Sherman
June 8, 1861

To Ellen Ewing Sherman
June 12, 1861
To Ellen Ewing Sherman
June 17, 1861
To John Sherman
June 20, 1861
To Charles Ewing
June 22, 1861
To Ellen Ewing Sherman
July 3, 1861
To Ellen Ewing Sherman
July 6, 1861
To Maria Boyle Ewing Sherman
July 14, 1861

CHAPTER THREE
To Ellen Ewing Sherman
July 15, 1861
To Ellen Ewing Sherman
July 16, 1861
To John Sherman
July 16, 1861
To Ellen Ewing Sherman
July 19, 1861
To John Sherman
July 19, 1861
To Ellen Ewing Sherman
July 24, 1861
To Ellen Ewing Sherman
July 28, 1861
To Ellen Ewing Sherman
August 3, 1861
To Ellen Ewing Sherman
August 3, 1861
To Ellen Ewing Sherman
[August 12, 1861]
To Maria Boyle Ewing Sherman
August 13, 1861
To Ellen Ewing Sherman
August 17, 1861
To Ellen Ewing Sherman
August 19, 1861
To John Sherman
August 19, 1861
To Ellen Ewing Sherman
[August 20–27, 1861]

To John Sherman
  September 9, 1861
To Thomas Ewing Sr.
  September 15, 1861
To Ellen Ewing Sherman
  September 18, 1861
To Thomas Ewing Sr.
  September 30, 1861
To John Sherman
  October 5, 1861
To Ellen Ewing Sherman
  October 6, 1861
To Abraham Lincoln
  October 10, [1861]
To Ellen Ewing Sherman
  October 12, 1861
To Salmon P. Chase
  October 14, 1861
To Lorenzo Thomas
  October 22, 1861
To Ellen Ewing Sherman
  October 23, 1861
To John Sherman
  October 26, 1861
To Ellen Ewing Sherman
  November 1, 1861
To William Dennison Jr.
  November 6, 1861
To Lorenzo Thomas
  November 6, 1861
To Robert Anderson
  November 21, 1861
To John Sherman
  November 21, 1861
To Thomas Ewing Sr.
  December 12, 1861
To Henry W. Halleck
  December 12, 1861

CHAPTER FOUR
To Ellen Ewing Sherman
  December [18 or 19], 1861
To Thomas Ewing Sr.
  December 24, 1861
To John Sherman
  December 24, 1861

To Ellen Ewing Sherman
  January 1, 1862
To John Sherman
  January 4, 1862
To John Sherman
  January 8, 1862
To John Sherman
  January 9, 1862
To Ellen Ewing Sherman
  January 11, 1862
To Philemon B. Ewing
  January 20, 1862
To Ellen Ewing Sherman
  January 29, 1862
To John Sherman
  February 3, 1862
To Robert Anderson
  February 6, 1862
To Ellen Ewing Sherman
  February 17, 1862
To Ellen Ewing Sherman
  February 21, 1862
To John Sherman
  February 23, 1862
To Charles Ewing
  February 27, 1862
To Ellen Ewing Sherman
  March 6, 1862
To Ellen Ewing Sherman
  March 12, 1862
To Ellen Ewing Sherman
  March 17/18, 1862
To Ellen Ewing Sherman
  April 3, 1862
To Thomas Ewing Sr.
  April 4, 1862
To Ellen Ewing Sherman
  April 11, 1862
To Ellen Ewing Sherman
  April 14, 1862
To John Sherman
  April 16, 1862
To William T. Sherman Jr.
  April 19, 1862
To John Sherman
  April 22, 1862

To Ellen Ewing Sherman
  April 24, 1862
To Charles Ewing
  April 25, 1862
To Thomas Ewing Sr.
  April 27, 1862
To Thomas Ewing Sr.
  May 3, 1862
To John Sherman
  May 7, 1862
To John Sherman
  May 12, 1862
To Philemon B. Ewing
  May 16, 1862
To Ellen Ewing Sherman
  May 23, 1862
To Ellen Ewing Sherman
  May 26, 1862

CHAPTER FIVE
To John Sherman
  [May 31, 1862]
To Ulysses S. Grant
  June 6, 1862
To Ellen Ewing Sherman
  June 6, 1862
To Thomas Ewing Sr.
  June 7, 1862
To Ellen Ewing Sherman
  June 10, 1862
To Benjamin Stanton
  June 10, 1862
To Ellen Ewing Sherman
  June 27, 1862
To S. S. L'Hommedieu
  July 7, 1862
To Charles Ewing
  July 8, 1862
To Philemon B. Ewing
  July 13, 1862
To Philemon B. Ewing
  July 14, 1862
To Henry W. Halleck
  July 16, 1862
To E. S. Plummer et al.
  July 23, 1862

To Samuel Sawyer
  July 24, 1862
To John Park
  July 27, 1862
To Ellen Ewing Sherman
  July 31, 1862
To Maria Boyle Ewing Sherman
  August 6, 1862
To Thomas Ewing Sr.
  August 10, 1862
To Andrew Johnson
  August 10, 1862
To Ellen Ewing Sherman
  August 10, 1862
To James Wickersham
  August 10, 1862
To Salmon P. Chase
  August 11, 1862
To Ulysses S. Grant
  August 11, 1862
To John Sherman
  August 13, 1862
To Gideon J. Pillow
  August 14, 1862
To John A. Rawlins
  August 14, 1862
To Isaac F. Quinby
  August 15, 1862
To Ulysses S. Grant
  August 17, 1862
To Henry W. Halleck
  August 18, 1862
To Ellen Ewing Sherman
  August 20, 1862
To the Editors of the *Memphis Bulletin*
  and *Memphis Appeal*
  August 21, 1862
To Thomas Hunton
  August 24, 1862
To William H. H. Taylor
  August 25, 1862

CHAPTER SIX
To John Sherman
  August 26, 1862
To John Sherman
  September 3, 1862

To Ellen Ewing Sherman
    September 12, 1862
To New York Gentlemen
    [September] 17, 1862
To the Editor of the *Memphis Bulletin*
    September 21, 1862
To John Sherman
    September 22, 1862
To Thomas Tasker Gantt
    September 23, 1862
To Ellen Ewing Sherman
    September 25, 1862
To John A. Rawlins
    September 26, 1862
To Thomas C. Hindman
    September 28, 1862
To Ellen Ewing Sherman
    October 1, 1862
To John Sherman
    October 1, 1862
To Ellen Ewing Sherman
    October 4, 1862
To Maria Boyle Ewing Sherman
    October 4, 1862
To Thomas C. Hindman
    October 17, 1862
To Miss P. A. Fraser
    October 22, 1862
To Philemon B. Ewing
    November 2, 1862
To Valeria Hurlbut
    November 6, 1862
To Ulysses S. Grant
    November 8, 1862
To John T. Swayne
    November 12, 1862
To Henry W. Halleck
    November 17, 1862
To F. G. Pratt
    November 17, 1862
To Joseph Tagg
    November 17, 1862
To John C. Pemberton
    November 18, 1862
To John A. Rawlins
    November 19, 1862

To John Sherman
    November 24, 1862
To John Sherman
    December 6, 1862
To the Sherman Children
    December 8, 1862
To Irvin McDowell
    December 14, 1862
To Ellen Ewing Sherman
    December 14, 1862
To John Sherman
    December 14, 1862
To Edwin M. Stanton
    December 16, 1862
To John Sherman
    December 20, 1862
To Ellen Ewing Sherman
    January 4, 1863
To John Sherman
    January 6, [1863]
To Ellen Ewing Sherman
    January 12, 1863
To Thomas Ewing Sr.
    January 16, 186[3]
To Ellen Ewing Sherman
    January 16, 1863
To Ulysses S. Grant
    January 17, 1863
To John Sherman
    January 17, 1863
To Ellen Ewing Sherman
    January 24, 1863
To Ethan A. Hitchcock
    January 25, 1863

CHAPTER SEVEN
To John Sherman
    January 25, 1863
To Edwin M. Stanton
    January 25, 1863
To Ellen Ewing Sherman
    January 28, 1863
To John Sherman
    January 31, 1863
To David Dixon Porter
    February 1, 1863

To Frank P. Blair
February 2, 1863
To Frank P. Blair
February 3, 1863
To Ulysses S. Grant
February 3, 1863
To John A. Rawlins
February 3, 1863
To David Dixon Porter
February 4, 1863
To John Sherman
February 4, 1863
To Thomas Ewing Sr.
February 6, 1863
To Ellen Ewing Sherman
February 6, 1863
To Maria Boyle Ewing Sherman
February 6, 1863
To Benjamin H. Grierson
February 9, 1863
To John Sherman
February 12, 1863
To Thomas Ewing Sr.
February 17, 1863
To John Sherman
February 18, 1863
To Edward O. C. Ord
February 22, 1863
To Ellen Ewing Sherman
February 22, 1863
To John A. Rawlins
February 23, 1863
To Frank J. Bramhall
February 24, 1863
To Ellen Ewing Sherman
February 26, 1863
To Philemon B. Ewing
March 3, 1863
To Thomas Ewing Sr.
March 7, 1863
To David Tod
March 12, 1863
To Ellen Ewing Sherman
March 13, 1863
To John Sherman
March 14, 1863

To Maria Boyle Ewing Sherman
March 15, 1863
To Stephen A. Hurlbut
March 16, 1863

CHAPTER EIGHT
To John Sherman
April 3, 1863
To Thomas W. Knox
April 7, 1863
To Ulysses S. Grant
April 8, 1863
To Murat Halstead
April 8, 1863
To John A. Rawlins
April 8, 1863
To Ellen Ewing Sherman
April 10, 1863
To John Sherman
April 10, 1863
To Ellen Ewing Sherman
April 17, 1863
To Ellen Ewing Sherman
April 23, 1863
To John Sherman
April 23, 1863
To John Sherman
April 26, 1863
To Maria Boyle Ewing Sherman
April 26, 1863
To Ellen Ewing Sherman
April 29, 1863
To Ellen Ewing Sherman
May 2, 1863
To Ellen Ewing Sherman
May 6, 1863
To Ellen Ewing Sherman
May 9, 1863
To Ellen Ewing Sherman
May 19, 1863
To Ellen Ewing Sherman
May 25, 1863
To John Sherman
May 29, 1863
To Ulysses S. Grant
June 2, 1863

To Ellen Ewing Sherman
June 2, 1863
To Ellen Ewing Sherman
June 11, 1863
To John T. Swayne
June 11, 1863
To Maria Boyle Ewing Sherman
June 13, 1863
To Thomas Ewing Sr.
June 14, 1863
To David Dixon Porter
June 14, 1863
To John A. Rawlins
June 17, 1863
To William T. Sherman Jr.
June 21, 1863
To Ellen Ewing Sherman
June 27, 1863
To John Sherman
[ca. June 27, 1863]
To Ulysses S. Grant
July 3, 1863
To Ulysses S. Grant
July 4, 1863

CHAPTER NINE
To Ellen Ewing Sherman
July 5, 1863
To Ellen Ewing Sherman
July 15, 1863
To David Dixon Porter
July 19, 1863
To John Sherman
July 19, 1863
To Philemon B. Ewing
July 28, 1863
To John Sherman
July 28, 1863
To Charles Anderson
[ca. August 1863]
To David Stuart
August 1, 1863
To Edward O. C. Ord
August 3, 1863
To Jesse Reed and W. B. Anderson
August 3, 1863

To John Sherman
August 3, 1863
To John A. Rawlins
August 4, 1863
To Philemon B. Ewing
August 5, 1863
To Thomas Ewing Sr.
August 13, 1863
To Ulysses S. Grant
August 15, 1863
To Thomas Ewing Sr.
August 20, 1863
To James W. Tuttle
August 20, 1863
To Lew Wallace
August 27, 1863
To James B. McPherson
September 1, 1863
To John M. Wright
September 2, 1863
To Frederick A. P. Barnard
September 4, 1863
To James B. McPherson
September 4, 1863
To H. W. Hill
September 7, 1863
To John Sherman
September 9, 1863
To James B. McPherson
September 10, 1863
To Dennis Hart Mahan
September 16, 1863
To Henry W. Halleck
September 17, 1863
To John A. Rawlins
September 17, 1863
To Charles C. Smith
October 4, 1863
To Ellen Ewing Sherman
October 6, 1863
To Ellen Ewing Sherman
October 8, 1863
To Henry W. Halleck
October 10, 1863
To Ellen Ewing Sherman
October 10, 1863

To Mary Elizabeth Hoyt Sherman
 [ca. October 10, 1863]
To Thomas Ewing Sherman
 [ca. October 10, 1863]
To David Dixon Porter
 October 14, 1863
To Ellen Ewing Sherman
 October 14, 1863
To John M. Wright
 October 14, 1863
To Philemon B. Ewing
 October 24, 1863
To Ellen Ewing Sherman
 October 24, 1863
To John Sherman
 October 24, 1863
To the Editors of the *Memphis Bulletin*
 October 27, 1863
To Ellen Ewing Sherman
 October 28, 1863
To James B. Bingham
 November 9, 1863
To James E. Yeatman
 November 9, 1863
To Ellen Ewing Sherman
 November 17, 1863
To James B. McPherson
 November 18, 1863
To John A. Logan
 December 21, 1863
To John Sherman
 December 29, 1863
To John Sherman
 December 30, 1863

CHAPTER TEN
To Maria Boyle Ewing Sherman
 January 6, 1864
To Ellen Ewing Sherman
 January 11, 1864
To Ellen Ewing Sherman
 January 19, 1864
To Maria Boyle Ewing Sherman
 January 19, 1864
To John A. Logan
 January 20, 1864

To Ulysses S. Grant
 January 24, 1864
To James B. Bingham
 January 26, 1864
To Ellen Ewing Sherman
 January 28, 1864
To John Sherman
 January 28, 1864
To Maria Boyle Ewing Sherman
 January 28, 1864
To Roswell M. Sawyer
 January 31, 1864
To Ellen Ewing Sherman
 February 7, 1864
To Ulysses S. Grant
 March 10, 1864
To Ellen Ewing Sherman
 March 10, 1864
To Ellen Ewing Sherman
 March 12, 1864
To John Sherman
 March 24, 1864
To Mason Brayman
 April 2, 1864
To Ulysses S. Grant
 April 2, 1864
To John Sherman
 April 5, 1864
To Joseph Holt
 April 6, 1864
To James B. Fry
 April 10, 1864
To Ulysses S. Grant
 April 10, 1864
To John Sherman
 April 11, 1864
To Lorenzo Thomas
 April 12, 1864
To Thomas Ewing Jr.
 April 18, 1864
To Charles A. Dana
 April 21, 1864
To Philemon B. Ewing
 April 21, 1864
To Ellen Ewing Sherman
 April 22, 1864

To John Sherman
April 22, 1864
To Edwin M. Stanton
April 23, 1864
To Thomas Ewing Sherman
April 25, 1864
To Thomas Ewing Sr.
April 27, 1864
To Ellen Ewing Sherman
April 27, 1864
To Maria Boyle Ewing Sherman
May 1, 1864
To Ellen Ewing Sherman
May 4, 1864

CHAPTER ELEVEN
To Ellen Ewing Sherman
May 20, 1864
To Ellen Ewing Sherman
May 22, 1864
To John Sherman
May 26, 1864
To Emily Hoffman
June 9, 1864
To Ellen Ewing Sherman
June 9, 1864
To John Sherman
June 9, 1864
To Ellen Ewing Sherman
June 12, 1864
To Henry Coppée
June 13, 1864
To Henry Coppée
June 13, 1864
To Ulysses S. Grant
June 18, 1864
To James B. Steedman
June 23, 1864
To Ellen Ewing Sherman
June 26, 1864
To Lorenzo Thomas
June 26, 1864
To Henry W. Halleck
June 27, 1864
To Ellen Ewing Sherman
June 30, 1864

To Maria Boyle Ewing Sherman
June 30, 1864
To Henry W. Halleck
July 7, 1864
To Ellen Ewing Sherman
July 9, 1864
To Hugh B. Ewing
July 13, 1864
To Philemon B. Ewing
July 13, 1864
To Henry W. Halleck
July 13, 1864
To Ellen Ewing Sherman
July 13, 1864
To George H. Thomas
July 20, 1864
To Lorenzo Thomas
July [23], 1864
To Ellen Ewing Sherman
July 26, 1864
To Henry W. Halleck
July 27, 1864
To Abraham Lincoln
July 27, 1864
To John A. Logan
July 27, 1864
To Ellen Ewing Sherman
July 29, 1864
To John A. Spooner
July 30, 1864
To John Sherman
July 31, 1864
To Ellen Ewing Sherman
August 2, 1864
To Emily Hoffman
August 5, 1864
To Ulysses S. Grant
August 7, 1864
To Ellen Ewing Sherman
August 9, 1864
To Daniel Martin
August 10, 1864
To Thomas Ewing Sr.
August 11, 1864
To Schuyler Colfax
August 12, 1864

To John Sherman
   August 12, 1864
To James Guthrie
   August 14, 1864
To Henry W. Halleck
   September 3, 1864
To Ellen Ewing Sherman
   September 3, 1864
To Henry W. Halleck
   September 4, 1864
To Henry W. Halleck
   September 4, 1864

CHAPTER TWELVE
To John Bell Hood
   September 7, 1864
To Ulysses S. Grant
   September 10, 1864
To John Bell Hood
   September 10, 1864
To James M. Calhoun et al.
   September 12, 1864
To John Bell Hood
   September 12, 1864
To John Bell Hood
   September 14, 1864
To Thomas Ewing Sr.
   September 15, 1864
To Eugene Casserly
   [September 17, 1864]
To Edward Everett
   September 17, 1864
To Thomas Ewing Jr.
   September 17, [1864]
To Abraham Lincoln
   September 17, 1864
To Ellen Ewing Sherman
   September 17, 1864
To John Sherman
   September 17, 1864
To T. S. Bell
   September 18, 1864
To Maria Boyle Ewing Sherman
   September 18, 1864
To Ulysses S. Grant
   September 20, 1864

To Philemon B. Ewing
   September 23, 1864
To Thomas Ewing Sr.
   September 23, 1864
To Abraham Lincoln
   September 28, 1864
To William M. McPherson
   [ca. September 15–30, 1864]
To Ulysses S. Grant
   October 1, 1864
To Ellen Ewing Sherman
   October 1, 1864
To George H. Thomas
   October 2, 1864
To Ulysses S. Grant
   October 9, 1864
To George H. Thomas
   October 9, 1864
To Ulysses S. Grant
   October 10, 1864
To Ulysses S. Grant
   October 11, 1864
To John Sherman
   October 11, 1864
To John M. Schofield
   October 17, 1864
To George H. Thomas
   October 17, 1864
To Henry W. Halleck
   October 19, 1864
To Ellen Ewing Sherman
   October 19, 1864
To Ellen Ewing Sherman
   October 21, 1864
To Joseph P. Thompson
   October 21, 1864
To Edwin M. Stanton
   October 25, 1864
To Ellen Ewing Sherman
   October 27, 1864
To George H. Thomas
   October 29, 1864
To Ulysses S. Grant
   November 1, 1864
To Ulysses S. Grant
   November 2, 1864

To Ulysses S. Grant
November 2, 1864
To Ulysses S. Grant
November 2, 1864
To Ulysses S. Grant
November 6, 1864
To Philip H. Sheridan
November 6, 1864
To John E. Smith
November 8, 1864
To Maria Boyle Ewing Sherman
and Mary Elizabeth Sherman
November 9, 1864
To Charles A. Dana
November 10, 1864
To Philemon B. Ewing
November 10, 1864
To Thomas Ewing Sherman
November 10, 1864
To Henry W. Halleck
November 11, 1864
To George H. Thomas
November 11, 1864
To Ellen Ewing Sherman
November 12, 1864

CHAPTER THIRTEEN
To Henry W. Halleck
December 13, 1864
To Ulysses S. Grant
December 16, 1864
To Ellen Ewing Sherman
December 16, 1864
To William J. Hardee
December 17, 1864
To Ulysses S. Grant
December 18, 1864
To Ulysses S. Grant
December 22, 1864
To Abraham Lincoln
December 22, 1864
To Ulysses S. Grant
December 24, 1864
To Henry W. Halleck
December 24, 1864
To Ellen Ewing Sherman
December 25, 1864

To Maria Boyle Ewing Sherman
December 25, 1864
To George H. Thomas
December 25, 1864
To P. J. Stanfield, A. J. Pagett, and others
December 28, 1864
To Thomas Ewing Sr.
December 31, 1864
To Ulysses S. Grant
December 31, 1864
To Ellen Ewing Sherman
December 31, 1864
To John Sherman
December 31, 1864
To Ellen Ewing Sherman
January 2, 1865
To Edwin M. Stanton
January 2, 1865
To Ellen Ewing Sherman
January 5, 1865
To Abraham Lincoln
January 6, 1865
To Salmon P. Chase
January 11, 1865
To Henry W. Halleck
January 12, 1865
To Ellen Ewing Sherman
January 15, 1865
To John Sherman
January 19, 1865
To Edwin M. Stanton
January 19, 1865
To Caroline Carson
January 20, 1865
To Ulysses S. Grant
January 21, 1865
To Thomas Ewing Sherman
January 21, 186[5]
To George H. Thomas
January 21, 1865
To John Sherman
January 22, 1865
To Henry W. Halleck
January 27, 1865
To Philemon B. Ewing
January 29, 1865

To Ulysses S. Grant
  January 29, 1865
To Oliver O. Howard
  February 23, 1865
To Hugh Judson Kilpatrick
  February 23, 1865
To Wade Hampton
  February 24, 1865

CHAPTER FOURTEEN
To Ulysses S. Grant
  March 12, 1865
To Ellen Ewing Sherman
  March 12, 1865
To Edwin M. Stanton
  March 12, 1865
To Alfred H. Terry
  March 12, 1865
To Ulysses S. Grant
  March 23, 1865
To Ellen Ewing Sherman
  March 23, 1865
To Ulysses S. Grant
  March 24, 1865
To Frederick F. Low
  March 24, 1865
To William M. McPherson
  March 24, 1865
To Maria Boylc Ewing Sherman
  March 24, 1865
To Thomas Turner
  March 25, 1865
To Ellen Ewing Sherman
  March 26, 1865
To Ellen Ewing Sherman
  March 31, 1865
To Edwin M. Stanton
  March 31, 1865
To George F. Granger
  April 3, 1865
To Robert Anderson
  April 5, 1865
To John A. Dahlgren
  April 5, 1865
To Thomas Ewing Sr.
  April 5, 1865

To Michael Hahn
  April 5, 1865
To Ellen Ewing Sherman
  April 5, 1865
To Ellen Ewing Sherman
  April 5, 1865
To John Sherman
  April 5, 1865
To Ellen Ewing Sherman
  April 6, 1865
To Ulysses S. Grant
  April 8, [1865]
To Philemon B. Ewing
  April 9, 1865
To Ellen Ewing Sherman
  April 9, 1865
To Thomas Ewing Sherman
  April 9, 1865

CHAPTER FIFTEEN
To Ulysses S. Grant
  April 12, 1865
To Ulysses S. Grant
  April 13, 1865
To Hugh Judson Kilpatrick
  April 14, 1865
To Joseph E. Johnston
  April 14, 1865
To Ulysses S. Grant
  April 15, 1865
To Joseph D. Webster
  April 17, 1865
To Ulysses S. Grant
  April 18, 1865
To Henry W. Halleck
  April 18, 1865
To Ellen Ewing Sherman
  April 18, 1865
To Sewall L. Fremont
  April 21, 1865
To Joseph E. Johnston
  April 21, 1865
To Ellen Ewing Sherman
  April 22, 1865
To David L. Swain
  April 22, 1865

To Joseph E. Johnston
  April 23, 1865
To Joseph E. Johnston and
  William J. Hardee
  April 23, 1865
To Joseph E. Johnston
  April 23, 1865
To Joseph E. Johnston
  April 24, 1865
To Joseph E. Johnston
  April 24, 1865
To Ulysses S. Grant
  April 25, 1865
To Edwin M. Stanton
  April 25, 1865
Terms of a Military Convention
  April 26, 1865
To Joseph E. Johnston
  April 27, 1865
To Ulysses S. Grant
  April 28, 1865
To Ellen Ewing Sherman
  April 28, 1865
To John A. Rawlins
  April 29, 1865
To George H. Thomas
  May 2, 1865
To John M. Schofield
  May 5, 1865
To Salmon P. Chase
  May 6, 1865

To Salmon P. Chase
  May 6, 1865
To Henry W. Halleck
  May 7, 1865
To Ellen Ewing Sherman
  May 8, 1865
To Ulysses S. Grant
  May 10, 1865
To Henry W. Halleck
  May 10, 1865
To Ellen Ewing Sherman
  May 10, 1865
To John A. Logan
  May 12, 1865
To Oliver O. Howard
  May 17, 1865
To John A. Rawlins
  May 19, 1865
To Theodore S. Bowers
  May 26, 1865
To Ulysses S. Grant
  May 28, 1865
To Ulysses S. Grant
  May 28, 1865
To John M. Schofield
  May 28, 1865
Special Field Order No. 76
  May 30, 1865

List of Letters by Recipient

Charles Anderson
  [ca. August 1863]
Robert Anderson
  May 20, 1861; November 21, 1861; February 6, 1862; April 5, 1865
Frederick A. P. Barnard
  September 4, 1863
T. S. Bell
  September 18, 1864
James B. Bingham
  November 9, 1863; January 26, 1864
Frank P. Blair
  February 2, 1863; February 3, 1863
Theodore S. Bowers
  May 26, 1865
David F. Boyd
  February 23, 1861; April 4, 1861; May 13, 1861
Frank J. Bramhall
  February 24, 1863
Mason Brayman
  April 2, 1864
James Calhoun et al.
  September 12, 1864
Simon Cameron
  May 8, 1861
Caroline Carson
  January 20, 1865
Eugene Casserly
  [September 17, 1864]
Salmon P. Chase
  October 14, 1861; August 11, 1862; January 11, 1865; May 6, 1865; May 6, 1865
Schuyler Colfax
  August 12, 1864
Henry Coppée
  June 13, 1864; June 13, 1864
John A. Dahlgren
  April 5, 1865
Charles A. Dana
  April 21, 1864; November 10, 1864
William Dennison Jr.
  May 8, 1861; November 6, 1861
The Editor(s) of the *Memphis Bulletin*
  September 21, 1862; October 27, 1863

The Editors of the *Memphis Bulletin* and *Memphis Appeal*
    August 21, 1862
Edward Everett
    September 17, 1864
Charles Ewing
    February 3, 1861; June 22, 1861; February 27, 1862; April 25, 1862; July 8, 1862
Hugh B. Ewing
    December 18, 1860; January 12, 1861; July 13, 1864
Philemon B. Ewing
    January 20, 1862; May 16, 1862; July 13, 1862; July 14, 1862; November 2, 1862;
    March 3, 1863; July 28, 1863; August 5, 1863; October 24, 1863; April 21, 1864; July 13, 1864;
    September 23, 1864; November 10, 1864; January 29, 1865; April 9, 1865
Thomas Ewing Sr.
    December 1, 1860; January 8, 1861; May 17, 1861; May 27, 1861; May 31, 1861;
    September 15, 1861; September 30, 1861; December 12, 1861; December 24, 1861;
    April 4, 1862; April 27, 1862; May 3, 1862; June 7, 1862; August 10, 1862;
    January 16, 186[3]; February 6, 1863; February 17, 1863; March 7, 1863; June 14, 1863;
    August 13, 1863; August 20, 1863; April 27, 1864; August 11, 1864; September 15, 1864;
    September 23, 1864; December 31, 1864; April 5, 1865
Thomas Ewing Jr.
    February 3, 1861; April 26, 1861; May 1, 1861; May 11, 1861; May 23, 1861; June 3, 1861;
    April 18, 1864; September 17, [1864]
Miss P. A. Fraser
    October 22, 1862
Sewall L. Fremont
    April 21, 1865
James B. Fry
    April 10, 1864
Thomas Tasker Gantt
    September 23, 1862
George Mason Graham
    [December 25,] 1860; January 5, 1861; January 16, 1861; January 20, 1861
George F. Granger
    April 3, 1865
Ulysses S. Grant
    June 6, 1862; August 11, 1862; August 17, 1862; November 8, 1862; January 17, 1863;
    February 3, 1863; April 8, 1863; June 2, 1863; July 3, 1863; July 4, 1863; August 15, 1863;
    January 24, 1864; March 10, 1864; April 2, 1864; April 10, 1864; June 18, 1864;
    August 7, 1864; September 10, 1864; September 20, 1864; October 1, 1864;
    October 9, 1864; October 10, 1864; October 11, 1864; November 1, 1864;
    November 2, 1864; November 2, 1864; November 2, 1864; November 6, 1864;
    December 16, 1864; December 18, 1864; December 22, 1864; December 24, 1864;
    December 31, 1864; January 21, 1865; January 29, 1865; March 12, 1865; March 23, 1865;
    March 24, 1865; April 8, [1865]; April 12, 1865; April 13, 1865; April 15, 1865; April 18, 1865;
    April 25, 1865; April 28, 1865; May 10, 1865; May 28, 1865; May 28, 1865
Benjamin H. Grierson
    February 9, 1863

James Guthrie
    August 14, 1864
Michael Hahn
    April 5, 1865
Henry W. Halleck
    December 12, 1861; July 16, 1862; August 18, 1862; November 17, 1862; September 17, 1863;
    October 10, 1863; June 27, 1864; July 7, 1864; July 13, 1864; July 27, 1864;
    September 3, 1864; September 4, 1864; September 4, 1864; October 19, 1864;
    November 11, 1864; December 13, 1864; December 24, 1864; January 12, 1865;
    January 27, 1865; April 18, 1865; May 7, 1865; May 10, 1865
Murat Halstead
    April 8, 1863
Wade Hampton
    February 24, 1865
William J. Hardee
    December 17, 1864; April 23, 1865
H. W. Hill
    September 7, 1863
Thomas C. Hindman
    September 28, 1862; October 17, 1862
Ethan A. Hitchcock
    January 25, 1863
Emily Hoffman
    June 9, 1864; August 5, 1864
Joseph Holt
    April 6, 1864
John Bell Hood
    September 7, 1864; September 10, 1864; September 12, 1864; September 14, 1864
Oliver O. Howard
    February 23, 1865; May 17, 1865
Thomas Hunton
    August 24, 1862
Stephen A. Hurlbut
    March 16, 1863
Valeria Hurlbut
    November 6, 1862
Andrew Johnson
    August 10, 1862
Joseph E. Johnston
    April 14, 1865; April 21, 1865; April 23, 1865; April 23, 1865; April 23, 1865; April 24, 1865;
    April 24, 1865; April 27, 1865
Hugh Judson Kilpatrick
    February 23, 1865; April 14, 1865
Thomas W. Knox
    April 7, 1863
S. S. L'Hommedieu
    July 7, 1862

Abraham Lincoln
October 10, [1861]; July 27, 1864; September 17, 1864; September 28, 1864;
December 22, 1864; January 6, 1865
John A. Logan
December 21, 1863; January 20, 1864; July 27, 1864; May 12, 1865
Frederick F. Low
March 24, 1865
Irvin McDowell
December 14, 1862
James B. McPherson
September 1, 1863; September 4, 1863; September 10, 1863; November 18, 1863
William M. McPherson
[ca. September 15–30, 1864]; March 24, 1865
Dennis Hart Mahan
September 16, 1863
Daniel Martin
August 10, 1864
Thomas O. Moore
January 18, 1861; January 18, 1861
New York Gentlemen
[September] 17, 1862
Edward O. C. Ord
February 22, 1863; August 3, 1863
John Park
July 27, 1862
John C. Pemberton
November 18, 1862
Gideon J. Pillow
August 14, 1862
E. S. Plummer et al.
July 23, 1862
David Dixon Porter
February 1, 1863; February 4, 1863; June 14, 1863; July 19, 1863; October 14, 1863
F. G. Pratt
November 17, 1862
Isaac F. Quinby
August 15, 1862
John A. Rawlins
August 14, 1862; September 26, 1862; November 19, 1862; February 3, 1863;
February 23, 1863; April 8, 1863; June 17, 1863; August 4, 1863; September 17, 1863;
April 29, 1865; May 19, 1865
Jesse Reed and W. B. Anderson
August 3, 1863
Roswell M. Sawyer
January 31, 1864
Samuel Sawyer
July 24, 1862

John M. Schofield
    October 17, 1864; May 5, 1865; May 28, 1865
Philip H. Sheridan
    November 6, 1864
Ellen Ewing Sherman
    November 3, 1860; November 10, 1860; November 23, 1860; November 26, 1860;
    November 29, 1860; December 18, 1860; December 23, 1860; January 5, 1861;
    January 8, 1861; [January 16, 1861]; January 20, 1861; January 27, 1861; February 1, 1861;
    February 16, 1861; February 23, 1861; [February 25, 1861]; June 8, 1861; June 12, 1861;
    June 17, 1861; July 3, 1861; July 6, 1861; July 15, 1861; July 16, 1861; July 19, 1861;
    July 24, 1861; July 28, 1861; August 3, 1861; August 3, 1861; [August 12, 1861];
    August 17, 1861; August 19, 1861; [August 20–27, 1861]; September 18, 1861;
    October 6, 1861; October 12, 1861; October 23, 1861; November 1, 1861;
    December [18 or 19], 1861; January 1, 1862; January 11, 1862; January 29, 1862;
    February 17, 1862; February 21, 1862; March 6, 1862; March 12, 1862; March 17/18, 1862;
    April 3, 1862; April 11, 1862; April 14, 1862; April 24, 1862; May 23, 1862; May 26, 1862;
    June 6, 1862; June 10, 1862; June 27, 1862; July 31, 1862; August 10, 1862;
    August 20, 1862; September 12, 1862; September 25, 1862; October 1, 1862;
    October 4, 1862; December 14, 1862; January 4, 1863; January 12, 1863; January 16, 1863;
    January 24, 1863; January 28, 1863; February 6, 1863; February 22, 1863;
    February 26, 1863; March 13, 1863; April 10, 1863; April 17, 1863; April 23, 1863;
    April 29, 1863; May 2, 1863; May 6, 1863; May 9, 1863; May 19, 1863; May 25, 1863;
    June 2, 1863; June 11, 1863; June 27, 1863; July 5, 1863; July 15, 1863; October 6, 1863;
    October 8, 1863; October 10, 1863; October 14, 1863; October 24, 1863; October 28, 1863;
    November 17, 1863; January 11, 1864; January 19, 1864; January 28, 1864;
    February 7, 1864; March 10, 1864; March 12, 1864; April 22, 1864; April 27, 1864;
    May 4, 1864; May 20, 1864; May 22, 1864; June 9, 1864; June 12, 1864; June 26, 1864;
    June 30, 1864; July 9, 1864; July 13, 1864; July 26, 1864; July 29, 1864; August 2, 1864;
    August 9, 1864; September 3, 1864; September 17, 1864; October 1, 1864;
    October 19, 1864; October 21, 1864; October 27, 1864; November 12, 1864;
    December 16, 1864; December 25, 1864; December 31, 1864; January 2, 1865;
    January 5, 1865; January 15, 1865; March 12, 1865; March 23, 1865; March 26, 1865;
    March 31, 1865; April 5, 1865; April 5, 1865; April 6, 1865; April 9, 1865; April 18, 1865;
    April 22, 1865; April 28, 1865; May 8, 1865; May 10, 1865
John Sherman
    December 1, 1860; December 9, 1860; December 18, 1860; December 29, 1860;
    January 16, 1861; January 18, 1861; February 1, 1861; March 9, 1861; March 21, 1861;
    March 22, 1861; April 8, 1861; April 18, 1861; April 22, 1861; April 25, 1861; May 11, 1861;
    May 20, 1861; May 22, 1861; May 24, 1861; June 8, 1861; June 20, 1861; July 16, 1861;
    July 19, 1861; August 19, 1861; September 9, 1861; October 5, 1861; October 26, 1861;
    November 21, 1861; December 24, 1861; January 4, 1862; January 8, 1862; January 9, 1862;
    February 3, 1862; February 23, 1862; April 16, 1862; April 22, 1862; May 7, 1862;
    May 12, 1862; [May 31, 1862]; August 13, 1862; August 26, 1862; September 3, 1862;
    September 22, 1862; October 1, 1862; November 24, 1862; December 6, 1862;
    December 14, 1862; December 20, 1862; January 6, [1863]; January 17, 1863;
    January 25, 1863; January 31, 1863; February 4, 1863; February 12, 1863; February 18, 1863;
    March 14, 1863; April 3, 1863; April 10, 1863; April 23, 1863; April 26, 1863; May 29, 1863;

[ca. June 27, 1863]; July 19, 1863; July 28, 1863; August 3, 1863; September 9, 1863;
October 24, 1863; December 29, 1863; December 30, 1863; January 28, 1864;
March 24, 1864; April 5, 1864; April 11, 1864; April 22, 1864; May 26, 1864; June 9, 1864;
July 31, 1864; August 12, 1864; September 17, 1864; October 11, 1864; December 31, 1864;
January 19, 1865; January 22, 1865; April 5, 1865

Maria Boyle Ewing Sherman
December 15, 1860; July 14, 1861; August 13, 1861; August 6, 1862; October 4, 1862;
December 8, 1862; February 6, 1863; March 15, 1863; April 26, 1863; June 13, 1863;
January 6, 1864; January 19, 1864; January 28, 1864; May 1, 1864; June 30, 1864;
September 18, 1864; November 9, 1864; December 25, 1864; March 24, 1865

Mary Elizabeth Hoyt Sherman
December 8, 1862; [ca. October 10, 1863]; November 9, 1864

Thomas Ewing Sherman
December 8, 1862; [ca. October 10, 1863]; April 25, 1864; November 10, 1864;
January 21, 186[5]; April 9, 1865

William T. Sherman Jr.
April 19, 1862; December 8, 1862; June 21, 1863

Charles C. Smith
October 4, 1863

John E. Smith
November 8, 1864

John A. Spooner
July 30, 1864

P. J. Stanfield, A. J. Pagett, and others
December 28, 1864

Benjamin Stanton
June 10, 1862

Edwin M. Stanton
December 16, 1862; January 25, 1863; April 23, 1864; October 25, 1864; January 2, 1865;
January 19, 1865; March 12, 1865; March 31, 1865; April 25, 1865

James B. Steedman
June 23, 1864

David Stuart
August 1, 1863

David L. Swain
April 22, 1865

John T. Swayne
November 12, 1862; June 11, 1863

Joseph Tagg
November 17, 1862

William H. H. Taylor
August 25, 1862

Alfred H. Terry
March 12, 1865

George H. Thomas
July 20, 1864; October 2, 1864; October 9, 1864; October 17, 1864; October 29, 1864;
November 11, 1864; December 25, 1864; January 21, 1865; May 2, 1865

Lorenzo Thomas
    October 22, 1861; November 6, 1861; April 12, 1864; June 26, 1864; July [23], 1864
Joseph P. Thompson
    October 21, 1864
David Tod
    March 12, 1863
Thomas Turner
    March 25, 1865
James W. Tuttle
    August 20, 1863
Lew Wallace
    August 27, 1863
Joseph D. Webster
    April 17, 1865
James Wickersham
    August 10, 1862
John M. Wright
    September 2, 1863: October 14, 1863
James E. Yeatman
    November 9, 1863

Index

Abner (horse), 488, 491, 560

Adams, Charles Francis, 702–3

Adams, Henry, 702–3

Adams, Wirt (CSA), 872, 873n

Almenay, Joseph, 267

Anderson, Charles, 28, 510, 511n

Anderson, Elizabeth Clinch, 86–87, 159, 190

Anderson, John, 28

Anderson, Larz, 28, 254, 584, 595

Anderson, Robert (USA), 20, 21n, 22, 23, 27, 31, 34, 35–36, 39, 43, 49, 50, 69, 113, 114, 131, 132, 134, 135, 140, 141, 142, 143, 145, 147, 157, 158, 161, 174, 247, 653, 840; letter from, 190n

Anderson, William, 28

Andersonville Prison (Ga.), 680–81, 685, 690

Anthony, DeWitt Clinton (USA), 280, 303, 321, 347, 557

Appler, Jesse J. (USA), 243, 245n, 650

Arkansas Post, Ark., 290, 350, 352, 353, 360, 361, 379, 381

Atkins, Smith D. (USA), 873

Atlanta Campaign, 632, 635–701 passim, 715; and evacuation of the city, 702–13 passim, 717; limited success of, 702

Audenreid, Joseph C. (USA), 632, 859

Augur, Christopher Columbus (USA), 904, 905n

Ayres, Romeyn B. (USA), 115, 116n, 117, 120

Babcock, Orville E. (USA), 617, 763, 767n, 769, 771, 772

Bache, George M. (USN), 505, 506n

Badger, George E., 862, 872

Bagley, Lieutenant (USA), 115, 116n, 124

Baker, Edward D. (USA), 41, 236

Baker, Laurence S. (CSA), 869, 870n

Baltimore, Md., riots in, 72

Banks, Mary Palmer, 606, 608n

Banks, Nathaniel P. (USA), 96, 97, 127, 135, 231, 358, 360, 362, 363, 371, 372, 377, 380, 444, 457, 460, 476, 500, 517, 582, 590, 591, 597, 605, 606, 607, 612, 614, 618, 621, 626, 634, 637, 638, 639, 640, 645, 690

Banks and banking, 16, 264–65, 336–37, 397

Barnard, Frederick A. P., 534n

Barnard, John G. (USA), 103, 104n, 119, 534, 578, 787

Barnard, Margaret McMurray, 534

Barry, Henry W. (USA), 720, 721n

Barry, William F. (USA), 682, 683n

Bartlett, William J. C., 513, 514n

Bartley, Susan Denman Sherman, 100, 101n, 454, 579

Bartley, Thomas Wells, 491, 493n

Bates, Edward, 67, 69

Baton Rouge, La., U.S. arsenal at, 35, 37, 38, 510

Beauregard, Pierre Gustave Toutant (CSA), 97, 98n, 103, 107, 115, 117, 121, 125, 126–39 passim, 191, 196, 201, 202, 207, 210, 212, 216, 217, 219, 229, 234, 242, 248, 253, 285, 399, 404, 649, 687, 748, 749, 751, 757, 758, 777, 805, 819

Beauter, Saul, 307, 308n. See also Berry, Samuel

Beckwith, Amos (USA), 827

Beebe, George M., 53, 54n

Bell, John, 6, 7n, 66

Bell, T. S., 720n; letter from, 721n

Benham, Henry W. (USA), 125, 126n

Benjamin, Judah P., 36n, 483

Benton Barracks (Mo.), 166, 171, 173, 189

Berry, Samuel, 308n. See also Beauter, Saul

Biddle, Charles J. (USA), 125, 126n

Bingham, James B., 571n, 592n, 595

Blacks, 260, 264, 274–75, 276, 280, 285, 292–93, 302–3, 320, 435, 461, 528, 573–74, 613, 620–21, 699–700, 702, 727, 740–41, 778, 794–98, 797–98, 869–70, 888–89, 897, 899–901; and nonmilitary jobs, 535, 537, 589, 621, 628, 659, 699–700; as soldiers, 586, 589, 658–59, 677–78, 719, 783, 794–95; WTS sets aside land for, 760, 801

Blair, Francis Preston, Jr. "Frank" (USA), 61, 62n, 64, 68n, 69–70, 73, 74, 76, 87, 91, 93, 95, 96, 139, 348, 363, 370, 379, 388, 392, 411, 415, 447, 458, 467, 468, 470, 472, 473, 485, 486, 487, 512, 539, 568, 570, 611, 643, 652, 789, 804, 814, 845, 850; letter from, 382–83n

Blair, Montgomery, 60, 64, 67, 68n, 93, 94n, 95, 100

Blanck, Henry (USA), 518

Boicourt, Captain (USA), 332, 333, 334–35

Booth, John Wilkes, 874

Boris, Justers A. (USA), 108, 116

Bowers, Theodore S., 903n, 904

Bowie, Alexander J., 469, 713

Bowie, Allen T., 468–69

Bowman, Samuel M. (USA), 187, 188n, 197, 203, 741; letter from, 848; writes biographical sketch of WTS, 651, 664, 667, 676, 846

Boyce, Henry, 6n, 27, 607

Boyce, Louise, 5, 6n, 26, 39, 607

Boyd, David F., 3, 9, 10n, 27, 65, 84, 606, 607; letter from, 84n

Boyer (orderly, USA), 488, 491, 560

Brady, Mathew, 579–80

Bragg, Braxton (CSA), 32, 33n, 37, 57, 68, 97, 196, 201, 210, 212, 217, 253, 270, 273, 282, 296, 304, 306, 309–10, 314n, 363, 476, 483, 510, 546, 569, 577, 649, 687, 693, 694, 695; letter from, 50n

Bramhall, Frank J., 410n

Bramlette, Thomas E., 695

Brant, Joshua, 137, 140n

Brayman, Mason (USA), 610

Breckinridge, John C. (CSA), 6, 7n, 13, 149, 202, 255, 295, 296, 306, 686, 758, 856, 863–64

Breese, K. Randolph (USN), 485, 505

Brough, John, 511

Brown, Joseph E., 703, 716, 717n, 726

Buchanan, James C., 21n, 22, 23, 27, 28, 35, 442

Buckland, Ralph P. (USA), 198, 199n, 219, 221, 254, 276, 323, 447, 524, 545, 585, 590, 767

Buckner, Simon Bolivar (CSA), 142–60 passim, 179, 180, 191, 192, 193, 219, 248, 683

Buell, Don Carlos (USA), 17, 18n, 114, 127, 168, 169, 174, 177, 178, 179, 185, 189, 200–213 passim, 219, 223, 227, 231, 252, 273, 279, 281, 282, 285, 293, 296, 301, 309, 312, 313, 314, 362, 393, 498, 529–30, 555, 561–62, 564, 611, 616, 617, 648–50, 694; replaces WTS in Kentucky, 156n, 159, 160, 163, 166, 172, 173, 175, 176, 182; WTS's opinion of, 229, 253, 312, 562

Bull Run, First Battle of, 112–30 passim, 653; performance of volunteers at, 119, 121, 124–25, 126, 135, 137, 172

Burbank, Sidney (USA), 104, 105, 139, 194, 235

Burbridge, Stephen G. (USA), 381, 383n, 386, 695

Bureau of Freedmen, Refugees, and Abandoned Lands, 899, 901

Burnside, Ambrose (USA), 104, 132, 134, 348, 362, 363, 499, 564, 567, 577

Butler, Benjamin F. (USA), 105, 106n, 107, 597, 713, 775, 798, 800, 805, 821, 832; WTS offers to replace in New Orleans, 339

Butler, Matthew C. (CSA), 885

Butterfield, Daniel (USA), 608

Byers, Samuel H. M., 824

Byrd, Robert K. (USA), 175, 180n

Calhoun, James M., 707, 728

Cameron, Simon, 60, 68n, 73, 75n, 78, 79, 80n, 86, 90, 95, 98–99, 103, 113, 132, 147, 148, 153, 154n, 157, 162, 174, 522

Campbell, Robert, 93, 94n

Canby, Edward R. S. (USA), 697, 700, 722, 723, 751, 808, 816, 817n, 851, 903

Carroll, William H. (CSA), 268

Carson, Caroline, 803n, 804n

Carson, James, 803, 804n

Carter (stablehand), 488, 502

Carter, Samuel P., 175, 180, 199

Carter, William B., 178, 180–81n

Casey, James, 21n, 89n

Cass, Lewis, 20, 21n, 22

Casserly, Eugene, 586, 587n, 718, 872; letter from, 873n
Chalmers, James R. (CSA), 557, 558n, 568
Chase, Daniel (USA), 343, 365, 417
Chase, Salmon P., 35, 36n, 41, 59, 62, 68n, 101, 102, 103, 105, 157, 278, 375n, 466, 517, 546, 760, 786, 798, 907; letters from, 148, 150n, 795n, 889n, 891n
Chattanooga, Battle of, 576–77, 631
Church, Albert E., 664, 665n
Churchill, Thomas J. (CSA), 353
City Point, Va.: WTS, USG, and Lincoln meet at, 821, 836–37
Clare, William (CSA), 728
Clark (assassin), 866, 895–96
Clark, Charles (CSA), 532, 534n
Clark, Luke (USA), 75, 76n, 395, 422, 472, 626
Clark, Powhatan, 5, 6n, 9, 26, 27, 36, 607
Clark, William T. (USA), 682, 683n
Clay (horse), 5, 18, 20, 22, 30, 36
Clay, Cassius Marcellus (USA), 311, 312n
Clay, Henry, 46
Cobb, Howell (CSA), 890, 891n
Cockerill, Joseph R. (USA), 254, 255n, 276, 626, 627, 767
Cockrill, Sterling M., 559, 561n, 585
Cohen, Solomon, 789
Colfax, Schuyler, 691–92, 718, 787
Comyn, John (USA), 625, 626n
Confiscation acts, 272, 273n, 276, 285, 293, 302–3, 325–26
Consaul, J. T. (USA), 308n
Conscription, 397–98, 697, 700, 701, 715, 719–20, 738, 743–44; laws concerning, 397, 413, 415–16, 417, 419–20, 437–38, 458–59
Coolbaugh, George (USA), 553, 585, 587
Cooper, Samuel (CSA), 67, 69n, 90n, 257n
Coppée, Henry, 651n, 664, 667
Corcoran, Michael (USA), 106, 107n
Corinth, Miss., 229, 231, 234, 235
Corse, John M. (USA), 343, 344n, 535, 553, 672, 676, 735, 737, 743, 804, 846
Cosby, George Blake (CSA), 533, 534n, 546, 553

Cotton, trade in, 788–90, 799, 801–2
Cox, Jacob D. (USA), 135, 908
Crittenden, John J., 66, 155
Crocker, Marcellus M. (USA), 611, 612n
Crook, George (USA), 897
Cullum, George W. (USA), 578, 579n
Cunningham, Nathaniel B. (USA), 332, 334–35
Curtis, Samuel R. (USA), 189, 224, 264, 273, 274–75, 280, 303, 307, 308, 316, 343, 344, 362, 363, 580

Dahlgren, John A. (USN), 763, 764, 767, 770, 772, 773, 810, 815, 841
Dahlgren, Ulric (USA), 841
Dana, Charles A., 448n, 450, 451n, 459, 461, 754
Davidson, J. L. (USA), 726
Davis, Charles H. (USA), 301, 302n
Davis, Jefferson, 63, 80, 82, 86, 97, 102, 127, 129, 149, 217, 226n, 343, 413, 457, 506, 513, 518, 532, 566–67, 597, 683, 686, 692, 715, 716, 726, 740, 742, 746, 747, 748, 749, 750–51, 767, 768, 775, 776, 777, 801, 824n, 835, 856, 861, 863, 866, 875, 884, 885, 890, 897
Davis, Jefferson C. (USA), 314, 696, 699, 730, 780, 804, 809–10
Davis, Joseph, 532, 534n
Dayton, Lewis Mulford (USA), 246, 260, 359, 445, 457, 467, 477, 501, 560, 592, 608, 632, 663, 718, 742, 762, 778, 834, 845
DeCourcey, John F. (USA), 386
Dennis, Elias S. (USA), 512, 513n
Dennison, William, Jr., 27, 29, 31, 35, 74, 75, 77, 79, 144n
Denver, James W. (USA), 228, 258, 342, 343, 418, 532
Derby, Nelson W., 310, 311n, 315
Deserters, 276, 349, 366
Dick (horse), 725
Dickey, T. Lyle (USA), 207, 208n, 218
Dix, John A. (USA), 894, 895n
Dodge, Grenville M. (USA), 574, 577, 611, 672, 676
Dolly (horse), 340, 470, 488, 491, 560, 565
Douglas, Stephen A., 6, 7n, 686

Duff, William L. (USA), 589, 590n
Duggan, James, 845, 848n, 854
Duke (horse), 491, 560, 569, 728, 853
Duncan, Johnson Kelly (CSA), 868, 869n
Dunn, William M., Jr. (USA), 763, 766, 827, 830
Du Pont, Samuel Francis (USN), 457

Early, Jubal A. (CSA), 684
Easton, Langdon C. (USA), 764, 766n, 770, 788, 827
Emancipation Proclamation, 312
Etheridge, Emerson, 200, 201n
Everett, Edward, 497, 713–14
Ewing, Charles (USA), 50, 52, 58, 61, 75, 76, 77, 79, 80, 81, 82, 89, 92, 95, 98, 103, 105, 108, 116, 139, 170, 187, 206, 340, 343, 353, 358, 359, 364, 377, 394, 395, 407, 408, 412, 417, 422, 457, 464–78 passim, 488, 490, 491, 502, 504, 509, 520, 521, 522, 554, 560, 563, 566, 585, 598, 604, 606, 623, 634, 646, 663, 666, 672, 676, 680, 685, 715, 716, 741, 753, 768, 778, 779, 783, 787, 797, 799, 834, 837, 846, 852, 854; arrives at WTS's command, 342; does not answer EES's letters, 445, 448, 728, 739, 824, 848, 854–55; expects a promotion, 625, 737, 742, 813–14, 842, 845; wants his regiment placed under WTS's command, 192, 194, 204, 209, 210, 225, 235, 238–39, 240–41n, 248–50, 261, 262, 267, 310, 319
Ewing, Henrietta Young, 20, 21n, 110, 117–18, 666
Ewing, Hugh Boyle (USA), 6n, 21, 25, 34, 48, 79, 80, 81, 110, 145, 206, 225, 235, 310, 343, 358, 359, 363, 364, 378, 394, 395, 408, 412, 417, 421, 422, 457, 467, 468, 470, 471, 490, 504, 509, 512, 521–22, 553, 554, 560, 598, 604, 623, 784, 834, 837; demands promotion, 606, 624–25, 626–27; drinking problem of, 448, 608n; wants to become a cotton broker, 678–79; wants to return to military service, 813, 814, 842, 845–46, 852
Ewing, Maria Theresa, 106, 107n, 117, 208, 210n, 261, 377, 554, 560, 573, 669

Ewing, Maria Willis Boyle, 117, 118n, 206, 208, 508, 521, 522, 604
Ewing, Mary Gillespie, 186, 659, 667, 754, 814, 834
Ewing, Philemon Beecher, 7, 21, 74, 76, 156n, 185, 191, 206, 225, 229, 289, 296, 584, 608, 609, 646, 656, 659, 660, 669; defends WTS against newspaper attacks, 172n, 223, 225, 240, 251, 254
Ewing, Thomas, Jr. (USA), 2, 3, 54n, 63–64, 67, 95, 100, 102, 103, 121, 122, 128, 633, 783, 837; letters from, 77n, 80n, 85, 310
Ewing, Thomas, Sr., 1, 2, 14n, 19, 20, 21, 33, 46, 48, 55, 61, 68, 74, 76, 117, 121, 128, 166, 168, 185, 187, 204, 206, 208, 230, 234–35, 236, 240, 249, 254, 262, 358, 464, 467, 508, 554, 556, 572–73, 580, 595, 631, 664, 667, 686, 717, 755, 784, 792, 846, 872; defends WTS, 236, 354, 755; letters from, 85n, 172n
Ewing, Thomas "Tommy" (Philemon's son), 186–87, 464, 488, 489, 509, 667, 721, 834, 855

Farragut, David G. (USN), 690, 713, 722
Fessenden, William Pitt, 63–64, 65n
Fisher, J. M. (USA), 276
Fitch, Henry S. (USA), 268, 269n, 276–77, 594
Floyd, John B. (CSA), 683
Foote, Andrew Hull (USN), 190n, 195
Foote, Henry Stuart, 597
Forrest, Nathan Bedford (CSA), 218, 546, 550n, 582, 584, 590, 610, 622, 626, 628, 629, 647, 728, 731, 732, 746, 750, 805, 807, 808, 872
Fort Donelson (Tenn.), 167, 191, 193, 196, 200, 233, 236
Fort Henry (Tenn.), 167, 190n
Fort Jackson (La.), 35, 37, 38, 40
Fort Moultrie (S.C.), 23, 28–29
Fort Pickens (Fla.), 72, 77
Fort Pike (La.), 35, 37, 38, 40
Fort Pillow (Tenn.), 628, 629
Fort St. Philip (La.), 35, 37, 38, 40
Fort Sumter (S.C.), 28–29, 34, 35–36, 59, 510
Fort Wood (La.), 40

Foster, John G. (USA), 757, 762–75 passim, 783, 790, 798, 802, 804, 805, 810, 815, 817
Fouke, Philip B. (USA), 224n
Franklin, William B. (USA), 393, 394n, 413
Fraser, William D., 780
Frémont, John C. (USA), 96, 97, 138, 144, 145, 306, 311; Frémont's Proclamation, 137–38
Fremont, Sewall L., 839, 868–69
Frost, Daniel M. (CSA), 79, 80, 81, 82
Fry, James B. (USA), 203, 204n, 648
Fugitive Slave Law, 24

Gaither, Edgar Basil, 284, 286n
Gales, Joseph, 247, 248n
Gamble, Hamilton R., 139, 140n
Gantt, Thomas Tasker, 61, 62n; letter from, 304n
Gardner, Franklin (CSA), 697
Garesche, Julius P. (USA), 127, 128n, 358
Garfield, James A. (USA), 293, 294n
Garrard, Kenner (USA), 612, 618, 654–55, 662–63, 735
Garrard, Theophilus T. (USA), 175, 180n
Geary, John W. (USA), 801, 802n
Gibson, William H. (USA), 143, 144n
Giddings, Joshua Reed, 832, 833n
Giesy, Henry H. (USA), 644
Gilbert, Charles C. (USA), 193, 216
Gillem, Alvan C. (USA), 807, 808n
Gillespie, Eliza "Sister Angela," 195, 235, 239, 261n, 282, 310, 315, 316, 341, 395, 422, 482, 721, 754, 834, 855
Gillmore, Quincy A. (USA), 457n, 597, 884
Goddard, Charles, 61, 254
Gorman, Willis A. (USA), 354, 357n
Graham, George Mason, 7n, 12, 22, 32, 39, 42, 46, 55, 607; letters from, 38n, 45n
Graham, William A., 862
Grand Review of the Armies of the United States, 858, 883, 895–97, 902, 906–7
Granger, George F. (USA), 839
Granger, Mary Reese, 61, 62n
Granger, Moses M. (USA), 61, 206, 211
Granger, Robert S. (USA), 577, 579n, 611, 625

Grant, Julia Dent, 464
Grant, Ulysses S. (USA), 103n, 167, 168, 169, 190n, 191n, 192, 197, 198, 202–12 passim, 217–29 passim, 236, 241, 242, 243, 244, 254, 263, 267, 268, 271n, 275, 277, 278n, 281, 285, 290, 296, 304, 319, 328, 332, 333, 336, 337, 338, 340–509 passim, 515, 517, 519, 520, 522, 523, 526, 531, 536, 538, 539, 541, 542, 551, 559, 560, 563–64, 565, 569, 572, 574, 575, 576, 577, 581, 597, 605, 607, 608, 609, 611, 614, 616, 619, 622, 631, 635, 636, 644–45, 646, 647–50, 660, 676, 679, 698, 700, 703, 713, 715, 735–36, 743, 752, 755, 759, 760, 775, 776, 785, 786, 787, 788, 793, 800, 809, 811, 821, 823, 825, 828–29, 836, 837, 838, 845, 847, 851, 852, 853, 857, 863, 878, 884, 885, 892, 893, 897, 902, 903, 906, 907; at Appomattox, 856, 859–60, 861, 862; assumes command as general in chief, 581, 604n; helps WTS with peace negotiations, 857, 858, 876–77, 901; letters from, 304n, 324n, 462, 469n, 559, 604n, 684, 722, 724n, 732n, 733n, 747–48, 749n, 766–67n, 774n, 817n, 823n, 828n, 851n, 860n, 877–78n, 905n; relationship with WTS, 167, 169, 232–33, 523, 542, 603–4, 784, 805–6; takes command in Tennessee, 229; takes command of Military Division of the Mississippi, 563; in Virginia, 638, 640, 646, 647, 681, 728, 849; wife visits camp, 464; WTS's opinion of, 193, 205, 229, 236, 253, 290, 341, 415, 439, 466, 498, 501, 526, 542, 564, 567, 581, 603, 610, 613
Greeley, Horace, 683
Green, William Mercer, 531–32, 534n
Grierson, Benjamin H. (USA), 322, 324n, 334, 383, 470
Grover, Cuvier (USA), 801, 802n, 804
Guthrie, James, 695n
Gwin, William (USN), 350, 351n

Hahn, Michael, 843, 844n
Halleck, Elizabeth Hamilton, 171
Halleck, Henry W. (USA), 114, 152, 153n, 156n, 159, 161–73 passim, 177, 183–97 pas-

sim, 202–21 passim, 226–27, 229, 230, 235, 237, 238–39, 247, 248–49, 250, 251, 252, 253, 254, 255, 267, 273, 276, 277, 284, 285, 287, 290, 298, 304, 311, 351, 352, 361, 362, 392, 399, 405, 419, 452, 500–501, 523, 550, 551, 581, 589, 603, 604, 608–9, 636n, 640, 654, 703, 726, 783, 842, 871; end of friendship with WTS, 858, 887, 892–907 passim; letters from, 171n, 191, 204n, 205n, 210, 211n, 212, 237, 251, 253n, 254, 256n, 281n, 306n, 523, 543, 550, 589, 608, 617, 866n, 892n, 895n, 896n; promoted to general in chief, 229, 255–56; reaction to terms of Sherman-Johnston peace agreement, 858; and transfer of Charles Ewing's regiment to WTS's command, 192, 194, 238, 239, 248–49; WTS's opinion of, 167, 193, 205, 214–15, 229, 234–35, 253, 255–56, 273, 305, 405, 581

Halstead, Murat, 443n, 451–52
Hamilton, Schuyler, 92, 104, 194n, 235
Hammond, Charles, 247, 248n
Hammond, John Henry (USA), 170, 171n, 191, 260, 261, 359, 418, 445, 477, 502, 570
Hampton, Wade (CSA), 761, 820, 851, 872, 885; letter from, 820n
Hanford, William C. (USN), 403
Hanlon, Sister Ann, 267, 305
Hanson, Roger W. (CSA), 149, 150n
Hardee, William J. (CSA), 160, 161n, 162, 180, 242, 682, 696, 698–99, 717, 762, 766, 769–70, 771, 772, 777, 782, 784, 792, 892; letter from, 769n
Hardie, James A. (USA), 578, 579n
Harker, Charles Garrison (USA), 659
Harney, William S. (USA), 87, 88n, 93, 96
Harper, James (USA), 720, 721n
Harris, Leonard (USA), 151, 152n
Harris, West (CSA), 308n
Hartshorn, Dana (USA), 206, 208n, 359
Hascall, Milo S. (USA), 196
Haskin, Joseph A. (USA), 35, 36n, 38, 483
Hatch, Edward (USA), 810
Hawkins, John P. (USA), 573, 574n, 586, 590, 719
Hawley, Joseph R. (USA), 868, 869n

Hazen, William B. (USA), 761, 763n, 805, 846
Hazzard, George Washington (USA), 151, 152n
Heintzelman, Samuel P. (USA), 115, 116n, 120, 122, 123
Herron, Francis Jay (USA), 485
Hewit, Henry S. (USA), 203, 204n, 226, 400
Hicks, Stephen G. (USA), 221, 224n, 355, 512
Hildebrand, Jesse (USA), 198, 199n, 218, 221, 467, 767
Hill, John, 110, 111n, 115, 117, 130, 364, 470, 471, 491, 502, 685, 718, 744
Hill, Joshua, 726
Hill, Thomas H., 528, 529
Hillyer, William S. (USA), 323, 324n
Hindman, Thomas C. (CSA), 160, 161n, 304, 310
Hitchcock, Ethan Allen (USA), 93, 94n, 100, 188–89, 191n, 556, 578, 792, 875; letter from, 793n
Hitchcock, Henry (USA), 94n, 828, 829n, 834, 845, 867, 869, 871
Hoffman, Emily, 635, 642n
Hoffman, William (USA), 685
Holliday, Thomas D. (USA), 201, 203n, 214, 243
Holmes, Theophilus Hunter (CSA), 304, 319
Holt, Joseph (USA), 616n
Hood, John Bell (CSA), 635, 636, 676–707 passim, 713, 715, 716, 717, 723–52 passim, 759, 762, 763, 766, 769, 774, 776, 779, 782, 791, 805, 815–16, 817; letters from, 707n, 710n, 711n, 769n
Hooker, Joseph (USA), 407, 408n, 423, 455, 474, 500, 564, 611, 631, 639, 673; WTS's opinion of, 452, 676, 681, 700
Hosea, Louis M. (USA), 886
Hovey, Alvin P. (USA), 256, 257n, 323, 329, 338, 674
Howard, Oliver O. (USA), 611, 612n, 670, 672, 673, 675, 676, 695, 699, 730, 770, 804, 816, 826, 827, 860–61, 894; WTS's opinion of, 676, 681, 700, 814
Howe, James H. (USA), 322

Hoyt, Alfred, 566, 606
Hoyt, Charles, 186n
Hoyt, Samuel, 800
Hudson, Peter T. (USA), 815, 817n
Hunter, David (USA), 106, 107n, 115, 122, 123, 127, 306, 311, 457
Hunter, John, 52, 76, 77, 79, 80, 81
Hunter, Tom, 103, 104n
Hunton, Thomas, 286n
Hurlbut, Stephen A. (USA), 196, 207, 222–23, 225, 241, 242, 243, 245, 249, 251, 273, 276, 294, 310, 346, 406, 421, 448n, 479–80, 568, 569, 573, 585, 593, 610, 611, 626, 649–50

Irvin, William, 284, 286n
Isham, Warren P., 279, 280n
Iverson, Alfred (CSA), 758

Jackson, Claiborne F., 69, 70, 71n, 82, 87
Jackson, James S. (USA), 146
Jackson, Thomas Jonathan "Stonewall" (CSA), 232n, 346n
Jackson, William H. (CSA), 249, 251, 279, 280n, 514, 546, 553
Jackson, Miss., 471, 498–515 passim
Jarreau, Benjamin, 22, 23n, 27, 66
Jefferson Barracks (Mo.), 90, 94
Jenney, William LeBaron (USA), 575, 576n
Johnson, Andrew, 132, 133n, 134, 162, 175, 184, 200, 591, 595, 857, 863, 872, 878, 906, 907
Johnson, Bushrod Rust (CSA), 868, 869n
Johnson, J. Neely, 21n
Johnson, Mary Mackall Bowie, 469
Johnson, Reverdy, 469, 556
Johnson, Richard W. (USA), 146
Johnston, Albert Sidney (CSA), 142n, 148, 149, 150n, 160, 168, 179, 191, 192, 200, 202, 219, 247
Johnston, Joseph Eggleston (CSA), 97, 98n, 115, 125, 193, 399, 404, 472, 476, 479, 484, 489–507 passim, 513, 532, 553, 588, 605, 617, 618, 622, 625, 635–76 passim, 705, 726, 821, 824, 826, 830, 835, 836, 837, 841, 842, 850–62 passim, 884, 885, 886, 893,

903; letter from, 862n; negotiates peace agreement with WTS, 856–57, 861–68, 869–70, 874–76, 878, 879–80, 881; returned to command, 824
Jones, Wells S. (USA), 650, 651n

Kearny, Philip (USA), 447, 448n, 450
Keating, John, 22
Keeler, William B. (USA), 518
Kelley, Abby, 727
Kentucky, 113, 114, 131–66 passim, 171, 174–85, 187
Keyes, Erasmus D. (USA), 115, 116n, 122, 123
Kilburn, Charles Lawrence (USA), 792, 793n
Kilpatrick, Hugh Judson (USA), 698, 764, 765, 766n, 772, 783, 818, 827
King, Rufus (USA), 247, 248n
King, Susan Petigru, 802, 803n
Klein, George, 491, 495
Klein, Mr., 491, 495
Klein, Mrs., 491, 495, 607
Knox, Thomas W., 370, 371, 378, 381–82, 386–89, 396, 435, 438, 441, 442; letters from, 390n, 440–41n

Lagow, Clark B. (USA), 323, 324n
Lane, James Henry, 540, 541n
Lange, Father, 604, 608n
Lauman, Jacob G. (USA), 276, 278n, 342, 343, 418, 484
Lay, George W. (CSA), 84
Lee, Albert Lindley (USA), 447, 448n
Lee, John, 117
Lee, Robert E. (CSA), 110, 111n, 452, 507, 518n, 520, 546, 582, 597, 622, 647, 659, 686, 695, 724, 728, 751, 762, 768, 774, 776, 805, 815, 817, 821, 823n, 824, 825, 830, 835, 836, 841, 847, 849, 850, 853, 857; surrender of, 856, 859, 861, 862, 876, 886
Lee, Stephen Dill (CSA), 546, 550n, 553, 699
Leggett, Mortimer D. (USA), 611, 612n, 845
L'Hommedieu, S. S., 248n, 254, 584, 595
Lightburn, Joseph Andrew Jackson (USA), 512, 513n
Lincoln, Abraham, 3, 6, 7n, 8, 14, 15–16n, 16,

31, 44, 56–77 passim, 83, 86, 88, 96, 97,
100, 102, 103, 109n, 112, 121, 131, 132, 134,
136, 137, 150, 157, 171, 180, 188n, 199, 200,
210, 212, 216, 231, 261n, 266, 272, 289, 290,
291, 292, 293, 306n, 307, 311, 312, 336, 345,
348, 350, 354, 362, 364, 369, 372, 375, 378,
405, 411, 414, 416, 419, 420, 435, 437, 438,
440, 441, 442, 443, 445, 450, 452, 457, 458,
463, 474, 475, 482, 501, 511n, 517, 566, 567,
579, 580, 611, 619, 627, 653, 701, 702, 708,
715, 716, 724, 742, 743, 759, 777, 778, 782,
785, 796, 842, 844, 847, 876, 881; assassination of, 857, 863, 866, 867, 874–75; letters from, 668n, 674, 686–87, 699, 793–
94n; WTS's opinion of, 59, 69, 77, 91, 217,
733–34, 821
Lindsey, Daniel W. (USA), 353
Logan, John A. (USA), 415, 573, 611, 625,
626, 673, 675, 676, 793, 845, 858, 899
Long, Eli (USA), 575, 576n
Longstreet, James (CSA), 577, 579n, 611
Loomis, Cyrus O. (USA), 626, 627
Loudon, D. W. C. (USA), 385, 386n
Lovejoy, Owen, 112, 683
Lovell, Mansfield (CSA), 227, 228n
Low, Frederick F., 831
Lucas, James H., 40, 68, 99, 117, 138, 145, 170,
187
Lynch, Ellen, 669
Lyon, Nathaniel (USA), 79, 81n, 87, 91, 93,
96, 139

McArthur, John (USA), 209, 210n, 497, 648
McClellan, George (USA), 75, 88, 98, 105,
108, 113–14, 115, 125–39 passim, 144, 145,
156n, 158, 174, 176, 177, 182, 193, 199, 204,
211, 226, 227, 231, 246, 248, 251, 253n, 285,
287, 290, 292, 298, 305, 311, 312, 348, 393,
405, 458, 555, 564, 715, 733, 743; letter
from, 743; runs for the presidency, 701,
733–34, 742; WTS's opinion of, 74, 77, 79,
88, 193, 204, 305, 312, 452, 742–43
McClernand, John A. (USA), 196, 200, 207,
209, 213, 215, 217, 220, 222, 227, 233, 237,
242, 244, 252, 279, 290, 337, 350–64 passim, 370, 371, 372, 375, 377, 379, 392, 393,

395, 400, 406, 415, 417, 421, 435, 436, 439,
440, 453, 460, 465, 471, 478–79, 485–87,
499, 501, 582, 650; relieved of command,
487n, 494–95; supersedes WTS in Vicks-
burg campaign, 350, 362, 363–64; WTS's
opinion of, 253, 359, 415, 456–57, 465,
472, 473, 501
McComb, Amelia Sherman, 100, 101n
McComb, Robert, 100, 101n
McCook, Alexander (USA), 146, 147, 148n,
155, 178, 198, 209, 219, 255, 670
McCook, Daniel (USA), 53, 54n, 88, 89, 92,
98, 106, 659
McCook, Edward Moody (USA), 680, 681n
McCoy, James C. (USA), 196, 197n, 201, 358,
418, 491, 632, 837
McCracken, John, 261
McCullagh, Joseph B., 586, 587n, 679
McDowell, Helen Burden, 128
McDowell, Irvin (USA), 60, 80n, 88, 91,
103–4, 106, 108, 112–28 passim, 137, 211,
295, 306, 341, 399, 404, 413, 653
McDowell, John A. (USA), 198, 199n, 219,
267, 323, 341–42, 355, 418
McDowell, Malcolm (USA), 195, 355
Macfeely, Robert (USA), 405, 406–7n, 594
McLane, Louis, Jr., 641, 642n
McLane, Sophie Hoffman, 641, 642n
McLaws, Lafayette (CSA), 792, 793n
McLean, John, 17
McLean, Nathaniel H. (USA), 203n
McMillan, Charles (USA), 359n, 382, 400
McPherson, James Birdseye, 341, 406, 415,
460, 486, 500, 506, 509, 512, 515, 522, 523,
539, 541, 542, 551, 569, 573, 585, 587, 588,
589, 593, 602, 603, 605, 608, 609, 611, 617,
618, 631, 632, 634, 636, 639, 645, 646, 654,
659, 667, 675, 679; death of, 635, 670–71,
672, 676, 681, 682–83, 868; engagement to
Emily Hoffman, 635, 641–42, 682–83;
WTS's opinion of, 415, 439, 472, 672
McPherson, William, 76, 77n, 79; letter
from, 833n
McQuesten, James F. (USA), 110, 111n, 115
Magoffin, Beriah, 149, 150n
Magrath, Andrew G., 835, 836n

Magruder, John B. (CSA), 590

Mahan, Dennis Hart, 513, 514n, 550, 786, 792; letters from, 543n, 550, 787n

March through the Carolinas, 760, 765, 773–74, 798–99, 821–28, 831, 833–34, 836–37, 842–43; plans for, 775–77, 804–6, 807–9, 813, 814, 815–16

March to the Sea, 759–61, 762, 764, 767; plans for, 703, 722–23, 728–58 passim, 809–10

Markland, Absalom H. (USA), 379, 380n, 389, 777

Martin, Daniel, 686–89, 717–18; letter from, 689n

Mason, John S. (USA), 312, 313n

Mason, Rodney (USA), 221, 222, 223, 224n, 225

Maynard, Horace, 132, 133n, 134, 162, 175, 180, 184, 200

Meade, George G. (USA), 518n, 858, 871, 898

Meagher, Thomas (USA), 137, 138n

Meigs, Montgomery (USA), 99, 100, 102, 452, 576, 783–84

Memminger, Christopher G., 835, 836n

Memphis, Tenn., 229–30, 251, 255–88 passim, 328, 376–77, 480

Meridian Campaign, 581, 585–608 passim

Meriwether, Elizabeth Avery, 277, 278n, 346–47

Merritt, Wesley (USA), 897

Miles, Dixon S. (USA), 115, 116n, 120

Miller, Gertrude, 25, 26n

Miller, Joe, 4, 5, 6n, 7, 25, 46, 47, 84

Miller, Silas P., 227, 228n, 608

Mitchel, Ormsby M. (USA), 157, 219, 252

Moore, Marshall F. (USA), 211, 725, 729, 737

Moore, Thomas O., 10, 11, 22, 23, 24, 26, 32, 37, 38, 39, 44–53 passim, 57, 687, 693; letters from, 48–49, 50n, 51, 53, 482–83; orders seizure of federal military property, 37–39, 40, 42–46, 52, 53, 482–83, 510, 693; WTS suggests trying for treason, 483

Morgan, George W. (USA), 295, 296, 301, 342, 345, 346n, 384–85, 386, 731

Morgan, John Hunt (CSA), 322, 507n, 509, 512, 520, 546, 647

Morton, Charles A. (USA), 405, 407n

Morton, Oliver P., 138, 140, 146, 225

Moss, Samuel, Jr., 713

Moulton, Charles W. (USA), 109, 606, 619, 679

Moulton, Frances Beecher Sherman, 109n, 449, 451n, 454

Mower, Joseph Anthony (USA), 487, 634, 645, 684, 737, 743, 745, 746, 805

Muldrough's Hill (Ky.), 141, 143, 145, 147, 309

Mungen, William (USA), 242, 251, 342

Myers, Abraham C. (CSA), 68, 69n

Myers, Frederick (USA), 119

Myers, John B. (USA), 241, 242

Negley, James S. (USA), 151, 152n

Nelson, Thomas A. R., 726

Nelson, William (USA), 143, 144n, 151, 156, 157, 161, 178, 198, 223, 314

Newell, Cicero (USA), 322

Newspapers and reporters, 216, 221, 229, 230, 233, 236–37, 240, 247–48, 257–58, 279, 283, 287, 357, 378, 379–81, 395–96, 411–12, 413, 438–39, 445–46, 451, 465, 467, 568, 754, 814; and Shiloh, 206–8, 211–12, 216, 244–45. *See also* Knox, Thomas W.

Newton, John (USA), 611, 612n, 731

Ord, Edward O. C. (USA), 284, 286n, 484, 496, 497, 499, 512, 515, 875, 897; letter from, 514n

Osterhaus, Peter J. (USA), 81n, 494, 495n, 568, 674

Otey, James Hervey, 467, 468n

Paducah, Ky., 191–97

Palmer, John M. (USA), 611, 612n, 617

Palmer, Joseph C., 138, 140n

Park, John, 259n

Parke, John B. (USA), 484, 485n, 496, 497, 499

Patterson, Coos, 103, 117

Patterson, H. J., 170, 187

Patterson, Mrs. H. J., 109, 111n

Patterson, Robert (USA), 99–100n, 100,

104, 105, 107, 115, 125, 215; letters from, 216n, 219, 506
Pearce, James, 528
Peck, Harry W. (USA), 115, 116n
Pemberton, John C. (CSA), 290, 333n, 334, 335, 338, 363, 532; letter from, 333–34n
Penham, Calhoun, 713
Petigru, James Louis, 802, 803n
Phelps, Seth L. (USN), 301, 302n
Pillow, Gideon J. (CSA), 179, 180, 181n, 277, 871
Piper, Alexander (USA), 110, 111n, 115
Pitzman, Julius (USA), 477, 569
Poe, Orlando M. (USA), 630, 721, 765
Polk, Leonidas (CSA), 179, 181n, 194, 588, 605
Pope, John (USA), 97, 98n, 164, 165, 169, 170, 209, 213, 221, 227, 231, 234, 238, 295, 306, 380, 403, 422, 457, 465, 503; WTS's opinion of, 253
Porter, David Dixon (USN), 329, 344, 350, 505, 585, 589, 590, 605, 815, 821, 841
Porter, Fitz John (USA), 104, 393, 564
Porter, Horace (USA), 722, 724, 732
Prentice, George D., 238n
Prentiss, Benjamin M. (USA), 169, 207, 208n, 209, 215, 216, 219, 220, 221, 222, 223, 241, 242, 243–44, 311, 650
Preston, William (CSA), 149, 150n
Price, Sterling (CSA), 93, 94n, 170, 174, 177, 184, 185, 189, 279, 306, 338, 590, 715, 723, 734
Prime, Frederick E. (USA), 102, 103, 119, 140, 145, 155, 156n, 227, 235, 309, 377, 456
Proclamation of Amnesty and Reconstruction, 578
Purcell, Edward, 729
Purcell, John B., 729

Quinby, Isaac F. (USA), 115, 116n

Randolph, Tenn., 306–7, 347
Rankin, James L., 284, 286n, 780
Rawlins, John A. (USA), 210n, 220n, 271n, 272n, 278n, 296n, 334n, 617, 747–48n
Rawson, E. E., 707

Reeder, Andrew H., 91, 92n, 96, 97
Rees, David, 800
Reese, Doly, 61, 62n
Reese, Henry, 93, 94n, 110, 291, 449, 454, 606
Reese, Mary, 450, 451n
Reese, Mary Elizabeth Sherman "Elizabeth," 62n, 93, 94n, 100, 291, 304–5, 310, 345, 449–50, 454, 474
Reese, Rose, 449, 451n, 566
Reid, Hugh Thompson, 607, 608n
Reid, Whitelaw, 204n
Reynolds, John F. (USA), 868
Reynolds, Thomas C., 69, 71n
Rice, Americus V. (USA), 251, 253n, 659
Richardson, Israel B. (USA), 115, 116n, 120
Ridgely, Randolph, 780
Rives, William C., 66
Roddey, Philip D. (CSA), 746
Roler, Edwin O. F., 558, 559, 561n
Rose, William A. (USA), 842, 848, 849
Rosecrans, William S. (USA), 127, 128n, 135, 136, 348, 358, 362, 363, 365, 423, 455, 474, 689–90; WTS's opinion of, 452–53, 476, 500, 564, 565, 567, 569, 689–90, 715, 746
Roswell, Ga., 662–63
Rousseau, Lovell H. (USA), 141, 142n, 668

St. Ange, E. Berte, 5, 6n, 9, 27, 56, 65
St. Louis, Mo., riots in, 79–82, 91
Sam (horse), 488, 491, 560
Sanger, William D. "Dan" (USA), 196, 220, 222, 244, 261, 262–63, 389, 477, 585
Savannah, Ga., 759, 760, 762–74, 778, 782–83
Sawyer, Roswell M. (USA), 570, 602n, 620, 632, 853, 902
Saxton, Rufus, Jr. (USA), 762, 763n, 764
Schenck, Robert C. (USA), 108, 109n, 115, 122, 123
Schleich, Newton (USA), 75, 76n, 96
Schoepf, Albin F. (USA), 150, 152n, 181
Schofield, John M. (USA), 323, 324n, 605, 611, 616, 617, 618, 632, 634, 635, 639, 654, 667, 670, 676, 695, 699, 730, 745–46, 750, 758, 759, 779, 815, 817, 821, 823, 826, 827, 828, 837, 842, 852, 864, 867, 872, 879–80,

883, 885, 903; letter from, 887; WTS's
opinion of, 700
Scott, Winfield (USA), 35, 36n, 43, 60, 68n,
91, 92, 97–98, 102, 103, 104, 105, 110, 132
Secession, 5–111 passim
Selfridge, Thomas O. (USN), 505, 506n
Selover, Abia A., 138, 140n
Seward, Frederick, 874
Seward, William Henry, 24, 35, 36n, 121, 373,
375n, 517, 874
Seymore, Jane, 375–77
Seymour, Truman (USA), 608, 609n
Shelby, Joseph O. (CSA), 723
Shepherd, Oliver L. (USA), 101
Shepley, George F. (USA), 889, 891n
Sheridan, Philip H. (USA), 684, 703, 728,
743, 752–53, 788, 823n, 827, 851, 858, 860,
861, 863, 871
Sherman, Charles (father), 1, 579–80, 651
Sherman, Charles Celestine (son), 635, 646,
647n, 656, 659, 661, 669, 680, 729, 744,
754, 755, 779; death of, 760, 784–85, 787,
791, 807
Sherman, Charles T. (brother), 61, 62n, 91,
92, 100, 101–2, 114, 254, 304, 346n, 454,
515, 576
Sherman, Eleanor Mary "Elly" (daughter),
18–19, 36, 107, 184, 263, 310, 315, 407, 482,
488, 630, 721, 744, 754, 854, 867; visits
WTS in camp, 535, 539
Sherman, Ellen Ewing (wife), 2, 14, 17, 18–
19, 27, 35, 41, 64, 67, 68, 69, 81, 92, 95, 96,
97, 98, 101, 113, 114, 118, 121, 130, 137, 166,
171, 186, 190, 194, 201, 205, 206, 212, 218,
238, 239, 249, 251, 261, 262, 273, 291, 294,
301, 314, 316, 319, 320, 337, 340, 345, 349,
354, 395, 398, 414, 421, 423, 449–50, 464,
474n, 482, 488, 507, 509, 516, 519–20, 521,
523–24, 535, 539, 579, 580, 609, 610, 630,
635, 652, 661, 712, 713, 716, 755–56, 779,
806, 807, 808, 809, 811, 812, 834, 842, 852,
854; comments on the press, 393, 394n,
411, 625; letters from, 12, 22n, 23n, 39n,
47, 48n, 55–56, 148n, 156n, 186n, 188n,
192, 194, 199, 204–5, 239–40, 261n, 292n,
304, 306n, 344n, 365n, 394n, 403n, 407,
408n, 412n, 469, 478, 521n, 558, 561n, 565,
604, 607n, 608n, 627n, 656, 672n, 681n,
718n, 738n, 744n, 829–30n; relationship
with WTS, 187–88, 191–92, 196, 202, 273,
464–65, 585, 606, 685; told to remain in
Lancaster, Ohio, 126, 133, 140, 147, 148,
166, 185, 186, 343; visits WTS in camp,
319–20, 340, 515–16, 517, 519–20, 521, 535,
539; worries about WTS's mental health,
156n, 171n, 186n
Sherman, Francis C., 871, 873n
Sherman, Francis T. (USA), 606
Sherman, Henry S. (nephew), 345, 346n,
353, 375, 421, 450, 495, 504, 515, 560
Sherman, Hoyt (brother), 450, 451n
Sherman, James (brother), 450, 451n, 677
Sherman, John (brother), 2, 15n, 33, 39, 49,
55, 66, 75, 92, 98, 103, 106, 107, 108, 110,
116, 117, 118, 121, 128, 129, 130, 131, 133, 147,
156n, 166, 167, 185, 187, 188n, 202, 254,
289, 303, 304, 305, 344n, 381, 452, 454, 522,
586, 635, 652, 691, 784, 838, 839, 846–47,
848, 853, 885; defends WTS against newspaper attacks, 152n, 217; elected U.S. Senator, 61, 62–63; helps WTS find a job, 59,
63–64, 77, 91, 92–93, 95; letters from, 17n,
26n, 29n, 68n, 71n, 82, 144n, 186n, 193n,
294n, 337–38n, 375n, 419, 421n, 474n,
518n, 567n, 620n, 629n, 680n, 719n, 787n,
800n; serves in military, 99–101
Sherman, Margaret Cecilia Stewart (sister-
in-law), 29, 100, 193, 216, 220, 292, 567,
597, 610, 800
Sherman, Maria Boyle Ewing "Minnie"
(daughter), 2, 4, 10, 12n, 19n, 24, 25, 36,
55, 57, 65, 116, 129, 135, 185, 206, 230, 240,
263, 310, 358, 378, 407, 422, 467, 478, 493,
560, 561, 566, 570, 594, 631, 634, 664, 669,
671, 676, 716, 717, 744, 754, 784, 785, 828,
838, 847, 854, 855, 867, 872; visits WTS in
camp, 535, 539
Sherman, Mary (niece), 193
Sherman, Mary Elizabeth "Lizzie" (daughter), 2, 18–19, 25, 36, 39, 55, 65, 110, 130,
184, 185, 187–88, 206, 240, 263, 282, 310,
315, 454, 464, 478, 482, 488, 493, 504, 560,

561, 566, 572, 581, 585, 594, 630, 633, 634,
661–62, 664, 669, 676, 713, 716, 721, 744,
754, 779, 784, 824, 829, 834, 838, 847, 854,
855, 867, 872; visits WTS in camp, 535, 539
Sherman, Mary Hoyt (mother), 1, 580, 651
Sherman, Rachel Ewing (daughter), 114,
116n, 130, 310, 630, 744, 754, 854, 867;
visits WTS in camp, 535, 539
Sherman, Thomas E. "Tommy" (son), 2,
18–19, 25, 36, 57, 130, 205, 209, 240, 263,
319, 340, 343, 344, 407, 454, 464, 468, 482,
489, 493, 560, 561, 570, 572, 584–85, 594,
605, 657, 664, 669, 717, 744, 792, 799, 847,
854, 867; visits WTS in camp, 535, 539
Sherman, Thomas W. (USA), 115, 133, 134n
Sherman, William T.
—autobiography of, 651–54
—comments on Vicksburg campaign, 406,
414–15, 420, 435–34, 439, 444, 446, 452–
53, 459–62, 520
—complains about lack of support for the
war in the North, 372–74, 413–14, 416–17,
447, 613
—concerned about his historical reputation, 154–55, 636, 647–54, 665, 667, 755,
791–92, 798, 810–11, 828, 846, 859
—and death of James McPherson, 635, 670–
71, 672, 676, 681, 682–83
—and death of Willy, 498–99, 551–68 passim, 646, 756
—fears Confederate Army will break up
into guerrilla bands, 871–72, 883–84, 886
—fights Stanton's allegations about his fitness to command, 880–82, 884–85
—financial difficulties of, 2, 21–22, 25, 31, 32,
33, 67–68, 145
—gives credit to USG for successes at
Vicksburg, 472, 473, 477
—health of, 140, 145, 147, 246, 457, 753–54,
786
—in Louisiana, 1–58 passim
—mental health of, 114, 142–65 passim,
171n, 173–74, 217
—military career: appointed colonel of
Thirteenth U.S. Infantry, 88–104 passim;
asks to be relieved of command in Ken-

tucky, 156n, 158, 159, 163; commissioned
brigadier general of regular army, 522,
523; considers rejoining the army, 40–59
passim; contemplates resignation, 413,
419, 579, 593; despondency over performance, 121–22, 173–75, 179, 183, 185; negotiates peace agreement with Joseph E.
Johnston, 856–58, 861–68, 869–70, 874–
76, 879–80, 886, 902–3; offers services to
secretary of war, 78–79, 82, 86; promoted
to brigadier general of volunteers, 112,
126, 127, 131; promoted to major general
of volunteers, 226, 228n; receives field
command after Kentucky debacle, 168;
refuses to consider commission to the
rank of lieutenant general, 800, 805–6,
809, 811; replaces USG as commander of
Military Division of the Mississippi, 581–
82; success as occupation commander of
Memphis, 339, 343, 376–77; takes command of Army of the Tennessee, 499
—offers to replace Benjamin Butler in New
Orleans, 339
—and the press, 161, 165, 166, 171, 203–4,
206–8, 212, 217, 221, 229, 230, 233, 236–37,
240, 241, 247–48, 257–58, 279, 283, 287,
337, 357, 370, 378, 381–82, 386–92, 395–97,
398–403, 404–5, 408–9, 411–12, 413, 415,
418, 420, 423, 438–39, 441, 442–43, 467,
517, 568, 570–71, 643, 729, 814
—refuses to act against U.S. interests, 24–
58, 71
—relationship with USG, 167, 169, 232–33,
523, 542, 603–4, 784, 805–6
—relationship with wife, 12, 25, 31, 55, 117,
119, 154–55, 173, 187–88, 191–92, 196, 202,
464–65, 585, 606, 685; asks her to remain
in Lancaster, Ohio, 126, 133, 140, 147, 148,
185, 343
—resigns from Louisiana State Seminary of
Learning and Military Academy, 41–46,
687
—in St. Louis, 51, 52, 53, 55, 58, 61, 65, 89
—seeks new job after Louisiana, 17, 28, 37,
39, 40, 46, 47–48, 52, 55, 75
—views on: abolition, 91; blacks, 292–93,

320, 528, 573–74, 613, 620–21, 628, 677–78, 688, 699–700, 727, 740–41, 760, 778, 794–98, 832–33, 888–89, 899–901; black soldiers, 454, 461, 582, 586, 589, 657–58, 700, 783, 794–95; Catholicism, 117, 267, 314; conduct of the war, 87–88, 90, 108, 166; Confederate troop strength, 145, 153, 164, 223, 232, 234, 249, 252–53; confiscation of rebel property, 279–80; consolidation of regiments, 455–56, 458–59, 462, 463, 474–76; Copperheads, 510, 720; death penalty for court-martials, 615–16; democracy, 126, 239, 293–94, 295, 480, 512; depredations by troops, 145, 153–54, 249, 253, 262, 283–84, 289, 298–300, 305, 316–17, 328, 367, 369, 373, 376, 468–69, 518–19, 528–29, 531–32, 540, 694; destructive war, 230, 261, 262, 289, 492–93, 498, 525, 551, 582, 629, 697, 702, 703, 736, 759–60, 761, 778; duration and severity of the war, 117, 126, 140, 202, 224, 246, 249, 251, 255, 273, 297, 311, 352, 377, 397–98, 404, 407, 619; eastern theater of the war, 500; elections, 564, 566, 593, 691–92, 733–34; elective office, 715, 716, 738, 809, 833; enlistment, 133, 136, 137, 140, 147; establishing civil governments in occupied territory, 324–27, 331–32; Federal troop numbers and strength, 217–18, 220, 225, 233, 249–50, 253, 266, 272, 309, 312, 336, 345, 363, 368, 540, 548–49, 614, 697, 743; foragers, 818–20; guerrillas, 229, 231, 269, 281, 283–84, 305, 306–8, 315–19, 320, 321–22, 332–35, 346–47, 753; importance of the West and the western theater in the war, 37–38, 72, 84, 96, 126, 136, 149, 189, 194, 231, 240, 255–56, 328–29, 533, 544, 608–9; inevitability of war, 44–45, 83–84, 312; loyalty oaths, 268–69, 276–77; making room for civilian personnel on military transportation, 623–24, 627–28, 689–90, 739–40; military preparedness of the North, 160, 289; the nature of the war, 38, 180, 183, 202, 208–9, 302, 571, 582, 641–42, 687–88, 693–95, 697, 706–9; need for secrecy about military move-

ments, 107, 605, 608, 638, 643, 662, 754; the North, 16, 63, 180, 207–8, 230, 517; political appointments, 59–104 passim; politicians, 230, 241, 652, 686–88, 905–6; politics and the war effort, 66, 113, 435, 460; prisoner exchange, 709–10; railroads and war, 172–73, 180, 250, 827; reconstruction of the Union, 514–15, 536–50 passim, 555–56, 582, 591, 595–96, 598–602, 645, 889–90; repopulation of the South by Northerners, 183, 263, 272–73, 289; return of sick and wounded soldiers to home front, 225, 282, 288, 291–92; rule of law, 24, 26, 29–30, 31, 32, 33, 54, 75, 235, 239, 258–59, 288, 293, 297, 303, 324–27, 337, 380–81, 480, 516, 534, 540–41, 654, 694, 832–33, 905–6; secession, 3–111 passim, 117, 239, 284–86, 544, 592–93, 598–602, 641–42, 652–53, 686–88, 694–95, 840, 843–44, 868; slavery, 3, 8, 11, 16, 63, 65–66, 74, 91, 126, 229, 260, 264, 280, 285, 289, 292–93, 326, 517, 591, 755, 844; the South, 16, 63, 86, 190, 203, 544–46; South Carolina, 761, 771, 776–77, 798; Southern hatred of the North, 193, 196, 198, 230, 231, 246, 250, 260–61, 262, 263, 269, 287–88, 297, 309, 319, 373, 525, 558, 851–52; Southern seizure of Federal property, 37–39, 40, 42–46, 50, 53, 510, 592, 694–95; Southern support of the war effort, 166, 172, 179–80, 186, 187, 266, 311, 313, 352, 373, 375, 439, 620, 813, 816–17; speculators, 230, 260, 266, 269–70, 278, 279, 288, 329–30, 345; state recruiting agents, 668, 677–78, 703, 712, 719, 797; stragglers, 197, 300; substitutes, 727; trade with Confederacy, 230, 260, 269–72, 277, 278, 281, 283, 295, 313, 322–23, 678–79, 801; the Union, 60, 61, 190, 714; volunteer soldiers, 60, 70, 76, 89, 112, 119–37 passim, 141, 142, 166, 174, 210, 362–63
—worries about EES's health, 635, 656–69 passim
Sherman, William T., Jr. "Willy" (son), 2, 18–19, 25, 36, 39, 57, 65, 79–82, 110–11, 117, 129, 130, 133, 135, 148, 185, 188, 202, 208,

209, 240, 263, 315, 359, 378, 395, 422, 464, 467, 478, 481, 482, 493, 504, 598, 657, 661, 760, 785, 792, 847; death of, 498–99, 551–68 passim, 594, 604–5, 635, 646, 736–37, 754, 756, 760, 785, 791; visits father in camp, 535, 539

Shiloh, Battle of, 168, 169, 201–28 passim, 241–45, 636, 647–50; and newspaper reporters, 169, 206–8, 211–12, 216, 237, 241, 244–45

Ship Island (Miss.), 87–88, 93

Shiras, Alexander E. (USA), 17, 18n, 145; letter from, 146n

Sibley, Caleb (USA), 100, 101n

Sickles, Daniel E. (USA), 447, 448n, 450

Sill, Joshua W. (USA), 151, 152n

Sixty-Ninth New York Volunteer Infantry, 115, 137

Slaves, 229, 260, 264, 274–75, 285, 292–93, 302–3, 325–27, 502, 591. *See also* Blacks

Slidell, John, 36n, 483, 890

Slocum, Henry W. (USA), 611, 612n, 621, 730, 761, 765, 770–71, 780, 796, 804, 809, 810, 814, 816, 826, 827, 898

Smith, Andrew J. (USA), 342, 345, 346n, 379, 381, 384, 386, 605, 611, 612, 617, 618, 621, 645, 647, 715, 745, 746, 748, 758

Smith, Charles C. (USA), 353, 554, 560

Smith, Charles F. (USA), 168, 191, 196, 197, 355, 649–50

Smith, Edmund Kirby (CSA), 295, 296, 301, 308, 309, 322, 626, 907

Smith, Francis W., 9–10, 26, 27, 48, 51, 52, 65

Smith, Frederick W., 264, 265n

Smith, Giles A. (USA), 364, 365n, 456, 487

Smith, Gustavus W. (CSA), 142, 777, 784, 792

Smith, J. Condit (USA), 509, 510n, 585

Smith, John E. (USA), 804

Smith, Martin L. (CSA), 310, 311n, 495

Smith, Morgan L. (USA), 228, 258, 276, 342, 345, 350, 351, 358, 364, 376, 378, 379, 568

Smith, Persifor F., 452, 652

Smith, S. A., 12, 13, 15, 26, 29, 30, 32, 33, 37, 38–39, 40, 42–44, 48, 49, 54, 56, 57, 65, 84, 607; letters from, 49, 50n, 56

Smith, Thomas Kilby (USA), 222, 224n, 242, 254, 393–94, 417, 456

Smith, William Sooy (USA), 589, 590, 591n, 630–31; WTS's opinion of, 605

Speculators, 260, 269–70, 278, 279, 319, 329–30

Speed, Fry (USA), 152n

Spiegel, Marcus M. (USA), 515, 518n

Spooner, John A., 703

Stambaugh, Susan, 659

Stanbery, Henry, 595, 597n

Stanley, David S. (USA), 655, 699, 730, 746, 750, 758

Stanton, Benjamin, 225, 226n, 230, 240, 246, 251, 254–55, 305, 354, 559; letters from, 241–42, 245n, 251, 354

Stanton, Edwin M., 204n, 205, 211n, 347, 348, 375n, 419, 457, 527n, 576, 662, 669, 699, 700, 701, 760, 786, 794, 795–96, 797–98, 805, 823, 842, 847, 889; and end of friendly relations with WTS, 884–97 passim, 901, 903, 904, 906–7; letters from, 790n, 839n; objects to terms of Sherman-Johnston peace agreement, 857–58, 878; releases documents to the press, 857–58, 880–82

Stanton, Sidney S. (CSA), 162, 165n

Steedman, James B. (USA), 150, 152n, 710, 752

Steele, Clement F. (USA), 573

Steele, Frederick (USA), 304, 310, 323, 350, 379, 381, 383–84, 388, 392, 415, 447, 467, 468, 491, 494, 497, 512, 541, 589, 590, 612, 621

Stephens, Alexander, 714, 716

Stevens, Isaac I. (USA), 284, 286n

Stewart, Warren (USA), 364, 365n

Stone, Charles P. (USA), 205n, 225–26, 606, 634

Stoneman, George (USA), 125, 126n, 611–12, 617–18, 654–55, 668, 670, 680–81, 685, 690, 807, 823, 851, 861, 866, 881, 885, 893, 896

Strong, William E. (USA), 899

Stuart, David (USA), 198, 199n, 221, 222, 242, 276, 323, 350, 364, 379, 381, 421, 422, 447, 450, 467–68

Stuart, James Ewell Brown "Jeb" (CSA), 322, 324n, 546

Sumner, Charles, 727, 832

Sumner, Edwin V. (USA), 393, 394n, 413

Swain, David L., 874n

Swayne, John T., 327n, 330, 331

Swayne, Noah H. 254, 255n

Sweeny, Thomas William (USA), 559, 560n, 639

Swords, Thomas (USA), 100, 101n, 102, 147, 452

Sykes, George (USA), 100–101n

Talmadge, Theodore, 61, 793, 811, 814

Taylor, Ezra (USA), 644

Taylor, John (USA), 196, 197n, 418

Taylor, Joseph P. (USA), 17, 101

Taylor, Richard (CSA), 17, 590

Taylor, Zachary, 17, 91, 466, 648, 872

Tebow, James O. (USA), 518

Tennessee: bridge burning expedition in, 162, 179–81, 185, 199–200; affairs in eastern part of, 174–84, 189

Terry, Alfred H. (USA), 800, 801n, 805, 815, 821, 827, 828, 830; letter from, 827n

Thayer, John Milton (USA), 440, 441n

Thielemann, Christian (USA), 233, 328

Thomas, Frances Lucretia Kellogg, 779, 780n

Thomas, George H. (USA), 100–101, 132, 134, 140, 143, 149, 150, 155, 156, 157, 161, 162, 174–75, 178–79, 180, 181–82, 183, 198, 219, 227, 231, 252, 314n, 565n, 576, 605, 611, 612, 617, 618, 631, 634, 635, 636, 638, 639, 659, 667, 673, 676, 695, 699, 703, 704, 724, 732, 734, 736, 746, 747, 748, 750–51, 757, 759, 762, 765–66, 772, 774, 775, 776, 778, 782, 784, 785, 788, 791, 805, 806, 814, 816, 821, 823n, 871, 893; WTS's instructions to, 807–8; WTS's opinion of, 229, 253, 655, 700, 766, 814

Thomas, Lorenzo (USA), 89, 90n, 95, 106, 108, 113, 147, 148, 152n, 154n, 162, 163, 165n, 187, 271n, 320, 435, 447, 454, 459, 461, 462, 586

Thompson, Jacob (CSA), 532, 534n, 897

Thompson, Joseph P., 740n

Thompson, M. Jeff (CSA), 279, 280n

Tilghman, Lloyd (CSA), 160, 161n

Tod, David, 254, 355, 356, 357n

Toombs, Robert A., 683, 890

Torbett, Granville C., 265

Townsend, Edward D. (USA), 17

Tumlin, Lewis, 639

Turner, Henry S., 39, 40n, 49, 50, 52, 56n, 58, 59, 64, 66–67, 69, 73, 82, 93, 100, 117, 126, 138–39, 186n, 187, 835–36; letters from, 50n, 65n, 836n

Turner, India, 117

Turner, Julia, 103

Turner, Julia Maria Hunt, 109, 111n, 246, 835

Turner, Thomas (USN), 836n

Turner, Thomas T. (CSA), 66–67, 68n, 69, 73, 82, 138, 140n, 835

Turner, Wilson Price (CSA), 138, 140n, 835

Tuttle, James Madison (USA), 467, 468, 497, 512, 524–25

Twiggs, David E. (CSA), 67, 68–69n

Tyler, Daniel (USA), 108, 109n, 115, 117, 118, 119, 120, 121, 122, 123

United States Military Academy, 541–43, 577–78

Vallandigham, Clement Laird, 510, 511n, 540, 720, 742

Vallas, Anthony, 5, 6n, 9, 37, 39, 46

Vance, Zebulon, 860, 861n, 862

Van Dorn, Earl (CSA), 270, 271n, 310, 338

Van Rensselaer, C. (USA), 387

Van Vliet, Frederick (USA), 73, 75n

Van Vliet, Stewart (USA), 53, 54n, 73, 125

Van Vliet, Mrs. Stewart, 128

Veatch, James Clifford (USA), 589, 590, 610

Vicksburg Campaign, 290, 313, 337–497 passim

Villepigue, John B. (CSA), 279, 280n

Wade, Benjamin, 61, 62n, 458, 558

Wainwright, Samuel A. (USA), 365

Walcutt, Charles C. (USA), 307, 355, 357n

Walker, John G. (USN), 505, 506n

Walker, S. P., 274, 277
Wallace, Lewis (USA), 117, 196, 237, 244,
    250, 252, 355, 410, 498, 648, 649, 650;
    seeks to regain command, 526–27
Wallace, Sergeant, 415–16, 417n
Wallace, William H. L. (USA), 210n, 650,
    651n
Ward, William T. (USA), 151, 152n
Warner, Willard (USA), 707, 709–10, 743,
    908
Washburn, Cadwallader C. (USA), 626,
    627n
Washburn, Elihu B., 805
Washington, Edward C. (USA), 471, 472,
    477
Washington Peace Conference, 56, 57–58n
Waterhouse, Allen C. (USA), 243, 245n
Watts, N. (CSA), 445, 447, 448n, 451
Webster, Daniel, 2, 214, 714
Webster, Joseph D. (USA), 632, 677, 780n,
    846, 853
Weitzel, Godfrey (USA), 869, 870n, 878, 881
Wells, S. C., 707
Wheeler, Joseph (CSA), 710, 731, 746, 796,
    819, 885
Wherry, William M. (USA), 906, 908n
Whitaker, Walter C. (USA), 719, 720n
White, William H., 332–36
White, Mrs. William H., 332–36
Whitfield, John W. (CSA), 546, 550n
Whiting, William H. C. (CSA), 225, 226n
Wilcox, Cadmus C. (CSA), 160, 161n
Wilkes, Charles (USN), 172n

Wilkie, Franc B., 370
Wilkinson, Mary F., 492, 493n
Wilkinson, Robert A. (CSA), 492, 493n
Wilkinson, Robert A., Jr. (CSA), 492, 493n
Williams, Alpheus Starkey (USA), 809
Williams, John S. (USA), 162, 165n
Williams, Seth (USA), 97, 98n
Willock, Julia Ann Sherman, 464
Wilson, James H. (USA), 732, 746, 748, 758,
    807, 851, 866, 869, 874, 880, 884, 886, 893
Wolford, Frank (USA), 151, 152n
Women, Southern, 246, 262, 266, 281, 318–
    19, 492, 502, 662, 717, 792
Wood, Thomas J. (USA), 146, 655, 743
Woods, Charles R. (USA), 485, 805, 846
Woods, Isaah C. (USA), 138, 140n, 145
Wool, John E. (USA), 88–89n, 144
Worthington, Thomas P. (USA), 221, 224n,
    305, 354–56
Wright, Augustus R., 716, 717n, 726
Wright, Horatio G. (USA), 295, 296n, 309,
    311, 312
Wright, John M. (USA), 530n

Yancey, William Lowndes, 683
Yates, Richard, 138, 140n
Yeatman, James E., 477, 478n
Yorke, Louis E. (USA), 394
Young, George Washington, 5, 6n, 107, 117–
    18

Zollicoffer, Felix K. (CSA), 143, 144n, 148,
    149, 150, 156, 157, 161, 162, 175, 181, 199